When should I travel to get the best airfare?
Where do I go for answers to my travel questions?
What's the best and easiest way to plan and book my trip?

frommers.travelocity.com

Frommer's, the travel guide leader, has teamed up with **Travelocity.com**, the leader in online travel, to bring you an in-depth, easy-to-use resource designed to help you plan and book your trip online.

At **frommers.travelocity.com**, you'll find free online updates about your destination from the experts at Frommer's plus the outstanding travel planning and purchasing features of Travelocity.com. Travelocity.com provides reservations capabilities for 95 percent of all airline seats sold, more than 47,000 hotels, and over 50 car rental companies. In addition, Travelocity.com offers more than 2,000 exciting vacation and cruise packages. Travelocity.com puts you in complete control of your travel planning with these and other great features:

> **Expert travel guidance from Frommer's** - over 150 writers reporting from around the world!
>
> **Best Fare Finder** - an interactive calendar tells you when to travel to get the best airfare
>
> **Fare Watcher** - we'll track airfare changes to your favorite destinations
>
> **Dream Maps** - a mapping feature that suggests travel opportunities based on your budget
>
> **Shop Safe Guarantee** - 24 hours a day / 7 days a week live customer service, and more!

Whether traveling on a tight budget, looking for a quick weekend getaway, or planning the trip of a lifetime, Frommer's guides and Travelocity.com will make your travel dreams a reality. You've bought the book, now book the trip!

Travelocity.com
A Sabre Company

Frommer's®

A New Star-Rating System & Other Exciting News from Frommer's!

In our continuing effort to publish the savviest, most up-to-date, and most appealing travel guides available, we've added some great new features.

Frommer's guides now include a new **star-rating system.** Every hotel, restaurant, and attraction is rated from 0 to 3 stars to help you set priorities and organize your time.

We've also added **seven brand-new features** that point you to the great deals, in-the-know advice, and unique experiences that separate travelers from tourists. Throughout the guide, look for:

Finds	Special finds—those places only insiders know about
Fun Fact	Fun facts—details that make travelers more informed and their trips more fun
Kids	Best bets for kids—advice for the whole family
Moments	Special moments—those experiences that memories are made of
Overrated	Places or experiences not worth your time or money
Tips	Insider tips—some great ways to save time and money
Value	Great values—where to get the best deals

We've also added a **"What's New"** section in every guide—a timely crash course in what's hot and what's not in every destination we cover.

Other Great Guides for Your Trip:

Frommer's Tokyo

Frommer's Hong Kong

Frommer's Beijing

Frommer's China: The 50 Most Memorable Trips

Japan
6th Edition

by Beth Reiber with Janie Spencer

Here's what the critics say about Frommer's:

"Amazingly easy to use. Very portable, very complete."
—*Booklist*

"The only mainstream guide to list specific prices. The Walter Cronkite of guide-books—with all that implies."
—*Travel & Leisure*

"Complete, concise, and filled with useful information."
—*New York Daily News*

"Hotel information is close to encyclopedic."
—*Des Moines Sunday Register*

"Detailed, accurate, and easy-to-read information for all price ranges."
—*Glamour Magazine*

Hungry Minds™

Best-Selling Books • Digital Downloads • e-Books • Answer Networks
e-Newsletters • Branded Web Sites • e-Learning
New York, NY • Cleveland, OH • Indianapolis, IN

About the Authors

Beth Reiber lived and worked for 4 years in Germany and 3 years in Japan selling travel articles to the *Los Angeles Times, Chicago Tribune, Washington Post,* and many other newspapers. She also worked in Tokyo as editor of the *Far East Traveler.* Now residing in Lawrence, Kansas, with her husband and two sons, she's the author of several Frommer's guides, including *Frommer's Tokyo* and *Frommer's Hong Kong.* She also contributes to *Frommer's Europe from $70 a Day, Frommer's Southeast Asia,* and *Frommer's USA.*

Janie Spencer spent 7 years in Japan working for the *Tokyo Journal* and *Kyodo News Service.* A freelance writer, she now lives near Paris with her husband and daughter.

Published by:

Hungry Minds, Inc.

909 Third Ave.
New York, NY 10022

ISBN 0-7645-6554-0
ISSN 1045-6899

Editor: Margot Weiss
Production Editor: M. Faunette Johnston
Photo Editor: Richard Fox
Cartographer: Elizabeth Puhl
Production by Hungry Minds Indianapolis Production Services

Front cover photo: Kyoto: Woman at a shrine, wearing a traditional kimono.
Back cover photo: Men and women walking on Kawaramachi Street.

Special Sales

For general information on Hungry Minds' products and services, please contact our Customer Care department; within the U.S. at 800-762-2974, outside the U.S. at 317-572-3993, or fax 317-572-4002. For sales inquiries and reseller information, including discounts, bulk sales, customized editions, and premium sales, please contact our Customer Care department at 800-434-3422.

Manufactured in the United States of America

5 4 3 2 1

Contents

Appendix A: Japan in Depth 602

Appendix B: A Glossary of Useful Japanese Terms 635

Appendix C: A Japanese-Character Index of Establishment Names 641

Index 650

List of Maps

An Invitation to the Reader

In researching this book, we discovered many wonderful places—hotels, restaurants, shops, and more. We're sure you'll find others. Please tell us about them so that we can share the information with your fellow travelers in upcoming editions. If you were disappointed with a recommendation, we'd love to know that, too. Please write to:

Frommer's Japan, 6th Edition
Hungry Minds, Inc. • 909 Third Avenue • New York, NY 10022

An Additional Note

Please be advised that travel information is subject to change at any time—and this is especially true of prices. We therefore suggest that you write or call ahead for confirmation when making your travel plans. The authors, editors, and publisher cannot be held responsible for the experiences of readers while traveling. Your safety is important to us, however, so we encourage you to stay alert and be aware of your surroundings. Keep a close eye on cameras, purses, and wallets, all favorite targets of thieves and pickpockets.

New! Frommer's Star Ratings & Icons

Every hotel, restaurant, and attraction listing in this guide has been ranked for quality, value, service, amenities, and special features using a star-rating scale. In country, state, and regional guides, we also rate towns and regions to help you narrow down your choices and budget your time accordingly. Hotels and restaurants in the Very Expensive and Expensive categories are rated on a scale of one (highly recommended) to three stars (exceptional). Those in the Moderate and Inexpensive categories rate from zero (recommended) to two stars (very highly recommended). Attractions, towns, and regions are rated according to the following scale: zero stars (recommended), one star (highly recommended), two stars (very highly recommended), and three stars (must-see).

In addition to the rating system, we also use seven icons to highlight insider information, useful tips, special bargains, hidden gems, memorable experiences, kid-friendly venues, places to avoid, and other useful information:

(Finds   (Fun Fact   (Kids   (Moments   (Overrated   (Tips   (Value

The following abbreviations are used for credit cards:

AE American Express	DISC Discover	V Visa
DC Diners Club	MC MasterCard	

FROMMERS.COM

Now that you have the guidebook to a great trip, visit our website at **www.frommers.com** for travel information on nearly 2,000 destinations. With features updated regularly, we give you instant access to the most current trip-planning information available. At Frommers.com, you'll also find the best prices on airfares, accommodations, and car rentals—and you can even book travel online through our travel booking partners. At Frommers.com, you'll also find the following:

- Daily Newsletter highlighting the best travel deals
- Hot Spot of the Month/Vacation Sweepstakes & Travel Photo Contest
- More than 200 Travel Message Boards
- Outspoken Newsletters and Feature Articles on travel bargains, vacation ideas, tips & resources, and more!

What's New in Japan

PLANNING A TRIP TO JAPAN
Money For visitors to Japan, one major problem has always been finding ATMs that accepted foreign-issued credit cards. No longer. Now, all 21,000 post offices across Japan have ATMs that accept foreign bankcards operating on the Cirrus (MasterCard) and PLUS (Visa) systems. Hours of operation are limited, however, until 6 or 7pm weekdays and 5pm weekends.

When to Go Several national holidays are moving to Mondays to take advantage of three-day weekends. **Coming-of-Age Day** has already moved to the second Monday in January; **Health Sports Day** is now celebrated the second Monday in October. Beginning in 2003, other holidays moving to Monday are **Marine Day** (3rd Mon in July) and **Respect-for-the-Aged Day** (3rd Mon in Sept).

Fast Facts In an ongoing effort to attract foreign visitors, Japan has abolished its 3% local tax formerly added to hotel and restaurant bills. Now, only a **5% consumption tax** is added to all goods and services. Higher-end restaurants and hotels also add a **service charge.**

Access to the Internet and cell phones is becoming more wide spread. Many first-grade hotels in larger cities offer in-room, **high-speed Internet access,** often through multi-functional TV sets equipped with keyboards. Many also rent **cell phones** through their business center. Passengers flying Japan Airlines or All Nippon Airways from North America should check whether a recent program allowing complimentary use of a domestic cell phone is still in place and whether they qualify (ANA's rental applies only to first- and business-class passengers). There are also **cell-phone rental companies,** but business travelers and those staying more than a few weeks may find it cheaper to purchase a phone.

SETTLING INTO TOKYO Getting Around A new subway line, called the **Oedo Line,** makes a meandering loop around the city and is convenient for traveling between Roppongi and Shinjuku. However, existing subway lines necessitated that the new line be buried so deeply that despite the escalators, station platforms take a while to reach.

Fast Facts Although Tokyo remains one of the safest cities in the world, crime, including the theft of luxury cars and apartment burglaries, is on the increase. Of more concern to visitors is a rise in **pickpocketing,** especially in crowded subway trains and in areas popular with tourists, such as Tsukiji and Asakusa.

Accommodations Long an accommodations-wasteland, Shibuya welcomed several new hotels the past year. First to open, and closest to the station, is the **Shibuya Excel Hotel Tokyu,** 1–12–2 Dogenzaka (© **03/ 5457-0109**), located above a shopping center and connected to the station by an overhead passage. It offers a variety of rooms, including those geared to business travelers and to women, some with great city views.

Dining For those times when only a burger will do, Tokyoites now have **Kua' Aina,** 5-10-1 Minami Aoyama (© 03/3407-8001), a Hawaiian import, whose giant burgers and sandwiches have met with huge success.

EXPLORING TOKYO The **Edo-Tokyo Museum,** 1-4-1 Yokoami (© 03/3626-9974) now offers free guided tours in English from 10am to 3pm (last tour). Depending on individual interest, museum tours last one to two hours but are too rushed to take in everything. Still, participants can always follow up with a more leisurely tour on their own.

The **National Museum of Modern Art,** 3 Kitanomaru Koen Park (© 03/3214-2561) has finally reopened after several years of renovation. It houses the nation's largest collection of modern Japanese art, including works by Munahata Shiko, Kuroda Seiki, and Yokoyama Taikan.

Tokyo DisneySea, 1-1 Maihama (© 045/683-3333), is Tokyo's newest theme park, Located next to Tokyo Disneyland it offers seven "ports of call" featuring 33 attractions, including a submarine adventure and the *Indiana Jones* ride.

Shopping Odaiba, a manmade island in Tokyo Bay, is Tokyo's newest hot spot for shopping, especially **Venus Fort,** an Italian-themed indoor mall with fountains, plazas, and imported Italian goods. In the Ginza, the huge **Sogo** department store succumbed to the recession and closed. Taking its place is **Bic Camera,** 1-11-1 Yurakucho (© 03/3981-8437), with six floors of merchandise ranging from cameras to computers.

The **Japan Traditional Craft Center,** Tokyo's best shop for beautifully designed Japanese crafts from all over Japan, has moved from its Aoyama location to Ikebukuro's Tobu department store, 1-11-1 Nishi-Ikebukuro (© 03/5954-6066). It's now closed on Wednesday instead of Thursday.

SIDE TRIPS FROM TOKYO
Kamakura Volunteer student guides are on hand most weekends between 10am and noon outside the East exit of Kamakura Station to provide free tours of the city's major sights. Try to arrive a little before 10am, before other visitors whisk them away.

Hakone Yunessun, Kowakudani (© 0460/2-4141), is a luxurious new hot-spring spa offering a variety of indoor and outdoor baths. It's especially good for the shy, since it's geared toward families and everyone wears bathing suits. There's also a section, however, for purists who prefer to bathe in the buff.

THE JAPAN ALPS Takayama Sadly, two of Takayama's best ryokan have closed—the **Hida Gasshoen** and **Kinkikan.**

THE REST OF WESTERN HONSHU Nagoya The **Noritake Craft Center,** 3-1-36 Noritake Shinmachi (© 052/561-7114), has temporarily closed while undergoing a complete renovation to bring it up to snuff for its 100-year anniversary bash, to be held in 2004. It has also changed its name to Noritake Square; contact the Nagoya tourist office for updated information on its reopening, expected in 2002.

Osaka Osaka's bay area is hopping, especially since the opening of the hugely popular **Universal Studios Japan,** 2-1-33 Sakurajima (© 06/4790-7000), with the usual Hollywood-themed rides and entertainment. Unfortunately, most of the attractions have been dubbed from the original English into Japanese.

Kurashiki Toyoko Inn is a chain of business hotels that goes the extra kilometer in trying to attract guests, including lobby computers with free Internet access, free movies (unfortunately only in Japanese) and complimentary breakfast. In Kurashiki, you'll find the new **Toyoko Inn Kurashikieki Minamiguchi** centrally located on Chuo Dori, 1–10–20 Achi (© 086/430-1045).

Matsue   The newly opened **Louis C. Tiffany Garden Museum,** 369 Nishihamasada-cho (© 0852/36-3000), offers a stunning collection of one of the finest Tiffany collections in the world, including paintings, furniture, ceramics, jewelry, and stained-glass windows, just one more reason to head to this out-of-the-way town on Honshu's northern coast.

SHIKOKU Takamatsu   If it's been a while since you've been to Taka-matsu, you'll be surprised by its new state-of-the-art train station, part of a new waterfront development that includes the town's newest and most expensive hotel, **ANA Hotel Clement Takamatsu,** 1–1 Hamano-cho (© 087/811-1111). Rising 21 stories high, it offers sea-view rooms and good restaurants, including a top-floor Italian restaurant that seems more Tokyo than this once-sleepy backwater.

Matsuyama   Ehime Prefecture spent big bucks constructing a cycling path that follows the **Shimanami Kaido Bridge** as it hopscotches across six islands in the Seto Inland Sea 69km (43 miles) to Hiroshima Prefecture. The result is one of Japan's **best bike rides,** with great views, beaches and sights along the way, and best of all, inexpensive bike rentals.

HOKKAIDO Sapporo Hotel Monterey Edelhof, N2 W1 (© 011/242-7111), is part of a growing chain of hotels that targets Japanese women with its European-inspired decor, but this one takes the cake with its Otto Wagner–inspired architectural details that hark back to early 1900s Vienna. Its Wagner House Restaurant looks like it was airlifted straight out of Vienna.

1

The Best of Japan

Hardly a day goes by that you don't hear something about Japan, whether the subject is trade, travel, scandal, natural disaster, cuisine, the arts, or the nation's worst economic recession since World War II. Yet Japan remains something of an enigma to people in the Western world. What best describes this Asian nation? Is it the giant producer of cars, computers, and a whole array of sleek electronic goods that compete favorably with the best in the West? Or is it still the land of the geisha and bonsai, the punctilious tea ceremony, and the delicate art of flower arrangement? Has it become, in its outlook and popular culture, a country more Western than Asian? Or has it retained its unique ancient traditions while forging a central place in the modern industrialized world?

In fact, Japan is an intricate blend of East and West. Its cities may look Westernized—often disappointingly so—but beyond first impressions there's very little about this Asian nation that could lull you into thinking you're in the West. Yet Japan also differs greatly from its Asian neighbors. Although it borrowed much from China in its early development, including Buddhism and its writing system, the island nation remained steadfastly isolated from the rest of the world throughout much of its history, usually deliberately so. Until World War II, it had never been successfully invaded; and for more than 200 years, while the West was stirring with the awakenings of democracy and industrialism, Japan completely closed its doors to the outside world and remained a tightly structured feudalistic society with almost no outside influence.

It's been just a little more than a century since the Japanese opened their doors, embracing Western products wholeheartedly, yet at the same time altering them and making them unquestionably their own. Thus, that modern highrise may look Western, but inside it may contain a rustic-looking restaurant with open charcoal grills, corporate offices, a pachinko parlor, a high-tech bar with views of Mt. Fuji, a McDonald's, an acupuncture clinic, a computer showroom, and a rooftop shrine. Your pizza may come with octopus, beer gardens are likely to be fitted with Astroturf, and "parsley" refers to unmarried women older than 25 (because parsley is what's left over on a plate). City police patrol on bicycles, garbage collectors attack their job with the vigor of a well-trained army, and white-gloved elevator operators, working in some of the world's swankiest department stores, bow and thank you as you exit.

Because of this unique synthesis of East and West into a culture that is distinctly Japanese, Japan is not easy for Westerners to comprehend. Discovering it is like peeling an onion—you uncover one layer only to discover more layers underneath. Thus, no matter how long you stay in Japan, you never stop learning something new about it—and to me that constant discovery is one of the most fascinating aspects of being here.

1 The Best Travel Experiences

Long ago, the Japanese ranked the "best three" of almost every natural wonder and attraction in their country: the three best gardens, the three best scenic spots, the three best waterfalls, even the three best bridges. But choosing the "best" of anything is inherently subjective, and decades—even centuries—have passed since some of the original "best three" were so designated. Still, lists can be useful for establishing priorities. To help you get the most out of your stay, I've compiled this list of what I consider the best Japan has to offer based on our many combined years of traveling through the country. From the weird to the wonderful, the profound to the profane, the obvious to the obscure, these recommendations should fire your imagination and launch you toward discoveries of your own.

- **Making a Pilgrimage to a Temple or Shrine:** From mountaintop shrines to neighborhood temples, Japan's religious structures rank among the nation's most popular attractions. Usually devoted to a particular deity, they're visited for specific reasons: Shopkeepers call on Fushimi-Inari Shrine outside Kyoto, dedicated to the goddess of rice and therefore prosperity, while couples wishing for a happy marriage head to Kyoto's Jishu Shrine, a shrine to the deity of love. Shrines and temples are also the sites for most of Japan's major festivals. See chapter 2, the regional chapters, and "The Best Temples & Shrines" section, below.

- **Taking a Communal Hot-Spring Bath:** No other people on earth bathe as enthusiastically, as frequently, and for such a long duration as the Japanese. Their many hot-spring resorts—thought to cure all sorts of ailments as well

as simply making you feel good—range from hangar-like affairs to outdoor baths with views of the countryside. No matter what the setup, you'll soon warm to the ritual of soaping up, rinsing off, and then soaking in near-scalding waters. See "The Best Spas & Public Baths," later in this chapter, for specific recommendations.

- **Participating in a Festival:** With Shintoism and Buddhism as its major religions and temples and shrines virtually everywhere, Japan has festivals literally every weekend. These celebrations, which range from huge processions of wheeled floats to those featuring horseback archery and ladder-top acrobatics, can be lots of fun; you may want to plan your trip around one. See the "Calendar of Events," in chapter 2.

- **Dining on Japanese Food:** There's more to Japanese cuisine than sushi, and part of what makes travel here so fascinating is the variety of national and regional dishes. Every prefecture, it seems, has its own style of noodles, its special vegetables, and delicacies. If money is no object, order *kaiseki*, a complete meal of visual and culinary finesse. See appendix A, the "Where to Dine" sections in the regional chapters, and "The Best Culinary Experiences," later in this chapter.

- **Viewing the Cherry Blossoms:** Nothing symbolizes the coming of spring so vividly to the Japanese as the appearance of the cherry blossoms—and nothing so amazes visitors as the way the Japanese gather under the blossoms to celebrate the season with food, drink, dance, and karaoke. See the "Calendar of Events," in chapter 2.

- **Riding the Shinkansen Bullet Train:** Asia's fastest train whips you across the countryside at more than 290km (180 miles) an hour as you relax, see the country's rural countryside, and dine on boxed meals filled with local specialties of the area you're speeding through. See "Getting Around Japan," in chapter 2.

- **Staying in a Ryokan:** Japan's legendary service reigns supreme in the *ryokan,* a traditional Japanese inn. Staying in a ryokan is the height of both luxury and simplicity: You'll bathe in a Japanese tub, dine in your own room on a futon laid out on a *tatami* (rice-mat floor covering) floor, sleep on a futon, awaken to lovely views (usually a Japanese garden) past the shoji screens, and breakfast in your room to start the day. See "Tips on Accommodations," in chapter 2, and the "Where to Stay" sections in the regional chapters.

- **Shopping in a Department Store:** Japan's department stores are among the best in the world, offering everything from food to designer clothing to electronics to kimono and traditional crafts. Service also is among the best in the world: If you arrive as the store opens, staff will be lined up at the front door to bow as you enter. See "Shopping," in chapter 4 and in the regional chapters.

- **Attending a Kabuki Play:** Based on universal themes and designed to appeal to the masses, Kabuki plays are extravaganzas of theatrical displays, costumes, and scenes—but mostly they're just plain fun. See "Tokyo After Dark," in chapter 4.

- **Strolling Through Tokyo's Nightlife District:** Every major city in Japan has its own nightlife district, but probably none is more famous, more wicked, or more varied than Tokyo's Kabuki-cho in Shinjuku, which offers everything from hole-in-the-wall bars to strip joints, discos, and gay clubs. See "Tokyo After Dark," in chapter 4.

- **Seeing Mt. Fuji:** It may not seem like much of an accomplishment to see Japan's most famous and tallest mountain, visible from 100 miles away. But the truth is: It's hardly ever visible except during the winter months and rare occasions when the air is clear. Catching your first glimpse of the giant peak is truly breathtaking and something you'll never forget, whether you see it from aboard the Shinkansen, from a Tokyo skyscraper, or from a nearby national park. If you want to climb it, be prepared for a group experience— 400,000 people climb Mt. Fuji every year. See "Climbing Japan's Most Famous Mountain: Mt. Fuji," in chapter 5.

- **Spending a Few Days in Kyoto:** If you see only one city in Japan, Kyoto should be it. Japan's capital from 794 to 1868, Kyoto is one of Japan's finest ancient cities, boasting some of the country's best temples, Japanese-style inns, traditional restaurants, shops, and gardens. See chapter 7.

2 The Best Temples & Shrines

- **Sensoji Temple** (Tokyo): The capital's oldest temple is also its liveliest. Throngs of visitors and stalls selling both traditional and kitschy items lend it a festival-like atmosphere. This is the most important temple to see in Tokyo. See p. 164.

- **Meiji Jingu Shrine** (Tokyo): Tokyo's most venerable and refined Shinto shrine honors the Emperor Meiji and his empress with simple yet dignified architecture surrounded by a dense forest. This is a great refuge in the heart of the city. See p. 164.

- **Kotokuin Temple** (Kamakura): This temple is home to the Great Buddha, Japan's second-largest bronze image, which was cast in the 13th century and sits outdoors against a magnificent wooded backdrop. The Buddha's face has a wonderful expression of contentment, serenity, and compassion. See p. 218.

- **Hase Kannon Temple** (Kamakura): Although this temple is famous for its 30-foot-tall Kannon of Mercy, the largest wooden image in Japan, it's most memorable for its thousands of small statues of Jizo, the guardian deity of children, donated by parents of miscarried, stillborn, or most frequently, aborted children. It's a rather haunting vision. See p. 219.

- **Toshogu Shrine** (Nikko): Dedicated to Japan's most powerful shogun, Tokugawa Ieyasu, this shrine is the nation's most elaborate and opulent, with 2.4 million sheets of gold leaf. It's set in a forest of cedar. See p. 222.

- **Kiyomizu Temple** (Kyoto): One of Japan's best-known temples with a structure imitated by lesser temples around the country, Kiyomizu commands an exalted spot on a steep hill with a sweeping view over Kyoto. The pathway leading to the shrine is lined with pottery and souvenir shops, and the temple grounds have open-air pavilions where you can drink beer or eat noodles. Don't neglect the smaller **Jishu Shrine** on its grounds—it's dedicated to the god of love. See p. 315.

- **Sanjusangendo Hall** (Kyoto): Japan's longest wooden building contains the spectacular sight of more than 1,000 life-size wood-carved statues, row upon row of the thousand-handed Kannon of Mercy. See p. 316.

- **Kinkakuji** (Temple of the Golden Pavilion; Kyoto): Constructed in the 14th century as a shogun's retirement villa, this three-story pavilion shimmers in gold leaf and is topped with a bronze phoenix; it's a beautiful sight when the sun shines and the sky's blue. See p. 317.

- **Todaiji Temple** (Nara): Japan's largest bronze Buddha sits in the largest wooden structure in the world, making it the top attraction in this former capital. Although not as impressive as the Great Buddha's dramatic outdoor stage in Kamakura, the sheer size of Todaiji Temple and its Buddha make this a sight not to be missed if you're in the Kansai area. See p. 339.

- **Ise Grand Shrines** (Ise): Although there's not much to see, these shrines are the most venerated Shinto shrines in all of Japan, and pilgrims have been flocking here for centuries. Amazingly, the Inner Shrine, which contains the Sacred Mirror, is razed and reconstructed on a new site every 20 years according to strict rules governing purification in the Shinto religion. Follow the age-old route of former pilgrims after you visit the shrines, and stop for a meal in the nearby Okage Yokocho District. See p. 358.

- **Itsukushima Shrine** (Miyajima): The huge red *torii* (the traditional entry gate of a shrine) standing in the waters of the Seto Inland Sea is one of the most photographed landmarks in Japan and signals the approach to this shrine. Built over the tidal flats on a gem of an island called Miyajima, it's considered one of Japan's most scenic spots. At night, the shrine is illuminated. See p. 458.

- **Kotohiragu Shrine** (Kotohira, on Shikoku): One of Japan's oldest and most popular shrines beckons at the top of 785 granite steps on the Yashima Plateau with great

views of the Seto Inland Sea, but for most Japanese, it's the "I made it!" that counts. See p. 466.

- **Dazaifu Tenmangu Shrine** (Fukuoka): Established in 905 to deify the god of scholarship, this immensely popular shrine has a festive atmosphere and is popular with students wishing to pass school exams. The road leading to the shrine is lined with souvenir and craft shops. See p. 486.

3 The Best Gardens

- **Hama Rikyu Garden** (Tokyo): Considered by some to be the best garden in Tokyo, this peaceful oasis has origins stretching back 300 years when it served as a retreat for a former feudal lord and as duck-hunting grounds for the Tokugawa shoguns. Surrounded by water on three sides, it contains a tidal pool, moon-viewing pavilions, and teahouses. See p. 172.

- **Sankei-en Garden** (Yokohama): Historic villas, tea arbors, a farmhouse, a pagoda, and other authentic buildings, all set in a century-old landscaped garden with ponds and streams, make this one of the most interesting and picturesque gardens in Japan. See p. 232.

- **Ryoanji Temple** (Kyoto): Japan's most famous Zen rock garden, laid out at the end of the 15th century, consists of moss-covered boulders and raked pebbles enclosed by an earthen wall. It is said that it's impossible to see all 15 rocks from any vantage point; see if you can. Come early in the morning for some peaceful meditation. See p. 317.

- **Katsura Imperial Villa** (Kyoto): Designed by Japan's most famous gardener, Kobori Enshu, the garden surrounding this imperial

villa is, in my view, Japan's most beautiful. A "stroll garden," its view changes with every step but is always complete, perfectly balanced, and in harmony. It's well worth the extra effort involved to see it. See p. 327.

- **Saihoji** (Kyoto): Popularly known as the Moss Temple, Saihoji is Japan's most famous moss garden, with more than 100 varieties spread throughout the grounds, giving off an iridescent glow. It's especially beautiful after a rainfall. See p. 329.

- **Kenrokuen Garden** (Kanazawa): Considered by some to be Japan's grandest landscape garden (and rated one of the "best three"), Kenrokuen is also one of the largest. The garden took 150 years to complete and consists of ponds, streams, rocks, mounds, trees, grassy expanses, and footpaths. See p. 366.

- **Koko-en** (Himeji): It isn't old (it was laid out in 1992), but this is a wonderful surprise package of nine small gardens, each one different but typical of gardens during the Edo Period, which lasted from 1603 to 1867. Upon seeing what can be accomplished with skill and money in only a decade, some gardeners may turn green with envy. See p. 418.

- **Korakuen Garden** (Okayama): Rated one of Japan's three most beautiful gardens, Korakuen was completed in 1700 and incorporates the surrounding hills and Okayama Castle into its design. It's definitely worth a visit if you're in the vicinity, though personally I like Kenrokuen more. See p. 422.
- **Ritsurin Park** (Takamatsu): Dating from the 17th century, this former private retreat of the ruling Matsudaira clan is an exquisite stroll garden that incorporates Mt. Shiun in its landscaping and boasts 1,600 pine trees and 350 cherry trees. Stop for tea in the Feudal-Era teahouse and contemplate the view in leisure. See p. 465.
- **Senganen** (Kagoshima): Laid out more than 300 years ago by the Shimazu clan, this summer retreat with a 25-room villa was known for its poem-composing parties, held beside a rivulet that still exists. After touring the garden and villa, be sure to visit the nearby museum with relics belonging to the Shimazu family. This garden is one of my favorites. See p. 509.

4 The Best Castles, Palaces & Villas

- **Matsumoto Castle** (Matsumoto): Popularly known as the Crow Castle due to its black color, this small castle boasts the oldest *donjon* (keep) in Japan (it's 400 years old). A moon-viewing room was added in 1635, and exhibited inside the castle is a collection of Japanese matchlocks and samurai armor dating from the mid–16th century through the Edo Period. See p. 252.
- **Kyoto Imperial Palace** (Kyoto): Home to Japan's imperial family from the 14th to 19th centuries, this palace is praised for its Heian design and graceful garden. Good news for travelers: Guided tours of the palace are free. See p. 312.
- **Nijo Castle** (Kyoto): One of the few castles built by the mighty Tokugawa shogunate as a residence rather than for defense, Nijo Castle is where the shogun stayed whenever he was in Kyoto. It's famous for its creaking floorboards that warned of enemy intruders and is considered the quintessence of Momoyama architecture. See p. 313.
- **Katsura Imperial Villa** (Kyoto): Built in the 1600s by a brother of the emperor, this villa and garden are considered to be among the best—if not the best—in traditional architecture and landscape gardening. More than anyplace else, it illustrates the life of refinement enjoyed by 17th-century nobility, when leisure pursuits included such activities as moon viewing. See p. 327.
- **Osaka Castle** (Osaka): Although just a reproduction of what was once the mightiest castle in the land, Osaka Castle still impresses with its sheer size. Inside you'll find a high-tech museum detailing the life and times of Toyotomi Hideyoshi, the warrior general who built the castle. See p. 380.
- **Himeji Castle** (Himeji): Said to resemble a white heron poised in flight over the plains, this is quite simply Japan's most beautiful castle. With its extensive gates, moats, turrets, and maze of passageways, it has survived virtually intact since feudal times. If you see only one castle in Japan, make it this one. See p. 417.
- **Matsue Castle** (Matsue): This 17th-century castle is one of Japan's few remaining original castles (not a reconstruction), and it

features a five-story donjon with samurai gear and artifacts belonging to the ruling Matsudaira clan. See p. 437.

- **Matsuyama Castle** (Matsuyama): Occupying a hill above the city, this is also one of the few original castles left in Japan. It boasts good views over Matsuyama from its three-story donjon as well as a collection of armor and swords of the Matsudaira clan. See p. 472.

- **Kumamoto Castle** (Kumamoto): Although a ferroconcrete reconstruction not nearly as huge as the original, this massive castle is still an impressive sight, especially at night when it's illuminated. It's famous for its curved walls, which made invasion virtually impossible. The interior houses a museum with palanquins, armor, swords, and other artifacts of the former ruling clans. See p. 521.

5 The Best Museums

- **Tokyo National Museum** (Tokyo): Even professed museum-phobes should make a point of visiting the National Museum, the largest repository of Japanese arts in the world. Lacquerware, china, kimono, samurai armor, swords, woodblock prints, religious art, and more are on display, making this the best place in Japan for viewing Japanese antiques and decorative objects. If you visit only one museum in Japan, this should be the one. See p. 165.

- **Edo-Tokyo Museum** (Tokyo): Housed in a high-tech modern building, this ambitious museum chronicles the fascinating and somewhat tumultuous history of Tokyo (known as Edo during the Feudal Era) with models, replicas, artifacts, and dioramas. See p. 168.

- **Hakone Open-Air Museum** (Chokoku-no-Mori, Hakone): Beautifully landscaped grounds and spectacular scenery showcase approximately 700 20th-century sculptures, from Giacomo and Rodin to Henry Moore. Here, too, is the Picasso Pavilion, housing 200 of the artist's works. See p. 240.

- **Silk Museum** (Yokohama): The role silk played in Japan's export market at the turn of the century cannot be overemphasized, as this interesting museum clearly shows with its displays of live silk worms, silk panels, gorgeous kimono, and more. Oddly, the museum is usually empty because crowds rush to Yokohama's more modern attractions—but I think this is the city's finest museum. See p. 232.

- **Japan Ukiyo-e Museum** (Matsumoto): One of the best woodblock-print museums in Japan, this museum displays the largest collection of prints in the world on a rotating basis. A must-see in Matsumoto. See p. 254.

- **Hida Minzoku Mura Folk Village** (Takayama): Picturesquely situated around a pond with flowers, more than 30 shingled and thatched farmhouses—many transported from the surrounding Japan Alps—are filled with farm implements and objects of daily life, providing fascinating insight into the life and times of the extended families that once inhabited them. See p. 261.

- **Inro Museum** (Takayama): Of Takayama's many specialty museums, this one is my favorite: It houses Japan's largest collecti on of *inro* and *netsuke,* small containers with toggles that were once standard accessories of the kimono. You could spend hours looking at these miniature works of art. See p. 264.

- **Museum Meiji Mura** (Nagoya): This open-air architectural museum is an absolute treasure with more than 60 original buildings and structures dating from the Meiji Period situated on 250 beautifully landscaped acres on the shore of a lake. Western-style homes, churches, a Kabuki theater, a bathhouse, a prison, a brewery, and much more are open for viewing and filled with furniture and household items. Mail a postcard from an authentic post office, buy candy from an old candy store, and drink tea in the lobby of the original Imperial Hotel, which was designed by Frank Lloyd Wright. See p. 350.
- **Ohara Museum of Art** (Kurashiki): Founded in 1930, this museum just keeps getting better, with works by both Western and Japanese greats, spread through several buildings. Its location in the picturesque Kurashiki historic district is a bonus. See p. 430.
- **Adachi Museum** (Matsue): This museum near Matsue combines two of my passions—art and gardens—making it a winner. Japanese modern art is the focus indoors, while the perfectly landscaped garden comes into view through framed windows, making it part of the art in a very surreal way. See p. 441.
- **Louis C. Tiffany Garden Museum** (Matsue): This, one of the world's best collections of Tiffany paintings, furniture, ceramics, stained-glass windows, and jewelry, will take your breath away—and make you wonder how much insurance the museum pays in this earthquake-prone land. See p. 439.
- **Peace Memorial Museum** (Hiroshima): Japan's most thought-provoking museum contains exhibits examining Hiroshima's militaristic past, the events leading up to the explosion of the world's first atomic bomb, the city's terrible destruction, and its active antinuclear movement. See p. 448.
- **Fukuoka Asian Art Museum** (Fukuoka): This fascinating museum is devoted to contemporary and modern art from around Asia, including the Philippines, Indonesia, Malaysia, Thailand, China, Korea, and India. See p. 485.

6 The Best Small Towns & Villages

- **Takayama:** Located in the Japan Alps and surrounded by mountain peaks, this former castle town has a delightful historic quarter with 18th-century merchant homes, sake breweries, special-interest museums, craft shops, restaurants, and Japanese inns, all easy to explore on foot. Another highlight is the **Hida Minzoku Mura Folk Village,** an open-air museum illustrating how local farmers once lived (see "The Best Museums," above). See "Takayama, Little Kyoto of the Mountains," in chapter 6.
- **Ogimachi** (Shirakawago): With its thatch-roofed farmhouses, rice paddies trimmed with flower beds, roaring river, and pine-covered mountains rising on all sides, Ogimachi is one of the most picturesque rural villages in Japan. Many of the large, thatched farmhouses are now inexpensive *minshuku* (family-run inns), where you can stay and sample the local mountain cuisine. See "Rural Shirakawago & Ogimachi," in chapter 6.
- **Tsumago:** Nestled in the Japan Alps, Tsumago served as an old

post town for *daimyo* (feudal lords) and their samurai traveling between Kyoto and Edo (now Tokyo). Virtually untouched by the 20th century, it has many authentic feudal-age wooden buildings, some of which are open to the public. See "Along the Nakasendo Highway: Tsumago & Magome," in chapter 6.

- **Nara:** This ancient capital boasts a large park with temples, shrines, museums, the country's largest bronze Buddha, plus friendly free-ranging deer. See "A Side Trip to Nara," in chapter 7.

- **Mt. Koya:** This mountaintop enclave of 120 Shingon Buddhist temples is one of Japan's most sacred places. It contains the mausoleum of Kobo Daishi, one of the most revered figures in Japanese Buddhist history, as well as an extensive burial ground of daimyo, samurai, and others who wished to be close to their leader

for all of eternity. Following in the footsteps of emperors, nobles, and commoners who've made pilgrimages here over the last thousand years, you can even spend the night in one of the temples. See "The Temples of Mt. Koya," in chapter 8.

- **Uchiko** (Shikoku): This well-preserved village boasts a number of buildings dating from the Edo Period and the turn of the century, including several homes now open to the public and a 1916 Kabuki theater. See "An Easy Side Trip," in chapter 9.

- **Chiran** (Kyushu): One of 102 castle towns that once bordered a feudal kingdom during the Edo Period, this small town has a delightful road called Samurai Lane that's lined with walled compounds including six samurai houses with gardens open to the public. See "A Side Trip to the Gardens of Chiran," in chapter 10.

7 The Best National Parks

- **Nikko National Park:** This 200,000-acre national park centers on the sumptuous Toshogu Shrine with its mausoleum of Tokugawa Ieyasu, majestic cedars, and lakeside resorts. See p. 221.

- **Fuji-Hakone-Izu National Park:** Boasting magnificent Mt. Fuji at its core, this popular weekend getaway beckons vacationing Tokyoites with its many hot-spring spas, stunning close-up views of Mt. Fuji, sparkling lakes, historic attractions relating to the famous Feudal-Era Tokaido Highway, and coastal areas of Izu Peninsula. One of the best ways to see Hakone is via a circular route that involves travel on a two-car mountain tram, a cable car, a ropeway, and a boat; it's a delightful journey with wonderful scenery and interesting sights along the way. See p. 235.

- **Japan Alps National Park:** Encompassing Honshu's most impressive mountain ranges and the site of the 1998 Winter Olympics, this national park offers skiing as well as unique villages worth a visit in their own right. See p. 251.

- **Ise-Shima National Park:** Boasting a rugged seascape of capes, inlets, and islets, this park is the birthplace of cultivated pearls. It's famous for its bays dotted with pearl-cultivating oyster rafts, its female divers, a pearl museum, plus a top-notch aquarium and the Ise Grand Shrines, Japan's most venerable shrines. For fun, there are also two theme parks here. See p. 356.

- **Seto-Naikai (Inland Sea) National Park:** Covering 251

square miles of water, islands, islets, and coastline, this sea park stretches from Kobe in the east to Beppu in the west. It's studded with numerous islands of all sizes, the most famous of which is Miyajima, home of the Itsukushima Shrine. Cruises ply the waters of the Seto Inland Sea, as do regular ferries sailing between Honshu, Shikoku, and Kyushu. The adventuresome can even cycle across the Seto Inland Sea via the Shimanami Kaido Bridge linking Honshu with Shikoku (see "The Best Outdoor Adventures," later in this chapter). See p. 457.

- **Unzen-Amakusa National Park:** At western Kyushu's high-altitude national park, you can climb Mt. Fugen (4,462 ft. above sea level), relax in a hot-spring bath, golf at one of Japan's oldest public courses, and take a walk through the Hells, the park's extra-steamy sulfur springs. See p. 543.
- **Towada-Hachimantai National Park:** Tohoku's most popular park beckons with scenic lakes, rustic

hot-spring spas, hiking, and skiing. See p. 560.
- **Shikotsu-Toya National Park:** This 381-square-mile park in eastern Hokkaido encompasses lakes, volcanoes, and famous hot-spring resorts like Noboribetsu. See p. 584.
- **Daisetsuzan National Park:** The largest of Japan's 28 national parks—and some say Hokkaido's most beautiful—Daisetsuzan boasts three volcanic chains, fir- and birch-covered hillsides, the impressive Sounkyo Gorge, and plenty of skiing and hiking opportunities. See p. 591.
- **Akan National Park:** Popular for hiking, skiing, canoeing, and fishing, Akan National Park in Hokkaido is characterized by dense forests of sub-arctic primeval trees and caldera lakes, the most famous of which are Kussharo, one of Japan's largest mountain lakes, and Mashu, considered one of Japan's least-spoiled lakes and one of the world's clearest. See p. 595.

8 The Best of Old Japan

- **Splurging on a Night in a Ryokan:** If you can afford to, splurge at least one night on a stay in one of the country's best ryokan, where the service is impeccable, the kaiseki meals are out of this world, and glorious views outside your tatami room are of miniature landscaped gardens. You'll be pampered in a manner fit for an emperor—many of the nation's oldest ryokan were indeed born to serve members of the imperial court as they traveled Japan's Feudal-Era highways. See "Tips on Accommodations," in chapter 2, the "Where to Stay" sections in the regional chapters

and "The Best Traditional Ryokan," later in this chapter.
- **Attending a Sumo Match:** There's nothing quite like watching two monstrous sumo wrestlers square off, bluff, and grapple as they attempt to throw each other on the ground or out of the ring. Matches are great cultural events, but even if you can't attend a match, you can watch one on TV during one of the six annual 15-day tournaments. See "Spectator Sports," in chapter 4, and "Sumo," in appendix A.
- **Strolling through a Japanese Garden:** Most of Japan's famous gardens are relics of the Edo

Period, when the Shogun, daimyo feudal lords, the imperial family, and even samurai and Buddhist priests developed private gardens for their own viewing pleasure. Each step in a strolling garden brings a new view to die for. See "The Best Gardens," earlier in this chapter, and the "Attractions" sections in the regional chapters to see which are heaven on earth.

- **Participating in Zazen Meditation in a Buddhist Temple:** Zazen, or sitting meditation, is practiced by Zen Buddhists as a form of spiritual training and by laymen as a way to relieve stress and clear the mind. Several temples in Japan are willing to take in foreigners for Zazen sessions. See "Five Unforgettable Ways to Immerse Yourself in Japanese Culture," in chapter 4, and the "Here and *Zazen:* Buddhism in Japan" in appendix A.

- **Taking Lessons in Ikebana:** Japanese flower arranging is respected around the world. It takes years of instruction to become masterful at it; however, you can learn the basics at several ikebana schools in Tokyo. See "Five Unforgettable Ways to Immerse Yourself in Japanese Culture," in chapter 4 and "Floral & Landscape Arts," in appendix A.

- **Attending a Traditional Tea Ceremony:** Developed in the 16th century as a means to achieve inner harmony with nature, the tea ceremony is a highly ritualized ceremony carried out in teahouses throughout the country, including those set in Japan's many parks and gardens. Several Tokyo hotels offer instruction in the tea ceremony in English. See p. 171.

- **Getting a Shiatsu Massage:** Shiatsu, or pressure-point massage, is available in virtually all first-class accommodations in Japan and at most moderately priced ones as well. After a hard day of work or sightseeing, nothing beats a relaxing massage and a hot bath. Tokyo has several clinics that are used to foreigners. See "Five Unforgettable Ways to Immerse Yourself in Japanese Culture," in chapter 4.

- **Seeing an Acupuncturist:** Whether it's a crick in your neck or a stomachache, acupuncture can relieve pain, relax muscles, and generally make you feel better—and it doesn't hurt despite the needles! As with shiatsu, there are several Tokyo clinics that are used to foreigners. See "Five Unforgettable Ways to Immerse Yourself in Japanese Culture," in chapter 4.

- **Relaxing at a Hot-Spring Resort:** No country in the world boasts more natural hot springs than Japan, which has 19,500 different springs. Hot-spring spas are found in virtually all regions of the country and feature everything from hot-sand baths to open-air baths. See the regional chapters.

- **Spending a Day in Asakusa** (Tokyo): Asakusa is the best place to experience Tokyo's old downtown with its popular Sensoji Temple, Nakamise shopping lane with crafts and kitsch, and casual traditional restaurants. As in days of yore, arrive by boat on the Sumida River. See chapter 4.

- **Exploring Kyoto's Higashiyama-ku District:** Kyoto's eastern sector is a lovely combination of wooded hills, temples, shrines, museums, shops, and traditional restaurants, making it one of the best neighborhoods in Japan for a stroll. See "A Stroll Through Higashiyama-ku," in chapter 7.

- **Visiting Kyoto's Gion District:** Japan's most famous geisha houses may be off limits to anyone without a proper introduction, but an early-evening stroll through this solemn-looking enclave of wooden homes and plain facades is like a journey back in time. You might even catch a glimpse of an elaborately made-up *maiko* (apprentice) on her way to an appointment or hear strains of *shamisen* (a traditional three-stringed Japanese instrument) played behind closed doors. See chapter 7.

- **Watching Cormorant Fishing:** Every night in summer, wooden boats gaily decorated with paper lanterns will take you out on rivers outside Kyoto and Nagoya for an up-close look at cormorant fishing. The birds, maneuvered by fishermen in traditional garb, have tight collars around their necks to prevent them from swallowing their catch. Drinking and dining on board contribute to the festive air. See "A Summer Spectacle: Cormorant Fishing," in chapter 7, and "Watching Cormorant Fishing," in chapter 8.

- **Walking to Kobo Daishi's Mausoleum on Mt. Koya:** Ever since the 9th century when Buddhist leader Kobo Daishi was laid to rest at Okunion on Mt. Koya, his faithful followers have followed him to their graves—and now tomb after tomb line a 1-mile pathway to Daishi's mausoleum. Cypress trees, moss-covered stone lanterns, and thousands upon thousands of tombs make this the most impressive graveyard stroll in Japan, especially at night. See "Exploring Mt. Koya," in chapter 8.

9 The Best of Modern Japan

- **Attending a Baseball Game** (Tokyo): After sumo, baseball is Japan's most popular spectator sport. Watching a game with a stadium full of avid fans can be quite fun and can shed new light on America's favorite pastime. See "For It's Ichi, Ni, San Strikes You're Out . . .," in chapter 4 and "Take Me Out to the Ballgame," in chapter 10.

- **Visiting Tsukiji Fish Market** (Tokyo): One of the largest wholesale fish markets in the world, this indoor market bustles with activity from about 3am on as frozen tuna is unloaded from boats, auctions are held, and vendors sell octopus, fish, squid, and everything else that's edible from the sea to the city's restaurants. Be sure to bring your camera. See p. 169.

- **Seeing Tokyo from the TMG:** On the 45th floor of the Tokyo Metropolitan Government Office (TMG), designed by well-known architect Kenzo Tange, an observatory offers a bird's-eye view of Shinjuku's cluster of skyscrapers, the never-ending metropolis, and, on fine winter days, Mt. Fuji. Best of all, it's free. See p. 177.

- **Hanging Out in Harajuku** (Tokyo): Nothing beats Sunday in Harajuku, where you can begin the day leisurely with brunch and then stroll the promenade of Omote Sando Dori, shop the area's many boutiques, take in a museum or two and perhaps a flea market, and then relax over drinks at a sidewalk cafe and watch the never-ending parade of humanity. See "Frommer's Favorite Tokyo Experiences," in chapter 4.

- **Shopping for Japanese Designer Clothes** (Tokyo): Japanese designer clothing is often outrageous, occasionally practical, but mostly just fun. Department stores and designer boutiques in Aoyama are the places to try on the styles if you have both the money and the figure for them. See "Shopping," in chapter 4.

- **Spending an Evening in an Entertainment District:** A spin through one of Japan's famous nightlife districts, such as **Shinjuku** or **Roppongi** in Tokyo or **Dotombori** in Osaka, is a colorful way to rub elbows with the natives as you explore narrow streets with their whirls of neon, tiny hole-in-the-wall bars and restaurants, and all-night amusement spots. See "Tokyo After Dark," in chapter 4, and "Osaka After Dark," in chapter 8.

- **Taking Center Stage in a Karaoke Bar** (Tokyo, Osaka): Believe it or not, spending an evening in a karaoke bar can be lots of fun. They're usually tiny affairs with only a few stools at a counter, a *mama-san* or host, and a regular, appreciative clientele. Corny music videos, including English-language hits, are displayed with text on a screen so you can sing along; no matter how bad you are, everyone claps when you're done (or maybe just because you're done). A good place to shake your inhibitions. See "Tokyo After Dark," in chapter 4, and "Osaka After Dark," in chapter 8.

- **Seeing Fish Eye-to-Eye in an Aquarium** (Tokyo, Nagoya, Toba, Osaka, Kagoshima): Because Japan is surrounded by sea, it's no surprise that it has more than its fair share of aquariums. Several have made splashy debuts in the past decade with innovative displays that put you eye-to-eye with the creatures of the deep. Among the best are those in Toba and Osaka. See pgs. 361 and 381.

- **Visiting Holland, Spain, Outer Space, or the Edo Period Without Leaving Japan:** Theme parks are big business in Japan, many of them quite sophisticated and realistic down to the tiniest detail. **Huis Ten Bosch** (Nagasaki) is a reproduction Dutch village with shops, restaurants, museums, and much more; **Shima Spain Mura** (Ise-Shima) takes a similar approach but with a Spanish theme. **Sengoku Jidaimura** (Ise-Shima) evokes the Warring States Period of Japanese history, while the **Noboribetsu-Date Historic Village** (Noboribetsu) is an Edo-Era park; both have staff dressed in period costumes, theatrical events, and museums. **Space World** (Kita-Kyushu) is an amusement park based on space travel, while **Ocean Dome** (Miyazaki) is the world's largest indoor water park. All of these are great fun and a must if you're traveling with children. See pgs. 535, 362, 359, 586, 486, and 501.

10 The Best Spas & Public Baths

- **Hakone:** Hakone abounds in hot-spring spas and ryokan along the old Tokaido Highway, which originated to serve the needs of feudal lords traveling to Edo (now Tokyo). Its proximity to Tokyo makes it my number one choice for a weekend hot-spring getaway. The most famous public bathhouse in Hakone is the state-of-the-art **Yunessun,** with its wide variety of indoor and outdoor baths. The timid should take heart—you wear a bathing suit to most of them. See "Hakone: By Mountain Tram, Cable Car, Ropeway & Boat," in chapter 5.

- **Spa World** (Osaka): You could easily spend a whole day at this lavishly decorated, international-themed, hot-spring bathing facility: Travel the world with a bath in the German sector, a sauna in the Finnish room, and an outdoor soak in the Japanese area. Swim in the rooftop pool, relax on the sun terrace, and have a massage. See p. 381.

- **Thalassa Shima:** Set on the dramatic coastline of Ise Shima Bay, this modern resort combines the Japanese love for taking the waters with French thalassotherapy (seawater, sea mud, and seaweed treatments). A pool overlooking the bay, rooms with seaside views, and French and Japanese restaurants make this a great sophisticated getaway. See p. 363.

- **Dogo Onsen Honkan** (Matsuyama): Located in Japan's oldest hot-spring spa, this century-old bathhouse gets my vote for the country's most delightful. It's a wonderful traditional wooden structure with baths and a communal tatami area where you can relax afterwards in a *yukata* (cotton robe) and drink tea. Very civilized. See p. 473.

- **Beppu:** This king of hot-spring spas offers 168 public bathhouses and baths in water, mud, and sand. **Suginoi Palace** is Beppu's most elaborate—a huge, hangar-like affair with lush tropical plants, pools of various sizes and temperatures, an adjoining water park, and even variety shows. **Takegawara Bathhouse,** built in 1879, is the place to go for hot black sand—you'll be buried up to your neck. See pgs. 492 and 493.

- **Nyuto Onsen:** This valley in Tohoku's Towada-Hachimantai National Park is about as remote as you can get, with a string of rustic Japanese inns and outdoor baths nestled in the wooded hills. Difficult to get to, but an experience you won't easily forget. See "Lake Tazawa and Nyuto Onsen," in chapter 11.

- **Noboribetsu Onsen:** Hokkaido's most popular resort and one of Japan's best-known spas, Noboribetsu offers 11 different kinds of hot water. Foremost among the many public bathing facilities is **Daiichi Takimotokan** with some 20 pools. See p. 584.

11 The Best Outdoor Adventures

- **Climbing Mt. Fuji:** Okay, so climbing Japan's tallest—12,388 feet high—and most famous mountain is not the solitary, athletic pursuit you may have envisioned—but with 400,000 people climbing it annually, it's a great, culturally enriching group activity. The most recent trend is to climb through the night with a flashlight and then cheer the sunrise from the top of the mountain. See "Climbing Japan's Most Famous Mountain: Mt. Fuji," in chapter 5.

- **Hiking the Old Nakasendo Highway** (Japan Alps): Back in the days of the shogun, feudal lords were required to return to Edo (now Tokyo) every other year, traveling designated highways. Nakasendo was one of these highways, and a 5-mile stretch through a valley still exists between the old post towns of **Magome** and **Tsumago.** It's a beautiful walk, and the towns are historic relics. See "Walking the Nakasendo Highway Between Tsumago & Magome," in chapter 6.

- **Skiing in Honshu and Hokkaido:** Host of two winter Olympics (in Sapporo in 1972 and Nagano in 1998) and riddled with mountain chains, Japan is a great destination for skiing, the most popular winter sport in the country. The Japan Alps in Central Honshu and the mountains of

> **Tips Active Vacations**
>
> Want to go on a vacation where hiking, canoeing, fishing, skiing, or hunting is the focus? Head straight for **Hokkaido,** Japan's wilderness. Dameon Takada, who speaks English, organizes active vacations, which include airfare (from Tokyo), accommodations, and meals at his Japanese-style hot-spring resort on volcanic Lake Akan (see chapter 12). Write to him with a proposal and he'll tailor a trip to suit your needs. **Dameon Takada,** Hotel Emerald, 4–6–5 Akan Onsen, Akancho, Akan-gun 085-0467 (℃ **0154/ 67-2011;** fax 0154/67-2864).
>
> For more information on outdoor activities in Japan, including hiking, skiing, cycling, windsurfing, rock climbing, and even hot-spring spas, see www.outdoorjapan.com.

Tohoku and Hokkaido are common destinations. See chapters 6, 11, and 12.

If you'd rather leave the planning to someone else, join a trip sponsored by the **Shinyi Ski Club;** contact Julia Nolet, 3–6–4 Nishi Azubu, Minato-ku, Tokyo 106 (℃ **03/3423-8858** from 10am to 10pm Tokyo time; fax 03/3423-8859; jnworwor@ gol.com).

- **Cycling** (Matsuyama): Hard to believe, but you can bike from Shikoku to Hiroshima Prefecture via the 43-mile Shimanami Kaido Bridge, which is actually comprised of 10 bridges and six islands in the Seto Inland Sea. A well-maintained, dedicated biking path makes this one of Japan's best outdoor activities. See "Cycling the Shimanami Kaido Bridge," in chapter 9.
- **Shooting the Kumagawa Rapids** (Kumamoto): You can glide down one of Japan's most rapid rivers in a long, traditional wooden boat or opt for a more adventurous journey on a raft guided by professionals. Either way, the scenery is great. See "Shooting the Kumagawa Rapids," in chapter 10.
- **Swimming and Snorkeling:** Because Japan is a nation of islands you'd think swimming would be the paramount summer activity. Most of Japan's beaches, however, are unattractive and incredibly crowded. Exceptions are those in southern Kyushu. See chapter 10.
- **Fishing:** Most foreigners laugh when they see Japanese fishing spots—a stocked pool in the middle of Tokyo or a cement-banked river, lined elbow to elbow with fishermen. For more sporting conditions, head to Lake Akan in Hokkaido's **Akan National Park,** where you can fish for rainbow trout or white spotted char. See "Akanko Spa & Akan National Park," in chapter 12.

12 The Best Traditional Ryokan

- **Hiiragiya Ryokan** (Kyoto; ℃ **075/221-1136**): If ever there was an example of the quintessential ryokan, Hiiragiya is it. Located in the heart of old Kyoto, it's the ultimate in tatami luxury: a dignified enclave of polished woods and rooms with antique furnishings overlooking private gardens. Six generations of the same family have provided impeccable service and hospitality to countless guests since 1861. See p. 288.

- **Kinmata** (Kyoto; ☎ **075/ 221-1039**): Open since the early 1800s, this beautiful, traditional wooden inn in the heart of old Kyoto is now in its seventh generation of innkeepers; the present owner is a renowned kaiseki chef. With just six rooms, this ryokan is personable and intimate. See p. 289.
- **Tawaraya** (Kyoto; ☎ **075/ 211-5566**): This venerable inn has been owned and operated by the same family since it opened in the first decade of the 1700s; it's now in its 11th generation of innkeepers. Located in old Kyoto, its guest list reads like a Who's Who of visitors to Japan, including Leonard Bernstein, the king of Sweden, Alfred Hitchcock, and Saul Bellow. See p. 288.
- **Ryokan Kurashiki** (Kurashiki; ☎ **086/422-0730**): Located right beside the willow-lined canal of Kurashiki's famous historic district, this ryokan occupies an old mansion and three 250-year-old, antique-filled warehouses. It's a great place for exploring as you wander the corridors and peek into nooks and crannies, admiring all the antiques. See p. 432.
- **Mitakiso** (Hiroshima; ☎ **082/ 237-1402**): The tatami rooms of this traditional inn are spread along an exquisite landscape garden with stunted pines, ponds, Japanese maples, stone lanterns, and meandering streams. See p. 452.
- **Iwaso Ryokan** (Miyajima; ☎ **0829/44-2233**): The setting here is as romantic as you'll find anywhere in Japan. If you can afford it, stay in one of the ryokan's 80-year-old cottages, where you'll have a view of maples and a gurgling brook on one of Japan's most scenic and famous islands. If staying here doesn't make you feel like a samurai or a geisha, nothing will. See p. 459.
- **Kannawaen** (Beppu; ☎ **0977/ 66-2111**): This century-old ryokan spreads through lush and carefully tended gardens. Its tatami rooms with shoji screens look out onto hot springs, bamboo, streams, bonsai, stone lanterns, and flowers. A perfect place to escape the crowds and relax in the traditional bathhouse or the open-air hot springs. See p. 494.

13 The Best Western-Style Hotels

- **Park Hyatt Tokyo** (Tokyo; ☎ **800/233-1234** in the U.S. and Canada): Occupying the 39th to 52nd floors of a skyscraper designed by Kenzo Tange, this might well be the most gorgeous and sophisticated hotel in all of Japan, if not the world. Offering unparalleled views of the city, one of Tokyo's hottest restaurants, rooms you could live in, and legendary service, it's a must for anyone who can afford it. See p. 110.
- **Four Seasons Hotel Chinzan-so** (Tokyo; ☎ **03/3943-2222**): Surrounded by a lush, 17-acre garden, this top-rated hotel is a wonderful respite in one of the world's most crowded cities, with impeccable service and a terrific spa and health club free for hotel guests. See p. 111.
- **Nikko Kanaya Hotel** (Nikko; ☎ **0288/54-0001**): Dating from the 19th century, this rambling, old-fashioned hotel combines the rustic charm of a European country lodge with design elements of old Japan—and it's just a 15-minute walk from Toshogu Shrine. See p. 225.

- **The Fujiya Hotel** (Miyanoshita, Hakone; ✆ **0460/2-2211**): Established in 1878 and nestled on a wooded hillside, the Fujiya is one of Japan's oldest, grandest, and most majestic Western-style hotels. Resembling a Japanese ryokan from the outside, it boasts a comfortable interior of detailed woodwork, old-fashioned antique-filled guestrooms, a delightful 1930s dining hall, indoor/outdoor pools, extensive landscaping, and hot-spring baths. Staying here makes you feel like you've traveled not just to Hakone but to another decade. See p. 243.

- **Kawana Hotel** (Ito; ✆ **0557/ 45-1111**): Built in 1936 to resemble an English country estate, this relaxed yet refined hotel boasts large, manicured lawns that slope to the sea and two famous 18-hole golf courses. A great getaway from Tokyo. See p. 249.

- **Kyoto Hotel** (Kyoto; ✆ **075/ 223-2333** for reservations): First built in 1888 but now completely rebuilt as Kyoto's tallest building, this hotel nonetheless exudes an old-world atmosphere and impresses with its excellent service, a lobby designed to resemble the hotel's original 1920s ballroom,

and rooms that are the ultimate in comfort and grandeur with views over the Kamo River and Higashiyama Mountains. See p. 289.

- **Nara Hotel** (Nara; ✆ **0742/ 26-3300**): From far away, this 1909 building overlooking several ponds just a short walk from Nara Park, resembles a palace. Rooms in the main building have high ceilings with antique light fixtures and old-fashioned decor. See p. 341.

- **Ritz-Carlton** (Osaka; ✆ **800/ 241-3333** in the U.S. and Canada): This chain's first venture in Japan has the company's trademark antiques, artwork, and intimate public spaces, as well as such pluses as free access to its fitness center and large, well-appointed rooms. It's not far from Osaka Station. See p. 388.

- **Unzen Kanko Hotel** (Unzen; ✆ **0957/73-3263**): This rustic mountain lodge of ivy-covered wood and stone was built in 1935 to cater to foreigners in search of Mt. Unzen's cooler climate. It offers a casual and relaxed atmosphere, hot-spring baths, and comfortable, old-fashioned rooms not far from the Hells. See p. 546.

14 The Best Affordable Japanese-Style Places to Stay

- **Ryokan Shigetsu** (Tokyo; ✆ **03/ 3843-2345**): With a great location in the colorful and traditional Asakusa neighborhood, this modern ryokan offers simple yet elegant Japanese- and Western-style rooms, an inexpensive restaurant serving delicious Japanese meals, and a public bath with views of a pagoda. If I had relatives coming to Tokyo who wanted to stay in an inexpensive Japanese inn, this is where I'd send them. See p. 22.

- **Sumiyoshi** (Takayama; ✆ **0577/ 33-0288**): Located in the heart of Takayama on the banks of the Miyagawa River, this 90-year-old former silkworm factory features an *irori* (open-hearth fireplace) in the high-ceilinged communal room, antiques and painted screens throughout, and simple but delightfully old-fashioned tatami rooms overlooking the river. See p. 266.

- **Minshuku Shirakawago's Ogimachi:** Nestled in a narrow valley of the Japan Alps, Ogimachi is a small village of paddies, flowers, irrigation canals, and 200-year-old thatched farmhouses, about two dozen of which offer simple tatami accommodations and meals featuring local cuisine. A great, inexpensive escape. See p. 272.

- **Matsubaya Ryokan** (Kyoto; ✆ **075/351-3727** or 075/351-4268): Opened in 1885 and owned and managed by friendly Mrs. Hayabashi, the fifth generation of innkeepers, this wooden ryokan has rooms with balconies facing a miniature inner courtyard and rooms facing a tiny enclosed garden. See p. 286.

- **Seikan-so** (Nara; ✆ **0742/22-2670**): Although this 80-year-old ryokan is beginning to show its age, it has something no other accommodation in this price range offers: a beautiful landscaped garden of manicured azalea bushes, trees, and flowers. It's also within walking distance of Nara Park. See p. 341.

- **Temple Accommodations on Mt. Koya:** If your vision of Japan includes temples, towering cypress trees, shaven monks, and religious chanting at the crack of dawn, head for the religious sanctuary atop Mt. Koya, where some 50 Buddhist temples offer tatami accommodations—some with garden views—and two vegetarian meals a day. See "The Temples of Mt. Koya," in chapter 8.

- **International Villas** (Okayama Prefecture): Financed and maintained by Okayama Prefecture, International Villas are six

exceptional—and exceptionally inexpensive—accommodations in delightful rural settings. One, located in a mountain village, is modeled after a traditional soy-sauce warehouse; two are in 19th century–renovated thatched farmhouses; two more are in open and airy modern buildings with views of the Seto Inland Sea; and the last is at a hot-spring spa. See "Countryside Delights: Okayama Prefecture's International Villas," in chapter 8.

- **Miyajima Morinoyado** (Miyajima; ✆ **0829/44-0430**): This public people's lodge on picturesque Miyajima island is modern yet traditional and would easily cost four times as much if it were privately owned. See p. 460.

- **Matsushima Kanko Hotel** (Matsushima; ✆ **022/354-2121**): Popularly known as Matsushima-jo because it looks like a castle, Matsushima's oldest ryokan is a delightful airy building with a traditional tiled roof, red railings, and inexpensive, simple rooms. Nowadays, most Japanese seem to prefer the town's newer and more luxurious hotels, but no place better conveys the town's past than this. See p. 555.

- **Tsuru-no-yu Onsen** (Nyuto Onsen; ✆ **0187/46-2139**): This rustic inn, with a history stretching back to the Edo Period, thatched-roof building, and outdoor hot-spring baths, is as close as you can get to time travel. To really save money, opt for the self-cooking wing and prepare your own meals. See p. 562.

15 The Best Culinary Experiences

- **Experiencing a Kaiseki Feast:** The ultimate in Japanese cuisine, *kaiseki* is a feast for the senses and

the spirit. Consisting of a variety of exquisitely prepared and arranged dishes, a kaiseki meal is a multi-course event to be savored slowly. Both the ingredients and the dishes they comprise are chosen with great care to complement the season. There are hundreds of exceptional kaiseki restaurants in Japan, from old-world traditional to sleek modern; two standouts are **Takamura** in Tokyo and **Kagetsu** in Nagasaki. Traditional ryokan also serve kaiseki. See chapters 3 and 10 and "Japanese Cuisine," in appendix A.

- **Spending an Evening in a Robatayaki:** Harking back to the olden days when the Japanese cooked over an open fireplace, a *robatayaki* is a convivial place for a meal and drinks. One of the most famous is **Inakaya** in Tokyo, where diners sit at a counter; on the other side are two cooks, grills, and mountains of food. You'll love the drama of this place. See chapter 3 and "Japanese Cuisine," in appendix A.

- **Dining on Western Food in Modern Settings:** Japan has no lack of great Western food, and some of the best places to dine are at its first-class hotels. The **New York Grill,** on the 52nd floor of the Park Hyatt in Tokyo, epitomizes the best of the West with its sophisticated setting, great views, great food, and great jazz. See p. 143.

- **Buying Prepared Meals at a Department Store:** The basement floors of department stores are almost always devoted to foodstuffs including take-out foods. Shopping for your meal is a fun experience: Hawkers yell their wares, samples are set out for you to nibble, and you can choose anything from tempura and sushi to boxed meals. See chapter 4, the regional chapters, and "Japanese Cuisine," in appendix A.

- **Slurping Noodles in a Noodle Shop:** You're supposed to slurp when eating Japanese noodles, which are prepared in almost as many different ways as there are regions. Noodle shops range from standup counters to traditional restaurants; one of my favorites is **Raitei** in Kamakura. See p. 220, "Japanese Cuisine," in appendix A, and the "Where to Dine" sections in regional chapters

- **Rubbing Elbows in a Yakitori-ya:** Yakitori-ya are the pubs of Japan—usually tiny affairs with just a counter, serving up skewered grilled chicken. They're a good place to meet the natives and are inexpensive as well. You'll find them in every nightlife district in the country. See the regional chapters and "Japanese Cuisine," in appendix A.

16 The Best Destinations for Serious Shoppers

- **For Everything:** Japanese department stores are microcosms of practically everything Japan produces, from the food halls in the basement to departments selling clothing, accessories, office supplies, souvenirs, pottery, household goods, and cameras to rooftop garden centers. What's more, service is great—one of the many sales clerks on hand will take your money and return with your change and a beautifully wrapped package. You'll be spoiled for life. See "Shopping," in chapter 4.

- **For Designer Fashions:** Tokyo's **Shibuya District** has the most designer boutiques in town, while **Aoyama** boasts main shops for all the big-name designers, including Issey Miyake and lines from Comme des Garçons. Department stores also carry big-name designers; their annual summer sales are mob scenes. See "Shopping," in chapter 4.

- **For Souvenirs:** The Japanese are avid souvenir shoppers when they travel, so souvenirs are sold literally everywhere, even near shrines and temples. **Nakamise Dori,** a pedestrian lane leading to Tokyo's Sensoji Temple, is one of Japan's most colorful places to shop for paper umbrellas, toys, and other souvenirs. The two best places for one-stop memento shopping are the **Oriental Bazaar** (p. 195) in Tokyo and the **Kyoto Handicraft Center** (p. 331), both of which offer several floors of everything from fans to woodblock prints.

- **For Traditional Crafts:** Japan treasures its artisans so highly that it designates the best as National Living Treasures. The two best shops for a varied inventory of traditional crafts, from knives and baskets to lacquerware and ceramics, are the **Japan Traditional Craft Center** in Tokyo and the **Kyoto Craft Center.** Department stores also offer an excellent collection of traditional crafts. See "Shopping" in chapters 4 and 7.

- **For Antiques and Curios:** Flea markets are great for browsing; you'll see everything from used kimono to Edo-Era teapots for sale. Japan's largest and one of its oldest monthly markets is at **Toji Temple** in Kyoto, held the 21st of each month (with a lesser flea market held the first Sun of each month). **Tokyo** also has great weekend markets. See chapters 4 and 7.

- **For Electronics:** Looking for that perfect digital camera, CD player, calculator, or rice cooker? Then join everyone else in the country by going to one of the nation's two largest electronics and electrical-appliance districts. In Tokyo, it's **Akihabara,** where open-fronted shops beckon up to 50,000 weekday shoppers with whirring fans, blaring radios, and sales pitches. In Osaka, head to **Den Den Town.** Be sure to comparison shop and bargain. See "Shopping," in chapters 4 and 8.

- **For Kitchenware: Kappabashi-dougugai Dori** in Tokyo and **Doguya-suji Street** in Osaka are the nation's largest wholesale districts for restaurant items: dishes, trays, lacquerware, disposable chopsticks, *noren* (shop-door curtains), even those plastic-food displays you see in restaurant windows. Stock up for your next party. See chapters 4 and 8.

- **For Local Specialties:** Many prefecture capitals have a government-owned exhibition hall where local products are on display for sale. Often called a *kanko bussankan,* the hall may have everything from locally produced pottery to folk toys and foodstuffs. Cities with kanko bussankan include **Kanazawa, Okayama, Matsuyama, Kumamoto,** and **Kagoshima.** If you don't have time to go to the cities themselves, drop by their Tokyo branch offices near Tokyo Station—many have local products for sale in addition to tourist brochures. See chapters 4, 8, 9, and 10.

- **For Porcelain and Pottery:** Pottery and porcelain is produced seemingly everywhere in Japan. Some of the more famous centers include **Nagoya,** home to Noritake, Japan's largest chinaware company; **Matsuyama,** famous for its Tobe pottery (white porcelain with cobalt-blue designs); and **Kagoshima** with its Satsuma pottery, which comes in white (used by the upper class in feudal Japan) and black (used by the common people). See chapters 8, 9 and 10.

2

Planning Your Trip to Japan

This book is designed to guide you through your own discoveries of Japan, however brief or extended your visit may be. From experience, I know that the two biggest concerns for visitors to Japan are the language barrier and the high cost of living. To help alleviate fears about the first, I've provided the Japanese symbols for establishments that do not have English signs so you can recognize their names (see appendix C), given brief instructions on how to reach most of the places I recommend, made suggestions for ordering in restaurants without English menus, and provided prices for everything from subway rides to admission to museums.

As for costs, probably everyone has heard horror stories about Japan's high prices. After the dramatic fall of the dollar against the yen in the 1980s and 1990s, Tokyo did indeed become one of the world's most expensive cities, with food and lodging costing as much as in New York or London, maybe more. But since Japan's economic bubble burst more than a decade ago, something happened that would have been unthinkable during the heady spending days of the 1980s—the Japanese became bargain-conscious. There are now inexpensive French bistros, secondhand clothing stores, and hotels that haven't raised their rates in more than 7 years. Some hotels and restaurants—in a desperate bid to stay alive—have even lowered their prices.

Still, it's difficult not to suffer an initial shock about Japan's high prices, which will seem especially exorbitant if you insist on living and eating exactly as you do back home. The secret is to live and eat as the Japanese do. This book will help you do exactly that, with descriptions of out-of-the-way eateries and Japanese-style inns that cater to the native population. By following this book's advice and exercising a little caution on your own, you should be able to cut down on needless expenses and learn even more about Japan in the process. While you may never find Japan cheap, you'll find it richly rewarding for all the reasons you chose Japan as a destination in the first place.

Despite the difficulties inherent in visiting any foreign country, I think you'll find Japan very easy to navigate. There are many more signs in English than there were even just a decade ago. And Japan remains one of the safest countries in the world; in general, you don't have to worry about muggers, pickpockets, or crooks. In fact, I sometimes feel downright coddled in Japan. Everything runs like clockwork: Subway trains are on time, all the public telephones work, and the service—whether in hotels, restaurants, or department stores—ranks among the best in the world. I know if I get truly lost, someone will help me and will probably even go out of his or her way to do so. The Japanese are honest and extremely helpful toward foreign visitors. Indeed, it's the people themselves who make traveling in Japan such a delight.

This chapter will help you with the what, when, where, and how of travel to Japan—from what documents you should take with you to how to get around easily and economically.

Japan

1 The Regions in Brief

Separated from mainland China and Korea by the Sea of Japan, the nation of Japan stretches in an arc about 1,800 miles long from northeast to southwest, yet it is only 250 miles wide at its broadest point. Japan consists primarily of four main islands—**Honshu, Hokkaido, Shikoku,** and **Kyushu.** Surrounding these large islands are more than 4,000 smaller islands and islets, most of them uninhabited; farther to the south are the **Okinawan islands,** perhaps best known for the fierce fighting that took place there during World War II and for their continued (and controversial) use as an American military base. If you were to superimpose Japan's four main islands onto a map of the United States, they would stretch all the way from Maine down to Florida, which should give you an idea of the diversity of Japan's climate, flora, and scenery—Hokkaido in the north is subarctic, while southern Kyushu is subtropical. Honshu, Japan's most populous island and home to Tokyo, Kyoto, and Osaka, is connected to the other three islands by tunnel or bridge, which means you can travel to all four islands by train.

As much as 75% of Japan consists of **mountains.** They are found on all four main islands and most are volcanic in origin. Altogether, there are some 265 **volcanoes,** more than 30 of them still considered active. Mt. Fuji (on Honshu), dormant since 1707, is Japan's highest and most famous volcano, while Mt. Aso (on Kyushu) boasts the largest caldera in the world. Because of its volcanic origins, earthquakes have plagued Japan throughout its history. In the 20th century, the two most destructive earthquakes were the 1923 Great Kanto Earthquake, which killed more than 100,000 people in the Tokyo area, and the 1995 Great Hanshin Earthquake, which claimed more than 6,000 lives in Kobe.

Japan is divided into 47 regional divisions, or **prefectures.** Each prefecture has its own prefectural capital and is comparable to the U.S. state or the British county. Japan's total land mass is slightly smaller than California in area, yet Japan has almost half the population of the United States. And because ¾ of Japan is mountainous and therefore uninhabitable, its people are concentrated primarily in only 10% of the country's landmass, with the rest of the area devoted to agriculture. In other words, imagine almost half the U.S. population living in California—primarily in San Diego County—and you get an idea of how crowded Japan is. For this island nation—isolated physically from the rest of the world; struck repeatedly through the centuries by earthquakes, fires, and typhoons; and possessed of only limited space for harmonious living—geography and topography have played a major role both in determining its development and in shaping its culture, customs, and arts.

HONSHU

Of the four main islands, Honshu is the largest and most populated. Because it's also the most important historically and culturally, it's where most visitors spend the bulk of their time.

KANTO DISTRICT

Located in east-central Honshu and comprising metropolitan **Tokyo** and six prefectures, this district is characterized by the Kanto Plain, the largest flatland in Japan. Although development of the district didn't begin in earnest until the establishment of the shogunate government in Edo (present-day Tokyo) in 1603, Tokyo and surrounding giants like **Yokohama** and its port make this the most densely populated region in Japan.

KANSAI DISTRICT

Also called the Kinki District and encompassing seven prefectures, this is Japan's most historic region. **Nara** and **Kyoto**—two of Japan's ancient capitals—are here, as are two of Japan's most important port cities, **Kobe** and **Osaka.** With the opening of Kansai International Airport outside Osaka in 1994, many foreign visitors now opt to bypass Tokyo altogether in favor of Kansai's many historic spots, including **Mt. Koya** with its many temples, **Himeji** with what I consider to be Japan's most beautiful castle, **Ise-Shima National Park** with Japan's most revered Shinto shrine, Nara with its Great Buddha and temples, and, of course, Kyoto, the former capital for more than 1,000 years with so many temples, imperial villas, and gardens that it ranks as Japan's foremost tourist destination.

CHUBU DISTRICT

The Chubu (Central) District lies between Tokyo and Kyoto and straddles central Honshu from the Pacific Ocean to the Japan Sea, encompassing nine prefectures. **Nagoya,** Japan's fourth-largest city, is Chubu's most important city and a gateway to its other destinations. The district is marked by great variety—mountain ranges (including the **Japan Alps,** see below), volcanoes (including **Mt. Fuji**), large rivers, and coastal regions on both sides of the island. It's popular for skiing and hiking, for quaint mountain villages such as **Takayama,** and for tourist attractions that include the open-air Museum Meiji Mura (near Nagoya), the castle in **Matsumoto,** and Kenrokuen Garden in **Kanazawa,** considered one of Japan's finest.

THE JAPAN ALPS

Spreading over central Honshu in the Chubu District, the Japan Alps are among Japan's most famous mountain ranges, especially since hosting the 1998 XVIII Winter Olympics in **Nagano. Chubu-Sangaku National Park** (also called the Japan Alps National Park) contains some of the nation's most beautiful mountain scenery, while destinations like **Takayama** and **Shirakawago** provide everything from quaint historic districts to thatched-roof farmhouses.

ISE-SHIMA

Shima Peninsula, in Mie Prefecture, juts out into the Seto Inland Sea and is famous for **Ise-Shima National Park,** noted for its coastal scenery and Ise Jingu Shrines. **Toba,** birthplace of the cultured pearl, is popular for its Mikimoto Pearl Island and the Toba Aquarium. Shima Peninsula also boasts two theme parks, one fashioned after Japan's Warring States Era and the other an amusement park with a Spanish theme.

CHUGOKU DISTRICT

Honshu's western district has five prefectures and is divided by the Chugoku Mountain Range. Industrial giants such as **Hiroshima** and **Okayama** lead as the major cities, drawing tourists with reconstructed castles, Korakuen Garden, and the sobering Peace Memorial Park in Hiroshima, dedicated to victims of the world's first atomic bomb. **Kurashiki** is a must for its photogenic, historic warehouse district, while **Miyajima,** part of the Seto-Naikai (Inland Sea) National Park, is considered one of Japan's most beautiful islands.

TOHOKU DISTRICT

Northeastern Honshu, with **Sendai** as its regional center, encompasses six prefectures. Known as the Tohoku District, it isn't nearly as developed as the central and southern districts of Honshu, due in large part to its rugged, mountainous terrain and harsh climate. **Matsushima,** about halfway up the coast between Tokyo and the tip of Honshu, is the district's major tourist destination; with its pine-clad islets dotting the bay, it's considered one of Japan's most scenic spots. **Kakunodate,** located inland, is a former castle town offering preserved samurai houses and, during cherry blossom season, a stunning show of pink flowers to travelers willing to take a road less traveled. **Towada-Hachimantai National Park,** which extends over three prefectures, boasts scenic lakes, rustic hotspring spas, hiking, and skiing.

SHIKOKU

Shikoku, the smallest of the four main islands, is fairly undeveloped and off the beaten path for many foreign visitors. It's famous for its 88 Buddhist temples founded by one of Japan's most interesting historical figures, the Buddhist priest Kukai, known posthumously as Kobo Daishi. Other major attractions are Ritsurin Park in **Takamatsu,** Matsuyama Castle in **Matsuyama,** and **Dogo Spa,** one of Japan's oldest hot-spring spas. For active travelers, the **Shimanami Kaido Bridge** offers 43 scenic miles of dedicated biking trails that connect Shikoku with Hiroshima via six islands in the Seto Inland Sea.

KYUSHU

The southernmost of the four main islands, Kyushu boasts a mild subtropical climate, active volcanoes, and hotspring spas. Because it's the closest to Korea and China, Kyushu served as a gateway to the continental mainland throughout much of Japan's history, later becoming the springboard for both traders and Christian missionaries from the West. **Fukuoka,** Kyushu's largest city, serves as the rail gateway from Honshu, dispersing travelers to hot springs in **Beppu, Unzen,** and **Ibusuki** and to such major attractions as Kumamoto Castle in **Kumamoto** and Iso Garden in **Kagoshima. Nagasaki,** victim of the world's second atomic bomb, is one of Japan's most cosmopolitan cities and one of my favorites. In recent years, Kyushu has become a major destination for tourists from Taiwan, Korea, and Hong Kong, who flock to the region's many theme parks including Ocean Dome in **Miyazaki** and Huis Ten Bosch outside Nagasaki.

HOKKAIDO

Japan's second-largest island, Hokkaido lies to the north of Honshu and is regarded as the country's last frontier with wide-open pastures, evergreen forests, mountains, gorges, crystal-clear lakes, and wildlife, much of it preserved in national parks. Originally occupied by the indigenous Ainu, it became colonized by Japanese settlers mostly after the Meiji Restoration in 1868. Today it's home to 5.6 million people, 1.6 million of whom live in **Sapporo.** With a land mass that accounts for 22% of Japan's total area, Hokkaido has the nation's lowest population density: less than 5% of the total population. That, together with the island's cold, severe winters but mild summers and its unspoiled natural beauty, makes this island a nature-lover's paradise.

2 Visitor Information

The **Japan National Tourist Organization (JNTO)** publishes a wealth of free, colorful brochures and maps covering Japan as a whole, Tokyo, and various regions of the country. For general information about Japan, ask for "Your Traveling Companion," which includes "Tips for Budget Travel" and money-saving advice on traveling, lodging, and dining in the Tokyo and Kansai areas; and "The Tourist's Language Handbook," a phrase booklet to help foreign visitors communicate with the Japanese. JNTO even has a free reservation service for select budget hotels and

Japanese-style inns throughout Japan, several of which are reviewed in this guide; ask for the latest "Directory of Welcome Inns" pamphlet. JNTO has offices in the following locations.

In the **United States:** 401 N. Michigan Ave., Suite 770, Chicago, IL 60611 (© **312/222-0874;** info@jntochi.org); 515 S. Figueroa, Suite 1470, Los Angeles, CA 90071 (© **213/623-1952;** info@jnto-lax.org); One Rockefeller Plaza, Suite 1250, New York, NY 10020 (© **212/757-5640;** info@jntonyc.org); and 1 Daniel Burnham Court, Suite 250C, San Francisco, CA 94109 (© **415/292-5686;** info@jntosf.org).

In **Canada:** 165 University Ave., Toronto, ON M5H 3B8, Canada (© **416/366-7140;** info@jntoyyz.com).

In the **United Kingdom:** Heathcoat House, 20 Savile Row, London W1X 1AE, England (© **020/7734-9638;** www.seejapan.co.uk).

In **Australia:** Level 33, The Chifley Tower, 2 Chifley Sq., Sydney, NSW 2000, Australia (© **02/9232-4522**).

THE JNTO ONLINE   You can also reach JNTO via the Internet at **www.jnto.go.jp**, where you can read up on what's new, view maps of more than 20 major cities, check train and flight schedules and fares around Japan, get the latest weather report, and browse through information ranging from reasonable accommodations and hints on budget travel to regional events, museums, and attractions. By clicking on "Reasonable Accommodations," you can even request a reservation at one of the participating Welcome Inn accommodations (described later in "Tips on Accommodations").

THE JNTO IN JAPAN   In Japan, your best bet for general or specific information is at one of the JNTO's four excellent **Tourist Information Centers (TICs).** The TIC maintains offices in Tokyo and Kyoto as well as at Narita Airport outside Tokyo and at Kansai International Airport outside Osaka (see chapters 4, 8, and 9 for locations and open hours). All distribute leaflets on destinations throughout Japan that are not available at the destinations themselves. (If you're going to Hiroshima, for example, you can get JNTO's "Hiroshima and Miyajima" leaflet only at a TIC.) They also can provide train, bus, and ferry schedules and leaflets on major attractions and sights—for example, Japanese gardens, Japanese hot springs, and museums and art galleries. Unfortunately, these leaflets are almost never available at the destinations themselves, so be sure to pick them up at a TIC before beginning your journey. JNTO maintains a toll-free Japan **Travel-Phone,** available daily from 9am to 5pm at © **0088/22-4800** everywhere except Tokyo and Kyoto. In Tokyo, call © **03/3201-3331** (not available Sat afternoons, Sun, and national holidays); in Kyoto, call © **075/371-5649.** From these two cities, you must pay for the local call.

LOCAL INFORMATION   You'll also find locally run tourist offices in nearly all cities and towns, most of them conveniently located at or near the main train station. Look for the logo of a red question mark with the word "information" written below. Although the staff at a particular tourist office may not speak English (many do), they can point you in the direction of your hotel, perhaps provide you with a map in English, and, in many cases, even make hotel bookings for you. Note, however, that they're not equipped to provide you with information on other regions of Japan (for that, go to a TIC). I've included information on local tourist offices throughout this book including how to reach them when disembarking from the train and their open hours; see "Visitor Information," in the regional chapters.

3 Entry Requirements & Customs

ENTRY REQUIREMENTS

Americans traveling to Japan as tourists with the intention of staying 90 days or less need only a valid passport to enter the country; visa requirements have been waived by a reciprocal visa-exemption agreement.

Note that only American *tourists* don't need a visa—that is, those in the country for sightseeing, sports activities, family visits, inspection tours, business meetings, or short study courses. Tourists cannot work in Japan or engage in any remunerative activity including the teaching of English (though many young people ignore the law). No extensions of stay are granted, which means American tourists must absolutely leave the country after 90 days. If you're going to Japan to work or to study for longer than 90 days, you'll need a visa; contact the Japanese embassy or consulate nearest you.

Australians and **New Zealanders** do not need a visa for stays of up to 90 days. **Canadians** can stay up to three months without a visa, while citizens of the **United Kingdom** and **Ireland** can stay for up to 6 months without a visa.

CUSTOMS

WHAT YOU CAN BRING INTO JAPAN If you're 20 or older, you can bring duty-free into Japan up to 400 non-Japanese cigarettes, 500 grams of tobacco, or 100 cigars; three bottles (760cc each) of alcohol; and 2 ounces of perfume. You can also bring in gifts and souvenirs whose total market value is less than ¥200,000 ($1,667).

WHAT YOU CAN TAKE HOME Returning **U.S. citizens** who have been away for 48 hours or more are allowed to bring back, once every 30 days, $400 worth of merchandise duty-free including (for those 21 and older) 1 liter of wine or spirits. Beyond that, the next $1,000 worth of goods is assessed at a flat rate of 10% duty. Be sure to have your receipts handy. For packages, you're allowed to send per day by mail up to $200 worth of goods to yourself duty free; mark the package "Personal Purchases." You can also mail to other people up to $100 worth of goods per day; mark the package "Unsolicited Gift." You cannot bring fresh foodstuffs into the United States; tinned foods, however, are allowed. For more information, check the **U.S. Customs Service** website at **www.customs.gov** or write to them at P.O. Box 7407, Washington, DC 20044 to request the free pamphlet "Know Before You Go."

Citizens of the U.K. returning from Japan have a Customs allowance of 200 cigarettes; 2 liters of still table wine and 1 liter of spirits or strong liqueurs (over 22% volume) *or* 2 liters of fortified or sparkling wine; 60cc (ml) perfume; 250cc (ml) of toilet water; and £145 worth of all other goods including gifts and souvenirs. People under 17 cannot have the tobacco or alcohol allowance. For more information, contact **HM Customs & Excise House,** Berkeley House, 304 Regents Park Rd., Finchley, London N3 2JY (© **020/ 7865-4400;** www.hmce.gov.uk/).

For a clear summary of the rules for **Canadian citizens,** write for the booklet "I Declare" issued by **Revenue Canada,** 2265 St. Laurent Blvd., Ottawa K1G 4KE (© **800/461-9999** or 613/993-0534; www.ccra-adrc. gc.ca). Canada allows its citizens a C$750 exemption if you're gone for 7 days or longer (C$200 if you're gone between 48 hours and 7 days), and you're allowed to bring back duty-free 200 cigarettes, 50 cigars, and 1.5 liters of wine (or 1.14 liters of liquor or 8.5 liters of beer). In addition, you're

Tips An Important Note

At all times foreigners are required to carry either their passports or, for those who have been granted longer stays, their alien registration cards. The police generally do not stop foreigners, but if you're caught without the proper identification, you'll be taken to the local police headquarters. It happened to me once, and believe me, I can think of better ways to spend an hour and a half than explaining in detail who I was, what I was doing in Japan, where I lived, and what I planned on doing for the rest of my life. Safeguard your passport in an inconspicuous, inaccessible place like a money belt. If you lose it, visit the nearest consulate of your native country as soon as possible for a replacement.

allowed to mail gifts to Canada from abroad at the rate of C$60 a day, provided they're unsolicited and don't contain alcohol or tobacco. (Write on the package "Unsolicited gift, under $60 value").

The duty-free allowance for **Australian citizens** is A$400 or, for those under 18, A$200. Returning citizens can bring in 250 cigarettes or 250 grams of loose tobacco as well as 1,125ml of alcohol. If you're returning with valuable goods you already own, such as foreign-made cameras, you should file form B263. A helpful brochure, available from Australian consulates or Customs offices, is "Know Before You Go." For more information, contact **Australian Customs Services,** GPO Box 8, Sydney

NSW 2001 (© **1300-363-263;** www.customs.gov.au).

The duty-free allowance for **New Zealand citizens** is NZ$700. Citizens over 17 can bring in 200 cigarettes, 50 cigars, or 250 grams of tobacco (or a mixture of all three if their combined weight doesn't exceed 250 grams) plus 4.5 liters of wine *or* beer and 1.125 liters of liquor. New Zealand currency does not carry import or export restrictions. Most questions are answered in a free pamphlet available at New Zealand consulates and Customs offices, "Advice to Travellers." For more information, contact **New Zealand Customs,** 17-21 Whitmore St., Box 2218, Wellington (© **800/ 428-786,** or 04/473-6099; www. customs.govt.nz).

4 Money

CURRENCY The currency in Japan is called the *yen,* symbolized by ¥. Coins come in denominations of ¥1, ¥5, ¥10, ¥50, ¥100, and ¥500. Bills come in denominations of ¥1,000, ¥2,000, ¥5,000, and ¥10,000. You'll find all coins get used, and you'll want to keep plenty of change handy for riding local transportation such as buses or streetcars. Although change machines are virtually everywhere, even on buses where you can change larger coins and

¥1,000 bills, you'll find it faster to have the exact amount on hand.

Although the **conversion rate** varies daily and can fluctuate dramatically, the prices in this book are based on the rate of US$1 to ¥120, or ¥100 to US83¢.

Personal checks are not used in Japan. Most Japanese pay with either credit cards or cash—and because the country overall has such a low crime rate, you can feel safe walking around with money (though of course you

The Japanese Yen

For American Readers At this writing $1 = approximately ¥120, or ¥100 = 83¢. This was the rate of exchange used to calculate the dollar values given in this guide (rounded off to the nearest nickel for prices less than $10 and to the nearest dollar for prices more than $10). To roughly figure the price of something in dollars, calculate $8 for every ¥1,000 or multiply the yen amount by .008. For example, if something costs ¥2,000, that's approximately $16, which is close to the actual $16.65.

For British Readers At this writing £1 = approximately ¥175, or ¥100 = 57p; this was the rate of exchange used to calculate the pound values in the table below. The Euro is approximately worth ¥110.

¥	U.S.$	U.K.£	¥	U.S.$	U.K.£
10	.08	.06	1,500	12.50	8.55
25	.21	.14	2,000	16.65	11.45
50	.42	.28	2,500	20.85	14.30
75	.62	.43	3,000	25.00	17.15
100	.83	.57	4,000	33.35	22.85
200	1.65	1.15	5,000	41.65	28.55
300	2.50	1.70	6,000	50.00	34.30
400	3.35	2.30	7,000	58.35	40.00
500	4.15	2.85	8,000	66.65	45.70
600	5.00	3.45	9,000	75.00	51.45
700	5.85	4.00	10,000	83.35	57.15
800	6.65	4.55	15,000	125.00	85.70
900	7.50	5.15	20,000	166.65	114.30
1,000	8.35	5.70	25,000	208.35	142.85

A note on exchange rates: The most difficult task of writing a guide is to set the rate of exchange, especially for Japan; if I could advise you accurately on the future exchange rate, I'd be too rich to be a guidebook writer. Since these rates will surely fluctuate, check the rate again when you travel to Japan and use this table only as an approximate guide.

should always exercise caution). The only time you really need to be alert to possible pickpockets in Japan is when you're riding a crowded subway during rush hour or walking in heavily visited areas of Tokyo.

In any case, I suggest you bring some cash and traveler's checks (for those times when you might not have access to an ATM), but the bulk of your expenses can be paid with credit cards, including cash advances.

CURRENCY EXCHANGE You can exchange money at both **Narita** and **Kansai international airports.** In addition, all **banks** displaying an AUTHORIZED FOREIGN EXCHANGE sign can exchange currency, and exchange rates usually are displayed at the appropriate foreign-exchange counter. Banks are generally open Monday through Friday from 9am to 3pm, though business hours for exchanging foreign currency usually don't begin until 10:30 or 11am. If you need to exchange money outside of banking hours, inquire at one of the larger first-class **hotels**—some of them may cash traveler's checks or exchange money even if you're not their guest (you'll need to show your passport.) Likewise, large **department stores** in major cities also offer exchange services and are often open until 7:30 or 8pm. Note, however, that hotels and department stores may charge a handling fee, offer a slightly less favorable exchange rate, and require a passport for all transactions.

TRAVELER'S CHECKS Traveler's checks (which you can get before leaving home at almost any bank) in U.S. dollar and other denominations can be exchanged for yen at most banks with exchange services and at major hotels throughout Japan, but note that you'll need your passport every time you cash a check. Traveler's checks have a slight advantage in that they generally fetch a better exchange rate than cash; they also offer protection in case of theft and are useful for obtaining cash if ATMs are not easily accessible. Note, however, that in some very remote areas, even banks won't cash them. Before taking off for small towns, be sure you have enough cash with you.

CREDIT CARDS Credit cards are convenient for obtaining cash and for paying for accommodations, meals at expensive restaurants, and major purchases. The exchange rate is better than what you can get for either cash or traveler's checks at a bank (though fees charged by your bank or credit card company may cancel any real savings; before going abroad, ask your card issuer how it calculates the exchange rate and about applicable fees). They are a safe way to carry money and provide a convenient record of all your expenses.

The most readily accepted cards are **MasterCard** (also called Eurocard), **Visa,** and the Japanese credit card **JCB** (Japan Credit Bank); many tourist-oriented facilities also accept **American Express** and **Diners Club.** Shops and restaurants accepting credit and charge cards will usually post which cards they accept at the door or near the cash register. However, some establishments may be reluctant to accept cards for small purchases and inexpensive meals; inquire beforehand. In addition, note that the vast majority of Japan's smaller and least-expensive businesses—many restaurants, noodle shops, fast-food joints, mom-and-pop establishments, and some of the cheapest accommodations—as well as Japanese-style inns that may charge upward of more than $150 a night per person, do not accept credit cards.

GETTING CASH USING YOUR CREDIT CARD OR BANK ATM CARD You can also use bank-issued credit cards and ATM cards to get cash. Because most ATM machines in Japan accept only cards issued by Japanese banks, your best bet for obtaining cash is at a **post office.** All 21,000 post offices across Japan accept foreign bankcards operating on the Cirrus (MasterCard) or PLUS (Visa) systems. The catch is that even though the ATM may be located outside the main postal transaction area, machines are operable only limited hours (depending on the bank, that may be until 6 or 7pm weekdays and up to 5pm on weekends). Besides post offices, other places with ATMs that might accept foreign-issued cards include **Citibank** (which usually accepts both Visa and MasterCard and sometimes American Express as well), **large department stores,** and **airports.** Ask the local tourist office for the most convenient location. Note that there is no public American Express office in Japan.

To obtain cash from an ATM or credit card, you must have a personal identification number (PIN). If you've forgotten your PIN number or didn't even know you had one, call the phone number on the back of your card and ask the bank to send it to you. If you already have a PIN, it's a good idea to check with your card issuer to be certain your PIN will work in Japan. Ask, too, for a list of banks that will honor your card.

This goes also for bankcards using the Plus, Cirrus, or other ATM system for cash withdrawal. ATMs are linked to a national network that most likely includes your bank at home. **Cirrus,** accepted at ATMs linked to Master-Card (© **800/424-7787;** www.mastercard.com), and **PLUS,** linked with Visa (© **800/843-7587;** www.visa.com), are the two most popular networks; check the back of your ATM card to see which network your bank belongs to. Ask your bank for a list of places where your ATM card can be used in Japan or use the 800 numbers and websites above to locate ATMs in your destination.

5 When to Go

CLIMATE   Most of Japan's islands lie in a temperate seasonal wind zone similar to the East Coast of the United States, which means there are four distinct seasons. The Japanese are very proud of their seasons; they place much more emphasis on the seasons than people do in the West. Kimono, dishes and bowls used for kaiseki, and even Noh plays, change with the season. Certain foods are eaten during certain times of the year such as eel in summer and fugu in winter. Almost all haiku have seasonal references. The cherry blossom signals the beginning of spring, and most festivals are tied to seasonal rites. Even urban dwellers note the seasons; almost as though on cue, businessmen will change virtually overnight from their winter to summer attire.

Because Japan's four main islands stretch in an arc from northeast to southwest at about the same latitudes as Boston and Atlanta, you can travel in the country at virtually any time of year. Winters in southern Kyushu are mild, while summers in northern Hokkaido are cool. In addition, there's no rainy season in Hokkaido.

Summer, which begins in June, is heralded by the rainy season, which lasts from about mid-June to mid-July. Although it doesn't rain every day, it does rain a lot, sometimes quite heavily, and umbrellas are imperative. You'll also be more comfortable in light cottons, though you should bring a light jacket for unexpected cool evenings or air-conditioned rooms. As you walk through all the puddles, remember that this is when Japan's farmers are out planting rice seedlings. After the rain stops, it turns very hot (in the 80s) and uncomfortably humid throughout the country, with the exception of the northern island of Hokkaido, such mountain-top resorts as Hakone, and the Japan Alps. If you're not used to high heat and humidity, try to stay out of the sun during the hottest time of the day and be sure to drink plenty of liquids.

The period from the end of August through September is **typhoon season,** although most storms stay out at sea and generally vent their fury on land only in thunderstorms.

Autumn, which lasts until about November, is one of the best times to travel in Japan. The days are pleasant and slightly cool, with the changing reds and scarlets of leaves giving brilliant contrast to the deep-blue skies. There are also many chrysanthemum shows in Japan at this time, popular maple-viewing spots, and many autumn festivals. Be sure to pack a jacket in autumn.

Winter, lasting from December to March, is marked by snow in much of Japan, especially in the mountain ranges where the skiing is superb. Many tourists also flock to hot-spring resorts. The climate is generally dry, and on the Pacific coast the skies are often blue. Tokyo, where the mean winter temperature is about 40°F, doesn't get much snow, though it can be crisp and cold. Northern Japan's weather, in Tohoku and Hokkaido, can be quite severe, while southern Japan, especially Kyushu, enjoys generally mild, warm weather. Wherever you are, you'd be wise to bring a coat and warm clothing.

Spring arrives with a magnificent fanfare of plum and cherry blossoms in March and April, an exquisite time when all of Japan is ablaze in whites and pinks. The **cherry-blossom season** starts in southern Kyushu toward the end of March and reaches northern Japan about mid-April. The blossoms themselves last only a few days, symbolizing to the Japanese the fragile nature of beauty and of life itself. Other flowers also bloom through May or June, including azaleas and irises, and there are numerous festivals throughout Japan celebrating the rebirth of nature.

Tokyo's Average Daytime Temperatures & Rainfall

	Jan	Feb	Mar	Apr	May	June	July	Aug	Sept	Oct	Nov	Dec
Temp. (°F)	37	39	45	54	65	71	77	80	73	62	51	41
Temp. (°C)	3	4	7	13	18	22	25	27	23	17	11	5
Days of Rain	4.3	6.1	8.9	10	9.6	12.1	10	8.2	10.9	8.9	6.4	3.8

BUSY SEASONS The Japanese have a passion for travel, and they all generally travel at the same time, resulting in jam-packed trains and hotels. The worst times of year to travel in Japan are the **New Year's** period, from December 27 to January 4; **Golden Week,** from April 29 to May 5; and during the **Obon Festival,** about a week in mid-August. Avoid traveling on these dates at all costs since all long-distance trains, domestic airlines, and most accommodations are booked solid. The weekends before and after these holidays are also likely to be crowded or booked. Exceptions are major cities like Tokyo or Osaka— since the major exodus is back to hometowns or the countryside, holidays such as Golden Week can be almost blissful in a metropolis. Note, however, that during New Year's all museums and many restaurants in Japan are closed, often for 3 or 4 days.

Another busy time is during the **school summer vacation,** from about July 19 through August. It's best to reserve train seats and book accommodations during this time in advance. In addition, you can expect destinations to be packed during major festivals, so if one of these is high on your list, be sure to make plans in advance.

HOLIDAYS National holidays are January 1 (New Year's Day), 2nd Monday in January (Coming-of-Age Day), February 11 (National Foundation Day), March 20 or 21 (Vernal Equinox Day), April 29 (Greenery Day), May 3 (Constitution Memorial Day), May 5 (Children's Day), July 20 (Marine Day; from 2003 it will be celebrated the 3rd Mon in July), September 15 (Respect-for-the-Aged Day; from 2003 it will be celebrated on the 3rd Mon in Sept); September 23 or 24 (Autumn Equinox Day); 2nd Monday in October (Health Sports

Day); November 3 (Culture Day), November 23 (Labor Thanksgiving Day); and December 23 (Emperor's Birthday).

When a national holiday falls on a Sunday, the following Monday becomes a holiday. Although government offices (including JNTO's Tourist Information Centers) and some businesses are closed on public holidays, restaurants and most stores remain open. The exception is during the New Year's celebration, January 1 through 3, when almost all restaurants, public and private offices, and stores close up shop; during that time, you'll have to dine in hotels.

All museums close for New Year's for 1 to 4 days, but most major museums remain open for the other holidays. If a public holiday falls on a Monday (when most museums are closed), many museums will remain open but will close instead the following day, Tuesday. Note that privately owned museums, such as art museums or special-interest museums, generally close on public holidays. To avoid disappointment, be sure to phone ahead if you plan on visiting a museum on or the day following a holiday.

FESTIVALS With Shintoism and Buddhism as the major religions in Japan, it seems as though there's a festival going on somewhere in the country almost every day, especially in summer. Every major shrine and temple has at least one annual festival with events that might include traditional dances, colorful processions, and booths selling souvenirs and food. Such festivals are always free, though admission may be charged for special exhibitions such as flower shows. There are also a number of national holidays observed throughout the country with events and festivals, as well as such annual seasonal events as cormorant fishing and cherry-blossom viewing.

The larger, better-known festivals are exciting to attend but do take some planning since hotel rooms may be booked 6 months in advance. If you haven't made prior arrangements, you may want to let the following schedule be your guide in avoiding certain cities on certain days. You won't find a hotel room anywhere near Takayama, for example, on the days of its two big festivals (and if you do, you'll pay top prices).

If you do plan your trip around a certain festival, be sure to double-check the exact dates with the Japan National Tourist Organization since these dates can change. In Japan, stop by one of the TIC offices in Tokyo, Kyoto, or Narita or Kansai airports for a leaflet called "Calendar Events," which comes out monthly and describes major festivals in Tokyo and the rest of Japan. You can also call the local tourist office of the city hosting each festival (see the regional chapters), though the staff does not always speak English.

CALENDAR OF EVENTS

January

New Year's Day, the most important national holiday in Japan. Because this is a time when Japanese are together with their families and because almost all businesses, restaurants, museums, and shops close down, it's not a particularly rewarding time of the year for foreign visitors. January 1.

Tamaseseri (Ball-Catching Festival), Hakozakigu Shrine, Fukuoka. The main attraction here is a struggle between two groups of youths who try to capture a sacred wooden ball. The winning team is supposed to have good luck the whole year. January 3.

Dezomeshiki (New Year's Parade of Firemen), Odaiba, Tokyo. Agile firemen dressed in traditional costumes prove their worth with acrobatic stunts atop tall bamboo ladders. January 6.

Usokae (Bullfinch Exchange Festival), Dazaifu Temmangu Shrine, outside Fukuoka. The trick here is to get a hold of the bullfinches made of gilt wood passed from person to person. Given away by priests, they're supposed to bring good luck. January 7.

Coming-of-Age Day, a national holiday. This day honors young people who have reached the age of 20, when they can vote and assume other responsibilities. They visit shrines throughout the country to pray for their future. In Tokyo, the most popular shrine for the occasion is Meiji Shrine near Harajuku Station. 2nd Monday in January.

Toka Ebisu Festival, Imamiya Ebisu Shrine, Osaka. Ebisu is considered the patron saint of business and good fortune, so this is the time when businesspeople pray for a successful year. The highlight of the festival is a parade of women dressed in colorful kimono and carried through the streets in palanquins (covered litters). January 9 to 11.

Ame-Ichi (Candy Fair), Matsumoto. Formerly a salt fair, this lively festival has featured traditional candy for the past century. Second weekend in January.

Grass Fire Ceremony, Nara. As evening approaches, Wakakusayama Hill is set ablaze and fireworks are displayed. The celebration marks a time more than 1,000 years ago when a dispute over the boundary of two major temples in Nara was settled peacefully. January 15.

Toshi-ya, Kyoto. This traditional Japanese archery contest is held in the back corridor of Japan's longest wooden structure, Sanjusangendo Hall. January 15.

February

Sounkyo Ice Festival, Sounkyo Onsen. Ice sculptures, ice slides, frozen waterfalls lit in various colors, and evening fireworks are the highlights of this small-town festival. Month of February.

Oyster Festival, Matsushima. Matsushima is famous for its oysters, and this is the time they're considered to be at their best. Oysters are given out free at booths set up at the seaside park along the bay. First Sunday in February.

Setsubun (Bean-Throwing Festival), at leading temples throughout Japan. According to the lunar calendar, this is the last day of winter; people throng to temples to participate in the traditional ceremony of throwing beans to drive away imaginary devils, yelling "Evil go out, good luck come in." February 3 or 4.

Lantern Festival, Kasuga Shrine, Nara. A beautiful sight in which more than 3,000 stone and bronze lanterns are lit. February 3 or 4.

Snow Festival, Odori Avenue, Sapporo. This famous Sapporo festival features huge, elaborate statues and figurines carved in snow and ice. Competitors come from around the world. February 5 to 11.

Hari-kuyo, Tokyo. To show respect for the needles that have done them great service, women bring broken pins and needles to Awashimado near Sensoji Temple in Asakusa and to Shojuin Temple on this day to stick them into squares of tofu, a custom since the Edo Period. February 8.

March

Omizutori (Water-Drawing Festival), Todaiji Temple, Nara. This festival includes a solemn evening rite in which young ascetics brandish large burning torches and draw circles of fire. The biggest ceremony takes place on March 12; on the next day, the ceremony of drawing water is held to the accompaniment of ancient Japanese music. March 1 to 14.

Hinamatsuri (Doll Festival), observed throughout Japan. It's held in honor of young girls to wish them a future of happiness. In homes where there are girls, dolls dressed in ancient costumes representing the emperor, empress, and dignitaries are set up on a tier of shelves along with miniature household articles. March 3.

Kasuga Matsuri, Kasuga Shrine, Nara. This 1,100-year-old festival features traditional costumes and classical dances. March 13.

Vernal Equinox Day, a national holiday. Throughout the week, Buddhist temples hold ceremonies to pray for the souls of the departed. Varies between March 19 to 22.

Cherry-Blossom Season (Sakura Matsuri). This rite of spring begins in late March in Kyushu and Shikoku, travels up Honshu through April, and reaches Hokkaido by the beginning of May; early to mid-April is when the blossoms bloom in Tokyo and Kyoto. Popular cherry-viewing spots in Kyoto include Maruyama Park, the garden of Heian Shrine, the Imperial Palace, Nijo Castle, Kiyomizu Temple, and Arashiyama. In Tokyo, people throng to Ueno Park (where there's also a potted-plant fair and an antiques market), Yasukuni Shrine, Aoyama Cemetery, and the moat encircling the Imperial Palace. Late March to May.

April

Kanamara Matsuri, Kanayama Shrine, Kawasaki (just outside Tokyo). This festival extols the joys of sex and fertility (and, more recently raises awareness about AIDS). It features a parade of giant phalluses, some carried by transvestites. Needless to say, it's not your average festival, and you can get some unusual photographs here. 1st Sunday in April.

Buddha's Birthday (also called Hana Matsuri), observed throughout Japan. Ceremonies are held at all Buddhist temples. April 8.

Kamakura Matsuri, Tsurugaoka Hachimangu Shrine, Kamakura. This festival honors heroes from the past including Minamoto Yoritomo, who made Kamakura his shogunate capital back in 1192. Highlights include horseback archery (truly spectacular to watch), a parade of portable shrines, and sacred dances. Second to third Sunday of April.

Takayama Spring Festival, Takayama. Supposedly dating back to the 15th century, this festival is one of Japan's grandest with a dozen huge, gorgeous floats that are wheeled through the village streets. April 14 to 15.

Gumonji-do (Firewalking Ceremonies), Miyajima. Walking on fire is meant to show devotion and is also for purification; these rites and ancient shrine dances called *bugaku* are held atop Mt. Misen. Mid-April.

Yayoi Matsuri, Futarasan Shrine, Nikko. Yayoi Matsuri features a parade of decorated floats. April 16 to 17.

Golden Week, a major holiday period throughout Japan. Many Japanese offices and businesses close down, and families go on vacation. It's a crowded time to travel; reservations are a must. April 29 to May 5.

May

Hakata Dontaku, Fukuoka. Citizens dressed as deities ride through the streets on horseback to the accompaniment of flutes, drums, and traditional instruments. May 3 to 4.

Children's Day, a national holiday honoring young boys. The most common sight throughout Japan is colorful streamers of carp—which symbolize perseverance and strength, attributes desirable for boys—flying from poles. May 5.

Takigi Noh Performances, Kofukuji Temple, Nara. These Noh plays are presented outdoors after dark under the blaze of torches. May 11 to 12.

Kanda Festival, Kanda Myojin Shrine, Tokyo. This festival began during the Feudal Era as the only time townsmen could enter the shogun's castle and parade before him; today it features a parade of dozens of portable shrines carried through the district plus a tea ceremony. Held in odd-numbered years on the Saturday and Sunday before May 15.

Aoi Matsuri (Hollyhock Festival), Shimogamo and Kamigamo Shrines, Kyoto. This is one of Kyoto's biggest events, a colorful pageant commemorating the days when the imperial procession visited the city's shrines. May 15.

Kobe Matsuri, Kobe. This relatively new festival celebrates Kobe's international past with fireworks at Kobe Port, street markets, and a parade on Flower Road with participants wearing native costumes. Mid-May.

Grand Festival of Toshogu Shrine, Nikko. Commemorating the day in 1617 when Tokugawa Ieyasu's remains were brought to his mausoleum in Nikko, this festival re-creates that drama with more than 1,000 armor-clad people escorting three palanquins through the streets. May 17 and 18.

Sanja Matsuri, Asakusa Shrine, Tokyo. Tokyo's most celebrated festival features about 100 portable shrines carried through the district on the shoulders of men and women in traditional garb. Third Friday and the following Saturday and Sunday in May.

Mifune Matsuri, Arashiyama, on the Oi River outside Kyoto. The days of the Heian Period, when the imperial family used to take pleasure rides on the river, are re-enacted. Third Sunday in May.

June

Takigi Noh Performances, Kyoto. Evening performances of Noh are presented on an open-air stage at the Heian Shrine. June 1 to 2.

Hyakumangoku Matsuri (One Million Goku Festival), Kanazawa. Celebrating Kanazawa's production of 1 million *goku* (5.119 bushels) of rice, this extravaganza features folk songs and traditional dancing in the streets, illuminated paper lanterns floating downriver, public tea ceremonies, Geisha performances, and—the highlight—a parade that winds through the city in re-enactment of Lord Maeda Toshiie's triumphant arrival in Kanazawa on June 14, 1583, with lion dances, ladder-top acrobatics by Kaga firemen, and a torch-lit outdoor Noh performance. June 8 to 14.

Sanno Festival, Hie Shrine, Tokyo. This Edo-Period festival is held on even years and features the usual portable shrines, transported through the busy streets of the Akasaka District. June 10 to 16.

Rice-Planting Festival, Sumiyoshi Shrine, Osaka. In hopes of a successful harvest, young girls in traditional farmers' costumes transplant rice seedlings in the shrine's rice paddy to the sound of music and traditional songs. June 14.

Hyakuman-goku Festival, Kanazawa. Held only since 1952, this festival commemorates the arrival of Maeda—a feudal lord who laid the foundations of the

Kaga clan—in this castle town. The highlight is a procession, and, in the evening, paper lanterns float down the Asano River. Mid-June.

Cormorant Fishing, Nagara River near Gifu, Kiso River in Inuyama (near Nagoya), and Oi River near Kyoto. Visitors board small wooden boats after dark to watch cormorants dive into the water to catch *ayu,* a kind of trout. Generally June to September.

July

Ueki Ichi (Potted-Plant Fair), Fuji Sengen Shrine, Tokyo. Held near Asakusa, this fair displays different kinds of potted plants and *bonsai* (miniature, dwarfed trees) as well as a miniature Mt. Fuji that symbolizes the opening of the official climbing season. July 1.

Hakata Yamagasa, Fukuoka. The main event takes place on the 15th, when a giant fleet of floats, topped with elaborate decorations that range from miniature castles to dolls, is paraded through the streets. July 1 to 15.

Tanabata (Star Festival), celebrated throughout Japan. According to myth, the two stars Vega and Altar, representing a weaver and a shepherd, are allowed to meet once a year on this day. If the skies are cloudy, however, the celestial pair cannot meet and must wait another year. Celebrations may differ from town to town, but in addition to parades and food/souvenir stalls, look for bamboo branches with colorful strips of paper bearing children's wishes. July 7.

Hozuki Ichi (Ground Cherry Pod Fair), Tokyo. This colorful affair at Sensoji Temple in Asakusa features hundreds of stalls selling ground cherry pods and colorful wind bells. July 9 to 10.

Yamakasa, Fukuoka. Just before the crack of dawn, seven teams dressed in loincloths and happi coats (short, colorful kimono-like jackets) race through town, bearing 1-ton floats on their shoulders. In addition, elaborately decorated, 30-foot-tall floats designed by Hakata doll masters are on display throughout town. July 15.

Gion Matsuri, Kyoto. One of the most famous festivals in Japan, it dates back to the 9th century when the head priest at Yasaka Shrine organized a procession in an attempt to ask the gods' assistance against a plague that was raging in the city. Although celebrations continue throughout the month, the highlight is on the 17th, when more than 30 spectacular, wheeled floats wind their way through the city streets to the accompaniment of music and dances. Many visitors plan their trip to Japan around this event. July 16 and 17.

Marine Day. Dedicated to those employed in the marine industry, this national holiday celebrates the importance the sea plays in the livelihood of Japan. July 20 in 2002; 3rd Monday in July from 2003.

Kobe Summer Festival, Kobe. Community groups, including many national and international samba teams, parade through the streets of Sannomiya and Motomachi. This is followed by fireworks displays over Kobe Port along with many staged events throughout the city. July 20.

Obon Festival. This national festival commemorates the dead who, according to Buddhist belief, revisit the world during this period. Many Japanese return to their hometowns for the religious rites, especially if a family member has died recently. As one Japanese whose grandmother had died a few months before told me, "I have to go back to my hometown—it's my grandmother's first Obon." Mid-July or mid-August, depending on the area in Japan.

Tenjin Matsuri, Temmangu Shrine, Osaka. One of the city's biggest festivals, it dates back to the 10th century when the people of Osaka visited Temmangu Shrine to pray for protection against the diseases prevalent during the long, hot summer. They would take pieces of paper cut in the form of human beings and, while the Shinto priest said prayers, would rub the paper over themselves in ritual cleansing. Afterward, the pieces of paper were taken by boat to the mouth of the river and disposed of. Today, events are re-enacted with a procession of more than 100 sacred boats making their way down river, followed by a fireworks display. There's also a parade of some 3,000 people in traditional costume. July 24 and 25.

Matsuri-Miyazaki Festival, on the riverside by City Hall, Miyazaki. Miyazaki Prefecture's largest festival attracts more than 300,000 people with its performing arts and stalls selling food and local products. Late July.

Kangensai Music Festival, Itsukushima Shrine, Miyajima. There is classical court music and bugaku dancing, and three barges carry portable shrines, priests, and musicians across the bay along with a flotilla of other boats. Because this festival takes place according to the lunar calendar, the actual date changes each year. Late July or early August.

Hanabi Taikai (Fireworks Display), Tokyo. This is Tokyo's largest summer celebration, and everyone sits on blankets along the banks of the Sumida River near Asakusa.

Great fun! Last Saturday of July or early August.

August

Oshiro Matsuri, Himeji. This celebration is famous for its Noh dramas lit by bonfire and performed on a special stage on the Himeji Castle grounds, as well as a procession from the castle to the city center with participants dressed as feudal lords and ladies in traditional costume. First Friday and Saturday of August.

Peace Ceremony, Peace Memorial Park, Hiroshima. This ceremony is held annually in memory of those who died in the atomic bomb blast of August 6, 1945. In the evening, thousands of lit lanterns are set adrift on the Ota River in a plea for world peace. A similar ceremony is held on August 9 in Nagasaki. August 6.

Tanabata Festival, Sendai. Sendai holds its Star Festival 1 month later than the rest of Japan. It's the country's largest, and the whole town is decorated with colored paper streamers. August 6 to 8.

Matsuyamam Festival, Matsuyama. Jubilant festivities include dances, fireworks, a parade, and a night fair. August 11 to 13.

Takamatsu Festival, Takamatsu. About 6,000 people participate in a dance procession that threads its way along the Chuo Dori Avenue; anyone can join in. There's also a fireworks display. August 12 to 14.

Toronagashi and Fireworks Display, Matsushima. First there's a fireworks display, followed by the setting adrift on the bay of about 5,000 small boats with lanterns, which are meant to console the souls of the dead; another 3,000 lanterns are lit on islets in the bay. Evening of August 15.

Daimonji Bonfire, Mt. Nyoigadake, Kyoto. A huge bonfire in the shape of the Chinese character *dai,* which means "large," is lit near the peak of the mountain; it's the highlight of the Obon Festival (see July above). Mid-August.

September

Yabusame, Tsurugaoka Hachimangu Shrine, Kamakura. Archery performed on horseback recalls the days of the samurai. September 16.

October

Okunchi Festival, Suwa Shrine, Nagasaki. This 350-year-old festival, one of Kyushu's best, illustrates the influence of Nagasaki's Chinese population through the centuries. Highlights include a parade of floats and dragon dances. October 7 to 9.

Marimo Matsuri, Lake Akan, Hokkaido. This festival is put on by the native Ainu population to celebrate Marimo (a spherical weed found in Lake Akan) and includes dances. Mid-October.

Takayama Matsuri (Autumn Festival), Takayama. Similar to the festival held here in April, huge floats are paraded through the streets. October 9 and 10.

Nagoya Festival. Nagoya's biggest event commemorates three of its heroes—Tokugawa Ieyasu, Toyotomi Hideyoshi, and Oda Nobunaga—in a parade that goes from City Hall to Sakae and includes nine floats with mechanical puppets, marching bands, and a traditional orchestra. Second weekend in October.

Oeshiki Festival, Hommonji Temple, Tokyo. In commemoration of Buddhist leader Nichiren (1222–82), people march toward the shrine carrying large lanterns decorated with paper flowers. October 11 to 13.

Nada Kenka Matsuri (Roughhouse Festival), Matsubara Shrine, Himeji. Youths shouldering portable shrines jostle each other as they attempt to show their skill in balancing their heavy burdens. October 14 and 15.

Doburoku Matsuri Festival, Ogimachi, Shirakawago. This village festival honors unrefined sake, said to represent the spirit of god, with a parade, an evening lion dance, and plenty of eating and drinking. October 14 to 19.

Nikko Toshogu Shrine Festival, Nikko. A parade of warriors in early-17th-century dress are accompanied by spear-carriers, gun-carriers, flag-bearers, Shinto priests, pages, court musicians, and dancers as they escort a sacred portable shrine. October 17.

Fire Festival, Yuki Shrine, Kyoto. Long rows of torches are embedded along the approach to the shrine to illuminate a procession of children. October 22.

Jidai Matsuri (Festival of the Ages), Heian Shrine, Kyoto. Another of Kyoto's grand festivals, this is one of the city's most interesting. Held in commemoration of the founding of the city in 794, it features a procession of more than 2,000 people dressed in ancient costumes representing different epochs of Kyoto's 1,200-year history. October 22.

November

Ohara Matsuri, Kagoshima. About 15,000 people parade through the town in cotton *yukata,* dancing to the tune of popular local folk songs. A sort of Japanese Mardi Gras, this event attracts several hundred thousand spectators a year. November 2 to 3.

Daimyo Gyoretsu, Hakone. The old Tokaido Highway that used to link Kyoto and Tokyo comes alive again with a faithful reproduction of a feudal lord's procession in the olden days. November 3.

Shichi-go-san (Children's Shrine-Visiting Day), held throughout Japan. Shichi-go-san literally means "seven-five-three" and refers to children of these ages who are dressed in their kimono best and taken to shrines by their elders to express thanks and pray for their future. In Tokyo, the most popular sites are Asakusa Shrine, Kanda Myojin, and Meiji Shrine. November 15 (or the nearest Sun).

Tori-no-Ichi (Rake Fair), Otori Shrine, Tokyo. This fair in Asakusa features stalls selling rakes lavishly decorated with paper and cloth, which are thought to bring good luck and fortune. Based on the lunar calendar, the date changes each year. Mid-November.

December

Gishi-sai, Sengakuji Station, Tokyo. This memorial service honors 47 *ronin* (master-less samurai) who avenged their master's death by killing his rival and parading his head; for their act, all were ordered to commit suicide. Forty-seven men dressed as the ronin travel to Sengakuji Temple (the site of their and their master's burial) with the enemy's head to place on their master's head. December 14.

On-Matsuri, Kasuga Shrine, Nara. This festival features a parade of people dressed as courtiers, retainers, and wrestlers of long ago. Mid-December.

Hagoita-Ichi (Battledore Fair), Sensoji Temple, Tokyo. Popular since Japan's feudal days, this Asakusa festival features decorated paddles of all types and sizes. Most have designs of Kabuki actors—images made by pasting together padded silk and brocade—and make great souvenirs and gifts. December 17 to 19.

New Year's Eve. At midnight, many temples ring huge bells 108 times to signal the end of the old year and the beginning of the new. Families visit temples and shrines throughout Japan to pray for the coming year. In Tokyo, Meiji Shrine is the place to be for this popular family celebration, as thousands throng to the shrine to usher in the new year at midnight; many of the area coffee shops and restaurants stay open all night, and trains operate the entire night. December 31.

6 Health & Insurance

STAYING HEALTHY You don't need any inoculations to enter Japan. **Prescriptions** can be filled at Japanese pharmacies only if they're issued by a Japanese doctor. To avoid the hassle, bring more prescription medications than you think you'll need, clearly labeled in their original vials, and be sure to pack them in your carry-on luggage. Over-the-counter items are easy to obtain, though name brands are likely to be different from back home, some ingredients allowed elsewhere may be forbidden in Japan, and prices are likely to be higher.

Contact the **International Association for Medical Assistance to Travelers (IAMAT)** (© 716/754-4883 in the U.S. or 416/652-0137 in Canada; www.sentex.net/~iamat) for information regarding local English-speaking doctors. In Japan, the local consulate and sometimes even the local tourist office can provide a list of area doctors who speak English. If you do get sick, you may want to ask the concierge at your hotel—some hotels even have in-house doctors or clinics. If you can't find a doctor who can help you right away, try the emergency room at the local hospital. Many emergency rooms have walk-in-clinics for emergency cases that are not life-threatening, though there are usually set hours of operation.

JET LAG A major consideration for visitors flying to Japan, especially on long flights from North America, is jet lag. Flying west has slightly less effect than flying east, which means the harder flight to recover from is the journey from Japan back to North America.

To minimize the adverse effects of jet lag—primarily fatigue and slow adjustment to your new time zone—refrain from consuming carbonated drinks or alcohol during the flight. In addition, eat light meals high in vegetable and cereal content the day before, during, and the day after your flight and drink plenty of water to prevent dehydration. Further, exercise your body during the flight by walking around the cabin every so often and by flexing your arms, hands, legs, and feet. It also helps to set your watch (and your mental clock) to the time zone of your destination as soon as you board the plane. Upon reaching your destination, try to stay awake until your usual bedtime (based on the destination time zone); a brisk walk in bright sunshine or vigorous exercise also helps.

TRAVEL INSURANCE There are three kinds of travel insurance: trip cancellation, medical, and lost-luggage coverage. Trip-cancellation insurance is a good idea if you have paid a large portion of your vacation expenses up front. The other two types of insurance, however, don't make sense for most travelers. Rule number one: Check your existing policies before you buy any additional coverage.

Medical and hospital services can be quite expensive in Japan. Before leaving home, check whether your existing health insurance covers you if you should get sick (especially if you have an HMO); Medicare does not cover travel outside North America. If you need hospital treatment, most health insurance plans and HMOs will cover out-of-country hospital visits and procedures, at least to some extent. However, most make you pay the bills up front at the time of care, and you'll get a refund after you've returned and filed all the paperwork. Be sure to carry your identification card in your wallet.

Your homeowner's insurance should cover stolen luggage. The airlines are responsible for $2,500 on domestic flights if they lose your luggage ($9 per pound on international flights); if you plan to carry anything more valuable than that, keep it in your carry-on bag.

Some credit- and charge-card companies may insure you against travel accidents if you buy plane, train, or bus tickets with their cards. Before purchasing additional insurance, read your policies and agreements over carefully. Call your insurers or credit/charge-card companies if you have any questions.

If you do require additional insurance, try one of the companies listed below. But don't pay for more than you need. For example, if you need only trip-cancellation insurance, don't purchase coverage for lost or stolen property. Trip-cancellation insurance costs approximately 6% to 8% of the total value of your vacation.

Reputable issuers of travel insurance include **Access America,** 6600 W. Broad St., Richmond, VA 23286-4991 ⓒ **800/284-8300;** www.accessamerica.com); **Travel Guard International,** 1145 Clark St., Stevens Point, WI 54481 (ⓒ **800/826-1300;** www.travel-guard.com); **Travel Insured International, Inc.,** P.O. Box 280568, East Hartford, CT

06128-0568 (© **800/243-3174;** www.travelinsured.com); and, for British travelers, **Columbus Travel Insurance,** 17 Devonshire Square, London EC2M 4SQ (© **020/ 7375-0011**).

7 Tips for Travelers with Special Needs

FOR TRAVELERS WITH DISABILITIES For travelers with disabilities, traveling can be a nightmare in Japan, especially in Tokyo and other large metropolises. In Tokyo, for example, most subways are accessible only by stairs and lots of them; many sidewalks can be so jam-packed that getting around on crutches or in a wheelchair is exceedingly difficult. Although Tokyo's subway trains have seating for handicapped passengers—located in the first and last compartments of the train and indicated by a white circle with a blue seat—subways can be so crowded that there's barely room to move. In addition, the seats for the handicapped are almost always occupied by commuters—so unless you're visibly handicapped, no one is likely to offer you his or her seat. Even Japanese homes are not very accessible since the main floor is always raised about a foot above the entrance-hall floor. Not surprisingly, people with mobility limitations are a rare sight in the larger cities.

When it comes to facilities for the blind, however, Japan has a very advanced system. Throughout subway stations and on many major sidewalks in Tokyo and other cities, there are raised dots and lines on the ground to guide blind people at intersections and toward subway platforms. In some cities, street lights chime a certain song when the signal turns green east-west and another for north-south greens. Even Japanese yen notes are identifiable by a slightly raised circle—the ¥1,000 note has one circle in a corner, while the ¥10,000 note has two. And finally, many elevators have floors indicated in Braille.

In any case, a disability shouldn't stop anyone from traveling. Because Tokyo can be confusing and frustrating even for the able-bodied, travelers with disabilities may wish to travel to Japan's smaller cities and rural villages. Those using a wheelchair should travel with a compact one. There are more resources out there than ever before. Consider joining the **Society for Accessible Travel and Hospitality (SATH),** 347 Fifth Ave. Suite 610, New York, NY 10016 (© **212/447-7284;** fax 212/725-8253; www.sath. org) for $45 annually, $30 for seniors and students, to gain access to their vast network of connections in the travel industry. They provide information sheets on travel destinations and referrals to tour operators that specialize in traveling with disabilities. Their quarterly magazine, *Open World for Disability and Mature Travel,* is full of good information and resources. A year's subscription is $13 ($21 outside the United States).

FOR GAY & LESBIAN TRAVELERS While there are many gay and lesbian establishments in big cities like Tokyo, the gay community in Japan is not a vocal one, and, in any case, information in English is hard to come by. The **International Gay & Lesbian Travel Association (IGLTA)** (© **800/448-8550** or 954/776-2626; fax 954/776-3303; www.iglta.org) links travelers with the appropriate gay-friendly service organization or tour specialist. With around 1,200 members, it offers quarterly newsletters, marketing mailings, and a membership directory that's updated quarterly. Membership often includes gay or lesbian businesses but is open to individuals for $200 yearly plus a $100 administration fee for new members. Members are kept informed of gay and gay-friendly hoteliers, tour operators, and airline and cruise-line representatives. Contact the IGLTA for a list of its member agencies, which will be tied into IGLTA's information resources.

A general gay and lesbian travel agency is **Islanders/Kennedy Travels,** 314 Jericho Turnpike, Floral Park, NY, 11001, (② **800/988-1181;** www.kennedytravel.com).

FOR SENIORS   A few museums in Tokyo, including the Tokyo National Museum, offer free admission to senior citizens over 65 (be sure to have your passport handy). Many other museums in Tokyo and elsewhere offer discounts. In general, however, seniors do not receive a discount for admission to museums and other attractions (be sure to ask, since discounts might not be written in English). In addition, visitors to Japan should be aware that there are many stairs to navigate in metropolitan areas, particularly in subway and train stations and even pedestrian overpasses.

Before leaving home, you might consider becoming a member (the annual fee is $10) of **AARP** (formerly the American Association of Retired Persons) 601 E St. NW, Washington, DC 20049 (② **800/424-3410** or 202/434-2277; www.aarp.org), which brings a wide range of special benefits including *Modern Maturity* magazine, a monthly newsletter, and discounts on airfares.

If you want something more than the average vacation or guided tour, try **Elderhostel,** 11 Avenue de Lafayette, Boston, MA 02110-1746 (② **877/426-8056;** www.elderhostel. org) or the University of New Hampshire's **Interhostel** (② **800/733-9753**), both variations on the same theme: educational travel for senior citizens. On these escorted tours, the days are packed with seminars, lectures, and field trips, and academic experts guide the sightseeing. Elderhostel arranges study programs for those 55 and over (and a spouse or companion of any age) in the United States and in 77 countries around the world including Japan. Most courses last about 3 weeks and many include airfare, accommodations in student dormitories or modest inns, meals, and tuition. Write or call for a free catalog, which lists upcoming courses and destinations. Interhostel takes travelers 50 and over (with companions over 40) and offers 2- and 3-week trips, mostly international. The courses in both these programs are ungraded, involve no homework, and often focus on the liberal arts. They're not luxury vacations, but they're fun and fulfilling.

FOR FAMILIES   The Japanese are very fond of children, which makes traveling in Japan with children a delight. All social reserve seems to be waived for children. While the average Japanese will not approach foreign adults, if you bring a child with you, the Japanese will not only talk with you but may even invite you home. Taking along some small and easy-to-carry gifts for your kids to give out to other children you meet is a great icebreaker.

While children may not like such foreign customs as eating raw fish, they will find many other Japanese customs to their taste. What child could resist taking baths en famille and actually getting to splash? If you go to a ryokan, chances are your kids will love wearing *yukata* (cotton kimono) and clattering around in *geta* (wooden sandals). Your children will be pampered and played with and will receive presents and lots of attention. Udon- and soba-noodle shops are inexpensive and ubiquitous, and the transition from kid-favorite spaghetti to udon is easy. In addition, most family-style restaurants, especially those in department stores, offer a special children's meal that often includes a small toy or souvenir. Tourist spots in Japan almost always have a table or counter with a stamp and ink pad so that visitors can commemorate their trip; you might wish to give your children a small notebook so they can collect imprints of every attraction they visit.

Children 6 to 11 years old generally are charged half price for everything from temple admission to train tickets, while children under six are often admitted free. If your child under six sleeps with you, you generally won't even have to pay for him or her in most hotels and ryokan. However, it's always advisable to ask in advance.

Safety also makes Japan a good destination for families. Still, plan your itinerary with care. To avoid crowds, visit tourist sights on weekdays. Never travel on city transportation during rush hour or on trains during popular public holidays. And remember that, with all the stairways and crowded sidewalks, strollers are less practical than baby backpacks.

FOR STUDENTS   Students sometimes receive discounts at museums, though occasionally discounts are available only to students enrolled in Japanese schools. Furthermore, discounted prices are often not displayed in English. Your best bet is to bring along an International Student Identity Card (ISIC; see below) along with your university student ID and show them at museum ticket windows.

The best resource for students is the **Council on International Educational Exchange,** or CIEE (© **800/2COUNCIL;** www.ciee.org). Its travel branch, **Council Travel Service (CTS)** (www.counciltravel.com), is the biggest student travel agency operation in the world, offering discounts on plane tickets and the like. Ask them for a list of CTS offices in major cities so you can keep the discounts flowing (and aid lines open) as you travel.

From CIEE, you can obtain the student traveler's best friend, the $22 **International Student Identity Card (ISIC).** It's the only officially acceptable form of student identification good for discounts to museums and attractions. It also provides you with basic health and life insurance and a 24-hour help line. If you're no longer a student but are still under 26, you can get an **International Youth Travel Card** from CIEE; it will get you the insurance and some of the discounts but not student admission prices in museums.

In Canada, **Travel CUTS,** 200 Ronson St., Ste. 320, Toronto, ONT M9W 5Z9 (© **886/246-9762** or 416/614-2887; www.travelcuts.com) offers similar services. **Campus Travel,** 52 Grosvenor Gardens, London SW1W 0AG (© **0870/240-1010**), opposite Victoria Station, is Britain's leading specialist in student and youth travel, with about 50 branches spread throughout the UK.

FOR SINGLES   Traveling alone poses no difficulty, even for women. The main obstacle is expense since the price of accommodations is usually cheaper for couples and groups. Single travelers, therefore, should do what traveling businessmen do: Stay at so-called business hotels. With their large number of single rooms, they cater almost exclusively to solo businessmen.

An alternative is to register with **Travel Companion Exchange** (© **631/454-0880**), one of the nation's oldest roommate finders for single travelers. You can find a trustworthy travelmate who will split the cost of the room with you and be around as little, or as often, as you like during the day.

8 Getting There

BY PLANE

Japan has two international airports. Outside Tokyo is **Tokyo International Airport** in Narita (usually referred to as the Narita Airport), where you'll want to land if your main business is in the capital, the surrounding region, or points north or east such as Hokkaido. Japan's other international airport, **Kansai International Airport** (KIX) outside Osaka, is convenient if your destination is Osaka, Kobe, Nara, Kyoto, or western or southern Japan; it is also convenient for domestic air travel within Japan, since most domestic flights out of Tokyo depart from Haneda Airport, necessitating an airport transfer if you're arriving at Tokyo International Airport. Some international flights also serve Nagoya, Fukuoka, and Sapporo airports.

THE MAJOR CARRIERS

Since the flying time to Tokyo is about 12 hours from Los Angeles and 13½ hours from Chicago or New York, you'll want to consider on-board services and even mileage programs (you'll earn lots of miles on this round-trip) as well as ticket price when choosing your carrier. Airlines flying to Japan from North America, Europe, Australia, and New Zealand include:

Air Canada (© 888/247-2262; www.aircanada.com) offers flights from Vancouver to Tokyo daily and to Nagoya several times a week and from Toronto to Tokyo (via Vancouver) daily.

Air New Zealand (© 0800/737-000 in New Zealand, 800/262-1234 in the U.S.; www.airnewzealand.com) flies from Auckland to Tokyo, Osaka, and Nagoya.

All Nippon Airways (© 800/235-9262; www.fly-ana.com) is Japan's largest domestic carrier. It offers daily round-trip service from New York, Washington, D.C., Chicago, Los Angeles, and San Francisco to Tokyo, as well as a direct flight from Honolulu to Osaka. It also flies from London and Sydney to Tokyo and Osaka. ANA has a code-share alliance with United Airlines (meaning that both airlines can sell each other's tickets; you can also earn United frequent-flier miles with ANA). Since combining international flights with domestic flights is cheaper than purchasing tickets separately, it's prudent to discuss your travel plans with an ANA or United Airlines agent if your final destination lies beyond Tokyo or Osaka. ANA passengers can also receive discounts at ANA hotels in Japan with free baggage transfers. For first- and business-class passengers flying roundtrip from Canada or the United States, another perk is complimentary domestic-use cell phone rentals for a maximum of 2 weeks, with passengers paying only the calling charges; phones can be picked up at airports upon arrival.

American Airlines (© 800/433-7300; www.im.aa.com) offers flights daily from Seattle, Dallas, San Jose and Chicago to Tokyo, as well as from Dallas to Osaka, and code shares with Japan Airlines.

British Airways (© 0845/77-333-77 in Britain; www.britishairways.com) flies from London to Tokyo.

Continental Airlines (© 800/523-3273; www.continental.com) offers flights several times weekly from Newark and Houston to Tokyo.

Delta Airlines (© 800/241-4141; www.delta.com) offers daily flights from Atlanta to Tokyo.

Japan Airlines (© 800/525-3663; www.japanair.com), Japan's flagship carrier, offers more international flights to Japan than any other carrier and is noted for its excellent service. Another plus to flying Japan Airlines is that JAL international passengers can make advance seat reservations at JAL overseas offices for Shinkansen bullet trains, a great convenience if you're traveling during peak times, and can purchase Japan Rail Passes (see "Getting Around Japan," below). Furthermore, all passengers can apply for complimentary, domestic-use cell phones that can be picked up upon arrival at the airport in Japan. Female travelers will appreciate the women-only toilets with Shiseido skin-care products and other women's toiletries. JAL flies to Tokyo from New York, Chicago, San Francisco, Los Angeles, Las Vegas, and Vancouver, and to Osaka from Chicago and Los Angeles. It also connects Japan with England, New Zealand, and Australia.

KLM Royal Dutch Airlines (© **020/4747-747** in the Netherlands, 800/447-4747 in the U.S.; www.klm.com) flies from Amsterdam to Tokyo, Osaka, and (once a week) Nagoya. It is also the only European carrier that flies to Sapporo, with twice weekly service, making it convenient for trips to Hokkaido. KLM has connecting flights from London, Paris, and most other European capitals and is included in Northwest Airlines' mileage program.

Northwest Airlines (© **800/447-4747;** www.nwa.com), operating across the Pacific for more than 50 years (longer than any other airline), offers more nonstop service between North America and Japan than any other American carrier, with nonstop flights to Tokyo, Osaka, and Nagoya. North American gateways to Japan are Los Angeles, San Francisco, Seattle, Detroit, New York, Minneapolis–St. Paul, and Honolulu; Japan-bound flights also offer connecting service to 10 cities in Asia. The fact that Northwest (which shares mileage programs with KLM and Continental) flies to so many Asian destinations makes it easy to coordinate onward travel plans to, say, Hong Kong or Bangkok. Another

Northwest code-share alliance with Japan Air System, offers onward flights throughout Japan. The airline's stellar service has even attracted the hard-to-please Japanese, who regularly fly Northwest.

Qantas (© **800/227-4500;** © 13-13-13 in Australia; www.qantas.com) flies from Sydney, Melbourne, and Brisbane to Tokyo and Osaka.

United Airlines (© **800/538-2929;** www.united.com) has daily flights from San Francisco, Los Angeles, Seattle, Chicago and New York to Tokyo and daily flights from San Francisco to Osaka. It shares codes with ANA to and within Japan.

AIRFARES

Because the flight to Japan is such a long one, you may wish to splurge on upgraded service and a roomier seat. But we're talking about a serious splurge: Northwest's round-trip business-class fare to Tokyo is $6,644 from New York. Northwest recently expanded its international business class by eliminating first class and reconfiguring its seats to provide a roomier seat pitch of 60 inches (the distance between seat rows).

Full-fare economy-class tickets on Northwest cost $2,788 from New York and $2,038 from the West Coast to Tokyo. APEX (Advance Purchase Excursion) fares are less expensive still but are usually loaded with restrictions and are based on the seasons. There are three fare seasons: peak season (summer) is the most expensive, basic season (winter) is the least expensive, and shoulder season is between the other two in time and in price. In all three seasons, APEX fares are a little higher on weekends. Northwest's APEX fares have run as low as $448 for a winter weekday roundtrip flight between Los Angeles and Tokyo. Fares quoted are as of October 2001, and are subject to change.

> ### *Tips* Flying for Less: Tips for Getting the Best Airfares
>
> Passengers within the same airplane cabin rarely pay the same fare for their seats. You'll save money by purchasing your ticket in advance, for example, and by flying on a weekend. Here are a few other easy ways to save:
>
> 1. **Check your newspaper for advertised discounts** or call the airlines directly and ask whether any promotional rates or special fares are available. Periodically, airlines lower prices on their most popular routes. If your schedule is flexible, ask if you can secure a cheaper fare by staying an extra day or by flying midweek. (Many airlines won't volunteer this information.) If you already hold a ticket when a sale breaks, it may even pay to exchange your ticket, which usually incurs a $50 to $75 charge. Note, however, that the lowest-priced fares are often nonrefundable, require an advance purchase of 21 days, and carry penalties for changing dates of travel.
>
> 2. **Look for discount fares.** Some companies provide deeply discounted tickets—sometimes saving you more than 50% on economy fares and around 30% on APEX fares—with no restrictions, depending on availability. You can buy your ticket through them well in advance or, if you're lucky, at the last moment. Among such firms that deal with travel to Japan are **Nippon Travel,** in Rockville, MD (tel] **301/279-0026**) and **Japan Associates Travel,** 2000 17th St. NW, Washington, DC 20009 (© **202/939-8853**).
>
>   Consolidators, also known as bucket shops, are another good place to find low fares. Consolidators buy seats in bulk from the airlines and then sell them back to the public at prices below even the airlines' discounted rates. Their small, boxed ads usually run in the Sunday travel section at the bottom of the page. Before you pay, however, ask for a confirmation number from the

9 Escorted & Package Tours

ESCORTED TOURS

If you're the kind of traveler who doesn't like leaving such arrangements as accommodations, transportation, and itinerary to chance, you may wish to join an escorted tour of Japan. Among the many companies offering group tours are **Pacific Bestour,** 228 River Vale Rd., River Vale, NJ 07675 (© **800/688-3288** or 201/664-8778; www.bestour.com) and **TBI Tours,** 53 Summer St., Keene, NH 03431 (© **800/223-0266;** www.general tours.com). For active travelers, **Esprit**

Travel, 2101 Wilshire Blvd., Santa Monica, CA 90403 (© **800/377-7481;** www.espritravel.com) specializes in walking, hiking, and special-interest trips in Japan. **Japan Airlines,** Japan's flagship carrier, operates JALPAK (© **800/221-1081;** www.jalpak.com), which offers complete travel packages to Japan; call the airline or a travel agent for details.

PACKAGE TOURS

Package tours are not the same thing as escorted tours. They are simply a way consolidator and then call the airline itself to confirm your seat. Be prepared to book your ticket with a different consolidator—there are many to choose from—if the airline can't confirm your reservation. Also be aware that bucket-shop tickets are usually nonrefundable or rigged with stiff cancellation penalties, often as high as 50% to 75% of the ticket price.

Council Travel (**©** **800/2COUNCIL;** www.counciltravel.com) caters especially to young travelers, but their bargain-basement prices are available to people of all ages. Other reliable consolidators include **1-800-FLY-CHEAP** (www.flycheap.com) and **Cheap Tickets** (**©** **800/377-1000;** www.cheaptickets.com), which serves as a clearinghouse for unused seats.

3. **Search the Internet for cheap fares** and check out the great last-minute deals available through free e-mail services, provided directly by the airlines.

4. **Book a seat on a charter flight.** Discounted fares have pared the number available, but they can still be found. Most charter operators advertise and sell their seats through travel agents, thus making these local professionals your best source of information for available flights. Before deciding to take a charter flight, however, check the restrictions on the ticket: You may be asked to purchase a tour package, to pay in advance, to be amenable if the day of departure is changed, to pay a service charge, to fly on an airline you're not familiar with (this usually is not the case), and to pay harsh penalties if you cancel but be understanding if the charter doesn't fill up and is canceled up to 10 days before departure. Summer charters fill up more quickly than others and are almost sure to fly, but if you decide on a charter flight, seriously consider cancellation and baggage insurance.

to buy airfare and accommodations at the same time. For destinations like Japan, they are a smart way to go because they save you a lot of money. In many cases, a package that includes airfare, hotel, and transportation to and from the airport will cost you less than just the hotel alone would have cost had you booked it yourself. That's because packages are sold in bulk to tour operators who then resell them to the public at a cost that drastically undercuts standard rates.

Packages, however, vary widely. Some offer a better class of hotels than others, while others offer the same hotels for lower prices or a range of hotel choices at different prices. Some offer flights on scheduled airlines, while others book charters. In some packages, your choice of accommodations and travel days may be limited. Some packages let you choose between escorted vacations and independent vacations; others allow you to add on just a few excursions or escorted day trips (also at lower prices than you could locate on your own) without booking an entirely escorted tour. Each destination usually has one or two packages that are cheaper than the rest because they buy in even greater bulk. If you spend the time to shop around, you will save in the long run.

FINDING A PACKAGE DEAL

The best place to start your search is the travel section of your local Sunday newspaper. Also check the ads in the back of national travel magazines like *Travel & Leisure, National Geographic Traveler,* and *Condé Nast Traveler.* Among the many tour companies offering independent packages to Japan, check **Japan & Orient Tours** (✆ 800/377-1080), **Orient Flexi-Pax Tours** (✆ 800/545-5540; www. orientflexipax.com), **Pacific Bestour** (✆ 800/688-3288; www.bestour.com),

and **TBI Tours** (✆ 800/223-0266; www.generaltours.com).

Another good resource is the airlines themselves, which often package their flights with accommodations. **All Nippon Airways** (✆ 800/ 235-9262; www.fly-ana.com), Japan's largest domestic carrier, offers discounts at ANA hotels and can save you money on domestic flights planned in conjunction with your international flight. **Northwest Airlines World Vacations** (✆ 800/ 800-1504; www.nwaworldvacations. com) offers flight-and-hotel packages to Tokyo and beyond that allow you to choose from a range of hotels and to tailor your trip from 3 to 20 nights.

10 Getting Around Japan

Japan has an extensive public transport system, the most convenient segment of which is the nation's excellent rail service. You can also travel by plane (good for long-distance hauls), bus (the cheapest mode of travel), ferry, and car.

BY TRAIN

The most efficient way to travel around Japan is by train. Whether you're being whisked through the countryside aboard the famous Shinkansen bullet train or are winding your way up a wooded mountainside in a two-car electric tram, trains in Japan are punctual, comfortable, dependable, safe, and clean. All trains except locals have washrooms, toilets, and drinking water. Bullet trains even have telephones. And because train stations are usually located in the heart

of the city next to the city bus terminal or a subway station, arriving in a city by train is usually the most convenient method. What's more, most train stations in Japan's major cities and resort areas have tourist offices to help with hotel directions. The staff may not speak English, but the office usually has maps or brochures in English. Train stations also often have a counter where hotel reservations can be made free of charge. Most of Japan's trains are run by the **Japan Railways (JR) Group,** which operates as many as 27,000 trains daily, including more than 500 Shinkansen bullet trains.

SHINKANSEN (BULLET TRAIN)

The **Shinkansen** is probably Japan's best-known train. With a front car that resembles a space rocket, the

---

(*Tips* **Travel Tip**

In the following chapters, to help you reach the hotels, restaurants, and sights I've recommended in this book, I've included the nearest train or subway station or bus or tram information followed in parentheses by the number of minutes it takes to walk from the station or bus stop to your destination.

Shinkansen hurtles along at a maximum speed of 300kmph (187 mph) through the countryside on its own special tracks. Among the most luxurious Shinkansen trains are the *Grand Hikari,* a double-decker train that travels between Tokyo and Kyushu, and the *Twilight Express,* a luxury hotel on wheels that runs from Osaka to Sapporo.

Four Shinkansen lines operate in Japan. The most widely used line for tourists is the **Tokaido-Sanyo Shinkansen,** which runs from Tokyo Station west to such cities as Nagoya, Kyoto, Osaka, Kobe, Himeji, Okayama, and Hiroshima before reaching its final destination of Hakata/Fukuoka on the island of Kyushu. Trains run so frequently—as often as every 10 or 15 minutes during peak times—that it's almost like catching the local subway. The **Tohoku Shinkansen Line** runs from Tokyo and Ueno stations to Morioka, Kakunodate, and Akita in eastern Honshu. The **Joetsu Shinkansen** connects Tokyo and Ueno stations with Niigata on the Japan Sea coast. The newest line is the **Nagano Shinkansen,** completed in time for the 1998 Winter Olympics and connecting Tokyo and Ueno stations with Nagano in the Japan Alps.

Shinkansen running along these lines offer two kinds of service—trains that stop only at major cities (Nozomi and Hikari trains) and trains that make more stops and are therefore slightly slower (Kodoma). If your destination is a smaller city on the Shinkansen line, make sure the train you take stops there. As a plus, information on stops is broadcast in English. Telephone calls can be made to and from bullet trains, but to make a call you must have a magnetic telephone card (see "Fast Facts: Japan," later in this chapter).

REGULAR SERVICE   In addition to bullet trains, there are also two types of long-distance trains that operate on regular tracks. The **limited-express trains,** or L'EX (*Tokkyu*) branch off the Shinkansen system and are the fastest after the bullet trains, while the **express trains** (*Kyuko*) are slightly slower and make more stops. Slower still are **rapid express trains** (*Shin-Kaisoku*) and the even slower **rapid trains** (*Kaisoku*). To serve the everyday needs of Japan's commuting population, **local trains** (*Futsu*) stop at all stations and are the trains most widely used for side trips outside the major cities.

There are also some privately owned lines that operate from major cities to tourist destinations. **Kintetsu (Kinki Nippon Railway)** lines, for example, are useful for traveling in the Kansai area and to the Ise Shima Peninsula.

INFORMATION   For information on rail service throughout Japan, stop by the **Tourist Information Centers** in Tokyo, Kyoto, or the international airports in Narita or Osaka (see "Visitor Information," earlier in this chapter) for the *Railway Timetable,* published annually in English and providing train schedules for the Shinkansen and some other major lines. To be on the safe side, I also stop by the train information desk or the tourist information desk as soon as I arrive in a new destination to check on train schedules onward to my next destination.

No matter which train you ride, be sure to hang on to your ticket—you'll be required to give it up at the end of your trip as you exit through the gate. And pack lightly since porters are virtually nonexistent, overhead luggage space is small, and most rail stations have lots of stairs. Even if you're a woman traveling alone, don't expect anyone to help you with your luggage—it's happened to me three times in some 15 years.

TRAIN DISTANCES/TRAVELING TIME Because Japan is an island nation, many people erroneously believe that the traveling time between destinations is of little concern. However, the country is much longer than most people imagine. Its four main islands, measured from the northeast to the southwest, cover roughly the distance from Maine to Florida. (Thank goodness for the Shinkansen bullet train!) In addition, transportation can be slow in mountainous regions, especially if you're on a local train.

The chart below measures the distances and traveling times from Tokyo to principal Japanese cities. Since Tokyo is located approximately in the middle of Japan, you'll most likely change trains there when traveling from east to west and vice versa. Traveling times do not include the time needed for transferring and are calculated for the fastest trains available, excluding the *Nozomi Super Express* (Shinkansen). (I have excluded the *Nozomi Super Express* because most tourists to Japan use the JR Rail Pass, which is not valid on the *Nozomi*.)

Train Travel from Tokyo to Principal Cities

City	Distance (Miles)	Travel Time
Aomori*	458	4 hr. 38 min.
Atami	60	50 min.
Beppu*	762	8 hr.
Fukuoka (Hakata Station)	730	6 hr. 30 min.
Hakodate*	559	6 hr. 56 min.
Hiroshima	554	4 hr. 50 min.
Ito	75	1 hr. 45 min.
Kagoshima	927	12 hr.
Kamakura	32	53 min.
Kanazawa*	386	5 hr.
Kobe (Shin-Kobe Station)	365	3 hr. 30 min.
Kumamoto*	804	8 hr. 07 min.
Kyoto	318	2 hr. 36 min.
Matsue*	570	6 hr.
Matsumoto	146	2 hr. 30 min.
Matsuyama*	587	7 hr.
Miyazaki*	899	12 hr. 10 min.
Nagasaki*	825	8 hr. 30 min.
Nagoya	227	1 hr. 55 min.
Narita	42	1 hr.
Niigata	207	1 hr. 40 min.
Nikko	90	1 hr. 50 min.
Okayama	455	3 hr. 51 min.
Osaka (Shin-Osaka Station)	341	2 hr. 30 min.
Sapporo*	731	12 hr.
Shimoda	103	2 hr. 45 min.
Takamatsu*	496	5 hr. 10 min.
Takayama*	330	4 hr. 52 min.
Toba*	289	3 hr. 50 min.
Yokohama	20	30 min.

*Destination requires a change of trains.

Tips   Train Travel Tips

Your best source for train schedules is the *Railway Timetable* available at JNTO's **Tourist Information Centers.** For routing information and questions about train times once you've begun your trip, you can call the Tourist Information Center's toll-free **Travel-Phone** at ✆ **0088/22-4800** daily from 9am to 5pm; call the TIC at ✆ **03/3201-3331** in Tokyo and at ✆ **075/371-5649** in Kyoto. You can also call **Japan Rail's English-Language Telephone Service** in Tokyo for information (✆ **03/3423-0111**) daily from 10am to 6pm. (No reservations are accepted by phone.)

TRAIN FARES & RESERVATIONS

Trains are expensive in Japan; ticket prices are based on the type of train (Shinkansen bullet trains are the most expensive), the distance traveled, whether your seat is reserved, and the season, with slightly higher prices (usually a ¥200/$1.65 surcharge) during peak season (Golden Week, July 21–Aug 31, Dec 25–Jan 10, and Mar 21–Apr 5). I've included train prices from Tokyo for many destinations covered in this book (see individual cities for more information). Unless stated otherwise, prices are for non-reserved seats on the fastest train available during regular season. You can buy JR tickets and obtain information at any Japan Railways station for JR trains going throughout Japan, including those along the Yamanote Line, which loops around Tokyo.

Seat Reservations   If you wish, you can reserve a seat in advance for the Shinkansen, as well as for limited-express and express trains, at any major Japan Railways station for a small fee (¥510/$4.25 for the Shinkansen). The larger stations have special reservation counters called **Midori-no Madoguchi** (Green Window) or Travel Service Centers, easily recognizable by their green signs with RESERVATION TICKETS written on them. They are generally open daily from 10am to 6pm. If you're at a JR station with no special reservation office, you can reserve your seats at one of the regular ticket windows. You can also purchase and reserve seats at several travel agents including the giant **Japan Travel Bureau (JTB),** which has offices all over Japan. It's a good idea to reserve your seats for your entire trip through Japan as soon as you know your itinerary, especially if you'll be traveling during peak times; however, you can only reserve 1 month in advance. If it's not peak season, you'll probably be okay using a more flexible approach to traveling—note that all trains also have non-reserved cars that fill up on a first-come, first-seated basis. You can also reserve seats on the day of travel up to departure time. I hardly ever reserve a seat when it's not peak season, preferring instead the flexibility of being able to hop on the next available train. If you want to sit in the no-smoking car of the Shinkansen bullet train, ask for the *kinensha.*

Tips for Saving Money   If your ticket is for travel covering more than 100km (62 miles), you can make as many stopovers en route as you wish as long as you complete your trip within the validity period of the ticket. Tickets up to 200km (124 miles) are valid for 2 days, with 1 day added for each additional 200km. Note, too, that stopovers are granted only if your trip does not originate or end in Tokyo, Yokohama, Osaka, Nagoya, Kyoto, Kobe, Hiroshima, Kitakyushyu, Fukuoka, Sendai, or Sapporo. You can, however, purchase a ticket, say, in Takayama bound for Nagasaki (a total of about 1,860km or 1,155 miles), stopping in Kyoto and Hiroshima along the way. You can save money by purchasing tickets for long distances even though you plan to break up your journey.

You can also save money by purchasing a round-trip ticket for long distances. A round-trip by train on distances exceeding 600 km (373 miles) one-way costs 20% less than two one-way tickets.

There are also regional tickets good for sightseeing. The **Hakone Free Pass,** for example, offered by Odakyu railways, includes round-trip transportation from Tokyo and unlimited travel in Hakone for a specific number of days.

JAPAN RAIL PASS   The Japan Rail Pass is without a doubt the most convenient and most economical way to travel around Japan. With the rail pass, you don't have to worry about buying individual tickets, and you can reserve your seats on all JR trains for free. The rail pass entitles you to unlimited travel on all JR train lines including the Shinkansen (except the *Nozomi Super Express*), as well as on JR buses and ferries.

There are several types of rail passes available; make your decision based on

your length of stay in Japan and the cities you intend to visit. You might even find it best to combine several passes to cover your travels in Japan, such as a 1-week standard pass for longer journeys, say, to Kyushu, plus a regional Kansai Area Pass for visiting Kyoto and other destinations in the Kansai area.

The Standard Pass   If you wish to travel throughout Japan, your best bet is to purchase the standard Japan Rail Pass. It's available for ordinary coach class and for the first-class Green Car, and you can purchase passes good for 1, 2, or 3 weeks. Rates for the ordinary pass, as of October 2001, are ¥28,300 ($236) for 7 days, ¥45,100 ($375) for 14 days, and ¥57,700 ($481) for 21 days. Rates for the Green Car are ¥37,800 ($315) for 7 days, ¥61,200 ($510) for 14 days, and ¥79,600 ($633) for 21 days. Children (under 12, over 6) are charged half fare. Personally, I have never traveled first class in Japan and do not consider it necessary. However, during peak travel times (New Year's, Golden Week, and the Obon season in mid-Aug), you may find it easier to reserve a seat in the first-class Green Car, which you can also do with an ordinary pass by paying a surcharge.

Regional Passes   If you plan to travel only to eastern or western

---

(Value   Japan Rail Pass

You can save quite a bit by purchasing a rail pass, even if you only plan to travel a little. How economical is a Japan Rail Pass? For example, if you were to buy a round-trip reserved-seat ticket on the Shinkansen from Tokyo to Kyoto, it would cost you ¥26,440 ($220), which is almost as much as a week's ordinary rail pass. If you plan to see more than just Tokyo and Kyoto, it pays to use a rail pass.

Another advantage to a rail pass is that it offers a 10% discount or more off room rates at many JR Hotel Group hotels, including the Hotel Granvia in Kyoto, Okayama, and Hiroshima, the Crowne Plaza Metropolitan and Tokyo Station Hotel in Tokyo, and Hotel Kurashiki. A Japan Rail Pass booklet, which comes with your purchase of a rail pass, lists member hotels.

Honshu or Kyushu, you'll probably find it more economical to purchase one of several regional rail passes available for ordinary coach class. If, for example, you are arriving by plane at the Kansai Airport outside Osaka and intend to remain in western Honshu, you may wish to opt for one of two different **JR-West Passes** offered. The **Kansai Area Pass,** which can be used for travel between Osaka, Kyoto, Kobe, Nara, Himeji, and other destinations in the Kansai area, is available as a 1-day pass for ¥2,000 ($17) or a 4-day pass for ¥6,000 ($50); children pay half fare. Travel is restricted to JR local trains (that is, Shinkansen and limited express trains are not included in the pass) and unreserved seating.

The other JR-West Pass available is the **Sanyo Area Pass,** which covers a larger area, allows travel via Shinkansen (including the super-fast Nozomi) and JR local trains from Osaka as far as Hakata (in the city of Fukuoka on Kyushu), and includes Hiroshima, Okayama, Kurashiki, Himeji, and Kobe. It's available for 4 days for ¥20,000 ($167) and for 8 days for ¥30,000 ($250); children's passes are half price.

Though not as popular as western Honshu, eastern Honshu also offers its own **JR-East Pass,** which includes travel from Tokyo to parts of the Japan Alps and throughout the Tohoku District, including Sendai, Kakunodate, and Aomori via Shinkansen and local JR lines. Passes for travel in ordinary coach cars are available for 5 days for ¥20,000 ($167), 10 days for ¥32,000 ($267), and a 4-day flexible pass (which is valid for any 4 consecutive or nonconsecutive days within a month) for ¥20,000 ($167). Half-fare children's passes and Green Car passes are also available.

If your travels are limited to the island of Kyushu, consider the **JR-Kyushu Rail Pass,** valid for 5 days for ¥15,000 ($125) and for 7 days for ¥20,000 ($167).

Before You Leave Home   The Japan Rail Pass is available only to foreigners visiting Japan as tourists and *can be purchased only outside Japan*. It's available from most travel agents (chances are your travel agent sells them) including the **Japan Travel Bureau** (JTB) (✆ 212/698-4919). If you're flying **Japan Airlines** (JAL) (✆ 800/ 525-3663 in the U.S. and Canada) or All Nippon Airways (ANA; ✆ 800/ 235-9262 in the U.S. and Canada), you can also purchase a rail pass from them.

With the exception of JR-West Passes, which may be purchased in Japan only by tourists, you cannot buy a rail pass once you're in Japan, so you must arrange for one before you leave home. You'll be issued a voucher (called an **Exchange Order**), which you'll then exchange for the pass itself after you arrive in Japan. Note that once you purchase your Exchange Order, you must exchange it in Japan for the pass itself within 3 months from the date of issue of the Exchange Order. When obtaining your actual pass, you must then specify the date you wish to start using the pass within a 1-month period. Note, too, that you cannot reserve seats in advance outside Japan with a rail pass.

Once You've Arrived   In Japan, you can exchange your voucher for a Japan Rail Pass at more than 40 Japan Rail Pass exchange offices, at which time you must present your passport and specify the date you wish to begin using the pass; most offices are open daily from 10am to 6pm, some even longer.

At both Narita Airport (daily 7am–9pm) and Kansai International Airport (daily 5:30am–11pm), you can pick up Japan Rail Passes at either the Travel Service Center or the Ticket

Office. Other Travel Service Centers or Ticket Offices, all located in JR train stations, include those at Tokyo (open daily 5:30am–10:30pm), Ueno, Shinjuku, Ikebukuro, and Shibuya stations in Tokyo; Kyoto Station; Shin-Osaka and Osaka stations; and Hiroshima, Sapporo, Okayama, Takamatsu, Matsuyama, Hakata, Nagasaki, Kumamoto, Miyazaki, and Nishi-Kagoshima stations. Vouchers can be exchanged for the JR-Kyushu Rail Pass at stations in Kyushu (including Hakata and Nagasaki), while vouchers for the JR East Pass can be exchanged at Narita Airport, many stations in Tokyo, and some stations in Tohoku. A list of exchange offices is provided with your voucher.

BY PLANE

Because it takes the better part of a day and night to get by train from Tokyo down to southern Kyushu or up to northern Hokkaido, you may find it more convenient to fly at least one stretch of your journey in Japan. You may, for example, fly into Osaka and then onward to Fukuoka on Kyushu, from which you can take a leisurely 2 weeks to travel by train through Kyushu and Honshu before returning to Osaka. I don't, however, advise flying short distances—say, from Tokyo to Osaka—simply because the time spent getting to and from airports is longer and costlier than traveling by Shinkansen.

Almost all domestic flights from Tokyo leave from the much more conveniently located **Haneda Airport.** However, if you're arriving on an international flight at Narita Airport, this means you'll probably have to transfer to Haneda Airport via the Airport Limousine Bus (see chapter 3 for details). On the other hand, if you're already in Tokyo you can easily reach Haneda Airport via monorail from Hamamatsucho Station on the Yamanote Line.

Three major domestic airlines are **Japan Airlines (JAL)** (℃ **0120/25-5971** in Japan; see "Getting There," earlier in this chapter for U.S. phone numbers), **All Nippon Airways (ANA)** (℃ **0120/029-222** in Japan), and **Japan Air Systems (JAS)** (℃ **0120/5-11283** in Japan), with networks that stretch all the way from Okinawa to northern Hokkaido. Regular fares are generally the same no matter which airline you fly domestically. However, fares change often, with the most expensive fares charged for peak season including New Year's, Golden Week, and summer vacation. However, bargains do exist. Some flights early in the day or late at night may be cheaper than flights during peak time. In addition, some small, regional airlines, such as **Skymark** (℃ **03/3433-7670** in Tokyo; 092/736-3131 in Fukuoka), operating out of Fukuoka on the island of Kyushu and **Air Do** (℃ **03/5350-7333** in Tokyo, ℃ 011/200-7333 in Sapporo) out of Sapporo on the island of Hokkaido, sometimes offer cheaper fares than those on JAL or ANA (see chapters 10 and 11). It pays, therefore, to shop around. Although it's subject to change, the regular fare for a one-way flight aboard JAL, ANA, and JAS from Tokyo to Kagoshima (or vice versa) is about ¥33,000 ($275) during the regular season. JAL, however, offers an evening flight from Kagoshima back to Tokyo for as low as ¥20,500 ($171) during the regular season. Roundtrip tickets are also slightly cheaper. For comparison, a train ticket between the two cities is ¥25,350 ($211) one way. Where airline fares are provided in this book, fares are for regular tickets during the regular season. Tickets can be purchased directly through the airline or through a travel agent such as **Japan Travel Bureau (JTB),** which has offices virtually everywhere in Japan.

If you know your itinerary in advance, it's cheaper to plan ahead and purchase your domestic flight in conjunction with your international flight to Japan. For example, if you plan to visit Tokyo and Sapporo from Los Angeles, you should purchase a Los Angeles–Sapporo ticket with a Tokyo stopover. Such throughfares are available to the following cities from the United States: Tokyo, Osaka, Sapporo, Nagoya, Fukuoka, and Okinawa. If you fly JAL or ANA internationally between North America and Japan, you can save more than 30% on the cost of your inner-Japan domestic flight by purchasing your domestic ticket in conjunction with your international ticket on the same carrier. Likewise, if you're coming from Europe, you may find it cheaper to fly KLM from Amsterdam to Osaka or Tokyo and then depart from Sapporo directly for Amsterdam. Contact the airlines directly or through your travel agent.

BY BUS

Buses often go where trains don't and thus may be the only way for you to get to the more remote areas of Japan—such as, for example, Shirakawago in the Japan Alps. In Hokkaido, Tohoku, and Kyushu, and other places, buses are used extensively.

Some buses require you to purchase your ticket in advance at the ticket counter at the bus terminal. For others, when you board a bus, you'll generally find a ticket machine by the entry door. Take a ticket, which is number-coded with a board displayed at the front of the bus. The board shows the various fares, which increase with the distance traveled. You pay your fare when you get off.

In addition to serving the remote areas of the country, **long-distance buses** (called *chokyori basu*) also operate between major cities in Japan and offer the cheapest mode of transportation.

Although **Japan Railways** operates almost a dozen bus routes eligible for JR Rail Pass coverage, the majority of buses are run by private companies. Many long-distance buses travel during the night and offer reclining seats and toilets, thus saving passengers the price of a night's lodging. For example, special buses depart from **Tokyo Station's** Yaesu south side every night for Kyoto (¥8,180/$68), Osaka (¥8,610/$72), Hiroshima (¥12,060/$100.50), Matsuyama (¥12,000/$100), and Takamatsu (¥10,500/$87.50), arriving at those cities' main train stations the next morning. Night buses also depart from **Shinjuku Station's** new south exit or from the **Shinjuku Highway Bus Terminal** (a 3-min. walk from Shinjuku Station's west exit) bound for Nagoya, Okayama, Kurashiki, and Hakata. Night buses also travel from these cities in reverse back to Tokyo. Slight discounts are given for round-trip travel completed within 6 to 10 days, depending on the city. A round-trip ticket to Hiroshima, for example, costs ¥22,000 ($183) if completed within 7 days, compared to ¥12,060 ($100) one-way.

For more information on local and long-distance bus service, refer to individual cities covered in this guide or contact the **Tourist Information Center** in Tokyo or Kyoto (see "Visitor Information," earlier in this chapter).

BY CAR

With the exception, perhaps, of Izu Peninsula, the Tohoku region, and Hokkaido, driving is not recommended for visitors wishing to tour Japan. Driving is British style (on the left side of the road), which may be hard for those not used to it; traffic can be horrendous; and it's not even economical. Not only is gas expensive (about ¥95 for one liter, or approximately 80¢ for a quarter of a gallon), but all of Japan's expressways charge high tolls—the one-way toll from Tokyo to Kyoto is almost the same price as a ticket to Kyoto on the Shinkansen. And whereas the Shinkansen takes only 3 hours to get to Kyoto, driving takes about 8 hours. In addition, you may encounter few signs in English in remote areas. Driving in cities is even worse: Streets are often hardly wide enough for a rickshaw, let alone a car, and many roads don't have sidewalks so you have to dodge people, bicycles, and telephone poles. Free parking is hard to find, and garages are expensive. Except in remote areas, it just doesn't make sense to drive.

There are approximately a dozen major car-rental companies in Tokyo alone, with branch offices throughout the city and at the Narita Airport, including **Nippon Rent-A-Car Service** (C 03/3485-7196 for the English Service Desk), **Toyota Rent-A-Car** (C 03/3264-0100), **Nissan Rent-A-Car** (C 0120/00-4123) and **Avis** (C 03/5397-8915); these companies also have branches throughout Japan. In almost every city with a JR train station, there is also a **JR Eki Rent-A-Car** office, offering 20% discounts on car rentals booked in conjunction with train tickets; you can reserve these cars at any JR Travel Service Center (located in train stations) anywhere in Japan. Rates vary, but the average cost for 24 hours with unlimited mileage begins at ¥6,000 ($50) for a subcompact including insurance but not gas; in some tourist areas, such as Hokkaido, rates are more expensive in peak season.

If you do intend to drive in Japan, you'll need either an **international** or a Japanese driving license. Remember, cars are driven on the left side of the road, and signs on all major highways are written in both Japanese and English. It is against the law to drink alcohol and drive, and you must wear seat belts at all times. Be sure to purchase a bilingual map since back roads often have names of towns written only in Japanese. Recommended is the *Shobunsha Road Atlas Japan,* available in bookstores with English books and with maps of major cities as well, including Tokyo, Sapporo, Hiroshima, and others.

BREAKDOWNS/ASSISTANCE
The **Japan Automobile Federation (JAF)** maintains emergency telephone boxes along Japan's major arteries to assist drivers whose cars have broken down or drivers who need help. Calls from these telephones are free and will connect you to the operation center of JAF.

BY FERRY
Because Japan is an island nation, it has an extensive ferry network linking the string of islands. Although it takes longer to travel by ferry, it's also cheaper and can be a pleasant, relaxing experience. For example, you can take a ferry from Tokyo to Kochi on Shikoku, departing Tokyo at 7:50pm and arriving in Kochi the next day at 4:20pm, with fares starting at ¥11,000 ($92) one-way. Other routes link Osaka with Shikoku and Kyushu. Contact the **Tourist Information Center** (see "Visitor Information," earlier in this chapter) for more details concerning ferries, prices, schedules, and telephone numbers of the various ferry companies.

11 Tips on Accommodations

Accommodations available in Japan range from inexpensive Japanese-style inns to large Western-style hotels. Although you can travel throughout Japan without making reservations beforehand, it's essential to book in advance if you're traveling during peak travel seasons and is recommended at other times (see "When to Go," earlier in this chapter for peak travel times).

If you arrive in a town without reservations, most local tourist offices—generally located in or near the main train station—will find accommodations for you at no extra charge. Note that in popular resort areas, most accommodations raise their rates during peak times. Some also charge more on weekends.

A note on reservations: When making reservations, especially at a Japanese-style accommodation, it's best if the call is conducted in Japanese or by fax, as written English is always easier for most Japanese to understand.

A note about taxes: In figuring out your bill, remember that a 5% consumption tax will be added (some business hotels and inexpensive inns include the tax in their rates). There will also be a 10% to 15% service charge added to your bill in upper-end hotels, while expensive ryokan will add a 10% to 20% service charge (sometimes included in room rates). No service charge is levied at business hotels, pensions, and minshuku for the simple reason that no services are provided. Unless otherwise stated, tax and service charges are not included in room rates quoted in this book.

JAPANESE-STYLE INNS

A stay at a traditional ryokan or Japanese inn can prove very expensive. Yet the unique experience makes it worth it, for nothing quite conveys the simplicity and beauty—indeed the very atmosphere—of old Japan more than these inns with their gleaming polished wood, tatami floors, rice-paper sliding doors, and meticulously pruned gardens. Personalized service by kimono-clad hostesses and exquisitely prepared kaiseki meals are the trademarks of such inns, some of which are of ancient vintage. Indeed, staying in one is like taking a trip back in time.

If you want to experience a Japanese-style inn but can't afford the prices of a ryokan, there are a number of alternatives described below. Although they don't offer the same personalized service, beautiful setting, or memorable cuisine, they do offer the chance to stay in a simple tatami room, sleep on a futon, and, in some cases, eat Japanese meals. As at a ryokan, prices are per person and often include two meals as well. English, however, is rarely spoken.

RYOKAN   Ryokan developed during the Edo Period, when *daimyo* (feudal lords) were required to travel to and from Edo (present-day Tokyo) every 2 years. They always traveled with a full entourage including members of their family, retainers, and servants. The best ryokan, of course, were reserved for the daimyo and members of the imperial family. Some of these exist today, passed down from generation to generation.

Traditionally, ryokan are small, only one or two stories high, contain about 10 to 30 rooms, and are made of wood with a tile roof. Most guests arrive at their ryokan between 4 and 5pm. The entrance is often through a gate and small garden; upon entering, you're met by a bowing woman in a kimono. Take off your shoes, slide on the proffered plastic slippers, and follow your hostess down the long wooden corridors until you reach the sliding door of your room. After taking off your slippers, step into your tatami room, which is almost void of furniture. What you'll find is a low table in the middle of the room, floor cushions, an antique scroll hanging in an alcove, a simple flower arrangement, and, best of all, a view past rice-paper sliding screens of a Japanese landscaped garden with bonsai, stone lanterns, and a meandering pond filled with carp. Notice there's no bed in the room.

Almost immediately, your hostess brings you welcoming hot tea and a sweet served at your low table so you can sit there for a while, recuperate from your travels, and appreciate the view, the peace, and the solitude. Next comes your hot bath, either in your own room (if you have one in your room) or in the communal bath. Since many ryokan are clustered around hot springs (*onsen*), many offer the additional luxury of bathing in thermal baths including outdoor baths. (For bathing, be sure to follow the procedure outlined in "Minding Your Ps & Qs," in appendix A—soaping and rinsing *before* getting into the tub.) After bathing and soaking away all tension, aches, and pains, change into your *yukata,* a cotton kimono provided by the ryokan.

When you return to your room, you'll find the maid ready to serve your *kaiseki* dinner, which consists of locally grown vegetables, sashimi (raw fish), grilled or baked fish, tempura, and various regional specialties, all spread out on many tiny plates; the menu is determined by the chef. Admire how each dish is in itself a delicate piece of artwork; it all looks too wonderful to eat, but finally hunger takes over. If you want, you can order sake or beer to accompany your meal (but you'll pay extra for drinks).

After you've finished eating, your maid will return to clear away the dishes and to lay out your bed. The bed is really a futon, a kind of mattress with quilts, and it is laid out on the tatami floor. The next morning, the maid will wake you, put away the futon, and serve a breakfast of fish, pickled vegetables, soup, dried seaweed, rice, and a raw egg to be mixed with the rice. Feeling rested, well fed, and pampered, you're then ready to pack your bags and pay your bill. Your hostess sees you off at the front gate, smiling and bowing as you set off for the rest of your travels.

Such is life at a good ryokan. Sadly, however, the number of upper-class ryokan diminishes each year. Unable to compete with more profitable high-rise hotels in these days of recession, many ryokan in Japan have closed down, especially in large cities; very few remain in such cities as Tokyo and Osaka. If you want to stay in a Japanese inn, it's best to do so in Kyoto or at a resort or hot-spring spa. Altogether, there are approximately 70,000 ryokan still operating in Japan in a variety of different price ranges.

In addition, although ideally a ryokan is an old wooden structure that once served traveling daimyo or was perhaps the home of a wealthy merchant, many today—especially those in hot-spring resort areas—are actually modern concrete affairs with as many as 100 or more rooms. Meals are served in dining rooms. What they lack in intimacy and personal service, however, is made up for in slightly cheaper prices and such amenities as modern bathing facilities and perhaps a bar and outdoor recreational facilities. Most guest rooms are fitted with a color TV, a telephone, a safe for locking up valuables, and a cotton yukata, as well as such amenities as soap, shampoo, a razor, a toothbrush, and toothpaste.

Rates are per person rather than per room and include breakfast, dinner, and often service; tax is extra. Thus, while rates may seem high, they're actually competitively priced compared to what you'd pay for a hotel room and comparable meals in a restaurant. Although rates can vary from ¥9,000 to an astonishing ¥150,000 ($75–$1,250) per person, the average cost is generally ¥12,000 to ¥20,000 ($100–$167). Even within a single ryokan the rates can vary greatly, depending on the room you choose, the dinner courses you select, and the number of people in your room. If you're paying the highest rate, you can be certain you're getting the best room, the best view of the garden or perhaps even your own private garden, and a much more elaborate meal than lower-paying guests. All the rates for ryokan in this book are based on double occupancy; if there are more than two of you in one room, you can generally count on a slightly lower per-person rate.

Although I heartily recommend you try spending at least 1 night in a ryokan, there are a number of **disadvantages** to this style of accommodation. The most obvious problem is that you may find it uncomfortable sitting on the floor. And because the futon is put away during the day, there's no place to lie down for an afternoon nap or rest, except on the hard, tatami-covered floor. In addition, some of the older ryokan, though quaint, are bitterly cold in the winter and may have only Japanese-style toilets. As for breakfast, you might find it difficult to swallow raw egg, rice, and seaweed in the morning. (I've even been served grilled grasshopper—quite crunchy.) Sometimes you can get a Western-style breakfast if you order it the night before, but more often than not the fried or scrambled eggs will arrive cold, leading you to suspect they were cooked right after you ordered them.

A ryokan is also quite rigid in its **schedule.** You're expected to arrive sometime after 4pm, take your bath, and then eat at around 6 or 7pm. Breakfast is served early, usually by 8am, and checkout is by 10am. That means you can't sleep in, and because the maid is continually coming in and out, you have a lot less privacy than you would in a hotel.

Another drawback of the ryokan is that some will not take you. They simply do not want to deal with the problems inherent in accepting a foreign guest, including the language barrier and differing customs. I've seen a number of beautiful old ryokan I'd like to include in this book, but I've been turned away at the door. Sadly, I've also lost ryokan that once accepted foreigners but have stopped doing so following unacceptable behavior (such as climbing in the win-dow at midnight). On the bright side, the recession has convinced other ryokan to open their doors to foreigners for the first time. In any case, those recommended in the pages that follow do welcome Westerners.

You should always make a **reservation** if you want to stay in a first-class ryokan (and even in most medium-priced ones), because the chef has to shop for and prepare your meals. The ryokan staff members often do not look kindly upon unannounced strangers turning up on their doorstep (though I did this on a recent weekday trip to Nikko without any problems at all). You can make a reservation for a ryokan through any travel agency in Japan or by calling or faxing a ryokan directly. You may be required to pay a deposit. For more information on ryokan in Japan, including destinations not covered in this guide, pick up the *Japan Ryokan Guide* at one of the Tourist Information Centers in Japan. In addition, check out www.eryokan.co.jp, a Tokyo-based travel reservations company with 300 member inns that can be booked online.

MINSHUKU Technically, a *min-shuku* is inexpensive Japanese-style lodging in a private home—the Japanese version of a bed-and-breakfast. Minshuku can range from thatched farmhouses and rickety old wooden buildings to modern concrete structures often located in resort and tourist areas and generally including two meals in their rates. Because minshuku are family-run affairs, there's no personal service, which means you're expected to lay out your own futon at night, stow it away in the morning, and tidy up your room. Most also do not supply a towel or yukata, nor do they have rooms with a private bathroom. There is, however, a public bathroom, and meals are served in a communal dining room. And since minshuku cater primarily to Japanese travelers, they're often excellent places to meet the locals.

Officially, what differentiates a ryokan from a minshuku is the level of service and corresponding price, but the differences are sometimes very slight. I've stayed in cheap ryokan providing almost no service and in minshuku too large and modern to be considered private homes. The average per-person cost for 1 night in a minshuku is generally ¥7,000 to ¥9,000 ($58–$75) and includes two meals.

KOKUMIN SHUKUSHA   A *kokumin shukusha* can be translated as a People's Lodge—public lodging found primarily in national parks and resort and vacation areas. Established by the government, there are more than 300 of these facilities throughout Japan. Catering largely to Japanese school groups and families, they offer basic, Japanese-style rooms at an average daily rate of about ¥6,500 ($54) per person including two meals. Although you don't have to have a reservation to stay in these places, they're usually full during the summer and peak seasons. Reservations can be made through a travel agency; many are also in the *Directory of Welcome Inns* (see "Helping Hands," below). The drawback to many of these lodges is that, because they're often located in national parks and scenic spots, the best way to reach them is by car.

SHUKUBO   These are lodgings in a Buddhist temple, similar to inexpensive ryokan, except they're attached to temples and serve vegetarian food. There's usually an early-morning service at 6am, which you're welcome—in some shukubo, required—to join. Probably the best place to experience life in a temple is at Mt. Koya (see chapter 8). Prices generally range from about ¥7,000 to ¥15,000 ($50–$125) per person, including two meals.

WESTERN-STYLE ACCOMMODATIONS

Western-style lodgings range from large first-class hotels to inexpensive ones catering primarily to Japanese businessmen.

When selecting and reserving your hotel room, call or fax the hotel directly to inquire about rates, even if a toll-free 800 number is provided; sometimes there are special packages, such as weekend or honeymoon packages that central reservations desks will not be aware of. Special rates are also sometimes offered on the hotel's website. Always ask what kinds of rooms are available. Almost all hotels in Japan offer a wide range of rooms at various prices; room size is the most important factor in pricing. Rooms with views—whether of the sea or a castle—are also generally more expensive, as are rooms on higher floors. In Japan, a **twin room** refers to a room with twin beds, and a **double room** refers to one with a double bed; most hotels charge more for a twin room, but others charge more for doubles. Some of the upper-priced hotels also offer executive floors, which are generally on the highest floors and offer such perks as a private lounge with separate check-in, more in-room amenities such as fax machines or dataports, complimentary breakfast and evening cocktails, extended checkout time, and privileges that can include free use of the health club.

Once you decide on the type of room you want, ask for the best in that category. For example, if you want a standard room and deluxe rooms start on the 14th floor, ask for a standard on the 13th floor. In addition, be specific about the kind of room you want, whether it's a nonsmoking room, a room with a view of Mt. Fuji, or a room with a dataport for your computer modem.

Be sure to give your approximate time of arrival, especially if it's after 6pm when they might give your room away. Check-in ranges from about noon or 1pm for first-class hotels to 3 or 4pm for business hotels. Checkout is generally about 10am for business hotels and 11am or noon for upper-range hotels. In any case, it's perfectly acceptable to leave your luggage with the front desk or the bell captain if you arrive early or want to sightsee after checking out.

HOTELS Both first-class and medium-priced hotels in Japan are known for excellent service and cleanliness. The first-class hotels in the larger cities can compete with the best hotels in the world and offer a **wide range of services,** from health clubs and massage services to business centers and restaurant and shopping arcades. Unfortunately, health clubs and swimming pools usually cost extra—anywhere from ¥2,000 to an outrageous ¥5,000 ($17–$42) per single use. In addition, outdoor pools are generally open only in July and August. Rooms in upper-range hotels and many moderate hotels in large cities catering to tourists come with such **standard features** as a minibar, bilingual cable TV with pay movies and English channels like CNN or BBC, a clock, a radio, cotton kimono, a hot-water pot and tea (and occasionally coffee), a hair dryer, and a private bathroom with a tub-and-shower combination. (Since Japanese are used to soaping down and rinsing off before bathing, it would be rare to find tubs without showers; similarly, showers without tubs are practically nonexistent in this nation of bathers.) Several also have "washlet" toilets, which are combination toilets and spray bidets with a controllable range of speeds and temperatures. Because they're accustomed to foreigners, most hotels in this category employ an English-speaking staff and offer nonsmoking floors or rooms. Services provided include room service, same-day laundry and dry cleaning, and English-language newspapers (often complimentary) delivered to your room. Note that in medium-range hotels, same-day laundry service is not available Sundays and holidays and you must turn in your laundry by 10am to receive it by 5pm that day.

The most expensive hotels in Japan are in Tokyo, where you'll pay at least ¥25,000 ($208) for a double or twin room in a first-class hotel and ¥14,000 to ¥25,000 ($117–$208) for a medium-priced hotel. Outside the major cities, rooms for two people generally range from about ¥16,000 to ¥20,000 ($133–$167) for first-class hotels and ¥12,000 to ¥15,000 ($100–$125) for medium-priced hotels.

BUSINESS HOTELS Catering primarily to traveling Japanese businessmen, a "business hotel" is a no-frills establishment with tiny, sparsely furnished rooms, most of them singles but usually with some twin or double rooms also available. Primarily just a place to crash for the night, these rooms usually have everything you need but in miniature form—minuscule bathroom, tiny bathtub, small bed (or beds), and barely enough space to unpack your bags. If you're a large person, you may have trouble sleeping in a place like this. There are no bellhops, no room service, and sometimes not even a lobby or coffee shop, although usually there are vending machines selling beer, soda, cigarettes, and snacks. Usually, business hotels do not have no-smoking rooms. The advantages of staying in business hotels are price—starting as low as ¥6,000 or ¥7,000 ($50 or $58) for a single—and location—usually near major train and subway stations. Check-in is usually not until 3 or 4pm, and checkout is usually at 10am; you can leave your bags at the front desk.

The most sophisticated business hotels are in Tokyo, where, because of high prices, they make up the bulk of medium-priced accommodations. Some business hotels also offer membership clubs for frequent guests. Sunroute, for example, has a membership

Tips Tips for Saving on Your Hotel Room

Although Japanese hotels have traditionally remained pretty loyal to their published **rack rates,** which are always available at the front desk, the recession has opened possibilities for bargains.

- **Always ask politely whether a less expensive room is available than the first one mentioned.** Ask whether there are corporate discounts. If there are two of you, ask whether a double or a twin room is cheaper.

- **Dial direct.** When booking a room in a chain hotel, call the hotel's local line as well as the toll-free number to see where you get the best deal.

- **Ask about promotions and special plans.** Hotels frequently offer special "plans," including "Spring Plans," "Ladies' Plans," and even "Shopping Plans" that provide cheaper rates and services.

- **Check the Internet.** If the hotel has a website, check to see whether discounts or special promotions are offered. Some hotels offer discounts exclusively through the Internet.

- **Remember the law of supply and demand.** Resort hotels are more crowded and therefore more expensive on weekends and during peak travel periods such as Golden Week. Discounts, therefore, are often available for midweek and off-season stays.

- **Avoid extra charges.** Find out before you dial whether your hotel imposes a surcharge on local or long-distance calls. A pay phone, however inconvenient, may save you money. Also, instead of using the minibar in your room, save money by buying drinks and snacks from convenience stores or vending machines.

- **Ask about hotel membership plans.** Some chain business hotels offer hotel memberships with discounts on meals and free stays after a certain number of nights. Others, such as the New Otani and the Imperial in Tokyo, allow free use of the hotel swimming pool simply by becoming a member at no extra charge. Inquire at the front desk.

- **Ask the local tourist office whether there's a Welcome Card.** Nine tourist regions around Japan, including Kagawa Prefecture (Shikoku), Fukuoka, Aomori Prefecture (Tohoku District), and Hiroshima, offer a free **Welcome Card** to foreign visitors that provides discounts in room rates in participating hotels.

club you can join for ¥1,000 ($8.35), which gives a 15% to 30% discount on hotel rates depending on the day of the week, a 10% discount on its restaurants after 5pm, and a late 3pm checkout. When making your reservation, ask whether such a membership is available.

PENSIONS Pensions are like minshuku, except that accommodations are Western-style with beds instead of futon and the two meals served are usually Western. Often managed by a young couple or a young staff, they cater to young Japanese and are most often located in ski resorts and in the countryside, sometimes making access a problem. Averaging 10 guest rooms, many seem especially geared to young Japanese women and are thus done up in rather feminine-looking decor with lots of pinks and flower prints. The average cost is ¥8,000 to ¥10,000 ($67–$83) per person per night including two meals.

YOUTH HOSTELS There are some 350 youth hostels in Japan, most of them privately run and operating in locations ranging from temples to concrete blocks. There's no age limit (though children younger than 4 may not be accepted), and although most of them require a youth hostel membership card from the Japan Youth Hostel Association, they often let foreigners stay without one at no extra charge or for about ¥600 ($5) extra per night. Youth hostels are reasonable, costing about ¥3,500 ($29) per day including two meals, and can be reserved in advance. However, there are usually quite a few restrictions such as a 9 or 10pm curfew, a lights-out policy shortly thereafter, an early breakfast time, and closed times through the day, generally from about 10am to 3pm. In addition, rooms generally have many bunk beds or futon, affording little privacy. On the other hand, they're certainly the cheapest accommodation in Japan.

Because youth hostels are often inconveniently located, I have included only a couple in this guide, but if you plan on staying almost exclusively in hostels, pick up a pamphlet called "Youth Hostel Map of Japan," available at the **Tourist Information Centers** in Tokyo, Kyoto, and Narita and Kansai airports. You should also get a youth hostel membership card. In the U.S., contact **Hostelling International/American Youth Hostels,** 733 15th St. NW, Suite 840, Washington, DC 20005 (✆ **202/783-6161;** www.hiayh.org), which also offers a directory of low-cost accommodations around the country and abroad. Cards cost $25 for adults, $15 for seniors older than 54, and are free for children younger than 17.

If you fail to obtain a youth hostel card in your own country, you can get one in Tokyo for ¥2,500 ($21) from the **Japan Youth Hostel Association,** located in the Suidobashi Nishiguchi Kaikan, 2–20–7 Misaki-cho, Chiyoda-ku, Tokyo 101 (✆ **03/3288-0260**); open Monday through Saturday from 10am to 5pm, closed the second and fourth Saturday of the month and national holidays, a 1-minute walk from the Suidobashi Station's west exit. You can also buy a youth hostel card in Tokyo at the **Youth Hostel information counter** on the eighth floor of Seibu department store in Ikebukuro.

CAPSULE HOTELS Capsule hotels, which became popular in the early 1980s, are used primarily by Japanese businessmen who have spent an evening out drinking and missed the last train home—costing about ¥3,000 to ¥4,000 ($25–$33) per person, a capsule hotel is sometimes cheaper than a taxi to the suburbs. The units are small—no larger than a coffin and consisting of a bed, a private color TV, an alarm clock, and a radio—and are usually stacked two deep in rows down a corridor; the only thing separating you from your probably inebriated neighbor is a curtain. A cotton kimono and a locker are provided, and baths and toilets are communal. Most capsule hotels do not accept women.

INTERNATIONAL VILLAS International Villas are such a great deal for foreigners that I want to give them special mention here. These small country inns are financed and maintained by the Okayama prefectural government and are open only to foreigners, although accompanying Japanese guests are welcome. Each villa is small, with a half dozen or so guest rooms, (usually without private bathroom), and is equipped with public bathroom and kitchen facilities. No meals are served, but you can cook your own or visit one of the local restaurants. There are six International Villas, most of them in small villages or rural settings: Fukiya, Koshihata (currently closed), Ushimado, Hattoji, Shiraishi Island, and Takebe. Most rooms are Western-style twins, but some Japanese-style rooms are also available. The cost for staying at one of the villas is ¥3,000 ($25) per person for nonmembers and ¥2,500 ($21) for members. To become a member, simply pay ¥500 ($4.15) for a membership card upon check-in at any villa. For more information, see "Okayama: Gateway to Shikoku," in chapter 8.

LOVE HOTELS Finally, a word about Japan's so-called "love hotels." Usually found close to entertainment districts and along major highways, such hotels do not provide sexual services themselves; rather, they offer rooms for rent by the hour to couples. Altogether, there are an estimated 35,000 such love hotels, usually gaudy structures shaped like ocean liners or castles and offering such extras as rotating beds and mirrored walls. You'll know that you've wandered into a love-hotel district when you notice hourly rates posted near the front door.

HELPING HANDS

WELCOME INNS If you find all my recommendations for a certain city fully booked, there are several ways of finding alternative accommodations. Top on my list would be to book a room through one of four **Welcome Inn Reservation Centers,** located at the Tourist Information Centers (TICs) in Tokyo, Kyoto, Narita Airport outside Tokyo, and Kansai Airport outside Osaka (see "Visitor Information," earlier in this chapter).

Some 750 modestly priced hotels and Japanese-style inns throughout Japan are members of Welcome Inns (several of these are also recommended in this book). Room rates are ¥8,000 ($67) or less for a single and ¥13,000 ($108) or less for a double. No fee is charged for the reservation service, though you are asked to guarantee your reservation with a credit card.

For more information, contact your nearest Japan National Tourist Organization office (again, see "Visitor Information," earlier in this chapter) and request the *Directory of Welcome Inns,* which not only lists all the properties but also contains a reservation request form that you should then mail or fax to the Tokyo TIC at least 3 weeks prior to your departure; you'll then receive a confirmation slip and detailed information and access maps to your selected accommodations. If you have access to the Internet, you can also access the e-mail reservation request form through JNTO's home page at **www.jnto.go.jp**; click on "Accommodations" and then click "Welcome Inn Reservation Assistance." Alternatively, you can also make reservations directly with Welcome Inn members offering online bookings by going to www.jnto.go.jp, entering WI followed by the code number of the establishment you are interested in in the Search box, and following instructions.

If you're already in Japan, you can apply by mailing, faxing, or e-mailing your reservation request form (telephone reservations are not accepted) or by appearing in person at one of the four TIC offices during the following hours:

- **Tokyo TIC,** in the Tokyo International Forum, 3–5–1 Marunouchi (reservations accepted Monday through Friday 9:15–11:30am and 1–4:45pm)
- **Narita Airport TIC,** in the arrivals lobby of Terminal 2 (daily 9am–7:30pm)

- **Kyoto TIC,** a minute's walk from Kyoto Station's north side (take the Karasuma central exit) at the Kyoto Tower Building, Higashi-Shiokoji-cho, Shimogyo-ku (Mon–Fri 9–11:30am and 1–4:30pm)
- **Kansai International Airport,** Osaka, at the north end of the International Arrivals Lobby (daily 9am–8:30pm)

All centers are closed on public holidays.

JAPANESE INN GROUP In addition to Welcome Inns, there's another great organization called the Japanese Inn Group, a special organization of more than 80 Japanese-style inns and hotels throughout Japan offering inexpensive lodging and catering largely to foreigners. Although you may balk at the idea of staying at a place filled mainly with foreigners, remember that many inexpensive Japanese-style inns are not accustomed to guests from abroad and may be quite reluctant to take you in. I have covered many of these Japanese Inn Group members in this guidebook through the years and have found the owners for the most part to be an exceptional group of friendly people eager to offer foreigners the chance to experience life on tatami and futon. In many cases, these are good places in which to exchange information with other world travelers, and they are popular with both young people and families.

Although many of the group members call themselves ryokan, they are not ryokan in the true sense of the word because they don't offer personalized service and many of them don't serve food. However, they do offer simple tatami rooms that generally come with a TV and an air conditioner (sometimes both are coin-operated); most also have towels and a cotton *yukata* robe for your use. Some offer Western-style rooms as well, and though rooms without a private bathroom are more common, some do

offer private bathrooms. Facilities generally include a coin-operated washer and dryer and a public bathroom. The average cost of a 1-night stay is about ¥4,500 to ¥7,500 ($37.50–$62.50) per person without meals. Breakfast is usually available for an extra charge; dinner is also sometimes available.

Upon your arrival in Japan, head to one of the four Tourist Information Centers (see above) where you can pick up a pamphlet called "Japanese Inn Group," which lists the members of this organization. You should make reservations directly with the ryokan in which you wish to stay (most have faxes and many have e-mail). In some cases, you'll be asked to pay a deposit (equal to 1 night's stay), which you can do with a personal check, traveler's check, money order, or bank check, but the easiest way is with American Express. For more information, contact the Inn Group's headquarters at Ryokan Asakusa Shigetsu, 1–31–11 Nishi-Asakusa, Taito-ku, Tokyo 111-0032 (© **03/3843-2345;** fax 03/3843-2348); there's also a Kyoto office at Hiraiwa Ryokan, 314, Hayao-cho, Kaminoguchi-agaru, Ninomiyacho-dori, Shimogyo-ku, Kyoto 600-8114 (© **075/351-6748;** fax 075/351-6969). Some member inns belong to the Welcome Inn group as well, which means you can also make reservations through one of the TIC offices listed above.

LOCAL RESERVATION AGENTS If you arrive at your destination and then discover you need help obtaining accommodations, you may inquire about a place to stay at the hotel and ryokan reservation office or the tourist information office, both found in most train stations. Although policies may differ from office to office, you generally don't have to pay a fee for their services, but you usually do have to pay a percentage of your overnight charge as a deposit. The disadvantage is that you don't see the locale beforehand,

and if there's space left at a ryokan even in peak tourist season, there may be a reason for it. The two worst places I've stayed in Japan were booked through one of these reservation offices at a train station in peak season (don't worry, I don't recommend them in this book). Although these offices can be a real lifesaver in a pinch and in most cases may be able to recommend quite reasonable and pleasant places in which to stay, it certainly pays to plan in advance.

You can also book room reservations through a travel agency such as the **Japan Travel Bureau (JTB),** found everywhere in Japan.

12 Packing Tips

The first thing you'll want to do when packing is select the smallest bag you can get away with and **pack as lightly as you can.** Storage space is limited on Japan's trains, including the Shinkansen bullet train, business hotels sometimes lack closets, and there are multitudes of stairs and overhead and underground passageways to navigate in virtually every train station in the country.

The most important item is **a good pair of walking shoes,** well-broken-in. You will probably be walking much more than you do at home and because shoe sizes in Japan are smaller than in the West, you can't count on finding a pair that will fit. Keep in mind, too, that because you have to remove your shoes to enter Japanese homes, inns, shrines, and temples, you should bring a pair that's easy to slip on and off. And since you may be walking around in stocking feet, save yourself embarrassment by packing socks and hose without holes.

As for **clothes,** you'll need a coat in winter and very light clothing for the hot and humid summer months. Jackets are necessary for spring and autumn; I've seen it snow in March in Tokyo, and even May can be quite crisp. Japan's top French restaurants usually require jackets and ties. It's considered inappropriate for women to wear dresses without hose or tops without sleeves, though I've noticed that the younger generation ignores this, especially in resort areas. Jeans are okay for casual dining and sightseeing, but shorts are uncommon in Japan outside hiking and sports areas.

Virtually all hotels and Japanese-style inns—save youth hostels and some budget-priced inns—provide towels, soap, washcloths, toothbrushes, toothpaste, shampoo, a cotton kimono (called a *yukata* and not a giveaway), and usually razors. If you run out of something, you'll have no problem finding it in Japan. Most hotels and inns also provide a thermos of hot water or a water heater as well as some tea bags. If you're a coffee addict, you can save money by buying instant coffee and drinking your morning cup in your hotel room. Hair dryers are a standard feature in almost all rooms with private bathrooms, including business hotels.

Tips Help with Heavy Bags

If your bag becomes a burden but you don't want to mail items home, an alternative is to send a bag onward to your next or last stop by *takkyu-bin*, available at larger hotels or from most convenient stations. Bags reach most destinations in one or two nights, with the cost of an average-size bag less than $20.

It's also good to carry a supply of **pocket tissues,** which you can pick up at newspaper stands near and in train stations, because some public rest rooms do not have toilet paper. It's also a good idea to carry change for local buses (faster than trying to change ¥1,000 notes), a folding umbrella, and a compass for getting your bearings and following directions using local maps. Finally, pack small, inexpensive gifts from home that can be given to those who show unexpected kindness, including candy, postcards, and hometown souvenirs.

13 Suggested Itineraries for Seeing Japan

Japan, with its rich culture and varied geography, has much to offer the curious visitor, not only in and around the major cities but in many of the outlying regions as well. If you want to see *everything,* you should plan on spending at least a year in Japan. More likely, your time will be limited to a week or two, so you'll have to be selective; this section will help you decide on an itinerary.

My suggested itineraries are divided into two sections. The first one is useful for first-time visitors who have only 1 or 2 weeks in Japan and want to see the highlights of central and southern Honshu. The second section consists of regional itineraries, giving you an idea of how to plan your travels if you're interested in touring, for example, the Japan Alps or Hokkaido. If you're in Japan for several weeks, you can fashion your own personalized itinerary by combining several of my suggested itineraries. You might, for example, wish to combine my 1-week tour with a trip to Kyushu.

Regardless of what itinerary you plan, I am adamant about one thing: *Kyoto is a must.* In addition to having served as the nation's capital for more than 1,000 years, it has more temples, shrines, and historic sights than any other Japanese city. As a base, it's also useful for touring other attractions in the Kansai area. Other **top favorites include Nara,** another ancient capital near Kyoto; **Tokyo,** for its wealth of museums, design, and fashion; **Mt. Koya,** Japan's most revered religious center where you can sleep in a Buddhist temple; **Nikko,** the site of Shogun Tokugawa Ieyasu's mausoleum; **Takayama and Shirakawago,** two picturesque villages in the Japan Alps; **Hiroshima,** with its famous Peace Memorial Park and a museum of the atomic bomb; **Kurashiki** with its picture-perfect historic warehouse district; and Japan's numerous hot-spring spas.

FOR FIRST-TIMERS

If You Have 1 Week in Japan

Day 1 Arrive at Narita Airport and head to your hotel in Tokyo (it's about a 2-hr. trip). Recuperate from your flight, settle in, and get a feel for the city. Top off the day with a meal in a traditional restaurant. Try to stay up as late as you can to adjust to the new time zone.

Day 2 Because of the difference in time zones, you'll probably be wide awake in the wee hours of the morning, so get up and head for Tsukiji Fish Market. After a breakfast of fresh sushi, take the Hibiya Line to Ueno, where you'll find the Tokyo National Museum. From Ueno, hop on the Ginza Line for Asakusa and its famous Nakamise Dori Lane with shops selling traditional products and Sensoji Temple. If you have time, stroll down Ginza's fashionable shopping district or head toward Harajuku with its inexpensive clothing boutiques and Oriental Bazaar. Spend the evening in Shinjuku, Roppongi, or another of Tokyo's famous nightlife areas or attend a Kabuki play.

Day 3   Take the 40-minute Shinkansen bullet train to Odawara or the 1½-hour Odakyu Romance Car to Hakone Yumoto, gateways to the wonderful Fuji-Hakone-Izu National Park (if possible, leave your luggage at Odawara Station and travel overnight only with a small bag). Here you can travel through some of Japan's most scenic countryside via a circuitous route that includes a two-car tram, a cable car, ropeway, and a boat while seeing such sights as a wonderful open-air sculptural museum and, if you're lucky, the elusive Mt. Fuji. Spend the night in the Fujiya Hotel, one of my favorites in all of Japan, or in a Japanese inn.

Day 4   Complete your trip through Hakone, return to Odawara, and transfer to the 3-hour Shinkansen bullet train to Kyoto. End the day with a stroll through Kyoto's central shopping area and a visit to the Museum of Kyoto, topped with a walk through the Gion geisha district and the Pontocho nightlife area. Spend the night in one of Kyoto's many traditional Japanese-style inns.

Day 5   Start the day with a self-guided walk through eastern Kyoto, seeing Sanjusangendo Hall, Kiyomizu Temple, and perhaps Heian Shrine with its garden, followed by shopping at the Kyoto Handicraft Center. If it's summer, spend the evening watching cormorant fishing in nearby Arashiyama.

Day 6   Visit Kyoto's other main attractions—Nijo Castle, Kyoto Imperial Palace, Ryoanji Temple with its famous rock garden, and the Golden Pavilion. If you have a rail pass, you should also consider taking the 1-hour Shinkansen bullet train from Kyoto to Himeji, where you can tour what's arguably Japan's most beautiful feudal castle.

Day 7   Depart Japan.

If You Have 2 Weeks in Japan

This is something of a whirlwind trip, but it allows you to take in some of the best that Honshu Island has to offer. If you have 1 or 2 extra days, you might wish to devote more time to Kyoto or one of the other destinations. Also, if you're landing at Kansai International Airport outside Osaka instead of at Narita Airport near Tokyo, you'll want to modify the itineraries; if you have no desire to see Tokyo, see the Kansai area itinerary below.

Day 1   As above.

Day 2   Rise in the wee hours and head to Tsukiji Fish Market, followed by a walk through the nearby lovely Hama Rikyu Garden. From the garden, board a boat for a cruise down the Sumida River to the historic district of Asakusa, where you can shop for souvenirs on Nakamise Dori and visit Sensoji Temple. In late afternoon, head to the Ginza for a visit to one of Japan's legendary department stores, followed perhaps with a performance of Kabuki at the nearby Kabukiza theater.

Day 3   Visit Tokyo's two most important museums—the Tokyo National Museum with its decorative arts and the Edo-Tokyo Museum, which outlines the capital's history. Next, go to Harajuku to see Meiji Shrine, Tokyo's most popular shrine, and to do some shopping at Oriental Bazaar, great for Japanese souvenirs. Take in some of Tokyo's crazy nightlife after dark.

Day 4   Take a day trip outside of Tokyo. Good choices include the ancient capital Kamakura or Nikko, which is famous for the sumptuous mausoleum of Shogun Tokugawa Ieyasu. Or take an overnight trip to

Hakone (see Day 3 in the 1-week itinerary above).

Day 5   Early in the morning, take the Shinkansen to Nagoya (about 2 hr.) and then a 3-hour train ride to Takayama in the Japan Alps (if you don't have a rail pass, there's also a direct bus from Tokyo's Shinjuku Station). Explore the picturesque, narrow streets of this old castle town and its many interesting museums.

Day 6   Before departing Takayama, visit the morning market by the river. Take the 2-hour bus ride along a winding mountain road to Shirakawago, a tiny village of rice paddies and thatched farmhouses. Spend the night in one of these farmhouses.

Day 7   From Shirakawago, it takes the better part of a day to reach Kyoto, but the scenery is magnificent. Take a bus to either Takayama or Nagoya and then transfer to a train for Kyoto.

Day 8   Start the day with a self-guided walk through eastern Kyoto, seeing Sanjusangendo Hall, Kiyomizu Temple, and perhaps Heian Shrine, followed by shopping at the Kyoto Handicraft Center. In late afternoon, walk through central Kyoto's shopping district, visit the Museum of Kyoto, and end the day with a stroll through the Gion geisha district and Pontocho.

Day 9   Visit the Kyoto Imperial Palace, Nijo Castle, Ryoanji Temple, and the Golden Pavilion. If it's summer, spend the evening watching cormorant fishing in nearby Arashiyama.

Day 10   Early in the morning, head for Nara, one of Japan's ancient capitals, where you'll want to spend at least 3 hours seeing the Great Buddha and Kasuga Shrine in the expansive Nara Park. From Nara, you can take the Kintetsu Railways private line (departing from Nara Kintetsu Station) to Kintetsu Namba Station in Osaka, transferring there to the Nankai Koya Line bound for Mt. Koya. (If you have a rail pass, you can take Japan Railways trains to Hashimoto and transfer there to the private Nankai Koya Line.) Mt. Koya is Japan's most sacred religious site, achingly beautiful with more than 120 Buddhist temples spread through the forests. Spend the night in one of these temples, dining on vegetarian food.

Day 11   After visiting Okunoin, the burial grounds of Kobo Daishi, return to Osaka and transfer to the Shinkansen bullet train at Shin-Osaka Station or to a JR train at Osaka Station bound for Kurashiki. En route, make a 2-hour stopover in Himeji to see the beautiful Himeji Castle. Spend the night in Kurashiki and take an evening stroll along the canal.

Day 12   Take in the sights of Kurashiki including its many museums. Leave for Hiroshima late in the day (it's about an hour away by Shinkansen).

Day 13   Spend the morning at Peace Memorial Park with its museum and statues, followed by an afternoon excursion to the tiny island of Miyajima with its famous Itsukushima Shrine.

Day 14   Depart Japan.

REGIONAL TOURS
The Kansai Area in 7 Days

Day 1   Arrive in Osaka by train or by plane and transfer to Osaka Station (a 30-min. trip from the airport). Settle into your hotel and then head for Spa World, one of Japan's most sophisticated hot-spring spas, where you can swim and relax in whirlpools and hot baths; maybe you'll even opt for a massage to smooth out those travel kinks. Afterwards, walk through the adjacent festivalgate, a fairy tale–like amusement park popular with families and young people.

Day 2 Spend the day in Osaka, visiting Osaka Castle, the aquarium, and maybe even the new Universal Studios. In the evening, explore the Dotonburi nightlife area or take in a Bunraku puppet performance.

Day 3 From Kintetsu Namba Station, take the Nankai Koya Line to Mt. Koya, Japan's most sacred temple village, to spend the night in a Buddhist temple and dine on vegetarian food.

Day 4 Return to Shin-Osaka Station and transfer for a train to Himeji (a 40-min. trip by Shinkansen), where you can tour the magnificent Himeji Castle and delightful Koko-en Garden. In late afternoon, take the Shinkansen to Kyoto, where you should stay in one of Kyoto's many tradional Japanese-style inns.

Day 5 In Kyoto, visit Ryoanji Temple with its rock garden, the Golden Pavilion, the Kyoto Imperial Palace, and Nijo Castle. Top off the day with a walk through Kyoto's central shopping area, stopping off to see the Museum of Kyoto. In the evening, take a walk in Gion and along Pontocho.

Day 6 Start the day with a self-guided walk through eastern Kyoto, seeing Sanjusangendo Hall, Kiyomizu Temple, and Heian Shrine, followed by shopping at the Kyoto Handicraft Center. If it's summer, spend the evening watching cormorant fishing in nearby Arashiyama.

Day 7 Take a day trip to Nara, where you can see the Great Buddha and Kasuga Shrine in Nara Park.

The Kanto Area in 7 Days

Days 1–3 See "If You Have 2 Weeks in Japan," above.

Day 4 Take a day trip to Kamakura, the ancient capital with many temples.

Day 5 Visit Nikko, famous for the sumptuous mausoleum of Shogun Tokugawa Ieyasu, for the day.

Day 6 Take the 40-minute Shinkansen bullet train to Odawara or the 1½-hour Odakyu Romance Car to Hakone Yumoto, gateways to the wonderful Fuji-Hakone-Izu National Park (if possible, travel only with an overnight bag, leaving your luggage at your Tokyo hotel). You'll travel through some of Japan's most scenic countryside via a circuitous route that includes a two-car tram, a cable car, ropeway, and a boat while seeing such sights as a wonderful open-air sculptural museum and, if you're lucky, elusive Mt. Fuji. Spend the night in the Fujiya Hotel, one of my favorites in all of Japan, or a Japanese inn.

Day 7 Complete your trip through Hakone and return to Tokyo.

The Japan Alps & Chubu (Central Honshu) District in 8 Days

Day 1 Settle into Nagoya, gateway to the region's many destinations. Take in Nagoya Castle and the Tokugawa Art Museum with its outstanding collection of Tokugawa memorabilia.

Day 2 Spend the morning seeing a few more Nagoya attractions such as the Port of Nagoya Public Aquarium or Noritake Square. In the afternoon, head to Inuyama City and its Meiji Mura open-air architectural museum, one of my favorite museums in all of Japan. If it's summer, stay in Inuyama to observe the evening cormorant fishing.

Day 3 Get up early and take the 1½-hour train ride to Ise-Shima

National Park, where you'll see Japan's most revered Shinto shrine. Afterwards, stroll through the nearby Oharai-machi historic district. After lunch, have some fun at the Sengoku Jidaimura, a theme park centered on Japan's Warring States Period, or head to Toba for its famous Mikimoto Pearl Island and Toba Aquarium. Spend the night in Ise-Shima National Park or return to your hotel in Nagoya.

Day 4 Depart Nagoya by train on the Chuo Honsen Line to either Nagiso or Nakatsugawa Station (about an hour's ride) and then board a bus for either Tsumago or Magome. Here you can have a pleasant 3-hour hike along the old Nakasendo Highway, one of feudal Japan's several highways connecting Edo with the provinces, and tour the old post towns of Tsumago and Magome. Afterwards, continue onward to Matsumoto in the Japan Alps, where you'll spend the night.

Day 5 Spend the morning seeing Matsumoto's two most important sights—Matsumoto Castle, with Japan's oldest existing donjon, and the Japan Ukiyo-e Museum, one of the best woodblock-print museums in Japan. In the afternoon, take the train north to Kanazawa on the Sea of Japan.

Day 6 Spend the day in Kanazawa. Be sure to stroll through Kenrokuen Garden, considered one of Japan's finest, and tour the nearby Seisonkaku Villa and the excellent Ishikawa Prefectural Museum for Traditional Products.

Day 7 Take the train onward to Takayama, a gem of a village in the Japan Alps. Spend the afternoon strolling through its picturesque historic district and visiting a few of its many unique museums. Spend the night in a traditional Japanese-style inn.

Day 8 Before departing Takayama, visit the colorful morning market by the river. Take the 2-hour bus ride along a winding mountain road to Shirakawago, a tiny village of rice paddies and thatched farmhouses. Spend the night in one of these farmhouses.

The Chugoku (Western Honshu) District in 4 Days

Day 1 Four hours west of Tokyo or an hour west of Osaka, Okayama is a major stop on the Tokaido-Sanyo Shinkansen Line. En route, stop off in Himeji for a tour of Japan's loveliest castle. Spend the night in Okayama.

Day 2 Take in Okayama's sights especially Okayama Castle, deliberately painted black to contrast with white Himeji Castle, and the nearby Korakuen Garden, considered one of Japan's most beautiful landscaped gardens. Depart Okayama for a night in one of Okayama Prefecture's six International Villas, beautifully constructed and situated in rural communities.

Day 3 Take the train to Kurashiki, 26km (16 miles) west of Okayama and one of Japan's most photogenic towns. Stroll along the willow-lined canal of its famous historic district, stopping in at the Ohara Museum of Art, the Kurashiki Folkcraft Museum, and the Japanese Rural Toy Museum. Spend the night here.

Day 4 Take the Shinkansen 1 hour farther west to Hiroshima and spend a couple of sobering hours at Peace Memorial Park. Afterward, take a 45-minute train to Miyajima, a scenic island in the Seto Inland Sea with the famous Itsukushima Shrine.

Shikoku Island in 4 Days

You can easily combine this tour with the Chugoku tour above.

Day 1 From Okayama, take a train over the long Seto Ohashi

Bridge for the 1-hour ride to Taka-matsu, where you'll spend the night. Visit Ritsurin Park, a beautiful stroll garden, and then head to Shikoku Mura Village, an open-air Edo-Period museum.

Day 2 Take the train 1 hour west to Kotohira, where you can visit Kotohiragu Shrine and the nearby Kompira Grand Playhouse, one of Japan's oldest Kabuki theaters. Head onward to Matsuyama, where you should spend a couple relaxing hours at the delightful Dogo Onsen Honkan bathhouse before retiring to your hotel.

Day 3 Tour Matsuyama Castle, one of Japan's few original castles, and then take a 20-minute train to the picturesque village of Uchiko, which boasts some fine old homes and buildings dating from the Edo Period.

Day 4 For an up-close and personal tour of the Seto Inland Sea, head to the nearby Shimanami Kaido Bridge with its dedicated hiking and biking trail (rental bikes available) connecting six islands and extending 43 miles all the way to Hiroshima Prefecture. Stop off at the Shiyoden Treasure Museum with its astounding collection of samurai armor and swords.

Kyushu Island in 9 Days

Day 1 Take the bullet train to Hakata Station in Fukuoka (a 6-hr. trip from Tokyo). If you feel up to it, tour one or two of the town's attractions. My favorites are the Fukuoka Asian Art Museum and Daizafu Tenmangu Shrine.

Day 2 Take the train 2½ hours south to Beppu, one of Japan's most famous hot-spring resorts. Tour the Hells, boiling ponds that boast unique features—one spouts one of the largest geysers in Japan; another

is used as breeding grounds for crocodiles. Afterwards, soothe your travel-weary muscles at Suginoi Palace, one of Japan's largest and most interesting hot-spring public baths, or by being buried up to your neck in hot sand at the Takegawara Bathhouse. Spend the night in Beppu.

Day 3 Take the train 3 hours farther south to Miyazaki. Be sure to visit Haniwa Garden with its striking replica burial mounds and 400 haniwa clay figures. Top off the day at Ocean Dome, Japan's largest all-weather indoor water park.

Day 4 It's about a 2-hour train ride farther south to Kagoshima, where you can wander through the lava fields of Mt. Sakurajima and visit lovely Senganen with its Feudal-Era garden, villa, and museum. Spend the night in Kagoshima.

Day 5 Take the bus 31km (19 miles) south to Chiran, a castle town dating from the Edo Period. Continue southward to Ibusuki, Kyushu's southernmost tip, where you can have yourself buried up to your neck in hot black sand at Surigahama Public Beach. Spend the night in Ibusuki.

Days 6–7 Take the train 3½ hours northward along Kyushu's western coast to Kumamoto and check into your hotel. Or take the bus to Hitoyoshi on the Kumagawa River for some white-water rafting. Tour the massive Kumamoto Castle and then go shopping at the Kumamoto Traditional Crafts Center next door. Visit Suizenji Garden, which replicates the 53 stages of the Tokaido Highway in its landscaping.

Day 8 Board the train for the cosmopolitan Nagasaki, where you should spend the day seeing the sights, including Glover Garden and the Peace Park, dedicated to those who died in the atomic blast.

Day 9   Take a 2-hour bus ride to Unzen Spa, where you can walk through the Hells, hike to the top of Mt. Fugen, and enjoy the indoor and outdoor baths of Unzen Spa House.

The Tohoku District in 4 Days

Day 1   Take the Shinkansen from Tokyo to Sendai (about 2 hr.) and then board a sightseeing boat for a 50-minute trip to Matsushima, famous for its scenic coastline of pine-studded islets. Visit the venerable Zuiganji Temple, northern Japan's most famous Zen temple, Entsuin Temple with its nice gardens, and a museum or two. Spend the night in Matsushima.

Day 2   Return to Sendai and take the Shinkansen onward to Kakunodate, a small and relatively unspoiled castle town famous for its samurai district and cherry trees. Be sure to see the Aoyagi Samurai Manor, a compound of traditional buildings packed with Edo-Period memorabilia. Spend the night in Kakunodate.

Days 3–4   Backtrack one stop on the Shinkansen to Tazawako and board a bus for Nyuto Onsen, a secluded valley of hot springs and rustic inns. It's a good base from which to explore the many wonders of the Towada-Hachimantai National Park, including hiking, skiing, and swimming.

Hokkaido Island in 7 Days

Day 1   Take the train to Hakodate (about a 7-hr. trip from Tokyo). Take a cable car to the top of Mt. Hakodate, famous for its night view of Hakodate.

Day 2   Visit Hakodate's morning market and then depart for Noboribetsu Onsen. Hike through Hell Valley for a view of the bubbling hot water that has made Noboribetsu famous, and then experience its magic at the Daiichi Takimotokan hot-spring baths (open to non-hotel guests until 3pm). Spend the night in Noboribetsu Onsen.

Day 3   Visit the Noboribetsu-Date Historic Village, an early Edo-Period theme park, or the Noboribetsu Marine Park. In late afternoon, depart for Sapporo, about 1½ hours away, where you'll spend the night.

Day 4   Take a walk through Sapporo's downtown district and then tour the Sapporo Beer Museum, followed by lunch at the Sapporo Factory. Afterward, take a bus 50 minutes to Nopporo Forest Park where you can visit the Historical Museum of Hokkaido and see vintage homes and buildings at the Historical Village of Hokkaido. Spend the night in Sapporo.

Day 5   Depart Sapporo by train to Kamikawa (a 2½-hr. ride), followed by a 30-minute bus ride to Sounkyo in the Daisetsuzan National Park. Rent a bike to the pretty Sounkyo Gorge and then take the cable car to the top of Kuro-dake Mountain for the view or some hiking. Spend the night in Sounkyo.

Day 6   Depart Sounkyo early in the morning by bus back to Kamikawa and then by train 2½ hours to Bihoro. There, board a sightseeing bus for a 5-hour tour of Akan National Park, ending up in Akanko where you'll spend the night.

Day 7   Take a boat cruise of Lake Akan, famous for its marimo, a spongelike ball of duckweed, and tour the marimo museum. Visit Ainu Kotan Village with its shops and traditional Ainu dancing.

FAST FACTS: Japan

American Express There are no American Express customer service offices in Japan.

Banks & ATM Networks See "Money," earlier in this chapter.

Business Hours Government offices and private companies are generally open Monday through Friday from 9am to 5pm. Banks are open Monday through Friday from 9am to 3pm, while neighborhood post offices are open Monday through Friday from 9am to 5pm. Major post offices, however, are open Monday through Friday from 9am to 7pm and sometimes Saturday mornings as well.

Department stores are open from about 10am to 7:30 or 8pm, with irregular closing days one to four times a month (but always the same day of the week). Since closed days differ for each department store, you can always find several that are open, even on Sunday. Smaller stores are generally open from about 10am to 8pm and are closed one day a week. Convenience stores are open 24 hours.

Keep in mind that museums, gardens, and most attractions stop selling admission tickets at least 30 minutes before the actual closing time. Similarly, restaurants take their last orders at least 30 minutes before the posted closing time (even earlier for kaiseki restaurants) and are sometimes closed between 2 and 5pm.

Customs See "Entry Requirements and Customs," earlier in this chapter.

Doctors & Dentists For medical emergencies, dial ⓒ 119 from any phone; an ambulance will deliver you to the nearest hospital. (Be sure to push a red button before dialing.) Otherwise, contact your embassy or the Tourist Information Center (see "Visitor Information," earlier in this chapter) for a list of English-speaking doctors. In addition, the AMDA International Medical Information Center (ⓒ 03/5285-8088; available Mon–Fri 9am–5pm) can provide information on English-speaking staff. See "Fast Facts: Tokyo," in chapter 3 for more information on doctors, dentists, clinics, and hospitals in Tokyo.

Documents Required See "Entry Requirements & Customs," earlier in this chapter. Be sure to carry your passport with you at all times (or, if you live in Japan, your alien registration card).

Drugstores Drugstores, called *kusuri-ya,* are found readily in Japan. However, note that you cannot have a prescription filled in Japan without first consulting a doctor in Japan, so it's best to bring an adequate supply of important medicines with you. No drugstores in Japan stay open 24 hours. However, convenience stores, open day and night throughout Japan, carry such nonprescription items as aspirin.

Earthquakes Kobe's tragic 1995 earthquake brought attention to the fact that Japan is earthquake-prone, but, in reality, most earthquakes are too small to detect. However, in case of an earthquake you can feel, there are a few precautions you should take. If you're indoors, take cover under a doorway or against a wall and do not go outdoors. If you're outdoors, stay away from trees, power lines, and the sides of buildings; if you're surrounded by tall buildings, seek cover in a doorway. Never use elevators during a quake. Other precautions include noting emergency exits wherever you stay; all hotels supply flashlights, usually found attached to your bedside table.

Electricity The electricity throughout Japan is 100 volts AC, but there are two different cycles in use: In Tokyo and in regions northeast of the capital, it's 50 cycles, while in Nagoya, Kyoto, Osaka, and all points to the southwest, it's 60 cycles. Leading hotels in Tokyo often have two outlets, one for 110 volts and one for 220 volts; many of them also have hair dryers in the rooms. You can use many American appliances in Japan because the American standard is 110 volts and 60 cycles, but they may run a little slowly. Note, too, that the flat, two-legged prongs used in Japan are the same size and fit as in North America, but three-pronged appliances are not accepted. For sensitive equipment, either have it adjusted or use batteries if it's also battery-operated.

Internet Access Most upper-range hotels in the big cities are used to catering to international business travelers and therefore offer in-room dataports for computer hookups as well as adapters to let you access the Internet. Some even have interactive TVs that provide Internet access. Many offer business centers as well, most of which are equipped with computers for guest use (a fee may be charged). Otherwise, Nippon Telegraph & Telephone (NTT) operates newer public telephone models equipped with a modular jack for portable computer hookups, making it possible to scan websites and receive e-mail. Look for gray ISDN telephones—readily available in lobbies of major hotels, airports, and train stations—which have English explanations on how to use them and accept prepaid telephone cards. Finally, most major cities in Japan have Internet cafes where you can check e-mail either by paying a fee or by purchasing a drink or a meal. **Kinko's,** with more than 50 locations in Japan, also has computers for customer use (call toll-free © **0120-001-966** for the nearest location). Check individual city and regional chapters for information on Internet cafes and hotels with Internet access.

Embassies & Consulates The embassies of most countries are located in Tokyo.

- **U.S. Embassy:** 1–10–5 Akasaka, Minato-ku, near Toranomon subway station (© **03/3224-5000**; consular section open Mon–Fri 8:30am–12:30pm and 2–4pm; telephone inquiries accepted Mon–Fri 8:30am–1pm and 2–5:30pm).
- **Canadian Embassy:** 7–3–38 Akasaka, Minato-ku, near Aoyama-Itchome Station (© **03/3408-2101**; consular section open Mon–Fri 9am–12pm and 1:30–5pm).
- **British Embassy:** 1 Ichibancho, Chiyoda-ku, near Hanzomon Station (© 03/3265-5511; consular section open Mon–Fri 9am–noon and 2–4pm).
- **Embassy of Ireland:** 5th floor, 2–10–7 Kojimachi, Chiyoda-ku, near Hanzomon Station, exit 4 (© **03/3263-0695**; open Mon–Fri 10am–12:30pm and 2–4pm; telephone inquiries accepted Mon–Fri 9:30am–5:30pm).
- **Australian Embassy:** 2–1–14 Mita, Minato-ku (© **03/5232-4111**; open Mon–Fri 9am–12:30pm and 1:30–4:30pm; make an appointment for the consular section). A 15-minute walk from Shiba-koen Station or take a taxi from Kamyacho, Mita, Hamamatsucho, or Tamachi.

• **New Zealand Embassy:** 20–40 Kamiyama-cho, Shibuya-ku, a 15-minute walk from Shibuya Station (✆ **03/3467-2271;** consular section open Mon–Fri 9am–12:30pm and 1:30–5pm).

Since most visa or passport sections are open only at certain times during the day, it's best to call in advance.

The U.S. Embassy, British Embassy, and several other embassies maintain consulates in some other major cities; for information regarding location, inquire at the respective embassies.

Emergencies The national emergency numbers are ✆ **110** for calling police and ✆ **119** for calling an ambulance and for reporting a fire. You do not need to insert any money into public telephones to call these numbers, but you must push a red button before dialing. Be sure to speak slowly and precisely. See also "Doctors & Dentists," above.

Holidays & Peak Travel Seasons See "When to Go," earlier in this chapter.

Information See "Visitor Information," earlier in this chapter and regional chapters for local information offices. If you need assistance while traveling in Japan, your best bet is to call the Japan National Tourist Organization's toll-free **Travel-Phone** at ✆ **0088/22-4800** (available daily 9am–5pm); in Tokyo, call the TIC at ✆ **03/3201-3331;** in Kyoto, call ✆ **075/371-5649.**

Laundry/Dry Cleaning All upper-bracket and most medium-range hotels offer laundry and dry-cleaning service. For same-day service, you are usually required to hand over your laundry by 10am; many hotels do not offer laundry service on Sundays and holidays. Several Japanese-style accommodations in the budget category have coin-operated washers and dryers. Otherwise, launderettes are abundant.

Liquor Laws The legal drinking age is 20. You'll find vending machines dispensing beer and whiskey in almost every neighborhood in Japan, but they close down at 11pm. *Note:* If you intend to drive in Japan, you are not allowed even one drink.

Mail If your hotel cannot mail letters for you, ask the concierge where the nearest post office is. Post offices are easily recognizable by the red logo of a capital T with a horizontal line over it. Mailboxes are bright orange-red. It costs ¥110 (90¢) to airmail letters weighing up to 25 grams and ¥70 (60¢) for postcards to North America and Europe. Domestic mail costs ¥80 (65¢) for letters weighing up to 25 grams and ¥50 (40¢) for postcards.

Although all **post offices** are open Monday through Friday from 9am to 5pm, international post offices (often located close to the central train station) are open much later; often until 7pm and sometimes on Saturday from 9am to 5pm. It is only at these larger post offices that you can mail packages abroad. Conveniently, they sell cardboard boxes in four sizes with the necessary tape and string. Packages mailed abroad cannot weigh more than 20 kilograms (about 44 pounds). A package weighing 10 kilograms (about 22 pounds) will cost ¥6,750 ($56) to North America via surface mail and will take about a month. Express packages, which take three days to North America and can weigh up to 30 kilograms (66 pounds), cost ¥142,900 ($107.50) for 10 kilograms (22 pounds).

Maps The Japan National Tourist Organization publishes a free *Tourist Map of Japan* showing the four main islands and the major highway and railway lines, with maps of 11 cities on the reverse side. It also distributes free maps of Tokyo and Kyoto, available at Tourist Information Centers. In addition, free city maps are available at local tourist offices throughout Japan. Unless you're living in Japan or plan on driving your own car, I consider these free maps offered by the Tourist Information Center and local city offices adequate for trips through the country. If for some reason you need more detailed maps, atlases of Japan and maps of Tokyo and Kyoto are readily available at major bookstores that sell English-language books, including bookstores in Tokyo and Kyoto (see the "Fast Facts" section of each city for exact locations).

Measures & Weights Before the metric system came into use in Japan, the country had its own standards for measuring length and weight. One of these old standards is still common—rooms are still measured by the number of tatami straw mats that will fit in them. A six-tatami room, for example, is the size of six tatami mats; a tatami measures roughly 3 feet wide and 6 feet long.

Newspapers & Magazines Three English-language newspapers are published daily in Japan: the *Japan Times,* the *Daily Yomiuri* (with weekly supplements from the *Los Angeles Times, Washington Post,* and *Chicago Tribune*), and the *International Herald Tribune/Asahi Shimbun.* Hotels and major bookstores carry the international edition of such newsmagazines as *Time* and *Newsweek.* For regional publications detailing what's going on in a city, check with the local tourist information offices (see the regional chapters). You can also read the *Japan Times* online at www.japantimes.co.jp.

Pets There is no regulation for bringing a cat into Japan. If you intend to bring a dog with you, however, you must obtain a rabies certificate from the U.S. Department of Agriculture or, if you're a citizen of another country, from the appropriate ministry in your government. For more information, contact the Japanese Embassy or consulate nearest you.

Police The national emergency number for police is Ⓒ **110.**

Radio & TV For English-language radio programs, the American Forces Network, or AFN (at 810 kHz), is the English-language military station. It broadcasts music, talk shows, and sports events from the United States as well as Tokyo sumo matches. Tokyo's J-Wave (81.3 mHz) broadcasts programs in English with a wide range of music. InterFM (76.1 mHz) in Tokyo specializes in foreign-language broadcasts including adult contemporary music and information, mostly in English but also in French, Chinese, Korean, Spanish, and other languages.

If you enjoy watching television, you've come to the wrong country. Almost nothing is broadcast in English; even foreign films are dubbed in Japanese. However, if you have what's called a **bilingual television,** you can switch from Japanese to the original language to hear programs and movies in English. Most of the upper-range hotels offer bilingual TVs, though note that there are very few English movies and sitcoms broadcast each week (and most of these are fairly old). In my opinion, a major plus of bilingual TVs is that they allow you to listen to the nightly national news broadcast by NHK at 7 and 9pm. Otherwise, major hotels in larger cities also have cable TV with English-language programs including CNN broadcasts and BBC World as well as in-house pay movies. Note, however, that CNN is sometimes broadcast only in Japanese, particularly in outlying areas. On the other hand, even if you don't understand Japanese, I suggest that you watch TV at least once; maybe you'll catch a samurai series. Commercials are also worth watching.

A word on those **pay video programs** offered by hotels and many resort ryokan: Upper-range hotels usually have a few choices in English, and these are charged automatically to your bill. Most business hotels usually offer only one kind of pay movie; since the descriptions are usually in Japanese only, I'll clear up the mystery—they're generally "adult entertainment" programs. If you're traveling with children, you'll want to be extremely careful about selecting your TV programs. Many adult video pay channels appear with a simple push of the channel-selector button, and they can be difficult to get rid of.

In budget accommodations, you may come across televisions with coin boxes attached to their sides. Sometimes this means that the TVs can be activated only by inserting coins into the box; I call these coin-operated TVs. But if the TV functions without having to insert coins, the coin box is for those special adult entertainment videos. Now you know.

Restrooms   If you need a restroom, your best bet is at train and subway stations (though these tend to be dirty), big hotels, department stores, and fast-food restaurants. Use of restrooms is free in Japan, but since public facilities often do not supply toilet paper, it's a good idea to **carry a packet of tissues.**

To find out whether a stall is empty, knock on the door. If it's occupied, someone will knock back. Similarly, if you're inside a stall and someone knocks, answer with a knock back or else the person will just keep on knocking persistently and try to get in. And don't be surprised if you go into some rest rooms and find men's urinals and individual private stalls in the same room. Women are supposed to simply walk right past the urinals without noticing them.

Many toilets in Japan, especially those at train stations, are **Japanese style:** They're holes in the ground over which you squat facing the end that has a raised hood. Men stand and aim for the hole. Although Japanese lavatories may seem uncomfortable at first, they're actually much more sanitary because no part of your body touches anything.

Across Japan, the rage nowadays is **washlet toilets,** combination toilet/bidets with heated toilet seats and buttons and knobs directing sprays of water of various intensities and temperatures to various body parts. But alas, instructions are only in Japanese. The voice of experience: Don't stand up until you've figured out how to turn the darn spray off.

Smoking   In 1999, lung cancer surpassed stomach cancer as Japan's major cancer-related death. Still, it sometimes seems as though every adult in Japan smokes. Some 60% of Japanese men smoke (15% of women), and although this figure is down from 85% in 1965, those who do smoke have little consciousness of nonsmokers' rights. Few restaurants have no-smoking sections, and only the upper-range hotels are apt to have designated nonsmoking floors. If you want to sit in the no-smoking car of the Shinkansen bullet train, ask for the *kinensha*. During peak travel times, be sure to reserve a seat in the no-smoking car in advance.

Storage Lockers Coin-operated lockers are located at all major train stations as well as at most subway stations, but most lockers are generally not large enough to store big pieces of luggage (and those that are large enough are often taken). Lockers generally cost ¥300 to ¥700 ($2.50–$5.85) depending on the size. Some major stations also have check-in rooms for luggage, though these tend to be rare.

Taxes There's a 5% consumption tax imposed on goods and services in Japan, including hotel rates and restaurant meals. Some budget accommodations include the tax in their tariff, while others don't; be sure to ask whether rates include tax. In hot-spring resorts, accommodations with hot-spring baths also levy a nightly ¥150 ($1.25) hot-spring tax.

In addition to these taxes, a 10% to 15% **service charge** will be added to your bill in lieu of tipping at most of the fancier restaurants and at moderately priced and upper-end hotels. Thus, the 15% to 20% in tax and service charge that will be added to your bill in the more expensive locales can really add up. Most *ryokan,* or Japanese-style inns, include a service charge but not a consumption tax in their rates. If you're not sure, ask. Business hotels, *minshuku,* youth hostels, and inexpensive restaurants do not impose a service charge.

As for **shopping,** a 5% consumption tax is also levied on most goods. (Some of the smaller vendors are not required to levy tax.) Travelers from abroad, however, are eligible for an exemption on goods taken out of the country, although only the larger department stores and specialty shops seem equipped to deal with the procedures. In any case, most department stores grant a refund on the consumption tax only when the total amount of purchases for the day exceeds ¥10,000 ($83). You can obtain a refund immediately by having a sales clerk fill out a list of your purchases and then presenting the list to the tax-exemption counter of the department store; you will need to show your passport. Note that no refunds for consumption tax are given for food, drinks, tobacco, cosmetics, film, and batteries.

If you depart Japan from the Narita Airport outside Tokyo, the **service facility fee** is already included in the price of your ticket. However, at Kansai International Airport, you must pay the service facility fee when checking in. It costs ¥2,650 ($22) for adults and ¥1,330 ($11) for children.

Telephone & Fax For dialing Japan, the country code is **81.** In addition, all telephone area codes for all of Japan's cities begin with a zero: Tokyo's area code, for example, is 03, while Osaka's is 06. For other area codes, check the "Orientation" section of each city in this guide. Use the entire area code only when dialing from outside the area but from within Japan. When calling Japan from abroad, it is usually necessary to drop the zero in the area code. When calling from the United States, for example, dial 81 for Japan followed by only 3 for Tokyo (not 03) and 6 (not 06) for Osaka. If you have questions, call the international operator in the country from which you are placing your call.

If you're staying in a medium- or upper-range hotel, you can make local, domestic, and international calls from your room. Some of the best hotels even offer in-room fax machines, most have business centers, and almost all will let you send a fax. For telephone calls, however, it's prudent to ask first whether you can make the call directly, whether you must go through the operator, and whether a surcharge will be added to your bill.

You can find **public telephones** virtually everywhere—in telephone booths on the sidewalk, on stands outside shops, on train platforms, in restaurants and coffee shops, even on bullet trains (but these require a magnetic telephone card; see below). A local call costs ¥10 (8¢) for the first minute, after which a warning chime will ring to tell you to insert more coins or you'll be disconnected. I usually insert two or three coins at the start so I won't have to worry about being disconnected; ¥10 coins that aren't used are always returned at the end of the call. Some older, red models available for public use outside ma-and-pa shops accept only ¥10 coins, but most public phones accept both ¥10 and ¥100 coins. The latter is convenient for long-distance calls. All gray, ISDN telephones are equipped for international calls and have dataports for Internet access. **Toll-free numbers** in Japan begin with **0120** or **0088.**

If you think you'll be making a lot of calls from public telephones and don't want to deal with coins, purchase a magnetic, **prepaid telephone card.** These are available in values of ¥500 ($4.15) and ¥1,000 ($8.35) and are sold at vending machines (many of which are located right beside telephones), station kiosks, and even at tourist attractions, where cards are imprinted with photos of temples, castles, and other sights (but are also often more expensive than regular telephone cards since they double as collectors' items). Green and gray telephones accept telephone cards. In fact, many nowadays accept only telephone cards; simply insert the card into the slot. On the gray ISDN telephones, there's a second slot for a second telephone card, which is convenient if the first one is almost used up or if you think you'll be talking a long time. Domestic long-distance calls are 20% to 40% cheaper at night, on weekends, and on national holidays for calls of distances more than 60km (37 miles).

Of course, you can also avoid public telephones altogether by joining what seems like the rest of the population and using a **mobile phone,** a *keitai denwa.* If you're flying Japan Airlines or All Nippon Airways from North America, you might qualify for complimentary cell phone usage during your stay (contact the airlines). Otherwise, if you're in Japan for only a few days and are staying in an upper-class hotel in a major city, it's probably most convenient to rent a mobile phone from your hotel. The New Otani in Tokyo, for example, charges ¥2,000 ($17) per day, with calls charged an extra ¥330 ($2.75) per minute (there is no charge for incoming calls. Otherwise, there are various companies offering rental phones, including **Mova Rental Center,** on Sotobori Dori Avenue near Tokyo Station, 2–6–22 Yaesu, 3rd floor (✆ **03/3243-6801;** open Mon–Fri 9am–6pm), which charges ¥10,500 ($87.50) for a week's rental, plus ¥60 (50¢) per minute of calls. Clearly, for extended stays, you're better off purchasing a mobile phone. **Tu-Ka** and **Au** are two major cell phone companies, with outlets seemingly on every corner. Basic phones cost ¥4,800 to ¥5,800

($40–$48), plus you'll have to purchase special prepaid cards that are good for a limited number of calls within three months or so. There are many plans available.

There are several ways to make **international calls.** You can, for example, make a collect call or place a call through a KDD operator anywhere in Japan by dialing ✆ **0051.** From a public telephone, look for a specially marked International and Domestic Card/Coin Telephone. Although many of the specially marked green telephones, the most common public telephone, accept both coins and magnetic telephone cards for international calls, most in larger cities such as Tokyo do not (due to illegal usage of telephone cards). Thus, if you wish to use a magnetic telephone card, which is certainly easier than having a lot of coins on hand, look for a gray ISDN public phone, found in the lobbies of major hotels, train stations, and airports. These telephones have slots for two telephone cards, which is convenient for long conversations. They even have dataports for hooking up to the Internet. Some hotels also have a KDD Credit Phone, a KDD IC Global Phone, or a Japan Telecom Phone, which are special phones equipped to accept credit cards. NTT operates IC Card Payphones in many hotels, which are equipped to accept special cards costing ¥1,000 ($8.35) sold in adjacent vending machines.

In addition, several telephone companies sell prepaid international telephone cards that can be used with any telephone, including cell phones. The **KDD Global Phone Card** is available in values of ¥1,000 ($8.35) and ¥2,000 ($17) and can be purchased at major convenience stores and from vending machines located next to some KDD telephones. Similarly, IDC puts out its **0061 Love Home Card** and Telecom has a **Moshi Moshi Card,** both available at convenience stores and from vending machines. Essentially, they work like telephone cards issued by U.S. telephone companies. An access number must first be dialed followed by a secret telephone number and then the number you wish to dial.

International rates vary according to when you call, which telephone company you use, and what type of service you use. Direct-dial service is cheaper than operator-assisted calls and is offered by both international public telephones and by hotels that advertise the service (though remember to ask about the surcharge). You can also save money by calling between 11pm and 8am Japan time, when rates are up to 40% cheaper than calling during a weekday. From 7 to 11pm, rates are 20% cheaper than daytime rates on weekdays. Weekend day rates are also 20% cheaper than weekday rates. KDD's weekday prime-time rates are ¥450 ($3.75) for 3 minutes; after 11pm, it drops to ¥350 ($2.90) for 3 minutes.

To make a direct-dial international call, you must first dial one of the international access codes—**001** (KDDI), **0041** (Japan Telecom), or **0061** (IDC)—followed by **010** and then the country code. The country code for the United States and Canada is **1;** for the United Kingdom, it's **44;** for Australia, it's **61;** and for New Zealand, it's **64.** To call the United States, for example, simply dial an access code such as 001, followed by 010, the country code 1, the area code, and the telephone number. If you're dialing from your hotel room, you must first dial for an outside line, usually 0.

If you wish to be connected with an operator in your home country, you can do so from green international telephones by dialing ℂ **0039** followed by the country code. (For the United States, dial **0039-111**.) These calls can be used for collect calls or credit-card calls. Some hotels and other public places are equipped with special phones that will link you to your home operator with the push of a button, and there are instructions in English.

If you have a U.S. calling card, ask your phone company for the direct access number from Japan that will link you directly to the United States. If you have AT&T, for example, dial **00539-111**; if you're using MCI, however, it depends on which Japanese company you're using (for KDD, it's **0053-121**).

Your hotel probably can handle **faxes**. If not, you can send a fax from a **Kokusai Denshin Denwa** office (the name is equivalent to International Telephone & Telegraph); ask the hotel clerk where the office nearest your hotel is.

Time   Japan is 9 hours ahead of Greenwich mean time, 14 hours ahead of New York, 15 hours ahead of Chicago, and 17 hours ahead of Los Angeles. Since Japan does not go on daylight saving time, subtract 1 hour from the above times in the summer when calling from countries that have daylight saving time such as the United States.

Because Japan is on the other side of the international dateline, you lose a day when traveling from the United States to Asia. (If you depart the United States on Tues, you'll arrive on Wed.) Returning to North America, however, you gain a day, which means that you arrive on the same day you left. (In fact, it often happens that you arrive in the states at an earlier hour than you departed from Japan.)

Tipping   One of the delights of being in Japan is that there's no tipping— not even to waitresses, taxi drivers, or bellboys. If you try to tip them, they'll probably be confused or embarrassed. Instead, you'll have a 10% to 15% service charge added to your bill at higher-priced hotels and restaurants.

Tourist Offices   See "Visitor Information," earlier in this chapter.

Travel-Phone   If you're having problems communicating with someone in Japan, are lost, or need information, the Japan National Tourist Organization operates a nationwide telephone system, called Travel-Phone, that provides toll-free service every day throughout the year from 9am to 5pm. If you're outside Tokyo or Kyoto, all you have to do is insert a ¥10 coin or a card into a telephone (it will be returned to you at the end of the call) and dial ℂ **0888/22-4800**. Note that these toll-free calls can be made only if you're outside Tokyo or Kyoto. In Tokyo, dial ℂ **03/ 3201-3331** (Mon–Fri 9am–5pm and Sat 9am–noon); in Kyoto, dial ℂ **075/ 371-5649** (daily 9am–5pm). In these two cities, you have to pay for the call, which is ¥10 (8¢) per minute.

Water   The water is safe to drink anywhere in Japan, although some people claim it's too highly chlorinated. Bottled water is also readily available.

Weather   The *Japan Times* carries nearly a full page of weather information daily including forecasts for Tokyo and other major Japanese cities and a weekly outlook.

Settling into Tokyo

To the uninitiated, Tokyo may seem like a whirlwind of traffic and people, so confusing that visitors might think they have somehow landed on another planet. Little wonder first-time visitors are almost invariably disappointed. They come expecting an exotic Asian city, but instead they find a city Westernized and modernized to the point of ugliness, much of it a drab concrete jungle of unimaginative buildings clustered so close together there's hardly room in which to breathe.

Simply stated, Tokyo is a crush of humanity. Its subways are often packed, its sidewalks are crowded, its streets are congested, and its air is filled with noise, pollution, and what can only be called mystery smells. Approximately 12 million people live in its 800 square miles (many of them in bedroom towns from which they have to commute to work for an average of 2–3 hr. every day). No matter where you go in Tokyo, you're never alone. After you've been here for a while, Paris, London, and even New York will seem deserted.

Crowds and urban ugliness are all that you'll see if you don't bother to look beneath the surface. But Tokyo is alluring in its own way, and if you open yourself to it you'll find a place unlike any other in the world, humming with energy and vitality. People rush around here with such purpose, such determination, it's hard not to feel that you're in the midst of something important, that you're witnessing history in the making.

A LOOK AT THE PAST   Though today the nation's capital, Tokyo is a relative newcomer to the pages of Japanese history. For centuries it was nothing more than a rather unimportant village called Edo, which means simply "mouth of the estuary." In 1603, Edo was catapulted into the limelight when the new shogun, Tokugawa Ieyasu, made the sleepy village the seat of his government. He expanded Edo Castle, making it the largest and most impressive castle in the land, and surrounded it with an ingenious system of moats that radiated out from the castle in a great swirl, giving him easy access to the sea and thwarting enemy attack.

The town developed quickly, due largely to the shogun's decree requiring all *daimyo* (feudal lords) to permanently leave their families in Edo, a shrewd move to thwart insurrection in the provinces. There were as many as 270 daimyo in Japan in the 17th century, all of whom maintained several mansions in Edo, complete with elaborate compounds and expansive gardens. The daimyos' trusted samurai soon accounted for more than half of Edo's population, and the merchant class expanded as well. By 1787 the population had grown to 1.3 million, making Edo—even then—one of the largest cities in the world.

When the Tokugawas were overthrown in 1868, the Japanese emperor was restored to power and moved the capital from Kyoto to Edo, now renamed Tokyo (Eastern Capital). Japan's Feudal Era—and its isolation from the rest of the world—was over. As the capital city, Tokyo was the hardest hit in this new era of modernization, with fashion, architecture, food, and even people imported from the West. West was best, and things Japanese were forgotten or ignored.

It didn't help that Tokyo was almost totally destroyed twice in the first half of this century: In 1923, a massive earthquake measuring 7.9 on the Richter scale destroyed more than a third of the city and claimed more than 100,000 lives; disaster struck again in 1945, toward the end of World War II, when Allied incendiary bombs laid more than half the city to waste and killed another 100,000 people.

TOKYO TODAY I guess that's why most visitors are disappointed with Tokyo—there's almost nothing of historical importance to match Kyoto or Kamakura. So put your notions of quaint Japan out of your mind and plunge headfirst into the 21st century, because that's what Tokyo is all about.

As the financial nerve center of Japan, Tokyo has long set the pace for what happens in the rest of Asia. The city is so wired and electric you can feel it in the air. It's the reigning capital of Asian pop art and kitsch, fads and trends.

But even though the city has a fast-paced, somewhat zany side, it also has a quieter and often overlooked side that makes the city both loveable and liveable. Although formidable at first glance, Tokyo is nothing more than a series of small towns and neighborhoods clustered together, each with its own narrow, winding streets, mom-and-pop shops, fruit stands, and stores. Look for the details, and you'll notice carefully pruned bonsai adorning the sidewalks; women in kimono bowing and shuffling down the streets; old wooden houses tucked between massive apartment complexes; everywhere, neatness and order. Peer inside those concrete high-rises, and you're apt to find Japanese restaurants that are perfect replicas of wood-beamed farmhouses side-by-side with cocktail bars that epitomize high-tech avant-garde.

I personally love Tokyo. Despite its daily frustrations, Tokyo is exhilarating, often exciting, and unceasingly interesting. Best of all, it's one of the world's safest metropolises, with the lowest theft rate of any large city on the planet. Although common sense dictates I avoid public parks after dark when I'm out alone and watch my purse in crowded subways, I otherwise walk without fear anywhere and anytime in Tokyo, day or night. The city's safety is best illustrated by what an American friend living in Tokyo was told when her daughter started first grade in a Japanese school: Parents were to refrain from walking their children to or from school, allowing, instead, the children to walk on their own.

Perhaps the only thing in Tokyo you have to watch out for are those Japanese businessmen who've had too much to drink—reserve thrown off, they might want to practice their English on you.

1 Orientation

ARRIVING
BY PLANE

There are two airports serving Tokyo, but most likely you'll arrive at the New Tokyo International Airport in Narita (usually referred to as the **Narita Airport**), 64.5km (40 miles) outside Tokyo. If you're arriving in Tokyo from elsewhere in Japan, your flight will probably land at **Haneda Airport,** used primarily for domestic flights.

FACILITIES AT NARITA AIRPORT   The New Tokyo International Airport consists of two terminals, Terminal 1 and 2. Arrival lobbies in both terminals have banks for money exchange open daily 6am to 11pm as well as ATMs and are connected to all ground transportation to Tokyo.

A **Tourist Information Center (TIC),** managed by the Japan National Tourist Organization, is located in the arrival lobbies of both Terminal 1 (℡ **0476/30-3383**) and Terminal 2 (℡ **0476/34-6251**). The TIC offers free maps and pamphlets and can direct you to your hotel or inn. Both are open daily 9am to 8pm; if you don't yet have a hotel room and want one at a modest price, you can make reservations here free of charge Monday through Friday from 9am to 7:30pm.

If you've purchased a Japan Rail Pass, you can turn in your voucher at one of the **Japan Railways (JR) View Plazas** (Travel Service Centers), located in both Terminal 1 and Terminal 2 and open daily 6:45am to 9:45pm. Other facilities at both terminals include post offices and medical clinics and, in their departure lounges, shower rooms and day rooms for napping and children's playrooms. Terminal 2 also has an audio video room with personal TVs and Internet facilities (¥300/$2.50 for 30 min.), as well as a business center (open daily 7am–9pm).

GETTING TO TOKYO FROM NARITA AIRPORT   Jumping into a **taxi** is the easiest way to get to Tokyo, but it's also prohibitively expensive—and may not even be the quickest if you happen to hit rush hour. Expect to spend ¥24,000 to ¥25,000 ($200–$208) for a 1½ to 2-hour taxi ride from Narita.

By Bus   The most popular way to get from Narita to Tokyo is via the **Airport Limousine Bus** (℡ **03/3665-7220**), which picks up passengers and their luggage directly from just outside the arrival lobbies of terminals 1 and 2 and delivers them to downtown hotels. This is the best mode of transportation if you have heavy baggage or are staying at one of the many hotels served by the bus. Buses travel most frequently to the **Tokyo City Air Terminal (TCAT),** located in downtown Tokyo and reached in about 70 minutes. Buses also depart frequently—up to four or five times an hour during peak times—for Tokyo Station and Shinjuku Station. They also serve more than 40 major hotels on a slightly less frequent schedule—generally once or twice an hour—it can take almost 2 hours to reach a hotel in Shinjuku. Check with the staff at the Airport Limousine Bus counter in the arrival lobbies to inquire which bus stops nearest your hotel and the time of departure. Fares for the limousine bus average ¥2,700 to ¥3,000 ($22.50–$25), based on distance traveled; children 6 to 12 are charged half-fare; those under 6 ride free.

If you take a limousine bus into Tokyo, plenty of taxis are available at the end of the line. TCAT, Shinjuku Station, and Tokyo Station are also served by public transportation; TCAT is connected to the subway Hanzomon Line's end stop, Suitengu-mae, via moving walkways and escalators; Shinjuku and Tokyo stations are hubs for subway lines and commuter trains.

If the Airport Limousine Bus is full or there's a wait to your destination, try **Airport Shuttle Bus** (℡ **0476/35-6767**), also with counters in the arrival lobbies of both terminals. It also operates buses to approximately 24 hotels in Tokyo, though departures are not as frequent. Fares for this service average ¥2,900 ($24).

By Train   The quickest way to reach Tokyo is by train, with several options available. Trains depart directly from the airport's two underground stations, called Narita Airport Station (which is in Terminal 1) and Airport Terminal 2.

The JR **Narita Express (NEX)** is the fastest way to reach Tokyo Station, Shinagawa, Shinjuku, Ikebukuro, and Yokohama, with departures approximately once an hour, or twice an hour during peak hours. The trip to Tokyo Station takes 53 minutes and costs ¥3,140 ($26) one-way. The trip to Shinagawa, Shinjuku or Ikebukuro costs ¥3,310 ($28). Note, however, that if you have a validated JR Rail Pass, you can ride the NEX free (as mentioned above, you can validate your Rail Pass at the JR View Plaza, also called the JR Travel Service Center, located in both terminals). Because all seats are reserved, you must first stop by the NEX counter near the train terminal for a seat assignment before boarding the train. Seats are sometimes sold out in advance. (If you want to reserve a seat for your return trip to Narita Airport—and I strongly urge that you do—you can do so here at the NEX counter. Look for a sign that says JR RESERVATION TICKET OFFICE or VIEW PLAZA; in Tokyo you'll find them at major JR stations. Plan to arrive at Narita 2 hr. before departure.)

If the NEX is sold out and you're still determined to use your Rail Pass, you can take the slower **JR Airport Liner,** which will get you to Tokyo Station in 80 minutes. If you don't have a rail pass, this rapid train will cost you ¥1,280 ($11).

An alternative is the privately owned **Keisei Skyliner** train, which departs directly from both Narita Airport Station (Terminal 1) and Airport Terminal 2 and travels to Ueno Station in Tokyo in about 1 hour, with a stop at Nippori Station on the way. You'll find Keisei Skyliner counters in the arrival lobbies of both terminals. Trains depart approximately every 30 or 40 minutes between 7:49am and 9:58pm. The fare from Narita Airport to Ueno Station in Tokyo is ¥1,920 ($17) one-way; early-morning, and evening fares are cheaper. If you're on a strict budget, you can take one of Keisei's slower limited express trains to Ueno Station, with fares starting at ¥1,000 ($8.70) for the 75-minute trip. At Ueno Station you can take either the subway or the JR Yamanote Line to other parts of Tokyo. There are also plenty of taxis.

GETTING TO HANEDA AIRPORT If you're connecting to a domestic flight, more than likely you'll need to transfer to Haneda Airport. The **Airport Limousine Bus** makes runs between Narita Airport and Haneda Airport that cost ¥3,000 ($25). The trip takes about an hour.

GETTING FROM HANEDA AIRPORT INTO CENTRAL TOKYO If you're arriving by domestic flight at Haneda Airport, located closer to the center of Tokyo, you can take the **Airport Limousine Bus** to Shinjuku Station, Tokyo Station or the Tokyo City Air Terminal (TCAT) in downtown Tokyo, and hotels in Shinjuku, Ikebukuro, and Akasaka. Fares run from ¥900 to ¥1,200 ($7.50–$10). The locals, however, are more likely to take the **monorail** from Haneda Airport to Hamamatsucho Station on the Yamanote Line; the fare is ¥470 ($3.90) and the trip takes only 15 minutes. The Yamanote Line connects with major stations, including Tokyo Station and Shinjuku Station.

BY LAND OR SEA

BY TRAIN If you're arriving in Tokyo by the Shinkansen bullet train, you'll probably arrive at **Tokyo Station.** Tokyo Station is easily (though confusedly) connected to the rest of the city via JR commuter trains and the subway. Trains from northern Japan also stop at Ueno Station, and by autumn 2003, Shinagawa will be served by Shinkansen.

BY BUS Long-distance bus service from Hiroshima, Nagoya, Osaka, Kyoto, and other major cities delivers passengers to **Tokyo Station,** which is connected to the rest of the city via subway and commuter train. Other bus terminals serving the region outside Tokyo include Shinagawa and Shinjuku stations, both of which are served by the JR Yamanote Line, which loops around the city.

BY FERRY   Long-distance ferries arrive in Tokyo at the **Tokyo Ko Ferry Futo (Tokyo Port Ferry Terminal).** From there, you can board a bus for Shinkiba JR Station and catch a train to town.

VISITOR INFORMATION

The **Tourist Information Center (TIC),** 3-5-1 Marunouchi (℃ **03/ 3201-3331**), is buried in the Tokyo International Forum, near the JR Yuraku-cho Station and Hibiya subway station; it's in the basement 1 concourse of the Glass Hall Building, a dramatic glass structure that resembles the hull of a ship. Assuming you're able to find them, the TIC staff can answer all your questions regarding Tokyo and Japan, give you a map of the city plus various sightseeing materials, and will even book inexpensive hotels for you around the country, charging no fee for the service. They're courteous and efficient; I cannot recommend them highly enough. They also have more information than any other tourist office on the rest of Japan, including pamphlets and brochures on major cities and attractions. Be sure to stop off here if you plan to visit other destinations, because information in English may not be available at the destination itself. Open Monday through Friday from 9am to 5pm and on Saturday from 9am to noon; closed Sunday and national holidays. Note that the hotel reservation service is available only weekdays 9:15 to 11:30am and 1 to 4:45pm.

If it's a weekend or holiday, an alternative for information on Tokyo is the **Tokyo Tourist Information Center,** operated by the Tokyo Metropolitan Government's Tokyo Convention & Visitors Bureau. Located in the same complex as the TIC above, in the Tokyo International Forum's A Block on the ground floor (℃ **03/5221-9084**), it dispenses pamphlets and its own city map (which I consider better than the one issued by TIC). It's open daily 10am to 6:30pm. Another TCVB information counter is in Shinjuku Station near the east exit, also open daily 10am to 6:30pm.

Other TIC offices are located in the arrival lobbies of Terminal 1 and Terminal 2 at Narita Airport, open daily from 9am to 8pm.

If you want a quick rundown of what's happening in Tokyo, call ℃ **03/ 3201-2911** for a taped recording in English describing current exhibitions, performances, festivals, and events.

TOURIST PUBLICATIONS   English-language newspapers such as the *Japan Times* and the *Daily Yomiuri* carry information on the theater, films, and special events. *Tokyo Journal,* a quarterly available for ¥600 ($5) at foreign-language bookstores, covers Kabuki, concerts, gallery exhibitions, festivals, and more (events are also listed online at www.Tokyo.to). There are also free publications at hotels, restaurants, and other establishments. The best of these is *Tokyo Classified,* filled mainly with classifieds for the expat community but also containing nightlife information, events listings, movie reviews, and dining information. *Tokyo Weekender,* aimed at expats living in Tokyo, also carries a section on what's going on in the city. Other giveaways include the bilingual **Juice** with nightlife information and **JapanZine.**

CITY LAYOUT

Your most frustrating moments in Tokyo will probably occur when you find that you're totally lost. Maybe it will be in a subway or train station, when all you see are signs in Japanese, or on a street somewhere as you search for a museum,

Tokyo at a Glance

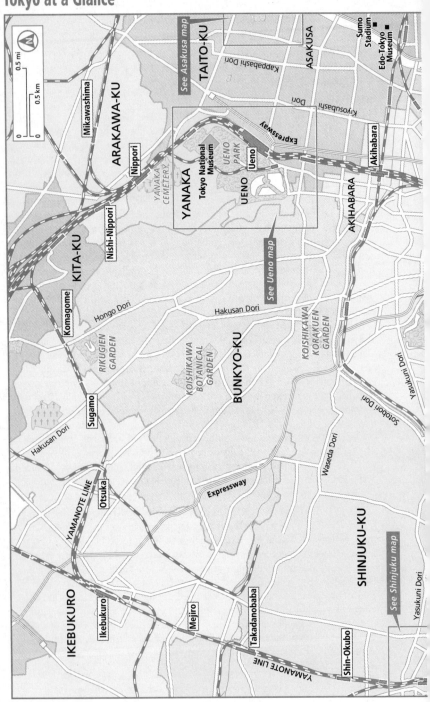

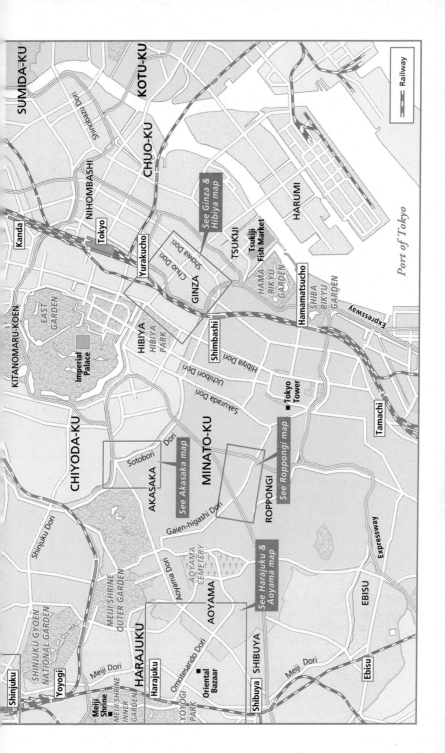

SUMIDA-KU

KOTU-KU

CHUO-KU

Kanda

Shinobazu Dori

NIHOMBASHI

Tokyo

Yurakucho

See Ginza & Hibiya map

Chuo Dori

Showa Dori

GINZA

TSUKIJI

Tsukiji Fish Market

HARUMI

KITANOMARU-KOEN

EAST GARDEN

Imperial Palace

HIBIYA

HIBIYA PARK

Shimbashi

Uchibori Dori

Hibiya Dori

Hamamatsucho

HAMA RIKYU GARDEN

SHIBA RIKYU GARDEN

Expressway

Port of Tokyo

CHIYODA-KU

Sakurada Dori

Tokyo Tower

Tamachi

Sotobori Dori

AKASAKA

See Akasaka map

MINATO-KU

ROPPONGI

See Roppongi map

Shinjuku Dori

Gaien-higashi Dori

Aoyama Dori

AOYAMA CEMETERY

See Harajuku & Aoyama map

MEIJI SHRINE OUTER GARDEN

EBISU

Expressway

Shinjuku

Yoyogi

SHINJUKU GYOEN NATIONAL GARDEN

HARAJUKU

AOYAMA

SHIBUYA

Meiji Dori

Harajuku

Omotesando Dori

Oriental Bazaar

Shibuya

Meiji Dori

Ebisu

Meiji Dori

Meiji Shrine

MEIJI SHRINE INNER GARDEN

YOYOGI PARK

━ ━ ━ Railway

93

restaurant, or bar. At any rate, accept it here and now: You *will* get lost if you are at all adventurous and strike out on your own. It's inevitable. But take comfort in the fact that Japanese get lost, too—even taxi drivers! And don't forget most of the hotel and restaurant listings in this book have the number of minutes (in parentheses) it takes to walk there from the nearest station; if you take note, you'll at least know the radius from the station to your destination. It's wise, too, to allow extra time to find your way around.

Tokyo, situated at one end of Tokyo Bay and spreading across the Kanto Plain, still retains some of its Edo- Period features. If you look at a map, you'll find a large green oasis in the middle of the city, site of the Imperial Palace and its grounds. Surrounding it is the castle moat; a bit farther out are remnants of another circular moat built by the Tokugawa shogun. The JR Yamanote Line forms another loop around the inner city; most of Tokyo's major hotels, nightlife districts, and attractions are near or inside this oblong loop.

For administrative purposes, Tokyo is broken down into **23 wards,** known as *ku.* Its business districts of Marunouchi and Hibiya, for example, are in Chiyoda-ku, while Ginza is part of Chuo-ku (Central Ward). These two ku are the historic hearts of Tokyo, for it was here that the city had its humble beginnings.

MAIN STREETS & ARTERIES   One difficulty in finding your way around Tokyo is that hardly any streets are named. Think about what that means—12 million people living in a huge metropolis of nameless streets. Granted, major thoroughfares and some well-known streets in areas like Ginza and Shinjuku received names after World War II at the insistence of American occupation forces, and a few more have been labeled or given nicknames that only the locals know, but for the most part Tokyo's address system is based on a complicated number scheme that must make the postal worker's job here a nightmare. To make matters worse, most streets in Tokyo zigzag—an arrangement apparently left over from olden days, to confuse potential attacking enemies. Now they confuse Tokyoites and visitors alike.

Among Tokyo's most important named streets are **Meiji Dori,** which follows the loop of the Yamanote Line and runs from Ebisu in the south through Shibuya, Harajuku, Shinjuku, and Ikebukuro in the north; **Yasukuni Dori** and **Shinjuku Dori,** which cut across the heart of the city from Shinjuku to Chiyoda-ku; and **Sotobori Dori, Chuo Dori, Harumi Dori,** and **Showa Dori,** which pass through Ginza. (*Dori* means avenue or street, as does *michi.*)

Intersections in Tokyo are called a crossing; it seems every district has a famous crossing. **Ginza 4-chome Crossing** is the intersection of Chuo Dori and Harumi Dori. **Roppongi Crossing** is the intersection of Roppongi Dori and Gaien-Higashi Dori.

ADDRESSES   Because streets did not have names when Japan's postal system was established, the country has a unique address system. A typical Tokyo address might read 7-8-4 Roppongi, Minato-ku, which is the address of the Inakaya restaurant. Minato-ku is the name of the **ward.** Wards are further divided into **districts,** in this case Roppongi. Roppongi itself is broken down into **chome** (numbered subsection), here 7-chome. Number 8 refers to a smaller area within the chome—often an entire block, sometimes larger. Thus, houses on one side of the street will usually have a different middle number from houses on the other side. The last number, in this case 4, refers to the actual building. Although it seems reasonable to assume that next to a number 4 building will be a number 5, that's not always the case; buildings were assigned numbers as they were constructed, not according to location.

Addresses are usually, but not always, posted on buildings beside doors, on telephone poles, and by streetlights, but often they are written only in kanji. In recent years Roman letters have been added to addresses posted below stop lights at major intersections. But one frustrating trend is for new, modern buildings to omit posting any address whatsoever on their facade.

FINDING YOUR WAY AROUND   If you're traveling by subway or JR train, the first thing you should do upon reaching your destination is to look for **signs** posted on every platform that tell which exit to take for particular buildings, attractions, and chome. At Roppongi Station, for example, you'll find yellow signboards that tell you which exit to take for Roppongi 7-chome, which will at least get you pointed in the right direction once you emerge from the station. Stations also have maps of the area either inside the station or at the exit; these are your best plan of attack when trying to find a particular address.

As you walk around Tokyo, you will also notice **maps** posted beside sidewalks giving a breakdown of the postal number system for the area. The first time I tried to use one, I stopped one Japanese, then another, and asked them to point out on the map where a particular address was. They both studied the map and pointed out the direction. Both turned out to be wrong. Not very encouraging, but if you learn how to read these maps, they're invaluable.

Another invaluable source of information is the numerous **police boxes,** called *koban,* located in every neighborhood throughout the city. Police officers have area maps and are very helpful. You should also never hesitate to ask a Japanese the way, but be sure to ask more than one. You'll be amazed at the con-flicting directions you'll receive. Apparently, the Japanese would rather hazard a guess than impolitely shrug their shoulders and leave you standing there. The best thing to do is ask directions of several Japanese and then follow the major-ity opinion. You can also duck into a shop and ask someone where a nearby address is, although in my experience employees do not even know the address of their own store. They may, however, have a map of the area.

MAPS   Before setting out on your own, arm yourself with a few maps. Maps are so much a part of life in Tokyo they're often included in a shop or restaurant advertisement, on a business card, and even in private party invitations. Even though I've spent several years in Tokyo, I rarely venture forth without a map. The Tourist Information Center issues a *Tourist Map of Tokyo,* which includes a subway map. Better, in my opinion, is the free map given away by the Tokyo Convention & Visitors Bureau, which also has smaller, detailed maps of several districts (such as Shinjuku). Armed with both these maps, you should be able to locate at least the general vicinity of every place mentioned in this chapter and the next.

For a detailed map, however, head for **Tower Books, Kinokuniya,** or another English-language bookstore (see "Shopping from A to Z," in chapter 4). My own personal favorite is Nippon Kokuseisha's *Map of Central Tokyo,* a compact

---

Tips **Take Your Time**

You should always allow more time to reach a destination than you think you'll need. Once you learn how to use the subway and the layout of the city, finding your way around becomes an interesting challenge, with every success a major victory. It's almost like being 4 years old all over again.

folding map listing chome and chome subsections for major areas. Another useful tome is Shobunsa's *Tokyo Metropolitan Atlas,* which covers all 23 of Tokyo's wards with specific postal maps, as well as greater Tokyo and its vicinity, along with expressway and Tokyo area road maps. If you plan on spending a lot of time in Tokyo, consider Kodansha's heftier *Tokyo City Atlas,* which has both Japanese and English place names, along with rail and subway maps, district maps, and an index to important buildings, museums, and other places of interest.

TOKYO'S NEIGHBORHOODS IN BRIEF

Taken as a whole, Tokyo seems formidable and unconquerable. It's best, therefore, to think of it as nothing more than a series of villages scrunched together, much like the pieces of a jigsaw puzzle. Holding the pieces together, so to speak, is the **Yamanote Line,** a commuter train loop around central Tokyo that passes through such important stations as Yuraku-cho, Tokyo, Ueno, Shinjuku, Ikebukuro, Harajuku, and Shibuya.

Hibiya This is not only the business heart of Tokyo, but its spiritual heart as well. This is where the Tokugawa shogun built his magnificent castle, and was thus the center of old Edo. Today, Hibiya is no less important as the home of the **Imperial Palace,** built on the ruins of Edo Castle and the residence of Japan's 125th emperor. Bordering the palace is the wonderful East Garden, open free to the public. Hibiya is also home to the **Tourist Information Center** (see "Visitor Information," above). Hibiya is located in the Chiyoda-ku Ward.

Ginza Ginza is the swankiest and most expensive **shopping area** in all Japan. When the country opened to foreign trade in the 1860s, following two centuries of self-imposed seclusion, it was here that Western imports and adopted Western architecture were first displayed. Today, Ginza is where you'll find a multitude of department stores, boutiques, exclusive restaurants, hotels, art galleries, hostess clubs, and drinking establishments. On the edge of Ginza is **Kabukiza,** venue for Kabuki productions.

Nihombashi Back when Edo became Tokugawa's shogunate capital, Nihombashi is where merchants settled and set up shop. It became the commercial center of the city and therefore of all of Japan. Nihombashi, which stretches east of **Tokyo Station,** serves as Tokyo's financial center, home of the computerized **Tokyo Stock Exchange** and headquarters for major companies and banks. The area takes its name from an actual bridge, Nihombashi, which means "Bridge of Japan" and served as the starting measuring point for all main highways leading out of the city to the provinces during the Edo Period.

Tsukiji Located only two subway stops from Ginza, Tsukiji was born from reclaimed land during the Tokugawa shogunate; its name, in fact, means "reclaimed land." Today it's famous for the **Tsukiji Fish Market,** one of the largest wholesale fish markets in the world. Nearby is the Hama Rikyu Garden, considered by some to be the best garden in Tokyo.

Asakusa In the northeastern part of central Tokyo, Asakusa served as the pleasure quarters for old Edo. Today it's known throughout Japan as the site of the famous **Sensoji Temple,** one of Tokyo's top and oldest attractions. It also has a wealth of tiny shops selling traditional Japanese crafts. When Tokyoites talk about *shitamachi* (old downtown), they are referring to the traditional homes and tiny narrow streets of the Asakusa and Ueno areas.

Ueno Located just west of Asakusa, on the northern edge of the JR Yamanote Line loop, Ueno is also part of the city's old downtown. Ueno boasts **Ueno Park,** a huge green space comprising a zoo, a concert hall, and several acclaimed museums, including the **Tokyo National Museum,** which houses the largest collection of Japanese art and antiquities in the world. Ueno Station serves as a stop for major train lines heading north and eastward, including some lines of the Shinkansen bullet train. Under the train tracks of the JR Yamanote Line loop is a thriving market for food, clothing, and accessories.

Shinjuku Originating as a post town in 1698 to serve the needs of feudal lords and their retainers traveling between Edo and the provinces, Shinjuku was hardly touched by the 1923 Great Kanto Earthquake, making it an attractive alternative for businesses wishing to relocate following the destruction. In 1971, Japan's first skyscraper was erected with the opening of the Keio Plaza Hotel in western Shinjuku, setting a dramatic precedent for things to come. Today more than a dozen skyscrapers, including several hotels, dot the Shinjuku skyline, and with the opening of the Tokyo Metropolitan Government Office (TMG) in 1991, Shinjuku's transformation into the capital's upstart business district was complete. Eastern Shinjuku is known for its shopping, particularly the huge **Takashimaya Times Square**

complex, and for its nightlife, especially in **Kabuki-cho,** a thriving amusement center, and in **Shinjuku 2-chome,** Tokyo's premier gay nightlife district. Separating Eastern and Western Shinjuku is **Shinjuku Station,** the nation's busiest commuter station and located on the western end of the Yamanote Line loop. An oasis in the middle of Shinjuku madness is Shinjuku Gyoen Park, a beautiful garden for strolling.

Harajuku The mecca of Tokyo's younger generation, Harajuku swarms throughout the week with teenagers in search of fashion and fun. At its center is **Omotesando Dori,** a fashionable tree-lined avenue flanked by trendy shops, sidewalk cafes, and restaurants. Nearby is **Takeshita Dori,** a narrow pedestrian lane packed with young people looking for the latest in inexpensive clothing and cosmetics. Harajuku is also the home of one of Japan's major attractions, **Meiji Jingu Shrine,** built in 1920 to deify Emperor and Empress Meiji. Another drawing card is the **Oriental Bazaar,** a great shop specializing in products and souvenirs of Japan.

Aoyama While Harajuku is for teenyboppers, Aoyama is a yuppified playground and shopping mecca for Tokyo's trendsetters, chic and upscale and boasting more designer fashion outlets than anywhere else in the city. Located on the eastern end of Omotesando Dori (and an easy walk from Harajuku), Aoyama boasts a number of fine shops and a great array of tempting restaurants.

Ikebukuro Located north of Shinjuku on the Yamanote Line loop, Ikebukuro is the working man's Tokyo, less refined and a bit rougher around the edges. Ikebukuro is where you'll find **Seibu**

and **Tobu,** two of the country's largest department stores, as well as the **Japan Traditional Craft Center** with its beautifully crafted traditional items. The **Sunshine City Building,** one of Tokyo's tallest skyscrapers, is home of a huge indoor shopping center and aquarium.

Akihabara Tokyo's center for electronic and electrical appliances, with more than 600 shops offering a look at the latest in gadgets and gizmos. A stop on the Yamanote Line, this is a fascinating place for a stroll, even if you aren't interested in buying anything.

Shibuya Located on the southwestern edge of the Yamanote Line loop, Shibuya serves as an important nightlife and shopping area for the young. With a plethora of neon and video billboards around Shibuya Station that earn it the nickname "Times Square of Tokyo," it is home to as many as a dozen department stores specializing in everything from designer clothing to housewares.

Ebisu One station south of Shibuya on the JR Yamanote Line, Ebisu was a minor player in Tokyo's shopping and nightlife league until the 1995 debut of **Yebisu Garden Place,** a smart-looking complex of apartments, concert halls, two museums, restaurants, a department store, and a first-class hotel, all connected to Ebisu Station via moving walkway. The vicinity east of Ebisu Station, once a sleepy residential and low-key shopping district, has recently blossomed into a small but thriving nightlife mecca popular with expats who find Roppongi too crass or commercial.

Roppongi Tokyo's best-known nightlife district for young Japanese and foreigners, Roppongi has more bars and nightclubs than any other district, as well as a multitude of restaurants serving international cuisines. The action here continues until dawn.

Akasaka With its several large hotels and small nightlife district, Akasaka caters mostly to businessmen but is otherwise of little interest to visiting tourists. It does, however, boast some good restaurants; in recent years, so many Korean restaurants and establishments have set up shop here that it could be nicknamed "Little Korea."

Shinagawa Once an important post station on the old Tokaido Highway, Shinagawa remains an important crossroad due to **Shinagawa Station,** a major hub of the JR railway network located on the southern end of the Yamanote Line loop. Starting in autumn 2003, it will also be a stop on the Shinkansen bullet train, which should give the area a developmental push. It's home to several major hotels, some of which offer fantastic views of Tokyo Bay.

Odaiba This is Tokyo's newest district, quite literally—it was constructed from reclaimed land in Tokyo Bay. Connected to the mainland by the **Rainbow Bridge** (famous for its chameleon colors after nightfall), the Yurikamome Line monorail, and a vehicular harbor tunnel, Odaiba is home to a few hotels, Japan's largest convention space, several shopping complexes (including the very fancy Venus Fort), the **Museum of Maritime Science,** a man-made sandy beach complete with a boardwalk, a monolithic Ferris wheel, and **Megaweb,** a huge multimedia car amusement and exhibition center sponsored by Toyota. For young Japanese, it's one of Tokyo's hottest date spots.

2 Getting Around

The first rule of getting around Tokyo: It will always take longer than you think.

For short-time visitors, calculating travel times in Tokyo is tricky business. Taking a taxi is expensive and involves the probability of getting stuck interminably in traffic, with the meter ticking away. Taking the subway is usually more efficient, even though it's more complicated and harder on your feet: Choosing which route to take isn't always clear, and transfers between lines are sometimes quite a hike in themselves. If I'm going from one end of Tokyo to the other by subway, I usually allow anywhere from 30 to 60 minutes, depending on the number of transfers and the walking distance to my final destination. If you don't have to change trains, you can travel from one end of Tokyo to the other in about 30 minutes or less. In any case, travel times to destinations within each line are posted on platform pillars.

Your best bet for getting around Tokyo is to take the subway or Japan Railways (JR) commuter train to the station nearest your destination. From there you can either walk, using a map and asking directions along the way, or take a taxi.

BY PUBLIC TRANSPORTATION

If you think you'll be using a combination of public transportation systems in one day—subway, JR train, and bus—you might consider purchasing a **Tokyo Free Kippu,** which, despite its name, costs ¥1,580 ($13). This combination ticket allowing unlimited travel for one day on all JR lines, subways, and Toei buses (with the exception of double-decker buses) is available at all JR stations, JR View Plazas, and most subway stations.

BY SUBWAY & JR TRAIN

BY SUBWAY   Tokyo's subway system is efficient, modern, clean, and easy to use, and all station names are written in English. Some cars also post the next station in English. Altogether, there are 13 subway lines crisscrossing underneath the

---

Value Saving on Transportation

If you think you'll be using Tokyo's subway system a lot or simply wish to avoid having to purchase an individual ticket for each ride, I strongly urge you to invest in an **SF Metro Card,** a prepaid card also sold at vending machines for ¥1,000 ($8.35), ¥3,000 ($25), and ¥5,000 ($42) worth of rides. Insert the card into the automatic ticket gates when you enter and exit the subway wickets; the charge for the ride will be deducted automatically from your card. You can also use your Metro Card in the vending machine to purchase regular single tickets. Since rides on the subway can really add up, you'll find the ¥1,000 Metro Card useful even if you're staying in Tokyo just 3 or 4 days. Although other types of tickets and passes are available, I find them too complicated for short-time visitors.

If you'll be using the JR lines frequently, consider purchasing an **IO Card,** a prepaid card similar to the SF Metro Card that allows you to pass through automatic fare gates without having to purchase a separate JR ticket each time. IO cards come in values of ¥3,000 ($25) and ¥5,000 ($42). There's also a **JR 1-Day Tokyo Rail Pass** (Tokunai Free Kippu), which allows unlimited travel on JR trains for one day for ¥730 ($6).

> **Tips**   **Subway Information**
>
> For more information on tickets, passes, and lines for the subway, stop by information desks located at Ginza, Shinjuku, Nihombashi, and Otemachi stations.

city, and each line is color-coded. The Ginza Line, for example, is orange, which means all its coaches and signs are orange. If you're transferring to the Ginza Line from another line, just follow the orange signs and circles to the Ginza Line platform. Before boarding, however, make sure the train is going in the right direction; otherwise you'll end up in the opposite end of the city. Tokyo's newest line, the Oedo Line, makes a zigzap loop around the city and is useful for traveling between Roppongi and Shinjuku (be aware, however, that it's buried deep underground and stations take a while to reach, despite escalators).

Tickets   Vending machines at all subway stations sell tickets; fares begin at ¥160 ($1.35) for the shortest distance and increase according to how far you're traveling, with ¥300 ($2.50) charged for the longest distance. Children under 6 ride free; children 6 to 11 pay half-fare. Vending machines give change, and most accept ¥1,000, ¥5,000 and ¥10,000 notes. **To purchase your ticket,** insert money into the vending machine until the fare buttons light up, then push the amount for the ticket you want. Your ticket and change will drop onto a little platform at the bottom of the machine.

Fares are posted on a large subway map above the vending machines, but they're generally in Japanese only; major stations also post a smaller map listing fares in English, but you may have to search for it. An alternative is to look at your Tourist Information Center subway map—it lists stations in both Japanese and English. Once you know what the Japanese characters look like, you may be able to locate your station and the corresponding fare. If you still don't know the fare, just buy a basic-fare ticket for ¥160 ($1.35) and insert it into the automatic entrance gate. When you exit at your destination, look for the **fare adjustment machine;** insert your ticket to find out how much more you owe, or look for a **fare adjustment window** where a subway employee will tell you how much extra you owe.

In any case, be sure to hang on to your ticket, since you must give it up at the end of your journey.

Hours   Most subways run from about 5am to midnight, although the times of the first and last trains depend on the line, the station, and whether it's a weekday or weekend. Schedules are posted in the stations, and through most of the day trains run every 3 to 5 minutes.

Avoid taking the subway during the weekday morning **rush hour,** from 8 to 9am—the stories you've heard about commuters packed into trains like sardines are all true. There are even "platform pushers," men who push people into compartments so that the doors can close. If you want to witness Tokyo at its craziest, go to Shinjuku Station at 8:30am—but go by taxi unless you want to experience the crowding firsthand.

Exiting the Subway   Once you reach your destination, look for the yellow signs designating which exit to take for major buildings, museums, and addresses. If you're confused about which exit to take from the station, ask someone at the window near the ticket gate. Taking the right exit can make a world of difference, especially in Shinjuku, where there are more than 60 station exits.

BY TRAIN   In addition to subway lines, electric commuter trains operated by **Japan Railways (JR)** run above ground. These are also color-coded, with fares beginning at ¥130 ($1.10). Buy your ticket from vending machines the same as you would for the subway.

The **Yamanote Line** (green-colored coaches) is the best-known and most convenient JR line. It makes an oblong loop around the city, stopping at 29 stations along the way. In fact, you may want to take the Yamanote Line and stay on it for a roundup view of Tokyo; the entire trip takes about an hour, passing stations like Shinjuku, Tokyo, Harajuku, Akihabara, and Ueno on the way.

Another convenient JR line is the **Chuo Line,** whose coaches are orange-colored; it cuts across Tokyo between Shinjuku and Tokyo stations. The yellow-colored **Sobu Line** runs between Shinjuku and Akihabara and beyond to Chiba. Other JR lines serve outlying districts for the metropolis' commuting public. Since the Yamanote, Chuo, and Sobu lines are rarely identified by their specific names at major stations, look for signs that say "JR Lines."

For more information on JR lines and tickets, stop by one of JR's **Information Centers** at Tokyo Station (central passage; open daily 9am–7pm) and Shinjuku Station (the east side; open daily 10am–6:30pm). You can also call the JR's English-language telephone service at ℂ **03/3423-0111,** available Monday through Friday from 10am to 6pm.

A NOTE ON TRANSFERS   You can transfer between subway lines without buying another ticket, and you can transfer between JR train lines on one ticket. However, your ticket or prepaid card does not allow a transfer between subway lines, JR train lines, and private train lines connecting Tokyo with outlying destinations such as Nikko. You usually don't have to worry about this, though, because if you exit through a wicket and have to give up your ticket, you'll know you have to buy another one.

There are instances, however, when you pass through a ticket wicket to transfer between subway lines (for example, when you transfer from the Yurakucho Line to the Hibiya Line at Hibiya Station). In this case, simply show your ticket when you pass through the wicket or insert it into the automatic gate, whereupon it will be returned. The general rule is that if your final destination and fare are posted above the ticket vending machines, you can travel all the way to your destination with only one ticket. But don't worry about this too much— the ticket collector will set you straight if you've miscalculated. Note, however, that if you pay too much for your ticket, the portion of the fare that's left unused is not refundable—so, again, the easiest thing to do if in doubt is to buy the cheapest fare.

BY BUS

Buses are difficult to use in Tokyo because destinations are sometimes written only in Japanese and most bus drivers don't speak English. However, they are sometimes convenient for short distances. If you're feeling adventurous, board the bus at the front and drop the exact fare into the box by the driver. If you don't have the exact fare (usually ¥200/$1.65), a slot located next to the driver will accept coins only; your change will come out below, minus the fare. Another slot will accept ¥1,000 bills only; the change, minus the fare, comes out in the same place as if you insert a coin. A sign board at the front of the bus displays the next stop. When you wish to get off, press one of the buttons on the railing near the door or the seats. You can pick up an excellent **Toei Bus Route Guide map** showing all major bus routes at one of the Tokyo Tourist Information Centers operated by the Tokyo Convention and Visitors Bureau (see "Visitor Information," earlier in this chapter).

BY TAXI

Taxis are shamefully expensive in Tokyo. **Fares** start at ¥660 ($5.50) for the first 2km (1¼ miles) and increase ¥80 (65¢) for each additional 274m (904 ft.) or 40 seconds of waiting time. There are also smaller, more compact taxis that start out slightly less at ¥640 ($5.35) for the first 2km (1¼ miles) but then increase ¥80 for each additional 290m (957 ft.). In 1997, when controls regulating taxi fares became less restrictive, some taxis began offering fares cheaper than the standard rates for short distances. Fares are posted on the back of the front passenger seat. If you're like me, however, you probably won't shop around—you'll just gratefully jump into the first taxi that stops. Note that from 11pm to 5am, an extra 30% is added to your fare.

With the exception of some major thoroughfares in the downtown area, you can **hail a taxi** from the street or go to a taxi stand or a major hotel. A red light will show above the dashboard if a taxi is free to pick up a passenger; a green light indicates the taxi is occupied. Be sure to stand clear of the back door—it swings open automatically. Likewise, it shuts automatically once you're in. Taxi drivers get upset if you try to manhandle it yourself.

Unless you're going to a well-known landmark or hotel, it's best to **have your destination written out in Japanese,** since most taxi drivers don't speak English. But even that may not help. Tokyo is so complicated even taxi drivers may not know a certain area, although they do have detailed maps. If a driver doesn't understand where you're going, he may refuse to take you. Otherwise, don't be surprised if he jumps out of the cab to ask for directions at a nearby shop—with the meter ticking.

There are so many taxis cruising Tokyo that one is always around and available—except when you need it most. That is, when it's raining and sometimes just after 1am on weekends, after all subways and trains have stopped. However, one valuable result of the recession is the number of available taxis now cruising late at night; now that companies no longer pay for employees' expensive after-the-last-train taxi fares, nighttime revelers no longer have to stay out until 3am just to find a taxi.

One of these major taxi companies can be called for a pick-up: **Nihon Kotsu** (© 03/3586-2151), **Kokusai** (© 03/3491-6001), **Daiwa** (© 03/3563-5151), or **Hinomaru** (© 03/3814-1111). Note, however, that only Japanese is spoken, and you'll be required to pay extra (usually not more than ¥500/$4.35). I've never telephoned for a taxi—just like in the movies, a taxi usually cruises by just when you raise your hand.

 FAST FACTS: Tokyo

If you can't find answers to your questions here, check "Fast Facts: Japan," in chapter 2. If you still can't find an answer, call the **Tourist Information Center** (© 03/3201-3331) daily from 9am to 5pm. If you're staying in a first-class hotel, another valuable resource is the concierge or guest-relations desk; the staff there can tell you how to reach your destination, answer general questions, and will even make restaurant reservations for you.

American Express There is no public American Express office in Japan.

Area Code If you're calling a Tokyo number from outside Tokyo but within Japan, the area code for Tokyo is 03. For details on calling Tokyo from outside Japan, see "Telephone & Fax," in "Fast Facts: Japan," in chapter 2.

Babysitters Most major hotels can arrange babysitting services, but expect to pay about $80 for 2 hours. A very few also provide in-house day-care centers. **Tokyo Domestic Service** (© 03/3584-4769) can provide bilingual sitters. There's a 3-hour minimum charge of ¥5,500 ($46), then ¥1,500 ($12) per hour after that. Parents are also required to pay transportation (¥1,000/$8.35 during the day, ¥1,500/$12 from 9 to 11pm, and ¥3,000/$25 after 11pm) and to provide meals.

Business Hours Government offices and private companies are generally open Monday through Friday 9am to 5pm. Banks are open Monday through Friday 9am to 3pm, while neighborhood post offices are open Monday through Friday 9am to 5pm. Some major post offices, however, (located in each ward) are open Monday through Friday from 9am to 7pm.

Department stores are open from about 10am to 7:30 or 8pm, with irregular closing days one to four times a month (but always the same day of the week). Since closed days differ for each department store, you can always find several that are open, even on Sunday. Smaller stores are generally open from about 10am to 8pm, closed one day a week. Convenience stores such as 7-Eleven are open 24 hours.

Keep in mind that museums, gardens, and most attractions stop selling admission tickets at least 30 minutes before the actual closing time. Similarly, restaurants take their last orders at least 30 minutes before the posted closing time (even earlier for kaiseki restaurants).

Currency Exchange You can exchange money in major banks throughout Tokyo, often indicated by a sign in English near the front door. Banks give a slightly better exchange rate for traveler's checks than for cash; *you'll need your passport to exchange traveler's checks*. If you need to exchange money outside banking hours, inquire at one of the larger first-class hotels—some of them will cash traveler's checks or exchange money even if you're not a guest, though note that you'll need a passport to change money in a hotel. At Narita Airport (which also has ATMs for major credit cards), exchange counters are open from 6am to 11pm. At Shinjuku Station, the Odakyu Sightseeing Service Center, located at the Odakyu Shinjuku Station west exit concourse, can exchange notes (not traveler's checks) into yen daily from 8am to 6pm.

Otherwise, the most convenient ATMs are located in post offices, available for Visa, MasterCard, and Plus and Cirrus cards during regular post office hours. You can also get cash advances using Visa credit cards at any Sumitomo Bank and from MasterCard at Union Credit (UC) banks and some Sumitomo banks, Citibanks, Mitsubishi-Tokyo banks, and affiliated banks, with branches all over town; you'll have to show your passport for cash advances.

Dentists & Doctors Many first-class hotels offer medical facilities or an in-house doctor. Otherwise, your embassy can refer you to English-speaking doctors, specialists, and dentists. In addition, the **AMDA International Medical Information Center** (✆ **03/5285-8088**), available Monday through Friday 9am to 5pm, can provide information on English-speaking staff. The following are clinics with some English-speaking staff that are popular with foreigners living in Tokyo: **The International Clinic,** 1–5–9 Azabudai, Minato-ku, within walking distance of Roppongi or Azabu Juban stations (✆ **03/3582-2646**; open Monday through Friday 9am to noon and 2:30 to 5pm, Saturday 9am to noon; walk-ins only); the **Ishikawa Clinic,** Azabu Sakurada Heights, Room 201, 3–2–7 Nishi-Azabu, Minato-ku, near Roppongi Station (✆ **03/3401-6340**; open Monday to Friday 9am to 12:30pm, as well as Monday 3:15 to 4:30pm, Tuesday and Thursday 3 to 6:30pm, and Wednesday and Friday 3 to 6pm; both walk-ins and appointments accepted, though appointments are preferred); **Tokyo Medical & Surgical Clinic,** 32 Mori Building, 3–4–30 Shiba-koen, Minato-ku, near Kamiyacho, Onarimon, or Shiba-koen stations and across from Tokyo Tower (✆ **03/3436-3028**; open Monday to Friday 9am to 1pm and 2 to 5pm, Saturday 9am to noon; appointments only). At the Tokyo Medical & Surgical Clinic, above, is also the **Tokyo Clinic Dental Office** (✆ **03/ 3431-4225**), open Monday, Wednesday, Thursday, and Friday from 9am to 6pm and Saturday 9am to 5pm. You can also make appointments to visit doctors at the hospitals listed below.

Drugstores There is no 24-hour drugstore in Tokyo, but ubiquitous 24-hour convenience stores such as 7-Eleven, Lawson, and FamilyMart carry things like aspirin. If you're looking for specific pharmaceuticals, a good bet is the **American Pharmacy,** Hibiya Park Building, 1–8–1 Yurakucho, Chiyoda-ku (✆ **03/3271-4034**; open Monday through Saturday 9:30am to 8pm, Sunday and holidays 10am to 6:30pm), which has many of the same over-the-counter drugs you can find at home (many of them imported from the United States) and can fill American prescriptions—but note that you must first visit a doctor in Japan before foreign prescriptions can be filled, so it's best to bring an ample supply of any prescription medication with you.

Embassies & Consulates See "Fast Facts: Japan," in chapter 2.

Emergencies The national emergency numbers are ✆ **110** for police and ✆ **119** for ambulance and fire. You do not have to insert a coin or telephone card for an emergency number from a public phone, but you do have to push a red button before placing the call.

Hospitals In addition to going to these hospitals for an emergency, you can also make appointments at their clinics to see a doctor: **The International Catholic Hospital** (Seibo Byoin), 2–5–1 Naka-Ochiai, Shinjuku-ku, near Meijiro Station on the Yamanote Line (✆ **03/3951-1111**; clinic hours Monday through Saturday 8 to 11am; closed third Saturday of each month; appointments required); **St. Luke's International Hospital** (Seiroka Byoin), 9–1 Akashi-cho, Chuo-ku, near Tsukiji Station on the Hibiya Line (✆ **03/3541-5151**; Monday through Friday 8:30 to 11am; appointments necessary for some treatments); and the **Japan Red Cross Medical Center**

(Nihon Sekijujisha Iryo Center), 4–1–22 Hiroo, Shibuya-ku (✆ **03/ 3400-1311;** Mon–Fri 8:30–11am; walk-ins only), whose closest subway stations are Roppongi, Hiroo, and Shibuya—from there, you should take a taxi.

Hotlines In addition to the Tourist Information Center (see "Visitor Information," earlier in this chapter), the Tokyo Metropolitan Government maintains a **Foreign Residents' Advisory Center** (✆ **03/5320-7744**) that can answer questions ranging from problems of daily life to Japanese customs and culture, Monday to Friday from 9:30am to noon and 1 to 4pm. For criminal matters or concerns, the Metropolitan Police Department has a telephone counseling service for foreigners (✆ **03/3503-8484**), available daily 8:15am to 5:15pm.

Information See "Visitor Information," earlier in this chapter.

Internet Access If your hotel doesn't provide Internet access, **Kinko's** has more than 25 locations throughout Tokyo, including 1–2–12 Yurakucho (✆ **03/5251-4808;** near Hibiya Station), opposite the Imperial Hotel; 7–14–16 Ginza (✆ **03/5565-0441,** near Higashi Ginza Station); and in the Odakyu Southern Tower Building, 2–2–1 Yoyogi (✆ **03/3377-5711;** near Shinjuku Station's south exit). All are open 24 hours and charge ¥400 ($3.35) per 15 minutes of computer time. Cheaper are cybercafes. I like **Necca,** located on the third floor of the Chitose Kaikan Building at 13–8 Udagawa-cho, on Inokashira Dori near the police box in Shibuya (✆ **03/5728-2561;** near Shibuya Station). Offering high-speed Internet access and games, it's open Sunday to Wednesday from 9am to 11pm and 24 hours Thursday through Saturday. It costs ¥200 ($1.65) to become a lifetime member, after which it costs ¥500 ($4.15) per hour.

Lost Property If you've forgotten something on a subway, in a taxi, or on a park bench, don't assume it's gone forever—if you're willing to trace it, you'll probably get it back. If you can remember where you last saw it, the first thing to do is telephone the establishment or return to where you left it; there's a good chance it will still be sitting there. If you've lost something on the street, go to the nearest police box (*koban*); items found in the neighborhood will stay there for 3 days or longer. After that, you should contact the **Central Lost and Found Office of the Metropolitan Police Board,** 1–9–11 Koraku, Bunkyo-ku (✆ **03/3814-4151**).

If you've lost something in a taxi, contact the **Taxi Kindaika Center,** 7-3-3 Minamisuma, Koto-ku (✆ **03/3648-0300**). For JR trains, have someone who speaks Japanese call or go to the **Lost and Found Sections** at Tokyo JR Station (✆ **03/3231-1880**) or at Ueno JR Station (✆ **03/3841-8069**); or you can call the **JR East Infoline** at (✆ **03/3423-0111**). If you've lost something on a subway or bus, call the lost and found section of the **Tokyo Metropolitan Government,** 2-3-29 Hamamatsucho, Minato-ku (✆ **03/ 3431-1515**).

Luggage Storage/Lockers Coin-operated lockers are located at all major JR stations, such as Tokyo, Shinjuku, and Ueno, as well as at most subway stations. Lockers cost ¥200 to ¥700 ($1.65–$5.85), depending on the size.

Newspapers & Magazines Three English-language newspapers are published daily in Japan (see "Fast Facts: Japan," in chapter 2). For what's going on in Tokyo, pick up a copy of *Tokyo Journal* or *Tokyo Classified*.

If you're interested in seeing the latest edition of your favorite magazine back home, your best bet is to drop in on the **World Magazine Gallery,** 3–13–10 Ginza, behind the Kabuki-za near Higashi-Ginza Station (© 03/3545-7227; open Mon–Fri 11am–7pm), which displays more than 900 magazines from 55 countries around the world. Magazines are for reading here only and are not for sale, but there is a coffee shop where you can peruse them at your leisure.

Police The national emergency telephone number is © 110.

Post Offices If your hotel cannot mail letters for you, ask the concierge where the nearest post office is. The **Central Post Office,** just southwest of Tokyo Station at 2–7–2 Marunouchi, Chiyoda-ku (© 03/3284-9527), has longer business hours than most: Monday through Friday 9am to 7pm, Saturday 9am to 5pm, Sunday and public holidays 9am to 12:30pm. An after-hours counter remains open throughout the night for mail and packages, making this the only 24-hour service facility in town.

For English-language postal information call © 03/5472-5851 Monday through Friday between 9:30am and 4:30pm. Also see "Mail," under "Fast Facts: Japan," in chapter 2.

Radio & TV See "Fast Facts: Japan," in chapter 2.

Restrooms If you're in need of a restroom in Tokyo, your best bets are train and subway stations, big hotels, department stores, and fast-food chains like McDonald's. For an explanation of using Japanese toilets, see "Fast Facts: Japan," in chapter 2.

Safety Tokyo is one of the safest cities in the world. However, crime is on the increase, and there are precautions you should always take when traveling: Stay alert and be aware of your immediate surroundings. Be especially careful with cameras, purses, and wallets, particularly in crowded subways, department stores, or tourist attractions (such as the retail district around Tsukiji Fish Market), especially as pickpocketing has been on the rise. Some Japanese also caution women against walking through parks alone at night.

Taxes See "Fast Facts: Japan," in chapter 2.

Telephone & Fax For information on how to make calls, see "Fast Facts: Japan," in chapter 2. For assistance on directory telephone listings in Tokyo, dial © 104.

There are several English telephone directories providing addresses and telephone numbers for many businesses, companies, shops, and restaurants in Tokyo: the **English Telephone Directory, Townpage,** the **Japan Times Directory,** and the **Japan Telephone Book Yellow Pages.** The latter comes out twice a year and provides both telephone and fax numbers for every business and organization you are likely to need. If your hotel does not have one on hand and you're interested in buying one, they're available at the bookstores listed under "The Shopping Scene," in chapter 4.

3 Where to Stay

Tokyo has no old, grand hotels in the tradition of Hong Kong's Peninsula or Bangkok's Oriental; it has hardly any old hotels, period. But what the city's hotels may lack in quaintness or old grandeur is more than made up for by the excellent service for which the Japanese are legendary; cleanliness, and efficiency. Be prepared, however, for small rooms. Space is at a premium in Tokyo, so with the exception of some of the upper-range hotels, rooms seem to come in only three sizes: minuscule, small, and adequate.

Unfortunately, Tokyo also doesn't have many first-class ryokan, or Japanese-style inns. I suggest, therefore, that you wait for your travels around the country to experience a first-rate ryokan. Otherwise, there are moderate and inexpensive Japanese-style inns in Tokyo. In fact, if you're traveling on a tight budget, a simple Japanese-style inn is often the cheapest way to go, though don't expect much in the way of service or amenities. In addition, most of the upper-bracket hotels (like the Miyako) offer at least a few Japanese-style rooms, with tatami mats, a Japanese bathtub (deeper and narrower than the Western version), and futon. Although these rooms tend to be expensive, they're usually large enough for four people.

For more on available types of accommodations, see "Tips on Accommodations," in chapter 2.

PRICE CATEGORIES   The recommended hotels which follow are arranged first according to price, then by location. After all, since attractions are spread throughout the city and Tokyo's public transportation service is fast and efficient (I've provided nearest subway or train stations for each listing)—and since this is one of the most expensive hotel cities in the world—the overriding factor in selecting accommodations will likely be one of cost. I've divided Tokyo's hotels into price categories based upon two people per night, excluding tax and service charge: **Very Expensive** hotels charge ¥35,000 ($292) and above, **Expensive** hotels charge ¥25,000 to ¥35,000 ($208–$292), **Moderate** hotels offer rooms for ¥14,000 to ¥25,000 ($117–$208), and **Inexpensive** accommodations offer rooms for ¥13,000 ($108) and less. Unless otherwise indicated, rooms are with private bath.

TAXES & SERVICE CHARGES   In addition to quoted prices, upper-class hotels and most medium-range hotels will add a service charge of 10 to 15%. Further, all hotels add an additional 5% tax. Unless otherwise stated, the prices given in this chapter do not include tax or service.

Tips Mapping out Tokyo's Hotels

Once you've chosen a hotel or inn that appeals to you, you can locate it using the following neighborhood maps:

- To locate accommodations in **Akasaka,** p. 109.
- To locate accommodations in **Ueno,** p. 114.
- To locate accommodations in **Shinjuku,** p. 116 to 117.
- To locate accommodations in **Asakusa,** p. 121.
- To locate accommodations in **Hibiya** and **Ginza,** p. 134 to 135.
- To locate accommodations in **Harajuku,** p. 147.
- To locate accommodations in **Roppongi,** p. 153.

> **Tips A Note on Prices**
>
> The prices quoted in this book were figured at ¥120 = US$1. However, because of fluctuations in the exchange rate of the yen, the U.S. dollar equivalents given will probably vary during the lifetime of this edition. Be sure to check current exchange rates when planning your trip. In addition, the rates given below may increase, so be sure to ask the current rate when making your reservation.

RESERVATIONS   Although Tokyo doesn't suffer from a lack of hotel rooms during peak holidays (when most Japanese head for the hills and beaches), rooms may be in short supply because of conventions and other events. If possible, avoid coming to Tokyo in mid-February unless you book well in advance—that's when university entrance exams bring aspiring high-school students and their parents flocking to the capital for a shot at one of the most prestigious universities in the country. And in summer, when most foreign tourists visit Japan, the cheaper accommodations are likely to fill up first.

It's always best, therefore, to make your hotel reservations in advance, especially if you're arriving in Japan after a long transoceanic flight and don't want the hassle of searching for a hotel room. If you've arrived in Tokyo without reservations, stop by the **Tourist Information Center** (TIC; see "Visitor Information," earlier in this chapter) where its Welcome Inn Reservation Center will book an inexpensive room free of charge.

VERY EXPENSIVE
HIBIYA & GINZA

Imperial Hotel ★★ *(Kids)*   Located across from Hibiya Park, within walking distance of Ginza and the Imperial Palace, this modern structure is one of Tokyo's best-known hotels, with foreigners (mostly business executives) making up about 40% of the guests. The Imperial's trademark is impeccable service: Guests are treated like royalty. Although the Imperial's history goes back to 1922, when it opened as a much smaller hotel designed by Frank Lloyd Wright, the present hotel dates from 1970, with a 31-story tower added in 1983. (Part of the original structure survives at Meiji-Mura, an architectural museum outside Nagoya.) Wright's legacy lives on, unfortunately, only in the hotel's Art-Deco Old Imperial Bar. On the plus side, it's one of the few hotels with a children's day-care center.

Rooms in the main building are quite large for Tokyo. Tower rooms, while slightly smaller, are higher up, have floor-to-ceiling bay windows, and offer fantastic views of either the Imperial Palace or, my preference, Ginza and Tokyo Bay. All come equipped with the amenities you expect from a first-class hotel, as well as such appreciated extras as a hand-free phone, bedside controls for the curtains, and a private e-mail address for each guest. *A tip:* Become a member of the Imperial Club (membership is free), and you can use the pool and gym free of charge.

1–1–1 Uchisaiwaicho, Chiyoda-ku, Tokyo 100-8558. ⓒ **800/223-6800** in the U.S. and Canada or 03/3504-1111. Fax 03/3581-9146. www.imperialhotel.co.jp. 1,059 units. ¥30,000–¥56,000 ($250–$467) single; ¥35,000–¥61,000 ($292–$508) double or twin; from ¥110,000 ($917) suite. AE, DC, JCB, MC, V. Station: Hibiya (1 min.). **Amenities:** 13 restaurants, 4 bars; 20th-floor indoor pool with breathtaking views (fee: ¥1,000/$8.35; free for Imperial Club members), fitness room (fee: ¥1,000/$8.35; free for Imperial Club members), sauna; day-care center for children aged 2 weeks to 6 years (fee: ¥5,000/$42 for 2 hr.); concierge;

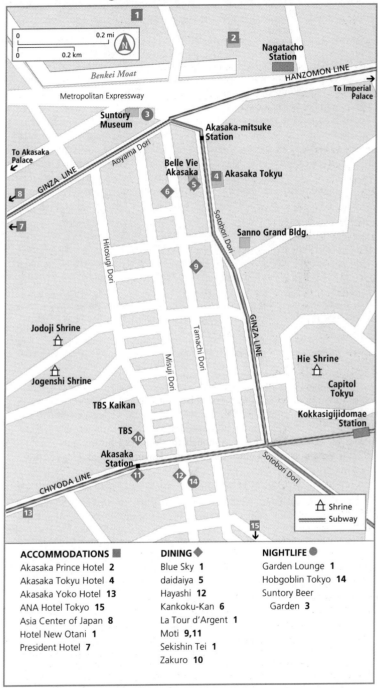

Nightlife & Where to Stay & Dine in Akasaka

0.2 mi
0.2 km

Benkei Moat

Metropolitan Expressway

Nagatacho Station

HANZOMON LINE

To Imperial Palace

Suntory Museum

Akasaka-mitsuke Station

To Akasaka Palace

Aoyama Dori

GINZA LINE

Belle Vie Akasaka

Akasaka Tokyu

Sotobori Dori

Sanno Grand Bldg.

Hitosugi Dori

Jodoji Shrine

Jogenshi Shrine

Tamachi Dori

GINZA LINE

Misuji Dori

Hie Shrine

Capitol Tokyu

TBS Kaikan

Kokkasigijidomae Station

TBS

Akasaka Station

CHIYODA LINE

Sotobori Dori

⌂ Shrine
— Subway

ACCOMMODATIONS ■
Akasaka Prince Hotel **2**
Akasaka Tokyu Hotel **4**
Akasaka Yoko Hotel **13**
ANA Hotel Tokyo **15**
Asia Center of Japan **8**
Hotel New Otani **1**
President Hotel **7**

DINING ◆
Blue Sky **1**
daidaiya **5**
Hayashi **12**
Kankoku-Kan **6**
La Tour d'Argent **1**
Moti **9,11**
Sekishin Tei **1**
Zakuro **10**

NIGHTLIFE ●
Garden Lounge **1**
Hobgoblin Tokyo **14**
Suntory Beer
  Garden **3**

limousine and car-rental services; extensively equipped business center; impressive shopping arcade; salon; 24-hr. room service; in-room massage; babysitting; same-day dry cleaning/laundry service; nonsmoking rooms; in-house doctor and dentist; tea-ceremony room; post office. *In room:* A/C, cable TV with pay movies, fax, dataport, minibar, hot-water pot with tea and coffee, hair dryer, large safe, bathroom scale.

SHINJUKU

Park Hyatt Tokyo ★★★ Located in West Shinjuku on the 39th to 52nd floors of Kenzo Tange's granite-and-glass Shinjuku Park Tower, the Park Hyatt is among the most gorgeous and sophisticated hotels in Japan, a perfect reflection of high-tech, avant-garde Tokyo in the 21st century. If you can afford it, stay here. Check-in, on the 41st floor, is comfortably accomplished at one of three sit-down desks. Elevators reserved only for the guest-room floors offer privacy; if you do see other guests, they're likely to be personalities, fashion designers, or CEOs. In contrast to Shinjuku's other hotels, there's no off-the-street foot traffic here; rather, a hushed, soothing atmosphere prevails. Be sure to book early for the 52nd-floor New York Grill, one of Tokyo's best and offering a spectacular setting (see "Where to Dine," later in this chapter).

All rooms average at least 538 square feet (the largest in Tokyo) and offer original art work, stunning and expansive views (including Mt. Fuji on clear days), bathrooms to die for with a deep tub (plus separate shower), and a TV, a walk-in closet, remote-control curtains, and more, including a Japanese/English dictionary.

3–7–1–2 Nishi-Shinjuku, Shinjuku-ku, Tokyo 163-1055. ✆ **800/233-1234** in the U.S. and Canada or 03/5322-1234. Fax 03/5322-1288. www.parkhyatttokyo.com. 178 units. ¥49,000–¥60,000 ($408–$500) single or double; from ¥94,000 ($783) suites. AE, DC, JCB, MC, V. Station: Shinjuku (a 13-min. walk, or 5-min. free shuttle ride); Hatsudai on the Keio Line (7 min.); Tochomae (8 min.). **Amenities:** 4 restaurants, 2 bars; dramatic, 20-meter indoor swimming pool with great views (free for hotel guests); health club and spa (fee: ¥4,000/$33); concierge; salon; 24-hr. business center; 24-hr. room service; in-room massage; babysitting; same-day dry cleaning/laundry service; nonsmoking rooms; CD, laser disc, and book libraries; free shuttle service to Shinjuku Station one to three times an hour; complimentary shoeshine. *In room:* A/C, VCR and wide-screen TV with cable and pay movies that can also be used to access the Internet, CD and laser disc players (with free rentals), fax, dataport with high-speed access, minibar, hot-water pot with tea, hair dryer, safe, bathroom scale, washlet toilet.

EBISU

Westin Tokyo ★★ A black marble floor, neoclassical columns and statuary, huge floral bouquets, and palm trees set this smart-looking hotel apart from other Tokyo hotels—it would fit right in in Hong Kong. Opened in 1995 and set in the attractive Yebisu Garden Place (Tokyo's first planned community), it's still a hike from Ebisu Station, even with the aid of the elevated moving walkways. It's also far from Tokyo's business center. But the largely Japanese clientele favors it for its European ambience, relaxed atmosphere, the Westin name, and the facilities of Yebisu Garden Place, including restaurants and shopping.

The spacious, high-ceilinged rooms blend 19th-century Biedermeier styles with contemporary furnishings and boast high ceilings, either king-size (in the double rooms) or two double beds (in twins), over-size desks, separate lighted vanities, and large bathrooms with separate shower and tub areas. Guest Office rooms provide such additional features as a laser printer, fax machine, and office supplies. Rooms with the best view are those facing Tokyo Bay, though in winter those facing west are treated to views of Mt. Fuji.

1–4–1 Mita, Meguro-ku, Tokyo 153-8580. ✆ **800/WESTIN-1** in the U.S. and Canada or 03/5423-7000. Fax 03/5423-7600. www.westin.co.jp. 445 units. ¥42,000 ($350) single; ¥47,000 ($392) double or twin; from ¥100,000 ($833) suite. Guest Office or Executive Club, ¥49,000 ($408) single; ¥54,000 ($500) double or twin. AE, DC, JCB, MC, V. Station: Ebisu (7 min. via Yebisu Sky Walk). **Amenities:** 6 restaurants, 3 bars and lounges;

access to nearby health club with heated indoor pool and gym (fee: ¥4,000/$33); concierge; business center; 24-hr. room service; in-room massage; babysitting; same-day dry cleaning/laundry service; nonsmoking rooms; executive-level rooms. *In room:* A/C, cable TV with pay movies, dataport, minibar, hot-water pot with tea, hair dryer.

ROPPONGI & AKASAKA

Hotel Okura ⟨★★⟩   Tokyo's most venerable hotel, located across the street from the U.S. Embassy, is the favorite home-away-from-home of visiting United States dignitaries and top-level executives, as well as celebrities from the Rolling Stones to Yo-Yo Ma. Service is dignified, gracious, and impeccable. Rich decor elegantly combines ikebana and shoji screens with old-fashioned Western spaciousness. The atmosphere is low key, with none of the flashiness of some of the city's newer hotels. All rooms are comfortable, with a convenient gauge showing outdoor temperature and humidity, though some rooms are rather small and have a slightly weird mix of fabric designs. My favorites are the renovated rooms in the main building facing the garden; those on the 5th floor have balconies overlooking the garden and pool. *A tip:* Although fees are charged for use of the health club, hotel guests can use facilities free simply by becoming a member of Okura Club International—there's no charge to become a member and membership starts immediately upon filling out an application at the hotel guest relations desk.

2-10-4 Toranomon, Minato-ku, Tokyo 105-0001. © **800/223-6800** in the U.S. or 03/3582-0111. Fax 03/3582-3707. www.hotelokura.co.jp. 858 units. ¥29,000–¥42,500 ($242–$354) single; ¥37,500–¥59,000 ($312–$492) double; ¥40,000–¥59,000 ($333–$492) twin; from ¥89,000 ($742) suite. AE, DC, JCB, MC, V. Station: Toranomon or Kamiyacho (5 min.). **Amenities:** 9 restaurants, 2 bars; nicely landscaped outdoor pool (free for hotel guests); health club (fee: ¥3,500/$29 to use everything; ¥2,000/$17 for indoor pool only); concierge; tour desk; comprehensive business center; shopping arcade; salon; 24-hr. room service; in-room massage; same-day dry cleaning/laundry service; nonsmoking rooms; free shuttle service to the nearest subway (daily 1–9:30pm); tea-ceremony room; private museum showcasing Japanese art; pharmacy; in-house doctor; post office; packing and shipping service. *In room:* A/C, bilingual satellite TV with on-demand pay movies and which doubles as a computer with Internet access, fax, high-speed dataport, minibar, hot-water pot with tea, hair dryer, bathroom scale.

NEAR IKEBUKURO

Four Seasons Hotel Tokyo at Chinzan-So ⟨★★★⟩   A bit off the beaten track (about a 15-min. taxi ride from Ikebukuro), the Four Seasons is set in the luscious 17-acre, 100-year-old Chinzan-So Garden, making it extremely inviting after a bustling day in Tokyo. It also has one of Tokyo's best health clubs and spas, including a gorgeous glass-enclosed indoor pool surrounded by greenery with a glass ceiling that opens in summer, indoor and outdoor Jacuzzis (the outdoor one overlooks a small Japanese garden), and Japanese hot-springs bath (the water is shipped in from Izu Peninsula)—all free for hotel guests. The health club, open 24 hours and with personal-sized TVs at most work stations, even offers free Continental breakfasts. Stunning interiors also make it one of the most beautiful European-style hotels in Japan. Since the hotel embraces the park, almost all rooms have peaceful garden views from their bay windows. Even the smallest rooms, which occupy the lower floors, boast king-size beds and are twice the size of most Japanese hotel rooms. Be sure to ask the concierge for a walking guide of the surrounding area; and don't miss a stroll through the garden.

2-10-8 Sekiguchi, Bunkyo-ku, Tokyo 112-8667. © **800/332-3442** in the U.S., 800/268-6282 in Canada, or 03/3943-2222. Fax 03/3943-2300. www.fourseasons-tokyo.com/. 286 units. ¥37,000–¥49,000 ($308–$408) single; ¥42,000–¥54,000 ($350–$450) double or twin; from ¥67,000 ($558) suite. Club Floor Room, ¥47,000–¥54,000 ($392–$450) single; ¥54,000–¥61,000 ($450–$508) twin or double. AE, DC, JCB, MC, V. Station: Edogawabashi (exit 1a, a 10-min. walk or a 2-min. ride). **Amenities:** 4 restaurants, 1 bar, 1 lounge;

Kids Family-Friendly Hotels

Crowne Plaza Metropolitan Tokyo *(p. 123)* This medium-priced hotel gets kudos for letting children under 20 stay free in their parents' room (maximum of three persons per room). It also has an outdoor pool.

Hotel New Otani *(p. 118)* This huge hotel has both indoor and outdoor swimming pools, but best for parents is the babysitting room for children aged 1 month to 5 years. For a small fortune, you can even leave the darlings overnight.

Imperial Hotel *(p. 108)* Although oriented to business travelers, this famous hotel makes it easier to bring the family along with its day-care center for children aged 2 weeks to 6 years, its babysitting service, and indoor pool.

National Children's Castle Hotel *(p. 129)* The absolute best place to stay with kids, since the same building contains Tokyo's best indoor/outdoor playground and activity rooms for all ages, offering everything from building blocks to computer games.

Sakura Ryokan *(p. 126)* This modern Japanese-style inn offers a large family room that sleeps up to eight people in traditional Japanese style, on futon laid out on tatami mats.

indoor pool, health club, and spa (free for hotel guests); concierge; business center; 24-hr. room service; in-room massage; same-day laundry/dry cleaning service; nonsmoking rooms; executive-level rooms; complimentary shoe-shine; complimentary chauffeured service (I love this) to anywhere in Tokyo (weekdays 8am–5pm). *In room:* A/C, satellite TV with on-demand pay movies and mini TV in bathroom, high-speed dataport, minibar, hot-water pot with tea, hair dryer, safe, bathroom scale, washlet toilet.

EXPENSIVE
GINZA

Renaissance Tokyo Hotel Ginza Tobu ♣ This small, classy, and personable hotel, located on Showa Dori behind the Ginza Matsuzakaya department store and within easy walking distance to the Kabuki theater, employs an efficient and helpful full-time staff of 200, many of whom are foreigners. Because the modern hotel has an association with Marriott, as many as 60% of its hotel guests are foreign as well. Facilities are limited; you're clearly paying for location here. Interestingly, the cheapest singles (which have single-size beds) are not offered to foreigners—they're considered too small—but if you insist they'll let you have one (contact the hotel directly). Though these rooms are indeed small, I personally find them more nicely appointed than those offered by most business hotels.

6–14–10 Ginza, Chuo-ku, Tokyo 104-0061. (✆) **800/228-9898** in the U.S. and Canada or 03/3546-0111. Fax 03/3546-8990. www.renaissancehotels.com. 206 units. ¥17,000–¥23,000 ($142–$192) single; ¥28,000 ($233) double or twin. Renaissance floor ¥30,000 ($250) single; ¥35,000 ($292) double or twin. AE, DC, JCB, MC, V. Station: Ginza (4 min.) or Higashi-Ginza (1 min.). **Amenities:** 3 restaurants, 1 bar; concierge; business center; salon; room service (6:30am–11:45pm); in-room massage; same-day dry cleaning/laundry service; nonsmoking rooms; executive-level rooms. *In room:* A/C, bilingual cable TV with on-demand pay videos, dataport, minibar, hot-water pot with tea, hair dryer.

NIHOMBASHI & AROUND TOKYO STATION

Palace Hotel ★★   This hotel has an enviable location across the street from the Imperial Palace and its lovely gardens. But it's also close to Tokyo's business district, making it a favorite with foreign business travelers; in fact, foreigners account for fully half of its guests. If you can, spring for a deluxe twin—they're large, have spacious bathrooms with separate shower and tub areas and washlet toilets, are equipped with VCRs, and, best of all, face the gardens with glass-sliding doors that open onto balconies. For added security and prompt service, attendants are on call at service stations on each floor. Repeat guests are rewarded with monogrammed slippers.

1–1–1 Marunouchi, Chiyoda-ku, Tokyo 100-0005. © **800/457-4000** U.S. and Canada or 03/3211-5211. Fax 03/3211-6987. www.palacehotel.co.jp. 389 units. ¥24,000–¥29,000 ($200–$242) single; ¥33,000–¥45,000 ($275–$375) double; ¥32,000–¥60,000 ($267–$500) twin; from ¥100,000 ($833) suite. AE, DC, JCB, MC, V. Station: Otemachi (2 min.), Tokyo Station (7 min.). **Amenities:** 7 restaurants; access to nearby health club (¥3,150/$26); concierge; business center; shopping arcade; salon; 24-hr. room service; in-room massage; same-day dry-cleaning/laundry service; nonsmoking rooms. *In room:* A/C, satellite TV with pay movies, dataport, minibar, hot-water pot with tea and coffee, hair dryer, safe, bathroom scale.

Royal Park Hotel ★★★   Opened in 1989, the Royal Park is located east of Tokyo Station (about a 10-min. ride by taxi), not far from the Tokyo Stock Exchange, Japan's financial center, and Suitengu Shrine (popular with expectant mothers hoping for a safe delivery). One of its greatest assets, however (aside from its friendly and superbly efficient staff), is that it's connected via an enclosed walkway to the Tokyo City Air Terminal, the main terminus of the Airport Limousine Bus (which shuttles passengers to and from Narita Airport), making this the most convenient place for visitors with only a night or two to spend in Tokyo. It's also the first hotel I've seen with a Woman's Traveler Desk, offering check in and other special services. But what makes it particularly attractive to business travelers (including many Americans) are its up-to-date guest rooms, which have a sophisticated computerized TV system that allows guests to access the Internet, send e-mail, check airline schedules, watch videos on demand, play computer games, and more. The best views are from twins facing the Sumida River or upper-floor rooms facing the city skyline to the north.

2–1–1 Nihonbashi-Kakigara-cho, Chuo-ku, Tokyo 103-8520. © **800/457-4000** in the U.S. or 03/3667-1111. Fax 03/3667-1115. www.royalparkhotels.co.jp/nihonbashi/index-e.html. 450 units. ¥22,000–¥26,000 ($183–$217) single; ¥30,000–¥43,000 ($250–$358) double or twin; Executive floor, from ¥26,000 ($217) single, ¥34,000 ($283) double. AE, DC, JCB, MC, V. Station: Suitengu-mae (underneath the hotel). **Amenities:** 8 restaurants, 2 bars; health club with 20-meter indoor pool (fee: ¥3,000/$25; ¥1,500/$12.50 for pool alone); concierge; tour desk; 24-hr. business center; small shopping arcade; convenience store; salon; 24-hr. room service; in-room massage; babysitting; same-day dry cleaning/laundry service; nonsmoking rooms; executive-level rooms. *In room:* A/C, cable TV with pay movies and Internet access, fax (executive-level rooms only), high-speed broadband dataport, minibar, hot-water pot with tea, hair dryer, safe, bathroom scale, washlet toilet.

UENO

Hotel Sofitel ★★★ *(Finds)*   Located across from Shinobazu Pond in the heart of Ueno, this French-owned hotel is easily recognizable by its unique architecture: five pyramid-shaped trapeziums, stacked on top of each other. Inside, it's an oasis of refined beauty, excellent service, and great views. And with only a handful of rooms on each floor, it has the atmosphere of an intimate, luxury boutique hotel. Its restaurant, Provence, with a French chef, is drawing rave reviews. Chic rooms, with rates based on size, boast original artwork and TVs, but there's nothing that beats the view over Shinobazu Pond, with its bird refuge

Where to Stay & Dine in Ueno

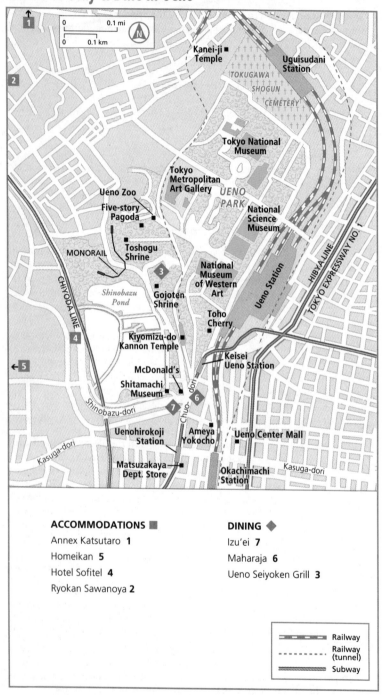

ACCOMMODATIONS ■
Annex Katsutaro **1**
Homeikan **5**
Hotel Sofitel **4**
Ryokan Sawanoya **2**

DINING ◆
Izu'ei **7**
Maharaja **6**
Ueno Seiyoken Grill **3**

Railway
Railway (tunnel)
Subway

and the adjoining zoo (some rooms facing the opposite side do, however, have occasional views of Mt. Fuji). I'm partial to the superior rooms on the 25th floor. All in all, a great place for its uniqueness, and easy accessibility to Ueno Park with its many museums make it a natural for joggers and art lovers alike.

2–1–48 Ikenohata, Taito-ku, Tokyo 110-0008. ⓒ **800/221-4542** in the U.S. and Canada or 03/5685-7111. Fax 03/5685-6171. www.sofiteltokyo.com. 83 units. ¥24,000–¥29,000 ($200–$242) single; ¥30,000–¥35,000 ($250–$292) double or twin. AE, DC, JCB, MC, V. Station: Yushima (7 min.), Ueno (10 min.). **Amenities:** 1 French restaurant, 1 bar; exercise room (free); 24-hr. room service; in-room massage; same-day dry cleaning/laundry service; nonsmoking rooms. *In room:* A/C, cable TV with pay movies and Internet access, dataport, minibar, hot-water pot with tea, hair dryer, safe.

SHINJUKU

Century Hyatt Tokyo ⭐   Located on Shinjuku's west side next to Shinjuku Central Park (popular with joggers), this 28-story hotel features an impressive seven-story atrium lobby with three of the most massive chandeliers you're likely to see anywhere. The excellent staff is used to the many foreigners (mostly American) who pass through the hotel's doors, which means you'll be treated to the usual high Hyatt standards. Room rates are based on size, though even the cheapest are adequate; ask for one on a high floor overlooking the park (in winter, you might also have a view of Mt. Fuji). Single rooms don't let in much sunshine; the twins are better, with big bay windows. Only a quarter of the rooms cater to business travelers with fax machines, dataports, and a two-line, hand-free speakerphone, a reflection of the fact that the hotel attracts leisure travelers as well.

2–7–2 Nishi-Shinjuku, Shinjuku-ku, Tokyo 160-0023. ⓒ **800/233-1234** in the U.S. and Canada, 03/3349-0111. Fax 03/3344-5575. www.centuryhyatt.co.jp. 766 units. ¥23,000–¥32,000 ($192–$267) single; ¥32,000–¥36,000 ($267–$300) double or twin. Regency Club, from ¥36,000 ($300) single or double. AE, DC, JCB, MC, V. Station: Tochomae (1 min), Nishi-Shinjuku (3 min.) or Shinjuku (a 10-min. walk, or a free 3-min. shuttle ride). **Amenities:** 6 restaurants, 1 bar, 1 lounge; health club with indoor pool (fee: ¥2,000/$17); concierge; tour desk; business center; shopping arcade; salon; 24-hr. room service; in-room massage; same-day dry cleaning/laundry service; nonsmoking rooms; executive-level rooms; free shuttle service to Shinjuku Station every 20 min. *In room:* A/C, cable TV with pay movies, minibar, hot-water pot with tea, hair dryer.

Tokyo Hilton ⭐   Located on Shinjuku's west side, the 38-story Tokyo Hilton opened in 1984 as the largest Hilton in the Asia/Pacific area. Today it keeps a lower profile than most of the other Shinjuku hotels, with a quiet, subdued lobby, and remains popular with business and leisure travelers alike. Rooms are up-to-date and adequate in size, and as with all Hiltons, the room decor here reflects traditional native style, with shoji screens instead of curtains and simple yet elegant furnishings. Business-floor rooms come with the extras free — high-speed Internet access, fax, and safe; there's also a business lounge.

6–6–2 Nishi-Shinjuku, Shinjuku-ku, Tokyo 160-0023. ⓒ **800/HILTONS** in the U.S. or Canada or 03/3344-5111. Fax 03/3342-6094. www.hilton.com. 806 units. ¥29,000–¥37,000 ($242–$308) single; ¥35,000–¥43,000 ($292–$358) twin or double. Business floor, ¥32,000–¥40,000 ($267–$333) single; ¥38,000–¥46,000 ($317–$383) twin or double. Executive floor, ¥35,000–¥44,000 ($292–$367) single; ¥41,000–¥50,000 ($342–$417) twin or double; from ¥70,000 ($583) suite. Children stay free in parents' room. AE, DC, JCB, MC, V. Station: Nishi-Shinjuku (2 min.), Tochomae (3 min.), or Shinjuku (10-min walk or free shuttle bus). **Amenities:** 5 restaurants, 1 bar, 1 lounge; 2 outdoor tennis courts; health club with indoor pool (fee: ¥1,500/$12 for either pool or gym alone, ¥2,000 ($17) for sauna; or ¥2,000/$17 for pool and gym, ¥4,000 ($33) for everything); concierge; tour desk; Kinko's (open 24 hr.); small shopping arcade; convenience store; salon; 24-hr. room service; in-room massage; same-day dry cleaning/laundry service; nonsmoking rooms; executive-level rooms; complimentary shuttle service to Shinjuku Station three to six times an hour. *In room:* A/C, satellite TV with pay movies, minibar, hot-water pot with tea, hair dryer.

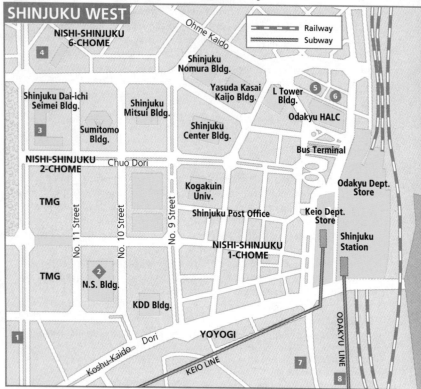

Ohme Kaido

Railway
Subway

NISHI-SHINJUKU
6-CHOME

4

Shinjuku
Nomura Bldg.

Yasuda Kasai
Kaijo Bldg.

L Tower
Bldg.

5   6

Shinjuku Dai-ichi
Seimei Bldg.

Shinjuku
Mitsui Bldg.

Odakyu HALC

3

Sumitomo
Bldg.

Shinjuku
Center Bldg.

Bus Terminal

NISHI-SHINJUKU
2-CHOME   Chuo Dori

Odakyu Dept.
Store

TMG

Kogakuin
Univ.

Keio Dept.
Store

Shinjuku Post Office

Shinjuku
Station

No. 11 Street

No. 10 Street

No. 9 Street

NISHI-SHINJUKU
1-CHOME

TMG

2

N.S. Bldg.

KDD Bldg.

1

YOYOGI

Koshu-Kaido   Dori

KEIO LINE

7

8

ODAKYU LINE

ROPPONGI & AKASAKA

Akasaka Prince Hotel ★★   This 40-story ultramodern white skyscraper—
an Akasaka landmark with a facade that reminds me of an unfolding fan—
caused quite a stir when it opened in 1983, with some Tokyoites complaining it
was too cold and sterile. I think the Akasaka Prince, designed by Kenzo Tange,
was just ahead of its time. The lobby is intentionally spacious and empty, lined
with almost 12,000 slabs of white marble, so as not to compete with brilliant
Japanese kimono (weddings are big business in Japanese hotels). The hotel's sig-
nature restaurant, Le Trianon, is located in a stately 70-year-old European-style
building that once belonged to the imperial family.

The good-sized guest rooms are set on a 45 degree angle from the center axis
of the building's core, giving each one a corner view with expansive windows
overlooking the city and letting in lots of sunshine; request one overlooking the
Akasaka side, and you'll have a view of neon lights down below and Tokyo Tower
in the distance. The single rooms are among the nicest in Tokyo, with three
windows forming a pleasant alcove around a sofa.

1–2 Kioi-cho, Chiyoda-ku, Tokyo 102-8585. ✆ **800/542-8686** in the U.S. and Canada or 03/3234-1111. Fax
03/3262-5163. www.princehotels.co.jp/english/. 761 units. ¥27,000–¥36,000 ($225–$300) single;
¥34,000–¥40,000 ($283–$333) twin; ¥37,000–¥42,000 ($308–$350) double; from ¥90,000 ($750) suite. AE,
DC, JCB, MC, V. Station: Akasaka-mitsuke or Nagatacho (2 min.). **Amenities:** 9 restaurants, 2 bars, 2 lounges;
outdoor heated pool open May through September (fee: ¥1,000/$8.35); small exercise room (fee:
¥500/$4.15); concierge; tour desk; excellent business center, with a spectacular 20th-floor view; convenience

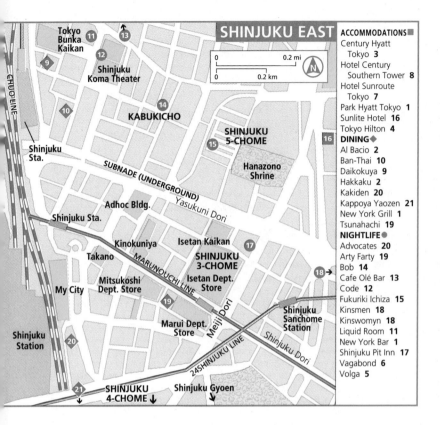

store; salon; 24-hr. room service; in-room massage; babysitting; same-day dry cleaning/laundry service; nonsmoking rooms. *In room:* A/C, cable TV with pay movies, highspeed dataport, minibar, hot-water pot with tea, hair dryer, safe; washlet toilet.

ANA Hotel Tokyo ⭐ A gleaming white, triangular building rising 37 stories above the crossroads of Akasaka, Roppongi, Toranomon, and Kasumigaseki, the ANA Hotel Tokyo (an affiliate of All Nippon Airways and referred to by the Japanese as the Zenniku hotel) has given the Hotel Okura stiff competition since its 1986 opening and caters mostly to Japanese with a friendly, accommodating staff. Rooms are large, with those on the upper floors offering views of the American Embassy and Tokyo Bay (I consider this the best view), Mt. Fuji (visible usually only in winter), or the Imperial Palace. If you're on a lower floor without much of a view, have a drink in Astral Bar on the 37th floor. While within walking distance to the nightlife districts of both Roppongi and Akasaka, its location appeals mainly to business travelers.

1–12–33 Akasaka, Minato-ku, Tokyo 107-0052. ☏ **800/262-4683** in the U.S. and Canada or 03/3505-1111. Fax 03/3505-1155. www.anahotels.com/tokyo. 901 units. ¥24,000–¥27,000 ($200–$225) single; ¥31,000–¥38,000 ($258–$317) double or twin; from ¥60,000 ($500) suite. Executive Floor, ¥39,000–¥42,000 ($325–$350) twin or double. AE, CB, DC, JCB, MC, V. Station: Tameike Sanno (1 min.); Roppongi, Akasaka, Kamiyacho, Toranomon, or Kokkai Gijido-mae (5–10 min.). **Amenities:** 8 restaurants, 2 bars, 2 lounges; outdoor pool (fee: ¥1,000/$8.35) exercise room (fee: ¥1,500/$12); sauna (men only); concierge; tour desk; business center; shopping arcade; salon; room service (6am–2am); in-room massage; babysitting; same-day dry cleaning/laundry service; nonsmoking rooms; executive-level rooms. *In room:* A/C, cable TV with pay movies, highspeed dataport, minibar, hot-water pot with tea, hair dryer.

Hotel New Otani ★★ *Kids*　If you like quiet, small hotels, this place is not for you. Like a city unto itself, the New Otani is so big that two information desks assist lost souls searching for a particular restaurant or one of the shops in the meandering arcade; there are even two check-in desks. Its most splendid feature is its garden, the best of any Tokyo hotel—a 400-year-old Japanese garden that once belonged to a feudal lord, with 10 acres of ponds, waterfalls, bridges, bamboo groves, and manicured bushes. Parents will also appreciate the day-care center.

A variety of rooms, in a main building and a newer tower, are available. Those in the main building are comfortable, with shoji-like screens on the windows and bedside controls for the curtains, air conditioner, and do not disturb sign; more expensive rooms have such extras as bathroom scales, walk-in closets, and fax machines (otherwise, fax machines are available free of charge). In the tower, rooms range from chic ones done in jade, black, and chrome and boasting washlet toilets and fax machines, to "fusui healing" rooms that have such extras as an in-room humidifier, foot bath, and compact CD/MD player. The tower offers the best views—of the garden, the skyscrapers of Shinjuku, and, on clear days, Mt. Fuji in the distance. Since rates are the same no matter which way you face, be sure to request a room overlooking the garden.

4–1 Kioi-cho, Chiyoda-ku, Tokyo 102-8578. ✆ **800/421-8795** in the U.S. and Canada or 03/3265-1111. Fax 03/3221-2619. www.newotani.co.jp/en/. 1,541 units. ¥28,500–¥36,000 ($237–$300) single; ¥33,500–¥57,000 ($279–$475) double; ¥41,000–¥57,000 ($342–$475) twin; from ¥75,000 ($625) suite. AE, DC, JCB, MC, V. Station: Akasaka-mitsuke or Nagatacho (3 min.). **Amenities:** 28 restaurants, 5 bars and lounges; outdoor pool (fee: ¥2,000/$17; free if you become a New Otani Hotel Club member at no extra charge); small exercise room (free for hotel guests); health club with indoor tennis courts (fee: ¥5,000/$42); day-care center for children from 1 month to 5 years old (fee: ¥6,000/$50 for 2 hr.); concierge; tour desk; business center; shopping arcade with 120 stores; convenience store; salon; medical and dental clinics; post office; tea-ceremony room; chapel with daily services; art museum (free for hotel guests; pick up tickets at the guest relations desk); 24-hr. room service; in-room massage; same-day dry cleaning/laundry service; nonsmoking rooms. *In room:* A/C, cable TV with pay movies, highspeed dataport, minibar, hot-water pot with tea, hair dryer, safe. washlet toilet.

SHINAGAWA

Le Meridien Pacific Tokyo ★　This graceful and dignified hotel across the street from Shinagawa Station occupies grounds that once belonged to Japan's imperial family, a reminder of which remains in the peaceful, tranquil garden with a pond and a waterfall that serves as a dramatic backdrop of the lobby lounge. Approximately 60% of hotel guests are foreigners, mostly French. Its location on the Yamanote Line make it convenient for travel in the city; trains to Kamakura and other points west and south also depart Shinagawa Station (at the end of 2003, it will also be a stop on the Shinkansen bullet train). Room rates are based on a variety of factors: for single rooms it's the size of the bed; for doubles it's the size of the room, size of the bed, and whether the room faces the garden or the bay (more expensive); for twins it's the height (the best views are those from the highest floors overlooking Tokyo Bay). Most bathrooms are surprisingly small, however, with almost no counter space to speak of.

3–13–3 Takanawa, Minato-ku, Tokyo 108-8567. ✆ **800/225-5843** in the U.S. or 03/3445-6711. Fax 03/3445-5733. www.htl-pacific.co.jp. 954 units. ¥22,000–¥25,500 ($183–$212.50) single;¥25,000–¥33,000 ($208–$275) twin or double; from ¥50,000 ($412) suite. AE, DC, JCB, MC, V. Station: Shinagawa (1 min.). **Amenities:** 6 restaurants, 2 bars, 2 lounges; outdoor pool (free); access to fitness center at Le Meridien Grand Pacific in Odaiba (fee: ¥1,050/$8.75); concierge; business center; small shopping arcade, salon; room service (6am–midnight); in-room massage; babysitting; same-day dry cleaning/laundry service; nonsmoking rooms; free shuttle bus to Le Meridien Grand Pacific Tokyo Hotel in Odaiba. *In room:* A/C, cable TV with pay movies, highspeed dataport (not in all rooms), minibar, hot-water pot with tea, hair dryer, washlet toilet.

Miyako Hotel Tokyo ★★ (*Value*)   A Radisson affiliate, this hotel is one of our favorites in Tokyo, for its calm peacefulness as well as its small-luxury-hotel service (when one of us didn't have time to go to the post office, the concierge offered to go herself during her lunch hour). This sister hotel of the famous Miyako Hotel in Kyoto was designed by Minoru Yamasaki, the architect of New York's World Trade Center and Los Angeles' Century Plaza. Because it's a bit off the beaten path, it has a quieter, more relaxed atmosphere than more centrally located hotels, as well as more competitive rates. Japanese account for 60% of guests.

The rooms are large with huge floor-to-ceiling windows overlooking the hotel's own lush garden, a famed garden next door, or Tokyo Tower. The singles are a good deal but are often fully booked. Rooms on the eighth floor have fax machines.

1–1–50 Shiroganedai, Minato-ku, Tokyo 108-8640. (*C*) **800/333-3333** in the U.S and Canada or 03/ 3447-3111. Fax 03/3447-3133. www.miyako-hotel-tokyo.co.jp/. 498 units. ¥18,000–¥24,000 ($150–$200) single; ¥30,000–¥38,000 ($250–$317) double; ¥25,000–¥38,000 ($208–$317) twin; from ¥80,000 ($667) suite. AE, DC, JCB, MC, V. Station: Shiroganedai (4 min.) or Shirokane-Takanawa (5 min.) or free shuttle from Meguro or Shinagawa Station. **Amenities:** 5 restaurants, 1 bar, 1 lounge; health club with 25-meter indoor heated pool (fee: ¥700/$5.85 for either pool or gym; ¥2,800/$23 for everything); concierge; tour desk; shopping arcade; convenience store; salon; dental/medical clinics; room service (7am–midnight); in-room massage; same-day dry cleaning/laundry service; nonsmoking rooms; free shuttle service to Meguro Station every 15 minutes and to Shinagawa Station (mornings only). *In room:* A/C, cable TV with pay movies, dataport, minibar, hot-water pot with tea, hair dryer, safe, washlet toilet.

ON OR NEAR ODAIBA

Hotel Nikko Tokyo ★★   Opened in 1996, this grand, elegant hotel offers great views of the Tokyo skyline and Rainbow Bridge from its location on Odaiba, an island of reclaimed land with a convention center, shopping malls, beaches, and sightseeing attractions. Surrounded by parks and gardens that give it a relaxed, resort-evoking atmosphere, it bills itself as an "urban resort" and is especially popular with young well-to-do Japanese in search of an exotic weekend getaway. With a wooden walkway linking it to the Tokyo Decks shopping mall and a sandy beach, it's by far the most un-Tokyolike hotel in the city. A curved facade assures waterfront views from most rooms, which have the added benefit of private balconies with two chairs. The most expensive rooms offer commanding views of Tokyo Bay, Rainbow Bridge, and the city skyline, while the least expensive rooms, smaller in size, face another hotel or the Maritime Museum and Haneda Airport across the bay. This is a great choice if you want to get away from the bustle of Tokyo, but the location can be a disadvantage; it's served only by the monorail Yurikamome Line and the inconvenient Rinkai Fukutoshin Line, which can be quite crowded on weekends, as can bus and taxi travel via the Rainbow Bridge or harbor tunnel.

1–9–1 Daiba, Minato-ku, Tokyo 135-8625. (*C*) **800/645-5687** in the U.S. and Canada or 03/5500-5500. Fax 03/5500-2525. info@hnt.co.jp. 453 units. ¥27,000–¥40,000 ($225–$333) single; ¥32,000–¥45,000 ($267–$375) double or twin; from ¥80,000 ($667) suite. AE, DC, JCB, MC, V. Station: Daiba (1 min.). **Amenities:** 8 restaurants, 1 bar, 1 lounge; outdoor pool; spa with indoor pool connected to outdoor heated tub, Jacuzzi and sun terrace overlooking Rainbow Bridge (fee: ¥3,000/$25 the first day; thereafter ¥1,000/$8.35); concierge; business center; room service (6am–11pm); in-room massage; same-day dry cleaning/laundry service; nonsmoking rooms. *In room:* A/C, satellite TV with pay movies, dataport, minibar, hot-water pot with tea, hair dryer, safe, washlet toilet.

MODERATE
GINZA
Hotel Ginza Daiei ★   A redbrick building located behind the Kabukiza theater, this business hotel offers minuscule but well-equipped rooms, with lots of

extras not usually found in this price range, including three telephones in each room, bedside controls for the air-conditioning, room lights, curtains, and do not disturb sign, cable TV with CNN, and radios wired for 440 stations. The most expensive twins are so-called "Healthy Twins," corner rooms with larger bathrooms featuring jet baths and mini-TV.

3–12–1 Ginza, Chuo-ku, Tokyo 104-0061. ✆ 03/3545-1111. Fax 03/3545-1177. info@Ginza-daiei.co.jp. 106 units. ¥11,400–¥13,300 ($95–$111) single; ¥15,600 ($130) double; ¥17,500–¥20,800 ($146–$173) twin. AE, DC, JCB, MC, V. Station: Higashi-Ginza (3 min.), or Yurakucho (10 min). **Amenities:** In-room massage; same-day dry cleaning/laundry service; nonsmoking rooms. *In room:* A/C, cable TV, minibar, hot-water pot with tea, hair dryer, trouser press, washlet toilet.

Mitsui Urban Hotel Ginza ✪   Because of its great location, convenient to the Ginza and to the Hibiya and Kasumigaseki business centers, this attractive hotel caters to both business travelers and tourists. The lobby, on the second floor, has a friendly staff. The bright and modern guestrooms are tiny, but feature a few amenities found usually only at more expensive hotels. In addition, bathrooms are larger than in other business hotels, with a decent-size tub and a no-fog mirror. I suggest asking for a room away from the highway overpass beside the hotel.

8–6–15 Ginza, Chuo-ku, Tokyo 104-0061. ✆ 03/3572-4131. Fax 03/3572-4254. www.mitsuikanko.co.jp. 265 units. ¥14,000–¥17,000 ($117–$142) single; ¥21,000–¥24,500 ($175–$204) double; ¥21,000–¥30,000 ($175–$250) twin. AE, DC, JCB, MC, V. Station: Shimbashi (2 min.). **Amenities:** 3 restaurants, 2 lounges; room service (Mon–Fri 10pm–1am); same-day laundry service. *In room:* A/C, TV, hot-water pot with tea, hair dryer, washlet toilet.

AROUND TOKYO STATION

Hotel Yaesu Ryumeikan *(Value*   This 30-year-old, nondescript hotel is your best bet for reasonably priced lodging just minutes away from Tokyo Station. From the north Yaesu exit, turn left onto Sotobori Dori; it will be on your right, just before Eitai Dori. It offers both Japanese-style tatami rooms and Western-style rooms with beds. I personally prefer the Japanese-style rooms, especially the most expensive tatami rooms, which have a nice, traditional feel and come with a sitting alcove and Japanese-style deep tub. Only Japanese breakfasts are available; if you can't stomach rice and fish in the morning, opt for a room without breakfast and subtract ¥1,000 ($8.35) per person from the rates below.

1–3–22 Yaesu, Chuo-ku 103-0028. ✆ 03/3271-0971. Fax 03/3271-0977. www.ryumeikan.co.jp/yaesu.html. 30 units (25 with bathroom). ¥8,000–¥9,500 ($67–$79) single without bathroom, ¥10,000–¥13,000 ($83–$108) single with bathroom; ¥14,000 ($117) double without bathroom; ¥17,000–¥18,000 ($142–$150) double with bathroom. Rates include Japanese breakfast. AE, DC, MC, V. Station: Tokyo Station (3 min. from the north Yaesu exit), or Nihombashi (1 min., exit A3). On the corner of Eitai Dori and Sotobori Dori. **Amenities:** 2 restaurants (Japanese, coffee shop). *In room:* A/C, TV, hot-water pot with tea.

ASAKUSA

Asakusa View Hotel   This is the only upper-bracket and modern hotel in the Asakusa area, and it looks almost out of place rising among this famous district's older buildings. It's a good place to stay if you want to be in Tokyo's old downtown but don't want to sacrifice any creature comforts. The medium-size guest rooms are very pleasant, with sleek contemporary Japanese furnishings and bay windows that let in plenty of sunshine (and smaller windows that can be opened, a rarity in Tokyo); rooms facing the front have views over the famous Sensoji Temple. Eight Japanese-style rooms are also available, sleeping up to five people; on the same floor is a small, rooftop Japanese garden and Japanese-style public baths featuring tubs made of 2,000-year-old cypress.

3–17–1 Nishi-Asakusa, Taito-ku, Tokyo 111-8765. ✆ 03/3847-1111. Fax 03/3842-2117. www.viewhotels. co.jp. 337 units. ¥13,000–¥18,000 ($108–$150) single; ¥21,000–¥31,000 ($175–$258) double;

Nightlife & Where to Stay & Dine in Asakusa

Railway
Subway

ASAKUSA 3-CHOME

NISHI-ASAKUSA
3-CHOME

Kototoi Dori

ASAKUSA 2-CHOME

Hisago Dori

Kokusai Dori

HANAYASHIKI
AMUSEMENT
PARK

Asakusa
Shrine

Sensoji
Temple

HANAKAWADO
2-CHOME

Five-storied
Pagoda

France-Za

Horizon
Gate

HANAKAWADO
1-CHOME

NISHI-ASAKUSA
2-CHOME

Dempoin
Temple

Umamichi Dori

Sushiya Dori

TOBU ASAKUSA
LINE

ASAKUSA 1-CHOME

Orange Dori

Chinyoko Dori

Nakamise Dori

Kannon Dori

Asakusa
Station

Edo Dori

SUMIDA PARK

Matsuya
Dept.
Store

Kaminarimon
Dori

Ferry
Pier

KAMINARIMON 1-CHOME

Asakusa
Information
Center

Asakusa
Station

Tarawamachi
Station

AZUMA BRIDGE

Asakusa Dori

GINZA LINE

ASAKUSA LINE

Sumida River

METROPOLITAN EXPWY.

Asahi
Building

Asakusa
Station

KOMAGATA BRIDGE

0   0.1 mi
0   0.1 km
N

ACCOMMODATIONS ■

Asakusa View Hotel **2**
Hotel Sunroute Asakusa **8**
Kikuya Ryokan **4**
Ryokan Shigetsu **5**
Sakura Ryokan **1**

NIGHTLIFE ●

Sky Room **10**

DINING ◆

Chinya **6**
Daikokuya **3**
Kamiya Bar **7**
Komagata Dojo **12**
La Ranarita Azumabashi **10**
Mugitoro **11**
Namiki Yabusoba **9**

¥26,000–¥31,000 ($217–$258) twin; ¥34,000 ($283) triple. Japanese-style rooms, from ¥40,000 ($333) for 2. Executive floor, ¥32,000 ($267) single or double. AE, DC, JCB, MC, V. Station: Tawaramachi (8 min.). On Kokusai Dori. **Amenities:** 5 restaurants, 1 bar, 1 lounge; 20-meter indoor pool, with retractable roof (fee: ¥3,000/$25, but request a 50% discount coupon at the front desk); shopping arcade; salon; Japanese-style public baths (fee: ¥1,050/$8.75); room service (7am–2am); same-day dry cleaning/laundry service; nonsmoking rooms; executive-level rooms. *In room:* A/C, TV, minibar, hot-water pot with tea, hair dryer.

Ryokan Shigetsu ★★★ *Finds*   Whenever a foreigner living in Tokyo, soon to play host to first-time visitors to Japan, asks me to recommend a moderately priced ryokan in Tokyo, this is the one I suggest most often. It has a great location in Asakusa just off Nakamise Dori, a colorful, shop-lined pedestrian street leading to the famous Sensoji Temple—an area that gives you a feel for the older Japan. A member of the Japanese Inn Group, it represents the best of modern yet traditional Japanese design—simple yet elegant, with shoji, unadorned wood, and artwork throughout. Traditional Japanese music or the recorded chirping of birds plays softly in the background of public spaces. Two public Japanese baths have views of the nearby five-storied pagoda. A Japanese restaurant serves excellent Japanese breakfasts, as well as mini-kaiseki dinners (discounts given to hotel guests; reserve 5 days in advance) and lunches. There are 11 Western-style rooms, 7 singles and 3 double or twins, but I prefer the slightly more expensive 12 Japanese-style tatami rooms, which include Japanese-style mirrors and comfortable chairs for those who don't like relaxing on the floor. In short, this establishment costs no more than a regular business hotel but has much more class.

1–31–11 Asakusa, Taito-ku 111-0032. ℂ **03/3843-2345.** Fax 03/3843-2348. www.shigetsu.com. 22 units. ¥7,300–¥9,000 ($61–$75) single; ¥14,000–¥16,000 ($117–$133) twin. Japanese or Western breakfast ¥1,200 ($10) extra, Japanese dinner ¥3,000 ($25) extra. AE, MC, V. Station: Asakusa (4 min.). **Amenities:** 1 restaurant (Japanese); Apple laptop in lobby providing free Internet access; nonsmoking rooms. *In room:* A/C, TV, minibar, hot-water pot with tea, hair dryer.

SHINJUKU

Hotel Century Southern Tower ★★   Opened in 1998 and a welcome addition to the Shinjuku hotel scene, this sleek, modern hotel is located just south of the station and just a footbridge away from the huge Takashimaya Times Square shopping complex. Because it occupies the top floors of a sleek white building, it seems far removed from the hustle and bustle of Shinjuku below. Its 20th-floor lobby is simple and uncluttered and boasts almost surreal views of Tokyo stretching in the distance. Also on the 20th floor is Tribecks, a contemporary restaurant offering Asian- and European-influenced American food and great views of Shinjuku. Ask for a room on a high floor. Rooms facing east are considered best (and are therefore more expensive), especially at night when neon is in full regalia. Rooms facing west have views of Shinjuku's skyscrapers and, on clear days (mostly in winter), of Mt. Fuji. A playful touch is the maps in each room outlining the important buildings visible from your windows.

2–2–1 Yoyogi, Shibuya-ku, Tokyo 151-8583. ℂ **03/5354-0111.** Fax 03/5354-0100. www.hotelbook.com/ 375 units. ¥16,000–¥18,000 ($133–$150) single; ¥22,000–¥24,000 ($183–$200) twin; ¥22,000–¥28,000 ($183–$233) double. AE, DC, JCB, MC, V. Station: Shinjuku (2 min.). **Amenities:** 3 restaurants (Japanese, Chinese, contemporary American), 1 lounge; exercise room (free); convenience store; 24-hr. Kinko's; same-day dry cleaning/laundry service; nonsmoking rooms. *In room:* A/C, cable TV with pay movies, dataport, fridge, hot-water pot with tea, hair dryer, safe, washlet toilet.

Hotel Sunroute Tokyo *Value*   Conveniently located just a short walk southeast of Shinjuku Station, this no-frills hotel attracts a large foreign clientele and calls itself a "city hotel." While it does boast a couple restaurants, facilities, and services, its guest rooms resemble those in a business hotel rather than tourist accommodations, with just the basics. Essentially, a place to sleep in a convenient location without spending a fortune.

2–3–1 Yoyogi, Shibuya-ku, Tokyo 151-0053. ℂ **03/3375-3211**. Fax 03/3379-3040. sunroute.aska.or.jp. 538 units. ¥12,500–¥15,500 ($104–$129) single; ¥17,500 ($146) double; ¥18,000–¥25,000 ($150–$208) twin. Rates include service charge. AE, DC, JCB, MC, V. Station: Shinjuku (3 min.). **Amenities:** 3 restaurants (Japanese, Chinese, Italian), 1 bar; convenience store; salon; room service (11am–10:30pm); same-day dry cleaning/laundry service; nonsmoking rooms. *In room:* A/C, TV, minibar, hot-water pot with tea, hair dryer.

AOYAMA

President Hotel ⭐ *Value*   This small hotel is a good choice for the budget-conscious business traveler, not only because it's a respected address in Tokyo but also thanks to its reasonable prices and great location, between Akasaka, Shinjuku, Aoyama, and Roppongi. It also offers some of the same conveniences and services as the larger and more expensive hotels. The unpretentious lobby has a comfortable European atmosphere—you don't have to be embarrassed about meeting business clients here. Rooms themselves are tiny but cheerful; ask for a room facing the front on a high floor.

2–2–3 Minami Aoyama, Minato-ku, Tokyo 107-8545. ℂ **03/3497-0111**. Fax 03/3401-4816. www.president-hotel.co.jp. reservation@president-hotel.co.jp. 210 units. ¥12,000–¥13,000 ($100–$108) single; ¥17,000 ($142) double; ¥17,000–¥21,000 ($142–$175) twin. AE, DC, JCB, MC, V. Station: Aoyama-Itchome (1 min.). On Aoyama Dori. **Amenities:** 2 restaurants (Japanese, French), 1 coffeeshop; room service (7–9am and 5–9pm); same-day dry cleaning/laundry service. *In room:* A/C, cable TV, dataport, minibar, hot-water pot with tea, hair dryer.

IKEBUKURO

Crowne Plaza Metropolitan Tokyo ⭐ *Kids*   This brick building, just a couple minutes' walk southwest of Ikebukuro Station but a bit out of the way for most Tokyo attractions, offers the kind of service and amenities that Americans (who make up 10% of the hotel's guests) will find familiar, though rooms are much smaller than their U.S. counterparts. Rates are based on size and floor height; those facing west have views of Mt. Fuji in winter. The hotel compensates for any shortcomings by offering a few perks—of particular note are the business center's computers offering free Internet access. In addition, all beds are double size or larger, even in the single and twin rooms, and children stay free in parents' room, a rarity in Japanese hotels.

1–6–1 Nishi-Ikebukuro, Toshima-ku, Tokyo 171-8505. ℂ **800/227-6963** in the U.S. and Canada or 03/3980-1111. Fax 03/3980-5600. www.crowneplaza.com. 815 units. ¥16,500–¥19,500 ($137–$154) single; ¥22,000–¥26,500 ($183–$221) double; ¥22,000–¥30,000 ($183–$250) twin. Children under 20 stay free in parents' room (maximum of 3 persons in a room). AE, DC, JCB, MC, V. Station: Ikebukuro (west exit, 3 min.). **Amenities:** 8 restaurants, 1 bar, 2 lounges; outdoor pool (fee: ¥1,000/$8.35); access to nearby health club (fee: ¥2,000/$17); sauna (men only); business center, with free Internet access; convenience store; salon; room service (6am–1am); in-room massage; babysitting; same-day dry cleaning/laundry service; nonsmoking rooms. *In room:* A/C, cable TV with pay movies on demand, dataport (not in all rooms), minibar, hot-water pot with tea, hair dryer.

ROPPONGI & AKASAKA

Akasaka Tokyu Hotel   This business hotel catering mostly to Japanese boasts a high occupancy rate thanks to its ideal location in the middle of Akasaka and its reasonable rates. Built in 1969, it's easily recognizable by its candy-striped exterior (it's called the "Pajama Building" by the locals). Rooms, in a corresponding pink-and-white color scheme, include shoji screens and window panels that slide shut for complete darkness (even in the middle of the day), as well as windows that can be opened (a rarity in Tokyo). There are 200 single rooms, but the lower-priced ones are pretty small. Front-facing rooms look upon the whirl and neon of Akasaka; those in the back are quieter and face a steep slope of greenery.

2–14–3 Nagata-cho, Chiyoda-ku, Tokyo 100. © **800/428-6598** in the U.S. or 03/3580-2311. Fax 03/3580-6066. www.tokyuhotel.com. 535 units. ¥15,000–¥22,000 ($125–$183) single; ¥28,000 ($233) double; ¥22,000–¥35,000 ($183–$293) twin. AE, DC, JCB, MC, V. Station: Akasaka-mitsuke (1 min.). **Amenities:** 1 restaurant (Japanese), 1 coffee shop, 1 lounge; business center; shopping arcade; room service (7am–midnight); same-day dry cleaning/laundry service; nonsmoking rooms. *In room:* A/C, cable TV with pay movies, minibar, hot-water pot with tea, hair dryer.

Hotel Ibis   The Ibis is about as close as you can get to the night action of Roppongi, oddly lacking in hotels. It caters to both businessmen and couples who come to Roppongi's discos and don't make (or want to make) the last subway home. The lobby, with computers available for accessing the Internet (and costing ¥500/$4.15 for 25 minutes) is on the fifth floor, with the guest rooms above. Small but comfortable, they feature modern furniture and windows that can be opened (though with a freeway nearby, I'm not sure you'd want to). On the 13th floor is a branch of the well-known Italian restaurant Sabatini, with views of the city.

7–14–4 Roppongi, Minato-ku, Tokyo 106-0032. © **03/3403-4411.** Fax 03/3479-0609. www.ibis-hotel.com. 182 units. ¥11,500–¥16,000 ($96–$133) single; ¥14,100–¥23,000 ($117–$192) double; ¥19,000–¥23,000 ($158–$192) twin; ¥24,000 ($200) triple. AE, DC, JCB, MC, V. Station: Roppongi (1 min.). **Amenities:** 2 restaurants (Italian, pizza/pasta), 1 coffee shop; room service (Mon–Fri 12:30–8pm); same-day dry cleaning/laundry service; nonsmoking rooms. *In room:* A/C, cable TV, minibar, hot-water pot with tea, hair dryer.

Roppongi Prince Hotel   This is a good choice if you want to be close (about a 6-min. walk) to Roppongi's night action. Opened in 1984 (a welcome event in Roppongi, still woefully lacking in hotels), the hotel attracts Japanese businessmen on weekdays and vacationers aged 20 to 25 on weekends and caters to them with a young and cheerful staff, modern designs with bold colors, and a resort-like atmosphere. The hotel is built around an inner courtyard, which features a pool with a Jacuzzi and heated deck—a solar mirror on the roof directs sun rays toward the sunbathers below, making it Tokyo's only outdoor heated pool open year-round. Unfortunately for the shy, sides of the raised pool are clear, see-through acrylic, giving diners at the adjacent outdoor patio unique ringside views. Rooms are small but bright and modern, with either black or white decor. Empty refrigerators let you stock up yourself.

3–2–7 Roppongi, Minato-ku, Tokyo 106-0032. © **800/542-8686** in the U.S. and Canada or 03/3587-1111. Fax 03/3587-0770. www.princehotels.co.jp/Roppongi-e/. 216 units. ¥19,500 ($162) single; ¥23,000–¥26,500 ($192–$221) twin; ¥24,500–¥26,500 ($204–$221) double. AE, DC, JCB, MC, V. Station: Roppongi (8 min.). **Amenities:** 4 restaurants, 1 bar, 1 lounge; outdoor heated pool open year-round (free); outdoor Jacuzzi; sauna; room service (7am–2am); same-day dry cleaning/laundry service; nonsmoking rooms. *In room:* A/C, cable TV with pay movies and video games, fridge, hot-water pot with tea, hair dryer.

Tokyo Prince Hotel 🐧 Set in Shiba Park near Zozoji Temple and Tokyo Tower, this is the Prince Hotel chain's oldest Tokyo property, built in 1964 for the Olympic Games and now passed over as visitors flock to the city's newer, glitzier hotels. Still, the friendly service is that of a small, luxury hotel, with facilities rivaling those of much more expensive choices. Its central location makes it possible to walk to Roppongi for nightlife (the walk home is sobering) or to Hibiya or the Tokyo Trade Center on business. Ask for the sightseeing map in English showing nearby attractions. Guests include many foreign business executives. Parts of the hotel show its age (particularly in corridors and some of the lowest-priced rooms), but rooms have all the basics. The most expensive rooms are larger and face the front of the hotel and a parking lot; opt for a cheaper, smaller room on a top floor with a view of the park and Tokyo Tower. Non-smokers will like the fact that there's a no-smoking lounge on the 11th floor with an up-close view of the Tower.

3–3–1 Shibakoen, Minato-ku, Tokyo 105-8560. © **800/542-8686** or 03/3432-1111. Fax 03/3434-5551. www.princehotels.co.jp/english/. 484 units. ¥24,000–¥25,000 ($200–$208) single; ¥25,000–¥35,000 ($208–$292) double or twin. AE, DC, JCB, MC, V. Station: Onarimon (1 min.), Daimon or Akabanebashi (both 7 min.), Kamiyacho or Hammamatsucho (both 10 min.). **Amenities:** 10 restaurants (including an all-weather beer garden), 1 no-smoking lounge, 2 bars; outdoor pool (fee: ¥1,000/$8.35); concierge; tour desk; business center; small shopping arcade; convenience store; salon; 24-hr. room service; in-room massage; same-day dry cleaning/laundry service; nonsmoking rooms. *In room:* A/C, cable TV with pay movies, high-speed dataport (in 300 rooms), fridge, hot-water pot with tea, hair dryer.

SHIBUYA

Shibuya Excel Hotel Tokyu ⭐ Across from bustling Shibuya Station and connected by a footbridge and underground passage, this busy, modern hotel opened in 2000, the first new hotel to debut in Shibuya in many years. It's been so successful (I don't know why no one thought of locating hotels in Shibuya before), Tokyu promptly built another one farther from the station. With an excellent location above Mark City shopping mall (reception is on the 5th floor), the Excel tries hard to appeal to everyone: for business travelers, there are "Excel" twin rooms that feature a fax/copier machine and high-speed dataports. For women, there are two floors reserved only for females and accessed by a special key; in-room amenities, such as face cream, are also geared to women. There are also handicap-accessible rooms, and almost half the rooms are for nonsmokers. Rooms, on the 7th to 24th floors, are comfortable. Ask for an upper-floor room facing Shinjuku: the night view is great. In-room refrigerators are empty so you can stock up yourself from hotel vending machines, which, by the way, management claim are the largest in Japan.

1–12–2 Dogenzaka, Shibuya-ku 150-0043. © **03/5457-0109.** Fax 03/5457-0309. www.tokyu.co.jp/inn/e. 408 units. ¥17,000–¥23,000 ($142–$192) single; ¥22,000–¥24,000 ($183–$200) double; ¥24,000–¥36,000 ($200–$300) twin. AE, DC, JCB, MC, V. Station: Shibuya (1 min. by footbridge). **Amenities:** 2 restaurants (Japanese, French), plus many more in Mark City mall; public fax and copy machine; shopping mall beneath hotel; room service (9pm–midnight); same-day dry cleaning/laundry service; nonsmoking rooms. *In room:* A/C, satellite TV, dataport, fridge, hot-water pot with tea, hair dryer, trouser press.

SHINAGAWA

Shinagawa Prince Hotel With four gleaming white buildings added at various stages, the Shinagawa Prince is the largest hotel in Japan. This place is a virtual city within a city, with more than a dozen food and beverage outlets, a large sports center with nine indoor tennis courts, 104-lane bowling center, indoor golf practice center, billiards, video games, indoor and outdoor pools, and a fitness center. It caters to Japanese businessmen on weekdays and students and family vacationers on weekends and holidays. Rooms vary widely depending upon which building you select: The Main Tower has only very small singles, at the cheapest rates; the Annex has singles, twins, and doubles in a medium price range; the New Tower and a new addition have the best rooms, the highest prices, and the best views, including great views of Rainbow Bridge and Tokyo Bay from its upper floors. Be sure to have a drink or meal at the 39th-floor Top of Shinagawa; its views of Tokyo Bay and the rest of Tokyo are among the best in the city. With its many diversions, this hotel is like a resort getaway, but it's too big and too busy for my taste.

4–10–30 Takanawa, Minato-ku, Tokyo 108-8611. © **800/542-8686** in the U.S. or Canada or 03/3440-1111. Fax 03/3441-7092. 3,686 units. ¥8,000–¥18,000 ($67–$150) single; ¥14,100–¥27,500 ($117–$229) twin; ¥14,600–¥26,500 ($122–$221) double. DC, JCB, MC, V. Station: Shinagawa (2 min.). **Amenities:** 12 restaurants,

2 bars; sports center (various fees charged; ¥1,000/$8.33 for indoor pool); tour desk; business center; convenience store; same-day dry cleaning/laundry service; nonsmoking rooms. *In room:* A/C, TV, fridge, hot-water pot with tea, hair dryer.

INEXPENSIVE
ASAKUSA

Hotel Sunroute Asakusa ⭐ Located on Kokusai Dori, this modern, pleasant hotel opened in 1998 as a business hotel but is a good choice for leisure travelers as well. Not only does it boast a good location near the sightseeing attractions of Asakusa, but it is also classier than most business hotels, with Miró reprints in the lobby and modern artwork in each guestroom. Though small, rooms come with all the comforts. The mostly single rooms have slightly larger beds and bathrooms than found at most business hotels. The hotel's one coffee shop, a chain called Jonathan's serving both Japanese and Western food, is open daily 24 hours.

1–8–5 Kaminarimon, Taito-ku, Tokyo 111-0034. ② **03/3847-1511.** Fax 03/3847-1509. www.sunroute-asakusa.co.jp/english/index.htm. 120 units. ¥7,800–¥8,600 ($65–$72) single; ¥13,000 ($108) double; ¥15,000–¥17,000 ($125–$142) twin. AE, DC, MC, V. Station: Tawaramachi (1 min.); Asakusa (8 min.). **Amenities:** 1 restaurant; same-day laundry service; nonsmoking rooms (singles only). *In room:* A/C, TV, hot-water pot with tea, hair dryer, washlet toilet.

Kikuya Ryokan This friendly establishment is located in Asakusa in a modern redbrick building about a 10-minute walk from Sensoji Temple, just off Kappabashi Dori (a street lined with shops specializing in wholesale restaurant cookware and tableware). It's a member of the Japanese Inn and Welcome Inn groups—which may explain why it's filled only with foreigners, nary a Japanese guest is in sight. The simple tatami rooms, while clean, lack the character of a more traditional ryokan. There's a communal refrigerator where you can store food and drinks; otherwise, most of the rooms with bath have their own fridge. Guests are requested to leave during the daily cleaning (10:30am–3pm).

2–18–9 Nishi-Asakusa, Taito-ku, Tokyo 111-0035. ② **03/3841-4051.** Fax 03/3841-6404. 10 units (7 with bathroom). ¥4,800 ($40) single without bathroom; ¥5,600–¥6,500 ($47–$54) single with bathroom; ¥8,000 ($67) double without bathroom; ¥8,400–¥8,600 ($70–$72) double with bathroom; ¥11,000 ($92) triple without bathroom, ¥12,000 ($100) triple with bathroom. American breakfast ¥800 ($6.65) extra. AE, MC, V. Station: Tawaramachi (8 min.). *In room:* A/C, TV, hot-water pot with tea, no phone.

Sakura Ryokan *Kids* A member of Japanese Inn and Welcome Inn groups, this modern concrete establishment with an elevator is a combination business-tourist hotel and has both Japanese and foreign guests. It's located in Asakusa just northwest of the Kappabashi Dori and Kototoi Dori intersection, about a 10-minute walk from Sensoji Temple. The reception area is on the second floor, and the friendly owner speaks some English. Rooms are spotless, and all come with a sink and an alarm clock. Almost half are Western style; both Western- and Japanese-style rooms are available with or without private bathroom. The single rooms are quite spacious compared to those in business hotels. There's one Japanese-style room, complete with a terrace, large enough for a family of six or seven.

2–6–2 Iriya, Taito-ku, Tokyo 110-0013. ② **03/3876-8118.** Fax 03/3873-9456. www.sakura-ryokan.com. 18 units (8 with bathroom). ¥5,300–¥5,500 ($44–$46) single without bathroom, ¥6,300 ($52) single with bathroom; ¥9,600 ($80) double without bathroom; ¥10,600 ($88) double with bathroom; 12,600–¥13,500 ($105–$112) triple without bathroom; ¥13,800–¥15,600 ($115–$130) triple with bathroom. Japanese or Western breakfast ¥800 ($6.65) extra; Japanese dinner ¥1,600 ($13) extra (reservations required). AE, MC, V. Station: Iriya (5 min.; exit 1 or 2). **Amenities:** Computer with Internet access free for guest use; coin-op washer and dryer. *In room:* A/C, cable TV, hot-water pot with tea.

UENO

Annex Katsutaro ⊛ Opened in 2001, this thoroughly modern concrete ryokan is a standout for its simple yet chic designs, spotless Japanese-style rooms (all with bathroom), and location—right in the heart of Yanaka with its old-fashioned neighborhood atmosphere and about a 20-minute walk northwest of Ueno Park. The Keisei Skyliner from Narita Airport stops at nearby Nippori Station. If you have your own laptop, you can tap into the Internet free of charge from your own room, though for those without, there's a public computer guests can use for free. There should be more places like this, but if it's full, don't let management talk you into taking a room in its much older and dingier main Ryokan Katsutaro; it's not nearly as nice as the annex.

3–8–4 Yanaka, Taito-ku, Tokyo 110-0001. ℭ **03/3828-2500.** Fax 03/3821-5400. www.katsutaro.com. 17 units. ¥6,000 ($50) single; ¥10,000–¥12,000 ($83–$100) twin; ¥14,000–¥16,000 ($117–$133) triple. Continental breakfast ¥800 ($6.65) extra. AE, MC, V. Station: Sendagi (2 min.) or Nippori (7 min.). **Amenities:** Computer with Internet access free for guest use; coin-op washers and dryers; free coffee service. *In room:* A/C, TV, fridge, hot-water pot with tea.

Homeikan ⊛⊛ *Finds* Although a bit of a hike from Ueno Park (about 30 min.), this is a lovely place to stay if you wish to experience an authentic, traditional ryokan in a traditional neighborhood. It consists of three separate buildings, acquired over the last century by the present owner's grandfather. Homeikan, the main building (Honkan), was purchased almost 100 years ago; today it is listed as a "Tangible Cultural Property" and is used mainly by groups of students and senior citizens. Across the street is Daimachi Bekkan, built after World War II to serve as the family home. A beautiful, 31-room property, it boasts a private Japanese garden with a pond, nice public baths (including one open 24 hr.), and wood-inlaid and pebbled hallways leading to very nice tatami rooms adorned with such features as gnarled wood trim and sitting alcoves, as well as simpler tatami rooms for budget travelers. This is where most foreigners stay, and if you opt for meals, it will be served in your room in true ryokan fashion. The third building, Morikawa Bekkan, about a 5-minute walk away, was built about 45 years ago and, with 35 rooms, is the largest.

5–10–5 Hongo, Bunkyo-ku, Tokyo 113-0033. ℭ **03/3811-1181** or 3811-1187. Fax 03/3811-1764. www1. odn.ne.jp/homeikan/. 91 units (none with bathroom). ¥6,400 ($53) single; ¥11,200 ($93) double; ¥14,400 ($120) triple. Western or Japanese breakfast ¥1,000 ($8.35); Japanese dinner ¥2,000 ($17; not available first night of stay). AE, DC, MC, V. Station: Hongo Sanchome (8 min.) or Kasuga (5 min.). *In room:* A/C, TV, minibar, hot-water pot with tea, safe.

Ryokan Sawanoya ⊛ Although this ryokan is relatively modern looking and unexciting, it's delightfully located in a wonderful residential area of old Tokyo, northwest of Ueno Park and within walking distance of the park's many attractions and Nezu Shrine. The owner, English-speaking Sawa-san, gives out a map outlining places of interest in the vicinity, as well as pamphlets on inexpensive accommodations throughout Japan; if you pay for the call, he'll even make your next reservation with another Japanese Inn Group inn. Upon your arrival, Sawa-san will give a short tour of the establishment before taking you to your tatami room, and throughout are written explanations to help the ryokan novice. Once a week or so, Sawa-san's son provides guests with a special treat— a traditional Japanese lion dance, free of charge. His daughter-in-law sometimes gives demonstrations of the tea ceremony. In short, this is a great place to stay thanks to Sawa-san's enthusiastic devotion to his neighborhood, which he readily imparts to his guests. Highly recommended.

2–3–11 Yanaka, Taito-ku, Tokyo 110-0001. ☎ **03/3822-2251.** Fax 03/3822-2252. www.sawanoya.com. 12 units (2 with bathroom). ¥4,700–¥5,000 ($39–$42) single without bathroom; ¥8,800 ($73) double without bathroom; ¥9,400 ($78) double with bathroom; ¥12,000 ($100) triple without bathroom, ¥13,500 ($112.50) triple with bathroom. Breakfast of toast and fried eggs ¥300 ($2.50) extra; Japanese breakfast ¥900 ($7.80) extra. AE, MC, V. Closed Dec 29–Jan 3. Station: Nezu (exit 1, 7 min.). **Amenities:** Computer with Internet access free for guest use; coin-op washers and dryers (free laundry detergent); ironing board, iron and trouser press (on 3rd floor); free coffee/tea service, public fridge. *In room:* A/C, TV, hot-water pot with tea, hair dryer.

SHINJUKU

Sunlite Hotel In 1985 this business hotel moved across the street from its old location into a new building, turning the older building into the Hotel Sunlite Annex (the cheaper rates below are in the older annex). A plus to staying here are the weekly antiques flea markets held at nearby Hanazono Shrine. Rooms are cheerful and clean, although annex rooms are small (its singles are minuscule). Feelings of claustrophobia are somewhat mitigated by windows that can be opened. The main (new) building's corner twins with windows on two sides are the best. *Note:* If you like to stay out late, beware: Doors close at 2am and don't reopen until 5:30am.

5–15–8 Shinjuku, Shinjuku-ku, Tokyo 160-0022. ☎ **03/3356-0391.** Fax 03/3356-1223. 197 units. ¥8,300–¥8,900 ($69–$74) single; ¥13,500–¥15,000 ($112.50–$125) twin; ¥14,000 ($117) double. AE, DC, JCB, MC, V. Station: Shinjuku (12 min.) or Shinjuku Sanchome (5 min.). The hotel is on the east side of Shinjuku Station, on Meiji Dori. **Amenities:** 1 restaurant (Western), 1 coffee shop; same-day laundry service; washer and dryer free of charge. *In room:* A/C, TV, hot-water pot with tea, hair dryer.

Tokyo International Youth Hostel *Value* This spotless hostel, in a highrise, is definitely the best place to stay in its price range—it offers fantastic Tokyo views; in winter you can even see Mt. Fuji from rooms on the west side. Even the public baths boast good views (especially at night). All beds are dormitory style, with two, four, or five bunk beds to a room. The rooms are very pleasant, with big windows, and each bed has its own curtain for privacy. There are also rooms accessible for travelers with disabilities, and two Japanese-style tatami rooms for families that sleep up to six persons. If there are vacancies, you can stay longer than the normal 3-day maximum. In summer, it's a good idea to reserve about 3 months in advance. Closed from 10am to 3pm and locked at 10:30pm (lights out at 11pm).

1–1 Kagura-kashi, Shinjuku-ku, Tokyo 162-0823. ☎ **03/3235-1107.** Fax 03/3264-4000. 158 beds. ¥3,100 ($26) per person. Breakfast ¥400 ($3.35); dinner ¥800 ($6.65). No youth-hostel card required; no age limit. No credit cards. Closed Dec 29–Jan 3. Station: Iidabashi (2 min.). Reception is on the 18th floor of the Central Plaza Building. **Amenities:** Shopping mall on 1st & 2nd floors of same building; washer and dryer free of charge. *In room:* A/C, no phone.

HARAJUKU & AOYAMA

Hotel Harajuku Trim With its front desk on the second floor and only 27 single rooms and 14 twins available, it would be easy to pass this brick building on Meiji Dori and not even know there was a business hotel here. This is the only choice in this hotel-barren shopping paradise. Rooms are clean and functional, with just the basics. The cheapest available twins are actually singles with an added bed. The most expensive singles are a bargain for single travelers. However, the main reason to stay here is because youthful Harajuku is a fun place to be.

6–28–6 Jingumae, Shibuya-ku, Tokyo 150-0001. ☎ **03/3498-2101.** Fax 03/3498-1777. 41 units. ¥8,700–¥10,000 ($72–$83) single; ¥13,600–¥16,700 ($113–139) twin. No credit cards. Station: Meiji-Jingumae (3 min.). **Amenities:** 1 restaurant (Japanese), 1 coffee shop. *In room:* A/C, TV, hot-water pot with tea.

National Children's Castle Hotel (Kodomo-no-Shiro Hotel) *(Kids)*   The National Children's Castle, or Kodomo-no-Shiro, situated on Aoyama Dori about halfway between Aoyama and Shibuya (and a bit of a trek from the station), is a great place to stay if you're traveling with children. Although the hotel itself, located on the seventh and eighth floors, is plain rather than playful and isn't child–theme oriented, the complex boasts Tokyo's best and most sophisticated indoor/outdoor playground for children, complete with a clinic and restaurants. Guests range from businesspeople on weekdays to families and young college students on weekends. The rooms—mainly twins—are simple and of adequate size, with large windows. The most expensive twins, which face Shinjuku, have the best views. The hotel's three singles do not have windows, but you can pay extra to stay in a twin. The three Japanese-style rooms, available for three or more people, are a good way for families to experience the traditional Japanese lifestyle. Make reservations at least six months in advance, especially if you plan on being in Tokyo in the summer. Note that there's an 11pm curfew and check-in isn't until 3pm.

5–53–1 Jingumae, Shibuya-ku, Tokyo 150-0001. *(C)* **03/3797-5677.** Fax 03/3406-7805. 27 units. ¥6,400 ($53) single; ¥14,000–¥15,400 ($117–$128) twin; ¥20,400–¥68,000 ($170–$567) Japanese-style room. AE, DC, JCB, MC, V. Station: Omotesando (8 min.) or Shibuya (10 min.). The front desk is on the 7th floor. **Amenities:** 3 restaurants; National Children's Castle; nonsmoking rooms. *In room:* A/C, TV, hot-water pot with tea.

IKEBUKURO

Kimi Ryokan *(★)*   This has long been a Tokyo favorite for inexpensive Japanese-style lodging. Spotlessly clean and with such Japanese touches as sliding screens, flower arrangements in public spaces, and traditional Japanese music playing softly in the hallways, it caters almost exclusively to foreigners (mostly twentysomethings) and is so popular there's sometimes a waiting list to get in. A bulletin board lists job opportunities (primarily teaching English); a lounge with TV and vending machines is a popular hangout, making it a good place to network with other travelers. Rooms are all Japanese style, with singles the size of 4½ tatami mats and the larger twins the size of 6 tatami mats (a single tatami measures about 3 ft. by 6 ft.).

2–36–8 Ikebukuro, Toshima-ku, Tokyo 171-0014. *(C)* **03/3971-3766.** Fax: 03/3987-1326. 38 units (none with bathroom). ¥4,500 ($37) single; ¥6,500–¥7,500 ($54–$62) double. Rates include tax. No credit cards. Station: Ikebukuro (west exit, 5 min.). The police station near the west exit of the station has maps that will guide you to Kimi. *In room:* A/C.

AKASAKA

Akasaka Yoko Hotel   In a handy location close to the nightlife of both Roppongi (a 15-min. walk) and Akasaka (a 4-min. walk), this pleasant small business hotel caters primarily to Japanese. There are only singles and twins; for a couple of dollars more in each category, you can get a slightly larger room, which may be worth it if you're claustrophobic. If you're on a budget, two people can stay in the highest-priced single with its semi-double-size bed for ¥13,000 ($113). In any case, the bathrooms are barely large enough for even one person. Basically, this is just a place to lay your head down at night.

6–14–12 Akasaka, Minato-ku, Tokyo 107-0052. *(C)* **03/3586-4050.** Fax 03/3586-5944. yokohotl@ sepia.ocn.ne.jp. 245 units. ¥8,900–¥9,800 ($74–$82) single; ¥14,000–¥15,500 ($117–$129) twin. AE, JCB, MC, V. Station: Akasaka (4 min., on Akasaka Dori). **Amenities:** 1 restaurant (Franco-Japanese); same-day dry cleaning/laundry service; nonsmoking rooms. *In room:* A/C, TV, fax, dataport, hot-water pot with tea, hair dryer.

Asia Center of Japan *(Value)*   Great rates make this the top choice if you're looking for inexpensive Western-style accommodations in the center of town. However, it's so popular that it's often fully booked; be sure to reserve 6 months in advance. Everyone—from businessmen to students to travelers to foreigners teaching English—stays here; I know one teacher who lived here for years. Resembling a college dormitory, the Asia Center is popular with area office workers for its inexpensive cafeteria with outdoor seating and snack bar. Accommodations are basic, no frills, and in the singles you can almost reach out and touch all four walls. The cheapest doubles have small, semi-double-size beds (not quite full size but larger than single/twin size). Female travelers should avoid rooms on the ground floor—the windows can open and in Japan there are no screens. Tucked on a side street off Gaien-Higashi Dori not far from Aoyama Dori, the center is about a 15-minute walk to the nightlife of Roppongi or Akasaka or one stop by subway.

8–10–32 Akasaka, Minato-ku, Tokyo 107-0052. (℃ **03/3402-6111.** Fax 03/3402-0738. http://jcha.yado-jozu.ne.jp. 166 units (149 with bathroom). ¥5,100 ($42) single without bathroom, ¥7,500 ($62) single with bathroom; ¥10,500 ($87) twin with bathroom; ¥8,500–¥9,500 ($71–$79) double with bathroom; ¥14,100 ($117) triple with bathroom. Rates include tax. JCB, MC, V. Station: Aoyama-Itchome (6 min.), Nogizaka (6 min.). **Amenities:** 1 restaurant, 1 snack bar; coin-op washers and dryers. *In room:* A/C, coin-operated TV.

SHINAGAWA

Family Inn Fifty's   Despite its catchy name, almost no English is spoken at this wannabe American 1950s-style motel. Opened in 2000, it sports red bar stools in its lobby and photos of Marilyn Monroe and other American icons in the rooms, but otherwise this is a no-nonsense but cheerful accommodation, offering identical, small rooms with one double bed, a sofa-bed, and tiled bathrooms but no closet. A machine handles check-in (you'll need a credit card; the front desk staff will guide you through the process). And you'll save ¥1,000 ($8.35) per night on the rates below if you book your reservation online. If you want a smoking room, you'll pay ¥1,000 more than the quoted rates. There aren't many places this cheap, this straightforward, and this streamlined in Japan. A motel chain in the making?

1–3–25 Osaki, Shinagawa-ku, Tokyo 141-0032. (℃ **03/3490-0050.** www.fiftys.com. 50 units. ¥6,000 ($50) single; ¥9,000 ($75) twin; ¥10,000 ($83) triple. Rates include Continental breakfast. MC, V. Station: Osaki (2 min.); take the stairs down the east exit, cross under the highway, and then turn left. **Amenities:** Non-smoking rooms. *In room:* A/C, TV.

4 Where to Dine

From stand-up noodle shops and pizzerias to exclusive kaiseki restaurants and sushi bars, there are at least 80,000 restaurants in Tokyo—which gives you some idea of how fond the Japanese are of eating out. In a city where apartments are so small and cramped that entertaining at home is almost unheard of, restaurants serve as places for socializing, meeting friends, and wooing business associates—as well as great excuses for drinking a lot of beer, sake, and whiskey.

HOW TO DINE IN TOKYO WITHOUT SPENDING A FORTUNE   I know people in Tokyo who claim they haven't cooked in years—and they're not millionaires. They simply take advantage of one of the best deals in Tokyo—the fixed-price lunch, usually available from 11am to 2pm. Called a *teishoku* in a Japanese restaurant, a fixed-price meal is likely to include a soup, a main dish such as tempura or whatever the restaurant specializes in, pickled vegetables, rice, and tea. In restaurants serving Western food, the fixed-price lunch is variously referred to as a set lunch, *seto coursu* or simply *coursu,* and usually includes an appetizer, a main course with one or two side dishes, coffee or tea, and sometimes dessert. Even restaurants listed under **very expensive**—where you'd otherwise spend at least ¥12,000 ($100) or more for dinner (including tax and service charge but excluding drinks)—and **expensive**—where you can expect to pay ¥8,000 to ¥12,000 ($67–$100) for dinner—usually offer set-lunch menus, allowing you to dine in style at very reasonable prices. To keep your costs down, therefore, try having your biggest meal at lunch, avoiding, if possible, the noon to 1pm weekday crush when Tokyo's army of office workers flood area restaurants. Since the Japanese tend to order fixed-price meals rather than a la carte, set dinners are also usually available (though they're not as cheap as set lunches). All-you-can-eat buffets, offered by many hotel restaurants, are also bargain meals for hearty appetites.

So many of Tokyo's good restaurants fall into the **moderate** category that it's tempting to simply eat your way through the city—and the range of cuisine is so great you could eat something different at each meal. A dinner in this category will average ¥4,000 to ¥8,000 ($33–$67). Lunch is likely to cost half as much.

Many of Tokyo's most colorful, noisy, and popular restaurants fall into the **inexpensive** category, where meals usually go for less than ¥4,000 ($33); many offer meals for less than ¥2,000 ($17) and lunches for ¥1,000 ($8.35) and less. The city's huge working population heads to these places to catch a quick lunch or to socialize with friends after hours. In the past few years, a number of excellent yet inexpensive French bistros and Italian trattorie have burst onto the culinary scene. Ethnic restaurants, particularly those serving Indian, Chinese, and other Asian cuisine, are also plentiful and usually inexpensive. Hotel restaurants are also good bargains for inexpensive set lunches. Finally, remember to see "Tokyo After Dark," in chapter 4 for suggestions on inexpensive drinking places that serve food.

OTHER DINING NOTES   The restaurants listed below are organized first by neighborhood and then by price category.

Note that a 5% consumption tax will be added to restaurant bills. In addition, many first-class restaurants, as well as hotel restaurants, will add a 10% to 15% service charge. Unless otherwise stated, the prices I've given do not include the extra tax and service charge.

Note that restaurants that have no signs in English letters are preceded by a numbered icon, which is keyed to a list of **Japanese symbols** in appendix C.

Tips **Mapping Out Tokyo's Restaurants**

You can locate the restaurants reviewed below using the following neighborhood maps:

- To locate restaurants in **Akasaka**, p. 109.
- To locate restaurants in **Ueno**, p. 114.
- To locate restaurants in **Shinjuku,** p. 116 to 117.
- To locate restaurants in **Asakusa**, p. 121.
- To locate restaurants in **Hibiya** and **Ginza**, p. 134 to 135.
- To locate restaurants in **Harajuku**, p. 147.
- To locate restaurants in **Roppongi**, p. 153.

Finally, keep in mind that the **last order** is taken at least 30 minutes before the actual closing time, sometimes even an hour before at the more exclusive restaurants.

HIBIYA & GINZA
VERY EXPENSIVE

Kamon ★★ TEPPANYAKI   Kamon, which means "Gate of Celebration," has an interior that could be a statement on Tokyo itself—traditionally Japanese yet ever so high-tech. Seating is at one of several large counters (some with views over Hibiya), with grills in the middle where expert chefs prepare excellent teppanyaki before your eyes. Japanese sirloin steaks or filet, cooked to perfection, are available, as well as seafood ranging from fresh prawns and scallops to crabmeat and fish, and seasonal vegetables. The service is, of course, imperial.

On the 17th floor of the Imperial Hotel, 1–1–1 Uchisaiwai-cho. ⓒ 03/3504-1111. Reservations recommended for dinner. Set dinners ¥12,000–¥18,000 ($100–$150); set lunches ¥3,500–¥5,000 ($29–$42). AE, DC, JCB, MC, V. Daily 11:30am–2:30pm and 5:30–9:30pm. Station: Hibiya (1 min.).

① **Sushiko** ★★ SUSHI   If you're in pursuit of top-quality sushi, your search will eventually take you here, considered by some to be one of the best sushi bars in town. There's no written menu, and the counter seats 11 customers only. Owned by a fourth-generation restaurateur, this establishment doesn't display its fish as in most sushi bars but rather keeps it freshly refrigerated until the moment it meets the swift blade of the expert chefs. Unless you know your sushi, you're best off telling the chef how much you want to spend and letting him take it from there.

6–3–8 Ginza. ⓒ 03/3571-1968. Reservations required. Meals ¥12,000–¥15,000 ($100–$125). AE, JCB, MC, V. Daily 11:30am–10:30pm. Station: Ginza or Hibiya (4 min.). A block east of the elevated tracks of the JR Yamanote Line, on the Ginza side on Sukiyabashi Dori.

EXPENSIVE

② **Ohmatsuya** ★★ *Finds* JAPANESE GRILL   Enter this second-floor restaurant in a nondescript building and you're instantly back in time: after being greeted by waitresses clad in traditional countryside clothing, you'll find yourself surrounded by an old farmhouse atmosphere. (Part of the decor is from a 17th-century samurai house in northern Japan.) Even the style of cooking is traditional, as customers grill their own food over a hibachi. Sake is served in a length of bamboo, and dinner menus include such delicacies as grilled fish, skewered meat, and vegetables. A true find—and easy to find at that—located on Sony Street, the small side street behind the Sony Building.

6–5–8 Ginza. ⓒ 03/3571-7053. Reservations required. Set dinners ¥6,500–¥9,000 ($54–$75). AE, JCB, DC, MC, V. Mon–Fri 5–10pm (last order 9:30pm); Sat 4:30–9:30pm (last order 8:30pm). Closed holidays. Station: Ginza (3 min.). On the second floor of the modern Ail D'Or Building behind the Sony Building on Sony St.

Ten-ichi ★ TEMPURA   In this restaurant, located on Namiki Dori in the heart of Ginza's nightlife, you can sit at a counter to watch the chef prepare your meal. This is the main shop of a 70-year-old restaurant chain that helped the tempura style of cooking gain worldwide recognition by serving important foreign customers. Today Ten-ichi still has one of the best reputations in town for serving the most delicately fried foods, along with its special sauce (or, if you prefer, you can dip the morsels in lemon juice with a pinch of salt).

There are 10 Ten-ichi restaurants in Tokyo, including the Ginza Sony Building at the intersection of Harumi Dori and Sotobori Dori (ⓒ **03/3571-3837;**

station: Hibiya or Ginza), the Imperial Hotel's Tower basement (✆ 03/
3503-1001; station: Hibiya), and 3–19–3 Akasaka on Misujidori Street (✆ 03/
3583-0107; station: Akasaka or Akasaka-mitsuke).

6–6–5 Ginza, on Namiki Dori. ✆ 03/3571-1949. Reservations recommended for lunch, required for dinner.
Set dinners ¥10,000–¥15,000 ($83–$125); set lunches ¥7,000–¥10,000 ($58–$83). AE, DC, JCB, MC, V. Daily
11:30am–9:30pm. Station: Ginza (3 min.).

MODERATE

③ **Donto** 🎌🎌 VARIED JAPANESE   Located in Hibiya on Harumi Dori,
this is a great place for lunch. Popular with the local working crowd (and therefore best avoided between noon and 1pm), it's pleasantly decorated in a rustic
style with shoji screens, wooden floors, and an open kitchen. Take off your shoes
at the entryway and put them into one of the wooden lockers. Choose what you
want from the plastic display case, which shows various teishoku and set meals.
Everything from noodles, sashimi, tempura, and obento to kaiseki is available.
Unfortunately, the best deals are daily specials written in Japanese only; ask
about them or look around at what others are eating.

There's another Donto on the 49th floor of the Sumitomo Building in Shinjuku (✆ 03/3344-6269; station: Tochomae).

Yurakucho Denki Bldg. basement, 1–7–1 Yurakucho, on Harumi Dori. ✆ 03/3201-3021. Set dinners
¥3,500–¥7,500 ($29–$62); set lunches ¥880–¥1,000 ($7.35–$8.35). AE, DC, JCB, MC, V. Mon–Sat 11am–2pm
and 5–10:30pm. Closed holidays. Station: Hibiya (1 min.).

④ **Ginza Daimasu** KAISEKI/OBENTO   This 65-year-old restaurant has a
simple, modern decor with Japanese touches. Experienced, kimono-clad
waitresses serve artfully arranged set meals from the English menu. The
Fukiyose-zen obento—many delicate dishes served in three courses—includes
beautiful tempura delicacies served in an edible basket and a menu (in Japanese)
explaining what you're eating. A plastic-food display in the front window will
help you recognize the restaurant. Set lunches are served until 3pm.

6–9–6 Ginza. ✆ 03/3571-3584. Reservations required for kaiseki. Kaiseki ¥5,000–¥12,000 ($42–$100);
obento ¥2,300–¥3,800 ($19–$32); set lunches ¥2,000–¥2,500 ($17–$21). DC, JCB, MC, V. Daily
11:30am–9:30pm (last order 8:30pm). Station: Ginza (2 min.). Across from Matsuzakaya department store on
Chuo Dori.

⑤ **Kushi Colza** 🎌 YAKITORI/KUSHIYAKI   Kikkoman, a well-known
producer of soy sauce, maintains a few restaurants, including this one. It serves
yakitori and *kushiyaki* (grilled meats and vegetables on skewers), delicately
seasoned with—what else?—Kikkoman soy sauce. Small, pleasant, and with an
open counter where you can watch friendly chefs prepare your food, Kushi
Colza has an English menu that lists three set dinners consisting of various skewered filets of beef, fish, eel, or pork served with an appetizer, salad, soup, and
dessert. There's also a special weekend and holiday set dinner for ¥3,000 ($25).
A la carte selections for skewered specialties average ¥480 to ¥800 ($4–$6.65)
per skewer. My favorite accompaniment is the seasonal salad with soy sauce
dressing. Lunch specials featuring beef or fish dishes are also available, though
the menu is only in Japanese.

6–4–18 Ginza. ✆ 03/3571-8228. Reservations recommended. Set dinners ¥3,300–¥4,500 ($27–$37); set
lunches ¥850–¥1,500 ($7.10–$12.50). AE, DC, JCB, MC, V. Mon–Fri 11:30am–1pm and 5–10pm; Sat, Sun and
holidays 4:30–9pm. Station: Hibiya (5 min.), Ginza (10 min.). Located on a small side street between and paralleling Sotobori Dori and the elevated JR Yamanote Line tracks, behind Sukiyabashi Hankyu department
store; look for its sign, which says KUSHI & WINE.

Nightlife & Where to Stay & Dine in Hibiya & Ginza

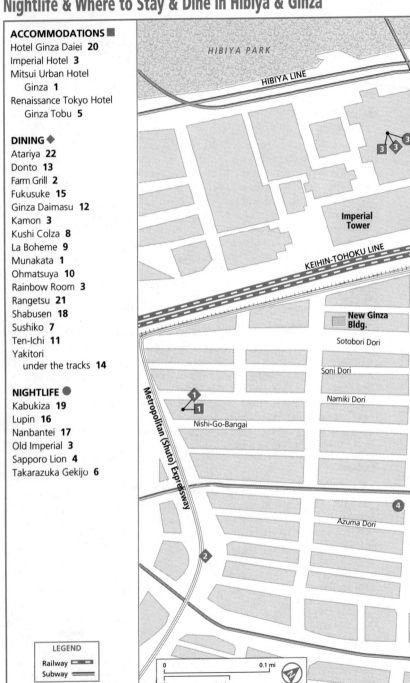

ACCOMMODATIONS ■
Hotel Ginza Daiei **20**
Imperial Hotel **3**
Mitsui Urban Hotel
    Ginza **1**
Renaissance Tokyo Hotel
    Ginza Tobu **5**

DINING ◆
Atariya **22**
Donto **13**
Farm Grill **2**
Fukusuke **15**
Ginza Daimasu **12**
Kamon **3**
Kushi Colza **8**
La Boheme **9**
Munakata **1**
Ohmatsuya **10**
Rainbow Room **3**
Rangetsu **21**
Shabusen **18**
Sushiko **7**
Ten-Ichi **11**
Yakitori
    under the tracks **14**

NIGHTLIFE ●
Kabukiza **19**
Lupin **16**
Nanbantei **17**
Old Imperial **3**
Sapporo Lion **4**
Takarazuka Gekijo **6**

HIBIYA PARK

HIBIYA LINE

Imperial
Tower

KEIHIN-TOHOKU LINE

New Ginza
Bldg.

Sotobori Dori

Soni Dori

Namiki Dori

Nishi-Go-Bangai

Metropolitan (Shuto) Expressway

Azuma Dori

LEGEND
Railway
Subway

0   0.1 mi
0   0.1 km

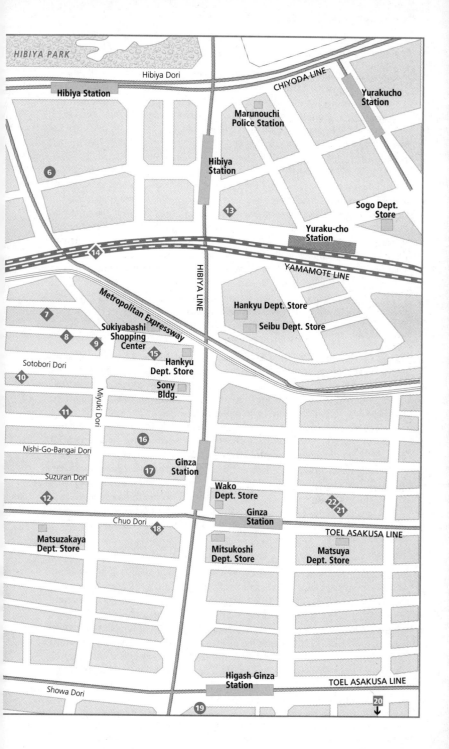

(*Tips*) **A Note on Japanese Symbols**

Many establishments and attractions in Japan do not have signs in Roman (English-language) letters. Those that don't are indicated in this guide with an oval with a number that corresponds to a number in appendix C showing the Japanese symbols. Thus, to find the Japanese symbol for, say, Rangetsu (below), refer to no. 6 in appendix C.

Munakata ⭐ KAISEKI/OBENTO   Kaiseki is one of the most expensive meals you can have in Japan, but there are some lunch specials here (served until 2pm) that make it quite reasonable. This basement restaurant is cozy, with slats of wood and low lighting that give customers a sense of privacy even in the middle of the day. In addition to mini-kaiseki meals, there are also tempura and various obento lunch boxes like the Shokado bento for ¥1,300 ($11). If you come before 6:30pm on weekdays and 7pm on weekends, you can take advantage of a special kaiseki meal for ¥5,000 ($42). A great place for lunch or for a dinner splurge: English menus are available.

Mitsui Urban Hotel basement, 8–6–15 Ginza. ☎ **03/3574-9356.** Main dishes ¥1,200–¥4,000 ($10–$33); kaiseki set meals ¥8,000–¥15,000 ($67–$125); mini-kaiseki lunches ¥2,500 ($21). AE, DC, JCB, MC, V. Mon–Fri 11:30am–3pm and 5–10pm; Sat, Sun, and holidays 11:30am–10pm. Station: Shimbashi (2 min.), Hibiya (10 min.).

Rainbow Room ⭐ INTERNATIONAL   Lots of Tokyo hotels now offer all-you-can-eat buffets, but this 17th-floor restaurant has been serving buffets for more than 40 years. Its spread features more than 40 dishes, mostly European and some international, which vary according to seasonal food promotions spotlighting a country's cuisine, from Indonesian to Swiss. Views are of Ginza and Hibiya Park, and there's live jazz music in the evenings. This restaurant has enjoyed great popularity for decades, making reservations a must. To save money, come for an early dinner before 8:30pm weekdays (except holidays), when ¥2,500 ($21) buys five "points," which you then use to order various dishes valued at different points: drinks and appetizers are one point, while main dishes ranging from lamb chops with potatoes or club sandwich to beef stew cost two to four points each.

Imperial Hotel, 17th floor, 1–1–1 Uchisaiwai-cho. ☎ **03/3504-1111.** Reservations recommended. Buffet dinner ¥7,500 ($62.50); buffet lunch ¥5,000 ($42). AE, DC, JCB, MC, V. Daily 11:30am–2:30pm and 5–9:30pm. Station: Hibiya (1 min.).

(6) **Rangetsu** ⭐ SUKIYAKI/SHABU-SHABU/KAISEKI/OBENTO   This well-known Ginza restaurant has been dishing out sukiyaki, shabu-shabu, obento (traditional box meals), and steaks for almost five decades. It uses only Matsuzaka beef (bought whole and carved up by the chefs), which ranges from costlier fine-marbled beef to cheaper cuts with thick marbling. There are also various crab dishes (including a crab sukiyaki), kaiseki, sirloin steaks, and eel dishes. Especially good deals are the obento box meals, available day and night and offering a variety of small dishes, and the various set lunches served until 2:30pm. In the basement is a sake bar with more than 80 different kinds of sake from all over Japan, which you can also order with your meal. Outside the door is a plastic display case with descriptions in English.

3–5–8 Ginza. ☎ **03/3567-1021.** Reservations recommended. Beef sukiyaki or shabu-shabu ¥4,500 ($37); obento meals ¥2,200–¥4,000 ($18–$33); set lunches ¥1,200–¥1,700 ($10–$14). DC, JCB, MC, V. Mon–Sat 11:30am–10pm; Sun and holidays 11:30am–9pm. Station: Ginza (3 min.). On Chuo Dori across from the Matsuya department store.

INEXPENSIVE

(7) **Atariya** ✯ YAKITORI   Because it's open mostly at night and serves yakitori, this is technically a drinking establishment, but it also makes a good choice for inexpensive dining in Ginza. You have your choice of table or counter seating on the first floor, while up on the second floor you take off your shoes and sit on split-reed mats. Since set courses will include most parts of the chicken, including the liver, gizzard, and skin, you might wish to order a la carte for your favorites. Mine include asparagus wrapped in grilled pork, *tskune* (ground chicken meatballs on a skewer), and *shoniku* (chicken breast yakitori). The shop's name means "to be right on target, to score a bull's-eye," and according to its English pamphlet, eating here is certain to bring you good luck.

3–5–17 Ginza. ✆ **03/3564-0045.** Yakitori set courses ¥1,500–¥2,500 ($12–$21); individual skewers ¥150–¥300 ($1.25–$2.50). No credit cards. Tues–Fri 4:30–10:15pm (last order); Sat 2–9:30pm; Sun 2–8:30pm. Station: Ginza (3 min.). Near Ginza 4-chome Crossing. Take the small side street that runs between Wako department store and Wako Annex; Atariya is in the 2nd block on the right.

Farm Grill (*Value*) AMERICAN   After all of Tokyo's cramped, tiny restaurants, what strikes you first about this place is the space—enough for 260 widely placed tables. And with its simple wood decor and (for Tokyo) reasonable prices, the second thing that will come to mind is that it's just like millions of casual restaurants in the States, which is exactly what makes this restaurant so unusual. Such a variety of American food in Japan is hard to come by, and at these prices, it's otherwise nonexistent outside hotels. Overflowing buffets, offering a variety of vegetables, casseroles, meats, and desserts, invite gluttony, but it's gluttony, thank goodness, with a time limit—90 minutes for lunch and 2 hours for dinner. Add ¥1,000 ($8.35) to your meal, and you can drink all you want of a variety of beverages including wine, cocktails, and beer.

Ginza Nine Building 3, 8–5 Ginza. ✆ **03/5568-6156.** Dinner buffet ¥2,500 ($21); lunch buffet ¥970 ($8.10) weekdays, ¥1,200 ($10) Sat, Sun and holidays. AE, JCB, MC, V. Daily 11:30am–4:30pm and 5–11pm. Station: Shimbashi (exit 1, 4 min.). Near the Ginza Dai-Ichi Hotel, on the second floor of a building underneath the Shuto Expressway.

(8) **Fukusuke** SUSHI   In this basement full of cheap restaurants, called Ginza Palmy, walk all the way to the back (away from Harumi Dori) to this very inexpensive sushi bar, popular with area office workers. It has an exceptionally long counter, which makes it a good choice if you're looking for an empty seat

---

(Kids) **Family-Friendly Restaurants**

Cafe Creperie Le Bretagne (*p. 148*)   If sweet bean paste is not your child's idea of dessert, then perhaps the crepes at this casual establishment will do the trick, filled with fruit, chocolate, and other yummy concoctions.

Hard Rock Cafe (*p. 156*)   This internationally known establishment should pacify grumbling teenagers. They can munch on hamburgers, gaze at famous guitars and other rock 'n' roll memorabilia, and most important, buy that Hard Rock Cafe T-shirt.

Kua' Aina (*p. 149*)   When your kids start asking for "real food," take them here for the best burgers in town.

during the noon-to-1pm rush (a branch of the same restaurant is catty-corner). It has a display counter outside with various choices of set meals as well as an illustrated card showing various a la carte sushi. Easiest, however, is to order one of the set meals. The ¥850 ($7.10) set lunch includes soup, various sushi, Japanese pickles, and tea.

Toshiba Building B2, 5–2–1 Ginza. (C) 03/3573-0471. Sushi a la carte ¥120–¥500 ($1–$4.15); set dinners ¥1,300–¥4,500 ($11–$37.50); set lunches ¥850–¥1,300 ($7.10–$11). AE, DC, JCB, MC, V. Mon–Sat 11am–10pm; Sun and holidays 11:30am–9pm. Station: Ginza or Hibiya (4 min.). In the second basement below the Sukiyabashi Hankyu department store on Sotobori Dori at Sukiyabashi Crossing.

La Boheme ITALIAN   The food here is passable, but what sets La Boheme apart is that it's open every day until 5am. I also like its huge, open kitchen in the middle of the room, surrounded by a U-shaped counter that provides a ringside view of the action. The pasta ranges from lasagna to bolognese along with some Japanese-style versions that include steamed breast of chicken with Japanese baby leek, spinach, and sesame oil; and fresh shrimp and basil with garlic, olive oil, and shimeji mushrooms.

You'll find other La Boheme restaurants in Harajuku at 6–7–18 Jinguma ((C) **03/3400-3406**) and 5–8–5 Jingumae ((C) **03/5467-5666**) and in Shibuya at 1–6–8 Jinnan ((C) **03/3477-0481**), both open daily from 11:30am to 5am.

6–4–1 Ginza ((C) 03/3572-5005). Pizza and pasta ¥500–¥1,300 ($4.15–$11); set lunches ¥580–¥1,250 ($4.85–$10). AE, DC, JCB, MC, V. Daily 11:30am–5am. Station: Hibiya (5 min.), Ginza (10 min.). Behind Sukiyabashi Hankyu department store, on a corner.

(9) **Shabusen** (Value) SHABU-SHABU   Located on the second floor of a fashion department store just a stone's throw from Ginza 4-chome crossing (the Harumi Dori–Chuo Dori intersection), this is a fun restaurant where you can cook your own sukiyaki or shabu-shabu in a boiling pot as you sit at a round counter. It's also one of the few shabu-shabu restaurants that caters to individual diners (this dish is usually shared by a group). Orders are shouted back and forth among the staff, service is rapid, and the place is lively. There's an English menu complete with cooking instructions, so it's user-friendly. The special shabu-shabu dinner for ¥3,950 ($32), with appetizer, tomato ("super dressing") salad, beef, vegetables, noodles or rice porridge, and dessert, is enough for most voracious appetites.

You'll find a branch of Shabusen in the basement of the TBS building at 5–3–3 Akasaka ((C) **03/3582-8161**).

Core Bldg. 2F, 5–8–20 Ginza. (C) 03/3571-1717. Set dinners ¥2,200–¥5,600 ($18–$47); set lunches ¥850–¥3,000 ($7.10–$25). AE, DC, JCB, MC, V. Daily 11am–10pm. Station: Ginza (1 min.). On Chuo Dori next to the Nissan building.

Yakitori Under the Tracks (Finds) YAKITORI   This is not a restaurant but rather a place—underneath an arch of the elevated Yamanote railway tracks. Although there are several fancier establishments that occupy an entire arch, look for the one arch located about halfway between Harumi Dori and the Imperial Hotel Tower with a handful of tiny yakitori stands, each with a few tables and chairs. They cater to a rather boisterous working-class clientele, mainly men. The atmosphere, unsophisticated and dingy, harks back to prewar Japan, somewhat of an anomaly in the otherwise chic Ginza. Dining here can be quite an experience, and on my last visit, several stall owners enthusiastically beckoned me to join them.

Under the Yamanote Line tracks separating Ginza from Hibiya. No phone. Skewers ¥180–¥400 ($1.50–$3.35). No credit cards. Mon–Sat 5pm–midnight. Station: Hibiya or Yurakucho (3 min.).

TSUKIJI

Since Tsukiji is home to the nation's largest wholesale fish market, it's not surprising that this area abounds in sushi and seafood restaurants. In addition to the recommendations here, don't neglect the many stalls in and around the market where you can eat everything from noodles to fresh sashimi.

MODERATE

⑩ **Tentake** FUGU   People who really know their *fugu*, or blowfish, will tell you that the only proper time to eat it is from October through March when it's fresh. You can eat fugu year-round, however, and a good place to try this Japanese delicacy is Tentake, a place popular with the Tsukiji working crowd. There's an English menu listing fugu dishes such as tempura fugu; a complete fugu dinner with all the trimmings costs ¥9,000 ($75). Otherwise, if you want suggestions, try the fugu-chiri for ¥3,800 ($32), a do-it-yourself meal in which you cook raw blowfish, cabbage, dandelion leaves, and tofu in a pot of boiling water in front of you—this was more than I could eat, but you can make a complete meal of it by ordering the fugu-chiri course for ¥5,900 ($49), which adds tempera, yakitori, and other dishes. If someone in your party doesn't like fugu, I'd recommend the crab set menu for ¥3,900 ($32). And yes, that's fugu swimming in the fish tank.

Tip: Before you eat here, be sure you read about fugu in "Tips on Dining, Japanese Style" in appendix A.

6–16–6 Tsukiji. ✆ 03/3541-3881. Fugu dishes ¥1,000–¥3,900 ($8.35–$32); fugu set courses ¥3,900–¥13,500 ($32–$112); set lunches ¥800–¥1,000 ($6.65–$8.35). JCB, MC, V. Daily 11:30am–9:30pm (last order). Closed Wed Mar and Oct; 1st and 3rd Wed Feb and Nov. Station: Tsukiji (7 min.). From the Harumi Dori/Shinohashi intersection, walk on Harumi Dori in the opposite direction of Ginza; the restaurant is on the left just before the bridge in a modern building.

INEXPENSIVE

⑪ **Edogin** SUSHI   There are four Edogin sushi restaurants in Tsukiji, all located within walking distance of one another. Since they're close to the famous fish market, you can be assured the fish will be fresh. There's nothing aesthetic about the main Edogin, first established about 80 years ago—the lights are bright, it's packed with the locals, and it's noisy and busy. It's particularly packed during lunch- and dinnertime because the food is dependably good and plentiful. The menu is in Japanese only, but there's a glass case outside with some of the dishes displayed, with prices for most ¥3,000 ($25) or less. As an alternative, look at what the people around you are eating or, if it's lunchtime, order the teishoku (served until 2pm). The *nigiri-zushi* for ¥1,000 ($8.35) offers a variety of sushi, along with soup and pickled vegetables; if you're really hungry, order the more plentiful ¥1,400 ($12) nigiri-zushi teishoku.

4–5–1 Tsukiji. ✆ 03/3543-4401. Set meals ¥1,000–¥3,500 ($8.35–$29); lunch teishoku ¥1,000–¥1,400 ($8.35–$12). AE, DC, MC, V. Mon–Sat 11am–9:30pm; Sun and holidays 11:30am–9pm. Station: Tsukiji (3 min.). Located near the Harumi and Shinohashi Dori intersection behind McDonald's; anyone in the neighborhood will be able to point you in the right direction.

⑫ **Sushi Dai** ⭐ SUSHI   Located right in the Tsukiji Fish Market, this restaurant boasts some of the freshest fish in town. The easiest thing to do is order the seto, a set sushi course that usually comes with tuna, eel, shrimp, and other morsels plus six rolls of tuna and rice in seaweed (*onigiri*). If you're here for breakfast and can't stomach sushi so early, order *tamago* (a slice of layer-fried omelet).

Tsukiji Fish Market. ✆ 03/3547-6797. Sushi a la carte ¥200–¥1,000 ($1.65–$8.35); sushi seto ¥1,500–¥3,000 ($12.50–$25). No credit cards. Mon–Sat 5am–2pm. Closed holidays. Station: Tsukiji (10 min.).

Located in a row of barracks housing other restaurants and shops beside the covered market. Cross the bridge that leads to the market grounds, take a right and then your first left; to your right will be the barracks. Sushi Dai is in Building 6 on the 3rd alley (just past the mail box), the 3rd shop on the right.

ASAKUSA
MODERATE

⑬ **Komagata Dojo** ⊕ *Finds* DOJO Following a tradition spanning 200 years and now in its 6th generation of owners, this old-style dining hall specializes in *dojo*, a tiny sardinelike river fish that translates as a "loach." It's served in a variety of styles, from grilled to stewed. Easiest is to order one of the set meals, which includes a popular *dojo nabe*, cooked on a charcoal burner at your table (dojo nabe ordered a la carte costs ¥1,400/$12). Otherwise, look around and order what someone else is eating. The dining area is simply one large room of tatami mats, with ground-level boards serving as tables and waitresses in traditional dress moving quietly about. A restaurant very much out of the Edo Period.

1–7–12 Komagata, Taito-ku. ✆ 03/3842-4001. Reservations recommended for dinner. Dojo dishes ¥1,200–¥1,400 ($10–$12); set meals ¥2,000–¥6,300 ($17–$52.50). DC, JCB, MC, V. Daily 11am–9pm. Station: Asakusa (3 min.). To reach the restaurant, walk south on Edo Dori (away from Kaminarimon Gate and Sensoji Temple); the restaurant—a large, old-fashioned wood house on a corner, with blue curtains at its door—is on the right side of the street, about a 5-min. walk from Kaminarimon Gate, past the Sanwa Bank.

La Ranarita Azumabashi ⊕ ITALIAN The Asahi Beer Tower may not mean anything to you, but if I mention the building with the golden hops poised on top, you'll certainly know it when you see it (the building was designed by Philippe Starck). The Asahi Beer Tower is the high-rise beside the golden hops and looks like . . . a beer mug with foam on top? On the top floor (in the foam), is this Italian-managed restaurant with soaring walls and great views of Asakusa. It's a perfect perch from which to watch barges on the river or the sun set over Asakusa as you dine on everything from pizza or pasta (available in half sizes) to grilled scampi. The set lunches, which begin at ¥1,200 ($10) on weekdays and ¥2,500 ($21) on weekends and holidays, include an antipasto, salad, main dish, and coffee. If you want a ringside seat, make a reservation at least 3 days in advance or avoid the weekends.

Asahi Beer Tower (on the opposite side of the Sumida River from Sensoji Temple), 22nd floor, 1–23–1 Azumabashi. ✆ 03/5608-5277. Reservations recommended on weekends. Pizza ¥1,300–¥1,800 ($11–$15); pasta ¥650–¥1,800 ($5.40–$15); main dishes ¥1,600–¥2,900 ($13–$24). AE, DC, JCB, MC, V. Mon–Sat 11:30am–2pm (last order) and 5–9pm (last order); Sun and holidays 11:30am–2pm and 4–8pm (last order). Station: Asakusa (4 min.).

⑭ **Mugitoro** YAM KAISEKI Founded about 60 years ago but now housed in a new building, this restaurant specializes in *tororo-imo* (yam) kaiseki and has a wide following among middle-aged Japanese women. Popular as a health food, the yams used here are imported from the mountains of Akita Prefecture and are featured in almost all the dishes. The menu changes monthly, and there's an English menu. If you're on a budget or want a quick meal, come for the weekday lunch buffet offered until 1pm that includes fish, yam, a vegetable, soup, and rice; simply deposit your ¥1,000 ($8.35) into the pot on the table.

2–2–4 Kaminarimon. ✆ 03/3842-1066. Reservations recommended. Set dinners ¥6,000–¥13,000 ($50–$108); set lunches ¥2,500–¥5,000 ($21–$42). AE, DC, JCB, MC, V. Mon–Sat 11:30am–9pm (last order); Sun and holidays 11am–9pm. Station: Asakusa (2 min.). From Sensoji Temple, walk south (with your back to Kaminarimon Gate) until you reach the 1st big intersection with the stoplight. Komagata-bashi Bridge will be to your left; Mugitoro is right beside the bridge on Edo Dori, next to a tiny temple and playground. Look for the big white lantern hanging outside.

INEXPENSIVE

(15) **Chinya** *Value* SHABU-SHABU/SUKIYAKI   Established in 1880, Chinya is an old sukiyaki restaurant with a new home in a seven-story building to the left of Kaminarimon Gate. The entrance to this place is open-fronted; all you'll see is a man waiting to take your shoes and a hostess in a kimono ready to lead you to one of the tatami-floored dining areas above. It offers very good shabu-shabu or sukiyaki set lunches for less than ¥2,000 ($17), available until 4pm and including soup and side dishes. Otherwise, dinner set meals of shabu-shabu or sukiyaki, including rice and soup, begin at ¥2,500 ($21). There's a display case out front showing a few options, but the very good English menu includes instructions, making this a good bet for the sukiyaki/shabu-shabu novice.

1–3–4 Asakusa. © 03/3841-0010. Set meals ¥2,500–¥7,000 ($21–$58). AE, DC, JCB, MC, V. Mon–Sat 11:45am–9:15pm; Sun and holidays 11:30am–9pm. Station: Asakusa (1 min.). On Kaminarimon Dori; located to the left of the Kaminarimon Gate if you stand facing Asakusa Kannon Temple (look for the sukiyaki sign).

(16) **Daikokuya** TEMPURA   This simple tempura restaurant has been popular with the locals since 1887, and though it does not offer the most refined tempura, it has atmosphere and its huge portions are legendary. It specializes in Edo-style tempura and *tendon* (tempura on a bowl of rice, usually ebi, or prawn), prepared using sesame oil. Although there's no English menu, there are photographs of many of the dishes. There's an annex around the corner to handle the overflow crowd.

1–38–10 Asakusa. © 03/3844-1111. Set courses ¥3,000–¥4,300 ($25–$36). No credit cards. Daily 11:10am–8:30pm. Closed irregularly once or twice a month. Station: Asakusa (5 min.). Off Nakamise Dori to the west; take the small street that passes by the south side of Dempoin Temple (also spelled Demboin); the restaurant is at the 1st intersection on the left, a white corner building with a Japanese-style tiled roof and sliding front door.

Kamiya Bar JAPANESE/WESTERN   This inexpensive eatery, established in 1880 as the first Western bar in Japan, serves both Japanese and Western fare on its three floors. The first floor is the bar, popular with tobacco-smoking older Japanese men. The second floor offers Western food of a sort (that is, the Japanese version of Western food), including fried chicken, smoked salmon, spaghetti, fried shrimp, and hamburger steak; the third floor serves Japanese food ranging from udon noodles and yakitori to tempura, and sashimi. I personally prefer the third floor for both its food and its atmosphere. Although the menus are in Japanese only, there are extensive plastic-food display cases showing set meals costing ¥1,500–¥3,500 ($12–$29). This is a very casual restaurant, very much a place for older locals, and can be quite noisy and crowded.

1–1–1 Asakusa. © 03/3841-5400. Main dishes ¥610–¥1,300 ($5.10–$11). No credit cards. Wed–Mon 11:30am–9:30pm (last order). Station: Asakusa (1 min.). Located on Kaminarimon Dori in a plain, brown-tiled building between Kaminarimon Gate and the Sumida River.

(17) **Namiki Yabusoba** ★ NOODLES   Asakusa's best-known noodle shop, founded in 1913, offers plain buckwheat noodles in cold or hot broth as well as more substantial tempura with noodles, all listed in an English menu. Seating is at tables or on tatami mats, but since it's small you won't be able to linger if people are waiting.

2–11–9 Kaminarimon. © 03/3841-1340. Dishes ¥650–¥1,600 ($5.40–$13). No credit cards. Fri–Wed 11:30am–7:30pm. Station: Asakusa (2 min.). From Kaminarimon Gate, walk south (away from Sensoji Temple); Namiki is on the right side of the street in the 2nd block, a brown building with some bamboo trees, a small maple, and a stone lantern by the front door.

UENO

EXPENSIVE

Ueno Seiyoken Grill 🐾 CLASSIC FRENCH   Seiyoken opened in 1876 as one of Japan's first restaurants serving Western food. Now a nondescript building dating from the 1950s, it nonetheless remains the best place to eat in Ueno Park, serving pricey but quite good classic French cuisine, with a relaxing view of greenery outside its large windows and classical music playing softly in the background. The English menu, which changes often (the set menus change either daily or weekly), includes seafood such as sole stuffed with shrimp in white wine sauce, lobster Thermidor, or grilled scallops in carrot sauce, as well as meat dishes ranging from filet mignon in red wine sauce to roasted duck in green pepper sauce. There's a varied selection of French wines as well as wines from Germany, California, and Australia. The Grill is located to the right as you enter the building and is not to be confused with the much cheaper utilitarian restaurant to the left.

In Ueno Park between Kiyomizu Temple and Toshogu Shrine. 🕿 03/3821-2181. Main dishes ¥3,000–¥7,000 ($25–$58); set dinners ¥7,000–¥12,000 ($58–$100); set lunches ¥4,000–¥5,000 ($33–$42). AE, DC, JCB, MC, V. Daily 11am–8pm (last order). Station: JR Ueno (6 min.).

MODERATE

⑱ **Izu'ei** EEL   Put aside all your prejudices about eels and head for this modern yet traditionally decorated restaurant with a 260-year history dating back to the Edo Period. Since eels are grilled over charcoal, the Japanese place a lot of stock in the quality of the charcoal used, and this place boasts its own furnace in the mountains of Wakayama Prefecture, which produces the best charcoal in Japan. *Unagi donburi* (rice with strips of eel on top), tempura, and sushi are available, as well as set meals. There's no English menu, but there's a display case outside, and the menu has some pictures.

2–12–22 Ueno. 🕿 03/3831-0954. Reservations recommended. Main dishes ¥1,500–¥3,000 ($12–$25); set meals ¥2,000–¥8,000 ($17–$67). AE, DC, JCB, MC, V. Daily 11am–9:30pm. Station: JR Ueno (3 min.). On Shinobazu Dori, across the street from Shinobazu Pond and the Shitamachi Museum, next to KFC Home Kitchen.

INEXPENSIVE

Maharaja INDIAN   Decorated in peach and pink with etched mirrors and lots of brass, this spotless modern restaurant offers curries and tandoori at inexpensive prices including a good all-you-can-eat lunch buffet served from 11am to 3pm.

Nagafuji Bldg. Annex, 3rd floor, 4–9–6 Ueno. 🕿 03/3835-0818. Main dishes ¥1,150–¥1,950 ($9.60–$16); set meals ¥1,500–¥2,500 ($12.50–$21); lunch buffet ¥950 ($7.90) on weekdays, ¥1,270 ($11) weekends and holidays. AE, DC, JCB, MC, V. Daily 11am–9:30pm (last order). Station: JR Ueno (2 min.). In the annex of a modern building situated between Chuo Dori and the north end of Ameyokocho shopping street.

SHINJUKU

In addition to the suggestions below, be sure to check out the restaurant floors of several buildings in Shinjuku, where you can find restaurants in all price categories serving a variety of Japanese and international cuisine, some with very good views. These include the 29th and 30th floors of the **N.S. Building,** where in addition to Al Bacio and Hakkaku (described below) there are restaurants serving tempura, tonkatsu, teppanyaki, sushi, and Italian, German, and French food; the top four floors of the **Sumitomo Building,** where in addition to Donto (see review under "Hibiya & Ginza," earlier in this chapter) you'll find more than 20 outlets offering everything from tempura to Chinese cuisine; and the 12th, 13th, and 14th floors of **Takashimaya Times Square,** where in addition to Kappoya Yaozen (described below) there are restaurants serving sushi, tonkatsu, noodles, and more.

VERY EXPENSIVE

New York Grill ★★★ AMERICAN   On the 52nd floor of Tokyo's most exclusive hotel, the New York Grill has remained *the* place to dine ever since its 1994 opening; some swear it's the most sophisticated restaurant in all of Japan. Surrounded on four sides by glass, it features stunning views (especially at night), artwork by Valerio Adami, live jazz in the evenings, and a 1,600-bottle wine cellar (with an emphasis on California wines). The restaurant backs up its dramatic setting with generous portions of U.S. and Japanese steaks, seafood, and other fare ranging from delectable roast duck to rack of "certified organically raised" lamb, all prepared in an open kitchen. Both the set lunch and the weekend and holiday brunch are among the city's best and most sumptuous (reservations required)—and are great options for those who don't want to pawn their belongings to eat dinner here. I wouldn't miss it.

Park Hyatt Hotel, 3–7–1–2 Nishi-Shinjuku. ℭ 03/5322-1234. Reservations required. Main dishes ¥3,500–¥8,000 ($29–$67); set lunch ¥4,600 ($38); set dinners ¥10,000–¥15,000 ($83–$125); Sat, Sun, and holiday brunch ¥5,800 ($48). AE, DC, JCB, MC, V. Mon–Sat 11:30am–2:30pm and 5:30–10:30pm; Sun and holidays 11:30am–2:30pm and 5:30–10pm. Station: Shinjuku (west exit, a 13-min. walk or a 5-min. free shuttle ride), Hatsudai on the Keio Line (7 min.), Tochomae on Oedo Line (8 min.).

EXPENSIVE

⑲ **Kakiden** ★★ KAISEKI   Although located on the eighth floor of a rather uninspired building, Kakiden has a relaxing teahouse atmosphere with low chairs, shoji screens, bamboo trees, and soothing traditional Japanese music playing softly in the background. Sibling to another Kakiden in Kyoto that was founded more than 260 years ago as a catering service for the elite, this kaiseki restaurant serves set meals that change with the seasons according to what's fresh and available. There's an English menu listing the various set meals available, but probably the best thing to do is simply pick a meal to fit your budget. The set lunch is available until 3pm. Set dinners include box kaiseki starting at ¥5,000 ($42), mini-kaiseki for ¥8,000 ($67), and kaiseki courses ranging from ¥8,000 to ¥15,000 ($67–$125). Some of the more common dishes here include fish, seasonal vegetables, eggs, sashimi, shrimp, and mushrooms, but don't worry if you can't identify everything—I've found that even the Japanese don't always know what they're eating.

3–37–11 Shinjuku, 8th floor. ℭ 03/3352-5121. Reservations recommended for lunch. Set dinners ¥5,000–¥15,000 ($42–$125); set lunch ¥4,000 ($33). AE, DC, JCB, MC, V. Daily 11am–9pm (last order). Station: Shinjuku (east exit, 1 min.). On the east side of Shinjuku Station next to My City shopping complex.

MODERATE

Ban-Thai THAI   One of Tokyo's longest-running Thai restaurants and credited with introducing authentic Thai food to the Japanese, Ban-Thai still prepares excellent Thai dishes, with 90 mouth-watering items listed on the menu. My favorites are the cold and spicy meat salad, the chicken soup with coconut and lemon grass, and the *pat Thai* (Thai fried rice). *Note:* If you make a reservation, there's a ¥300 ($2.50) per-person table charge; also, portions are not large, so if you order several portions and add beers, your tab can really climb.

1–23–14 Kabuki-cho, 3rd floor. ℭ 03/3207-0068. Main dishes ¥1,200–¥1,800 ($10–$15); set dinners ¥2,500–¥6,000 ($21–$50); set lunches ¥600–¥900 ($5–$7.50) weekdays, ¥1,600–¥2,200 ($13–$18) weekends and holidays. AE, JCB, MC, V. Mon–Fri 11:30am–3pm and 5–11pm (last order); Sat–Sun and holidays

11:30am–11pm. Station: Shinjuku (east exit, 7 min.). In East Shinjuku in the seediest part of Kabuki-cho (don't worry, the interior is nicer than the exterior) on a neon-lit pedestrian street connecting the Koma Building with Yasukuni Dori (look for the red neon archway and Pronto coffee shop), about halfway down.

20 **Kappoya Yaozen** ⭑ KAISEKI Established 280 years ago, this Shinjuku branch in a department store has a rather plain interior, but the hostesses in kimono are friendly, and the view of surrounding Shinjuku is pleasant. It's also a very good choice for inexpensive kaiseki. A display case gives an approximation of some of the set meals available (they change with the seasons); otherwise, there's a pamphlet with pictures—or order simply according to your budget. This place is popular with older shoppers at the humongous Takashimaya Times Square, who, probably exhausted, come here for a civilized break.

Takashimaya Times Square, 14th floor, 5–24–2 Sendagaya. ✆ 03/5361-1872. Set meals ¥1,800–¥15,000 ($15–$125); set lunches ¥1,500–¥4,500 ($12.50–$37.50). AE, JCB, MC, V. Daily 11am–11pm (last order 9:30pm). Station: Shinjuku (south exit, 1 min.).

21 **Tsunahachi** TEMPURA A small, old-fashioned, brown building in the heart of fashionable East Shinjuku, this is the main shop of a restaurant that has been serving tempura since 1923. Now there are more than 40 branch restaurants in Japan, including three in Shinjuku Station alone, and others in Ginza and Akasaka. Hours may vary, but most shops are open daily from 11:30am to 10pm. This is the largest outlet, and it has an English menu; but the easiest option is to order the teishoku, the least expensive of which includes six pieces of tempura, including deep-fried shrimp, cuttlefish, white fish, green pepper, conger eel, and Japanese pickles. The most expensive teishoku has 10 pieces of tempura.

3–31–8 Shinjuku. ✆ 03/3352-1012. Reservations recommended. Tempura a la carte ¥450–¥1,200 ($3.75–$10); teishoku ¥1,100–¥1,800 ($9.15–$15). AE, JCB, V. Daily 11:15am–10pm. Station: Shinjuku San-chome (2 min.), Shinjuku (east exit, 5 min.). Off Shinjuku Dori on the side street that runs along the east side of Mitsukoshi department store.

INEXPENSIVE

Al Bacio ITALIAN This is a good place for inexpensive European-style fish in a West Shinjuku high-rise, and the N.S. Building, which has a hollow core and catwalks on upper floors, is one of my favorites. A friendly greeting, Italian contemporary music, and a view of the nearby TMG Government Offices are what you get at this casual 29th-floor restaurant. Pasta portions are large enough to serve two. A large blackboard at the door lists daily specials of fresh fish, available baked, grilled, or in papillote; a fish for two persons generally averages ¥3,000 ($25).

N.S. Building, 29th floor, 2–4–1 Nishi-Shinjuku. ✆ 03/3348-1393. Pastas ¥900–¥1,400 ($7.50–$12); main dishes ¥1,600–¥2,100 ($13–$17.50); set dinners ¥3,500 and ¥4,800 ($29 and $40); set pasta lunch ¥900 ($7.50). AE, DC, JCB, MC, V. Daily 11:30am–3pm and 5–9:30pm. Station: Tochomae (3 min.), Shinjuku Station (west exit, 8 min.).

Daikokuya *Value* SHABU-SHABU/SUKIYAKI/YAKINIKU If you're a big eater traveling on a budget, you won't want to miss dining here. This place offers only three main dishes—shabu-shabu, sukiyaki, and yakiniku—and serves up as much of it as you can consume in a 2-hour period. If you want to drink beer, whiskey, or shochu with your meal, add ¥1,100 ($9.15) to the prices, and you'll be able to drink to your heart's content as well. Popular with students and young office workers, Daikokuya is a rather strange place (its interior is kind of cavernous—maybe harking back to cave-age gluttony?) and, needless to say, can be quite rowdy.

Naka-Dai Building, 4th floor, 1–27–5 Kabuki-cho. ✆ **03/3202-7272.** All-you-can-eat main dishes ¥1,650–¥1,950 ($14–$16). No credit cards. Sun–Thurs 5–11:30pm; Fri–Sat 3pm–midnight. Station: Shinjuku (east exit, 10 min.). In Kabuki-cho, 1 block. west of Koma and across from Hotel Kent.

㉒ Hakkaku ⭐ *Finds* VARIED JAPANESE   This lively, crowded establishment has a lot going for it: a corner location in a skyscraper with expansive views over Yoyogi Park, inexpensive dishes and meals, and Kirin beer on tap. Although its decor and food resemble that of a bar, it's open for lunch and offers more variety. At lunch, only set meals are available; choose grilled fish, hirekatsu (breaded pork cutlet), or from the display case. Dinner offers a wider range of possibilities, including sashimi, grilled fish, *nikujaga* (a very tasty beef and potato stew), and salads. Yakitori, beginning at ¥300 ($2.50) per skewer, includes asparagus wrapped in bacon and tsukune, two of my favorites. Since the menu is only in Japanese, perhaps you'll want to sit at the robatayaki counter where you can point at various dishes, watch them be prepared on the open grill, and then receive them from a wooden paddle passed in your direction.

N.S. Building, 29th floor, 2–4–1 Nishi-Shinjuku. ✆ **03/3345-1848.** Main dishes ¥480–¥800 ($4–$6.65); set lunches ¥750–¥850 ($6.25–$7.10). AE, DC, JCB, MC, V. Daily 11am–3pm and 5–10pm. Station: Tochomae (3 min.), Shinjuku Station (west exit, 8 min.).

HARAJUKU & AOYAMA
EXPENSIVE

Nobu ⭐⭐ NOUVELLE JAPANESE/PACIFIC RIM   Sister restaurant to New York's Nobu, this classy, modern establishment is the place to see and be seen—and you can count on being seen since the staff yells "Irashaimase!" ("Welcome!") the minute anyone is ushered into the dining room, noisily announcing each arrival. Jazz plays softly in the background, flowers sit atop each table, and the efficient staff keeps everything running smoothly. The food, beautifully presented and served one dish at a time, is a unique blend of Pacific Rim ingredients (not quite Japanese) with decidedly American/Latin influences. Sushi and sashimi are served, as well as sushi rolls like California rolls (with avocado) and soft-shell crab rolls. Other dishes include yellowtail sashimi with jalapeño, scallop sashimi with Peruvian red chili paste, and black cod with miso. If ordering is too much of a chore, you can leave your meal to the discretion of Chef Matsuhisa by ordering the Omakase, a complete chef's-choice dinner starting at ¥10,000 ($83). Prices are less expensive at lunch; in fine weather, you can dine on an outdoor patio with a retractable roof.

6–10–17 Minami Aoyama. ✆ **03/5467-0022.** Reservations recommended. Sushi and sashimi (per piece) ¥400–¥1,400 ($3.35–$12); tempura a la carte (per piece) ¥300–¥1,400 ($2.50–$12); set dinners ¥5,000–¥20,000 ($42–$167); set lunches ¥2,800–¥7,000 ($23–$58). AE, DC, JCB, MC, V. Mon–Fri 11:30am–2pm; daily 6–10pm. Station: Shibuya or Omotesando (15 min.). On Roppongi Dori near Komazawa Dori and Kotto Dori.

Sabatini ⭐ ITALIAN   This restaurant, with its Italian furniture and tableware and strolling musicians, seems as if it has been moved intact from the Old World. In fact, the only thing to remind you that you're in Tokyo is your Japanese waiter. The Italian brothers who own Sabatini have had a restaurant in Rome for more than 40 years and take turns overseeing the Tokyo restaurants, so one of them is always here. The menu includes seafood, veal, steak, lamb, and a variety of vegetables; many of the ingredients, like olive oil, ham, salami, tomato sauce, and parmesan, are flown in fresh from Italy. Naturally, there's a wide selection of Italian wines.

Suncrest Bldg., 2–13–5 Kita-Aoyama. ✆ **03/3402-3812.** Reservations recommended for dinner. Pasta ¥1,800–¥3,200 ($15–$27); main dishes ¥2,100–¥6,500 ($17.50–$54); set dinner ¥15,000 ($125); set lunch

¥3,500–¥5,000 ($29–$42). AE, DC, JCB, MC, V. Daily 11:30am–2:30pm and 5:30–11pm. Station: Gaienmae (2 min.). On Aoyama Dori near Gaien-Nishi Dori.

MODERATE

Aux Bacchanales FRENCH   A real French sidewalk cafe, right in Tokyo's favorite people-watching neighborhood of Harajuku. Actually, the restaurant consists of two sections, both of which are packed on weekends: a brasserie with sandwiches and omelets priced at less than ¥650 ($5.40), strong espresso, and good cheap wine (counter prices are slightly cheaper than at one of the sit-down tables, just like in France); and a restaurant with both outdoor and indoor seating offering such dishes as grilled lobster, steak tartare, *lapin à la moutarde,* and lamb with thyme.

Palais France Building, 1–6–1 Jingumae (on Meiji Dori). ℂ **03/5474-0076.** Main dishes ¥2,400–¥2,800 ($20–$23). AE, DC, JCB, MC, V. Cafe daily 10am–11pm (last order); restaurant daily 6:30–10:30pm (last order). Station: Meiji-Jingumae (2 min.), Harajuku (7 min.). On Meiji Dori near Takeshita Dori.

Daini's Table ✿ NOUVELLE CHINESE   This elegant Chinese restaurant, located next to the Blue Note jazz club off Kotto Dori, serves intriguing dishes that are nicely presented one dish at a time rather than all at once as in most Chinese restaurants. It offers both traditional dishes (roast Peking duck, steamed chicken with sesame sauce, boiled prawns with red chili sauce, and hot-and-sour Peking-style soup) and more unusual combinations (stir-fried tiger prawns with spinach and garlic and stir-fried shredded beef with soy-bean paste in a pancake roll). Everything I've had here has been delicious. Expect to spend about ¥7,000 ($58) per person.

6–3–14 Minami Aoyama. ℂ **03/3407-0363.** Reservations recommended. Main dishes ¥1,800–¥3,800 ($15–$32); set dinners ¥5,000–¥12,000 ($42–$100). AE, DC, MC, V. Daily 5:30–11pm (last order). Station: Omotesando (6 min.).

El Castellano CASTILIAN   Señor Vicente Garcia is El Castellano and a true host; leave Tokyo, return 4 years later—and he still remembers who you are. And we, his faithful clients, how can we forget his smiling face? The walls of this very tiny place are covered in signatures of happy customers, some of whom (having drunk a little too much red wine) may be dancing on the tables to flamenco music. In short, this place lets diners feel at home. The custom is to let Señor Garcia order for you (although not de rigeur); he'll choose the best appetizer (tortilla or gambas, perhaps), one of the changing regional dishes, and, of course, paella, the best this side of Sevilla. Though you can eat for less, expect to spend ¥5,000 ($42) per person for dinner with wine.

2–9–11 Shibuya. ℂ **03/3407-7197.** Reservations recommended. Main dishes ¥2,300–¥2,500 ($19–$21). No credit cards. Mon–Sat 6–11pm. Station: Omotesando or Shibuya (10 min.). On Aoyama Dori about halfway between Aoyama and Shibuya, across and down the street from the National Children's Castle (not a big sign, so look).

Lunchan AMERICAN   Good American food is the forte of this contemporary, open, and airy bistro, with a dinner menu that includes pasta, pizza, sandwiches, and meat entrees. Choose from among such dishes as pizza al forno with Italian smoked ham, fresh mushrooms, oregano, and hot peppers; meat loaf; grilled snapper with lentil saffron sauce; steak; or a smoked-chicken pita sandwich. A wide selection of lunch specials is offered including sandwiches with all the trimmings. Sunday brunch, which includes a glass of champagne and is served until 3pm, features breakfast treats like eggs Benedict and pancakes, ordered from a menu.

Nightlife & Where to Stay & Dine in Harajuku

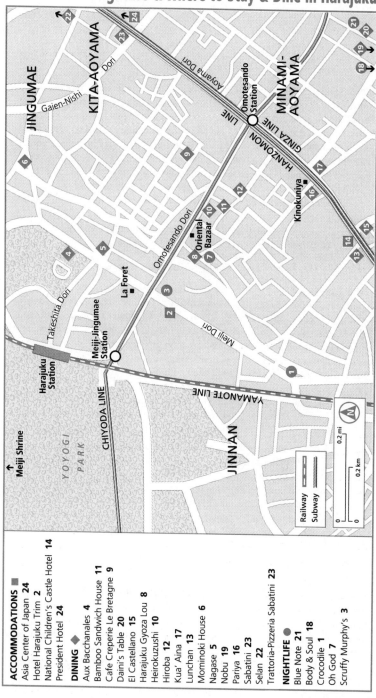

ACCOMMODATIONS ■
Asia Center of Japan **24**
Hotel Harajuku Trim **2**
National Children's Castle Hotel **14**
President Hotel **24**

DINING ◆
Aux Bacchanales **4**
Bamboo Sandwich House **11**
Cafe Creperie Le Bretagne **9**
Daini's Table **20**
El Castellano **15**
Harajuku Gyoza Lou **8**
Heirokuzushi **10**
Hiroba **12**
Kua' Aina **17**
Lunchan **13**
Mominoki House **6**
Nagase **5**
Nobu **19**
Pariya **16**
Sabatini **23**
Selan **22**
Trattoria-Pizzeria Sabatini **23**

NIGHTLIFE ●
Blue Note **21**
Body & Soul **18**
Crocodile **1**
Oh God **7**
Scruffy Murphy's **3**

1–2–5 Shibuya. ✆ 03/5466-1398. Reservations required for Sun brunch. Pizza ¥1,400–¥1,600 ($12–$13); main dishes ¥1,600–¥2,800 ($13–$23); set lunches ¥1,200–¥2,800 ($10–$23); Sunday brunch ¥2,500 ($21). AE, DC, JCB, MC, V. Mon–Sat 11:30am–10pm; Sun 11am–9pm. Station: Omotesando or Shibuya (10 min.). Easy to find, halfway between Shibuya and Aoyama and just off Aoyama Dori on the side street south of the National Children's Castle.

Selan ITALIAN   This restaurant enjoys one of the most envied spots in all of Tokyo—on a gingko-lined street that serves as the entrance to Meiji-Jingu-gaien Park. The food, Italian with Japanese and French influences, is rather ordinary, featuring main dishes like grilled Japanese steak and stewed chicken with olives, plus an assortment of pizzas and pastas—but on a warm summer's day, there's nothing more sublime than sitting on the outdoor terrace and reveling in all the greenery. The hours below are for the first-floor restaurant with its large picture windows; the ground-floor cafe, which offers the same menu, boasts an outdoor terrace open throughout the day—make that throughout the year, thanks to outdoor heaters.

2–1–19 Kita-Aoyama. ✆ 03/3478-2200. Pasta and pizza ¥1,200–¥2,200 ($10–$18); main dishes ¥2,200–¥2,800 ($18–$23); set lunches ¥1,800–¥5,000 ($15–$42). AE, DC, JCB, MC, V. Mon–Fri 11:30am–2:30pm and 6–9:30pm; Sat 10am–2:30pm and 6–9:30pm; Sun 10am–2:30pm and 6–8:30pm. Station: Gaienmae or Aoyama-Itchome (5 min.). Off Aoyama Dori, at the entrance to Meiji-Jingu-gaien Park.

INEXPENSIVE

In addition to the choices below, also consider the Aoyama branch of **Honoji,** 5–50–2 Jingumae (✆ **03/5467-6770;** open Mon–Sat 11:30am–2pm and 5:30–11pm), serving up good home-style Japanese cooking. It's off Aoyama Dori on the second side street past Kinokuniya grocery, on the right as you walk from Omotesando Station (the closest station) in the direction of Shibuya (see "Roppongi," below, for a review). Also, **La Boheme** has two locations in Harajuku: 6–7–18 Jingumae (✆ **03/3400-3406**) and 5–8–5 Jingumae (✆ **03/5467-5666**) on Omotesando Dori, both serving pizza and pasta and open daily from 11:30am to 5am (see earlier in this chapter).

Bamboo Sandwich House SANDWICHES   This is a good bet for a sandwich break in a cheerful setting. It offers 20 sandwich fillings on your choice of bread. Though the fillings can be a bit odd (unless you've been searching for chicken with tuna sauce or a potato-and-meat-sauce gratin filling), but there are also more mundane choices like tuna or roast pork, and with great outdoor seating, even a weird sandwich seems okay here.

5–8–8 Jingumae. ✆ 03/3407-8427. Sandwiches ¥340–¥700 ($2.85–$5.85). No credit cards. Daily 11am–10pm. Station: Omotesando or Meiji-Jingumae (5 min.), Harajuku (8 min.). Off Omotesando Dori on a side street that runs beside the Paul Stuart shop.

Cafe Creperie Le Bretagne (Kids CREPES   With an inviting open-fronted shop, posters of Brittany, natural wood and brick, and a French staff, this is *the* place for authentic buckwheat galettes and crepes filled with yummy fruit or chocolate or such irresistible combinations as banana, chocolate, and rum. Kids love this place, too.

4–9–8 Jingumae. ✆ 03/3478-7855. Crepes ¥700–¥1,200 ($5.85–$10). No credit cards. Tues–Thurs 11:30am–11pm; Fri–Sat 11:30am–midnight; Sun 11:30am–10pm (last order). Station: Omotesando. Off Omotesando Dori; take the side street opposite the Hanae Mori building (the one between McDonald's and Ito Hospital, with a HARAJUKU sign above it), walk to the end of the block, and turn left.

23 **Harajuku Gyoza Lou** GYOZA   If you like gyoza (pork dumplings), you owe yourself a meal here. Unlike most greasy spoons that specialize in fast-food Chinese (and tend to be on the dingy side), this restaurant in the heart of

Harajuku is hip yet unpretentious and draws in a young crowd with its straight-forward menu posted on the wall. Only four types of gyoza are offered: boiled (sui-gyoza) or fried (yaki-gyoza), with or without garlic (ninniku). A few side dishes like cucumber, boiled cabbage with vinegar, sprouts with a spicy meat sauce, and rice are available, as is beer and sake. A U-shaped counter encloses the open kitchen, giving diners something to watch as they chow down on the very good gyoza.

6–2–4 Jingumae. ℂ 03/3406-4743. Gyoza ¥290 ($2.40) for a plate of 6. No credit cards. Mon–Sat 11:30am–4:30am; Sun and holidays 11am–11:30pm. Station: Meiji-Jingumae (3 min.) or Harajuku (5 min.). From the Meiji/Omotesando Dori intersection, walk on Omotesando Dori toward Aoyama and turn right at Café de Rope; it's at the end of this street, on the right.

24 **Heirokuzushi** SUSHI   Bright (a bit too bright), clean, and modern, this is one of those fast-food sushi bars where plates of food are conducted along the counter on a conveyor belt. Customers help themselves to whatever strikes their fancy. To figure your bill, the cashier simply counts the number of plates you took from the conveyor belt: pink plates cost ¥120 ($1), green ones ¥160 ($1.35), blue ones ¥240 ($2), and black ones ¥350 ($2.90). There's a plastic display case of take-out sushi, which you might want to eat in nearby Yoyogi Park.

5–8–5 Jingumae. ℂ 03/3498-3968. Sushi ¥120–¥350 ($1–$2.90) each. No credit cards. Daily 11am–9pm. Station: Meiji-Jingumae (2 min.), Omotesando (5 min.). On Omotesando Dori close to the Oriental Bazaar.

Hiroba JAPANESE HEALTH FOOD   Located in the basement of the Crayon House, which specializes in Japanese children's books, this natural-food restaurant offers a buffet lunch of organic veggies, fish, brown rice, and other health foods. For dinner, only set meals are available. The dining hall is very simple (its atmosphere reminds me of a potluck supper in a church basement), and because of the upstairs bookstore, there are likely to be families here.

Crayon House, 3–8–15 Kita Aoyama. ℂ 03/3406-6409. Lunch buffet ¥1,200 ($10); set dinner ¥1,200 ($10). No credit cards. Daily 11am–2pm and 5–10pm. Station: Omotesando (2 min.). Off Omotesando Dori on the side street to the right of the Hanae Mori building.

Kua' Aina ⚡ *Kids* HAMBURGERS/SANDWICHES   How far will you go for a great burger? Quite simply, the best burgers in town make this Hawaiian import a smashing success, and if you come at meal time you'll probably have to wait for a table at one of the upstairs, tiny dining rooms. Burgers come as third- and whopping half-pounders, and there are also sandwiches ranging from BLT with avocado and roast beef to tuna. A good, carnivore fix.

5–10–21 Minami Aoyama. ℂ 03/3407-8001. Burgers and sandwiches ¥580–¥1,230 ($4.85–$10). No credit cards. Mon–Sat 11am–11pm; Sun 11am–10:30pm. Station: Omotesando (2 min). On Aoyama Dori at its busy intersection with Kotto Dori, catty-corner from Kinokuniya grocery store.

Mominoki House NOUVELLE JAPANESE/MACROBIOTIC   Mominoki House dishes could be described as French, except they're the creations of a very busy chef (who is also the owner) who uses lots of soy sauce, ginger, Japanese vegetables, and macrobiotic foods. This alternative restaurant, in a category by itself, features hanging plants and split-level dining, allowing for more privacy than one would think possible in such a tiny place. Its recorded jazz collection is extensive, and on most Saturday nights there's live music beginning at 8pm (music charge: ¥1,000–¥1,500/$8.35–$12.50). Dinner features approximately 50 dishes a la carte and may include the likes of tofu steak, roasted, organic chicken with rosemary, sole, eggplant gratin (delicious), salads, and homemade sorbet. Note that there's a dinner table charge of ¥300 ($2.50) per person. Especially good deals are the five daily lunch specials featuring brown rice, miso soup, seasonal vegetables, fish or another main dish, and a glass of wine. There's an English menu, but daily specials are written on the blackboard in Japanese only. The chef, Mr. Yamada, speaks English, so if in doubt ask him what he recommends.

2–18–5 Jingumae. ℂ 03/3405-9144. Main dishes ¥1,000–¥2,000 ($8.35–$17); set lunches ¥1,000–¥1,500 ($8.35–$12.50). No credit cards. Mon–Sat 11am–10:30pm (last order). Closed Golden Week. Station: Meiji-Jingumae (10 min.), Harajuku (15 min.). From the Meiji Dori/Omotesando intersection, walk north on Meiji Dori and turn right at the pedestrian overpass; it will be on the left at the 2nd street on the corner.

Nagase (★ (Finds FRENCH   This is another one of those casual neighborhood bistros offering great food at very reasonable prices that made its debut following the economic recession. Like most of the others, a cut in prices means a crowding of tables to accommodate as many diners as possible, but except for the most special of occasions, I'll gladly settle for cheaper prices over spaciousness. A French menu lists set menus that give a choice of a half-dozen main dishes, which might include the fish of the day, beef Burgundy, *confit de canard* (duck confit), or *noisettes de lamb au thym* (lamb with thyme), along with a salad or side dish, bread, and coffee. My ¥1,000 ($9) lunch was one of the best Western meals I've ever had in Japan at that price—a salad with boiled egg, chicken, mushrooms, and tomato followed by white fish on mashed potatoes with an eggplant-tomato sauce subtly flavored with curry.

3–21–12 Jingumae. ℂ 03/3423-1925. Reservations required on weekends. Set dinners ¥2,300–¥3,500 ($19–$29); set lunches ¥1,000–¥2,300 ($8.35–$19). No credit cards. Tues–Sat 11:30am–2pm and 5:30–9:30pm; Sun and holidays 11:30am–2pm and 5:30–8:30pm (last order). Station: Meiji-Jingumae (3 min.), Harajuku (8 min.). On the opposite side of Meiji Dori from Takeshita Dori, on a side street nicknamed Harajuku Dori; it's on the left side of the street, up on the second floor.

Pariya (★ VARIED JAPANESE/INTERNATIONAL   What a clever concept—design a chic, airy restaurant sure to draw in the fashionable Aoyama crowd and then keep them coming with set lunches that change weekly and let diners compose their own meals with choices of a main course, one side dish, a salad, genmai (unpolished brown rice) or hakumai (polished white rice), soup, and coffee and tea. Ethnic-influenced offerings have included grilled chicken, salmon, and sukiyaki beef, while side dishes have ranged from sweet potatoes to pasta. At dinner, the establishment is a combination bar/restaurant, with a la carte main dishes ranging from chicken in coconut sauce to shrimp gratin.

3–12–14 Kita Aoyama. ℂ 03/3486-1316. Set lunches ¥1,100 ($9.15) with genmai, ¥1,000 ($8.35) with hakumai; dinner main courses ¥900–¥1,500 ($7.50–$12.50). AE, JCB, MC, V. Mon–Sat noon–3pm and 6–9pm (last order). Station: Omotesando (4 min.). On a side street off Aoyama Dori, past Kinokuniya grocery store.

Trattoria-Pizzeria Sabatini ITALIAN   This basement restaurant, opened in 1984 and owned by two brothers from Rome who also operate Sabatini, an expensive Italian restaurant in the same building (see review above), offers the closest thing to real pizza in town. Many ingredients are flown in from Italy, including olive oil, huge slabs of Parmesan and other cheeses, as well as the restaurant's large wine selection; they've even shipped in a pasta machine. In addition to pizzas, there's also spaghetti, lasagne, fettuccine, and meat and seafood dishes. All you need order, however, is pizza.

Suncrest Bldg., 2–13–5 Kita-Aoyama. ℂ 03/3402-2027. Pasta and pizza ¥1,300–¥1,800 ($11–$15); main dishes ¥2,200–¥3,000 ($18–$25); set lunches ¥1,500–¥3,200 ($12.50–$27). AE, DC, JCB, MC, V. Mon–Sat 11:30am–2:30pm and 5:30pm–3am; Sun and holidays 11:30am–2:30pm and 5:30–11pm. Station: Gaienmae (1 min.). At the intersection of Aoyama Dori and Gaien-Nishi Dori.

SHIBUYA

Serving as a major commuter nucleus and boasting the largest concentration of fashion department stores in Tokyo, Shibuya caters primarily to students and young office workers with a lively nightlife scene offering inexpensive dining and drinking. In addition to the suggestions below, consider **Honoji,** 1–11–3 Shibuya (℃ **03/3407-4430;** open Mon–Sat 11:30am–2pm and 5:30–11pm; closed holidays; look under "Roppongi," below, for a review), as well as **La Boheme,** 1–6–8 Jinnan (℃ **03/3477-0481;** open daily 11:30am–5am; see earlier in this chapter).

INEXPENSIVE

The Aegean GREEK   This is the only Greek-owned-and-operated restaurant in Tokyo, surprising for a metropolis with so many Mediterranean-influenced restaurants. A small, basement establishment, with room for only 30 diners, it seems a bit cluttered and claustrophobic, but the limited menu includes all the Greek classics, from dolmade and Greek salad to moussaka, gyros, souvlaki and swordfish steak, along with the requisite Baklava and Greek wines. There's no regular closing date, except when owner Nik Biniari gets tired, shutters his doors, and goes on vacation. How Greek.

3–18–3 Shibuya. ℃ **03/3407-1783.** Main dishes ¥1,900–¥2,700 ($16–$22.50). AE, DC, MC, V. Daily 5:30–10:30pm. Station: Shibuya (east exit, 2 min.). On Meiji Dori avenue in the direction of Ebisu, just past the circular pedestrian overpass, on the right.

ROPPONGI

Because Roppongi is such a popular nighttime hangout for young Tokyoites and foreigners, it boasts a large number of both Japanese and Western restaurants. To find the location of any of the Roppongi addresses below, stop by the tiny police station on Roppongi Crossing (Roppongi's main intersection of Roppongi Dori and Gaien-Higashi Dori), where you'll find a map of the area. If you still don't know where to go, ask one of the policemen.

About a 10-minute walk west of Roppongi (via Roppongi Dori in the direction of Shibuya) is another popular nighttime area—**Nishi-Azabu.** Once primarily a residential neighborhood, Nishi-Azabu has slowly changed over the years as it began absorbing the overflow of Roppongi. It has restaurants and bars yet remains mellower and much less crowded than Roppongi.

VERY EXPENSIVE

㉕ **Inakaya** ★★ ROBATAYAKI   Whenever I'm playing hostess to foreign visitors in Tokyo, I always take them to this festive restaurant, and they've never been disappointed. Although tourist-oriented and pricey, it's still great fun; the drama of the place alone is worth it. Customers sit at a long, U-shaped counter, on the other side of which are mountains of fresh vegetables, beef, and seafood. And in the middle of all that food, seated in front of a grill, are male chefs—ready to cook whatever you point to in the style of robatayaki. Orders are yelled out by your waiter and are repeated in unison by all the other waiters, with the result that there's always this excited yelling going on. Sounds strange, I know, but actually it's a lot of fun. Food offerings may include yellowtail, red snapper, sole, king crab legs, giant shrimp, steak, meatballs, gingko nuts, potatoes, eggplant, and asparagus, all piled high in wicker baskets and ready for the grill. There's another nearby branch at 5–3–4 Roppongi (℃ **03/3408-5040**), open the same hours.

7–8–4 Roppongi. ℃ **03/3405-9866.** Meals average ¥12,000 ($100). AE, DC, JCB, MC, V. Daily 5pm–5am. Station: Roppongi (4 min.). On Gaien-Higashi Dori in the direction toward Akasaka, just past the Ibis Hotel on the left.

26 **Takamura** ★★★ *Finds* KAISEKI Takamura is a must for anyone who can afford it. Located on the edge of Roppongi, this wonderful 60-year-old house, perched on a hill and hidden by greenery, is like a peaceful oasis that time forgot. Each of its eight rooms is different, with bamboo and charcoal hearths built into the floor and windows looking out onto miniature gardens. Takamura has a very Japanese feeling, which intensifies proportionally with the arrival of your meal—seasonal kaiseki food arranged so artfully you almost hate to destroy it. Your pleasure increases, however, as you savor the various textures and flavors of the food. Specialties may include quail, sparrow, or duck, grilled on the hearth in your own private tatami room. Seating is on the floor, as it is in most traditional Japanese restaurants, but with leg wells. The price of dinner here usually averages about ¥27,000–¥33,000 ($225–$275) by the time you add drinks, tax, service charge, and table charge (¥2,000/$17 per person) Dinner is for parties of two or more, while lunch is available only for parties of four or larger.

3–4–27 Roppongi. ⓒ 03/3585-6600. Reservations required (1 day in advance for lunch, a week in advance for dinner, at which time you must order your meal). Set dinners ¥17,000, ¥20,000, and ¥25,000 ($142, $165, and $208); set lunches ¥13,000, ¥15,000, and ¥17,000 ($108, $125, and $142). AE, DC, JCB, MC, V. Tues–Sat noon–3pm and Mon–Sat 5–10:30pm. Closed for lunch the day following a holiday, 1st week in Jan. and 1 week in mid-Aug. Station: Roppongi (4 min.). The restaurant has 2 entrances, each marked by wooden gate with a little roof. The sign on the restaurant is in Japanese only, but look for the credit-card signs. From Roppongi Crossing, take Roppongi Dori in the direction of Kasumigaseki; turn right after the Fuji photo shop.

EXPENSIVE

27 **Fukuzushi** ★★ SUSHI This is one of Tokyo's classiest sushi bars, attracting a cosmopolitan crowd. Although it has a traditional entrance through a small courtyard with lighted lanterns and the sound of trickling water, the interior is slick and modern with bold colors of black and red. Some people swear it has the best sushi in Tokyo, although with 7,000 sushi bars in the city, I'd be hard-pressed to say which one is tops. Certainly, you can't go wrong here. Five different set lunches are available that feature sushi, *chirashi-zushi* (assorted sashimi with rice), or eel as the main course. Dinners are more extensive, with the ¥8,000 ($72) set course consisting of salad, sashimi, steamed egg custard, grilled fish, sushi, miso soup, dessert, and coffee.

5–7–8 Roppongi. ⓒ 03/3402-4116. Reservations recommended, especially for dinner. Set dinners ¥6,000–¥8,000 ($50–$67); set lunches ¥2,500–¥4,500 ($21–$37.50). AE, DC, JCB, MC, V. Mon–Sat 11:30am–2pm and 5:30–11pm; holidays 5:30–10pm. Station: Roppongi (4 min.). From Roppongi Crossing, walk toward Tokyo Tower on Gaien-Higashi Dori, turning right after McDonald's and left in front of Hard Rock Cafe.

Kisso ★★ KAISEKI I love eating here because Kisso represents all that is best about modern Japan—understated elegance and a successful marriage between the contemporary and the traditional. There should be more places like this in Tokyo. This establishment sells Japanese gourmet cookware, including expensive ceramics, utensils, and lacquerware of contemporary design, in its shop on the third floor. The restaurant, in the basement of an interesting building filled with shops dedicated to the best in interior design, is simple but elegant with heavy tables, sprigs of flowers, and soft lighting. The food is kaiseki and comes only in set meals, served (as you might guess) on beautifully lacquered bowls and trays and ceramic plates.

Axis Bldg., 5–17–1 Roppongi. ⓒ 03/3582-4191. Reservations recommended for dinner. Set dinners ¥6,000–¥13,000 ($50–$108); set lunches ¥1,200–¥5,000 ($10–$42). AE, DC, JCB, MC, V. Mon–Sat 11:30am–2pm and 5:30–9pm (last order). Closed holidays. Station: Roppongi (5 min.). From Roppongi Crossing, walk toward Tokyo Tower on Gaien-Higashi Dori; the Axis Building will be on your right.

Nightlife & Where to Stay & Dine in Roppongi

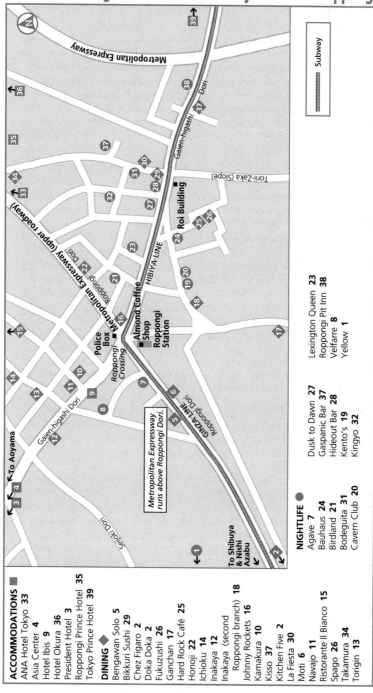

ACCOMMODATIONS ■
ANA Hotel Tokyo **33**
Asia Center **4**
Hotel Ibis **9**
Hotel Okura **36**
President Hotel **3**
Roppongi Prince Hotel **35**
Tokyo Prince Hotel **39**

DINING ◆
Bengawan Solo **5**
Bikkuri Sushi **29**
Chez Figaro **2**
Doka Doka **2**
Fukuzushi **26**
Ganchan **17**
Hard Rock Café **25**
Honoji **22**
Ichioku **14**
Inakaya **12**
Inakaya (second
  Roppongi branch) **18**
Johnny Rockets **16**
Kamakura **10**
Kisso **37**
Kitchen Five **2**
La Fiesta **30**
Moti **6**
Navajo **11**
Ristorante Il Bianco **15**
Spago **26**
Takamura **34**
Torigin **13**

NIGHTLIFE ●
Agave **7**
Bauhaus **24**
Birdland **21**
Bodeguita **31**
Cavern Club **20**
Dusk to Dawn **27**
Gaspanic Bar **37**
Hideout Bar **28**
Kento's **19**
Kingyo **32**
Lexington Queen **23**
Roppongi Pit Inn **38**
Velfarre **8**
Yellow **1**

--- Subway

Metropolitan Expressway

Metropolitan Expressway (upper roadway)

Roppongi Dori

Gaien-higashi Dori

Torii-zaka (Slope)

Roi Building

HIBIYA-LINE

Almond Coffee Shop

Roppongi Station

Police Box

Roppongi Crossing

GINZA-LINE

Roppongi Dori

Metropolitan Expressway runs above Roppongi Dori.

Gaien-higashi Dori

Seijo-Dori

To Aoyama

To Shibuya & Nishi Azabu

MODERATE

Chez Figaro TRADITIONAL FRENCH This Tokyo old-timer has been serving the same authentic, traditional French cuisine since 1969, and it's still popular with both foreigners and Japanese. A small and cozy place that has changed little over the decades, it offers such specialties as homemade paté, escargots, saffron-flavored fish soup, pepper steak, and duckling with orange sauce.

4–4–1 Nishi Azabu. ℂ 03/3400-8718. Reservations recommended. Main dishes ¥2,500–¥4,500 ($21–$37.50); set dinners ¥3,800–¥8,000 ($32–$67); set lunches ¥2,500–¥3,500 ($21–$29). AE, DC, JCB, MC, V. Daily noon–2pm and 6–9:30pm (last order). Station: Hiroo (7 min.), Roppongi (15 min.). From Hiroo, take exit 3 and walk straight toward Nishi-Azabu Crossing; the restaurant is on your left. From Roppongi, walk toward Shibuya on Roppongi, turning left onto Gaien-Nishi Dori; it will be on your right.

Doka Doka ☆ NOUVELLE JAPANESE Opened in 1996, this restaurant/drinking establishment is a curious blend of the traditional and quirky, but it's done so well that the atmosphere intrigues rather than annoys. The traditional interior features mud-textured walls, heavy wood beams, and an open coal fire in the middle of the small first floor. Balcony seating upstairs rings a hand-carved balustrade and antique shoji dating from the early Showa Period (retrieved from a former geisha house in the Yoshiwara red-light district of yore). Soft jazz plays in the background, and seating is on an odd assortment of tiny chairs imported from Africa, Tibet, Bali, and other exotic lands. The food, on a handwritten Japanese-only menu (ask the manager for explanations), changes every 3 months according to what's fresh and available. Past dishes have included duck with miso salad, fish nabe, and an excellent chicken cassoulet. The bread is homemade. Expect to spend at least ¥5,000 ($42) per person.

4–2–14 Nishi Azabu. ℂ 03/3406-1681. Reservations recommended on weekends. Main dishes ¥1,000–¥3,200 ($8.35–$27); set dinner ¥5,000 ($42). AE, DC, JCB, MC, V. Mon–Sat 6pm–3am (last order). Closed holidays. Station: Hiroo (7 min.), Roppongi (15 min.). On a small side street across Gaien-Nishi Dori from the gas station, next to Kitchen Five (see below).

Navajo ☆☆ Value PACIFIC RIM This restaurant's name is somewhat of a puzzle, but everything else falls into place once you're inside this pleasant, upscale modern establishment with its warm, natural woods, silhouette lighting, and jazz music playing softly in the background. The menu lists so many interesting choices, having to make a decision seems grossly unfair—do you start with the crab- and scallop-stuffed spring rolls in Hollandaise sauce, the rice salad with boiled crab and shrimp, or the Caesar salad? Do you go for the Southern fried catfish, served either Japanese or Cajun style, the sirloin steak in a garlic, onion, and red wine sauce, or the roasted chicken with vermouth sauce? Luckily, the friendly, multi-lingual staff, used to indecision, is knowledgeable about its unique, Japanese-Californian fusion cuisine and is not afraid to make recommendations. Best of all, prices are reasonable. No wonder people come back.

4–11–5 Roppongi. ℂ 03/3470-1717. Main dishes ¥2,200–¥3,800 ($18–$32); set lunches ¥900–¥2,500 ($7.50–$21). AE, DC, JCB, MC, V. Mon–Fri 11:30am–2pm and 6pm–5am; Sat 6–11pm. Station: Roppongi (2 min.) Off Gaien-Higashi Dori, on a side street opposite Ibis Hotel; from Roppongi Crossing, walk on Gaien-Higashi Dori in the direction of Aoyama and take the 2nd right.

Spago ☆☆ CALIFORNIAN Like its sister restaurant in Los Angeles, Spago serves innovative California cuisine popularized by its owner, world-famous Austrian-born chef Wolfgang Puck. The atmosphere here is bright, airy, and cheerful—very California—with huge bouquets of flowers, potted palms, and ferns. The menu changes every 3 months to reflect what's in season; expect the likes of angel-hair pasta with fresh thyme in goat cheese sauce and broccoli, grilled swordfish with jalapeno-cilantro-cumin vinaigrette, and roasted baby lamb with marsala wine sauce and mashed potatoes (small portions are available). If you order pizza, it will come not with tomato sauce but with olive oil, making it much lighter, so the emphasis is on the toppings. Needless to say, the main dishes are always imaginative, and the service is great. Dining here is a pleasure; I especially like the no-smoking terrace. As you might expect, Spago has one of the largest selections of California wines in town. For dessert, try the homemade ice cream.

5–7–8 Roppongi. (*C*) 03/3423-4025. Reservations required. Pizza and pasta ¥1,900–¥2,000 ($16–$17); main dishes ¥3,000–¥4,900 ($25–$41); set lunches ¥1,900–¥5,000 ($16–$42). AE, DC, JCB, MC, V. Mon–Fri 11:30am–2pm and 6–10pm; Sat–Sun 11:30am–2pm and 6–9:30pm; holidays 6–9:30pm. Station: Roppongi (4 min.). From Roppongi Crossing, walk toward Tokyo Tower on Gaien-Higashi Dori, turning right after McDonald's and left in front of Hard Rock Cafe.

INEXPENSIVE

Bengawan Solo INDONESIAN   This was one of the first ethnic restaurants to open in Tokyo (in 1957), and you're likely to find some old Tokyo hands dining here. Friendly Indonesian waiters and decor add to the spicy goodness of Bengawan's traditional Indonesian food, with perennial favorites including beef in hot sauce and shrimp in coconut cream. There are lots of healthy vegetarian choices, too, such as *tempeh* (Indonesian tofu) and gado-gado salad (with peanut sauce).

7–18–13 Roppongi. (*C*) 03/3408-5698. Main dishes ¥1,200–¥1,800 ($10–$15); set lunches ¥800–¥1,200 ($6.65–$10); set dinners ¥3,500–¥5,500 ($29–$46). AE, JCB, MC, V. Daily 11:30am–3pm and 5–11pm (last order 10pm). Station: Roppongi (C2 exit, 2 min.). On Roppongi Dori on the right side of the street if you're walking from Roppongi Crossing toward Shibuya, across from the Wave Building.

(28) **Bikkuri Sushi** (*Value* SUSHI   This is one of the cheapest places to eat in this popular nightlife district. Plates of sushi move along a conveyor belt past customers seated at the counter, who simply help themselves to whichever plates strike their fancy; this makes dining a cinch since it's not necessary to know the name of anything. The white plates of sushi are all priced at ¥130 ($1.10), while the colored dishes run ¥250 ($2.10) and ¥650 ($5.40). Your bill is tallied according to the number of plates you've taken.

3–14–9 Roppongi. (*C*) 03/3403-1489. Dishes ¥130–¥650 ($1.10–$5.40). No credit cards. Daily 11am–5am. Station: Roppongi (3 min.). On the left-hand side of Gaien-Higashi Dori (the road leading to Tokyo Tower), across the street from the Roi Building.

(29) **Ganchan** ✿ YAKITORI   This is one of my favorite yakitori-ya, and I've spent many a night here. Small and intimate, it's owned by a friendly and entertaining man who can't speak English worth a darn but keeps trying with the help of a worn-out Japanese-English dictionary he keeps behind the counter. His staff is young and fun loving. There's an eclectic cassette collection—I never know whether to expect Japanese pop tunes or Simon and Garfunkel. Seating is along just one counter with room for only a dozen or so people. Though there's an English menu, it's easiest to order the yakitori seto, a set course that comes with salad and soup and eight skewers of such items as chicken, beef, meatballs, green peppers, and asparagus with rolled bacon. Be aware that there's a table charge of ¥600 ($5) per person, which includes an appetizer.

6–8–23 Roppongi. (*C*) 03/3478-0092. Yakitori skewers ¥200–¥400 ($1.65–$3.35); yakitori set course ¥2,500 ($21). AE, JCB, V. Mon–Sat 5:30pm–2am; Sun and holidays 5:30pm–midnight. Station: Roppongi (7 min.). From Roppongi Crossing, take the small street going downhill to the left of the Almond Coffee Shop; Ganchan is at the bottom of the hill on the right.

Hard Rock Cafe *Kids* AMERICAN   Founded by two American expatriates in London in 1971, Hard Rock Cafe now has half a dozen locations in Japan; this was the first. If you have disgruntled teenagers in tow, bring them to this world-famous hamburger joint dedicated to rock-and-roll to ogle the memorabilia on the walls, chow down on a burger, and look over the T-shirts for sale. In addition to hamburgers, the menu includes salads, sandwiches, steak, barbecued ribs, barbecued chicken, a fish of the day, and fajitas. The music, by the way, is loud.

5–4–20 Roppongi. ✆ **03/3408-7018.** Main dishes ¥1,380–¥3,000 ($12–$25). AE, DC, JCB, MC, V. Sun–Thurs 11:30am–2am; Fri–Sat 11:30am–4am; holidays 11:30am–11:30pm. Station: Roppongi (3 min.). From Roppongi Crossing, walk on Gaien-Higashi Dori toward Tokyo Tower and take a right at McDonald's.

③⓪ **Honoji** ★ *Finds* JAPANESE   A plain wooden facade and a no-nonsense interior of concrete walls with wire-mesh screens set the mood for what this restaurant offers: good, home-style Japanese cooking, along with some Japanese interpretations of Western food. Although it looks small at first glance (an open kitchen takes up half the space), there are backroom nooks and crannies that give diners a sense of privacy as they enjoy grilled fish, sashimi, yakitori, grilled eggplant with miso, deep-fried tofu, and a few Western dishes like a creamed spinach and scallop gratin. It serves the kinds of food offered by neighborhood *nomiya* (drinking establishments) all over Japan, which isn't exactly the kind of fare you'd expect to find in trendy Roppongi. Still, the crowds that wait at the door, especially on weekend nights, attest to its success. There's an English menu, but probably the best deal is the set dinner, which includes sashimi, a main dish such as grilled fish, seasonal vegetables, and several other side dishes. Otherwise, expect to spend ¥3,000 to ¥3,500 ($27–$31.50) per person; note that there's a ¥450 ($3.75) table charge at night. The lunch teishoku, available for ¥900 ($7.50) and the only item offered for lunch, draws Japanese from all walks of life.

You'll find other branches in Harajuku at 5–50–2 Jingumae (✆ **03/5467-6770;** open Mon–Sat 11:30am–2pm and 5:30–11pm) and in Shibuya at 1–11–3 Shibuya (✆ **03/3407-4430;** open Mon–Sat 11:30am–2pm and 5:30–11pm).

3–4–33 Roppongi. ✆ **03/3588-1065.** Main dishes ¥400–¥680 ($3.35–$5.65); set dinner ¥3,000 ($25). AE, DC, MC, V. Mon–Fri 11:30am–1:30pm (last order); Mon–Sat 5:30–11pm (last order 10:15pm). Station: Roppongi (3 min.). On the right side of Roppongi Dori as you walk from Roppongi Crossing in the direction of Akasaka.

③① **Ichioku** ★ JAPANESE ORIGINALS   This is one of my favorite restaurants in Tokyo for casual dining. It's a tiny, cozy place with only eight tables, and you fill out your order yourself from the menu in English, complete with pictures, glued onto your table underneath clear glass. The food, featuring organically grown vegetables, can best be called Japanese nouvelle cooking, with original creations offered at very reasonable prices. There's tuna and ginger sauté, mushroom sauté, shrimp spring rolls, Thai curry, asparagus salad, fried potatoes, and a dish of crumbled radish and tiny fish. I recommend the tofu steak (fried tofu and flakes of dried fish) as well as the cheese *gyoza* (a fried pork dumpling with cheese melted on it). The average check here is ¥2,500 to ¥3,000 ($21–$25).

4–4–5 Roppongi. ✆ **03/3405-9891.** Main dishes ¥800–¥2,450 ($6.65–$20). AE, DC, MC, V. Mon–Fri 11:30am–2pm and 5pm–midnight (last order); Sat 5pm–midnight; holidays 5–10pm. Station: Roppongi (4 min.). On a side street in the neighborhood behind the police station; look for the Rastafarian colors and a yin/yang sign.

Johnny Rockets HAMBURGERS   This used to be the best hamburger joint in town til Kua' Aina (see review earlier in this chapter) opened up shop, but the burgers are still very good. Since the regular burgers are huge (I've seen sumo wrestlers stocking up here), I was glad when smaller versions were added to the menu. Perched on the second floor of a building at Roppongi Crossing with views of the madness below, Johnny Rockets is decorated like an American 1950s diner. Seating is on a first-come, first-served basis at the counters, and smoking is not allowed. Other goodies on the menu include sandwiches, fries (which you can get topped with chili), malts, shakes, floats, and pie à la mode. It definitely hits the spot, especially after a night of carousing. From 11am to 4pm daily, a fixed-price lunch offers a hamburger or sandwich, fries, and a drink (unlimited refills).

3–11–10 Roppongi, Roppongi Crossing. ℂ 03/3423-1955. Hamburgers ¥600–¥1,200 ($5–$10); set lunches ¥800–¥1,100 ($6.65–$9.15). No credit cards. Sun–Thurs 11am–11pm; Fri and Sat 11am–5am. Station: Roppongi.

Kamakura YAKITORI   More refined than most yakitori-ya, this basement establishment is decorated with paper lanterns and sprigs of fake but cheerful spring blossoms, with traditional koto music playing softly in the background. The English menu lists yakitori set courses, and a la carte sticks include those with shrimp, meatballs, gingko, squid, eggplant, and mushrooms.

4–10–11 Roppongi. ℂ 03/3405-4377. Yakitori skewers ¥180–¥280 ($1.50–$2.35); set dinners ¥2,300–¥4,300 ($19–$36). AE, DC, JCB, MC, V. Mon–Sat 5pm–midnight. Station: Roppongi (2 min.). Off Gaien-Higashi Dori on a side street opposite Ibis Hotel; from Roppongi Crossing, walk on Gaien-Higashi Dori in the direction of Aoyama and take the 2nd right.

Kitchen Five ★ *Finds* MEDITERRANEAN/ETHNIC   If it's true that cooking with love is the best spice, then perhaps that's why Yuko Kobayashi's 15-year-old, 16-seat restaurant is so popular. She goes to market every morning to fetch ingredients for a dozen main dishes, which can include stuffed eggplant, moussaka, and various other casseroles and curries. Every summer Kobayashi goes off to search for recipes in Sicily, South America, northern Africa, and other countries that feature garlic, tomatoes, and olive oil in their cuisine. The love for what she does shines in her eyes as she cooks, serves, and walks you through the menu of daily dishes displayed. *A word of warning:* The food is so delicious, it's tempting to overorder. Highly recommended.

4–2–15 Nishi-Azabu. ℂ 03/3409-8835. Dishes ¥1,300–¥1,900 ($11–$16). No credit cards. Tues–Sat 6–9:45pm (last order). Closed holidays, Golden Week, and late July–early Sept. Station: Hiroo (7 min.), Roppongi (15 min.). Opposite Gaien-Nishi Dori from the gas station, down a side street.

La Fiesta MEXICAN   While there are an ever-growing number of Mexican restaurants in Tokyo, the majority serve only passable food. This one, however, is better than most, and while its renditions may not be what you're used to, they're usually very tasty in their own right and are good for a spicy fix. Colorfully decorated with South-of-the-Border memorabilia and with lively, Mexican music to set the pace, it offers quesadillas, enchiladas, tacos, chimichangas, fajitas, and very good burritos. And of course, everything goes down better with a margarita; Mexican beers and a good selection of tequilas are also available.

3–15–23 Roppongi. ℂ 03/3475-4412. Main dishes ¥800–¥2,280 ($7–$19); fixed-price meals ¥1,580–¥2,850 ($13–$24). AE, DC, JCB, MC, V. Station: Roppongi (4 min.). From Roppongi Crossing, walk down Gaien-Higashi Dori in the direction of Tokyo Tower, turning left after passing McDonald's on your right.

Moti INDIAN   This is my favorite Indian restaurant in town. Dishes include vegetable curries, chicken and mutton curries (I usually opt for the sag mutton—lamb with spinach), and tandoori chicken. Set lunches, served until 2:30pm, offer a choice of vegetable, chicken, or mutton curry along with Indian bread (naan) and tea or coffee.

6–2–35 Roppongi. ✆ 03/3479-1939. Main dishes ¥1,300–¥1,500 ($11–$12.50); set dinners ¥2,600–¥3,000 ($22–$25); set lunches ¥950–¥1,350 ($7.90–$11) Mon–Sat, ¥1,250–¥1,650 ($10–$14) Sun and holidays. AE, DC, JCB, MC, V. Mon–Sat 11:30am–10pm (last order); Sun and holidays noon–10pm. Station: Roppongi (3 min.). From Roppongi Crossing, walk toward Shibuya on Roppongi Dori; it will be on the left.

Ristorante Il Bianco ITALIAN   My friends and I don't know how they do it (or why, considering they probably lose money on us), but this very tiny Italian restaurant offers inexpensive wines (mostly from Chile) beginning at ¥1,000 ($8.35) for a bottle. More amazing, you can bring in your own favorite bottle without paying a corkage fee. Pasta comes in three sizes, with the smallest size perfect as a starter for one person. The larger sizes can be shared. Main courses include veal and spinach gratin, roast chicken, wrapped white fish with potato, wild roast duck, and grilled filet mignon. The only problem is finding the place—stop at the police station at Roppongi Crossing to look at the map or ask for directions. And once you get there, be sure to take the stairs to the second-floor restaurant unless you want a cheap thrill—the elevator deposits you directly into the kitchen.

4–5–2 Roppongi. ✆ 03/3470-5678. Reservations a must for dinner. Pasta ¥1,300–¥1,400 ($11–$12); main dishes ¥1,500–¥2,000 ($12.50–$17); set dinners ¥4,000–¥5,000 ($33–$67); set lunches ¥1,000–¥2,800 ($8.35–$23). AE, DC, MC, V. Mon–Fri 11:30am–2pm and 5–10pm (last order); Sat 5–10pm. Station: Roppongi (3 min.). From Roppongi Crossing, take Roppongi Dori in the direction toward Akasaka, turning left at the stop light with a small park and water fountain; it's down this street, on the left.

㉜ **Torigin** YAKITORI/RICE CASSEROLES   Part of a chain of yakitori establishments, this no-frills place is typical of the smaller Japanese restaurants all over the country patronized by the country's salarymen, who stop off for a drink and a bite to eat before boarding the commuter trains for home. An English menu includes skewers of grilled chicken, gingko nuts, green peppers, quail eggs, and asparagus with rolled bacon as well as various *kamameshi* (rice casseroles cooked and served in their own little pots and topped with chicken, bamboo shoots, mushrooms, crab, salmon, or shrimp).

4–12–6 Roppongi. ✆ 03/3403-5829. Yakitori skewers ¥140–¥250 ($1.15–$2.10); kamameshi ¥800–¥1,200 ($6.65–$10). No credit cards. Mon–Sat 11:30am–2pm and 5–11pm. Station: Roppongi (2 min.). From Roppongi Crossing, take Gaien-Higashi Dori in the direction of Akasaka and take the 3rd right.

AKASAKA
VERY EXPENSIVE

La Tour d'Argent ✿✿ CLASSIC FRENCH   Here's the place to dine if you're celebrating a very special occasion, are on a hefty expense account, or fancy yourself a jet-setter. Opened in 1984, La Tour d'Argent is the authentic sister to the one in Paris, which opened back in 1582 and was visited twice by Japan's former emperor Hirohito. Entrance to the Tokyo restaurant is through an impressive hallway with a plush interior and displays of tableware used in the Paris establishment throughout the centuries. The dining hall looks like an elegant Parisian drawing room. The service is superb, and the food is excellent. The specialty here is roast duckling—it meets its untimely end at the age of 3 weeks and is flown to Japan from Brittany. Other dishes on the menu, which changes seasonally, may include sea bass, frog legs, lobster casserole, young pigeon, or Kobe beef sirloin.

Hotel New Otani, 4–1 Kioi-cho. ⓒ 03/3239-3111. Reservations required. Main dishes ¥6,500–¥12,000 ($54–$100). AE, CB, DC, JCB, MC, V. Tues–Sun 5:30–10:30pm (last reservation accepted for 8:30pm). Station: Akasaka-mitsuke or Nagatacho (3 min.).

Sekishin Tei ★★ TEPPANYAKI Nestled in the New Otani's 400-year-old garden (and the reason it's the hotel's most popular restaurant), this teppanyaki restaurant is composed of three glass-enclosed pavilions, all with the same menu of Kobe beef, fish, lobster, and vegetables cooked on a grill right in front of you. If you order a salad, try the soy-sauce dressing; it's delicious. You'll eat surrounded by peaceful views, making this place a good lunchtime choice.

Hotel New Otani, 4–1 Kioi-cho, Chiyoda-ku. ⓒ 03/3238-0024. Reservations required. Set dinners ¥13,000–¥18,000 ($108–$150); set lunches ¥3,500–¥6,000 ($29–$50). AE, DC, JCB, MC, V. Mon–Fri 11:30am–2pm and 6–9pm; Sat–Sun and holidays 11:30am–3pm and 6–9pm. Station: Nagatacho or Akasaka-mitsuke (3 min.).

EXPENSIVE

㉝ **Hayashi** ★★★ JAPANESE GRILL/RICE CASSEROLES One of the most delightful old-time restaurants I've been to, this cozy, rustic-looking place serves home-style country cooking and specializes in grilled food that you prepare yourself over your own square hibachi. Altogether, there are 10 grills in this small, two-story restaurant, some of them surrounded by tatami mats and some by wooden stools or chairs. As the evening wears on, the one-room main dining areas can get quite smoky, but somehow that just adds to the ambience. Other nice touches are the big gourds and memorabilia hanging about and the waiters in traditional baggy pants. Hayashi serves three set menus, which change with the seasons. The ¥6,000 ($50) meal—which will probably end up being closer to ¥8,000 ($67) by the time you add drinks, tax, and service charge—may include such items as sashimi and vegetables, chicken, scallops, and gingko nuts, which you grill yourself. At lunch, only *oyakodomburi* is served: literally, "parent and child," a simple rice dish topped with egg and chicken.

Sanno Kaikan Bldg., 3rd and 4th floors, 2–14–1 Akasaka. ⓒ 03/3582-4078. Reservations required for dinner. Set dinners ¥6,000, ¥8,000, and ¥10,000 ($50, $67, and $83). AE, DC, JCB, MC, V. Mon–Fri 11:30am–2pm and 5:30–11pm; Sat 5:30–11pm. Closed holidays. Station: Akasaka (exit 2, 1 min.). Just south of Misuji Dori on the 3rd and 4th floors of a nondescript, improbable-looking building.

㉞ **Zakuro** ★ SHABU-SHABU/SUKIYAKI Zakuro, a local chain, is one of several restaurants claiming to have introduced shabu-shabu in Japan. It serves Kobe beef, and is decorated with folk art (including works by famous Japanese artists Shiko Munakata and Shoji Hamada). Friendly, kimono-clad hostesses serve shabu-shabu, sukiyaki, tempura, and teriyaki beef, all available as set dinners with various side dishes. At lunch there are set meals of tempura, sashimi, sukiyaki, and teriyaki beef. Since Zakuro (which means "pomegranate") has an English menu, ordering is no problem. It's a popular place to bring visiting foreign clients.

You'll find other Zakuro restaurants in front of the American Embassy (ⓒ 03/3582-2661), in Nihombashi south of the Takashimaya department store (ⓒ 03/3271-3791), and in Ginza south of Matsuya department store (ⓒ 03/3535-4221).

TBS Kaikan Bldg. basement, 5–3–3 Akasaka. ⓒ 03/3582-6841. Reservations recommended. Set dinners ¥6,800–¥16,000 ($57–$133); set lunches ¥1,500–¥3,800 ($12.50–$32). AE, DC, JCB, MC, V. Daily 11am–10pm (last order). Station: Akasaka (TBS exit, 1 min.).

MODERATE

Blue Sky CHINESE   Located on the 17th floor of the New Otani's main building with great views of the city, this revolving restaurant provides panoramic views and all-you-can eat buffets, primarily Chinese. The food, tasty and varied, consists of approximately 40 different items for lunch and 50 for dinner and includes spicy Szechuan cuisine, dim sum, Japanese food, and freshly baked pizza. My only complaint is that the restaurant revolves at a breakneck speed that matches fast-paced Tokyo, making a complete turn every 45 minutes. If the thought makes you dizzy, there's another buffet-style restaurant called **Top of the Tower** on the 40th floor of the New Otani's tower, also with spectacular views of the city and offering continental buffet lunches for ¥4,800 ($40) and dinners for ¥7,500 ($62.50).

Hotel New Otani, 4–1 Kioi-cho, Chiyoda-ku. (℃ **03/3238-0028**. Dinner buffet ¥6,300 ($52.50); lunch buffet ¥3,500 ($29). AE, DC, JCB, MC, V. Daily 11:30am–2pm and 5–9pm. Station: Akasaka-mitsuke or Nagatacho (3 min.).

daidaiya *Finds* VARIED JAPANESE/NOUVELLE JAPANESE   You'd be forgiven upon stepping out of the elevator for confusedly thinking you've landed in a nightclub rather than a restaurant—the daidaiya's theatrical, dark entrance is the first clue that this is not your ordinary Japanese restaurant. The dining room, a juxtaposition of the modern and traditional with a slate stone floor, shoji screens, warm woods, and black furniture, is rather like the cuisine—a curious mix of traditional Japanese food and original nouvelle creations, all mouthwateringly good. Jazz music plays in the background; tatami seating is also available, with views over Akasaka. An English menu lists such intriguing entrees as deep-fried tilefish—crunchy on the outside—topped with spring onions and served with a miso dipping sauce, and Okinawan pork, simmered in sweet sauce and served with a risotto of mustard and wild plants. Lunch sets, including obento, are equally satisfying. I love this place.

Bellevie Akasaka Building, 9th floor, 3–1–6 Akasaka. (℃ **03/3588-5087**. Reservations recommended for dinner. Main dishes ¥1,200–¥2,500 ($10–$21); set dinners ¥5,000–¥7,000 ($42–$58); set lunches ¥800–¥2,000 ($6.65–$17). AE, DC, JCB, MC, V. Mon–Fri 11:30am–2pm and 5pm–midnight (last order); Sat–Sun 11:30am–11pm. Station: Akasaka-mitsuke (1 min., underneath Bellevie Akasaka Building).

INEXPENSIVE

Don't forget to consider **Hayashi,** on the fourth floor of the Sanno Kaikan Building, 2–14–1 Akasaka, described above as an expensive restaurant. I mention it again here simply because I don't want those of you on a budget to miss it. This is one of the coziest and most delightful restaurants in town. Although dinner is costly, you can enjoy the same atmosphere for much, much less at lunch when only one dish, *oyakodomburi* (rice with chunks of chicken and omelet on top), is served with pickled vegetables, clear soup, and tea for ¥900 ($7.50). Open for lunch Monday through Friday from 11:30am to 2pm.

Akasaka is also home to two branches of **Moti,** my favorite Indian restaurant in town, with branches on the second floor of the Akasaka Floral Plaza, 3–8–8 Akasaka (℃ **03/3582-3620**), and on the third floor of the Kinpa Building, 2–14–31 Akasaka (℃ **03/3584-6640**). See p. 158 for a complete review. Finally, a branch of **Shabusen,** which specializes in inexpensive shabu-shabu, is located in the basement of the TBS building at 5–3–3 Akasaka (℃ **03/3582-8161**). See p. 138 for a complete review.

㉟ **Kankoku-Kan** KOREAN   Akasaka is home to many Korean restaurants, saunas, and shops. This one is one of the most accessible, with an easy-to-find location and a friendly staff. Try the yakiniku, a cook-it-yourself meal of beef, pork, or chicken; chapche, a noodle and vegetable dish; chagaemonchun, a kind of potato pancake; or ask the staff for a recommendation. If you like spicy foods, you shouldn't pass up the kimchi, a fiery cabbage side dish.

3–9–6 Akasaka. ✆ **03/3582-2989.** Main dishes ¥800–¥3,500 ($6.65–$29). AE, DC, JCB, MC, V. Daily 11:30am–midnight. Station: Akasaka-mitsuke (1 min.). Across from Bellevie Akasaka Building; look for the WELCOME TO KOREA sign.

4

Exploring Tokyo

Tokyo hasn't fared very well over the centuries. Fires and earthquakes have taken their toll, old buildings have been torn down in the zeal of modernization, and World War II left most of the city in ruins. The Tokyo of today has very little remaining of historical significance. Save your historical sightseeing for places like Kyoto, Nikko, and Kamakura and consider Tokyo your introduction to the newest of the new in Japan, the showcase of the nation's accomplishments in the arts, technology, fashion, and design. It's also the best place in the world for taking in Japan's performing arts, such as Kabuki, and such diverse activities as the tea ceremony, flower arranging, and sumo. Tokyo also has more museums than any other city in Japan, as well as a wide range of other attractions, including parks and temples. Here you can explore mammoth department stores, experiment with restaurants, walk around the various neighborhoods, revel in pop art and kitsch, and take advantage of glittering nightlife. There's so much to do in Tokyo that I can't imagine being bored—even for a minute.

SEEING THE CITY BY GUIDED TOUR
With the help of this book and a good map, you should be able to visit Tokyo's major attractions easily on your own. However, if you are pressed for time, consider taking one of several group tours of Tokyo and its environs offered by the **Japan Travel Bureau (JTB)** (© 03/5796-5454) and such tour companies as the **Japan Gray Line** (© 03/3433-5745 and 03/3436-6881). Day tours may include Tokyo Tower, the Imperial Palace district, Asakusa Sensoji Temple, Meiji Jingu Shrine, a harbor or river cruise, and the Ginza. There are also a number of organized evening tours that take in such activities as Kabuki or entertainment by Geisha. Be warned, however, that tours are very tourist-oriented and are more expensive than touring Tokyo on your own. Prices range from about ¥4,000 ($33) for a morning tour to about ¥9,800 ($82) for a night tour with dinner and Kabuki. You can easily book tours through most tourist hotels and travel agencies.

For more personalized, one-on-one tours of Tokyo, contact **Jun's Tokyo Discovery Tours,** managed by Tokyoite Junko Matsuda, which offers tailored sightseeing trips to Tsukiji, Asakusa, Yanaka, Harajuku, Aoyama, Shibuya, and Shinjuku, as well as shopping trips (like to Sunday morning flea markets held at local shrines) and special-interest trips according to your interests. Tours, which are especially useful if you wish to communicate with shopkeepers and the locals, learn more about what you're seeing, or are timid about finding your way on public transportation (if you wish, you'll be met at your hotel), cost ¥2,000 ($17) per hour (minimum of 3 hr.) and are available for up to four adults or a family. Reserve tours at least three days in advance (1 week preferred) by fax (fax 03/3749-0445) or e-mail (me2@gb3.so-net.ne.jp), stating your desired date, approximate number of hours, and what you'd like to see; messages can also be left at © 03/3749-0445.

SUGGESTED ITINERARIES FOR SEEING THE CITY

There are two things to remember in planning your sightseeing itinerary: The city is huge, and it takes time to get from one end to the other. Plan your days so you cover Tokyo neighborhood by neighborhood, coordinating sightseeing with dinner and evening plans. The suggested itineraries below will guide you to the most important attractions, but note that some attractions are closed 1 day of the week.

If You Have 1 Day   Start by getting up in the wee hours of the morning (if you've just flown in from North America, you'll be suffering from jet lag anyway and will find yourself wide awake by 5am) and head for the **Tsukiji Fish Market,** Japan's largest wholesale fish market (closed Sun, holidays, and some Wed). Be brave and try a breakfast of the freshest sushi you'll ever have. By 9am you should be on the Hibiya Line on your way to Ueno, where you should head to the **Tokyo National Museum,** the country's largest and most important museum of Japanese art (closed Mon). From there, you should head to Asakusa for lunch in one of the area's traditional Japanese restaurants, followed by a walk on Nakamise Dori (good for souvenirs) to **Sensoji Temple.** In the late afternoon, you might want to go to Ginza for some shopping, followed by dinner in a restaurant of your choice. Drop by a yakitori-ya, a typical Japanese watering hole, for a beer and a snack. You might be exhausted by the end of the day, but you'll have seen some of the city's highlights.

If You Have 2 Days   On the first day, get up early and go to **Tsukiji Fish Market.** Next, head for the nearby **Hama Rikyu Garden,** which opens at 9am. It's about a 20-minute walk from Tsukiji or a short taxi ride away. After touring the garden, one of the city's best, board the ferry that departs from inside the grounds for a trip up the Sumida River to Asakusa, where you can visit **Sensoji Temple** and shop along Nakamise Dori, followed by lunch in a traditional Japanese restaurant. You might even wish to follow "A Walking Tour of Asakusa," described later in this chapter. In the afternoon, head to the Ginza with its many department stores. If there's a performance, drop by the **Kabukiza theater** for part of a Kabuki play. Have dinner at a Ginza restaurant.

On your second day, go early in the morning to the **Edo-Tokyo Museum** (located next to the sumo stadium), a great museum that illuminates the city's tumultuous history. Next, head to Ueno, where you should walk through Ueno Park to the **Tokyo National Museum.** From there, board the JR Yamanote Line to Harajuku, where you can visit **Meiji Jingu Shrine,** Tokyo's most famous Shinto shrine; the **Ota Memorial Museum of Art** with its collection of woodblock prints; and the **Oriental Bazaar,** a great place to shop for souvenirs. Spend the evening in one of Tokyo's famous nightlife districts such as Shinjuku or Roppongi.

If You Have 3 Days   Spend the first 2 days as outlined above; on the 3rd day head for **Kamakura,** one of Japan's most important historical sites. Located an hour south of Tokyo by train, Kamakura served as the capital back in the 1100s and is packed with temples and shrines, one of which features the Great Buddha outdoor bronze statue.

If You Have 4 or 5 Days   Consider yourself lucky. Spend the first 3 days as outlined above; devote the 4th day to pursuing your own interests, such as taking a trip to one of Tokyo's numerous art or specialty museums, making an appointment with an acupuncturist, shopping, or following one of the recommended walking tours in this chapter. This may be the evening to spend in wild partying, staying out until the first subways start running at 5am.

If you have a 5th day, you might visit **Nikko,** approximately 2 hours north of Tokyo, to see the sumptuous mausoleum of Tokugawa Ieyasu, the shogun who succeeded in unifying Japan in the 1600s. Or you might consider a 2-day trip to **Hakone,** famous for its fantastic open-air sculpture museum and home to some of the best old-fashioned Japanese inns near Tokyo. Hakone also offers unparalleled views of Mt. Fuji if the weather is clear. See chapter 5 for more ideas on side trips from Tokyo.

1 The Top Attractions

The Imperial Palace (Kyokyo)   The Imperial Palace is the heart and soul of Tokyo. Built on the very spot where Edo Castle used to stand during the days of the Tokugawa shogunate, it became the imperial home upon its completion in 1888 and is now the residence of Emperor Akihito, 125th emperor of Japan. Destroyed during air raids in 1945, the palace was rebuilt in 1968 using the principles of traditional Japanese architecture. But don't expect to get a good look at it; most of the palace ground's 284 acres are off-limits to the public, with the exception of 2 days a year when the royal family makes an appearance before the throngs: New Year's Day and on the Emperor's birthday (Dec 23). Still, all Japanese tourists make brief stops here to pay their respects. You'll have to console yourself with a camera shot of the palace from the southeast side of **Nijubashi Bridge** with the moat and the palace turrets showing above the trees. The wide moat, lined with cherry trees, is especially beautiful in the spring. You might even want to spend an hour strolling the 3 miles around the palace and moat.

But the most important thing to do in the vicinity of the palace is to visit its **Higashi Gyoen** (East Garden), where you'll find what's left of the central keep of old Edo Castle, the stone foundation; see "Parks & Gardens," later in this chapter.

Hibiya Dori Ave. Station: Nijubashi-mae (1 min.) or Hibiya (5 min.).

Sensoji Temple ★★★   This is Tokyo's oldest and most popular temple, with a history dating back to 628. That was when, according to popular lore, two brothers fishing in the nearby Sumida River netted the catch of their lives—a tiny golden statue of Kannon, the Buddhist goddess of mercy and happiness who is empowered with the ability to release humans from all suffering. Sensoji Temple (also popularly known as Asakusa Kannon) was erected in her honor, and although the statue is housed here, it's never shown to the public. Still, through the centuries, worshippers have flocked here, seeking favors of Kannon; and when Sensoji Temple burned down during a 1945 bombing raid, the present structure was rebuilt with donations by the Japanese people.

Colorful **Nakamise Dori,** a pedestrian lane leading to the shrine, is lined with traditional shops and souvenir stands, while nearby **Demboin Garden** remains an insider's favorite as a peaceful oasis away from the bustling crowds. Asakusa is one of my favorite neighborhoods, and you can easily spend half a day here; see the walking tour later in this chapter for more on this fascinating part of old Tokyo.

2–3–1 Asakusa, Taito-ku. ✆ 03/3842-0181. Free admission. Open 24 hours. Station: Asakusa (2 min.).

Meiji Jingu Shrine ★★   This is Tokyo's most venerable Shinto shrine, opened in 1920 in honor of Emperor and Empress Meiji, who were instrumental in opening Japan to the outside world more than 120 years ago. Japan's two largest *torii* (the traditional entry gate of a shrine), built of cypress more than 1,700 years old, give dramatic entrance to the grounds, once the estate of a *daimyo* (feudal lord). The shaded pathway is lined with trees, shrubs, and a dense woods. In late May/June, the **Iris Garden** is in spectacular bloom (separate admission fee charged). The shrine itself, about a 10-minute walk from the first torii, is a fine example of dignified and refined Shinto architecture. It's made of plain Japanese cypress and topped with green-copper roofs. Meiji Jingu Shrine is the place to be on New Year's Eve, when more than 2 million people crowd onto the grounds to usher in the New Year.

Meiji Shrine Inner Garden, 1–1 Kamizono-cho, Yoyogi, Shibuya-ku. © 03/3379-5511. Free admission. Daily sunrise–sunset (until 4:30pm in winter). Station: Harajuku (2 min.).

Tokyo National Museum (Tokyo Kokuritsu Hakubutsukan) ★★★   The National Museum not only is the largest and oldest museum in Japan, it also boasts the largest collection of Japanese art in the world. This is where you go to see antiques from Japan's past—old kimono, samurai armor, priceless swords, lacquerware, metalworks, pottery, scrolls, screens, ukiyo-e (woodblock prints), calligraphy, ceramics, archaeological finds, and more. Items are shown on a rotating basis with about 4,000 on display at any one time—so no matter how many times you visit the museum, you'll always see something new. You'll need 2 hours to do it justice.

The museum comprises five buildings. The **Main Gallery** (Honkan), straight ahead as you enter the main gate, is the most important one, devoted to Japanese art. Here you'll view Japanese ceramics; Buddhist sculptures dating from about A.D. 538 to 1192; samurai armor, helmets, and decorative sword mountings; swords, which throughout Japanese history were considered to embody spirits all their own; textiles and kimono; lacquerware; and paintings, calligraphy, ukiyo-e, and scrolls. Be sure to check out the museum shop in the basement; it sells reproductions from the museum's collections as well as traditional crafts by contemporary artists.

The **Gallery of Eastern Antiquities** (Toyokan) houses art and archaeological artifacts from everywhere in Asia outside Japan. There are Buddhas from China and Gandhara, stone reliefs from Cambodia, embroidered wall hangings and cloth from India, Iranian and Turkish carpets, Thai and Vietnamese ceramics, and more. Chinese art—including jade, paintings, calligraphy, and ceramics—makes up the largest part of the collection, illustrating China's tremendous influence on Japanese art, architecture, and religion. You'll also find Egyptian relics, including a mummy dating from around 751 to 656 B.C. and wooden objects from the 20th century B.C.

The **Heiseikan Gallery,** opened in 1999, is where you'll find archaeological relics of ancient Japan, including pottery and Haniwa clay burial figurines of the Jomon Period (10,000 B.C.–1,000 B.C.) and ornamental, keyhole-shaped tombs from the Yayoi Period (400 B.C.–A.D. 200). The **Gallery of Horyuji Treasures** (Horyuji Homotsukan) displays priceless Buddhist treasures from the Horyuji Temple in Nara, founded by Prince Shotoku in 607. Although the building's stark modernity (designed by Taniguchi Yoshio, who also designed the expansion of the New York Museum of Modern Art) seems odd for an exhibition of antiquities, the gallery's low lighting and simple architecture lend dramatic effect to the museum's priceless collection of bronze Buddhist statues, ceremonial Gigaku masks used in ritual dances, lacquerware, and paintings. The

Tokyo Attractions

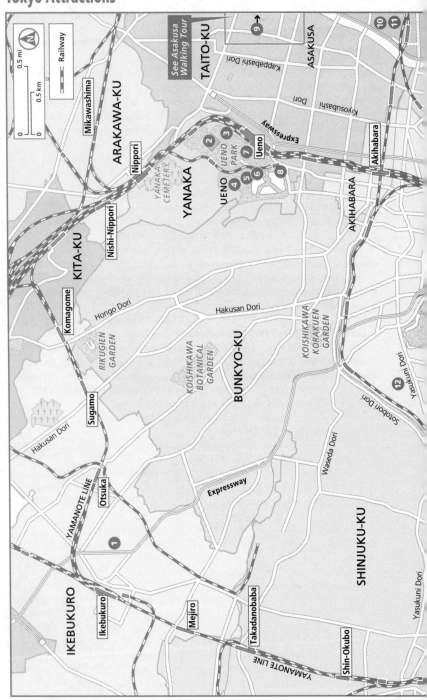

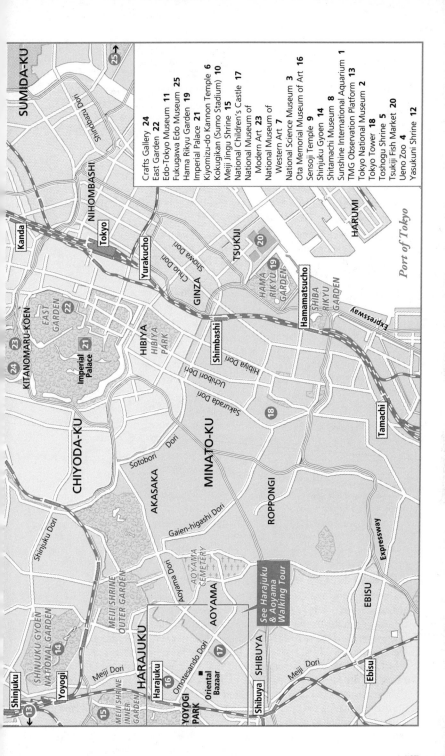

Crafts Gallery **24**
East Garden **22**
Edo-Tokyo Museum **11**
Fukugawa Edo Museum **25**
Hama Rikyu Garden **19**
Imperial Palace **21**
Kiyomizu-do Kannon Temple **6**
Kokugikan (Sumo Stadium) **10**
Meiji Jingu Shrine **15**
National Children's Castle **17**
National Museum of
  Modern Art **23**
National Museum of
  Western Art **7**
National Science Museum **3**
Ota Memorial Museum of Art **16**
Sensoji Temple **9**
Shinjuku Gyoen **14**
Shitamachi Museum **8**
Sunshrine International Aquarium **1**
TMG Observation Platform **13**
Tokyo National Museum **2**
Tokyo Tower **18**
Toshogu Shrine **5**
Tsukiji Fish Market **20**
Ueno Zoo **4**
Yasukuni Shrine **12**

See Harajuku & Aoyama Walking Tour

Frommer's Favorite Tokyo Experiences

Strolling Through Asakusa. Asakusa conveys the atmosphere of old Tokyo better than any other place in the city. Sensoji Temple is the city's oldest and most popular temple, and Nakamise Dori, the pedestrian lane leading to the temple, is lined with open-fronted stalls selling souvenirs and traditional Japanese goods.

Taking in the Early-Morning Action at Tsukiji Fish Market. Get up early your first morning in Japan (you'll be wide awake with jet lag anyway) and head straight for the country's largest fish market, where you can watch the tuna auctions, browse through stalls of seafood, and sample the freshest sushi you'll ever have.

Spending an Evening in a Yakitori-ya. There's no better place to observe Tokyo's army of office workers at play than at a yakitori-ya, a drinking place that serves skewered foods and bar snacks. Fun, noisy, and boisterous.

Watching a Kabuki Play at the Kabukiza Theater. Kabuki has served as the most popular form of entertainment for the masses since the Edo Period. Watch the audience members as they yell their approval; watch the stage for gorgeous costumes, stunning stage settings, and easy-to-understand dramas of love, duty, and revenge.

Viewing the Treasures at the Tokyo National Museum. It's a feast for the eyes at the world's largest museum of Japanese art, packed with everything from samurai armor and lacquerware to kimono and wood-block prints. If you visit only one museum in Tokyo, this should be it.

Hanging Out in Harajuku on Sunday. Start with brunch and then stroll Omotesando Dori for people-watching. Shop the area's boutiques, visit

Hyokeikan, built in 1909 to commemorate the marriage of Emperor Taisho, holds special exhibitions.

Ueno Park, Taito-ku. ⓒ 03/3822-1111. Admission ¥420 ($3.50) adults, ¥130 ($1.10) students, ¥70 (60¢) children, free for senior citizens (except during special exhibitions). Free for everyone 2nd Sat of every month (except during special exhibitions). Oct–March, Tues–Sun 9:30am–5pm (enter by 4:30pm); Apr–Sept, Tues–Thurs and Sat–Sun 9:30am–5pm and Fri 9:30am–8pm. Closed Dec 26–Jan 3. Station: Ueno (10 min.).

Edo-Tokyo Museum (Edo-Tokyo Hakubutsukan) ★★★ *Kids*   The building housing this impressive museum is said to resemble a rice granary when viewed from afar, but to me it looks like a modern *torii*, the entrance gate to a shrine. This is the metropolitan government's ambitious attempt to present the history, art, disasters, science, culture, and architecture of Tokyo from its humble beginnings in 1590—when the first shogun, Tokugawa Ieyasu, made Edo (old Tokyo) the seat of his domain—to 1964, when Tokyo hosted the Olympics. All in all, the museum's great visual displays create a vivid portrayal of Tokyo through the centuries. I wouldn't miss it. Expect to spend at least 2 hours here.

After purchasing your tickets and taking the escalator to the sixth floor, you'll enter the museum by walking over a replica of Nihombashi Bridge, the starting point for all roads leading out of old Edo. Exhibits covering the Edo Period portray the lives of the shoguns, merchants, craftsmen, and townspeople. The a couple of museums and the Meiji Shrine, or just sit back and take in all the action from a sidewalk cafe.

Seeing Sumo.   Nothing beats watching huge sumo wrestlers (most weigh well over 300 lb.), throw each other around. Matches are held in Tokyo in January, May, and September; catch one on TV if you can't make it in person.

Shopping the Department Stores.   Tokyo's department stores are huge, spotless, and filled with merchandise, some of which you never knew existed; many also have first-rate art galleries. Shibuya and Ginza boast the greatest concentration of department stores. Tobu, in Ike-bukuro, is the city's largest—a virtual city in itself. Be there when the doors open in the morning and you can witness a sight you'll never see back home: employees lined up in a row, bowing to incoming customers.

Feasting on a Kaiseki Meal.   A *kaiseki* meal, consisting of dish after dish of artfully displayed delectables, goes for big bucks—but it may well be the most beautiful and memorable meal you'll ever have. Splurge at least once on the most expensive kaiseki meal you can afford, and you'll feel like royalty.

Taking a Spin Through Kabuki-cho.   Shinjuku's Kabuki-cho has the craziest nightlife in all of Tokyo with countless strip joints, porn shops, restaurants, bars, and the greatest concentration of neon you're likely to see anywhere. A fascinating place for an evening's stroll.

Clubbing in Roppongi.   You can dance and party the night away in the madness that's Roppongi; most revelers party 'til dawn.

explanations are mostly only in Japanese, but there's plenty to look at including a replica of an old Kabuki theater, a model of a daimyo's mansion, portable floats used during festivals, maps and photographs of old Edo, and—perhaps most interesting—a rowhouse tenement where Edo commoners lived in cramped quarters measuring only 10 square meters. Other displays cover the Meiji Restoration, the Great Kanto Earthquake of 1923, and the bombing raids of World War II (Japan's own role as aggressor is disappointingly glossed over).

If you have time, consider taking advantage of a **free guided tour** service, offered by volunteers daily 10am to 3pm (last tour). Most tours last 1–2 hours, depending on the level of visitor interest, and are insightful for their explanations of the Japanese-only displays. My guide, for example, picked out fascinating scenes depicted on a screen of 1630s Edo, from a bathhouse to military training grounds. Tours are not comprehensive; you may wish to explore the museum afterwards on your own. Kids can find much to interest them here.

1–4–1 Yokoami, Sumida-ku. ✆ **03/3626-9974.** Admission ¥600 ($5) adults, ¥300 ($2.50) students through high school. Tues–Wed and Sat–Sun 10am–6pm; Thurs–Fri 10am–8pm. Station: Ryogoku on the JR Sobu and Oedo lines (2 min.).

Tsukiji Fish Market ★★★   This huge wholesale fish market—the largest in Japan and one of the largest in the world—is a must for anyone who has never seen such a market in action. And the action here starts early: At about 3am, boats begin arriving from the seas around Japan, from Africa, and even from America, with enough fish to satisfy the demands of a nation where seafood reigns supreme. To give you some idea of its enormity, this market handles almost all the seafood consumed in Tokyo. The king is tuna, huge and frozen, unloaded from the docks, laid out on the ground, and numbered. Wholesalers then walk up and down the rows, jotting down the numbers of the best-looking tuna, and by 5:15am, the tuna auctions are well under way. The wholesalers then transfer what they've bought to their own stalls in the market, subsequently selling the fish to their regular customers, usually retail stores and restaurants.

The market is held in a cavernous, hangarlike building, which means you can visit it even on a dismal rainy morning. There's a lot going on—men in black rubber boots rushing wheelbarrows and carts through the aisles, hawkers shouting, knives chopping and slicing. Wander the aisles and you'll see things you never dreamed were edible. This is a good place to bring your camera if you have a flash: The people working here burst with pride if you single them out for a photograph. The floors are wet, so leave your fancy shoes at the hotel.

Tsukiji is also a good place to come if you want sushi for breakfast. Beside the covered market are rows of barracklike buildings divided into **sushi restaurants and shops** related to the fish trade. In addition, as you walk the distance between the Tsukiji Station and the fish market, you'll find yourself in a delightful district of tiny retail shops and stalls where you can buy the freshest seafood in town, plus dried fish and fish products, seaweed, vegetables, knives, and other cooking utensils. There are also a lot of pottery shops and stores that sell plastic and lacquered trays, bowls, and cups. Although they sell in great quantities to restaurant owners, shopkeepers will usually sell to the casual tourist as well. *A word of warning:* While walking through the retail district on our way from Tsukiji Market, my Japanese friend and I were warned several times by local shopkeepers to keep watch over our purses, advice we didn't take lightly. Apparently, pickpockets have been at work here on unsuspecting tourists.

5–2–1 Tsukiji, Chuo-ku. ℂ 03/3542-1111. Free admission. Mon–Sat 5–11am (best time 5–8am). Closed some Wed, holidays, New Year's, and Aug 15–16. Station: Tsukiji (Honganji Temple exit, 10 min.) or Tsukijijo (6 min).

2 Five Unforgettable Ways to Immerse Yourself in Japanese Culture

Just walking down the street could be considered a cultural experience in Japan, but there are more concrete ways to learn more about this country's cultural life: The best is by participating in some of its time-honored rituals and traditions. For some background information on Japanese flower arranging, the tea ceremony, and other activities recommended below, see "Cultural Snapshots: Japanese Arts in a Nutshell," in appendix A.

IKEBANA Instruction in *ikebana,* or Japanese flower arranging, is available at a number of schools in Tokyo, several of which offer classes in English on a regular basis. (Note that you should call beforehand to enroll.) **Sogetsuryu Ikebana School,** 7–2–21 Akasaka (ℂ 03/3408-1151; station: Aoyama-Itchome, a 5-min. walk from exit 4), offers instruction in English on Monday from 10am to noon (closed in Aug). The cost of one lesson for first-time participants is ¥4,850 ($41), including the cost of the flowers and materials. The **Ohararyu Ikebana School,** 5–7–17 Minami Aoyama (ℂ 03/3499-1200; station: Omotesando, 3 min.), offers 2-hour instruction in English at 10am on

Wednesday and Thursday and at 1:30pm on Tuesday, charging ¥4,000 ($33) for instruction and materials. You can also come just to observe for ¥800 ($6.65). Finally, the **Ikenobo Ochanomizu Gakuin,** 2–3 Kanda Surugadai (© **03/ 3292-3071;** station: Ochanomizu, a 3-min. walk), offers 1½-hour classes on Wednesday at 11am and 2pm, charging ¥3,700 ($31) including the cost of the flowers.

If you wish to see ikebana, ask at the **Tourist Information Office** whether there are any special exhibitions. Department stores sometimes have special ikebana exhibitions in their galleries. Another place to look is **Yasukuni Shrine,** located on Yasukuni Dori northwest of the Imperial Palace (closest station: Ichigaya or Kudanshita). Dedicated to Japanese war dead, the shrine is also famous for ongoing ikebana exhibitions on its grounds.

TEA CEREMONY   Several first-class hotels hold tea-ceremony demonstrations in special tea-ceremony rooms. Reservations are usually required, and since they're often booked by groups, you'll want to call in advance to see whether you can participate. **Seisei-an,** on the seventh floor of the Hotel New Otani, 4–1 Kioi-cho, Chiyoda-ku (© **03/3265-1111,** ext. 2443; station: Nagatacho or Akasaka-mitsuke, a 3-min. walk from both), holds 20-minute demonstrations Thursday through Saturday from 11am to 4pm. The cost is ¥1,050 ($8.75), including tea and sweets. **Chosho-an,** on the seventh floor of the Hotel Okura, 2–10–4 Toranomon, Minato-ku (© **03/3582-0111;** station: Toranomon or Kamiyacho, a 10-min. walk from both), gives 30-minute demonstrations anytime between 11am and noon and between 1 and 4pm Monday through Saturday. Appointments are required; the cost is ¥1,050 ($8.75) for tea and sweets. At **Toko-an,** on the fourth floor of the Imperial Hotel, 1–1–1 Uchisaiwaicho, Chiyoda-ku (© **03/3504-1111;** station: Hibiya, 1 min.), demonstrations are given from 10am to noon and 1 to 4pm Monday through Saturday except holidays. Reservations are required. The fee is ¥1,500 ($12.50) for tea and sweets.

Lessons in the tea ceremony conducted in English are held several times weekly at the **Waraku-an,** located just behind the Canadian Embassy in Minato Ward. A one-time membership fee is ¥5,000 ($42), while monthly fees are ¥5,000 ($42) for two lessons and ¥8,000 ($67) for three lessons. For more information, contact the **International Chado Culture Foundation** at © **03/3512-2566.**

ACUPUNCTURE & SHIATSU   Although most Westerners have heard of acupuncture, they may not be familiar with *shiatsu* (Japanese pressure-point massage). Most first-class hotels in Japan offer shiatsu in the privacy of your room. There are acupuncture clinics everywhere in Tokyo, and the staff of your hotel may be able to tell you of one nearby. As it's not likely the clinic's staff will speak English, it might be a good idea to have the guest relations officer at your hotel not only make the reservation but specify the treatment you want.

For acupuncture, try **Ido-no-Nihonsha** on the second floor of the Kokushin Building, 1–10–2 Sinjuku (© **03/3341-3470;** station: Shinjuku-Gyoenmae, 5 min.). Hours here are 10am to 6pm Monday through Friday; call for an appointment and fees, but note that no English is spoken. For shiatsu, try **Namikoshi Shiatsu Center,** which has several branches in Tokyo. Those where some English is spoken include the **Shibuya branch** on the second floor of No. 2 Okuno Building, 2–18–8 Shibuya (© **03/3409-1731;** station: Shibuya, 5 min.), open Monday through Saturday from 10am to 7pm. It charges ¥8,200 ($68) an hour for the first visit and ¥7,200 ($60) per hour on subsequent visits.

Some English is also spoken at the **Asakusabashi branch** on the second floor of the Isoe Building, 1–29–7 Yanagibashi (✆ **03/3861-3963;** station: Asakus-abashi, 5 min.), open Monday through Saturday from 9am to 7pm. The rates here are ¥7,000 ($58) per hour for the first visit and ¥6,000 ($50) per hour on subsequent visits. Although no English is spoken, there's a more convenient branch in Yurakucho on the third floor of the Kotsu Kaikan Building, 2–10–1 Yurakucho (✆ **03/3211-8008;** station: Yurakucho, 1 min.). It's open Monday through Saturday from 10am to 6:30pm and charges ¥7,800 ($65) per hour.

PUBLIC BATHS If you don't have the chance to visit a hot spring, I suggest that you go at least once to a neighborhood *sento* (public bath). Altogether, Tokyo has an estimated 1,400 sento—which may sound like a lot but is nothing compared to the 2,687 the city used to have just 30-some years ago. Easily recognizable by a tall chimney and shoe lockers just inside the door, a sento sells just about anything you might need at the bathhouse—soap, shampoo, towels, even underwear.

Since there are many public baths spread throughout the city, it's best simply to go to the one most convenient to you. If you prefer a suggestion, however, the **Azabu Juban Onsen,** 1–5 Azabu Juban, Minato-ku (✆ **03/3404-2610;** station: Roppongi), is one of the more luxurious and is the one I used to go to when I lived for a while in an apartment without a tub or shower. Its brownish water actually comes from a hot spring 500 meters (¼ mile) underground. It's closed on Tuesday but is open the rest of the week from 11am to 9pm; admission is ¥1,260 ($10.50) until 6pm; ¥940 ($7.85) after 6pm.

ZAZEN A few temples in the Tokyo vicinity occasionally offer sitting medita-tion with instruction in English. Approximately 30 minutes east of Akihabara on the Sobu Line is **Ida Ryogoku-do zazen Dojo** of the Sotoshu Sect, 5–11–20 Minami Yawata, Ichikawa City (✆ **0473/79-1596;** station: Moto-Yawata, 5 min.). Zazen is held daily at 5:30 and 10am and 3 and 8:30pm, generally for 45 minutes. A Dogen-Sangha meeting is held the fourth Saturday of the month from 1 to 2:30pm, consisting of 30 minutes for zazen followed by a 1-hour lec-ture. Participation is free, and if you call from Moto-Yawata Station, someone will come for you. You can also stay here for longer stays to practice zen; call Mr. Nishijima at ✆ 03/3435-0701 for more information.

In addition, the **Young Men Buddhist Association of Tokyo University,** of the Sotoshu Sect, second floor of the Nippon Shimpan Building, 3–33–5 Hongo (✆ **03/3235-0701;** station: Hongo-Sanchome, 3 min.) holds a Dogen-Sangha meeting the first, third, and fifth Saturday of each month from 1 to 2:30pm, which includes 30 minutes of zazen and a 1-hour lecture in English. There's a ¥400 ($2.50) fee. This one, too, allows long-term stays.

3 Parks & Gardens

Although Japan's most famous gardens are not in Tokyo, the first three places listed below use traditional principles of landscaping and give visitors an idea of the scope and style of Japanese gardens. The fourth listing, Ueno Park, is Tokyo's largest city park and contains a number of museums and attractions, making it one of the city's most visited places.

Hama Rikyu Garden ★★ Considered by some to be the best garden in Tokyo, this peaceful oasis has origins stretching back 300 years, when it served as a retreat for a former feudal lord and as duck-hunting grounds for the Tokugawa shoguns. In 1871, possession of the garden passed to the imperial family, who used it to entertain such visiting dignitaries as General Ulysses S. Grant. Come here to see how the upper classes enjoyed themselves during the Edo Period. Located on Tokyo Bay and surrounded by water on three sides, the garden contains an inner tidal pool, spanned by three bridges draped with wisteria. There are also other ponds; a refuge for ducks, herons, and migratory birds; a promenade along the bay lined with pine trees and offering views of Rainbow Bridge; a 300-year-old pine; moon-viewing pavilions; and teahouses. Plan on at least an hour's stroll to see everything. From a boarding pier inside the garden's grounds, ferries depart for Asakusa every hour (or more often) between 10:15am and 4:05pm; the fare is ¥620 ($5.15) one-way.

1–1 Hamarikyuteien, Chuo-ku. ✆ 03/3541-0200. Admission ¥300 ($2.50). Daily 9am–5pm. Station: Shimbashi (10 min.).

East Garden (Higashi Gyoen) ⚜⚜   The 53 acres of the formal Higashi Gyoen—once the main grounds of Edo Castle and located next to the Imperial Palace—are a wonderful respite in the middle of the city. Yet surprisingly, this garden is hardly ever crowded. **Ninomaru,** my favorite part, is laid out in Japanese style with a pond, stepping stones, and winding paths; it's particularly beautiful when the wisteria, azaleas, irises, and other flowers are in bloom. Near Ninomaru is the **Sannomaru Shozokan,** which displays changing exhibitions of art treasures belonging to the imperial family free of charge.

On the highest spot of Higashi Gyoen is the **Honmaru** (inner citadel)**,** where Tokugawa's main castle once stood. Built in the first half of the 1600s, the castle was massive, surrounded by a series of whirling moats and guarded by 23 watchtowers and 99 gates around its 10-mile perimeter. At its center was Japan's tallest building at the time, the five-story castle keep, soaring 168 feet above its foundations and offering an expansive view over Edo. Today all that remains of Tokugawa's castle are a few towers, gates, stone walls, moats, and the stone foundations of the keep.

1–1 Chiyoda, Chiyoda-ku. ✆ 03/3213-1111. Free admission. Mar–Oct, Tues–Thurs and Sat–Sun 9am–4:30pm (enter by 4pm); Nov–Feb, Tues–Thurs and Sat–Sun 9am–4pm (enter by 3:30pm). Closed Dec 23–Jan 3; open other national holidays. Station: Otemachi, Takebashi, or Nijubashi-mae.

Shinjuku Gyoen ⚜   Formerly the private estate of a feudal lord and then the imperial family, this is considered one of the most important parks of the Meiji Era. It's wonderful for strolling because of the variety of its planted gardens; styles range from French and English to Japanese traditional. This place amazes me every time I come here. The park's 144 acres make it one of the city's largest, and each bend in the pathway brings something completely different: Ponds and sculpted bushes give way to a promenade lined with sycamores that opens up into a rose garden. Cherry blossoms, azaleas, chrysanthemums, and other flowers provide splashes of color from spring through autumn. There are also wide grassy expanses, popular for picnics and playing, and a greenhouse filled with tropical plants.

11 Naitocho, Shinjuku-ku. ✆ 03/3350-0151. Admission ¥200 ($1.65). Tues–Sun 9am–4:30pm (enter by 4pm). Station: Shinjuku Gyoen-mae (2 min.).

Ueno Park   Ueno Park—on the northeast edge of the Yamanote Line—is one of the largest parks in Tokyo and one of the most popular places in the city for Japanese families on a day's outing. It's a cultural mecca with a number of attractions, including the prestigious Tokyo National Museum, the National Museum of Western Art, the delightful Shitamachi Museum with its displays of old

Tokyo, Ueno Zoo, and Shinobazu Pond, a bird sanctuary. For a map of the Ueno area, see p. 166.

A landmark in the park is the small **Toshogu Shrine.** Erected in 1651, it's dedicated to Tokugawa Ieyasu, founder of the Tokugawa shogunate. Stop here to pay respects to the man who made Edo (present-day Tokyo) the seat of his government and thus elevated the small village to the most important city in the country. The pathway to the shrine is lined with massive stone lanterns, as well as 50 copper lanterns donated by *daimyo* (feudal lords) from all over Japan. Entrance to the shrine itself is to the left of the main building, where you can see a couple examples of exquisite art, including murals by a famous Edo artist, Kano Tan-yu, and samurai armor worn by Ieyasu. The shrine is open daily from 9am to 6pm (to 5:30pm in winter); admission is ¥200 ($1.65). On a more somber note, there's also a display on the shrine grounds appealing for world peace, with photographs of Hiroshima following its destruction by the atom bomb and of victims dead and alive.

Also in the park is **Kiyomizu Kannon-do Temple,** completed in 1631 as a copy of the famous Kiyomizu Temple in Kyoto (but on a much less grand style). It enshrines Kosodate Kannon, protectress of childbearing and child-raising. Women hoping to become pregnant come here to ask for the goddess' blessing; those whose wishes have been fulfilled return to pray for their child's good health and protection. Many leave behind dolls as a symbol of their child—if you take your shoes off and walk to the door to the right of the inner shrine, you'll see some of those dolls. Once a year, a requiem service is held for all the dolls at the temple, after which they are cremated.

The busiest time of the year at Ueno Park is in April, during the **cherry-blossom season,** when people come en masse to celebrate the birth of the new season. It's not the spiritual communion with nature that you might think, however. On weekends and in the evenings during cherry-blossom time (which only lasts for a few days), havoc prevails as office workers break out of their winter shells. Whole companies converge on the park to sit under the cherry trees on plastic or cardboard, and everyone drinks sake and beer and gets drunk and rowdy and—worst of all—sings karaoke. At any rate, visiting Ueno Park during cherry-blossom season is an experience no one should miss. More than likely, you'll be invited to join one of the large groups and by all means do.

Taito-ku. Free admission to the park; separate admissions to each of its attractions. Open daily 24 hours. Station: Ueno (1 min.).

4 More Museums

In addition to the museums listed below, Tokyo has a wealth of small museums specializing in everything from papermaking to swords; for a more complete list of Tokyo museums, see *Frommer's Tokyo.* For details on the **Tokyo National Museum** and the **Edo-Tokyo Museum,** see "The Top Attractions," earlier in this chapter.

Crafts Gallery (Bijutsukan Kogeikan)   Housed in a handsome Gothic-style brick building constructed in 1910 as headquarters of the Imperial Guard, this gallery exhibits contemporary crafts including pottery, ceramics, kimono, metalworks, glassware, lacquerware, bamboo works, and more; objects are changed approximately four times a year to reflect the changes of the seasons. Most exhibitions concentrate on a specific theme such as bamboo ware or the works of a single artist, usually one noted for skill in traditional arts. Unfortunately, exhibition space is very limited; you can tour the place in 45 minutes or less.

Kitanomaru Koen Park, Chiyoda-ku. © **03/3211-7781.** Admission ¥420–¥830 ($3.50–$6.90) adults, ¥130–¥450 ($1.10–$3.75) students, ¥70–¥330 (60¢–$2.75) children; price depends on the exhibit. Tues–Sun 10am–5pm. Station: Takebashi (7 min.).

Fukagawa Edo Museum (Fukagawa Edo Shiryokan) ★ *Kids*   This is the Tokyo of your dreams, the way it appears in all those samurai flicks on Japanese TV: A reproduction of a 19th-century neighborhood in Fukagawa, a prosperous community on the east bank of the Sumida River during the Edo Period. This delightful museum is located off Kiyosumi Dori on a pleasant tree-lined, shop-filled street called Fukagawa Shiryokan Dori. The museum's hangarlike interior contains 11 full-scale replicas of traditional houses, vegetable and rice shops, a fish store, two inns, a fire watchtower, and tenement homes, all arranged to resemble an actual neighborhood. There are lots of small touches and flourishes to make the community seem real and believable—a cat sleeping on a roof, a snail crawling up a fence, a dog relieving itself on a pole, sounds of birds, a vendor shouting his wares, horses' hooves clattering, and a dog barking. Of Tokyo's museums, this one is probably the best for children; plan on spending about an hour here. Don't confuse this museum with the much larger Edo-Tokyo Museum, which traces the history of Tokyo.

1-3-28 Shirakawa, Koto-ku. © **03/3630-8625.** Admission ¥300 ($2.50) adults, ¥50 (40¢) children 6–14. Daily 9:30am–5pm. Closed 2nd and 4th Mon of each month. Station: Kiyosumi-Shirakawa (3 min.).

Hara Museum of Contemporary Art (Hara Bijutsukan) ★★   Japan's oldest museum devoted to contemporary international and Japanese art is housed in a 1930s tiled, Bauhaus-style Art Deco home that once belonged to the current director's grandfather; the building alone is worth the trip. The museum stages three or four exhibitions annually; some are on the cutting edge of international art, but at least one features works from its own collection, which focuses on paintings and sculptures mainly from the 1950s and 1960s by Japanese and foreign artists and includes works by Andy Warhol, Roy Lichtenstein, Claes Oldenburg, Jackson Pollock, Karel Appel, Robert Rauschenberg, and Frank Stella. Be sure to check out the downstairs toilet by Morimura Yasumasu. Afterward, relax at the lovely greenhouse-like cafe with outdoor seating. You'll spend at least an hour at this great museum.

4-7-25 Kita-Shinagawa, Shinagawa-ku. © **03/3445-0651.** Admission ¥1,000 ($8.35) adults, ¥700 ($5.85) students 16 and older, ¥500 ($4.15) children, free for seniors. Tues, Thurs–Sun, and holidays 11am–5pm; Wed 11am–8pm. Closed during exhibition changes. Station: Shinagawa (15 min.).

Tips Museum Tips

Note that most museums in Tokyo are closed on Mondays and for New Year's; generally the last few days in December and the first 3 days of January. If a Monday happens to be a national holiday, however, most museums will remain open but will close Tuesday instead. Some of the privately owned museums may also be closed the day following every national holiday as well as for exhibition changes. Call beforehand to avoid disappointment. Remember, too, that you must enter museums at least 30 minutes before closing time. For a listing of current special exhibitions, including those being held at major department stores, consult the *Tokyo Journal,* published quarterly.

Museum of Contemporary Art, Tokyo (MOT; Tokyo-to Gendai Bijutsukan) ⚞ The MOT is inconveniently located but is well worth the trek

if you're a fan of the avant-garde (you'll pass the Fukagawa Edo Museum, described above, on the way, so you may wish to visit both). This modern structure of glass and steel, with a long corridor entrance that reminds me of railroad trestles, houses both permanent and temporary exhibits of Japanese and international postwar art in large rooms that lend themselves to large installations. Although temporary exhibits, which occupy most of the museum space, have ranged from Southeast Asian art to a retrospective of Jasper Johns, the smaller permanent collection presents a chronological study of 50 years of contemporary art, beginning with Japanese postwar avant-garde and continuing with anti-artistic trends and pop art in the 1960s, Minimalism, and art after the 1980s. Included are works by Andy Warhol, Gerhard Richter, Roy Lichtenstein, David Hockney, Frank Stella, Sandro Chia, and Julian Schnabel, with individual works changed frequently during the year. Depending on the number of exhibits you visit, you'll spend anywhere from 1–2 hours here.

4-1-1 Miyoshi, Koto-ku. ℭ 03/5245-4111. Admission to permanent collection ¥500 ($4.15) adults, ¥250 ($2.10) students and children; special exhibits ¥700–¥1,000 ($5.85–$8.35). Tues–Thurs and Sat–Sun 10am–6pm; Fri 10am–9pm. Station: Kiyosumi-Shirakawa (exit A3, 13 min.). On Fukagawa Shiroyokan-dori Street.

National Museum of Modern Art (Tokyo Kokuritsu Kindai Bijutsukan)

This newly renovated museum houses the largest collection of modern Japanese art under one roof, including both Japanese- and Western-style paintings, prints, watercolors, drawings, and sculpture, all dating from the Meiji Period to World War II. Names to look for include Munahata Shiko, Kuroda Seiki, and Yokoyama Taikan. To provide a wider context, a few Western artists are also represented, among them Klee and Kandinsky. Expect to spend about 90 minutes here.

3 Kitanomaru Koen Park, Chiyoda-ku. ℭ 03/3214-2561. Admission ¥420 ($3.50) adults, ¥130 ($1.10) students, ¥70 (60¢) children; special exhibits cost more. Tues–Sun 10am–5pm (to 8pm Fri in summer). Station: Takebashi (5 min.).

National Museum of Western Art (Kokuritsu Seiyo Bijutsukan) Japan's

only national museum dedicated to Western art is housed in a main building designed by Le Corbusier and two more recent additions. It presents a chronological study of sculpture and art from the end of the Middle Ages through the 20th century, beginning with works by Old Masters, including Lucas Cranach the Elder, Rubens, El Greco, Murillo, and Tiepolo. French painters and Impressionists of the 19th and 20th centuries are well represented, including Delacroix, Monet (with a whole room devoted to his work), Manet, Renoir, Pissarro, Sisley, Courbet, Cezanne, and Gauguin. The museum's 20th-century collection includes works by Picasso, Max Ernst, Miro, Dubuffet, and Pollock. The museum is also famous for its 50-odd sculptures by Rodin, one of the largest collections in the world, encompassing most of his major works including *The Kiss, The Thinker, Balzac,* and *The Gates of Hell.*

Ueno Park, Taito-ku. ℭ 03/3828-5131. Admission ¥420 ($3.50) adults, ¥130 ($1.10) students, ¥70 (60¢) children; special exhibits require separate admission fee. Free admission to permanent collection 2nd and 4th Sat of the month. Tues–Thurs and Sat–Sun 9:30am–5pm; Fri 9:30am–8pm. Station: Ueno (4 min.).

National Science Museum (Kokuritsu Kagaku Hakubutsukan) 𝘒𝘪𝘥𝘴

This is a sprawling complex, comprising three buildings and covering everything from the evolution of life to electronics in Japan. Unfortunately, most displays are in Japanese (be sure to pick up the museum's English pamphlet), but the museum is worth visiting for its exhibits relating to Japan. There are also plenty of exhibits geared toward children. Dinosaurs greet visitors on the ground floor of the main hall, while up on the third floor plants and animals of Japan are featured, including the Japanese brown bear, the Japanese crested ibis, the Japanese monkey, and marine life such as huge king crabs. Other highlights include a display on the origin, development, and history of the Japanese people; a hands-on discovery room for children exploring sound, light, magnetism, and other scientific phenomena; a map of Japan showing the location of all its active volcanoes; recreated wood and marine habitats; and an amazing room of stuffed and preserved animals, including a gorilla and other primates, bears, alligators, and a giant squid. You'll want to spend about 2 hours here, more if you have children in tow.

Ueno Park, Taito-ku. © 03/3822-0111. Admission ¥420 ($3.50) adults, ¥70 (60¢) children; more for special exhibits. Tues–Sun 9am–4:30pm. Station: Ueno (5 min.).

Open-Air Folk House Museum (Nihon Minka-en) ⭐ *Finds*   Located in the neighboring city of Kawasaki, 30 minutes by express train on the Odakyu Line from Shinjuku, this open-air museum is highly recommended if you won't have a chance to visit other similar museums (such as those in Takayama, Shirakawa, and Takamatsu). In a lovely setting of wooded hillsides are 23 traditional thatched houses and other historical buildings, all open to the public so you can wander in and inspect the various rooms, gaining insight into the way rural Japanese lived in centuries past. Most of the buildings are heavy-beamed thatched houses, but there are also warehouses, a samurai's residential gate, a waterwheel, and a Kabuki stage from a small fishing village, all originally from other parts of Honshu and reconstructed here. The oldest houses date from about 300 years ago and were usually homes for extended families. An English pamphlet tells about each of the buildings, and there are also many explanations throughout in English. Plan on spending a half day here, including transportation back and forth.

7-1-1 Masugata, Tama-ku, Kawasaki. © 044/922-2181. Admission ¥300 ($2.50) adults, ¥100 (85¢) students and children. Tues–Sun 9:30am–4pm. Station: Mukogaoka Yuen (15 min.)

Ota Memorial Museum of Art (Ota Kinen Bijutsukan) ⭐   This great museum features the private ukiyo-e (woodblock print) collection of the late Ota Seizo, who early in life recognized the importance of ukiyo-e as an art form and dedicated himself to its preservation. Although the collection contains 12,000 prints, only 80 to 100 are displayed at any given time, in thematic exhibitions that change monthly and include English descriptions. The museum itself is small but delightful, with such traditional touches as bamboo screens and stone pathways. You can tour the museum in about 30 minutes.

1-10-10 Jingumae, Shibuya-ku. © 03/3403-0880. Admission ¥500–¥900 ($4.15–$7.50) adults, ¥400–¥700 ($3.35–$5.85) high school and college students, ¥300–¥500 ($2.50–$4.15) junior high students, ¥100–¥300 (85¢–$2.50) children; price depends on the exhibit. Tues–Sun 10:30am–5:30pm (enter by 5pm). Closed from the 1st to 4th of each month. Station: Harajuku (2 min.) or Meiji-Jingumae (1 min.). Near the Omotesando Dori and Meiji Dori intersection, behind La Forêt.

5 Spectacular City Views

Tokyo Metropolitan Government Office (TMG) ⭐⭐⭐   Tokyo's new city hall—designed by one of Japan's best-known architects, Kenzo Tange—is an impressive addition to the skyscrapers of West Shinjuku. Three buildings comprise the complex—TMG No. 1, TMG No. 2, and the Metropolitan Assembly Building—and together they contain everything from Tokyo's Disaster Prevention

Center to the governor's office. Most important for visitors, however, is TMG No. 1, the tall building to the north that offers one of the best views of Tokyo. This 48-story, 800-foot structure, the tallest building in Shinjuku, boasts two observatories located on the 45th floors of both its North and South Towers, with access from the first floor. Both observatories offer the same spectacular views—on clear winter days you can even see Mt. Fuji—as well as a small souvenir shop and coffee shop.

2-8-1 Nishi-Shinjuku. (✆ 03/5321-1111. Free admission. Daily 9:30am–10pm. Closed Dec 29–Jan 3. Station: Tochomae (1 min.), Shinjuku (10 min.), or Nishi-Shinjuku (4 min.).

Tokyo Tower 🌟 *Kids*   Japan's most famous observation tower was built in 1958 and was modeled after the Eiffel Tower in Paris. Lit up at night, this 1,099-foot tower, a relay station for TV and radio stations, is a familiar and beloved landmark in the city's landscape; but with the construction of skyscrapers over the past few decades (including the TMG, above, with its free observatory), it has lost some of its appeal as an observation platform and seems like an attraction relic of the 1950s. With its tacky souvenir shops and assorted small-time attractions, this place is as about as kitsch as kitsch can be.

The tower has two observatories: the main one at 495 feet and the top observatory at 825 feet. The best time of year for viewing is said to be during Golden Week at the beginning of May. With many Tokyoites gone from the city and most factories and businesses closed down, the air at this time is thought to be the cleanest and clearest. There are several offbeat tourist attractions in the tower's base building, including a wax museum (where you can see the Beatles, a wax rendition of Leonardo's *Last Supper*, Hollywood stars, and a medieval torture chamber), a small aquarium, a museum of holography, and a trick art gallery, all with separate admission fees and appealing mainly to children.

4-2 Shiba Koen, Minato-ku. (✆ 03/3433-5111. Admission to main observatory ¥820 ($6.85) adults and ¥460 ($3.85) children; top observatory ¥1,420 ($11.85) adults and ¥860 ($7.15) children. Daily 9am–8pm (to 9pm in Aug). Station: Onarimon or Kamiyacho (5 min.).

6 City Strolls

SEARCHING FOR OLD EDO   A WALKING TOUR OF ASAKUSA

Start:	Hama Rikyu Garden (near Shimbashi Station) or Asakusa Station (exit 1 or 3).
Finish:	Kappabashi Dori (station: Tawaramachi).
Time:	Allow approximately 5 hours, including the boat ride.
Best Times:	Tuesday through Friday, when the crowds aren't as big.
Worst Times:	Sunday, when Demboin Garden and the shops on Kappabashi Dori are closed.

If anything remains of old Tokyo, Asakusa is it. This is where you'll find narrow streets lined with small residential homes, women in kimono, Tokyo's oldest and most popular temple, and quaint shops selling boxwood combs, fans, kitchen knives, sweet pastries, and other products of yore. With its temple market, old-fashioned amusement park, traditional shops, and restaurants, Asakusa preserves the charm of old downtown Edo better than anyplace else in Tokyo. For many

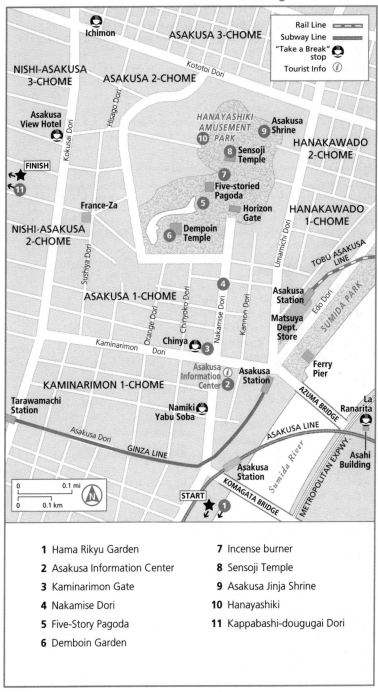

Ichimon

ASAKUSA 3-CHOME

NISHI-ASAKUSA 3-CHOME

ASAKUSA 2-CHOME

Kototoi Dori

Hisago Dori

Kokusai Dori

Asakusa View Hotel

FINISH

11

France-Za

NISHI-ASAKUSA 2-CHOME

Sushiya Dori

HANAYASHIKI AMUSEMENT PARK

10

Asakusa Shrine

9

HANAKAWADO 2-CHOME

8 Sensoji Temple

7

Five-storied Pagoda

5

Horizon Gate

Dempoin Temple

6

HANAKAWADO 1-CHOME

Umamichi Dori

TOBU ASAKUSA LINE

ASAKUSA 1-CHOME

4

Chiyoko Dori

Orange Dori

Nakamise Dori

Kannon Dori

Asakusa Station

Edo Dori

SUMIDA PARK

Matsuya Dept. Store

Kaminarimon Dori

Chinya

3

Asakusa Information Center

2

Asakusa Station

Ferry Pier

KAMINARIMON 1-CHOME

AZUMA BRIDGE

La Ranarita

Tarawamachi Station

Namiki Yabu Soba

Asakusa Dori

GINZA LINE

ASAKUSA LINE

Sumida River

Asahi Building

0   0.1 mi
0   0.1 km

START

Asakusa Station

1

KOMAGATA BRIDGE

METROPOLITAN EXPWY.

Legend

Rail Line
Subway Line
"Take a Break" stop
Tourist Info ⓘ

1 Hama Rikyu Garden
2 Asakusa Information Center
3 Kaminarimon Gate
4 Nakamise Dori
5 Five-Story Pagoda
6 Demboin Garden

7 Incense burner
8 Sensoji Temple
9 Asakusa Jinja Shrine
10 Hanayashiki
11 Kappabashi-dougugai Dori

older Japanese, a visit to Asakusa is like stepping back to the days of their child-hood; for tourists, it provides a glimpse of the way things were.

Pleasure-seekers have been flocking to Asakusa for centuries. Originating as a temple town back in the 7th century, it grew in popularity during the Tokugawa regime as merchants grew wealthy and whole new forms of popular entertain-ment arose to cater to them. Theaters for Kabuki and Bunraku flourished in Asakusa, as did restaurants and shops. By 1840, Asakusa had become Edo's main entertainment district. In stark contrast to the solemnity surrounding places of worship in the West, Asakusa's temple market had a carnival atmosphere reminiscent of medieval Europe, complete with street performers and exotic animals. It retains some of that festive atmosphere even today.

The most dramatic way to arrive in Asakusa is by boat from Hama Rikyu Garden (see stop no. 1 below), just as people used to arrive in the olden days. If you want to forgo the boat ride, take the subway to Asakusa Station and start your tour from there. Otherwise, head to:

❶ Hama Rikyu Garden

The garden is at the south end of Tokyo (station: Shimbashi, then a taxi ride or 13-min. walk). Considered by some to be Tokyo's finest garden, it was laid out during the Edo Period in a style popular at the time, in which surrounding scenery was incorporated in its composition. (See "Parks & Gar-dens," earlier in this chapter for more details.)

Boats depart the garden to make their way along the Sumida River hourly or more frequently between 10:15am and 4:05pm, with the fare to Asakusa costing ¥620 ($5.15). Although much of what you see along the working river today is only con-crete embankments, I recommend the trip because it affords a different per-spective of Tokyo—barges making their way down the river and high-rise apartment buildings with laundry fluttering from balconies, warehouses, and superhighways. The boat passes under approximately a dozen bridges during the 40-minute trip, each one completely different. During cherry blossom season, thousands of cherry trees lining the bank make the trip particularly memorable.

Upon arrival in Asakusa, walk away from the boat pier a couple of blocks inland, where you'll soon see the colorful Kaminarimon Gate. Across the street is the:

❷ Asakusa Information Center

Located at 2–18–9 Kaminarimon (☎ **03/3842-5566**) the center is open daily from 9:30am to 8pm and is staffed by English-speaking volunteers from 10am to 5pm. Stop here to pick up a map of the area and to ask direc-tions to restaurants and sights. In addition, note the huge Seiko clock on the center's facade—a music clock that performs every hour on the hour from 10am to 7pm. Mechanical dolls re-enact scenes from several of Asakusa's most famous festivals. Then it's time to head across the street to the:

❸ Kaminarimon Gate

The gate is unmistakable with its bright red colors and a 220-pound lantern hanging in the middle. The statues inside the gate are the gods of wind to the right and thunder to the left, ready to protect the deity enshrined in the temple. The god of thunder is particularly fearsome—he has an insatiable appetite for navels. Once past the gate, you'll find yourself immediately on a pedestrian lane called:

❹ Nakamise Dori

The lane leads straight to the temple. Nakamise means "inside shops," and historical records show that vendors have sold wares here since the late

17th century. Today Nakamise Dori is lined on both sides with tiny stall after tiny stall, many owned by the same family for generations. If you're expecting austere religious artifacts, however, you're in for a surprise: sweets, shoes, barking toy dogs, Japanese crackers (called *sembei*), bags, umbrellas, Japanese dolls, T-shirts, fans, masks, and traditional Japanese accessories are all sold. How about a brightly colored straight hairpin—and a black hairpiece to go with it? Or a temporary tattoo in the shape of a dragon? This is a great place to shop for souvenirs, gifts, and items you have no earthly need for—a little bit of unabashed consumerism on the way to spiritual purification.

TAKE A BREAK
If you're hungry for lunch, there are a number of possibilities in the neighborhood. **Chinya**, 1–3–4 Asakusa, just west of Kaminarimon Gate on Kaminarimon Dori, has been serving sukiyaki and shabu-shabu since 1880. To the south of Kaminarimon Gate is **Namiki Yabu Soba**, 2–11–9 Kaminarimon, Asakusa's best-known noodle shop. For Western food, head to the other side of the Sumida River, where on the 22nd floor of the Asahi Beer Tower is **La Ranarita**, 1–23–1 Azumabashi, a moderately priced Italian restaurant with great views of Asakusa. (See chapter 3 for complete reviews.)

Near the end of Nakamise Dori, as you head toward the temple, you'll pass a kindergarten on your left, followed by a:

⑤ Five-story red-and-gold pagoda.
It's a 1970 remake of one constructed during the time of the third shogun, Iemitsu, in the 17th century.

A low-lying building connected to the pagoda is the gateway to the gem of this tour: a **hidden garden,** one of Asakusa's treasures, just a stone's throw

from Nakamise Dori but barely visible on the other side of the kindergarten. Most visitors to Asakusa pass it by, unaware of its existence, primarily because it isn't open to the general public. And yet, anyone can visit it simply by asking for permission, which you can obtain by entering the building connected to the pagoda at the left. Go inside, turn right, and walk to the third door to the left; you'll be asked to sign your name and will be given a map showing the entrance to the garden, which is open Monday through Saturday from 9am to 3pm. However, because the garden is on private grounds belonging to the Demboin Monastery, it's occasionally closed for functions (call ℭ **03/3842-0181** to see whether it's open, or trust to luck). Once you've obtained permission, retrace your steps down Nakamise past the kindergarten, take the first right onto Demboin Dori, and then enter the second gate on your right. This is the entrance to:

⑥ Demboin Garden
The gate to Demboin Garden (also spelled Dempoin Garden) may be locked. If so, ring the doorbell to be let in. Soon you'll find yourself in a peaceful oasis in the midst of bustling Asakusa, in a countryside setting that centers on a pond filled with carp and turtles. Enshu Kobori, a tea-ceremony master and famous landscape gardener who also designed a garden for the shogun's castle, designed the garden in the 17th century. Because most people are unaware that the garden exists or that it's accessible, you may find yourself the sole visitor. The best view is from the far side of the pond, where you can see the temple building and pagoda above the trees.

Return to Nakamise Dori and resume your walk north to the second gate, which opens onto a square filled with pigeons and a large:

7 Incense burner

This is where worshippers "wash" themselves to ward off or help cure illness. If, for example, you have a sore throat, be sure to rub some of the smoke over your throat for good measure. But the dominating building of the square is:

8 Sensoji Temple

Sensoji is Tokyo's oldest temple. Founded in the 7th century and therefore already well established long before Tokugawa settled in Edo, Sensoji Temple is dedicated to Kannon, the Buddhist goddess of mercy, and is therefore popularly called the Asakusa Kannon Temple. According to legend, the temple was founded after two fishermen pulled up a golden statue of Kannon from the sea. The sacred statue is still housed in the temple, carefully preserved inside three boxes; even though it's never on display, people still flock to the temple to pay their respects.

Within the temple is a counter where you can buy your fortune by putting a 100-yen coin into a wooden box and shaking it until a long bamboo stick emerges from a small hole. The stick will have a Japanese number on it, which corresponds to one of the numbers on a set of drawers. Take out the fortune, written in both English and Japanese, from the drawer that has your number. But don't expect the translation to clear things up; my fortune contained such cryptic messages as "Getting a beautiful lady at your home, you want to try all people know about this" and "Stop to start a trip." If you find that your fortune raises more questions than it answers or you simply don't like what it has to say, you can conveniently negate it by tying it to one of the wires provided for this purpose just outside the main hall.

If you walk around the temple to the right, on the northeast corner of the grounds is a small orange shrine, the:

9 Asakusa Jinja Shrine

The shrine was built in 1649 by Iemitsu Tokugawa, the third Tokugawa shogun, to commemorate the two fishermen who found the statue of Kannon and their village chief. From Asakusa Jinja Shrine, walk around the back side of Sensoji northwest to:

10 Hanayashiki

This is a small and corny amusement park that first opened in 1853 and still draws in the little ones. (See "Especially for Kids," below for more details.)

Most of the area west of Sensoji Temple (the area to the left if you stand facing the front of the temple) is a small but interesting part of Asakusa popular among Tokyo's older working class. This is where several of Asakusa's old-fashioned pleasure houses remain, including bars, restaurants, strip shows, traditional Japanese vaudeville, and so-called "love hotels," which rent rooms by the hour. If you keep walking west, within 10 minutes you'll reach:

11 Kappabashi-dougugai Dori

This district is generally referred to simply as Kappabashi Dori. This is Tokyo's wholesale district for restaurant items. Shop after shop sells pottery, chairs, tableware, cookingware, lacquerware, rice cookers, noren, and everything else needed to run a restaurant. And yes, you can even buy those models of plastic food you've been drooling over in restaurant displays. Ice cream, pizza, sushi, mugs foaming with beer—they're all here, looking like the real thing (stores close about 5:30pm).

WINDING DOWN
The Asakusa View Hotel, on Kokusai Dori Avenue between Sensoji Temple and Kappabashi Dori, has several restaurants and bars. In the basement is the clubby Ice House, the hotel's main bar, while on the ground floor is a casual coffee shop. There are also Japanese, Chinese, and French restaurants.

IN THE HEART OF TRENDY TOKYO	A STROLL THROUGH HARAJUKU & AOYAMA

Start:	Meiji Jingu Shrine (station: Harajuku).
Finish:	Japan Traditional Craft Center (station: Gaienmae).
Time:	Allow approximately 4 hours.
Best Times:	The first and fourth Sundays of every month, when there's an antiques/flea market at Togo Shrine.
Worst Times:	Monday, from the first to fourth of every month (when the Ota Memorial Museum of Art is closed), and Thursday (when the Oriental Bazaar is closed).

Harajuku is one of my favorite neighborhoods in Tokyo, though I'm too old to really fit in. In fact, anyone over 25 is apt to feel ancient here, since this is Tokyo's most popular hangout for Japanese high school and college students. The young come here to see and be seen; you're sure to spot Japanese punks, girls decked out in the fashions of the moment, and young couples looking their best. I like Harajuku for its vibrancy, its sidewalk cafes, its street hawkers, and its trendy clothing boutiques. It's also the home of Tokyo's most important Shinto shrine, as well as a delightful woodblock-print museum and an excellent souvenir shop of traditional Japanese items.

Nearby is **Aoyama**, a yuppified version of Harajuku, where the upwardly mobile dine and shop for designer clothing. Connecting Harajuku and Aoyama is **Omotesando Dori,** a wide, tree-lined, European-style shopping boulevard that forms the heart of this area; its many sidewalk cafes make it a popular promenade for people-watching.

From Harajuku Station, take the south exit (the one closer to Shibuya) and turn right over the bridge, where you will immediately see the huge cypress torii marking the entrance to:

❶ Meiji Jingu Shrine

This is the most venerable shrine in Tokyo, dedicated to Emperor and Empress Meiji (p.164). On the 10-minute walk along the tree-shaded path to the shrine, stop off at the Iris Garden, spectacular for its irises in June.

TAKE A BREAK
If the hike to Meiji Shrine has made you thirsty, stop off at the rustic, outdoor snack pavilion just inside the entranceway to the shrine grounds. It offers coffee, beer, and ice cream and is open daily from 9am to sunset.

After visiting the shrine, retrace your steps back to Harajuku Station. If it's Sunday, you'll see groups of teenagers—many bizarrely dressed—gathered on the bridge over the train tracks. They're all that's left of the masses of teens that used to congregate on nearby Yoyogi Dori back when it was closed to vehicular traffic on Sundays. Sadly, authorities decided to open Yoyogi and Omotesando Dori streets to traffic, thereby putting an end to Tokyo's most happening Sunday scene. At Harajuku Station, continue walking north beside the station to its north exit. Across the street from Harajuku Station's north exit is:

❷ Takeshita Dori

This pedestrian-only street is lined nonstop with stores that cater to teenagers. It's packed—especially on Sunday afternoons—with young people hunting for bargains on inexpensive clothing, shoes, music, sunglasses, jewelry, watches, cosmetics, and more.

After inching your way through the flow of humanity along this narrow lane, you'll eventually find yourself on a busy thoroughfare, Meiji Dori. If it's the first or fourth Sunday of the month, turn left (north) onto Meiji Dori. In a couple minutes, on your left you'll see:

❸ Togo Shrine

Togo Shrine is dedicated to Admiral Togo, who was in charge of the fleet that defeated the Russian navy in 1905 in the Russo-Japanese War. Nowadays, the shrine is most popular for its flea market held the first and fourth Sundays of every month, when everything from old chests, dolls, porcelain, and kimono are for sale, all spread out on a tree-shaded sidewalk that meanders around the shrine.

Head back south on Meiji Dori. To your right, just before the big intersection, is:

❹ La Forêt

La Forêt is filled with trendy shoe and clothing boutiques. The less expensive boutiques tend to be on the lower floors; the more exclusive are higher up. (See "Shopping," later in this chapter for details on many of the shops and department stores listed in this walking tour.) Behind La Forêt is one of my favorite museums, the:

❺ Ota Memorial Museum of Art

The museum is at 1–10–10 Jingumae and features the private ukiyo-e (woodblock prints) collection of the late Ota Seizo. (See review earlier in this chapter for more.)

Across Omotesando Dori is:

❻ Chicago

This store specializes in used American clothing but also stocks hundreds of used and new kimono and yukata in a corner of its basement.

Near La Forêt is Harajuku's major intersection, Meiji Dori and Omotesando Dori. Here,

on the intersection near Chicago, is one of Harajuku's more unusual shops:

❼ Condomania

This store at 6–30–1 Jingumae, sells condoms in a wide range of sizes, colors, and styles, from glow-in-the-dark to scented. It's open daily 11am to 11pm.

Heading east on Omotesando Dori (away from Harajuku Station), you'll soon see, to your right:

❽ Kiddy Land

Located at 6–1–9 Jingumae, this store sells gag gifts and a great deal more than just toys, including enough to amuse non-discerning adults. You could spend an hour browsing here, but the store is so crowded with teenagers that you may end up rushing for the door.

Continue east on Omotesando Dori (where sidewalk vendors selling jewelry and ethnic accessories set up shop on weekends), to your right will soon be Harajuku's most famous store:

❾ Oriental Bazaar

At 5–9–13 Jingumae, you'll find the Oriental Bazaar, Tokyo's best one-stop shopping for Japanese souvenirs. Four floors offer antique chinaware, old kimono, Japanese paper products, fans, jewelry, woodblock prints, screens, chinaware, and much more, all at reasonable prices. I always stock up on gifts here for the folks back home.

As you continue walking east on Omotesando Dori, on your left are buildings that probably wouldn't catch your attention anywhere else but look highly unusual in this part of Tokyo:

❿ Dojunkai Apartments

The apartments were built in the mid-1920s following the Great Kanto Earthquake. Several such apartment complexes were built for the middle class, but few from that era remain. With their ivy-covered walls and clump of shady trees, the apartments look quite cozy; some have been turned into galleries and shops. With

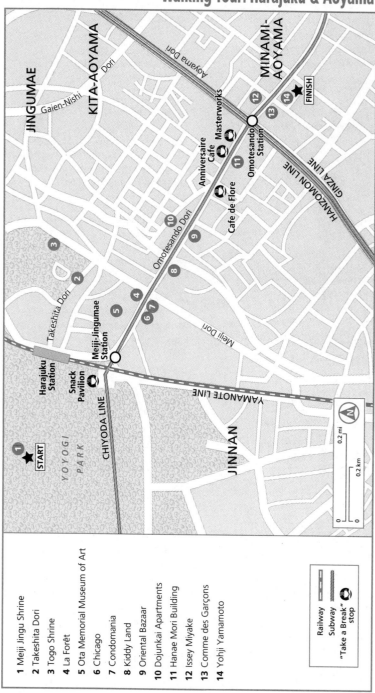

1 Meiji Jingu Shrine
2 Takeshita Dori
3 Togo Shrine
4 La Forêt
5 Ota Memorial Museum of Art
6 Chicago
7 Condomania
8 Kiddy Land
9 Oriental Bazaar
10 Dojunkai Apartments
11 Hanae Mori Building
12 Issey Miyake
13 Comme des Garçons
14 Yohji Yamamoto

Railway
Subway
"Take a Break" stop

land prices the way they are, however, the Dojunkai Apartments' days are numbered; by the time you read this, it could be a major construction site.

> **TAKE A BREAK**
> Harajuku and Aoyama have more sidewalk cafes than any other part of Tokyo. Most conspicuous is the fancy **Anniversaire Café,** 3–5–30 Kita-Aoyama, across from the Hanae Mori Building (see number 11, below). **Café de Flore,** 5–1–2 Jingumae, just before the Hanae Mori Building, is a multi-level cafe overlooking the Omotesando promenade and a branch of a Parisian cafe of the same name on Boulevard Saint-Germain. **Masterworks,** 3–5–28 Kita-Aoyama, is a simple, open-fronted cafe located just before the Aoyama and Omotesando Dori intersection.

Near the end of Omotesando Dori, to your right, is the:

⓫ Hanae Mori Building

This building was designed by Japanese architect Kenzo Tange (who also designed the Akasaka Prince Hotel and the TMG city hall in Shinjuku). It houses the entire collection of Hanae Mori, from casual wear to evening wear. In the basement is the Antique Market with individual stallkeepers selling china, jewelry, clothing,

watches, swords, and items from the 1930s.

At the end of Omotesando Dori, where it connects with Aoyama Dori, is Omotesando Station. You can board the subway here or, for more shopping, cross Aoyama Dori and continue heading east, where you'll pass a number of designer shops. First comes:

⓬ Issey Miyake

The store is on the left at 3–18–11 Minami-Aoyama. Its clothes are known for their richness in texture and fabrics. To the right is:

⓭ Comme des Garçons

At 5–2–1 Minami-Aoyama Comme des Garçons showcases Rei Kawakubo's designs for both men and women. Farther down the street, on the right, is:

⓮ Yohji Yamamoto

As with all Yamamoto shops, this store at 5–3–6 Minami-Aoyama has an interesting avant-garde interior.

> **WINDING DOWN**
> The cafes listed above are just a few minutes' walk away, but if you're dying for a burger, look no farther than **Kua' Aina,** 5–10–21 Minami Aoyama, on the corner of Aoyama Dori and Kotto Dori intersection. It boasts the most satisfying burgers in town, along with sandwiches and soft drinks.

7 Especially for Kids

In addition to its observatories, **Tokyo Tower** (see "Spectacular City Views," earlier in this chapter) contains a few other attractions that might be worth a visit if you have children in tow including a small **aquarium** and a **wax museum.** Other attractions listed earlier that are good for children include the **Edo-Tokyo Museum, Fukagawa Edo Museum,** and **National Science Museum.**

Hanayashiki   Opened in 1853, this small and rather corny amusement park is Japan's oldest. It offers a small roller coaster, a kiddie Ferris wheel, a carousel, a haunted house, a 3D theater, and other diversions that appeal to children. Note, however, that after paying admission, you must still buy tickets for each ride; tickets are ¥100 (85¢) each, and most rides require 2 or 3.

2–28–1 Asakusa (northwest of Sensoji Temple), Taito-ku. ✆ 043/3842-8780. Admission ¥900 ($7.50) adults, ¥400 ($3.35) children 5–12 and senior citizens, free for children 4 and younger. Wed–Mon 10am–6pm (5pm in winter). Station: Asakusa (7 min.).

Joypolis Sega Bored teenagers in tow, grumbling at yet another temple or shrine? Bring them to life at Tokyo's most sophisticated virtual amusement arcade, outfitted with the latest in video games and high-tech virtual-reality attractions, courtesy of Sega. Video games include sledding and car races, in which participants maneuver curves utilizing virtual-reality equipment, as well numerous aeronautical battle games. There's also a 3D sightseeing tour with seats that move with the action on the screen, several virtual reality rides, and much, much more. Most harmless are the Print Club machines, which have taken Japan by storm and will print your face on stickers with the background (Mt. Fuji, perhaps?) of your choice. If you think your kids will want to try everything, you can buy them a passport for ¥3,300 ($27.50).

Tokyo Decks, 3rd floor, Odaiba. (© 03/5500-1801. Admission ¥500 ($4.15) adults, ¥300 ($2.50) for children; individual attractions an additional ¥200–¥700 ($1.65–$5.85) each. Daily 10am–10:30pm. Station: Odaiba Kaihin Koen (2 min.).

National Children's Castle (Kodomo-no-Shiro) ⭐ Here's a great place to bring the kids. Conceived by the Ministry of Health and Welfare to commemorate the International Year of the Child in 1979, the Children's Castle holds various activity rooms designed to appeal to children of all ages. The third floor, designed for spontaneous and unstructured play, features a large climbing gym, a computer play room, building blocks, a play house, dolls, books, and a teen corner with table tennis and other age-appropriate games; there's also an art room staffed with instructors to help children with projects suitable to their ages. On the fourth floor is a music room, which holds mini-concerts and special events and also has instruments the kids are invited to play (during my last visit, a band composed of junior-high-aged kids was playing for an enthusiastic audience of dancing toddlers) as well as a video room with private cubicles where visitors can make selections from a stocked library of English and Japanese videos. On the roof is an outdoor playground complete with tricycles and a small, toddler wading pool. Various programs are presented throughout the week, including puppet shows, fairy tales, and origami presentations.

5–53–1 Jingumae, Shibuya-ku. © 03/3797-5666. Admission ¥500 ($4.15) adults, ¥400 ($3.35) children 3–17, free for children under 3; ¥200 ($1.65) extra for wading pool. Tues–Fri 12:30–5:30pm; Sat–Sun and holidays (including school holidays) 10am–5:30pm. Station: Omotesando (exit B2, 8 min., on Aoyama Dori in the direction of Shibuya) or Shibuya (10 min.).

Sunshine International Aquarium Claiming to be the world's highest aquarium, this Sunshine City complex is the unlikely home to more than 20,000 fish and animals, including dolphins, octopuses, eels, piranhas, sea horses, sea otters, seals, giant crabs, and rare—and rather weird—species of fish. There are several shows, including performances by seals and what's probably the world's only "fish circus," featuring an electric eel and an archer fish.

World Import Mart Bldg., 10th floor, Sunshine City, 3–1–3 Higashi Ikebukuro. © 03/3989-3466. Admission ¥1,600 ($13.35) adults, ¥800 ($6.65) children 4–15, free for children 4 and younger. Mon–Sat 10am–6pm; Sun and holidays 10am–6:30pm. Station: Higashi Ikebukuro (3 min.) or Ikebukuro (7 min.).

Tokyo Disneyland ⭐⭐⭐ If you (or your kids) have your heart set on visiting all the world's Disney parks, head to Tokyo Disneyland. Virtually a carbon copy of the back-home version, this one also boasts the Jungle Cruise, Pirates of the Caribbean, Haunted Mansion, and Space Mountain. Other hot attractions include Toontown, a wacky theme park where Mickey, Minnie, Donald, and other Disney characters work and play; MicroAdventure, which features 3D glasses and various special effects; and Star Tours, a thrill adventure created by Disney and George Lucas.

1–1 Maihama, Urayasu-shi, Chiba. ℂ **045/683-3333**. Disneyland Passport, including entrance to and use of all attractions ¥5,500 ($46) adults, ¥4,800 ($40) senior citizens and junior high and high school students, ¥3,700 ($31) children 4–11, free for children under 4. Starlight admission after 5pm or 6pm, ¥4,500 ($37.50), ¥3,900 ($31), and ¥3,000 ($25) respectively. Daily 8 or 9am–9 or 10pm, with slightly shorter hours in winter. Schedule is subject to change, so call in advance or check www.tokyodisneyresort.co.jp. Tickets can be purchased in advance at the Tokyo Disneyland Ticket Center, Hibiya Mitsui Building, 1–1–2 Yurakucho (station: Hibiya). Station: Maihama Station on the JR Keiyo Line from Tokyo Station (1 min.).

Tokyo DisneySea 🎡🎡   Opened in 2001 adjacent to Disneyland, this theme park based on ocean lore centers on seven distinct "ports of call," including the futuristic Port Discovery marina with its StormRider which flies straight into the eye of a storm; Lost River Delta with its Indiana Jones Adventure; Mermaid Lagoon based on the film *The Little Mermaid;* and the Arabian Coast, with its Sindbad's Seven Voyages boat ride.

1–1 Maihama, Urayasu-shi, Chiba. ℂ **045/683-3333**. One-day passport, ¥5,500 ($46) adults, ¥4,800 ($40) senior citizens and junior high and high school students, ¥3,700 ($31) children 4–11, free for children under 4. Daily 8am–10pm in summer, 10am–7pm in winter. Schedule subject to change, so call in advance or go to www.tokyodisneyresort.co.jp. Tickets can be purchased in advance at the Tokyo Disneyland Ticket Center, Hibiya Mitsui Building, 1–1–2 Yurakucho (station: Hibiya). Station: Maihama Station on the JR Keiyo Line from Tokyo Station (1 min.).

Ueno Zoo   Founded back in 1882, Japan's oldest zoo is small by today's standards but remains one of the most well-known zoos in Japan, due in part to its giant pandas, donated by the Chinese government to mark the re-establishment of diplomatic relations between the two countries following World War II. A vivarium, opened in 1999, houses amphibians, fish, and reptiles including Komodo dragons, green tree pythons, and dwarf crocodiles. Personally, I can't help but feel sorry for some of the animals in their small spaces, but children will enjoy the Japanese macaques, polar bears, California sea lions, penguins, gorillas, giraffes, zebras, elephants, deer, and tigers.

Ueno Park, Taito-ku. ℂ **03/3828-5171**. Admission ¥600 ($5) adults, ¥200 ($1.65) children 12–14, free for children under 12 and senior citizens. Tues–Sun 9:30am–5pm (enter by 4pm). Closed some holidays. Station: Ueno (4 min.).

8 Spectator Sports

For information on current sporting events taking place in Tokyo, ranging from kickboxing and pro wrestling to soccer, table tennis, and golf classics, check the quarterly magazine *Tokyo Journal* or contact the Tourist Information Center.

MARTIAL ARTS   If you're interested in the martial arts including kendo and aikido, stop by the **Tourist Information Center** for its list of schools that allow you to watch practice. You can also join on a monthly basis for instruction. Otherwise, contact the various federations directly: **International Aikido Federation** (ℂ **03/3203-9236**); the **All-Japan Judo Federation** (ℂ **03/ 3818-4199**); the **Japan Karate-do Federation** (ℂ **03/3503-6640**); and the **All Japan Kendo Federation** (ℂ **03/3211-5804** or 03/3211-5805). All have member schools in Tokyo; call for an appointment.

SUMO   Sumo matches are held in Tokyo at the **Kokugikan,** 1–3–28 Yokoami, Sumida-ku (ℂ **03/3623-5111;** station: Ryogoku, then a 1-min. walk). Matches are held in January, May, and September for 15 consecutive days, beginning at around 10am and lasting until 6pm; the top wrestlers

For It's Ichi, Ni, San Strikes You're Out...

The Japanese are so crazy about baseball, you'd think they invented the game. Actually, it was introduced to Japan by the United States way back in 1873. Today, it's as popular among Japanese as it is among Americans. Even the annual high school play-offs keep everyone glued to the TV set.

As with other imports, the Japanese have added their own modifications: Some of the playing fields are smaller (new ones tend to have American dimensions) and, borrowing from American football, each team has its own cheerleaders. There are several American players who have proved very popular with local fans; but according to the rules, no more than four foreigners may play on any one team. On the other hand, recent years have also seen an exodus of top Japanese players defecting to American teams, including the hugely popular and successful Suzuki Ichiro, leadoff hitter and rightfielder for the Seattle Mariners. In fact, Japanese fans have been so mesmerized by the Mariners (whose games are broadcast on Japanese TV), that television ratings for Japanese games has fallen.

Although playing one's hardest is at a premium in the United States, in Japan, any attempt at excelling individually is frowned upon. As in other aspects of life, it is the group, the team that counts. To what extent that's so may be illustrated by the case of an American player: When he missed opening day at training camp due to a life-or-death operation on his son at a hospital, his contract was immediately canceled. And rather than let a foreign player excel by breaking the hitting record set by a Japanese, American Randy Bass was thrown only balls and walked.

There are two professional leagues, the Central and the Pacific, which play from April to October and meet in the final Japan Series play-offs. In Tokyo, the home teams are the **Yomiuri Giants** and the **Nippon Ham Fighters,** both of which play at the Tokyo Dome (✆ **03/ 3811-2111;** station: Suidobashi); and the **Yakult Swallows,** which play at Jingu Stadium (station: Gaienmae). Other teams playing in the vicinity of Tokyo are the **Chiba Lotte Marines,** who play at Kawasaki Stadium, Kanagawa (✆ **044/244-1171;** station: Kawasaki on the JR Tokaido Line, then by bus no. 16, 19, 21, 22, or 23); the **Seibu Lions,** Seibu Lions Stadium, Tokorozawa City (✆ **0429/24-1151;** station: JR to Seibu Kyujo-mae on the Seibu Sayama Line); and the **Yokohama Bay Stars,** Yokohama Stadium, Yokohama (✆ **045/661-1251;** station: Kannai on the JR Keihin Tohoku Line). Advance tickets go on sale on Friday, 2 weeks prior to the game, and can be purchased at the stadium or, for Tokyo teams, at any **Playguide** ticket outlet (✆ **03/3257-9999,** with counters throughout the city). Prices for the Tokyo Dome and Jingu Stadium begin at about ¥1,500 ($12.50) for an unreserved seat in the outfield and ¥1,900 ($16) for an unreserved seat in the infield.

compete after 3:30pm. The best seats are ringside box seats, but they're bought out by companies and by friends and families of sumo wrestlers. Usually available are balcony seats, which can be purchased at any **Playguide** ticket outlet (© **03/3257-9999,** with counters throughout Tokyo) or at ticket counters in several department stores, including Matsuya in Ginza, Isetan in Shinjuku, and Seibu or Tobu in Ikebukuro. You can also purchase tickets directly at the Kokugikan ticket office beginning at 9am every morning of the tournament. Prices range from about ¥2,100 ($17.50) for an unreserved seat (sold on the day of the event) to ¥8,200 ($68) for a good reserved seat.

If you can't make it to a match, watching on TV is almost as good. Tournaments in Tokyo, as well as those that take place annually in Osaka, Nagoya, and Fukuoka, are broadcast on the NHK channel from 4 to 6pm daily during matches.

9 Shopping

One of the delights of being in Japan is the shopping. It won't take you long to become convinced that shopping is the number one pastime in Tokyo. Women, men, couples, and even whole families go on buying expeditions in their free time, making Sunday the most crowded shopping day of the week.

THE SHOPPING SCENE

BEST BUYS Tokyo is the country's showcase for everything from the latest in camera, computer, or stereo equipment to original woodblock prints. Traditional Japanese crafts and souvenirs that make good buys include toys (both traditional and the latest in technical wizardry), kites, Japanese dolls, carp banners, swords, lacquerware, bamboo baskets, ikebana accessories, ceramics, chopsticks, fans, masks, knives, scissors, sake, and silk and cotton kimono. And you don't have to spend a fortune: You can pick up handmade Japanese paper (washi) products, such as umbrellas, lanterns, boxes, stationery and other souvenirs for a fraction of what they would cost in import shops in the United States. In Harajuku, it's possible to buy a fully lined dress in the latest fashion for $60, and I can't even count the number of pairs of fun, casual shoes I've bought in Tokyo for a mere $35. Used cameras can be picked up for a song, reproductions of famous woodblock prints make great inexpensive gifts, and many items—from pearls to electronic video and audio equipment—can be bought tax free (see "Taxes," below).

Japan is famous for its electronics, but if you're buying new you can probably find these products just as cheaply, or even more cheaply, in the United States. If you think you want to shop for electronic products while you're in Tokyo, it pays to do some comparison shopping before you leave home so you can spot a deal when you see one. On the other hand, one of the joys of shopping for electronics in Japan is discovering new, advanced models; you might decide you want that new Sony MP3 player simply because it's the coolest thing you've ever seen, no matter what the price.

GREAT SHOPPING AREAS Another enjoyable aspect of shopping in Tokyo is that specific areas are often devoted to certain goods, sold wholesale but also available to the individual shopper. **Kappabashi Dori** (station: Tawaramachi), for example, is where you'll find shops specializing in kitchenware, while **Kanda** (station: Jimbocho) is known for its bookstores. **Akihabara** (station: Akihabara) is packed with stores selling the latest in electronics. **Ginza** (station: Ginza) is the chic address for clothing boutiques as well as art galleries. **Aoyama** (station: Omotesando) boasts the city's largest concentration of designer clothing stores, while nearby **Harajuku** (stations: Harajuku, Meiji-Jingumae, or Omotesando) is the place to go for youthful, fun, and inexpensive fashions.

SALES   Department stores have sales throughout the year, during which you can pick up bargains on everything from electronic goods and men's suits to golf clubs, toys, kitchenware, food, and lingerie; there are even sales for used wedding kimono. The most popular sales are for **designer clothing,** usually held twice a year in July and December or January. Here you can pick up fantastic clothing at cut-rate prices—but be prepared for the crowds. To find out about current sales, check the *Tokyo Journal,* the quarterly guide to what's going on in Tokyo.

Items on sale in department stores are usually found on one of the top floors in what's usually labeled the "Exhibition Hall" or "Promotion Hall" in the store's English brochure, which you can obtain by stopping by the information desk located near the main entrance. Sometimes an entire floor is devoted to a sale.

TAXES   Remember that a 5% consumption tax will be added to the price marked, but all major department stores in Tokyo will refund the tax to foreign visitors if total purchases amount to more than ¥10,001 ($83.35) on that day. Exemptions include food, beverages, tobacco, pharmaceuticals, cosmetics, film, and batteries. When you've completed your shopping, take the purchased goods and receipts to the tax-refund counter in the store. There are forms to fill out (you will need your passport). Upon completion, a record of your purchase is placed on the visa page of your passport and you are given the tax refund on the spot. When leaving Japan, make sure you have your purchases with you; you may be asked by Customs to show them (pack them in your carry-on).

SHIPPING IT HOME   Many first-class hotels in Tokyo provide a packing and shipping service. In addition, most large department stores, as well as tourist shops such as the Oriental Bazaar and antiques shops, will ship your purchases overseas.

If you wish to ship packages yourself, the easiest method is to go to a post office and purchase an easy-to-assemble cardboard box, available in three sizes (along with the necessary tape and string). Keep in mind that packages mailed abroad cannot weigh more than 20kg (about 44 lb.) and that only the larger international post offices accept packages to be mailed overseas. Remember, too, that mailing packages from Japan is expensive. Ask your hotel concierge for the closest international post office.

SHOPPING FROM A TO Z
ANTIQUES & CURIOS
In addition to the listings here, other places to look for antiques include the **Antique Market** in the basement of the Hanae Mori Building on Omotesando Dori (*©* **03/3406-1021;** station: Omotesando, 1 min.); **Mayuyama,** housed in a distinguished stone building between Kyobashi and Takaracho within walking distance of Tokyo Station (*©* **03/3561-5146**), one of the best-known names in fine—and expensive—antiques; and the **Oriental Bazaar** and Tokyo's outdoor **flea markets** (later in this chapter).

Fuji-Torii   Open since 1948, this shop in Harajuku specializes in traditional works of art and antiques, including screens, scrolls, lacquerware, ceramics, furniture, and woodblock prints. 6–1–10 Jingumae (next to Kiddy Land). *©* **03/3400-2777.** Wed–Mon 11am–6pm. Closed 3rd Mon. Station: Meiji-jingumae (2 min.).

Kurofune *(Finds)*   Located in a large house in Roppongi, Kurofune is owned by an American, John Adair, who for more than 22 years has specialized in Japanese antique furniture in its original state. The largest collection here is of mid- to top-quality pieces. Browsing is a delight even if you can't afford to buy;

stock includes hibachi, fabrics, prints, maps, lanterns, baskets, screens, and folk art. 7–7–4 Roppongi. © 03/3479-1552. Mon–Sat 10am–6pm. Station: Roppongi (5 min.). From Roppongi Crossing, walk away from Tokyo Tower on Gaien-Higashi Dori, take the diagonal street to the left and then take a right at 7-Eleven.

Tokyo Antique Hall (Komingu Kottokan) This is one of the best places for one-stop hunting, with approximately 32 dealers offering mostly Japanese antiques and bric-a-brac. Although most articles are marked, it's okay to try bargaining. You could spend hours here, looking over everything from woodblock prints and lacquerware to hairpins, jewelry, ceramics, pottery, and samurai gear. 3–9–5 Minami Ikebukuro. © **03/3982-3433** or 03/3980-8228. Fri–Wed 11am–7pm (some stalls may close early if business is slow). Station: Ikebukuro (10 min.). Take a right out of the station's east side and walk south on Meiji Dori; the shop will be on your left.

ARCADES & SHOPPING MALLS

IN HOTELS Shopping arcades are found in several of Tokyo's first-class hotels. Although they don't offer the excitement and challenge of going out and rubbing elbows with the natives, they do offer convenience, English-speaking clerks, and consistently top-quality merchandise. The **Imperial Hotel Arcade** (station: Hibiya) is one of the best, with shops selling pearls, woodblock prints, porcelain, antiques, and expensive name-brand clothing like Hanae Mori. The **Okura** and **New Otani** hotels also have extensive shopping arcades.

UNDERGROUND ARCADES Underground shopping arcades are found around several of Tokyo's train and subway stations; the biggest are at **Tokyo Station** (the Yaesu side) and **Shinjuku Station** (the east side). They often have great sales and bargains on clothing, accessories, and electronics. My only complaint is that once you're in them, it sometimes seems like you'll never find your way out again.

DUTY-FREE ARCADES Other good places to shop if you're short of time are duty-free stores. To qualify, you must present your passport, whereupon you'll be issued a piece of paper to surrender at the Customs desk when departing Japan (the Customs desk at the Narita Airport is well marked, so you can't miss it). At that time, you may also be requested to show your purchases to Customs officials, so be sure to put them in your carry-on.

The best-known tax-free arcade is the **International Arcade** near the Imperial Hotel under the elevated JR Yamamote train tracks (© **03/3571-1528;** station: Hibiya). It features merchandise from pearls to electronics. Narita Airport's duty-free shops, located past the security machines and customs, are also good places to shop for alcohol. Prices aren't cheaper and selections are limited, but I usually buy my sake here before boarding the plane just so I don't have to lug it around.

SHOPPING MALLS **Sunshine City** (station: Higashi Ikebukuro or Ikebukuro) is one of Tokyo's oldest shopping malls, with more than 300 shops and restaurants spread through several adjoining buildings. Its popularity, however, is now challenged by newer and grander shopping malls in recently developed Odaiba (station: Odaiba Kaihin Koen). Palette Town is an amusement/shopping center that contains the Italian-themed **Venus Fort,** an indoor mall that evokes scenes from Italy with its store-fronted lanes, painted sky, fountains, plazas, and Italian name-brand boutiques. Nearby **Tokyo Decks** specializes in international household goods, including imports from the United States, Europe, China, and Hong Kong.

BOOKS

Yasukuni Dori in Jimbocho-Kanda (station: Jimbocho) is lined with bookstores selling both new and used books, with several dealing in English-language books. Keep in mind, however, that English-language books are usually more expensive in Japan than back home. Still, no bibliophile should pass this street up. Stores are closed on Sunday; most are closed holidays as well. **Kitazawa** (✆ 03/3263-0011), the most spacious of the three listed here, boasts an overwhelming selection of books, including the most recently published novels, American and English classic literature, topical books ranging from history to politics, books on Japan, and antiquarian books. **Tuttle Book Shop** (✆ 03/3291-7071), the Tokyo branch of a Vermont firm, carries a wide selection of books on Japan and the Far East written in English, including English translations of Japanese novels. Established in 1882, **Ohya Shobo** (✆ 03/3291-0062) doesn't have any English-language books, but it does claim to have the world's largest stock of 18th- and 19th-century Japanese illustrated books, woodblock prints, and maps, including maps from the Edo Period.

Kinokuniya   This is one of Tokyo's best-known bookstores, with one of the city's largest selections of books and magazines in English—including books on Japan, dictionaries and textbooks for students of Japanese, and novels—on its sixth floor. Takashimaya Annex, Takashimaya Times Square complex. ✆ 03/5361-3301. Daily 10am–8pm. Closed some Weds. Station: Shinjuku (south exit, 2 min.).

Maruzen   This is Japan's oldest bookstore, founded in 1869. Its English-language section is on the second floor, with everything from dictionaries and travel guides to special-interest books on Japan. It also carries books on science, politics, and history, as well as magazines and paperbacks. The basement contains an office-supply shop with printing and copying services, while the fourth-floor Craft Center sells traditional handmade products of Japan. 2-3-10 Nihombashi. ✆ 03/3272-7211. Mon–Sat 10am–7:30pm; Sun 10am–6pm. Closed some Suns. Station: Kyobashi (3 min.). On Chuo Dori across from Takashimaya department store, within walking distance of the Ginza and Tokyo stations.

Tower Records and Books   My friends in Tokyo don't shop anywhere else for their books and magazines, as prices are usually lower here than elsewhere. The seventh floor is devoted to imported publications, with a good selection of English-language books, more than 3,000 different kinds of magazines, and the Sunday editions of major newspapers. 1–22–14 Jinnan. ✆ 03/3496-3661. Daily 10am–10pm. Closed some Mon. Station: Shibuya (Hachiko exit, 5 min.).

CAMERAS & FILM

You can purchase cameras at many duty-free shops, including those in Akihabara, but if you're really serious about photographic equipment or want to stock up on film, make a trip to a shop dealing specifically in cameras. If purchasing a new camera is too formidable an expense, consider buying a used camera. New models come out so frequently in Japan that older models can be grabbed up for next to nothing.

Bic Camera   A huge, six-floor store near the Tourist Information Center offering not only single-lens reflex, large and medium format, and digital cameras but also computers, watches, toys, and much more. Note, however, that it caters primarily to Japanese; English-speaking sales clerks are scarce and and export models are limited. Ask for the English brochure. 1–11–1 Yurakucho, Chiyoda-ku. ✆ 03/5221-1112. Daily 10am–8pm. Station: Yurakucho (1 min.)

㊱ **Camera No Kimura**   This store, west of Ikebukuro Station, has a small but good selection of used cameras and lenses. Since there's no telling what may be available, camera bugs stop by frequently just to look over the stock. 1–18–8 Nishi Ikebukuro, Toshima-ku. ℂ 03/3981-8437. Mon–Sat 8am–8pm; Sun and holidays 10am–7pm. Station: Ikebukuro (1 min.).

Matsuzakya Camera   A great place to head for used Japanese and foreign cameras. It also stocks new equipment. 1–27–34 Takanawa, Minato-ku. ℂ 03/3443-1311. Mon–Sat 10am–7pm; Sun and holidays 10am–6pm. Station: Shinagawa or Meguro (15 min.).

Yodobashi Camera   Shinjuku is the photographic equipment center for Tokyo, and this store, 1 block west of the station, is the biggest in the area. In fact, it ranks as one of the largest discount camera shops in the world, with around 30,000 items in stock, and it reputedly sells approximately 500 to 600 cameras daily. Although prices are marked, you can bargain here. This is the place to stock up on film; you can also have film developed here. In addition to cameras, it sells watches, calculators, computers and other electronic equipment, though if you're interested specifically in watches, clocks, audio/video equipment, games, and other wares, there are branches nearby that specialize in these (ask at the head shop for a map of the area). 1–11–1 Nishi-Shinjuku, Shinjuku-ku. ℂ 03/3346-1010. Daily 9:30am–9pm. Station: Shinjuku (west exit, 3 min.).

CRAFTS & TRADITIONAL JAPANESE PRODUCTS

If you want to shop for traditional Japanese folk crafts in the right atmosphere, nothing beats **Nakamise Dori** (station: Asakusa; 1 min.), a pedestrian lane leading to Sensoji Temple in Asakusa. It's lined with stall after stall selling souvenirs galore, from wooden geta shoes and hairpins worn by geisha to T-shirts, fans, toy swords, and dolls. Most are open from 10am to 6pm; some may close 1 day a week.

Another good place to search for traditional crafts are **department stores,** which usually have sections devoted to ceramics, pottery, bambooware, flower-arranging accessories, and fabrics.

Japan Sword   This is the best-known sword shop in Tokyo, with an outstanding collection of fine swords, daggers, sword guards and fittings, and other sword accessories, as well as some antique samurai armor. Coming here is like visiting a museum. The place also sells copies and souvenir items of traditional swords at prices much lower than the very expensive historic swords. You can also have swords cleaned and polished here. 3–8–1 Toranomon, Minato-ku. ℂ 03/3434-4321. Mon–Fri 9:30am–6pm; Sat 9:30am–5pm. Closed holidays. Station: Toranomon (exit 2, 5 min.).

Japan Traditional Craft Center (Zenkoku Dentoteki Kogeihin Senta) *Finds*   This store is worth a trip even if you can't afford to buy anything. Established to publicize and distribute information on Japanese crafts and to promote the country's artisans, the center is a great introduction to both traditional and contemporary Japanese design. It sells various top-quality crafts from all over Japan on a rotating basis, so there are always new items on hand. Crafts for sale usually include lacquerware, ceramics, fabrics, paper products, bamboo items, writing brushes, metalwork, stone lanterns, and more. Prices are high, but rightfully so. Tobu department store, Metropolitan Plaza, 1–11–1 Nishi-Ikebukuro. ℂ 03/5954-6066. Thurs–Tues 11am–7pm. Station: Ikebukuro (1 min.).

Kokkusai Kanko Kaikan *(Finds)*   What finds these two places are! Located right beside each other, practically on top of Tokyo Station, they contain tourism promotional offices for almost every prefecture in Japan. In addition to stocking tourist brochures and pamphlets, many of the offices also sell a few goods and products unique to their prefecture. Altogether, there are several dozen of these little shops, most on the first through fourth floors of the Kokusai Kanko Kaikan Building and a few on the ninth floor of the Daimaru department store. You won't find such a varied collection of regional goods anywhere else in Japan—and prices are very reasonable, cheaper than at department stores. What's more, no one shops here. You don't have time to go to Okayama to buy its famous Bizen pottery? You forgot to buy your clay ningyo doll while in Fukuoka? You can find those here, as well as toys, lacquerware, pottery, glassware, paper products, sake, food items, kokeshi dolls, bamboo ware, pearls, china, and everything else Japan makes. 1–8–3 Marunouchi, Chiyoda-ku, and on the 9th floor of the Daimaru department store. ℂ 03/3215-1181. Mon–Fri 9am–5pm. Closed holidays. Station: Tokyo (north Yaesu exit, 1 min.). Look for Kokusai Kanko Kaikan on the small square with the clock; its entrance is opposite the JR Travel Service Center. In Daimaru, take the left-hand elevator just off the square with the clock.

Oriental Bazaar   If you have time for only one souvenir shop in Tokyo, this should be it. This is the city's best-known and largest souvenir/crafts store, selling products at reasonable prices and offering four floors of souvenir and gift items, including cotton yukata, kimono (new and used), woodblock prints, paper products, wind chimes, stationery, fans, chopsticks, lamps and vases, Imari chinaware, sake sets, Japanese dolls, pearls, and even books on Japan and a large selection of antique furniture. This store will also ship things home for you. There's a smaller branch on the fourth floor of Terminal 1 at Narita Airport (ℂ 0476/32-9333), open daily 7:30am to 8:30pm. 5–9–13 Jingumae, Shibuya-ku. ℂ 03/3400-3933. Fri–Wed 10am–7pm. Station: Meiji-Jingumae (3 min.), Harajuku (4 min.), or Omotesando (5 min.). On Omotesando Dori in Harajuku; look for an Asian-looking facade of orange and green.

Sakai Kokodo Gallery   This gallery claims to be the oldest woodblock print shop in Japan. The first shop was opened back in 1870 in the Kanda area of Tokyo by the present owner's great-grandfather, and altogether four generations of the Sakai family have tended the store. It's a great place for original prints, as well as for reproductions of such great masters as Hiroshige. (If you're really a woodblock print fan, you'll want to visit the Sakai family's excellent museum, Japan Ukiyo-e Museum, in the small town of Matsumoto in the Japan Alps; see "Matsumoto, Gateway to the Japan Alps," in chapter 6.) 1–2–14 Yurakucho, Chiyoda-ku (across from the Imperial Hotel's Tower). ℂ 03/3591-4678. Daily 11am–6pm. Station: Hibiya (1 min.).

DEPARTMENT STORES

Japanese department stores are institutions in themselves. Usually enormous, well-designed, and chock-full of merchandise, they have about everything you can imagine, including museums and art galleries, pet stores, rooftop playgrounds or greenhouses, travel agencies, restaurants, grocery markets, and flower shops. You could easily spend a whole day in a department store—eating, attending cultural exhibitions, planning your next vacation, and, well, shopping. Microcosms of Japanese society, these department stores reflect the affluence of modern Japan, offering everything from elaborate wedding kimono to fashions by the world's top designers.

One of the most wonderful aspects of the Japanese department store is the **courteous service.** If you arrive at a store as its doors open at 10 or 10:30am, you'll witness a daily rite: Lined up at the entrance are staff who bow in welcome. Some Japanese shoppers arrive just before opening time so as not to miss this favorite ritual. Sales clerks are everywhere, ready to help you. In many cases, you don't even have to go to the cash register once you've made your choice; just hand over the product, along with your money, to the sales clerk, who will return with your change, your purchase neatly wrapped, and an "*arigatoo gozaimashita*" (thank you very much). A day spent in a Japanese department store could spoil you for the rest of your life.

The basement of the store is usually devoted to **foodstuffs:** fresh fish, produce, and pre-prepared snacks and dinners. There are often free samples of food; if you're feeling slightly hungry, walking through the food department could do nicely for a snack. Many department stores include **boutiques** by such famous Japanese and international fashion designers as Issey Miyake, Rei Kawakubo (creator of Comme des Garçons), Hanae Mori, Christian Dior, Calvin Klein, and Brooks Brothers, as well as a department devoted to the kimono. Near the **kimono department** may also be the section devoted to **traditional crafts;** department stores are convenient places to shop for these. To find out what's where, stop by the store's information booth located on the ground floor near the front entrance and ask for the floor-by-floor pamphlet in English. Be sure, too, to ask about **sales** on the promotional floor—you never know what bargains you may chance upon.

Hours are generally from 10 or 10:30am to 7, 7:30, or 8pm. Department stores used to close 1 day a week, but now they close irregularly, always on the same day of the week (say, on Tues) but in no apparent pattern. One month they may be closed the second and third Tuesday of the month, but the next month only the first or not at all. In any case, you can always find several department stores that are open, even on Sundays and holidays (major shopping days in Japan). All major credit and charge cards are accepted.

Isetan Isetan is a favorite among foreigners living in Tokyo. It has a good line of conservative clothing appropriate for working situations, as well as contemporary and fashionable styles, including designer clothes (Issey Miyake, Yohji Yamamoto, Tsumori Chisato, Vivienne Westwood, Paul Smith) and large dress sizes (on the 2nd floor). It also has a great kimono section along with all the traditional accessories (obi, shoes, purses), a well-known art gallery on the eighth floor of its annex, and an arts and crafts section with changing exhibits. In the annex, which carries mostly men's clothing, is also a New Creator's Space on the ground floor, unique among Japanese department stores (which are generally reluctant to carry anything but the tried and true), that showcases clothing by up-and-coming Japanese designers. 3–14–1 Shinjuku, Shinjuku-ku. (C) **03/3352-1111.** Mon–Thurs 10am–7:30pm; Fri–Sun 10am–8pm. Closed some Wed. Station: Shinjuku Sanchome (1 min.) or Shinjuku (east exit, 6 min.). On Shinjuku Dori, east of Shinjuku Station.

Matsuya This is one of my favorite department stores in Tokyo; if I were buying a wedding gift, Matsuya is one of the first places I'd look. It has a good selection of Japanese folkcraft items, kitchenware, kimono, and beautifully designed contemporary household goods in addition to the usual clothes and accessories. I always make a point of stopping by the seventh floor's Design Collection, which displays items from around the world selected by the Japan Design Committee as examples of fine design, from the Alessi teapot to Braun razors. 3–6–1 Ginza, Chuo-ku. © 03/3567-1211. Daily 10am–8pm. Station: Ginza (2 min.). On Chuo Dori Ave., just a long block north of Ginza 4-chome Crossing.

Mitsukoshi   This Nihombashi department store is one of Japan's oldest and grandest, founded in 1673 by the Mitsui family as a kimono store. In 1683, it became the first store in the world to deal only in cash sales; it was also one of the first stores in Japan to begin displaying goods on shelves rather than having merchants fetch bolts of cloth for each customer, as was the custom of the time. Yet another first: It was also one of the first shops to employ female clerks. Today, housed in a building dating from 1914, it remains one of Tokyo's loveliest department stores, with a beautiful and stately Renaissance-style facade and an entrance guarded by two bronze lions, replicas of the lions in Trafalgar Square. It carries many name-brand boutiques, including Givenchy, Dunhill, Chanel, Hanae Mori, Oscar de la Renta, Christian Dior, and Tiffany. Its kimono, by the way, are still hot items.

Another branch, located right on Ginza 4-chome Crossing (© 03/3562-1111; Mon–Sat 10am–8pm; Sun 10am–7:30pm), is popular with young shoppers. 1–4–1 Nihombashi Muromachi, Chuo-ku. © 03/3241-3311. Daily 10am–7pm. Closed some Mon. Station: Mitsukoshimae (1 min.).

Seibu   Once the nation's largest department store—and still one of the biggest—Seibu has 47 entrances, thousands of sales clerks, dozens of restaurants, 12 floors, 31 elevators, and an average of 170,000 shoppers a day. Two basement floors are devoted to foodstuffs—you can buy everything from taco shells to octopus to seaweed. Dishes are set out so you can nibble and sample the food as you move along, and hawkers yelling out their wares give the place a marketlike atmosphere. Fast-food counters sell salads, grilled eel, chicken, sushi, and other ready-to-eat dishes. The rest of the floors offer clothing, furniture, art galleries, kitchenware, and a million other things. Loft, Seibu's department for household goods and interior design, and Wave, Seibu's CD department, occupy the top four floors of the main building. Many of the best Japanese and Western designers have boutiques here; Size World and Queen's Coordination, both on the fourth floor, specialize in large and petite women's sizes respectively.

There's another Seibu in **Ginza** near the elevated tracks of the JR Yamanote Line, between the Hibiya and Ginza subway stations (© 03/3286-0111; daily 11am–8pm; closed some Tues; station: Yurakucho, 1 min.). It specializes in men's and women's clothing and accessories, from casual to formal wear. Next to it is Hankyu, another large department store.

Also look for Seibu in **Shibuya** at 21–1 Udagawacho (© 03/3462-0111; open Sun–Wed 10am–8pm; Thurs and Fri 10am–9pm; closed some Wed; station: Shibuya, Hachiko exit, 2 min.), which is similar to the main store in Ikebukuro. This Seibu consists of two buildings connected by pedestrian skywalks, and it offers lots of designer boutiques; a branch of Loft (behind Seibu B), Seibu's interior design and household goods shop; and Parco and Movida fashion department stores. 1–28–1 Minami Ikebukuro, Toshima-ku. © 03/3981-0111. Sun–Tues 10am–8pm; Wed–Sat 10am–9pm. Closed some Tues. Station: Ikebukuro (underneath the store).

Takashimaya   With a history just as long, this attractive department store provides stiff competition for Mitsukoshi (above). It was founded as a kimono shop in Kyoto during the Edo Period and opened in Tokyo in 1933. It features boutiques by such famous designers as Chanel, Laroche, Dunhill, Céline,

Lanvin, Louis Vuitton, Gucci, Christian Dior, Issey Miyake, and Kenzo. 2–4–1 Nihombashi (on Chuo Dori Ave.), Chuo-ku. ℭ 03/3211-4111. Daily 10am–7pm. Closed some Wed. Station: Nihombashi (1 min.).

Takashimaya Times Square   Since its opening in 1996, Takashimaya Times Square has been the number one draw in Shinjuku and is packed on weekends. Much larger than Takashimaya's Nihombashi flagship, this huge complex is anchored by Takashimaya department store, which boasts 10 floors of clothing and restaurants. There's also Tokyu Hands with everything imaginable for the home hobbyist; Kinokuniya bookstore with English-language books on the sixth floor; and Tokyo IMAX Theater, a huge screen with 3D films. 5–24–2 Sendagaya, Shinjuku-ku. ℭ 03/5361-1122. Daily 10am–7:30pm. Closed some Weds. Station: Shinjuku (1 min.). Across the street from Shinjuku Station's south exit.

Tobu/Metropolitan Plaza   Once overshadowed by nearby Seibu, this flagship of the Tobu chain expanded and reopened in 1993 as Japan's largest department store, employing 3,000 clerks to serve the 180,000 customers who enter its doors daily. It consists of a main building, a connecting central building, and Metropolitan Plaza. It offers everything from luxury goods and the latest international fashions to hardware, software, toys, daily necessities, and traditional Japanese products (good for souvenirs). Its basement food floor is massive—food accounts for nearly 20% of Tobu's total sales. Here, too, is the new home of the Japan Traditional Craft Center, a must for anyone interested in traditional and contemporary handmade Japanese crafts. 1–1–25 Nishi-Ikebukuro, Toshima-ku. ℭ 03/3981-2211. Daily 10am–8pm. Closed some Wed. Station: Ikebukuro (west exit, 1 min.).

Wako   This is one of Ginza's smallest department stores but also one of its classiest, housed in one of the few area buildings that survived World War II. It was erected in 1932 and is famous for its distinctive clock tower, graceful curved facade, and innovative window displays. The owners are the Hattori family, founders of the Seiko watch company. The store's ground floor carries a wide selection of Seiko watches and clocks, while the upper floors carry imported and domestic fashions and luxury items with prices to match. It caters to older, well-to-do customers; you won't find hordes of young Japanese girls shopping here. 4–5–11 Ginza (at Ginza 4-chome Crossing), Chuo-ku. ℭ 03/3562-2111. Mon–Sat 10:30am–6pm. Closed holidays. Station: Ginza (1 min.).

ELECTRONICS

The largest concentration of electronics and electrical-appliance shops in Japan is in an area of Tokyo called **Akihabara Electric Town** (Denkigai), centered around Chuo Dori. Although you can find good deals on video and audio equipment elsewhere, Akihabara is special simply for its sheer volume. With more than 600 multilevel stores, shops, and stalls, Akihabara accounts for one-tenth of the nation's electronics and electrical-appliance sales. An estimated 50,000 shoppers come here on a weekday, 100,000 per day on a weekend. Even if you don't buy anything, it's great fun walking around. If you do intend to buy, make sure you know what the item would cost back home. Or, you may be able to pick up something that's unavailable back home. Most of the stores and stalls are open-fronted, and many are painted neon green and pink. Inside, lights are flashing, fans are blowing, washing machines are shaking and shimmying, and stereos are blasting. Salesmen yell out their wares, trying to get customers to look at their rice cookers, refrigerators, computers, cellular phones, video equipment, digital cameras, CD and DVD players, TVs, calculators, and watches. This is the best place to go to see the latest models of everything electronic, an educational experience in itself.

If you are buying, be sure to bargain and don't buy at the first place you go to. One woman I know who was looking for a portable cassette player bought it at the third shop she went to for ¥4,000 ($33) less than what was quoted to her at the first shop. Make sure, too, that whatever you purchase is made for export—that is, with instructions in English, an international warranty, and the proper electrical connectors. All the larger stores have duty-free floors where products are made for export. Two of the largest are **Yamagiwa,** 3–13–10 Soto-Kanda (© 03/3253-2111) and **Laox,** 15–3 Soto-Kanda (© 03/3255-5301). If you're serious about buying, check these stores first.

The easiest way to get to Akihabara is via the Yamanote Line or Sobu Line to the JR Akihabara Station. You can also take the Hibiya subway line to Akihabara Station, but it's farther to walk. In any case, take the Akihabara Electric Town exit. Most shops are open daily from about 10am to 7pm.

FASHIONS

The department stores listed above are all good places to check out the latest trends. Otherwise, Harajuku and Shibuya are the places to go for hundreds of small shops selling inexpensive designer knockoffs, as well as fashion department stores, multistoried buildings filled with concessions of various designers and labels. The stores below are two of the most well known and largest.

La Forêt   This is not only the largest store in Harajuku but also one of the most fashionable, appealing mostly to teenage and twentysomething shoppers. Young and upcoming Japanese designers are here as well as names like Plantation by Issey Miyake. You'll find the most reasonably priced fashions and accessories in the basement and on the fourth floor. There's also an annex. There's so much to see, you could easily spend a few hours here. 1–11–6 Jingumae, Shibuya-ku. © 03/ 3475-0411. Daily 11am–8pm. Station: Meiji-Jingumae (1 min.) or Harajuku (3 min.). Just off Harajuku's main intersection of Omotesando Dori and Meiji Dori.

Parco   A division of Seibu, Parco is actually three buildings clustered together and called Parco Part 1, Part 2, and Part 3. Parco Part 1 is the place to go for designer boutiques for men and women, with clothes by such avant-garde Japanese designers as Yohji Yamamoto, Issey Miyake, Tsumori Chisato, Junya Watanabe, and Takeo Kikuchi. Part 2 has children's clothing, while Part 3 is devoted to sports clothes and casual clothing. Parco has two sales a year that you shouldn't miss if you're here—one in January and one in July. 15–1 Udagawacho, Shibuya-ku. © 03/3464-5111. Daily 10am–8:30pm. Station: Shibuya (Hachiko exit, 4 min.)

Designer Boutiques

The block between Omotesando Crossing and the Nezu Museum in **Aoyama** (station: Omotesando, 2 min.) has become the Rodeo Drive of Japan, the showcase of top designers. Even if you can't buy here (steep prices for most pocketbooks), a stroll is *de rigeur* for clothes hounds and those interested in design. Most shops are open daily from 11am to 8pm. **Comme des Garçons,** on the right side as you walk from Aoyama Dori (© 03/3406-3951), is Rei Kawakubo's showcase for her daring—and constantly evolving—men's and women's designs. The goddess of Japanese fashion and one of the few females in the business, Kawakubo has remained on the cutting edge of design for almost 2 decades. Across the street is **Issey Miyake** (© 03/3423-1408) with two floors of cool, spacious displays of Miyake's interestingly structured designs for men and women (His very popular Pleats Please line is around the corner on Aoyama Dori, 3–13–21 Minami Aoyama, © 03/5772-7750). One of Japan's newer designers, **Tsumori Chisato,** has a shop on the left side of the street (© **03/ 3423-5170**). Also worth seeking out along this stretch is **Yohji Yamamoto** across the street (© **03/3409-6006**), where Yamamoto's unique, classically wearable clothes are sparingly hung, flaunting the avant-garde interior space.

FLEA MARKETS

Flea markets are good opportunities to shop for antiques as well as delightful junk. You can pick up secondhand kimono at very reasonable prices, as well as kitchenware, vases, cast-iron tea pots, small chests, dolls, household items, and odds and ends. (Don't expect to find any good buys in furniture.) The markets usually begin as early as dawn or 6am and last until 3 or 4pm or so, but go early if you want to pick up bargains. Bargaining is expected.

In addition to these regularly scheduled markets, check the *Tokyo Journal* for a list of others. Note that, since most are outdoors, they tend to be canceled if it rains. Tokyo also has huge antiques fairs several times a year, including the Heiwajima Antique Fair, held for several days in May, June, July, September, and December near Ryutsu Center Station on the Tokyo Monorail Line and an antique fair held at Ueno Shinobazu Pond for several weeks in April, July/August, and the month of October. Contact the Tourist Information Center for an update.

Togo Shrine, on Meiji Dori in Harajuku (near Meiji-Jingumae or Harajuku stations), has an antiques market on the first, fourth, and when there is one, fifth Sunday of every month from 4am to 2pm, and it is great for used kimono as well as small furniture and curios. It's one of my favorites. **Nogi Shrine,** a 1-minute walk from Nogizaka Station, has an antiques flea market from dawn to about 2pm the second Sunday of each month except November.

Fun Fact **Nogi Shrine**

Nogi Shrine has a lovely setting and commemorates General Nogi and his wife, both of whom committed suicide on September 13, 1912, to follow the Meiji Emperor into the afterlife. Their simple home and stable are on shrine grounds.

Hanazono Shrine, near the Yasukuni Dori/Meiji Dori intersection east of Shinjuku Station (a 5-min. walk from Shinjuku Sanchome Station), has a flea market every Sunday from dawn to about 2pm (except in May and Nov due to festivals).

Finally, the closest thing Tokyo has to a permanent flea market is **Ameya Yokocho** (also referred to as Ameyokocho or Ameyacho), a narrow street near Ueno Park that runs along and underneath the elevated tracks of the JR Yamanote Line between Ueno and Okachimachi stations. There are about 400 stalls here selling discounted items ranging from fish, seaweed, and vegetables to handbags, tennis shoes, cosmetics, watches, and casual clothes. The scene retains something of the *shitamachi* spirit of old Tokyo. Although housewives have been coming here for years, young Japanese recently discovered the market as a good bargain spot for fashions, accessories, and cosmetics. Some shops close on Wednesdays, but hours are usually daily from 10am to 7pm; early evening is the most crowded time. Don't even think of coming here on a holiday—it's a standstill pedestrian traffic jam.

KIMONO

Chicago, on Omotesando Dori in Harajuku (✆ **03/3409-5017;** station: Meiji-Jingumae, 1 min. or Harajuku, 2 min.), is the place to go for used kimono. It stocks hundreds of affordable used kimono, cotton yukata, and obi (sashes) towards the back left corner of the basement shop, past the 1950s clothes, in its Kimono Corner. Open daily from 11am to 8pm. The nearby **Oriental Bazaar** (see "Crafts & Traditional Japanese Products," earlier in this chapter) also has a decent selection of new and used kimono at affordable prices, including elaborate wedding kimono.

In addition, department stores sell new kimono, notably **Takashimaya** and **Mitsukoshi** in Nihombashi and **Isetan** in Shinjuku. They also hold sales for rental wedding kimono. Flea markets are also good for used kimono and yukata, particularly the antiques market at **Togo Shrine.**

Established in 1913, **Hayashi Kimono** (✆ **03/3501-4012**), with two locations in the International Arcade (see "Arcades & Shopping Malls," earlier in this chapter), sells all manner of kimono, including antique kimono, cotton yukata, and *tanzen* (the heavy winter overcoat that goes over the yukata). If you're buying a gift for someone back home, this is the best place to start. Open daily from 10am to 6:45pm (to 6pm on Sun).

KITCHENWARE & TABLEWARE

In addition to the department stores listed above, there are two areas in Tokyo with a number of shops filled with items related to cooking and serving. In **Tsukiji,** along the streets stretching between Tsukiji Station and Tsukiji Fish Market, are shops selling pottery, serving trays, bowls, dishes, wonderful fish knives, and lunch boxes. The second place to look is **Kappabashi-dougugai Dori** (station: Tawaramachi), popularly known as Kappabashi; this is Japan's largest wholesale area for cookware. There are approximately 150 specialty stores here selling cookware, including sukiyaki pots, woks, lunch boxes, pots and pans, aprons, knives, china, lacquerware, rice cookers, and disposable wooden chopsticks in bulk. Although stores in Tsukiji and Kappabashi are wholesalers selling mainly to restaurants, you're welcome to browse and purchase as well. Stores in both areas are closed on Sunday.

PEARLS

Mikimoto, on Chuo Dori not far from Ginza 4-chome Crossing, past Wako department store (✆ **03/3535-54611;** station: Ginza, 1 min.), is Japan's most famous pearl shop. It was founded by Mikimoto Koichi, the first to produce a really good cultured pearl, in 1905. Open daily 10:30am to 6:30pm, closed the third Wednesday of every month. Otherwise, there's a Mikimoto branch (✆ **03/3591-5001**), in the **Imperial Hotel Arcade,** under the Imperial Hotel (station: Hibiya), where you'll also find **Asahi Shoten** (✆ **03/3503-2528**), with a good selection in the modest-to-moderate price range, and **K. Uyeda Pearl Shop** (✆ **03/3503-2587**), with a wide selection of pearls in many different price ranges.

10 Tokyo After Dark

By day, Tokyo is arguably one of the least attractive cities in the world. A congested mass of concrete, it has too many unimaginative buildings, too many cars and people, and not enough trees and greenery.

Come dusk, however, Tokyo comes into its own. The drabness fades, the city blossoms into a profusion of giant neon lights and paper lanterns, and its streets fill with millions of overworked Japanese out to have a good time. If you ask me, Tokyo at night is one of the craziest cities in the world. It never gives up and never seems to sleep. The entertainment district of Roppongi, for example, is more crowded at 3am than it is at 3pm. Many establishments stay open until the first subways start running after 5am. Whether it's jazz, reggae, gay bars, sex shows, discos, mania, or madness that you're searching for, Tokyo has it all.

GETTING TO KNOW THE SCENE   Tokyo has several nightlife districts spread throughout the city, each with its own atmosphere, price range, and clientele. Most famous are probably **Ginza, Kabuki-cho** in Shinjuku, and **Roppongi.** Before visiting any of the locales suggested below, be sure to just walk around one of these neighborhoods and absorb the atmosphere. The streets will be crowded, the neon lights will be overwhelming, and you never know what you might discover on your own.

Although there are many bars, discos, and restaurants packed with young Japanese women, nightlife in Japan is still pretty much a man's domain, just as it has been for centuries. At the high end of this domain are the **geisha bars,** where highly trained women entertain by playing traditional Japanese instruments, singing, and holding witty conversations—nothing more risqué than that. Generally speaking, such places are outrageously expensive and closed to outsiders. As a foreigner, you'll have little opportunity to visit a geisha bar unless you're invited by a business associate, in which case you should consider yourself extremely fortunate.

More common than geisha bars, and generally not quite as expensive, are the so-called **hostess bars,** many of which are located in Ginza and Akasaka. A woman will sit at your table, talk to you, pour your drinks, listen to your problems, and boost your ego. You buy her drinks as well, which is one reason the tab can be so high. Hostess bars in various forms have been a part of Japanese society for centuries. Most of you will probably find the cost of visiting a hostess bar not worth the price since hostesses usually speak only Japanese, but such places provide Japanese males with sympathetic ears and the chance to escape the world of both work and family. Men usually have their favorite hostess bar, often a small place with just enough room for regular customers. In the more exclusive hostess bars, only those with an introduction are allowed entrance.

The most popular nightlife spots are **drinking establishments,** where the vast majority of Japan's office workers, college students, and expatriates go for an evening out. These places include Western-style bars as well as Japanese-style watering holes, called *nomi-ya*. Yakitori-ya, restaurant-bars that serve yakitori and other snacks, are included in this group. Dancing and live-music venues are also hugely popular with young Tokyoites.

At the low end of the spectrum are Tokyo's topless bars, sex shows, massage parlors, and porn shops, with the largest concentration of such places in Shinjuku's **Kabuki-cho District.**

In addition to the establishments listed below, be sure to check the restaurants listed in the inexpensive category under "Where to Dine," in chapter 3 for a relatively cheap night out on the town. Many places serve as both eateries and watering holes, especially yakitori-ya.

EXTRA CHARGES & TAXES   One more thing you should be aware of is the "table charge" that some bars and many cocktail lounges charge their customers. Included in the table charge is usually a small appetizer—maybe nuts, chips, or a vegetable. For this reason, some locales call it an *otsumami*, or a snack charge. At any rate, the charge is usually between ¥300 and ¥500 ($2.70 and $4.50) per person. Some establishments levy a table charge only after a certain time in the evening; others may add it only if you don't order food from the menu. If you're not sure and it matters to you, be sure to ask before ordering anything. Remember, too, that a 5% consumption tax will be added to your bill. Some higher-end establishments, especially nightclubs, hostess bars, and some dance clubs, will also add a 10% to 20% service charge.

FINDING OUT WHAT'S ON   To find out what's happening in the entertainment scene—contemporary and traditional music and theater, exhibitions in museums and galleries, films, and special events—buy a copy of the *Tokyo Journal.* It's published quarterly and is available for ¥600 ($5) at foreign-language bookstores, restaurants, and bars. Keep an eye out also for the free *Tokyo Classified,* which carries a nightlife section covering concerts and events and is available at bars and other venues around town. For alternative live-music venues complete with ticket prices and times, look for the free giveaway *Juice* at clubs and bars.

GETTING TICKETS FOR EVENTS   If you're staying in one of the higher-class hotels, the concierge or guest-relations manager can usually get tickets for you. Otherwise, you can always head to the theater or hall itself. An easier way is to go through one of many ticket services available. **Ticket PIA (℘ 03/5237-9999)** is probably your best bet because it has an English-language service. Other services include **Ticket Saison (℘ 03/5990-9999)** and **CN Playguide (℘ 03/5802-9999)**.

THE PERFORMING ARTS

For descriptions of Japanese traditional performance arts such as Kabuki and Noh, see "Cultural Snapshots: Japanese Arts in a Nutshell," in appendix A. In addition to the performance art listings below, Tokyo also has occasional shows of more avant-garde or lesser-known performance art productions, including highly stylized Butoh dance performances from companies like Sankai Juku and percussion demonstrations by Kodo drummers and other Japanese drum groups. See *Tokyo Journal* for complete listings.

KABUKI   Of the several theaters in Tokyo with regular showings of Kabuki, none is more well known or prestigious than Kabukiza ✮✮✮, 4–12–15 Ginza (℘ **03/3541-3131,** 03/5565-6000 for advance reservations). Conveniently located within easy walking distance of the Ginza 4-chome Crossing (directly above the Higashi-Ginza Station), this impressive theater with a Momoyama-style facade (influenced by 16th-century castle architecture) is a remake of the 1924 original building. It seats almost 2,000 and features the usual Kabuki stage fittings, including a platform that can be raised and lowered below the stage for dramatic appearances and disappearances of actors, a revolving stage, and a runway stage extending into the audience.

The Kabukiza stages about eight or nine Kabuki productions a year. Each production begins its run between the first and third of each month and runs about 25 days, with performances daily from 11 or 11:30am to about 9pm (there are no shows in Aug). Usually, there are two different programs being shown; matinees run from about 11 or 11:30am to 4pm, and evening performances run from about 4:30 or 5pm to about 9pm. It's considered perfectly okay to come for only part of a performance.

Of course, you won't be able to understand what's being said, but that doesn't matter; the productions themselves are great entertainment. For an outline of the plot, you can purchase an **English program,** which costs ¥1,000 ($8.35);

you also can rent **English earphones** for ¥650 ($5.40), plus a ¥1,000 ($8.35) refundable deposit—these provide a running commentary on the story, music, actors, stage properties, and other aspects of Kabuki. Buying a program or renting earphones will add immensely to your enjoyment of the play.

Tickets generally range from ¥2,400 to ¥16,000 ($20–$133), depending on the program and seat location. Advance tickets can be purchased at the **Advance Ticket Office** to the right side of Kabukiza's main entrance from 10am to 6pm. You may also make advance reservations by phone (same-day bookings are not accepted). Otherwise, tickets for each day's performance are placed on sale 1 hour before the start of each performance.

If you don't have time for an entire performance or you wish to view Kabuki only for a short while, it's possible to watch only one act, with tickets costing only ¥600 to ¥1,000 ($5–$8.35), depending on the time of day and length of the show. One-acts generally last about 1 or 1½ hours; note that English-language earphones are not available here, but you can buy a program. Note also that seats are a bit far from the stage, on the very top two rows of the theater (on the 4th floor; there is no elevator). On the other hand, I have seen several acts this way, sometimes simply dropping by when I'm in the area. Tickets, sold at the smaller entrance to the left of the main entrance, are available on a first-come, first-served basis and go on sale 20 minutes prior to each act. If you liked the act so much that you wish to remain for the next one, it's possible to do so if the act is not sold out; tickets in these cases are usually available on the fourth floor.

If you're in Tokyo in August, you can usually see Kabuki instead at the **National Theater of Japan** (Kokuritsu Gekijo), 4–1 Hayabusacho, Chiyoda-ku (✆ **03/3265-7411;** station: Hanzomon, 6 min.). Kabuki is scheduled here throughout the year except during May, September, and December, when Bunraku (see below) is being staged instead. Matinees usually begin at noon and evening performances at 5pm. Most tickets range from about ¥1,500 to ¥3,800 ($12.50–$32).

NOH   Noh performances are given at many locations in Tokyo, with tickets ranging from about ¥2,300 to ¥6,000 ($19–$50). Performances are usually in the early afternoon at 1pm or in the late afternoon at 5 or 6:30pm; check the *Tokyo Journal* for exact times. The **National Noh Theater** (Kokuritsu Nohgakudo), 4–18–1 Sendagaya, Shibuya-ku (✆ **03/3423-1331;** station: Sendagaya, 5 min.), is Tokyo's most famous. Other Noh theaters worth checking out are **Hosho Nohgakudo,** 1–5–9 Hongo, Bunkyo-ku (✆ **03/3811-4843;** station: Suidobashi, 5 min.); **Kanze Nohgakudo,** 1–16–4 Shoto, Shibuya-ku (✆ **03/3469-5241;** station: Shibuya, 10 min.); **Kita Nohgakudo,** 4–6–9 Kami-Osaki, Shinagawa-ku (✆ **03/3491-8813;** station: JR Meguro, 10 min.); and **Tessenkai Nohgaku-do Kenshujo,** 4–21–29 Minami Aoyama, Minato-ku (✆ **03/3401-2285;** station: Omotesando, exit A4, 5 min.).

BUNRAKU   Three Bunraku performances a year—in May, September, and December—are staged at The National Theater of Japan (Kokuritsu Gekijo), 4–1 Hayabusacho, Chiyoda-ku (✆ **03/3265-7411;** station: Hanzomon, 6 min.). There are usually two to three performances daily at 11am, 2:30pm, and 6pm, with tickets averaging ¥5,000 ($42). Earphones with English explanations are available for ¥650 ($5.40).

TAKARAZUKA KAGEKIDAN   This world-famous, all-female troupe stages elaborate musical revues with dancing, singing, and gorgeous costumes, with performances ranging from Japanese versions of Broadway hits to original

Japanese works based on local legends. The first Takarazuka troupe, formed in 1912 at a resort near Osaka, gained instant notoriety because all its performers were women, in contrast to the all-male Kabuki. When I went to see this troupe perform, I was surprised to find that the audience also consisted almost exclusively of women; indeed, the troupe has an almost cult-like following.

Performances, with story synopses available in English, are held generally in March, April, July, August, November, December, and sometimes in June at **Tokyo Takarazuka Gekijo,** 1–1–3 Yurakucho (© **03/5251-2001;** station: Hibiya, 1 min.). Tickets, available at the box office or through Ticket Pia (© **03/5237-9999**), generally range from about ¥3,000 to ¥10,000 ($25–$83).

Kingyo ★ This sophisticated nightclub stages one of the most high-energy, visually charged acts I've ever seen—nonstop action of ascending and receding stages and stairs, fast-paced choreography, elaborate costumes, and loud music. There are a few female dancers, but most of the dancers are males assuming female parts, just like in Kabuki. In fact, many of the performances center on traditional Japanese themes with traditional dress and kimono, but the shows take place in a very technically sophisticated setting. There are also satires: One recent performance included a piece on Microsoft vs. Apple; another featured aliens from outer space. Great fun. It's located in the heart of the Roppongi nightlife district at 3–14–17 Roppongi (© **03/3478-3000;** station: Roppongi, 4 min.), near the Roppongi cemetery. Cover is ¥4,000 ($33) for daily shows at 7:30 and 10pm, with additional shows Friday and Saturday at 1:30am. Reservations are advised, as this is a very popular show.

THE CLUB & MUSIC SCENE
THE MAJOR ENTERTAINMENT DISTRICTS

GINZA A chic and expensive shopping area by day, Ginza transforms itself into a dazzling entertainment district of restaurants, bars, and first-grade hostess bars at night. It's the most sophisticated of Tokyo's nightlife districts and is also one of the most expensive. Almost all the Japanese businessmen you see out carousing in Ginza are paying by expense account; the prices are ridiculously high.

Since I'm not wealthy, I prefer Shinjuku and Roppongi. However, because Ginza does have some fabulous restaurants and several hotels, I've included some recommendations for a drink in the area if you happen to find yourself here after dinner. The cheapest way to absorb the atmosphere in Ginza is simply to wander about, particularly around **Namiki Dori** and its side streets.

SHINJUKU Northeast of Shinjuku Station is an area called **Kabuki-cho,** which undoubtedly has the craziest nightlife in all of Tokyo, with block after block of strip joints, massage parlors, pornography shops, peep shows, bars, restaurants, and, as the night wears on, lots of drunk Japanese men. A world of its own, it's sleazy, chaotic, crowded, vibrant, and fairly safe. Despite its name, Shinjuku's primary night hot spot has nothing to do with Kabuki. At one time, there was a plan to bring some culture to the area by introducing a Kabuki theater; the plan never materialized but the name stuck. Although Kabuki-cho was always the domain of businessmen out on the town, in recent years young Japanese, including college-age men and women, have claimed parts of it as their own and now outnumber businessmen; the result is that there are a growing number of inexpensive drinking establishments well worth a visit.

To the east of Kabuki-cho is a smaller district called **Goruden Gai,** which is "Golden Guy" mispronounced. It's a neighborhood of tiny alleyways leading past even tinier bars, each consisting of just a counter and a few chairs. Generally

---

Tips   Shinjuku Safety

A word of warning for women traveling alone: Forgo the experience of Shinjuku. The streets are crowded and therefore relatively safe, but you may not feel comfortable with so many inebriated men stumbling around. If there are two of you, however, go for it. I took my mother to Kabuki-cho for a spin around the neon, and we escaped relatively unscathed. You're also fine walking alone to or meeting someone at one of my recommended restaurants.

---

closed to outsiders, these bars cater to regular customers. On hot summer evenings, the mama-san of these bars sit outside on stools and fan themselves, with soft red lights melting out of the open doorways. Things aren't as they appear, however. These aren't brothels—they're simply bars, and the "mama"-san are as likely to be men as women. Unfortunately, Goruden Gai sits on such expensive land that many of the bar owners sold their shops to land developers in the 1980s. But then the economic bottom fell out, and these shops remain boarded up, awaiting their future. Still, approximately 100 drinking dens remain, making this tiny enclave one of the most fascinating in all of Tokyo.

Even farther east is **Shinjuku 2-chome** (pronounced "knee-chomay"), officially recognized as the gay-bar district of Shinjuku. Its lively street scene of mostly gays and some straights of all ages (but mostly young) make this one of the most vibrant nightlife districts. It's here that I was once taken to a host bar featuring young men in crotchless pants. The clientele included both gay men and groups of young, giggling office girls. That place has since closed down, but Shinjuku is riddled with other spots bordering on the absurd.

The best thing to do in Shinjuku is to simply walk about. In the glow of neon light, you'll pass everything from smoke-filled restaurants to hawkers trying to get you to step inside so they can part you from your money. If you're looking for strip joints, topless or bottomless coffee shops, peep shows, or porn, I leave you to your own devices, but you certainly won't have any problems finding them. In Kabuki-cho alone, there are an estimated 200 sex businesses in operation, including bathhouses where women are available for sex, usually at a cost of around ¥30,000 ($250). Although prostitution is illegal in Japan, everyone seems to ignore what goes on behind closed doors. Just be sure you know what you are getting into; your bill at the end may add up to much more than you figured.

ROPPONGI   To Tokyo's younger crowd, Roppongi is the city's most fashionable place to hang out. It's also a favorite with the foreign community, including models, business types, and English teachers. Roppongi has more than its fair share of live-music houses, restaurants, discos, expatriate bars, and pubs. Some Tokyoites complain that Roppongi is too crowded, too trendy, and too commercialized (and has too many foreigners), but for the casual visitor, I think Roppongi offers an excellent opportunity to see what's new and hot in the capital city and is easy to navigate because nightlife activity is so concentrated.

The center of Roppongi is **Roppongi Crossing** (the intersection of Roppongi Dori and Gaien-Higashi Dori), at the corner of which sits the garishly pink Almond Coffee Shop. The shop itself has mediocre coffee and desserts at terribly inflated prices, but the sidewalk in front of the store is the number one meeting spot in Roppongi.

If you need directions, there's a conveniently located **koban** (police box) catty-corner from the Almond Coffee Shop and next to the Bank of Tokyo-Mitsubishi. It has a big map of the Roppongi area showing the address system, and someone is always there.

Recently, the action of Roppongi has spilled over into neighboring **Nishi-Azabu,** which has several restaurants and bars catering to both Japanese and foreigners. The center of Nishi-Azabu is the next big crossroads, Nishi-Azabu Crossing (the intersection of Roppongi Dori and Gaien-Nishi Dori). Nishi Azabu is about a 10-minute walk from Roppongi Station; walk on Roppongi Dori in the direction of Shibuya.

LIVE MUSIC

The live-music scene exploded in the 1990s and is now throughout the metropolis. In addition to the dedicated venues below, several bars offer live music most nights of the week, including What the Dickens! and Scruffy Murphy's (see "The Bar Scene," below).

Bauhaus   This small club, featuring mostly 1970s and 1980s British and American hard rock (Deep Purple, Pink Floyd, Jimi Hendrix, the Rolling Stones, Led Zeppelin), is owned and operated by the house band, which plays 30-minute sets every hour on the hour from 8pm and then serves drinks to the regular clientele, mostly foreigners. The band is led by singer Kay-chan, a kind of Japanese David Bowie, who puts on quite a show—a bit raunchy at times. Reine Roppongi, 2nd floor, 5–3–4 Roppongi. ✆ 03/3403-0092. Cover ¥3,500 ($29) including 1 drink, plus 20% service charge. Mon–Sat 7pm–1am; music begins at 8pm. Station: Roppongi (3 min.). From Roppongi Crossing, walk toward Tokyo Tower on Gaien-Higashi Dori and turn right at McDonald's.

Birdland   Down to earth and featuring good jazz performed by Japanese musicians, Birdland has been a welcome refuge from Roppongi's madding crowd for more than a quarter of a century. It's small and cozy with candles and soft lighting and attracts an older, knowledgeable, and appreciative crowd. Square Bldg. (in the basement), 3–10–3 Roppongi. ✆ 03/3478-3456. Cover ¥1,500 ($12.50) plus ¥800 ($6.65) drink minimum and 10% service charge. Mon–Thurs 6pm–midnight; Fri–Sat 6pm–1am (music begins at 7pm). Station: Roppongi (2 min.). From Roppongi Crossing, walk toward Tokyo Tower on Gaien-Higashi Dori and take the first left.

Blue Note   Tokyo's most expensive, elegant jazz venue is cousin to the famous Blue Note in New York and has proven so popular it outgrew its original 1988 location and moved into this larger location 10 years later. Still, with 300 seats, it follows the frustrating practice of selling tickets good for only one set (there are 2 sets nightly). The musicians are top notch; Oscar Peterson, Sarah Vaughan,

---

Tips   Mapping Out Tokyo's Nightlife

Once you've chosen a nightlife spot that appeals to you, you can locate it using the following neighborhood maps:

- To locate bars and clubs in **Akasaka**, p. 109.
- To locate bars and clubs in **Shinjuku**, p. 116.
- To locate bars and clubs in **Asakusa**, p. 121.
- To locate bars and clubs in **Harajuku**, p. 147.
- To locate bars and clubs in **Roppongi**, p. 153.

Tony Bennett, David Sanborn, and the Milt Jackson Quartet have all performed here. 6–3–16 Minami Aoyama. ✆ **03/5485-0088.** Cover ¥7,000–¥8,000 ($58–$67) for most performances, more for top names. Mon–Sat 5:30pm–1am with shows at 7 and 9:30pm. Station: Omotesando (8 min.). Off Kotto Dori.

Body & Soul   This low-ceilinged, tiny but cozy basement club with only a few tables and a long bar gives everyone a good view of its mostly jazz performances by Japanese and foreign musicians. 6–13–9 Minami Aoyama. ✆ **03/5466-3348.** Cover ¥3,500 ($29) and up. Mon–Sat 7pm–midnight. Station: Omotesando (7 min.). Off Kotto Dori, near Nobu.

Cavern Club   If you know your Beatles history, you'll know Cavern is the name of the Liverpool club where the Fab Four got their start. The Tokyo club features Beatles memorabilia and house bands performing Beatles music exclusively and very convincingly at that. Close your eyes—and you'll swear you're listening to the real thing. Extremely popular with both Japanese and foreigners, it's packed on weekends—expect long lines. Reservations are taken but are good for only two sets—then you have to leave. 5–3–2 Roppongi. ✆ **03/ 3405-5207.** Cover ¥1,300 ($11), plus a 1 drink minimum and 22% service charge. Mon–Sat 6pm–2:30am; Sun and holidays 6pm–midnight. Station: Roppongi (4 min.). Take the side street going downhill on the left side of Almond Coffee Shop and then take the first left; the club will be on the right.

Crocodile   Popular with a young Japanese crowd, the eclectic Crocodile describes itself as a casual rock 'n' roll club, with live bands ranging from rock and blues to jazz-fusion, reggae, soul, experimental, and even country and salsa. It's a good place to check out new Japanese bands. It has an interesting interior and a good, laid-back atmosphere; depending on the music, the clientele ranges from Japanese with bleached-blond hair and earrings to a grunge crowd. 6–18–8 Jingumae, on Meiji Dori between Harajuku and Shibuya. ✆ **03/3499-5205.** Cover ¥2,000–¥3,000 ($17–$25), occasionally more for big acts. Daily 6pm–2am; music starts at 8pm. Station: Meiji-Jingumae or Shibuya (8 min.).

Liquid Room   This is one of Tokyo's longest-running live venues, home to some of the hottest Japanese and international bands. DJs hold court when there's no live music. As seating is very limited, most people come to keep moving, making this a good place to join the dancing crowd. Humax Pavilion, 7th floor, 1-20-1 Kabuki-cho. ✆ **03/3200-6831.** Cover ¥3,000–¥3,500 ($25–$29) for most acts. Open most (but not all) nights from about 6pm. Station: Shinjuku (east exit, 10 min.). Across from Koma Stadium's northwest side.

New York Bar   This is one of Tokyo's most sophisticated venues, boasting Manhattan-style jazz and breathtaking views of glittering West Shinjuku. Unfortunately, it's also one of the city's smallest. Consider coming for dinner in the adjacent **New York Grill** (p. 143); you'll save the cost of the cover. Park Hyatt Hotel, 52nd floor, 3–7–1–2 Nishi-Shinjuku. ✆ **03/5322-1234.** Cover ¥2,000 ($17). Daily from 5pm, with live music 8pm–midnight. Station: Shinjuku (13 min.), Hatsudai on the Keio Line (7 min.), or Tochomae (8 min.).

Roppongi Pit Inn   Another well-known music house, this no-frills joint has been catering to a younger crowd of jazz enthusiasts for almost 25 years. It boasts some of the finest in native and imported jazz, as well as fusion and jazz rock. 3–17–7 Roppongi (in the basement). ✆ **03/3585-1063.** Cover ¥3,000–¥4,000 ($25–$33), including 1 drink. Daily from 6:30pm with shows about 7:30. Station: Roppongi (7 min.).

Shinjuku Pit Inn This is one of Tokyo's most famous and longest-running jazz, fusion, and blues clubs, featuring both Japanese and foreign musicians. There are two programs daily—at 2:30 and 7:30—making it a great place to stop for a bit of music in the middle of the day. Since only a few snacks (such as potato chips and sandwiches) are available, eat before you come. 2–12–4 Shinjuku, southeast of the Yasukuni Dori/Meiji Dori intersection. ✆ 03/3354-2024. Cover from ¥1,300 ($11), including 1 drink, for the 2:30pm show (¥2,500/$21 weekends and holidays), ¥3,000–¥4,000 ($25–$33) for the evening shows. Station: Shinjuku Sanchome (4 min.).

DANCE CLUBS & DISCOS

Discos have lost their popularity since their heyday in the 1980s, but with the rise of almost cult-figure DJs, dance clubs have witnessed a resurgence in recent years, with Roppongi still boasting more dance clubs than anywhere else in the city. Sometimes the set cover charge includes drinks and occasionally even food, which makes for an inexpensive way to spend an evening. Keep in mind, however, that prices are usually higher on weekends and are sometimes higher for men than for women. Although discos are required by law to close at midnight, many of them ignore the rule and simply stay open until dawn.

Code Known for its frequent trance and techno events, this Shinjuku venue brings in both Japanese and foreign DJs to keep things hopping. Once a month (check the schedule), it's for men only. Shinjuku Toho-Kaikan, 4th floor, 1–19–2 Kabuki-cho. ✆ 03/3209-0702. Depending on the event, cover ¥2,500–¥3,500 ($21–$29) Mon–Thurs including 2 drinks; ¥3,500 ($29) Fri including 1 or 2 drinks; ¥3,000 ($25) Sat–Sun including 2 drinks. Daily 7pm–midnight. Station: Shinjuku (east exit, 10 min.). Beside Koma Stadium, a Shinjuku landmark.

Kento's Kento's was one of the first places to open when the wave of 1950s nostalgia hit Japan in the 1980s; it has even been credited with creating the craze. This is the place to come to if you feel like dancing the night away to tunes of the 1950s and 1960s played by live bands. Although there's hardly room to dance, that doesn't stop the largely over-30 Japanese audience from twisting in the aisles to the tunes of Elvis, Little Richard, The Temptations, Chuck Berry and others. Daini Reine Bldg., 5–3–1 Roppongi. ✆ 03/3401-5755. Also at 6–7–12 Ginza. ✆ 03/3572-9161. Cover ¥1,500 ($12.50) plus 20% service charge and 1 drink minimum. Mon–Sat 6pm–2:30am; Sun and holidays 6pm–midnight. Station: Roppongi (4 min.). Take the side street going downhill on the left side of Almond Coffee Shop and then take the first left; the club will be on the right.

Lexington Queen Opened in 1980, Lexington Queen has been the reigning queen of disco in Tokyo for more than 2 decades. In fact, it's so much smaller than the newer, glitzier discos, it seems almost quaint. Its list of past guests reads like a Who's Who of foreign movie and rock stars to have visited Tokyo, from Rod Stewart to Stephen Dorff to Dustin Hoffman to Marilyn Manson; one night when I was there, Duran Duran walked in. This is the best place to be on Halloween and New Year's if you can stand the crowds. Women are admitted free Mondays and Thursdays. Daisan Goto Bldg., 3–13–14 Roppongi. ✆ 03/3401-1661. Cover ¥3,000 ($25) for women, ¥4,000 ($33) for men, including 2 drinks. Daily 8pm–midnight (sometimes as late as 5am). Station: Roppongi (3 min.). From Roppongi Crossing, walk toward Tokyo Tower on Gaien-Higashi Dori and take the second left.

Milk This split-level, psychedelic basement disco packs 'em in with loud, loud, loud hard rock and alternative music. On Thursday, Friday, and Saturday nights, it features live bands from 10:30pm. In the same building is the very popular **What the Dickens** expat bar (see below). 1–13–3 Ebisu Nishi.

ⓒ **03/5458-2826.** Cover usually ¥2,000 ($17) Sun–Thurs; ¥3,000 ($25) Fri and Sat. Daily 8pm–4am. Station: Ebisu (west exit, 2 min.). Take the side street beside Wendy's; Milk will be on your left.

Velfarre If you're looking for the disco scene, search no further. This huge, plush venue—run by a record group famous for its Eurobeat recordings—claims to be Japan's largest disco and has all the latest technical gadgetry to match. Tokyo's disco of the moment, it attracts young Japanese dressed to kill. Even the staff is stylishly dressed. The dance floor is absolutely gigantic; stage dancers help set the pace. Leading DJs from Tokyo and abroad play everything from pop and retro to techno, hard house, and—what else?—Eurobeat. *Note:* Unlike other discos, this one closes promptly at closing time. 7–14–22 Roppongi. ⓒ **03/3402-8000.** Cover ¥2,000 ($17) for women and ¥3,000 ($25) for men Thurs including 2 drinks; ¥2,500 ($21) for women and ¥3,500 ($29) for men Fri and Sat including 2 drinks; free for women and ¥3,000 ($25) for men Sun including 2 drinks. Sun and Thurs 6pm–midnight; Fri–Sat 6pm–1am. Station: Roppongi (3 min.). From Roppongi Crossing, take the first left after Ibis Hotel.

Yellow Closed on and off by the boys in blue in its early days, this is the closest thing Tokyo has to a true underground disco, staging the city's most progressive events from butoh performances (a modern minimalist form of dance) to gay nights. Guest DJs from abroad make appearances, playing a variety of music from salsa and reggae to hip-hop, soul, and techno. Only those in the know are supposed to come here, so there's no sign—just a blank, yellow neon square. 1–10–11 Nishi-Azabu. ⓒ **03/3479-0690.** Cover ¥3,000–¥3,500 ($25–$29) including 1 or 2 drinks, depending on the DJ and the event. Daily 9pm–midnight (often until 4am); occasionally closed for private functions so call ahead. Station: Roppongi (10 min.). From Roppongi Crossing, head toward Shibuya on Roppongi Dori. Turn right at the next-to-last street before Gaien-Nishi Dori; it's in the 2nd. blk. on the right.

THE BAR SCENE

GINZA If you're looking for a quiet place for a drink, you can't do better than ㊲ **Lupin** ⚑, 5–5–11 Ginza (ⓒ **03/3571-0750;** station: Ginza, 2 min.), located in a tiny alley behind Ketel, a German restaurant on Namiki Dori. This tiny basement bar first opened back in 1928 and has changed little over the decades. Even the staff looks like they've been here since it opened. Because no music is played, it's is a good place to come if you want to talk (closed Sun). Another good bar is the **Old Imperial** in the Imperial Hotel (ⓒ **03/3504-1111;** station: Hibiya, 1 min.); the bar is the hotel's tribute to its original architect, Frank Lloyd Wright, and is the only place in the hotel with some Wright originals, including an art deco terra-cotta wall and a mural. With its low lighting and comfortable chairs and tables that are copies of Wright originals, it has a clubby, masculine atmosphere.

Nanbantei, just off Harumi Dori on Suzuran Dori near the Ginza 4-chome Crossing (ⓒ **03/3571-5700;** station: Ginza, 2 min.), is one of a chain of yakitori-ya with English menus, friendly staff, good yakitori, and lots of beer, making it a great choice for foreign visitors. Another good yakitori-ya is **Atariya,** on the small street that runs behind Wako department store (ⓒ **03/3564-0045;** station: Ginza, 3 min) and also with an English menu for its yakitori (closed Sun).

Sapporo beer is the draw at **Sapporo Lion,** a large beer hall with a mock Gothic ceiling, on Chuo Dori not far from Matsuzakaya department store (ⓒ **03/3571-2590;** station: Ginza, 3 min.). A large display of plastic foods and an English-language menu help you choose from snacks ranging from yakitori to sausage and spaghetti.

ASAKUSA   Sky Room, on the 22nd floor of the Asahi Beer Tower, across the Sumida River from Sensoji Temple and next to the building that looks like a mug of beer (✆ **03/5608-5277;** station: Asakusa, 4 min.), is a great place for an inexpensive drink after an active day in historic Asakusa. This inexpensive bar— a simple cafeteria-type place—offers great views over the area as well as different kinds of Asahi beer, wine, coffee, tea, and cider, all priced at only ¥500 ($4.15); it can be crowded on weekends, and note that the last order is taken at 8:30pm.

SHINJUKU   Tiny ③⑧ **Fukuriki Ichiza,** 1–1–10 Kabuki-cho ((✆**03/ 5291-5139);** station: Shinjuku Sanchome, 8 min.), with room for less than a dozen people, is typical of a multitude of miniature establishments that line the alleyways of Goruden Gai (see "The Major Entertainment Districts," earlier in this chapter). However, unlike most of the establishments here, it welcomes foreigners and is a small, funky bar that attracts a young clientele with its Latin American music, Ganja High dark beer brewed in Osaka, pictures of Che Guevera, and kitsch. Nearer the station, in the heart of Kabuki-cho a block north of Koma Stadium, **Café Ole Bar,** 22–38–2 Kabuki-cho (✆ **03/ 3200-2249;** station: Shinjuku east exit, 10 min.) is a cozy, small establishment patronized by both Japanese and foreigners and is a good stop for a drink (happy hour is 8–9pm daily).

Although most of Shinjuku's night action is east of the station, **Vagabond,** 1–4–20 Nishi-Shinjuku on the second floor in the second alley behind—north of—Odakyu Halc (✆ **03/3348-9109,** station: Shinjuku, west exit, 2 min.), is on the west side. It features a jazz pianist nightly and is popular with foreigners (especially Brits, who come for the Guinness). The place has been in operation for more than 20 years and is owned by the effervescent Mr. Matsuoka, who became enamored with jazz after seeing Louis Armstrong perform in Tokyo in the 1950s and who recently opened a sophisticated cocktail lounge on the ground-floor bar in the same building, with soft lighting and soft jazz playing in the background. Just down the street is ③⑨ **Volga,** 1–4–18 Nishi Shinjuku (✆ **03/3342-4996,** station: Shinjuku, west exit, 2 min.), a yakitori-ya in an ivy-covered, two-story brick building on the corner. Its unrefined atmosphere has changed little since its opening in the 1950s; the place is popular with middle-aged and older Japanese (closed Sun).

Finally, **karaoke** pros will love **Bob** 🎤, 1–9–1 Kabuki-cho (✆ **03/ 3208-0051;** station: Shinjuku east exit, 9 min.), a tiny basement bar with room for only a dozen people or so, a gracious host and an extensive library of English-language hits from Elvis to Bob Dylan to Bon Jovi. Bob, who lived abroad in the United States and Taiwan for 27 years, loves having foreign guests; I've seen even anti-karaoke diehards melt after a few hours here and end up singing their hearts out. A fun place to spend an evening. It's located east of Koma Stadium, on a tiny side street (closed Sun).

HARAJUKU   Mellow, dimly lit **Oh God,** 6–7–18 Jingumae (✆ **03/ 3406-3206;** station: Meiji-Jingumae, 4 min.), features a mural of a city at sunset and shows free foreign films every night at 9pm (6pm on Fri, Sat, Sun and holidays) with subsequent shows at midnight and 3am. I've seen everything from James Bond to Fassbinder to grade-B movies here; most of the "recent" releases are from the 1990s. There are also two pool tables. A godsend for travelers on a budget and a good place to hang out. Nearby, on Meiji Dori in the direction of Shibuya, is **Scruffy Murphy's,** 6–5–6 Jingumae (✆ **03/3499-3145;** station: Meiji-Jingumae, 1 min.; Harajuku: 4 min.), an Irish pub with good pub grub (shepherd's pie, fish and chips, roast beef), good beer, and live music on Fridays.

EBISU Beer Station, located at the entrance to Yebisu Garden Place if you're arriving via the moving walkway from Ebisu Station (© **03/3442-5111**), is an attractive beer hall that's a good imitation of a century-old brewery, just like you'd find in good old Bavaria; Bavarian oompah music even greets you at the entrance. There are several floors of dining and drinking, but the best place is the huge basement beer hall with its vaulted ceiling and huge pillars. There is also outdoor terrace seating, good for people-watching.

If the weather is fine, there's no better place to be than **Hanezawa Beer Garden,** 3–12–15 Hiroo (© **03/3400-6500;** station: Ebisu, Omotesando, or Shibuya, then a taxi). This traditional Japanese outdoor garden, spread under trees and paper lanterns, is a lovely place for drinks and a meal of shabu-shabu, barbecued beef, and snacks.

Ebisu's most popular bar (especially with expats) is **What the Dickens!,** 1–13–3 Ebisu Nishi (© **03/3780-2088;** station: Ebisu, west exit, 2 min.), which features free live bands nightly, English and Irish beer, and British pub grub. Take the side street that runs between Wendy's and KFC; the bar is at the end of the second block on the left on the 4th floor (closed Mon). But personally my favorite bar is the inimitable **Enjoy House,** 2–9–9 Ebisu Nishi (© **03/5489-1591;** station: Ebisu, west exit, 3 min.), with its 1960s-reminiscent decor, efficient yet relaxed and funky staff, friendly atmosphere, and tiny dance floor. Everyone here seems high and happy; the place is aptly named (closed Mon and 1st Sun of every month).

ROPPONGI Gaspanic Bar, 3–15–24 Roppongi (© **03/3405-0633;** station: Roppongi, 3 min.), epitomizes Roppongi frenzy, attracting foreign and Japanese twentysomethings. The music is loud, and after midnight, this place can get so crowded that women have been known to dance on the countertops. Thursdays are especially crowded since all drinks go for only ¥300 ($2.50). **Gaspanic Cafe,** downstairs, sells pizza by the slice, while in the basement is **Club Panic 99,** open only on Thursday, Friday, and Saturday for dancing. Large bouncers at the door serve as clues that this place can get rough. From Roppongi Crossing, walk towards Tokyo Tower on Gaien-Higashi Dori, turning left at Hamburger Inn. Similar is the nearby **Hideout Bar,** on Gaien-Nishi Dori across from the Roi Building at 3–14–9 Roppongi (© **03/3497-5219**). With its loud music and strong U.S. military presence, this place packs in twentysomethings like the Yamanote Line during rush hour.

If you like to dance but feel intimidated by the meat markets above, a fun choice is **Bodeguita,** 3–14–7 Roppongi (© **03/3796-0232;** station: Roppongi, 3 min.), a small, crowded Cuban club featuring Latin music, Cuban cocktails, and good food, including *arroz con frijoles* (the classic rice and beans) and *arroz saltado* (rice, fried potatoes, and meat). There's live music Wednesdays, but the real crowd pleaser is the Cuban party held the last Saturday of most months. It's across from Gaspanic (above).

For a drink, I'm partial to **Dusk to Dawn,** 3–13–8 Roppongi (© **03/ 5771-2258;** Roppongi, 3 min.), on the left side of Gaien-Higashi Dori as you walk toward Tokyo Tower, catty-corner from Starbuck's. It attracts an older, professional, international crowd with its convivial atmosphere (closed Sun). But the most sane, sophisticated place for a drink is surely **Agave,** 7–15–10 Roppongi (© **03/3497-0229;** station: Roppongi, 3 min.), a cellar bar boasting

Japan's largest selection of tequila (more than 400 kinds), as well as cigars from the Dominican Republic, Nicaragua, Honduras, Mexico, and Jamaica (closed Sun).

AKASAKA   In fine weather from June through August, one of my favorite places for a beer is atop the Suntory Building, where you'll find the **Suntory Beer Garden** (© 03/3401-4367; station: Akasake-mitsuke, 1 min.) with its great views of surrounding Akasaka, refreshing beer, barbecued meals, and snacks (closed Sun). If you'd rather rest your eyes on a Japanese landscape garden than on neon lights, head to the **Garden Lounge** at the Hotel New Otani (© 03/3265-1111; station: Nagatacho or Akasaka-mitsuke, 3 min.) before sunset. You can look out over a 400-year-old garden complete with a waterfall, a pond, bridges, and manicured bushes. Cocktails are on the expensive side, but there's live music from 5pm with a ¥300 ($2.50) cover charge. For a more casual setting, try **Hobgoblin Tokyo Brewery Pub and Restaurant,** 2–13–19 Akasaka (© 03/3585-3681; station: Akasaka, exit 2, 2 min.), a British chain offering more draft beers than any other bar in town, major sporting events from its satellite TVs, darts, and the hearty pub meals, including a traditional British roast on Sundays.

GAY & LESBIAN BARS

Shinjuku 2-chome (station: Shinjuku Sanchome), southeast of the Yasukuni-Gyoen Dori intersection, is Tokyo's gay and lesbian quarter, with a lively street scene and numerous establishments catering to a variety of age groups and preferences. The following are some good starting points, but you'll find a lot more in the immediate area by just exploring on your own. Attracting both gays and straights, **Advocates,** 2–18–1 Shinjuku (© 03/3358-3988), is a small bar open to the street with a few sidewalk tables, making this a good vantage for watching the street action. **Kinsmen,** on the second floor at 2–18–5 Shinjuku (© 03/3354-4949), welcomes customers of all persuasions. It's a pleasant oasis, small and civilized, with a huge flower arrangement dominating the center of the room (closed Tues). Nearby **Arty Farty,** 2–17–4 Shinjuku (© 03/3356-5388), behind Bygs on a corner, allows only men except on Sundays when women with gay partners are welcome. Finally, the casual, laid-back, women-only **Kinswomyn,** 2–15–10 Shinjuku (© 03/3354-8720), attracts a regular clientele of mainly Japanese lesbians and has a friendly, welcoming atmosphere (closed Tues).

5

Side Trips from Tokyo

If your stay in Tokyo is long enough, you should consider taking an excursion or two. **Kamakura** and **Nikko** rank as two of the most important historical sites in Japan, while the **Fuji-Hakone-Izu National Park** serves as a huge recreational playground for the residents of Tokyo. **Yokohama,** with its thriving port, waterfront development, and several museums and attractions, is an interesting day trip from Tokyo. For overnight stays, I recommend **Hakone** or **Izu Peninsula** since these resorts boast Japanese-style inns

(*ryokan*) where you'll be able to experience the atmosphere of old Japan.

Before departing Tokyo, stop by the Tourist Information Center (TIC) for a color brochure called "Side Trips from Tokyo," which carries information on Kamakura, Nikko, Hakone, and the Mt. Fuji area. The TIC also has a map of Tokyo's vicinity, as well as pamphlets on individual destinations, some of which give train schedules and other useful information; see "Visitor Information," in chapter 3 for the TIC location.

1 Kamakura, Ancient Capital ★★★

51km (32 miles) S of Tokyo

If you take only one day-trip outside Tokyo, it should be to Kamakura, especially if you're unable to include the ancient capitals of Kyoto and Nara in your travels. Kamakura is a delightful hamlet with no fewer than 65 Buddhist temples and 19 Shinto shrines spread throughout the village and surrounding wooded hills. Most of these were built centuries ago, when a warrior named Yoritomo Minamoto seized political power and established his shogunate government in Kamakura back in 1192. Wanting to set up his seat of government as far away as possible from what he considered to be the corrupt imperial court in Kyoto, Yoritomo selected Kamakura because it was easy to defend. The village is enclosed on three sides by wooded hills and on the fourth by the sea—a setting that lends a dramatic background to its many temples and shrines.

Although Kamakura remained the military and political center of the nation for a century and a half, the Minamoto clan was in power for only a short time. After Yoritomo's death, both of his sons were assassinated, one after the other, after taking up military rule. Power then passed to the family of Yoritomo's widow, the Hojo family, who ruled until 1333, when the emperor in Kyoto sent troops to crush the shogunate government. Unable to stop the invaders, 800 soldiers retired to the Hojo family temple at Toshoji, where they all disemboweled themselves in ritualistic suicide known as *seppuku.*

Today a thriving seaside resort with a population of 175,000, Kamakura— with its old wooden homes, temples, shrines, and wooded hills—makes a pleasant 1-day trip from Tokyo. (There's also a beach in Kamakura called Yuigahama

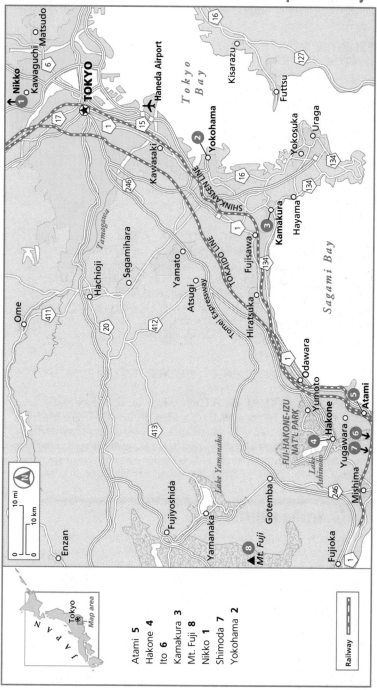

Atami **5**
Hakone **4**
Ito **6**
Kamakura **3**
Mt. Fuji **8**
Nikko **1**
Shimoda **7**
Yokohama **2**

Railway

Beach, but I find it unappealing; it's often litter-strewn and unbelievably crowded in summer. Skip it.)

ESSENTIALS

GETTING THERE Take the **JR Yokosuka Line** bound for Zushi, Kurihama, or Yokosuka; it departs every 10 to 15 minutes from the Yokohama, Shinagawa, Shimbashi, and Tokyo JR stations. The trip takes almost 1 hour from Tokyo Station and costs ¥890 ($7.40) one-way to Kamakura Station (free if you have a Japan Rail Pass).

VISITOR INFORMATION In Kamakura, there's a **tourist information window** (© 0467/22-3350; open daily 9am–6pm, 5pm in winter) immediately to the right outside Kamakura Station's east exit in the direction of Tsurugaoka Hachimangu Shrine. It sells a color brochure with a map of Kamakura for ¥200 ($1.65); there's also a free map (in both English and Japanese), but it's not always in stock. Ask here for directions on how to get to the village's most important sights by bus.

ORIENTATION & GETTING AROUND Kamakura's major sights are clustered in two areas: **Kamakura Station,** the town's downtown with the tourist office, souvenir shops spread along Komachi Dori and Wakamiya Oji, restaurants, and Tsurugaoka Hachimangu Shrine; and **Hase,** with the Great Buddha and Hase Kannon Temple. You can travel between Kamakura Station and Hase Station via the **Enoden Line,** a wonderful small train, or you can walk the distance in about 15 minutes. Destinations in Kamakura are also easily reached by buses that depart from Kamakura Station.

SEEING THE SIGHTS

Keep in mind that most temples and shrines open at about 8 or 9am and close between 4 and 5pm.

AROUND KAMAKURA STATION About a 10-minute walk from Kamakura Station, **Tsurugaoka Hachimangu Shrine** ★★★ (© 0467/22-0315) is the spiritual heart of Kamakura and one of its most popular attractions. It was built by Yoritomo and dedicated to Hachiman, the Shinto god of war who served as the clan deity of the Minamoto family. The pathway to the shrine is along Wakamiya Oji, a cherry tree–lined pedestrian lane that was also

---

Tips Touring Kamakura

If you wish, an English-speaking **volunteer student guide** will escort you for free to Kamakura's major sights. They can be found most weekends outside the east exit of Kamakura Station between 10am to noon (try to arrive a little before 10am, before other visitors whisk them away). You can also reserve a guide by calling at least three days prior to your visit, with the contact number different each day of the week: on Monday call © 090-1031-3504; Tuesday © 090-7245-7724; Wednesday © 090-1775-6945; Thursday © 070-5006-2142; and Friday © 090-7175-9673. Since these are student guides, numbers may change during the lifetime of this book. In return for the student's service, it would be a nice gesture to reimburse him or her for transportation costs and to pay for lunch and admission fees.

Kamakura

To Yokohama/Tokyo/Ofuna

Kita-Kamakura Station

■ Engakuji Temple

■ Kenchoji Temple

Tokeiji Temple ■

J A P A N

Tokyo

Kamakura

OGIGAYATSU

YOKOSUKA LINE

Modern Art Museum ■

Kamakura Municipal Museum

Gempei Pond

1

2 ■ 3rd torii

3

2nd torii ■

YUKINOSHITA

4

5

Komachi Dori

Wakamiya Oji

Kamakura Station

ⓘ Information

☒ Post Office

KOMACHI

6

O-MACHI

7

Yuigahama Dori

To Fujisawa

8

HASE

1st torii ■

YUMIGAHAMA

ENODEN LINE

Nameri River

GOKURAKU-JI

Yuigahama Beach

ZAIMOKUZA

Sagami Bay

ⓘ Information

☒ Post Office

▬▬ Railway

To Zushi

ATTRACTIONS ●

Great Buddha (Daibutsu) **6**

Hase Kannon Temple **8**

Tsurugaoka Hachimangu Shrine **1**

Zeniarai-Benten Shrine **4**

DINING ◆

Kamakura Oboro **2**

Milano a Riccione **3**

Miyokawa **7**

Raitei **5**

Fun Fact **Murder and Betrayal at Tsurugaoka Hachimangu Shrine**

As you ascend the 62 steps to the vermilion-painted shrine, note the **gingko tree** to the left that's thought to be about 1,000 years old. This is supposedly the site where Yoritomo's second son was ambushed and murdered back in 1219; his head was never found. Such stories of murder and betrayal were common in feudal Japan. Fearful that his charismatic brother had designs on the shogunate, Yoritomo banished him and ordered him killed. Rather than face capture, the brother committed *seppuku*. When the brother's mistress gave birth to a boy, the baby was promptly killed. Today, the lotus ponds, arched bridge, pigeons, and bright vermilion sheen of the shrine give little clue to such violent history.

---

constructed by Yoritomo back in the 1190s so that his oldest son's first visit to the family shrine could be accomplished in style with an elaborate procession. The lane stretches from the shrine all the way to Yuigahama Beach, with three massive torii gates set at intervals along the route to signal the approach to the shrine. On both sides of the pathway are souvenir and antiques shops selling lacquerware, pottery, and folk art.

At the top of the stairs, which afford a panoramic view toward the sea, is the shrine with its small **shrine museum.** The museum is worth the ¥100 (85¢) admission only if you're interested in seeing portable shrines from the Muromachi Period, a few Edo-Period screens depicting fight scenes from the Kamakura Period, and a handful of other relics like kimono and samurai armor. It's open daily 9:30 am to 4:15pm. Otherwise, shrine grounds are free to the public and are always open.

Although it's a bit out of the way, it might pay to visit **Zeniarai-Benten Shrine** (© 0467/25-1081), about a 20-minute walk west of Kamakura Station. This shrine is dedicated to the goddess of good fortune. On Asian zodiac days of the snake, worshippers believe that if you take your money and wash it in spring water in a small cave on the shrine grounds, it will double or triple itself later on. This being modern Japan, don't be surprised if you see a bit of ingenuity; my Japanese landlady told me that when she visited the shrine she didn't have much cash on her, so she washed something that she thought would be equally as good—her credit card. As a shrine dedicated to the goddess of fortune, it's fitting that admission is free. Open daily 8am to 5pm.

AROUND HASE STATION To get to these attractions, you can go by bus, which departs from in front of Kamakura Station (take any bus from platform 1 or 6 to the Daibutsuen-mae stop). Or, for a more romantic adventure, you can go by the **JR Enoden Line,** a tiny train that putt-putts its way seemingly through backyards on its way from Kamakura Station to Hase and beyond. Since it's mostly only one track, trains have to take turns going in either direction. I would suggest taking the bus from Kamakura Station directly to the Great Buddha, walking to Hase Shrine, and then taking the Enoden train back to Kamakura Station.

Probably Kamakura's most famous attraction is the **Great Buddha** ★★★ (© 0467/22-0703), called the *Daibutsu* in Japanese and located at **Kotokuin Temple.** Thirty-seven feet high and weighing 93 tons, it's the second-largest bronze image in Japan. The largest Buddha is in Nara, but in my opinion, the

Kamakura Daibutsu is much more impressive. For one thing, the Kamakura Buddha sits outside against a dramatic backdrop of wooded hills. Cast in 1252, the Kamakura Buddha was indeed once housed in a temple like the Nara Buddha, but a huge tidal wave destroyed the wooden structure—and the statue has sat under sun, snow, and stars ever since. I also prefer the face of the Kamakura Buddha; I find it more inspiring and divine, as though with its half-closed eyes and calm, serene face it's somehow above the worries of the world. It seems to represent the plane above human suffering, the point at which birth and death, joy and sadness merge and become one. Open daily from 7am to 6pm (to 5:30pm in winter). Admission is ¥200 ($1.65) for adults and ¥150 ($1.25) for children, and your entry ticket is a bookmark, a nice souvenir. If you want, you can pay an extra ¥20 (15¢) to go inside the statue—it's hollow.

About a 10-minute walk from the Daibutsu is **Hase Kannon Temple** ⭐⭐⭐ or Hasedera (✆ **0467/22-6300**), located on a hill with a sweeping view of the sea. This is the home of an 11-headed gilt statue of Kannon, the goddess of mercy, housed in the Kannon-do (Kannon Hall). More than 30 feet high and the tallest wooden image in Japan, it was made from a single piece of camphor wood back in the 8th century. The legend surrounding this Kannon is quite remarkable. Supposedly, two wooden images were made from the wood of a huge camphor tree. One of the images was kept in Hase, not far from Nara, while the second was given a short ceremony and then duly tossed into the sea to find a home of its own. The image drifted 300 miles eastward and washed up on shore but was thrown back in again because all who touched it became ill or incurred bad luck. Finally, the image reached Kamakura, where it gave the people no trouble. This was interpreted as a sign that the image was content with its surroundings, and Hase Kannon Temple was erected at its present site. Note how each face has a different expression, representing the Kannon's compassion for various kinds of human suffering. In the Kannon-do, you'll also find the **Treasure House** with relics from the Kamakura, Heian, Muromachi, and Edo periods.

Another statue housed here is of **Amida,** a Buddha who promised rebirth in the Pure Land to the West to all who chanted his name. It was created by orders of Yoritomo Minamoto upon his 42nd birthday, which is considered an unlucky year for men. You'll find it housed in the Amida-do (Amida Hall) beside the Kannon-do.

As you climb up the steps to the Kannon-do, you'll encounter statues of a different sort. All around you will be likenesses of **Jizo,** the guardian deity of children. Although parents originally came to Hase Temple to set up statues to represent their children in hopes the deity would protect and watch over them, through the years the purpose of the Jizo statues has changed. Now they represent miscarried, stillborn, or most frequently, aborted children. More than 50,000 Jizo statues have been offered here since the war, but the thousand or so you see now will remain only a year before being burned or buried to make way for others. Some of the statues, which can be purchased on the temple grounds, are fitted with hand-knitted caps and sweaters. The effect is quite chilling.

Hase Temple is open daily 8am to 6pm (to 5pm in winter); admission is ¥300 ($2.50) for adults, ¥100 (85¢) for children.

WHERE TO DINE

In addition to the choices below, there's also a pavilion at Hase Kannon Temple (see above) that serves inexpensive oden, noodles, beer, and soft drinks, with indoor and outdoor seating. Its great view makes it a good place for a snack on a fine day.

④⓿ **Kamakura Oboro** TOFU/VEGETARIAN   Built in the traditional style of a *kura* (warehouse) with its whitewashed walls and dark wooden beams, this tofu restaurant offers simple but delicious vegetarian meals, including udon noodles with tofu, soba noodles with tofu and vegetables, and tofu kaiseki, as well as sweets made from red bean paste. You can watch tofu being made at the entranceway; the dining room is upstairs.

1–8–25 Yukinoshita. Ⓒ **0467/61-0570.** Main dishes ¥780–¥1,800 ($6.50–$15). No credit cards. Daily 10am–6pm. Station: Kamakura (8 min.). Between Komachi Dori and Wakamiya Oji streets, at the very end just before Tsurugaoka Hachimangu Shrine.

Milano a Riccione ITALIAN   This is the Japanese branch of a restaurant from Milan known for its handmade pasta, seafood, and good selection of wines. Although located in a basement, it opens onto a subterranean courtyard, making it brighter and more cheerful than one would expect. There's an English seasonal menu, but the best bargain is the daily set lunch for ¥1,300 ($11.70), which gives you a choice of pasta, an appetizer, and coffee, espresso, or tea. It's also the quickest meal you can order; otherwise, if you're in a hurry, you should dine elsewhere, as care and time are devoted to the preparation of such meals as grilled scallops and leeks and roast chicken with zucchini and ham.

2–12–30 Komachi. Ⓒ **0467/24-5491.** Pizza and pasta ¥950–¥1,700 ($7.90–$14); main dishes ¥1,800–¥2,400 ($15–$20); set dinner ¥3,800 ($32); set lunches ¥1,300–¥2,500 ($11–$21). AE, DC, JCB, MC, V. Thurs–Tues 11:30am–3:30pm and 5:30–9:30pm (last order). Station: Kamakura (6 min.). On the left side of Wakamiya Oji when walking from Kamakura Station to Tsurugaoka Hachimangu Shrine.

④① **Miyokawa** MINI-KAISEKI/OBENTO   This modern, casual restaurant specializes in *kaiseki,* including beautifully prepared mini-kaiseki set meals that change with the seasons. It also offers a great obento lunch box, the least expensive of which is served in a container shaped like a gourd, as well as a set meal featuring steak prepared Japanese style. It also offers take-out obento, priced at ¥700 to –¥1,500 ($5.85–$12.50), which you could eat at the pavilion at Hase Temple.

1–16–17 Hase. Ⓒ **0467/25-5556.** Reservations recommended. Mini-kaiseki ¥5,500–¥10,000 ($46–$83); obento ¥2,000–¥5,000 ($17–$42); Japanese steak set meal ¥3,500 ($29). MC, V. Daily 11am–9pm. Station: Hase (5 min.). On the main road leading from Hase Station to the Great Buddha (about a 5-min. walk from each).

④② **Raitei** ★★★ *Finds* NOODLES/OBENTO   Though it's a bit inconveniently located, this is the absolute winner for a meal in Kamakura. Visiting Raitei is as much fun as visiting the city's temples and shrines. The restaurant is situated in the hills on the edge of Kamakura, surrounded by verdant countryside, and the wonder is that it serves inexpensive soba (Japanese noodles) as well as priestly kaiseki feasts, which you must reserve in advance. If you're here for soba or one of the obento lunch boxes, go down the stone steps on the right to the back entry, where you'll be given an English menu with such offerings as noodles with chicken, mountain vegetables, tempura, and more. The pottery used here comes from the restaurant's own specially made kiln, and you'll dine sitting on roughly hewn wood stools or tatami.

Takasago. Ⓒ **0467/32-5656.** Reservations required for kaiseki. Noodles ¥700–¥1,200 ($5.85–$10); obento lunch boxes ¥3,500–¥4,500 ($29–$37.50); soba set meals ¥2,500 ($21); kaiseki feasts from ¥6,000 ($50). At the front gate, you must pay an entry fee of ¥500 ($4.15), which counts toward the price of your meal. AE, DC, JCB (on meals costing more than ¥10,000/$83 only). Daily 11am–sundown (about 7pm in summer). Bus: 4 or 6 from platform 6 at Kamakura Station to Takasago stop (or a 15-min. taxi ride).

Moments A Special Stroll

When you've finished your meal at Raitei, be sure to walk the path circling through the garden past a bamboo grove, stone images, and a miniature shrine. The stroll takes about 20 minutes, unless you stop for a beer at the refreshment house, which has outdoor seating and a view of the countryside.

---

2 Shogun Country: Nikko ★★★

144km (90 miles) N of Tokyo

Since the publication of James Clavell's novel _Shogun,_ many people have become familiar with Tokugawa Ieyasu, the powerful real-life shogun of the 1600s on whom Clavell's fictional shogun was based. Quashing all rebellions and unifying Japan under his leadership, Tokugawa established such a military stronghold that his heirs continued to rule Japan for the next 250 years without serious challenge.

If you'd like to join the millions of Japanese who through the centuries have paid homage to this great man, travel 90 miles north of Tokyo to Nikko, where **Toshogu Shrine** ★★★ was constructed in his honor in the 17th century and where Tokugawa's remains were laid to rest in a mausoleum. Nikko means "sunlight"—an apt description of the way the sun's rays play upon this sumptuous shrine of wood and gold leaf. Another mausoleum containing Tokugawa's grandson, a temple, a shrine, and a garden are nearby. Surrounding the sacred grounds, designated a World Heritage Site by UNESCO in 1999, are thousands of majestic cedar trees in the 200,000-acre **Nikko National Park** ★★.

I've included a few recommendations for an overnight stay. Otherwise, you can see Nikko in a full day.

ESSENTIALS

GETTING THERE The easiest, fastest, and most luxurious way to get to Nikko is on the privately owned Tobu Line's Limited Express, called the **Spacia,** which departs every hour or more frequently from Asakusa Station and costs ¥2,740 ($23) one-way for the 2-hour trip. All seats are reserved, which means you are guaranteed a seat; if you're traveling on a holiday or a summer weekend, you may wish to purchase and reserve your ticket in advance. Another plus is that there's usually an English-speaking hostess on board who passes out pamphlets on the area and can answer sightseeing questions about Nikko.

Otherwise, you can also reach Nikko on Tobu's slower **rapid train** from Asakusa, which costs ¥1,320 ($11) one-way and takes 2 hours and 10 minutes, with trains departing every hour or more frequently. There are no reserved seats, which means you might have to stand if trains are crowded.

If you have a Japan Rail Pass, take the Shinkansen bullet train from Ueno to Utsunomiya (there are departures every 20 to 40 min., and the trip takes about 50 min.) and change there for a rapid JR train to Nikko (45 min.).

VISITOR INFORMATION Before leaving Tokyo, pick up the leaflet "Nikko" from the Tourist Information Center (TIC). It gives the train schedule for both the Tobu Line, which departs from Asakusa Station, and the JR trains that depart from Ueno Station. The TIC also has some color brochures with maps of the Nikko area.

Nikko's Tobu and JR stations are located almost side by side in the village's downtown area. The **Nikko Tobu Station tourist information counter** (© **0288/53-4511**), located inside Tobu Station to the right after passing through the wicket gate, is staffed by a friendly woman who speaks enough English to give you a map, answer basic questions, and point you in the right direction. You can also make hotel and ryokan reservations here for free. Open daily 8:30am to noon and 1 to 5pm.

Another tourist office, the **Nikko Information Center** (© **0288/54-2496**), is located on the main road leading from the train station to Toshogu Shrine. It has English-speaking staff and lots of information in English about Nikko including information on public hot springs. Open daily from 8:30am to 5pm.

GETTING AROUND   Toshogu Shrine and its mausoleum are on the edge of town, but you can walk from either the JR or Tobu train stations to the shrine in less than half an hour. Simply head straight out the main exit, pass the bus stands, and then turn right. There are signs pointing the way in English throughout town. Keep walking on this main road (you'll pass the Nikko Information Center about halfway down on the left side, as well as souvenir shops) until you come to a **T** intersection with a vermilion-colored bridge spanning a river (about a 15-min. walk from the train stations). The stone steps opposite lead up the hill into the woods and to Toshogu Shrine. You can also travel from Tobu Station by bus, getting off at either the Shinkyo (a 5-min. ride) or Nishi Sando (a 7-min. ride) bus stop.

SEEING THE SIGHTS

ON THE WAY TO THE SHRINE   The first indication that you're nearing the shrine is the vermilion-painted **Sacred Bridge (Shinkyo)** arching over the rushing Daiyagawa River. It was built in 1636, and for more than 3 centuries only shoguns and their emissaries were allowed to cross it. Even today, mortal souls like us are prevented from completely crossing it because of a barrier at one end. It is presently under restoration until 2003.

Across the road from the Sacred Bridge are some steps leading uphill into a forest of cedar where, after a 5-minute walk, you'll see a statue of **Shodo,** a priest who founded Nikko 1,200 years ago at a time when mountains were revered as gods. Behind him is the first major temple, Rinnoji Temple, where you can buy a **combination ticket** for ¥1,000 ($8.35) that allows entry to Rinnoji Temple, Toshogu Shrine, neighboring Futarasan Shrine, and the other Tokugawa mausoleum, Taiyuinbyo. Once at Toshogu Shrine, you'll have to pay an extra ¥520 ($4.35) to see Ieyasu's tomb. Combination tickets are also sold at the entry to Toshogu Shrine, which already include Ieyasu's tomb. It doesn't really matter where you buy your combination ticket since you can always pay the extra fee to see sights not covered. A note for bus riders: If you take the bus to the Nishi Sando bus stop, the first place you'll come to is the Taiyuinbyo Mausoleum, where you can also purchase a combination ticket.

RINNOJI TEMPLE   Rinnoji Temple was founded by the priest Shodo in the 8th century, long before the Toshogu clan came onto the scene. Here you can visit the **Sanbutsudo Hall,** a large building that enshrines three 28-foot-high, gold-plated, wooden images of Buddha. Perhaps the best thing to see at Rinnoji Temple, however, is its **Shoyo-en Garden** (opposite Sanbutsudo Hall), which requires a separate ¥300 ($2.50) admission. Completed in 1815 and typical of Japanese landscaped gardens of the Edo Period, this small strolling garden provides a different vista with each turn of the path, making it seem much larger than it actually is.

Nikko

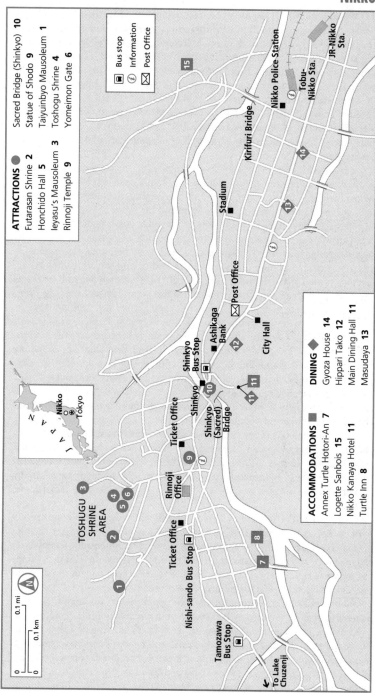

ATTRACTIONS ●
Futarasan Shrine **2**
Honchido Hall **5**
Ieyasu's Mausoleum **3**
Rinnoji Temple **9**
Sacred Bridge (Shinkyo) **10**
Statue of Shodo **9**
Taiyuinbyo Mausoleum **1**
Toshogu Shrine **4**
Yomeimon Gate **6**

🚌 Bus stop
ⓘ Information
✉ Post Office

ACCOMMODATIONS ■
Annex Turtle Hotori-An **7**
Logette Sanbois **15**
Nikko Kanaya Hotel **11**
Turtle Inn **8**

DINING ◆
Gyoza House **14**
Hippari Tako **12**
Main Dining Hall **11**
Masudaya **13**

TOSHUGU SHRINE AREA

Rinnoji Office

Ticket Office

Nishi-sando Bus Stop

Tamozawa Bus Stop

To Lake Chuzenji

Shinkyo (Sacred) Bridge

Shinkyo Bus Stop

Shinkyo

Ashikaga Bank

Post Office

City Hall

Stadium

Kirifuri Bridge

Nikko Police Station

Tobu-Nikko Sta.

JR-Nikko Sta.

JAPAN
Nikko ⊛
Tokyo

0   0.1 mi
0   0.1 km

TOSHOGU SHRINE 🕊🕊🕊   The most important and famous structure in Nikko is Toshogu Shrine, built by Tokugawa's grandson (and 3rd Tokugawa shogun), Tokugawa Iemitsu, as an act of devotion. It seems that no expense was too great in creating the monument: Some 15,000 artists and craftspeople were brought to Nikko from all over Japan, and after 2 years' work, they erected a group of buildings more elaborate and gorgeous than any other Japanese temple or shrine. Rich in colors and carvings, Toshogu Shrine is gilded with 2.4 million sheets of gold leaf (they could cover an area of almost 6 acres). The mausoleum was completed in 1636, almost 20 years after Ieyasu's death, and was most certainly meant to impress anyone who saw it as a demonstration of the Tokugawa shogunate's wealth and power.

Toshogu Shrine is set in a grove of magnificent ancient **Japanese cedars** planted over a 20-year period during the 1600s by a feudal lord named Matsudaira Masatsuna. Some 13,000 of the original trees are still standing, adding a sense of dignity to the mausoleum and the shrine.

You enter Toshogu Shrine via a flight of stairs that passes under a huge stone torii gateway, one of the largest in Japan. On your left is a 5-story, 115-foot-high **pagoda.** Although normally pagodas are found only at temples, this pagoda is just one example of how both Buddhism and Shintoism are combined at Toshogu Shrine. After climbing a second flight of stairs, turn left and you'll see the **Sacred Stable,** which houses a sacred white horse. Horses have long been dedicated to Shinto gods and are kept at shrines. Shrines also kept monkeys as well, since they were thought to protect horses from disease; look for the three monkeys carved above the stable door, fixed in the pose of "see no evil, hear no evil, speak no evil"—they're considered guardians of the sacred horse. Across from the stable is **Kami-Jinko,** famous for its carving by Kano Tanyu, who painted the images of the two elephants after reading about them but without ever seeing what they actually looked like.

At the next flight of stairs is **Yomeimon Gate,** considered to be the central showpiece of Nikko and popularly known as the Twilight Gate, implying that it could take you all day (until twilight) to see everything carved onto it. Painted in red, blue, and green and decorated with gilding and lacquerwork, this gate has about 400 carvings of flowers, dragons, birds, and other animals. It's almost too much to take in at once and is very un-Japanese in its opulence, having more in common with Chinese architecture than the usual austerity of most Japanese shrines.

To the left of the Yomeimon Gate is the hall where the portable shrines are kept, as well as **Honchido Hall,** famous for its dragon painting on the ceiling. If you clap your hands under the painting, the echo supposedly resembles a dragon's roar. You also can visit the shrine's main sanctuary, the **Hai-den,** comprising three halls: one was reserved for the imperial family, one for the shogun, and one (the central hall) for conducting ceremonies.

To the right of the main hall is the entrance to **Tokugawa Ieyasu's mausoleum.** If it's not already included in your combination ticket, admission is ¥520 ($4.35). After the ticket counter, look for the carving of a sleeping cat above the door, dating from the Edo Period and famous today as a symbol of Nikko (you'll find many reproductions in area souvenir shops). Beyond that are 200 stone steps leading past cedars to Tokugawa's tomb. After the riotous colors of the shrine, the tomb seems surprisingly simple.

Toshogu Shrine is open daily April to October from 8am to 5pm (to 4pm the rest of the year); you must enter at least 30 minutes before closing time.

FUTARASAN SHRINE   Directly to the west of Toshogu Shrine is Futarasan Shrine, the oldest building in the district (from 1617), which has a pleasant garden and is dedicated to the gods of mountains surrounding Nikko.

On the shrine's grounds is the so-called **ghost lantern,** enclosed in a small wooden structure. According to legend, it used to come alive at night and sweep around Nikko in the form of a ghost. It apparently scared one of the guards so much that he struck it with his sword, the marks of which are still visible on the lamp's rim.

Past Futarasan Shrine is **Taiyuinbyo Mausoleum** ⚘, the final resting place of Iemitsu, the third Tokugawa shogun. Completed in 1653, it's not nearly as ornate as Toshogu Shrine—nor as crowded—but is serenely elegant nonetheless, making it a pleasant last stop on your tour of Nikko.

WHERE TO STAY

If it's peak season or a weekend, it's best to reserve a room in advance, which you can do by calling directly or through a travel agency in Tokyo. Otherwise, if it's not peak season, you can also make a reservation upon arrival at Nikko Tobu Station, either at the **tourist information counter,** where the service is free, or at the **accommodation-reservation window** (✆ **0288/54-0864**), which charges a ¥200 to ¥500 ($1.65–$4.15) fee but is familiar with the accommodations in the area and will make all arrangements for you. Open daily 9am to 5pm.

MODERATE

Nikko Kanaya Hotel ⚘⚘ *Finds*   This distinguished-looking, old-fashioned place on a hill above the Sacred Bridge is the most famous hotel in Nikko, combining the rustic heartiness of a European country lodge with elements of old Japan. It was founded in 1873 by the Kanaya family, who wished to offer accommodations to foreigners, mainly missionaries and businessmen looking to escape the heat and humidity of Tokyo. The present complex, built in spurts over the past 100 years, has a rambling, delightfully old-fashioned atmosphere that fuses Western architecture with Japanese craftsmanship. Through the decades it has played host to a number of VIPs from Charles Lindbergh to Indira Gandhi to Shirley MacLaine; Frank Lloyd Wright left a sketch for the bar fireplace, which was later built to his design and is still here. Even if you don't stay here, you might want to drop by for lunch (see review below).

All rooms are Western-style twins, with the differences in price based on room size, view, and facilities. They're rather simple but cozy and have character; some have antiques. None have air-conditioning because the high altitude of Nikko rarely warrants it. If you want to stay in the best room in the house, a corner room in the 62-year-old wing where the emperor once stayed, you'll pay the highest price below.

1300 Kami-Hatsuishi, Nikko City, Tochigi 321-1401. ✆ **0288/54-0001.** Fax 0288/53-2487. www.kanayahotel. co.jp/. 76 units (65 with shower/tub and toilet, 11 with toilet only). ¥8,000 ($67) single with toilet only, ¥10,000 ($83) single with shower and toilet, ¥11,000–¥35,000 ($92–$292) single with bathroom; ¥10,000 ($83) twin with toilet only, ¥12,000 ($100) twin with shower and toilet, ¥13,000–¥40,000 ($108–$333) twin with bathroom. ¥3,000 ($25) extra on Sat and eve before national holidays; ¥5,000–¥10,000 ($42–$83) extra in peak season. AE, DC, JCB, MC, V. Bus: From Nikko Tobu Station to the Shinkyo stop, a 5-min. ride. On foot: 15 min. from Tobu Station. **Amenities:** 3 restaurants (shabu-shabu, Western, and coffee shop); 1 bar; small outdoor heated pool (open only in summer and free for hotel guests); outdoor skating rink (in winter); souvenir shops; in-room massage. *In room:* TV, minibar.

INEXPENSIVE

Annex Turtle Hotori-An ⚘   Owned by the friendly family that runs Turtle Inn (see below), this is one of my favorite places to stay in Nikko. One dip in the hot-springs bath overlooking the river will tell you why; at night, you're lulled to sleep by the sound of the rushing waters. A simple, modern structure, it's located in a nice rural setting on a quiet street with a few other houses. All its rooms except one are Japanese style. A plentiful Western-style breakfast costs ¥1,000 ($8.35) in the pleasant living area/dining room. For dinner, you can go to the nearby Turtle Inn (not available Sun; reservations should be made by 10am) or buy a pizza from the freezer and microwave it yourself. There's also a communal refrigerator where you can store your food.

8–28 Takumi-cho, Nikko City, Tochigi 321-1433. © 0288/53-3663. Fax 0288/53-3883. .or.jp/facility/3/facil/30913.html. . 11 units (all with bathroom). ¥5,800 ($48) per person. AE, MC, V. Bus: From Nikko Station to the Sogo Kaikan-mae stop, a 7-min. ride; then a 9-min. walk. **Amenities:** Hot-spring baths; coin-op washer and dryer. *In room:* TV.

Logette Sanbois   This two-story wooden establishment with a rustic, cabin-like interior has an idyllic spot on a mountainside surrounded by forest and is owned by the friendly Ogihara family. A disadvantage, however, is its rather isolated location. Two of the rooms are Japanese style with a private bathroom and even a balcony. The rest are Western style with and without bathrooms. Even if you have a private bathroom, you might want to use the public one—it boasts a large window overlooking the woods.

1560 Tokorono, Nikko City, Tochigi 321-1421. © 0288/53-0082. Fax 0288/53-5212. 9 units (4 with bathroom). ¥5,000 ($42) single without bathroom; ¥5,500 ($46) single with bathroom; ¥9,000 ($75) twin without bathroom, ¥10,000 ($83) twin with bathroom. Japanese breakfast ¥800 ($6.65) extra; Japanese dinner ¥2,700 ($22.50) extra. AE, DC, JCB, MC, V. A 15-min. walk from Tobu Station on the opposite side of the Daiyagawa River. *In room:* A/C.

Turtle Inn   This excellent pension, a Japanese Inn Group member, is located within walking distance of Toshogu Shrine in a newer two-story house on a quiet side street beside the Daiyagawa River. It's run by the friendly Fukuda family. Mr. Fukuda speaks English and is very helpful in planning a sightseeing itinerary for the area. Rooms are bright and cheerful in both Japanese and Western styles; the five tatami rooms are without bathroom. Excellent Western dinners (with Japanese touches) and Japanese dinners are available for ¥2,000 ($17), as are Western breakfasts for ¥1,000 ($8.35). Mashiko pottery is used for tableware. Be sure to order dinner by 10am and note that it's not available on Sunday.

2–16 Takumi-cho, Nikko City, Tochigi 321-1433. © 0288/53-3168. Fax 0288/53-3883. http://www.itcj.or.jp/facility/3/facil/309004.html . turtle@sunfield.ne.jp. 10 units (3 with bathroom). ¥4,200 ($35) single without bathroom, ¥5,000 ($42) single with bathroom; ¥8,400 ($70) double without bathroom, ¥10,000 ($83) double with bathroom. AE, MC, V. Bus: From Nikko Station to the Sogo Kaikan-mae stop, a 7-min. ride; then a 5-min. walk. *In room:* TV, no phone.

WHERE TO DINE
MODERATE
Main Dining Hall at Nikko Kanaya Hotel ★★ *Finds* CONTINENTAL Even if you don't spend the night here, you might want to come for a meal in the hotel's quaint dining hall with its wood-carved pillars. It's one of the best places in town for lunch. Since it's beside the Sacred Bridge, only a 10-minute walk from Toshogu Shrine, you can easily combine it with your sightseeing tour of Nikko. I suggest Nikko's specialty, locally caught rainbow trout available in three different styles of cooking. I had mine cooked Kanaya style, covered with soy sauce, sugar, and sake, grilled and served whole. The best bargain is the set lunch available until 3pm, which comes with soup, salad, a main dish such as

trout, bread or rice, and dessert. Lobster, salmon, chicken, and other Western fare are also listed on the English menu.

Nikko Kanaya Hotel, 1300 Kami-Hatsuishi. ✆ **0288/54-0001.** Reservations recommended during peak season. Main dishes ¥2,800–¥6,000 ($23–$50); set lunches ¥2,800–¥3,000 ($23–$25). AE, DC, JCB, MC, V. Daily noon–3pm and 6–8pm. A 15-min. walk from Nikko Tobu Station.

Masudaya ⚘ YUBA   Only two fixed-price meals are served at this Japanese-style, 80-year-old restaurant, both featuring *yuba*. A high-protein food made from soybeans, yuba is a local specialty produced only in Kyoto and Nikko. Until 100 years ago, it could be eaten only by priests and members of the imperial family. Now you can enjoy it, too, along with such sides as rice, sashimi, soup, fried fish, and vegetables. Dining is either in a common dining hall (make reservations 2 days in advance) or, for the more expensive meals, in private tatami rooms upstairs, for which you should make a reservation one week in advance.

439 Ichiyamachi. ✆ **0288/54-2151.** Reservations required. Set meals ¥3,950 ($33) and ¥5,340 ($44.50). No credit cards. Fri–Wed 11am–4pm (open Thurs if a holiday). A 5-min. walk from Nikko Tobu Station. On the left side of the main street leading from Tobu Station to Toshogu Shrine, just before the fire station.

INEXPENSIVE

Gyoza House GYOZA   This simple restaurant serving up *gyoza* (Chinese dumplings) and *ramen* (noodle-and-vegetable soup) is easy to spot with its red awning and bright green facade. An English menu and pictures on the wall make ordering a cinch, whether it's the typical *yaki-gyoza* (sautéed gyoza) or one of the more unique dishes like curry gyoza, *shoyu gyoza* (in a soup broth), or spicy ramen.

257 Matsubara-cho. ✆ **0288/53-0494.** Main dishes ¥450–¥1,050 ($3.75–$8.75). No credit cards. Sat–Thurs 11am–8pm (to 7:30pm in winter). A 2-min. walk from Nikko Tobu Station. On the left side of the main street leading from Tobu Station to Toshogu Shrine.

㊸ **Hippari Tako** NOODLES   This tiny, three-table establishment is under the caring supervision of motherly Miki-san, who serves a limited selection of noodle dishes, including ramen and stir-fried noodles with vegetables as well as *onigiri* (rice balls) and yakitori. There's an English menu, and the walls, covered with business cards and messages left by appreciative guests from around the world, are testimony to both the tasty meals and Miki-san's warm hospitality.

1011 Kami-Hatsuishi. ✆ **0288/53-2933.** Main dishes ¥500–¥800 ($4.15–$6.65). No credit cards. Daily 11am–8pm. A 15-min. walk from Nikko Tobu Station. On the left side of the main street leading from Toshogu Shrine, 1 min. before the Nikko Kanaya Hotel and the Sacred Bridge.

3 Yokohama, City of the 21st Century

32km (20 miles) S of Tokyo

There are few attractions in Yokohama to warrant a visit if you're just in Japan for a short time. However, if you find yourself in Tokyo for an extended period, Yokohama is a pleasant destination for an easy day trip. Be sure to make time for wonderful Sankei-en Garden; although a mere 90-some years old, it ranks on my long list as one of the top gardens in Japan.

A rather new city in Japan's history books, Yokohama was nothing more than a tiny fishing village when Commodore Perry arrived in the mid-1800s and demanded that Japan open its doors to the world. The village was selected by the shogun as one of several ports to be opened for international trade, transforming it from a backwater to Japan's most important gateway. Yokohama subsequently grew by leaps and bounds and was a pioneer when it came to Western goods and services, boasting Japan's first bakery (1860), photo studio (1862), telephone (1869), beer brewery (1869), cinema (1870), daily newspaper (1870), public rest room (1871), and ice cream (1879).

Now Japan's second-largest city with a population of 3.4 million, Yokohama remains the nation's largest international port and supports a large international community, with many foreigners residing in the section called the Bluff. Yokohama has an especially large Chinese population and Japan's largest Chinatown, whose restaurants serve as a mecca for hungry Tokyoites. Befitting a city known for its firsts, Yokohama has been developing Japan's largest urban development project to date, the **Minato-Mirai 21,** with a conference center, museums, hotels, and restaurants. In addition to Sankei-en Garden, Yokohama also boasts a handful of specialty museums. Hard to imagine that a mere 140-some years ago, Yokohama was a village of 100 houses.

ESSENTIALS

GETTING THERE   Because many Yokohama residents work in Tokyo, it's as easy to get to Yokohama as it is to get around Tokyo. Fares average ¥300 to ¥450 ($2.50–$4.15), depending on which line you take and which station you start from. Most convenient is probably the **JR Keihin-Tohoku Line,** which travels through Ueno, Tokyo, Yurakucho, Shimbashi, and Shinagawa stations before continuing on to Yokohama and Kannai stations, with the journey from Tokyo Station to Yokohama Station taking approximately 40 minutes. The **JR Yokosuka Line** and **JR Tokaido Line** are the quickest, traveling between Tokyo Station and Yokohama Station in about 30 minutes, with stops in Shimbashi and Shinagawa along the way. The **Keihinkyuko Line** (also shortened to Keikyu) stops at Asakusa, Shimbashi, and Shinagawa stations before continuing to Yokohama Station, with the trip from Shinagawa taking about 50 minutes. From Shibuya, take the express (not the local, which makes too many stops) **Tokyu-Toyoko Line** to Yokohama in about 30 minutes.

VISITOR INFORMATION   There are several tourist information centers in Yokohama. At Yokohama Station, take the east exit to the front of Sogo department store, where to the right you'll find the **Yokohama Tourist Information office** (© 045/441-7300; open daily 10am–6pm). Probably the most convenient and easiest-to-find branch of the **Yokohama Municipal Tourist Association** (© 045/211-0111; open Sun–Thurs 9am–6pm; Fri, Sat, and holidays except New Year's 9am–8pm) is in a kiosk outside the Sakuragi-cho subway station in the direction of Minato-Mirai 21 and its Landmark Tower. The main office is located in the Sangyo Boeki Center, 2 Yamashita-cho, Naka-ku (© 045/641-4759; open Mon–Fri 10am–6pm), an easy walk from Kannai Station and close to the Silk Center and Yamashita Park. All offices are among the best and most efficient I've come across in Japan, and the English-language map and city brochure are excellent. The staff speaks English, gives directions, and can give you all kinds of brochures on the city.

Next door to the city tourist office, in the Silk Center, is the **Kanagawa Prefectural Tourist Office** (© 045/681-0007; open Mon–Fri 9am–5:30pm), where you can also get information on Hakone and Kamakura, both in Kanagawa Prefecture.

GETTING AROUND   Yokohama Station is connected to Sakuragi-cho and Kannai stations, which are close to most of Yokohama's attractions by commuter train, subway, bus, and boat. Both the **JR Keihin-Tohoku Line** and the

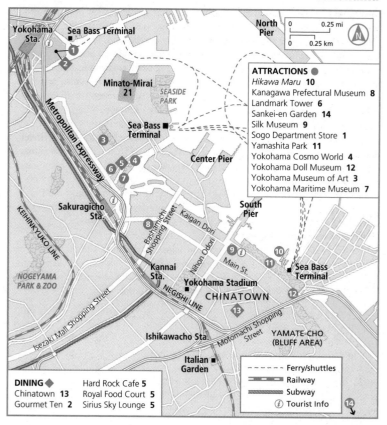

Tokyu-Toyoko Line from Tokyo pass through Yokohama Station and continue on to Sakuragi-cho and Kannai stations. Sakuragi-cho Station is the second stop from Yokohama Station by train or subway, Kannai the third. Bus no. 8, which travels to Sankei-en Garden, also passes Minato-Mirai 21, Chinatown, and Yamashita Park.

The most fun way to get from Yokohama Station to the attractions around Sakuragi-cho and Kannai is via the ***Sea Bass* shuttle boat** (*C* **045/671-7719**). Take the east exit from Yokohama Station and follow the signs; boats depart every 15 to 30 minutes from a pier outside the second floor of Sogo department store. They deposit passengers at Minato-Mirai 21 (near Sakuragi-cho Station) in 10 minutes or at Yamashita Park (near Kannai Station) in 20 minutes, with fares costing ¥350 ($2.90) and ¥600 ($5) respectively (children pay half fare). The trip affords a good view of Yokohama's skyline, especially the ongoing development of Minato-Mirai 21, and is considerably cheaper than the harbor cruises offered.

SEEING THE SIGHTS

A good plan for sightseeing would be to visit Sogo department store with its *ukiyo-e* (woodblock print) museum and maybe some shopping, take the *Sea Bass* shuttle boat to Minato-Mirai 21 to see the sights there, take the subway or walk to Kannai and Yamashita Park, and then board the bus for Sankei-en Garden.

AROUND YOKOHAMA STATION The biggest attraction here is **Sogo,** 2–18–1 Takashima (*©* **045/465-2111;** take the east exit from the station), Japan's second-largest department store (Tokyo's Tobu in Ikebukuro is the largest, while Ikebukuro's Seibu is third). It employs 5,000 sales clerks who serve as many as 150,000 customers a day—a number that can swell to double that on weekends. On the sixth floor is the **Sogo Museum of Art,** which features changing exhibitions as well as a traditional crafts department where you can shop for pottery, traditional blue-dyed clothing, kimono, chopsticks, and souvenirs. On the 10th floor are branches of famous restaurants.

But probably the best thing to do in Sogo is to visit the sixth-floor **Hiraki Ukiyo-e Museum** or Hiraki Ukiyo-e Bijitsukan (*©* **045/465-2233**), a delightful museum devoted exclusively to woodblock prints. Although it boasts an impressive 8,000 prints in its collection, only a few are on display at any one time in the one-room museum, in thematic exhibitions which change monthly; you can tour it in about 20 minutes. Tickets, purchased at vending machines outside the museum entrance, cost ¥500 ($4.15) for adults, ¥400 ($3.35) for students, and ¥300 ($2.50) for children.

Sogo is open daily from 10am to 8pm (closed some Tues). Hiraki Ukiyo-e Museum is open Wednesday to Monday from 10am to 7:30pm. From here, you can take the *Sea Bass* shuttle boat, described above, to Minato-Mirai 21 or Yamashita Park, or you can take the subway or commuter train.

AROUND SAKURAGI-CHO STATION There's no mistaking the **Minato-Mirai 21** when you see it. If you approach from the harbor via the *Sea Bass,* it will look like a vision of the future, a city not of this planet with its awe-inspiring monolithic buildings. Already boasting a huge state-of-the-art convention facility, three first-class hotels, Japan's tallest building, office buildings, two great museums, and an amusement park, the area is still under construction; upon completion, it will encompass 460 acres housing 10,000 residents and employing 190,000. It's all a bit too sterile for my taste, but its two museums make a visit here worthwhile.

If you arrive by train or subway, take the moving walkway that connects Sakuragi-cho Station to the Landmark Tower in Minato-Mirai 21 in 5 minutes.

There are several shopping malls in Minato-Mirai 21, including Queen's Square, Yokohama World Porter's, Landmark Plaza, and Jack Mall, but the area's most conspicuous building is the **Landmark Tower,** Japan's tallest building. The fastest elevator in the world will whisk you up 900 feet in about 40 seconds to the 69th floor, where there's an observation room called **Sky Garden** (*©* **045/222-5030**), open daily from 10am to 9pm (to 10pm Sat). From here you can see the harbor with its container port and Yokohama Bay Bridge, as well as almost the entire city and even, on clear days in winter, Mt. Fuji. However, its admission of ¥1,000 ($8.35) for adults, ¥800 ($6.65) for seniors, ¥500 ($4.15) for elementary and junior-high students, and ¥200 ($1.65) for children make it too expensive in my book. Better is the Landmark Tower's 70th-floor **Sirius Sky Lounge;** although there's a cover charge, its atmosphere is more relaxing. (See below).

It would be hard to miss **Yokohama Cosmo World** (*©* **045/641-6591**), an amusement park spread along both sides of a canal: It boasts one of the largest Ferris wheels in the world. Other diversions include a roller coaster that looks like it dives right into a pond (but vanishes instead into a tunnel), a haunted house, a simulation theater with seats that move with the action, kiddie rides, a games arcade, and much more. Admission is free but rides cost extra, usually

¥300 to ¥600 ($2.50–$5) each. It's open daily 11am to 8pm (11am–10pm July 20–Aug).

The most important thing to see at Minato-Mirai 21 is the **Yokohama Museum of Art** ⊛, 3–4–1 Minato-Mirai (© **045/221-0300**), which emphasizes works by Western and Japanese artists since the 1850s. The museum's ambitious goal is to collect and display works reflecting the mutual influence between the modern art of Europe and that of Japan since the opening of Yokohama's port in 1859. The light and airy building, designed by Kenzo Tange and Urtec Inc., features exhibits from its permanent collection—which includes works by Cézanne, Picasso, Matisse, Leger, Max Ernst, Dalí, and Japanese artists—that change three times a year, as well as special exhibits on loan from other museums. Open Friday through Wednesday from 10am to 6pm (closed the day following a national holiday). Admission for the permanent collection is ¥500 ($4.15) for adults, ¥300 ($2.50) for high-school and college students, and ¥100 (85¢) for children. Special exhibitions cost more. You'll spend at least an hour here.

Maritime buffs should check out the **Yokohama Maritime Museum,** 2–1–1 Minato-Mirai (© **045/221-0280**), which concentrates on Yokohama's history as a port, beginning with the arrival of Perry's "Black Ships." Other displays chart the evolution of ships from Japan and around the world from the 19th century to the present, with lots of models of everything from passenger ships to oil tankers. Kids like the three telescopes connected to cameras placed around Yokohama and the captain's bridge with a steering wheel; sailing fans enjoy touring the 320-foot, 4-masted *Nippon-Maru* moored nearby, built in 1930 as a sail-training ship for students of the merchant marines. Admission is ¥600 ($5) for adults and ¥300 ($2.50) for children. Open Tuesday through Sunday from 10am to 5pm (to 6:30pm in July and Aug, to 4:30pm Nov–Feb). Closed days following national holidays (except Sat and Sun). It takes more than an hour to see everything.

History buffs should wander over to the **Kanagawa Prefectural Museum of Cultural History,** or Kanagawa Kenritsu Rekishi Hakubutsukan, 5–60 Minaminaka-dori (© **045/201-0926**), about a 7-minute walk from either Sakuragi-cho or Kannai Station. It's housed in a Renaissance-style building constructed in 1904 as the nation's first modern foreign-exchange bank, but the interior has been completely renovated. Start by taking the escalator up to the third floor, where you'll begin a chronological odyssey through Kanagawa Prefecture's history from the Paleolithic Period 30,000 years ago to the opening of Yokohama Port and the modernization of Japan. I found the model villages throughout the various periods especially fascinating. Check out the four large-scale drawings of foreigners dating from the 19th century—they have distinct Japanese features despite the blue eyes. (The one on the left is Commodore Perry.) There are also models of both Perry's ships and Japan's first train, which ran between Tokyo and Yokohama. Open Tuesday through Sunday from 9:30am to 5pm; admission is ¥300 ($2.50) for adults, ¥200 ($1.65) for students, and free for seniors and children. Plan on about 45 minutes to an hour here.

IN & AROUND YAMASHITA PARK   Kannai Station is three stops by subway from Yokohama Station. A more picturesque method of transportation is the *Sea Bass* shuttle boat, which connects Yamashita Park with Yokohama Station and Minato-Mirai 21. (See "Getting Around," above.)

Laid out after the huge 1923 earthquake that destroyed much of Tokyo and Yokohama, Yamashita Park is Japan's first seaside park, a pleasant place for a stroll along the waterfront where you have a view of the city's mighty harbor and Bay Bridge. Moored alongside the park is the *Hikawa-Maru* (© 045/ 641-4361), a 1930 ocean liner that transported 25,000 passengers between Yokohama and North America before being called to military service during World War II. One of the few Japanese ships to survive the war, it now serves as a museum, with its engine room, bridge, sleeping quarters (including the captain's room and a state room once occupied by Charlie Chaplin), deck, and more on display. In summer from 5 to 9pm daily, the city's most unique beer garden sprawls on a top deck. *Hikawa-Maru* is open daily 9:30am to 9:30pm in summer and 9:30am to 6:30pm in winter. Admission is ¥800 ($6.65) for adults, ¥400 ($3.35) for children 6 to 15 years old, and ¥300 ($2.50) for children 3 to 5. It takes about 30 minutes to walk through the ship.

Across the gingko-lined street from Yamashita Park are two worthwhile special-interest museums. At the west end (closest to Minato-Mirai 21) is the Silk Center, where you'll find both the prefectural tourist office and the excellent **Silk Museum** ★★, 1 Yamashita-cho, Naka-ku (© 045/641-0841). For many years after Japan opened its doors, silk was its major export, and most of it was shipped to the rest of the world from Yokohama, the nation's largest raw-silk market. In tribute to the role silk has played in Yokohama's history, this museum has displays showing the metamorphosis of the silkworm and the process by which silk is obtained from cocoons, all well documented in English; from April to October you can even observe live cocoons and silk worms at work (compared to the beauty they produce, silk worms are amazingly ugly). The museum also displays various kinds of silk fabrics, as well as gorgeous kimono and reproduction Japanese costumes from the Nara, Heian, and Edo periods. Don't miss this museum, which takes about 30 minutes to see; surprisingly, it's never crowded. Open Tuesday through Sunday from 9am to 4:30pm; admission is ¥500 ($4.15) for adults, ¥300 ($2.50) for seniors, ¥200 ($1.65) for students, and ¥100 (85¢) for children 6 to 11.

At the opposite end of Yamashita Park is the **Yokohama Doll Museum,** 18 Yamashita-cho (© 045/671-9361), which houses approximately 9,000 dolls from 130 countries around the world. Its main floor displays antique dolls, including those produced by such famous doll makers as Lenci and Jumeau, as well as dolls from around the world dressed in native costume. The upstairs floor is devoted to Japanese dolls including folk dolls traditionally sold at shrines and temples, classical Edo-Period dolls, *hina* (elaborate dolls representing the empress and emperor, used for the March Hina Festival), and *kokeshi* (simple wooden dolls). Open Tuesday through Sunday 10am to 5pm (to 7pm mid-July through Aug); admission is ¥300 ($2.50) for adults and ¥150 ($1.25) for children. Plan on spending about 30 to 45 minutes here.

Not far from Yamashita Park is **Chukagai,** Japan's largest Chinatown with hundreds of souvenir shops and restaurants; see "Where to Dine," below.

SANKEI-EN GARDEN ★★★ In my opinion, **Sankei-en Garden** (© 045/ 621-0634) is the best reason to visit Yokohama. Although not old itself, this lovely park contains more than a dozen historical buildings that were brought here from other parts of Japan including Kyoto and Nara, all situated around streams and ponds and surrounded by Japanese-style landscape gardens. In 1906 Tomitaro Hara, a local millionaire who made his fortune exporting silk, laid out the park, which is divided into an Inner Garden and Outer Garden. As you wander along the gently winding pathways, you'll see a villa built in 1649 by the Tokugawa shogunate clan, tea arbors, a 500-year-old three-story pagoda, and a farmhouse built in 1750 without the use of nails. The gardens are well known for their blossoms of plums, cherries, wisteria, azaleas, irises, and water lilies, but no matter what the season, the views here are beautiful.

Plan on at least 2 hours to see both gardens. Sankei-en is open daily from 9am to 5pm (you must enter the Inner Garden by 4pm, the Outer Garden by 4:30pm); admission is ¥300 ($2.50) for the Outer Garden and another ¥300 ($2.50) for the Inner Garden (¥60/50¢ and 120/$1 respectively for children). The easiest way to reach Sankei-en Garden is by bus no. 8, which departs from platform No. 2 at Yokohama Station's east exit (near Sogo department store) and winds its way past Sakuragi-cho Station, Chinatown, and through Kannai before reaching the Honmoku-Sankeien-mae bus stop 30 minutes later (the bus stop is announced in English).

WHERE TO DINE

AROUND YOKOHAMA STATION   The most convenient place for a meal close to the station is **Gourmet Ten** on the 10th floor of Sogo department store (℃ **045/465-2111;** open 11am–10pm, closed some Tues), which you can reach by taking the east exit from Yokohama Station. It features branches of many famous restaurants including Tenichi, serving tempura; Shisen, a Chinese restaurant; Chikuyotei, a famous eel restaurant; and Sabatini, an Italian restaurant from Rome with another branch in Tokyo. Other restaurants serve a range of Japanese specialties from udon to Kobe beef. Since all restaurants have plastic-food displays outside their doors, ordering is easy. Set meals average ¥1,200 to ¥4,500 ($10–37.50). Most restaurants accept credit cards (those that do display them on the door).

LANDMARK TOWER   For casual, inexpensive, and fast dining, head to the Landmark Plaza shopping mall at the base of Landmark Tower. On the fifth floor, you'll find the large, American-style **Royal Food Court** (℃ **045/ 222-5566**) with a half-dozen self-serve counters offering different kinds of foods. You can dine here for less than ¥1,200 ($10). Among the options are pizza, a salad bar, and Chinese. Some seats have a view of the harbor and Yokohama Bay Bridge. Open daily from 11am to 8pm.

For even more sophisticated surroundings or just a romantic evening cocktail, take the elevator up to the 70th floor of Landmark Tower, where you'll find the Yokohama Royal Park Hotel Nikko's **Sirius Sky Lounge** ✿ (℃ **045/221-1111**) with stunning seaside views. It serves a buffet lunch daily from 11:30am to 2:30pm, with choices of Asian and continental dishes that may range from sautéed chili shrimp to pizza, costing ¥4,000 ($33) Monday through Friday and ¥5,000 ($42) weekends and holidays. After lunch, you can also come for a drink during teatime until 5pm. From 5pm to 1am daily, Sirius is a cocktail lounge and levies a cover charge: ¥1,000 ($6.65) per person from 5 to 7pm and again from 11pm to 1am; ¥2,000 ($17) for live music from 7 to 11pm.

Finally, another good place for a drink or a hamburger is the local branch of the **Hard Rock Cafe,** located on the first floor of Queen's Square Yokohama Tower A (℃ **045/682-5626;** open daily 11am–11pm or later).

CHUKAGAI (CHINATOWN)   Located in Yamashita-cho, a couple blocks inland from Yamashita Park, Chinatown has more than 500 restaurants and shops lining one main street and dozens of offshoots. Tokyoites have long been coming to Yokohama just to dine here; many of the restaurants have been owned by the same families for generations. Most serve Cantonese food and have plastic-food displays, English menus, or pictures of their dishes, so your best bet is to simply wander around and let your budget be your guide. Most dishes run ¥800 to ¥3,000 ($6.65–$25), and set lunches go for ¥800 to ¥1,200 ($6.65–$10). Larger restaurants accept credit cards; those that do display them on the front door. Most Chinatown restaurants are open from 11am or 11:30am to 9:30pm or later; some close Tuesday or Wednesday, but there are always restaurants open. Chinatown is about a 15-minute walk from Kannai Station or a 10-minute walk from Ishikawacho Station.

4 Climbing Japan's Most Famous Mountain: Mt. Fuji ⟨★⟨★

62 miles SW of Tokyo

Mt. Fuji, affectionately called "Fuji-san" by the Japanese, has been revered since ancient times. Throughout the centuries Japanese poets have written about it, painters have painted it, pilgrims have flocked to it, and more than a few people have died on it. Without a doubt, this mountain has been photographed more than anything else in Japan.

Mt. Fuji is stunningly impressive. At 12,388 feet the tallest mountain in Japan, it towers far above anything else around it, a cone of almost perfectly symmetrical proportions. Mt. Fuji is majestic, grand, and awe-inspiring. To the Japanese, it symbolizes the very spirit of their country. Though it's visible on clear days (mostly in winter) from as far as 100 miles away, Fuji-san is, unfortunately, almost always cloaked in clouds. If you catch a glimpse of this elusive mountain (which you can sometimes do from the bullet train between Tokyo and Nagoya), consider yourself extremely lucky. One of the best spots for views of Mt. Fuji is **Hakone** (see below).

ESSENTIALS

There are six ascending trails to the summit of Mt. Fuji (and 6 descending trails), each divided into 10 stages of unequal length with most climbs starting at the Go-go-me, or the Fifth Stage. From Tokyo, **Kawaguchiko Trail** is the most popular and most easily accessible, as well as the least steep. Although the "official" climbing season is from mid-July to the end of August, you can climb Mt. Fuji from April through October.

GETTING THERE   The easiest way to reach Kawaguchiko Trail's Fifth Stage is by **bus** from Shinjuku Station, and most trips require a change of buses at Kawaguchiko Station. There are some 18 buses a day in operation between Shinjuku and Kawaguchiko Station from mid-July to the end of August, with less frequent service April through mid-July and September through October. The bus ride from Shinjuku Station, with departures a 2-minute walk from the west side of the station in front of the Yasuda Seimi No. 2 Building, takes about 1 hour and 45 minutes and costs ¥1,700 ($14) one-way to Kawaguchiko Station. Note that you must make a reservation for this bus through **Keio Teito Dentetsu** (© 03/5376-2222) or a travel agency.

From Kawaguchiko Station there are buses onward to the Fifth Stage, with the trip taking approximately 45 minutes and costing another ¥1,700 ($14). During the official climbing season, there are also three buses daily that travel directly from Shinjuku Station to Kawaguchiko Trail's Fifth Stage, costing ¥2,600 ($22) one-way and taking almost 2½ hours. Note that bus service is suspended in winter, when Mt. Fuji is blanketed in snow and is considered too dangerous for novice climbers. Otherwise, buses generally run from April through October to the Fifth Stage unless there is inclement weather (including snow), though far less frequently than during the official season.

If you want to use your Japan Rail Pass, you can leave from Tokyo's Shinjuku Station via the **JR Chuo Line** to Otsuki, where you change to the **Fuji Kyuko Line** for Kawaguchiko Station. The entire trip takes about 2 hours. From Kawaguchiko Station, you can then take the 45-minute bus ride onward to the Fifth Stage.

VISITOR INFORMATION   More information and train and bus schedules can be obtained from the **Tokyo Tourist Information Center,** including a leaflet called "Mt. Fuji and Fuji Five Lakes." See "Visitor Information," in chapter 3.

CLIMBING MT. FUJI

Mt. Fuji is part of a larger national park called **Fuji-Hakone-Izu National Park** ★★. Of the handful of trails leading to the top, most popular for Tokyoites is the **Kawaguchiko Trail,** which is divided into 10 different stages; the Fifth Stage, located about 8,250 feet up and served by bus, is the usual starting point. From here it takes about 6 hours to reach the summit and 3 hours for the descent.

PREPARING FOR YOUR CLIMB   You don't need climbing experience to ascend Mt. Fuji (you'll see everyone from grandmothers to children making the pilgrimage), but you do need stamina and a good pair of walking shoes. It's possible to do it in tennis shoes, but if the rocks are wet, they can get awfully slippery. You should also bring a light plastic raincoat (which you can buy at souvenir shops at the Fifth Stage) since it often rains on the mountain, a sun hat, a bottle of water, a sweater for the evening, and a flashlight if you plan on hiking at night. It gets very chilly on Mt. Fuji at night. Even in August, the average temperature on the summit is 42.5°F.

Because of snow and inclement weather from fall through late spring, the best time to make an ascent is during the "official" climbing season from mid-July to August 31. It's also when buses run most frequently. However, it's also the most crowded time of the year. Consider the fact that there are more than 120 million Japanese, most of whom wouldn't dream of climbing the mountain outside the "official" 1½ months it's open, and you begin to get the picture. About 600,000 people climb Fuji-san every year, mostly in July and August and mostly on weekends—so if you plan on climbing Mt. Fuji on a Saturday or a Sunday in summer, go to the end of the line, please.

Don't be disappointed when your bus deposits you at **Kawaguchiko Fifth Stage,** where you'll be bombarded with souvenir shops, restaurants, and busloads of tourists; most of these tourists aren't climbing to the top. As soon as

---

(*Fun Fact* **The First Climbers**

The first documented case of someone scaling Mt. Fuji is from the early 8th century. During the Edo Period, pilgrimages to the top were considered a purifying ritual, with strict rules governing dress and route. Women, thought to defile sacred places, were prohibited from climbing mountains until 1871.

you get past them and the blaring loudspeakers, you'll find yourself on a steep rocky path, surrounded only by scrub brush and the hikers on the path below and above you. After a couple hours, you'll probably find yourself above the roily clouds, which stretch in all directions. It will be as if you were on an island, barren and rocky, in the middle of an ocean.

STRATEGIES FOR CLIMBING TO THE TOP   The usual procedure for climbing Mt. Fuji is to take a morning bus, start climbing in early afternoon, spend the night near the summit, get up early in the morning to climb the rest of the way to the top, and then watch the sun rise (about 4:30am) from atop Mt. Fuji (you can, of course, also wake up in time to see the sun rise and then continue climbing). At the top is a 1-hour hiking trail that circles the crater. Hikers then begin the descent, reaching the Fifth Stage about noon.

There are about 20 **mountain huts** along the Kawaguchiko Trail above the Fifth Stage, but they're very primitive, providing only a futon and toilet facilities. The cost is ¥5,000 ($42) per person without meals, ¥7,000 ($58) with meals. When I stayed in one of these huts, dinner consisted of dried fish, rice, bean-paste soup, and pickled vegetables; breakfast was exactly the same. Still, unless you want to carry your own food, I'd opt for the meals. Note that huts are open only July and August; book as early as you can to assure a place. I recommend the **Toyokan Hut** at the Seventh Stage (© **0555/22-1040**) or the **Taishikan Hut** at the Eighth Stage (© **0555/22-1947**). Call the **Fujiyoshida Tourist Information Service** at © **0555/22-7000** for more information.

In recent years, there's been a trend in which climbers arrive at the Fifth Stage late in the evening and then climb to the top through the night with the aid of flashlights. After watching the sunrise, they then make their descent. That way, they don't have to spend the night in one of the huts.

Climbing Mt. Fuji is definitely a unique experience, but there's a saying in Japan: "Everyone should climb Mt. Fuji once; only a fool would climb it twice."

5 Hakone: By Mountain Tram, Cable Car, Ropeway & Boat ★★★

60 miles SW of Tokyo

Part of the **Fuji-Hakone-Izu National Park** ★★, **Hakone** is one of the closest and most popular destinations for residents of Tokyo. Beautiful Hakone has about everything a vacationer could wish for—hot-spring resorts, mountains, lakes, breathtaking views of Mt. Fuji, and interesting historical sites. You can tour Hakone as a day trip if you leave early in the morning and limit your sightseeing to a few key attractions, but adding an overnight stay—complete with a soak in a hot-spring tub—is much more pleasant. If you plan to return to Tokyo, I suggest leaving your luggage in storage at your Tokyo hotel or Shinjuku Station and traveling to Hakone with only an overnight bag. If you're traveling onward, say, to Kyoto, leave your bags at a check-in counter at Hakone Yumoto Station.

ESSENTIALS

GETTING THERE & GETTING AROUND   Getting to and around Hakone is half the fun! There's an easy, circular tour you can follow through Hakone that includes various forms of unique transportation: Starting out by train from Tokyo, you then switch to a small two-car tram that zigzags up the mountain, change to a cable car and then to a smaller ropeway, and end your trip with a boat ride across Lake Ashi, stopping off to see major attractions along

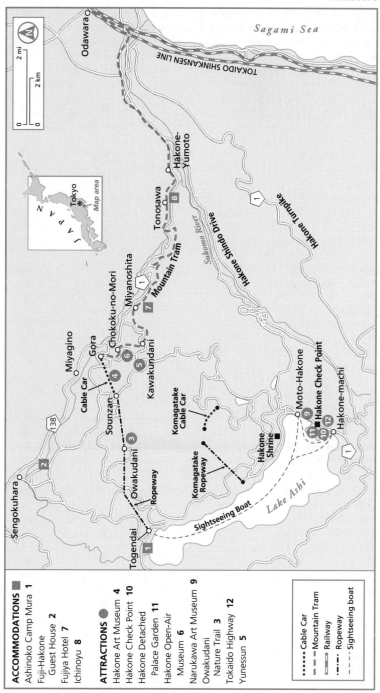

Hakone

Sagami Sea

TOKAIDO SHINKANSEN LINE

Odawara

Map area

JAPAN

Tokyo

Hakone-Yumoto

Hakone Turnpike

Tonosawa **8**

Sukomo River

Hakone Shindo Drive

Miyanoshita

Chokoku-no-Mori

7 Mountain Tram

Miyagino

Gora

Cable Car

6

Kawakundani **5**

Sounzan **4**

138

Owakudani **3**

Komagatake Cable Car

Moto-Hakone **9**

Hakone Check Point

Hakone-machi

2

Sengokuhara

Ropeway

Komagatake Ropeway

Hakone Shrine

11 10 12

Togendai **1**

Sightseeing Boat

Lake Ashi

ACCOMMODATIONS ■
Ashinoko Camp Mura **1**
Fuji-Hakone
   Guest House **2**
Fujiya Hotel **7**
Ichinoyu **8**

ATTRACTIONS ●
Hakone Art Museum **4**
Hakone Check Point **10**
Hakone Detached
   Palace Garden **11**
Hakone Open-Air
   Museum **6**
Narukawa Art Museum **9**
Owakudani
   Nature Trail **3**
Tokaido Highway **12**
Yunessun **5**

······· Cable Car
━ ━ ━ Mountain Tram
▭▭▭ Railway
─·─·─ Ropeway
─ ─ ─ Sightseeing boat

the way. From Lake Ashi (that is, from the villages of Togendai, Hakone-machi, or Moto-Hakone), you can then board a bus bound for Odawara Station (an hour's ride), where you can then board the train back to Tokyo. These same buses also pass all my recommendations listed below, useful if you wish to complete most of your sightseeing the first day before going to your hotel for the evening. There is also a bus that travels directly between Togendai and Shinjuku.

Odakyu (② 03/3481-0103) operates the most convenient network of trains, buses, trams, cable cars, and boats to and around Hakone. The most economical and by far easiest way to see Hakone is with Odakyu's **Hakone Free Pass,** which, despite its name, isn't free but does give you a round-trip ticket on the express train from Shinjuku Station to Odawara or Hakone Yumoto and includes all modes of transportation in Hakone listed above and covered below. The pass avoids the hassle of having to buy individual tickets and also provides nominal discounts on most of Hakone's attractions. Several variations of the pass are available; the most common, valid for 3 days, costs ¥5,500 ($46) for adults (half fare for children). The trip from Shinjuku to Odawara takes 1½ hours, and trains run approximately every 30 minutes. In Odawara, you then transfer to the electric mountain tram. Some express trains go all the way to Hakone Yumoto, where you can then board the mountain tram, with the trip from Shinjuku taking 2 hours.

If you can, travel on a weekday. The **Hakone Weekday Pass,** which is good only Monday through Thursday, is valid for 2 days and costs ¥4,700 ($39) for adults, half-price for children. Not only are weekdays less crowded, but some hotels offer cheaper weekday rates, which means you'll save all around. Note, however, that the Weekday Pass is not available during peak times, including Golden Week and summer school vacation (mid-July–Aug).

If time is of the essence or you want to be assured a seat during peak season, I recommend reserving a seat on the faster and more luxurious **Odakyu Romance Car,** which travels from Shinjuku all the way to Hakone Yumoto in 1½ hours and costs an extra ¥870 ($7.25) one-way.

If you have a **Japan Rail Pass,** you should take the Shinkansen bullet train from Tokyo Station to Odawara (not all bullet trains stop there, so make sure yours does). From there, you can buy a Hakone Free Pass that includes travel on Odakyu private railways, cable cars, buses, and boats for ¥4,130 ($34.40); it's valid for 3 days. The Weekday Pass costs ¥3,410 ($26).

All passes described above can be purchased at any station of the Odakyu Railway, including Shinjuku Station and Odawara.

VISITOR INFORMATION   Before leaving Tokyo, pick up the "Hakone and Kamakura" leaflet available from the Tourist Information Center; it lists the schedules for the extensive transportation network throughout the Hakone area. There's also a color brochure called "Hakone National Park," which includes sightseeing information and contains a map of the Hakone area. See "Visitor Information," in chapter 3 for TIC locations.

In Shinjuku Station, be sure to stop by the **Odakyu Sightseeing Service Center** (located on the ground floor near the west exit of Odakyu Shinjuku Station ② 03/5321-7887; www.odakyu-group.co.jp/english; open daily 8am–6pm), where you can obtain sightseeing information, purchase Hakone Free Pass tickets, exchange money, and if you wish, buy one- or two-day do-it-yourself package tours that include round-trip transportation to Hakone, meals, sightseeing, and hotel stays.

In Hakone Yumoto, there's the **Yumoto Tourist Office** (② 0460/5-8911; open daily 9am–5pm), which is staffed by English-speaking volunteers only on weekdays. You can pick up more pamphlets on Hakone here and can ask directions. It's a 2-minute walk from the Hakone Yumoto Station. Take a right out of the station onto the town's main street; the office is on the left.

EXPLORING HAKONE

STRATEGIES FOR SEEING HAKONE If you plan on spending only a day in Hakone, you should leave Tokyo very early in the morning and plan on visiting only a few key attractions—I recommend the **Hakone Open-Air Museum,** the **Owakudani nature trail,** and if time permits, the **Hakone Check Point** and/or **Narukawa Art Museum.**

Fun Fact Goblins & Good-Luck Talismans

Japan has its share of goblins and spirits. The **kappa** is a water creature about the size of a 12-year-old child, with scales and webbed feet and hands. Its most distinguishing characteristic, however, is a saucer-like indentation on top of its head that contains water; if the water pours out, the kappa loses its supernatural powers. The kappa preys on animals and people; its most disgusting habit is tearing out victims' livers through their anuses. On the other hand, kappa are fond of sumo.

A **tengu** is a goblin that looks like a human being but has wings and a long nose. Considered the guardian of mountains, he has been known to kidnap Buddhist priests, tie them to the tops of trees, and feed them dung disguised as delicious food. The **oni**, a demon with horns, fangs, and only a loincloth for clothing, is fond of humans—for dinner—but can also be seen at festival processions, sweeping away evil influences.

The Japanese also have **talismans** to keep away evil influences or to bring general good luck on a daily basis. As you travel in Japan, no doubt you'll see them in restaurants and shops. Most common is probably the **maneki-neko,** or beckoning cat, with one paw raised as though beckoning to people. It's usually displayed prominently at the entrance to a restaurant, bar, or other establishment and is thought to bring good business and fortune. Another common talisman is the **daruma,** an oblong-shaped doll without arms and legs. It's thought to derive from a Zen Buddhist who lost the use of his limbs after meditating for 9 years in a cave. During the Edo Period, daruma were though to protect against smallpox. Today, Japanese praying for the fulfillment of a wish will often buy a daruma and paint in one of the eyes. If the wish comes true, they'll paint in the other eye. No politician would ever run for office in Japan without buying a daruma and painting in the first eye; not doing so would be flirting with failure.

As for animals, you'll want to beware of **foxes.** They're considered not only clever but also bewitching—many folk tales relate how foxes turn into beguiling and seductive women. **Raccoons,** on the other hand, though also crafty, are considered amusing rather than fearsome.

If you're spending the night—and I strongly urge that you do—you can arrange your itinerary in a more leisurely fashion and devote more time to Hakone's attractions. You may wish to travel only as far as your hotel the first day, stopping at sights along the way and in the vicinity. The next day you could continue with the rest of the circuit through Hakone. Or, you can opt to complete most of your sightseeing the first day, and then backtrack to your accommodation or reach it by bus from Togendai, Hakone-machi, or Moto-Hakone.

SCENIC RAILWAY TO GORA Regardless of whether you travel via Shinkansen, the Odakyu Romance Car, or the ordinary Odakyu express, you'll end up at either Odawara Station, considered the gateway to Hakone, or a bit farther at Hakone Yumoto Station, located in Hakone itself. At either station, you can transfer to the **Hakone Tozan Railway,** a delightful, mountain-climbing, two-car electric tram that winds its way through forests and over streams and ravines as it travels upward to Gora, making several switchbacks along the way. The entire trip from Hakone Yumoto Station to Gora takes only 45 minutes, but it's a beautiful ride on a narrow track through the mountains. This is my favorite part of the whole journey. The trains, which run every 10 to 15 minutes, make about a half-dozen stops before reaching Gora, including **Tonosawa** and **Miyanoshita,** two hot-spring spa resorts with a number of old ryokan and hotels. Some of these ryokan date back several centuries, to the days when they were on the main thoroughfare to Edo, called the old Tokaido Highway. Miyanoshita is also the best place for lunch. See "Where to Dine" and "Where to Stay," below.

As for things to do along the way, you can begin your trip with some relaxing, hot-spring bathing at the thoroughly modern, sophisticated public bath called **Yunessun** ★★ (© **0460/2-4141**). About a 15-minute taxi or bus ride from Kowakudani stop on the Hakone Tozan Railway, this self-described "Mediterranean Style Spa Resort" offers a variety of both indoor and outdoor family baths, which means you wear your bathing suit. In addition to indoor Turkish, Roman, and salt baths, there's also a small children's play area with slides and a large outdoor area with a variety of small baths, including those mixed with coffee, sake, rose petals, or healthy minerals. For those who desire more traditional bathing, there's the Mori No Yu, with both indoor and outdoor baths separated for men and women (you don't wear your suit here). Most people who come stay 2–3 hours. Admission is ¥3,500 ($29) to Yunessun, ¥1,800 ($15) to Mori No Yu, and ¥4,000 ($33) to both; children pay half fare. Upon admission, you'll be given a towel, robe, and wristband to pay for drinks and extras (rental suits are available), so you can leave all valuables in your assigned locker. It's open daily 9am to 8pm (to 10pm in peak season).

The most important stop on the Hakone Tozan Railway is the next-to-the-last stop, Chokoku-no-Mori, where you'll find the famous **Hakone Open-Air Museum (Chokoku-no-Mori Bijutsukan)** ★★★, (© **0460/2-1161**) a minute's walk from the station. With the possible exception of views of Mt. Fuji, this museum is, in my opinion, Hakone's number one attraction. Using nature itself as a dramatic backdrop, it showcases sculpture primarily of the 20th century in a spectacular setting of glens, formal gardens, ponds, and meadows. There are 700 sculptures on display, both outdoors and in several buildings, with works by Carl Milles, Manzu Giacomo, Jean Dubuffet, Willem de Kooning, Barbara Hepworth, Joan Miró, and more than 20 pieces by Henry Moore. The Picasso Pavilion contains more than 200 works by Picasso from pastels to ceramics (it's one of the world's largest collections), while the Picture Gallery displays paintings by Miró, Renoir, Kandinsky, Vlaminck, Utrillo, and Takeshi Hayashi. There are several installations geared toward children where they can climb and play. I could spend all day here; barring that, count on staying at least 2 hours. When you're done, an informal cafe provides a peaceful view. Open daily from 9am to 5pm (until 4:30pm Dec–Feb); admission is ¥1,600 ($13) for adults, ¥1,100 ($9.15) for university and high school students and seniors, and ¥800 ($6.65) for children. Your Hakone Free Pass gives you a ¥100 (85¢) discount.

BY CABLE CAR TO SOUNZAN   Cable cars leave Gora every 20 minutes or so and arrive 9 minutes later at the end station of Sounzan, making several stops along the way as they travel steeply uphill. One of the stops is Koen-Kami, from which it's only a minute's walk to the **Hakone Art Museum** (© 0460/2-2623). This five-room museum displays Japanese pottery and ceramics from the Jomon Period (around 4000–2000 B.C.) to the Edo Period, including terracotta *haniwa* burial figures, huge 16th-century Bizen jars, and Imari ware. What makes this place particularly rewarding is the bamboo grove and small but lovely moss garden with a teahouse where you can sample some Japanese tea for ¥630 ($5.25). It is most beautiful in autumn. Open Friday through Wednesday from 9am to 4:30pm (to 4pm in winter); admission is ¥900 ($7.50) for adults, ¥400 ($4.15) for university and high school students and seniors, and free for children. The Hakone Free Pass gives a ¥100 (85¢) discount. Plan on spending about a half hour here, more if you opt for tea.

BY ROPEWAY TO TOGENDAI   From Sounzan, you board a ropeway with gondolas for a long, 30-minute haul over a mountain to Togendai on the other side, which lies beside Lake Ashi, known as Lake Ashinoko in Japanese. Note that the ropeway stops running at 5 or 5:30pm in summer and 4pm in winter.

Before reaching Togendai, however, get off at the first stop, Owakudani, the ropeway's highest point, to hike the 30-minute **Owakudani Nature Trail** ✿. Owakudani means "Great Boiling Valley," and you'll soon understand how it got its name when you see (and smell) the sulfurous steam escaping from fissures in the rock, testimony to the volcanic activity still present here. Most Japanese commemorate their trip here by buying boiled eggs cooked in the boiling waters, available at the small hut midway along the trail.

ACROSS LAKE ASHI BY BOAT   From Togendai you can take a pleasure boat across Lake Ashi, also referred to as "Lake Hakone" in some English brochures. Believe it or not, one of the boats plying the waters is a replica of a man-of-war pirate ship. It takes about half an hour to cross the lake to Hakone-machi (also called simply Hakone; *machi* means city) and Moto-Hakone, two resort towns right next to each other on the southern edge of the lake. This end of the lake affords the best view of Mt. Fuji, one often depicted in tourist publications. Boats are in operation all year (though they run less frequently in winter and not at all in stormy weather); the last boat departs around 5pm from the end of March to the end of November. There are also buses that connect Togendai with Moto-Hakone, Odawara, and Shinjuku.

If you're heading back to Tokyo, buses depart for Odawara near the boat piers in both Hakone-machi and Moto-Hakone. Otherwise, for more sightseeing, get off the boat in Hakone-machi, turn left, and walk about 5 minutes on the town's main road, following the signs and turning left to the **Hakone Check Point** ✿ (Hakone Seki-sho) (© **0460/3-6635**), on a road lined with some souvenir shops. This is a reconstructed guardhouse originally built in 1619 to serve as a checkpoint along the famous Tokaido Highway, which connected Edo (present-day Tokyo) with Kyoto. In feudal days, local lords, called *daimyo,* were required to spend alternate years in Edo; their wives were kept on in Edo as virtual hostages to discourage the lords from planning rebellions while in their home-lands. This was one of several points along the highway to guard against the transport of guns, spies and female travelers trying to flee Edo. Passes were nec-essary for travel, and although it was possible to sneak around it, male violators who were caught were promptly executed, while women suffered the indignity of having their heads shaved and then being given away to anyone who wanted them. Inside the reconstructed guardhouse you'll see life-size models re-enacting scenes inside a checkpoint. Your ticket also allows admission to a small museum with displays relating to the Edo Period, including items used for travel, samu-rai armor, and gruesome articles of torture. Open daily from 9am to 5pm (until 4:30pm in winter); admission is ¥300 ($2.50) for adults and ¥150 ($1.25) for children. It shouldn't take more than 30 minutes to see everything.

Just beyond the Hakone Check Point, at the big parking lot with the tradi-tional gate, is the **Hakone Detached Palace Garden** (Onshi-Hakone-Koen), which lies on a small promontory on Lake Ashi and has spectacular views of the lake and, sometimes, Mt. Fuji. Originally part of an imperial summer villa built in 1886, the garden is open free to the public 24 hours daily. It's a great place for wandering. On its grounds is the **Lakeside Observation Building** (open daily 9am–4:30pm) with displays relating to the Hakone Palace, which was destroyed by earthquakes.

If you take the northernmost exit from the garden, crossing a bridge, you'll see the neighboring resort town, **Moto-Hakone.** Across the highway and lined with ancient and mighty cedars is part of the old **Tokaido Highway** itself. During the Edo Period, more than 400 cedars were planted along this impor-tant road, which today stretches 1½ miles along the curve of Lake Ashi and makes for a pleasant stroll (unfortunately, though, a modern road has been built right beside the original one). Moto-Hakone is a 5-minute walk from the Detached Palace Garden.

In Moto-Hakone, the **Narukawa Art Museum** ★★ (© **0460/3-6828**), is very worthwhile and located just after entering town, up the hill to the right when you reach the orange torii gate. It specializes in modern works of the *Nihonga* style of painting, developed during the Heian period (794–1185) and is sparser than Western paintings (which tend to fill in backgrounds and every inch of canvas). Large paintings and screens by contemporary Nihonga artists are on display, including works by Yamamoto Kyujin, Maki Susumu, Kayama Matazo, Hirayama Ikuo, and Hori Fumiko. Changing exhibitions feature younger up-and-coming artists, as well as glassware. I wouldn't miss it; views of Lake Ashi and Mt. Fuji are a bonus. Open daily 9am to 5pm; admission is ¥1,200 ($10) for adults and ¥600 ($5) for children.

WHEN YOU'RE DONE SIGHTSEEING FOR THE DAY Buses depart for Hakone Yumoto and Odawara from both Hakone-machi and Moto-Hakone two to four times an hour. Be sure to check the time of the last departure; generally, it's around 8pm, but this can change with the season and the day of the week. (The bus also passes 2 of the accommodations recommended below, the Fujiya Hotel and Ichinoyu, as well as Yunessun hot-spring baths; another bus will take you to Fuji-Hakone Guest House.) Otherwise, the trip from Moto-Hakone takes approximately 30 minutes to Hakone Yumoto, where you can catch the Romance Car bound for Shinjuku, or 50 minutes to Odawara, where you can then catch the Odakyu express train or Romance Car back to Shinjuku or the Shinkansen back to Tokyo Station.

WHERE TO STAY

Ashinoko Camp Mura *Kids* Since you're in a national park, you might be inclined to enjoy nature by roughing it in a cabin beside Lake Ashi, just a 10-minute walk from the ropeway to Sounzan and boat to Hakone-machi. Operated by Kanagawa Prefecture and also with tent camping, it offers row and detached (more expensive and closer to the lake) cabins that sleep up to six persons, each with two bedrooms, bathroom, a living room with cooking facilities and tableware, and a deck with picnic table. However, there is no supermarket in nearby Togendai, so you'll either want to bring your own food or dine on Japanese breakfast and dinner in the camp restaurant (reservations required). There's a hiking trail around the lake. A great place for kids.

164 Hakone-machi, Moto-Hakone, Ashigarashimo-gun, Kanagawa 250-0522. *C* **0460/4-8279.** Fax 0460/4-6489. 36 units. Peak season, ¥26,250 ($218) row cabin; ¥31,500 ($262) detached cabin. Off season, ¥15,750 ($131) row cabin; ¥21,000 ($175) detached cabin. No credit cards. Bus: Togendai, from Odawara (1 hr) or Shinjuku (2 hrs), then a 10-min. walk. **Amenities:** 1 restaurant; rental bikes; barbecue grills. *In room:* Kitchenette, fridge.

Fuji-Hakone Guest House It's a bit isolated, but this Japanese Inn Group member offers inexpensive, spotlessly clean lodging in tatami rooms, all non-smoking. A newer house, situated in tranquil surroundings set back from a tree-shaded road, is run by a man who speaks very good English and is happy to provide sightseeing information, including a map of the area with local restaurants. Some of the rooms face the Hakone mountain range. Pluses are the communal lounge area with TV and even a piano and guitar and the outdoor hot-spring bath (for which there's an extra ¥500/$4.15 charge).

912 Sengokuhara, Hakone, Kanagawa 250-0631. *C* **0460/4-6577.** Fax 0460/4-6578. www.fujihakone.com. 14 units (none with bathroom). ¥5,000–¥6,000 ($42–$50) single; ¥10,000–¥12,000 ($83–$100) double; ¥14,000–¥16,000 ($117–$133) triple. Plus ¥150 ($1.25) local tax per person. Peak season and weekends ¥1,000–¥2,000 ($8.35–$17) extra. Minimum 2-night stay preferred. Western breakfast ¥800 ($6.65) extra. AE, MC, V. Bus: Hakone Tozan (included in the Hakone Free Pass) from Togendai (15 min.) or from Odawara Station (50 min.) to the Senkyoro-mae stop (announced in English), then a 1-min. walk. **Amenities:** Hot-spring bath; coin-op laundry and dryer; communal refrigerator and microwave. *In room:* A/C, TV.

The Fujiya Hotel ★★★ *Finds* The Fujiya, which was established in 1878, is quite simply the grandest, most majestic old hotel in Hakone; indeed, it might be the loveliest historic hotel in Japan. I love this hotel for its comfortably old-fashioned atmosphere, including such Asian touches as a Japanese-style roof, lots of windows, and long wooden corridors with photographs of famous guests. Staying here transports me to a gentler, and more genteel, past. There are five separate buildings, all different and added on at various times in the hotel's long history, but management has been meticulous in retaining its historic traditions. A landscaped garden out back, with a waterfall, a pond, a greenhouse, and stunning views over the valley, is great for strolls and meditation. An outdoor pool, fed by river water, occupies a corner of the garden, and there's also an indoor thermal pool and hot-spring public baths. Even the private bathroom in each room has piped in hot-spring water.

Except for rooms in the Forest Lodge (built in 1960 and rather ordinary), rooms are old-fashioned and spacious with high ceilings and antique furnishings; some even have claw-foot tubs. The most expensive rooms are the largest, but my favorite are those in the Flower Palace, which has an architectural style that reminds me of a Japanese temple and seems unchanged since its 1936 construction. Even if you don't stay here, do come for a meal or tea. Highly recommended.

Note that the special rate for foreigners below, is higher on weekends and is not available during Golden Week, the month of August, or New Year's (but if there's room, you can even stay in the Flower Palace).

359 Miyanoshita, Hakone-machi, Ashigarashimo-gun 250-0404. ℂ **0460/2-2211.** Fax 0460/2-2210. www.fujiyahotel.co.jp. 146 units. Special foreigners' rate, $120 single or double; $50 extra Sat or night before holiday. Regular rates, ¥18,000–¥25,000 ($150–$208) single or double; ¥5,000 ($42) extra on Sat or night before holiday; ¥10,000 ($83) extra mid-Aug and New Year's. AE, DC, JCB, MC, V. Station: Miyanoshita, Hakone Tozan Railway (5 min.). Bus: From Odawara or Moto-Hakone to Miyanoshita Onsen stop (1 min.). **Amenities:** 3 restaurants (see "Where to Dine," below), 1 bar; indoor and outdoor pools (free for hotel guests); hot-spring baths; Jacuzzi; sauna; landscaped garden; souvenir shops; game room; golf course; room service (9am–10pm); in-room massage; same-day laundry service. *In room:* A/C, TV, minibar, hair dryer.

㊹ **Ichinoyu** ★★ Located near Tonosawa Station (on the Hakone Tozan Line) next to a roaring river, this delightful, rambling, wooden building stands on a tree-shaded winding road that follows the track of the old Tokaido Highway. First opened more than 370 years ago, Ichinoyu is now in its 15th generation of owners. It claims to be the oldest ryokan in the area and was once honored by the visit of a shogun during the Edo Period. Old artwork, wall hangings, and paintings decorate the place.

The ryokan has only tatami rooms. The oldest date from the Meiji Period, more than 100 years ago. My favorite is the Take, old-fashioned and consisting mainly of seasoned and weathered wood; it faces the river and even has its own private outdoor bath, also with views of the river. Ditto for the Kotobuki room (rooms with private *rotenburo*, an outdoor hot-spring bath, cost ¥5,000/$42 extra). Both the communal tubs and the tubs in the rooms have hot water supplied from a natural spring. The price you pay depends on your room, the meals you select, and the time of year.

90 Tonosawa, Hakone-machi, Ashigarashimo-gun 250-0315. ℂ **0460/5-5331.** Fax 0460/5-5335. www. ichinoyu.co.jp. 24 units (12 with bathroom). ¥8,800–¥14,800 ($73–$123) per person including 2 meals. ¥3,000 ($25 extra per person in Aug and on Sat and holidays). AE, DC, JCB, MC, V. Station: Tonosawa, Hakone Tozan Railway (6 min.). Bus: From Odawara or Moto-Hakone to Tonosawa bus stop (2 min.). **Amenities:** Indoor and outdoor hot-spring baths. *In room:* A/C, TV, fridge, safe.

WHERE TO DINE

For casual dining while sightseeing, the Hakone Open-Air Museum has a pleasant cafe overlooking the park's fantastic scenery. Also sporting a view is the even less formal restaurant at the Owakudani Ropeway Station, serving spaghetti, curry rice, noodles, and other inexpensive fare.

Main Dining Room ★★ CONTINENTAL Hakone's grandest, oldest hotel, conveniently located near a stop on the two-car Hakone Tozan Railway, is a memorable place for a good Western meal. The main dining hall, dating from 1930, is very bright and cheerful with a high, intricately detailed ceiling, large windows with Japanese screens, a wooden floor, and white tablecloths. The views of the Hakone hills are impressive, and the service by the bow-tied wait staff is attentive. For lunch you can have such dishes as spaghetti, sandwiches, fried chicken, rainbow trout, and sirloin steak. The excellent dinners feature elaborate set courses or a la carte dishes ranging from scallops and sole to grilled lamb, chicken, rainbow trout, and steaks. Afterward, be sure to tour the landscaped garden.

In the Fujiya Hotel, 359 Miyanoshita. ℂ **0460/2-2211.** Reservations required for dinner. Main dishes ¥2,200–¥6,800 ($18–$57); set dinners ¥10,000–¥15,000 ($83–$125); lunch main dishes ¥1,500–¥5,800

($12.50–$48). AE, DC, JCB, MC, V. Daily noon–2pm and 6–8:30pm. Station: Miyanoshita on the Hakone Tozan Railway (5 min.).

Restaurant Peacock Boat House WESTERN   This casual restaurant, which is decorated (as its name implies) as a boathouse, sits on the shore of Lake Ashi. It offers inexpensive set meals, as well as a few a la carte items from its English menu such as rainbow trout, prawn gratin, and sirloin steak. Manager Nakamura, who has been at the helm for 30 years, will also whip up vegetarian dishes on request. The food is secondary, however, to the view; in summer, you can relax on the deck and watch the boats come and go and maybe even catch a sunset or a glimpse of Mt. Fuji.

3 Lake View Dr., Moto-Hakone. ⓒ **0460/3-6668.** Main dishes ¥1,500–¥1,800 ($12.50–$15; set meals ¥1,700–¥2,300 ($14–$19). AE, DC, V. Fri–Wed 11am–7pm (last order). Go right if exiting from the boat dock; if you're walking from Hakone-machi, it's to the left just after you've emerged from the old Tokaido Highway, next to the Hakone Ashinoko Museum of Fine Art.

6 Izu Peninsula, Tokyo's Playground

Atami: 96km (60 miles) SW of Tokyo; Ito: 120km (75 miles) SW of Tokyo

Whenever Tokyoites want to spend a few days at a hot-spring spa on the seashore, they head for the Izu Peninsula. Jutting out into the Pacific Ocean southwest of Tokyo, Izu boasts some fine beaches, verdant and lush countryside, and a dramatic coastline marked in spots by high cliffs and tumbling surf. Even though the scenery is at times breathtaking, there's little of historical interest to lure a short-term visitor to Japan; make sure you've seen both Kamakura and Nikko before you consider coming here. Keep in mind also that Izu's resorts are terribly crowded during the summer vacation period from mid-July to the end of August.

The best way to enjoy Izu Peninsula, which is in Shizuoka Prefecture, is to drive, making this one of the few times when it may be worthwhile to rent your own car. There's a road that hugs the coast all the way around the peninsula; you can drive it easily in a day. Rather than rent a car in Tokyo, however, I suggest you wait until you reach Atami or Ito, both of which have many car-rental agencies near their train stations. Ito, especially, warrants a car because attractions are rather far-flung and poorly served by public transportation.

If you're traveling during the peak summer season (July–Aug), you should make accommodation reservations at least several months in advance. Otherwise, there are hotel, ryokan, and minshuku reservation offices in all of Izu's resort towns that will arrange accommodations for you. Be aware, however, that if a place has a room still open at the last minute in August, there's probably a reason for it—poor location, poor service, or unimaginative decor.

Before leaving Tokyo, be sure to pick up the leaflet "The Izu Peninsula" at the Tourist Information Center.

ATAMI

Atami means "hot sea." According to legend, a long time ago a hot geyser spewing forth in the sea killed a lot of fish and marine life. The concerned fishermen asked a Buddhist monk to intervene on their behalf and to pray for a solution to the problem. The prayers paid off when the geyser moved itself to the beach; not only was the marine life spared, but Atami was blessed with hot-spring water the townspeople could henceforth bathe in.

Today, Atami—with a population of 44,000—is a conglomeration of hotels, ryokan, restaurants, pachinko parlors, souvenir shops, and a sizable red-light district, spread along narrow, winding streets that hug steep mountain slopes around Atami Bay. The city itself isn't very interesting, but it's the most easily accessible hot-spring resort from Tokyo, and it has a wide beach and a wonderful art museum that many Tokyoites make a day trip to see.

ESSENTIALS

GETTING THERE   From Tokyo Station, it's 55 minutes by **Shinkansen bullet train;** since not all bullet trains stop in Atami, be sure to check beforehand. If you don't have a Japan Rail Pass, the fare is ¥3,570 ($30) for an unreserved seat. You can also take the slower, 2-hour **JR Tokaido Local Line** for ¥1,890 ($16).

VISITOR INFORMATION   The **Atami Tourist Information Office** is to the left as you exit the train station (℃ **0557/81-6002;** open daily 10am–1:30pm and 2:50–5:30pm). No English is spoken, but English literature and a map are available.

GETTING AROUND   Buses serve major sightseeing attractions in Atami. If you're spending the day here, you might wish to purchase a one-day ticket for the **Atami Round Bus** (nicknamed the YuYu Bus), which makes a circuitous 1-hour-and-20-minute trip through town, departing Atami Station approximately every 30 minutes and passing most sights along the way, including the MOA Art Museum, Sun Beach, Sun Kurino Museum of Art, and Atami Castle. You can leave and reboard as often as you wish, or you can stay on for a tour of the city. The cost is ¥800 ($6.65) for adults and ¥400 ($3.35) for children. There's also a **Toyota Rental Car** office in front of Atami Station (℃ **0557/81-0100**), open daily 8am to 8pm.

SEEING THE SIGHTS

Atami's must-see is the **MOA Art Museum** ✿, 26–2 Momoyama-cho (℃ **0557/ 84-2511**), housed in a modern building atop a hill with sweeping views of Atami and the bay. It's a 15-minute bus ride away from Atami Station. Take the bus from platform 4 to the last stop; one-way fare is ¥160 ($1.35). The museum's entrance is dramatic—a long escalator ride through a tunnel followed by a 7-minute long laser show (given every hr.). The museum itself, however, concentrates on traditional Oriental art, including woodblock prints by Hokusai, Hiroshige, and their contemporaries; Chinese ceramics; Japanese bronze religious art; and lacquerware. Although some 200 items from the 3,500-piece private collection are changed monthly, look for two National Treasures almost always on display: a tea-storage jar with a wisteria design by Edo artist Ninsei and a gold-leaf screen of red and white plum blossoms by Ogata Korin. It takes about an hour to tour the museum, open Friday through Wednesday from 9:30am to 5pm (you must enter by 4:30pm); admission is ¥1,600 ($13) for adults, ¥1,200 ($10) for senior citizens, ¥800 ($6.65) for university and high-school students, and free for children. You can buy your tickets for ¥200 ($1.65) less at The Atami Tourist Information Office at the train station (see above).

   Another museum worth checking out if you have an hour to spare is the **Sunkurino Museum of Art** (℃ **0557/81-3367**), located a 15-minute walk from Atami Station near the Ginza Dori shopping street and Sun Beach. It displays glassware by Emile Galle, a leading French artist of art nouveau. Open daily 9:30am to 5:30pm; admission is ¥1,300 ($11) for adults, ¥700 ($5.85) for university and high-school students, and ¥300 ($2.50) for children.

WHERE TO STAY

㊸ **Taikanso** ★★   Located on a pine-shaded mountain slope above the city, this beautiful ryokan was built in 1938 as the private villa of a steelworks owner and was named after his friend Yokoyama Taikan, a famous Japanese painter. Ten years later it was converted to a Japanese inn; since then, it's been expanded into several buildings connected by covered pathways and meandering streams, adhering to a Kyoto style of architecture popular in the 16th century. Various styles of rooms are available, with the most expensive offering the best views, the most space, and the best meals. The ultimate in luxury is the oldest, a three-room suite with a sitting alcove and cypress tub. Queen Beatrix of the Netherlands stayed here with her husband and three sons. Although all the rooms boast hot-spring water for the tubs, there are three public baths with open-air bathing, including one made of cypress and another with a view of a waterfall and pond.

7–1 Hayashigaoka-cho, Atami City, Shizuoka 413-0031. ✆ 0557/81-8137. Fax 0557/83-5308. 44 units. ¥28,000–¥70,000 ($233–$583) per person. Rates include 2 meals and a service charge. AE, DC, JCB, V. Take a taxi from Atami Station, a 4-min. ride. **Amenities:** 1 sushi bar, 1 coffee shop, 1 night club with live band; outdoor swimming pool (free for hotel guests); in-room massage. *In room:* A/C, hot-water pot with tea.

WHERE TO DINE

㊻ **Home Run Sushi** SUSHI   For excellent sushi, head to this simple, one-room restaurant with both counter and table seating. There's no English menu, but pictures show various kinds of sushi a la carte. Or you can order the sushi set meal, which comes with various kinds of sushi, soup, and side dishes. I have no idea why this place is called Home Run—one of Japan's many mysteries.

5–4 Nagisacho. ✆ 0557/82-7300. Sashimi or sushi set meals ¥1,000–¥2,000 ($8.35–$17); sushi a la carte ¥200–¥600 ($1.65–$5). No credit cards. Open daily 11:30am–11pm. A 13-min. walk from Atami Station on Kaigandori (Rte. 135), catty-corner from Atami Fujiya Hotel. Look for the sign SUSHI BAR.

ITO

Just 11 miles south of Atami, Ito is also a hot-spring spa, hemmed in on one side by steeply wooded mountains and on the other by the sea. Its 75,000 inhabitants are unusually spread along the coast in a string of hamlets, separated by beautiful scenery but connected by winding roads, private railway, and buses. What makes this town truly unique, however, is that it supports an astonishing number of private museums, most of them Western and some quite odd. I don't think I could come up with a more bizarre collection of museums even if I tried.

ESSENTIALS

GETTING THERE   From Tokyo Station it's approximately 1 hour and 45 minutes to Ito Station aboard the **JR Odoriko** (¥4,090/$34) or 1 hour and 20 minutes aboard the **Super View Odoriko JR** (¥4,390/$37). Otherwise, there's a slower local line that takes approximately 2½ hours and costs ¥2,210 ($18) one-way. From Atami, the trip costs ¥320 ($2.65) and takes almost a half hour aboard the **JR Ito Local Line.**

VISITOR INFORMATION   The **Ito Tourist Information Office** is located across the street from the train station's exit (✆ **0557/37-6105;** open daily 9am–5pm).

⌐ *Fun Fact* **Ito's Restrooms**

Ito is very proud of its public restrooms dotting the city, each in a different architectural style. Check them out!

GETTING AROUND   The Ito Local Line travels south from Ito Station to **Jogasaki,** the site of Izu's famous Jogasaki Coast. However, since most museums are located inland from Jogasaki, it's best to rent a car. There are many agencies around Ito Station, including **Toyota Rental Car** (✆ **0557/37-0100**). Otherwise, a **bus** departing Ito Station for Shaboten Koen makes stops at both the Ikeda Museum of 20th Century Art and the Izu Glass & Craft Museum. You can also buy the **Free Pass** for ¥1,300 ($11), which allows unlimited one-day travel by bus, including the so-called Artistogo museum route, which departs Ito Station at 10:05am and returns at 5:26pm. In between, it makes seven circular routes past most of Ito's museums, stopping at museums almost hourly. Ask the tourist office for a map.

SEEING THE SIGHTS

Of Ito's 2 dozen museums, the most well-known and one of the oldest is the **Ikeda Museum of 20th Century Art** ⊛⊛, 614 Totari (✆ **0557/45-2211;** bus stop: Ikeda Nijuseki Bijutsukan). Though small, it boasts an impressive collection by both Western and Japanese artists, including Warhol, Salvador Dalí, Picasso, Renoir, Roy Lichtenstein, Edvard Munch, Emil Nolde, Willem de Kooning, Miró, Kokoshka, Matisse, and Chagall as well as Kimura Issho, Tatsuoki Nambata, and Junzo Watanabe. Plan on spending about 40 minutes here. Open daily 10am to 5pm; admission is ¥900 ($7.50) for adults, ¥700 ($5.85) for university and high-school students, and ¥500 ($4.15) for elementary and junior-high students.

Another personal favorite is the **Izu Glass & Craft Museum** ⊛, 11–300 Omurokogen (✆ **0557/51-7222;** bus stop: Risokyo), with its exquisite collection of Art Nouveau and Art Deco glass art, including figurines, perfume bottles, jewelry, vases, and lamps by such artists as Galle, Lalique, Erté, and Daum. Although at first thought it seems strange to find such a collection here, the use of dragonflies, water lilies, orchids, and other motifs show decided Japanese influence. You'll want to spend at least an hour here. Open 9am to 5pm daily; admission is ¥850 ($7.75) for adults and ¥450 ($3.75) for children.

Other art and decorative-art museums include the **Izu Lake Ippeki Museum** with works by Jean-Pierre Cassigneaul (✆ 0557/45-5500), the **Izukogen Museum of Pottery and Glass** (✆ 0557/54-9600) with Chinese works, the **Izu Lake Ippeki Museum of Perfume** (✆ 0557/45-7700) with early 20th-century American and European perfume bottles, the **Brian Wild Smith Museum** (✆ 0557/51-7330) with original pictures and books including *Mother Goose,* the **Bohemian Glass Museum** (✆ 0557/53-4630), and the **Antique Jewelry Museum** (✆ 0557/54-5566) with Victorian brooches, rings, and more. There are also special-interest museums with collections dedicated to Santa, the Teddy bear, angels, dolls, dollhouses, music boxes and automatic musical instruments, stained glass, antique clocks, aviation, ammonites, cats, and even penguins. A wax museum boasts likenesses of Elvis, the Beatles, Charlie Chaplin, Michael Jackson, presidents Lincoln and Clinton, and other celebrities. Contact the **Ito Tourist Office** for more information.

To see the **Jogasaki Coast** with its dramatic, rugged, cliff-lined coast and hiking paths, take the train to Jogasaki Station; from there it's a 20-minute walk. For bathing, there's the **Ito Orange Beach** not far from Ito Station.

WHERE TO STAY

Hotel Spa Ito   Hotel Spa Ito is a rather grandiose name for this simple business-hotel-like establishment with a friendly staff. It does, however, have one thing most business hotels don't—a hot-spring public bath including an outdoor tub. Although it's close to the coast, there are no views from the rather small rooms, which mercifully face away from the train tracks (in any case, there are no trains at night).

3–10 Yubata-cho, Ito City, Shizuoka 414-0005. ℂ **0557/38-9111.** Fax 0557/38-3091. 36 units. ¥7,000 ($58) single; ¥10,000 ($83) double; ¥12,000 ($100) twin. AE, DC, JCB, V. A 3-min. walk from Ito Station. Take a right out of the station. *In room:* A/C, TV, hot-water pot with tea.

Kawana Hotel ★★   This grand old hotel is a good choice for relaxation, golf, and swimming. With its whitewashed walls, red roof tiles, and manicured lawns sloping gently toward the sea, the place seems little changed since it opened in 1936. Even the lobby lounge, built on the theme of an English country estate, remains faithful to the era with its soaring ceiling, large fireplace, coat of arms, heavy wood detailing, and antique furniture. The hotel's seclusion drew Joe Dimaggio and Marilyn Monroe on their honeymoon. Today, its two 18-hole golf courses make it famous among golfers—the hotel is often fully booked a half year in advance. In contrast to the old-fashioned ambiance of the hotel's public spaces, rooms have kept up with the times with contemporary furnishings, automatic curtain controls (on rooms facing the sea), and large bathrooms, most with two sinks. The least expensive rooms are smaller in size and face inland toward the mountains; double rooms are a bit cramped for two large people. Don't forget to climb to the top of the hotel's observation tower for a view of the grounds and their 10,000 cherry trees. Since the hotel is rather isolated, you'll probably want to dine at one of its restaurants: the old-fashioned main dining room serving continental cuisine; a 370-year-old, thatched-roof farmhouse specializing in Japanese food; and the casual, oval-shaped Sun Parlor with windows on three sides and offering views of the sea and, on clear days, Mt. Fuji rising above the mountains.

1459 Kawana, Ito City, Shizuoka 414-0044. ℂ **0557/45-1111.** Fax 0557/45-3834. 140 units. ¥25,000 ($208) single; ¥32,000–¥36,000 ($267–$300) double; ¥28,000–¥50,000 ($233–$417) twin. AE, DC, JCB, MC, V. A 15-min. taxi ride from Ito Station. **Amenities:** 3 restaurants; 2 18-hole golf courses (greens fees: ¥16,000/$133 weekdays, ¥23,000/$192 weekends and holidays; 3 outdoor swimming pools, including a children's pool (fee: ¥1,600/$13); tennis courts; in-room massage. *In room:* Satellite TV, minibar, hot-water pot with tea.

(47) **Ryokan Inaba** ★★   This 80-year-old, traditional ryokan, a registered National Treasure, has a lovely spot on the Matsukawa river not far from Ito Orange Beach. Each room is different (a different kind of wood is even employed in each room), with such traditional touches as sitting balconies over the river or wood carvings adorning windows, transoms, or shoji screens. All rooms boast river views (making this the best place for viewing the annual tub race held here the first Sun in July). Meals are served either in your room or in a communal dining room facing the river, according to your preference. The owner speaks English.

12–13 Higashimatsubara-cho, Ito City, Shizuoka 414-0022. ℂ **0557/37-3178.** Fax 0557/37-3180. www.inaba-r.co.jp. inaba-r@mxn.mesh.ne.jp. 16 units (2 with bathroom, 6 with toilet only). Peak season, Sat, and holidays, ¥15,000–¥25,000 ($125–$208) per person; off-season and Sun–Fri, ¥13,000–¥20,000 ($108–$167) per person. Rates include 2 meals and service charge. MC, V. A 10-min. walk from Ito Station. Go straight out of the station, turn left at the third stoplight, and keep to the left; it will be to your right. **Amenities:** Hot-spring public baths; in-room massage. *In room:* A/C, TV, minibar, hot-water pot with tea, hair dryer.

WHERE TO DINE
(48) **Fujiichi** FISH   This family-owned establishment near the public fish market operates a fish shop on the ground floor and a simple restaurant on the first floor with views of the small Ito harbor. Popular with the locals, it also

attracts tourists who have heard about its reputation for fresh fish. You can even select a fish from a downstairs tank and grill it yourself at the table. The *teishoku* gives a choice of main dish (like grilled fish, tempura, or sashimi) along with rice and soup, while set courses include more side dishes.

7–6 Shizumicho. ⓒ **0557/36-7669**. Teishoku ¥1,000–¥2,280 ($8.35–$19); set courses ¥2,880–¥4,380 ($24–$36.50); donburi rice casseroles ¥1,200–¥2,500 ($10–$21). JCB, MC, V. Open Mon–Fri 10am–3pm; Sat–Sun 10am–7pm (last order). Closed holidays and 4th Wed of every month. From Ito Station, walk to the coast and turn right. After crossing the bridge, it will be on the right across from Denny's.

The Japan Alps

The several volcanic mountain ranges that lie in central Honshu together comprise the **Japan Alps National Park** ★★★ (called Chubu Sangaku National Park in Japanese). With the exception of Japan's tallest mountain, Mt. Fuji (see chapter 5), all of Japan's loftiest mountains are in these ranges, making the Japan Alps a popular destination for hikers in summer and skiers in winter (Nagano, near Matsumoto, hosted the XVIII Winter Olympics in 1998). In addition, since some of the villages nestled in these mountains retain much of their traditional architecture, the Japan Alps provide a unique look at mountain life both past and present.

A GOOD STRATEGY FOR SEE-ING THE JAPAN ALPS Because towns and villages in this region are spread out—with lots of mountains in between—traveling isn't as fast in this part of the country as on Honshu's broad plains. If you're coming from Tokyo, your best strategy for visiting all the destinations covered in this chapter is to start with a direct train from Shinjuku Station to Matsumoto. From there, take the Chuo Honsen Line's Wide View Shinano early in the morning to Nakatsugawa, where you can then board a bus for Magome and spend the day hiking to Tsumago. By late afternoon, you should be back on the Chuo Line bound for Nagoya (see chapter 8), where you then change trains for Takayama, reaching it in time for dinner. Takayama is the best starting point for bus rides to Ogimachi (in Shirakawago); in peak season, buses also connect Ogimachi with Nagoya. From about June to November, there's also a bus between Matsumoto and Takayama.

See "Suggested Itineraries for Seeing Japan," in chapter 2, "Planning Your Trip to Japan" for more information on sightseeing routes through the Japan Alps.

1 Matsumoto, Gateway to the Japan Alps ★

234km (146 miles) NW of Tokyo

Located in the middle of a wide basin about 660 feet above sea level and sur-rounded on all sides by mountain ranges, **Matsumoto** ★ boasts a fine feudal castle with the oldest existing *donjon* (keep) in Japan, as well as an outstanding woodblock-print museum. Although the city itself (pop. 202,000) is modern with little remaining from its castle days, I find Matsumoto pleasant, the air fresh, and its people among the nicest I've encountered in Japan.

Encircled with towering peaks, sparkling mountain lakes, and colorful wild flowers, Matsumoto serves as the gateway to the hiking trails of the Japan Alps National Park; most travelers heading to the more remote regions of the Japan Alps pass through here on their way.

ESSENTIALS

GETTING THERE   By Train   The **JR Chuo Honsen Line** runs directly to Matsumoto from Tokyo's Shinjuku Station. Its *Limited Express Azusa,* departing every hour or less, reaches Matsumoto in about 2½ to 3 hours and costs ¥6,200 ($52) one-way. There's also a direct train from Nagoya, which takes about 2 hours and costs ¥5,360 ($45).

By Bus   From Tokyo's Shinjuku Station, buses depart for Matsumoto approximately every hour, taking about 3¼ hours and costing ¥3,400 ($28). From Nagoya, it's a 2½-hour ride at ¥3,460 ($29); from Osaka, it's 5½ hours and ¥5,710 ($48); from Takayama, it's 2¼ hours and ¥3,100 ($26).

VISITOR INFORMATION   Before departing from Tokyo, pick up a sheet called "Nagano" at the **Tourist Information Center** (see "Orientation," in chapter 3). It provides bus and train information to Matsumoto, as well as information on sights in and around Matsumoto. It also recommends 2- to 4-hour hiking trips from **Kamikochi** ⊛, the Japan Alps' most popular destination for serious hikers; the small village is a little more than 2 hours via train and bus from Matsumoto.

In Matsumoto, you'll find the **Matsumoto Tourist Information** window (ⓒ **0263/32-2814;** open daily 9:30am–6pm Apr–Oct, to 5:30pm Nov–Mar) by taking the main (east) exit out of Matsumoto Station and turning right. It has a good pamphlet and a map of the city in English. Its excellent English-speaking staff will also help with accommodations.

GETTING AROUND   You can **walk** to Matsumoto Castle, about a mile northeast of the station, in about 20 minutes. Alternatively, the Town Sneaker Bus makes a circular trip to all the sights (you can board it from Ekimae Dori in front of the station); it costs ¥100 (85¢) each time you get off, and buses run every 30 minutes. To visit the Japan Ukiyo-e Museum, however, you'll have to go by **train** or **taxi.** You can rent a **bike** from JR Eki Rent-A-Car beside the station for ¥1,500 ($12.50) per day.

SEEING THE SIGHTS

All directions are from Matsumoto Station unless otherwise noted.

MATSUMOTO CASTLE & ENVIRONS

Matsumoto Castle ⊛⊛   Originally built in 1504 when Japan was in the throes of continuing bloody civil wars, Matsumoto Castle is a fine specimen of a feudal castle with a 400-year-old donjon that's the oldest existing keep in the country. Surrounded by a moat with ducks and white swans and lined with willow and cherry trees, the outside walls of the donjon are black, earning the place the nickname of Karasu-jo, or Crow Castle. It's rather small as castles go and dark and fairly empty inside. Take your shoes off at the entrance and walk in stocking feet over worn wooden floors and up steep and narrow steps until you finally reach the sixth floor, from which you have a nice view of the city. This would have served as the *daimyo's* (feudal lord's) headquarters in case of enemy attack, while the fifth floor, with views in all directions, was where the generals would have conferred during war. Although the Ishikawa clan rebuilt the castle in 1593 in anticipation of gun warfare (guns were introduced to Japan in 1543) with many arrow and gun slots and walls thick enough to withstand bullets, the castle was never attacked because the civil wars ended with the coming of the Edo Period (1603–1867). A moon-viewing room was added in 1635, and on exhibition inside the castle is a collection of Japanese matchlocks and samurai armor dating from the mid-16th century through the Edo Period.

The Japan Alps

Sea of Japan

Takojima

Suzu

Wajima

Noto

Anamizu

Toyama-wan

Nanao

Hakiu

Himi

Takaoka

Toyama

Tsubata

Kanazawa

Matto

Komatsu

Ogimachi

Shirakawago

Sho-gawa

Kaga

Yamanaka

Katsuyama

HAKUSAN
NATIONAL
PARK

Hokuno

Fukui

Ono

Kuzuryu-gawa

Nagara-gawa

Imago

Tsuruga

Ibigawa

Gifu

Mihama

Imazu

Biwa-ko

Imazu

Moriyama

Komono

Ohara

Ise-wan

KOGEN
NATIONAL
PARK

Hime-kawa

Chikuma-gawa

Tokamachi

Nakano

Nagano

Suzaka

Koshoku

Ueda

Kurobe-gawa

CHUBU
SANGAKU
NATIONAL
PARK

Sai-gawa

Matsumoto

Kamikochi

Kamioka

Furukawa

Okaya

Ina

Takayama

Kisofukushima

Gero

Kiso-gawa

Tsumago

Magome

Tsukechi

Nakatsugawa

Namiai

Yaotsu

Tenryu-gawa

Seki

Akechi

Seto

Shitara

Nagoya

Yahagi-gawa

Toyota

Tsushima

Chiryu

Tokai

Kuwana

Nishio

Toyokawa

Mikawa-wan

Enshu-nada

Kamioka

Tokyo

Map area

JAPAN

0   25 mi

0   25 km

Tips A Note on Japanese Symbols

Many establishments and attractions in Japan do not have signs in Roman (English-language) letters. Those that don't are indicated in this guide with an oval with a number that corresponds to a number in appendix C showing the Japanese symbols. Thus, to find the Japanese symbol for, say, the **Matsumoto Folkcraft Museum** (below), refer to no. 49 in appendix C.

Included in your castle ticket is admission to the **Japan Folklore Museum** (Nihon Minzoku Shiryokan) 🐸 next to the castle. This rather eclectic museum has displays relating to archaeology, history, and folklore of the surrounding region including samurai armor, an ornate palanquin, farming equipment, animals of the Japan Alps, and dolls used for the Tanabata Festival. You can tour both the castle and museum in about 1½ hours.

4–1 Marunouchi. ✆ 0263/32-2902. Admission ¥520 ($4.35) adults, ¥250 ($2.10) children. Free 1-hour tours in English on weekdays, but call ahead to reserve. Daily 8:30am–5pm. Town Sneaker Bus: Stop 5, Matsumotojo Kuromon. To walk, take Ekimae Dori, the main road leading away from the station, and turn left onto Honmachi Dori.

Kaichi Gakko Primary School   Built in 1876, this handsome white mortar building of black tile topped by an octagonal turret is a fine example of Meiji Era architecture. It's the oldest Western-style school in Japan and served as an elementary school for 90 years. The school remains much as it was, with displays of books, games, desks, abacuses, and other items. Most fascinating are the photographs of former pupils, showing how many young girls came to school with young siblings strapped to their backs since parents were hard at work. You can see everything in about 30 minutes.

2–4–12 Kaichi. ✆ 0263/32-5725. Admission ¥310 ($2.60) adults, ¥150 ($1.25) children. Daily 8:30am–5pm. Closed Sun and holidays Dec–Feb. Town Sneaker Bus: Stop 7, Takajomachi. Behind the castle, about a 5-min. walk north.

MORE TO SEE & DO

Japan Ukiyo-e Museum 🐸🐸🐸 _Finds_   Quite simply, one of the best museums of woodblock prints in Japan. The ultramodern building houses the private collection of the Sakai family. With more than 100,000 prints, it's believed to be the largest collection of its kind in the world and includes representative masterpieces of all known ukiyo-e artists. The exhibition changes every 2 months with approximately 100 to 150 prints on display at any one time. A 10-minute slide show with explanations in English introduces the current exhibition, and a pamphlet in English describes the history of the collection and how woodblock prints are made. I wouldn't miss it—you'll want to spend at least an hour here.

2206–1 Koshiba, Shimadachi. ✆ 0263/47-4440. Admission ¥1,000 ($8.35) adults, half price for children. Tues–Sun 10am–5pm. From platform 7, take the Kamikochi Line 10 min. to Oniwa Station (¥170/$1.40; JR Rail Pass not accepted) and then walk 15 min. (turn left out of the station, left at the post office; after passing under the bridge, take the 2nd right at the small cemetery and continue straight on); or take a ¥1,500 ($12.50) taxi ride.

(49) **Matsumoto Folkcraft Museum (Matsumoto Mingei-kan)** 🐸 Here's one more museum worth visiting if you have an extra 45 minutes or so. It contains folk art made primarily of wood, glass, bamboo, and porcelain from Japan and other countries. Particularly beautiful are the wooden chests.

1313–1 Satoyama. 0263/33-1569. Admission ¥210 ($1.75) adults, ¥100 (85¢) children. Tues–Sun 9am–5pm. About 15 min. by bus (¥290/$2.40; take the platform 1 bus and get out at the Shimoganai Mingeikan Guchi) or taxi.

Suzuki Shin-ichi Talent Education Institute ✮   If you studied violin when you were young, maybe you were one of the countless children around the world who learned by the Suzuki Method. Matsumoto is home to this famous institute where young and old alike from around the world come to study violin, piano, cello, and flute. It was founded by Dr. Suzuki (who died in 1998 at the age of 99) and is renowned for its group and private lessons held throughout the week for both pupils and teachers of the Suzuki Method; guests are welcome to watch, but you must make advance reservations. There are also periodic concerts given by graduating musicians of the institute. Call Monday through Saturday between 9am and 5pm for more information and reservations.

3–10–3 Fukashi. ✆ **0263/32-1611.** By reservation only. Town Sneaker Bus: Stop 11, Ohashi Dori Minami.

WHERE TO STAY

Because Matsumoto is popular primarily with hikers used to roughing it along nature trails, accommodations are geared mainly toward convenience, but there is one luxury hotel. Directions are from Matsumoto Station.

EXPENSIVE

Buena Vista ✮✮   Matsumoto's biggest and fanciest hotel is a white gleaming structure built to blend with the city. Constructed primarily as a conference hotel and to accommodate those attending the Saito Kinen Festival (see the "Calendar of Events," in chapter 2), it has more facilities than other hotels in Matsumoto. The singles are very small, and there are no doubles, but windows can be opened. The rates reflect the seasons, with singles priced at ¥11,000 ($92) and twins starting at ¥21,000 ($175) in peak season (July–Oct).

1–2–1 Honjo, Matsumoto, Nagano 390-0184. ✆ **0263/37-0111.** Fax 0263/37-0666. 200 units. ¥9,000–¥11,000 ($75–$92) single; ¥17,000–¥28,000 ($142–$233) twin. AE, DC, JCB, MC, V. Turn right onto Shirakaba Dori and walk 5 min. **Amenities:** 5 restaurants, 2 bars; business center; gift shop with a good selection of Nagano Prefecture crafts; salon; room service (7:30–10am and 5:30–10pm); in-room massage; same-day laundry/dry cleaning. *In room:* A/C, cable TV with pay movies, dataport, minibar, hot-water pot with tea, hair dryer, washlet toilet.

㊿ **Ichiyama Yado** ✮✮✮ *(Finds)*   In a Meiji-Era stone *kura* (warehouse) which has been remodeled (and modernized with elevator access to added stories), this spotlessly clean inn boasts dark wooden beams, Asian artwork, and architectural features common to the region. Both Japanese- and Western-style rooms are available, all with heavy shades to block light and windows that can be opened. Japanese rooms, with such pleasing touches as wood and bamboo ceilings and extras like room safes, are more expensive than the five Western-style rooms. Full Western breakfasts are served in the pleasant ground-floor dining room. Though Ichiyama has more charm than other listings here, note that check out time is 10am and check in 4pm.

2–1–17 Chuo, Matsumoto, Nagano 390-0811 ✆ **0263/32-0122.** Fax 0263/32-3968. 13 units. ¥10,000–¥12,000 ($83–$100) single; ¥16,000– ¥22,000 ($67–$183) double. Winter discounts available. Rates include breakfast and service charge. AE, DC, MC, V. From the station, take the third left off Ekimae Dori; (3 min.). **Amenities:** Laundry/dry cleaning service. *In room:* A/C, TV, fridge, hot-water pot with tea, hair dryer.

MODERATE

Matsumoto Tokyu Inn ✮   Visible from the station, the Matsumoto Tokyu Inn is a practical, clean, and convenient business hotel, though its rates are a bit higher than one would expect in Matsumoto. The majority of rooms are singles and twins, all with semi-double-size beds with feather quilts. There are also six doubles and five deluxe twins, the latter with sofa, chairs, and a separate vanity area with its own sink. On clear days, rooms facing west have views of the Japan Alps.

1–3–21 Fukashi, Matsumoto, Nagano 390-0185. ✆ **0263/36-0109.** Fax 0263/36-0883. 169 units. ¥8,500–¥9,700 ($71–$81) single; ¥14,000–¥18,200 ($117–$151.70) double or twin; ¥26,600–¥28,200 ($221.70–$235) deluxe twin. AE, DC, JCB, MC, V. Turn right out of the station, then a 2-min. walk. **Amenities:** 1 restaurant (Western/Japanese/Chinese dishes), 1 bar; salon; same-day laundry/dry cleaning service. *In room:* A/C, TV, minibar, hot-water pot with tea, hair dryer, washlet toilet.

Matsumoto Tourist Hotel This spotless business hotel boasts a comfortable second-floor lobby and small, mainly single rooms with wood furniture, windows that open, and panels that slide shut for complete darkness. A studio single with a sofa bed is just about right for one person, but if you're low on funds, two people can stay here for the cheapest double rate given below. Some rooms face another building; ask for one on a higher floor facing south with mountain views beyond the city.

2–4–24 Fukashi, Matsumoto, Nagano 390-0815. ✆ **0263/33-9000.** Fax 0263/36-6435. 201 units. ¥5,800–¥7,300 ($48–$61) single; ¥10,300–¥12,000 ($86–$100) double; ¥12,000 ($100) twin. Rates include tax and service charge. AE, JCB, MC, V. Take the main road leading away from the station (Ekimae Dori), walk to the third stoplight (Honmachi Dori), and turn right; (6-min.). **Amenities:** 1 restaurant serving *kushiage* (deep-fried skewered foods); coin-op washers and dryers. *In room:* A/C, TV, hot-water pot with tea, hair dryer.

INEXPENSIVE

Enjyoh Bekkan Although it's a bit far from the center of Matsumoto in a community called Utusukushigara Onsen (Utusukushigara Spa), this member of the Japanese Inn Group is worth recommending for its nearby hot spring. The modern ryokan offers simple but clean and spacious tatami rooms, eight of which have toilets and sinks, the rest with bathrooms. Best, however, is the nearby hot-spring bathing in a large public bath overlooking the garden (open 24 hr.).

110 Utsukushigahara-onsen, Satoyamabe-ku, Matsumoto, Nagano 390-0221. ✆ **0263/33-7233.** Fax 0263/36-2084. www.mcci.or.jp/www/enjyoh/. 19 units (11 with bathroom). ¥5,300 ($44) single without bathroom, ¥6,300 ($52.50) single with bathroom; ¥9,800 ($82) twin without bathroom, ¥11,400 ($95) twin with bathroom; ¥13,200 ($110) triple without bathroom, ¥15,400 ($128) triple with bathroom. Spa tax ¥150 ($1.25) extra. Breakfast ¥800 ($6.65) extra; Japanese-style dinner ¥4,500 ($37.50) extra. AE, MC, V. Bus: 20 min. to Utsukushigahara-onsen bus terminal, then a 5-min. walk. **Amenities:** Hot-spring baths; in-room massage; laundry service. *In room:* A/C, TV, fridge, hot-water pot with tea.

Hotel Ikkyu A bit on the old side but very reasonably priced and run by friendly people, the Hotel Ikkyu is actually more like a *minshuku,* with mostly tatami rooms but a few Western-style rooms available as well. (The best Western-style rooms are in the annex, which has been recently renovated.) Note, however, that there are four floors and no elevator.

1–11–13 Honjo, Matsumoto, Nagano 390-0814. ✆ **0263/35-8528.** Fax 0263/35-9500. 19 units (8 with toilet only). ¥4,500 ($37.50) per person without meals, ¥7,000 ($58) per person including breakfast and dinner. No credit cards. Turn right onto Shirakabe Dori, turn left at the Green Hotel, and then right at the intersection where the street narrows; it's down the side street to the left just before the bridge (12 min.). **Amenities:** 1 restaurant (Japanese); coin-op fax machine. *In room:* A/C, coin-op TV, minibar, hot-water pot with tea.

WHERE TO DINE

Matsumoto is famous for its buckwheat noodles, which are fairly thick with a hearty flavor and can be served hot or cold, with several kinds of dips and sauces.

(51) **Kura** ★★★ *Finds* TEMPURA This convivial restaurant in one of the largest *kura* (warehouses) in Matsumoto is known for its delicious tempura, though it also offers sushi, grilled fish, and the local *zaru soba* (cold noodles) on its English menu. The kura, which was built in the late Meiji Period, is unusual

for its height. Enter the dining room through the thick vault-like door and sit at the dark wood counter (an excellent way to meet the locals), at one of the tables, or, with advance reservations, in private tatami rooms on the second floor.

2–2–15 Chuo. ✆ 0263/33-6444. Main dishes ¥600–¥2,000 ($5–$17); set dinners ¥1,500–¥6,000 ($12.50–$50); set lunches ¥700–¥1,200 ($5.85–$10). AE, DC, JCB, V. Thur–Tues 11:30am–2pm and 5–10pm. From the station, take the third left off Ekimae Dori (3 min.).

Naja ⭑ VEGETARIAN/NATURAL   If you're a vegetarian or a fan of natural foods, head for Naja. A small place with plain wooden decor and music from the 1960s playing in the background, it looks and sounds as if it was transported from a commune in the woods of California. Its English menu lists a daily brown-rice set dinner, as well as such offerings as soybean curry with yogurt, noodles, tofu steak, and brown-rice porridge.

4–7–10 Chuo. ✆ 0263/36-9096. Main dishes ¥700–¥900 ($5.85–$7.50); set dinner ¥900 ($7.50). No credit cards. Mon–Sat 7–11pm. Walk down Ekimae Dori and turn left at Honmachi Dori; take the second right and continue for 5 blocks.

㊻ Nomugi ⭑ NOODLES   In this small eatery, popular among the locals, handmade buckwheat noodles are made and served until they run out, which is why they have a flexible closing time. You'll be given a sauce to pour into a cup; add onion, wasabi, and daikon radish, then dip your soba into the mix. At the end of your meal, make a soup from the soba water stock (served in a teapot) and the soba sauce. In winter, the soba is served with boiled toppings.

2–9–11 Chuo. ✆ 0263/36-3753. Soba ¥1,000 ($8.35); half portion ¥600 ($5). No credit cards. Wed–Mon 11:30am–4pm or 5pm. Closes at about 3pm in winter. Town Sneaker Bus stop: Honmachi. Walk up Ekimae Dori to Honmachi Dori and turn left, take the next right, then take the next left; it's just north of the Fujimori Hospital.

㊾ Shikimi ⭑ EEL/SUSHI   For inexpensive Japanese fare close to Matsumoto Station, try this place specializing in eel and sushi. An atmosphere of old Japan is evoked by its traditional tiled roof, cast-iron lanterns, and interior with wooden sliding doors, small tatami rooms, a wooden counter, and paper lanterns. I recommend the *unagi donburi* (strips of eel on rice), which comes with soup and pickled vegetables. If sushi is more to your liking, try one of Shikimi's platters of assorted sushi, called *moriawase*.

1–5–5 Chuo. ✆ 0263/35-3279 or 0263/36-7716. Unagi donburi ¥1,600–¥1,900 ($13–$19); platters of assorted sushi (moriawase) ¥1,600–¥3,000 ($13–$25). No credit cards. Mon–Wed and Fri 11:45am–3pm and 4:30–9:30pm; Sat–Sun 11:45am–9pm. Take the main road leading east (Ekimae Dori) 1 block, turn left, and walk 3 blocks; it will be on the left (3 min.)

Taiman ⭑⭑⭑ FRENCH   If you feel like treating yourself, this is an excellent choice. Wonderful French cuisine is served in rustic yet elegant surroundings near Matsumoto Castle. A changing menu of set dinners is available, as well as less-expensive fixed-price meals of either sole or stewed beef, which are always on the menu and come with soup and dessert. My ¥5,000 ($42) lunch—which included bread or rice plus salad, dessert, and coffee—started with an hors-d'oeuvre plate of marinated squid, lox, cream cheese, capers, and grated onion; the next course was crab gratin cooked in a cheese-and-tomato base resembling lasagne, and the main dish was sautéed pork wrapped in bacon and topped with cheese.

4–2–4 Ote. ✆ 0263/32-0882. Reservations recommended. Main dishes ¥3,000–¥9,000 ($25–$75); set dinners ¥5,000–¥18,000 ($42–$150); set lunches ¥5,000–¥9,000 ($42–$75). AE, DC, JCB, MC, V. Thurs–Tues 11:30am–2pm and 5–9pm (last order 8pm). Walk east on Ekimae Dori and turn left on Honmachi Dori with its post office; after the bridge, turn right at the second stoplight where the NTT building is (12 min.).

2 Along the Nakasendo Highway: Tsumago & Magome

About 98km (61 miles) E of Nagoya; 88km (55 miles) SW of Matsumoto

If you're traveling between Nagoya and Matsumoto, you'll most likely pass through Kiso Valley in mountainous Nagano Prefecture. Formed by the Kiso River, the valley has always served as a natural passageway through the Japan Alps and was, in fact, one of two official roads linking Kyoto with Edo (Tokyo) back in the days of the Tokugawa shogunate (the other route was the Tokaido Highway, which passes through Hakone). Called the **Nakasendo Highway** 🎎🎎, it was the route of traveling *daimyo* (feudal lords) and their entourages of samurai retainers journeying between Japan's two most important towns. To serve their needs, 11 post towns sprang up along the Nakasendo Highway. Back then, it took 3 days to travel through the valley.

Of the old post towns, **Tsumago** 🎎🎎 and **Magome** are two that still survive, with many of the old buildings left intact. A 5-mile pathway skirting the Kiso River links the two villages, providing hikers with the experience of what it must have been like to travel the Nakasendo Highway back in the days of the shogun. You can easily visit the two picturesque villages and take the hike in a 1-day excursion from Nagoya or Matsumoto.

ESSENTIALS

GETTING THERE   Since neither Magome nor Tsumago is directly on a train line, you'll have to make the final journey by bus.

To reach **Magome,** take the **JR Chuo Line Shinano** (which connects Nagoya and Matsumoto) to Nakatsugawa Station. Trains from Nagoya take about 50 minutes and cost ¥2,940 ($25); from Matsumoto it takes about 75 minutes and costs ¥1,890 ($16). The 30-minute bus ride onward to Magome costs ¥540 ($4.50).

To reach Tsumago, take the **JR Chuo Line Shinano** to Nagiso Station and then take a 10-minute bus ride (¥350/$2.90).

Note that not all trains stop in Nagiso or Nakatsugawa, so make certain your train does. Note also that buses are infrequent; be sure to inquire about bus schedules beforehand (the Matsumoto Station tourist office has information on bus schedules; see "Visitor Information," earlier in this chapter).

VISITOR INFORMATION   The best way to obtain information about Kiso Valley is to stop by the **Tourist Information Center** in Tokyo, Kyoto or Narita or Kansai international airports to pick up a leaflet called "Kiso Valley," which provides a rough sketch of the 5-mile hiking path between Magome and Tsumago and gives some basic information about the villages; you can also stop by the tourist office in Matsumoto.

Otherwise, there's a tourist office in Tsumago (© **0264/57-3123**) and one in Magome (© **0264/59-2336**). Both are open daily from 9am to 5pm.

TRAVELING BETWEEN TSUMAGO & MAGOME   If you can't walk the entire distance between Tsumago and Magome, there's also a **bus** that travels between the two villages. You could, therefore, walk around Tsumago and then take a bus to Magome (¥650/$5.40).

Especially useful for hikers is a **luggage-transfer service** available between Magome and Tsumago on weekends and national holidays from mid-April to mid-November (offered daily during peak season, July 20–Aug). Luggage is accepted at either town's tourist office no later than 11:30am, and deliveries take approximately an hour and cost ¥500 ($4.15) per bag. It would be prudent, however, to call and verify this beforehand with the Magome or Tsumago tourist office, but note that only Japanese is spoken.

WALKING THE NAKASENDO HIGHWAY BETWEEN TSUMAGO & MAGOME

Allow about 3 hours for the hike between Tsumago and Magome, although you can probably do it in 2 hours. It doesn't matter which town you start from, though starting from Tsumago is a bit easier because the path leads slightly downhill. In any case, the trail is mainly a footpath tracing the contours of the Kiso Valley and crisscrossing the stream over a series of bridges. At times, the trail follows a paved road.

Since signs along the way are only in Japanese, familiarize yourself with the Japanese characters for (54) **Tsumago** and (55) **Magome.** Since the trail does go up some steep inclines, be sure to wear your walking shoes. And have fun—this is a great walk!

TSUMAGO ★★ Tsumago, the second post town from the south, is the more beautiful and authentic of the two towns. Threatened with gradual decline and desertion after the Chuo Line was constructed in 1911, bypassing Tsumago, the town experienced decades of neglect—and that's probably what ultimately saved it. Having suffered almost no modernization in the rebuilding zeal of the 20th century, Tsumago was a perfect target for renovation and restoration in the early 1970s, and in a rare show of insight, electrical wires, TV antennas, and telephone poles were hidden from sight along the main road. Thus, Tsumago looks much as it did back in the days of Edo.

On the main street of Tsumago, be sure to stop off at **Waki-honjin Okuya** (✆ **0264/57-3322**), an officially appointed inn that once served as a way station for daimyo and court nobles; it was also home to a sake brewery. The present house dates from 1877 and was rebuilt with *hinoki* cypress trees, a fact that has a special significance for this region. For centuries, all the way through the Edo Period, the people of the Kiso Valley were prohibited from cutting down trees, even if they were on private property. When the Meiji Period dawned and the ban was finally lifted, wealthy landowners were quick to rebuild in a more stately manner. This house, rebuilt in the style of a grand old castle, was visited by Emperor Meiji himself in 1880. Be sure to check out the daimyo's bathtub and toilet. Next door is the **Rekishi Shiryokan,** which serves as a local museum with displays of rice bowls, hair combs, books with ukiyo-e prints, and other items relating to the Edo Period.

Across the lane is the **Tsumagojuku Honjin** (✆ **0264/57-4100**), another recently restored inn where feudal lords and other nobles stayed. Apparently, the Shimazaki family had plans drawn up to rebuild their inn back in 1830. Renovation, however, didn't take place until 160 years later when an heir discovered the plans and gave them to the township, which rebuilt the inn according to the original plans using techniques dating from the period. You'd swear it was original. A ¥700 ($5.85) ticket allows admission to all three museums; all are open daily 9am to 5pm.

MAGOME The southernmost post town, Magome has old inns and souvenir shops that line both sides of a gently sloping road. It takes about 20 minutes to stroll through the town. It also has a restored inn, **Waki-honjin** (✆ **0264/59-2108;** open daily 9:30am–5pm), filled with artifacts showing the everyday life of a post town. Admission here is ¥200 ($1.65) for adults and ¥100 (85¢) for children.

WHERE TO DINE

There are a number of restaurants serving noodles and other simple fare along the main streets of both Magome and Tsumago. One I like is ⑤⑥ **Tawaraya** ((**©** 0264/57-2257; open mid-Mar to Dec, Thurs–Sun 10am–4:30pm) in Tsumago, which offers *sansai soba* (a filling bowl of hot buckwheat noodles in soup with mushrooms and mountain vegetables) for ¥900 ($7.50), two skewers of *gohei* (grilled rice cakes with sauce) for ¥500 ($4.15), and *anmitsu* (a traditional dessert) for ¥400 ($3.35). Seating is at tables (wooden slabs with irregular natural edges) or on tatami. The women working here couldn't be nicer.

3 Takayama, Little Kyoto of the Mountains 👁👁👁

528km (330 miles) NW of Tokyo, 165km (103 miles) NE of Nagoya

Located in the Hida Mountains (part of the Japan Alps National Park), **Takayama** 👁👁👁 is surrounded by 10,000-foot peaks, making the train ride here breathtaking. The village, situated along a river on a wide plateau, was founded back in the 16th century by Lord Kanamori, who selected the site because of the impregnable position afforded by the surrounding mountains. Modeled after Kyoto but also with strong ties to Edo (Tokyo), Takayama borrowed from both cultural centers in developing its own architecture, food, and crafts, all well preserved today thanks to centuries of remote isolation. With a rich supply of timber provided by surrounding forests, its carpenters were legendary, creating not only beautifully crafted traditional merchants' homes in Takayama but also the Imperial Palace and temples in Kyoto.

Today, Takayama boasts a delightful and elegant historic district, called **San-machi Suji,** with homes of classical design typical of 18th-century Hida. The streets are narrow and clean and are flanked on both sides by tiny canals of running water, which in centuries past were useful for fire prevention, washing clothes, and dumping winter snow but which now give the town its own distinct character. Rising up from the canals are one- and two-story homes and shops of gleaming dark wood with overhanging roofs; latticed windows and slats of wood play games of light and shadow in the white of the sunshine. In the doors of many shops, strips of blue cloth flutter in the breeze.

With its quaint old character, great shopping (including a lively city market), and museums, Takayama is a town that invites exploration. As you walk down the streets, you'll also notice huge cedar balls hanging from the eaves in front of several shops, indicating one of Takayama's sake factories. Altogether there are eight of them in Takayama, most small affairs. Go inside, sample the sake, and watch the men stirring rice in large vats. There are also a surprising number of museums, most housed in traditional homes and filled with historic relics and antiques.

ESSENTIALS

GETTING THERE   By Train   The easiest way to reach Takayama is by direct train from Nagoya, with about eight departures daily for the 2¼-hour trip that costs ¥5,360 ($45) for an unreserved seat. There's also one direct train a day from Osaka via Kyoto, which takes 5½ hours and costs ¥7,560 ($63).

By Bus   Buses depart Tokyo's Shinjuku Station four times daily from mid-March to the end of November, arriving in Takayama 5½ hours later and costing ¥6,500 ($54). There are fewer departures in winter and more frequent departures from mid-July through August. From Matsumoto, the **Nouhi Bus** ((**©** 0577/32-1160) passes through magnificent mountain scenery on the 2¼-hour trip and costs ¥3,100 ($26).

VISITOR INFORMATION   Before departing Tokyo, Kyoto or Narita or Kansai airports, stop by the **Tourist Information Center** for the excellent "Takayama and Shirakawago" leaflet, which contains maps and travel and sight-seeing information. In Takayama, the local **tourist office** (✆ **0577/32-5328;** open daily 8:30am–6:30pm, to 5pm Nov–Mar) is housed in a wooden booth just outside the main (east) exit of Takayama Station. You can pick up an English brochure with a map of the town showing the location of all museums and attractions.

More information is available at **www.hidanet.ne.jp/takayama/e-taka.htm** and there is free Internet access at the tourist office in front of the station (open same hours) and at Takayama City Hall (2–18 Hanaoka-machi, ✆**0577/32-3333;** open Mon–Fri 8:30am–5pm).

GETTING AROUND   Takayama is one of Japan's easiest towns to navigate. Most of Takayama's attractions lie to the east of the train station in **San-machi Suji** and are easily reached from the station in about 10 to 15 minutes **on foot.** Throughout the town are signs in English pointing directions to the many attractions; they're even embedded in sidewalks and streets.

An alternative to walking is to rent a **bicycle** from one of the many shops ringing the station; the cost averages ¥300 ($2.50) per hour or ¥1,300 ($11) for the whole day.

To reach Hida Folk Village and Hida Takayama Art Museum, you'll have to go by bus, which departs from platform 6 at the bus station to the left of the main exit of the train station. Consider purchasing a "Free Jo Shakin" for ¥550 ($4.15), a **one-day bus pass** allowing you to reboard as often as you wish.

SEEING THE SIGHTS

Takayama's main attraction is its old merchants' houses, which are clustered together in San-machi Suji on three narrow streets called **Ichino-machi, Nino-machi,** and **Sanno-machi.** Be sure to allow time for just wandering around. In addition to the district's many museums, there are also shops selling Takayama's specialties, including sake, yew wood carvings, and a unique lacquerware called *shunkei-nuri.*

Be sure, too, to visit the **Miyagawa Morning Market,** which stretches on the east bank of the Miyagawa River between Kajibashi and Yayoibashi bridges. Held every morning from 7am (6am in summer) to noon, it's very picturesque with cloth-covered stalls selling fresh vegetables, flowers, pickled vegetables, children's clothing, and toys.

THE TOP ATTRACTIONS

Note that the attractions listed below are closed during the New Year's holidays.

Hida Minzoku Mura Folk Village (Hida no Sato) ★★★   This is an open-air museum of more than 30 old thatched and shingled farmhouses, sheds, and buildings, many of which were brought here from other parts of the region to illustrate how farmers and artisans used to live in the Hida Mountain range. The whole village is picturesque with swans swimming in the central pond, green moss growing on the thatched roofs, and flowers blooming in season. Some of the houses have *gassho-zukuri*-style roofs, built steeply to withstand the region's heavy snowfalls; the tops of the roofs are said to resemble hands joined in prayer. All the structures, which range from 100 to 500 years old, are open to the public and are filled with furniture, old spindles and looms, utensils for cooking and dining, instruments used in the silk industry, farm tools, sleds, and straw boots and snow capes for winter.

Workshops have been set up in one corner of the village grounds to demonstrate Takayama's well-known carving and lacquerwork industries. Among the other attractions here are the **Hida Folklore Museum** (Hida Minzoku-kan) with more displays on life in the Hida region, and souvenir shops selling pottery and other craft items. You'll probably want to spend about 1½ hours here, but if you're heading to Shirakawago, skip it; there's a similar, more easily accessible open-air museum there.

© 0577/33-4714. Admission ¥700 ($5.85) adults, ¥200 ($1.65) children under 15. Daily 8:30am–5pm. Take the bus from platform 6 next to Takayama Station (a 10-min. ride) or walk 30 min. SW from the train station.

Merchants' Houses ⭐⭐⭐   In contrast to other castle towns during the Edo Period, Takayama was under the direct control of the Tokugawa government rather than a feudal lord, which meant its homes were built and owned by merchants and commoners rather than the samurai class that dominated other Japanese cities. Located side by side in San-machi Suji and easily toured in less than an hour, **Yoshijima-ke** or Yoshijima House (© **0577/32-0038**) and **Kusakabe Mingeikan** (© **0577/32-0072**) are merchants' mansions that once belonged to two of the richest families in Takayama. Of the two, the Yoshijima House is my favorite: With its exposed attic, heavy crossbeams, sunken open-hearth fireplace, and sliding doors, it's a masterpiece of geometric design. It was built in 1908 as both the home and factory of the Yoshijima family, well-to-do brewers of sake. Notice how the beams and details of the home gleam, a state attained through decades of polishing as each generation of women did their share in bringing the wood to a luster. Yoshijima-ke is also famous for its lattices, typical of Takayama yet showing an elegance influenced by Kyoto. Lovers of contemporary Japanese art will want to keep a lookout for lithographs of the well-known female artist Shinoda Toko; at the back of the house is a small gallery-cum-coffee shop.

The Kusakabe Mingeikan, built in 1879 for a merchant dealing in silk, lamp oil, and finance, is more refined and imposing. Its architectural style is considered unique to Hida but has many characteristics common during the Edo Period, including a two-story warehouse with open beams and an earthen floor. On display are personal items from Japan and imports from other countries, handed down through the generations and arranged just as they would have been in the 18th and 19th centuries.

North end of Nino-machi St., 1–52 Ojimachi. Separate admission to each house: ¥500 ($4.15) for adults, ¥300 ($2.50) for children. Summer: both open daily 9am–5pm. Winter (Dec–Feb): Yoshijima-ke, Wed–Mon 9am–4:30pm; Kusakabe Mingeikan, daily 9am–4:30pm.

MORE MUSEUMS

Fujii Art Gallery (Fujii Bijutsu Mingei-Kan) ⭐   This gallery occupies a traditional merchant's storehouse; its entrance is a copy of an outer gate that once led to Takayama Castle. The varied collection from the Edo Period includes beautiful *tansu* (chests) inlaid with mother-of-pearl, sake and wine glasses, Imari and Kutani porcelain, tortoise-shell combs, ceremonial dolls, kimono, tea kettles, paper lanterns, rice barrels, smoking utensils, farming tools, spinning wheels, and more. Many items are identified in English, making this a very worthwhile museum; you can see it all in about 30 minutes.

Sanno-machi St., 69 Kamisanno-machi. © 0577/35-3778. Admission ¥700 ($5.85) adults, ¥400 ($3.35) children. Daily 9am–5pm. Just down the street from the Hida Folk Archeological Museum (below), a 10-min. walk from the train station.

57 **Hida Folk Archeological Museum (Hida Minzoku Kokokan)** This interesting old house in the heart of San-machi Suji is more than 200 years old. It once belonged to a retainer of Lord Kanamori and is reputed to have had some association with ninja—look for the display window outside the entrance with grappling hooks. The house contains several trick devices, including secret passageways and a hanging ceiling. Imagine inviting an enemy to your home, offering him the best room in the house, and then sneaking upstairs to chop the rope that holds up the suspended ceiling! The ceiling plunges down with a loud thud, neatly crushing your enemy to death. Rather dramatic, don't you think? And, of course, very effective. You'll see the mechanics of the ceiling by peeking through a hole in an upstairs room. The house, which can be toured in less than 30 minutes, also serves as an archaeological museum for finds dating from the Jomon Period, including stone implements and earthware.

Sanno-machi St., 82 Kamisanno-machi. **0577/32-1980.** Admission ¥400 ($3.35) adults, ¥250 ($2.10) high-school and junior-high students, ¥150 ($1.25) children. Mar–Nov, daily 8:30am–6pm; Dec–Feb, daily 9am–5pm. A 10-min. walk from the train station.

58 **Hida Takayama Museum of Art** Serious glass lovers will not want to miss this museum with its collection of mostly European and Asian glassware from the 16th to the 20th centuries, including works by Tiffany, Lalique, and Gallé. Several rooms are furnished in turn-of-the-century decorative and applied arts by masters like Louis Majorelle, Mackintosh, and Vienna's Secessionist artists. Plan on spending about 45 minutes here.

1–124–1 Kamiokamoto-cho. © **0577/35-3535.** Admission ¥1,300 ($11) adults, ¥1,000 ($8.35) university and high-school students, ¥800 ($6.65) junior-high age and younger. Apr–Nov, daily 9am–5pm; Dec–Mar, Tues–Sun 9am–5pm. Take the bus from platform 6 to Hida Takayama Bijutsukan (or a 10-min. walk from Hida Minzoku Mura).

Hirata Folk Art Museum (Hirata Kinen-kan) ★★ Here you'll find what is probably Takayama's most varied and extensive collection of folk art. It vividly conveys what life was like during the Edo Period by displaying household utensils, crafts, and fine arts found in a typical middle-class home; the house itself, built in 1897 in the traditional style with a sunken hearth and both living and working quarters, belonged to a candlemaker. Items are identified in English. On display are folk toys, coin boxes, mirrors, toiletry sets, geta, spectacles, hair adornments, *shunkei* lacquerware, and paper and kerosene lamps; my favorite is the room outfitted with items used for travel, including guide maps, portable abacuses, compasses, a traveling pillow, a folding lantern, and even a folding hat. Depending on your interest, you'll spend anywhere from 30 to 50 minutes here.

Ichino-machi St., 39 Kaminino-machi. © **0577/33-1354.** Admission ¥300 ($2.50) adults, ¥150 ($1.25) children. Daily 9am–5pm.

Historical Government House (Takayama Jinya) ★★★ I highly recommend a visit here to anyone interested in Japanese history. The building served as the Tokugawa government's administrative building for 177 years (1692–1868). Of some 60 local government offices that were once spread throughout Japan, this is the only one still in existence. Like a miniature palace with an outer wall and an imposing entrance gate, the sprawling complex consists of both original buildings and reconstructions. In addition to administrative offices, chambers, and courts, the complex contained living quarters, a huge kitchen, an interrogation room with torture devices, and a 400-year-old rice granary, the oldest and biggest in Japan.

What makes a visit here especially educational are the free guided tours available in English, which last about 30 to 40 minutes and provide fascinating insight into administrative life during the Edo Period. When tours are not available (just ask at the desk), audiophones are available free of charge.

1–5 Hachi-ken-machi. ℂ **0577/32-0643.** Admission ¥420 ($3.50) for adults, free for high-school age and younger. Apr–Oct, daily 8:45am–5pm; Nov–Mar, daily 8:45am–4:30pm. A 10-min. walk from the train station.

Inro Museum (Inro Bijitsukan) ★★★ (finds) If you're an enthusiast of the tiny, intriguing *inro,* a small portable medicine case, you must not miss this museum. If you're not yet a fan, you probably will be after visiting here. It displays Japan's largest collection of 18th-century inro and *netsuke,* toggles or counterweights used for hanging inro (as well as purses and tobacco pouches) from kimono sashes. All inro are displayed with their original and thematically matching netsuke intact, and some of the designs display a great sense of humor. More than 300 rare inro and netsuke are on display, and they're all wonderful works of art. I could spend hours here.

1–98 Ojimachi. ℂ **0577/32-8500.** Admission ¥500 ($4.15) for adults, ¥300 ($2.50) for high-school, junior-high, and elementary students. Wed–Mon 9am–5pm. Closed Dec–Mar. In a beautiful *kura* (storehouse) just off Omotesando Dori, not far from Yoshijima-ke.

Lacquerware Museum (Hida Takayama Shunkei Kaikan) This museum, which can be toured in a half hour, displays Takayama lacquerware, known for the transparency of its finish, which enhances the grain of the wood. Takamaya lacquerware is admired all over Japan for its honey-colored sheen. The museum displays some 1,000 items dating from the 17th century to the present, including beautifully crafted trays, furniture, vases, rice containers, and lunch boxes; one exhibit explains the multistage production technique and tools of the craft. There's also a shop—and after seeing the time-consuming process to produce shunkei ware, you'll know why prices are high.

1–88 Kanda-cho. ℂ **0577/32-3373.** Admission ¥300 ($2.50) adults, ¥200 ($1.65) high-school and junior-high students, free for children. Summer, daily 8am–5:30pm; winter, daily 9am–5pm. A 15-min. walk from the train station.

㊸ **Lion Dance Ceremony Exhibition Hall (Shishi-Kaikan)** More than 800 lion masks from all over Japan, used to perform the lion dance in Japanese festivals, are on display here, as well as Edo-Period screens, ceramics, scrolls, coins, samurai armor, and swords. Best, however, are the 15-minute performances given every half hour by marionettes, which decorate many of Takayama's floats in its two festivals; they're capable of wonderful acrobatics.

53–1 Sakura-machi. ℂ **0577/32-0881.** Admission ¥600 ($5) adults, ¥400 ($3.35) junior-high age and younger. Summer, daily 8:30am–5:30pm; winter, daily 9am–5pm. A 1-min. walk from Takayama Festival Floats Exhibition Hall (below).

Takayama Festival Floats Exhibition Hall (Takayama Yatai Kaikan) ★ This exhibition hall displays four of the huge, elaborate floats used for Takayama's famous Takayama Matsuri (Autumn Festival). Dating mostly from the 17th century and colorfully decorated with carvings, hanging lanterns, and some with marionettes, floats are as high as 23 feet and are mounted on wheels. Free 20-minute guided tours in English are available, making the festival hall an interesting stop if you're unable to see the festival itself.

The admission price also allows entrance to **Sakurayama Nikko Kan** next door, which houses a replica of the Toshogu Shrine in Nikko (see chapter 5), built at one-tenth the scale. I was initially skeptical, but the 28 buildings—complete with computerized sunsets and sunrises—are works of art.

178 Sakura-machi. ✆ **0577/32-5100.** Admission ¥820 ($6.85) adults, ¥510 ($4.25) high-school students, ¥410 ($3.40) junior-high age and younger. Summer, daily 8:30am–5pm; winter, daily 9am–4:30pm. In the precincts of Sakurayama Hachimangu Shrine, about a 10-min. walk north of San-machi Suji or a 25-min. walk from the train station.

Takayama Museum of Local History (Kyodokan)　This city-owned local history museum is housed in a former sake brewery and a 100-year-old storehouse. It displays objects relating to Takayama's history, including items formerly used in the brewing of sake, equipment used by the city's volunteer fire department, marionettes and replica floats used in Takayama's festivals, personal items of the Kanamori clan (rulers of the Hida region from 1586–1692), and examples of local crafts, including yew carvings, shunkei lacquerware, and pottery.

75 Kami-Ichino-machi. ✆ **0577/32-1205.** Admission ¥300 ($2.50) adults, ¥150 ($1.25) children. Apr–Oct, daily 8:30am–5pm; Nov–Mar, Tues–Sun 9am–4:30pm. On Ichino-machi St., a 10-min. walk from the train station.

WHERE TO STAY

There are more minshuku and ryokan in Takayama than hotels, making it the perfect place to stay in a traditional inn. In fact, staying in a tatami room and sleeping on a futon is the best way to immerse yourself in the life of this small community, and the best news is that there are places to fit all budgets.

You should be aware that in peak season—Golden Week (Apr 29–May 5), August, at festival times in April and October, and New Year's—prices will be higher, generally between 10% and 20%.

All directions are from Takayama Station.

EXPENSIVE

⑥⓪ **Nagase** ★★★　The Nagase family has been running this traditional inn for 250 years, spanning 10 generations. A renovated merchant's home that highlights the region's strong architectural identity, it's filled with antiques. Each of the tatami guest rooms is unique, made special by carved wooden transoms, bamboo detailing, shunkei lacquer furniture, flower arrangements, and hanging scrolls in alcoves. Best of all, each room has views of one of six perfectly crafted miniature gardens, complete with small waterfalls and streams fed by natural springs that provide their own serenade throughout the ryokan. Kyoto-style cuisine and local specialties, served on beautiful lacquerware and ceramics, is brought to your room. If you are looking for an authentic Japanese experience (not to mention Takayama's most venerable inn), look no further.

10 Kami-Nino-machi, Takayama, Gifu 506-0845. ✆ **0577/32-0068.** Fax 0577/32-1068. 10 units (8 with bathroom, 2 with toilet only). ¥15,000–¥17,000 ($125–$142) per person with toilet only; ¥18,000–¥30,000 ($150–$250) per person with bathroom. Rates include breakfast, dinner, and service. MC, V. Just south of San-machi Suji, on Nino-machi St., a 10-min. walk from the train station. **Amenities:** Jacuzzi; in-room massage. *In room:* A/C, TV, minibar, hot-water pot with tea, safe.

MODERATE

Four Seasons *Value*　Although this modern-looking building with an arched roof looks out of place in Takayama, the hotel is a good choice in terms of price. Catering to business travelers during the week and tourists on weekends, it has an accommodating staff, free coffee and tea in the lobby, and a slightly feminine touch in its public spaces and rooms, which come with all the basics. Those on the sixth floor have wooden furniture and wooden floors (important for the allergy conscious). A large Japanese bath with Jacuzzi and sauna overlooking a small garden is a plus. (By the way, as you may have guessed by its rates, this place is not part of the famous Four Seasons hotel chain.)

Kanda-machi 1–1, Takayama, Gifu 506-0006. ✆ **0577/36-0088.** Fax 0577/36-0080. 46 units. ¥6,900–¥7,480 ($57.50–$62) single; ¥13,100–¥14,300 ($109–$119) twin. AE, MC, V. A 10-min. walk NE. **Amenities:** 1 restaurant (local Japanese food); hot-spring indoor bath; Jacuzzi; sauna; rental bikes; in-room massage; coin-op washers and dryers; same-day laundry/dry cleaning service. *In room:* A/C, TV with pay movies, minibar, hot-water pot with tea, hair dryer, washlet toilet.

(61) **Hachibei** ★ This minshuku, a big older house with a newer addition, has a pleasant open hearth (*irori*) where guests (mostly young Japanese) can sit and socialize in the evening. The corridors, tatami rooms, and dining hall have a slight youth-hostel feel to them—functional and simple. Ask for a corner room or, in the off-season, one of the larger combination rooms that usually are reserved for four but are available for two for the same price and that have both tatami areas and Western beds with down covers. The public baths are large and include an open-air bath. The front garden features a red arched bridge, a koi pond, and marble table and seats.

Kamiokamoto-machi 1–389, Takayama, Gifu 506-0055. ✆ **0577/35-2111.** Fax 0577/35-2389. 27 units (none with bathroom). ¥7,000 ($58) per person. Rates include breakfast, dinner, and service. AE, DC, JCB, MC, V. A few minutes' walk from Hida Minzoku Mura Folk Village; call from the station for shuttle bus pickup. **Amenities:** In-room massage; coin-op washers and dryers. *In room:* A/C, TV, hot-water pot with tea, safe.

Minshuku Sosuke ★ The entryway of this warm and friendly minshuku is filled with country knickknacks. There's an *irori* (open hearth) in the communal room to the left as you enter—if it's chilly, you'll be invited to sit down and warm yourself. The cuisine served includes local specialties, and meals are plentiful and delicious (Western breakfasts are available). Mealtimes are especially fun: Everyone is seated around one long table, and since most of the guests are Japanese, this is a good opportunity to learn about other parts of the country. Although the building housing the minshuku is 170 years old, the inside has been remodeled, and all the rooms, though simple, are clean and are nonsmoking.

Okamoto-machi 1–64, Takayama, Gifu 506-0054. ✆ **0577/32-0818.** Fax 0577/33-5570. http://www.irorisosuke.com. Email: info@irori-sosuke.com. 13 units (none with bathroom). ¥7,500–¥10,000 ($62.50–$83) per person. Rates include breakfast, dinner, and service. No credit cards. An 8-min. walk west of the station. Turn right out of the station and then take the first right (at the T intersection); it's over the bridge on the right side of the street, across from the Green Hotel. **Amenities:** Coin-op washers and dryers. *In room:* A/C, TV, hot-water pot with tea, no phone.

(62) **Sumiyoshi** ★★★ *Finds* It calls itself a ryokan, but its price and homey atmosphere make it seem more like a minshuku. Built more than 90 years ago by a well-known local carpenter to house a silkworm industry, it opened in 1950 as a ryokan and probably hasn't changed a bit since then. An open-hearth fireplace, samurai armor, and antiques fill the reception area, where you are invited to have tea or coffee, and on the second floor there's an outdoor deck facing the river. Rooms are comfortable and old-fashioned, and many have painted screens and antiques; request one facing the river. The older women running the place don't speak English, but they're very sweet.

Hon-machi 4, Takayama, Gifu 506-0011. ✆ **0577/32-0228.** Fax 0577/33-8916. 10 units (1 with bathroom). ¥8,000–¥13,000 ($67–$108) per person. Rates include breakfast, dinner, and service. No credit cards. Across from historic San-machi Suji on the Miyagawa River, a 10-min. walk NE. **Amenities:** In-room massage; laundry/dry cleaning service. *In room:* A/C, TV, minibar, hot-water pot with tea, safe.

Yamakyu ★ This minshuku has a deserved reputation for serving the best meals in town in its price range. Although it's a bit far from the station—in a quiet residential area about a 20-minute walk or a 5-minute taxi ride—it's only a 10-minute walk to the historic district. As with most minshuku, the Japanese-style rooms—nicely done with natural woods and artwork—are without private bathrooms, but the public baths are large and pleasant and feature turning waterwheels.

Tenshoji-machi 58, Takayama, Gifu 506-0832. ✆ **0577/32-3756.** Fax 0577/35-2350. 28 units (none with bathroom). ¥7,000 ($58) per person; ¥500 ($4.15) extra for special meals featuring festival favorites at twice-yearly festival times (mid-Apr, Oct). Rates include breakfast, dinner, and service. No credit cards. Walk straight up San-machi Suji, (20 min.). **Amenities:** In-room massage; laundry/dry cleaning service. *In room:* A/C, TV, hot-water pot with tea, safe.

INEXPENSIVE

Rickshaw Inn ★★ In a modern house, centrally located between the train station and San-machi Suji, the Rickshaw Inn is welcoming and homey, due in no small part to the friendly owner, Setoyama Eiko, a Takayama native who lived in the United States and speaks flawless English. A communal living room—with sofas, TV, newspapers, a table, and an adjoining kitchen complete with refrigerator, hotplate, microwave, and toaster—is a good place to relax with fellow guests. Simple Japanese- and Western-style rooms are available, with Asian artwork on the walls and batik shades to block out light. No meals are served, but Eiko-san is happy to recommend nearby restaurants (ask for her map) and is also knowledgeable about museums, crafts, and Takayama's history.

Suehiro-cho 54. Takayama, Gifu 506-0016. ✆ **0577/32-2890.** Fax 0577/32-2469. 9 units (7 with bathroom). ¥4,200 ($35) single without bathroom, ¥6,000 ($50) single with bathroom; ¥9,800–¥11,000 ($82–$92) double or twin. AE. A 6-min. walk east, just off Kokubunji St. **Amenities:** Coin-op washer and dryer; nonsmoking rooms; communal kitchen. *In room:* A/C, TV, no phone.

WHERE TO DINE

Since most ryokan and minshuku serve breakfast and dinner, lunch is most visitors' only concern. Takayama has some local specialties you should try while you're here (they may well be served at your ryokan or minshuku). The best known is *hoba miso,* which is soybean paste mixed with dried scallions, ginger, and mushrooms and cooked on a dry magnolia leaf at your table above a small clay burner. *Sansai* are mountain vegetables, including edible ferns and other wild plants, and *ayu* is river fish, grilled with soy sauce or salt. Other favorite dishes include Takayama's own style of *soba* (buckwheat noodles), *mitarashi-dango* (grilled rice balls with soy sauce), and *Hida beef.*

All directions given are from Takayama Station.

EXPENSIVE

(63) **Kakusho** ★★★ VEGETARIAN For a big splurge, dine at Kakusho, established 180 years ago and offering local vegetarian fare called *shojin-ryori,* typically served at Buddhist temples. Situated on the slope of a hill in the eastern part of the city, a 5-minute walk from San-machi Suji, this delightful restaurant serves meals either in small, private tatami rooms dating from the Edo Period or in a larger room from the Meiji Period that can be opened to the elements on three sides, all of which overlook a dreamy, mossy garden enclosed by a clay wall. You must make a reservation to dine here; the least expensive meals consist of various mountain vegetables, mushrooms, nuts, and tofu, with more dishes added for the more expensive set meals.

2–98 Babacho. ✆ **0577/32-0174.** Reservations required. Set dinners ¥7,000–¥12,000 ($58–$100); set lunches ¥5,500–¥10,000 ($46–$83). No credit cards. Daily 11:30am or 1:30pm (2 lunch seatings) and 5:30–about 7pm (flexible closing time). Closed some Wed, some Thurs. Just north off of San-machi and 1 block east of Kami-ichino-machi, (15 min.).

MODERATE

Osteria de la Fourcetta ✦ ITALIAN   Although this small, peach-toned restaurant is cozy and inviting, the best seats are out on the back terrace overlooking the Miyogawa river. The chef, trained in Italy, prepares delicious dishes like *carre di anello alla grigia* (grilled lamb) and *pollo di bresse alla chiantigiana* (marinated breast of chicken) and will even whip up vegetarian meals on request. A small quibble: pasta portions are small; even our accompanying 11-year-old reviewer had to order two plates to be satisfied.

3–18 Honmachi. ✆ **0577/37-4064.** Pasta ¥900–¥1,400 ($7.50–$12); main dishes ¥1,500–¥2,700 ($12.50–$22.50); set lunches ¥1,000–¥2,000 ($8.35–$17); set dinner ¥4,500 ($37.50); MC, V. Wed–Mon 11:30am–2pm, 6–9pm. Closed 1st and 3rd Wed. Open daily in July and Aug. On Honmachi St. north of Kajibashi Bridge, (10 min.).

64 Suzuya ✦✦ LOCAL SPECIALTIES   Darkly lit with traditional Takayama country decor, this restaurant specializing in Takayama cuisine is so popular that if you come for lunch between noon and 1pm, you'll probably have to wait for a table. There's an English-language menu complete with photographs and explanations of each dish, including such local specialties as mountain vegetables, hoba miso, Takayama-style buckwheat noodles, Hida beef, and *tobanyaki,* which is a stew of leeks, Japanese green peppers, mushrooms, and various chicken parts (including liver, gizzard, skin, and meat) that you cook at your table in your own personal cooker. Also cooked at the table is *sansai-miso-nabe,* a stew of Chinese cabbage, chicken, and various mountain vegetables flavored with miso. Highly recommended.

Hanakawa-cho 24. ✆ **0577/32-2484.** Reservations recommended in summer and during festivals. Set meals ¥1,300–¥4,150 ($11–$35). AE, V. Wed–Mon 11am–3pm and 5–7:30pm. Just off Kokubunji St., halfway between the station and the Miyagawa River (6 min.); look for the curtains with bells hanging above the front door and the cedar ball hanging from the eaves.

INEXPENSIVE

Agura ✦✦ *Finds* LOCAL SPECIALTIES/PIZZA   A converted rice *kura* (warehouse) with a high-beamed ceiling, wooden floors, slabs of wood for tables, and locally crafted bent-wood chairs make for a lovely, airy setting, heightened by eclectic cuisine, hip waiters in Asian pajamas, and jazz music. The English menu has lots of great salads, pizzas fired in a wood-burning stove, and local specialties like Hida beef prepared at the table accompanied by regional vegetables.

4–7 Shinmeicho ✆ **0577/37-2666.** Pizzas ¥880–¥980 ($7.35–$8.15); main dishes ¥680–¥1,500 ($5.65–$12.50). No credit cards. Tues–Sun 6pm–midnight. South of Takayama City Memorial Hall, (12 min.).

Atomboy SUSHI   If you're hungry for sushi, head to this conveyor belt restaurant not far from the station. The Japanese pop music might drive you nuts, but the sushi is good and inexpensive.

7–21 Kami Okamoto ✆ **0577/32-8007.** Plate with two pieces ¥100–¥500 (85¢–$4.15). No credit cards. Daily 11am–10pm. Turn left out of the station, left at the first street and right after the bridge, (5 min.).

65 Myogaya VEGETARIAN   Just a minute's walk east of the train station, this tiny shop sells health foods and offers vegetarian set meals from an English menu, which include side dishes such as brown rice, miso soup, salad, and pickles and offer a choice of such main dishes as potato croquette, deep-fried tofu, gyoza, and samosas. Drinks range from organic coffee to plum juice and wine made from organic grapes.

Hanasato-cho 5–15. ✆ **0557/32-0426.** Set meals ¥900–¥1,000 ($7.50–$8.35). No credit cards. Mon–Sat 11:30am–2pm and 5–7:30pm.

4 Rural Shirakawago & Ogimachi

555km (347 miles) NW of Tokyo

With its thatched-roof farmhouses, paddies trimmed with flower beds, roaring river, and pine-covered mountains rising on all sides, **Shirakawago** is one of the most picturesque regions in Japan. Admittedly, it has its share of tour buses (especially in May, Aug, and Oct), but because of its rather remote location and because it's accessible only by car or bus, Shirakawago still remains off the beaten path for most tourists. A visit to this rural region could well be the highlight of your trip.

Although Shirakawago stretches about 39km (24 miles) beside the Shokawa River and covers 142 square miles, mountains and forest account for 95% of the region, and Shirakawago's 2,000 residents and cultivated land are squeezed into a valley averaging less than 2 miles in width. Thus, land in Shirakawago for growing rice and other crops has always been scarce and valuable. As a result, farmhouses were built large enough to hold extended families, with as many as several dozen family members living under one roof. Because there wasn't enough land available for young couples to marry and build houses of their own, only the eldest son was allowed to marry; the other children were required to spend their lives living with their parents and helping with the farming. But even though younger children weren't allowed to marry, a man was allowed to choose a young woman, visit her in her parents' home, and father her children. The children then remained with the mother's family, becoming valuable members of the labor force.

Before the roads came to Shirakawago, winter always meant complete isolation as snow 6 feet deep blanketed the entire region. Open-hearth fireplaces (*irori*) in the middle of a communal room were commonplace. They were used both for cooking and for warmth, and because there were no chimneys, smoke simply rose into the levels above. The family lived on the ground floor, and the upper floors were used for silk cultivation and storage of utensils. Because of the heavy snowfall, thatched roofs were constructed at steep angles, known as *gassho-zukuri* in reference to the fact that the tops of the roofs look like hands joined in prayer. The steep angle also allowed rain to run off quickly, and the thatch (Japanese pampas grass) dried quickly in the sun, preventing decay.

Today, there are about 150 thatched farmhouses, barns, and sheds in Shirakawago, most of them built about 200 to 300 years ago. The thatched roofs are about 2 feet thick and last some 40 years. The old roofs are replaced in Shirakawago every April, when one to four roofs are replaced on successive weekends. The whole process involves about 200 people, who can replace one roof in a couple of days.

Shirakawago's inhabitants live in several small villages. Of these, the village of **Ogimachi** ★★★, declared a UNESCO World Cultural and Natural Heritage site in 1995, is the most important for visitors. With just 700 residents, it's a delightful hamlet of narrow lanes winding past thatched-roof farmhouses, which stand like island sentinels surrounded by paddies. Many of the farmhouses have been turned into minshuku, souvenir shops, restaurants, and museums, including an **open-air museum** that depicts life in the region before roads opened it up to the rest of the world.

ESSENTIALS

GETTING THERE   The most common way to reach Ojimachi is **by bus** from Takayama with a change of buses in Makido. The entire trip takes about 2 hours and costs ¥3,360 ($28). If you have a **JR Rail Pass,** you can use it between Makido and Ogimachi, in which case you'll need to buy a ticket only for the stretch between Takayama and Makido (¥1,930/$16). There are usually three departures from Takayama daily depending on the season; though buses run throughout the year, heavy winter snowfall sometimes renders the road impassable.

You can also reach Ogimachi from Nagoya via the **JR Tokai Bus** (your JR Rail Pass is valid for this, too); the fare is ¥4,760 ($40) one-way. Note, however, that buses operate only from the first Saturday in April through November. From Kanazawa, a bus operates daily from mid-March through November; fare for this is ¥1,800 ($15).

VISITOR INFORMATION   The **tourist office** (© 05769/6-1751 or 05769/6-1013; open Thurs–Tues 9am–5pm) is located beside a parking lot in the center of town. You can reserve a room in a minshuku here if you haven't already done so, and you can pick up a map in English. If you want to make the tourist office your very first stop upon arrival from Takayama, get off at the bus stop called Gassho-Shuraku; the tourist office is about a minute's walk away. There is another tourist office on the other side of the river near the Gassho-zukuri Minkaen (below) with the same open hours.

GETTING AROUND   Your own two feet can do it best. You can **walk** from one end of the village to the other in about 15 minutes, and throughout are English signs directing you to the various attractions.

SEEING THE SIGHTS IN & AROUND OGIMACHI

In addition to an open-air museum, several old farmhouses in Ogimachi are open to the public.

66 **Doburoku Matsuri no Yakata (Festival Hall)** ★★   Not far from Myozenji (below) is Festival Hall, erected in honor of the Doburoku Matsuri Festival held in Shirakawago every year from October 14 to 19. Centering on a locally produced, potent sake, the festival is held just outside the museum's grounds at Hachimanjinja Shrine. Any time of the year, you can come here to see some of the costumes worn during the festival and to try some of the festive sake. The highlight of the museum, however, is the 30-minute video that depicts Shirakawago through the seasons including heavy snowfall in winter, reroofing of thatched roofs, and the festival. It's in Japanese only, but I found it highly entertaining.

© 05769/6-1655. Admission ¥300 ($2.50) adults, ¥100 (85¢) junior-high and elementary students. Daily 9am–4pm. Closed Oct 14–15 and Dec–Mar.

Moments A View of Ogimachi

For an overview of the village, walk along the gently sloping road that leads from the north of Ogimachi to the **Shirayama Viewing Point** ★★. There's a restaurant up here, but the best thing to do is to turn left at the crest of the hill and walk to the hill's westernmost point (toward the river) where there are some secluded benches. From here, you'll have a marvelous view of the whole valley. If you're thirsty or hungry, go to the restaurant to buy a drink or a snack and then take it with you to the lookout.

Tips **A Note on Japanese Symbols**

Many hotels, restaurants, attractions, and other establishments in Japan do not have signs giving their names in Roman (English-language) letters. Appendix C lists the Japanese symbols for all such places described in this guide. Each set of characters representing an establishment name has a number in the appendix that corresponds to the number that appears inside the oval before the establishment's name in the text. Thus, to find the Japanese symbol for, say, the **Myozenji** museum (below), refer to no. 67 in appendix C.

---

(67) **Myozenji**   This 180-year-old thatched house displays farm equipment, straw raincoats, palanquins, and other relics of rural life in the Japan Alps. You can walk around upstairs and inspect the roof from the inside; if a fire is burning in the downstairs irori, you'll see how smoky the upstairs can get. On the ground floor, be sure to go straight down the hall to the attached main building of Myozenji Temple, which is more than 2 centuries old. You can tour the home in about 20 minutes.

© **05769/6-1009.** Admission ¥300 ($2.50) adults, ¥100 (85¢) children. Daily 9am–5pm (until 4pm in Winter). Closed when used by the owners.

(68) **Gasshozukuri Seikatsu Shiryokan** 🏵   This is the best museum in town for seeing farm and household implements and folkcrafts, including cooking utensils, lacquerware, pottery, and clothing. Note the bamboo pipe for bringing running water into the house, the Buddhist family altar, the samurai outfits, and photographs of the imperial family. The upstairs is crammed with all kinds of farming tools and items used in everyday life, from mountain backpacks and handmade skis to the wooden hammers used for pounding rice and implements for silk cultivation. Plan on 15 to 20 minutes here.

© **05769/6-1818.** Admission ¥300 ($2.50) adults, ¥150 ($1.25) children. Apr–Nov, daily 9am–5pm. Closed Dec–Mar. Located on the southern edge of town past the Jyuemon minshuku (see "Where to Stay," below).

Shirakawago Gassho Zukuri Minkaen 🏵🏵🏵   To see how rural people lived in centuries past, visit this open-air museum with 25 *gassho-zukuri* houses and sheds filled with the tools of everyday life. The museum also serves as an artist colony, with artisans engaged in such traditional handicrafts as woodworking, pottery, weaving, ink drawing, and straw basket- and hatmaking, with their products for sale on-site. The buildings are picturesquely situated around ponds, paddies, flowerbeds, and streams, a photographer's dream. You can easily spend an hour here.

© **05769/6-1231.** Admission ¥700 ($5.85) adults, ¥300 ($2.50) children 7–15. Apr–July and Sept–Nov, daily 8:40am–5pm; Aug, daily 8am–6pm; Dec–Mar, Fri–Wed 9am–4pm. If Thurs is a national holiday, the museum remains open but closes Wed instead. Across the Shokawa River from Ogimachi, over a pedestrian suspension bridge.

(69) **Wada Ke** 🏵   This thatched-roof home is as fine as any you'll find in Takayama, not surprising since it belonged to the wealthy Wada family who served as the region's top officials. Still occupied by the Wada family, the 300-year-old house boasts carved transoms, painted sliding doors, lacquerware passed down through generations, and tatami rooms overlooking a private

garden. Upstairs you can see how the heavy roof beams are held together using only rope.

ⓒ **05769/6-1058.** Admission ¥300 ($2.50) adults, ¥150 ($1.25) children. Daily 9am–5pm. Closed sometimes. Just north of the main street.

WHERE TO STAY

Because huge extended families living under one roof are a thing of the past, many residents of Ogimachi have turned their gassho-zukuri homes into minshuku. Staying in one gives you the unique chance to lodge in a thatched farmhouse with a family that might consist of grandparents, parents, and children. English is limited to the basics of "bath," "breakfast," and "dinner," but smiles go a long way. Most likely, the family will drag out their family album with its pictures of winter snowfall and the momentous occasion when their thatched roof was repaired. What I like best about staying overnight in Ogimachi is that most Japanese tourists are day-trippers, which means you have the village pretty much to yourself after late afternoon. Be sure to take an evening or early-morning stroll.

Most minshuku are fairly small with about four to nine tatami rooms open to guests. Rooms are basic without bathroom or toilet (the communal toilets are sometimes nonflush style), and you're expected to roll out your own futon. Privacy may be limited, as only a flimsy sliding partition may separate you from the guest next door. In addition, note that you will be awakened at 7am when a public address system connected to speakers in all these farmhouses announces daily activities for senior citizens and weather reports. All recommended minshuku below are in thatch-roofed homes; rates include breakfast and dinner (add ¥300/$2.50 in winter for heating charges), and none accept credit cards or have private bathrooms. The tourist office can make a reservation for you at these or any of the others around town.

⑦⓪ **Furusato** ⍟   With lanterns hanging off its eaves, many flowers and shrubs, and antiques, this is one of the more attractively decorated minshuku in Ogimachi. Another plus are the meals, all made from scratch.

Shirakawa Mura, Ogimachi, Ono-gun, Gifu 501-5627. ⓒ **05769/6-1003.** 4 units (none with bathroom). ¥8,000 ($67) per person. Bus: to Jinja-mae stop. *In room:* hot-water pot with tea.

⑦① **Jyuemon** ⍟⍟   Jyuemon is a favorite among foreigners traveling in Japan. This attractive minshuku, in a 270-year-old farmhouse, features a stone-ringed pond with flowering shrubs and a couple of benches where you can relax and enjoy the view. In addition, there's an irori in the dining room, and the recently remodeled bathroom facilities feature flush toilets. The outgoing Mrs. Sakai who runs this place is quite a character; she sometimes serenades guests with a *shamisen.*

Shirakawa Mura, Ogimachi, Ono-gun, Gifu 501-5627. ⓒ **05769/6-1053.** 6 units. ¥8,000 ($76) per person. Bus: to Jinja-mae stop; on the south edge of Ogimachi near Doburoku Festival Hall.

⑦② **Nodaniya** ⍟⍟   Life in this minshuku centers around the irori, where you dine on what Janie, my coauthor, considers to be some of the best food she's ever had in a minshuku. The family is very friendly and the minshuku provides flush toilets and a communal cedar wood bath.

Shirakawa Mura, Ogimachi, Ono-gun, Gifu 501-5627. ⓒ **05769/6-1011.** 5 units. ¥7,700 ($64) per person. Bus: to Jinja-mae stop; across from Hachimanjinja Shrine.

WHERE TO DINE

Since all minshuku and ryokan serve breakfast and dinner, you'll only need to find a place for lunch.

⑦ **Irori** LOCAL SPECIALTIES   A huge block of gnarled wood sets outside Irori's front door. Inside, this gassho-zukuri house is appropriately rustic and has an irori. The menu, in Japanese only, includes fresh river fish (*ayu*), wild mountain vegetables (*sansai*), *hoba miso* (soybean paste cooked on a magnolia leaf over a small clay pot), and sansai soba. I opted for the yakidofu teishoku set meal, which consisted of fried tofu covered with fish flakes, vegetables, rice, and soup.

ⓒ**05769/6-1737.** Set meals ¥1,200–¥2,000 ($10–$17). No credit cards. Wed–Mon 9am–5pm. On Ogimachi's main road, a 3-min. walk from the main tourist office (in the direction of the Shirayama Viewing Point) and across from a gas station.

7

Kyoto & Nara

If you go to only one place in all of Japan, **Kyoto** ✿✿✿ should be it. Not only is it the most historically significant town in the nation, this former capital was also the only major Japanese city spared from the bombs of World War II. As such, it's rife with temples, shrines, imperial palaces, and traditional wooden homes. In nearby **Nara** ✿✿, another former capital—one even more ancient than Kyoto—is Japan's largest bronze Buddha and more historic temples.

Even though its well-preserved architecture and relics are what put Kyoto on the sightseeing map, I've always felt that its scenes from daily life are what make the city exceptional. As you walk its narrow streets and along its tiny canals, you'll be struck with images of yesterday. An old woman in kimono bent over her "garden," a couple of gnarled bonsai beside her front door. An open-fronted shop where a man makes tatami, the musty smell of the rice mats reminiscent of earth itself. A geisha shuffling to her evening appointment in Gion, where the sounds of laughter and traditional Japanese music waft past shoji screens and down the narrow alleyways. Couples enjoying a warm summer evening on the banks of the Kamo River, which cuts through the heart of the city. And spread throughout, an incredible 1,700 Buddhist temples and 300 Shinto shrines. Kyoto is home to 20% of Japan's national treasures.

As your Shinkansen bullet train glides toward Kyoto Station, however, your first reaction is likely to be one of great disappointment. There's Kyoto Tower looming in the foreground like some misplaced spaceship. Kyoto Station itself is strikingly modern and unabashedly high tech, looking as though it was airlifted straight from Tokyo. Modern buildings and hotels surround the station on all sides, making Kyoto look like any other Japanese town.

In other words, as Japan's seventh-largest city with a population of about 1½ million people, Kyoto hasn't escaped the afflictions of the modern age. Yet it has always led a rather fragile existence, as a look at any of its temples and shrines will tell you. Made of wood, they've been destroyed through the years by man, fire, and earthquake and have been rebuilt countless times. Come and explore—you'll soon understand why I consider Kyoto to be Japan's most romantic city despite modernization. No one who comes to this country should miss the wealth of experiences this ancient capital has to offer.

A LOOK AT THE PAST Kyoto served as Japan's capital for more than 1,000 years from 794 to the Meiji Restoration in 1868. Originally known as Heian-kyo, it was laid out in a grid pattern borrowed from the Chinese with streets running north, south, east, and west. Its first few hundred years—from about 800 A.D. to the 12th century—were perhaps its grandest, a time when culture blossomed and court nobility led luxurious and splendid lives dotted with poetry-composing parties and moon-gazing events. Buddhism flourished and temples were built. A number of learning institutions were set up for the sons and daughters of aristocratic families, and scholars were versed in both Japanese and Chinese.

Toward the end of the Heian Period, military clans began clashing for power as the samurai class grew more powerful, resulting in a series of civil wars that eventually pushed Japan into the Feudal Era of military government that lasted nearly 680 years—until 1868. The first shogun to rise to power was Minamoto Yoritomo, who set up his shogunate government in Kamakura. With the downfall of the Kamakura government in 1336, however, Kyoto once again became the seat of power. The beginning of this era, known as the Muromachi and Azuchi-Momoyama periods, was marked by extravagant prosperity and luxury, expressed in such splendid shogun villas as Kyoto's

Gold Pavilion and Silver Pavilion. Lacquerware, landscape paintings, and the art of metal engraving came into their own. Zen Buddhism was the rage, giving rise to such temples as Saihoji Temple and the Ryoanji rock garden. And despite the civil wars that rocked the nation in the 15th and 16th centuries and destroyed much of Kyoto, culture flourished. During these turbulent times, Noh drama, the tea ceremony, flower arranging, and landscape gardening gradually took form.

Emerging as victor in the civil wars, Tokugawa Ieyasu established himself as shogun and set up his military rule in Edo (presently Tokyo) far to the east. For the next 250 years, Kyoto remained the capital in name only, and in 1868 (which marked the downfall of the shogunate and the restoration of the emperor to power), the capital was officially moved from Kyoto to Tokyo.

1 Orientation

GETTING THERE

FROM KANSAI AIRPORT If you're arriving in Japan at Kansai International Airport (KIX) outside Osaka, **the JR Haruka Limited Express train** has direct service every 30 minutes to Kyoto Station; the trip takes approximately 75 minutes. It costs ¥3,490 ($29) for a reserved seat (recommended during busy departure times or peak season) and ¥2,980 ($25) for a nonreserved seat, or you can ride free with your JR Rail Pass. A cheaper (¥1,830/$15), though less convenient, alternative is the **JR Kanku Kaisoku,** which departs every 30 minutes or so from Kansai Airport and arrives in Kyoto 90 to 110 minutes later with a change at Osaka Station.

If you have a lot of luggage, I recommend taking the **Airport Limousine Bus** (© 075/682-4400) from Kansai Airport; buses depart every hour or less for the 105-minute trip to Kyoto Station. Fare is ¥2,300 ($19) one-way.

BY TRAIN FROM ELSEWHERE IN JAPAN Kyoto is one of the major stops on the Shinkansen bullet train; trip time from **Tokyo** is 2½ hours. The fare for a nonreserved seat is ¥12,710 ($106) one-way if you don't have a rail pass. Kyoto is only 20 minutes from Shin-Osaka Station in **Osaka,** but you may find it more convenient to take one of the local commuter lines that connect Kyoto directly with Osaka Station. From **Kobe,** you can reach Kyoto from Sannomiya and Motomachi stations. **Kyoto Station,** which is like a city in itself with tourist offices, restaurants, a hotel, department store, shopping arcade, art gallery, theater, and stage events, is connected to the rest of the city by subway and bus.

Frommer's Favorite Kyoto Experiences

Spending a Night in a Ryokan. Kyoto is one of the best places in Japan to experience the traditional inn, where you'll sleep on a futon in a tatami room and be treated to a beautifully presented multicourse kaiseki feast. Though expensive, it's the utmost in simple elegance.

Dining on a Tofu Vegetarian Meal in a Garden Setting. *Shojin ryori,* vegetarian meals served at Buddhist temples, are one of Kyoto's specialties. There are a number of rustic restaurants with outdoor garden seating.

Visiting a Japanese Garden. Kyoto has a wide range of traditional gardens, from austerely beautiful Zen rock gardens used by Buddhist priests for meditation to the miniature bonzai-like landscape gardens of the ruling classes.

Strolling Through Eastern Kyoto. Temples, shrines, gardens, shops, traditional neighborhoods—these are highlights of a day spent walking through this historic part of Kyoto. A slice of old Japan that you won't find in other Japanese cities.

Shopping for Traditional Crafts. Traditional arts and crafts thrive in Kyoto, where skills are passed down from generation to generation. You'll find small specialty shops selling everything from fans to wooden combs.

Seeing How the Upper Class Lived. Kyoto has more imperial palaces and villas than any other Japanese city. Walk through the shogun's digs at Nijo Castle, and if you have time, visit the Kyoto Imperial Palace, Katsura Imperial Villa, or Shugakuin Imperial Villa with their splendid gardens.

Exploring Gion. Kyoto's traditional pleasure quarter is fascinating for its austere architecture, hushed atmosphere, and the sight of heavily made-up geishas in traditional kimono hurrying to their evening appointments. Get an insider's look at this world at Gion Corner, where you can see performances of traditional dance, puppetry, and other cultural presentations.

Watching Cormorant Fishing Along the Oi River. There's no more romantic way to spend a summer's evening than drifting down the river in a wooden boat decorated with paper lanterns, watching the fishermen and their cormorants at work. Simply magical.

Taking an Evening Stroll Through Pontocho. A small, narrow pedestrian lane, Pontocho is lined with a dazzling collection of brightly lit hostess bars, restaurants, and drinking establishments. If it's a warm night, finish by sitting for a while along the banks of the nearby Kamo River, a popular spot for Kyoto's young couples.

BY BUS FROM TOKYO There are night buses that depart from Tokyo every evening for Kyoto, arriving the next morning; the fare is ¥8,180 ($68) one-way or ¥14,480 ($121) round-trip. Buses depart from Tokyo Station at both 10 and 10:50pm, arriving in Kyoto at 6 and 6:50am respectively, and from Shinjuku

Station at 11:10 and 11:50pm, arriving in Kyoto at 6:20am and 7am. Contact the **Tourist Information Center (TIC)** in Tokyo for more information (see "Visitor Information," in chapter 3).

VISITOR INFORMATION

Kyoto Station has two tourist-information facilities that provide maps and pamphlets and can direct you to your hotel. On the south side of the station, near the Hachijo exit and the terminus for the Shinkansen bullet train, is the **JR Tourist Office** (℃ 075/691-1000), staffed with English-speaking volunteers daily from 10am to 4pm. Bigger and better equipped is the **Kyoto City Tourist Information Office** (℃ 075/343-6656), located on the opposite (north) side of the station but up on the second floor near the pedestrian passage that runs through the building. It's open daily from 8:30am to 7pm.

Although these two facilities can provide you with basic information about Kyoto, the best place for information not only about Kyoto but about the rest of Japan is the **Tourist Information Center (TIC),** a minute's walk from Kyoto Station's north side (take the Karasuma exit out of Kyoto Station). It's located on the ground floor of the **Kyoto Tower Building,** the one topped by what looks like a spaceship (℃ 075/371-5649); the entrance is around the corner on Kara-suma Dori. It's open Monday through Friday from 9am to 5pm and Saturday from 9am to noon, and the staff speaks excellent English. On weekdays, you can also make reservations here for inexpensive lodging throughout Japan free of charge.

ON THE WEB   Check out the city's websites at www.city.kyoto.jp/ sankan/kankoshinko/visitor/index.html and raku.city.kyoto.jp/sight.html.

TOURIST PUBLICATIONS   In addition to the brochures and leaflets distributed by the TIC and Kyoto City Tourist Information offices, a monthly tabloid distributed free at hotels and restaurants is the *Kyoto Visitor's Guide,* which contains maps, a calendar of events, and information on sightseeing and shopping. In addition, a monthly English magazine, *Kansai Time Out,* carries information and articles on Kyoto, Osaka, and Nara. It's available in Kyoto for ¥300 ($2.50) at Maruzen bookstore, located in the heart of Kyoto on Kawara-machi Dori just north of Kawaramachi-Shijo Dori (℃ 075/241-2169; open daily 10am–8pm, closed 3rd Wed of every month).

CITY LAYOUT

Most of Kyoto's attractions and hotels are north of Kyoto Station (take the Kara-suma exit), spreading like a fan toward the northeast and northwest. The **northern and eastern edges** of the city contain the most famous temples. The largest concentration of restaurants, shops, and bars is in **Central Kyoto,** which radiates outward from the intersection of Kawaramachi Dori and Shijo Dori. It includes a narrow street called Pontocho, a nightlife mecca that runs along the western bank of the Kamo River, and the ancient geisha district of Gion.

FINDING AN ADDRESS   Kyoto's streets are laid out in a grid pattern with named streets and an address system that's actually quite easy to understand once you get to know the directional terms. Streets north of Kyoto Station that run east-west are numbered; for example, the *shi* of Shijo Dori means "Fourth Avenue." *Agaru* means "to the north," *sagaru* means "to the south," *nishi-iru* means "to the west," and *higashi-iru* means "to the east." Thus, an address that reads Shijo-agaru means "north of Fourth Avenue."

Many addresses also indicate which cross streets a building is near. Take the Hotel Gimmond, for example: Its address is Takakura Oike Dori, which tells you that the hotel is near the intersection of Takakura Dori and Oike Dori. Complete addresses include the ward, or *ku*, such as Higashiyama-ku.

KYOTO'S NEIGHBORHOODS IN BRIEF

The following are Kyoto's main tourist areas; to locate them, see the "Where to Stay in Kyoto" map on p. 282.

Around Kyoto Station The southern ward of **Shimogyo-ku,** which stretches from Kyoto Station north to Shijo Dori Avenue, caters to tourists with its cluster of hotels and to commuters with its shops and restaurants. Kyoto Station, which caused quite a controversy when built because of its size, height, and futuristic appearance, is now this area's top attraction with Isetan department store, a shopping arcade, restaurants, a cinema, a theater, an art gallery, and dramatic public spaces, including a rooftop plaza.

Central Kyoto The central part of Kyoto west of the Kamo River and north of Shimogyo-ku, **Nakagyo-ku** embraces Kyoto's main shopping and nightlife districts with most of the action on **Kawaramachi** and **Shijo Dori** avenues. In addition to its many shopping arcades, restaurants, and bars, Nakagyo-ku also has a number of exclusive ryokan tucked away in delightful neighborhoods typical of old Kyoto, and it is home to Nijo Castle. Nakagyo-ku is one of the most desirable places to stay in terms of convenience and atmosphere.

Pontocho, a narrow lane that parallels the Kamo River's western bank not far from the Kawaramachi-Shijo Dori intersection, is Kyoto's most famous street for nightlife. It's lined with exclusive hostess clubs, bars, and restaurants that boast outdoor verandas that extend over the Kamo River.

Eastern Kyoto East of the Kamo River, the wards of **Higashiyamaku** and **Sakyo-ku** boast a number of the city's most famous temples and shrines, as well as a number of restaurants specializing in Kyoto cuisine and Buddhist vegetarian dishes and shops selling local pottery and other crafts. Eastern Kyoto is a great area for walking and shopping, particularly Higashiyama-ku, and boasts several ryokan as well.

Gion, Kyoto's most famous geisha entertainment district, is part of Higashiyama-ku. Customers are entertained in traditional wooden geisha houses that are not open to the public—but the area makes for a fascinating stroll.

Northern Kyoto Embracing the **Kita-ku, Kamigyo-ku,** and **Ukyoku** wards, northern Kyoto is primarly residential but contains a number of Kyoto's top sights, including the Kyoto Imperial Palace, Kinkakuji (Temple of the Golden Pavilion), and Ryoanji Temple, home to Kyoto's most famous Zen rock garden.

2 Getting Around

BY PUBLIC TRANSPORTATION Kyoto has subway and bus networks that are efficient and quite easy to use, but one of the best ways to explore is by foot.

By Subway Kyoto is growing by leaps and bounds—there are now two subway lines. The older **Karasuma Line** runs north and south, from Takeda in the south to Kokusai Kaikan in the north, with stops at Kyoto Station and Imadegawa

Station (convenient for visiting the Imperial Palace). The newer **Tozai Line** runs in a curve from east to west and is convenient for visiting Nijo Castle and Higashiyama-ku. The subway lines intersect in Central Kyoto at Karasuma Oike Station. Fares start at ¥200 ($1.65), and service runs from 5:30am to about 11:30pm. Although buses are generally more convenient (they usually get you closer to where you want to go), I sometimes opt for the subway even if I have to walk a bit, simply to avoid hassling with buses and unknown stops.

By Bus   The easiest way to get around Kyoto and to most of its attractions is by bus. Buses depart from Kyoto Station's north (Karasuma) exit. The TIC and Kyoto City Tourist Information Office give out a city map showing major bus routes (see "Visitor Information," above). Some of the buses travel in a loop around the city, while others go back and forth between two destinations. For tourists, old-fashioned buses nicknamed the **Chin-Chin** bus (bus no. 100) make runs every 30 minutes from Kyoto Station with stops in central and east Kyoto that are convenient to major attractions, including Kyoto National Museum, Gojo-zaka, Gion, and Nanzenji. Chin-Chin buses depart Kyoto Station on the hour and half hour from 8am to 4pm; the fare is the same as for other local buses: ¥220 ($1.85) for a single fare or ¥500 ($4.15) for a one-day pass (good for all local buses). Chin-Chin bus no. 101 travels a different route from Kyoto Station northward to Nijo Castle, the Temple of the Golden Pavilion, and beyond.

Board the bus at the rear entrance. If the bus is traveling a **long distance** out to the suburbs, there will be a ticket machine right beside the back door—take the ticket and hold on to it. It has a number on it and will tell the bus driver when you got on and how much you owe. You can see for yourself how much you owe by looking for your number on a lighted panel at the front of the bus; the longer you stay on the bus, the higher the fare.

If you're on a **local loop bus,** however, the fare is the same no matter how long you stay on—¥220 ($1.85)—and you pay when you get off. Exact fare is required, which you drop into the machine box next to the driver. There's also a change machine for ¥500 coins and ¥1,000 bills next to the driver; after getting your change, drop the fare into the box. There are no transfer tickets, so you have to pay separately for each ride.

TRANSIT PASSES   If you think you'll be doing a lot of sightseeing in 1 or 2 days, it may pay to buy a pass. A **day pass** for buses only costs ¥500 ($4.15); a day pass for both buses and subways costs ¥1,200 ($10). A **2-day pass** valid for both buses and subways costs ¥2,000 ($17). You can purchase passes at subway stations, the city bus center at Kyoto Station, and major hotels. Finally, there are also **prepaid cards** that come in different values and can be used for the subway and most city buses. Because there is no time limit, they're convenient if you're staying in Kyoto for several days.

BY TAXI   Taxis in Kyoto come in two different sizes with only slightly different fares. Small ones are ¥580 ($4.85) for the first 2km (1¼ miles), and large ones are ¥660 ($5.50). Taxis can be waved down or, in the city center, boarded at marked taxi stands or at hotels. **MK Taxi** (© 075/721-2237) has the cheapest fares and also offers individualized guided tours in English.

BY BICYCLE   A popular way to get around Kyoto is by bike, made easy because there are few hills and most streets are named. You do, however, have to be on guard for vehicular traffic. **Muji's Rent-a-cycle** (© 075/353-7711), located just north of Kyoto Station in the Kintetsu department store, rents bicycles for ¥1,000 ($8.35) a day. It's open daily 10am to 6pm.

FAST FACTS: **Kyoto**

Area Code If you're calling a Kyoto number from outside Kyoto but within Japan, the area code for Kyoto is **075**. For details on calling Kyoto from outside Japan, see "Telephone & Fax," in "Fast Facts: Japan," in chapter 2.

Business Hours **Banks** are open Monday through Friday from 9am to 3pm; one with longer hours is the **High Touch Plaza** of the Kyoto Shinkin Bank on Shijo Dori, Yanaginobanba, Shimogyo-ku (© **075/255-3646**), open Thursday through Tuesday from 10am to 5pm including holidays. **Department stores** stay open from 10am to 7:30pm, while smaller **shops** in the downtown area remain open from about 10am to 8pm.

Climate Kyoto is generally hotter and more humid than Tokyo in summer and colder than Tokyo in winter. For more information, see "When to Go," in chapter 2.

Currency Exchange In addition to banks, a good place to exchange money after banks close is at large department stores like Isetan, Takashimaya, Daimaru, and Kintetsu. When changing money, be sure to bring your passport.

In addition to ATMs located at post offices (see "Post Offices," below), there are cash machines in Central Kyoto at the **All Card Plaza,** on the west side of Teramachi Street just north of Shijo Dori.

Dentists & Doctors The **Tourist Information Center** (© 075/371-5649) has a list of about a half-dozen dentists and about a dozen doctors who speak English. If the TIC is closed or you'd rather talk to a doctor directly, call **Dr. Sakabe,** Gokomachi, Nijo-sagaru, Nakagyo-ku (© 075/231-1624), an internist who speaks excellent English; he can refer you to other doctors as well.

Electricity In both Kyoto and Nara it's 100 volts, 60 cycles, almost the same as in the United States (110 volts, 60 cycles); your two-pronged appliances should work, but they'll run a little slowly (there are no three-pronged plugs in Japan).

Emergencies The national emergency numbers are © **110** for police and © **119** for ambulance and fire.

Hospitals Most hospitals are not equipped to handle emergencies 24 hours a day, but a system has been set up in which hospitals handle emergencies on a rotating basis. If you go by ambulance, it must take you to one of these: The **Kyoto Second Red Cross Hospital (Daini Sekijuji Byoin),** Marutamachi-sagaru, Kamanza Dori, Kamikyo-ku (© 075/231-5171), is staffed 24 hours a day, but a referral by a doctor who knows your problem is expected. English is spoken at **Japan Baptist Hospital (Nihon Baputesuto Byoin),** 47 Yamanomoto-cho, Kitashirakawa, Sakyo-ku (© 075/781-5191). Also in Kyoto are **Kyoto University Hospital (Kyoto Daigaku Byoin),** Shogoin Kawahara-cho, Sakyo-ku (© 075/751-3111), and **Kyoto Municipal Hospital (Kyoto Shiritsu Byoin),** Gojo Dori Onmae, Nakagyo-ku (© 075/311-5311). There's also a **holiday emergency clinic** on Shichihonmatsu Street, north of Marutamachi (© 075/811-5072).

Internet Access **Aspirin,** in Central Kyoto on the west side of the Teramachi covered shopping arcade just north of a pachinko parlor on the third floor (© **075/251-2351**), is an Internet cafe open daily 10am to 9pm (to 11pm on Fri). It charges either ¥100 (85¢) for the first 10 minutes and ¥50 (42¢) for each 5 minutes after that or ¥500 ($4.15) per hour. There is a ¥100 (85¢) charge for non-members.

Lost Property   If you leave something on the **Shinkansen bullet train,** call © **075/691-1000** to see whether it has been found. Items lost at **Kyoto Station** are turned in to the lost-and-found office (© **075/371-0134**). If you lost something along a street or outside, contact the **Shichijo Police Station** (© **075/371-2111**). **Taxi Kyodo Center** (© **075/672-1110**) handles lost and found for all taxi companies. If you're still having problems, the **TIC** suggests that you visit their office.

Luggage Storage/Lockers   Kyoto Station has lockers for storing luggage beginning at ¥300 ($2.50) for 24 hours, including lockers large enough for big suitcases on its south (Shinkansen) side.

Police   The national emergency telephone number is © **110.**

Post Offices   The **Kyoto Central Post Office,** located just west of Kyoto Station's Karasuma (north) exit (© **075/365-2471**), has ATM machines for cards operating on the Cirrus or Plus systems and is open Monday to Friday 9am to 7pm, Saturday 9am to 5pm, Sunday and holidays 9am to 12:30pm. You can mail packages bound for international destinations here. To the south of the Central Post Office's main entrance is a counter offering 24-hour service (but not for packages or currency exchange); stamps for letters are sold from vending machines. The **Nakagyo-ku Post Office,** at Sanjo and Higashinotoin streets in Central Kyoto, also with an ATM, is open Monday to Friday 9am to 7pm and Saturday 9am to 3pm.

Taxes   See "Fast Facts: Japan," in chapter 2.

3 Where to Stay in Kyoto

If you've never stayed in a **ryokan,** Kyoto is probably the best place to do so. With the exception of hot-spring resorts, Kyoto has more choices of ryokan in all price categories than any other city in Japan. Small, usually made of wood, and often situated in delightfully quaint neighborhoods, these ryokan can enrich your stay in Kyoto by putting you in direct touch with the city's traditional past. Remember that in upper- and medium-priced ryokan, the room charge is per person, and though the prices may seem prohibitive at first glance, they do include two meals and usually a service charge. These meals are feasts, not unlike kaiseki meals you'd receive at a top restaurant where they could easily cost ¥10,000 ($90). Ryokan in the budget category, on the other hand, usually don't serve meals unless stated otherwise, and they often charge per room rather than per person.

Kyoto also has excellent choices in all price ranges for those who decide to stay in a hotel (many hotels have Japanese-style rooms available in addition to Western-style rooms). Whichever type of accommodation you select, be sure to make reservations in advance, particularly in July and August, since Kyoto is a favorite holiday destination for the Japanese.

Because Kyoto is relatively small and has such good bus and subway systems, no matter where you stay you won't be too far away from the heart of the city (I've included transportation information for each establishment, followed in

Where to Stay in Kyoto

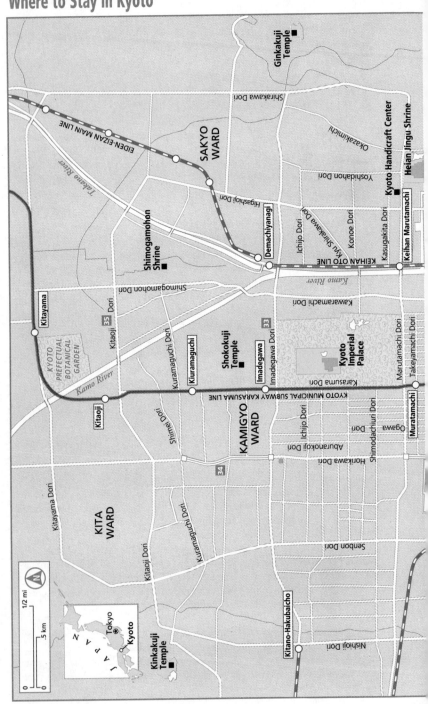

Ginkakuji Temple

Shirakawa Dori

SAKYO WARD

EIDEN-EIZAN MAIN LINE

Takano River

Kyoto Handicraft Center

Heian Jingu Shrine

Okazakimichi

Yoshidahon Dori

Higashioji Dori

Kyu Shirakawa Dori

Konoe Dori

Kasugakita Dori

Keihan Marutamachi

Demachiyanagi

Ichijo Dori

KEIHAN OTO LINE

Shimogamohon Shrine

Kitayama

Shimogamohon Dori

Kamo River

Kawaramachi Dori

Marutamachi Dori

Takeyamachi Dori

KYOTO PREFECTUAL BOTANICAL GARDEN

Kamo River

Kitaoji Dori

35

Kuramaguchi Dori

Kuramaguchi

Shokokuji Temple

Imadegawa

33

Imadegawa Dori

Kyoto Imperial Palace

Kitayama Dori

Kitaoji

Shimei Dori

Karasuma Dori

Muratamachi

KYOTO MUNICIPAL SUBWAY KARASUMA LINE

Ichijo Dori

Ichijo Dori

Aburanokoji Dori

Shimodachiuri Dori

Ogawa Dori

KAMIGYO WARD

Horikawa Dori

34

KITA WARD

Kuramaguchi Dori

Kitayama Dori

Kitaoji Dori

Senbon Dori

Nishioji Dori

Kitano-Hakubaicho

1/2 mi

.5 km

N

JAPAN

Tokyo

Kyoto

Kinkakuji Temple

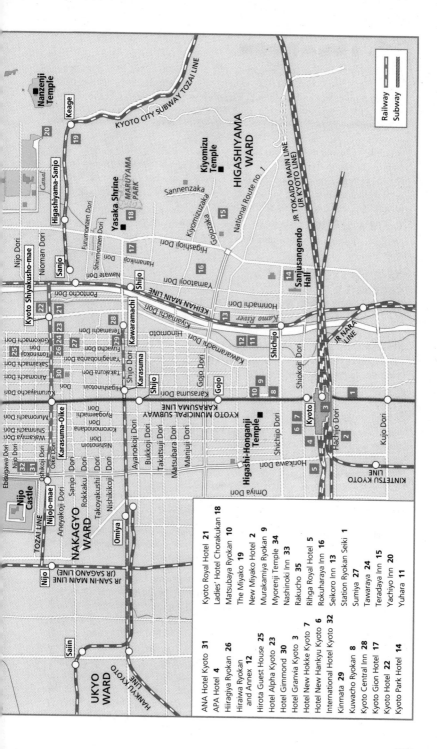

Railway
Subway

Nanzenji Temple
Keage
20
19
KYOTO CITY SUBWAY TOZAI LINE
Canal
Higashiyama-Sanjo
Nijo Dori
Nioman Dori
Sanjo
Furumonzen Dori
Shinmonzen Dori
MARUYAMA PARK
Yasaka Shrine
18
Sannenzaka
Kiyomizuzaka
Gojozaka
Kiyomizu Temple
15
HIGASHIYAMA WARD
National Route no. 1
JR TOKAIDO MAIN LINE (JR KYOTO LINE)
Hanamikoji Dori
Nawate Dori
17
Higashioji Dori
Shijo
22
21
Pontocho Dori
KEIHAN MAIN LINE
Kawaramachi
16
Yamatooji Dori
Sanjusangendo Hall
14
Hommachi Dori
Kamo River
28
Teramachi Dori
13
Kiyamachi Dori
Hinomoto
Kawaramachi Dori
23
24
26
27
29
Fuyacho Dori
Yanagibanba Dori
Takakura Dori
Higashinotoin Dori
Shichijo
12
11
JR NARA LINE
Gokomachi Dori
Tominokoji Dori
25
30
Karasuma
Shijo
Shijo Dori
Gojo Dori
Gojo
9
Shiokoji Dori
Karasuma Dori
Kurumayacho Dori
Sakaimachi Dori
Ainomachi Dori
Muromachi Dori
Shinmachi Dori
Wakamiya Dori
Koromonodana Dori
Nishinotoin Dori
Ayanokoji Dori
Bukkoji Dori
Takatsuji Dori
Matsubara Dori
Manjuji Dori
KYOTO MUNICIPAL SUBWAY KARASUMA LINE
Higashi-Honganji Temple
Karasuma-Oike
Oike Dori
Aneyakoji Dori
Sanjo Dori
Rokkaku Dori
Takoyakushi Dori
Nishikikoji Dori
Shichijo Dori
10
8
7
Kyoto
6
5
4
3
2
1
Hachijo Dori
Kujo Dori
Horikawa Dori
Omiya Dori
KINTETSU KYOTO LINE
Shijo
Omiya
Nijojo-mae
Nijo Castle
NAKAGYO WARD
Ebisugawa Dori
Nijo Dori
Oshikoji Dori
32
31
TOZAI LINE
Nijo
JR SAN-IN MAIN LINE (JR SAGANO LINE)
Saiin
HANKYU KYOTO LINE
UKYO WARD

ANA Hotel Kyoto **31**
APA Hotel **4**
Hiiragiya Ryokan **26**
Hiraiwa Ryokan and Annex **12**
Hirota Guest House **25**
Hotel Alpha Kyoto **23**
Hotel Gimmond **30**
Hotel Granvia Kyoto **3**
Hotel New Hokke Kyoto **6**
Hotel New Hankyu Kyoto **32**
International Hotel Kyoto **32**
Kinmata **29**
Kuwacho Ryokan **8**
Kyoto Central Inn **28**
Kyoto Gion Hotel **17**
Kyoto Hotel **22**
Kyoto Park Hotel **14**

Kyoto Royal Hotel **21**
Ladies' Hotel Chorakukan **18**
Matsubaya Ryokan **10**
The Miyako **19**
New Miyako Hotel **2**
Murakamiya Ryokan **9**
Myorenji Temple **34**
Nashinoki Inn **33**
Rakucho **35**
Rihga Royal Hotel **5**
Rokuharaya Inn **16**
Seikoro Inn **13**
Station Ryokan Seiki **1**
Sumiya **27**
Tawaraya **24**
Teradaya Inn **15**
Yachiyo Inn **20**
Yuhara **11**

283

Tips **A Note on Directions**

For all hotel, restaurant, and other listings in this chapter, directions provided are from Kyoto Station unless otherwise indicated. Numbers in parentheses after stations and bus stops refer to the time it takes to reach your destination on foot after alighting from public conveyance.

---

parentheses by the number of minutes it takes to walk from the subway or bus stop to the accommodation). Most hotels and ryokan are concentrated around Kyoto Station (Shimogyo-ku Ward), in Central Kyoto not far from the Kawaramachi-Shijo Dori intersection (Nakagyo-ku Ward), and east of the Kamo River (in the Higashiyama-ku and Sakyo-ku wards).

TAXES & SERVICE CHARGES   Remember, hotels levy a 5% tax on room rates. In addition, medium- and upper-range hotels add a 10% to 15% service charge.

AROUND KYOTO STATION
EXPENSIVE

Hotel Granvia Kyoto ★★   Opened in 1997 and owned by the Japan Railways group, this hotel boasts Kyoto's most convenient location for travelers arriving by train: It's right atop the new, futuristic-looking Kyoto Station. Only a minute's walk from city buses and trains, it's a great base for exploring Kyoto, Nara, and beyond. Thankfully, the hotel lobby is on the second floor, removed from the foot traffic of the station, and excellent insulation contributes to the tranquility. A very good guest-relations desk can help with everything from sightseeing to restaurant reservations, and although there's no business center, behind the guest-relations desk is a workstation and computer with free Internet access for hotel guests. Modern rooms are furnished with sleek, black furniture and have extensive bathroom counter space. If you can, avoid the least expensive rooms—they have rather unexciting views of the station's glass roof.

657 Higashi Shiokoji-cho, Karasuma Dori Shiokoji-sagaru, Shimogyo-ku, Kyoto 600-8216. ⓒ **075/344-8888.** Fax 075/334-4400. http://www.granvia-kyoto.co.jp/index2.html. 539 units. ¥14,000–¥24,000 ($117–$200) single; ¥18,000–¥28,000 ($150–$233) double; ¥20,000–¥30,000 ($167–$250) twin. Executive units from ¥25,000 ($208) single, ¥29,000 ($242) double, ¥33,000 ($275) twin. AE, DC, JCB, MC, V. Above Kyoto Station. **Amenities:** 12 restaurants, 2 bars; health club with indoor swimming pool, fitness gym, and sauna (fee: ¥1,000/$8.35); concierge; shopping arcade (in same building); salon; room service (6am–midnight); in-room massage; same-day laundry/dry cleaning service; nonsmoking rooms; executive level rooms. *In room:* A/C, bilingual cable TV, dataport, minibar, hot-water pot with tea, hair dryer, washlet toilet.

New Miyako Hotel ★   With the Miyako name behind it (it's a sister hotel to the famous Miyako in eastern Kyoto), this is one of the most popular hotels near Kyoto Station due in part to its convenient location near the terminus of both the Shinkansen and Kintetsu trains (the city bus terminus, however, is a 5-min. walk away on the other side of Kyoto Station). Opened in 1975 and recently updated and renovated, it has a nonfussy, almost Spartan lobby and rooms that vary in price according to floor and size, though the view is nothing special (children may like rooms facing the front, so they see the *Shinkansen* trains arrive) and even the standard rooms are of adequate size. A plus to staying here is the free shuttle to the Miyako, which is near the many temples of eastern Kyoto. I also like the rooftop summer beer garden.

Hachijo-guchi, Kyoto Station, Kyoto 601-8412. ℭ **800/336-1136** in the U.S. or 075/661-7111. Fax 075/661-7135. www.newmiyako.co.jp. 714 units. ¥9,000–¥11,000 ($75–$92) single; ¥18,000–¥28,000 ($150–$233) double; ¥19,000–¥27,000 ($158–$225) twin; ¥31,000 ($258) triple. Japanese-style units ¥40,000 ($333) for 2. AE, DC, JCB, MC, V. Across the street from Kyoto Station's south side (Hachijo Central exit). **Amenities:** 6 restaurants, 1 bar, 1 beer garden; concierge; business center; souvenir and gift shops; salon; room service (7–10pm); coin-op washer and dryer; same-day laundry/dry cleaning service; nonsmoking rooms. *In room:* A/C, cable TV with on-demand pay movies, dataport, minibar, hot-water pot with tea, hair dryer, trouser press, washlet toilet.

Rihga Royal Hotel ⭐

This has been one of Kyoto's grand hotels since 1969, a familiar landmark topped by the city's only revolving restaurant (see "Where to Dine in Kyoto," later in this chapter, for a review of the Top of Kyoto). The building's exterior railed ledges resemble traditional Japanese architecture, while the inside is a successful blend of traditional and modern, including standard rooms that feature shoji screens and window panels that close for complete darkness. The most expensive rooms—recently renovated and occupying the top two floors—have smart-looking Italian-style furnishings and spacious modern bathrooms. To aid the foreigners who make up about 30% of hotel guests, there's an English-language guest-relations coordinator on staff.

Horikawa-Shiokoji, Shimogyo-ku, Kyoto 600-8237. ℭ **075/341-1121.** Fax 075/341-3073. www.rihga.com. 494 units. ¥13,000–¥20,000 ($108–$167) single; ¥21,000–¥30,000 ($175–$250) double; ¥18,000–¥30,000 ($150–$250) twin; ¥35,000 ($292) quad. Japanese-style units ¥30,000 ($250) single or double. AE, DC, JCB, MC, V. Free shuttle bus every 15 min. 7:30am–9pm from Kyoto Station's Hachijo exit, or a 7-min. walk from Kyoto Station. **Amenities:** 7 restaurants, 1 bar, 1 lounge; indoor pool with sauna (men only) and Jacuzzi (fee: ¥2,000/$17); concierge; complimentary shuttle to station; salon; room service (6am–midnight); in-room massage; same-day laundry/dry cleaning service; nonsmoking rooms. *In room:* A/C, bilingual cable TV with pay movies, dataport, minibar, hot-water pot with tea, hair dryer, trouser press.

MODERATE

APA Hotel (Kyoto Ekimae) *Value*

Opened in 1999, this business hotel is a good choice for its location and rates. It's clean and smart looking and even boasts a no-smoking floor (a rarity for business hotels). Rooms are small (the cheapest singles are miniscule) but pleasantly decorated and, though close to the train tracks, relatively quiet.

553–7 Higashiaburakohji-machi, Shiokoji-sagaru, Aburakoji Dori, Shimogyo-ku, Kyoto 600-8235. ℭ **075/365-4111.** Fax 075/365-8720. 192 units. ¥7,000–¥8,500 ($58–$71) single; ¥13,000–¥15,000 ($108–$125) twin. AE, MC, V. A 3-min. walk from Kyoto Station's north (Karasuma) exit; turn left out of the station and walk between the post office and train station. **Amenities:** 1 restaurant (Western); in-room massage; same-day laundry/dry cleaning service; nonsmoking rooms. *In room:* A/C, TV with pay movies, fridge, hot-water pot with tea, hair dryer, washlet toilet.

Hotel New Hankyu Kyoto ⭐

This is a good choice in terms of price, convenient location, and service. The front-desk staff is very efficient and polite, and there's an information desk in the lobby with an English-speaking staff (foreigners account for about 10% of guests). A branch of the famous Minokichi restaurant is in the basement (see "Where to Dine in Kyoto," later in this chapter for a review), and in summer there's a rooftop beer garden with an all-you-can-eat buffet. Rooms are fairly standard, and the most expensive twins face the front of the hotel, which is noisy despite soundproof windows; all doubles face toward the back.

Shiokoji-dori, Shimogyo-ku, Kyoto 600-8216. ℭ **075/343-5300.** Fax 075/343-5324. 319 units. ¥12,000–¥14,000 ($108–$126) single; ¥22,000–¥26,000 ($198–$217) double or twin. AE, DC, JCB, MC, V. Across the street from Kyoto Station's north side (Karasuma exit). **Amenities:** 5 restaurants, 1 bar; concierge; room service (8–10pm); same-day laundry/dry cleaning service; nonsmoking rooms. *In room:* A/C, TV with pay movies, minibar, hot-water pot with tea, hair dryer.

INEXPENSIVE

Hiraiwa Ryokan and Annex ★★ This inexpensive ryokan is one of the best-known and oldest members of the Japanese Inn Group. The Hiraiwa family speaks almost no English and yet has been welcoming foreigners from all over the world for many years. The tatami guestrooms, spread through the 60-year-old traditional main building and a newer annex, are spotless. Breakfasts are communal affairs around the kitchen table, but note that Japanese breakfast, which includes *kamameshi* (rice casserole), miso soup, and tofu, must be ordered a day in advance. There are showers and two public baths, but better still is the neighborhood public bath and sauna just around the corner.

314 Hayao-cho, Kaminoguchi-agaru, Ninomiyacho Dori, Shimogyo-ku, Kyoto 600-8114. © **075/351-6748.** Fax 075/351-6969. www2.odn.ne.jp/hiraiwa/. 21 units (none with bathroom). ¥4,000–¥5,000 ($33–$42) single; ¥8,000–¥9,000 ($67–$75) double. Western breakfast ¥320–¥740 ($2.65–$6.15) extra; Japanese breakfast ¥1,050 ($8.75) extra. AE, MC, V. Bus: 17 or 205 (don't take the express 205) to Kawaramachi-Shomen (3rd stop) and then a 4-min. walk from the bus stop, or a 15-min. walk from Kyoto Station. **Amenities:** Coin-op washers and dryers. *In room:* A/C, TV, hot-water pot with tea.

Hotel New Hokke Kyoto *Value* Popular with tourists thanks to its favorable location and reasonable price, this older chain hotel recently underwent a much needed renovation and now offers clean and pleasantly decorated Western-style rooms, all with feather quilts, and smallish bathrooms. Note that all the singles have glazed windows (which could drive the claustrophobic over the brink) but do have semi-double size beds.

Shomen Chuoguchi, Karasuma, Kyoto-Eki-mae, Shimogyo-ku, Kyoto 600-8216. **075/361-1251.** Fax 075/361-1255. 190 units. ¥6,800–¥7,200 ($57–$60) single; ¥11,000 ($92) double; ¥13,000–¥20,000 ($108–$167) twin. AE, DC, JCB, MC, V. Across from Kyoto Station's Karasuma (north) exit. **Amenities:** 1 restaurant; business center; in-room massage; coin-op washers and dryers; same-day laundry/dry cleaning service; nonsmoking rooms (singles only). *In room:* A/C, TV with pay movies, dataport, fridge, hot-water pot with tea, hair dryer, washlet toilet.

Kuwacho Ryokan Despite its name, this conveniently located, family-run establishment is housed in a modern, concrete, three-story building (no elevator) and offers an equal number of Western- and Japanese-style rooms (all with bathroom). Personally, I prefer the Japanese-style rooms (somehow, bare rooms are more becoming to tatami than to Western styles). Rooms facing the front also have the plus of a small balcony. There's an international telephone with Internet access on the premises. Disadvantages: No meals are served, curfew is at 11pm, and if you pay by credit card, a 5% surcharge will be added to your bill.

231 Shichijo-agaru, Akezu Dori, Shimogyo-ku, Kyoto 600-8149. © **075/371-3191.** Fax 074/344-2228. www.kuwacho.com. 14 units. ¥5,000 ($42) single; ¥8,000 ($67) twin; ¥12,000 ($100) triple. ¥1,000 ($8.35) extra on holidays. AE, DC, JCB, MC, V. On Akezu Dori Street, a 4-min. walk north of Kyoto Station's Karasuma exit; walk north on Karasuma Dori, turn right at Shichijo Dori, and then take the 1st left. *In room:* A/C, TV, hot-water pot, safe.

Matsubaya Ryokan ★★★ *Finds* A member of the Japanese Inn Group, this traditional ryokan just east of Higashi Honganji Temple is a great choice in this category. First opened in 1885, it's now owned and managed by the friendly and irrepressibly energetic Mrs. Hayashi, representing the fifth generation of innkeepers. She'll talk on and on to you in Japanese even if you don't understand, making you wish you did. Her best, slightly higher-priced rooms have wooden balconies facing a miniature inner courtyard or face a tiny enclosed garden. All are tatami rooms with sitting alcoves. An international phone in the entryway accepts credit cards. Note that curfew here is 11pm, and when faxing to the ryokan, please be respectful of the time difference—Mrs. Hayashi isn't getting any younger, and she's been so kind to so many travelers. Highly recommended.

Higashinotouin Nishi, Kamijuzuyamachi Dori, Shimogyo-ku, Kyoto 600-8150. ☎ 075/351-3727 or 075/351-4268. Fax 075/351-3505. www.nmc.ne.jp/hp1/matsubayaryokan/. 11 units (none with bathroom). ¥4,500–¥5,000 ($37.50–$42) single; ¥9,000–¥10,000 ($75–$83) double; ¥12,600–¥14,000 ($105–$117) triple. Japanese breakfast ¥1,000 ($8.35) extra; Japanese dinner ¥4,500 ($37.50 extra). Reservations require a 1-night deposit, payable by cashier's check, international money order, or credit card. AE, MC, V. An 8-min. walk north of Kyoto Station's Karasuma exit; walk north on Karasuma Dori and take the 3rd right after passing Shichijo Dori. **Amenities:** Coin-op washer and dryer; communal fridge. *In room:* A/C, coin-op TV with CNN, hot-water pot with tea.

Murakamiya Ryokan 🏮🏮   Near the Matsubaya (above), this pleasant and spotlessly clean member of the Japanese Inn Group offers nicely decorated rooms—some with old-style ceilings and woodwork—in a 70-year-old traditional wooden building. The owner is friendly and accommodating and does her best to communicate, even though her English is limited. There's an international phone that accepts credit cards. A Japanese breakfast is available if you order it the night before. The ryokan locks its doors at 11pm.

270 Sasaya-cho, Shichijo-agaru, Higashinotouin Dori, Shimogyo-ku, Kyoto 600-8156. ☎ 075/371-1260. Fax 075/371-7161. www.mmn.co.jp/ryokanmurakamiya/. 8 units (none with bathroom). ¥4,500 ($37.50) single; ¥8,000–¥8,800 ($67–$73) double; ¥12,000–¥13,000 ($100–$108) triple. Japanese breakfast ¥1,000 ($8.35) extra. AE, MC, V. A 7-min. walk north of Kyoto Station's Karasuma exit; walk north on Karasuma Dori, take the 1st right after passing Shichijo Dori, and then take the 1st left. **Amenities:** Coin-op washer and dryer. *In room:* A/C, TV, hot-water pot with tea.

Station Ryokan Seiki   A member of the Japanese Inn Group, this relatively new, five-story concrete building houses tiny Japanese-style rooms (the single rooms measure four tatami mats). Avoid rooms facing Karasuma Dori because they're quite noisy. Although close to the station, city buses depart from the opposite side of the station, about a 5-minute walk away.

24–5 Kitakarasumaru-cho, Higashi-kujo, Minami-ku, Kyoto 601-8017. ☎ 075/682-0444. Fax 075/682-0171. www5.ocn.ne.jp/~seikis/. 17 units. ¥5,500 ($46) single; ¥9,000 ($75) double. AE, MC, V. A 3-min. walk straight south from Kyoto Station's south (Hachijo) exit, on Karasuma Dori (the one beside Avanti). **Amenities:** Coin-op washers and dryers. *In room:* A/C, cable TV, fridge, hot-water pot with tea.

Yuhara 🏮🏮🏮   This small ryokan has been welcoming guests from all over the world for more than 40 years and seems to be a favorite of visiting journalists, as evidenced by the many framed newspaper articles written about the ryokan that line the corridor walls. It has one of the most picturesque, pleasant settings in all of Kyoto—beside the tree-lined narrow Takasegawa canal in a quiet residential area that's a 13-minute walk from Kyoto Station—and is run by an enthusiastic woman who speaks some English. There are nice touches everywhere, from shoji screens and artwork in the rooms to plants and bamboo decorations in the hallways. One of the rooms is Western style, and three come with a sink. The largest room looks out onto a miniature courtyard. Guests are requested to vacate their rooms from 10am to 3pm, and there's an 11pm curfew.

188 Kagiyacho, Shomen-agaru, Kiyamachi Dori, Shimogyo-ku, Kyoto 600-8126. ☎ 075/371-9583. Fax 075/371-9583. 9 units (none with bathroom). ¥4,000 ($33) per person. AE, MC, V. Bus: 17 or 205 (don't take the express bus) to Kawaramachi-Shomen (the 3rd stop) and then a 2-min. walk (walk north to the traffic stop and turn right), or a 13-min. walk from the station. *In room:* A/C, coin-op TV, hot-water pot with tea, no phone.

Tips   **A Note on Japanese Symbols**

Many hotels, restaurants, attractions, and other establishments in Japan do not have signs giving their names in Roman (English-language) letters. Appendix C in this book lists the Japanese symbols for all such places described in this guide. Each set of characters representing an establishment name has a number in the appendix that corresponds to the number that appears inside the oval before the establishment's name in the text. Thus, to find the Japanese symbol for, say, the **Kinmata** (below), refer to no. 74 in appendix C.

CENTRAL KYOTO
VERY EXPENSIVE

Hiiragiya Ryokan ★★★   This exquisite ryokan is as fine an example of a traditional inn as you'll find in Japan. Situated in the heart of old Kyoto, it offers the ultimate in Japanese-style living, with a very accommodating staff that's helpful in initiating foreigners unfamiliar with Japan to the joys of a ryokan. Noteworthy former guests include princes of the Japanese royal family, Charlie Chaplin, and Pierre Cardin. If you're going to mortgage the house and splurge just once in Japan, this would be one of my top choices.

Built in 1818 and an inn since 1861—and under the same family's ownership for seven generations—Hiiragiya is a haven of simple design that makes artful use of wood, bamboo, screens, and stones in its spacious, traditionally arranged rooms. Even the remote controls for the lights and curtains are cleverly concealed in specially made lacquered boxes shaped like gourds (invented by the present owner's great grandfather). All rooms are outfitted with art and antiques, and most offer garden views. Dinners are exquisite multicourse kaiseki feasts; Western-style breakfasts are available upon request.

Fuyacho, Anekoji-agaru, Nakagyo-ku, Kyoto 604-8094. ✆ **075/221-1136.** Fax 075/221-1139. info@hiiragiya.co.jp. 33 units (28 with bathroom). ¥25,000 ($208) per person without bathroom ¥30,000–¥100,000 ($250–$833) per person with bathroom. Rates include 2 meals and service charge. AE, DC, JCB, MC, V. Located on the corner of Fuyacho and Oike sts. Subway: Kyoto Shiyakusho-mae (4 min.) or Karasuma-Oike (7 min.). Bus: 4, 17, or 205 to Kawaramachi Oike (4 min.). Taxi: 10 min. **Amenities:** In-room massage. *In room:* A/C, TV, minibar, hot-water pot with tea, hair dryer.

Tawaraya ★★★   Across the street from the Hiiragiya is another distinguished, venerable old inn, which has been owned and operated by the same family since it opened in the first decade of the 1700s (the present owner, Mrs. Toshi Okazaki Sato, is the 11th generation of innkeepers). Unfortunately, fire consumed the original building, so the oldest part of the ryokan now dates back only 175 years. This inn has had an impressive list of former guests, from former Canadian Prime Minister Pierre Trudeau to Alfred Hitchcock. Saul Bellow wrote in the ryokan's guest book, "I found here what I had hoped to find in Japan—the human scale, tranquility, and beauty."

With refined taste reigning supreme, each room is different and exquisitely appointed. Some, for example, have glass sliding doors opening onto a mossy garden of bamboo, stone lanterns, and manicured bushes, with cushions on a wooden veranda where you can sit and soak in the peacefulness.

Oike-Sagaru, Fuyacho, Nakagyo-ku, Kyoto 604-8094. ✆ **075/211-5566.** Fax 075/211-2204. 18 units. ¥35,000–¥75,000 ($292–$625) per person double including 2 meals. AE, DC, JCB, MC, V. Subway: Kyoto

Shiyakusho-mae (4 min.) or Karasuma-Oike (7 min.). Bus: 4, 17, or 205 to Kawaramachi Oike (4 min.). Taxi: 10 min. **Amenities:** In-room massage. *In room:* A/C, TV, minibar, hot-water pot with tea, hair dryer.

EXPENSIVE

ANA Hotel Kyoto ☆ Just across the street from Nijo Castle and offering rooms with castle views, this hotel has one of the most stunning lobby lounges in town, complete with a glass wall overlooking an impressive waterfall and tiny landscape garden, all to the accompaniment of Koto music (a Japanese stringed instrument). Rooms are attractive and comfortable with well-crafted, Asian-accented furniture and roomy bathrooms. None of the singles faces the castle; twin and double rooms that do so start at ¥24,000 ($200) during the regular season and ¥26,000 ($217) during April, May, October, November, and summer and New Year vacations.

Nijojo-mae, Horikawa Dori, Nakagyo-ku, Kyoto 604-0055. ℂ 800/ANA-HOTELS in the U.S. and Canada, or 075/231-1155. Fax 075/231-5333. http://www.ananet.or.jp/anahotels/e/direct/japan/kansai/kyoto.html. 304 units. ¥13,000 ($92) single; ¥19,000–¥24,000 ($158–$200) double; ¥19,000–¥26,000 ($158–$217) twin. ¥1,000 ($8.35) extra per person April, May, Oct, Nov, Sat and nights before holidays. AE, DC, JCB, MC, V. Subway: Nijojo-mae (1 min.). Bus: 9, 50, or 101 to Nijojo-mae. **Amenities:** 4 restaurants, 2 bars; indoor pool and sauna (fee: ¥3,000/$25); shopping arcade; room service (7am–11pm); in-room massage; same-day laundry/dry cleaning service; nonsmoking rooms. *In room:* A/C, cable TV with pay movies, minibar, hot-water pot with tea, hair dryer, bathroom scale, washlet toilet.

㉞ **Kinmata** ★★★ *Finds* With only six rooms, this beautiful, Meiji-Era, traditional wooden inn in the heart of Kyoto is exquisite inside and out, an oasis of the best Old Japan has to offer. First opened in the early 1800s, its earliest customers were medicine peddlers; an old sign announcing the house rules of past centuries—no gambling, no prostitution, no mah-jong, no noisy parties—still hangs in the hallway. The present owner, Mr. Ukai, represents the seventh generation of innkeepers here and is renowned as a chef, preparing wonderful kaiseki meals for his guests. Even if you don't stay here, you can come for a meal (lunch is ¥6,000/$50 and up for table seating, ¥8,000/$67 for Japanese-style seating). Pluses are the public cypress bath, an inner courtyard, and a peaceful garden. Note, however, that there's an 11pm curfew.

407 Gokomachi, Shijo-agaru, Nakagyo-ku, Kyoto 604-8044. ℂ 075/221-1039. Fax 075/231-7632. Kinmata@mbox.kyoto-inet.or.jp. 7 units (none with bathroom, 2 with toilet only). ¥15,000–¥18,000 ($125–$150) per person with breakfast; ¥25,000–¥35,000 ($208–$292) per person with 2 meals. Rates do not include service charge. AE, DC, JCB, MC, V. Just north of Shijo Dori Ave. on Gokomachi St. Subway: Shijo (7 min.). Bus: 4, 5, 17, or 205 to Shijo-Kawaramachi. *In room:* A/C, TV, hot-water pot with tea.

Kyoto Hotel ★★★ First built in 1888, one of Kyoto's oldest hotels underwent a complete transformation and reopened in 1994 as the city's tallest building, with 17 floors. Its height caused a stir of protest by those who advocate stricter height restrictions; though I usually side with historic preservationists, I must admit that no finer building could have violated the skyline. Its modern facade hints at traditional Japanese latticework, while the spacious lobby, designed after the hotel's original 1920s ballroom, exudes a gracefully elegant old-world ambience. Restaurants on the top floor offer stunning views.

Luxurious accommodations, a convenient location in the heart of Kyoto, and an English-speaking staff that makes a special effort to be hospitable (their motto is "Service with a Smile") come together to make this an excellent choice. Rooms, built around a central atrium, are the utmost in comfort and grandeur, with deep carpeting, rich textiles, and large bathrooms. The most expensive rooms are on upper floors with views over the Kamo River toward Higashiyama-ku. The only drawback is that the indoor pool and related facilities are open to guests only from 7 to 10am, after which they become a private club.

Kawaramachi-Oike, Nakagyo-ku, Kyoto 604-8558. © 075/211-5111 or 075/223-2333 for reservations. Fax 075/221-7770. www.kyotohotel.co.jp/. 322 units. ¥16,000–¥18,000 ($133–$150) single; ¥31,000–¥45,000 ($258–$375) double; ¥25,000–¥45,000 ($208–$375) twin; ¥50,000 ($417) quad; from ¥38,000 ($317) executive twin or double. AE, DC, JCB, MC, V. Subway: Kyoto Shiyakusho-mae (1 min., below the hotel). Bus: 4, 17, or 205 to Kawaramachi Oike. **Amenities:** 8 restaurants, 1 bar; indoor pool with jacuzzi and sauna (fee: ¥2,000/$17); concierge; shopping arcade; salon; room service (6:30am–2am); in-room massage; baby-sitting room; same-day laundry/dry cleaning service; nonsmoking rooms; executive-level rooms. *In room:* A/C, satellite TV, dataport, minibar, hot-water pot with tea, hair dryer, safe, washlet toilet.

Kyoto Royal Hotel   The main reason to stay here? Location, location, location. In the heart of Kyoto on Kawaramachi Dori, this typical tourist hotel has a friendly staff and tries hard to achieve a top-class atmosphere, but can't compete with the facilities and grandeur of Kyoto's other top hotels. Still, it's a convenient base for sightseeing and has an information desk to answer guest questions. Rooms are fairly basic, and note that most single rooms and some doubles face an inner courtyard, which cuts down on noise but also on sunshine. Rooms that face the Kamo River have better views but are minuscule. Standard twins have only two single-size beds rather than the semi-double-size beds now common in most medium-class hotels.

Sanjo-agaru Kawaramachi, Nakagyo-ku, Kyoto 604-8005. © 075/223-1234. Fax 075/223-1702. www.kyoto-royal.co.jp. 335 units. ¥10,000–¥17,000 ($83–$142) single; ¥18,000–¥25,000 ($150–$208) double; ¥22,000–¥24,000 ($183–$200) twin; ¥34,000 ($283) quad. AE, DC, JCB, MC, V. Subway: Kyoto Shiyakusho-mae (2 min.). Bus: 4, 17, or 205 to Kawaramachi Sanjo. **Amenities:** 5 restaurants, 2 bars; game room; concierge; salon; room service (7am–11pm); in-room massage; same-day laundry/dry cleaning service; nonsmoking rooms. *In room:* A/C, TV, minibar, hot-water pot with tea, hair dryer, washlet toilet.

Sumiya   Another traditional Japanese inn, this 100-year-old establishment offers excellent service amid simple yet elegant surroundings. Some rooms have wonderful views of tiny private gardens, which have outdoor benches and platforms for sitting. Like the other ryokan in this chapter, Sumiya has a great location in a typical Kyoto neighborhood but is less than a 5-minute walk from downtown Kyoto. Meals feature Kyoto kaiseki cuisine; Western breakfasts are also available.

Sanjo-sagaru, Fuyacho, Nakagyo-ku, Kyoto 604-8075. © 075/221-2188. Fax 075/221-2267. 23 units (17 with bathroom). ¥25,000–¥60,000 ($208–$500) per person. Rates include 2 meals and service charge. AE, DC, JCB, MC, V. On Fuyacho Dori just south of Sanjo St. Subway: Kyoto Shiyakusho-mae (5 min.) or Karasuma-Oike (8 min.). Bus: 4, 17, or 205 to Kawaramachi Oike (5 min.). Taxi: 10 min. **Amenities:** In-room massage. *In room:* A/C, TV, minibar, hot-water pot with tea, hair dryer, safe.

MODERATE

Hotel Gimmond   This small hotel on Oike Dori was built just 20-some years ago, but it achieves an older ambience in its lobby with the clever use of antique-looking lighting and decor. Though the hotel calls itself a tourist hotel and offers mainly twins, its accommodations place it in the category of business hotel. Rooms, which have been upgraded with new wallpaper, carpeting, and curtains, are soundproof, but I still think those that face away from Oike Dori are quieter; ask for one on a higher floor. The cheapest rooms are quite small.

Takakura Oike Dori, Nakagyo-ku, Kyoto 604-8105. © 075/221-4111. Fax 075/221-8250. www.gimmond.co.jp. 140 units. ¥8,300–¥9,300 ($69–$77.50) single; ¥14,000 ($117) double; ¥14,500–¥20,500 ($121–$171) twin. AE, DC, JCB, MC, V. Subway: Karasuma-Oike (2 min.). **Amenities:** 1 restaurant (Western), 1 bar; in-room massage; same-day laundry/dry cleaning service. *In room:* A/C, TV, fridge, hot-water pot with tea, hair dryer.

International Hotel Kyoto (Kyoto Kokusai Hotel) ⊛ I like this hotel because it offers a few surprises you wouldn't expect to find in medium-range accommodations. For one thing, its very nice lobby overlooks a pleasant, lush garden, which you can gaze upon from either the lobby tea lounge or the buffet-style restaurant, Azalea (see "Where to Dine in Kyoto," later in this chapter). Every evening at 7:30pm, the garden also serves as stage for a free 15-minute dance presentation given by *maiko* (geisha apprentices). There's also a summertime rooftop beer garden. Room rates are based on decor and amenities; recently renovated rooms cost more and offer such luxuries as washlet toilets and bathroom scales. All rooms are comfortable and are outfitted with shoji screens; approximately 60 twins and 2 doubles face Nijo Castle, but none of the singles do. Despite the hotel's name, more than 90% of its guests are Japanese.

Nijojo-mae, Horikawa Dori, Nakagyo-ku, Kyoto 604-8502. © 075/222-1111. Fax 075/231-9381. 274 units. ¥9,000–¥18,000 ($75–$150) single; ¥23,000–¥27,000 ($192–$225) double; ¥14,000–¥29,000 ($117–$242) twin; ¥23,000–¥33,000 ($192–$275) quad. AE, DC, JCB, MC, V. Subway: Nijojo-mae (2 min.). Bus: 9, 50, or 101 to Nijojo-mae (2 min.). Across from Nijo Castle. **Amenities:** 4 restaurants, 1 bar; concierge; shopping arcade; salon; room service (11:30am–9:45pm); in-room massage; laundry/dry cleaning service; nonsmoking rooms. *In room:* A/C, TV, minibar, hot-water pot with tea, hair dryer.

INEXPENSIVE

Hirota Guest House ⊛⊛ *(Finds)* This 120-year-old former sake brewery, not far from the Kawaramachi-Shijo Dori area, is the home of Hirota Harumi, a professional interpreter/tour guide who is happy to impart valuable sightseeing information about the town she knows so well. All of the rooms are tatami style, and while those facing the street are the least expensive, they are not as noisy as one might expect, since this is a quiet residential neighborhood. In the back of the house is a detached two-story cottage accommodating up to seven persons, ideal for families or groups. No meals are served.

665 Seimei-cho, Tominokoji-nishi, Nijo Dori, Nakagyo-ku, Kyoto 604-0951. © 075/221-2474. Fax 075/221-2627. h-hirota@msi.biglobe.ne.jp. 6 units (none with bathroom). ¥6,500–¥8,500 ($54–$71) single; ¥11,000–¥14,000 ($92–$117) double. Cottage with kitchen: ¥9,000 ($75) per person for 2, ¥8,000 ($67) per person for 3–4, ¥7,000 ($58) per person for 5–7. AE, MC, V. Subway: Oike Station (exit 1; 12 min.). **Amenities:** Rental bikes (¥1,000/$8.35 per day); in-room massage; babysitting; dry cleaning/laundry service; nonsmoking rooms. *In room:* A/C, TV, fridge, hot-water pot with tea and coffee.

Hotel Alpha Kyoto This small and unassuming but pleasant brick business hotel has a great location near the Kawaramachi-Shijo Dori intersection. I have always found the staff accommodating. Most rooms, including singles, are outfitted with double-size beds, but since the cheapest singles face an inner courtyard and are fairly dark, it may be worthwhile to dish out the extra yen for a brighter room. My favorite rooms are those that overlook a quiet temple and Buddhist cemetery—a fitting view in a town that boasts so many religious structures. The handmade origami crane in each room is a nice touch.

Kawaramachi, Sango-agaru, Nakagyo-ku, Kyoto 604-8006. © 075/241-2000. Fax 075/211-0533. hotelalpha@pop07.odn.ne.jp. 119 units. ¥6,800–¥8,500 ($57–$71) single; ¥11,800–¥15,300 ($98–$127.50) double; ¥12,500–¥17,200 ($104–$143) twin; Japanese-style units ¥22,300–¥27,300 ($186–$227.50) for 2. AE, DC, JCB, MC, V. Subway: Kyoto Shiyakusho-mae (2 min.). Bus: 4, 17, or 205 to Kawaramachi Sanjo (1 min.). Just off Kawaramachi Dori not far from Sanjo Dori; entrance is on a side street called Aneyakoji Dori. **Amenities:** 1 restaurant (Western/Kyoto cuisine). *In room:* A/C, TV, minibar, hot-water pot with tea, hair dryer.

Kyoto Central Inn As the name implies, this inn is centrally located in the heart of the city, near the intersection of Shijo Dori and Kawaramachi Dori. It resembles a business hotel, but thanks to its great location, about 50% of its guests are tourists; twins make up the vast majority of its rooms. Rooms are divided between older and newer wings, with the newer wing offering slightly larger rooms at higher prices. Since those facing the front or side of the building are plagued with traffic noise, ask for a room facing the back. A Starbucks coffee shop is next to the entrance.

Shijo Kawaramachi, Nishi-iru, Shimogyo-ku, Kyoto 600-8002. ✆ 075/211-1666. Fax 075/241-2765. kyocent@geisya.or.jp. 150 units. ¥7,000–¥9,000 ($58–$75) single; ¥11,000–¥13,000 ($92–$108) double or twin. AE, DC, JCB, MC, V. Bus: 4, 5, 17, or 205 to Shijo Kawaramachi (1 min.). *In room:* A/C, TV, hot-water pot with tea.

EASTERN KYOTO
VERY EXPENSIVE

The Miyako ★★ *Kids*　This is the place to stay if you're looking for a hotel with history. The Miyako, a member of the "Leading Hotels of the World" group, is one of the best-known hotels in Japan. First opened back in 1890, it boasts a guest list that reads like a Who's Who of visitors to Japan: Queen Elizabeth II, Prince Charles and Princess Diana, Anwar el-Sadat, Ted Kennedy, and Ronald Reagan. Even today, half of the guests staying here are foreigners.

Unfortunately, extensive renovations have obliterated all vestiges of the historic past in favor of a characterless marble lobby—but the service here is beyond reproof, and the setting is as good as it gets: The hotel sprawls over more than 16 hilltop acres at the northeastern end of the city, close to some of Kyoto's most famous temples and commanding a good view of the surrounding hills. Other pluses include a Japanese garden and a registration satellite at Kyoto Station where you can check in and deposit your bags (they'll be sent onward to your room), leaving you free to explore Kyoto or to take the complimentary bus to the hotel unencumbered by baggage. Families appreciate the day-care center and indoor and outdoor pools.

Western-style rooms come in a variety of styles and price ranges, with the least expensive rooms occupying the oldest wing and looking a bit dated. The best of the deluxe rooms have small balconies overlooking the valley. For those who wish to experience the pleasures of a traditional tatami room but with all the nearby conveniences of a first-rate hotel, the Japanese-style Kasui-en annex is a good bet for ryokan first-timers. Built in 1959, the annex offers 20 modern, elegant rooms with views of a Japanese garden and cypress baths.

Sanjo Keage, Higashiyama-ku, Kyoto 605-0052. ✆ 800/223-6800 in the U.S. and Canada, or 075/771-7111. Fax 075/751-2490. http://www.miyakohotel.co.jp/english/engl_a.html. 520 units. ¥17,000 ($142) single; ¥19,000–¥43,000 ($158–$358) double or twin; ¥43,000–¥48,000 ($358–$400) double or twin on executive Sky Floors; ¥30,000–¥50,000 ($250–$417) double in Kasui-en. ¥3,000 ($25) extra on Sat and nights prior to holidays and festivals. AE, DC, JCB, MC, V. Free shuttle from Kyoto Station. Subway: Keage (2 min.). **Amenities:** 7 restaurants, 1 cafe, 2 bars, 2 tea ceremony rooms; indoor and outdoor pools, Jacuzzi and sauna (fee: ¥1,500/$12.50); grass tennis court (¥5,000/$42 per hr.); sundecks (available also for moon viewing during full moon); observation deck; wild-bird sanctuary and bird-watching trail; tea ceremony (fee: ¥1,000/$8.35); concierge; shuttle bus (every 30 min. from Kyoto Station's Hachijo Central exit); business center; shopping arcade; salon; room service (6:30am–midnight); in-room massage; baby-sitting room for children up to 5 (open daily 10am–9pm; ¥5,000/$42 for 2 hr.); same-day dry/cleaning laundry; nonsmoking rooms; executive level rooms. *In room:* A/C, satellite TV, dataport, minibar, hot-water pot with tea, hair dryer.

Seikoro Inn ★★　This ryokan just east of the Kamo River was established in 1831, but the present building dates from about a century ago. After passing through a traditional front gate and small courtyard, you'll find yourself in a cozy parlor replete with an eclectic mix of Japanese and Western antiques, including an old grandfather clock. The rooms, also decorated in antiques, are very homey and comfortable; some open onto a garden with sliding doors and shoji screens. Rooms in an annex built just before the 1964 Olympics are high enough that you can see over the surrounding rooftops, but most of these don't have garden views so I prefer the ones in the oldest buildings. The owner, who speaks good English, doesn't mind if you take your meals elsewhere, especially if you're going to be here for a while.

Gojo-sagaru, Tonyamachi, Higashiyama-ku, Kyoto 605-0907. ✆ 075/561-0771. Fax 075/541-5481. 22 units. ¥25,000–¥50,000 ($208–$417) per person double including 2 meals; 30% less for room without meals. AE, DC, JCB, MC, V. Bus: 17 or 205 to Kawaramachi Gojo and then a 5-min. walk; cross the bridge over the Kamo River and after Kawabata Dori take the 1st right. Keihan Electric Railway: Gojo Station (2 min.). *In room:* A/C, TV, hot-water pot with tea, hair dryer, washlet toilet.

EXPENSIVE

Yachiyo Inn ⭐⭐ Situated on the approach to Nanzenji Temple, this inn attracts a large foreign clientele. Formerly a villa (it became a ryokan after World War II), the building is about 100 years old but has been remodeled so that parts of it seem almost new. Still, I prefer the 10 rooms here to those in the newer annex, especially the four on the ground floor with sitting alcoves that open onto a small garden. Most rooms have wooden bathtubs along with showers and Western-style toilets, as well as transom carvings and ikebana flower arrangements.

This ryokan doesn't mind if you prefer to take your meals elsewhere. If you're staying in Kyoto for a few days, you might want to first take breakfast and dinner at the ryokan and then later start going out to Kyoto's many restaurants. Breakfast is served communally in a pleasant room overlooking a garden and pond, while dinners are served in your room.

34 Nanzenji-Fukujicho, Sakyo-ku, Kyoto 605-8435. ✆ 075/771-4148. Fax 075/771-4140. 20 units (17 with bathroom). ¥30,000 ($250) double without bathroom; ¥36,000–¥50,000 ($300–$417) double with bathroom. Rates include 2 meals and service charge; 30% less without meals. AE, DC, JCB, MC, V. Bus: 5 or 100 to Nanzenji-Eikando-michi (2 min.). **Amenities:** 1 restaurant. *In room:* A/C, TV, hot-water pot with tea, hair dryer, safe.

MODERATE

Kyoto Gion Hotel This older, simple hotel has no frills but a great location in the heart of Gion, within easy walking distance of shops, nightlife, and the many sights in Higashiyama-ku. Rooms were renovated in 2001, though the singles rooms are still among the smallest I've seen (I'm not sure there's even room to unpack). There's no view to speak of, but I prefer the rooms facing west, which have floor-to-ceiling windows overlooking the quaint tiled roofs of Gion. A plus is the rooftop beer garden, open in summer.

555 Gion, Higashiyama-ku, Kyoto 605-0074. ✆ 075/551-2111. Fax 075/551-2200. 154 units. ¥8,000–¥8,500 ($77.50–$83) single; ¥14,000–¥20,000 ($137.50–$146) twin. AE, DC, JCB, MC, V. Bus: 206 to Gion (2 min.). On Shijo Dori beside Starbucks, near Yasaka Shrine. **Amenities:** 1 restaurant. *In room:* A/C, TV, minibar, hot-water pot with tea.

Kyoto Park Hotel ⭐ *(Value)* Well-located and offering good value for your money, this hotel is a good starting point for strolls through eastern Kyoto (including the pleasant walk to Kiyomizu Temple recommended later in this chapter). With its stained-glass windows, plants, and statues, it's reminiscent of a European hotel with grounds that include both a rock garden and a garden with a waterfall, cliff, and pond. Rooms, however, could do with a bit of updating, especially the furniture; but I'm partial to the twin rooms on the fifth floor, each of which has a balcony overlooking the garden.

644–2 Mawarimachi, Sanju-sangendo, Higashiyama-ku, Kyoto 605-0941. ✆ 075/525-3111. Fax 075/553-1101. http://www.kyopark.co.jp/index_e.htm. 268 units. ¥8,500–¥9,500 ($71–$79) single; ¥18,000 ($150) double; ¥15,500–¥36,000 ($129–$300) twin. ¥1,000–¥3,000 ($8.35–$25) more per person per day on

Sat, holidays, festivals, and peak season. Rates include tax and service charge. AE, DC, JCB, MC, V. Bus: 100, 206, or 208 to Hakubutsukan Sanjusangendo-mae (1 min.). Across the street from the National Museum and beside Sanjusangendo Hall. **Amenities:** 4 restaurants (including the Grand Rêve, under "Where to Dine in Kyoto," later in this chapter), 1 bar; shopping arcade; salon; in-room massage; same-day laundry/dry cleaning service; nonsmoking rooms. *In room:* A/C, cable TV, minibar, hot-water pot with tea, hair dryer.

INEXPENSIVE

⑧ **Rokuharaya Inn** This inexpensive ryokan on a small residential street typical of Kyoto, offers just the basics. Two rooms have coin-operated TV, but otherwise there's not much more—just your average Japanese tatami room. The best rooms are on the second floor of this two-story, wooden building, but do note that the stairs are very steep. More foreigners stay here than Japanese. The front doors are locked at 10pm.

147 Takemuracho Rokuhara, Higashiyama-ku, Kyoto 605-0845. ℂ **075/531-2776.** Fax 075/531-8261. 6 units (none with bathroom). ¥5,000–¥5,500 ($42–$46) per person. Breakfast ¥1,000 ($8.35) extra. AE, MC, V. Bus: 206 to Gojozaka and then a 3-min. walk. **Amenities:** Coin-op washers and dryers. *In room:* A/C, hot-water pot with tea.

Teradaya Inn Under the same ownership as the Rokuharaya Inn (above), this concrete inn has a great location in eastern Kyoto near Kiyomizu Temple. Rooms on the second floor are the brightest. Curfew is at 11pm.

583 Gojobashi-higashi 6-chome, Higashiyama-ku, Kyoto 605-0846. ℂ **075/561-3821.** Fax 075/561-3333. 5 units (none with bathroom). ¥5,500–¥7,000 ($46–$58) per person. Breakfast ¥1,000 ($8.35) extra; dinner ¥3,500 ($29) extra. AE, MC, V. Bus: 206 to Gojozaka stop and then a 3-min. walk. Just off the sloping approach to Kiyomizu Temple about halfway up (look for the large sign in English). **Amenities:** Coin-op washers and dryers. *In room:* A/C, TV, hot-water pot with tea (coffee on request).

FOR WOMEN ONLY

Ladies' Hotel Chorakukan ★★ *Finds* This small, eccentric-looking hotel for women, pleasantly located on the edge of Maruyama Park, is brimming with personality. The interior of the imposing Western-style building, built just after the turn of the 20th century as a private residence, has been modified so much through the decades that the atmosphere is comically bizarre—a thorough mix of grand and gaudy. The lobby, for example, has a chandelier and a high gilded ceiling, but the rest of the room sports plastic moldings and accents. Each guest room is slightly different (though they all seem to have a strange mix of wall coverings) and come with a sink, one to five beds, and great views of the park. This place would make a great set for a comedy—or an Agatha Christie play. Highly recommended.

Maruyama Park, Higashiyama-ku, Kyoto 605-0071. ℂ **075/561-0001.** Fax 075/561-0006. 20 units (all with toilet only). ¥5,000 ($42) single; ¥9,000 ($75) twin. No credit cards. Bus: 206 to Gion and then a 7-min. walk. **Amenities:** 1 Western restaurant (Chorakukan, see "Where to Dine," later in this chapter), 1 tea lounge. *In room:* A/C, TV, hot-water pot with tea, hair dryer.

NORTHERN KYOTO
INEXPENSIVE

⑦ **Myorenji Temple** ★★ *Finds* If you don't mind the austerity of life in a temple (early to bed, early to rise), you'll like the tranquility of this place. Located northwest of the Horikawa-Ternanouchi intersection in a pleasant, quiet neighborhood, Myorenji Temple was founded more than 650 years ago and is now run by a jolly woman named Chizuko-san, who speaks a little English. Since she manages this place virtually single-handedly, she prefers guests who stay 2 or 3 days and requests that they make reservations at least a week in advance (a month in advance would be even better). The temple buildings, about 200 years old and containing several important cultural properties, are beautifully laid out, and there's even a rock garden with raked pebbles. Rooms are simple but adequate; note that there's no air-conditioning, and since there are no bathing facilities on the temple grounds, you're given a ticket to use the neighborhood bath. Services are held every morning at 6:30am.

Teranouchi Omiya Higashi-iru, Horikawa, Kamigyo-ku, Kyoto 602-8418. **075/451-3527.** 6 units (none with bathroom). ¥3,800 ($32) per person. Rates include tax and a ticket for the neighborhood public bath. No credit cards. Bus: 9 to Teranouchi stop. *In room:* No phone.

Nashinoki Inn ★ *(Kids*   In a quiet, peaceful neighborhood north of the Kyoto Imperial Palace, this ryokan is run by a warm, friendly older couple who speak some English. Staying here is like living with a Japanese family since the home looks very lived in and is filled with the personal belongings of a lifetime. Some of the tatami rooms, which feature touches such as vases, Japanese dolls, and pictures, are quite large and adequate for families. Breakfast is served in your room.

Agaru Imadegawa Nashinoki St., Kamigyo-ku, Kyoto 602-0838. **℃ 075/241-1543.** Fax 075/211-0854. 7 units (1 with bathroom). ¥5,000 ($42) single; ¥8,800 ($73) double; ¥13,200 ($110) triple. Japanese or Western breakfast ¥900 ($7.50) extra. No credit cards. Subway: Imadegawa Station (13 min.). *In room:* A/C, coin-op TV.

Rakucho   This member of the Japanese Inn Group isn't as conveniently situated as most of the other inns listed above, but all of the rooms are pleasant and clean with a view of a small, peaceful garden; some also have a refrigerator. Entrance to the ryokan is through a well-tended tiny courtyard filled with plants. There's an international phone that accepts credit cards plus a refrigerator, a toaster, a microwave, and free instant coffee.

67 Higashihangi-cho, Shimogamo, Sakyo-ku, Kyoto 606-0824. **℃ 075/721-2174.** Fax 075/791-7202. www.rakucho-ryokan.com/. 8 units (none with bathroom). ¥4,500–¥5,000 ($37.50–$42) single; ¥8,000–¥8,800 ($67–$73) double; ¥12,000 ($100) triple. AE, MC, V. Subway: Kitaoji Station (10 min.). Bus: 205 to Furitsudaigaku-mae (2 min.; turn north at the post office). **Amenities:** Coin-op washers and dryers. *In room:* A/C, TV, hot-water pot and tea, safe.

4 Where to Dine in Kyoto

Kyoto cuisine, known as ***Kyo-ryori,*** is linked to Kyoto's long history and to seasonal foods produced in the surrounding region. Among the various types of Kyo-ryori available, most famous are probably the vegetarian dishes, which were created to serve the needs of Zen Buddhist priests and pilgrims making the rounds of Kyoto's many temples. Called ***shojin ryori,*** these vegetarian set meals include tofu simmered in a pot at your table (***yudofu***) and an array of local vegetables. Kyoto is also renowned for its own style of kaiseki (***Kyo-kaiseki***), originally conceived as a meal to be taken before the tea ceremony but eventually becoming an elaborate feast enjoyed by the capital's nobility with its blend of ceremonial court cuisine, Zen vegetarian food, and simple tea-ceremony dishes. Today, Kyoto abounds in restaurants serving both vegetarian tofu dishes and kaiseki meals fit for an emperor (Kyoto's better ryokan also serve kaiseki as the evening meal). Simpler restaurants specialize in ***Obanzai,*** homestyle Kyoto cooking using traditional seasonal ingredients. Otherwise, any restaurant advertising that it serves Kyo-ryori generally offers a variety of Kyoto specialties. For more on kaiseki and other Japanese-style meals, see "Tips on Dining, Japanese Style," in appendix A.

Remember: Last orders are taken 30 to 60 minutes before the restaurant's actual closing time, even earlier for some kaiseki restaurants (which often require a reservation).

Where to Dine in Kyoto

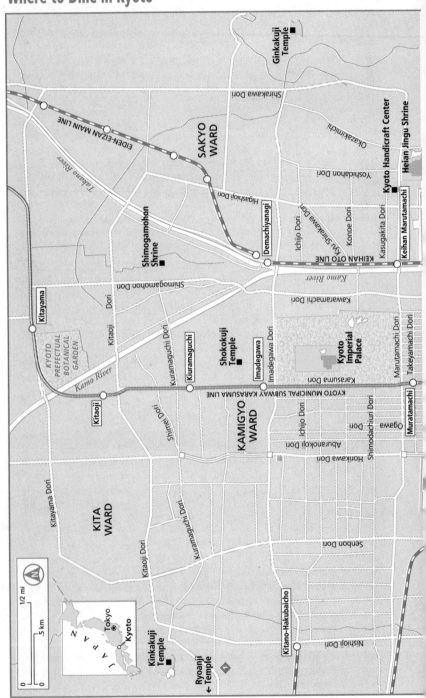

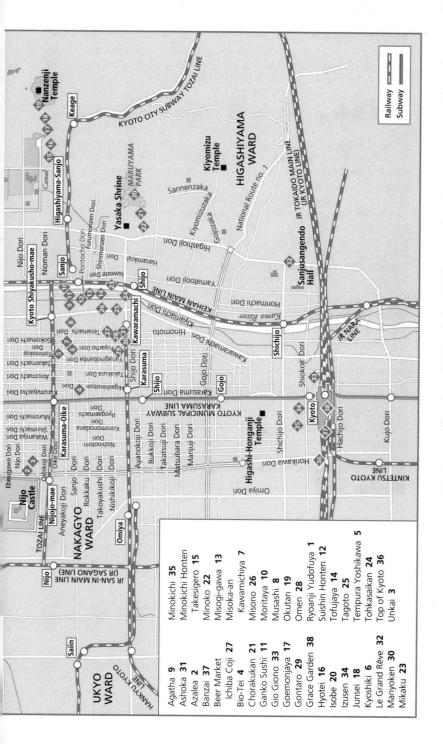

KYOTO CITY SUBWAY TOZAI LINE

Nanzenji Temple

Keage

HIGASHIYAMA WARD

Kiyomizu Temple

MARUYAMA PARK

Higashiyama-Sanjo

Yasaka Shrine

Sannenzaka

Sanjo

Kiyomizuzaka
Gojozaka

JR TOKAIDO MAIN LINE (JR KYOTO LINE)

National Route no. 1

Kyoto Shiyakusho-mae

Shijo

KEIHAN MAIN LINE

Sanjusangendo Hall

Kamo River

Nijo Castle

Nijojo-mae

Karasuma-Oike

TOZAI LINE

JR SAN-IN MAIN LINE (JR SAGANO LINE)

Nijo

Saiin

Omiya

Karasuma

Shijo

KYOTO MUNICIPAL SUBWAY KARASUMA LINE

Gojo

Shichijo

JR NARA LINE

Higashi-Honganji Temple

Kyoto

KINTETSU KYOTO LINE

Kujo Dori

HANKYU KYOTO LINE

NAKAGYO WARD

UKYO WARD

Railway
Subway

Agatha **9**
Ashoka **31**
Azalea **2**
Banzai **37**
Beer Market
  Ichiba Coji **27**
Bio-Tei **4**
Chorakukan **21**
Ganko Sushi **11**
Gio Giono **33**
Goemonjaya **17**
Gontaro **29**
Grace Garden **38**
Hyotei **16**
Isobe **20**
Izusen **34**
Junsei **18**
Kyoshiki **6**
Le Grand Rêve **32**
Manyoken **30**
Mikaku **23**

Minokichi **35**
Minokichi Honten
  Takesigero **15**
Minoko **22**
Misogi-gawa **13**
Misoka-an
Kawamichiya **7**
Misono **26**
Moritaya **10**
Musashi **8**
Okutan **19**
Omen **28**
Ryoanji Yudofuya **1**
Suishin Honten **12**
Tofujaya **14**
Tagoto **25**
Tempura Yoshikawa **5**
Tohkasaikan **24**
Top of Kyoto **36**
Unkai **3**

297

AROUND KYOTO STATION

In addition to the restaurants listed here, a good place for inexpensive dining is **Kyoto Station,** which houses various restaurants serving a wide variety of inexpensive meals and includes a food court on the 10th floor.

EXPENSIVE

Top of Kyoto CONTINENTAL Kyoto's only revolving restaurant, located on the 14th floor, is a good choice for a romantic dinner. Unlike most other revolving restaurants in Japan, which usually move so fast that one fears being flung against the windows by centrifugal force, this one, I'm happy to report, takes a leisurely 90 minutes to revolve, affording excellent views over the tops of Kyoto's temples to the mountains surrounding the city. With a smart Italian marble decor, it offers a seasonal menu that may include lobster with sweetbreads and caviar, smoked Norwegian salmon with papaya, rack of lamb, and steaks.

Rihga Royal Hotel, Horikawa-Shiokoji. ℂ 075/341-2311. Reservations recommended. Set lunches ¥2,500–¥4,500 ($21–$37.50); set dinners ¥6,000–¥12,000 ($50–$100). AE, DC, MC, V. Daily 11:30am–2:30pm and 5–9:30pm (last order). Free shuttle bus every 15 min. until 9pm from Kyoto Station's Hachijo (south) exit, or a 7-min. walk west of Kyoto Station to the Horikawa-Shiokoji intersection.

MODERATE

Grace Garden CONTINENTAL This smart-looking restaurant is trendier and more upbeat than most hotel restaurants that specialize in buffets (which tend toward the utilitarian) and is also smaller, with fewer than 100 seats. Bright and airy with large windows overlooking southern Kyoto, warm woods and peach-colored decor that give it an earthy glow, and an open kitchen, it offers a little of everything from its plentiful buffet spreads. All-you-can-drink menus are available starting at ¥1,500 ($12.50), and luckily for the less discerning among us, they come with a one-and-a-half-hour time limit. After dinner, retire to the Southern Court cocktail lounge on the same floor, which offers the same view over Kyoto and live piano music (best of all, there's no cover or music charge).

15th floor, Hotel Granvia Kyoto, Kyoto Station. ℂ 075/342-5522. Buffet dinner ¥3,500 ($29); Buffet lunch ¥2,200 ($18). AE, DC, JCB, MC, V. Daily 11:30am–2:30pm and 5:30–9:30pm. Above Kyoto Station.

Minokichi Value KYO-KAISEKI/KYO-RYORI A branch of the famous Minokichi restaurant first established in Kyoto 280 years ago, this place is designed to resemble a lane in a typical traditional Japanese village; waitresses are dressed in kimono and Japanese music plays in the background to help set the mood. The menu includes Kyo-kaiseki cuisine and typical Kyoto dishes, as well as such Japanese favorites as obento lunch boxes and eel. Set lunches, served daily until 2pm, are especially good bargains, featuring everything from eel to mini-kaiseki.

Hotel New Hankyu Kyoto, Shiokoji Dori. ℂ 075/343-5300. Reservations recommended. Set meals ¥2,000–¥12,000 ($17–$100); set lunches ¥1,800 ($15). AE, DC, JCB, MC, V. Daily 11:30am–9pm (kaiseki last order 6:30pm). Across the street from Kyoto Station's Karasuma (north) exit.

INEXPENSIVE

Banzai KYOTO HOMESTYLE COOKING As befitting a casual restaurant specializing in Obanzai, this restaurant is small and has room for only 29 diners to elbow up to the long counter and the few tables. Although there's an English menu listing such choices as crab boiled in a fish stock; *mochi* (pounded rice balls) filled with boiled fish; pork cooked in soy sauce, fish stock, and sugar; and green-tea noodles, the traditional way to choose your meal here is from the half dozen or so platters placed along the counter. Or you can order the obento lunch box (*Banzai Shokuzen*) or the *Banzai Iroha-bocho* set course, washing it down with local sake.

M3F floor of Hotel Granvia Kyoto, Kyoto Station. ℂ **075/342-5527.** Main dishes ¥650–¥1,800 ($5.40–$15); lunch obento ¥1,900 ($16); set course ¥3,900 ($32.50). AE, DC, JCB, MC, V. Daily 11:30am–2:30pm and 5:30–9pm. Above Kyoto Station.

Gio Giono ITALIAN   The modern, gray Renaissance Building next to Kyoto Station features several restaurants, including a coffee shop, a Chinese restaurant, and a beer hall. Best for a meal is this informal Italian restaurant on the second floor serving pizza, pasta, and such main dishes as sautéed scallops, tuna fish with tomato and capers, and grilled veal with vegetables and mozzarella. An especially good deal is the ¥950 ($7.90) set lunch, available until 2:30pm and offering a choice of daily pasta or pizza, soup, bread, salad, and coffee. Unfortunately, service is erratic; some of the staff acts like we're there to serve them.

Renaissance Bldg., 2nd floor, 849 Higashi Shiokojicho. ℂ **075/365-0202.** Pasta and pizza ¥1,300–¥2,000 ($11–$17); meat dishes ¥2,100–¥2,800 ($17.50–$23); set lunches ¥950 and ¥2,000 ($7.90 and $17). AE, DC, JCB, MC, V. Daily 11:30am–2:30pm and 5:30–9:15pm (last order). On Shiokoji Dori; turn right out of Kyoto Station's Karasuma (north) exit and walk 1 min. east.

⑦⑦ **Izusen** ✿✿✿ KYO-RYORI/VEGETARIAN   Although located in a nondescript building and with a very simple decor, this is one of my favorite restaurants in Kyoto. The food, which features local and vegetarian dishes, is delicious and beautifully presented. There's an English menu as well as a plastic-food display, and seating is either at tables or on tatami mats. You can choose from a variety of fixed-price meals offering soup, appetizer, rice, a main dish, and side dishes. A vegetarian meal for ¥1,800 ($15), for example, is the kind of light meal usually served at a tea ceremony. I usually opt for the Hana course (¥2,700/$22.50), which features Kyoto cuisine, including tempura, sashimi, various vegetables, broiled fish, rice, and soup.

Surugaiya Bldg., 2nd floor, Karasuma Shichijo Dori-sagaru. ℂ **075/343-4211.** Set meals ¥1,800–¥4,000 ($15–$33). No credit cards. Daily 11am–8pm. On Karasuma Dori between the Tourist Information Center and Kintetsu department store and above a McDonald's, a 1-min. walk from Kyoto Station's Karasuma (north) exit.

CENTRAL KYOTO

The heart of Kyoto's shopping, dining, and nightlife district is Nakagyo-ku, especially on Kawaramachi and Shijo Dori and along the many side streets. In summer, restaurants on the west bank of the Kamo River erect large wooden outdoor platforms that extend out over the water and offer open-air dining. For a cup of coffee, head to **Starbucks,** located on the corner of Shijo Dori and Yanaginobanba (ℂ **075/231-5008**).

EXPENSIVE

Manyoken ✿✿ FRENCH   Kyoto's first fully Western-style restaurant, Manyoken remains one of Kyoto's best known, with more than 90 years of experience serving traditional French cuisine. With its chandeliers, fresh roses, white tablecloths, drawing-room atmosphere, and attentive staff, this elegant restaurant offers a menu that changes monthly including set meals. A typical meal may start out with escargots in bourguignonne sauce or an eggplant and goose liver gratin followed by onion soup, beef filet with morels, and then baked Alaska or soufflé in Curaçao or chocolate. A la carte selections include steak, lobster, fish, and chicken.

Shijo Dori, Fuyacho Higashi-iru. © **075/221-1022.** Reservations recommended. Main dishes ¥3,600–¥12,000 ($30–$100); set meals ¥5,000–¥20,000 ($42–$165). AE, DC, JCB, MC, V. Wed–Mon 11:30am–2:30pm and 5–8:30pm (last order). Bus: 5 to Shijo-Fuyacho (1 min.). Just east of Fuyacho on the north side of Shijo Dori.

78 Misogi-gawa ★★★ *Finds* FRENCH KAISEKI   Dining here could well be the culinary highlight of your trip. Serving nouvelle French cuisine that utilizes the best of Japanese style and ingredients in what could be called French kaiseki, this lovely and exclusive restaurant stands on narrow Pontocho, which parallels the Kamo River and is one of Kyoto's most famous nightlife districts. Located in a century-old renovated wooden building that once belonged to a geisha, Misogi-Gawa is owned by master chef T. Inoue, who trained in Paris and successfully blends the two cuisines into dishes artfully prepared and served on Japanese tableware. One of the delights of eating here lies in receiving the various courses that are part of fixed-price meals, each one exquisitely arranged as though a work of art. The menu (written in French and changing regularly) includes lobster, sole, scallops, and various beef dishes, including a set steak course for ¥12,000 ($100). Seating options include a U-shaped counter with tatami seating and leg wells, another informal counter for customers who prefer to order a la carte dishes one by one, private tatami rooms, and my favorite, an outdoor summer veranda overlooking the river. A great place for a splurge.

Sanjo-sagaru, Pontocho. © **075/221-2270.** Reservations required. Main dishes ¥3,000–¥5,000 ($25–$42); set dinners ¥12,000–¥30,000 ($100–$250). AE, DC, JCB, MC, V. Tues–Sun 4:30–9pm (last order). Bus: 4, 17, or 205 to Sanjo Kawaramachi (5 min.).

Misono ★ TEPPANYAKI   Ths is a branch of the famous Kobe restaurant, which claims to have invented teppanyaki. You can bet with a reputation like that, it will live up to its good name. Your waiter prepares your meal in front of you (though with less fanfare than in other teppanyaki places) in a comfortable, dark wood–wainscoted room with a city view. If you're on a budget, come for the ¥1,200 ($10) set lunch, which includes steak, rice, and soup. There's an English menu.

Petit Monde Bldg., 5th floor, Takoyakushi, Kawaramachi. © **075/255-2981.** Set dinners ¥6,500–¥16,000 ($54–$133); set lunches ¥1,200–¥7,500 ($10–$62.50). AE, DC, JCB, MC, V. Wed–Mon 11:30am–3pm and 5–9:30pm (last order). Bus: 4, 5, 17, or 205 to Shijo Kawaramachi (1 min.). On the east side of Kawaramachi Dori just south of Maruzen bookstore and Takoyakushi St.

79 Moritaya ★★ SUKIYAKI, SHABU-SHABU   This restaurant on the Kamo River, located north of Sanjo Dori on a small street called Kiyamachi, was established in 1869 and specializes in beef from its own ranch. In addition to sukiyaki and shabu-shabu, teppanyaki courses starting at ¥8,000 ($67), steaks, and other beef dishes are available. But the best thing about dining here is the outdoor veranda on stilts over the river, open from June through September.

There's a branch on the 11th floor of Isetan department store at Kyoto Station (© **075/365-7788**), open daily 11am to 11pm (last order); closed some Tuesdays.

Kiyamachi Dori, Sanjo-agaru. © **075/231-5118.** Reservations required. Sukiyaki ¥3,800–¥7,500 ($32–$62.50); shabu-shabu ¥4,800–¥7,500 ($40–$62.50). AE, DC, JCB, MC, V. Daily noon–9pm (last order). Subway: Kyoto Shiyakusho-mae (3 min.). Bus: 4, 17, or 205 to Kawaramachi Sanjo (2 min.).

Tempura Yoshikawa ★★ TEMPURA   If you're hungering for tempura, this restaurant has a sign in English and is easy to find. Located in an old-fashioned part of Kyoto that boasts a number of expensive ryokan, it's a tiny, intimate place with a traditional atmosphere. The tempura counter seats only 12 and offers tempura lunches beginning at ¥2,000 ($17) and dinners beginning at ¥6,000 ($50). Meals in tatami rooms are more expensive, with tempura lunches beginning at ¥6,000 ($50), tempura dinners at ¥12,000 ($100), and Kyo-kaiseki meals costing ¥20,000 ($167).

Tominokoji Dori, Oike-sagaru. ☎ **075/221-5544.** Reservations required. Set dinners ¥6,000–¥20,000 ($50–$167); set lunches ¥2,000–¥6,000 ($17–$50). AE, DC, JCB, MC, V. Daily 11am–2pm and 5–8:30pm (last order). Counter seating closed Sun. Subway: Karasuma Oike Station (6 min.). On Tominokoji St. just south of Oike Dori.

Unkai ☺ KAISEKI/SHABU-SHABU/VEGETARIAN A convenient place for a meal if you're visiting Nijo Castle (across the street), Unkai has a modern and refined decor, floor-to-ceiling windows overlooking greenery, and kimono-clad waitresses. The English menu has photos illustrating a varied selection of shabu-shabu, kaiseki, tempura, and *shojin ryori* (a vegetarian set meal typical of Kyoto). The ¥5,000 ($42) Miyako Course is the one most often recommended for foreigners and includes an appetizer, sashimi, custard, grilled fish, tempura, miso soup, and rice.

ANA Hotel Kyoto, Nijojo-mae, Horikawa Dori. ☎ **075/231-1155.** Set dinners ¥4,000–¥12,000 ($33–$100); set lunches ¥3,000–¥6,000 ($25–$50). AE, DC, JCB, MC, V. Daily 11:30am–2:30pm and 5–10pm. Subway: Nijojo-mae (1 min.). Bus: 9, 50, or 101 to Nijojo-mae. On Horikawa Dori across from Nijo Castle's main entrance.

MODERATE

Agatha ☺☺ KUSHIYAKI Soothing jazz, playful decor, excellent food, and an enthusiastic, English-speaking staff make this a good choice in the heart of the city. Its namesake is none other than that great dame of mystery writers, with many set meals named after Agatha Christie characters. More than 50 different kinds of skewered food are available, including vegetables, seafood, and meat.

Kawaramachi-aneyakoji Higashi-iru, Nakagyo-ku. ☎ **075/223-2379.** Skewers ¥220–¥900 ($1.75–$7.50); set meals ¥2,500–¥5,500 ($21–$46). Daily 5pm–midnight. Subway: Kyoto Shiyakusho-mae (2 min.). Bus: 4, 17, or 205 to Kawaramachi Sanjo.

Ashoka ☺ INDIAN One of Kyoto's most popular Indian restaurants serves vegetarian and meat curries prepared by Indian chefs, including mutton, chicken, fish, vegetable, and shrimp selections, as well as tandoori. I started my meal here with mulligatawny Madrasi, a South Indian soup, and followed with Indian bread stuffed with minced meat along with mutton *sagwala* (mutton and spinach).

Kikusui Bldg., 3rd floor, Teramachi Dori. ☎ **075/241-1318.** Main dishes ¥1,400–¥2,200 ($12–$18); set dinners ¥2,000–¥5,800 ($17–$48); set lunches ¥900–¥2,000 ($7.50–$17). AE, DC, JCB, MC, V. Mon–Sat 11:30am–2:30pm and 5–9pm (last order); Sun and holidays 11:30am–9pm (last order). Closed 3rd Wed of the month. Bus: 4, 5, 17, or 205 to Shijo Kawaramachi (1 min.). Just north of Shijo Dori at the entrance to the Teramachi covered shopping arcade.

Azalea CONTINENTAL Azalea is a pleasant place for a casual Western meal if you're visiting nearby Nijo Castle. Offering an English menu and a view of its small, Japanese landscaped garden, it has inexpensive set lunches that may include a pasta or risotto dish as the main course, set dinners, and light a la carte selections such as sandwiches or beef curry rice for less than ¥2,000 ($17).

International Hotel Kyoto, Nijojo-mae, Horikawa Dori. ☎ **075/222-1111.** Set dinners ¥1,800–¥10,000 ($15–$83); set lunches ¥1,300–¥5,000 ($11–$42). AE, DC, JCB, MC, V. Daily 11:30am–2:30pm and 5–9pm. Subway: Nijojo-mae (2 min.). Bus: 9, 50, or 101 to Nijojo-mae. On Horikawa Dori across from Nijo Castle's main entrance.

Kyoshiki ✮ KAISEKI/KYO-RYORI   This reasonably priced kaiseki restaurant was converted from a Meiji-Era private home more than 20 years ago. I recommend the Hisago obento for ¥3,000 ($25) offered on the English-language menu; it consists of a variety of seasonal foods served in individual dishes that stack neatly on top of one another to form a gourd; you take the bowls apart to eat. The atmosphere here is relaxed and comfortable with both tatami and table seating.

Fuyacho Dori, Sanjo-agaru (just north of Sanjo Dori). ✆ **075/221-4840**. Set meals ¥3,000–¥10,000 ($25–$83); set lunches ¥3,000–¥3,300 ($25–$27.50). AE, DC, JCB, MC, V. Tues–Sun 11:40am–3pm and 5–8:30pm (last order). Bus: 5 to Shijo-Fuyacho (1 min.).

⑧⓪ **Tagoto** ✮ KYO-RYORI/KAISEKI/OBENTO   Nestled in an inner courtyard off busy Shijo Dori and offering a peaceful retreat in the heart of downtown Kyoto, this restaurant has been serving a variety of Japanese dishes at moderate prices since 1868. The English menu (with photos) includes Kyo-ryori set meals, tempura, obento lunch boxes, seasonal kaiseki courses, and *yuba* (a low-calorie curd made from soy milk). Inexpensive noodles and set lunches for less than ¥1,500 ($12.50) are served until 4pm. Seating is either at tables or on tatami.

Shijo-Kawaramachi, Nishi-iru, Kitagawa. ✆ **075/221-1811**. Set meals ¥3,000–¥10,000 ($25–$83). AE, DC, JCB, MC, V. Daily 11:30am–8:30pm (last order). Bus: 4, 5, 17, or 205 to Shijo Kawaramachi (1 min.). The entrance is off Sanjo Dori near the Kyoto Central Inn (look for a tiny door with a white sign; step through it and follow the passageway to the back courtyard).

⑧① **Tofujaya** (Finds) TOFU   After inheriting a tofu shop, owner Hamano-san opened this small, casual restaurant to promote tofu's nutritious qualities. Look for a tiny tofu shop on narrow Pontocho; the entrance to the second-floor restaurant is around the corner to the right. The restaurant, with room for only a dozen or so diners, has an open kitchen and an English menu listing *dengaku* (broiled tofu with a miso coating), fried tofu, sesame tofu, and other dishes priced under ¥900 ($7.50). It's easiest, however, to order one of the tofu kaiseki courses, which come with a variety of tofu and side dishes. I sure felt healthy after eating here.

Shijo-agaru, Pontocho. ✆ **075/212-7706**. Reservations required. Set courses ¥3,000–¥4,500 ($25–$37.50); set lunches ¥1,800–¥2,500 ($15–$21). No credit cards. Daily 11:30am–2pm and 5–9pm (until 9:30pm Sat–Sun and holidays). Closed some Tues. Bus: 4, 5, 17, or 205 to Shijo Kawaramachi (4 min.). On Pontocho's western side about halfway between Shijo and Sanjo streets (south of the playground and opposite Hunan Restaurant).

INEXPENSIVE

Beer Market Ichiba Coji ✮ (Value) CHINESE/ASIAN   It's difficult to classify this place, which calls itself a "Kyoto minibrewery" and serves its own original beer, claiming to have more beers on tap than any other establishment in Kyoto. But it's certainly much more than just a brewery. Visually, it's the most interesting and exciting new-age restaurant I've seen in Kyoto, reminding me of high-tech places in Tokyo with bare concrete walls, white pebbles on the floor, black furniture, an elevated dining platform above a running stream, and waitresses and cooks decked out in baggy Asian pants. The food is eclectic, although it's more Chinese than anything else. A specialty of the house is *pao,* morsels wrapped in lettuce leaves; also available are deep-fried *gyoza* (dumplings), deep-fried crab, *kushikatsu* (skewered foods), salads, and rice dishes. All the food is seasonal and fresh.

Withyou Bldg., Teramachi, Shijo-agaru. ✆ **075/252-2008**. Main dishes ¥450–¥2,000 ($3.75–$17); pao course ¥2,480 ($20). AE, DC, JCB, MC, V. Mon–Fri 11:30am–2pm and 5–10:15pm; Sat–Sun 11am–10:15pm (last order). Bus: 4, 5, 17, or 205 to Shijo Kawaramachi (3 min.). In the Teramachi covered shopping arcade just north of Nishikikoji Dori in the basement of the Withyou Bldg.

82 **Bio-Tei** VEGETARIAN/HEALTH FOOD   If you're yearning for a meal in a health-food restaurant, head to this very informal second-floor restaurant down the street from the Museum of Kyoto and catty-corner from the post office. It serves only one thing at lunch: a great lunch teishoku. Last time I was there it came with *genmae* (brown rice), salad, miso soup, pickles, and a curry-based tofu stew with potatoes and carrots. For dinner, vegetarian a la carte dishes are offered from a Japanese menu. Seating is at sturdy wooden tables hewn from Japanese cypress, and meals are served on tableware from local kilns. As befits a health-food restaurant, smoking is not allowed.

On the SW corner of Sanjo-Higashinotouin on the 2nd floor. ✆ **075/255-0086.** Lunch teishoku ¥800 ($6.65); dinner main courses ¥600–¥700 ($5–$5.85). No credit cards. Tues–Fri 11:30am–2pm; Tues–Wed and Fri–Sat 5–8:30pm (last order). Closed holidays. Subway: Karasuma-Oike (exit 5, 3 min.).

83 **Ganko Sushi** SUSHI   This popular, lively sushi restaurant offers the usual raw fish selections, as well as such items as grilled yakitori and kushikatsu, shabu-shabu, tempura, tofu (ranging from fried to grilled), and shrimp or crab dishes on an English menu. Behind the sushi counter is a fish tank with some rather large specimens swimming around happily until their numbers come up. On the second floor is a robatayaki restaurant that is popular with office workers after work; an English-language menu here lists grilled vegetables and meats.

Kawaramachi-Sanjo, Higashi-iru. ✆ **075/255-1128.** Sushi a la carte ¥50–¥780 (40¢–$6.35); set meals ¥1,000–¥2,580 ($8.35–$21.50). JCB, MC, V. First floor, daily 11:30am–10pm; second floor, daily 4:30–10pm. Subway: Kyoto Shiyakusho-mae (4 min.). Bus: 4, 17, or 205 to Kawaramachi Sanjo (2 min.). On Sanjo Dori just west of the Kamo River (look for its logo of a face with glasses and a bandana).

84 **Gontaro** NOODLES   This noodle shop has been serving its own hand-made noodles for a mere 70-some years. A small place with a modern yet traditional interior and an English menu, it offers various noodle dishes of either *soba* (buckwheat) or *udon* (a thicker, wheat noodle) with such toppings as tempura, as well as *donburi* (a rice casserole with tempura, yakitori, or other topping) and *nabe* (udon boiled in broth with seafood, chicken, and vegetables).

Fuyacho Dori, Shijo-agaru. ✆ **075/221-5810.** Noodles ¥700–¥1,500 ($5.85–$12.50); donburi ¥800–¥1,500 ($6.65–$12.50); nabe ¥3,800 ($32). JCB. Thurs–Tues 11:30am–10pm. Bus: 5 to Shijo-Fuyacho (1 min.). On the west side of Fuyacho Dori just north of Shijo Dori; look for a tiny recessed courtyard, white curtains, and a lone pine tree.

Misoka-An Kawamichiya ★★ NOODLES   Charming and delightful with a central courtyard and cubbyhole rooms, this tiny, 300-year-old noodle shop makes a great place for an inexpensive meal in the heart of traditional Kyoto. It offers plain buckwheat noodles as well as noodles with such adornments as tempura and chicken and onions. Its specialty is a one-pot noodle dish called *hokoro,* which includes chicken, tofu, mushrooms, and vegetables for two. There's an English menu.

Fuyacho Dori, Sanjo-agaru. ✆ **075/221-2525.** Noodles ¥550–¥1,380 ($4.60–$11.50); Hokoro ¥7,600 ($63) for 2 people. AE, MC, V. Fri–Wed 11am–8pm. Bus: 5 to Shijo-Fuyacho (2 min.). On the west side of Fuyacho Dori just north of Sanjo Dori.

85 **Musashi** *Value* SUSHI   For a cheap meal of raw fish, this conveniently located restaurant can't be beat. Morsels of sushi ranging from tuna to octopus are served up via a conveyor belt that moves plates along the counter; simply reach out and take whatever strikes your fancy. Sushi is priced at ¥120 ($1) a plate. Take-out sushi is also available from the sidewalk front counter.

On the NW corner of the Kawaramachi-Sanjo intersection. © 075/222-0634. ¥120 ($1) per plate. No credit cards. Daily 11am–9:40pm (last order). Bus: 4, 17, or 205 to Kawaramachi Sanjo (1 min.).

(86) **Omen** UDON   A casual atmosphere and healthy food at reasonable prices make this place popular. Vegetable udon (Omen) is the specialty, and the house's traditional style is to serve the wheat noodles in a flat wooden bowl, the sauce in a pottery bowl, the vegetables delicately arranged (sushi style) on a handmade platter with a bowl of sesame seeds alongside. You dip and mix yourself, unlike at other udon shops where it all arrives like a stew swimming in one bowl. Tempura, lightly fried tofu, and *kamonasu dengaku* (fried eggplant topped with a rich miso sauce) are among the other dishes offered on the English menu. Another branch is located just south of Ginkakuji (© **075/771-8994**); there's also one in New York.

Gokomachi Dori, Shijo-agaru. © **075/255-2125.** Main dishes ¥600–¥1,000 ($5–$8.35); set meals ¥1,300–¥2,500 ($11–$20.85). No credit cards. Fri, Mon–Wed 11am–3:30pm and 4:30–10pm; Sat and Sun 11am–10pm. Subway: Shijo (5 min.). Bus: 4, 5, 17, or 205 to Shijo Kawaramachi (3 min.). On the east side of Gokomachi Dori, north of Shijo.

(87) **Suishin Honten** YAKITORI   Although it's technically a drinking establishment, this inexpensive yakitori-ya is a great place to dine as well. Popular with young Japanese, it offers yakitori, sushi, and other Japanese bar foods. Be sure to remove your shoes at the entryway and place them in one of the lockers provided; you might want to choose your meal from the display case first or simply look around at what others are eating once you're settled.

Pontocho, Sanjo Dori-sagaru. © 075/221-8596. 2 skewers of yakitori ¥280 ($2.35); sushi set ¥650 ($5.40). AE, DC, JCB, MC, V. Daily 4–11:30pm (last order). Subway: Kyoto Shiyakusho-mae (4 min.). Bus: 4, 17, or 205 to Kawaramachi Sanjo (2 min.). On the west side of Pontocho just south of Sanjo Dori; look for a big white sign and a large display case of plastic food with a kite above it.

Tohkasaikan BEIJING CHINESE   This Beijing-style Chinese restaurant started life as a Western restaurant. The old building features an ancient, manually operated elevator, lots of wood paneling, high ceilings, old-fashioned decor, and a friendly staff. From June to mid-September, you can sit outside on a wooden veranda over the Kamo River, one of the cheapest places along the river to do so. If it's winter or raining, consider sitting in the fifth-floor dining room, which has nice views of the city. The best views, however, are from the rooftop garden (open in summer), where you can order mugs of beer and dine on dishes from the extensive English-language menu including sweet-and-sour pork, cooked shrimp with arrowroot, and chicken and green pepper. The second floor is reserved for groups of two or more ordering set courses. The service tends to be slow, and I've had better Chinese food, but the atmosphere is great and is reminiscent of another era. Popular with families.

Nishizume, Shijo Ohashi. © **075/221-1147.** Main dishes ¥1,300–¥2,700 ($11–$22.50); set meals ¥5,000–¥10,000 ($42–$83). AE, DC, JCB, MC, V. Daily 11:30am–9pm (last order). Bus: 4, 5, 17, or 205 to Shijo-Kawaramachi (2 min.) On Shijo Dori just west of the bridge spanning the Kamo River in a large, yellow, stone building.

EASTERN KYOTO

In addition to the restaurants discussed below, there are a lot of informal and inexpensive places near **Kiyomizu Temple.** If the weather is fine, you might wish to stop for noodles and a beer on the Kiyomizu Temple grounds, where you'll find several open-air tatami pavilions.

EXPENSIVE

88 Hyotei ★★★ *Finds* KAISEKI/OBENTO This 300-year-old restaurant first opened its doors as a teahouse to serve pilgrims and visitors on their way to Nanzenji Temple. Today it consists of two parts: one offering expensive Kyo-kaiseki, which originated with the tea ceremony but is now associated with Kyoto cooking, and the other offering seasonal obento lunch boxes. The kaiseki meals are served in separate tiny houses situated around a beautiful garden with a pond, maple trees, and bushes; the oldest house, which resembles a small tea-house, is more than 3 centuries old. Seating is on cushions on a tatami floor in your own private room with your food brought to you by kimono-clad women. The other part of the restaurant serves lunch boxes (Shokado Bento) until 4pm; the menu depends on the season, and seating here is at tables and chairs. Hyotei is also renowned for its seasonal breakfast, served until 11am Friday to Wednesday. For the cold winter months (Dec–Mar), the Uzuragayu set breakfast warms the body and soul with a quail rice gruel, grilled skewers, sashimi, soup, and other dishes, while the Asagayu features lighter fare including a rice porridge.

35 Kusakawa-cho, Nanzenji. ✆ 075/771-4116. Reservations required for kaiseki, recommended for obento. Kaiseki lunches from ¥18,000 ($150), dinners from ¥20,000 ($167); obento lunch boxes ¥4,000 ($33); breakfast including service and tax ¥4,150 ($34). AE, DC, JCB, MC, V. Fri–Wed 8am–7:30pm (last order); Thur 11:30am–7:30pm. Closed the 2nd and 4th Tues of month. Subway: Keage (5 min.). Bus: 5 or 100 to Nanzenji-Eikando-michi (2 min.). West of Shirakawa Dori on a road leading to Nanzenji Temple; look for a plain facade hidden behind a bamboo fence with a sign shaped like a gourd.

89 Mikaku ★ JAPANESE STEAK HOUSE Established almost a century ago by the present owner's grandfather, this restaurant in the heart of Gion is housed in a 100-year-old renovated building that was once a private home. The house specialty is an *aburayaki* meal, which consists of beef filet cooked with various vegetables and seasoned with soy sauce and wine. Sukiyaki, *mizudaki* (similar to shabu-shabu but stronger in taste), and teppanyaki are also available from the English menu. If you order sukiyaki or mizudaki, you'll sit in your own private tatami room on the second floor; if you order teppanyaki, seating is at a counter where the chef (the first female teppanyaki chef we've seen) will prepare your food in front of you on a hot griddle. Outside the window is a pleasant view of the Shirakawa River.

Nawate Dori, Shijo-agaru, Gion. ✆ 075/525-1129. Reservations recommended. Steak and shabu-shabu meals ¥6,500–¥15,000 ($54–$125); set lunch ¥2,500 ($21). AE, DC, JCB, MC, V. Mon–Sat 11:30am–1:30pm (last order) and 5–9:30pm (last order). Bus: 100 or 206 to Gion (5 min.) or 4, 5, 17, or 205 to Shijo Kawara-machi (5 min.). From Shijo Dori, go 1 block north on Nawate Dori and take the 1st left.

Minokichi Honten Takesigero ★★ KYO-KAISEKI One of Japan's best-known restaurants for Kyoto cuisine, Minokichi was founded in 1719 as one of eight restaurants licensed to serve freshwater fish and is now in its 10th generation of restaurateurs. With several branches in Japan, including a handful in Kyoto, Osaka, and Tokyo, this flagship restaurant consists of various dining venues in several buildings, including a 200-year-old thatched-roof farmhouse and an elegantly simple modern building reminiscent of tea-ceremony rooms, all with magnificent views of a graceful bamboo garden. The specialty is Kyoto-style kaiseki (*Kyo-kaiseki*); emphasis is on the appearance of the food, and great care is given to the selection and preparation of seasonal ingredients. Although the dishes themselves change, a kaiseki meal here always consists of 10 items:

appetizer, raw fish, soup, food cooked in delicate broth, steamed food, broiled food, deep-fried food, and vinegared food, fruit, and green tea with a sweet.

65 Torii-cho, Awataguchi (Sanjo-agaru, Dobutsuen-mae Dori). ☎ 075/771-4185. Reservations required for dinner, recommended for lunch. Kyo-kaiseki dinners ¥15,000–¥30,000 ($125–$250); kaiseki lunches ¥7,000–¥15,000 ($58–$125). AE, DC, JCB, MC, V. Daily 11:30am–2pm and 5–7:30pm (last order). Subway: Keage (10 min.). North of Sanjo Dori on the road to the Zoological Gardens.

(90) **Minoko** ✸✸✸ KAISEKI/OBENTO   This former villa is an enclave of traditional Japan with a simple, austere exterior and an interior of winding wooden corridors, tatami rooms, and a garden. Opened about 70 years ago by the present owner's father, Minoko does its best to retain the spirit of the tea ceremony, specializing in an elaborate kind of kaiseki dinner called *cha-kaiseki,* usually served at tea-ceremony gatherings and utilizing seasonal ingredients that are beautifully arranged to please both the palate and the eye. If you come for dinner, when only kaiseki is served, you'll eat in your own private tatami room. Lunch, which is served communally in a large tatami room with a view of a beautiful garden, is more economical and less formal but still draws on the tea ceremony for inspiration. The obento lunch box, for example, called *chabako-bento,* is named after the lacquered box it's served in, which is traditionally used to carry tea utensils to outdoor tea ceremonies. A *hiru-kaiseki,* or mini-kaiseki set meal, is also available at lunch.

480 Kiyoi-cho, Shimogawara-dori, Gion. ☎ 075/561-0328. Reservations recommended for lunch, required for dinner. Kaiseki ¥13,000 ($108); mini-kaiseki lunch ¥10,000 ($83); obento lunch box ¥4,500–¥6,000 ($37.50–$50). AE, DC, JCB, MC, V. Daily 11:30am–2:30pm and 5–10pm (last order 8pm). Closed irregularly 3 days a month. Bus: 100 or 206 to Gion (3 min.). A short walk south of Yasaka Shrine.

MODERATE

(91) **Isobe** KAISEKI/VARIED JAPANESE   A convenient place to stop for lunch if you're walking from Kiyomizu Temple to Heian Shrine, this modern, pleasant restaurant offers a nice view of Maruyama Park from its dining room and has an English menu with photographs listing a variety of set meals featuring sashimi, tempura, and kaiseki.

Maruyama Park, Ikenohata. ☎ 075/561-2216. Set meals ¥3,000–¥14,000 ($25–$117). AE, DC, JCB, MC, V. Daily 11am–10pm. Bus: 100 or 206 to Gion (10 min.). On the southeastern edge of the park (if you're walking from Kiyomizu, take a right at the park entrance; if you're coming from Gion, walk past Yasaka Shrine and keep to the right); look for the outdoor red umbrella (up only in dry weather but also depicted on the sign).

Junsei ✸ TOFU/KAISEKI/OBENTO   Specilizing in tofu dishes, Junsei opened in 1961, but the grounds and garden were originally part of a private institution established in the 1830s during the shogun era. Although tourist-oriented and popular with tour groups, the food is good and an English-language menu makes ordering easy. There are several buildings spread throughout the grounds, and what you want determines where you go; as soon as you arrive, you'll be given a menu and asked what you'll be eating. I chose the house specialty, a *yudofu* (tofu) set meal, and was directed to an older building filled with antiques and tatami mats. My meal came with vegetable tempura and various tofu dishes, including fried tofu on a stick and tofu boiled in a pot at my table. Other set meals include kaiseki (by reservation only), shabu-shabu or sukiyaki (¥8,000/$67), and obento box lunches (¥3,500 and ¥5,000/$29 and $42). After your meal, be sure to take a stroll through the garden.

60 Kusakawa-cho, Nanzenji. ☎ 075/761-2311. Reservations required for kaiseki. Tofu set meals ¥3,000–¥4,000 ($25–$33); kaiseki set meals ¥10,000–¥20,000 ($83–$167). AE, DC, JCB, MC, V. Daily 11am–7:30pm (last order). Subway: Keage (8 min.). Bus: 5 or 100 to Nanzenji-Eikando-michi (4 min.). East of Shirakawa Dori on the road to Nanzenji Temple.

Le Grand Rêve FRENCH   There aren't many restaurants in this vicinity, so this is a good choice for lunch or dinner if you're visiting nearby Sanjusangendo Hall or the Kyoto National Museum. This formal dining hall is small and intimate, overlooking a beautiful garden with a waterfall and pond. In addition to a la carte dishes, there are also set meals including a French *kaiseki* meal (French food prepared with the imagination of kaiseki and eaten with chopsticks). The menu changes with the seasons, but past main dishes have included sautéed chicken and grilled duck with lemon-and-honey sauce.

Kyoto Park Hotel at Shichijo Dori and Higashioji Dori. ✆ **075/525-3111.** Main dishes ¥1,500–¥2,200 ($12.50–$18); set dinners ¥6,000–¥10,000 ($50–$83); set lunches ¥2,000–¥3,000 ($17–$25). Daily 11am–2pm and 5–9pm. Bus: 100, 206, or 208 to Hakubutsukan Sanjusangendo-mae (1 min.).

92 **Okutan** ★★★ *Finds* TOFU/VEGETARIAN   This is one of the oldest, most authentic, and most delightful tofu restaurants in Kyoto. Founded about 350 years ago as a vegetarian restaurant serving for Buddhist monks, this thatched-roof wooden place in a peaceful setting with pond and garden serves just one thing: a tofu set meal (yudofu). Okutan is very simple and rustic with seating either in tatami rooms or outdoors on cushioned platforms, making it especially delightful in fine weather. Women dressed in traditional rural clothing bring your food. The set meal, which changes slightly with the seasons, includes a pot of tofu boiled at your table, fried tofu on a stick, vegetable tempura, yam soup, and pickled vegetables. Highly recommended.

86–30 Fukuchi-cho, Nanzenji. ✆ **075/771-8709.** Reservations recommended. Yudofu set meal ¥3,000 ($25). No credit cards. Fri–Wed 11am–5:30pm (last order). Bus: 5 or 100 to Nanzenji-Eikando-michi (6 min.). Just north of Nanzenji Temple's main gate (the San Mon Gate).

INEXPENSIVE

93 **Chorakukan** WESTERN   This informal place, a good stop if you're walking from Kiyomizu Temple to Heian Shrine, is one of the few Western restaurants in eastern Kyoto. The building, which dates from the Meiji Period and also houses the Ladies' Hotel Chorakukan (see "Where to Stay in Kyoto," earlier in this chapter), features elaborate woodwork and marble. Although the inexpensive downstairs restaurant is nothing fancy, it's restful: Classical music plays in the background, and there's a view of some maple trees. Dishes include fried shrimp, grilled chicken with bacon, spaghetti, curry, and sandwiches. Lunch specials are served from 11am to 2pm, when you have your choice of either a Western-style lunch or a Japanese-style box lunch. After lunch, you may wish to retire to the building's coffee shop, a beautiful room reminiscent of European coffee shops. Although the set dinners can be expensive, the set dinner for ¥3,000 ($25) is a good choice for the budget-conscious—it even includes a glass of wine.

In the SW corner of Maruyama Park. ✆ **075/561-0001.** Main dishes ¥1,000–¥1,800 ($8.35–$15); set dinners ¥3,000–¥8,000 ($25–$67); set lunches ¥1,500–¥1,800 ($12.50–$15). No credit cards. Daily 11am–7:30pm (last order). Bus: 100 or 206 to Gion (7 min); after passing Yasaka Shrine, look to the right for a large stone-and-brick, Western-style building with a huge stone lantern in its driveway.

94 **Goemonjaya** TOFU/TEMPURA/NOODLES   This typical Japanese restaurant specializes in tofu dishes and tempura. With tatami seating, a small garden, and a waterfall and carp-filled pond, it offers a yudofu (tofu) set meal, a shrimp or vegetarian tempura teishoku, and in summer only, inexpensive noodle dishes ranging in price from ¥650 ($5.40) for *somen* (thin vermicelli served cold) to ¥800 ($6.65) for *zarusoba* (cold, buckwheat noodles).

67 Kukasawa-cho, Nanzenji. ✆ 075/751-9638. Set meals ¥2,200–¥2,900 ($18–$24). No credit cards. Daily 11am–7pm (last order). Closed some Tues. Bus: 5 or 100 to Nanzenji-Eikando-michi (2 min.). Across the street from Yachiyo Inn on the road leading to Nanzenji Temple. Look for a red lantern beside the road and a display case of plastic food; the restaurant is back off the main road past a smiling Buddha and a red paper umbrella (open only in dry weather).

NORTHERN KYOTO

Ryoanji Yudofuya ★★ *Finds* TOFU/VEGETARIAN If you're visiting Ryoanji Temple in northeastern Kyoto, there's no lovelier setting for a meal than this traditional restaurant, which calls itself the Ryoanji Seven Herb Tofu Restaurant in honor of its *yudofu* (tofu) dish: boiled tofu and vegetables topped with seven herbs. Entrance to the restaurant, situated beside the Kyoyoike Pond, is along a small path that takes you past a stream, a small pond, a grove of maple and pine, and moss-covered grounds, which is also what you look out on as you dine, seated on tatami. You'll know you're getting close to the restaurant when you hear the thonk of a bamboo trough fed by a stream, which fills and hits against stone as it empties. Note that if you wish to come here only for a beer after visiting the temple, you'll be charged an extra ¥300 ($2.50) table charge in addition to the cost of the ¥500 ($4.15) beer.

Ryoanji Temple. ✆ 075/462-4742. Yudofu ¥1,500 ($12.50); yudofu vegetarian set meal ¥3,300 ($27.50). No credit cards. Daily 10am–5pm. Bus: 50 to Ritsumeikan Daigaku-mae (4 min.).

5 Exploring the City

Because Kyoto has so many worthwhile sights, you must plan your itinerary carefully. Even the most avid sightseer can become jaded after days of visiting yet another temple or shrine, no matter how beautiful or peaceful, so be sure to temper your visits to cultural and historical sights with time spent simply walking around. Kyoto is a city best seen on foot; take time to explore small alleyways and curio shops, pausing from time to time to soak in the beauty and atmosphere. If you spend your days in Kyoto racing around in a taxi or a bus from one temple to another, the essence of this ancient capital and its charm may literally pass you by.

Before setting out, be sure to stop by **Kyoto City Tourist Information** on the second floor of Kyoto Station near the Karasuma exit (✆ **075/343-6655**) or the **Tourist Information Center (TIC)** across from Kyoto Station's Karasuma exit in the Kyoto Tower Building (✆ **075/371-5649**) to pick up a detailed map of the city and a colorful sightseeing brochure listing Kyoto's most important sites. You can also pick up a leaflet called "Kyoto Walks," which contains five maps for strolling tours of Kyoto, including the walk from Kiyomizu Temple to Heian Shrine and on to the Silver Pavilion, which I've outlined below in more detail.

Keep in mind, too, that you must enter Kyoto's museums, shrines, and temples at least a half hour before closing time.

SUGGESTED ITINERARIES

If You Have 1 Day If you have only a single day to spend in Kyoto and want to see its most famous attractions, take a bus or a taxi to Gojo-zaka and then walk uphill past pottery and souvenir shops to **Kiyomizu Shrine.** Back at Gojo-zaka, board another bus (the 100 Chin-Chin bus) for **Heian Shrine,** where you should be sure to stroll the garden. Behind Heian Shrine is the **Kyoto Handicraft Center,** the best place in town for one-stop souvenir shopping. From here, take bus no.

204 to the stunning **Kinkakuji** (Temple of the Golden Pavilion) and, if time permits, take bus no. 12 to **Ryoanji Temple,** with the most famous rock garden in all of Japan. In the evening, dine at a traditional Japanese restaurant serving Kyoto cuisine, followed by a stroll through **Gion** and along the Kamo River.

If You Have 2 Days Spend the first day in eastern Kyoto, following the walking tour through Higashiyama-ku outlined later in this chapter; be sure to include a visit to Heian Shrine and a shopping trip to either the Kyoto Handicraft Center or the **Kyoto Craft Center** in Gion. In the evening, dine at a restaurant specializing in Kyoto cuisine, followed by a stroll along the Kamo River and Pontocho.

On the second day, visit the **Kyoto Imperial Palace** and **Nijo Castle** in central Kyoto, **Ryoanji Temple** with its famous rock garden, and **Kinkakuji (Temple of the Golden Pavilion)** in northwestern Kyoto. End the day with a visit to the **Museum of Kyoto** and shopping in the **Shijo-Kawaramachi** shopping district, followed by a stroll through Gion and an evening performance at **Gion Corner** with its cultural demonstrations.

If You Have 3 Days Spend the first 2 days in and around Kyoto as outlined above. On the third day, head for **Nara,** Japan's ancient capital, and its many temples and historical attractions. If it's summer, spend the evening in **Arashiyama,** where you can board a wooden boat and observe cormorant fishing (see "A Summer Spectacle: Cormorant Fishing," later in this chapter).

If You Have 4 or 5 Days (Or More) Spend the first 2 days in eastern Kyoto, following the two strolls described later in this section. On the third day, add **Nijo Castle,** the **Kyoto Imperial Palace, Ryoanji Temple,** and the **Temple of the Golden Pavilion** as outlined in "If You Have 2 Days," above. Spend the fourth day in **Nara.** If you have more time, visit the **Katsura Imperial Villa, Saihoji Moss Temple,** or one of the other recommended destinations close to Kyoto—or just spend more time exploring Kyoto, visiting the museums you haven't had time for, shopping, or pursuing your own interests.

AROUND KYOTO STATION

As strange as it sounds, the biggest tourist draw around Kyoto Station is **Kyoto Station** itself. Japan's largest station is a futuristic-looking building with soaring glass atriums, spage-age music, escalators rising to a rooftop observatory, and open stages for free concerts and other events. In a bold move to attract young Japanese (who nowadays prefer to take their vacations in more exotic or trendier climes), it also has a shopping center selling everything from clothing to Kyoto souvenirs, the fashionable Isetan department store, restaurants, and a Joypolis amusement arcade. I saw more tourists photographing Kyoto Station than any other modern building in town.

Just a 10- and 5-minute walk (respectively) north of Kyoto Station are two massive temple compounds, **Nishi-Honganji** and **Higashi-Honganji.** They were once joined as one huge religious center called Honganji, but they split after a disagreement several centuries ago. Higashi-Honganji is Kyoto's largest wooden structure, while Nishi-Honganji is an outstanding example of Buddhist architecture. But the best thing to do is visit Higashi-Honganji's garden, **Shosei-en** (✆ 075/371-2961), a 2-minute walk to the east. Once the private villa of Higashi-Honganji's abbot and designed in part by famous landscape architect

Kyoto Attractions

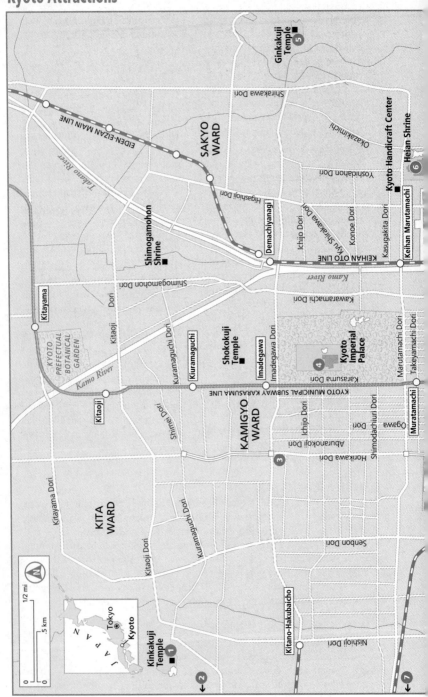

Ginkakuji Temple ⑤

Kyoto Handicraft Center

Heian Shrine ⑥

Shirakawa Dori

SAKYO WARD

Okazakimichi

Yoshidahon Dori

Kasugakita Dori

Konoe Dori

Keihan Marutamachi

Demachiyanagi

Higashioji Dori

Ichijo Dori

Kyu Shirakawa Dori

EIDEN-EIZAN MAIN LINE

Takano River

KEIHAN OTO LINE

Shimogamohon Shrine

Shimogamohon Dori

Kamo River

Kawaramachi Dori

Kitayama

Kitaoji Dori

KYOTO PREFECTUAL BOTANICAL GARDEN

Kamo River

Kuramaguchi Dori

Kuramaguchi

Shokokuji Temple

Imadegawa

Imadegawa Dori

Kyoto Imperial Palace ④

Marutamachi Dori

Takeyamachi Dori

Karasuma Dori

Marutamachi

Kitaoji

Shimei Dori

KYOTO MUNICIPAL SUBWAY KARASUMA LINE

KAMIGYO WARD

Ichijo Dori

Shimodachiuri Dori

Muratamachi

Ogawa Dori

Aburanokoji Dori

③

Horikawa Dori

KITA WARD

Kuramaguchi Dori

Kitaoji Dori

Kitayama Dori

Senbon Dori

Kitano-Hakubaicho

Nishioji Dori

1/2 mi

.5 km

JAPAN

Tokyo

Kyoto

Kinkakuji Temple ①

②

⑦

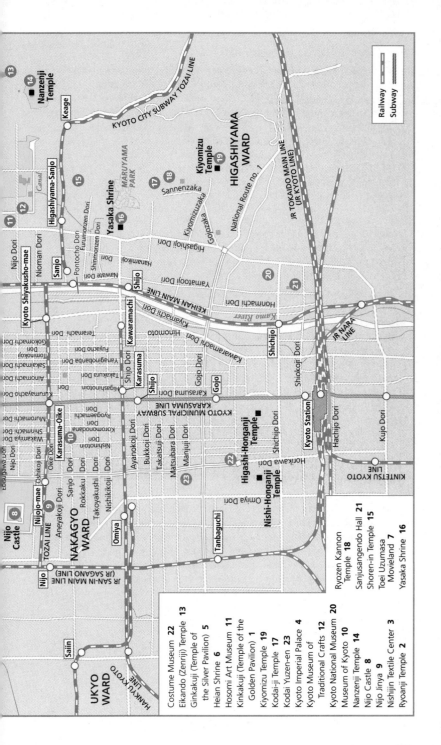

Railway ----
Subway ====

Nanzenji Temple

Keage

KYOTO CITY SUBWAY TOZAI LINE

Higashiyama-Sanjo

Sanjo

Kyoto Shiyakusho-mae

Nijo Dori
Nioman Dori
Pontocho Dori
Furumonzen Dori
Shinmonzen Dori
Nawate Dori
Hanamikoji Dori
Higashioji Dori
Yamatooji Dori
Honmachi Dori

MARUYAMA PARK

Yasaka Shrine

Sannenzaka
Kiyomizuzaka
Gojozaka

Kiyomizu Temple

HIGASHIYAMA WARD

National Route no. 1

JR TOKAIDO MAIN LINE (JR KYOTO LINE)

Shijo

KEIHAN MAIN LINE

Kawaramachi

Kawaramachi Dori
Kiyamachi Dori

Hinomoto

Kamo River

Karasuma
Shijo

Shijo Dori
Higashinotoin Dori
Takakura Dori
Yanaginobamba Dori
Fuyacho Dori
Teramachi Dori
Gokomachi Dori
Tominokoji Dori
Sakaimachi Dori
Ainomachi Dori
Kurumayacho Dori

Karasuma-Oike

Gojo
Gojo Dori

Shichijo

Shichijo Dori

Shiokoji Dori

JR NARA LINE

Kyoto Station

Hachijo Dori

Kujo Dori

KINTETSU KYOTO LINE

KYOTO MUNICIPAL SUBWAY KARASUMA LINE

Karasuma Dori
Shinmachi Dori
Muromachi Dori
Nishinotoin Dori
Koromonodana Dori
Ryogaemachi Dori
Ayanokoji Dori
Bukkoji Dori
Takatsuji Dori
Matsubara Dori
Manjuji Dori

Higashi-Honganji Temple

Nishi-Honganji Temple

Horikawa Dori
Omiya Dori

Tanbaguchi

Omiya

NAKAGYO WARD

Nijo Castle

Nijojo-mae

Nijo

JR SAN-IN MAIN LINE (JR SAGANO LINE)

TOZAI LINE

Oike Dori
Sanjo Dori
Rokkaku Dori
Takoyakushi Dori
Nishikikoji Dori
Aneyakoji Dori

Toshikoji Dori
Oshikoji Dori
Nijo Dori

Wakamiya Dori

Saiin

HANKYU KYOTO LINE

UKYO WARD

HANKYU KYOTO LINE

KINTETSU KYOTO

Ryozen Kannon Temple **18**
Sanjusangendo Hall **21**
Shoren-in Temple **15**
Toei Uzumasa Movieland **7**
Yasaka Shrine **16**

Costume Museum **22**
Eikando (Zenriji) Temple **13**
Ginkakuji (Temple of the Silver Pavilion) **5**
Heian Shrine **6**
Hosomi Art Museum **11**
Kinkakuji (Temple of the Golden Pavilion) **1**
Kiyomizu Temple **19**
Kodai-ji Temple **17**
Kodai Yuzen-en **23**
Kyoto Imperial Palace **4**
Kyoto Museum of Traditional Crafts **12**
Kyoto National Museum **20**
Museum of Kyoto **10**
Nanzenji Temple **14**
Nijo Castle **9**
Nishijin Textile Center **3**
Ryoanji Temple **2**

Moments   Cultural Immersion

If you're interested in learning firsthand about the tea ceremony, flower arranging, origami, Japanese calligraphy, Japanese cooking, simple phrases in Japanese, and other cultural pursuits, you can do so with the help of the members of the **Women's Association of Kyoto (WAK Japan)** in the privacy of their own homes or at your hotel. Contact Wak (✆ **075/752-9090;** www.wakjapan.com/) for information on private instruction, classes, and fees. Most classes run 1 to 2 hours and average ¥6,500 ($54) for one person, ¥10,000 ($83) for 2, and ¥5,000 ($42) per person for groups of three or four. Reservations should be made a couple days in advance, if possible.

Kobori Enshu in the 17th century, it features a pond and several buildings. Although there are many more beautiful and grander gardens in Kyoto, it provides a nice respite if you're in the area, and even better, it's free (donations are appreciated). It's open daily 9am to 4pm.

Costume Museum   This two-room museum is devoted to traditional Japanese clothing, ranging from ceremonial court dress to clothing worn by samurai, daimyo, and geisha. Note, however, that there's a special exhibit running through 2002 (and possibly longer) that has temporarily replaced the permanent exhibit with an elaborate, quarter-size replication of the Spring Palace as immortalized by Murasaki Shikibu in *The Tale of Genji,* complete with dolls wearing gorgeous kimono and miniature furniture of the Heian period. In any case, you can see everything in less than half an hour.

Izutsu Bldg., 5th floor, Shinhanayacho Dori, Horikawa Higashiiru (on the corner of Horikawa and Shinhanayacho sts. just northeast of Nishi-Honganji Temple). ✆ 075/342-5345. Admission ¥400 ($3.35) adults, ¥300 ($2.50) students, ¥200 ($1.65) children 7–12. Mon–Sat 9am–5pm. Bus: 9 to Nishi-Honganji-mae (2 min.), or a 15-min. walk north from Kyoto Station.

CENTRAL KYOTO

Much of Central Kyoto has been taken over by the 20th century, but there are a few interesting sites worth investigating.

If you've never been to a market in Japan, you'll probably want to take a stroll down **Nishiki-Koji Dori,** a fish-and-produce market right in the heart of town. A covered pedestrian lane stretching west from Teramachi Dori (and just north of Shijo Dori), Nishiki-Koji has been Kyoto's principal food market for more than 4 centuries. This is where the city's finest restaurants and inns buy their food; you'll find approximately 135 open-fronted shops and stalls selling seasonal vegetables, fish, beans, seaweed, pickled vegetables, and more. Shops are open from the early morning hours until about 6pm; many close on either Wednesday or Sunday.

Kyoto Imperial Palace (Kyoto Gosho) ⭐⭐   This is where the imperial family lived from 1331 until 1868 when they moved to Tokyo. The palace was destroyed several times by fire; the present buildings date from 1855. Modestly furnished with delicate decorations, the palace shows the restful designs of the peaceful Heian Period. The gardens are graceful. You can visit the palace only on a free, 1-hour guided tour, but fair warning: They're conducted quickly, leaving little time for dawdling or taking pictures.

Kyotogyoen-nai, Karasuma-Imadegawa. ✆ **075/211-1215**. Free admission. Tours in English Mon–Fri at 10am and 2pm, also 3rd Sat of every month and every Sat in Apr, May, Oct, and Nov. Permission must be obtained in person from the Imperial Household Agency Office (✆ **075/211-1215**), on palace grounds near the Inui Gomon Gate and open Mon–Fri 8:45am–noon and 1–4pm. Foreign visitors can apply in person in advance or on the day of the tour (before 9:40am for the 10am tour, before 1:40pm for the 2pm tour), but tours can fill up (especially in spring and fall); 1-day advance application required for all visitors 3rd Sat of every month and every Sat in Apr, May, Oct, and Nov. Must be 21 or older (or accompanied by an adult) and must present your passport; parties of no more than 9 may apply. Subway: Karasuma Line to Imadegawa (exit 3, 3 min.).

Museum of Kyoto (Kyoto Bunka Hakubutsukan) ✿

Through video displays, slides, and even holograms, this museum presents Kyoto's 1,200-year history from prehistoric relics to contemporary arts and crafts. I particularly like the various architectural models depicting a local market, merchants' homes, and a wholesale store, but best of all is the vermilion-colored Heian Shrine model with its holographic display of construction workers. The third floor features changing exhibitions of Kyoto arts and crafts as well as a Japanese-style room and garden. The annex, which occupies a 1906 bank with its original main hall (complete with teller cages), houses archaeological finds and folk crafts.

Unfortunately, explanations are in Japanese only, but the museum does offer free English guides every day from 10am to 5pm; personal tours last between 30 and 60 minutes depending on your interest (since guides are volunteers, it's a good idea to make a reservation for one). A special feature of the museum is its film library, which houses hundreds of Japanese classics from silent movies to films made up to 20 years ago (the Japanese movie industry was based in Kyoto for decades). Movies are shown twice a day Thursday through Sunday (at 1:30 and 5pm at last check, but you'd be wise to confirm the time).

At Sanjo and Takakura sts. ✆ **075/222-0888**. Admission ¥500 ($4.15) adults, ¥400 ($3.35) students, ¥300 ($2.50) children; movie admission included. Tues–Sun 10am–7:30pm. Subway: Karasuma-Oike (exit 5, 3 min.).

Nijo Castle (Nijojo) ✿✿✿

The Tokugawa shogun's Kyoto home stands in stark contrast to most of Japan's other remaining castles, which were constructed purely for defense. Built by the first Tokugawa shogun, Ieyasu, in 1603, Nijo Castle is considered the quintessence of Momoyama architecture, built almost entirely of Japanese cypress and boasting delicate transom wood carvings and paintings by the Kano School on sliding doors.

I prefer Nijo Castle to the Imperial Palace because you can explore its interior on your own. The main building, **Ninomaru Palace,** has 33 rooms, some 800 tatami mats, and an understated elegance, especially compared with castles being built in Europe at the same time. All the sliding doors on the outside walls of the castle can be removed in summer, permitting breezes to sweep through the building. Typical for Japan at the time, rooms were unfurnished, and the mattresses were stored in closets.

One of the castle's most intriguing features is its so-called **nightingale floors.** To protect the shogun from real or imagined enemies, the castle was protected by a moat and stone walls. How deep the shogun's paranoia ran, however, is apparent by the installation of these special floorboards, which creaked when trod upon in the castle corridors. The nightingale floors were supplemented by hidden alcoves for bodyguards.

Outside the castle is a **garden,** designed by the renowned gardener Kobori Enshu, that's famous in its own right. The original grounds of the castle, however, were without trees—supposedly because the falling of leaves in autumn reminded the shogun and his tough samurai of life's transitory nature, making them terribly sad.

Ironically, it was from Nijo Castle that Emperor Meiji issued his 1868 decree abolishing the shogunate form of government. Plan on spending an hour here.

On the corner of Horikawa Dori and Nijo Dori. © 075/841-0096. Admission ¥600 ($5) adults, ¥350 ($2.90) high-school students, ¥200 ($1.65) children. Audio guide ¥500 ($4.15) extra. Daily 8:45am–5pm (you must enter by 4pm). Subway: Nijojo-mae Station (1 min.). Bus: 9, 50, and 101 to Nijojo-mae (1 min.).

Nijo Jinya   This traditional house, built in the 17th century, served as an inn for out-of-town *daimyo* (feudal lords) visiting nearby Nijo Castle or the Imperial Palace. To ensure their safety, the 24-room house incorporated special features such as a secret, soundproof guard post located directly above the visitor's seat with a trap door that allowed the guard to drop directly on the guest if necessary, hidden stairways, secret chambers, and a narrow, dark hallway with a low ceiling to discourage sword fights and removable floor boards to trip intruders. Since the 55-minute tours are in Japanese only, I recommend coming here only if you've seen Kyoto's many other worthwhile sights. Be sure to purchase the English pamphlet for ¥100 (85¢); it describes the various rooms and their features. Better yet, arrange for a volunteer student guide who can interpret (arrangements can be made through the Tourist Information Center; you're expected to pay the student's admission and transportation fees). Incidentally, if you're heading for Kanazawa, skip this—Myoryuji Temple in Kanazawa is more interesting.

137 Oike-sagaru, Omiya Dori © 075/841-0972. Guided tours ¥1,000 ($8.35). Children under 15 not allowed. Reservations required at least 1 day in advance. Tours Thurs–Tues at 10am, 11am, 2pm, and 3pm. Subway: Nijojo-mae (exit 3, 3 min.). Head west on Oike Dori and take the second left; it's down this street in the 2nd block to the right. Bus: 9, 50, and 101 to Nijojo-mae (1 min.).

Nishijin Textile Center (Nishijin-Ori Kaikan) 🐾   About a 10-minute walk west of the Imperial Palace is this museum dedicated to the weavers who for centuries produced elegant textiles for the imperial family and nobility. The history of Nishijin silk weaving began with the history of Kyoto itself back in 794; by the Edo Period, there were an estimated 5,000 weaving factories in the Nishijin District. Today, the district remains home to one of Japan's largest handmade weaving industries. The museum regularly holds weaving demonstrations at its ground-floor handlooms, which use the Jacquard system of perforated cards for weaving. One of the most interesting things to do here is attend the **Kimono Fashion Show,** held six or seven times daily, showcasing kimono that change with the seasons. There's also, naturally, a shop selling textile products and souvenirs.

On Horikawa Dori just south of Imadegawa Dori. © 075/451-9231. Free admission. Daily 9am–5pm. Subway: Imadegawa (8 min.). Bus: 9 or 101 to Horikawa Imadegawa (2 min.).

EASTERN KYOTO

The eastern part of Kyoto, embracing the area of Higashiyama-ku with its Kiyomizu Temple and stretching up all the way to the Temple of the Silver Pavilion (Ginkakuji Temple), is probably the richest in terms of culture and charm. Although temples and gardens are the primary attractions, Higashiyama-ku also boasts several fine museums, forested hills and running streams, great shopping opportunities, and some of Kyoto's oldest and finest restaurants. I've included two **recommended strolls** through eastern Kyoto later in this chapter that will lead you to the region's best attractions as well as to some lesser-known sights that are worth a visit if you have the time.

Ginkakuji (The Temple of the Silver Pavilion) ★★   Ginkakuji, considered one of the more beautiful structures in Kyoto, was built in 1482 as a retirement villa of Shogun Ashikaga Yoshimasa, who intended to coat the structure with silver in imitation of the Golden Pavilion built by his grandfather. He died before this could be accomplished, however, so the Silver Pavilion is not silver at all but remains a simple, two-story, wood structure enshrining the goddess of mercy and Jizo, the guardian god of children. Note the sand mound in the garden, shaped to resemble Mt. Fuji.

Ginkakuji-cho. ⓒ 075/771-5725. Admission ¥500 ($4.15) adults, ¥300 ($2.50) junior-high and elementary students. Daily 8:30m–5pm Apr–Nov; 9am–4:30pm Dec–Mar. Bus: 5 or 17 to Ginkakuji-michi (5 min.).

Heian Shrine ★★   Although it dates only from 1895, Kyoto's most famous shrine was built in commemoration of the 1,100th anniversary of the founding of Kyoto and is a replica of the main administration building of the Heian capital. It also deifies two of Japan's emperors: Emperor Kanmu, 50th emperor of Japan, who founded Heian-kyo in 794; and Emperor Komei, the 121st ruler of Japan, who ruled from 1831 to 1866. Although the orange, green, and white structure is interesting for its Heian-Era architectural style, the most important thing to see here is **Shinen Garden** ★★★, the entrance to which is on your left as you face the main hall. Typical of gardens constructed during the Meiji Era, it's famous for its weeping cherry trees in spring, its irises and water lilies in summer, and its changing maple leaves in the fall. Don't miss it.

Nishi Tennocho, Okazaki. ⓒ 075/761-0221. Free admission to grounds; Shinen Garden ¥600 ($5) adults, ¥300 ($2.50) children. Daily 8:30am–5:30 in summer; 8:30am–5pm spring and autumn; 8:30am–4:30pm winter. Bus: 5 or 100 to Kyoto Kaikan Bijutsukan-mae (2 min.).

Hosomi Art Museum ★   This highly acclaimed private museum houses changing exhibits of Buddhist and Shinto art, primarily from temples and shrines in Kyoto and Nara, including Heian bronze mirrors, Buddhist paintings, lacquerware, tea-ceremonial objects, scrolls, folding screens, and pottery. In contrast to the objects it contains, the building itself is starkly modern, complete with automatic doors that open and clang shut with the finality of a prison. It's worth the 30 to 40 minutes it takes to walk through; be sure to browse through the gift shop of finely crafted goods.

6–3 Okazaki, Saishoji-cho. ⓒ 075/752-5555. Admission ¥700 ($5.85) adults, ¥500 ($4.15) senior-high, junior-high and elementary school students. Tues–Sun 10am–6pm. Subway: Higashiyama (exit 2, 5 min.). Catty-corner from the Kyoto Museum of Traditional Crafts (Fureaikan).

Kiyomizu Temple (Kiyomizudera) ★★★   This is Higashiyama-ku's most famous temple, known throughout Japan for the grand views afforded from its main hall. Founded in 798 and rebuilt in 1633 by the third Tokugawa shogun, Iemitsu, the temple occupies an exalted spot on Mt. Otowa, with its main hall constructed over a cliff and featuring a large wooden veranda supported by 139 pillars, each 49 feet high. The main hall is dedicated to the goddess of mercy and compassion, but most visitors come for the magnificence of its height and view, which are so well known to the Japanese that the idiom "jumping from the veranda of Kiyomizu Temple" means that they're about to undertake some particularly bold or daring adventure.

Also worth checking out are the three-story pagoda and Otowa Falls, but be sure not to spite the gods by neglecting to visit **Jishu Shrine** ★★ (ⓒ 075/541-2097), a vermilion-colored Shinto shrine behind Kiyomizu's main hall that has long been considered the dwelling place of the god of love and matchmaking. Ask for the English pamphlet and be sure to take the ultimate test: On the shrine's grounds are two "love-fortune-telling" stones placed 30 feet apart; if you're able to walk from one to the other with your eyes closed, your desires for love will be granted.

© 075/551-1234. Admission ¥300 ($2.50) adults, ¥200 ($1.65) children 7–15. Daily 6am–6pm. Bus: 100 or 206 to Gojo-zaka (10 min.).

Kodai-ji Temple   Located between Kiyomizu Temple and Yasaka Shrine, this temple was founded by Toyotomi Hideyoshi's widow, popularly referred to as Nene, to commemorate her husband and to pacify his spirit. Shogun Tokugawa Ieyasu, who served under Toyotomi before becoming shogun, financed its construction. It contains lovely gardens laid out by Kobori Enshu, as well as teahouses designed by Sen no Rikyu, a famous 16th-century tea master. A memorial hall enshrines wooden images of Hideyoshi (to the left) and Nene. Nene, by the way, became a Buddhist nun after her husband's death, as was the custom of noble women at the time.

Yasakatorii-mae-sagaru, Shimo-Kawaramachi. © 075/561-9966. Admission ¥500 ($4.15) adults, ¥300 ($2.50) children. Daily 9am–5pm. Bus: 206 to Higashiyama Yasui (5 min.).

Kyoto Museum of Traditional Crafts (Fureaikan) ⋆   Near Heian Shrine is this excellent museum dedicated to the many crafts that flourished during Kyoto's long reign as the imperial capital. Various displays and videos demonstrate the step-by-step production of crafts ranging from stone lanterns and fishing rods to textiles, paper fans, boxwood combs, lacquerware, and Noh masks. The displays are fascinating, the crafts beautiful, and explanations are in English, making even a 30-minute stop here well worth the effort.

In the basement of the Miyako Messe (International Exhibition Hall), 9–1 Seishoji-cho, Okazaki. © 075/762-2670. Free admission. Tues–Sun 10am–6pm. Bus: 5 or 100 to Kyoto Kaikan Bijutsukan-mae (2 min.).

Kyoto National Museum (Kokuritsu Hakubutsukan) ⋆⋆   This museum features changing exhibits highlighting magnificent art objects and treasures, many of which once belonged to Kyoto's many temples and the imperial court. Ceramics, sculpture, Japanese paintings, clothing and kimono, lacquerware, and metalworks are always on display, making this the best museum in town for viewing the ancient capital's priceless treasures. Plan on staying about an hour, but if you've seen the more extensive Tokyo National Museum, you may want to skip this.

527 Chaya-machi (across the street from Sanjusangendo Hall). © 075/541-1151. Admission ¥420 ($3.50) adults, ¥130 ($1.10) university and high-school students, ¥70 (60¢) junior-high and elementary students. Free admission 2nd and 4th Sat of the month. Tues–Sun 9am–4:30pm. Bus: 100, 206, or 208 to Hakubutsukan Sanjusangendo-mae (1 min.).

Sanjusangendo Hall ⋆⋆⋆   Originally founded as Rengeoin Temple in 1164 and rebuilt in 1266, Sanjusangendo Hall has one of the most visually stunning sights I've seen in a Japanese temple: 1,001 wooden statues of the thousand-handed Kannon. Row upon row, these life-size figures, carved from Japanese cypress in the 12th and 13th centuries, make an impressive sight; in the middle is a large seated Kannon carved in 1254 by Tankei, a famous sculptor from the Kamakura Period. Don't expect to actually see a thousand arms on each statue; there are only 40, the idea being that each hand has the power to save 25 worlds. To accommodate the thousand-handed Kannons as well as 30 other statues representing the Kannon's disciples, the hall stretches almost 400 feet, making it the longest wooden building in Japan. Its length was too hard to ignore—in the corridor behind the statues, archery competitions were held; standing here, you can easily imagine how hard it must have been to hit a piece of sacred cloth attached to the wall at the opposite end.

Shichijo Dori. © 075/525-0033. Admission ¥600 ($5) adults, ¥400 ($3.35) junior-high and high-school students, ¥300 ($2.50) children. Apr to mid-Nov, daily 8am–5pm; mid-Nov to Mar, 9am–4pm. Bus: 100, 206, or 208 to Hakubutsukan Sanjusangendo-mae (1 min.).

NORTHERN KYOTO

Two of Kyoto's most famous sights are in the northwestern corner of the city.

Kinkakuji (The Temple of the Golden Pavilion) ★★★   One of Kyoto's best-known attractions—and the inspiration for the Temple of the Silver Pavilion (above)—Kinkakuji was constructed in the 1390s as a retirement villa for Shogun Ashikaga Yoshimitsu and features a three-story pavilion covered in gold leaf and topped with a bronze phoenix on its roof. Apparently, the retired shogun lived in shameless luxury while the rest of the nation suffered from famine, earthquakes, and plague. If you come here on a clear day, the Golden Pavilion shimmers against a blue sky, its reflection captured in the waters of a calm pond. However, this pavilion is not the original; in 1950, a disturbed student monk burned Kinkakuji to the ground (the story is told by author Mishima Yukio in his famous novel, *The Temple of the Golden Pavilion*). The temple was rebuilt in 1955 and in 1987 was re-covered in gold leaf, five times thicker than the original coating. You almost need sunglasses. Be sure to explore the surrounding **park** with its moss-covered grounds and teahouses.

Kinkakuji-cho. © 075/461-0013. Admission ¥400 ($3.35) adults, ¥300 ($2.50) children. Daily 9am–5pm. Bus: 101 or 205 to Kinkakuji-michi (3 min.).

Ryoanji Temple ★★★   About a half-hour walk southwest of the Golden Pavilion is Ryoanji—home to what is probably the most famous **Zen rock garden** ★★★ in all of Japan—laid out at the end of the 15th century during the Muromachi Period. Fifteen rocks set in waves of raked white pebbles are surrounded on three sides by a clay wall and on the fourth by a wooden veranda. Sit down here and contemplate what the artist was trying to communicate. The interpretation of the rocks is up to the individual (Mountains above the clouds? Islands in the ocean?). My only objection to this peaceful place is that, unfortunately, it's not always peaceful—a loudspeaker on occasion extols the virtue of the garden, destroying any chance for peaceful meditation. If you get here early enough, you may be able to escape both the crowds and the noise.

After visiting the rock garden, be sure to take a walk around the 1,000-year-old **pond.** At one corner is a beautiful little restaurant, **Ryoanji Yudofuya** ★★ with tatami rooms and screens, where you can eat yudofu (see "Where to Dine in Kyoto," earlier in this chapter) or drink a beer and enjoy the view.

Goryoshita-cho. © 075/463-2216. Admission ¥400 ($3.35) adults, ¥200 ($1.65) children. Daily 8am–5pm in summer; 8:30am–4:30pm in winter. Bus: 50 to Ritsumeikan Daigaku-mae (4 min.).

Toei Uzumasa Eiga Mura (Toei Uzumasa Movieland) ★ *Kids*   If your kids are ready to mutiny because of yet another temple, get on their good side by coming to this studio park, one of Japan's three major film companies and where most of the samurai flicks are made. Don't expect the high-tech, polished glitz of American theme parks—rather, this is a working studio with indoor and outdoor movie sets re-creating the mood, setting, and atmosphere of feudal and turn-of-the-century Japan, complete with "villages" lined with shops, samurai houses, and old-time shops. Stagehands carry around props, hammers and saws, rework sets, and you may even see a famous star walking around dressed in samurai garb, or come upon a scene being filmed. There are, of course, other attractions, including a museum tracing the history of the film industry, a 20-minute Ninja show shown four times a day Monday through Friday, a special-effects show, a haunted house, a games arcade, and indoor rides and play areas for children. You can also have a photo taken of yourself decked out in a kimono or samurai gear. *Note:* Backlots are open only on weekends when there is no filming, but kids will prefer a weekday when there are Ninja shows and filming. Come here only if you have a lot of time (you'll probably spend a minimum of 2 hr. here), are a cinema buff, or have youngsters in tow.

10 Higashi-Hachigaokacho, Uzumasa, Ukyo-ku. ⓒ 075/864-7718. Admission ¥2,200 ($18) adults, ¥1,300 ($11) junior-high and high-school students, ¥1,100 ($9.15) children. Daily 9am–5pm (9:30am–4pm Dec–Feb). Closed Dec 21–Jan 1. Train: JR Line to Uzumasa or Hanazono Station (8 min.) or Keifuku Line to Uzumasa (5 min.). Bus: 75 to Uzumasa Eigamuramichi (4 min.).

WALKING TOUR **A STROLL THROUGH HIGASHIYAMA-KU**

Start:	Sanjusangendo Hall on Shichijo Dori a couple of blocks east of the Kamo River; to get there, walk 20 minutes from Kyoto Station or take bus no. 100, 206, or 208 to Hakubutsukan Sanjusangendo-mae.
Finish:	Kyoto Craft Center, Shijo Dori, Gion.
Time:	Allow approximately 6 hours, including stops for shopping and museums.
Best Times:	Weekdays, when temples and shops aren't as crowded.
Worst Times:	Monday, when the Kyoto National Museum is closed; Wednesday, when the Kyoto Craft Center is closed.

A stroll through Higashiyama-ku will take you to Kiyomizu Temple, one of Kyoto's most famous sights, and other worthwhile attractions like Sanjusangendo Hall and the Kyoto National Museum. It will also take you through some of Kyoto's most charming neighborhoods, with plenty of shopping opportunities en route.

Although the walking-tour leaflet ("Kyoto Walks") distributed by the TIC claims that you can walk from Kiyomizu Temple to Heian Shrine in 50 minutes, I don't see how it's possible unless you run the whole way. I've walked this route at least seven times, and it's always taken me the better part of a day—perhaps I'm slow, but it's a pace that I've found does justice to this wonderful area of Kyoto.

Note: The second walk, "The Philosophers' Stroll" (below), includes several attractions that could be combined with this walk if you don't have time for two walks. If you continue walking north from Maruyama Park instead of heading west for Gion, for example, you could take in Heian Shrine and the Kyoto Handicraft Center (covered at the end of the second walk). In any case, since eastern Kyoto has some of the city's most traditional and beautiful restaurants, be sure to read through the dining section to decide beforehand where you might want to eat lunch or dinner.

Start your stroll at:

❶ Sanjusangendo Hall

The hall dates from 1266 and is only about 50 feet wide, but stretches almost 400 feet, making it the longest wooden building in Japan. However, it's not the building itself that impresses but what it contains—1,001 life-size images of the thousand-handed Kannon. Seeing so many of them—row upon row of gold figures, glowing in the dark hall—is stunning. In the middle is an 11-foot-tall seated figure of Kannon carved in 1254. At

1 Sanjusangendo Hall
(Rengeoin Temple)
2 Kyoto National Museum
3 Kawai Kanjiro
Memorial House
4 Gojo-zaka
5 Kyoto Tojiki Kaikan
(Kyoto Ceramics Center)
6 Kiyomizu Temple
7 Jishu Shrine
8 Sannenzaka Slope
9 Ryozen Kannon Temple
10 Kodai-ji
11 Maruyama Park
12 Yasaka Shrine
(Gion Shrine)
13 Furumonzen Dori and
Shinmonzen Dori
14 Kyoto Craft Center
15 Gion

Subway
"Take a Break" stop

Kasugakita Dori
Marutamachi Dori

0   1/8 mile
0   100 meters

Biwako Sosui Canal

Kamo River

Nijo Dori

Niomon Dori

Higashiyama
Station

Sanjo Dori

Yoshida Hondori
Okazakamichi
Shirakawa Dori

Furumonzen Dori
Shinmonzen Dori

Higashioji Dori
Ingumichi Dori

MARUYAMA PARK

Shijo Dori

Gion
Hotel

FINISH HERE

Chorakukan   Isobe

Kodaiji Rakusho
Tea Room

Kiyomizu Zaka

Gojo Dori

Gojo-zaka

Taki-no-ya

Yamatooji Dori
Hanamikoji Dori

Gojo Dori

START HERE

Shichijo Dori

Le Grand Rêve

319

the back of the hall is a 130-yard-long archery range where a competition is held every January 15. (See "Exploring the City," earlier in this chapter, for more information on this and other major sights described in this stroll.)

Across the street is the:

❷ Kyoto National Museum (Kokuritsu Hakubutsukan)

The museum was established in the latter half of the last century as a repository for art objects and treasures that once belonged to Kyoto's temples and royal court. Individual items, most of which come from the museum's own collection, are rotated continuously, which means that no matter how many times you come here you'll always see something new. Always on display are ceramics, paintings, calligraphy, lacquerware, textiles, and sculptures. For ancient art, there's no better place in town than this.

TAKE A BREAK
Just past Sanjusangendo Hall is the Park Hotel, where you'll find the delightful **Le Grand Rêve**, a restaurant with views of a beautiful garden that serves French *kaiseki*—that is, French food served in courses and eaten with chopsticks. (See "Where to Dine in Kyoto," earlier in this chapter for details.)

Just east of the Park Hotel (toward the wooded hills) are Higashioji Dori and a stoplight; take a left and walk about 3 minutes until you come to the first intersection with a stoplight, where you'll see a sign advertising Kawai Kanjiro's House. Turn left here, take the first right down a narrow street, and to your right you'll soon see:

❸ Kawai Kanjiro Memorial House

Kawai Kanjiro Memorial House, Gojo-zaka (☎ 075/561-3585), the former home and studio of one of Japan's most well-known potters, Kawai Kanjiro (1890–1966). Inspired at a young age by Bernard Leach and one of the cofounders of the Japan Folk Crafts Museum in Tokyo, this versatile man hand made much of the furniture in this lovely home, which is a traditional Japanese house with an indoor open-pit fireplace and gleaming woodwork. Pottery, personal effects, and his outdoor clay kiln, built on a slope in the traditional Japanese method, are all on display, but I think this museum is worth seeing for the house alone, especially if you haven't had much opportunity to see the interiors of traditional homes. Admission is ¥900 ($7.50) for adults, ¥500 ($4.15) for students, and ¥300 ($2.50) for children. Open Tuesday through Saturday from 10am to 5pm.

Take a right out of the museum, walk to the busy road with the overpass, and turn right. When you get to the big intersection, look catty-corner across the intersection to the left and you'll see a slope leading uphill (to the left of the 2 big stone lanterns). It's called:

❹ Gojo-zaka

Gojo-zaka is lined with pottery shops including:

❺ Kyoto Tojiki Kaikan

This store to the right offers two floors of pottery from various artists (see "Shopping Kyoto," later in this chapter for more information).

After passing many more pottery and souvenir shops as the slope continues uphill (keep to the left when the road forks), you'll eventually reach stairs leading to:

❻ Kiyomizu Temple

The temple is the star attraction of this stroll. First founded in 798 and rebuilt in 1633 by the third Tokugawa shogun, Iemitsu, the temple occupies an exalted spot. The main hall is built over a cliff and features a large wooden veranda supported by 139 pillars, each 49 feet high. Take in the view of Kyoto from its deck, but to fully appreciate the grandeur of the main hall with its pillars and dark wood, be sure to walk to the three-story pagoda, which offers the best view of the main hall, built without the use of a single nail. From the pagoda, descend the stone steps to Otowa Falls where you'll see Japanese lined up to drink from the refreshing spring water. Kiyomizu's name, in fact, translates as "pure water."

TAKE A BREAK
On the grounds of Kiyomizu Temple, just beside Otowa Falls, is **Taki-no-ya,** an open-air pavilion, where you can sit on tatami and enjoy noodles and a beer or shaved ice colored with various flavors. This is a great place to stop (and now you know why this walk takes me all day). If you're lucky to be here in autumn, the fiery reds of the maple trees will set the countryside around you aflame. Open Friday through Tuesday from 10am to 5pm.

Before departing Kiyomizu Temple, be sure to make a stop at the vermilion-colored Shinto shrine located behind the temple's main hall:

⑦ Jishu Shrine

The shrine is regarded as a dwelling place of the deity in charge of love and matchmaking. Ask for the English-language leaflet that gives its history. Throughout the grounds are signs and descriptions in English telling about its various parts; for once, you're not left in the dark about the purpose of the various statues and memorials and what the Japanese are doing as they make their rounds. Very enriching. You can buy good-luck charms for everything from a happy marriage to easy delivery of a child to success in passing an examination. On the shrine's grounds are two stones placed about 30 feet apart—if you're able to walk from one stone to the other with your eyes closed, you're supposedly guaranteed success in your love life. It sure doesn't hurt to try. There's also a place where you can write down your troubles on a piece of paper and then

submerge it in a bucket of water, which supposedly will cause both the paper and your troubles to dissolve. If you failed the rock test, you might make a point of stopping off here.

From Kiyomizu Temple, retrace your steps downhill on the road directly in front of the temple's main gate. You'll again pass shop after shop selling sweets, pottery, fans, ties, hats, souvenirs, and curios. It's okay to go crazy shopping here, but remember that you're going to have to carry whatever you buy. After passing a couple of small shrines nestled in among the shops, you'll come to a split in the road and a small shrine on the right shaded by trees in front. Just beside this shrine are stone steps leading downhill (north) to a stone-cobbled street called:

⑧ Sannenzaka Slope

The slope leads past lovely antiques and curio shops and winds through neighborhoods of wooden buildings reminiscent of old Kyoto. Keep your eyes peeled for downhill stairs to the right leading to Maruyama Park; after taking these, the street will eventually end. Take the stairs straight ahead to:

⑨ Ryozen Kannon Temple

The temple has an 80-foot-high white statue dedicated to unknown soldiers who died in World War II. Memorial services are conducted four times daily at a shrine that contains memorial tablets of the 2 million Japanese who perished during the war. There's also a Memorial Hall commemorating the more than 48,000 foreign soldiers who died on Japanese territory. Open daily from 8:30am to 4:20pm; since admission is ¥200 ($1.65), you may just want to take a peek at the statue. Just past Ryozen Kannon Temple across the parking lot is:

⑩ Kodaiji Temple

Founded by the widow Nene in commemoration of her husband, Toyotomi Hideyoshi, who succeeded in unifying Japan at the end of the 16th century. In addition to teahouses and a memorial hall containing wooden images of the couple, there is a beautiful garden designed by master gardener Kobori Enshu.

Exit Kodai-ji Temple via the main steps leading downhill and turn right, continuing north.

TAKE A BREAK

Past Kodai-ji Temple and just before the street ends at a pagoda with a crane on top, keep your eyes peeled for a teahouse on your right with a garden, which you can glimpse from the street through a gate. The ⑨⑤ **Kodaiji Rakusho Tea Room,** 516 Washiochiyo (© **075/561-6892**), is a lovely place and one of my favorite tearooms in Kyoto. It has a 100-year-old miniature garden with a pond that's home to some of the largest and most colorful carp I've ever seen, some of which are 20 years old and winners of the many medals displayed in the back room. In summer, stop for *somen* (finely spun cold noodles), tea, or traditional desserts, and refresh yourself with views of the small but beautiful garden from one of the tables or from the back tatami room. If you're a gardener, you'll probably want to give up the hobby after you've seen what's possible—but rarely achieved. Open from 9:30am to 5:30pm (until 6pm in summer); closed 1 day a week but, unfortunately, not on a fixed day.

Continue on your stroll by taking a right out of the teahouse; turn right at the pagoda and then take an immediate left, which marks the beginning of:

⑪ Maruyama Park

This is one of Kyoto's most popular city parks, filled with ponds, pigeons, and gardens. In spring, it's one of the most popular spots for viewing cherry blossoms; to the left after entering the park is one of the oldest, most famous cherry trees in Kyoto. Also farther west is:

⑫ Yasaka Shrine

Yasaka Shrine is also known as Gion Shrine because of its proximity to the Gion District. Its present buildings date from 1654; the stone torii on the south side are considered among the largest in Japan. But the reason most people come here is one of practicality—the shrine is dedicated to the gods of health and prosperity, two universal concerns. This shrine, which is free to the public and open 24 hours, is packed during the Gion Festival and on New Year's Eve.

TAKE A BREAK

If you need a meal more substantial than the open-air pavilions at Kiyomizu and the teahouse were able to provide, a good choice for Japanese food is **Isobe**, located on the southeastern edge of Maruyama Park (turn right as soon as you enter the park from the south) and offering obento lunch boxes, tempura, shabu-shabu, and an assortment of Japanese cuisine. For Western food there's **Chorakukan**, located in a brick-and-stone Meiji-Era building at the southwest corner of Maruyama Park (to the left as you enter the park from the south). See "Where to Dine in Kyoto," earlier in this chapter for complete reviews.

Exit Yasaka Shrine to the west; this brings you to a busy street called Higashioji. Cross it and turn right, heading north on Higashi-oji until you reach a stream, the Shirakawa, where you should turn left and walk alongside the small river. This is a beautiful section of old Kyoto with many traditional and antiques shops on parallel streets north and south of the canal called respectively:

⑬ Furumonzen Dori and Shinmonzen Dori

You might wish to explore this small area. When you're done, take any street south; this brings you to busy Shijo Dori where you'll find the:

⑭ Kyoto Craft Center

The center carries beautifully crafted traditional items by local and famous artisans including glassware, pottery, jewelry, baskets, and more (see "Shopping Kyoto," later in this chapter for more information).

Across Shijo Dori is:

⑮ Gion

Gion is one of Japan's most famous nightlife districts. It's centered primarily on Hanamikoji Dori, which translates as "Narrow Street for Flower Viewing." This is Kyoto's long-standing geisha district, an enclave of discrete, traditional, and almost solemn-looking wooden homes that reveal nothing of the gaiety that goes on inside—drinking, conversation, and business dealings with dancing, singing, and music provided by geisha and their apprentices, called *maiko*. If it's early evening, you might glimpse one of these women as she small-steps her way in geta to an evening appointment, elaborately made up and wearing beautiful kimono. You might also wish to attend a performance at **Gion Corner** on Hanamikoji Dori, which offers performances of dance, puppetry, and other traditional arts nightly; see "Kyoto After Dark," later in this chapter for details.

☕ WINDING DOWN

If all this sightseeing and shopping has made you thirsty, there are a couple of easy-to-find locations right on Shijo Dori where you can quench your thirst. In the **Kyoto Craft Center**, described above, there's a stylish tea counter on the ground floor. Across the street at the **Gion Hotel**, there's a rooftop beer garden open in summer from 5:30 to 9pm. For more substantial dining, there are many restaurants and bars to the east across the Kamo River, on Pontocho, and near Shijo and Kawaramachi streets. See "Where to Dine in Kyoto," earlier in this chapter for many suggestions in this area.

WALKING TOUR | **THE PHILOSOPHERS' STROLL**

Start:	Ginkakuji, the Temple of the Silver Pavilion; take bus no. 5 or 17 from Kyoto Station to the Ginkakuji-michi stop.
Finish:	Kyoto Handicraft Center, Marutamachi Dori.
Time:	Allow about 5 hours including stops along the way.
Best Times:	Early on weekdays, when crowds aren't as thick.
Worst Times:	Monday, when the Kyoto Museum of Traditional Crafts and the Shishigatani Sabie teahouse are closed.

This stroll takes in the Temple of the Silver Pavilion, a couple of temples, a museum dedicated to Kyoto's traditional crafts, Kyoto's most well-known shrine and its garden, and the best place in town for one-stop souvenir shopping. Linking the Silver Pavilion with the other sights is a canal lined by trees—a path known as the **Philosophers' Pathway.**

From Kyoto Station, take bus no. 5 or 17 to the Ginkakuji-michi stop, head east (toward the wooded hills) along the canal, and continue east when the canal veers to the south. This takes you to:

❶ Ginkakuji, the Temple of the Silver Pavilion

This temple is the architectural jewel of this stroll. Contrary to its name, however, it isn't silver at all. It was built in 1482 as a retirement villa of Shogun Ashikaga Yoshimasa, who intended to coat the structure with silver in imitation of the Golden Pavilion built by his grandfather. He died before this could be accomplished, however, which is just as well—the wood of the Silver Pavilion is beautiful just as it is. The whole complex is designed for the enjoyment of the tea ceremony, moon viewing, and other aesthetic pursuits, with a beautiful garden of rippled sand, rocks, and moss. One of the small sand hills is easy to identify—it's in the image of Mt. Fuji. It's easy to imagine the splendor, formality, and grandeur of the life of Japan's upper class as you wander the grounds. A pathway takes you to a lookout point before you descend for a closer look at the pavilion (the interior is closed to the public).

Head back to that narrow canal heading south lined with cherry, willow, and maple trees and flanked by a small pathway. It's known as the:

❷ Philosophers' Pathway

The name Philosophers' Pathway refers to the fact that, throughout the ages, philosophers and priests have strolled this tranquil canal thinking deep thoughts. It's a particularly beautiful sight in spring during the cherry-blossom season. The pathway runs almost a mile, allowing you to think your own deep thoughts.

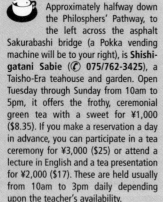

TAKE A BREAK
Approximately halfway down the Philosphers' Pathway, to the left across the asphalt Sakurabashi bridge (a Pokka vending machine will be to your right), is **Shishi-gatani Sabie** (© 075/762-3425), a Taisho-Era teahouse and garden. Open Tuesday through Sunday from 10am to 5pm, it offers the frothy, ceremonial green tea with a sweet for ¥1,000 ($8.35). If you make a reservation a day in advance, you can participate in a tea ceremony for ¥3,000 ($25) or attend a lecture in English and a tea presentation for ¥2,000 ($17). These are held usually from 10am to 3pm daily depending upon the teacher's availability.

At the end of the Philosphers' Pathway, near Nyakuoji Shrine, turn right and walk a few minutes through a residential area until you reach a street with some traffic on it (and a

wooden sign pointing toward Nanzenji). Here you should turn left. This brings you to:

❸ ⑨⑥ Ei Kando Temple

The temple is also known as **Zenrinji Temple** (© 075/761-0007), Founded in 856, it derives its popular name from the seventh head priest Eikan (1032–1111), who was loved by the people for attending to the impoverished sick and planting plum trees as a source of medicine. The temple is famous for a small statue of the Amida Buddha with his head turned, looking back over his shoulder. According to popular lore, it was carved after Eikan, who while walking and reciting chants he believed would propel him toward rebirth, was so astonished to see that the Amida Buddha had descended from the altar and was walking ahead of him that he stopped short in his tracks, whereupon the Buddha looked back over his shoulder and admonished, "Eikan, you are dawdling." How typically Zen. The Buddha facing backward is in the Amidado Hall. Otherwise, there isn't much to see here unless it's autumn and the many maples here are in their finest glory. The temple's pagoda, up on a hillside, offers a view over the city. Open daily from 9am to 4pm; admission is ¥500 ($4.15) except in September and October when it's ¥800 ($6.65), and in November when it's ¥1,000 ($8.35).

A minute's walk farther south brings you to the:

❹ Nomura Art Museum

The museum (© 075/751-0374) is on the right and features a private collection mainly of objects used in tea ceremonies, calligraphy, ceramics, and Noh masks. It's open only March to June and September to November, Tuesday to Sunday from 10am to 4:30pm. Admission is ¥700 ($5.85).

Just past the museum is:

❺ Nanzenji Temple

Nanzenji Temple (© 075/771-0365), is a Rinzai Zen temple set amid a

Walking Tour: The Philosophers' Stroll

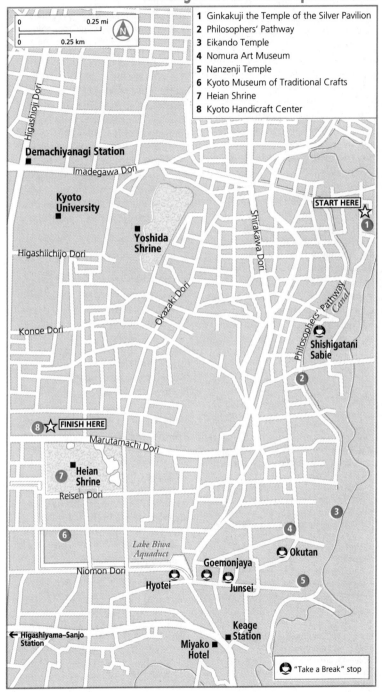

1 Ginkakuji the Temple of the Silver Pavilion
2 Philosophers' Pathway
3 Eikando Temple
4 Nomura Art Museum
5 Nanzenji Temple
6 Kyoto Museum of Traditional Crafts
7 Heian Shrine
8 Kyoto Handicraft Center

Higashioji Dori

Demachiyanagi Station

Imadegawa Dori

Kyoto University

Higashiichijo Dori

Yoshida Shrine

Okazaki Dori

Shirakawa Dori

START HERE
1

Philosophers' Pathway
Canal

Konoe Dori

Shishigatani Sabie

2

8 FINISH HERE

Marutamachi Dori

7 **Heian Shrine**

Reisen Dori

6

3

4

Okutan

Lake Biwa Aquaduct

Goemonjaya

Niomon Dori

Hyotei

Junsei

5

← Higashiyama–Sanjo Station

Keage Station

Miyako Hotel

"Take a Break" stop

grove of spruce. One of Kyoto's best known Zen temples, it was founded in 1293, and its present buildings date from the Momoyama Period. Attached to the main hall (Hojo) is a Zen rock garden attributed to Kobori Enshu; it's sometimes called "Leaping Tiger Garden" because of the shape of one of the rocks, but the association is a bit of a stretch for me. In the building behind the main hall is a sliding door with a famous painting by Kano Tanyu of a tiger drinking water in a bamboo grove. Spread throughout the temple precincts are a dozen other lesser temples and buildings worth exploring if you have the time, including Nanzen-in, which was built about the same time as Nanzenji Temple and served as the emperor's vacation house whenever he visited the temple grounds. The temple is open daily 8:40am to 5pm (4:30pm in winter); admission is ¥400 ($3.35) to the main hall and ¥200 ($1.65) to Nanzen-in.

TAKE A BREAK There are several traditional restaurants near Nanzenji that reflect the settings of the temples themselves. **Okutan,** just north of Nanzenji and with a view of a peaceful pond, has been serving vegetarian tofu meals for 350 years. On the road leading west from Nanzenji are **Junsei,** serving tofu, obento lunch boxes, and kaiseki in a beautiful garden setting; **Goemonjaya,** which serves moderately priced set meals and noodles; and **Hyotei,** which opened more than 300 years ago to serve pilgrims to Nanzenji, offering obento lunches as well as expensive kaiseki. See "Where to Dine in Kyoto," earlier in this chapter for details.

Head west from Nanzenji until you see a body of water on your right, the Lake Biwa Aqueduct. Continue west on Niomon Dori (the water will be on your right) to the

second bridge to your right, where you'll see a vermilion-colored torii gate. Turn right here and continue straight ahead to Nijo Dori, where you should turn left for one of my favorite museums, the:

⑥ Kyoto Museum of Traditional Crafts (Fureaikan)

This museum displays all the Kyoto crafts you can think of, from combs, umbrellas, and fans to textiles, sweets, bambooware, and masks. Explanations in English and videos describe how the crafts are made (mostly by hand). The best news: The museum is free. For more details, see "Exploring the City," earlier in this chapter.

Catty-corner across the street, it would be hard to miss:

⑦ Heian Shrine

If orange and green are your favorite colors, you're going to love Heian Shrine, one of Kyoto's most famous. Although it was built as late as 1895 in commemoration of the 1,100th anniversary of the founding of Kyoto, Heian Shrine is a replica of the city's first administrative quarters, built in Kyoto in 794, giving you some idea of the architecture back then. The most important thing to see here is the **garden,** the entrance to which is on your left as you face the main hall. Typical of gardens constructed during the Meiji Era, it's famous for its weeping cherry trees in spring, its irises and water lilies in summer, and its changing maple leaves in the fall. I love sitting on the bench in the wooden bridge topped by a phoenix; you'll probably want to dawdle.

Take a right out of the shrine's main exit onto Reisen Dori and then take the next right, which will bring you to the:

⑧ Kyoto Handicraft Center

The center is located behind the shrine on its north side. It's the best place in Kyoto for one-stop shopping for souvenirs of Japan, including pearls, kimono and yukata, fans, paper products, toys, and more; see "Shopping Kyoto," below for complete information. You may want to take advantage of the free hourly shuttle service the center provides to major hotels in Kyoto; the last bus departs at 6:05pm.

6 Imperial Villas & Temples Within Easy Reach of Kyoto

If this is your first visit to Kyoto and you're here for only a couple days, you should concentrate on seeing sights in Kyoto itself. If, however, this is your second trip to Kyoto, you're here for an extended period of time, or you have a passion for traditional Japanese architecture or gardens, there are a number of worthwhile attractions in the region surrounding Kyoto. Foremost on my list is **Katsura Imperial Villa.**

Note: The Katsura Imperial Villa, **Shugakuin Imperial Villa,** and **Saihoji** (popularly called the Moss Temple) all require advance permission to visit. To see the Katsura Imperial Villa or Shugakuin Imperial Villa, which are free, you must apply for permission in person at the **Imperial Household Agency Office** (© **075/221-1215;** no English is spoken and no reservations are accepted by phone, but you can call to see whether space is available), located on the west grounds of the **Kyoto Imperial Palace** near Inui Gomon Gate, a 3-minute walk from Imadegawa subway station. It's open Monday through Friday from 8:45am to noon and 1 to 4pm.

Tours of Katsura Imperial Villa are offered weekdays year-round and on Saturdays in April, May, October, and November (no tours on national holidays) at 10am, 11am, 2pm, and 3pm; tours of Shugakuin Imperial Villa are at 9am, 10am, 11am, 1:30pm, and 3pm. In the off-season, you may be able to make a reservation for a tour on the same day, though keep in mind that it takes an hour to reach Katsura Imperial Villa and 30 minutes to reach Shugakuin by taxi from the Imperial Household Agency Office. It's always better, therefore, to make a reservation a day or two in advance; in spring and fall, try to make a reservation a week in advance. The time of your tour will be designated when you apply. Parties are limited to 4 persons, everyone must present their passports, and participants must be at least 20 years old. Tours are conducted in Japanese only, but an English-language video is shown.

For tours of Saihoji, see below.

KATSURA IMPERIAL VILLA ✺✺✺   About a 15-minute walk from Katsura Station on the Hankyu railway line, or a 30-minute bus ride from Kyoto Station (take bus no. 33 to the Katsura Rikyu-mae stop) and then a 5-minute walk, this villa is considered the jewel of traditional Japanese architecture and landscape gardening. It was built between 1620 and 1624 by Prince Toshihito, brother of the emperor, with construction continued by Toshihito's son. The garden, markedly influenced by Kobori Enshu, Japan's most famous garden designer, is a "stroll garden" in which each turn of the path brings an entirely new view.

The first thing you notice upon entering Katsura is its simplicity—the buildings were all made of natural materials, and careful attention was paid to the slopes of the roofs and to the grain, texture, and color of the various woods used. A pavilion for moon viewing, a hall for imperial visits, a teahouse, and other buildings are situated around a pond; as you walk along the pathway, you're treated to views that literally change with each step you take. Islets; stone lanterns; various scenes representing seashores, mountains, and hamlets; manicured trees; and bridges of stone, earth, or wood that arch gracefully over the

A Summer Spectacle: Cormorant Fishing

If you're lucky enough to be in Kyoto between July 1 and September 15, I highly recommend that you spend one evening on the Oi River, drifting in a wooden boat and watching men fishing with trained cormorants, or seabirds. **Cormorant fishing** ★★★ takes place in Arashiyama every evening in summer (except when there's a full moon or during and after a heavy rain). There are two 1-hour shows, at 7 and 8pm in July and August and at 6:30 and 7:30pm September 1 to 15. For a fee of ¥1,700 ($14) for adults and ¥850 ($7.10) for children, you can board a narrow wooden boat gaily decorated with paper lanterns. Along with dozens of others, your boatman will pole you down the river so you can see the fishing boats lit by blazing torches. The cormorants, with rings around their necks so they don't swallow the fish they catch, dive under the water for *ayu*, a small river fish. Water taxis ply the river offering snacks and beer. I find the whole experience terribly romantic. If you're on a budget, however, you can watch from shore.

Cormorant fishing takes place near the **Togetsukyo Bridge** in Arashiyama, about 4½ miles from central Kyoto. You can reach it by taking the **JR Sagano Line** from Kyoto Station to Saga Arashiyama Station; from there, it's a 15-minute walk. There's also a local commuter line, the **Keifuku Arashiyama Line,** which you can catch on Shijo Dori at either Shijo-Omiya Station or Sai Station; take it to Arashiyama (the last stop), from which it's a 2-minute walk. Or catch **bus no. 71, 72, or 73** from the Kyoto Station and take it to Arashiyama, from which it's a 1-minute walk.

water—everything is perfectly balanced. No matter where you stand, the view is complete and in harmony. Every detail was carefully planned down to the stones used in the path, the way the trees twist, and how scenes are reflected in the water. Little wonder the Katsura Imperial Villa has influenced architecture not only in Japan but around the world. Sadly, tours are much too hurried (they last only 1 hr.), and no photography is allowed.

SHUGAKUIN IMPERIAL VILLA ★★   Northeast of Kyoto, about a 40-minute bus ride from Kyoto Station (take bus no. 5 from Kyoto Station to the Shugakuin Rikyu-michi bus stop) and then a 15-minute walk, this villa was built in the mid-1600s as a retirement retreat for Emperor Go-Mizunoo, who came to the throne at age 15 and suddenly abdicated 18 years later to beome a monk, passing the throne to his daughter in 1629. Amazingly, though the villa was only 2 hours from the Imperial Palace, the emperor came here only on day trips; he never once spent the night. I could live here! The 133-acre grounds, among Kyoto's largest, are situated at the foot of Mt. Hiei and are famous for the principle known as "borrowed landscape" in which the surrounding landscape is incorporated in the overall garden design. Grounds are divided into three levels: The **upper garden,** with its lake, islands, and waterfalls, is the most extensive of the three and offers grand views of the surrounding countryside from its hillside pavilion. The **middle garden,** built as a residence for the emperor's daughter, contains a villa with the famous "Shelves of Mist;" in keeping with the Japanese penchant for ranking the best three of everything, this is considered one of the three most beautiful shelves in Japan. The gardens are more spacious and natural than most Japanese-style gardens, which are often small and contrived. Tours, which take 1 hour and 15 minutes and cover 1.85 miles, allow ample time for photography.

SAIHOJI ★★   Popularly known as **Kokedera** (the Moss Temple), Saihoji was converted into a Zen temple in 1339 and is famous for its velvety-green moss garden spread underneath the trees. Altogether, there are more than 100 different varieties of moss throughout the grounds, giving off an iridescent and mysterious glow that's best just after a rain. Before being allowed to visit the grounds, tour participants must first listen to a lecture (in Japanese).

Note: Because the monks are afraid that huge numbers of visitors would trample the moss to death, prior permission is needed to visit Saihoji, and you can obtain it only by writing to the temple at least 10 days in advance. Write to Saihoji Temple, 56 Jigatani-cho, Matsuo, Nishikyo-ku, Kyoto 615-8286. (© 075/ 391-3631) and give your name, your address in Japan, your age, your occupation, and the date you'd like to visit (plus 2nd and 3rd choices). Include a self-addressed return envelope and International Reply Coupons for return postage. (If you're in Japan, you should send a double postcard or *ofuku hagaki*.) The cost of the visit, which includes a Sutra-writing demonstration, is a "donation" of at least ¥3,000 ($25; no change given), payable when you pick up your ticket. To reach Saihoji, take the Karasuma subway line to Shijo Station, transferring there to bus no. 29 to the Kokedera-michi stop.

BYODOIN TEMPLE ★   Located in the town of Uji, about 11 miles southeast of Kyoto, Byodoin Temple (© 0774/21-2861) is a good example of temple architecture of the Heian Period. Originally a villa, it was converted into a temple in 1053. Most famous is the main hall, known as **Phoenix Hall,** the only original building remaining. It has three wings, creating an image of the mythical bird of China, the phoenix; on the gable ends are two bronze phoenixes. On the temple grounds is one of the most famous bells in Japan as well as a monument to Minamoto Yorimasa, who took his own life here after being defeated by the rival Taira clan. Byodoin is best known to Japanese, however, for gracing the back of ¥10 coins. Byodoin is about a 10-minute walk from the Uji JR Station (there's a map of the town in front of the station). Admission to the grounds is ¥600 ($5), ¥500 ($4.15) more for Phoenix Hall. Temple grounds are open daily 9am to 5pm; Phoenix Hall daily 9am to 5pm (4pm in winter).

FUSHIMI-INARI SHRINE ★   Just a minute's walk from the JR Inari Station, Fushimi-Inari Shrine © 075/641-7331 has long been popular with merchants, who come here to pray for success and prosperity. One of Japan's most celebrated Shinto shrines, it was founded back in 711 and is dedicated to the goddess of rice. The 2½-mile-long pathway behind the shrine is lined with more than 10,000 red torii gates, presented by worshippers throughout the ages; there are also stone foxes, which are considered messengers of the gods. It's a glorious walk as you wind through the woods and the tunnel of torii gates and then gradually climb a hill, where you'll have a good view of Kyoto. At several places along the path are small shops where you can sit down for a bowl of noodles or other refreshment. Admission is free, and the expansive grounds never close. The most popular times to visit are on the first day of each month and New Year's.

Note: Both Byodoin Temple and Fushimi-Inari Shrine are on the same JR line that continues to Nara. If you plan on spending the night in Nara, you could easily take in these two attractions on the way.

7 Shopping Kyoto

As the nation's capital for more than 1,000 years, Kyoto spawned a number of crafts and exquisite art forms that catered to the elaborate tastes of the imperial court and the upper classes. Kyoto today is still renowned for its **crafts,** including Nishijin textiles, Yuzen-dyed fabrics, Kyo pottery (pottery fired in Kyoto), fans, dolls, cutlery, gold-leaf work, umbrellas, paper lanterns, combs, Noh masks, cloisonné, and lacquerware.

GREAT SHOPPING AREAS   The majority of Kyoto's tiny specialty shops are situated in central Kyoto along Shijo Dori and in the area of Kawaramachi Dori. The square formed by **Kawaramachi Dori, Shijo Dori, Sanjo Dori,** and **Teramachi Dori** includes a covered shopping arcade and specialized shops selling lacquerware, combs and hairpins, knives and swords, tea and tea-ceremony implements, and more—including, of course, clothing and accessories.

If you're looking for antiques, woodblock prints, and art galleries, head toward **Shinmonzen Dori** and **Furumonzen Dori** in Gion, which parallel Shijo Dori to the north on the eastern side of the Kamo River (see "A Stroll Through Higashiyama-ku," earlier in this chapter). You'll find pottery and souvenir shops in abundance on the roads leading to Kiyomizu Temple in **Higashiyama-ku.**

For clothing, accessories, and modern goods, Kyoto's many **department stores** are good bets. They're conveniently located near Kyoto Station or in the heart of Nakagyo-ku near the Shijo-Kawaramachi intersection. In addition, there's a big underground shopping mall called **Porta** that radiates from the Karasuma (north) side of Kyoto Station; its boutiques sell everything from clothing and shoes to stationery. And inside Kyoto Station itself, **The Cube** shopping mall in the first and second basements has dozens of boutiques selling clothing and accessories as well as local souvenirs and crafts.

CRAFTS & SPECIALTY SHOPS

(97) **Aritsugu**   The fact that this family-owned business is located at the Nishiki-Koji market is appropriate since it sells hand-wrought knives and other handmade cooking implements, including sushi knives, bamboo steamers, pots, pans, and cookware used in the preparation of traditional Kyoto cuisine. In business for 400 years, the shop counts the city's top chefs among its customers. Open daily 9am to 5:30pm. Nishiki-Koji Dori, Gokomachi Nishi-iru, Nakagyo-ku. ✆ 075/221-1091. 1 block north of Shijo Dori on the north side of Nishiki-Koji Dori, west of Gokomachi. Bus: 4, 5, 17, and 205 to Shijo Kawaramachi (5 min).

Kasagen   Kasagen has been making traditional umbrellas (*bangasa*) since 1861. They're more expensive than elsewhere but are of high quality and are made to last a lifetime. Open Thursday to Tuesday 10am to 8pm; opens at noon on holidays. 284 Gion-machi, Kitagawa. ✆ 075/561-2832. Bus: 206 or 208 to Gion.

Kikuya   Kikuya has a good selection of used kimono, haori, geta, and kimono accessories for both adults and children. Although they're not antiques as Kikuya advertises but simply secondhand, the goods here are beautiful and timeless. Everything is in good condition (Japanese wear kimono only for special occasions), but be sure to look thoroughly for any spots or defects. Prices seem high to us; expect to pay ¥3,000 ($25) for a silk haori or a child's kimono. No credit cards are accepted. Open Monday to Saturday 9am to 7pm. Manjuji Dori, Sakaimachi, Higashi-iru. © 075/351-0033. Take the Keihan Electric Line to Gojo (5 min.).

Kyoto Ceramics Center (Kyoto Tojiki Kaikan) This two-story shop is operated by an association of Kyoto potters who display their wares of Kyo pottery (pottery fired locally). Approximately 10,000 items are on display from sake cups and vases to bowls, plates, and chopstick rests. Daily 9:30am to 5pm. On Gojo-zaka on the way to Kiyomizu Temple. © 075/541-1102. Bus: 100 or 206 to Gojo-zaka (2 min.).

Kyoto Craft Center Whereas the Kyoto Handicraft Center (below) is good for souvenirs and inexpensive gifts for the folks back home, this craft center is the kind of place you head to buy a wedding gift or something really special for yourself. Featuring beautifully designed contemporary crafts by local and famous artisans, the Kyoto Craft Center devotes its two floors to a wide range of products, including jewelry, scarves, pottery, glass, fans, damascene, baskets, and much more. Since the products are continually changing, there's always something new. Open Thursday to Tuesday 11am to 7pm. 275 Gion, Kitagawa, Higashiyama-ku. © 075/561-9660. Bus: 201 to Ishidanshita or 100 and 206 to Gion (3 min.). On Shijo Dori east of the Kamo River in the heart of Gion.

Kyoto Handicraft Center For one-stop souvenir shopping, your best bet is Kyoto's largest craft, gift, and souvenir center. Five floors of merchandise contain almost everything Japanese imaginable: pearls, lacquerware, dolls, kimono, woodblock prints, pottery, cameras, cassette players, paper products, swords, lanterns, silk and textile goods, painted scrolls, and music boxes—and that's just for starters. You can even buy the socks to be worn with geta wooden shoes and the obi sashes to be worn with the kimono.

You can easily spend an hour or two here just wandering around; there are also demonstrations showing artisans at work on various crafts, including hand weaving, woodblock printing, and the production of damascene. You can even try your own hand at making woodblock prints, cloisonné, and dolls with instruction provided. For this you should plan at least 1 hour, and bookings are made at the information counter on the ground floor from 1 to 4pm daily; lessons cost ¥1,500 ($12.50) and are a great way for older children to get creative while you shop. Daily 10am to 6pm (to 7pm April and October, to 5:30pm December to February). Closed December 31 to January 3. Kumano Jinja Higashi, Sakyo-ku. © 075/761-5080. Bus: 206 to Kumano-jinja-mae (3 min.). Just north of Heian Shrine on Marutamachi Dori. Free hourly bus service (on the hour except noon) from the center to major hotels throughout Kyoto.

(98) **Miyawaki Baisen-an** This elegant, open-fronted shop has specialized in handmade fans since 1823, particularly fans characteristic of Kyoto. A little English is spoken. Prices range from ¥2,800 ($23) for a small, tea ceremonial fan to ¥370,000 ($3,083) for the best that money can buy. Open daily 9am to 6pm (to 7pm July and August). 102 Tominokoji-nishi, Rokkaku-dori, Nakagyo-ku. © 075/ 221-0181. Subway: Karasuma Oike (6 min.). On Rokkaku-dori just west of Tominokoji.

Yamato Mingei-Ten This shop has been selling folk crafts and folk art from all over Japan for more than 4 decades, including ceramics, glassware, lacquerware, textiles, paper products, baskets, and other hand-crafted items. Open Wednesday to Monday 10am to 8:30pm. On Kawaramachi Dori (just north of Maruzen bookstore), Nakagyo-ku. © 075/221-2641. Bus: 4, 5, 17, and 205 to Shijo Kawaramachi.

DEPARTMENT STORES

Department stores are good places to shop for Japanese items and souvenirs, including pottery, lacquerware, and kimono as well as clothing and everyday items. Since department stores are closed different days of the week, you'll always find several open.

JR Kyoto Isetan, located in Kyoto Station (© 075/352-1111; open daily 10am–7:30pm; closed some Tues), is Kyoto's most fashionable department store for young people, specializing in women's imported and domestic clothing. Across the street is **Kintetsu,** Karasuma Dori (© 075/361-1111; open daily 10am–7:30pm; closed some Thurs), convenient for all those necessities from film to toiletries and food.

In Central Kyoto, **Daimaru,** on Shijo Dori west of Takakura (© 075/211-8111; open daily 10am–7:30pm; closed some Wed), is Kyoto's largest department store with everything from clothing and food to electronic goods spread on nine floors. Nearby are **Hankyu,** on the southeast corner of Shijo-Kawaramachi intersection (© 075/223-2288; open daily 10:30am–8pm; closed some Tues) with seven floors of fashion, housewares, and food; and **Takashimaya,** across the street at the southwest corner of Shijo-Kawaramachi intersection (© 075/221-8811; open daily 10am–7:30pm; closed some Wed), one of Japan's oldest and most respected department stores with a good selection of traditional crafts.

MARKETS

On the 21st of each month, a flea market is held at **Toji Temple** (© 075/691-3325), about a 15-minute walk southwest of Kyoto Station. Japan's largest flea market, it's also one of the oldest; its history stretches back more than 700 years, when pilgrims began flocking to Toji Temple to pay their respects to Kobo Daishi, who founded the Shingon sect of Buddhism. Today, Toji Temple is still a center for the Shingon sect, and its market (popularly known as Kobo-san) is a colorful affair with booths selling Japanese antiques, old kimono, ethnic goods, odds and ends, and many other items. Worshippers come to pray before a statue of Kobo Daishi and to have their wishes written on wooden slats by temple calligraphers. Even if you don't buy anything, the festive atmosphere of the market and booths makes a trip here a memorable experience. The largest Kobo-san markets take place in December and January. Held from about 6am to 4pm. A smaller market, devoted entirely to Japanese antiques, is held at Toji Temple on the first Sunday of each month.

Held to commemorate the scholar and poet Sugawara Michizane, the **Tenjin-san market** held at **Kitano Tenmangu Shrine** (© 075/461-0005) the 25th of every month is a large market offering a little bit of everything—antiques, used clothing, ceramics, food—in a beautiful setting. It's open from about 8am to dusk, but go as early as you can. Kitano Shrine is on Imadegawa Dori between Nishi-oji and Senbon; take the Chin-Chin bus no. 101 to the Kitano Tenmangu-mae stop. Unlike the other temple markets, the **Chion-ji market** (© 075/691-3325), held the 15th of each month from 9am to 4pm, is devoted to handmade goods and crafts, including pottery and clothing. To reach it, take bus no. 206 to Hyakumanben at the Higashioji and Imadegawa intersection; **Chion-ji Temple** is just to the northeast.

Although you may not buy anything to take home with you, it's worth strolling through the **Nishiki-Koji Dori market** just for the atmosphere. Kyoto's 400-year-old city produce market, this covered shopping arcade 1 block north of Shijo Dori in the heart of old Kyoto, is lined with vendors selling fish, flowers, eggs, pickled vegetables, fruit, and take-out foods. Open from the 10am to about 6pm; some shops close on either Wednesday or Sunday.

8 Kyoto After Dark

Nothing beats spending a fine summer's evening strolling the streets of Kyoto. From the geisha district of Gion to the bars and restaurants lining Pontocho, Kyoto is utterly charming and romantic at night. Begin your evening with a walk along the banks of the Kamo River—it's a favorite place for young couples in love. In summer, restaurants stretching north and south of Shijo Dori along the river erect outdoor wooden platforms on stilts over the water.

FINDING OUT WHAT'S ON   There are many annual events and dances, including the very popular geisha area dances held in June, the only time of year you can see traditional dances performed by all five of Kyoto's traditional geisha districts; Gion Odori dances in October featuring *geiko* and *maiko* (geisha and apprentice geisha in Kyoto) dressed in elaborate costume; and Kabuki at the Minamiza Theater in December. To find out what's happening while you're in Kyoto, pick up the monthly magazine **Kansai Time Out,** available in Kyoto at the Maruzen bookstore on Kawaramachi Dori for ¥300 ($2.50). Although major concerts are infrequent in Kyoto (they're usually held in nearby Osaka), the magazine is the best source for finding out what's going on in the classical and contemporary music scene. In addition, the **Kyoto Visitor's Guide,** a monthly tabloid distributed free at tourist offices, hotels, and restaurants, contains a calendar of events and performances for the month.

THE MAJOR NIGHTLIFE DISTRICTS
GION ★★
A small neighborhood of plain wooden buildings in Higashiyama-ku on the eastern side of the Kamo River, Gion doesn't look anything like what you've probably come to expect from an urban Japanese nightlife district; in fact, there's no neon in sight. There's something almost austere and solemn about Kyoto's most famous geisha district, as though its raison d'être were infinitely more important and sacred than mere entertainment. Gion is a shrine to Kyoto's past, an era when geisha numbered in the thousands.

Contrary to popular Western misconceptions, geisha are not prostitutes. Rather, they're trained experts in the traditional arts, conversation, and coquettishness, and their primary role is to make men feel like kings when they're in the soothing enclave of the geisha house. There are now only a mere couple hundred geisha in Gion; after all, in today's high-tech world, few women are willing to undergo the years of rigorous training to learn how to conduct the tea ceremony, to play the *samisen* (a three-stringed instrument), or to perform ancient court dances.

Gion is about a 5-minute walk from the Shijo-Kawaramachi intersection; to reach it, walk east on Shijo Dori and then take a right on Hanamikoji Dori. Its narrow streets are great for strolling; a good time to take a walk through the neighborhood is around dusk when geisha are on their way to their evening appointments. Perhaps you'll see one—or a *maiko* (a young woman training to be a geisha)—clattering in her high wooden shoes (called *geta*). She'll be dressed in a brilliant kimono, her face a chalky white, and her hair adorned with hairpins and ornaments. From geisha houses, music and laughter lilt out from behind paper screens, sounding all the more inviting because you can't enter. Don't take it personally; not even the Japanese will venture inside without the proper introductions.

Gion Corner After strolling around Gion, visit Gion Corner, which stages special variety programs in the ancient cultural arts. You'll see short demonstrations of the tea ceremony, *ikebana* (flower arranging), *koto* (Japanese harp) music, *gagaku* (ancient court music and dance), *kyogen* (Noh comic play), *kyomai* (Kyoto-style dance) performed by maiko, and *bunraku* (puppetry). The shows cater to tourists, and none of the individual performances beat a full-scale production of the real thing, but this is a convenient and fast introduction to the traditional forms of Japanese entertainment. Yasaka Hall, Hanamikoji Dori, Shijo-sagaru, Gion. ✆ 075/561-1119. Tickets ¥2,800 ($23); available at most hotels, travel agencies, and at Gion Corner box office. Mar 1–Nov 29, programs held daily (except Aug 16) at 7:40pm and 8:40pm. Reservations not necessary but arrive early. Bus: 4, 5, 17, or 205 to Shijo Kawaramachi (8 min.); or from other than Kyoto Station, no. 12, 46, 80, or 207 to Shijo Keihan-mae (4 min.). Located on Hanamikoji Dori south of Shijo Dori.

PONTOCHO

Pontocho is a narrow street that parallels the Kamo River's western bank, stretching from Shijo Dori north to Sanjo Dori. Riddled with geisha houses, hostess bars, restaurants, and bars that fill every nook and cranny, Pontocho makes for a fascinating walk as you watch groups of Japanese enjoying themselves.

Note: Although many of these restaurants lining the river have outdoor verandas in summer, I was able to include only a couple of them in "Where to Dine in Kyoto," earlier in this chapter. Unfortunately, most of Pontocho's restaurants are unreceptive to foreigners, and I was turned away from establishment after establishment with the excuse that the place was full—even when I could see that it was not. The Kyoto Tourist Information Center (TIC) informed me that they don't recommend Pontocho to foreigners simply because of the cold reception. However, I think it's worth walking through Pontocho because the area is so interesting and so Japanese. Although many of the bars and clubs are virtually impossible to enter without an introduction, you might want to come here for a meal at one of the restaurants recommended in the dining section earlier in this chapter. And if you're feeling adventurous and are determined to find seating under the paper lanterns on one of the open verandas, you might get lucky. Once in a while, restaurants that don't want the publicity of a guidebook will accept the occasional foreigner or two, especially one versed in a little Japanese.

Another good place to look for nightlife is **Kiyamachi,** a small street that parallels Pontocho to the west and that runs beside a small canal.

THE CLUB & LIVE MUSIC SCENE

Kento's Rather out of place in the Gion geisha district, this chain specializes in the oldies but goldies of the 1950s and 1960s. Open daily 6:30 to 11:30pm. Hitotsume-nishi-iru, Hanamikoji Dori, Shijo-agaru. ✆ 075/551-2777. Cover ¥1,200 ($10) plus 20% service and a 1-drink, 1-dish minimum. Bus: 4, 5, 17, or 205 to Shijo Kawaramachi (5 min.); or from other than Kyoto Station, no. 12, 46, 80, or 207 to Shijo Keihan-mae (2 min.). From Shijo Dori, walk south on Hanamikoji Dori and take the first right.

Rag Depending on who's playing, the crowd here ranges from an older, more mellow audience to a younger, rowdier bunch. Mostly, however, it's a college-age crowd that comes here to listen to rock, jazz, acoustic, and fusion. Beer starts at ¥650 ($5.40), and snacks range from ¥500 to ¥900 ($4.15–$7.50). There's no music charge or minimum-dish requirement after the live music is over; you might want to come just for a drink at the backcorner bar where the view is pleasant. Open nightly with live music 7:30 to 10:30pm. Empire Bldg., 5th floor,

Kiyamachi Dori, Sanjo Agaru. 🕻 **075/241-0446** or 255-7273 (10am–7pm). Live music cover ¥1,000–¥5,000 ($8.35–$42) depending on the band plus a 1-drink, 1-dish minimum. Subway: Kyoto Shiyakusho-mae (3 min.). Bus: 5, 17, or 205 to Kawaramachi Sanjo (2 min.). On the east side of Kiyamachi north of Sanjo Dori.

99 **Taku Taku** If you're young and want to hear live music, head for this old sake warehouse with a plain decor. Featuring heavy metal, rock, soul, blues, reggae, jazz, and punk rock, it caters mainly to Kyoto's college students. Open nightly with live music usually 7 to 9pm. Tominokoji-Bukkoji. 🕻 **075/351-1321.** Cover for local bands ¥1,600 ($13) which includes 1 drink; more for big-name bands. Bus: 5 to Shijo-Fuyacho (5 min.). Walk south from Shijo Dori on Tominokoji Dori. It's just past the red-and-white spiral of a 2-seater corner barbershop, on the right side of the street behind a small parking lot; just listen for the music.

THE BAR SCENE

Bar Isn't It? Springing up all over Kansai and with a branch in Tokyo, this chain specializes in inexpensive food and drinks. The staff tends to be we-are-so-cool-we-work-in-Japan *gaijin* (foreigners), but it's cheap; and since this is where lots of foreigners hang out, it's a good place to meet them. Open Wednesday to Saturday from 6pm. Basement, Forum Bldg., Kawaramachi, Sanjo-sagaru. 🕻 **075/221-5399.** Subway: Kyoto Shiyakusho-mae (4 min.). Bus: 5, 17, or 205 to Kawaramachi Sanjo (2 min.). 2 blocks south of Sanjo Dori between Kawaramachi and Kiyamachi sts.

François Salon de Thé If evening entertainment to you means a cup of coffee or tea or a drink in quiet, intimate surroundings, this is the place for you. The small interior has the atmosphere of an old Viennese coffeehouse with a domed ceiling, dark-wood paneling, stained-glass windows, heavy red-cushioned chairs, and classical music. Open daily 10am to 11pm. Shijo Kobashi Nishizume-Minami. 🕻 **075/351-4042.** On a small street running along the west side of a tiny canal just a minute's walk southwest of the Shijo Ave. Bridge, which spans the Kamo River. Bus: 4, 17, or 205 to Shijo Kawaramachi.

Orizzonte Sky Lounge Located atop Kyoto's tallest building, this sophisticated cocktail lounge offers the city's best view of Higashiyama-ku's wooded hills. Cocktails start at ¥1,000 ($8.35), and there's no cover charge. Open nightly 5:30 to 11pm. Kyoto Hotel, 17th floor, Kawaramachi-Oike. 🕻 **075/223-2333.** Subway: Kyoto Shiyakusho-mae (1 min.).

Pig & Whistle Here's a traditional English pub where you can play darts, stand at the bar, or sit at a table with your mum. On the second and fourth Fridays of each month there's free, live music. Thursdays are Ladies' Night with reduced drink prices. It attracts an older, mixed crowd of both foreigners and Japanese, including foreigners who are networking for employment or business opportunities. The menu includes fish-and-chips, nachos, and the ubiquitous raisin butter—but most people come here to drink. Noisy and fun. Open nightly from 6pm. Shobi Bldg., 2nd floor, 115 Ohashi-cho, Ohashi, Higashi Iru, Sanjo Dori. 🕻 **075/761-6022.** Subway: Sanjo Keihan (2 min.).

9 A Side Trip to Nara ★★

42km (26 miles) S of Kyoto

In the beginnings of Japanese history, the nation's capital was moved to a new site each time a new emperor came to the throne. In 710, however, the first permanent Japanese capital was set up at **Nara.** Not that it turned out to be so permanent—

after only 74 years, the capital was moved first to Nagaoka and shortly thereafter to Kyoto, where it remained for more than 1,000 years. What's important about those 74 years, however, is that they witnessed the birth of Japan's arts, crafts, and literature, as Nara imported everything from religion to art and architecture from China. Even the city itself, laid out in a rectangular grid pattern, was modeled after Chinese concepts. It was during the Nara Period that Japan's first historical account, first mythological chronicle, and first poetry anthology (with 4,173 poems) were written. Buddhism flourished, and Nara grew as the political and cultural center of the land with numerous temples, shrines, pagodas, and palaces.

The Japanese flock to Nara because it gives them the feeling that they're communing with ancestors. Foreigners come here because Nara offers them a glimpse of a Japan that was. Remarkably enough, many of Nara's historic buildings and temples remain intact, and long ago someone had enough foresight to enclose many of these historical structures in the quiet and peaceful confines of a large and spacious park, which has the added attraction of free-roaming deer.

ESSENTIALS

GETTING THERE   Nara is easily reached from Kyoto Station on two lines: the JR Nara Line and the Kintetsu Limited Express. If you have a Japan Rail Pass, you'll probably want to take the commuter **JR Nara Line,** which departs about four times an hour and takes 45 to 60 minutes depending on the train; if you don't have a pass, the trip costs ¥690 ($5.75) one-way. If speed or luxury is of the utmost importance, the deluxe **Kintetsu Limited Express** whisks you to Nara in 35 minutes, guarantees you a seat (all seats are reserved), and costs ¥1,110 ($9.25) one-way; departures are every 30 minutes on the hour and half hour (if it's peak season, it's a good idea to buy your ticket in advance). A slower **Express Kintetsu** takes 45 minutes and costs ¥610 ($5.10).

You can also reach Nara from Osaka in about 30 to 50 minutes, depending on the train and the station from which you leave. The **Kintetsu Nara Line,** departing from Namba Station, takes 40 minutes and costs ¥540 ($4.50) one-way.

VISITOR INFORMATION   Pick up brochures and information on Nara before leaving Kyoto at the **Tourist Information Center (TIC)** across from Kyoto Station's Karasuma exit. The Kyoto map distributed here, called the "Tourist Map of Kyoto/Nara," has a good map of Nara on the reverse side (the Kyoto map distributed by the local Kyoto City Tourist Information Office does not). Be sure to pick up the leaflet "Nara Walks."

In Nara itself, there are tourist information offices at both **JR Nara Station** (© **0742/22-9821;** open daily 9am–5pm) and **Kintetsu Nara Station** (© **0742/24-4858;** open daily 9am–5pm). Both have good brochures and maps with useful information on how to get around Nara by bus. For more detailed information on Nara, visit the **Nara City Tourist Center,** 23–4 Kami-sanjo-cho (© **0742/22-3900;** open daily 9am–9pm), located in the heart of the city on Sanjo Dori between both stations and about a 5-minute walk from each. Finally, there's **Sarusawa Information Center** (© **0742/26-1991;** open daily 9am–5pm), located at Sarusawa-ike Pond, south of Nara Park and not far from Nara's many attractions.

GETTING AROUND   If you take the Kintetsu Line, you'll arrive at **Kintetsu Nara Station;** if you take the JR train, you'll arrive at **JR Nara Station.** Both stations are about a 10-minute walk from each other and are within walking

Nara

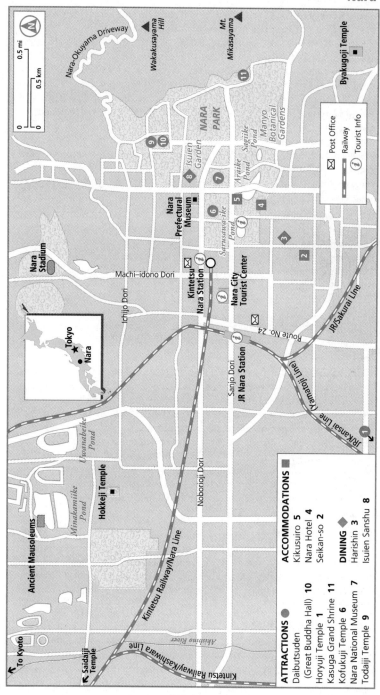

ATTRACTIONS ●
Daibutsuden
(Great Buddha Hall) **10**
Horyuji Temple **1**
Kasuga Grand Shrine **11**
Kofukuji Temple **6**
Nara National Museum **7**
Todaiji Temple **9**

ACCOMMODATIONS ■
Kikusuiro **5**
Nara Hotel **4**
Seikan-so **2**

DINING ◆
Harishin **3**
Isuien Sanshu **8**

⌧ Post Office
▬ Railway
ⓘ Tourist Info

distance of Nara Park. Kintetsu Station is slightly closer, about a 5-minute walk to the entrance of the park, while the JR Station is about a 10-minute walk to the park. Keep in mind, however, that Nara Park is quite large and its major attractions are far-flung; it takes about 20 minutes to walk from Kintetsu Nara Station to Todaiji Temple. Around the stations themselves is Nara's small downtown area, with Sanjo Dori serving as the main shopping street and running from JR Nara Station to Nara Park. If you prefer to ride rather than walk, **The World Heritage Loop Line Bus,** which stops at both stations and major attractions, costs ¥180 ($1.50) for one trip or ¥800 ($6.65) for the whole day. The number 1 bus travels counter clockwise and the number 2 bus clockwise. The bus operates Saturdays, Sundays and National Holidays year round and daily June through September.

IF YOU'RE HEADING TO HORYUJI   If you plan on visiting the Horyuji Temple Area (see below), the fastest way to get there is from JR Nara Station on the JR Kansai Yamatoji Line going in the direction of Namba in Osaka; departures are every 10 minutes or so and bring you to Horyuji Station in 12 minutes. From there, you can either walk to the temple area in about 17 minutes or take the bus (¥170/$1.40), which departs three times an hour.

Or, from either the JR or Kintetsu Station, you can take bus no. 60, which departs twice an hour and takes 39 minutes to reach the Horyuji-mae stop. There are also other buses—nos. 52, 97, and 98—that take 53 minutes to make the trip (¥760/$6.30).

Obviously, since it takes quite a bit of time getting to and from Horyuji, you must limit your sightseeing to only the major attractions if you plan on visiting both Nara Park and Horyuji in 1 day.

GUIDED TOURS OF NARA   **Goodwill Guides** will be glad to show you the sights in exchange for the chance to practice their English. A national organization of volunteers, Goodwill Guides range from students and housewives to retired people. One guide each is generally posted at both the JR and Kintetsu Station tourist offices and is available to the first tourists who show up any day except Sunday. Otherwise, if you want to be assured of having a guide, you can make reservations in advance by calling © 0742/45-5920 the day before to arrange a time. Guides are available daily from 9am to 5pm. There's no charge for these personal guides, but you are requested to pay their transportation to meet you, and I suggest you also pay for the guide's lunch (guides do not have to pay admission fares to attractions).

SEEING THE SIGHTS

The best way to enjoy Nara is to arrive early in the morning before the first tour buses start pulling in. If you don't have much time, the most important sites to see are **Todaiji Temple, Kasuga Shrine,** and **Kofukuji Temple's Treasure House,** which you can see in about 3 hours. If you have more time, add **Horyuji Temple.**

AROUND NARA PARK

With its ponds, grassy lawns, trees, and temples, Nara Park covers about 1,300 acres and is home to more than 1,000 deer, which are considered divine messengers and are therefore allowed to roam freely through the park. The deer are generally quite friendly; throughout the park you can buy "deer cookies," which all but the shyest fawns will usually take right out of your hand.

Kofukuji Temple ⭐   As you walk east from either the JR or Kintetsu Station, this is the first temple you reach. It was established in 710 as the family temple of the Fujiwaras, the second most powerful clan after the imperial family from the 8th to 12th centuries. At one time as many as 175 buildings were erected on the Kofukuji Temple grounds, giving it significant religious and political power up until the 16th century; through centuries of civil wars and fires, however, most of the structures were destroyed. Only a handful of buildings still remain, but even these were rebuilt after the 13th century. The **five-story pagoda,** first erected in 730, was burned down five times. The present pagoda dates from 1426 and is an exact replica of the original; at 164 feet tall, it's the second-tallest pagoda in Japan (the tallest is at Toji Temple in Kyoto). Also of historic importance is the **Eastern Golden Hall** (Tokondo), originally constructed in 726 by Emperor Shomu to speed the recovery of the ailing Empress Gensho. Rebuilt in 1415, it houses several priceless images including a bronze statue of Yakushi Nyorai, a Buddha believed to cure illnesses, which was installed by Emperor Shomu on behalf of his sick wife; a 12th-century wooden Bodhisattva of wisdom, long wor-shipped by scholar monks and today by pupils hopeful of passing university entrance exams; and guardians and assistants of Yakushi. But the best thing to see here is the temple's **Treasure House** (Kokuhokan) ⭐⭐, which displays many statues and works of art originally contained in the temple's buildings, many of them National Treasures. Most famous are a statue of Ashura carved in the 8th century and a bronze head of Yakushi Nyorai, but my favorites are the 12th-cen-tury carved wooden statues representing priests of the Kamakura Period with fas-cinating facial features that render them strikingly human.

Ⓒ **0742/22-7755.** Treasure House ¥500 ($4.50) adults, ¥400 ($3.60) junior- and senior-high students, ¥150 ($1.35) elementary students; Eastern Golden Hall ¥300 ($2.50) adults, ¥200 ($1.65) junior-high and high-school students, ¥100 (85¢) elementary students. Daily 9am–5pm.

Nara National Museum (Nara Kokuritsu Hakubutsukan) ⭐   To the east of Kofukuji, this museum opened in 1895 to house invaluable Buddhist art and archaeological relics and has since expanded into a second building. Many mas-terpieces originally contained in Nara's many temples are now housed here, including Buddhist sculptures from various periods in Japan's history, paintings, masks, scrolls, calligraphy, roof tiles, and archaeological objects obtained from temple ruins, tombs, and sutra mounds. Unfortunately, although items are iden-tified in English, explanations of their historical significance are not.

Ⓒ **0742/22-7771.** Admission ¥420 ($3.50) adults, ¥130 ($1.10) high-school and college students, ¥70 (60¢) junior-high and elementary students. Higher admission during special exhibitions. Tues–Sun 9:30am–5pm, Apr–Oct Fri 9:30am–7pm. Closed Dec 26–Jan 4.

Todaiji Temple ⭐⭐⭐   Nara's premier attraction is Todaiji Temple and its **Daibutsu** (Great Buddha). When Emperor Shomu ordered construction of both the temple and Daibutsu back in the mid-700s, he intended to make Todaiji the headquarters of all Buddhist temples in the land. As part of his plans for a Buddhist utopia, he commissioned work for this huge bronze statue of Buddha; it took eight castings to complete this remarkable work of art, which remains the largest bronze statue of Buddha in Japan. At a height of more than 50 feet, the Daibutsu is made of 437 tons of bronze, 286 pounds of pure gold, 165 pounds of mercury, and 7 tons of vegetable wax. However, thanks to Japan's frequent natural calamities, the Buddha of today isn't quite what it used to be. In 855, in what must have been a whopper of an earthquake, the statue lost its head. It was repaired in 861, but alas, the huge wooden building housing the

Buddha was burned twice during wars, melting the Buddha's head. The present head dates from 1692.

The wooden structure housing the Great Buddha, called **Daibutsuden,** was destroyed several times through the centuries; the present structure dates from 1709. Measuring 161 feet tall, 187 feet long, and 164 feet wide, it's the largest wooden structure in the world—but is only two-thirds its original size. Be sure to walk in a circle around the Great Buddha to see it from all different angles. Behind the statue is a model of how the Daibutsuden used to look, flanked by two massive pagodas as well as a huge wooden column with a small hole in it near the ground. According to popular belief, if you can manage to crawl through this opening, you'll be sure to reach enlightenment (seemingly a snap for children). You can also get your fortune in English for ¥150 ($1.25) by shaking a bamboo canister until a wooden stick with a number comes out; the number corresponds to a piece of paper. Mine told me that though I will win, it will be of no use, an illness will be serious, and the person for whom I am waiting will not come. And the monk who gave me the fortune said mine was a good one!

ⓒ **0742/22-5511.** Admission ¥500 ($4.15) adults, ¥300 ($2.50) children. Daily Mar 8am–5pm; Apr–Sept, 7:30am–5:30pm; Oct, 7:30am–5pm; Nov–Feb, 8am–4:30pm.

Kasuga Grand Shrine 🌟🌟   A stroll through the park will bring you to one of my favorite Shinto shrines in all Japan. Originally the tutelary shrine of the powerful Fujiwara family, it was founded in 768 and, according to Shinto concepts of purity, was torn down and rebuilt every 20 years in its original form until 1863. Since virtually all empresses hailed from the Fujiwara family, the shrine enjoyed a privileged status with the imperial family. Nestled in the midst of verdant woods, it's a shrine of vermilion-colored pillars and an astounding 3,000 stone and bronze lanterns. The most spectacular time to visit is in mid-August or the beginning of February when all 3,000 lanterns are lit. Here, too, you can pay ¥200 ($1.65) for an *onikuji,* a slip of paper on which your fortune is written in English. If the fortune is unfavorable, you can conveniently negate it by tying the piece of paper to the twig of a tree. Although admission to the grounds is free, if you want a closer view of the bronze lanterns (perhaps to photograph them) and the worship hall, pay the admission charge to the inner grounds.

ⓒ **0742/22-7788.** Free admission to grounds; inner grounds ¥420 ($3.50) adults, ¥315 ($2.60) high and junior-high school students, ¥210 ($1.75) elementary students. Daily 9am–4:30pm.

THE HORYUJI TEMPLE AREA 🌟🌟🌟

Founded in 607 by Prince Shotoku as a center for Buddhism in Japan, **Horyuji Temple** (ⓒ **07457/5-2555**) is one of Japan's most significant gems in terms of architecture, art, and religion. It was from here that Buddhism blossomed and spread throughout the land. Today, about 45 buildings remain, some of them dating from the end of the 7th century and comprising what are probably the oldest wooden structures in the world. For details on reaching Horyuji, see "Essentials," above.

At the western end of the grounds is the two-story, 58-foot-high **Golden Hall,** or Kondo, which is considered the oldest building at Horyuji Temple. Next to the main hall is a **five-story pagoda** dating from the foundation of the temple, which contains four scenes from the life of Buddha. The **Great Treasure House,** or Daihozoden, a concrete building constructed in 1941, contains temple treasures including statues and other works of art from the 7th and 8th centuries. On the eastern precincts of Horyuji Temple is an octagonal building built in 739 called **Yumedono Hall,** or the Hall of Dreams; supposedly, Prince Shotoku used this building for quiet meditation.

Admission to Horyuji Temple, the Treasure House, and the Hall of Dreams is ¥1,000 ($8.35) for adults and ¥500 ($4.15) for children. The grounds are open daily from 8am to 5pm (to 4:30pm from Nov 4–Feb 21).

East of Yumedono is **Chuguji Temple** (℅ 07457/5-2106), a nunnery built for members of the imperial family. It contains two outstanding works of art: The wooden statue of **Miroku-bosatsu,** dating from the 7th century, is noted for the serene and compassionate expression on its face. The **Tenjukoku Mandala,** the oldest piece of embroidery in Japan, was originally 16 feet long and was created by Shotoku's widow and her female companions with scenes depicting life of the times. Only a replica of the fragile embroidery is now on display. Open daily from 9am to 4:30pm (to 4pm Oct 1–Mar 20); admission is ¥400 ($3.35).

WHERE TO STAY

⑩ **Kikusuiro** ✦✦✦   You can't find a more beautiful example of a Japanese-style ryokan than this lovely 130-year-old inn, an imposing structure with an ornate Japanese-style roof surrounded by a white wall. The ryokan has been designated a private cultural asset by the Ministry of Culture. Rooms, some of which face Ara-ike Pond, are outfitted with scrolls and antiques and are connected to one another with rambling wooden corridors. There's also a beautiful garden. The manager, Mr. Itoh, speaks English.

1130 Takahata-cho Bodaimachi, Nara 630-8301. ℅ 0742/23-2001. Fax 0742/26-0025. 14 units, 8 with bathroom. ¥28,000 ($233) per person without bathroom, ¥30,000–¥50,000 ($250–$417) per person with bathroom. Rates include 2 meals. DC, JCB, MC, V. South of Nara Park's Kofukuji 5-story pagoda on Sanjo Dori (Route 308); a 10-min. walk from Kintetsu Nara Station, 15 min. from JR Nara Station. **Amenities:** 2 restaurants (Western, Japanese). *In room:* A/C, TV, fridge, hot-water pot with tea.

Nara Hotel ✦✦✦   One of the most famous places to stay in Nara (and with a front-desk staff eager to please), the Nara Hotel sits like a palace on top of a hill overlooking several ponds. Built in 1909 and similar to Japan's other hotels built around the turn of the 20th century to accommodate the foreigners who poured into the country following the Meiji Restoration, it's constructed as a Western-style hotel but has many Japanese features. You have your choice of accommodations in the old section of the hotel with its high ceilings, antique light fixtures, and comfortable old-fashioned decor or in the new addition, which opened in 1984 and offers larger modern rooms with dataports and verandas overlooking the old town. I personally prefer the atmosphere of the older rooms—those facing the city are less expensive than those in the new wing, while the higher-priced ones have a view of the pond.

Nara-Koennai, Nara 630-8301. ℅ 0742/26-3300. Fax 0742/23-5252. 132 units. ¥14,000 ($117) single; ¥23,000–¥27,000 ($192–$225) double; ¥22,000–¥50,000 ($183–$417) twin. AE, DC, JCB, MC, V. About a 4-min. walk south of Nara Park; an 8-min. taxi ride from train station. **Amenities:** 2 restaurants (Japanese, Western), 1 bar; souvenir shop; room service (4–10:30pm); in-room massage; same-day laundry/dry cleaning service . *In room:* A/C, satellite TV, minibar, hot-water pot with tea, hair dryer, washlet toilet.

Seikan-so ✦✦ *Value*   This is a lovely choice in inexpensive Japanese-style accommodations. It boasts the most beautiful garden of any Japanese Inn Group member I've seen, complete with azalea bushes and manicured trees—the kind of garden usually found only at ryokan costing twice as much. Located in a quiet neighborhood about a 10-minute walk south of Nara Park, it dates from 1916 and is owned by a friendly young couple who speak English. The traditional Japanese building wraps around the inner garden. Unfortunately, the rooms are beginning to show their age, but all is forgiven if you can get one of the six facing the garden—be sure to request one when making your reservation. A Japanese or Western breakfast is available.

29 Higashi-Kitsuji-cho, Nara 630-8327 ☏ **0742/22-2670.** Fax 0742/22-2670. seikanso@chive.ocn.ne.jp. 9 units (none with bathroom). ¥4,000 ($33) per person. Discounts available for children under 10. Breakfast ¥450–¥700 ($3.75–$5.85) extra. AE, MC, V. Loop bus 1 to Kitayobate stop (1 min.), or a 12-min. walk from Kintetsu Nara Station, 25 min. from JR Nara Station. **Amenities:** Nonsmoking rooms. *In room:* A/C, TV, hot-water pot with tea, no phone.

WHERE TO DINE

(101) **Harishin** ★★★ *Finds* OBENTO   Many tourists never see this lovely part of old Nara near Gangoji Temple and consisting of narrow lanes and traditional wooden homes and shops. The restaurant itself is a 200-year-old house of ochre-colored walls and a wood-slat facade, and dining is on tatami with a view of a garden. Only a mini-kaiseki meal and an obento that change with the season, the creation of chef-owner Nakagawa-san, are served. On my last visit, my obento included an aperatif wine, light tofu flavored with sesame, soup, rice, pickled vegetables, tempura, and various exquisitely prepared bite-size morsels of shrimp, chicken, potatoes wrapped in bacon, and scallops. Highly recommended.

15 Nakashinya-cho. ☏ 0742/22-2669. Obento ¥2,500 ($21), mini-kaiseki ¥3,500 ($29). AE, DC, JCB, MC, V. Tues–Sun 11:30am–2:30pm and 6–8pm (last order); if Mon is a national holiday, open Mon and closed Tues. A 5-min. walk south of Sarusawa-ike Pond on the road that leads south from the east edge of the pond (stop at the tourist office for directions).

Isuien Sanshyu ★★ EEL   Isuien Garden, established during the Edo Period and enlarged a century ago by a Nara merchant, is a strolling garden that uses the principles of borrowed landscape, incorporating the hills of Kasuga and Wakayama in its design. While nothing spectacular, it does have a wonderful thatched-roof restaurant overlooking part of the garden and a pond—a great, traditional place for a meal. It serves only one thing, a set meal of eel (*unagi*) basted with a yam paste, soup, rice, and pickled vegetables—considered very healthy. If you wish, you can pay the extra admission to see the entire garden (¥600/$5 for adults), but there are better gardens in Kyoto.

Isuien Garden, 74 Suimoncho. ☏ 0742/22-2173. Eel set meal ¥2,400 ($20). No credit cards. Wed–Mon 11:30am–2pm. North of Nara Park. Take the road between Kofukuji Temple and Nara National Museum (Rte. 369) north in the direction of Kyoto; after passing the busy street, take the first right. Isuien is at the end of this street.

The Rest of Western Honshu

In addition to Tokyo, Kyoto, and the Japan Alps, Honshu has numerous other cities, towns, and attractions in its western half that are well worth a visit. As the largest of Japan's islands and the home to 80% of the country's population, Honshu is where most of the country's important historical events took place; you'll find many castles, gardens, temples, shrines, and other famous sights linked to the past here. Honshu's climate ranges from snowy winters in the north and its mountain ranges to subtropical weather in the south, and the middle of the island is traversed by Japan's longest river, the Shinano. With all this to offer, it's little wonder that many travelers to Japan never make it off this central island.

1 Nagoya

363km (227 miles) W of Tokyo; 147km (92 miles) E of Kyoto; 186km (116 miles) E of Osaka

Nagoya was founded as a castle town more than 385 years ago on orders of Tokugawa Ieyasu, who considered its strategic position on the Tokaido Highway to be useful for controlling Osaka and other points west. Today, Nagoya is Japan's fourth-largest city with a population of 2.15 million—yet it's a place most foreigners never stop to see. True, it doesn't have the attractions of many of the nation's other cities, but it does have a castle originally built by the first Tokugawa shogun, as well as one of Japan's most important Shinto shrines. You can also stroll through an aquarium famous for its penguins and sea turtles, visit the world-famous Noritake chinaware factory, spend hours at an open-air architectural museum (one of my favorites in Japan), and watch cormorant fishing in summer. Nagoya, capital of Aichi Prefecture, also serves as the gateway to Takayama in the Japan Alps (see "Takayama, Little Kyoto of the Mountains," in chapter 6) and Ise-Shima National Park (covered later in this chapter).

ESSENTIALS

GETTING THERE   By Plane   If you're arriving at **Nagoya International Airport** on a domestic or international flight, you can take the airport shuttle bus to the **Melsa Meitetsu Bus Center,** in front of the Sakura Dori exit of Nagoya Station, for ¥870 ($7.25). Buses depart every 10 minutes from 8:20am to 10:05pm daily for the 30-minute ride.

By JR Train   The Shinkansen bullet train to **JR Nagoya Station** takes approximately 2 hours from Tokyo, 45 minutes from Kyoto, and 1 hour from Shin-Osaka Station. The fare from Tokyo Station is ¥10,070 ($84) for an unreserved seat.

By Bus   From Shinjuku Station in Tokyo, the Chuo Line bus costs ¥5,100 ($42.50) one way for the 6-hour trip, with several departures daily. From Kyoto, the Tomei Highway Bus costs ¥2,500 ($21) and takes 2¾ hours; from Osaka, it's just over 3 hours and ¥2,900 ($24).

VISITOR INFORMATION Before departing Tokyo, Kyoto, or Narita or Kansai international airports, stop by the Tourist Information Center for the leaflet "Nagoya and Vicinity," which contains a city map and transportation and sightseeing information. In Nagoya Station, you can pick up a map and pamphlets at the **Nagoya Tourist Information Center** (✆ 052/541-4301; open daily 9am–7pm) in the central concourse, opposite the Central exit wickets of the JR Line; look for the ? and JR signs.

For more detailed information about Nagoya, walk 8 minutes from Nagoya Station's Central exit straight down Sakura Dori (or take the subway one stop to Kokusai Center Station) to the **Nagoya International Center** on the third floor of the Nagoya International Center Building, 1–47–1 Nagono (✆ **052/ 581-0100;** open Tues–Sat 9am–8:30pm, Sun and holidays 9am–5pm; closed 2nd Sun in Feb and Aug). It's one of Japan's best facilities for foreign visitors and residents, with an English-speaking staff, a lounge area with a TV featuring CNN newscasts, Internet access, and lots of information on the city, including free monthly publications *Nagoya Calendar* and *Avenues*. Be sure to pick up a city map and a pamphlet entitled "Welcome to Aichi." The center also advises foreign residents on how to get a visa, where to find an apartment, and which doctors speak English. Here, too, you can apply to visit a Japanese family in their home in the local **Home Visit** system. You must apply in person no later than 5pm the day before you wish to visit; be sure to bring your passport.

For recorded information in English on events, concerts, festivals, and the arts, call ✆ **052/581-0400.**

INTERNET ACCESS The Nagoya International Center (see "Visitor Information," above) provides Internet access for ¥250 ($2.10) per 30 minutes or ¥500 ($4.15) for an hour. Café Quatre (✆ **052/562-1517;** open daily 11am–11pm), on the 12th floor of Towers Plaza above Nagoya Station charges ¥300 ($2.50) for 30 minutes. Kinko's, 2–3–31 Sakae, Naka-ku (✆ **052/ 231-9211**), is open daily 24 hours with self-serve computers costing ¥250 ($2.10) per 15 minutes.

ORIENTATION Almost completely destroyed during World War II, Nagoya was rebuilt with wide, straight streets, many of which are named.

The ultra-modern, twin-towered **JR Nagoya Station,** with its many train lines (including the Shinkansen), soars more than 50 stories above the skyline and contains Takashimaya department store, offices, a Marriott hotel, many restaurants and an observatory. Clustered nearby are the Meitetsu Bus Terminal, Meitetsu Shin-Nagoya Station, the city bus terminal, Kintetsu Station, a subway station for the Sakura Dori and Higashiyama lines, as well as many hotels and a huge underground shopping arcade that stretches 3.7 miles and includes about 600 shops.

Most of the city's attractions spread out east of Nagoya Station (take the Central/Sakuradori exit), including the city's downtown area, **Sakae,** with its many shops, restaurants, and department stores. Also in Sakae is **Higashi Dori,**

Tips **A Note on Directions**

All directions in the listings below are from Nagoya Station unless otherwise noted; the time in parentheses indicates walking time from the subway or bus stop indicated.

Nagoya

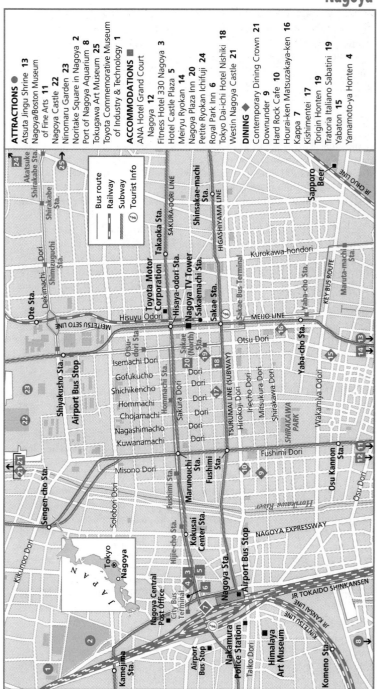

ATTRACTIONS ●
Atsuta Jingu Shrine **13**
Nagoya/Boston Museum
  of Fine Arts **11**
Nagoya Castle **22**
Ninomaru Garden **23**
Noritake Square in Nagoya **2**
Port of Nagoya Aquarium **8**
Tokugawa Art Museum **25**
Toyota Commemorative Museum
  of Industry & Technology **1**

ACCOMMODATIONS ■
ANA Hotel Grand Court
  Nagoya **12**
Fitness Hotel 330 Nagoya **3**
Hotel Castle Plaza **5**
Meiryu Ryokan **14**
Nagoya Plaza Inn **20**
Petite Ryokan Ichifuji **24**
Royal Park Inn **6**
Tokyo Dai-ichi Hotel Nishiki **18**
Westin Nagoya Castle **21**

DINING ◆
Contemporary Dining Crown **21**
Downunder **9**
Hard Rock Cafe **10**
Hourai-ken Matsuzakaya-ken **16**
Kappa **7**
Kishimentei **17**
Torigin Honten **19**
Tratoria Italiano Sabatini **19**
Yabaton **15**
Yamamoto-ya Honten **4**

a wide boulevard that stretches north and south with a park and a TV tower in its green meridian. North of Higashi Dori is **Nagoya Castle,** while south is **Atsuta Jingu Shrine.**

GETTING AROUND   The easiest way to get around is via the city's four-line **subway** system, which is simple to use because station names are written in both English and Japanese, and there are English announcements and digital signs in trains. Probably the most important line for tourists is the **Meijo Line,** which runs through Sakae underneath Higashi Dori and takes you to both Nagoya Castle (stop: Shiyakusho) and Atsuta Jingu Shrine (stop: Jingu-Nishi), with one branch terminating at Nagoya Port with its aquarium; if you take this line in the opposite direction, you'll eventually end up in Ozone (no kidding!). Individual tickets for the subway are ¥200 to ¥320 ($1.65–$2.65) depending on the distance.

To go where subway lines don't, such as the Tokugawa Art Museum, you'll find it convenient to take one of the **city buses,** for which you'll pay a flat fare of ¥200 ($1.65). City buses depart from Nagoya Station and from Sakae Bus Terminal on Higashi Dori just south of Sakae subway station. There's also the private **Meitetsu Bus Line** with a terminal located at Nagoya Station.

There are several **transportation passes** worth considering if you'll be traveling a lot within a single day. For subways, there's a one-day pass (**Ichinichi Jo-sha**) for ¥740 ($6.20) that allows you to ride as much as you want for a full day; for ¥850 ($7.10), you can ride as much as you want on both subways and city buses. Or you can buy a 1-day ticket and attraction pass (**Ikomai Kippu**) for ¥1,300 ($11), which allows you to ride subways and city buses all day with the added bonus of free entry to Nagoya Castle and discounts for most other attractions. You can purchase all passes at subway stations.

SEEING THE SIGHTS

Atsuta Jingu Shrine   Because it contains one of the emperor's Three Sacred Treasures, this is revered as one of the three most important shrines in Japan. Founded in the 2nd century and last rebuilt in 1935, it enshrines the Kusanagi-no-Tsurugi (Grass-Mowing Sword), which is one of the Three Regalia of the Emperor. The other two sacred treasures are the Sacred Mirror (in the Ise Grand Shrines) and the Jewels (in the Imperial Palace in Tokyo). According to legend, the Grass-Mowing Sword was presented to a prince named Yamato-Takeru, who used it during a campaign against rebels in eastern Japan; the rebels set a field of grass on fire, and the prince used the sword to mow down the grass, thereby quelling the fire. (*Atsuta* means "hot field" in Japanese.) Actually, there isn't much to see here—the sword is never on public display—yet Japanese make pilgrimages here to pay their respects, first purifying their hands or mouths with water, then throwing coins into the money box, clapping twice to gain the attention of the gods, and then bowing twice.

1–1–1 Jingu, Atsuta-ku. ℭ 052/671-4151. Free admission to the grounds. Open 24 hours. Station: Jingu-mae (4 min.).

Nagoya/Boston Museum of Fine Arts ★★   In partnership with the Museum of Fine Arts in Boston, this sister museum displays masterpieces on loan from the MFA, presented in both long-term exhibits that change every 5 years and in temporary exhibits that change twice a year. In a gleaming white building next to Kanayama Station, the museum gets high marks for curation and signage—the best we've seen in Japan. Unfortunately, there is only one small corner devoted to Japanese art in the long-term collection.

1–1–1 Kanayama-cho, Naka-ku. © 052/684-0101. Admission ¥1,200 ($10) adults, ¥900 ($7.50) university and high-school students, ¥500 ($4.15) children; admission only to long-term exhibition ¥400 ($3.35) adults, ¥300 ($2.50) high-school students. Tues–Sun 10am–5pm (to 9pm on Fri). JR, Meitetsu, or subway: Kanayama (1 min.).

Nagoya Castle ⭐   Built for his ninth son by Tokugawa Ieyasu, the first Toku-gawa shogun, Nagoya Castle was completed in 1612 and served as both a strategic stronghold and a residence for members of the Owari branch of the Tokugawa family for almost 250 years, until the Meiji Restoration ended their rule in 1868. A shrewd and calculating shogun, Tokugawa forced feudal lords throughout Japan to contribute to the castle's construction, thereby depleting their resources and making it harder for them to rebel. Although Nagoya Castle was largely destroyed in World War II (only 3 turrets and 3 gates escaped destruction), the main donjon and other structures, rebuilt in 1959, are almost a carbon copy of the original. Like most reconstructed castles in Japan, this replica is made of ferroconcrete, yet it's still impressive from afar. Inside, the 154-foot donjon is thoroughly modern and even has an elevator up to the fifth floor, where you have fine views of Nagoya and beyond. The castle houses treasures that escaped the bombing during World War II, including beautiful paintings on sliding doors and screens. There's also a model of Honmaru Palace (destroyed during WWII), the living quarters of the shogun when he visited Nagoya, and a high-tech exhibit that explores Nagoya Castle's construction and what life was like during the Edo Period.

Atop the donjon roof are two **golden dolphins,** replicas of those that per-ished during World War II and long thought to protect the castle from dreaded fires. The dolphins each weigh about 2,650 pounds and are made of cast bronze covered with 18-karat-gold scales. Incidentally, the dolphin on the south end— the favored, warmer side—is considered to be male, while the one relegated to the colder northern side is female.

East of the castle is **Ninomaru Garden,** laid out at the time of the castle's con-struction, converted to a dry Japanese landscape garden in 1716, and today one of the few remaining castle gardens in Japan. Besides providing a beautiful set-ting, it served as an emergency shelter for the lord in case of enemy attack. Stop by the **Ninomaru Tea House**—it's said that if you drink tea here, 5 years will be added to your life. Unless you linger, you should be able to tour the castle and grounds in less than 1½ hours.

1–1 Honmaru, Naka-ku. © 052/231-1700. Admission ¥500 ($4.15) adults, ¥100 (85¢) junior-high and ele-mentary school students. Daily 9am–4:30pm. Station: Shiyakusho (5 min.).

Noritake Square in Nagoya ⭐⭐   Nagoya has been a pottery and porcelain production center for centuries; today, the city and its vicinity manufacture 90% of Japan's total export chinaware. The largest chinaware company in Japan is Noritake, founded in 1904 and known the world over for its fine tableware. You can learn more about Noritake by spending about an hour or more here, begin-ning with an excellent film depicting the history of Noritake and describing the manufacturing and decorating processes involved in making porcelain. Unlike most modern-day factories, where work is largely automated, almost all the work here is still done by hand. Other highlights include a museum with exam-ples of all the Noritake chinaware ever produced and a shop selling Noritake (including an outlet for discounted products).

Note: As this book went to press, the Noritake Square was closed for remodeling in preparation for its 2004 100-year anniversary; check with the tourist office for updated information and possibly new open hours.

3–1–36 Noritake Shinmachi, Nishi-ku. ℂ 052/561-7114. Admission ¥500 ($4.15) adults, ¥300 ($2.50) high school students, free for children. Tues–Sun 10am–5pm. Subway: Kamejima (5 min.), or a 10-min. walk north of Nagoya Station.

Port of Nagoya Public Aquarium ★ *Kids*   Young Japanese flock to Nagoya's port area on weekends, drawn by a small amusement park, a maritime museum, a shopping complex, and believe it or not, a pleasure boat shaped like the golden dolphins of Nagoya Castle. But the Public Aquarium is the major draw for kids of all ages, with displays that concentrate on marine life from the seas around Japan. There's a 15-minute hologram show that transports you to the deep sea in a "submarine;" a touch tank with sea urchins, starfish, and other animals; and an IMAX theater with shows on the hour (included in the entry price). The aquarium is best-known, however, for its penguin tank, which copies the environment of the Antarctic with artificial falling snow and cold temperatures to maintain the penguins' reproductive cycle, and the loggerhead and green turtles with a sand beach to encourage them to lay eggs. You'll probably spend about 1½ hours here.

1–3 Minato-machi, Minato-ku. ℂ 052/654-7080. Admission ¥1,500 ($12.50) adults, ¥700 ($5.85) children. Tues–Sun 9:30am–5:30pm (to 8pm in Aug). Station: Nagoyako (exit 1, 7 min.).

Tokugawa Art Museum ★★★ *Finds*   Located on the grounds of a former mansion owned by the Owari branch of the Tokugawa family—with the original entry gate still intact—this worthwhile museum houses thousands of documents, samurai armor, swords, matchlocks, helmets, pottery, lacquerware, Noh costumes, and paintings that once belonged to the Tokugawa family, including objects inherited from the first Tokugawa shogun, Ieyasu. There are also replicas of structures and items that once adorned Nagoya Castle, including decorative alcoves, a teahouse, and a Noh stage. The museum's most famous exhibit is the 12th-century picture scrolls of *The Tale of Genji (Genji Emaki)*, but they're displayed only a few weeks a year in autumn (check with the tourist office); otherwise, replicas are on display. There are excellent English explanations throughout the museum that put the displays in historic context. You can easily spend an hour here.

1017 Tokugawa-cho, Higashi-ku. ℂ 052/935-6262. Admission ¥1,200 ($10) adults, ¥700 ($5.85) high-school students, ¥500 ($4.15) children; extra charge for special exhibits. Tues–Sun 10am–5pm. City bus: 2 to Shindeki stop (3 min.).

Toyota Commemorative Museum of Industry and Technology   This museum seems an odd marriage—it's devoted to both textile machinery and automobile production and technology. That's because the Toyota Group, founded by Toyoda Sakichi, the inventor of automatic looms, has a long history of producing both. Housed in an attractive brick building dating from the Taisho Period (1912–25), the museum displays approximately 80 looms and textile machinery, from wooden hand looms to airjet looms that utilize computer graphics. The automobile pavilion provides an historic chronology of automobile production, beginning with a replica of the first Toyota car (1936), early assembly lines using manpower, and automated assembly lines using industrial robots for everything from engine mounting to painting. There's also a display of both old and new Toyota cars. Expect to spend a minimum of an hour here.

P-Ping! Pachinko Parlors

Brightly lit and garish, pachinko parlors are packed with upright **pin-ball-like machines**—and row upon row of Japanese businessmen, housewives, and students sitting intently in front of them. Originating in Nagoya and popular since the 1950s, pachinko is a game in which ball bearings are flung into this vertical pinball machine one after the other. The player controls the strength with which the ball is released, but otherwise there's very little to do; some players even wedge a matchstick under the control and just watch the machine with folded arms. Points are amassed according to which holes the ball bearings fall into, just like in pinball. If you're good at it, you win ball bearings back, which you can subsequently trade in for food, cigarettes, watches, calculators, and other prizes.

It's illegal to win money in Japan, but outside many pachinko parlors and along back alleyways there are slots where you can trade in the watches, calculators, and other prizes for cash. The slots are so small that the person handing over the goods never sees the person who hands back money. Police, meanwhile, just look the other way.

Pachinko parlors compete in an ever-escalating war of themes, lights, and noise. Step inside one and you'll wonder how anyone could possibly think—the noise level of thousands of ball bearings clanking is awesome. Perhaps that's the answer to its popularity: It's an escapist pastime. Some people seem to be addicted to the mesmerizing game; newspaper articles talk of errant husbands who never come home anymore, while psychologists analyze its popularity.

Every hamlet seems to have a pachinko parlor, and cities like Tokyo and Nagoya are inundated with them. You'll see them in nightlife districts and clustered around train stations—but with their unmistakable clanging and clanking, you'll hear them long before you reach their neon-lit facades.

4–1–35 Noritake Shinmachi, Nishi-ku. © 052/551-6111. Admission ¥500 ($4.15) adults, ¥300 ($2.50) junior-high and high-school students, ¥200 ($1.65) children. Tues–Sun 9:30am–5pm. Train: Meitetsu Line to Sakou (3 min.). Subway: to Kamejima (10 min.). Just north of the Noritake Craft Center, about a 15-min. walk from Nagoya Station.

IN NEARBY INUYAMA CITY

Inuyama City has several worthwhile attractions, so I suggest coming here for a day of sightseeing and, in summer, topping it off with some cormorant fishing (see below). The **Inuyama Tourist Office** (© 0568/61-6000) is located in Inuyama Station (open daily 9am–5pm, to 6pm July 20–Aug), but for information by phone call the Inuyama International Tourist Center (© 0568/61-1000).

Inuyama Castle ⚐   Constructed in 1537 atop a bluff overlooking the Kiso River, miraculously surviving centuries of war and earthquake (part of it was damaged by an 1891 earthquake but then repaired), Japan's oldest castle is a designated National Treasure. The four-story keep—much smaller than most of

Japan's castles—is the nation's only privately owned castle, owned by the Naruse family since 1618. In addition to displaying a few samurai outfits, it offers a nice, expansive view over the river that's especially worth a look if you intend to join the nearby cormorant fishing. The castle is so diminutive you can see everything in 15 minutes.

Admission ¥400 ($3.35) adults, ¥100 (85¢) children. Daily 9am–5pm. From Meitetsu Shin-Nagoya Station, take the Inuyama Line 23 min. to Inuyama Yuen Station; from there it's about a 15-min. walk.

Museum Meiji Mura ★★★   Inuyama City's most important attraction is one of my favorite museums in Japan. In fact, it may well be the main reason for a Nagoya stopover. A 250-acre open-air architectural museum, it features more than 60 buildings and structures dating from the Meiji Period (1868–1912), all beautifully situated on landscaped grounds on the shores of a lake. Before Japan opened its doors in the mid-1800s, unpainted wooden structures dominated Japanese architecture; after Western influences began infiltrating Japan, however, stone, brick, painted wood, towers, turrets, and Victorian features came into play. Unfortunately, earthquakes, war, fire, and developer greed have destroyed most of Japan's Meiji-Era buildings, making this a priceless collection.

On the grounds are Western homes that once belonged to foreigners living in Nagasaki and Kobe, official government buildings and schools, two Christian churches, a post office, a bathhouse, a Kabuki theater, a brewery, bridges, and even a prison. Don't miss the front facade and lobby of the original Imperial Hotel in Tokyo, designed by Frank Lloyd Wright and containing some of the hotel's original Wright-designed furniture. In fact, most of the buildings display furniture and other items related to the building it's housed in. You can mail a postcard from the post office, buy candy at the old candy shop, have coffee or tea in the Imperial Hotel lobby, or stop for a drink in the brewery. Plan on spending at least 3 hours here, though you could easily spend the better part of a day.

© 0568/67-0314. Admission ¥1,600 ($13) adults, ¥1,100 ($9.15) high-school students, ¥700 ($5.85) children. Daily 9:30am–5pm (to 4pm Nov–Feb). Take the Meitetsu Line from Meitetsu Shin-Nagoya Station to Inuyama Station (¥540/$4.50 one-way), which takes about 30 min. by express; change there for a 20-minute direct bus to Meiji Mura (¥410/$3.40 one-way).

WATCHING CORMORANT FISHING ★★★

There are two places near Nagoya where you can watch **cormorant fishing** every night in summer (except during a full moon or the 2 or 3 days following a heavy rain). In this ancient, 300-year-old Japanese fishing method, trained *ukai* (seabirds) dive into the water in search of *ayu,* a small Japanese trout. At nightfall, wooden fires are lit in suspended cages at the front of long wooden boats to attract the ayu, whereupon leashed cormorants are released into the water. To ensure that the cormorants don't swallow the fish, the birds are fitted with neck rings.

In **Inuyama,** cormorant fishing takes place from June 1 to September 30 on the Kiso River. Spectators can board boats at 6:15, 6:45, and 7:15pm to observe the spectacle firsthand. While waiting for the full darkness that must descend before the fishing takes place (usually around 7:30pm), you can dine on set meals (ranging in price from ¥3,000–¥5,000/$25–$42, with Western food available) that you order when you make your reservations. You can also purchase drinks from boat vendors and can even buy and set off Japanese fireworks, which give the evening a celebratory atmosphere. The actual fishing itself occupies only

20 minutes. To participate, take the Inuyama Line of the Meitetsu Railways from Meitetsu Shin-Nagoya Station 23 minutes to Inuyama Yuen Station (¥590/$4.90); from there, it's a 5-minute walk. Call ahead to make reservations (© **0568/61-0057**); upon arrival, stop by the ticket office near the bridge. Tickets cost ¥2,500 ($21) for adults and ¥1,250 ($10.40) for children in June and September, ¥2,800 ($23) and ¥1,400 ($12) respectively in July and August.

The city of **Gifu** features cormorant fishing from May 11 to October 15 on the Nagaragawa River, where you can also dine and view the whole spectacle aboard a small wooden boat. To reach Gifu, take the Meitetsu Main Line train from Meitetsu Shin-Nagoya Station to Shin-Gifu Station (¥540/$4.50). From there, switch to a local train or bus (¥200/$1.65) heading for Nagarabashi Station. You'll see the ticket office (*Gifu-shi Ukai Kanransen Jimusho*) after exiting the station. You can call ahead to reserve your ticket (© **058/262-0104**) beginning in mid-April, daily between 8:45am and 8pm. Tickets cost ¥3,300 ($27.50) for adults and ¥2,900 ($24) for children. Boats depart at 6:15pm, 6:30pm, and 7:05pm.

WHERE TO STAY
EXPENSIVE
In addition to the hotels listed below, the **Nagoya Hilton,** 1–3–3 Sakae, Naka-ku, Nagoya 460-0008 (© **800/HILTONS** or 052/212-1111; fax 052/212-1225; www.hilton.com) offers 438 units to mostly foreign business travelers; while the new **Nagoya Marriott Associa Hotel,** 1–1–4 Meieki, Nakamura-ku, Nagoya 450-6002 (© **052/584-1113,** Fax 052/584-1112, www.associa.com/nma/), boasts restaurants, a health club, a business center and 780 rooms all conveniently located above Nagoya Station.

ANA Hotel Grand Court Nagoya ★★★
In an ultra-modern building that also houses the Nagoya/Boston Museum of Fine Arts (see earlier in this chapter; hotel guests receive a ¥200/$1.65 museum discount), this hotel seems intent on mirroring its artsy neighbor with plenty of artwork of its own, including what graces the walls of its marble-floored, sophisticated lobby and its guest rooms. An excellent concierge desk, eager to provide assistance, receives high marks for efficiency. Rooms are large, with every convenience. Since there are no single rooms, the rates below are for single use of a double room; deluxe doubles and twins have king-size beds. Suites and luxury rooms, on the 26th floor, add in-room fax machines, plush bathrobes, extra toiletries, and even flower arrangements. For a splurge, the 30th-floor Star Gate Restaurant and Bar offers spectacular views of Nagoya.

1–1–1 Kanayama-cho, Naka-ku, Nagoya 460-0023. © **800/262-4683** in the U.S. and Canada or 052/683-4111. Fax 052/683-4121. www.anahotels.com. 246 units. ¥17,000–¥23,000 ($142–$192) single; ¥24,000–¥31,000 ($200–$258) double; ¥28,000–¥31,000 ($233–$258) twin; ¥38,000 ($317) executive floor double. AE, DC, JCB, MC, V. JR, Meitetsu or Subway: Kanayama (1 min.). **Amenities:** 5 restaurants, 1 lounge, 1 bar; concierge; sundries shop; salon; room service (10am–midnight); in-room massage; babysitting; same-day laundry/dry cleaning service; nonsmoking rooms; executive-level rooms. *In room:* A/C, cable TV with pay movies, dataport, minibar, hot-water pot with tea, hair dryer, safe, bathroom scale, washlet toilet.

Westin Nagoya Castle ★★
Situated just west of Nagoya Castle, the chief attraction of this 30-year-old hotel—a local favorite for special occasions and meetings—is the wonderful views of the moat and castle from its rooms, especially at night when the castle is illuminated. Rooms are spacious, but it's worth staying here only if you get a room with a view (note that the cheapest singles

do not face the castle); otherwise, the location is rather inconvenient, though courtesy shuttle buses to Nagoya Station and Sakae are a big plus.

3–19 Hinokuchi-cho, Nishi-ku, Nagoya 451-8551. ℂ 800/Westin-1 in the U.S. and Canada or 052/521-2121. Fax 052/531-3313. 229 units. ¥13,000–¥30,000 ($108–$250) single; ¥24,000–¥35,000 ($200–$292) double or twin; from ¥22,000 ($183) executive single, from ¥27,000 ($225) executive double. AE, DC, JCB, MC, V. Subway: Tsurumai Line to Sengencho (10 min.), or courtesy shuttle bus from Nagoya Station. **Amenities:** 5 restaurants, 2 bars; indoor 5-lane, 25-meter pool and Jacuzzi (fee: ¥1,500/$12.50) with exercise room and sauna (fee: ¥3,000/$25 for everything); concierge; courtesy shuttle from Nagoya Station (on the hour 10am–5pm), courtesy shuttle from Sakae (on the half hour 10:30am–5:30pm); shopping arcade; salon; 24-hr. room service; in-room massage; babysitting; same-day laundry/dry cleaning service; nonsmoking rooms; executive-level rooms. *In room:* A/C, bilingual satellite TV with pay movies, minibar, hot-water pot with tea, hair dryer.

MODERATE

Fitness Hotel 330 Nagoya   Conveniently located near Nagoya Station, this business hotel has mostly single rooms (but with semi-double-size beds), with rates based on room size. All but the windows on Sakura Dori open, though the view is only of an office building a few feet away. Nonsmoking rooms are available—the only reason for its name that I could find, though I suppose you could take the stairs instead of the elevator.

3–25–6 Meieki, Nakamura-ku, Nagoya 450-0002. ℂ **052/562-0330.** Fax 052/562-0331. 100 units. ¥7,500–¥8,000 ($62.50–$67) single; ¥12,000–¥14,000 ($100–$117) twin; ¥11,000 ($92) double. AE, DC, JCB, MC, V. Station: Nagoya (3 min.); walk down the Unimall underground arcade to exit 8 or straight down Sakura Dori. **Amenities:** 1 restaurant (Japanese/Western), 1 coffee shop; business center; in-room massage; same-day laundry/dry cleaning service; nonsmoking rooms. *In room:* A/C, TV, fridge, hot-water pot with tea, hair dryer, washlet toilet.

Hotel Castle Plaza ✿   Under the same ownership as the Westin Nagoya Castle, this hotel has more facilities than you'd expect from its moderate price, including a dozen restaurants serving everything from shabu-shabu and noodles to Indian, Chinese, Italian, and French cuisine. It is also convenient to Nagoya Station. The cheapest twins are actually studio twins with a sofa bed—comfortable for one person, but cramped for two—and many face adjoining buildings. Better are the most expensive rooms on top floors facing east with good views of the city; some have been remodeled with such extras as dataports, safes, and washlet toilets.

4–3–25 Meieki, Nakamura-ku, Nagoya 450-0002. ℂ **052/582-2121.** Fax 052/582-8666. 262 units. ¥9,500–¥13,000 ($79–$108) single; ¥13,000–¥23,000 ($108–$192) twin; ¥15,000–¥18,000 ($125–$150) double. AE, JCB, MC, V. Station: Nagoya (5 min.). From the Central exit, walk straight down Sakura Dori; the hotel is on the right. **Amenities:** 12 restaurants, 1 bar; indoor 25-meter pool and health club with sauna (fee: ¥2,500/$21); travel agency; shopping arcade; salon; room service (9:30pm–midnight); in-room massage; same-day laundry/dry cleaning; nonsmoking rooms. *In room:* A/C, cable TV, minibar, hot-water pot with tea, hair dryer.

Royal Park Inn ✿✿ *Value*   Spotless and recently updated, this inn has a great location just minutes from Nagoya Station. Rooms are well appointed, offering better in-room amenities than most hotels in its price range, including TVs that provide Internet access, heavy curtains to block light, and a sitting area; note, however, that the cheapest double has only a semi-double-size bed. Best are the doubles on the 10th floor, with nicer amenities and some with city views.

3–27–5 Meieki, Nakamura-ku, Nagoya 450-0002. ℂ **052/581-4411.** Fax 052/581-4427. www.royalpark-nagoya.com. 314 units. ¥9,500–¥12,000 ($79–$100) single; ¥17,000–¥23,000 ($142–$192) twin; ¥15,000–¥21,000 ($125–$175) double. AE, DC, JCB, MC, V. Station: Nagoya (3 min.). From the Central exit, walk 1 block east on the 1st street north and parallel to Sakura Dori and then turn right. **Amenities:** 2 restaurants (Japanese, French), 1 bar, 1 lounge; in-room massage; same-day laundry/dry cleaning; nonsmoking rooms. *In room:* A/C, cable TV with pay movies, minibar, hot-water pot with tea, hair dryer, trouser press, washlet toilet.

Tokyo Dai-Ichi Hotel Nishiki ★★★ *Finds*   This smart-looking hotel is my top pick among Nagoya's moderately priced hotels. Located in the heart of Nagoya's nightlife and business district on Nishiki Dori, it opened in 1997 with prices comparable to a business hotel but with atmosphere and decor that's much classier. Targeting female travelers as well as businesspeople, it offers smartly decorated rooms with large desks and larger-than-usual bath towels; all but the cheapest singles, which are located next to elevator shafts, have dataports as well. The deluxe twins are separated into living and sleeping areas and even have two TVs. Although the hotel has a restaurant of its own, a handful of tenant restaurants in the same building are an added bonus.

3–18–21 Nishiki, Naka-ku, Nagoya 460-0003. ✆ 052/955-1001. Fax 052/953-6783. www.daiichi-hotel.co.jp/. 233 units. ¥8,000–¥10,000 ($67–$83) single; ¥13,000 ($108) double; ¥15,000–¥22,000 ($125–$183) twin. AE, DC, JCB, MC, V. Station: Sakae (4 min.). **Amenities:** 1 bar/restaurant (American); concierge; in-room massage; same-day laundry/dry cleaning service; nonsmoking rooms. *In room:* A/C, cable TV, minibar, hot-water pot with tea, hair dryer, safe, washlet toilet.

INEXPENSIVE

Meiryu Ryokan   A Japanese Inn Group member and family-owned for more than 40 years, this is a no-nonsense place. Most customers are Japanese businessmen, some of whom have lived here during the week for years, commuting home to families on weekends. Tatami rooms are spotless and cozy with more space and features than most others in this price category, including a closet and free coffee. The men's public bathroom has a sauna (they don't have many female guests at this ryokan, but there's a separate bathroom in case a lone female makes an appearance). The owners' son, who often clerks the front desk, speaks English well and is very helpful.

2–4–21 Kamimaezu, Naka-ku, Nagoya 463-0013. ✆ 052/331-8686. Fax 052/321-6119. www.japan-net.ne.jp/~meiryu. 23 units (none with bathroom). ¥5,000 ($42) single; ¥8,000 ($67) twin; ¥10,500 ($87.50) triple. Japanese breakfast ¥600 ($5) extra; Japanese dinner ¥2,200 ($18) extra. AE, V. Station: Kamimaezu (exit 3, 4 min.). **Amenities:** Coin-operated laundry. *In room:* A/C, bilingual TV, hot-water pot with tea and coffee.

Nagoya Plaza Inn *Value*   Although just a basic business hotel, with Japanese businessmen accounting for about 90% of its guests, it offers complimentary coffee and tea in its lobby throughout the day and breakfast rolls in the morning. The hallways could use some updating, but the rooms have been redone, the staff is friendly enough, and the location is convenient. The very small rooms come with a desk and panels to shut out light; the cheapest singles are rather dark and bare with glazed windows, just a bed, and wall hooks for clothes. If you want to make tea in your room, you'll have to ask for a hot-water pot.

3–8–21 Nishiki, Naka-ku, Nagoya 460-0003. ✆ 052/951-6311. Fax 052/951-6319. 176 units. ¥4,980–¥6,000 ($41.50–$50) single; ¥9,500 ($79) double; ¥9,700 ($81) twin. Rates include tax and service charge. 10% discount Sun. and holiday evenings. AE, DC, JCB, MC, V. Station: Sakae (3 min.). **Amenities:** Same-day laundry/dry cleaning service; coin-op washer and dryer. *In room:* A/C, TV with pay movies, minibar, trouser press.

Petit Ryokan Ichifuji ★★ *Kids*   Although this place is way out there in Ozone (pronounced *Ozon-ay* in Japanese), the young couple running this Japanese Inn Group ryokan has put so much heart and soul into the accommodations that it's well worth the subway ride out here. Ishida Tomiyasu, who speaks English, inherited the 40-year-old ryokan from his father and grandfather, and together with his wife, Yoko, has remodeled it to fit younger Japanese taste and has put in a cypress public bath. While the house's bright pink exterior and its

---

> ⌒*Tips* **A Note on Japanese Symbols**
>
> Many establishments and attractions in Japan do not have signs in Roman (English-language) letters. Those that don't are indicated in this guide with an oval with a number that corresponds to a number in appendix C showing the Japanese symbols. Thus, to find the Japanese symbol for, say, **Yamamoto-ya Honten** (below), refer to no. 102 in appendix C.

---

collection of bears and rabbits may be too cutesy for some, the youthful staff and the owners' two young children make this a welcoming, family-oriented retreat. Best of all, children under 7 years of age stay for free, while those under 18 are half price. All except one of the rooms is tatami, and a vending machine sells prepaid international telephone cards. Both Japanese and Western breakfasts and dinners are available. You'll feel right at home.

1–7 Saikobashi-dori, Kita-ku, Nagoya 462-0818. ☎ **052/914-2867.** Fax 052/981-6836. www.jin.ne.jp/ichi fuji. 13 units (none with bathroom). ¥4,800($40) single; ¥8,400–¥9,400 ($70–$78) double; ¥10,800–¥12,300 ($90–$102.50) triple. Breakfast ¥500 ($4.15) extra; dinner ¥1,500 ($12.50) extra. AE, MC, V. Station: Heiandori (exit 2, 3 min.); Ozone (8 min.). **Amenities:** Coin-o washer and dryer. *In room:* A/C, TV, hot-water pot with tea.

WHERE TO DINE

One of Nagoya's specialties is **kishimen,** fettuccine-like broad and flat white noodles usually served in a soup stock with soy sauce, tofu, dried bonito shavings, and chopped green onions. Nagoya is also famous for **miso nikomi udon**—udon noodles served in a bean-paste soup and flavored with such ingredients as chicken and green onions. **Cochin** (free-range) chicken and breaded pork cutlets (**tonkatsu**) are also Nagoya favorites.

AROUND NAGOYA STATION

Kappa ⭐ *Finds* SUSHI/VARIED JAPANESE   Clean and friendly, Kappa is really two restaurants, one serving varied Japanese cuisine and the other sushi. Since the sushi is delivered via a conveyor belt, choosing is no more difficult than reaching out for a passing plate, which is color-coded according to price. Adjacent to the sushi bar is a robatayaki offering grilled food and other meals. Seating here is at tables and chairs or on the floor at low tables with leg wells, some with nice city views. To find Kappa in the "city" that Nagoya Station has become, take the elevators next to the Takashimaya cloak room.

12th floor, Towers Plaza, Nagoya Station, 1–1–4 Meieki, Nakamura-ku. ☎ 052/541-7888. 2 pieces sushi ¥120–¥480 ($1–$4); set meals ¥1,280–¥1,800 ($11–$15). AE, DC, MC, V. Daily 11am–10:30pm (last order).

⑩⑫ **Yamamoto-ya Honten** UDON NOODLES   This chain noodle shop, a 2-minute walk from Nagoya Station, specializes in miso nikomi udon. Its noodles, all handmade, are thick, hard, and chewy and are served in a type of bean paste that's special to Nagoya. If you like your noodles spicy, add a mixture of spices to your food from the large bamboo container on your table. An English menu with explanations makes ordering easy.

25–9 Meieki, basement of the Horinouchi Bldg., Sakura Dori, Nakamura-ku. ☎052/565-0278. Udon dishes ¥1,200–¥1,950 ($10–$16). AE, DC, MC, V. Daily 11am–10pm. Station: Nagoya (exit 6, 2 min.); on Sakura Dori's north side.

IN SAKAE

In addition to the choices below, there's another branch of **Yamamoto-ya Honten** on the southwest corner of Hommachi Dori and Mitsukura Dori, not far from the Nagoya City Art Museum (© **052/201-4082;** open daily 11am–2am). And if you are collecting T-shirts or are hungry for a hamburger, there's a **Hard Rock Cafe** in the ZXY Building, third floor, 1–4–5 Sakae, Naka-ku (© **052/ 218-3220;** open daily from 11:30am–11pm; to 3am on Fri and Sat), with an entrance across from the Hilton Hotel.

Downunder 🍴 AUSTRALIAN   You'll feel right at home in this bar/restaurant where the friendly, mostly Australian and New Zealander staff chat with customers. The decor is very casual, and though customers are mainly Japanese, some foreigners make it their home away from home—at least while they're doing business in Nagoya. The unusual menu includes the Oz burger ("biggest in town!!!"), the traditional Downunder meat pie, and fresh salads. And, of course, there's Aussie beer.

Sakae Sky Building, 1–7–26 Sakae, Naka-ku. © 052/201-4300. Main dishes ¥1,000–¥1,500 ($8.35–$12.50). AE, MC, V. Sun and Tues–Thurs 5:30pm–midnight; Fri–Sat 5:30pm–1am. Station: Fushimi (5 min.). On a side street beside the Nagoya Hilton hotel.

Hourai-ken Matsuzakaya-ken EEL   This eel restaurant is a branch of two famous restaurants near Atsuta Shrine. There's no English menu, but you can't go wrong ordering one of the various unagi donburi (rice casserole with eel on top). Most famous is the Hitsumabushi, a set meal for ¥2,300 ($19) that includes unagi donburi, various condiments, miso soup, and Japanese pickles. Eating it involves a ritual: First, dish out some of the eel casserole into the smaller wooden bowl and eat it plain. For the next course, try it with some of the seaweed and green onions that come with it. Finally, add some of the soup and wasabi to the last mixture you tried.

The other, more elegant branches are both south of Atsuta Shrine at 2–10–26 Jingu, Atsuta-ku (© **052/682-5598;** open daily 11:30am–2:30pm and 4:30–8:30pm), and 503 Gondo-cho, Atsuta-ku (© **052/671-8686;** open Tues–Sun 11:30am–2pm and 4:30–8:30pm).

In Matsuzakaya department store, 10th floor, 3–16–1 Sakae, Naka-ku. © 052/264-3825. Unagi teishoku (set meal) ¥1,500–¥2,300 ($12.50–$19). AE, JCB, V. Daily 11am–9pm. Closed some Wed. Station: Yabacho (1 min.).

(103) **Kishimentei** *Value* KISHIMEN NOODLES   This small hole-in-the-wall has been offering Nagoya's specialty for more than 70 years—kishimen noodles. Its set lunch, served until 2pm, is a bargain at ¥620 ($5.15). Otherwise, meals include noodles with pork, tempura shrimp, or vegetables. There are even packages of noodles in case you want to take some home with you. There's no menu in English, but a plastic-food display is in the window.

Towa Bldg., 3–20–4 Nishiki, Naka-ku. © 052/951-3481. Noodles ¥500–¥1,400 ($4.15–$12); teishoku ¥700–¥1,400 ($5.85–$12). No credit cards. Mon–Sat 11am–8:30pm (last order). Station: Sakae or Fushimi (5 min.). Just north of the Money Museum of the Tokai Bank.

(104) **Torigin Honten** 🍴 CHOCHIN CHICKEN   In the heart of Nagoya, this 30-year-old casual restaurant with counter, tatami, or table seating is known for its *Nagoya cochin* (free-range chicken). It also serves yakitori, with a set menu of eight different skewers costing ¥1,680 ($14), as well as *miso-nabe* (rice cake, tofu, chicken, and vegetable stew) and kamameshi set meals (rice casseroles). An amiable staff makes it user-friendly; a black-and-white kura-style facade makes it easy to identify.

3–14–22 Nishiki, Naka-ku. © 052/973-3000. Set meals ¥950–¥4,900 ($7.90–$41). AE, DC, JCB, MC, V. Daily 5–11pm. Closed irregularly. Station: Sakae (4 min.).

Trattoria Italiano Sabatini ★★★ ITALIAN   Boasting an airy atrium with large mural "windows" opening onto an Italian town, this branch of the famous Tokyo restaurants run by three brothers from Rome is a welcome addition to the Nagoya dining scene. With staff and chef trained in the Tokyo store, it serves the same excellent, very Italian cuisine with many ingredients imported from Italy. Lunches change daily and dinners weekly, with a wide variety of antipasta and pasta always available. *Pollo alla cacciatorae* (chicken in a tomato and olive sauce) and *filetto al carpaccio* (thin slices of beef) are on the a la carte menu. My lunch menu consisted of antipasta; linguini with spicy tomato and mushroom sauce; grilled garlic, potatoes, spinach, and broccoli; two kinds of homemade gelato; pie; and coffee, after which I was ready to climb through that "window" in search of my siesta.

3–14–22 Nishiki, Naka-ku. ✆ **052/973-4560.** Main dishes ¥1,800–¥4,000 ($15–$33); pasta ¥1,400–¥2,400 ($12–$20); set lunches ¥1,600–¥3,500 ($13–$29); set dinners ¥6,000 and ¥8,000 ($50 and $67). AE, DC, JCB, MC, V. Daily 11:30am–2pm and 5:30–10pm (last order). Station: Sakae (4 min.).

(105) **Yabaton** ★★★ *Finds* TONKATSU   You'll recognize this everyman's eatery in Nagoya's old downtown district immediately by its curtains displaying comical pigs dressed like sumo wrestlers. The only thing served is tonkatsu (pork cutlet), and Yabaton is famous for it. You'll be asked whether you want yours with *sa-u-zu* (sauce) or miso katsudon; the former is thicker and sweeter, but the latter is the specialty here (if you can't decide, ask for a little of both). *Donburi,* a breaded and fried pork cutlet on rice, is the cheapest, but recommended is *hire,* a tender cut with less fat. Main dishes all come with cabbage; rice is ¥200 ($1.65) extra, while miso soup is ¥100 (85¢) extra.

3–6–23 Osu. ✆ **052/241-2409.** Main dishes ¥700–¥2,100 ($5.85–$17.50). AE, DC, MC, V. Tues–Sun 11am–9pm. Station: Yabacho (3 min.). From Wakamiya-Otsu Dori intersection, walk 1 short block south on Otsu Dori and turn right.

NEAR NAGOYA CASTLE

Contemporary Dining Crown ★★★ TEPPANYAKI/FRENCH-JAPANESE CROSSOVER CUISINE   This may well be Nagoya's best choice for celebrating a special occasion. A sophisticated dining venue with great views of the castle and live music in the evening, it offers a fusion of French and Japanese cuisine, with dishes that might include minced ostrich spiced with pepper. There's also a teppanyaki corner with views over the city, and a bar where you might wish to retire with a drink.

Westin Nagoya Castle 3–19 Hinokuchi-cho, Nishi-ku. ✆ **052/521-2121.** Reservations recommended for window seating. Set lunches ¥3,300–¥3,500 ($27.50–$29); set dinners ¥4,500–¥10,000 ($37.50–$83). AE, DC, MC, V. Daily 11am–2:30pm and 5pm–midnight. Subway: Sengencho (10 min.) or courtesy shuttle bus from Nagoya Station (see "Where to Stay," earlier in this chapter).

2 Ise-Shima National Park ★★

465km (289 miles) W of Tokyo; 100km (62 miles) S of Nagoya

Blessed with subtropical vegetation, small islands dotting its shoreline, and the most revered Shinto shrine in Japan, **Ise-Shima National Park** merits a 1- or 2-night stopover if you're anywhere near Nagoya. Located on and around Shima Peninsula and covering 200 square miles, this national park has bays and inlets that are the home of the Mikimoto pearl and thousands of pearl-cultivating rafts. Although you could conceivably cover the major attractions on a day's outing from Nagoya, I've recommended accommodations in case you'd like to take in the sights at a more leisurely pace.

Ise-Shima's major attractions are concentrated in the small towns of Ise, Futami-no-ura, Toba, and Kashikojima, all in Mie Prefecture. **Ise** (also called Ise-shi, which translates as Ise City) is where you'll find the Ise Grand Shrines. **Futami-no-ura** (also called simply Futami) is famous for a theme park based on Japan's history from 1477 to 1598. **Toba** contains Mikimoto Pearl Island, which offers a pearl museum and demonstrations by its famous women divers, as well as the impressive Toba Aquarium. Near **Kashikojima,** you can visit an amusement park with a Spanish theme or take boat trips around Ago Bay, which, with its islets and pearl-cultivating oyster rafts, is one of the most scenic spots in the park.

ESSENTIALS

GETTING THERE   By Train   The easiest way to get to Ise-Shima is from Nagoya on the private **Kintetsu Nagoya Line** (Kinki Nippon Railway), which departs about every 30 minutes or so from Kintetsu Station, next to the JR Nagoya Station. It takes about 1 hour and 20 minutes via limited express to reach Ise (with stops at both Ise-shi and Ujiyamada stations), about 1 hour and 40 minutes to reach Toba, and 2 hours to reach Kashikojima. Note that Kintetsu trains do not go to Futami-no-ura. A ticket from Nagoya to the end of the line in Kashikojima costs ¥3,480 ($29) one-way. There are also Kintetsu lines to the Shima Peninsula both from Kyoto (2 hr. and 15 min. to Toba) and from Osaka's Kintetsu Station in Uehonmachi (2 hr. to Toba).

If you're traveling on a **Japan Rail Pass,** you can also reach Ise-Shima by **JR Kaisoku (Rapid) Mie** trains, which depart hourly from Nagoya Station, but you'll be charged an extra ¥460 ($3.85). JR trains stop at Ise-shi and Futami-no-ura before terminating at Toba, where if you're heading to Kashikojima, you can change to the Kintetsu Line.

By Bus   There are buses that depart nightly from Tokyo's Ikebukuro Station's east exit at 10:20 and 11:20pm, arriving at Ise-shi Station at 6:20 and 7:20am respectively. The fare is ¥7,850 ($65) one-way.

VISITOR INFORMATION   Be sure to drop by the Tourist Information Centers in Tokyo, Kyoto, or international airports at Narita or Osaka to pick up the free leaflet "Ise-Shima," which lists train schedules from Osaka, Kyoto, and Nagoya and gives information on the park's main attractions. Otherwise, drop by the **Ise-shi City Tourist Information Center** located at Kintetsu Ujiyamada Station in Ise City (✆ **0596/23-9655;** open daily 9am–5:30pm) for sightseeing information.

GETTING AROUND   Transportation within Ise-Shima National Park is either by train or by bus. **Trains** are convenient if your destinations are Ise City, Toba, Futami-no-ura, and Kashikojima (see "Getting There," above). To travel to major sites, however, including the Outer and Inner Shrines, Ise Sengoku Era Village, and Mikimoto Pearl Island, your best bet is aboard the **CAN-Bus,** which you can board in front of the JR stations in Ise City and Toba. A one-day pass costs ¥1,000 ($8.35) for a one day pass and can be bought at any bus stop. There are also local buses that run between the Outer and Inner Shrine of the Ise Grand Shrines; you must also take a bus to reach Parque Espana.

EXPLORING ISE-SHIMA NATIONAL PARK

The easiest way to see the park's sights is to start in Ise City, the northern gateway to Ise-Shima National Park, and work your way down the peninsula to Kashikojima.

ISE CITY (ISE-SHI)

THE ISE GRAND SHRINES ★★   Considered the most venerable Shinto shrines in the nation, the Ise Grand Shrines (Ise Jingu) consist of the Outer Shrine and the Inner Shrine, plus more than 100 minor shrines and a forest of Japanese cypress. Since the Outer and Inner shrines are about 4 miles apart, your best bet is to first visit the Outer Shrine, which is a 5-minute walk from Ise-shi Station, and then take a bus to the Inner Shrine. In addition to the CAN-Bus (described above in "Getting Around"), local buses run between the two shrines every 10 to 15 minutes and cost ¥410 ($3.40) one way. Because of the distance between the shrines and their large grounds, plan on spending at least 2 hours exploring Ise.

The **Outer Shrine** (Geku) was founded in 477 and is dedicated to the Shinto goddess of harvest, agriculture, clothing, and housing. The **Inner Shrine** (Naiku) was founded a few centuries earlier and is dedicated to Amaterasu, the sun goddess. Both are among the few Shinto shrines in Japan without any Chinese Buddhist influences. Constructed of plain cypress wood with thick thatched roofs, they're starkly simple and have no ornamentation except for gold and copper facing on their beams and doors. In fact, if you've come all the way to Shima Peninsula just to see the shrines, you may be disappointed—there's nothing much to see. The shrines are so sacred that no one is allowed up close to them except members of the imperial family and high Shinto priests. Both shrines are surrounded by four wooden fences, and we lesser mortals are allowed only as far as the third gate.

The fences don't allow you to see much, but that doesn't stop the estimated six million Japanese who come here annually. They come because of what the shrines represent, which is an embodiment of the Japanese Shinto religion itself. The Inner Shrine is by far the more important because it's dedicated to the sun goddess, considered to be the legendary ancestress of the imperial family. It contains the Sacred Mirror (Yata-no-Kagami), one of the Three Sacred Treasures of the emperor.

According to legend, the sun goddess sent her grandson to Japan so that he and his descendants could rule over the country. Before he left, she gave him three insignia—a mirror, a sword, and a set of jewels. As she handed him the mirror, she is said to have remarked, "When you look upon this mirror, let it be as if you look upon me." The mirror, therefore, is said to embody the sun goddess herself and is regarded as the most sacred object in the Shinto religion. It's kept in the deep recesses of the Inner Shrine in a special casket and is never shown to the public. (The sword is in the Atsuta Shrine in Nagoya, and the jewels are in the Imperial Palace in Tokyo.)

Perhaps the most amazing thing about the Outer and Inner shrines is that, even though they were founded centuries ago, the buildings themselves have never been more than 20 years old—every 20 years they're completely torn down and rebuilt exactly as they were on neighboring sites. The present buildings were built in 1993 for the 61st time. No photographs of the shrines themselves are allowed.

Even though you can't see much of the shrines themselves, they're still the most important stops in Ise-Shima. The Inner Shrine is approached by crossing the elegant Uji Bridge and is surrounded by 800-year-old cypress trees. Watch how the Japanese stop after crossing the second small bridge on the approach to the shrine to wash and purify their hands and mouths with water from the Isuzu River. Its source lies on the Inner Shrine, and it's considered sacred. You'll also see a couple of white royal horses, kept near the shrine for the use of the sun goddess.

ISE'S HISTORIC DISTRICT ★★★   After visiting the Inner Shrine, turn right after recrossing Uji Bridge for the nearby historic district of **Oharai-machi,** whose main street is lined with beautiful wooden buildings including kura (storehouses), some dating from the Edo Period and others newly constructed but faithful to traditional architecture. It once served as the main pilgrimage road leading to the Grand Shrines of Ise. During the Edo Period, when travel was strictly controlled, joining a mass pilgrimage to Ise was for many Japanese a once-in-a-lifetime opportunity to venture beyond their homes; they took full advantage of it here. Today it's an interesting area for a stroll, shopping, or a meal.

About halfway down is **Okage-yokocho,** a re-created Meiji-Era village with teahouses, restaurants, and shops selling Japanese candies, traditional toys, folk crafts, and candles. If you have time, stop by the **Okageza** (☏ **0596/23-8838;** open daily 9:30am–5pm), a museum housed in an authentic Edo-Era building that captures the spirit of Oharai-machi during the Edo Period; its models and scenes convey what life was like for both the residents and the pilgrims passing through. Admission is ¥600 ($5) for adults and ¥300 ($2.50) for children; English earphones are included in the price.

Across from Okage-yokocho is ⑩⑥ **Akafuku** (☏ **0596/22-2154;** open daily 5am–5pm), the original makers (opened in 1707) of the sticky rice cakes for which Ise-Shima is famous. You'll recognize the shop by the *kamado* (huge, red, ginger jar–shaped ceramic cooking stoves) used to heat water for tea in the open entranceway. It has been a tradition to serve complimentary tea to shrinegoers for centuries, and this shop, built in 1887, still does. You pay only for the cakes—¥230 ($1.90) for three cakes with tea. First pay for your cakes at the old cash register on the dark-wood counter; the staff, in traditional dark-blue outfits, will then serve you on tatami mats around braziers or on benches in the back overlooking the river. You can watch cakes being made, and from May through August, you can also watch swallows fly in and out to their nests in the eaves.

FUTAMI-NO-URA

If you're at all sentimental, make a trip to Futami-no-ura (also called simply Futami), which you can reach by JR train in 10 minutes from either Ise-shi or Toba or by bus in 25 minutes from the Inner Shrine in Ise. There you'll find a pair of large rocks that jut out of the sea not far from shore. Known as the **Wedded Rocks,** they represent man and wife and are joined by a thick braided rope, the same kind you see extended from torii gates at Shinto shrines. The best time to visit is at dawn in summer: In this Land of the Rising Sun, the spectacle of the sun rising between these two rocks is a favorite among Japanese, especially during the solstice when the rising sun goes one better by also revealing the silhouette of Mt. Fuji. But you have to be an early bird to catch it—the sun rises as early as 4:30am in summer.

Ise Sengoku Era Village (Sengoku Jidaimura) ★★★ *Kids*   The castle you see on the hill from Futami-no-ura Station (which, by the way, is a mirrored building shaped like the Wedded Rocks) is not the former residence of a famous shogun but a replica of Azuchi Castle in Sengoku Jidaimura, one of Japan's many theme parks. If you have youngsters in tow or if you haven't seen one of these period theme parks elsewhere in Japan, go to one—they're fun! This one is among my favorites because, rather than trying to re-create a village in Holland or Spain, it's centered on a specific time in Japan's history, the Age of Warring States—the Sengoku Era (1477–1573), when local warlords struggled for supremacy, and the Azuchi-Momoyama Era (1573–98), when Oda Nobunaga gained control of the land and finally put an end to civil war. In keeping with the theme of this Japanese equivalent of Dodge City, all the staff are dressed in 16th-century costumes, and attractions reflect the pre-Edo Era. You can watch period dramas and theater ranging from a courtesan performance that includes singing, dancing, and the tea ceremony to the action-charged antics of a ninja troupe. A 3D movie captures the destruction of Toyotomi Hideyoshi's Osaka Castle by Tokugawa forces, while in the Ninja Labyrinth you can try to negotiate 11 challenging obstacles. There are also old-fashioned game centers, including shooting ranges using bows and arrows and other weaponry of the era. That gold-roofed castle is dedicated to Nobunaga—who built Azuchi Castle—and is filled with high-tech giant screens, dioramas, and lasers that depict famous attacks he staged to gain control; plenty of visual and audio effects will make you feel you're in the midst of war. The top-floor Gold Room, lined with real gold, has a great view of Ise-Shima. You'll probably spend about 3 hours here.

ⓒ **0596/43-2300.** Admission ¥4,900 ($41) adults, ¥2,500 ($21) children 4–12. Daily 9am–5pm; 9:30am–4pm Dec–Mar. A 15-min. walk from Futami-no-ura Station or a couple minutes' walk from the CAN-Bus Ise Sengoku Jidaimura bus stop.

TOBA

Mikimoto Pearl Island ★★ Toba's best-known attraction is touristy but is still quite enjoyable, especially if you have a weakness for pearls or have ever wondered how they're cultivated.

To learn about the man who toiled through years of adversity to produce the world's first cultured pearl, visit **Kokichi Mikimoto Memorial Hall,** built in 1993 to commemorate the 100th anniversary of Mikimoto's success. Born in Toba in 1858 as the eldest son of a noodle-shop owner, Kokichi Mikimoto went to Yokohama as a young man and was surprised to see stalls selling pearls with great success. He reasoned that if oysters produced pearls as the result of an irritant inside the shell, why couldn't man introduce the irritant himself and induce oysters to make pearls? It turned out to be harder than it sounded. It wasn't until 5 years after he started his research that Mikimoto finally succeeded in cultivating his first pearl, here on what is today called Mikimoto Pearl Island. In 1905, Mikimoto cultivated his first perfectly round pearl, after which he built what is probably the most successful pearl empire in the world.

Mikimoto, who died at the age of 93, was a remarkable man and a real character. In addition to chronicling his life, the Memorial Hall contains some of his earliest jewelry and models made with pearls, many of which were only recently re-acquired by Mikimoto & Co. Ltd. through auctions. My favorite is the brooch made for the 1937 Paris International Exhibition, which can be worn several different ways by employing various clasps. The Pearl Pagoda has 12,760 Mikimoto pearls and took 750 artisans 6 months to complete, after which it was exhibited at the Philadelphia World Exhibition in 1926. The Liberty Bell, a third the size of the original, has 12,250 pearls and was displayed at the New York World's Fair in 1939.

The **Pearl Museum** tells all you'd probably ever want to know about the creation of pearls, with live demonstrations that show the insertion of the round nucleus into the shell, a video of the harvesting of the pearls 2 years later, and more live demonstrations that explain the process of making a pearl necklace by hand, from the selection and sorting of pearls to the drilling and stringing. You can learn about the criteria used for pricing pearls (luster is the most important) and can see an exhibit that examines the relationship between people and pearls since ancient times. There are also more Mikimoto pearl creations like the Pearl Pavilion, which contains the world's largest pearl (1.6 inches in diameter) and resembles Nara's Hall of Dreams.

In addition, **women divers** (*Ama*) in traditional white outfits demonstrate how women of the Shima Peninsula have dived through the ages in search of abalone, seaweed, and other edibles. They were also essential to the pearl industry, diving to collect the oysters and then returning them to the seabed following insertion of the nucleus. At one time, there were thousands of Ama, known for their skill in going to great depths for extended periods of time. It is said that there are still more than 1,000 of these women divers left, but I've seen them only at demonstrations given for tourists. If you happen to see Ama working in earnest, consider yourself lucky. Here you can watch them from the air-conditioned comfort of a viewing room built especially for overseas guests.

There's also, of course, a shop selling Mikimoto pearl jewelry and a restaurant. You can easily spend 1½ hours on Pearl Island.

© **0599/25-2028.** Admission ¥1,500 ($12.50) adults, ¥750 ($6.25) children 7–15. Mid-Mar to May, mid-July to Aug, and Oct to mid-Nov, daily 8:30am–5:30pm; Jan to mid-Mar, June to mid-July, Sept, and mid-Nov, daily 8:30am–5pm; Dec, daily 9am–4:30pm. Just a few minutes' walk from Toba Station, connected to the mainland via a short pedestrian bridge.

Toba Aquarium ★★ *Kids*   Next to Pearl Island is one of Japan's largest and most sophisticated aquariums, containing more than 850 species of aquatic plants and animals. Various zones and themes make it easy to navigate. The display of marine animals around Ise-Shima and Japan includes giant spider crabs and the finless porpoise, the world's smallest whale. The exhibit of "living fossils"—creatures that have remained relatively unchanged since ancient times—includes sharks, horseshoe crabs, and the Nautilus (which are bred here), while the marine mammal kingdom includes Commerson's dolphins, seals, and sea lions, with sea-lion shows several times a day. The aquarium also boasts exotic and rare creatures such as dugongs, African manatees, and Amazonian turtles and frogs. Plan on spending at least an hour here, longer if you have kids.

© **0599/25-2555.** Admission ¥2,400 ($20) adults, ¥1,200 ($10) for children. Dec–mid-Mar, daily 9am–5pm; mid-Mar to mid-July and Sept through Nov, daily 8:30am–5pm; mid-July–Aug, daily 8am–6pm (to 9pm several weeks in Aug). A few minutes' walk from Toba Station.

KASHIKOJIMA

At the southern end of the Shima Peninsula, the last stop on the Kintetsu Line is Kashikojima.

One of the main attractions of Kashikojima for the Japanese is the **boat cruises of Ago Bay.** Vessels, built to resemble Spanish galleons or with other Spanish-based themes, depart from the town's boat dock, about a 2-minute walk from the train station. The cost of the cruise is ¥1,500 ($12.50) for adults, half-price for children. You'll pass pearl-cultivating rafts, fishing boats, and many small islands along the way. The trip lasts almost an hour, with boats departing every half hour or so between 9:30am and 4:30pm from March 21 through October, less frequently in winter. For more information or inquiries about the winter schedule, call the **Shima Marine Leisure Co.** (© **0599/43-1023**).

Parque España ★★ *Kids* You may wonder what this Spanish village, called Shima Spain Mura by the locals, is doing in southern Ise Shima—Mie Prefecture has a sister relationship with Valencia in Spain, a relationship that is exploited to the hilt in this ambitious theme park. A huge facility that employs about 80 Spanish-speaking natives, it's essentially a Spanish-themed amusement park that includes a shopping area specializing in products from Spain; a plaza that stages dances, festivals, and other outdoor entertainment; a coliseum that features folk dancing and singing; and amusement rides that range from an adventure lagoon ride through a world of fantasy to the fastest roller coaster I ever care to ride (and one of the longest, lasting more than 3 hair-raising minutes).

Most educational is the Museo Castillo de Xavier, a reproduction of the castle where Francis Xavier was born (Xavier later brought Christianity to Japan), which presents a brief overlook of highlights in Spanish history, though only in Japanese. Still, there's no mistaking the replica of prehistoric drawings from the Altamira caves, the model of the Santa Maria that Columbus sailed to America, and replicas of the Prado's most famous works. There are amusements geared to all ages as well as numerous restaurants. Plan on spending about 2 hours here.

ⓒ **0599/57-3333.** Passport to all attractions ¥4,800 ($40) adults, ¥3,800 ($32) children 12–17, ¥3,200 ($27) children 4–11; extra charge for gaming houses and flamenco show. Admission only, which includes the museum and most shows but no rides (which you can purchase separately for ¥200–¥600/$1.65–$5 per ride), ¥3,200 ($27) adults, ¥2,200 ($18) children 12–17, and ¥1,600 ($13) children 4–11. Daily 9am–9pm in Aug; daily 9:30am–5:30pm the rest of summer, spring, and autumn; 9:30am–5pm in winter. Take the special shuttle bus from Kashikojima Station; it departs every half hour on weekends and in July and Aug (hourly at other times of the year). Shuttles also run from Isobe Station on the Kintetsu Line every 10 min. at peak hours, 3 times per hour other times. Tickets ¥360 ($3); ride takes about 15 min. from either station.

WHERE TO STAY

Kashikojima is the best place to go if you want to escape the crowds and relax in a rural setting, while Toba and Ise have the greatest number of attractions.

ISE

⑩⑦ **Hoshidekan** ★★ *Finds* Catering to the health conscious, this inexpensive 80-year-old wooden Japanese Inn Group ryokan has several tatami rooms with windows framed with gnarled roots and bamboo (they simply don't make windows like this anymore) circling an inner courtyard. It's managed by a group of women who are strong advocates of macrobiotic vegetarian cooking, which they serve in a simple tatami room (both Japanese and Western meals are available). If you want the ¥1,000 ($9) vegetarian course for dinner (Genmai teishoku), be sure to reserve it by 3pm.

2–15–2 Kawasaki, Ise-shi, Mie 516-0009. ⓒ **0596/28-2377.** Fax 0596/27-2830. www.amigo.ne.jp/ ~hoshide/kan/. 12 units (none with bathroom). ¥4,800 ($40) single; ¥8,500 ($71) double; ¥12,000 ($100) triple. Rates include tax and service. Breakfast from ¥700 ($5.85) extra; dinner ¥1,000 ($8.35) extra. AE, MC, V. Station: Ise-Shi, then a 7-min. walk in the opposite direction from the shrine. **Amenities:** 1 macrobiotic restaurant (reservations required); in-room massage; coin-op washer and dryer; nonsmoking rooms. *In room:* A/C, TV, hot-water pot with organic tea, no phone.

TOBA

⑩⑧ **Awami** This small ryokan is in a three-story modern white building. All the rooms are Japanese-style—simple but fresh and clean—and have sinks and small sitting areas with windows, some with a view of the bay just across the road. Rooms with or without bathroom are the same price; foreigners are usually given a room with bathroom, which are smaller than miniscule.

300–7 Ohama-cho, Toba-shi 517-0015. © **0599/25-2423.** Fax 0599/25-2701. awami@e-net.or.jp. 10 units (5 with bathroom). ¥8,000 ($67) per person off-season, ¥10,000 ($83) per person in summer, including 2 meals and service charge. Room without meals, ¥6,000 ($50) per person off-season, ¥7,000 ($58) per person summer. No credit cards. Station: Toba (8 min.). Turn left out of the Kintetsu side of the station; it will be just off this road to the left. *In room:* A/C, TV, hot-water pot with tea.

Thalassa Shima ★★★ *Value* Although the approach to this luxury hotel doesn't seem to promise much, inside it's another story. Everything about this sophisticated seaside luxury hotel is focused on the stunningly beautiful setting on the sea, with nary another building in sight. It has a soothing, subdued atmosphere, fitting for a resort dedicated to healing. Thalassa Shima is a French-Japanese joint venture into thalasso therapy, consisting of seawater, seaweed, and sea-mud treatments. Thalasso therapy is popular in France, but this modern, striking, and elegant hotel is the first such resort in Japan. My co-author was skeptical that a 1-night stay involving a seaweed bath, an underwater-jet treatment, a massage bath, and pressure therapy could make much difference, but she has to admit she left the hotel much more relaxed and feeling beautiful! Rooms—all of which have small balconies facing the sea—are large, well appointed, and full of amenities. Upon check in, reserve a dinner table at either the **Lumiere** with its nouvelle French cuisine or the classic Japanese restaurant, both with views of the sea.

Shirahama, Uramura-cho, Toba-shi, Mie 517-0025. © **0599/32-1111.** Fax 0599/32-1109. 122 units. From ¥20,000 ($167) per person double occupancy, including breakfast and dinner, more on Sat and holidays. Thalasso therapy treatment ¥10,000–¥13,500 ($83–$112). 2-night Resort Plan packages from ¥58,000 ($485) per person, including 4 meals and thalasso therapy. AE, DC, JCB, MC, V. Free 25-min. shuttle bus every hour from JR or Kintetsu Toba Station. **Amenities:** 2 restaurants (French, Japanese), 1 bar; thalasso therapy center with pool overlooking the bay, exercise room, doctor, full French thalasso therapy equipment, massage aromatotherapy room, sauna and Jacuzzi; lounge/library; Shu Uemura aesthetic salon; sundries shop; limited room service; in-room massage; babysitting; dry cleaning/laundry service; nonsmoking rooms. *In room:* A/C, TV with free video movies, minibar, hot-water pot with herb tea and cookies, hair dryer, safe, bathroom scale.

KASHIKOJIMA

(109) **Ishiyama-So** ★ *Finds* If you're looking for an inexpensive, unusual place to stay, a good choice is this family-run Japanese Inn Group member located on a small island just a stone's throw from the Kashikojima pier. It can be reached only via the hotel's own private boat—call to let them know you've arrived at Kashikojima; the boat will arrive shortly, and you'll be delivered right to the ryokan's front door. Although the building itself is concrete, its location right on the water gives it a slightly exotic atmosphere, right up to the small crabs that scurry in through the front door. You can swim right off the dock here (because of boat traffic, though, you shouldn't go farther out than the dock), and footpaths crisscross the small island. All rooms are Japanese style and face the bay; meals are also Japanese. The owner speaks English.

Yokoyama-jima, Kashikojima, Ago-cho, Mie 517-0502. © 05995/2-1527. Fax 05995/2-1240. 6 units (3 with bathroom, 3 with toilet only). ¥5,500 ($46) single with toilet only, ¥6,000 ($50) single with bathroom; ¥10,000 ($83) double with toilet only, ¥11,000 ($92) double with bathroom. Breakfast ¥500 ($4.15) extra. Dinner ¥1,500 ($12.50) extra. AE, MC, V. A 2-min. walk from the station to Kashikojima pier, then a 2-min. boat trip. *In room:* A/C, coin-op TV, hot-water pot with tea, safe, no phone.

Shima Kanko Hotel ★★★ Sitting on a hill above Ago Bay, this is a resort hotel in the old tradition, established in 1951 and boasting impeccable service and great views. It was the hotel of choice of the Showa Emperor; he stayed here five times. Most rooms have views of the bay and are spacious, and despite periodic updating, they retain an old-fashioned atmosphere with their shoji screens and wooden furniture. The highest-priced twins facing the bay in the main building are the best; they offer splendid views, large bathrooms with two sinks, and a separate washlet toilet. The hotel boasts its own garden, and there's a pathway leading down to a private dock where you can sit and watch the pearl cultivators at work on their rafts. On the roof is an observatory, great for watching the beautiful sunsets; the coffee shop's outdoor terrace is another wonderful place to soak in the view.

Ago-cho, Kashikojima, Mie 517-0593. © **0599/43-1211.** Fax 0599/43-3538. skh-ms@mint.or.jp. 200 units. ¥13,500–¥20,500 ($112.50–$171) single; ¥15,000–¥30,000 ($125–$250) twin; ¥18,000–¥22,000 ($150–$183) double; ¥15,000–¥25,000 ($125–$208) Japanese-style rooms for 2. Peak season (Golden Week, end of July–Aug, New Year's) ¥5,000 ($42) extra; Sat and evenings before holidays ¥3,000 ($25) extra. AE, DC, JCB, MC, V. Station: Kashikojima (then free shuttle to hotel). **Amenities:** 4 restaurants, 1 bar, 1 lounge; outdoor pool with children's slides (free to hotel guests); free use of a nearby sister ryokan with beautiful public baths (ask at front desk); games arcade; concierge; souvenir shop; room service (2–9:30pm); in-room massage; next-day laundry/dry cleaning service. *In room:* A/C, bilingual TV, minibar, hot-water pot with tea, hair dryer.

WHERE TO DINE

In addition to the choices below, resorts and hotels throughout the Shima Peninsula offer wonderful seafood dining.

ISE

(110) **Okadaiya** NOODLES   This purveyor of Ise-Shima's specialty, Ise udon (a soft, thick, wheat noodle served in a black soy soup with green onions), has been in business since 1953. There's no English menu, but the udon teishoku, which comes with Ise udon, pickles, rice, and vegetables, is a good bet for ¥700 ($5.85).

31 Uji-Imazaike-cho, Ise-shi. © **0596/22-4554.** Noodles ¥400–¥850 ($3.35–$7.10). No credit cards. Fri–Wed 10:30am–5pm. Station: Ise-Shi (5 min.). A 5-min. walk from the Inner Shrine on the main street of the Oharai-machi historic district; look for the blue-and-white awning with the big wooden sign above and the flower pots below.

(111) **Sushi Kyu** ★★ *Kids* SUSHI/LOCAL SPECIALTIES   Located on the main street of Oharai-machi in a 130-year-old former ryokan, this traditional restaurant offers tatami seating at low tables with a view out over the river. Even the cashier sits on tatami behind an enclosure, just like the old days. Kimono-clad waitresses serve sushi and local cuisine from a Japanese menu. Try the tekoni sushi, raw bonito marinated with soy sauce and mixed with vinegared rice in a bowl, or the obento of various delicacies. Like many family-type restaurants, there's also a child's plate with rice, soup, fried shrimp, salad, desert and drink for ¥700 ($5.85).

20 Uji Nakanokiri-machi, Ise-Shi. © **0596/27-0120.** Set meals ¥900–¥2,000 ($7.50–$17). No credit cards. Tues–Sun 11am–8pm; Mon 11am–5pm. Closed 1st and last day of the month. Station: Ise-Shi (5 min.). A 5-min. walk from the Inner Shrine on the main street of the Oharia-machi historic district.

KASHIKOJIMA

La Mer ★★ FRENCH   One of Ise-Shima's most famous restaurants, La Mer has a reputation for serving its own delightful French cuisine with a decided Japanese twist. Since Kashikojima is surrounded by water, you can safely assume that the seafood here is fresh and excellent, though Matsuzaka beef, a house specialty, is also highly recommended. The restaurant is probably most famous for its abalone; if you've never had it, this is a great, albeit expensive, place to try it. Lobster, Matsuzaka, and abalone are all featured in the set dinners. Located in the well-known Shima Kanko Hotel, the dining hall mirrors the hotel with an old-fashioned atmosphere, an attentive staff, and tables overlooking the bay and oyster rafts. Reserve a window seat and get there before sunset if possible (sunset times are posted in the hotel lobby). Set lunches have beef or seafood as the main dish.

Shima Kanko Hotel, Kashikojima. ℂ **0599/43-1211.** Reservations required for set dinners. Main dishes ¥5,000–¥10,000 ($42–$83); set dinners ¥12,000–¥30,000 ($100–$250); set lunches ¥5,000–¥12,000 ($42–$100). AE, DC, MC, V. Daily 11:30am–2pm and 5:30–8:30pm. Station: Kashikojima (then free shuttle to hotel).

3 More of Old Japan: Kanazawa ★★

618km (386 miles) NW of Tokyo; 224km (140 miles) NE of Kyoto

On the northwest coast of Honshu on the Sea of Japan, Kanazawa is the gateway to the rugged, sea-swept Noto Peninsula. It was the second-largest city (after Kyoto) to escape bombing during World War II, and some of the old city has been left intact, including a district of former samurai mansions, old geisha quarters, and tiny narrow streets that run crookedly without rhyme or reason (apparently to confuse any enemies foolish enough to attack). Kanazawa is most famous for its **Kenrokuen Garden,** one of the most celebrated gardens in all of Japan. It's the main reason people come here, though there are several fine museums nearby that are also worth a visit.

Kanazawa first gained notoriety about 500 years ago, when a militant Buddhist sect joined with peasant fanatics to overthrow the feudal lord and establish its own autonomous government, an event unprecedented in Japanese history. The independent republic survived almost 100 years before it was attacked by an army of Oda Nobunaga, who was trying to unite Japan at a time when civil wars wracked the nation. Kanazawa was subsequently granted to one of Nobunaga's retainers, Maeda Toshiie, who constructed a castle and transformed the small community into a thriving castle town. The Maeda clan continued to rule over Kanazawa for the next 300 years, amassing wealth in the form of land and rice and encouraging development of the arts. Throughout the Tokugawa shogunate, the Maedas remained the second most powerful family in Japan and controlled the largest domain in the country. The arts of Kutani ware, Yuzen silk dyeing, and Noh theater flourished—and enjoy success and popularity in Kanazawa even today. Japan's fourth largest city at the end of the Feudal Era, Kanazawa now has a population of 440,000 and is capital of Ishikawa Prefecture.

ESSENTIALS

GETTING THERE   By JR Train   Direct trains from Osaka (via Kyoto) depart half-hourly or hourly; the ride takes less than 3 hours and costs ¥6,930 ($58) for an unreserved seat. From Nagoya, direct trains depart for Kanazawa every 2 hours and take about 3 hours; the cost is ¥6,620 ($55) for an unreserved seat.

From Tokyo, take the Joetsu Shinkansen to Echigoyuzawa and switch there for the limited express Hakutaka train to Kanazawa. The trip takes about 4½ hours and costs ¥11,690 ($97).

By Bus   Buses depart four times a day from Ikebukuro Station's east exit in Tokyo, arrive in Kanazawa 7½ hours later, and cost ¥7,840 ($65). Buses also depart daily from Nagoya and Kyoto stations, both take about 4 hours and cost ¥4,060 ($34).

VISITOR INFORMATION   Be sure to pick up the flyer "Kanazawa" at the Tourist Information Centers in Tokyo, Kyoto, Narita or Kansai international airports, or at the local **Tourist Information Center** (℃ **076/232-6200**) inside Kanazawa Station. To find the center, turn right after passing through the wicket (you'll be heading toward the East Gate exit); it will soon be on your left beside a shopping arcade. Open daily 9am to 7pm (with English-speaking volunteers on duty 10am–6pm), it distributes an excellent map and brochure in English. You can also book hotel rooms here.

GETTING AROUND   Kanazawa's attractions spread south and southeast from the station (take the East Gate exit). Sights are too far-flung to see everything on foot, so the easiest way to get around Kanazawa is by **bus.** All major lines depart from Kanazawa Station, and as many as 15 lines will take you to Kenrokuen Garden; a map showing all bus routes and where they depart from Kanazawa Station is on the map/pamphlet distributed by the tourist office (which may change once reconstruction of the bus area has been completed; reconfirm bus departures with the tourist office).

Take a ticket when boarding the bus and pay when you get off; it costs ¥200 ($1.65) to most sights in the city. Useful for visitors is the **Kanazawa Loop Bus,** which goes to all the tourist sites and costs ¥500 ($4.15) for a one-day pass. Or, if you want to use all of the city buses, the **Kanazawa Free Pass** (¥900/$7.50) gives you unlimited 1-day travel on buses as well as 10% to 50% discounts on admission to Seisonkaku Villa, the Honda Museum, Nomura Samurai House, and Saihitsu-an. The tourist office can help you decide which is most useful for you.

You can also travel around Kanazawa by **bicycle. JR Rental Cycle** (℃ **076/ 261-1721;** open daily 9am–6pm), at the west exit of Kanazawa Station, rents cycles for ¥1,200 ($10) per day.

EXPLORING KANAZAWA

Much of Kanazawa's charm lies in the atmosphere of its old neighborhoods. Be sure to wear your good walking shoes since the best way to explore various parts of the city is on your own two feet. One suggested itinerary for tackling the city's sights would be to take a bus to the Higashi Geisha district, then another bus onward to Kenrokuen and the sights in its vicinity, and then walk to the Naga-machi Samurai district. Directional signs in English to major sights are posted throughout the city. Note, however, that what is identified as Saigawa Odori Avenue on the map issued by the tourist office is called Chuo Dori by the locals and has street signs that identify it as such.

KENROKUEN GARDEN & VICINITY

In addition to Kenrokuen Garden, there is a cluster of museums just south of the garden that are worth a visit if you have time.

(112) **Gyokusen-en** *(Finds*   Not far from Kenrokuen Garden's north entrance, this 300-year-old landscape garden took 100 years and four generations to complete. Constructed on a steep slope and drawing on water from Kenrokuen for its two ponds and stream, the garden boasts the oldest tearoom in Kanazawa (300 years old), 47 stone lanterns, and 10 stone basins. Of special interest is the secret Christian stone lantern, which encases a hidden stone image of the Virgin Mary. (During the Edo Period, Christianity was forbidden, so followers had to worship in secrecy.) The garden is rather small and traffic from a nearby road is intrusive, but you might want to come here for some green tea and sweet bean

cakes (¥700/$5.85 extra) and contemplation if the crowds at Kenrokuen get you down.

8–3 Kosho-machi. Ⓒ **076/221-0181.** Admission ¥500 ($4.15) adults, ¥400 ($3.35) high-school students, ¥350 ($2.90) children. Daily 9am–4pm; closed Dec–Mar 10. Bus: Kenrokuenshita stop (2 min.).

Honda Museum (Honda Zohinkan)   This private museum, which you can tour in about 40 minutes, displays the personal effects of the Honda clan, Lord Maeda's chief retainer and amasser of great fortune and real estate during the Edo Period. One of Japan's few museums dedicated to a military family of the Edo Period and providing insight into a privileged life, it displays samurai out-fits, weapons (some of the arrow tips are truly wicked), glassware, ceramics, incense burners, sake cups, medicine chests, uniforms of the Maeda's personal firefighter brigade, a marriage trousseau, and treasures awarded to the clan by the Tokugawa shogun, including handwritten poems written by Ieyasu.

3–1 Dewa-machi. Ⓒ **076/261-0500.** Admission ¥500 ($4.15) adults, ¥350 ($2.90) students over 12 years, ¥250 ($2.10) children. Mar–Oct daily 9am–5pm; Nov–Feb Fri–Wed 9am–5pm. Bus: Dewa-machi Kokuritsu Byoin-mae or Kencho-mae stop (5 min.). Located between the prefecture's art and history museums (see below).

⑬ **Ishikawa Prefectural Art Museum (Ishikawa Kenritsu Bijutsukan)**   Founded to preserve Ishikawa Prefecture's most important cultural resources, this museum houses scrolls, paintings, Kutani ware, and items such as samurai costumes belonging to the Maeda family, as well as contemporary oil paintings and decorative art by artists living in Ishikawa, many of them National Living Treasures. One room is reserved solely for a pheasant-shaped incense burner by a 17th-century Kyoto potter, one of the most valuable pieces in the collection. You can see everything in about 45 minutes.

2–1 Dewa-machi. Ⓒ**076/231-7580.** Admission to permanent exhibit ¥350 ($2.90) adults, ¥280 ($2.35) stu-dents, free for children under 18; more for special exhibits. Daily 9:30am–5pm. Closed during exhibit changes. Bus: Dewa-machi Kokuritsu Byoin-mae or Kencho-mae stop (5 min.). Just south of Kenrokuen Park, not far from Ishikawa Prefectural Museum for Traditional Products and Crafts.

Ishikawa Prefectural History Museum (Kenritsu Reikishi Hakubut-sukan) 🌟 *(Kids)*   Housed in a handsome redbrick building built to stock guns and gunpowder before the turn of the 20th century, this museum exhibits arti-facts dealing with the history of the prefecture from prehistoric to modern times. Although explanations are in Japanese only, a thick notebook with English translations is available, giving you more information about Ishikawa's history than you ever wanted to know. Still, I spent a very enjoyable hour here, learn-ing that Lord Maeda had as many as 8,000 retainers, who in turn had their own retainers, making the samurai population here very large indeed. You'll see samurai outfits, a model of a samurai house, photographs of the Meiji Era, and a life-size model of a textile factory from the Industrial Age that's actually clang-ing and banging away. There's a hands-on room where children can dress in period clothing and try their hand at weaving, making bamboo screens, beating drums, and generating fire with a stick.

3–1 Dewa-machi. Ⓒ **076/262-3236.** Admission ¥250 ($2.10) adults, ¥200 ($1.65) students, free for children under 18. Daily 9am–5pm. Bus: Dewa-machi Kokuritsu Byoin-mae or Kencho-mae stop (5 min.).

Ishikawa Prefectural Museum for Traditional Products and Crafts (Ishikawa Kenritsu Dento Sangyo Kogeikan) 🌟🌟🌟   If you have time to visit only one museum in Kanazawa, this is the one to choose. It's by far the best place in town for viewing and learning about all the beautiful handcrafted items for which Kanazawa has long been famous. There are explanations in English and a detailed English pamphlet. Here you can see the famous Kutani pottery, first produced under the patronage of the Maeda clan in the 1600s, as well as displays of Kaga Yuzen dyeing and hand painting on silk (Kanazawa is known for its bold and clear picturesque designs). Also on display are Kanazawa lacquerware (which uses raised lacquer painting), paulownia woodcrafts, metalwork, family Buddhist altars, Kanazawa gold leaf, wooden molds for sweets, bambooware, fishing hooks and rods, folk toys, Japanese paper (washi), umbrellas, and even fireworks. Schedule about an hour to appreciate everything.

1–1 Kenroku-machi. ℂ **076/262-2020.** Admission ¥250 ($2.10) adults, free for children. Apr–Nov, daily 9am–5pm (closed 3rd Thurs of every month); Dec–Mar, Fri–Wed 9am–5pm. Bus: Dewa-machi Kokuritsu Byoin-mae stop (2 min.). Next to Seisonkaku Villa.

Kenrokuen Park ★★★   At one time, Kanazawa possessed an impressive castle belonging to the powerful Maeda clan, but it was destroyed by fire in 1881. Near the park entrance is one of the few structures remaining, the handsome **Ishikawamon** (Ishikawa Gate), which used to be the south entrance to the castle. Observing how big and grand the gate is, you can appreciate the size of the original Maeda castle. Remarkably, its roof tiles are actually lead in case emergency dictated they be melted down for musket balls. The area just beyond the gate is gradually undergoing transformation into a public park.

Just south of Ishikawamon is Kanazawa's main attraction, the 25-acre **Kenrouken Garden** ★★★. The largest of what are considered to be the three best landscape gardens in Japan—the other two are Kairakuen Garden in Mito and Korakuen Garden in Okayama—it's considered by some to be the grandest. Its name can be translated as "a refined garden incorporating six attributes"— spaciousness, careful arrangement, seclusion, antiquity, elaborate use of water, and scenic charm. Ponds, trees, streams, rocks, mounds, and footpaths have all been combined so aesthetically that the effect is spellbinding.

Altogether, it took about 150 years to complete the garden, which served as the outer garden of Kanazawa Castle. The fifth Maeda lord started construction in the 1670s, and successive lords added to it according to their own individual tastes. The garden as you now see it was finished by the 12th Maeda lord in 1822; only after the Meiji Restoration was it opened to the public. In addition to cherry trees, irises, ponds, and other elements of natural beauty, there are several historic structures, including a tea-ceremony house, a former samurai house, and most important, Seisonkaku Villa. Plan on 1½ hours to see everything.

In the southeast corner of Kenrokuen Park is **Seisonkaku Villa** ★★ (ℂ **076/221-0580;** open Thurs–Tues 8:30am–4:30pm), built in 1863 by the 13th Maeda lord as a retirement home for his widowed mother. Elegant and graceful, this villa has a distinctly feminine atmosphere with delicately carved wood transoms and painted shoji screens. The bedroom is decorated with tortoises painted on the shoji wainscoting; tortoises were associated with long life, and it must have worked—the mother lived to be 84. Admission to the villa is ¥600 ($5) for adults, ¥300 ($2.50) for junior-high and high-school students, ¥250 ($2.10) for children.

Tip: You may want to arrive at dawn or near the end of the day since Kenrouken Garden is a favorite destination of Japanese tour groups, led by guides who explain everything in detail—through loudspeakers.

1–4 Kenroku-machi. ℂ **076/221-5850.** Admission ¥300 ($2.50) adults, free for seniors over 65, ¥100 (85¢) children 6 to 18 years. Mar to mid-Oct, daily 7am–6pm; mid-Oct to Feb, daily 8am–4:30pm. Bus: Kenrokuenshita or Kencho-mae stop (both 3 min.).

THE NAGAMACHI SAMURAI DISTRICT

About a 15-minute walk west of Kenrokuen Garden, the Nagamachi Samurai district is basically a few streets lined with beautiful wooden homes hidden behind gold-colored mud walls. An unhurried stroll in the neighborhood will give you an idea of what a feudal castle town might have looked like.

Nomura Samurai House ★ Stop 30 minutes here to see how samurai lived back in the Edo Period. Occupied by members of the Nomura family for 10 generations, this traditional Japanese home boasts a drawing room made of Japanese cypress, with elaborate designs in rosewood and shoji screens painted with landscapes, and a tea-ceremony room. Rooms overlook a small, charming garden with a miniature waterfall, a winding stream, and stone lanterns. Personal effects of the Nomura family and other objects from the Edo Period are on display, including a samurai outfit, the family altar, and a nightingale box (deliberately dark so the nightingale would sing).

1–3–32 Nagamachi. ✆ 076/221-3553. Admission ¥500 ($4.15) adults, ¥400 ($3.35) high-school students, ¥250 ($2.10) children. Apr–Sept, daily 8:30am–5:30pm; Oct–Mar, daily 8:30am–4:30pm. Bus: Kohrinbo stop (5 min.).

Saihitsu-an This old home, built in the Taisho Era for the Japanese tea ceremony, has been converted into the Kaga Yuzen Silk Dyeing Studio, where you can watch artists at work painting intricate designs on silk. An English sheet explains the time-consuming dyeing technique in detail; it takes up to 3 months to make 13 yards of Yuzen handpainted silk, enough for one kimono. In addition to a display of Kaga Yuzen kimono, a small selection of scarves, bags, and handkerchiefs are for sale. I got a kick out of a sign by the entrance noting that CHILDREN AND DRUNKS ARE FORBIDDEN TO ENTER. Assuming you're neither, you can see everything in 30 minutes.

1–3–16 Nagamachi. ✆ 076/264-2811. Admission ¥500 ($4.15). Fri–Wed 9am–noon and 1–5pm (you must enter by 11:45am and 4:30pm). Bus: Kohrinbo stop (4 min.).

Shinise Memorial Hall This 120-year-old building once served as the Nakaya Chinese Pharmacy, which first opened in 1579 to dispense Chinese medicines and was a familiar landmark in the city. Donated to the city and moved here, it contains part of the old pharmacy, a tearoom, and a study. The second floor serves as a showcase for traditional crafts and tools of the Kanazawa people, with exhibitions changing about three times a year. Worth a 15-minute stop.

2–2–45 Nagamachi. ✆ 076/220-2524. Free admission. Daily 9:30am–5pm. Bus: Kohrinbo stop (4 min.).

OTHER SIGHTS

HIGASHI GEISHA DISTRICT Northeast of Korakuen Park (take bus no. 11 or 12 to the Hashiba-cho stop), this geisha district is one of three old entertainment quarters of the city. A walk here reveals rather solemn-looking, wood-slatted facades of geisha houses dating from the 1820s, where men of means came to be entertained with music, dancing, songs, the tea ceremony, poem reciting, and other pleasurable pursuits. The ⑭ **Shima Geisha House,** 1–13–21 Higashiyama (✆ 076/252-5675; open daily 9am–6pm), a typical tearoom where merchants as well as men of letters came to watch geisha perform, is open to the public. Inside, you'll find rooms that were allotted to personal use as well as to performing, along with displays of ordinary artifacts from combs, pipes, and game boards to cooking utensils. Admission is ¥400 ($3.35) for adults, ¥300 ($2.50) for children, but you'll probably want to stop for tea in the new addition facing a garden, which costs ¥500 to ¥700 ($4.15–$5.85) more. It takes only 20 minutes or so to tour the house.

⑪⑤ **MYORYUJI TEMPLE** ★★ Myoryuji Temple (1–2–12 Nomachi (℃ 076/241-2877), is popularly known as Ninja-dera (or Temple of the Secret Agents) because of its secret chambers, hidden stairways, tunnels, and trick doors. Built by the Maeda clan for family prayer in 1643, it looks rather small from the outside, just two stories high to comply with height restrictions during the Edo Period. Inside, four stories are evident, but even this is false—three more levels are concealed. The fortresslike structure contains an amazing 29 stairways and a labyrinth of corridors, along with such trick devices as pitfalls to trap unsuspecting intruders, slatted stairs where lances could make stabs at passing legs, escape hatches, and rooms that could be opened only from the outside—just one more example of how deep paranoia ran during the Edo Period. Although rumor has it that a tunnel once connected the temple to the castle, a river running between them makes it unlikely.

Myoryuji Temple can be seen only by phoning ahead for a reservation; chances are good that you'll be able to see it the same day you call. To ensure that you don't get lost (which would be quite easy because of all the trick doors), you'll be grouped with other visitors and led by a guide who, unfortunately, describes everything in Japanese only. However, demonstrations of the various trick devices are fairly self-explanatory. Tours, given daily from 9am to 4:30pm (to 4pm in winter), last 30 minutes and cost ¥800 ($6.65) for adults and ¥600 ($5) for children (only children over 6 are admitted). To reach it, take a bus to the Nomachi-Hirokoji stop, from which it's a 5-minute walk.

SHOPPING

Kanazawa's most famous products are its **Kutani pottery,** with bright five-color overglaze patterns, and its hand-painted **Yuzen silk.** Kanazawa also produces maki-e lacquerware, sweets, toys, wooden products, and almost all of Japan's gold leaf. For convenient shopping for these and other souvenirs, try **Omiyage Kan** right in Kanazawa Station.

For department stores, boutiques, and contemporary shops, visit the **Katamachi and Tatemachi shopping streets,** within walking distance of Kenrokuen Garden and the Nagamachi Samurai district. **Omicho Market,** just off Hyaku-mangoku Odori between the station and Kenrokuen Garden, is the city market with more than 200 stalls selling seafood, vegetables, and fruit.

Ishikawa Prefectural Products Center (Kanko Bussankan) This is the place to come for one-stop shopping. The ground floor sells local products ranging from lacquerware and pottery to glassware and toys, while the second floor houses a restaurant. Open daily 10am to 6pm (closed some Tuesdays). 2–20 Kenroku-machi. ℃ 076/222-7788. Just north of Kenrokuen Garden; if you're arriving at the garden via bus no. 10, 11, or 12, you'll get off the bus just a few steps away from here.

⑪⑥ **Kaga Yuzen** Whereas the Saihitsu-an (above) is primarily a workshop, this is a combination museum and shop. The museum (admission: ¥300/$2.50 adults, ¥200/$1.65 children) displays kimono and explains the process of Yuzen dyeing, but you can skip it if you like and simply take the stairs to the left of the entryway to the basement shop, where you can purchase scarves, purses, fans, ties, clothing, and other items made from Yuzen cloth, which heavily uses nature in its designs—mainly flowers, animals, and landscapes. Open daily 9am to

5:30pm (to 5pm and closed Thursdays in winter). 8–8 Kosho-machi. 𝄐 076/ 224-5511. Not far from the Ishikawa Prefectural Products Center, about a 5-min. walk from the Kenrokuenshita bus stop on the same street as Gyokusen-en garden.

Kutani Kosen Pottery Kiln (Kutani Kosengama)   If your interest lies in pottery, it's worth a visit to this Kutani ware shop not far from Myoruyji Temple. You can see the entire process of producing Kutani ware, including the kilns heated by pine and the painting. Open daily 9am to noon and 1 to 5pm. 5–3–3 Nomachi. 𝄐 076/241-0902. Bus: 20 min. from Kanazawa Station to the Nomachi stop.

⑪⑦ **Sakuda**   Thinking about wallpapering a room in gold leaf? Then you'll certainly want to pay a visit to Sakuda, located in a modern building in the Higashi Geisha district. You can watch artisans at work, pounding the gold leaf and spreading it until it's paper-thin and translucent. (As much as 98% of Japan's entire national output of gold leaf is produced in Kanazawa.) But most people come here to shop for gold-leafed vases, boxes, bowls, trays, screens, furniture, and—this being Japan—golf balls and clubs. Don't miss the second-floor bathrooms; the women's is done entirely in gold leaf, the men's in platinum. The staff was serving complimentary tea spiked with gold leaf to everyone who dropped by during my last visit. Open daily 9am to 6pm. 1–3–27 Higashiyama. 𝄐 076/251-6777. Bus: Hashiba-cho stop.

⑪⑧ **Tawaraya Ame** *Kids*   They've been selling Japanese confectionery from this traditional wood-slatted building for more than 160 years. Tawaraya makes two types of candy from rice and barley, using malt instead of sugar. One of the candies is soft like honey (¥800/$6.65 for 300g/10.5 oz.); the other is hard and comes in a wooden bucket (¥1,800/$15 for 750g/1.65 lb.). The staff recommends breaking the hard candy with a hammer (kids love this) and putting it in a refrigerator. Open Monday to Saturday 9am to 6pm; Sunday 10am to 5pm. 2–4 Kobashi-machi. 𝄐 076/252-2079. About a 10-min. walk from Higashi Geisha district, near the Kobashi Bridge.

WHERE TO STAY
EXPENSIVE
Most of the expensive accommodations and some of the moderately priced hotels add a surcharge averaging ¥1,000 ($8.35) per person during peak season—New Year's, Golden Week (Apr 29–May 5), mid-July through August, and October. We've indicated those that do in the listings below.

Directions are from Kanazawa Station; minutes in parentheses indicate the walking time required from the bus stop.

ANA Hotel Kanazawa *★★*   This sleek, curved, white building soaring next to Kanazawa Station is part of the ANA conglomerate that includes All Nippon Airways. It offers convenient access to the station, good service, and varied dining choices (including a summertime beer garden). The marbled lobby is filled with the sounds of a cascading waterfall and a river of chandeliers shimmers from the atrium above. Rooms are simple, comfortable, and uncluttered, with everything you'd expect from one of Kanazawa's best hotels.

16–3 Showa-machi, Kanazawa, Ishikawa 920-8518. 𝄐 800/ANA-HOTELS in the U.S. and Canada or 076/224-6111. Fax 076/224-6100. www.anahotels.com. 254 units. ¥12,000–¥14,000 ($100–$117) single; ¥19,000–¥25,000 ($158–$208) double; ¥23,000–¥46,000 ($192–$383) twin. Peak season ¥1,000 ($8.35) extra per person. AE, DC, JCB, MC, V. Station: Kanazawa (east exit, 1 min.). **Amenities:** 4 restaurants, 1 bar; tour desk; salon; room service (7am–11pm); in-room massage; same-day laundry/dry cleaning service; non-smoking floor. *In room:* A/C, cable TV with pay movies, minibar, hot-water pot with tea, hair dryer, washlet toilet.

Hotel Nikko Kanazawa ★★   Owned by rival Japan Airlines and giving the ANA Hotel across the street stiff competition, this 29-story high-rise was designed by a Japanese-French team. It exudes a French-colonial atmosphere with a lobby adorned with a bubbling fountain, rattan chairs stuffed with pillows, trees, antiques, and Oriental decorative art ranging from ginger jars to Japanese lacquered boxes. The English-speaking concierge staff receives high marks. Spacious rooms come with many extra comforts, including lighted closets and speakers for the TV and radio in the bathroom; there are special floors for nonsmokers and women travelers. Higher-priced rooms offer great views from Kanazawa's tallest building.

2–15–1 Hon-machi Kanazawa, Ishikawa 920-0853. 𝄢 **800/NIKKO-US** (800/645-5687) in the U.S. and Canada or 076/234-1111. Fax 076/234-8802. 260 units ¥13,000–¥16,000 ($108–$133) single; ¥24,000–¥28,000 ($200–$233) double; ¥26,000–¥30,000 ($217–$250) twin. AE, DC, JCB, MC, V. Across the street from the east exit. **Amenities:** 4 restaurants (Japanese, Chinese, international), 1 bar, 1 lounge; next-door health club with indoor pool (fee: ¥2,000/$17); concierge; shopping arcade; salon; room service (7am–10pm); in-room massage; babysitting; same-day laundry/dry cleaning service; nonsmoking rooms; executive-level rooms. *In room:* A/C, satellite TV with pay movies, minibar, hot-water pot with tea, hair dryer, bathroom scale, washlet toilet.

MODERATE

Kanazawa Citymonde Hotel   This modern-design hotel built in 1991 targets female travelers with its pastels-and-pink color scheme and a pre-existing tea-ceremony house that occupies part of a pleasant garden and is visible from the lobby coffee lounge. The cheapest singles are quite small, but the majority of rooms are perfectly adequate twins; higher-priced twins even boast two bathrooms—greatly appreciated by a pair trying to get ready for an outing at the same time. Some higher-floor rooms have a view of Kenrokuen with magnificent mountains in the background.

2–10 Hashiba-cho, Kanazawa, Ishikawa 920-0911. 𝄢 **076/224-5555.** Fax 076/224-5554. 207 units. ¥8,000–¥9,500 ($67–$79) single; ¥12,000–¥15,000 ($100–$125) double; ¥15,000–¥19,000 ($125–$158) twin. Peak season ¥500 ($4.15) extra per person. AE, DC, JCB, MC, V. Bus: 11 or 12 to Hashiba-cho. On Hyaku-mangoku Odori between Kenrokuen Garden and the Higashi Geisha district (within a 7-min. walk to each). **Amenities:** 4 restaurants (French, Chinese, Japanese), 1 bar; room service (5–11pm); in-room massage; same-day laundry/dry cleaning service. *In room:* A/C, TV, fridge, hot-water pot with tea, hair dryer.

Kanazawa Miyako Hotel ★ ⟨Value⟩   Don't be turned off by the hotel's cheerless exterior—all of the rooms have been nicely updated and are among the largest for their price in Kanazawa. Add to that the Miyako name (synonymous with quality service), a discount for Frommer's readers, and a convenient location (linked to the station via an underground passage), and you'll see why I like this lodging. Single and twin rooms feature semi-double beds with feather bed quilts, heavy curtains to shut out light, brightly lit rooms, blonde wood furniture and tiled bathrooms. Be sure to mention Frommer's when you make a reservation.

6–10 Konohanacho, Kanazawa Ishikawa 920-0852. 𝄢076/261-2111. Fax 076/261-2113. reservation@kanazawa.mykhtls.co.jp. 295 units. ¥10,000–¥12,000 ($83–$100) single; ¥16,000–¥24,000 ($133–$200) double; ¥18,000–¥28,000 ($150–$233) twin; ¥27,000–¥36,000 ($225–$300) triple. 10% discount and complimentary breakfast for Frommer's readers. AE, JCB, MC, V. Across the street from Kanazawa Station east exit (3 min.). **Amenities:** 2 restaurants (Japanese, Western), 1 bar/lounge, 1 summertime beer garden; tour desk; shopping arcade; salon; room service (7am–11:30pm); in-room massage; babysitting; same-day laundry/dry cleaning service; nonsmoking floor. *In room:* A/C, TV with pay movies, minibar, hot-water pot with tea, hair dryer, washlet toilet.

INEXPENSIVE

APA Hotel Kanazawa Station Square   Although just a business hotel, it does have a special feature that sets it apart—large public baths complete with

Jacuzzi, sauna, and a rooftop outdoor bath, all free to hotel guests. Another plus: its convenient location just steps away from Kanazawa Station. If you're not a fan of public baths, however, you might choose to stay elsewhere; the hotel is not geared toward tourists, little English is spoken, and rooms are so miniscule that if you open your luggage you may have to leap to reach your bed. But rooms are clean and have basic necessities, including small windows that open.

1–9–28 Hirooka, Kanazawa, Ishikawa 920-0031. (C) 076/231-8111. Fax 076/231-8112. 456 units. ¥7,000–¥8,000 ($58–$67) single; ¥11,000 ($92) double; ¥12,000–¥16,000 ($100–$133) twin. AE, JCB, MC, V. Just outside the west exit of Kanazawa Station. **Amenities:** 3 restaurants (French, Japanese), 1 bar; public baths with sauna and Jacuzzi; in-room massage; coin-op washer and dryer; nonsmoking floors. *In room:* A/C, TV, dataport, fridge, hot-water pot with tea, hair dryer, washlet toilet.

Ryokan Murataya   This Japanese Inn Group ryokan is in the heart of Kanazawa, not far from Katamachi and Tatemachi shopping streets and within walking distance of Kenrokuen. It's modern and rather uninteresting from the outside but comfortable and pleasant inside. All rooms are clean and are Japanese style without bathroom.

1–5–2 Katamachi, Kanazawa, Ishikawa 920-0981. (C) 076/263-0455. Fax 076/263-0456. murtaya@ spacelan.ne.jp. 11 units (none with bathroom). ¥4,500 ($37.50) single; ¥8,500 ($71) twin; ¥12,000 ($100) triple. Western breakfast ¥450 ($3.75) extra; Japanese breakfast ¥800 ($6.65) extra. AE, MC, V. Bus: From platform 7, 8, or 9 to Katamachi, then a 3-min. walk. From the bus stop walk down Tatemachi 1 block and turn right. **Amenities:** Coin-operated washer and dryer. *In room:* A/C, TV, hot-water pot with tea.

(119) **Yogetsu** 🌟🌟 *(Finds)*   This delightful little minshuku has a picturesque location right on the main street of the Higashi Geisha district. Run by a jovial older woman who understands some English, Yogetsu is a 100-year-old house that used to belong to a geisha. The rooms, in different sizes, are rather plain (I prefer those on the 2nd floor that face the front), but the quiet, quaint surroundings and cleanliness make up for the lack of decor. The second-floor rooms are air-conditioned.

1–13–22 Higashiyama, Kanazawa, Ishikawa 920-0831. (C)076/252-0497. 5 units (none with bathroom). ¥4,500 ($37.50) per person without meals, ¥5,000 ($42) with breakfast, ¥6,500 ($54) with 2 meals. No credit cards. Bus: 11 or 12 (platform 10 or 11) to Hashiba-cho, then a 4-min. walk; or a 20-min. walk east of the Kanazawa Station. *In room:* TV (some are coin-op), hot-water pot with tea.

WHERE TO DINE

Kanazawa's local specialties, known collectively as **Kaga Ryori,** consist of seafood, such as tiny shrimp and winter crabs, as well as freshwater fish, duck and mountain vegetables.

All directions are from Kanazawa Station.

AROUND KENROKUEN GARDEN

Hana Anzu   VARIED JAPANESE/KAGA   Convenient to Kenrokuen Garden's main (north) entrance and located at the Ishikawa Prefectural Products Center (where you'll probably want to do some shopping), this traditionally decorated restaurant specializes in Kaga cuisine. The most popular set lunch is the Hana Anzu bento for ¥1,800 ($15). More expensive is the Kaga mini-kaiseki, Jibu-Zen, which costs ¥3,000 ($25) and features a duck stew. Although the menu is in Japanese only, photos translate for you.

Ishikawa Prefectural Products Center, 2nd floor, 2–20 Kenrokumachi. (C) 076/222-5188. Set meals ¥1,000–¥3,000 ($8.35–$25). AE, DC, JCB, MC, V. Daily 11am–6pm (closed Tues Jan–Mar). Bus: Kenrokuen-shita stop (1 min.).

120 **Miyoshian** ★★★ *Finds* KAGA KAISEKI   A great place to try the local Kaga cuisine right in Kenrokuen Garden, this 100-year-old restaurant consists of three separate wooden buildings, the best of which is a traditional room extending over a pond. This is where you'll probably dine, seated on tatami with a view of an ancient pond (giant carp swim in the murky waters). Only set meals of Kaga cuisine are served, featuring *jibuni* (a duck-and-vegetable stew eaten primarily in winter) and other dishes. My ¥1,500 ($12.50) meal included soup, jibuni, sashimi, eel on rice, pickles, a Japanese sweet, and thick, green tea. From 9am to 2pm, you can also come just for green tea and sweets for ¥500 to ¥600 ($4.15–$5). In the evening only groups of six or more may dine here.

Kenrokuen Garden, 1–11 Kenrokumachi. ⓒ 076/221-0127. Reservations required for dinner, not accepted for lunch. Kaga teishoku ¥1,500–¥3,000 ($12.50–$25); Kaga kaiseki from ¥5,000 ($42). MC, V. Thurs–Tues 10:30am–2:30pm and 4:30–8:30pm. Bus: Kenrokuenshita stop, then turn right after entering park (5 min.).

KATAMACHI AREA

Just north of the Saigawa Ohashi Bridge is an area full of restaurants and drinking establishments, radiating out from Katamachi Shopping Street and Saigawa Odori (called Chuo Dori by the locals).

121 **Hamacho** ★ JAPANESE SEAFOOD   Hamacho offers seafood and vegetables in season; the menu, written on a blackboard but in Japanese only, changes according to what's fresh and available and may include *imo* (Japanese potatoes), freshly picked mushrooms, vegetables, various seafood selections, and sashimi. Just tell Mr. Ishigami, the owner and chief chef, how much you want to spend and he'll do the rest. If there's anything you don't like, be sure to tell him. Sit at the counter where you can watch the preparation of your set meal, which may include grilled fish or shrimp, noodles, tofu, sashimi, soup, and vegetables.

2–27–24 Katamachi. ⓒ 076/233-3390. Reservations recommended. Set meals ¥6,000–¥10,000 ($50–$83). AE, DC, JCB, MC, V. Mon–Sat 5pm–midnight. Closed holidays. Bus: to Katamachi (2 min.). Just off Chuo Dori (identified as Saigawa Dori on the map issued by the tourist office) beside a small canal.

Kincharyo VARIED JAPANESE   This, without a doubt, is Katamachi's easiest restaurant to find: it's located on the third floor of the very visible Tokyu Hotel. Sister restaurant to a famous 70-year-old restaurant in the Teramachi Temple district (near Myoryuji Temple), this one is popular with Japanese women. For lunch there's tempura, mini-kaiseki, sushi, and more, but most popular is the obento for ¥1,800 to ¥3,500 ($15–$29)—so popular, in fact, that it sometimes runs out. Set dinners include tempura, Kaga kaiseki, sushi, shabu-shabu, and more.

Tokyu Hotel, 2–1–1 Kohrinbo. ⓒ 076/231-2411. Set lunches ¥1,800–¥5,000 ($15–$42); set dinners ¥3,500–¥10,000 ($29–$83). AE, DC, MC, V. Daily 11:30am–2pm and 5–9pm. Bus: Kohrinbo (1 min.).

122 **Kitama** ★★ VARIED JAPANESE/KAGA   Sitting on tatami mats, you'll have a pleasant view of a small, moss-covered, 100-year-old garden of tiny pines, stone lanterns, and rocks. The Kojitsu obento, served in an upright lunch box, features sashimi, small pieces of pork and fish, fried shrimp, a soybean patty, and various seasonal vegetables. The jibuni teishoku, with duck stew, clear soup, pickled vegetables, rice, and hors d'oeuvres, is also quite satisfying.

2–3–3 Katamachi. ⓒ 076/261-7176. Set meals ¥1,500–¥3,800 ($12.50–$32). AE, DC, JCB, MC, V. Daily 11:30am–8:30pm. Closed irregularly. Bus: to Katamachi (1 min.). From the intersection of Katamachi and Chuo Dori (marked Saigawa Dori on the tourist map), walk 1 block west on Chuo Dori and turn right; the restaurant will be on your left with a display case and bamboo fence at its entrance.

AROUND KANAZAWA STATION

Benkay VARIED JAPANESE   With several locations around Japan, Benkay is dependable for good and varied Japanese cuisine, which includes mini-kaiseki, obento, tempura, and sushi for lunch and tempura, sushi, and kaiseki for dinner.

Hotel Nikko Kanazawa, 2–15–1 Hon-machi. © **076/234-1111.** Set lunches ¥2,500–¥5,000 ($21–$42); set dinners ¥6,000–¥10,000 ($50–$83). AE, DC, JCB, MC, V. Daily 11:30am–2pm and 5:30–9:30pm. A 1-min. walk from Kanazawa Station's east exit.

Daiwa *Value* STEAK/VARIED JAPANESE   A large display case outside helps you order from this convenient restaurant in the station's restaurant complex. The steak set meal for only ¥950 ($7.90) offering steak, rice and vegetables is an excellent value, while the kid's plate includes a drink and toy (¥750/$6.25). The *unagi seiro* (¥950/$7.90) is grilled eel on a bed of rice, with soup and pickles.

Kanazawa Station © **076/260-3726.** Set meals ¥850–¥1,380 ($7.10–$11.50). AE, DC. Daily 11am–8pm. In Kanazawa Station (number 7 on the local tourist map).

Le Grand Chariot ★★ INTERNATIONAL   This combination bar and restaurant is decorated in such a riot of colors that it looks like a kaleidoscope gone awry. The hotel describes it as "Arabic imagination"—whatever. The dining area, which occupies only a small end of the bar, is the highest spot in Kanazawa and offers great views, particularly at sunset. You can even see the Japan Sea in the distance. Live piano music sets the mood as you dine on seafood, pork, beef, or chicken main dishes along with soup, salad, and other sides.

Hotel Nikko Kanazawa, 30th floor, 2–15–1 Hon-machi. © **076/234-1111.** Set lunches ¥2,000–¥5,000 ($17–$42); set dinners ¥5,000–¥10,000 ($42–$83). AE, DC, JCB, MC, V. Daily 11:30am–2pm and 5–9:30pm. A 1-min. walk from the east exit.

NEAR THE HIGASHI GEISHA DISTRICT

(101) **Kotobuki-Ya** ★★★ *Finds* VEGETARIAN   Specializing in *shojin ryori* (Buddhist vegetarian cooking), Kotobuki-ya is in a beautiful 160-year-old merchant's house with a two-story airy entryway. Dining here, on beautiful lacquer and pottery tableware, is a wonderful experience—not surprisingly, they have had many fine reviews. For lunch, you can dine for ¥2,500 ($21) on the shojin ryori obento (not available on Sun); for ¥300 ($2.50) more per person, you can even have your own private tatami room. Lunch kaiseki costs ¥5,200 ($43), but the price already includes your own private room. Kaiseki dinners offer a choice of vegetarian or with fish, and private rooms cost ¥800 ($6.65) more per person. Two of the rooms have a view of the garden.

2–4–13 Owari-cho. © **076/231-6245.** Reservations required at least 1 day in advance. Set lunches ¥2,500–¥5,200 ($21–$43); kaiseki dinners ¥7,000–¥12,000 ($58–$100). No credit cards. Mon–Sat 11:30am–2pm; daily 5–7pm (last order). Bus: to Musashigatsuji (3 min.). On a side street north of Hyaku-mangoku Dori, behind Nisseki gas station.

4 Osaka

546km (341 miles) W of Tokyo; 42km (26 miles) SW of Kyoto; 339km (212 miles) E of Hiroshima

Although its history stretches back about 1,500 years, Osaka first gained prominence when Hideyoshi Toyotomi, the most powerful lord in the land, built Japan's most magnificent castle here in the 16th century. To develop resources for his castle town, he persuaded merchants from other parts of the nation to resettle in Osaka. During the Edo Period, the city became an important distribution center as feudal lords from the surrounding region sent their rice to merchants in Osaka, who in turn sent the rice onward to Tokyo and other cities.

As the merchants prospered, the town grew and such arts as Kabuki and Bunraku flourished. With money and leisure to spare, the merchants also developed a refined taste for food.

Nowadays, Osaka, capital of Osaka Prefecture on the southern coast of western Honshu, is an industrial city with a population of about 2.6 million, making it the third most-populated city in Japan (after Tokyo and Yokohama). The legacy of the city's commercial beginnings is still present—Osakans are usually characterized as being outgoing and clever at money affairs. An Osakan greeting is "Are you making any money?" Osaka has a reputation throughout Japan as an international and progressive business center and is known for its food, castle, port, and Bunraku puppet theater. Because of its international airport, it serves as a major gateway to the rest of Japan.

ESSENTIALS
GETTING THERE
BY PLANE   Osaka's **Kansai International Airport (KIX; ✆ 0724/ 55-2500)** receives both domestic and international flights; for details on the international carriers that fly here, see "Getting There," in chapter 2.

The two major domestic airlines that fly into KIX are **All Nippon Airways (ANA) (✆ 800/235-9262** in the U.S. and Canada, toll free 0120/029-222 in Japan) and **Japan Airlines (✆ 800/525-3663** in the U.S. and Canada, toll free 0120/25-5971 in Japan). From Tokyo's Haneda and Narita airports, flight time is about 1 to 1¼ hours; at press time, the average fare was ¥18,500 ($154) one-way.

Arriving at KIX   Arriving at KIX, one experiences Japan at its modern best. Constructed on a huge synthetic island 3 miles off the mainland in Osaka Bay and connected to the city by a six-lane highway and two-rail line bridge, this 24-hour airport boasts the latest in technology—glass elevators ferry passengers to the four floors of the complex in an atrium setting, touch screens provide information in many languages, and if you arrive on an international flight, you'll board the driverless, computer-controlled Wing Shuttle to get to the central terminal. And, like the city itself, it's user-friendly: Signs are clear and abundant, and facilities—which range from restaurants and shops to a **post office** (2nd floor south, near JAL counter; open daily 8am–7pm), **ATMs** that accept foreign credit cards, a children's **playroom** in the international departure area (free of charge), **Discovery Internet Café** (2nd floor south, ✆ 0724/56-8710); open daily 8am–8pm), and **dental and medical clinics**—are seemingly endless.

Getting from KIX to Osaka   Taxis are prohibitively expensive: expect to spend $200 for a cab to the city center. Easiest, especially if you have luggage, is the **Airport Limousine Bus** service to major hotels in Osaka; most fares cost ¥1,300 ($11). Tickets can be purchased at counters in the arrival lobby. Another transportation mode to and from KIX is by **OCAT Shuttle 880,** which serves the Osaka City Air Terminal, next to JR Namba Station in Osaka, for ¥880 ($7.35).

If you're taking the **train** into Osaka (stations: Osaka, Tennoji, or Shin-Osaka) or even farther to Kyoto, simply walk through KIX's second-floor connecting concourse (baggage carts are designed to go on escalators and as far as

---

Impressions

In trade it is a Chicago. In situation it is a Venice.
—John Foster Fraser, *Round the World on a Wheel* (1899), on Osaka

train ticket gates) and board the **JR Haruka,** which travels to Tennoji and Shin-Osaka stations before continuing to Kyoto. The fare to Shin-Osaka is ¥2,470 ($21) for the 48-minute trip, with departures generally twice an hour. Slower is the **JR rapid** (JR Kanku Kaisoku), which travels from the airport to Tennoji and Osaka stations before continuing to Kobe. The 60-minute trip to Osaka Station costs ¥1,160 ($9.70).

If you a have a **Japan Rail Pass,** you can ride these trains for free. Exchange your voucher in the Kansai Airport (rail) Station at the Green Window on the second floor (open daily 5:30am–11pm) or at the West Japan Railways Information Counter in the international arrivals lobby on the first floor of the passenger terminal (open Wed–Sun 9:30am–8pm and Mon–Tues 9:30am–6pm).

Next to the JR trains in the same station at the airport is the private **Nankai Line,** which has three types of trains to Namba Nankai Station. The sleek **rapi:t a** (pronounced *rapito alpha*) train reaches Namba in 30 minutes. There's one train an hour, and it costs ¥1,390 ($12) for ordinary reserved seats. The **rapi:t b** (*rapito beta*) at the same price stops at more stations, including Sakai, and takes 35 minutes. You can also take an ordinary **Nankai Express Line** for ¥890 ($7.40) and reach Namba in 42 minutes.

Returning to KIX When you depart from KIX by plane after your stay in Japan, you'll pay a passenger terminal use fee of ¥2,650 ($22) for adults, ¥1,330 ($11) for children, at the vending machines (credit cards accepted) before you can pass through security.

BY TRAIN Osaka is 2½ hours from Tokyo by Shinkansen bullet train; tickets are ¥13,240 ($110) for an unreserved seat (the Nozomi Shinkansen is more expensive). All Shinkansen bullet trains arrive at **Shin-Osaka Station** at the city's northern edge. To get from Shin-Osaka Station to Osaka Station and other points south, use the most convenient public transportation, the **Midosuji Line** subway; the subway stop at Osaka Station is called **Umeda Station. JR trains** also make runs between Shin-Osaka and Osaka stations.

If you haven't turned in your voucher for your **Japan Rail Pass** yet, you can do so at Osaka Station's or Shin-Osaka Station's Green Windows (open daily 5:30am–11pm), at Osaka Station at the Travel Information Satellite (TiS) on the main floor (daily 10am–7pm, to 6pm Sun and holidays), or at the Shin-Osaka Station TiS on the second floor (daily 7am–8pm).

If you're arriving in Osaka from Kobe or Kyoto, the commuter lines, which will deliver you directly to Osaka Station in the heart of the city, are more convenient than the Shinkansen, which will deposit you at out-of-the-way Shin-Osaka Station.

BY BUS JR night buses depart from both Tokyo (Yaesu exit) and Shinjuku (new south exit) stations every evening, arriving in Osaka the next morning. The trip from Tokyo takes about 9 hours and costs ¥8,610 ($80). The arrival terminal for long-distance buses is at the Osaka City Air Terminal, next to Namba Station with its many train and subway lines.

VISITOR INFORMATION
AT THE AIRPORT The **Kansai Tourist Information Center** (© 0724/ 56-6025; open daily 9am–9pm) is near the south end of the International Arrivals Lobby. The multilingual staff can help with general travel information about Japan and hotel reservations, and they offer brochures and maps.

IN TOWN   At **Osaka Station,** the **Visitors Information Center Umeda** (© **06/6345-2189;** open daily 8am–8pm) is at the east (Midosuji) exit of JR Osaka Station; the English-speaking staff gives out good maps of the city and assists in securing hotel rooms. Another center is just east of the central exit of **Shin-Osaka Station** on the third floor (© **06/6305-3311;** open daily 8am–8pm). Note that if you're arriving by Shinkansen, you'll be up on the fourth floor, so simply go down one flight to the tourist office. At **JR Namba Station,** you'll find the **Visitors Information Center Namba** (© **06/6643-2125;** open daily 8am–8pm) in the basement of the Osaka City Air Terminal (OCAT) building.

To find out what's going on in Osaka, pick up a copy of *Kansai Time Out,* a monthly magazine with information on sightseeing, festivals, restaurants, and other items of interest pertaining to Osaka, Kobe, and Kyoto. It sells for ¥300 ($2.50) at bookstores, restaurants, tourist information offices, and places frequented by English-speaking tourists, and it's sometimes available free at major hotels.

Another source of information available free at the tourist offices and at many hotels is *Meet Osaka,* a quarterly with information on sightseeing, Bunraku, festivals, concerts, and special exhibits and events. *Welcome to Osaka Tourist Guide* provides discount coupons and information on what to see and do; *Osaka How to Enjoy It* is also an excellent source of information. Finally, Osaka has a homepage in English at **www.city.osaka.jp/.**

CONSULATES   Several embassies maintain consulates in Osaka including **Australia** (© **06/6941-9271**); **Canada** (© **06/6212-4910**), **Great Britain** © **06/6281-1616**), and the **United States** (© **06/6315-5900**).

DRUG STORE   The American Pharmacy (© **06/4804-3811**) in Universal CityWalk (Konohana, Osaka Bay) carries a number of American drugs, cosmetics and health items and can fill American prescriptions (but note that you must first visit a Japanese doctor). It's open 10am to 10:30pm daily.

INTERNET ACCESS   Internet access is available at **Kinko's,** 3–2–14 Umeda, Kita-ku (© **06/6343-3980** or toll free 0120/001-966), across from Osaka Station. Open daily 24-hours, Kinko's charges ¥250 ($2.15) for 15 minutes of computer use. In Namba, try **Internet Salon Oval O. P.** (© **06/6634-5700**) at 4–2–1 Namba on the 8th floor of the Namba Midosuji Building (exit 13 of Namba Station). It charges ¥500 ($4.15) for 30 minutes and is open Monday through Friday noon to 10pm and Saturday and Sunday noon to 9pm.

MAIL   The Central Post Office, or *Osaka Chuo Yubinkyoku* (© **06/6347-8006**), a minute's walk west of Osaka Station, is open 24 hours for mail. For postal service information in English, call © **06/6944-6245** Monday to Saturday 9:30am to 4:30pm.

ORIENTATION

Osaka is divided into various wards, or *ku,* the most important of which for visitors are Kita-ku (North Ward), which encompasses the area around Osaka Station and the heart of the city, called Namba; Chuo-ku (Central Ward), where you'll find Osaka Castle; and Tennoji-ku.

AROUND OSAKA STATION   Kita-ku embraces the area around Osaka Station and the subway Umeda Station and includes many of the city's top hotels, the city's tallest buildings, lots of restaurants, and several shopping complexes, mostly underground.

AROUND OSAKA CASTLE   Osaka Castle, which lies to the east, is the historic center of the city. It's in **Chuo-ku,** the Central Ward, which stretches through the city center.

NAMBA   Four subway stops south of Umeda Station is Namba, with a cluster of stations serving subways, JR trains, and Kintetsu and Nankai lines, all of which are connected to one another via underground passageways. This is the heart of the city, bustling with a spirit of old Osaka, where you'll find more hotels, Osaka's liveliest eating and entertainment district centered on a narrow street called **Dotombori** (also written Dotonbori), and major shopping areas like the enclosed pedestrian street **Shinsaibashi-Suji** and **America-Mura** with imported goods from America. Farther south is **Den Den Town,** Osaka's electronics district and **Dogayasuji** famous for restaurant supplies. Connecting Kita-ku with Namba is Osaka's main street, **Midosuji Dori,** a wide boulevard lined with gingko trees.

AROUND TENNOJI PARK   At the south end of the JR Loop Line is **Tennoji-ku,** which was once a thriving temple town with **Shitennoji Temple** at its center. In addition to a park with a zoo, it boasts **festivalgate,** a theme park with many rides and amusements, and **Spa World,** Japan's biggest and most luxurious public bathhouse.

OSAKA BAY AND PORT   West of the city around Osaka Bay is where you will find **Universal Studios Japan** and Universal CityWalk; **Tempozan Harbour Village** with its first-class aquarium, shopping complex, and Suntory Museum; the **Maritime Museum,** and domestic and international ferry terminals.

GETTING AROUND

Despite its size, I find Osaka easier to get around than other large Japanese cities because there are lots of signs and information in English.

BY SUBWAY   Osaka's user-friendly subway network is easy to use because all lines are color-coded and the station names are in English (even announcements are in English on many lines). The red **Midosuji Line** is the most important one for visitors; it passes through Shin-Osaka Station and on to Umeda (the subway station next to Osaka Station), Shinsaibashi, Namba, and Tennoji.

Fares begin at ¥200 ($1.65) and increase according to the distance traveled. If you think you'll be traveling a lot by subway on a given day, consider purchasing a **One Day Pass** for ¥850 ($7.10), which allows unlimited rides on subways and buses all day.

BY JR TRAIN   There's also a Japan Railways train called the Osaka Kanjo Line, or **JR Loop Line,** which passes through Osaka Station and makes a loop around the central part of the city (similar to the Yamanote Line in Tokyo); take it to visit Osaka Castle. The One Day Pass is not valid on this line, but your **Japan Rail Pass** is. Otherwise, fares begin at ¥120 ($1).

(*Tips*   **A Note on Directions**

For all the attractions, accommodations, and restaurants listed below, I've included the nearest subway or JR station followed by the walking time to the establishment once you reach the indicated station (in parentheses).

SEEING THE SIGHTS
NEAR OSAKA STATION
Floating Garden Observatory (Kuchu Teien Tenbodai)   This is a futuristic observatory 557 feet in the air, and it seems to float between the two towers of the Umeda Sky Building. Take the super-fast glass elevator from the East Tower building's third floor; you'll then take a glass-enclosed escalator that also bridges the two towers before depositing you on the 39th floor. I'm not afraid of heights, but taking an escalator over thin air in an earthquake-plagued nation certainly caught my attention; it made the "floating" observatory feel safe in comparison. From here, you have an unparalleled view of all Osaka.

Umeda Sky Building, 1–1–88 Oyodo-naka, Kita-ku. (C) **06/6440-3901.** Admission ¥700 ($5.85) adults, ¥300 ($2.50) children. Daily 10am–10:30pm. Station: Osaka or Umeda (9 min.).

Museum of Oriental Ceramics ⭐   This modern facility, about a 15-minute walk south of Osaka Station on Nakanoshima Island in the Dojima River, was designed especially for viewing ceramics, with darkened rooms that utilize natural light and computerized natural-light simulation to spotlight the beautiful pieces. You'll find mostly Korean and Chinese antique ceramics, but the collection includes some Japanese pieces designated as National Treasures. If ceramics are your passion, you'll probably spend at least an hour here.

1–1–26 Nakanoshima, Kita-ku. (C) **06/6454-8600.** Admission ¥500 ($4.15) adults, ¥300 ($2.50) students, children free. Tues–Sun 9:30am–5pm. Closed during exhibition changes. Station: Yodoyabashi or Kitahama (5 min.).

Osaka Museum of Housing and Living ⭐ *Kids*   Kids love this life-size reproduction of Osaka as it might have looked in the 1830s; parents appreciate the English audio guide full of interesting tidbits. Highlights include miniature scenes of Osaka living conditions since the Meiji Period and a chronological look at one woman's housing history: born in the Karahori Shopping district, she lived in a converted bus after the war and eventually moved to a modern housing development. Plan on at least an hour here.

Housing Information Center, 8 floor, 6–4–20 Tenjinbashi, Kita-ku. (C) **06/6242-1170.** Adults ¥600 ($5), free for children 15 and younger. Wed–Mon 10am–5pm. Closed 3rd Mon of every month. Subway: Tenjinbashisuji-Rokuchome (exit 3, 1 min.).

AROUND OSAKA CASTLE
Osaka Castle (Osaka-jo) ⭐⭐   First built in the 1580s on the order of Hideyoshi Toyotomi, Osaka Castle was the largest castle in Japan, a magnificent structure used by Toyotomi as a military stronghold against rebellious feudal lords. By the time he died in 1598, Toyotomi had succeeded in crushing his enemies and unifying Japan under his command.

After Toyotomi's death, Tokugawa Ieyasu seized power and established his shogunate government in Edo. But Toyotomi's heirs had ideas of their own: Considering Osaka Castle impregnable, they plotted to overthrow the Tokugawa government. In 1615, Tokugawa sent troops to Osaka where they not only defeated the Hideyoshi insurrectionists but destroyed Osaka Castle. The Tokugawas rebuilt the castle in 1629, but the main tower was destroyed by lightning 36 years later, and the rest burned in 1868 as the shogunate made their last stand against imperial forces and what later became known as the Meiji Restoration.

The present Osaka Castle dates from 1931 and was extensively renovated in 1997. Built of ferroconcrete, it's not as massive as the original but is still one of Japan's most famous castles and is impressive with its white walls, black and gold-leaf trim, and copper roof. Its eight-story donjon (keep) rises 130 feet, with an observation platform on the top floor offering bird's-eye views of the city. The rest of the donjon houses a high-tech history museum that uses 3D pictures, videos, holograms, models, and artifacts to describe the life and times of Hideyoshi Toyotomi and the history of the castle, including the intense fighting that took place between Toyotomi and Tokugawa forces. Cultural assets on display include scrolls, folding screens, swords, and samurai armor; models include a full-scale reproduction of Toyotomi's Gold Tea Room and a model of Osaka Castle during the Toyotomi Era. You'll probably spend about 45 minutes here.

1–1 Osakajo, Chuo-ku. © **06/6941-3044.** Admission ¥600 ($5) adults, free for children under 12. Daily 9am–5pm. Station: Osakajo-Koen or Morinomiya (15 min.); or Tenmabashi of Osaka Business Park (10 min.).

AROUND TENNOJI PARK

festivalgate *Kids*   This indoor/outdoor amusement complex looks like a setting for a fantasy film, with an underwater theme and employing lush, tropical colors. Rides include a roller coaster that shoots throughout the complex at 62 miles an hour. There are also shooting galleries, virtual-reality games, and rides for small children.

3–2–36 Ebisu-higashi, Naniwa-ku. © **06/6635-1000.** Free admission; rides cost ¥300–¥700 ($2.50–$5.85) each. Daily 10am–10pm. Station: Shin-imamiya or Dobutsuenmae (1 min.).

Spa World *★★★*   This is the most luxurious and ambitious bathhouse I've ever seen. It can accommodate up to 5,000 people and draws upon hot springs brought up from 2,970 feet below the earth's surface. On its roof, in a large hangarlike room, is a covered swimming complex that includes a pool, a slide, a wave pool, a sunning terrace overlooking festivalgate (under the same ownership), and a wading pool (rental bathing suits available). The rest of the large complex is divided into themed, geographical bathing zones, which are rotated between the sexes and include luxurious locker rooms. At the Asian Zone, for example, Middle Eastern music and tiled mosaics set the tone for the Turkish bath, while China is represented by a medicinal bath. Massage is also available. If you're timid about going to a public bath, this one will convert you. If you're already a fan, you'll want to move in—note, however, that at 5am you're charged for a new day.

3–2–24 Ebisu-higashi, Naniwa-ku. © **06/6631-0001.** Admission weekdays, ¥2,700 ($22.50) adults, ¥1,500 ($12.50) children; weekends and holidays, ¥3,300 ($27.50) adults, ¥1,700 ($14) children. Daily 10am–9am. Station: Shin-Imamiya or Dobutsuenmae (2 min.). Next to festivalgate.

OSAKA BAY AREA

Osaka's well-developed waterfront offers a quick getaway for Osakans wishing to escape urban life, and, with the opening of **Universal Studios Japan,** has become one of Japan's major draws. In addition to the attractions below, in Konohana there's **Universal CityWalk,** a very upscale shopping venue with some world-renowned restaurants (see "Where to Dine," later in this chapter).

Osaka Aquarium (Kaiyukan) *★★★* *Kids*   Of all the aquariums in Japan, this is probably my favorite. One of the world's largest—encompassing 286,000 square feet and containing 2.9 million gallons of water—it's constructed around the theme "Ring of Fire," which refers to the volcanic perimeter encircling the Pacific Ocean. Tours begin with a video of erupting volcanoes followed by an escalator ride to the eighth floor; from there, you'll pass through 14 different habitats ranging from arctic to tropical as you follow a spiraling corridor back to the ground floor, starting with the daylight world above the ocean's surface and proceeding to the depths of the ocean floor. The walls of the aquarium tank are

Osaka Attractions & Nightlife

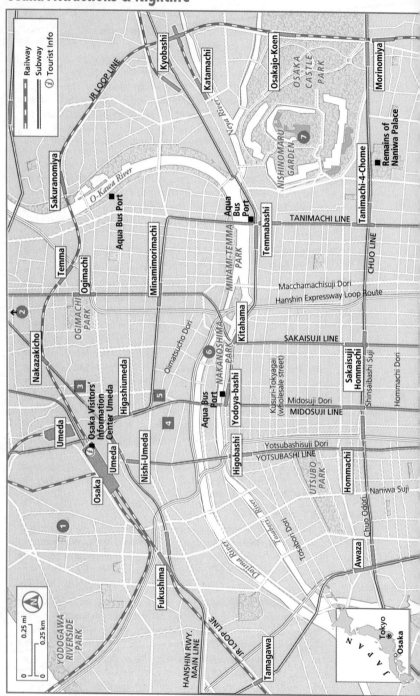

Legend:
- Railway
- Subway
- ⓘ Tourist Info

Labels and locations:

JR LOOP LINE

Kyobashi

Katamachi

Osakajo-Koen

OSAKA CASTLE PARK

Morinomiya

Sakuranomiya

NISHINOMARU GARDEN

⑦

Remains of Naniwa Palace

O-Kawa River

Aqua Bus Port

Tanimachi-4-Chome

Temma

Ogimachi

Minamimorimachi

MINAMI-TEMMA PARK

Aqua Bus Port

Temmabashi

TANIMACHI LINE

②

Nakazakicho

OGIMACHI PARK

Oimatsucho Dori

Macchamachisuji Dori

Hanshin Expressway Loop Route

CHUO LINE

Kitahama

SAKAISUJI LINE

③

Osaka Visitors' Information Center Umeda

Higashiumeda

⑤

⑥

NAKANOSHIMA PARK

Yodoya-bashi

Sakaisuji Hommachi

Shinsaibashi Suji

Hommachi Dori

Umeda

ⓘ

Umeda

④

Aqua Bus Port

Kusuri-Tokyagai (wholesale street)

Midosuji Dori

MIDOSUJI LINE

Osaka

Nishi-Umeda

Higobashi

Yotsubashisuji Dori

YOTSUBASHI LINE

Hommachi

UTSUBO PARK

Naniwa Suji

①

Tosabori River

Tosabori Dori

Chuo Odori

Awaza

Fukushima

Dojima River

YODOGAWA RIVERSIDE PARK

HANSHIN RWY. MAIN LINE

JR LOOP LINE

Tamagawa

N

0.25 mi

0.25 km

JAPAN

Tokyo

Osaka

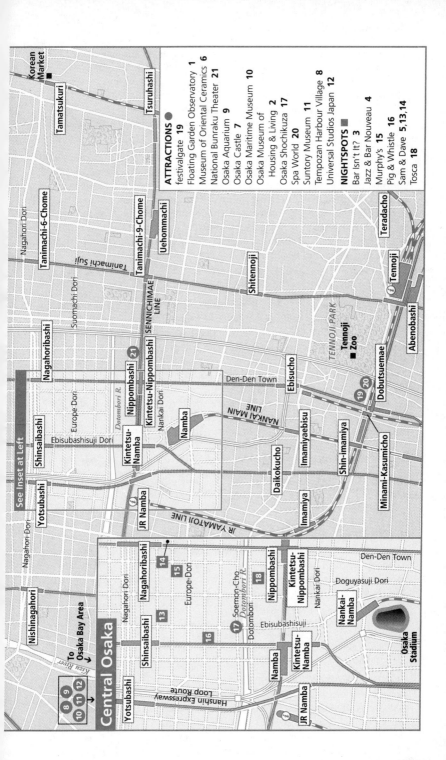

ATTRACTIONS ●
festivalgate **19**
Floating Garden Observatory **1**
Museum of Oriental Ceramics **6**
National Bunraku Theater **21**
Osaka Aquarium **9**
Osaka Castle **7**
Osaka Maritime Museum **10**
Osaka Museum of
  Housing & Living **2**
Osaka Shochikuza **17**
Spa World **20**
Suntory Museum **11**
Tempozan Harbour Village **8**
Universal Studios Japan **12**

NIGHTSPOTS ■
Bar Isn't It? **3**
Jazz & Bar Nouveau **4**
Murphy's **15**
Pig & Whistle **16**
Sam & Dave **5, 13, 14**
Tosca **18**

Central Osaka

To
Osaka Bay Area

Kizu River

Hanshin Expressway Loop Route

Nishinagahori
Yotsubashi
Shinsaibashi
Nagahoribashi
Nagahori Dori
Europe-Dori
Soemon-Cho
Dotombori R.
Dotombori
Ebisubashisuji
Nagahori Dori
Namba
Kintetsu-Nippombashi
Kintetsu-Namba
JR Namba
Nankai-Namba
Nippombashi
Nankai Dori
Den-Den Town
Doguyasuji Dori
Osaka Stadium

See Inset at Left

Nagahori Dori
Yotsubashi
Shinsaibashi
Nagahoribashi
Nagahori Dori
Suomachi Dori
Europe-Dori
Dotombori R.
Ebisubashisuji Dori
Kintetsu-Namba
JR Namba
Namba
Kintetsu-Nippombashi
Nippombashi
Nankai Dori
Den-Den Town
Daikokucho
Imamiyaebisu
Imamiya
Shin-imamiya
Minami-Kasumicho
Ebisucho

Tamatsukuri
Korean Market
Tsuruhashi
Tanimachi-6-Chome
Tanimachi-9-Chome
Uehommachi
Tanimachi Suji
Tanimachi Suji
SENNICHIMAE LINE
Shitennoji
Teradacho
Tennoji
TENNOJI PARK
Tennoji Zoo
Doubutsuemae
Abenobashi

JR YAMATOJI LINE
NANKAI MAIN LINE

383

constructed of huge acrylic glass sheets, making you feel like you're immersed in the ocean. You'll see 35,000 specimens representing 380 species including, whale sharks, the largest fish in captivity. Allow about 1 to 2 hours to tour the aquarium, avoiding weekends.

1–1–10 Kaigan-dori, Minato-ku. © **06/6576-5501.** Admission ¥2,000 ($17) adults, ¥900 ($7.50) children 7–15, ¥400 ($3.35) children 4–6. Daily 10am–8pm. Closed sometimes in June and in winter. Station: Osakako (5 min.).

Osaka Maritime Museum *(Kids)* This interesting museum that explores the relationship of people to the sea and Osaka's history as a port is housed in a futuristic dome on the water; access to the museum is through an underwater tunnel. There are lots of interactive displays that focus on Osaka's seafaring past and the use of navigational tools, but most interesting for children are probably the virtual reality sea adventure and a simulated sail through Osaka port (both of which cost extra) and the boardable, life-size replica of a 17th-century ship. You'll spend an hour or two here.

2–5–20 Nanko-kita, Suminoe-ku. © **06/4703-2900.** Admission: ¥600 ($5) adults, free for 15 and younger. Tues–Sun 10am–6pm. Subway: Cosmosquare (exit 1, 10 min.).

Suntory Museum *(icon)* The Suntory Museum, which you can tour in less than an hour, is that fantastically modern-looking structure you see near the aquarium, designed by well-known architect Tadao Ando. The museum—which hangs changing exhibitions against a dramatic background of the sea beyond its glass walls—is known for its impressive collection of 10,000 posters, including works by Toulouse-Lautrec, Mucha, and Casssandre, and glass objects, including some rare pieces by Emile Gallé. There's also a 3D IMAX theater with scenes so real you'll swear those fish on the screen are about to swim into your lap, a good museum shop, the Sky Lounge (perfect for taking a break), and a restaurant, the Sun Tempo (see "Where to Dine," later in the chapter).

1–5–10 Kaigan-dori, Minato-ku. © **06/6577-0001.** Admission ¥1,000 ($8.35) to museum, ¥1,000 ($8.35) to IMAX theater. Tues–Sun 10:30am–7:30pm. Station: Osakako (5 min.).

Universal Studios Japan *(stars)* *(Kids)* Following the tradition of Universal's Hollywood and Orlando theme parks, USJ takes guests on a fantasy trip through the world of American blockbuster movies, with rides, actual movie sets, live entertainment, and more. All the American favorites have been reproduced here, including amusements centered on *Jurassic Park, Jaws,* and *Back to the Future,* but there are also new attractions designed specifically for Japan, such as Snoopy's Sound Stage Adventure, an interactive playground. Unfortunately, most of the attractions have been dubbed into Japanese (I wonder why the original English isn't available on audioguide). Plan for a whole day here, but note that it is immensely popular. Arrive early.

2–1–33 Sakurajima, Konohana. © **06/4790-7000.** Studio Pass to all attractions ¥5,500 ($46) adults, ¥4,800 ($40) seniors, ¥3,700 ($31) children 4–11. Open daily, generally 9am–7pm, but can vary with the season. From Osaka Station take the JR Yumesaki Line (10 min.) to Universal City Station (5 min.). Direct buses depart from city-center hotels, including The Ritz-Carlton in Umeda and Nankai South Tower in Namba.

IN NEARBY TAKARAZUKA

Northwest of Osaka, the town of Takarazuka is synonymous with the all-female **Takarazuka Troupe.** Founded in 1914 to attract vacationers to Takarazuka, the troupe proved instantly popular with the general public, whose taste turned from traditional Japanese drama to lively Western musicals and entertainment. Performances are held at the **Takarazuka Revue Hall** (© **0797/86-7777**) most days throughout the year (closed Wed), usually at 1pm on weekdays and at 11am and 3pm on weekends and holidays. Tickets range from about ¥3,500 to ¥7,500 ($29–$62.50).

SHOPPING

Den Den Town (station: Nipponbashi or Ebisucho) is Osaka's electronics shopping region (*Den* is short for "electric"), similar to Tokyo's Akihabara and just as good. Some 200 shops here deal in electrical and electronic equipment from rice cookers to cassette players and personal computers. Most stores here are open daily 10am to 7pm.

If you're in the market for dolls or toys, you'll want to visit **Matsuyamachi-suji Street** (station: Matsuyamachi). It's lined with wholesale and retail outlets selling everything from elaborate Japanese dolls to yo-yos. Shops here are open from 9:30am to 5:30pm; some close different days of the week, but you're always sure to find some open.

Running north to south and a few blocks east of Nankai Namba Station is **Doguya-suji Street,** where you'll find about 40 shops selling wholesale restaurant supplies. From the comic (a shrimp sushi key ring) to the sublime (high-quality lacquerware), there are lots of gift ideas here at very inexpensive prices—not surprising since Osaka is known as the food capital of Japan.

Osaka must rank as one of the world's leading cities in underground shopping arcades. **Diamor Osaka** in Umeda (where the JR, Hanshin, subway, and Hankyu train lines intersect) has 73 shops and 16 galleries. This connects to Hankyu Sanbangai, which has two stories above ground and two beneath. They are both so massive and complicated that you'll probably get lost in the maze. **Crysta Nagahori,** connecting Nagahoribashi Station to Yotsubashi-suji, has a glass atrium ceiling and flowing streams of water, while Namba Walk connects Nipponbashi and Namba stations.

Other shopping areas include an above-ground covered shopping street near the **Shinsaibashi** subway station; paralleling Midosuji Dori to the east, it runs south all the way past Dotonbori to Namba. On the other side of Midosuji Dori is **America-Mura,** a popular spot for young Japanese shopping for T-shirts, Hawaiian shirts, ripped jeans, and other American fashions at inflated prices; its biggest marketplace is **Big Step** (open daily 11am–8pm; closed 2nd and 3rd Wed of the month). Osaka's newest shopping complex is the very upscale **Universal CityWalk** near Universal Studios, offering everything from Hello Kitty goods to Italian imports.

WHERE TO STAY

In the listings below, the nearest subway or JR station is indicated followed by the number of minutes it takes to walk from the station to the hotel (in parentheses).

AROUND OSAKA & SHIN-OSAKA STATIONS
Expensive

In addition to the choices listed below, also consider the **Hilton Osaka,** 1–8–8 Umeda, Kita-ku, Osaka 530-0001 (*©* **800/HILTONS** or 06/6347-7111; fax 06/6347-7001), a well-established branch of the Hilton chain with a wide range of services and facilities, including an adjacent shopping and dining complex; and the **Westin Osaka,** 1–1–20 Oyodonaka, Kita-ku, Osaka 531-0076 (*©* **800/WESTIN-1** or 06/6440-1111; fax 06/6440-1100), next to the Umeda Sky Building (with its Floating Garden Observatory) and offering some of the largest guest rooms in the city.

Where to Stay & Dine in Osaka

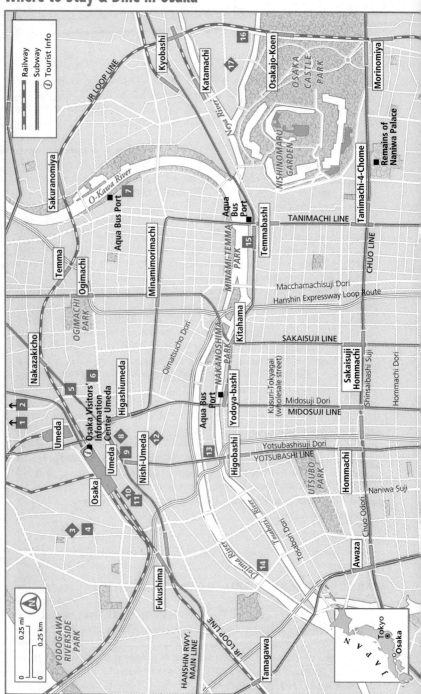

Railway
Subway
ⓘ Tourist Info

JR LOOP LINE
Kyobashi
Katamachi
16
17
Osakajo-Koen
OSAKA CASTLE PARK
Morinomiya
Sakuranomiya
NISHINOMARU GARDEN
Remains of Naniwa Palace
Neya River
O-Kawa River
Aqua Bus Port
7
Aqua Bus Port
Tanimachi-4-Chome
TANIMACHI LINE
Temma
Ogimachi
Minamimorimachi
MINAMI-TEMMA PARK
15
Temmabashi
CHUO LINE
OGIMACHI PARK
Macchamachisuji Dori
Hanshin Expressway Loop Route
Nakazakicho
Oimatsucho Dori
Kitahama
SAKAISUJI LINE
Higashiumeda
5
6
Osaka Visitors' Information Center Umeda
NAKANOSHIMA PARK
Kusuri-Tokyagai (wholesale street)
Sakaisuji Hommachi
Shinsaibashi Suji
Hommachi Dori
Umeda
Aqua Bus Port
Yodoya-bashi
Midosuji Dori
MIDOSUJI LINE
8
Nishi-Umeda
12
Osaka
9
Umeda
13
Higobashi
Yotsubashisuji Dori
YOTSUBASHI LINE
Hommachi
UTSUBO PARK
Naniwa Suji
10
11
3
4
Dojima River
14
Tosabori River
Tosabori Dori
Chuo Odori
Awaza
Fukushima
YODOGAWA RIVERSIDE PARK
0.25 mi
0.25 km
0
HANSHIN RWY. MAIN LINE
JR LOOP LINE
Tamagawa
JAPAN
Tokyo
Osaka

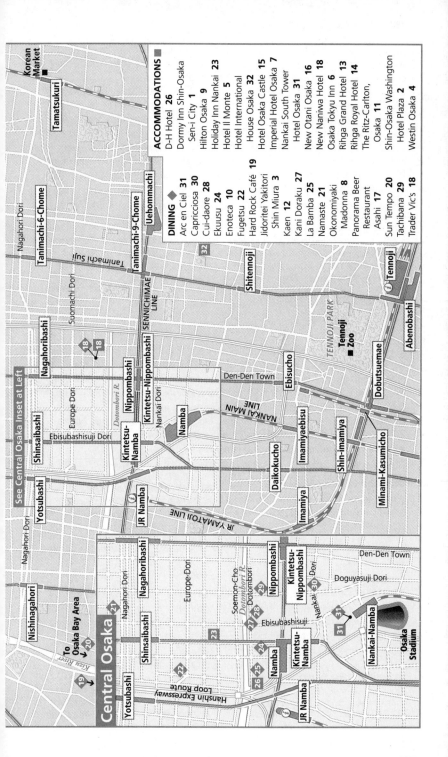

Central Osaka

Korean Market

Tamatsukuri

Tanimachi-6-Chome

Tanimachi-9-Chome

Uehommachi

Nagahori Dori

Tanimachi Suji

Suomachi Dori

SENNICHIMAE LINE

Shitennoji

Nagahoribashi

Nippombashi

Kintetsu-Nippombashi

Namba

Den-Den Town

Ebisucho

Ebisubashisuji Dori

Dotombori R.

Nankai Dori

Europe Dori

Kintetsu-Namba

NANKAI MAIN LINE

Imamiyaebisu

Shin-imamiya

Daikokucho

Imamiya

JR Namba

JR YAMATOJI LINE

Minami-Kasumicho

Dobutsuemae

Abenobashi

Tennoji

TENNOJI PARK

Tennoji Zoo

Shinsaibashi

Yotsubashi

See Central Osaka Inset at Left

ACCOMMODATIONS ■
D-H Hotel **26**
Dormy Inn Shin-Osaka
Sen-i City **1**
Hilton Osaka **9**
Holiday Inn Nankai **23**
Hotel Il Monte **5**
Hotel International
House Osaka **32**
Hotel Osaka Castle **15**
Imperial Hotel Osaka **7**
Nankai South Tower
Hotel Osaka **31**
New Otani Osaka **16**
New Naniwa Hotel **18**
Osaka Tokyu Inn **6**
Ringa Grand Hotel **13**
Ringa Royal Hotel **14**
The Ritz-Carlton,
Osaka **11**
Shin-Osaka Washington
Hotel Plaza **2**
Westin Osaka **4**

DINING ◆
Arc en Ciel **31**
Capricciosa **30**
Cui-daore **28**
Ekuusu **24**
Enoteca **10**
Fugetsu **22**
Hard Rock Café **19**
Jidoritei Yakitori
Shin Miura **3**
Kaen **12**
Kani Doraku **27**
La Bamba **25**
Namaste **21**
Okonomiyaki
Madonna **8**
Panorama Beer
Restaurant
Asahi **17**
Sun Tempo **20**
Tachibana **29**
Trader Vic's **18**

Central Osaka

To Osaka Bay Area

Kita River

Nishinagahori

Nagahori Dori

Nagahoribashi

Hanshin Expressway Loop Route

Yotsubashi

Shinsaibashi

Europe-Dori

Soemon-Cho

Dotombori R.

Dotombori

Ebisubashisuji

Namba

Kintetsu-Namba

Nippombashi

Kintetsu-Nippombashi

Nankai Dori

Den-Den Town

Doguyasuji Dori

JR Namba

Nankai-Namba

Osaka Stadium

Rihga Royal Hotel ★★   One of Osaka's most established and largest hotels, the Royal opened in 1935, expanded in 1973, and is now part of the Rihga chain. Located on Nakanoshima, an island in the middle of the Dojima River in the heart of Osaka (less than a 10-min. ride from Osaka Station), it boasts a friendly and helpful multilingual staff as well as one of my favorite lobby lounges in the city—a restful oasis where you can sip your drink, watch a cascading waterfall against a backdrop of cliffs and foliage, and be serenaded by piano music in the early evening. Comfortable rooms are nicely decorated in French drawing-room style, with large desks and other features that make them popular with business travelers. Of the hotel's many restaurants, most renowned is the Chambord, offering French cuisine and views from the 29th floor.

5–3–68 Nakanoshima, Kita-ku, Osaka 530-0005. ☎ **06/6448-1121.** Fax 06/6448-4414. www.rihga.co.jp. 993 units. ¥12,000–¥24,000 ($100–$200) single; ¥24,000–¥30,000 ($200–$250) twin; ¥26,000–¥45,000 ($217–$375) double. Presidential Towers executive floor from ¥33,000 ($275) double. AE, DC, JCB, MC, V. Station: Yodoyabashi, then free shuttle bus from exit 4 with departures every 15 min.; or Osaka Station north exit, free shuttle every 20 min. **Amenities:** 16 restaurants, 4 bars; a beautifully designed indoor pool, Jacuzzi, and sauna (fee: ¥2,100/$17.50); concierge; tour desk; business center; shopping arcade; salon; 24-hr. room service; in-room massage; babysitting; same-day laundry/dry cleaning service; nonsmoking rooms; executive-level rooms. *In room:* A/C, cable TV with pay movies, dataport, minibar, hot-water pot with tea, hair dryer, washlet toilet.

The Ritz-Carlton, Osaka ★★★   Opened in 1997, The Ritz-Carlton's first Japanese venture immediately gained a reputation as one of the nation's top hotels. Instead of the grandiose marble lobby most Japanese hotels seem to favor, the lobby here is small and intimate, done in Old World style with overstuffed sofas, fireplaces, and antiques. Hotel restaurants are all on the same lower floor to preserve the privacy of hotel guests. The hotel also wins kudos for offering complimentary use of the fitness center to all guests. Stylish rooms—among the largest in the city—offer panoramic views, especially from deluxe corner rooms, as well as goose-down pillows and comforters, terry robes, and marble bathrooms with magnifying mirrors and two sinks.

2–5–25 Umeda, Kita-ku, Osaka 530-0001. ☎ **800/241-3333** in the U.S. and Canada or 06/6343-7000. Fax 06/6343-7001. www.ritzcarlton.com. 292 units. ¥27,000–¥40,000 ($225–$333) single; ¥36,000–¥49,000 ($300–$408) twin or double. Club floors from ¥43,000 ($358) single; ¥49,000 ($408) double. AE, DC, JCB, MC, V. Station: Osaka, Umeda, or Nishi-Umeda (5 min.). **Amenities:** 4 restaurants, 1 bar, 1 lounge; state-of-the-art health club with indoor heated pool and indoor/ outdoor whirlpools (all free to hotel guests); children's day-care center; concierge; business center; shopping arcade; salon; 24-hr. room service; in-room massage; same-day laundry/dry cleaning service; nonsmoking rooms; executive-level rooms. *In room:* A/C, cable TV with pay movies, dataport, minibar, hot-water pot with tea and coffee, hair dryer, safe, bathroom scale, washlet toilet.

Moderate

Osaka Tokyu Inn   Part of a nationwide chain, this typical business hotel has quiet and clean rooms. The cheapest singles and some of the twins face an inner courtyard with absolutely no view; better are those facing the front, where you can look down on a small and tidy temple and cemetery seemingly out of place among Osaka's office buildings—typical Japan.

2–1 Doyama-cho, Kita-ku, Osaka 530-0027. ☎ **06/6315-0109.** Fax 06/6315-6019. www.tokyu.co.jp/inn/. 402 units. ¥8,500–¥12,000 ($71–$100) single; ¥17,500 ($146) double; ¥17,500–¥20,500 ($146–$171) twin. AE, DC, JCB, MC, V. Station: Osaka or Umeda (10 min.). Take the underground passageway lined with shops and follow the signs for OGIMACHI until you're above ground at the M10 exit; I suggest stopping by the tourist office to get a map showing the way. **Amenities:** 1 restaurant (Western), 1 lounge; business center; same-day laundry/dry cleaning service; nonsmoking rooms. *In room:* A/C, TV, minibar, hot-water pot with tea, hair dryer, washlet toilet.

Rihga Grand Hotel ⚜ This is a fine small hotel on the island of Nakanoshima in the heart of Osaka. Its location, next to Osaka's Festival Hall, makes it a favorite among concertgoers and musicians. Dating from 1960, it's also one of Osaka's older hotels, and it has aged gracefully. Rooms have recently been renovated with contemporary furnishings. I prefer the ones that face the river—although there's little boat traffic and nothing really to see, the view conveys a sense of spaciousness.

2–3–18 Nakanoshima, Kita-ku, Osaka 530-0005. ✆ **06/6202-1212.** Fax 06/6227-5054. www.rihga-grand.co.jp. 310 units. ¥12,000–¥15,000 ($100–$125) single; ¥22,000–¥30,000 ($183–$250) double or twin. AE, DC, JCB, MC, V. Station: Higobashi (5 min.). **Amenities:** 6 restaurants, 1 bar; salon; in-room massage; same-day laundry/dry cleaning service; nonsmoking rooms. *In room:* A/C, TV, minibar, hot-water pot with tea, hair dryer, washlet toilet.

Shin-Osaka Washington Hotel Plaza This modern, gray high-rise close to Shin-Osaka Station is a business hotel with mostly singles. All the rooms are clean, but the cheapest singles are very small, while the cheapest doubles offer only a semi-double bed. Some rooms also face an inner courtyard, rendering them dark even in the day. Better are rooms on higher floors, especially the deluxe rooms, which are slightly larger. Consider staying here only if you're traveling by Shinkansen and don't want to stay overnight far from the station.

5–5–15 Nishinakajima, Yodogawa-ku, Osaka 532-0001. ✆ **06/6303-8111.** Fax 06/6302-7007. www.wgh.co.jp. 490 units. ¥9,500–¥12,500 ($79–$104) single; ¥13,000–¥21,000 ($108–$175) double; ¥20,000–¥21,000 ($167–$175) twin. AE, DC, JCB, MC, V. Station: Shin-Osaka (Central Gate exit, 4 min.). Behind the Hewlett Packard building. **Amenities:** 5 restaurants, 1 bar; indoor pool, sauna, and gym (fee: ¥2,500/$21). *In room:* A/C, satelite TV, minibar, hot-water pot with tea, washlet toilet.

Inexpensive

Hotel Il Monte ⚜ New in 1997, this smart-looking corner hotel has a convenient location that brings in both business and leisure travelers. A small reception on the third floor has a helpful staff. Breakfast is the only meal available, and coffee is free to guests. Rooms are simple but modern and come with desks and ample counter space in the bathrooms.

7–13 Doyama-cho, Kita-ku, Osaka 530-0027. ✆ **06/6361-2828.** Fax 06/6361-3525. www.hotwire.co.jp/ilmonte/. 122 units. ¥8,500 ($71) single; ¥12,100 ($101) double; ¥14,300 ($108–$120) twin. AE, DC, JCB, MC, V. Station: Osaka, Umeda, or Higasahi Umeda (10 min.). East of Osaka Station on Shin-Midosuji Ave. beside the Hankyu-Higashi Dori shopping street. **Amenities:** Same-day laundry/dry cleaning service; non-smoking rooms. *In room:* A/C, cable TV with pay movies, minibar, hot-water pot with tea, hair dryer, washlet toilet.

(124) **Dormy Inn Sen-i City** *Value* This very simple business hotel, a 10-minute walk northwest of Shin-Osaka Station is easy to spot with its green-and-blue sign and a clock on top of the building. The lobby is on the sixth floor, and guest rooms are on the sixth and seventh floors. The rooms are a few decades away from being modern, but they're clean, good for the price, are fairly large as far as business hotels go, and include morning coffee and bread in their rates. Most are singles, none of which have bathrooms, and are available only to men since the public baths are also only for men. Single female travelers are given a double or a twin, both of which have private bathrooms with Western-style toilets and deep, Japanese-style tubs for ¥5,980 ($50).

2–2–17 Nishi-Miyahara, Yodogawa-ku, Osaka 532-0004. ✆06/6394-3331. Fax 06/6394-3335. 70 units (12 with bathroom). ¥4,980–¥5,980 ($40–$50) single without bathroom (for men only); ¥12,000 ($100) twin or double with bathroom. AE, DC, JCB, MC, V. Free shuttle bus departs every 10 min. or so from Shin-Osaka Station's Central Gate exit from 8am–7pm; go to the lowest level where shuttles leave from farthest stop to the right. **Amenities:** Courtesy shuttle; free coin-op washer and dryer; nonsmoking rooms. *In room:* A/C, TV, hot-water pot with tea.

AROUND OSAKA CASTLE
Expensive

New Otani Osaka ★★★ In a business park that's home to corporate head-quarters for KDD, NEC, Sumitomo, and other big companies, this Leading Hotel of the World member attracts both business and tourist clientele. Its proximity to Osaka Castle Park, popular with joggers, families, and young Japanese, and its varied public facilities, ranging from fine dining to casual dining to a fitness club, give the property something of an "urban resort" atmosphere. Everything about this hotel is visually pleasing, from the marbled, airy four-story atrium lobby to pleasant and comfortable rooms. Rates are based on room size and view, with the more expensive rooms providing a view of Osaka Castle. Service throughout the hotel is first class.

1–4–1 Shiromi, Chuo-ku, Osaka 540-8578. ⓒ **06/6941-1111.** Fax 06/6941-9769. www.newotani.co.jp. 540 units. ¥28,000–¥41,000 ($233–$342) single; ¥32,000–¥45,000 ($267–$375) twin or double. AE, DC, JCB, MC, V. Station: JR Loop Line to Osakajo-Koen (3 min.). Across the moat from Osaka Castle. **Amenities:** 12 restaurants, 3 bars; fitness club with indoor and outdoor pools and sauna (fee: ¥2,500/$21); outdoor tennis courts; children's day -care center; concierge; tourdesk; business center; shopping arcade; salon; room service (6am–1am); in-room massage; same-day laundry/dry cleaning service; nonsmoking rooms. *In room:* A/C, cable TV with pay movies, dataport, minibar, hot-water pot with tea, hair dryer, washlet toilet.

Moderate

Hotel Osaka Castle *Value* The rather plain rooms in this tourist hotel—popular with families and youth groups—offer value for the money thanks to the hotel's central location, a front-desk staff used to answering sightseeing questions, quick access to public transport, and proximity to Matsuzakaya department store (in the same building). Rooms are on the fifth, six, eighth, and ninth floors; the best ones face the river with floor-to-ceiling windows—wonderful when cherry blossoms line the river.

1–1 Tenmabashi-Kyomachi, Chuo-ku, Osaka 540-0032. ⓒ **06/6942-2401.** Fax 06/6946-9043. 120 units. ¥7,500–¥8,500 ($62.50–$71) single; ¥13,000–¥17,000 ($108–$142) twin; ¥13,000–¥15,000 ($108–$125) double. AE, DC, JCB, MC, V. Station: Tenmabashi (1 min.). On the banks of the Okawa River above Tenmabashi Station. **Amenities:** 2 restaurants (Chinese, Western); in-room massage; free use of washers and dryers; dry cleaning/laundry service; nonsmoking rooms. *In room:* A/C, cable TV with pay movies, fridge, hot-water pot; washlet toilet.

NAMBA
Expensive

Nankai South Tower Hotel Osaka ★★ This hotel makes a great base for exploring destinations throughout the Kansai area. Towering 36 stories above Namba Nankai Station, it's convenient to Kansai International Airport (just a 30-min. train ride away, which is why international airline crews stay here) and Shin-Osaka Station (15 min. away by subway). It's also a good location for day trips to Universal Studios Japan, Mount Koya, Kyoto, and Nara. Right in the center of the Namba shopping and nightlife district (connected to Takashimaya department store), the hotel offers rooms with large picture windows showing sprawling city views. Extras include in-bathroom telephones and heavy drapes to shut out light. *Tip:* Apply for a South Tower Club card (¥3,000/$25) at the time of your reservation, and you'll receive a 20% discount on your room, 10% discount in hotel restaurants, and a discount on pool and fitness club use.

5–1–60 Namba, Chuo-ku, Osaka 542-0076. ⓒ **800/457-4000** in the U.S. and Canada or 06/6646-1111. Fax 06/6648-0331. www.southtower.co.jp. 548 units. ¥17,000–¥22,000 ($142–$183) single; ¥28,000–¥39,000 ($233–$326) double/twin; executive-level doubles from ¥35,000 ($292) double/twin. AE, DC, JCB, MC, V. Station: Namba Nankai (1 min.). **Amenities:** 6 restaurants, 2 bars, 1 lounge; fitness center with indoor atrium pool, spa and sauna (fee: ¥5,000/$42); concierge; bus to Universal Studios Japan (¥400/$3.35); business center; shopping arcade; salon; 24-hr. room service; in-room massage; babysitting; same-day laundry/dry cleaning service; nonsmoking rooms; executive-level rooms. *In room:* A/C, cable TV with pay movies, dataport, minibar, hot-water pot with tea, hair dryer, washlet toilet.

Moderate

DH Hotel ★★ *(Finds)*   You can stay here in style for what you'd pay at an unexciting business hotel. This postmodern concrete hotel, designed by Takeyama Sei, is famous for its architecture (it's shaped like a **D**, hence its name). There are only two rooms on each floor; each is starkly decorated with cement walls, sleek black furniture, fresh flowers, an entertainment area with a bar, a stainless-steel sink, and a CD player to pop in your own tunes. There's a separate room for the toilet, but the raised tubs with Jacuzzi jets are divided from the sleeping area only by a curved wall of glass. More expensive rooms have a glass-encased personal sauna. Toiletries are provided in a drawstring pouch that you're encouraged to take with you when you leave. The hotel is popular with young Japanese couples who have come to Dotombori for a night on the town, so rates are higher on Friday and Saturday nights, the night before a national holiday, and during such peak times as New Year's, Golden Week, and mid-August. There are no single rooms, but on weekdays, lone travelers can stay in one of the double or twin rooms for ¥10,000 to ¥18,000 ($83–$150).

2–5–15 Dotonbori, Chuo-ku, Osaka 542-0071. ☎ **06/6212-2995.** Fax 06/6212-7462. 12 units. ¥16,000–¥26,000 ($133–$217) double; ¥20,000 ($167) twin. Peak season, weekends, and holiday evenings ¥2,000–¥3,000 ($17–$25) extra per room. AE, DC, JCB, MC, V. Station: JR Namba and Namba subway station (3 min.). West of Midosuji Dori and south of the Dotombori-gawa River on Dotombori's west end. **Amenities:** 1 restaurant/bar (dim sum), 1 Internet café; in-room massage. *In room:* A/C, TV, Jacuzzi, fridge, hot-water pot with tea, hair dryer, safe.

Holiday Inn Nankai *(Kids)*   Kids stay for free in their parents' rooms, making this a good family choice. Centrally located on tree-lined Midosuji Dori close to restaurants, shopping and nightlife, it has recently undergone complete renovation, with clean rooms offering comfortable furnishings, double-size beds (even in the twins), good bed-side lights, and heavy drapes to shut out light. The front desk is understaffed, but they do speak English.

2–15–5 Shinsaibashisuji, Chuo-ku Osaka 542-0085. ☎ **06/6213-8281.** Fax 06/6213-8640. www.six continentshotels.com. 229 units. ¥12,000–¥19,000 ($100–$158) single; ¥15,000–¥22,000 ($125–$183) twin; ¥22,000 ($183) double. AE, DC, JCB, MC, V. Subway: Namba (exit 14, 3 min.), Shinsaibashi (exit 4, 5 min.). **Amenities:** 2 restaurants (Japanese, coffee shop), 1 bar; exercise room (fee: ¥1,000/$9.15); shopping arcade; salon; room service (7am–10pm); in-room massage; dry cleaning/laundry service; nonsmoking rooms. *In room:* A/C, cable and satellite TV with pay movies, dataport, fridge, hot-water pot with tea, hair dryer.

Inexpensive

New Naniwa Hotel   Most of the rooms in this older but clean hotel offer a tatami mat with a small sitting area, small bathrooms, separate toilets, and separate sinks. Or, if you prefer, there are five Western-style rooms. Although views are only of rooftops, rooms on the fifth and sixth floor have more light. There is also a public bath. Breakfasts (Western or Japanese) are served in a small dining room, but elaborate-for-the-price Japanese dinners are served in rooms, ryokan-style. The owner's son speaks English well and is very helpful.

2–10–12 Shimanouchi Chuo-ku, Osaka 556-0082. ☎ **06/6213-1241.** Fax 06/6213-8098. www2.odn.ne.jp/~newnaniwahotel. 30 units (all with bathroom). ¥7,000 ($58) single; ¥12,000 ($100) Western twin; ¥13,000 ($108) Japanese twin. Breakfast ¥ 1,050 ($8.75) extra; dinner ¥4,200 ($35) extra. Rates include tax. AE, DC, JCB, MC, V. Station: Nipponbashi (exit 7, 5 min.). On Dotombori, 2 blocks east of Sakaisuji Dori. *In room:* A/C, TV, hot-water pot with tea.

ELSEWHERE IN THE CITY
Expensive

Imperial Hotel Osaka ★★★   Uniquely designed scents and soothing music conspire with dramatic use of light and Frank Lloyd Wright–inspired furnishings to create a luxurious yet comfortable 1930s atmosphere. Although a bit off the beaten track, the hotel's location, on the cherry-tree-lined Okawa River, is great for jogging and gives this luxury hotel a relaxing resort-like setting despite its corridor connection to the OAP, a large office building that attracts business travelers. And, of course, this Osaka property offers the same fine service as the famed Imperial in Tokyo. All standard rooms offer double beds, large windows with remote-control drapes and views of the river, aromatherapy cosmetics, magnifying mirrors, and both terry-cloth and cotton robes.

1–8–50 Temmabashi, Kita-ku Osaka 530-0042. ℂ **06/6881-1111.** Fax 06/6881-1200. 390 units. ¥25,000–¥31,000 ($208–$258) single; ¥30,000–¥36,000 ($250–$300) double or twin; Imperial floor from ¥26,000 ($217) single. AE, DC, JCB, MC, V. Station: JR Sakuranomiya west exit (5 min.); or Osaka Station north exit, free shuttle every 20 min. (more on weekends). **Amenities:** 8 restaurants, 2 bars; golf driving range (¥5,000/$42); Osaka's largest state-of-the-art health club with 3 outdoor tennis courts, 25-meter indoor pool, spa, Jacuzzi and sauna (fee: ¥2,000/$17 in the morning, ¥5,000/$42 in the afternoon); children's day-care center; concierge; business center; shopping arcade; salon; barbershop; 24-hr. room service; in-room massage; same-day laundry/dry cleaning service; nonsmoking floor; executive-level rooms; medical clinic; free bicycles (the castle is a 10-min. ride away). In room: A/C, cable TV with pay movies, fax, dataport, minibar, hot-water pot with tea, hair dryer, safe, bathroom scale, washlet toilet.

Inexpensive

Hotel International House Osaka (Value)   The International House is a facility used for international seminars, conventions, and meetings. It includes this hotel, used mainly by those attending seminars but also open to the public—try to book well in advance. Rooms are spartan with about as much personality as those in a business hotel, but they have everything you need, including tiny tiled bathrooms, yukata, and a small desk (there are no hair dryers in rooms, but ask for a loaner at the front). Some 40 of the 50 rooms are singles, making this a great choice for the single traveler. Note, however, that there's a midnight curfew.

8–2–6 Uehommachi, Tennoji-ku, Osaka 543-0001. ℂ **06/6773-8181.** Fax 06/6773-0777. 52 units. ¥6,500 ($54) single; ¥12,000 ($100) twin. Closed Dec 29–Jan3 and Aug 14–15. AE, DC, JCB, MC, V. Station: Uehommachi on the Kintetsu Line (5 min.); or the Tanimachi 9-chome (8 min.) or Shitennoji-mae subway station (5 min.). **Amenities:** 1 restaurant (Western), 1 cafe; same-day laundry/dry cleaning service. In room: A/C, cable TV, hot-water pot with tea.

WHERE TO DINE

There's a saying among Japanese that whereas a Kyotoite will spend his last yen on a fine kimono, an Osakan will spend it on food. You don't have to spend a lot of money, however, to enjoy good food in Osaka. Local specialties include *Oshi-zushi* (pressed square-shaped sushi), **udon** noodles with white soy sauce, and *takoyaki* (wheat-flour dumplings with octopus).

Osaka is probably best-known, however, for *okonomiyaki*, which literally means "as you like it." Its origins date from about 1700 when a type of thin flour pancake cooked on a hotplate and filled with miso paste was served during Buddhist ceremonies. It wasn't until this century that it became popular, primarily during food shortages, and gradually, other ingredients such as pork, egg, and vegetables were added. Today, Osaka is literally riddled with inexpensive okonomiyaki restaurants.

⌒Kids Family-Friendly Restaurants

Sushi Kyu (Ise, *p. 364*)   From the 100-year-old building to the kimono-attired cashier adding with his abacus, everything about this Japanese restaurant will take the kids back in time. The only modern touch is the special child's plate geared to please young palates.

Capricciosa (Osaka, *p. 395*)   Spaghetti and pizza are the specialties at this casual, inexpensive restaurant that's popular with both students and families.

Cui-daore (Osaka, *p. 396*)   This place pleases parents with its inexpensive meals, wide variety, and English menu, while the little ones are won over by the mechanical clown outside the front door and the kid's meal with toy.

Hard Rock Cafe (Nagoya, *p. 355*; Osaka, *p. 397*; Kobe, *p. 409*)   When nothing but a burger will do, take your grumbling teenager to this well-known rock 'n' roll chain for some "real" food (and maybe a T-shirt, too).

Old Spaghetti Factory (Kobe, *p. 410*)   Inexpensive set meals that include ice cream and soft drinks in the price, and a large choice of spaghetti dinners make this airy, casual place perfect for families.

AROUND OSAKA STATION
Expensive
⑫⑤ **Kaen** ★★★ FRENCH KAISEKI   This refined, modern restaurant, with seating for only 32 lucky diners, serves only set meals, which change once a month. The food is French, but each course is served in the kaiseki manner: separately, using Japanese plates and dishes; diners use chopsticks instead of forks. Each plate is chosen to enhance the food according to color, texture, and the seasons. Highly recommended.

Steak Ron Building, 3rd floor, 1–10–2 Sonnezaki-shinchi. © **06/6344-2929.** Reservations recommended. Set dinners ¥6,000–¥15,000 ($50–$125); set lunches ¥2,500–¥5,000 ($21–$42). AE, DC, JCB, MC, V. Mon–Sat 11:30am–2pm and 5–9pm (last order). Station: JR Kitashinchi (1 min.) or Nishi-Umeda (5 min.). South of Osaka Station across from the Ekimae Dai-Ni (Dai-2) Building.

Moderate
Enoteca ★ CONTINENTAL   Sharing quarters with a wine shop, this restaurant specializes in meals that complement our favorite form of the grape. A non-fussy decor and reasonably priced, tasty food drew us in (okay, so the wine had something to do with it). The menu runs the gamut from the classic *croque monsieur* (¥700/$5.85) and scallops with three kinds of pepper to beef stew and grilled chicken with balsamic sauce. Daily wine selections start at ¥450 ($3.35) by the glass; bottles begin at ¥2,600 ($22).

Herbis, 2nd floor, 2–5–25 Umeda. © **06/6343-7175.** Main dishes ¥700–¥1,000 ($5.85–$8.35). AE, DC, JCB, MC, V. Daily 11am–9:30pm (last order). Stations: Nishi-Umeda (3 min.). South of Osaka Station in the Herbis complex adjacent to The Ritz-Carlton.

Inexpensive
Jidoritei Yakitori Shin Miura ★ YAKITORI   Takimikoji Village, located in the same building as the Floating Garden Observatory (see "Seeing the Sights,"

earlier in this chapter), is a re-created Showa-Era 1920s–30s Japanese village, boasting everything from an old-fashioned sweets shop and a barbershop to a post office and a miniature shrine. There are also about a dozen restaurants here—branches of well-known Osaka establishments—serving okonomiyaki, kushikatsu, teppanyaki, noodles, and more. Most lunches cost less than ¥1,000 ($8.35) and dinners less than ¥2,000 ($17), making it very popular with those who work in the area. Among the choices, Jidoritei Yakitori Shin Miura is one of our favorites, offering three kinds of lunch teishoku (try the *donburi obento*, yakitori on rice with side dishes) and three yakitori dinner courses.

Takimikoji Village, Umeda Sky Building basement, 1–1–90 Oyodo-naka. 𝒞 **06/6440-5957.** Yakitori dinners ¥1,500 and ¥3,500 ($12.50 and $29); lunch teishoku ¥650–¥850 ($5.40–$7.10). AE, DC, JCB, MC, V. Daily 10am–2pm and 5–10:30pm. Station: Osaka or Umeda (11 min.).

Okonomiyaki Madonna OKONOMIYAKI   At this modern okonomiyaki restaurant with a young and friendly staff, ingredients change with the seasons but may include pork, beef, squid, octopus, shrimp, potato, mushroom, or oyster. Fried noodles are also available. Single diners will feel comfortable sitting around a counter watching food being prepared. Very casual.

Hilton Plaza, 1–8–8 Umeda. 𝒞 **06/6347-7371.** Set meals ¥1,200–¥2,800 ($10–$23). AE, DC, JCB, MC, V. Daily 11am–9:30pm (last order). Station: Umeda or Nishi-Umeda (2 min.), Osaka (4 min.). In the basement of Hilton Plaza (next to the Osaka Hilton hotel).

AROUND OSAKA CASTLE
Moderate

Trader Vic's INTERNATIONAL   This is a great lunch choice for Osaka Castle sightseers. Decorated in Polynesian style typical of Trader Vic's around the world, it offers dining with a view of the castle, the park, and the river. There's a lunch special (served Mon–Sat until 2:45pm) for ¥1,500 ($12.50), as well as alacarte lunch selections that include hamburgers, club sandwiches, pasta, and other international fare. Or come for the Sunday champagne brunch (served 11:30am–2:45pm), when for ¥1,000 ($8.35) extra you can drink unlimited sparkling wine. Dinners offer a wider, and more expensive, selection, including salads, a good selection of vegetable side dishes, curries, steaks, seafood, barbecued chicken, and Chinese dishes. There's an extensive cocktail menu.

New Otani Hotel, 1–4 Shiromi. 𝒞 **06/6941-1111.** Main dinner courses ¥6,500–¥9,500 ($54–$79); set lunch ¥1,500–¥3,500 ($12.50–$29); Sun brunch ¥3,500 ($29) adults, ¥2,000 ($17) children 7–12, ¥1,000 ($8.35) children 3–6. AE, DC, JCB, MC, V. Daily 11:30am–11:45pm. Station: Osakajo-Koen on the JR Loop Line (3 min.).

Inexpensive

Panorama Beer Restaurant Asahi *(Value)* VARIED WESTERN   For an inexpensive meal near the castle and a view of the city, head for this beer restaurant offering steak, lamb, and fried shrimp, as well as vegetarian dishes such as an eggplant, tomato and zucchini stew. Set lunches are a bargain and come with salad, rice, vegetables and all-you-can-drink tea, coffee or juice. And of course, you can also enjoy a mug of Asahi beer.

IMP Building, 26th floor, 1–3–7 Shiromi Chuo-ku. 𝒞 **06/6946-2595.** Main dishes ¥750–¥980 ($6.25–$8.15); set lunches ¥780–¥980 ($6.50–$8.15). AE, DC, JCB, MC, V. Daily 11:30am–2pm and 4:30–11pm. Subway: Osaka Business Park (1 min.); JR train: Osakajo-Koen (4 min.). In Osaka Business Park, across from the New Otani Hotel.

NAMBA

Dotombori (or Dotonbori), a narrow pedestrian lane just off Midosuji Dori that flanks the south bank of the Dotonbori Canal, is the center of Osaka's most famous nightlife district, which radiates out from Dotombori on both sides of the canal; you'll find lots of restaurants and bars here.

Expensive

Arc en Ciel ★★★ FRENCH/VARIED ASIAN   Towering 36 floors above the Namba nightlife district, this is a sophisticated venue for dining, enjoying live music, and taking in the panoramic view. In the evening, only seven-course French meals that change monthly are offered in the main dining room; the dinner for two (¥20,000/$167) includes half a bottle of wine, table charge, service charge, and tax. Diners with smaller appetites can opt for a la carte selections such as steak or seafood (¥2,400–¥3,500/$20–$29) in the lounge. More reasonable is the all-you-can-eat lunch buffets of French and Asian food; add ¥900 ($7.50) and you can also drink white wine and beer to your heart's content.

Nankai South Tower Hotel, 36th floor, 5–1–60 Namba. ✆ 06/6646-1111. Set dinner ¥12,000 ($100), set dinner for 2 ¥20,000 ($167); lunch buffet ¥3,300 ($27.50), but ¥300 ($2.50) extra Sat, Sun, and holidays. AE, DC, JCB, MC, V. Daily 11:15am–2:30pm and 5:30–8:30pm. Bar open daily 5:30pm–midnight; cover charge ¥1,200/$10 (free to hotel guests). Station: Namba Nankai (1 min.).

Moderate

⑫⑥ **Kani Doraku** CRAB   Specializing in *kani* (crab), this restaurant is difficult to miss—it has a huge model crab on its facade, moving its legs and claws. Part of a chain originating in Osaka a couple of decades ago, this is the main shop of more than 50 locations through-out Japan including another one just down the street at 1–6–2 Dotonbori (✆ **06/6211-1633**). Dishes range from crab-suki, crab-chiri (a kind of crab sukiyaki), and fried crab dishes to crab croquette, roasted crab with salt, crab salad, crab sushi, and boiled king crab. This main location occupies several floors, with some tables offering a view of the water.

1–6–18 Dotonbori. ✆ 06/6211-8975. Set dinners ¥4,800–¥10,000 ($40–$83); set lunches ¥2,500–¥3,500 ($21–$29). AE, DC, JCB, MC, V. Daily 11am–11pm. Station: Namba (exit 14, 2 min.). On Dotonbori beside the Ebisu-bashi Bridge.

⑫⑦ **Ekuusu** ★★★ *Finds* FRENCH-ASIAN CROSSOVER   There's room for only 15 blessed diners at this casual restaurant, who are treated to French food made with Asian ingredients, created by the chef-owner and served by his wife. The daily selections are written in Japanese on a stand-up blackboard at the entrance (look for it when searching for the restaurant); it's probably easiest to indicate how much you want to spend and your meal will be prepared accordingly. Everything is delicious, so you can't go wrong. Examples of past menus include a tomato and avocado salad with smoked shellfish and caviar, whole seabream with a roasted mushroom topping and herb cream sauce, and roast beef stuffed with vegetables. Typical French music (like Edith Piaf) plays in the background. Highly recommended.

Kamiya Building 2nd floor, 1–3–14 Domtonbori. ✆ 06/6213-6237. Reservations recommended weekends. Main dishes ¥1,200–¥2,600 ($10–$22). AE, DC, V. Mon–Sat 5:30–11pm. Subway: Nipponbashi (3 min.) Go east on Dotonbori to the Aioibashi Bridge and turn right; it's halfway down the block on your left.

Inexpensive

Capricciosa *Kids* PIZZA/PASTA   This chain restaurant is very popular with students and families for its huge portions large enough for two (I've never managed to finish a bowl of pasta alone) at inexpensive prices in a casual setting with

Italian decor. In addition to pizza and pasta (which is what most people order), the menu offers meat or fish daily specials like seafood risotto.

Namba Oriental Hotel Building, 2–8–17 Senichimae. ℭ **06/6644-8330.** Pizza and pasta ¥740–¥1,630 ($6.15–$14); main dishes ¥830–¥1,600 ($6.90–$13). AE, DC, MC, V. Daily 11am–10:30pm. Subway: Midosuji (exit 18, 5 min.).

Cui-daore ★★*Kids* VARIED JAPANESE   Cui-daore is famous for its clown model outside the front door, which began beating a drum and wiggling its eyebrows shortly after the place first opened in 1950. The restaurant's name means to "eat your way to bankruptcy" in reference to the Osakan joy of eating, but a look at the prices in the extensive plastic-food display case shows you can dine very reasonably here on a great variety of food ranging from tempura and yakitori to sushi, shabu-shabu, kaiseki, and even Western food. What's more, the restaurant is very user-friendly; items in the display cases are identified in English and by number for easy ordering, and there's also an English menu.

Altogether, there are eight floors of dining, and prices increase the higher up you go. On the ground floor is a modern, family-style dining area, serving everything from chicken curry and rice to a mixed seafood set. If you want to try Osaka's version of sushi, try the ¥1,000 ($8.35) combo. From the clown outside to the food inside, this is a great place to bring youngsters; a child's set meal (¥800/$6.65) includes a pair of black glasses just like the clown's. On the second floor is an *izakaya,* or Japanese-style pub, open from 4pm where you can order a beer, yakitori, and snacks. In winter, the third floor serves *nabe* (one-pot stews) in a quiet and comfortable setting, while the top floors have sukiyaki, shabu-shabu, and kaiseki meals that change monthly (kaiseki courses begin at ¥4,000/$33).

1–8–25 Dotonbori. ℭ **06/6211-5300.** Set meals ¥650–¥5,000 ($5.40–$42). AE, DC, JCB, MC, V. Daily 11am–10pm. Station: Namba (exit 14, 2 min.).

⑫⑧ **Fugetsu** OKONOMIYAKI   Big Step is the biggest shopping complex in America-Mura, young Osakans' favorite place to shop for American clothing. As such, this branch of a famous okonomiyaki restaurant appeals to young diners with its hip, modern interior, pop music, and individual booths for dining. I recommend the squid, octopus, and pork yakisoba (fried noodles) or the *butatama,* an okonomiyaki with pork and egg.

The main shop, with the same menu and open daily from 11:30am to 10pm, is a stark contrast to the America-Mura branch, with a real *shitamachi* downtown atmosphere. It's at 2–18 Ajiharacho Tennoji-ku (ℭ **06/6771-7938**), just a minute's walk from Tsuruhashi Station on the JR Loop Line. To find it, take the west exit (nishiguchi), go straight, and turn right at the second alleyway. In the Bay area you'll find Fugetsu in Universal CityWalk (ℭ **06/6463-0030**), open 11am to 10pm.

Big Step, 3rd floor, 1–6–14 Nishi Shinsaibashi. ℭ **06/6258-5189.** Okonomiyaki ¥550–¥950 ($4.60–$7.90); yakisoba ¥580–¥1,100 ($4.85–$9.15). AE, MC, V. Daily 11am–9:30pm (last order). Station: Shinsaibashi (2 min.).

La Bamba MEXICAN   Good for a quick fix if you're craving Mexican food, this tiny restaurant offers all the classics, from mole poblano and enchiladas to burritos, tostados, and tacos, as well as a vegetarian plate of chile relenos and cheese enchiladas. A basket of small chips and sauce arrive at your table free, and Mexican beers start at ¥600 ($5).

2–3–23 Dotonbori. ℭ **06/6213-9612.** Main dishes ¥500–¥1,680 ($4.15–$14); combination platters ¥1,350–¥2,200 ($11–$18). AE, JCB, MC, V. Tues–Fri 5–11pm; Sat–Sun 2–11pm. Station: Namba (5 min.). On the west end of Dotombori (west of Midosuji Dori) just past the Dotonbori Hotel.

Namaste ★★ INDIAN   This is a good place for hot and spicy Indian food, including tandoori and chicken, mutton, prawn, fish, and vegetable curries. The owner, who will wait on you, is so friendly and happy, one might think he's reached nirvana. You can reach yours by telling him how hot to make your food. The set lunches are a particularly great deal.

Rose Building 3–7–28 Minami Semba. ✆ 06/6241-6515. Main dishes ¥700–¥1,500 ($5.85–$12.50); set dinners ¥2,800–¥4,300 ($23–$36); set lunches ¥750–¥1,800 ($6.25–$15). AE, DC, MC, V. Daily 11:30am–3pm and 5:30–11pm. Station: Shinsaibashi (exit 1, 3 min.). Located just off Shinsaibashi-Suji, a covered pedestrian shopping street that parallels Midosuji Dori to the east, 3 blocks north of the Sony Tower building.

⑫⑨ **Tachibana** TOFU/VARIED JAPANESE   Whether you are sightseeing in Dotombori or viewing Kabuki, this restaurant, in a lovely, typical Japanese setting in the basement of the Shochikuza Theatre, is a good pick. A microbrewery (¥380/$3.15 for a glass of light or dark beer), Tachibana specializes in tofu, and most of the set meals include a dish of tofu. A changing daily lunch or a tempura teishoku are affordable and delicious. You can see famous Kabuki actors dining here, but how could you recognize them without their makeup?

Osaka Shochikuza Theater, 2nd basement, 1–9–19 Dotomburi. ✆ 06/6212-6074. Main dishes ¥480–¥1,300 ($4–$11); set dinners ¥2,300–¥5,300 ($19–$44); set lunches ¥1,050–¥2,500 ($8.75 and $21). AE, DC, JCB, MC, V. Daily 11am–2am. Station: Namba (exit 14, 2 min.).

OSAKA BAY AREA

In addition to the choices below, Universal CityWalk has lots of restaurants, most of which are open daily from 11am to 10pm, including **Bubba Gump's** (✆ 06/4804-3880), **Wolfgang Puck Cafe** (✆ 06/6465-7000), and a branch of Osaka's-own okomiyaki restaurant, **Fugetsu** (see above).

Moderate

Hard Rock Cafe *Kids*   This well-known rock 'n' roll restaurant, bar, and shop fits right in at the very popular Universal CityWalk complex. You'll find everything you expect from a Hard Rock here: rock music, lots of music memorabilia, T-shirts for sale, and a menu of burgers, steaks, sandwiches, and barbecue chicken. Despite the hype, the food is good and plentiful.

Universal CityWalk, 6–2–61 Shimaya, Konohana-ku ✆ 06/4804-3870. Main dishes ¥1,300–¥3,000 ($11–$25). Sun–Thurs 11am–11pm; Fri–Sat 11am–4am. Station: Universal City (3 min.).

Inexpensive

Sun Tempo PASTA/PIZZA   This casual, airy, and down-to-earth restaurant, with some tables offering a view of the harbor, is convenient if you're visiting the Suntory Museum or nearby Osaka Aquarium. The pasta is freshly made, but by far the best deal is the all-you-can-eat salad bar for a mere ¥300 ($2.50) on weekdays and ¥500 ($4.15) on weekends. After eating, you might want to retire to the museum's ninth-floor Sky Lounge (open Tues–Sun 11am–11pm), offering cocktails, beer, a limited menu, and views of the harbor.

Suntory Museum, Tempozan Harbour Village, 1–5–10 Kaigandori. ✆ 06/6577-0009. Pizza and pasta ¥900–¥1,400 ($7.50–$12). AE, DC, JCB, MC, V. Tues–Sun 11am–9pm. Closed when the museum is closed. Station: Osakako (5 min.).

OSAKA AFTER DARK
PERFORMING ARTS

BUNRAKU   The **National Bunraku Theater,** 1–12–10 Nipponbashi, Chuoku (✆ 06/6212-2531 for information; 06/6212-1122 for reservations), was completed in 1984 as the only theater in Japan dedicated to Japanese traditional puppet theater. Productions are staged five times a year, with most productions running for 2 to 3 weeks at a time and held daily from 11am. When Bunraku is not being performed, other traditional performing arts are often shown, including classical Japanese music. English programs are available. To find out whether a performance is being held, check *Meet Osaka* or contact one of the visitor information centers (see "Essentials," earlier in this chapter). Tickets usually run ¥4,600 to ¥5,800 ($38–$48) for adults; discounts are available for students and children. The National Bunraku Theater is located east of Namba and the Dotombori entertainment district, a 3-minute walk from exit 7 of Nipponbashi Station.

KABUKI   The **Osaka Shochikuza,** 1–9–19 Dotombori, Chuo-ku (✆ **06/ 6214-2211**), was built more than 50 years ago but was remodeled in 1997 as part of a revival of interest in Kabuki. Traditional kabuki is performed in January, July, and some other months of the year (the schedule changes yearly), and performances start usually at 11am and 4:30pm, with tickets averaging ¥4,200 ($35). Performance information is also listed in *Meet Osaka*. The theater is located on Dotombori just west of Ebisu-bashi Bridge.

THE BAR SCENE

Osaka's liveliest—and most economical—nightlife district radiates out from a narrow pedestrian lane called **Dotombori** (or Dotonbori), which flanks the south bank of the Dotonbori Canal. About a 2-minute walk from exit 14 of Namba Station or less than a 10-minute walk from Shinsaibashi Station, it's lined with restaurants and drinking establishments and is good for a lively evening stroll even if you don't wish to stop anywhere.

Bar Isn't It?   Part of a chain, Bar Isn't It? employs a *gaijin* (foreign) staff and attracts a mainly young Japanese clientele with its low prices—all food and drinks cost ¥500 ($4.15). No money is wasted on decor, and seating is at bar stools around dozens of high tables, but after midnight, it's standing room only. Live DJ sounds range from reggae to rock, and although there's no cover charge per se, on weekends there's a door charge of ¥1,000 ($8.35), which includes two drink tickets, apparently to keep out lowlifes who want to join in the fun but don't want to drink. There's another Bar Isn't It? near Shinsaibashi Station at 1–38–11 Shinsaibashi-Suji (✆ **06/6120-3861**), open nightly and also with a ¥1,000 ($8.35) door charge on weekends. Kakusho Building, 5th floor, 7–7 Doyamacho. ✆ **06/6363-4001.** Daily 6pm–2am, Fri–Sat to 4am. Station: Osaka, Umeda, or Higashi Umeda (10 min.). On the 5th floor above Shakey's, east of Osaka Station on Shin-Midosuji Ave. beside the Hankyu-Higashi Dori shopping street.

Jazz & Bar Nouveau   Lovers of jazz congregate at this live-music venue, fitted with art-nouveau-style lamps and cozy booths. In addition to the house trio, there's an open mike for vocalists wishing to belt out standard jazz tunes. A limited menu lists sandwiches and snacks. 1–8–3 Sonezaki Shinchi ✆ **06/6341-0348.** Cover ¥5,100 ($42.50), plus one dish and one drink minimum. Mon–Sat 6pm–2am. Subway: Higashi Umeda (5 min.); south of the station, off Midosuji Dori.

Murphy's   Of Osaka's several Irish pubs, this is probably the most popular (and our favorite), drawing a mixed crowd of both Japanese and foreigners and offering live Irish music on Wednesdays. Fish-and-chips or shepherd's pie are reasonable and surprisingly good, but you can also make a meal of the Guinness or Killkenny Ale. Lead Plaza Building, 6th floor, 1–6–31 Higashi Shinsaibashi. ✆ **06/ 6282-0677.** Mon–Thurs 5pm–1am; Fri–Sat 5pm to about 3am. Station: Nagahoribashi (1 min.) or Shinsaibashi (4 min.). On Suzuki St. 1 block north of Europa Dori, just west of the Minami Police Office, in a small building with lots of tiny bars.

Pig and Whistle   This is probably the best-known and one of the oldest expatriate bars in Osaka. Through the years, the number of foreign customers has fallen to less than 30% (I remember when it was almost exclusively foreign), but remaining are its friendly atmosphere, dartboards for entertainment, and munchies that include, of course, fish-and-chips.

There's also a branch in Umeda south of Osaka Station at 2–5 Sonezaki (© **06/6361-3198;** open daily 5pm to midnight). Across Building, 2nd floor, 2–6–14 Shinsaibashi-Suji. © **06/6213-6911.** Sun–Thurs 5pm–midnight; Fri–Sat 5pm–1am. Station: Namba or Shinsaibashi (4 min.). On Midosuji Street, near the Holiday Inn.

Sam & Dave   With exposed, wrapped pipes, fluorescent lighting, and a pool table, this bar with a dance floor and pool table also stages events several times a month, including performance art and poetry readings. Tuesday night is salsa night. It attracts both a Japanese and gaijin crowd.

Attracting a larger foreign clientele is **Sam & Dave Five** in Nagahoribashi, across from the post office (© **06/6251-5333**), which has an even bigger dance floor; upscale **Sam & Dave Two** Shinsaibashi, one block north of Sogo department store and one block east of Midosuji St (© **06/6243-6848**), is the hot spot for up-and-coming DJ's, with live bands performing most Saturdays. Plaza Umeshin Building, 4–15–19 Nishi-tenma. © **06/6365-1688.** Fri and Sat ¥1,000 ($8.35) cover, which includes 1 drink. Mon–Thurs 7pm–4am; Fri–Sat 7pm–5am; Sun 7pm–2am. Station: JR Kitashinchi (2 min.), Umeda (5 min.), Osaka (7 min.). SE of Osaka Station in a triangle-shaped parcel of land where Midosuji Dori curves southward before crossing the river and Nakanoshima Island.

(130) **Tosca**   Newcomers to Japan are forgiven for thinking that a *sunaku* ("snack") would be a good place to get a bite to eat. A *sunaku* is actually a drinking establishment, usually a small affair with a *mama-san* (female owner or manager) who coddles her clients, mostly men who stop regularly for drinks after work. Since outsiders must usually be introduced by an acquaintance to gain admittance, foreign visitors rarely get a glimpse into the world of *sunaku*. But the mama-san at Tosca happily welcomes foreign visitors and likes trying out her English, so even lone females will have a relaxed evening here. The convivial atmosphere is also good for meeting other customers; there's room for only 12. The mama-san serves snacks, pours drinks, smiles, and chats from behind the bar, never missing a beat. The bar's name stems from the fact that the mama-san is an accomplished pianist, but the only music here is **karaoke,** and as the evening wears on, even shy guests take a turn with the machine. The cover charge is waived for readers of this book, but there's a ¥500 ($4.15) snack charge, drinks cost ¥500 ($4.15), and karaoke is ¥200 ($1.65) a song. Senju Building basement, 1–6 Senmichimae. © **06/6211-1387.** Mon–Sat 7pm–midnight. Closed holidays. Station: Namba (exit 14, 2 min.). South of Dotombori in the block to the southeast of the Kadoza Building and on the same street as the tiny Hozenji Shrine. From Ebisu-bashi Bridge, walk east on Dotombori to the 2nd large crab, turn right, and walk down the covered shopping arcade to the 2nd alley left; it's down this narrow street on the left side in the 2nd block.

5 Kobe

584km (365 miles) W of Tokyo; 75km (47 miles) W of Kyoto; 31km (19 miles) W of Osaka

In January 1995, the world was riveted by news of one of the worst natural disasters of that decade: the Great Hanshin Earthquake that struck Kobe, killing more than 6,000 people and destroying much of the city. In the years since, Kobe has risen from the ashes with more attractions, hotels, and urban redevelopment than ever before and with only a few telltale signs of the city's grimmest hours. Indeed, if it weren't for an earthquake memorial, museum exhibitions, and a few remaining condemned buildings with cracked walls, visitors would never guess at the devastation of fewer than 10 years ago.

Blessed with the calm waters of the Seto Inland Sea, Kobe (the capital of Hyogo Prefecture) has served Japan as an important port town for centuries. Even today, its port is the heart of the city, its raison d'être. One of the first ports to begin accepting foreign traders in 1868 following Japan's 2 centuries of isolation, this vibrant city of 1½ million inhabitants is quite multicultural, with foreigners from almost 100 different nations residing here. Each group of immigrants has brought with them a rich heritage, and there are a number of fine restaurants serving every kind of cuisine—Western, Chinese, Korean, and Indian—as well as many steak houses offering that famous local delicacy, Kobe beef.

Equally famous is Kobe's wonderful nightlife, crammed into a small, navigable, and rather intimate quarter of neon lights, cozy bars, brawling pubs, and sophisticated nightclubs. As one resident of Kobe told me, "We don't have a lot of tourist sights in Kobe, so we make up for it in nightlife." Yet the attractions Kobe does offer are unique to Japan, including a neighborhood of Western-style residences built around the turn of the 20th century and a museum devoted to fashion. The people of Kobe are also proud of the 1998 opening of the world's longest suspension bridge, Akashi Kaikyo, one of a series of bridges linking Honshu with Shikoku.

ESSENTIALS

GETTING THERE **By Plane** If you're arriving at Kansai International Airport (KIX; see "Getting There," under Osaka, earlier in this chapter), there are several options for travel onward to Kobe. Fastest and most dramatic is to take a 3-minute shuttle to the Port Terminal ferry pier, where you can board the **K-Jet hydrofoil** for the 25-minute trip to the **Kobe City Air Terminal** (K-CAT; on your return you can check in here if you're flying ANA or JAL), located on Port Island. Departures are once or twice an hour. A shuttle bus from K-CAT to Sannomiya Station in the heart of Kobe is included in the fare of ¥2,400 ($20).

There are also **Limousine buses** departing KIX every 20 minutes bound for Sannomiya Station, costing ¥1,800 ($15) one-way and taking about 70 minutes. If you want to use your **Japan Rail Pass,** take a kaisoku (rapid train stopping only at major stops) to Osaka Station and change there for the JR Kobe Line's 20-minute ride to Sannomiya Station. If you're staying in a hotel closer to Shin-Kobe Station, take the JR Haruka train from the airport to Shin-Osaka Station and transfer there for a speedy Shinkansen connection to Shin-Kobe Station (see the Osaka section earlier in this chapter for detailed information).

By Train The **Shinkansen** bullet train takes 3¼ hours from Tokyo, 31 minutes from Kyoto, and about 14 minutes from Osaka; the fare from Tokyo for an unreserved seat is ¥13,760 ($115). All Shinkansen trains arrive at **Shin-Kobe Station,** which is linked to **Sannomiya Station** (considered the heart of the city) via a 3-minute subway ride (or a 20-min. walk). If you're arriving from nearby Osaka, Himeji, or Okayama, it may be easiest to take a local train stopping at Sannomiya Station if you're staying in one of the area's hotels.

By Bus Buses depart from Tokyo Station's Yaesu south exit for Kobe every night at 10:40, arriving in Kobe at 8:45am. The one-way fare is ¥8,690 ($72).

VISITOR INFORMATION   There are tourist information offices at **Shin-Kobe Station** (✆ **078/241-9550;** open daily 10am–6pm) and near **Sannomiya Station,** across the street and to the right from the south exit, on Flower Road (✆ **078/322-0220;** open daily 9am–7pm). The English-speaking staff can provide maps and sightseeing information and make hotel reservations. Limited tourist information is available online at www.city.kobe.jp/.

Information on Kobe's sights, festivals, and attractions appears in the monthly *Kansai Time Out,* available at bookstores, restaurants, and tourist-oriented locations for ¥300 ($2.50).

INTERNET ACCESS   A 6-minute walk from JR Sannomiya Station's east exit, **Kinko's,** behind Tokyu Inn at 4–2–2 Kumoidori (✆ **078/291-6731**), is open 24 hours and charges ¥200 ($1.65) per 10 minutes of Internet time. Although not as convenient, **Hyogo International Plaza,** 1–5–1 Kaigandori, Wakinohama, Chuo-ku (✆ **078/230-3060;** open Mon–Fri 9am–8pm, Sat 9am–5pm), a 10-minute walk from Nada Station, offers free Internet access.

ORIENTATION & GETTING AROUND   Squeezed in between hills rising in the north and the shores of the Seto Inland Sea to the south, Kobe stretches some 18 miles along the coastline, but in many places, it's less than 2 miles wide. It's made up of many wards (ku) such as Nada-ku, Chuo-ku and Hyogo-ku. The heart of the city lies around Sannomiya, Motomachi, and Kobe stations in the **Chuo-ku** (Central Ward). It's here you'll find the city's nightlife, its port, its restaurants, its shopping centers, and most of its hotels. Many of the major streets have names with signs posted in English.

Because the city isn't very wide, you can walk to most points north and south of Sannomiya Station. South of Sannomiya Station is the **Sannomiya Center Gai** covered-arcade shopping. North of Sannomiya Station are bars and restaurants clustered around narrow streets like **Higashimon Street.** Kitano-zaka leads to **Kitano-cho** with its Western-style houses, about a 15-minute walk north of Sannomiya Station. **Shin-Kobe Station** is a 20-minute walk north of Sannomiya. Running from Shin-Kobe Station south through Sannomiya all the way to the port is a flower-lined road—called, appropriately enough, **Flower Road.**

About a 10-minute walk west of Sannomiya Station is **Motomachi Station,** south of which lies the fashionable Motomachi covered-arcade shopping street, **Chinatown,** and Meriken Park. The next stop on the JR Line from Motomachi Station is **Kobe Station,** just south of which is **Harborland,** a waterfront region with hotels, restaurants, and the colorful Mosaic outdoor restaurant and shopping complex.

Because of restricted space, Kobe has constructed two artificial islands in its harbor, Port Island and Rokko Island.

A 13-kilometer **City Loop Line** bus, distinguishable by its old-fashioned appearance, passes all major attractions, including Kitano-cho, Chinatown, Meriken Park, and Harborland. Buses run every 15 to 20 minutes from about 9am to 6pm, with the route marked on the map distributed by the tourist office. It costs ¥250 ($2.10) for adults and ¥130 ($1.10) for children per ticket. A one-day pass, allowing you to get off and reboard as often as you like, costs ¥650 ($5.40) for adults and ¥330 ($2.75) for children.

You can also use the **JR Local Commuter Line,** which includes stops at Sannomiya, Motomachi, and Kobe stations, if you don't mind walking to destinations north and south of its stations (the City Loop Line buses will get you closer to major attractions). The subway is useful only for transportation between

Shin-Kobe and Sannomiya stations. The **Portliner Monorail** connects Sannomiya with Port Island, while the Rokko Liner travels between JR Sumiyoshi
Station and Rokko Island.

EXPLORING THE CITY

In addition to the sights below, ask the tourist office near Sannomiya Station
whether the next-door **Phoenix Plaza** (℃ **078/325-8558**) is still staging a special exhibit on the 1995 earthquake and its aftermath (it was slated to end in
2002 but may be extended). It's very informative and well documented in English; open free to the public daily 10am to 7pm.

KITANO-CHO

When Kobe was chosen as one of five international ports following the Meiji
Restoration, foreign traders and diplomats who settled here built homes in
much the same style as those they left behind in their native lands. Approximately 30 of these Western-style homes, called **ijinkan,** remain on a hill north
of Sannomiya Station called Kitano-cho. Because the area seems so exotic to
young Japanese, this is the number one draw for domestic visitors, who come
also to shop the area's many boutiques.

As of this writing, 22 Victorian- and Gothic-style homes are open to the public, many with lovely views of the sea from verandas and bay windows. Although
you may not be interested in visiting all of them, Kitano-cho is very pleasant for
an hour's stroll. It's located about a 15-minute walk north of Sannomiya Station
or a 10-minute walk west from Shin-Kobe Station. Or take the City Loop Line
to Kitano Ijinkan.

If all you want to do is take a quick look inside one of the former homes, the
Rhine no Yakata, 2–10–24 Kitano-cho (℃ **078/222-3403;** open Fri–Wed
9:30am–5pm), is open free of charge though it's unfurnished. Home of a
Frenchwoman, Madame Drewell, it's typical of European homes of the period
with an upper-floor sunroom overlooking the city and harbor.

Otherwise, the two I recommend are the **Moegi no Yakata,** 3–10–11 Kitano-
cho (℃ **078/222-3310;** open daily 9:30am–5pm in winter, 9am–6pm in summer; closed the 2nd Wed of every month), a pale-green, 100-year-old home
built for a former American consul general, Hunter Sharp, and filled with
antiques; and **Kasamidori-no-Yakata** ⚘, 3–13–3 Kitano-cho (℃ **078/
242-3223;** open daily 9:30am–5pm in winter, 9am–6pm in summer; closed 4th
Tues of every month), popularly referred to as the Weathercock House because
of its cock weathervane. This brick, 1909 residence was built by a German merchant and is probably Kobe's most famous home if not its most elaborate.
Admission to either home, located across from each other, is ¥300 ($2.50).

Finally, another home of note is **Uroko no Ie,** 2–20–4 Kitano-cho (℃ **078/
242-6530;** open daily 9am–6pm in summer, to 5pm in winter), which has a
castlelike exterior and contains lovely antiques, including Meissen porcelain and
Tiffany glass, as well as a small private museum of Western 18th- to 20th-
century art, with a few works by Andrew Wyeth, Utrillo, and others. Admission
is ¥1,000 ($8.35) for adults, ¥300 ($2.50) for children.

A GARDEN RETREAT   If you're a gardener, want a respite from city life, or
simply want to spend an hour in a cooler climate, take the Shin-Kobe ropeway
located next to Shin-Kobe Station for a 10-minute ride to the **Nunobiki Herb
Garden** ⚘ (℃ **078/271-1131**) with its lovely, meandering fragrant gardens

planted with various flowering shrubs and herbs and offering great views over Kobe. Be sure to take the ropeway to the end (don't get off at the first stop) and then walk downhill. It opens daily at 10am, closing at 5pm on weekdays, 8:30pm on Saturdays and during peak season (mid-July–August), and 7:30pm on Sundays (Dec–March, it closes daily at 4:30pm). It's closed the 2nd and 4th Monday of every month and for 2 weeks in February. Admission, including roundtrip by ropeway, is ¥1,200 ($12) for adults, half price for children.

CHINATOWN✿

Like the Kitano-cho area, **Chinatown** ✿ (called Nankin-machi), a 3-minute walk south of Motomachi Station (or to the Sakaemachi 1-chome stop on the City Loop Line bus), is worth a walk through for its lively street scene, with sidewalk vendors selling snacks and with open-fronted souvenir shops and produce stands. If the sidewalk vendors tempt you, eat your snack in the central square called **Nankin Park,** adorned with statues representing the animals of the 12-year Chinese astrological calendar. Chinatown's public rest room, called **Garyo-den,** which means "palace of a secluded wise man," is certainly one of Japan's most colorful—its outer wall is decorated with five-claw dragons and is based on a famous Chinese epic about a dragonlike hero; it's located a block off the main street. You may also want to come to Chinatown for a meal (see "Where to Dine," later in this chapter).

MERIKEN PARK

Meriken Park, a 10-minute walk south of Motomachi Station or a minute's walk from the Meriken Park stop on the City Loop Line bus, was established to commemorate the birthplace of Kobe Port. I find Kobe's port fascinating. Unlike many harbor cities where the port is located far from the center of town, Kobe's is right there, demanding attention and getting it. For a bird's-eye view of the whole operation, go to the **Kobe Port Tower** (✆ **078/391-6751**) on Nakatot-tei Pier (open daily 9am–8pm; to 6pm in winter, to 9pm in Aug). Opened in 1963, the tower is designed to resemble a Japanese drum, a cylindrical shape with the middle squeezed together. It's almost 600 feet tall, topped by a glass-enclosed five-story observatory.

Right beside the Port Tower is the **Kobe Maritime Museum,** 2–2 Hatobacho (✆ **078/391-6751;** Tues–Sun 10am–5pm), topped by a huge metal frame that resembles billowing sails or sea waves. Recounting the 130-year history of Kobe Port, it contains model ships, a "pilot room" complete with whistles and engine sounds, videos that explore Kobe's past and possible future, information on ports around the world, and a display of ancient vessels from a Venetian gondola to a South Pacific dugout canoe. But most interesting—and terrifying—are the English-language videos showing the aftermath of the 1995 earthquake with rampaging fires, buckled streets, overturned port containers, and crumpled buildings. You'll spend about an hour here.

A **combination ticket** for both the Port Tower and the Maritime Museum is ¥900 ($7.50) for adults, half-price for children. If you buy the tickets separately, they're ¥600 ($5) each for adults, half-price for kids.

By the way, on the eastern edge of Meriken Park is the **Port of Kobe Earthquake Memorial,** dedicated to the thousands of people who lost their lives. Established with the intent of preserving some of the quake's horrific force (298,000 buildings and homes were completely destroyed), it shows unrepaired damage, including tilted lampposts and a submerged and broken pier.

KOBE HARBORLAND

One of Kobe's newer leisure centers, Kobe Harborland is a fun place to stroll and browse. It's a few minutes' walk from either Kobe Station or Meriken Park, or you can take the City Loop Line to Harborland. For shopping, stop by Harbor Circus with its many boutiques or Kobe Hankyu department store, but best is **Mosaic,** an outdoor restaurant and shopping complex designed to resemble a Mediterranean village. Through the use of varying architectural and color schemes, it avoids the generic mall atmosphere, and by offering a diversity of ethnic goods and foods, it mirrors Kobe's international roots. Shops here are open daily from 11am to 8pm.

Beside it is **Mosaic Garden,** a small amusement park for younger children complete with kiddie rides, carousel, roller coaster, enclosed Ferris wheel, and games arcade. It's open from 11am to 10pm daily, with rides costing ¥300 to ¥600 ($2.50–$5).

MUSEUMS WORTH CHECKING OUT

Kobe Fashion Museum ★ *Finds*   Opened in 1997 and located on artificial Rokko Island, this is Japan's first museum devoted to fashion, housed in a contemporary, sophisticated setting that does justice to the high-brow costumes it contains. Temporary displays devoted to individual designers (there was a great show by John Galliano when I was there, in a setting designed by Japanese architect Tadao Ando) allow closer inspection than you could ever get at a fashion show. Other displays, which are imaginative tableaux complete with visual images, music, and lighting, may feature anything from 20th-century gowns by Christian Dior and Nina Ricci to extravagant Kabuki costumes or ethnic clothing worn by indigenous people from around the world. Displays change often, rotating the many costumes owned by the museum. In all, a very entertaining, unique museum, and a must-see if you're addicted to fashion and have an extra hour.

2–9 Koyocho-naka, Rokko Island. ℂ **078/858-0050.** Admission ¥500 ($4.15) adults, ¥250 ($2.10) children and senior citizens. Thurs–Tues 11am–6pm (to 8pm Fri). Take the local JR train to Sumiyoshi Station, transferring there for the Rokkoliner monorail to Island Center.

Hakutsuru Sake Brewery Museum ★   Everything you ever wanted to know about sake production is available at this former brewery, with English videos and pamphlets describing the various painstaking steps and comparing the old techniques to those used today. Hakutsuru, established in 1743, is one of many sake breweries in this part of Kobe; its actual brewery is now across the street (closed to the public). Plan on spending 45 minutes on your self-guided tour, which ends with hints on how to enjoy sake and—what would be a brewery tour without this?—free tastings.

4–5–5 Sumiyoshi-minami-machi, Higashinada-ku. ℂ **078/822-8907.** Admission free. Tues–Sun 9:30am–4:30pm. Station: Hanshin Sumiyoshi (5 min.); JR Sumiyoshi Station (15 min.)

WHERE TO STAY
EXPENSIVE

Hotel Okura Kobe ★★   This majestic 35-story hotel has the prestige of the Okura name, as well as a grand location right beside Meriken Park and the Port Tower within easy walking distance of the Motomachi covered shopping arcade and Chinatown. Its inviting lobby has views of a small garden (the only hotel garden in downtown Kobe), against a backdrop formed by the Maritime

Museum and the port. Each elegantly appointed room has all the comforts you'd expect of a first-class hotel. Pick up your phone and someone will answer "Yes, Ms. . . ." I like that kind of service (an appreciation shared apparently by the imperial family, who makes this their home base when in Kobe). As you'd expect, the best views are from those rooms facing the harbor; rooms on the 27th floor also offer highspeed Internet connection. *Tip*: Upon check in, ask for immediate free membership in the Okura Club International, which allows late check out, free use of the health club and indoor pool and other privileges.

2–1 Hatoba-cho, Chuo-ku, Kobe 650-8560. ℰ **800/526-2281** in the U.S. or 078/333-0111. Fax 078/333-6673. www.kobe.hotelokura.co.jp. 489 units. ¥14,000–¥21,000 ($117–$175) single; ¥20,000–¥36,000 ($167–$300) double or twin. AE, DC, JCB, MC, V. Station: Motomachi (10 min. south). Loop Line bus: Meriken Park (1 min.). **Amenities:** 5 restaurants, 2 bars; outdoor pool (fee: ¥1,000/$8.35); health club with gym, sauna and heated indoor lap pool (fee: ¥3,000–¥5,000/$25–$42); tennis courts; children's day-care center; concierge; tour desk; shopping arcade; salon; room service (7am–1am); in-room massage; same-day laundry/dry cleaning service; nonsmoking rooms. *In room:* A/C, cable TV with pay movies, minibar, hot-water pot with tea, hair dryer, bathroom scale, washlet toilet.

Portopia Hotel ⭐   Located on the artificial Port Island next to the convention center, this hotel caters primarily to the convention trade, except in summer when it's also popular with families. The most dramatic way to arrive here is via monorail—sleek, tall, and white, this hotel looks like some futuristic ship slicing through the landscape. Inside, it flaunts space and brightness with waterfalls, fountains, lots of brass, marble, and plants. Its rooms, whose large windows face either the sea or Kobe city (more popular for its night views), are elegantly designed with all the amenities. Rates are based on size and floor, with the best rooms (twins and doubles only) located in the south wing and boasting balconies. The main drawback to staying here is that it's a bit isolated from Kobe's center, though the monorail, with its interesting views of Kobe's port, is convenient, delivering passengers to Sannomiya Station. Even more convenient is the free shuttle service every 20 minutes to Sannomiya (10 min.) and Shin-Kobe stations (15 min.).

6–10–1 Minatojima, Nakamachi, Chuo-ku, Kobe 650-0046. ℰ **800/223-5652** in the U.S. and Canada or 078/302-1111. Fax 078/302-6877. www.portopia.co.jp. 778 units. ¥9,000–¥17,000 ($75–$142) single; ¥19,000–¥30,000 ($158–$250) twin or double. AE, DC, JCB, MC, V. Free shuttle service every 20 min. from Sannomiya and Shin-Kobe stations. Portliner monorail: 10 min. from Sannomiya Station to Shimin Hiroba Station (1 min.). **Amenities:** 10 restaurants, 3 bars; indoor and outdoor pools (fees: ¥2,000/$17 and ¥1,200/$10 respectively); health club with sauna (fee: ¥3,000/$25); tennis court; concierge; tour desk; business center; shopping arcade; salon; room service (6:30am–1am); in-room massage; same-day laundry/dry cleaning service; nonsmoking rooms. *In room:* A/C bilingual cable TV with pay movies; dataport, minibar, hot-water pot with tea, hair dryer, washlet toilet.

Shinkobe Oriental Hotel   This hotel is directly connected to Shin-Kobe Station—very convenient if you're arriving by Shinkansen. Rising 37 stories, it offers great views of Kobe and the bay or the Rokko mountains from fully equipped but rather plain rooms. Rates are based on room size and floor, with top floors commanding the grandest views. A plus is the large mall occupying the first four floors with many additional choices in dining.

1 Kitano-cho, Chuo-ku, Kobe 650-0002. ℰ **078/291-1121.** Fax 078/291-1154. 600 units. ¥13,000–¥19,000 ($108–$158) single; ¥23,000–¥34,000 ($192–$283) twin; ¥23,000–¥30,000 ($192–$250) double. AE, DC, JCB, MC, V. Station: Shin-Kobe (1 min.). **Amenities:** 9 restaurants, 2 bars; health club with indoor pool and sauna (fee: ¥5,000/$42); shopping arcade; salon; room service (6am–11am and 5pm–midnight); in-room massage; same-day laundry/dry cleaning service; nonsmoking rooms. *In room:* A/C, satellite TV with pay movies, minibar, hot-water pot with tea, hair dryer, washlet toilet.

MODERATE

Hotel Grand Vista ⭐⭐ 𝘝𝘢𝘭𝘶𝘦   A friendly, native-English-speaking staff greets you at this small and intimate boutique-like hotel, very conveniently located on the hill southwest of Shin-Kobe Station and near Kitano-cho, about a 15-minute walk from Sannomiya Station. The man who runs this place spent a lot of time in California and is eager to welcome foreigners. Guests with dimming eyesight will find communal reading glasses at the front desk to help with check-in, an unusual feature. There's also a computer in the lobby with free Internet access. Rooms are good for the price, small but modern and bright with city views. The cheapest singles have semi-double-size beds, while the biggest twins are large enough for three persons (costing ¥30,000/$250). All in all, this hotel has more class than its price range would suggest.

2–13–7 Kano-cho, Chuo-ku, Kobe 650-0001. ℂ 078/271-2111. Fax. 078/271-1171. www.grandvista.co.jp/. 108 units. ¥7,800–¥10,800 ($65–$90) single; ¥16,000–¥17,000 ($133–$142) double; ¥18,000–¥26,000 ($150–$217) twin. AE, DC, MC, JCB, V. Station: JR Shin-Kobe (5 min.) and Shin-Kobe subway (2 min.). From Shin-Kobe's south exit, walk past the Shin-Kobe Oriental Hotel and turn right (west) onto Kitano Rd.; it's on your left. **Amenities:** 1 restaurant (Italian); lobby computer with free Internet access; in-room massage; same-day laundry service. *In room:* A/C, satellite TV with pay movies, minibar, hot-water pot with tea, hair dryer.

Hotel Monterey Amalie ⭐   Taking its name from a long-ago Dutch sailing vessel, this property is part of a smart chain of boutique hotels that targets mostly female Japanese travelers with Old-World European decor and atmosphere. From its ivy-covered facade to whitewashed walls (some of which could use a fresh coat) and heavy-beamed ceilings, it looks much older than its 1992 construction date. Wood-floored guest rooms feature natural wooden furniture, sheer curtains and heavy wooden shutters, tiled bathrooms and free-standing wardrobes. Ask for a room overlooking Ikuta Shrine, but since occupancy is an enviable 85%, book early. Otherwise, try nearby sister hotel, Hotel Monterey Kobe (ℂ **078/392-7111**), with similar prices and a cloister-like atmosphere.

2–2–28 Nakayamate Dori, Chuo-ku, Kobe 650-0004. ℂ 078/334-1711. Fax 078/334-1788. 69 units. ¥8,000–¥10,000 ($67–$83) single; ¥18,000–¥21,000 ($150–$175) double; ¥19,000–¥25,000 ($158–$208) twin. AE, DC, JCB, MC, V. Station: Sannomiya (10 min). Just west of Ikuta Shrine. **Amenities:** 1 restaurant (French); access to exercise room and indoor pool at nearby Hotel Monterey Kobe (fee: ¥1,500/$12.50); in-room massage; same-day laundry/dry cleaning service; nonsmoking rooms. *In room:* A/C, TV with pay movies, minibar, hot-water pot with tea, hair dryer.

Maiko Villa Kobe ⭐   Located on a hill in West Kobe beside the world's longest suspension bridge, about a 20-minute train ride from Sannomiya Station, Maiko Villa is a bit far from the town center but its inconvenient location does offer some advantages, including cheaper prices than hotels in the center. Situated near the sea with the sound of seagulls and the faint scent of saltwater, it exudes a resortlike atmosphere, making it a good place to relax in a more leisurely setting—at the man-made sandy beach nearby or the hotel outdoor pool (open July and Aug). Its grounds are lovely, with ancient dwarf pines that date back to the early 1900s, when Emperor Meiji once had a second home here. Popular with vacationing Japanese and for marriage ceremonies (more than 700 a year), the modern hotel offers a variety of rooms, most with views of the sea, fishing boats, and the bridge (which changes color at night). Best are the deluxe twins—corner rooms, they boast heart-shaped tubs where you can bathe looking out at the sea. Avoid the 26 singles and doubles; facing inland, they are used mainly by bus drivers and tour guides. Better and almost as reasonable are the Japanese-style and combination (with both tatami rooms and twin beds) in the annex, almost all with balconies facing the sea.

11–18 Higashi Maiko-cho, Tarumi-ku, Kobe 655-0047. © 078/706-3711. Fax 078/705-0749. www.maikovilla.co.jp. 251 units. ¥7,500 ($62.50) single; ¥11,000 ($92) double; ¥15,000–¥20,000 ($125–$167) twin. Japanese-style rooms ¥12,800 ($107) double. Combination rooms ¥14,600–¥24,000 ($122–$200). AE, DC, JCB, MC, V. Station: From Sannomiya Station, take the JR Kobe Line rapid express (Kaisoku) to JR Maiko (5 min.). Follow signs and then take the hillside elevator. **Amenities:** 5 restaurants (Chinese, Japanese, French/Italian, coffee shop), 1 bar; outdoor pool (free to hotel guests); 300-seat concert hall with piano recitals twice a week; salon; in-room massage; same-day laundry/dry cleaning service; non-smoking rooms. *In room:* A/C, TV with pay movies, fridge, hot-water pot with tea, hair dryer, washlet toilet (main building only).

Hotel Tor Road ✰ An imitation fireplace, knickknacks on the mantle, antiques, a drop-leaf desk, and dark-wood wainscoting lend an English country atmosphere to this tourist hotel. The decent-size rooms are clean and tastefully decorated with larger-than-usual baths and double-size beds. Twin and double rooms have a separate sink area.

3–1–19 Nakayamate Dori, Chuo-ku, Kobe 650-0004. © 078/391-6691. Fax 078/391-6570. htorroad@oak.ocn.ne.jp. 78 units. ¥7,500–¥8,000 ($62.50–$67) single; ¥15,000–¥17,000 ($125–$142) double or twin. ¥1,000 ($8.35) more per room Sat, days before holidays, and peak season (Golden Week, mid-Aug, Christmas/New Year). Rates include buffet breakfast. AE, DC, JCB, MC, V. Station: Sannomiya or Motomachi (10 min.). On Tor Rd. just north of Ikuta Shinmichi Dori. **Amenities:** 1 restaurant (Italian), 1 bar; in-room massage; same-day laundry service. *In room:* A/C, TV, minibar, hot-water pot with tea, hair dryer.

INEXPENSIVE

Green Hill Hotel Urban Between Sannomiya and Shin-Kobe stations, this simple business hotel with mostly single rooms is primarily a place to park your head at night. Clean rooms are about as small as they come, with miniscule plastic-unit bathrooms and most without closets. About the only thing setting this hotel apart from thousands of other business hotels across the country is its automatic check-in via machine (you need a credit card); you can ask for assistance from the front desk, but English is limited. Don't confuse this with the older Green Hill Hotel around the corner.

2–5–16 Kano-cho, Chuo-ku, Kobe 650-0001. © 078/222-1221. Fax 078/242-1194. 120 units. ¥6,500 ($54) single; ¥11,500 ($96) twin or double. Rates include buffet breakfast and tax. AE, DC, MC, V. Station: Shin-Kobe or Sannomiya (10 min.); between the stations, on Flower Road. **Amenities:** 1 coffee shop. *In room:* A/C, TV, hot-water pot with tea, hair dryer.

Kobe YMCA Hotel This hotel is used primarily for banquets, weddings (yes, you can get married here at the YMCA), and teaching classes. But its location and facilities make it worth trying to get one of the four single rooms or 10 twins, all located on the fifth floor. Rooms are bare with a dormitory look to them and miniscule bathrooms, but there are some perks, including a health club. Men, women, and families are welcome.

2–7–15 Kano-cho, Chuo-ku, Kobe 650-0001. © 078/241-7205. Fax 078/231-1031. www.kobeymca.or.jp. 14 units. ¥5,700–¥7,500 ($47.50–$62.50) single; ¥11,000–¥14,000 ($92–$117) twin. ¥1,000 ($8.35) discount for YMCA members. Rates include breakfast. No credit cards. Station: Shin-Kobe or Sannomiya (10 min.). 1 block west of the main street leading from Sannomiya to Shin-Kobe Station (Flower Road), midway between the two. **Amenities:** 1 restaurant (breakfast and lunch only); health club with lane pool, sauna, exercise room, and jogging track (fee: ¥1,500/$12.50); free use of washer and dryer. *In room:* A/C, TV, no phone.

WHERE TO DINE

With its sizable foreign population, Kobe is a good place to dine on international cuisine, including Indian and Chinese food. The greatest concentration of Chinese restaurants is along a pedestrian lane in Chinatown, called **Nankin-machi** by the locals, just a couple minutes' walk south of Motomachi Station. If you're on a budget, you may just want to wander through and buy sticky buns or other inexpensive fare from street stalls.

EXPENSIVE

Alain Chapel ✿✿✿ FRENCH   For elegant French dining, Alain Chapel is an excellent choice. In a stately drawing-room setting with views of either Kobe city or the sea, this restaurant serves the creations of French chef Alain Chapel, whose set meals are popular with the Japanese clientele. If you decide to dine a la carte, you might start with lobster salad and then try Kobe beef, lamb, pigeon, or duck. Average dinner checks, including wine, tax, and service, are generally around ¥18,000 ($150) per person. Clearly, recession is a foreign word here, though set lunches are reasonable.

Kobe Portopia Hotel, 31st floor, 6–10–2 Minatojima, Port Island. ✆ 078/303-5201. Reservations recommended. Main dishes ¥3,200–¥4,000 ($27–$33); set dinners ¥7,500–¥18,000 ($62.50–$150); set lunches ¥3,800–¥8,000 ($32–$67). AE, DC, JCB, MC, V. Daily 11:30am–2pm and 5–9pm; Sat–Sun and holidays 11:30am–2:30pm and 5–9pm (last order). Portliner Monorail from Sannomiya Station to Shimin Hiroba Station (2 min.); or free shuttle service every 20 min. from Sannomiya and Shin-Kobe stations.

Kitano Club ✿ FRENCH   Located on a hill overlooking the city, this well-known restaurant with a country-club setting offers dining with a view. It's especially popular with middle-aged Japanese women, who come to take advantage of the daily lunch special, called Queen's Lunch, for ¥3,000 ($25)—and, yes, guys can order it, too. There are also set steak lunches and dinners. The dinner menu also includes fish of the day, lamb, chicken, and filet mignon.

1–5–7 Kitano-cho. ✆ 078/222-5123. Reservations recommended. Set dinners ¥6,000–¥10,000 ($50–$83); set lunches ¥3,000–¥7,000 ($25–$58). Daily 11:30am–2pm and 6–9pm (last order). Station: Shin-Kobe (7 min.). Go west on Kitano Rd. from Shinkobe Oriental Hotel, taking the 1st street on the right; it will be on your left.

Wakkoqu ✿ TEPPANYAKI STEAKS   This tiny, second-floor restaurant has room for only 30 diners at two counters, where expert chefs cook sirloin, tenderloin or other cuts of tender Kobe beef on the grill in front of them. Fixed-course meals come with side dishes like soup and fried vegetables. A good place to try Kobe's most famous product.

Hillside Terrace, 1–22–13 Nakayamate Dori. ✆ 078/222-0678. Reservations recommended. Set dinners ¥6,800–¥13,000 ($57–$108); set lunches ¥2,500–¥4,500 ($21–$37.50). AE, DC, JCB, MC, V. Daily noon–9pm (last order). Station: Sannomiya (7 min.). On the corner of Kitano-zaka and Pearl streets.

MODERATE

Gaylord ✿ INDIAN   One of Kobe's best-known and oldest (30 years) Indian restaurants, the elegantly decorated Gaylord belongs to the famous franchise (Bombay, New Delhi, Hong Kong, London, San Francisco, and Los Angeles) and attracts a large Indian clientele. The extensive menu includes such delights as shrimp cooked in mild gravy with coconut, marinated lamb pieces cooked in cream and spices, and tandoori fish, chicken, or mutton. Vegetarian selections vary and include saffron-flavored rice with nuts and fruit, chickpeas cooked in sharp spices, spiced lentils cooked with cream, and spinach and cheese cooked in spices. It's customary to order one dish per person and then share. If you're by yourself, you can order one of the set menus starting at ¥3,000 ($25). The mini-tandoori set, for example, comes with fish and chicken tandoori, shish kebab, Indian bread, salad, chicken curry, a dry vegetable dish, rice, and tea or coffee.

7th floor, Bacchus Building, 1–26–1 Nakayamate. ✆ 078/251-4359. Reservations recommended. Curries ¥1,500–¥2,400 ($12.50–$20); set dinners ¥3,000–¥6,000 ($27–$50.40); set lunches ¥1,500–¥2,000

($12.50–$17). AE, DC, JCB, MC, V. Mon–Fri 11:30am–2:30pm and 5:30–9:30pm; Sat–Sun 11:30am–2:30pm and 5–9:30pm. Station: Sannomiya (10 min.). On the north side of Nakayamate Dori (also called Yamate Kansen Dori) where it meets Higashimon St.

Hard Rock Cafe *Kids* AMERICAN   Japan's fifth Hard Rock Cafe offers the usual rock 'n' roll memorabilia, gold records, and items that once belonged to famous musicians as well as a straightforward American menu that includes burgers, barbecue chicken, grilled fajitas, steaks, and sandwiches. Its familiar foods are sure to please finicky young eaters; its long hours make it a good choice for a mid-afternoon or late-night meal.

Harbor Circus, 1–3–3 Higashi Kawasaki-cho. ✆ **078/366-5369.** Main dishes ¥1,380–¥2,780 ($11.50–$23). AE, DC, JCB, MC, V. Sun–Thurs 11am–11pm; Fri–Sat 11am–3am. Station: Kobe (3 min.). Take the DuoKobe underground shopping passage, keeping to the right and following signs to Harbor Circus.

Il Giappone VARIED JAPANESE   You have to be somewhat adventuresome to try this boisterous, lively drinking and eating establishment. After walking down pebbled, lamp-lit steps, you'll find yourself in a rustic but chic environment with gleaming wood floors, bamboo accents, and a warren of tatami rooms and counter seating (I prefer the counters, where you can watch food being prepared and have dishes handed to you via long-handled wooden paddles). The menu lists grilled fish, *harumaki* (spring rolls), fried shrimp, tofu, and other seasonal dishes, but it's only in Japanese. If that's too intimidating, easiest is probably to order the *osuzume course* (chef's selection) and leave the ordering to him.

1–5–8 Nakayamate Dori. ✆ **078/381-0033.** Main dishes ¥580–¥1,200 ($4.85–$10); osuzume courses ¥3,800 and ¥4,800 ($32 and $40). DC, JCB, MC, V. Daily 5–11pm. Station: Sannomiya (6 min.). On Higashimon Street, on the east side, just past Lawson convenience store.

⑬¹ **Steakland Kobe** STEAKS   If you want to eat teppanyaki steak but can't afford the high prices of Kobe beef, one of the cheapest places to go is Steakland Kobe, which is used to tourists and offers an English menu. Lunch specials, served from 11am to 3pm, feature steak (cooked on a hot plate in front of you), miso soup, rice, Japanese pickles, and a vegetable. More expensive Kobe beef is also available, with the least expensive fixed-price dinner offering Kobe sirloin costing ¥3,980 ($33).

1–8–2 Kitanagasa Dori. ✆ **078/332-1787.** Steaks ¥1,580–¥5,580 ($13–$46.50); steak dinner sets ¥2,480–¥6,780 ($21–$56.50); set lunches ¥950–¥2,980 ($7.90–$25). AE, DC, JCB, MC, V. Daily 11:30am–10pm (last order). Station: Sannomiya (2 min.). On the north side of Sunset Dori, the street that runs along the north side of Hankyu Sannomiya Station, diagonal across from McDonald's; look for the sign with the plaid ribbon.

Kobe Beef

Kobe is famous for its marbled beef, so tender that the best cuts virtually melt in your mouth. Unlike in countries such as Australia and the United States where cattle graze in open fields, in villages around Kobe cattle are hand-fed barley, corn, rice, bran, molasses, rapeseed oil, and soybean meal. The rumor that cattle are fed beer is untrue—they may, however, get one bottle each as a farewell present just before being sent off to the slaughterhouse. There are only a few head of cattle per household, so each gets a lot of individual attention. For exercise, the cattle are used for labor, and after the workout they are washed and massaged with water and straw brushes.

INEXPENSIVE

Brasserie Tooth Tooth ⭐ FRENCH   The music here may be classical, Latin, or ethnic Middle Eastern—but who knows what mood may strike in this eclectic, youthful cafe with French-style doors open to the street? Roast lamb with thyme, cassoulet (boiled pork and potatoes in red wine), fish, and steak are served from the French menu, as well as delicious homemade cakes made by a French-trained baker. The set dinner includes hor d'oeuvres, salad, a choice of the day's fish or meat, dessert, and coffee.

Tooth Tooth is so popular it has gone upscale with a second location south of Sannomiya Station, behind Sogo department store on the 11th floor of the International House (Kokusai Kaikan; ⓒ **078/230-3412**). With a curved glass facade overlooking a garden, **Tooth Tooth the Dining Garden** is open daily from 11am to 11pm.

Genryu Building, 3–12–3 Kitanaga Dori. ⓒ **078/332-3052**. Main dishes ¥1,700 ($14); set dinners ¥2,800–¥3,200 ($23–$27); set lunches ¥1,300–¥1,500 ($11–$12.50). JCB, V. Daily 11:30am–11:30pm. Station: Motomachi (5 min.). 1 block west of Tor Rd. and 1 block north of Sunset Dori. From the station, take the north exit and walk on Sunset Dori in the direction of Sannomiya, turning left 1 block before Tor Rd.

Italian Dining (Value) PIZZA/PASTA   Very popular with young Japanese for its inexpensive prices, hearty servings, and good food, this small, casual establishment offers two-dozen kinds of pizza, from calzone with tomato, onion, black olive, and Italian sausage to pizza with *kimchee* (spicy Korean cabbage), mushroom, and bacon. Pastas come in tomato, white wine, or cheese cream sauce as well as Japanese style with Japanese ingredients. A lively, noisy, and crowded place for dinner.

4–7–11 Kano-cho. ⓒ **078/327-2133**. Reservations recommended. Pizzas and pastas ¥880–¥1,780 ($7.35–$15); set lunches ¥780–¥1,000 ($6.50–$8.35). AE, DC, JCB, MC, V. Mon–Sat 11am–11pm; Sun and holidays 11am–midnight. Station: Sannomiya (3 min.). North of Sannomiya Station on the right side of Kitano-zaka; look for the mechanical music grinder.

Masaya Honten NOODLES   This well-known noodle restaurant has been dishing out noodles for more than 50 years. Since the menu is in Japanese only, make your choice from one of the display cases (there's one indoors and one out front) before sitting down. Dishes include tempura with noodles (tempura soba) and pork cutlet with noodles (tonkatsu soba). Although most dishes are under ¥1,000 ($8.35), meat dishes are more expensive. Sukiyaki served with noodles is ¥3,100 ($26).

1–8–21 Nakayamate Dori. ⓒ **078/331-4178**. Dishes ¥660–¥1,300 ($5.50–$11). No credit cards. Daily 11am–midnight. Station: Sannomiya Station (2 min.). North of Sannomiya Station on the left side of Kitano-zaka. Look for the waterwheel and plastic-food display case.

Nishimura COFFEE SHOP   In business for some 50 years, Nishimura is a Kobe landmark. It's on the north side of Yamate Kansen Dori across from Higashimon Street, but if you can't find it just follow your nose; the smell of roasting coffee broadcasts its location. At least 10 types of coffee are available, with seating at tables or counters.

1–26–1 Nakayamate Dori. ⓒ **078/261-3839**. Coffee from ¥450 ($3.75); cake and coffee ¥800 ($7.20). No credit cards. Daily 8:30am–11pm. Station: Sannomiya (10 min.).

Old Spaghetti Factory (Kids) (Value) SPAGHETTI   A branch of a U.S. chain founded in Portland in 1969, the Old Spaghetti Factory gets kudos for its renovation of an 1898 warehouse, complete with antiques and an airy setting. It offers inexpensive spaghetti with a choice of more than a dozen sauces from the usual meat sauce to sauteed bacon and spinach. Lunch sets (spaghetti, soup or salad, drink, and bread) are available on weekdays. Set dinners include the above and ice cream—a great deal, especially for families!

Harborland, 1–5–5 Higashi Kawasaki-cho. C 078/360-3911. Set lunches ¥680–¥980 ($5.65–$8.15); set dinners ¥980–¥1,380 ($8.15–$11.50). No credit cards. Mon–Fri 11am–2:30pm and 5–10pm; Sat–Sun 11am–10pm (last order). Station: Kobe (8 min.). From JR Kobe Station, take the C exit of DuoKobe and walk straight down Kobe Gas Light St. past Hankyu, following signs for BRICK WAREHOUSE RESTAURANT until you see the brick warehouse on your right.

KOBE AFTER DARK

Kobe has a wide selection of English-style pubs, bars, expatriate hangouts, and nightclubs. All the establishments below are easily accessible to foreigners, and most are within walking distance of Sannomiya Station.

THE CLUB & MUSIC SCENE

The Casablanca Club   This dinner club attracts a middle-aged clientele with its imported entertainment of soft vocals, piano music, and dancing. Set dinners range from ¥3,000 to ¥8,000 ($25–$67). If you don't want to eat here, there's a one-drink minimum per person. Beer costs ¥700 ($5.85); cocktails are ¥800 ($6.65). The interior is an elegant, cool white with a grand piano, palm trees, and pictures of Bogart and Bacall on the walls. Music starts at 6pm. Open Wednesday to Monday 5pm to midnight (last order 10:30pm). 3–1–6 Kitano-cho. C 078/241-0200. Station: Shin-Kobe or Sannomiya (10 min.). On Yamamoto Dori (also called Ijinkan Dori) between Hunter-zaka and Kitano-zaka.

Chicken George   This place is one of Kobe's most popular for well-known Japanese acts, including pop, jazz, and alternative. It's easy to spot with its grungy, graffiti-filled exterior; the inside is dark and cavernous. Though there's table seating for more mellow acts, sold-out sets means everyone stands. Check *Kansai Time Out* for concert listings. Open daily 6 or 6:30 to 10pm. 2–17–15 Shimo-Yamate Dori. C 078/392-0146. Cover ¥3,500–¥6,500 ($29–$54). Station: Sannomiya (5 min.). Just west of Ikuta Shrine.

Garage Paradise   Candlelight, gauzy curtains draping down from the high ceiling, Roman statues, a copper and stone bar, a spotlit pool table, and stone walls—yes, it would be paradise to redo your garage this way. Actually, it's a basement with five nightly sets of good, live soul music, along with DJs, and the interesting setting attracts the local foreigner clientele. If you're on a budget, come for happy hour Monday through Thursday before 8pm, when there's no cover; ladies get in free on Wednesdays. Open daily 6pmto 3am (Sunday and holidays to 1am). Kobe Yamashita Building, basement, 1–13–7 Nakayamate Dori. C 078/391-6640. Cover ¥500 ($4.15). Station: Sannomiya (10 min.). On Yamate Kansen Dori east of Higashimon, catty-corner from Nishimura coffee shop.

Kento's   With about 20 locations in Japan, Kento's has long been a great hit among the Japanese, with live bands playing oldies but goldies from the 1950s and 1960s. Snacks cost from ¥800 to ¥1,200 ($6.65–$10) and include the ubiquitous raisin butter (butter with raisins mixed in) and beer is ¥700 ($5.85). Open daily 6pm to 2:30am. 3–10–18 Shimoyamate Dori. C 078/392-2181. Cover ¥2,000 ($17) plus a 1-drink and 1-snack minimum. Station: Motomachi (5 min.). On Tor Rd. just north of Ikuta Shinmichi St., near the Washington Hotel.

Satin Doll   This traditional jazz club, in the same building as Gaylord (see "Where to Dine," above), first opened in 1972 and remains one of the city's top venues. Its sophisticated interior offers table and bar seating with some city views. There are three live music sets nightly, an English menu offering mainly snacks, and a wine list. A 10% service charge is added to your bill. Open daily 6pm to 2am. Bacchus Building, 1–26–1 Nakayama Dori. ✆ **078/242-0100**. Cover from ¥600 ($5), more for international acts. Station: Sannomiya (10 min.). On Yamate Kansen Dori opposite Higashimon Dori.

Sone   Kobe's oldest and and best-known jazz club has changed little since its 1969 opening, offering the same traditional jazz, including Dixieland ensembles and piano-vocalist duos, in a clubby, dated atmosphere. There are four stages nightly, and you're expected to eat; the Japanese menu lists pastas, pizza, fish, and Kobe steaks, with set meals starting at ¥3,500 ($29). Open daily 5pm to 12:30am. 1–24–10 Nakayamate Dori. ✆ **078/221-2055**. Cover usually ¥700 ($5.85). Station: Sannomiya (5 min.) North of the station on the left side of Kitano-zaka.

THE BAR SCENE

Ryan's Irish Pub   Alan Ryan is the ever-present owner and host at this very popular expatriate bar, the only Irish-owned pub in Kansai. Wednesday through Saturday features live music—everything from blues, country-and-western, and Irish—for which there's never a cover charge. There's Guinness on tap and food items like Irish stew and fish and chips to wash it all down. A good place to relax after a hard day of sightseeing; happy hour is til 8pm. Open daily 5pm to midnight (Friday to 1am, Saturday to 2am. Kondo Building, 7th floor, 4–3–2 Kano-cho. ✆ **078/391-6902**. Station: Sannomiya (1 min.). Across the north side of Sannomiya Station on the corner of Ikuta Shinmichi St., above a McDonald's.

Second Chance   This all-nighter is a small, one-room bar favored by night owls who don't mind the rather sparse furnishings with Hawaiian touches. Here is where people congregate when the other bars have had the good sense to close down for the night. Open daily 6pm to 5am. Takashima Building, 2nd floor, 2–1–12 Nakayamate Dori. ✆ **078/391-3544**. Station: Sannomiya (10 min.). On Yamate Kansen Dori west of Higashimon and catty-corner from Nishimura coffee shop.

Smokey   This place is one of a kind—a tiny bar with only eight seats at the counter, all under the watchful eye of 70-something bartender Kamogawa-san, who worked at several hotels (he even served Marilyn Monroe and Joe DiMaggio at the old Kobe Oriental Hotel) before opening his own bar in 1955. Now the oldest bar in Kobe, it's filled with memorabilia of a lifetime, and if you ask, Kamogawa-san will drag out his photographs of actors, actresses, comedians, baseball players, sumo wrestlers, and politicians who have sat here. He's also likely to show you a few of his magic tricks when he's not busy changing records on his old player. There's no cover or table charge, but the average bill is about ¥4,000 ($33). Since this place is tiny, even regular clientele often call to reserve a seat. Open Monday to Saturday 5 to 11:30pm. 1–9–1 Nakayamate Dori. ✆ **078/ 391-0257**. Station: Sannomiya (4 min.). North of the station on the left side of Kitano-zaka.

6 The Temples of Mt. Koya ★ ★ ★

730km (465 miles) W of Tokyo; 199km (124 miles) S of Osaka

If you've harbored visions of wooden temples nestled in among the trees whenever you've thought of Japan, the sacred mountain of **Mt. Koya** is the place to go. It's all here—head-shaven monks, religious chanting at the crack of dawn, the wafting of incense, temples, towering cypress trees, tombs, and early-morning mist rising above the treetops. Mt. Koya—called Koyasan by the Japanese— is one of Japan's most sacred places and the mecca of the Shingon Esoteric sect of Buddhism. Standing almost 3,000 feet above the world, the top of Mt. Koya is home to more than 115 Shingon Buddhist temples scattered through the mountain forests. Some 50 of these temples offer accommodations, making this one of the best places in Japan to observe temple life firsthand.

Koyasan became a place of meditation and religious learning more than 1,180 years ago when Kukai, known posthumously as Kobo Daishi, was granted the mountaintop by the imperial court in 816 as a place to establish his Shingon sect of Buddhism. Kobo Daishi was a charismatic priest who had spent 2 years in China studying Esoteric Buddhism before returning to his native land to spread his teachings among the Japanese. Revered for his excellent calligraphy, his humanitarianism, and his teachings, Kobo Daishi remains one of the most beloved figures in Japanese Buddhist history. When he died in the 9th century, he was laid to rest in a mausoleum on Mt. Koya. His followers believe Kobo Daishi is not dead but simply in a deep state of meditation, awaiting the arrival of the last Bodhisatva (Buddha messiahs). According to popular belief, priests opening his mausoleum decades after his death found his body still warm.

Through the centuries, many of Kobo Daishi's followers, wishing to be close at hand when the great priest awakens, have had huge tombs or tablets constructed close to Kobo Daishi's mausoleum, and many have had their ashes interred here. Pilgrims over the last thousand years have included emperors, feudal lords, samurai, and common people, all climbing to the top of the mountain to pay their respects. Women, however, were barred from entering the sacred grounds of Koyasan until 1872.

ESSENTIALS

GETTING THERE   The easiest way to get to Koyasan is from Osaka. Ordinary express (*kyuko*) trains of the **Nankai Line** depart from Osaka's Namba Station every half hour bound for Gokurakubashi, and the trip south takes about 1 hour and 40 minutes. If you want to ride in luxury, take one of the limited-express cars with reserved seats that take about 1 hour and 20 minutes. After arriving at the last stop, Gokurakubashi, you continue your trip to the top of Mt. Koya via a 5-minute ride in a cable car. The entire journey from Namba Station to Mt. Koya costs ¥1,230 ($10) one-way, including the cable car; if you take the faster limited express, it'll cost ¥760 ($6.35) extra.

VISITOR INFORMATION   At the top of Mt. Koya is Koyasan Station, where you'll find a booth of the local tourist office, the main office for which is located approximately in the center of Koyasan near Kongobuji Temple. You can pick up a map of Koyasan and book a room in a temple at either office, but it is recommended that you fax ahead for a reservation (see "Where to Stay," below). Both offices are open daily from 8:30am to 4:30pm in winter (Dec–Feb), to 5:30pm in summer (July–Sept) and to 5pm the rest of the year. For more information, contact the **Koyasan Tourist Association** at © **0736/ 56-2616.**

GETTING AROUND   Outside the cable car station, you must board a **bus** that travels 1¼ miles along a narrow, winding road to the village of Koyasan and then continues along the main street all the way through town to the Okunoin-mae or Ichinohashi (also called Ichinohashi-guchi) bus stop, the location of Kobo Daishi's mausoleum. The bus passes almost all the sites along the way, as well as most temples accommodating visitors and the Koyasan Tourist Association's main office. Buses depart every 30 minutes between 6:20am and 7:42pm, and the trip to Okunoin-mae takes 20 minutes and costs ¥400 ($3.35).

Otherwise, once you're settled in at your temple accommodation, you can probably walk to Okunoin and other locations mentioned below, but day-long bus passes, called Free Pass, are available for ¥800 ($6.65).

EXPLORING MT. KOYA

THE TOP ATTRACTION The most awe-inspiring and magnificent of Koyasan's many structures and temples, **Okunoin** ★★★ contains the mausoleum of Kobo Daishi. The most dramatic way to approach Okunoin is from the Ichinohashi bus stop, where a pathway leads 1 mile to the mausoleum. Swathed in a respectful darkness of huge cypress trees forming a canopy overhead are monument after monument, tomb after tomb—approximately 200,000 of them, all belonging to faithful followers from past centuries.

I don't know whether being here will affect you the same way, but I was awestruck by the sheer density of tombstones, the iridescent green moss, the shafts of light streaking through the treetops, the stone lanterns, and the gnarled bark of the old cypress trees. Together, they present a dramatic picture representing a thousand years of Japanese Buddhist history. If you're lucky, you won't meet many people along this pathway. Tour buses fortunately park at a newer entrance to the mausoleum at the bus stop called Okunoin-mae. I absolutely forbid you to take this newer and shorter route; its crowds lessen the impact of this place considerably. Rather, make sure you take the path farthest to the left, which begins near the Ichinohashi stop. Much less traveled, it's also much more impressive and is one of the main reasons for coming to Koyasan in the first place. And be sure to return to the mausoleum at night—the stone lanterns (now lit electrically) create a mysterious and powerful effect.

At the end of the pathway, about a 30-minute walk is the **Lantern Hall,** or Torodo, which houses about 21,000 lanterns, donated by prime ministers, emperors, and others. If you'd like to buy a lantern to dedicate to someone, it costs ¥500,000 to ¥1,000,000 ($4,166–$8,333). Two sacred fires, which reportedly have been burning since the 11th century, are kept safely inside. The mausoleum itself is behind the Lantern Hall. Buy a white candle, light it, and wish for anything you want. Then sit back and watch respectfully as Buddhists come to chant and pay respects to one of Japan's greatest Buddhist leaders.

MORE TO SEE & DO (132) **Kongobuji Temple** ★, located near the main Koyasan Tourist Association office in the center of town (© **0736/56-2011;** open daily 8:30am–4:30pm), is the central monastery headquarters of the Shingon sect in Japan. Although Kongobuji was originally built in the 16th century by Toyotomi Hideyoshi to commemorate his mother's death, the present building is 150 years old, reconstructed following a fire. The most important thing to see, however, is the temple's magnificent rock garden, reputedly the largest in Japan and said to represent a pair of dragons in a sea of clouds. If it's raining, consider yourself lucky—the wetness adds a sheen and color to the rocks. Admission is ¥500 ($4.15) for adults, ¥200 ($1.65) for children.

Another important site is the **Danjyo-Garan Complex** ★ (© **0736/56-3215;** open daily 8:30am–4:30pm), the first buildings constructed on Koyasan and still considered the center of religious life in the community. It's an impressive sight with a huge main hall (*kondo*); a large vermilion-colored pagoda (*daito*), which many consider to be Koyasan's most magnificent structure and which is very much worth entering (¥200/$1.65); and the oldest building on Mt. Koya, the Fudodo, which was built in 1197. Next to the complex is the

133 **Reihokan Museum** (© **0736/56-2029;** open daily 8:30am–4:30pm) with such treasures of Koyasan on display as wooden Buddha sculptures, scrolls, art, and implements spread through two buildings. Unfortunately, there are no English explanations, so come here only if you have 30 minutes to spare. Admission is ¥600 ($5) for adults, ¥350 ($2.90) for students, and ¥250 ($2.10) for children.

WHERE TO STAY

Although this community of 4,000 residents has the usual stores, schools, and offices of any small town, there are no hotels here—the only place you can stay is at a temple, and I strongly urge you to do so.

Japanese who come here have almost always made reservations beforehand, and you should do the same. You can make reservations by calling the temple directly or through travel agencies such as JTB. You can also make reservations upon arrival in Koyasan at either Tourist Association office (see "Essentials," above); I suggest faxing in advance to be sure you can get a space (fax **0736/56-2889**), especially during peak travel seasons.

WHAT IT'S LIKE TO STAY AT A KOYASAN TEMPLE   Prices for an overnight stay in one of the temples, including two vegetarian meals, range from ¥9,000 to ¥15,000 ($75–$125) per person, depending on the room. Tax is extra, and you should bring your own towel and toiletries. Check-in is around 3pm; check out is at 10am.

Your room will be tatami and may include a nice view of a garden. High-school and college students attending Koyasan's Buddhist university live at the temple; they'll bring your meals to your room, make up your futon, and clean your room. The morning service is at 6am; you don't have to attend, but I strongly recommend that you do. There's something uplifting about early-morning meditative chanting, even for nonbelievers. Both baths and toilets are communal, and meals are at set times. Because the students must leave for school, breakfast is usually served by 7:30am.

Buddhist monks are vegetarians, not teetotalers—since beer and sake are made of rice and grain, they're readily available at the temples for an extra charge.

Below are just a few of the dozens of area temples open to overnight guests. They're all located very near the indicated bus stop. All of them have public baths, but none offer rooms with bathrooms.

134 **Ekoin** ⭐   This 100-year-old temple, with origins stretching back almost 1,200 years ago when Kukai was said to have erected a stupa on this site, has nice grounds and is nestled in a wooded slope. For centuries it enjoyed support of the Shimazu clan of southern Kyushu. It's known for its excellent Buddhist cuisine, and the master priest will give zazen meditation lessons if his schedule permits. More than half the rooms have TVs and telephones; most also have nice sitting alcoves. There's always someone here who speaks a little English. Reservations should be made in advance especially for peak season.

Koyasan, Koya-cho, Ito-gun, Wakayama-ken 648-0201. © **0736/56-2514.** Fax 0736/56-2891. ekoin@mbox.co.jp. 36 units (none with bathroom). ¥9,000–¥12,000 ($75–$100) per person. Rates include 2 meals. JCB, V. Bus: Karukaya-do or Ichinohashi. *In room:* TV (some rooms), hot-water pot with tea, no phone in some rooms.

135 **Fudoin Temple**   Founded in 906, this temple's oldest existing building is 400 years old. Rooms, in new, modern buildings, look out on a garden and a

carp pond. The young head priest speaks English and offers towels and yukata to foreigners.

Koyasan, Koya-cho, Ito-gun, Wakayama-ken 648-0201. © **0736/56-2414.** Fax 0736/56-4700. 20 units (none with bathroom). ¥10,000–¥15,000 ($83–$125) per person. Rates include 2 meals. No credit cards. Bus: Rengedani. *In room:* TV (most rooms), hot-water pot with tea, safe, no phone.

(136) Rengejoin Temple ★★ This temple's head priest speaks English, so a lot of foreigners are directed here—it's a good place to meet people and to find out about Buddhism. It's also one of the few temples that may take you in without a reservation. Established 900 years ago, it was rebuilt 150 years ago after a fire. Rooms have views of a nice garden with a pond; a plus are the English videos placed in rooms that explore the history and significance of Mt. Koya and Kongobuji Temple. The disadvantage is that it's on the opposite end of town from Okunoin, about a 50-minute walk away.

Koyasan, Koya-cho, Ito-gun, Wakayama-ken 648-0201. © **0736/56-2233.** Fax 0736/56-4743. 48 units (none with bathroom). ¥9,000–¥15,000 ($75–$125) per person. Rates include 2 meals. No credit cards. Bus: Ishinguchi stop. *In room:* TV, hot-water pot with tea, no phone.

(137) Shojoshinin ★★★ This temple has a great location at the beginning of the tomb-lined pathway to Okunoin, making it convenient for your late-night stroll to the mausoleum. Originating as a thatched hut built by Kukai more than 1,150 years ago and once the second-largest temple in Koyasan after Kongobuji, today it boasts attractive 150-year-old buildings, including a large wooden structure with rooms overlooking a small garden and pond. It's usually full in August and peak seasons, so make reservations early.

Koyasan, Koya-cho, Ito-gun, Wakayama-ken 648-0201. © **0736/56-2006.** Fax 0736/56-4770. 20 units (none with bathroom). ¥9,000–¥12,000 ($75–$100). Rates include 2 meals. No credit cards. Bus: Ichinohashi. *In room:* TV (most rooms), hot-water pot with tea, no phone.

(138) Tentokuin The rooms of this temple, which dates from 1622, are located in a new annex. Most look out onto the garden, which in the 1930s was described as one of the most beautiful places in Japan. With a natural mountain background, the garden is of the "borrowed landscaping" type and retains its layout design dating from the Momoyama Period. Rates depend on room size and garden view. No English is spoken.

Koyasan, Koya-cho, Ito-gun, Wakayama-ken 648-0201. © **0736/56-2714.** Fax 0736/56-4725. 55 units (none with bathroom). ¥8,000–¥15,000 ($67–$125). Rates include 2 meals. AE, JCB, V. Bus: Honzanmae or Senjuinbashi. *In room:* TV, hot-water pot with tea, no phone.

7 Himeji, A Castle Town ⊛

640km (400 miles) W of Tokyo; 130km (81 miles) W of Kyoto; 87km (54 miles) E of Okayama

The main reason tourists come to Himeji, in Hyogo Prefecture, is to see its 400-year-old beautiful castle, which embodies better than any other castle the best in Japan's military architecture. If you were to see only one castle in Japan, this would be my pick.

Because of the castle's close proximity to Himeji Station, many tourists stop only long enough to see the castle and a few other sites before continuing their journey onward by Shinkansen. I've included a few recommendations, however, for those wishing to make an overnight stop.

ESSENTIALS

GETTING THERE A stop on the **Tokaido/Sanyo Shinkansen** bullet train, which runs between Tokyo and Kyushu, Himeji is about 3½ hours from Tokyo,

1 hour from Kyoto, and a half hour from Okayama. The fare from Tokyo is ¥14,700 ($122.50) for a nonreserved seat. Note that not all bullet trains stop in Himeji, so make sure yours does.

VISITOR INFORMATION   The **Himeji City Tourist Information Center** (© **0792/85-3792**) is located at the central exit of the station's north (castle) side, to the left after you exit from the ticket gate. It's open daily from 9am to 5pm, but foreigners are asked to visit the center between 10am and 3pm when an English-speaking volunteer is on hand to answer questions.

If you're stopping in Himeji only for a few hours to see the castle, deposit your luggage in the coin lockers just beside the tourist office or underneath the Shinkansen tracks.

ORIENTATION & GETTING AROUND   You can **walk** to Himeji's attractions. The main road in town is Otemae Dori, a wide boulevard that stretches from Himeji Station north to Himeji Castle. To the east (right) of Otemae Dori are two parallel streets, Miyukidori and Omizusuji, both covered shopping arcades. If you want, you can use a **bicycle** free of charge from 9am to 5:30pm. Just fill out an application form (before 4pm) at the station's tourist information counter and then exchange the ticket for a bicycle in front of the station or midway to the castle on Otemae Dori.

SEEING THE SIGHTS

Himeji Castle ★★★   As soon as you exit from Himeji Station, you'll see Himeji Castle straight ahead at the end of a wide boulevard called Otemae Dori. Perhaps the most beautiful castle in all of Japan, Himeji Castle is nicknamed "White Heron Castle" in reference to its white walls, which stretch out on either side of the main donjon and resemble a white heron poised in flight over the plain. Whether it looks to you like a heron or just a castle, the view of the white five-story donjon under a blue sky is striking, especially when the area's many cherry trees are in bloom. This is also one of the few castles in Japan that has remained virtually undamaged since its completion in 1618, surviving even the World War II bombings that laid Himeji city in ruins.

Originating as a fort in the 14th century, Himeji Castle took a more majestic form in 1581 when a three-story donjon was built by Toyotomi Hideyoshi during one of his military campaigns in the district. In the early 1600s, the castle became the residence of Ikeda Terumasa, one of Hideyoshi's generals and a son-in-law of Tokugawa Ieyasu. He remodeled the castle into its present five-story structure. With its extensive gates, three moats, turrets, and a secret entrance, it had one of the most sophisticated defense systems in Japan. The maze of passageways leading to the donjon was so complicated that intruders would find themselves trapped in dead ends. The castle walls were constructed with square or circular holes to allow muzzles of guns to poke through; the rectangular holes were for archers. There were also drop chutes where stones or boiling water could be dumped on enemies trying to scale the walls.

Allow at least 1½ hours here. On weekends (and occasionally on weekdays), volunteer guides usually hang around the castle ticket office and are willing to give you a guided tour of the castle for free. It gives them an opportunity to practice their English. Often college students, they can tell you the history of the castle and can relate old castle gossip. But even if you go on your own, you won't have any problems learning about the history of the castle since the city of Himeji has done a fine job of placing English explanations throughout the castle grounds. With or without a guide, you'll spend at least 2 hours here. *Tip:* A combination ticket, allowing discounted admission to both the castle and Koko-en (see below) is available at either entrance.

Honmachi. ☎ 0792/85-1146. Admission ¥600 ($5) adults, ¥200 ($1.65) children. Combination ticket to both Himeji Castle and Koko-en ¥720 ($6) adults, ¥280 ($2.35) children. Summer, daily 9am–6pm; winter, daily 9am–5pm. You must enter 1 hour before closing time. A 10-min. walk straight north of Himeji Station via Otemae Dori.

(139) **Koko-en** ★★ *Finds*   Although laid out only in 1992, this is a wonderful garden, occupying land where samurai mansions once stood at the base of Himeji Castle, about a 5-minute walk away. Actually it's composed of nine separate small gardens, each one different and enclosed by traditional walls, with lots of rest areas to soak in the wonderful views. The gardens, typical of those in the Edo Period, include a garden of deciduous trees, a garden of pine trees, a garden of flowers popular during the Edo Period, tea-ceremony gardens, and traditional Japanese gardens with ponds, waterfalls, and running streams. If you wish, relax at the Souju-an teahouse (¥500/$4.15 for tea and a sweet; open to 4pm) or dine at a restaurant overlooking a carp pond (see "Where to Dine," below). In any case, I wouldn't miss this special place. If you don't stop (but how could you resist?) you can stroll through all the gardens in about 45 minutes.

68 Honmachi. ☎ 0792/89-4120. Admission ¥300 ($2.50) adults, ¥150 ($1.25) children. Combination ticket to both Himeji Castle and Koko-en ¥720 ($6) adults, ¥280 ($2.35) children. Daily 9am–5pm (to 6pm in July and Aug). A 15-min. walk north of Himeji Station; turn left in front of Himeji Castle (the entrance will be on your right).

A PILGRIMAGE TO MT. SHOSHA AND ENGYOJI TEMPLE

If you're staying overnight, you might consider a half-day trip to **Mt. Shosha** (called Shoshazan in Japanese; ☎ 0792/66-3327), the 1,200-foot-high mountain retreat of Engyoji Temple, founded 1,000 years ago by a holy man who received enlightenment from the God of Wisdom and Intellect. Since then, Japanese have flocked to the mountain to seek purification in both body and spirit. Many make it a fun day's outing as well, bringing obento lunch boxes with them to enjoy under the wooded trees. I recommend this 3- to 4-hour excursion mainly for the lovely hike. The temple buildings spread along the mountaintop are a bonus.

To reach Shoshazan, take bus number 6 or 8 from in front of Himeji Station or Himeji Castle 25 minutes to the last stop (fare: ¥260/$2.15). From there, board a ropeway (cable car) that departs every 15 minutes and costs ¥900 ($7.50) round trip (half price for children). Make sure to check when the last ropeway departs the mountain (5pm in winter; 6 or 7pm in summer). After paying an admission of ¥300 ($2.50) for admission to temple grounds, you'll walk 20 minutes to reach the Maniden, the main temple building. An impressive, cliffside wooden structure dedicated to the Goddess of Mercy, it was first constructed in 970, burned to the ground almost 1,000 years later, and was reconstructed in 1932. Other highlights among the many other structures spread along the mountaintop are the Jikido, a former dormitory for priests-in-training, and the five mausolea of the Honda clan, rulers of Himeji Castle in the 17th century.

WHERE TO STAY
EXPENSIVE

Hotel Sungarden ★   This large, conspicuous hotel is considered Himeji's best. Personally, I think it lacks personality and charm, but its location (only a minute's walk from Himeji Station's Shinkansen side) is a definite plus, as are its many restaurants and its health club. In addition, some of its single and double rooms offer views of the castle; ask for a room on a higher floor facing north. Note, however, that it's popular with international tour groups and enjoys a high 85% occupancy rate.

100 Minami-ekimai-cho, Himeji 670-0962. ⓒ **0792/22-2231.** Fax 0792/24-3731. www.gardenhotels.co.jp/. 258 units. ¥9,000–¥13,000 ($75–$108) single; ¥16,000–¥19,500 ($133–$162.50) twin; ¥17,000 ($142) double. AE, DC, JCB, MC, V. A 1-min. walk from the south (Shinkansen) exit of Himeji Station. **Amenities:** 4 restaurants (Japanese, Chinese, Western), 1 bar, 1 lounge; health club with 20-meter indoor lane pool, sauna, whirlpool and exercise room (fee: ¥1,000/$8.35 before 9am; ¥2,000/$17 thereafter); salon; room service (7am–10pm); in-room massage; same-day laundry/dry cleaning service; nonsmoking rooms. *In room:* A/C, satellite bilingual TV with pay movies, fridge, hot-water pot with tea, hair dryer, washlet toilet.

MODERATE

Claire Higasa   This hotel is a good bet. Although distinctly a business hotel with its 50 single rooms, coin-operated fax and photocopy machine in the lobby, and soda and noodle vending machines, several pluses—like soothing music and flower arrangements in the lobby and an accommodating, English-speaking staff—take it out of the ordinary. Ask for a room with castle view on the sixth or seventh floor for the same price. The bathrooms are tiny and the shower/sink combination faucet a bit mind-boggling for the technically challenged, but who cares when the large seventh-floor public baths with Jacuzzi jets have castle views? Note that there's a 1am curfew.

22 Jyunishomae-cho, Himeji 670-0911. ⓒ **0792/24-3421.** Fax 0792/89-3729. higasa@skyblue.ocn.ne.jp. 60 units. ¥6,400–¥7,000 ($53–$58) single; ¥13,000 ($108) twin; ¥14,000 ($117) double. MC, V. A 5-min. walk from Himeji Station's north exit. Walk north on Otemae-Dori and take the 1st left after Junishomae (a large, one-way street with a traffic light); it's 4 short blocks farther on, on the left across from a small park. **Amenities:** 1 restaurant (Japanese); in-room massage; same-day laundry/dry cleaning service; nonsmoking rooms. *In room:* A/C, TV with free English movie, fridge, hot-water pot with tea, hair dryer, washlet toilet (except in cheapest singles).

Himeji Washington Hotel Plaza   The Washington is part of a chain of business hotels. Some of the staff speak a little English, and everyone is extremely helpful. Rooms are tiny but cheerful, with windows that open (some face another building), panels that close for complete darkness, and slippers that, so the hotel claims, are washed after every guests' use (my goodness, what do the other hotels do?). The lobby is on the second floor.

Omizusuji, Himeji 670-0926. ⓒ **0792/25-0111.** Fax 0792/25-0133. 149 units. ¥6,754–¥7,707 ($56–$64) single; ¥13,508 ($113) double or twin. AE, DC, JCB, MC, V. A 5-min. walk from Himeji Station's north exit. Walk north from the station on Otemae Dori, turning right at the 1st large street, Junishomae (a one-way street with a traffic light) and walk past 2 covered shopping arcades and Starbucks; it will be on the left. **Amenities:** 1 restaurant (Japanese); in-room massage; same-day laundry/dry cleaning service; nonsmoking rooms. *In room:* A/C, satellite TV with pay movies, minibar, hot-water pot with tea, hair dryer, washlet toilet.

INEXPENSIVE

Hotel Himeji Plaza   This business hotel on the south side of the station is a bit dingy, but the staff is friendly and courteous and the price is right. There are mostly singles and twins, most with single-size beds. Note, too, that some twins have no windows; Dracula wouldn't have minded, but you might. Best are the four doubles, recently renovated and a bit more up to date. The higher priced twins and doubles have empty fridges you can stock yourself, as do singles with bathrooms.

158 Toyozawa-cho, Himeji 670-0964. ⓒ **0792/81-9000.** Fax 0792/84-3549. h-plaza@memenet.or.jp. 213 units (50 with toilet only, 158 with bathroom). ¥5,900–¥6,000 ($49–$50) single without bathroom, ¥7,200–¥7,400 ($60–$62) single with bathroom; ¥12,300–¥13,800 ($102.50–$115) twin with bathroom; ¥12,300 ($102.50) double with bathroom. Rates include tax and service. AE, DC, JCB, MC, V. A 1-min. walk

from the south (Shinkansen) exit of Himeji Station, behind Sungarden Hotel. **Amenities:** 1 restaurant (Japanese/Western), 1 lounge; sauna (free for hotel guests); in-room massage; coin-op washers and dryers. *In room:* A/C, TV, fridge (some rooms), hot-water pot (except in cheapest singles).

WHERE TO DINE

Just east of Otemae Dori, the main drag from Himeji Station to the castle, is a parallel street called **Miyukidori,** a covered shopping arcade with lots of restaurants and coffee shops.

In the listings below, directions are from Himeji Station.

(140) **Asaka** SUSHI   This is sushi Himeji-style—you order by the plate, and then, using cups of sauce and brushes at your table, you brush on your sauce yourself. There's no menu, but there's a display case outside. The *nigiri* will give you one sushi each of octopus, squid, shrimp, tuna, and whitefish; the *anago* is five pieces of grilled conger on rice; the *tekka* is eight pieces of tuna and rice rolled in nori seaweed. Each plate costs ¥400 ($3.35).

106 Shiroganemachi. ✆ **0792/22-3835.** Sushi ¥400 ($3.35) a plate. No credit cards. Mon–Sat 10:30am–6pm. Walk north on Otemae Dori until you come to the 1st one-way street with a traffic light (Junishomae); turn left and then right. It'll be on your left (5 min.).

Coo's Italian PASTA/PIZZA   If you're hungering for something other than Japanese food, this casual eatery will do in a pinch. It has a convenient location on the main road between Himeji Station and the castle; choose a window seat for a view of the busy intersection. Unfortunately, the menu is only in Japanese and the food is mediocre. Offerings range from spaghetti in a tomato sauce with bacon and eggplant to pizza with bacon, salami and sausage. Lunch buffets give a choice of a main dish.

65 Minamimachi. ✆ **0792/89-4815.** Pizza and pasta ¥950–¥1,480 ($7.90–$12); set lunches ¥780–¥1,600 ($6.50–$13). No credit cards. Daily 11am–9pm (last order). Walk north on Otemae Dori to the 1st major street, Junishomae; it's on the corner to the left (3 min).

(141) **Fukutei** ★★ VARIED JAPANESE   This sophisticated restaurant with a simple but elegant interior and soothing Japanese instrumental music playing in the background is a popular refuge for shoppers from the nearby Miyukidori shopping arcade. It offers a wide variety of Japanese food, including sashimi, tempura, noodles, eel, and sushi. A great deal is the hearty teishoku obento (¥1,400/$12) served until 3pm. It usually includes sashimi, tempura, soup, rice, and pickled vegetables. There's also a mini-kaiseki available at lunch (¥1,400/$12) and dinner (¥2,500/$21). Fish swim in a black-marble pool in the center of the restaurant until their number comes up.

75 Kameimachi. ✆ **0792/23-0981.** Set lunches ¥1,400–¥2,000 ($12–$17); set dinners ¥2,000–¥8,000 ($17–$67). JCB, V. Fri–Wed 11am–3pm and 4–9:30pm. Walk north on Otemae Dori and take the 1st right after Junishomae (a large, one-way street with a traffic light); it's on your left just past Miyukidori (5 min.).

(142) **Kassui-ken** ★ EEL/NOODLES   This charmless restaurant would not have much to recommend it except for one overwhelming feature: it overlooks a waterfall and koi pond in lovely Koko-en Garden. It's certainly the most picturesque place in town to try Himeji's specialty, conger eel. If that's too exotic, however, it also serves a few noodle dishes, spaghetti, curry rice, and fried rice. Or you can stop just for a refreshing drink of beer, soda, or coffee, but avoid the busy lunchtime crowd.

Koko-en, 68 Honmachi. ✆ **0792/89-4131.** Main dishes ¥800–¥1,000 ($6.65–$8.35); set meals ¥1,500–¥2,000 ($12.50–$17). No credit cards. Daily 9:30am–4:30pm (10am–5:30pm June–Aug). Inside Koko-en (see "Seeing the Sights," above, for directions).

8 Okayama: Gateway to Shikoku

728km (455 miles) W of Tokyo; 218km (136 miles) W of Kyoto; 160km (100 miles) E of Hiroshima

Okayama is a major gateway to the island of Shikoku (see chapter 9), thanks to the Seto Ohashi Bridge, which measures almost 9.5km (6 miles) in length and connects Okayama Prefecture on Honshu island with Sakaide on Shikoku. Before the bridge was built in 1988, it took an hour by ferry to reach Shikoku, whereas traveling by train or car along the double-decker bridge cuts travel time down to just 15 minutes. Now there are two other bridges linking Honshu with Shikoku (one near Kobe and the other in Hiroshima Prefecture), but they're for vehicular travel only (no train service).

For those of you less interested in bridges, Okayama and its environs are important for other reasons as well. Okayama city, with a population of 1.9 million, boasts one of the most beautiful gardens in Japan. In nearby Kurashiki (see "Kurashiki, Market Town of Many Charms," later in this chapter), there's a historic quarter that ranks as one of the most picturesque neighborhoods in Japan. And scattered through Okayama Prefecture are so-called **International Villas,** built by the prefecture especially for foreigners and located primarily in rural areas, with amazingly low rates.

ESSENTIALS

GETTING THERE   Okayama is a major stop on the **Shinkansen** Tokaido/Sanyo Line, about 4 hours from Tokyo, 1 hour 15 minutes from Kyoto, and a little less than 1 hour from Hiroshima. The fare from Tokyo is ¥15,850 ($132) for a nonreserved seat.

A **bus** departs nightly from Shinjuku Station in Tokyo at 9:45pm, arriving at Okayama Station the next day at 8:05am. The fare is ¥10,200 ($85) one-way. For the same fare, you can also depart from Tokyo's Shinagawa Station at 9:15pm and arrive at 7:35am. There's also express bus service from Osaka.

VISITOR INFORMATION   Before departing Tokyo, Kyoto, or Kansai or Narita international airports, stop by the Tourist Information Center for the leaflet "Okayama, Kurashiki and Seto Ohashi Bridge," which contains useful information on train transportation to Okayama and important sites in the prefecture. In Okayama, the **Okayama City Tourist Information Office (② 086/ 222-2912;** open daily 9am–6pm) is inside Okayama Station near the central exit of the east side (look for the sign displaying a question mark). The office is well-prepared for foreign visitors, supplying maps in English of Okayama and Kurashiki and brochures.

Just a 4-minute walk from Okayama Station is the **Okayama International Center,** 2–2–1 Hokancho (② 086/256-2000;** open Tues–Sun 9am–5pm), where you can get more detailed information, obtain a better map of Okayama than those available at the station, take classes, log on to the Internet, peruse a library, and even stay overnight (see "Where to Stay," below). Although geared mainly toward foreign residents, classes offered that accept one-timers include instruction in tea ceremony, Japanese cooking, Japanese language, ikebana, and aikido. Check with the International Center for availability, times, and prices. The multilingual staff here is very helpful and is happy to steer you to Okayama Prefecture's International Villas, your hotel, or your next destination. To find the center, take the west exit of the station and turn right (north) onto the main street running in front of the station until you come to a 7-Eleven, where you should turn left; the center is the big building on your right. More information on Okayama Prefecture is available on the Internet via **www.pref.okayama.jp/**.

INTERNET ACCESS You can check and send e-mail at the Okayama International Center (see "Visitor Information," above), open every day except Monday. It costs ¥300 ($2.50) for 30 minutes of Internet time, but you may have to reserve the center's one computer in advance for busy times or be prepared to wait.

GETTING AROUND Okayama's sights are all clustered within walking distance of each other, due east of Okayama Station. The easiest way to sightsee is to board a **streetcar** from Okayama Station's east side bound for Higashiyama (platform 1) and disembark about 8 minutes later at the Shiroshita tram stop (the 3rd stop; to your right will be the very noticeable Okayama Symphony Hall building). Pay the ¥100 (85¢) fare when you get off. From here you can continue walking straight ahead (east) 8 minutes to Okayama Castle and then visit nearby Korakuen Garden and the Yumeji Art Museum.

SEEING THE SIGHTS

Okayama Castle *Overrated* Originally built in the 16th century, Okayamajo was destroyed in World War II and rebuilt in 1966. Thanks to its black exterior, it has earned the nickname "Crow Castle"; it was painted black to contrast with neighboring Himeji's famous White Heron castle. Unlike castles of yore, an elevator whisks you up to the fourth floor of the donjon. The top floor affords a good view of the park and the city beyond, while the other floors contain a few swords, samurai outfits, lacquerware and other Edo-Period items, most identified only in Japanese and quickly seen in 15 minutes or so. There's also a children's play area with old-fashioned toys, but probably the most rewarding thing to do here is to try on a kimono and have someone snap a picture of yourself with your camera. Donning costumes is free, but participants are limited to five hourly, accepted on the hour from 10am to 3pm (last suit-up). Frankly, if you've seen other Japanese castles, you might just want to photograph this one from the outside and move on. If you feel like indulging in a fairy-tale fantasy, you can rent paddleboats in the shape of swans in the river below the castle.

3–1–2 Marunouchi. (🕐 086/225-2096. Admission ¥300 ($2.50) adults, ¥120 ($1) children. Combination ticket to Okayama Castle and Korakuen Garden ¥520 ($4.35) adults, ¥260 ($2.15) children. Special exhibits cost more. Daily 9am–5pm. Streetcar stop: Shiroshita (8 min.). Continue walking east; it will be on your right.

Korakuen Garden ★★★ Okayama's claim to fame is this garden, considered one of Japan's three most beautiful landscaped gardens (the other 2 are in Kanazawa and Mito). Completed in 1700 by the Ikeda ruling clan after 14 years of work, its 28 acres are graced with a pond, running streams, pine trees, plum and cherry trees, flowering bushes like azaleas and hydrangeas, bamboo groves, teahouses, and tea plantations. The surrounding hills, as well as Okayama's famous black castle, are incorporated into the garden's design. Its name, Korakuen, means "the garden for taking pleasure later," which has its origins in an old saying: "Bear sorrow before the people; take pleasure after them." This garden differs from most Japanese gardens in that it has large expanses of grassy open areas—the first Japanese garden to do so and still a rarity in crowded Japan. Other unusual features worth seeking out are the Ryuten, a wooden pavilion that straddles a stream where poem-composing parties were held (participants had to complete poems before a cup of sake floated by), and an enclosure of red-crested cranes. You can easily spend an hour here.

Kids Joypolis

If you have children in tow, you might want to temper Okayama's cultural offerings with some good old-fashioned fun at **Joypolis,** 2–10–1 Shimoishii (© **086/232-8790;** open daily 10am–midnight), a chain of Japan's most sophisticated and largest video-game arcades. In addition to a toddler's play area, pachinko, video games, virtual horse races, and simulators (how good are you at skateboarding or racing cars?), there are 3D motion rides and other amusements. Entry is free, with most attractions individually priced between ¥300 and ¥600 ($2.50 and $5). With or without kids, it's worth at least visiting one of these eye-opening arcades.

1–5 Korakuen. © **086/272-1148.** Admission ¥350 ($2.90) adults, ¥140 ($1.15) children, free for seniors. Combination ticket to Okayama Castle and Korakuen Garden ¥520 ($4.35) adults, ¥260 ($2.15) children. Daily Apr–Sept 7:30am–6pm; Oct–Mar 8am–5pm. Streetcar stop: Shiroshita (11 min.). Continue walking straight east and then turn left for the footbridge.

(143) **Yumeji Art Museum (Yumeji-Kyodo Bijutsukan)** This museum, in a brick building topped by a cock weathervane just a few minutes' walk north of Korakuen, is dedicated to the works of Yumej Takehisa. Born in Okayama Prefecture in 1884, Yumeji is sometimes referred to as Japan's Toulouse-Lautrec and is credited with developing the fin de siècle Art-Nouveau movement in Japan. This collection includes some of his most famous works, mostly in the Nihonga style of painting. Beautiful women were his favorite subjects. The one-room exhibition can be toured in about 15 minutes.

2–1–32 Hama. © **086/271-1000.** Admission ¥700 ($5.85) adults, ¥400 ($3.35) students, ¥300 ($2.50) children. Tues–Sun 9am–5pm. Streetcar stop: Shiroshita (15 min.). Just north of Korakuen Park, a short walk across Horai-bashi Bridge.

SHOPPING

You can choose from a sampling of products and crafts made in Okayama Prefecture at the (144) **Okayama Prefectural Product Center** (Okayama-ken Kanko Bussan Sen-ta), 1–5–1 Omotecho (©**086/234-2270;** open daily 10am–8pm, closed 2nd Tues each month), conveniently located beside (south of) the Shiroshita streetcar stop on the first floor of Okayama Symphony Hall (a round purple building). Bizen pottery (unglazed pottery with a history stretching back 1,000 years), rush-grass mats (igusa), wooden trays, spirits, papier-mâché toys, and more are for sale.

For general shopping, there's a large underground shopping arcade called **Ichibangai** at Okayama Station, with boutiques selling clothing, shoes, and accessories. Across from the station and connected to Ichibangai is **Takashimaya** department store. In the heart of the city, just south of Shiroshita streetcar stop, is the 1-kilometer-long **Omotecho** covered shopping arcade, where you'll find **Tenmaya,** Okayama's largest department store.

WHERE TO STAY
EXPENSIVE

Hotel Granvia Okayama ★★ Value Owned by the East JR Railway Group and offering a discount for holders of a Japan Rail Pass, this is Okayama's best hotel in terms of luxury and location. Although connected to Okayama Station and the Ichibangai shopping center, it's probably easier to find if you go out the Central exit and look for it on your right. Rooms are large, with the best city views offered by the more expensive twins and doubles. Most singles, however, face another building. Piped into corridors is the sound of twittering birds, which you may like or find annoying. Among the hotel's several food-and-beverage outlets, best are those on the 19th floor with great views; among these, Applause, a classy cocktail lounge with a curved window facade, is a favorite for evening drinks (but note that there's a ¥1,000/$8.35 music cover charge after 8pm).

1–5 Ekimoto-machi, Okayama 700-8515. ℂ **086/234-7000.** Fax 086/234-7099. front-dp@granvia-oka.co.jp. 328 units. ¥8,500–¥15,000 ($71–$125) single; ¥17,000–¥30,000 ($142–$250) twin; ¥22,000–¥23,000 ($183–$192) double. 15% discount for JR Pass holders. AE, DC, JCB, MC, V. Connected to Okayama Station's east side by direct walkway (1 min.). **Amenities:** 4 restaurants (Japanese, French, Chinese, coffee shop), 1 bar, 2 lounges; 20-meter indoor pool, sauna and Jacuzzi (fee: ¥1,600 ($13); concierge; shopping arcade; salon; room service (6:30am–11:30pm); in-room massage; same-day laundry/dry cleaning service; nonsmoking rooms. *In room:* A/C, minibar, satellite TV, hot-water pot with tea, hair dryer, washlet toilet.

Okayama International Hotel ★★ This Western-style hotel (called the "Kokusai Hotel" in Japanese) is located on a hill above the city and has a resort-like holiday atmosphere. It's surrounded by greenery, and the lobby has a restive view of wooded hills and a waterfall. The lobby also boasts an impressive two-story wall made of Bizen-yaki ceramic tiles, for which Okayama Prefecture is famous. Comfortable, larger-than-average rooms face either the city or woods. City views are more dramatic; these rooms come with a map to help you pick out the speck of the castle, which you can just barely pick out if you squint. No matter—the night views are even better. Oddly enough, the most expensive twins face the woods; they're not worth the extra price, as the standard rooms are perfectly adequate. Restaurants also take advantage of the hotel's location with views of either greenery or city panoramas; best is the French L'Arc en Ciel (see "Where to Dine," below). The main drawback to staying here is one of access—the no. 12 bus leaving from Okayama Station's number 3 platform stops in front of the hotel, but it runs only nine times a day. Ask the tourist office for a schedule.

4–1–16 Kadota Honmachi, Okayama 703-8274. ℂ **086/273-7311.** Fax 086/271-0292. www.royalparkho-tels.co.jp. 177 units. ¥8,000–¥14,000 ($67–$117) single; ¥17,000–¥25,000 ($142–$208) twin; ¥18,000–¥20,000 ($150–$167) double. AE, DC, JCB, MC, V. Taxi: 15 min. **Amenities:** 4 restaurants (French, Japanese, Chinese, coffee shop), 1 bar; salon; room service (9–11:30pm); in-room massage; same-day laundry/dry cleaning service. *In room:* A/C, bilingual TV, minibar, hot-water pot with tea, hair dryer.

MODERATE

Ark Although this hotel with a good location near Okayama Station has a mostly business clientele, its spacious lobby is classier than in most business hotels and the staff is used to foreign guests. Rooms, however, are small, with only a tiny recessed alcove for the closet. The cheapest singles have a semi-double-size bed, while the more expensive ones have a double bed. Ask for a room on a higher floor with its better night view.

2–6–1 Shimoishii, Okayama 700-0907. ℂ **086/233-2200.** Fax 086/225-1663. info@arkhotel.co.jp. 183 units. ¥7,000–¥7,500 ($58–$62.50) single; ¥13,000–¥14,000 ($108–$117) twin; ¥13,000 ($108) double. AE, DC, JCB, MC, V. A 7-min. walk SE of Okayama Station (behind Hotel Granvia). Take the central (east) exit and then turn right (south) onto Shiyakusho-suji until you come to a gas station, where you should turn right; the Ark will be on your left. **Amenities:** 2 restaurants (Japanese, Italian), 1 bar, 1 lounge; in-room massage; same-day laundry/dry cleaning service; nonsmoking rooms. *In room:* A/C, TV, fridge, hot-water pot with tea, hair dryer, washlet toilet.

Value Countryside Delights: Okayama Prefecture's International Villas

If you're not on a tight schedule and you don't mind roughing it a bit, you might consider treating yourself to a few days in the countryside around Okayama at one of the prefecture's **International Villas.** Financed and maintained by the Okayama Prefectural Government, these small country inns are the brainstorm of a former Okayama governor, who wished to repay the kindness he received from foreigners during his trips abroad as a youth. Thus, these villas are open only to foreigners, though accompanying Japanese guests are welcome.

Altogether there are six International Villas, most in small villages or in rural settings 1 to 2 hours by train or bus from Okayama city. One, modeled after a traditional soy-sauce warehouse, is located in a mountain village named **Fukiya,** an old copper-mining town that has changed little since the mid–19th century. In **Koshihata** and **Hattoji,** accommodations are in 19th-century renovated thatched farmhouses, and in **Ushimado,** you'll stay in a modern exposed-beamed villa with sweeping views of the Seto Inland Sea—this one's probably the most popular among young backpackers craving isolation (though beware; it's a long, steep hike from the bus stop). Also offering great views is the villa on **Shiraishi Island** in the Seto Inland Sea, which features beaches, shrines, hiking trails, and accommodations in an airy glass-and-wooden building. In **Takebe,** known for its adjoining hot-springs bathhouse, you'll stay in an innovative wooden building designed to resemble a traditional wooden barge. All of these villas are remarkable; how wonderful it would be if other prefectures took a cue from Okayama and started building similar affordable lodgings!

Each villa is small, with only a half dozen or so simply furnished guest rooms (only those in Ushimado and Takebe have private bathrooms), and is outfitted with kitchen facilities so you can cook your own meals if you'd like a break from eating out (no meals are served), though you should do your grocery shopping before arriving at the villa, since stores may not be close at hand.

If these villas were privately owned, you'd easily pay more than twice what you'll be charged. The cost of staying at an International Villa is only ¥3,000 ($27) per person for nonmembers, ¥2,500 ($22.50) for members (add ¥500/$4.15 for single occupancy). Membership cards are easily available for ¥500 ($4.50) at check-in at any villa—certainly worth it if you're staying more than 1 night. Reservations can be made up to 3 months in advance by contacting the **Okayama International Center,** 2-2-1 Hokancho, Okayama 700-0026 or by calling © **086/256-2535** from 9am to noon and 1 to 5pm (Japan time) Tuesday through Sunday; you can also fax the center at 086/256-2576. More information is available via the Internet at www.harenet.ne.jp/villa/.

Mitsui Garden ⭐ Opened in 2000 near Okayama Station, this smart-looking business hotel distinguishes itself from most in this category with handsome public baths and rooms that are small but with an upbeat color scheme and modern decor. There are mostly singles and a few twins; since most face another building, you might want to request one that doesn't. There's a coin-operated fax and copy machine off the lobby.

1–7 Ekimoto-machi, Okayama 70-0024. ℂ **086/235-1131.** Fax 086/225-8831. 352 units. ¥6,500–¥8,000 ($54–$67 single; ¥14,500–¥16,000 ($121–$133) twin. AE, DC, JCB, MC, V. A 2-min. walk SE of Okayama Station. Take the central (east exit) and turn right; it's behind Hotel Granvia. **Amenities:** 1 buffet restaurant (Japanese/Western) open only for breakfast; in-room massage; same-day laundry/dry cleaning service; nonsmoking rooms. *In room:* A/C, TV with pay movies, fridge, hot-water pot with tea, hair dryer, washlet toilet.

INEXPENSIVE

⑭⑤ **Matsunoki** ⭐⭐ *Finds* This family-owned enterprise welcomes foreigners and gives them (to my mind) special treatment. Although it offers rooms with and without bathrooms in a cluster of three buildings, foreigners are automatically given rooms in the newer, main building, all with bathrooms at a price normally given only to bathless rooms (only if accommodations in the main building are full, which rarely happens, are foreigners shunted to the older buildings). Spotless rooms are mostly Japanese style, though three Western-style rooms are available, with glazed windows that open. The owners are earnestly learning English and offer a small gift to those who make reservations through Matsunoki's homepage. Meals are served in a cheerful communal dining hall (Western breakfasts are available), but even better is the ryokan's nearby Matsunoki-Tei (see "Where to Dine," below). You'll like this place, for all you Cinderella wannabe's, beware: There's a midnight curfew.

19–1 Ekimoto-machi, Okayama 700-0024. ℂ **086/253-4111.** Fax 086/253-4110. ww3.tiki.ne.jp/~matunoki. 58 units (24 with bathroom). ¥5,000 ($42) single with bathroom; ¥8,000 ($67) twin with bathroom. Rates include tax. Breakfast ¥700 ($5.85) extra; dinner ¥1,300 ($11) extra. No credit cards. A 2-min. walk from Okayama Station's west exit. Walk west on the street to the north of Tokyu Daiichi Hotel; it's just past the New Station Hotel, on the right across from Forum City. **Amenities:** 1 restaurant (Japanese); room service (11am–10:50pm); coin-op washer and dryer; free same-day laundry service for clothes that do not need ironing. *In room:* A/C, TV with free videos, hot-water pot with tea, hair dryer.

Okayama International Center These bright, spotless rooms on the sixth floor of the International Center have everything: proximity to Okayama Station, an English-speaking staff, use of a fully equipped kitchen, free laundry facilities, an international phone in the lobby with Internet capabilities in case you've brought your own computer (if you haven't, the center also has one computer you can use for a nominal fee; see "Essentials," earlier in this chapter). The catch? There are only two single rooms, four twins, and one triple (all are non-smoking), so occasionally no room is available. Your best bet is to call or reserve by fax several months in advance. There's an 11pm curfew.

2–2–1 Hokancho, Okayama 700-0026. ℂ **086/256-2000.** Fax 086/256-2226. 7 units (all with bathroom). ¥5,600 ($47) single; ¥8,000 ($67) twin; ¥10,500 ($87.50) triple. No credit cards. A 2-min. walk NW of Okayama Station's west exit. Turn right (north) onto the main street running in front of the station until you reach a 7-Eleven; turn left and the center is the big building on your right. **Amenities:** 1 coffee shop; kitchen; free use of washer and dryer; nonsmoking rooms. *In room:* A/C, satellite TV, no phone.

WHERE TO DINE

Okayama's most famous dish is Okayama *barazushi,* which features Seto Inland Sea delicacies and fresh mountain vegetables. Traditionally served during festive occasions, it consists of a rice casserole laced with shredded ginger and cooked egg yolk and topped with a variety of goodies, including conger eel, shrimp, fish, lotus root, and bamboo.

EXPENSIVE

L'Arc en Ciel ★★★ FRENCH   For a memorable meal in a romantic, intimate setting, head for L'Arc en Ciel, which sits atop a hill in the Okayama International Hotel (see "Where to Stay," above) with sweeping views of the city—beautiful at sunset. Chef Yuasa Shigeo, who learned his craft in France, changes the imaginative menu every 2 months. Dishes are works of art, creative and fun; I was surprised to see the filet of sole in white-cream sauce arrive with a small squid and a shrimp and topped with shredded crab and carrots. Another time, I opted for steak in a red wine sauce, cooked to perfection and served with tomato stuffed with ratatouille—with a clean, hollow beef bone serving as a cup for chives and other condiments. If you can't decide, the Chef's Menu for ¥4,000 ($33) offers very good value. A bit out of the way but worth it.

Okayama International (Kokusai) Hotel, 13th floor, 4–1–16 Kadota Honmachi. ✆ 086/273-7311. Reservations recommended. Main dishes ¥2,200–¥8,000 ($18–$67); set dinners ¥4,000–¥15,000 ($33–$125). AE, DC, JCB, MC, V. Daily 5–9:30pm. Taxi: 15 min. from Okayama Station.

MODERATE

⑭⑥ **Matsunoki-Tei** ★★ (Value) KAISEKI/SHABU-SHABU   The family who has long run the inexpensive Matsunoki ryokan (see "Where to Stay," above) also owns this very refined Japanese restaurant, located in an older house in a beautiful traditional setting. Dining here is a luxurious experience, as you sit in your own private tatami room (some with leg wells under the table) and enjoy well-prepared dishes brought by an efficient and courteous staff. Although kaiseki is one of the most expensive meals you can have in Japan, it's quite reasonable here, and the all-you-can-eat shabu-shabu has a 2-hour time limit (indicate whether you want kaiseki or shabu-shabu when making your reservation). Even more economical are the set lunches, which include noodle set meals for ¥800 ($6.65) and more elaborate mini-kaiseki meals.

20–1 Ekimotomachi. ✆ 086/253-5410. Reservations required. Kaiseki ¥3,000–¥10,000 ($25–$83); all-you-can-eat shabu-shabu ¥2,980 ($25); set lunches ¥800–¥3,500 ($6.65–$29). V. Daily 11am–2 and 5–10pm. See Matsunoki (under "Where to Stay," above) for directions.

Okayama Plaza WESTERN/JAPANESE   For Western fare near the castle and Korakuen, head for the Okayama Plaza Hotel's ninth-floor restaurant, which has the added benefit of castle views. Steak, sole, and salmon are on the menu, as well as less expensive pasta and sandwiches. Some Japanese set meals are also available, including a tempura set and an obento lunch box. Or, if it's not crowded, you can come just for a drink. A nice place to relax after a day of sightseeing.

Okayama Plaza Hotel, 2–3–12 Hama. ✆ 086/272-1201. Main dishes ¥1,200–¥6,500 ($10–$54); set lunches ¥2,000–¥2,500 ($17–$21); set dinners ¥3,500–¥6,000 ($29–$50). AE, DC, JCB, MC, V. Daily 7am–10pm. Bus: Okaden bus from gate 5 to Yumeiji-kyodo Bijutsukan-mae (1 min.). Streetcar stop: Shiroshita (15 min.). Just north of Korakuen Park, a short walk across Horai-bashi Bridge.

Petite Mariée ★ FRENCH   Brick walls, a beamed ceiling, French music, a large bouquet of flowers, and numerous European knickknacks set the mood at the tiny Petite Mariée, which serves inexpensive yet good French food. The set meals change monthly, but my ¥800 ($6.65) set lunch consisted of delicate red pepper soup, bread, whitefish crowned with fried shrimp and vegetables. A glass of wine with lunch costs only ¥100 (85¢) extra. Unfortunately, set meals are written in Japanese only, while the a la carte menu, which may include roast lamb or scallops, is in French. A civilized place for a meal.

1–3–8 Yanagimachi. ℂ **086/222-9066.** Main dishes ¥1,600–¥4,200 ($13–$35); set lunch ¥800 and ¥2,500 ($6.65 and $21); set dinners ¥2,800–¥5,000 ($23–$42). No credit cards. Thurs–Tues 11:30am–2pm and 5–8:30pm (last order). A 5-min. walk SE of Okayama Station. Take the central (east) exit, turning right (south) onto Shiyakusho-suji; go 1 block past the gas station (it will be on your right) and turn left onto Akura Dori. It's 2 blocks farther on your right.

INEXPENSIVE

In addition to the choices below, there are some inexpensive, rustic snack houses along the moat that separates Okayama Castle and Korakuen Garden, at Tsukimi Bridge, where you can order a drink, noodles, or ice cream and relax with a view of the castle. Most are open daily 8:30am to 5pm (to 4:30pm in winter).

⑭⑦ **Okabe** _Finds_ TOFU   This informal eatery in the heart of Okayama is a local institution, popular for its specialty, homemade tofu. There's no problem ordering since it serves only one teishoku, which consists of two kinds of tofu along with soup, rice, and pickled vegetables. Seating is along one long counter, behind which an army of women scurry to get out orders. Simple but atmospheric.

1–10–1 Omotecho. ℂ **086/222-1404.** Teishoku ¥700 ($5.85). No credit cards. Mon–Sat 11:30am–2:30pm. Closed national holidays. Streetcar: Shiroshita (2 min.). Walk south through the Omotecho covered shopping arcade to the stoplight and turn right (west); it's on the left, on a corner.

⑭⑧ **Shikisai** OKAYAMA   Located just outside the entrance to Korakuen Garden, this modern restaurant (its name translates as Four Seasons of Color), decorated with Bizen pottery and Japanese _ikebana,_ is a good place to try Okayama specialties, including _barazushi_ (¥1,500/$12.50), and seasonal dishes like nabe (a one-pot stew eaten in winter), anago (sea eel), ayu (a river fish), and mountain vegetables, as well as soba and udon noodles. The menu is written only in Japanese, so look at what others are eating. Top it off with Doppo, a locally brewed beer.

1–5 Korakuen. ℂ **086/273-3221.** Reservations required for dinner. Main courses ¥1,000–¥1,900 ($8.35–$16); set dinners from ¥3,500 ($29). No credit cards. Daily 11am–2pm and 6–10pm. Streetcar: Shiroshita (11 min.). Located just north of the 1st entrance gate, next to a souvenir shop.

⑭⑨ **Yamadome** ★ KUSHIKATSU   This 35-year-old restaurant has a homey Japanese atmosphere, with a local artist's work adorning the walls. It serves fried foods on a stick, from beef to fish to vegetables. The menu is only in Japanese, but the owner speaks English and there's a display case outside. A 10-stick kushikatsu course will set you back ¥1,350 ($12).

1–22 Tenjincho. ℂ **086/224-6886.** Kushikatsu sticks ¥110–¥170 (90¢–$1.40); set lunches ¥630–¥1,270 ($5.25–$11); kushikatsu sets ¥1,350–¥2,290 ($12–$19). No credit cards. Mon–Sat 11am–2:30pm and 5–9pm. Closed 1 week in mid-Aug. Shiroshita (1 min.). Just north of the streetcar stop, across the small street from the gas station (which you can see from the stop).

9 Kurashiki, Market Town of Many Charms ★ ★ ★

26km (16 miles) W of Okayama

If I were forced to select the most picturesque town in Japan, **Kurashiki** would certainly be a top contender. In the heart of the city, clustered around a willow-fringed canal, is a delightful area of old buildings and ryokan perfect for camera buffs.

As an administrative center of the shogunate in the 17th century, Kurashiki blossomed into a prosperous market town where rice, sake, and cotton were collected from the surrounding region and shipped off to Osaka and beyond. Back in those days, wealth was measured in rice, and large granaries were built to store the mountains of granules passing through the town. Canals were dug so that barges laden with grain could work their way to ships anchored in the Seto Inland Sea. Kurashiki, in fact, means "Warehouse Village."

It's these warehouses, which are still standing, that give Kurashiki its distinctive charm. Kurashiki is also known throughout Japan for its art museums, including the prestigious Ohara Museum of Art with its collection of European and Japanese art. For these reasons, Kurashiki is hardly undiscovered, and Japanese flock here in droves, especially in summer months. Yet despite its overcrowdedness, Kurashiki rates high on my list of places to see in Japan.

ESSENTIALS

GETTING THERE By Train If you're arriving in Kurashiki by **Shinkansen** (which takes about 4½ hours from Tokyo and costs ¥15,850/$132 for an unreserved seat; it's almost 2 hr. from Kyoto), you'll arrive at **Shin-Kurashiki Station,** about 9.5km (6 miles) west of **Kurashiki Station** and the heart of the city; the **local train** that runs between the two stations departs about every 15 minutes and takes 9 minutes. Note, however, that because Shin-Kurashiki Station is not the town's most convenient station for sightseeing and is not a major stop on the Shinkansen (not all trains stop here), if you're coming from the east it's much easier to disembark from the Shinkansen in Okayama and transfer to a local train for the 12-minute ride directly to Kurashiki Station. Your **JR Rail Pass** is good on all trains.

By Bus The same buses that depart from Tokyo's Shinjuku and Shinagawa stations for Okayama (see "Okayama, Gateway to Shikoku," earlier in this chapter) continue onward to Kurashiki, arriving in Kurashiki about 40 minutes after their Okayama stop and costing ¥10,400 ($87).

VISITOR INFORMATION There's a tourist information office on the second floor of **Kurashiki Station** (© 086/426-8681) near the ticket wicket, and it has maps in English and a leaflet, "Stroll around Kurashiki." Another information office, called the **Kurashiki-Kan** (© 086/422-0542), is right on the canal in the historic district; ironically the only Western-looking wooden building in the area (built in 1916), it also distributes a map and brochure and has a rest area with tables and vending machines. Both offices are open daily from 9am to 6pm (to 5pm in winter).

ORIENTATION The willow-lined canal called the **Bikan Historical Area** is only a 10-minute walk from Kurashiki Station; take the south exit and walk south on Chuo Dori, turning left just before the Kurashiki Kokusai Hotel. In fact, you can walk virtually everywhere of interest in Kurashiki; the Bikan Historical Area is zoned mostly pedestrian.

EXPLORING THE BIKAN HISTORICAL AREA & ENVIRONS

Kurashiki's **historic old town** is centered on a canal lined with graceful willows and 200-year-old granaries made of black-tile walls topped with white mortar. Many of the granaries have been turned into museums, ryokan, restaurants, and boutiques selling hand-blown glass, Bizen pottery, papier-mâché toys, women's ethnic clothing imported from Bali and India, and mats and handbags made of igusa (rush grass), a local specialty. Street vendors sell jewelry, their wares laid out beside the canal, and healthy young boys stand ready to give visitors rides in rickshaws.

A resident advised me that, because of the crowds that descend upon Kurashiki during the day (about 4 million tourists come here a year), I should get up early in the morning before the shops and museums open and explore this tiny area while it's still under the magic of the early-morning glow. "Real lovers of Kurashiki come on Monday," he added. "Because that's when most everything is closed, and there are fewer people." I've found that early evening is also a magical time to walk the streets.

Do try to avoid weekends, but no matter when you come, you're likely to fall under the city's spell. One of the most rewarding things to do in Kurashiki is simply to explore; even rain only enhances the contrasting black and white of the buildings.

THE MUSEUMS AND OTHER SIGHTS

Kurashiki Folkcraft Museum (Kurashiki Mingei-Kan) Under the slogan USABILITY EQUALS BEAUTY, this museum contains folkcrafts not only from Japan but from various other countries as well, giving unique insight into their cultural similarities and differences as reflected in the items they make and use in daily life. In its three old rice granaries are baskets made of straw, bamboo, and willow, as well as ceramics, glass, textiles, and woodwork from China, Korea, Taiwan, Indonesia, India, Mexico, Sweden, England, Portugal, Spain, Greece, Germany, and Japan. Unfortunately, items are not identified in English, so you'll just have to appreciate their beauty. Plan on spending about 30 minutes here.

1–4–11 Chuo. © 086/422-1637. Admission ¥700 ($5.85) adults, ¥400 ($3.35) university and high-school students, ¥300 ($2.50) children. Tues–Sun 9am–5pm (to 4:15pm Dec–Feb). On the canal, beside the Kurashiki-Kan tourist office.

Japan Rural Toy Museum (Nihon Kyodogangu-Kan) ★★ *Kids* Almost next to the Folkcraft Museum is this museum with its delightful and colorful display of traditional and antique toys, mostly from Japan but from other countries as well (the United States is represented by a cornhusk doll and a Raggedy Ann, among others). Opened in 1967, it has an astounding 12,000 items crammed into six rooms, including kites (200 of them!), miniature floats, antique Japanese dolls, masks, and spinning tops. Incidentally, the huge top in the corner helped the owner of the museum gain entry into the *Guiness World Book of Records*—by spinning 1 hour, 8 minutes, and 57 seconds. You can tour the museum in much less time than that—30 or 40 minutes. A large store at the entrance sells great traditional Japanese toys.

1–4–16 Chuo. © 086/422-8058. Admission ¥500 ($4.15) adults, ¥300 ($2.50) junior- and high-school students, ¥200 ($1.65) children. Daily 9am–5pm. On the canal.

Ohara Museum of Art (Ohara Bijutsukan) ★★★ This is by far Kurashiki's most impressive museum, a must-see even on a short list of sightseeing. Ohara Magosaburo, who believed that even people in remote Kurashiki should have the opportunity to view great works of art, founded it in 1930 as Japan's first museum of Western art. The main building, a two-story stone structure resembling a Greek temple, is small but manages to contain the works of such greats as Picasso, Matisse, Vlaminck, Chagall, Manet, Monet, Degas, Pissarro, Sisley, Toulouse-Lautrec, Gauguin, Cézanne, El Greco, Renoir,

Kandinsky, Klee, Pollack, Jasper Johns, Oldenburg, Frank Stella, Rothko, De Kooning, and Hundertwasser. The museum has expanded so much since its founding that several annexes have been added over the years. A craft gallery housed in a renovated granary contains works by some of my favorites, including ceramics by Hamada Shoji, Bernard Leach and Kawai Kanjiro and woodblock prints by Munakata Shiko, who lived in Kurashiki three years. Another building is devoted to Japanese artists painting in the Western style and contemporary Japanese artists, which makes for fascinating comparison. Allow for 1½ hours to see everything, but since your ticket is good all day, you don't have to see it all at once.

1–1–15 Chuo. ✆ 086/422-0005. Admission ¥1,000 ($8.35) adults, ¥600 ($5) university and senior-high students, and ¥500 ($4.15) children. Tues–Sun 9am–5pm. On the canal.

(150) **Ohashi House (Ohashi-tei)**   Built in 1796 by a wealthy rice merchant, this traditional mansion is typical of the era, with front rooms used for business and the entertaining of guests and the rear used as family living quarters. On display are Ohashi family heirlooms, but otherwise the rooms are fairly empty. It's the only merchant's house open to the public, but come for a 15-minute spin through only if you've never seen the inside of a traditional Japanese home.

3–21–31 Achi. ✆ 086/422-0007. Admission ¥500 ($4.15) adults, ¥300 ($2.50) senior citizens and children. Tues–Sun 9am–5pm. Across Chuo Dori from the Bikan Historical Area, behind the Heisa Hotel.

IVY SQUARE

A few minutes' walk from the canal and museums is a complex called **Kurashiki Ivy Square,** 7–1 Honmachi. Built as a cotton mill by a local spinning company in 1888, this handsome redbrick complex shrouded in ivy has been renovated into a hotel, restaurants, museums, and a few boutiques and galleries selling crafts. It's especially romantic in the evening when, from mid-June to the end of August, there's a beer garden in the inner courtyard (open daily 6–9:30pm). Classical music wafts from loudspeakers built into the brick floors of the courtyard.

Museums at Ivy Square include **Kurabo Memorial Hall (**✆ **086/422-0010),** which depicts the history of the old spinning company, Kurashiki's biggest employer for decades and providing jobs for many young women in the area; and **Torajiro Kojima Memorial Hall (**✆ **086/422-0011),** with paintings by local artist Torajiro Kojima, who went to Europe to purchase most of the pieces in the Ohara museum. Most unique, however, in my opinion is the (151) **Orgel Musée (**✆ **086/427-3904),** where 30-minute concerts on 30 antique organs, player pianos, and music boxes from Europe, the United States, and Japan are presented every hour on the hour from 10am to 5pm. Admission is ¥500 ($4.15) for adults and ¥300 ($2.50) for children.

A couple minutes' walk north of Ivy Square is the **Kurabo Orchid Center,** 16–1 Honmachi (✆ **086/421-3704;** open daily 9am–5pm), a greenhouse with 200 different varieties of orchids in every conceivable shape, color, and size. Admission is ¥350 ($2.90) for adults, ¥250 ($2.10) for students, ¥100 (85¢) for children.

ESPECIALLY FOR KIDS

Tivoli Park *(Kids)*   This branch of Copenhagen's Tivoli Park imitates the real thing with reproduction 19th-century buildings, flower beds, shows, and rides, including a Ferris wheel, carousel, roller coaster, kiddie rides, 3D motion theater, and water slide. Even a copy of the Little Mermaid herself is here. What makes it particularly attractive is that it's only a minute's walk from Kurashiki Station and, except during Golden Week and mid-August, is hardly ever crowded. Young Japanese come on dates, when it's all lit up at night.

12–1 Kotobuki Cho. ✆ 086/434-1111. Admission for everything ¥4,400 ($37) adults, ¥3,000 ($25) seniors, ¥4,100 ($34) junior- and high-school students, ¥3,100 ($26) elementary students, ¥1,050 ($8.75) children. Generally daily 10am–8pm, but vary with the season. Closed 2 weeks end of Jan. A 1-min. walk from Kurashiki Station's north exit.

WHERE TO STAY
EXPENSIVE

⑤ **Ryokan Kurashiki** ★★★ *Finds*　The best place to stay to get a feeling for old Kurashiki is right in the heart of it—in one of the old warehouses on Kurashiki's picturesque willow-lined canal. This venerable ryokan consists of an old mansion and three converted rice-and-sugar warehouses more than 250 years old. Filled with antiques and curios, it has long, narrow corridors, nooks and crannies, and the peaceful sanctuary of an inner garden. There's no other ryokan in Japan quite like this one—it's fun simply walking through the corridors and looking at all the antiques, including camera and clock collections. No two rooms are alike; some have views of the canal, while others look out over rooftops or the hotel garden. Western-style breakfasts are available, and at the adjoining Terrace de Ryokan Kurashiki, you can sip ceremonial green tea served by gracious, kimono-clad hostesses while looking out over a small garden. Even if you don't stay at this ryokan, you may wish to stop by for tea or coffee (look for the sign that reads ALBERGO DEL GIGLIO D'ORO around the corner from the main entrance).

4–1 Honmachi, Kurashiki 710-0054. ✆ 086/422-0730. Fax 086/422-0990. 16 units (10 with bathroom). ¥19,000–¥35,000 ($158–$292) per person without bathroom, ¥20,000–¥50,000 ($167–$417) per person with bathroom. Rates include 2 meals and service charge. AE, DC, MC, V. In the Bikan Historical Area, on the canal. **Amenities:** Tea lounge; in-room massage; same-day laundry/dry cleaning service; nonsmoking rooms. *In room:* A/C, TV, hot-water pot with tea.

⑤ **Tsurugata** ★★　Rustic furniture, gleaming wood, and high ceilings are trademarks of this ryokan, housed in a 250-year-old building on the canal that was once a merchant's house and shop selling rice, cotton, seafood, and cooking oil. The most expensive rooms have a view of the garden with its 400-year-old pine trees and stone lanterns, while the least expensive rooms are on the second floor without a view. All rooms, however, have private toilets, and there are public baths with instructions in English on how to use them, indicating that they're accustomed to foreign guests here. In fact, it's owned by the Kurashiki Kokusai Hotel, which has long been the most popular hotel for foreign visitors (see below).

1–3–15 Chuo, Kurashiki 710-0054. ✆ 086/424-1635. Fax 086/424-1650. 13 units (10 with toilet only, 3 with bathroom). ¥13,000–¥33,000 ($108–$275) per person. Rates include 2 meals and service. AE, DC, JCB, MC, V. In the Bikan Historical Area, on the canal. **Amenities:** 1 restaurant (Japanese); in-room massage; next-day laundry/dry cleaning service; nonsmoking rooms. *In room:* A/C, TV, hot-water pot with tea, washlet toilet.

MODERATE

Hotel Kurashiki　If you prefer a place near Kurashiki Station, you can't get any closer than this Japan Railways Group combination business-tourist hotel above the station. It also offers the advantage of discounts for Japan Rail Pass holders. The rooms in this modern, spotless, hotel are pleasantly decorated and have double-paned windows to shut out noise and nicely tiled bathrooms instead of the usual one-unit cubbyholes of most business hotels. The most expensive singles have double-size beds and sofas, making them quite roomy for

Japan, though cheapest rooms in all categories are quite small. Personally, I think it's a shame to come all this way and miss out staying in the Bikan Historical Area, but if it's convenience you want, this is your best bet.

1–1–1 Achi, Kurashiki 710-0055. ℭ **086/426-6111.** Fax 086/426-6163. 133 units. ¥8,500–¥13,000 ($71–$108) single; ¥16,000–¥20,000 ($133–$167) twin; ¥12,000–¥18,000 ($100–$150) double. 10% discount for holders of Japan Rail Pass. AE, DC, JCB, MC, V. Above Kurashiki Station's south exit. **Amenities:** 2 restaurants (Japanese, Western); shopping arcade; salon; in-room massage; same-day laundry/dry cleaning service. *In room:* A/C, bilingual TV, minibar, hot-water pot with tea, hair dryer, washlet toilet.

Kurashiki Ivy Square Hotel ⍟ An interesting place to stay and a good choice in this price category, this hotel is located in the brick converted cotton mill on Ivy Square. Much of the architectural style of the old mill has been left intact, and rooms have a rural, country atmosphere. Some rooms face a tiny expanse of green grass and an ivy-covered wall or a canal with koi fish. The Bikan Historical Area is just a few minutes' walk away.

7–2 Honmachi, Kurashiki 710-0054. ℭ **086/422-0011.** Fax 086/424-0515. info@ivysquare.co.jp. 161 units (67 with toilet only, 94 with bathroom). ¥7,000 ($58) single with toilet, ¥9,000–¥10,000 ($75–$83) single with bathroom; ¥11,500 ($96) twin with toilet, ¥14,500–¥18,000 ($121–$150) twin with bathroom; ¥16,000–¥17,000 ($133–$142) double with bathroom. ¥1,000 ($8.35) extra per person during peak holidays. AE, DC, JCB, MC, V. A few minutes' walk south of the Bikan Historical Area. **Amenities:** 1 restaurant (Japanese/Western), summer beer garden; shopping arcade; in-room massage; same-day laundry/dry cleaning service. *In room:* A/C, bilingual cable TV, fridge, hot-water pot with tea, hair dryer, washlet toilet.

Kurashiki Kokusai Hotel ⍟⍟ This has long been Kurashiki's most popular Western-style hotel—and it's easy to see why. This delightful hotel, built in 1963, blends into its surroundings with black-tile walls set in white mortar. Its atmosphere is decidedly old-fashioned, which only adds to the charm. Look for the two huge woodblock prints in the lobby, *Barriers of the Universe,* by Japanese artist Munakata Shiko (you can see more of his work at the Ohara Museum). Rooms have nice touches of locally made crafts that lift them out of the ordinary, including woven placemats, Kurashiki glass lampshades, and woodblock prints by a local artist. Female travelers receive a flower in their room. A newer annex offers slightly larger (mostly) twin rooms with larger bathrooms and washlet toilets, but best are the rooms facing the back with a pleasant view of the Ohara Museum, garden greenery, and the black-tile roofs of the old granaries.

1–1–44 Chuo, Kurashiki 710-0046. ℭ **086/422-5141.** Fax 086/422-5192. info@kurashiki-kokusai-hotel.co.jp. 106 units. ¥8,000–¥9,000 ($67–$75) single; ¥14,000–¥17,000 ($117–$142) double; ¥14,000–¥20,000 ($117–$167) twin. AE, DC, JCB, MC, V. A 10-min. walk south of Kurashiki Station, on Chuo Dori next to the Bikan Historical Area. **Amenities:** 1 restaurant (Western), 1 bar, 1 lounge, summer beer garden; in-room massage; same-day laundry/dry cleaning service. *In room:* A/C, bilingual cable TV, minibar, hot-water pot with tea, hair dryer; washlet toilet (annex only).

INEXPENSIVE

El Paso Inn The El Paso Inn, which opened in 1987 on a side street in the Bikan Historical Area, appeals mainly to the younger set with its simple, breezy architecture reminiscent of the American Southwest. Its Western-style rooms, which wrap around an open inner courtyard, are simple and tiny with even tinier bathrooms; only those on the third floor (there's an elevator) facing north have views. Double rooms have narrow, semi-double-size beds. A plus is that guests can use bicycles free of charge for up to 2 hours.

1–9–4 Chuo, Kurashiki 710-0046. ℭ **086/421-8282.** Fax 086/426-6030. 30 units. ¥5,500 ($46) single; ¥9,000 ($75) double; ¥10,000 ($83) twin; ¥15,000 ($125) triple; ¥20,000 ($167) quad. AE, DC, JCB, MC, V. A 13-min. walk south of Kurashiki Station; walk south on Chuo Dori, taking the 1st left past the Kokusai Hotel and then the 1st right; it's across from a kindergarten. **Amenities:** Free bicycles. *In room:* A/C, TV, fridge, hot-water pot with tea.

(154) **Kamoi** ✦   This minshuku, popular among young people, is located on the edge of the Bikan Historical Area, on a slope leading toward Tsurugatayama Park and Aichi Shrine. There's a small, front-yard garden, and although built only a decade ago, the minshuku follows an architectural style befitting old Kurashiki. A collection of Edo-Period firearms and chests grace the front entrance. Tatami rooms, where you're expected to lay out your own bedding at night, are simple. Fourth-floor rooms have good views of the city and have Western-style communal toilets, but beware that the hike up the many stairs can be cumbersome with heavy bags. Western-style breakfast is available if ordered the day before, and since the owner is also owner and chef of a restaurant with the same name (see "Where to Dine," below), the food served here is especially good. Not much English is spoken, but they're used to foreign guests. There's a 10pm curfew.

1–24 Honmachi, Kurashiki 710-0054. ℂ **086/422-4898.** Fax 086/427-7615. 17 units (none with bathroom). ¥4,500 ($37.50) per person without meals; ¥6,000 ($50) per person with breakfast and dinner. No credit cards. A 15-min. walk southeast of Kurashiki Station; walk south on Chuo Dori, turning left just before the Kurashiki Kokusai Hotel and left again when you reach the Ohara Museum; then turn right at Chugoku Bank and look for signs to Aichi Shrine. *In room:* A/C, coin-op TV, hot-water pot with tea, no phone.

Toyoko Inn Kurashikieki Minamiguchi *Value*   Opened in 2000, this inexpensive business hotel has a good location between Kurashiki Station and the Bikan Historical Area. It also tries harder than most business hotels to draw in customers, offering free Internet access from two computers in the lobby, free Internet access in guest rooms for those traveling with laptops, free movies (but only in Japanese), and free breakfast. Rooms are tiny, with most of the room taken up by double- or queen-size beds, but the price is right. Ask for a room on a top floor for unobstructed city views.

2–10–20 Achi, Kurashiki 710-0055. ℂ **086/430-1045.** Fax 086/430-1046. 154 units. ¥4,800 ($40) single; ¥7,300–¥7,800 ($61–$65) double. Rates include tax and breakfast. MC, V. A 3-min. walk south of Kurashiki Station, on Chuo Dori on the left side. **Amenities:** Free computer/Internet access in the lobby; in-room massage; same-day laundry/dry cleaning service. *In room:* A/C, TV with free movies, fridge, hot-water pot with tea, hair dryer, trouser press.

Young Inn Kurashiki   For inexpensive rooms close to the station, you might try this rather different kind of place (at least for Japan). A redbrick building, it has an informal youth-hostel feel and seems more European than Japanese. Painted in bright colors, it looks as though it might have been rather chic at one time but has faded somewhat. It caters mainly to young people and has two to three beds per room (all with sink); the beds are arranged on different levels in bunk-bed style. In fact, the three-bed rooms on the fifth floor have to be seen to be believed—the third bed (which is actually a semi-double, so four can stay here) is about 10 feet off the floor, and you have to climb a ladder to reach it. Definitely for the nimble who are unafraid of heights. The English-speaking owner also dabbles on the Internet; ask to check your e-mail on the computer in the coffee shop. There's a midnight curfew.

1–14–8 Achi, Kurashiki 710-0055. ℂ **086/425-3411.** Fax 086/427-8388. younginn@kurashiki.jp. 37 units (4 with bathroom). ¥4,000 ($33) single without bathroom, ¥6,000 ($50) single with bathroom; ¥7,000 ($58) twin without bathroom, ¥11,000 ($92) twin with bathroom; ¥12,000 ($100) triple without bathroom; ¥14,000 ($117) quad without bathroom. JCB. A 2-min. walk from Kurashi Station to the right (west) behind the Terminal Hotel. **Amenities:** Coffee shop. *In room:* A/C, coin-op TV, hot-water pot with tea, no phone in rooms without bathroom.

WHERE TO DINE
MODERATE

Kiyutei STEAKS   Enter through the front gate just off the canal, pass through the small courtyard, and go into a small room dominated by a counter with cooks grilling steaks, the specialty of the house. For lunch, there's a set meal served Tuesdays and Wednesdays until 2pm for ¥850 ($7.10) and Thursdays through Sundays until 3pm for ¥1,300/$11). There's an English-language menu.

1–2–20 Chuo. ✆ **086/422-5140.** Main dishes ¥800–¥3,700 ($6.65–$31); steak dinners ¥2,800 to ¥5,500 ($23–$46). AE, DC, JCB, MC, V. Tues–Sun 11am–9pm; June and Dec–Feb Tues–Sun 11:30am–8:30pm. On the canal, across from the main entrance of the Ohara Museum of Art.

Tsuta VARIED JAPANESE/WESTERN   Tsuta means "ivy" in Japanese, a reference to the fact that this restaurant is in Ivy Square. Set in the converted spinning factory, it has high ceilings and is airy and bright. Half of the restaurant serves local Kurashiki specialties, including special rice dishes, fish, obento, dishes that change with the season, and, for dinner, kaiseki and shabu-shabu. The other half of the restaurant, called Ivy, offers sandwiches and other Western fare.

Ivy Square, 7–2 Honmachi. ✆ **086/422-0011.** Set lunches ¥1,500–¥2,200 ($12.50–$18); set dinners ¥2,800–¥12,000 ($23–$100). AE, DC, JCB, V. Daily 11:30am–2pm and 5–9pm.

INEXPENSIVE

El Greco Coffeehouse COFFEEHOUSE   El Greco is Kurashiki's most famous coffee shop, open since 1959 and simply decorated with a wooden floor, wooden tables and benches, vases of fresh flowers, and El Greco prints. It serves coffee, fruit juice, milk shakes, ice cream, and cake from an English menu.

1–1–15 Chuo. ✆ **086/422-0297.** Coffee ¥450 ($3.75). No credit cards. Tues–Sun 10am–5pm. Next door to the Ohara Museum in an ivy-covered stone building.

Kamoi ✦ SUSHI   This sushi restaurant, occupying a 200-year-old rice granary on Kurashiki's willow-fringed canal, is run by the man who has a minshuku of the same name (see above). Its interior with stark-white walls and dark wooden beams is decorated with such antiques as cast-iron teapots, old rifles, gourds, and samurai hats. Since the menu is in Japanese, select from the plastic-food display outside the front door. In addition to sushi set meals, other set meals include a tempura teishoku, the Kamoi Teishoku (featuring sashimi and barazushi—a rice dish covered with vegetables and seafood and commonly served during festivals), and—my favorite—the Kurashiki Obento with tempura, tofu, vegetables, rice and soup.

1–3–17 Chuo. ✆ **086/422-0606.** Main dishes ¥900–¥1,200 ($7.50–$10); set meals ¥1,200–¥2,000 ($10–$17). No credit cards. Tues–Sun 10am–6:30pm. Catty-corner across the canal from the Ohara Museum of Art.

(155) **Kanaizumi** UDON   Kanaizumi, housed in a warehouse-style building with tall ceilings, is easy to spot—just look for its chef rolling out udon behind a large window open to the street (though he's on duty only from 11am–1pm daily). In addition to the thick, handmade wheat udon noodles, local cuisine is served. All its fixed-price meals come with udon. As the menu is only in Japanese, make your selection from the display case.

8–33 Honmachi. ✆ **086/421-7254.** Udon ¥500–¥1,550 ($4.15–$13); set meals ¥680–¥1,600 ($5.65–$13). No credit cards. Tues–Sun 11am–8pm. Behind (east of) Kurashiki Ryokan.

Ristorante Rentenchi PIZZA/PASTA This simple, tiny restaurant, run by a kind husband-and-wife team, is a good choice for inexpensive dining between Kurashiki Station and the Bikan Historical Area. Neapolitan-style, thick-crusted pizza from a wood-burning oven are the specialty, most with only one topping though several more can be added upon request. There's an English menu.

2-19-18 Achi. © 086/421-7858. Reservations recommended Sat nights. Pizza and pasta ¥800–¥1,500 ($6.65–$12.50); set lunches ¥650–¥1,800 ($5.40–$15). AE, JCB, MC, V. Wed–Mon 11:30am–2:30pm and 5–11pm. A 7-min. walk south of Kurashiki Station on Chuo Dori, on the left side (keep your eyes peeled; the sign is small).

10 Off the Beaten Path: Matsue ⊙

912km (570 miles) W of Tokyo; 186km (116 miles) NW of Okayama; 402km (251 miles) NE of Hakata (Fukuoka)

Capital of Shimane Prefecture and with a population of about 150,000, **Matsue** lies near the northern coast of western Honshu. It's off the beaten track for most foreign tourists, who tend to keep to a southerly route in their travels toward Kyushu. The Japanese, however, are quite fond of Matsue, and a fair number of them choose to spend their summer vacation in and around this pleasant small town, visiting its castle and other sights, including two outstanding museums—one devoted to Tiffany glass and the other highlighting contemporary Japanese art in a fantastic garden setting. Hugging the shores of Lake Shinji and Nakaumi Lagoon, cut in half by the Ohashi River, and crisscrossed by a network of canals, Matsue is a pretty castle town blessed with Edo-Era architecture, particularly along the castle moat where many samurai settled. All these things conspire to make a trip to Matsue—despite its out-of-the-way location—very worthwhile.

ESSENTIALS

GETTING THERE **By Train** The easiest way to reach Matsue is from Okayama via a 2½-hour **JR limited express train** ride that costs ¥4,850 ($41) for an unreserved seat. There's also one train a day, the **Isokaze,** that travels from Kokura in eastern Kyushu to Matsue in about 6 hours, costing ¥3,990 ($33) for an unreserved seat.

By Bus A bus departs from Tokyo's Shibuya Station (in front of Tokyu Inn) nightly at 8pm, arriving at Matsue Station at 6:40am and costing ¥11,550 ($96) one-way. From Hiroshima, there are 12 buses departing daily, taking 3½ hours and costing ¥3,950 ($33) one way.

VISITOR INFORMATION At the Tokyo, Kyoto, or Narita or Kansai Airport Tourist Information Centers, be sure to pick up the leaflet "Matsue and Izumo Taisha Shrine."

Upon arrival at **Matsue Station,** stop off at the **Matsue City Tourist Information** office (© **0852/21-4034;** open daily 9am–6pm), located in a kiosk in front of the station's north exit, where you can pick up English-language brochures on Matsue and Shimane Prefecture and a good map of the city. More information is available online at www.web-sanin.co.jp/matsue/kankou/e/e.htm.

INTERNET ACCESS **Idol,** 1–5–5 Nishitsuda (© **0852/23-1253;** open daily 10am–1am) is a members only Internet cafe (you can become a member for ¥200/$1.65) charging ¥490 ($4.10) for 1 hour. It's a 20-minute walk south of Matsue Station, or take bus no. 9 (ask the tourist office for directions).

MAIL   The main post office, where you can obtain cash from an ATM, is a 5-minute walk from the north exit of Matsue Station, on the street that runs in front of the station to your right (east).

ORIENTATION & GETTING AROUND   Matsue's attractions lie to the northwest of the station and across the Ohashi River, and although buses run virtually everywhere, you can easily cover most distances **on foot.** Matsue Castle is about a 30-minute walk from Matsue Station, with most attractions located just north of the castle along a picturesque moat on a street called Shiomi Nawate. To the west of Matsue Station, about a 10-minute walk away, is Lake Shinji, famous for its sunsets.

If you prefer to ride, ¥500 ($4.15) buys you an all-day pass for the **Lake Line,** which features red, old-fashioned buses running every 17 to 20 minutes in a loop through the city and stopping at most tourist sights daily between 8:40am and 6:26pm. Single trips cost ¥100 (85¢). Note that only major stops are flashed in roman letters inside the bus. Another bus, the red-and-green **Tiffany Line,** is useful for visiting the Louis C. Tiffany Garden Museum and costs ¥300 ($2.50) one-way.

GOODWILL GUIDES   Although Matsue's sights are concentrated in one area of town and are easy to find on your own, you may want a "goodwill guide" to show you around, especially if you're going to Izumo Taisha Shrine. Established by the Japan National Tourist Organization, the goodwill guide network is composed of volunteers with foreign-language abilities who act as guides in their city. All you have to do is pay their entrance fees into museums and sights—and it's nice if you buy them lunch, too. If you wish to have a guide, apply at the tourist information office 2 or 3 days in advance by phone (© **0852/21-4034**) or fax 0852/27-2598).

SEEING THE SIGHTS

To save money, note that you can buy a combination ticket for Matsue Castle, Hearn Memorial Hall, and Buke Yashiki for ¥920 ($7.65) for adults and ¥460 ($3.85) for children.

Matsue Castle ★★   First built in 1611 and partly reconstructed in 1642 and again in the 1950s, Matsue Castle is the only castle along this northern stretch of coast built for warfare as opposed to serving merely as a residence. It's also one of Japan's few remaining original castles—that is, it's not a ferroconcrete reconstruction. Rising up from a hill about a mile northwest of Matsue Station with a good view of the city, the five-story donjon (which actually conceals six floors to give its warriors a fighting advantage) houses the usual daimyo and samurai gear, including armor, swords, helmets, and lacquerware that belonged to the Matsudaira clan, who ruled for 10 generations.

Lafcadio Hearn, a European who lived in Matsue in the 1890s, adopted Japanese citizenship, and wrote extensively about Japan and the Japanese, said of Matsue Castle: "Crested at its summit, like a feudal helmet . . . the creation is a veritable architectural dragon, made up of magnificent monstrosities." As you walk through the castle up to the top floor, notice the staircase. Although it looks sturdy, it's light enough to be pulled up to halt enemy intrusions. Concealed holes on the second floor could serve as drop chutes for raining stones down on invaders. The top floor, with windows on all four sides from which the feudal lord could command his army, is the only such watchtower remaining in

Japan. And to think the castle almost met its demise during the Meiji Restoration when the ministry of armed forces auctioned it off, hoping to rid the city of its Feudal-Era landmark. Luckily, former vassals of the clan pooled their resources and bought the castle keep. In 1927, the grounds were donated to the city.

Also on castle grounds is the **Matsue Kyodo Kan,** a Western-style, Meiji-Era building, built in 1903 to accommodate Emperor Meiji should he ever turn up (he never did). Today it houses the Matsue Historical Museum, with free admission to its changing exhibits. You can tour this and the castle in less than an hour.

1–5 Tonomachi. ✆ **0852/21-4030.** Daily 8:30am–5pm (to 6:30pm Apr–Sept). Admission ¥550 ($4.60) adults, ¥280 ($2.35) children. Bus: Otemae-Matsuejo stop on the Lake Line (1 min.), or a 30-min. walk NW of Matsue Station.

ATTRACTIONS NEAR THE CASTLE

Most of these attractions are located on Shiomi Nawate, a small, picturesque street beside the castle's north moat. I've listed them in geographic order, walking from east to west.

⑮⑥ **Teahouse Meimei-an**   This is one of Japan's most renowned and well-preserved thatch-roofed teahouses, built in 1779 upon orders of a 29-year-old lord of the Matsudaira clan. It's located at the top of a flight of stairs, from which you have a good view of Matsue Castle (read: photo op). Note the waiting room (and its ancient toilet), for guests awaiting a summons to the teahouse. A separate building offers the bitter Japanese green tea and sweets for an additional ¥360 ($3), which you might find refreshing before moving off to your next destination.

278 Kitahoricho. ✆ **0852/21-9863.** Admission ¥300 ($2.50) adults, ¥200 ($1.65) children. Daily 9am–5pm. Lake Line bus: Hearn Kinenkan-mae (3 min.), or a 5-min. walk northeast of Matsue Castle, back from Shiomi Nawate on a small side street and up a flight of stairs to the left.

⑮⑦ **Buke Yashiki** ✬   This ancient samurai house, facing the castle moat, was built in 1730 and belonged to the Shiomi family, one of the chief retainers of the Matsudaira feudal clan residing in the castle. High-ranking samurai, the Shiomi family lived pretty much like kings themselves, having separate servants' quarters and even a shed for their palanquin. Compared with samurai residences in wealthier regions of Japan, however, this samurai house is considered rather austere. As you walk around it, peering into rooms with their wooden walls slid open to the outside breeze, you'll see furniture and objects used in daily life by samurai during the Edo Period. Plan on 20 minutes here.

305 Kitahoricho. ✆ **0852/22-2243.** Admission ¥300 ($2.50) adults, ¥150 ($1.25) children. Daily 8:30am–5pm (to 6pm Apr–Sept). Lake Line bus: Hearn Kinenkan-mae (3 min.). NE of Matsue Castle across the moat, on Shiomi Nawate.

Hearn Memorial Hall (Hearn Kinenkan)   Here you'll find memorabilia of writer Lafcadio Hearn (1850–1904) including his desk, manuscripts, photographs, and smoking pipes. The Japanese are fascinated with this man who married the daughter of a Matsue high-ranking samurai, became a Japanese citizen, and adopted the name Koizumi Yakumo. He was one of the first writers to give the Japanese the chance to see themselves through the eyes of a foreigner and to describe Japan to the outside world. His books still provide insight into Japanese life at the turn of the century and are available at all bookstores in Japan with an English section.

Since most Japanese will assume it's out of respect for Hearn that you've come to Matsue, you may want to read one of his books before coming here. His volume *Glimpses of Unfamiliar Japan* contains an essay called "In a Japanese Garden," in which he gives his impressions of Matsue, where he lived for 15 months before moving to Kumamoto to teach English.

Next to the memorial is **Lafcadio Hearn's Old Residence** (℃ 0852/ 23-0714; open daily 9am–5pm, to 4:40pm Nov–Feb), a Japanese-style house (and former samurai mansion) where Hearn lived in 1891. It has a pleasant, small garden immortalized in Hearn's essay, "In a Japanese Garden." Admission here is ¥250 ($2.10) for adults, ¥120 ($1) for children. You can tour both the museum and residence in less than an hour.

322 Okudanicho. ℃ 0852/21-2147. Admission ¥300 ($2.50) adults, ¥150 ($1.25) children. Daily 8:30am–5pm (to 6:30pm Apr–Sept). Lake Line bus: Hearn Kinenkan-mae (1 min.). On Shiome Nawate north of Matsue Castle.

(158) **Gesshoji Temple** ⚐   This is the family temple and burial ground of the Matsudaira clan, feudal lords of Matsue and the surrounding region. It was established back in 1664 by Matsudaira Naomasa, whose grandfather was the powerful Tokugawa Ieyasu. Nine generations of the Matsudaira clan are buried here, each in his own small compound spread throughout the solemn grounds (allow 20 min. to see all of them). At the grave of the sixth lord is a stone turtle (described by Hearn as "the monster tortoise") famous for midnight strolls that terrorized residents; if you rub its head, you'll have good luck. Stop for ceremonial green tea (¥400/$3.35) in a room of a modern building facing a great little garden. And in June, temple grounds are famous for stunning hydrangeas— don't miss it.

Sotonakabaracho. ℃ 0852/21-6056. Admission ¥400 ($3.35) adults, ¥200 ($1.65) university and high-school students, ¥150 ($1.25) children. Daily 8:30am–5:30pm (to 5pm Nov–Mar). Lake Line bus: Gesshoji-mae (4 min.). A 15-min. walk west of Matsue Castle.

MUSEUMS ON THE SHORES OF LAKE SHINJI

Louis C. Tiffany Garden Museum ⭐⭐⭐   Quite simply, this museum ranks among the finest collections of Tiffany in the world, in a gorgeous setting that does justice to the works it contains. Opened in 2001 in a building constructed expressly for the collection, the museum chronicles the rich and varied history of Tiffany's nearly 60 years of work in fine and decorative arts from the 1870s to the 1930s. Included are paintings, furniture, mosaics, ceramics, and the largest Tiffany jewelry collection in the world. The stained-glass works are in darkened rooms with natural lighting. Look for the museum's most valuable work, **Deer Window** ⭐⭐⭐, made in 1910 of 4,000 pieces of glass and a brilliant depiction of a deer drinking from a stream on an autumn day in late afternoon. You can easily spend 1½ spellbound hours here.

369 Nishihamasada-cho. ℃ 0852/36-3000. Admission ¥2,000 ($17) adults, ¥1,800 ($15) university and high-school students, ¥1,600 ($13) children. Daily 9am–5:30pm (to 4:30pm Oct–Mar). Bus: Tiffany-Bijutsukan-mae (1 min.).

Shimane Art Museum (Kenritsu Bijitsukan)   This modern museum with huge glass windows overlooking Lake Shinji showcases works by artists of Shimane Prefecture, as well as art that employs water as a theme. Though most of the permanent collection consists of Japanese artists, there are also a few pieces by Monet, Courbet, and Rodin. In addition to its many paintings, woodblock prints, photography, and ceramics, there's a rooftop terrace and an outdoor sculpture garden (free of charge) along Lake Shinji, perfect for a sunset stroll. In fact, the museum is so attuned to sunsets that in summer it remains open 30 minutes past sunset. You can see everything here in less than an hour.

1–5 Sodeshi-cho. © 0852/55-4700. Admission ¥300 ($2.50) adults, ¥200 ($1.65) university and high-school students, free for children. Special exhibitions cost extra. Tues–Sun 10am–6:30pm; from Mar–Sept, closes 30 min. after sunset. Lake Line bus: Kenritsu Bijitsukan-mae (in front of the museum). Or a 15-min. walk west of Matsue Station.

BOAT TRIPS

The **Horikawa Moat Tour** (Horikawa Meguri) (© **0852/27-0417**) is a tour of the castle moat aboard flat-bottom boats (take off your shoes and sit on tatami) with a rooftop canopy that lowers for tight squeezes under bridges. It's a picturesque, relaxing way to see the city, and the ticket price of ¥1,200 ($10) for adults and half-price for children is a day-pass allowing you to reboard as often as you wish. If you stay on board, it takes about an hour to circle the castle. Boarding spots are at Fureai Hiroba near the Hearn Memorial Hall, Kyomise Karakoro Hiroba Square near the Kyobashi Bridge, and Otemae-Matsuejo near Matsue Castle. Boats run every 15 minutes daily from 9am to 5pm (to 6pm in summer) March through November; every 20 minutes daily from 10am to 3pm December through February. Note, however, that commentary is only in Japanese.

From March through November, you can also take a boat over Lake Shinji, which is famous for its sunsets. **Hakucho Kanko** (© **0852/24-3218**) operates 1-hour boat tours of Lake Shinji six times a day, beginning at 11am and ending with the sunset cruise. Check with the tourist office for a monthly schedule. Trips cost ¥1,200 ($10) for adults and half-price for children. Boats depart from Daiichi Josenjo or Daini Josenjo (the latter is a stop on the Lake Line but is also just a 5-min. walk from Matsue JR Station).

SHOPPING

For one-stop shopping for locally crafted goods, visit the **Shimane Prefectural Products and Tourist Center** (Shimane-ken Bussankanko-kan), 191 Tono-machi (© **0852/22-5758**; open daily 9:30am–6pm), just southeast of Matsue Castle near the Ichibata department store (Lake Line bus to Otemae-Matsucjo, then a 1-min. walk). In a modern building that resembles the black-and-white structures typical of the region, the center sells everything from ceramics and abacuses (one of the few prefectures in Japan that still produces them) to toys, jewelry, and foodstuffs, all products of Shimane Prefecture. On the second floor are displays showing how various local products are produced, as well as an English-language video about the prefecture (instructions, however, are in Japanese only, so ask someone to help you).

Another interesting place to shop is the **Karakoro Art Studio,** Kyomise Karakoro Hiroba Square (© **0852/20-7000**; open Wed–Mon from 9:30am–6:30pm), a handsome, century-old former bank renovated into studios and shops selling locally made sweets, tea, jewelry, glassware, woodworking, and other crafts. Changing exhibitions are held in the basement vaults. It's located south of the castle on the moat; both the Lake Line bus and Horikawa Moat Tour boat stop here.

EASY SIDE TRIPS

IZUMO GRAND SHRINE (IZUMO TAISHA) *Overrated* The most important religious structure in the vicinity of Matsue is easy to see on a half-day side trip, but because there isn't a lot to see, come only if you have lots of extra time.

Izumo Taisha, 195 Kizuki Higashi, Taisha-cho (© **0853/53-3100;** open daily 8am–4:30pm), is considered one of Japan's holiest shrines because, according to popular lore, all the gods in the Shinto pantheon gather here for one month every autumn to determine the world's fate for the upcoming year. In Izumo this month is called the "Month of Gods." Everywhere else in Japan it's referred to as the "Month without Gods," since they're all away performing their duty, housed in those long buildings flanking both sides of the main shrine. Otherwise, like the Ise Grand Shrines, the main shrine here, reconstructed in 1744, is considered too sacred for mere mortals and is hidden away from close inspection. You'll have to content yourself with a picture showing how it looked 1,000 years ago, when it was reputedly 78 feet higher to heaven on top of huge pilings. This makes it the oldest site of a Shinto Grand Shrine displaying the Taisha style of architecture. It's dedicated to Okuninushi-no-kami, the Shinto deity responsible for medicine, farming, and happiness. To the left of the main shrine is the marriage shrine, where you'll see people throwing coins up into the bristled ends of thick, twisted rice ropes adorning the entrance—legend has it that if a coin gets stuck in the bushy end, the thrower will have good luck in marriage.

It's a 30- to 40-minute JR train ride from Matsue Station to Izumoshi Station (¥570/$4.75), followed by a 30-minute bus ride (¥460/$3.85) bound for Izumo Taisha ("Taisha-yuki"; get off at the last stop). Or, for a more atmospheric journey, you can also reach Izumo Taisha Shrine by taking the private Ichibata train from Matsue Onsen (departures are once or twice an hour) 55 minutes to Izumo Taisha-mae Station (only a couple of trains a day travel directly; otherwise you'll have to change trains in Kawato). The train stops at stations no larger than American closets and costs ¥790 ($6.60). From Izumo Taisha-mae Station it's a 15-minute walk to the shrine.

ADACHI MUSEUM 𝕬𝕬𝕬 *Finds*   I was blown away the first time I laid eyes on the Adachi Museum, 320 Furukawa-cho, Yasugi (© **0854/28-7111;** open daily 9am–5:30pm; to 5pm Oct–Mar), which houses one of Japan's premier collections of Japanese modern art (from the Meiji, Taisho, and Showa periods) amidst a meticulously sculpted garden. Exhibitions, which are changed four times a year to reflect the seasons, are comprised of 200 works and include the largest collection of distinguished painter Yokoyama Taikan, with at least 20 of his works always on display. A Ceramics Hall displays works by Kawai Kanjiro and Kitaoji Rasanjin. But what makes this museum truly unique is its perfectly landscaped garden, crafted to complement Taikan's masterpieces and continually visible through cleverly crafted windows to incorporate it into the museum's artwork. The effect is surreal, as though the garden is a still picture, a scroll, a Taikan painting. There are several outdoor viewing spots, as well as a coffee shop overlooking a koi pond and two teahouses serving traditional cakes and powdered green tea. You'll want to spend at least 2 hours here.

Admission to the museum is ¥1,100 ($9.15) for adults, ¥850 ($7.10) for university students, ¥450 ($3.75) for high-school students, and ¥200 ($1.65) for children. *Note:* This is a special rate available only to foreigners, so be sure to bring your passport. To get there using your JR pass, take the JR train from Matsue Station 20 minutes to Yasugi and then board a bus from in front of the station bound for Hirose (Hirose yuki); get off at the Saginoyu Onsen-mae stop (fare: ¥200/$1.65). Buses depart once an hour; otherwise, it's a 15-minute taxi ride. Upon departing the museum, make sure you get back on the right bus because different buses going elsewhere also stop in front of the Adachi

Museum. Since there are very few buses, it's best to work out a schedule with the Matsue tourist office. A certain travel writer got stranded out here and had to hitchhike.

WHERE TO STAY

Directions are from Matsue Station.

EXPENSIVE

⑮⑨ **Horaiso** ★★   Tucked away on a side street not far from Matsue Castle, this 50-year-old, family-run ryokan is guarded by a wall, an imposing wooden gateway, and an ancient pine tree. Each Japanese-style room is different, some with nice views of an inner courtyard garden. Although the ryokan is a bit worn, it has a certain charm missing in generic establishments. Don't be put off if there is an old man in the courtyard who tries to shoo you away; just find one of the women running it, all of whom are very kind.

Tonomachi, Matsue 690-0877. ☎ 0852/21-4337. Fax 0852/21-4338. 10 units (3 with bathroom). ¥15,000–¥20,000 ($125–$167) per person. Rates include 2 meals and service. No credit cards. Lake Line bus: Kenmin-kaikan-mae (1 min.). **Amenities:** In-room massage. *In room:* A/C, TV, hot-water pot with tea.

⑯⓪ **Minami-Kan** ★★ *Finds*   You'll be treated like royalty here at this ryokan, located right beside Lake Shinji. Although parts of the ryokan, including its lobby and rooms with private bath, are modern, the original building stems from 1888 and boasts several great tatami rooms with nice wood detailing (these have private toilets but no tubs). Most rooms have views of the lake, but if you really want to feel special, stay in the two-room garden cottage right beside the lake with views of the lake and a garden. Minami-Kan is also renowned for its cuisine.

14 Suetsugu Honmachi, Matsue 690-0843. ☎ 0852/21-5131. Fax 0852/26-0351. 7 units (3 with bathroom, 4 with toilet only); 1 cottage with bathroom. ¥20,000–¥50,000 ($167–$417) per person. Cottage from ¥30,000 ($250) per person. Rates include 2 meals. AE, DC, JCB, MC, V. Taxi: 8 min. Lake Line bus: Kyobashi Stop (2 min.). Off the Kyomise covered shopping arcade in the heart of Matsue. **Amenities:** 1 restaurant (Japanese); hot-spring baths; in-room massage; nonsmoking rooms. *In room:* A/C, TV, minibar, hot-water pot with tea, safe.

MODERATE

Hotel Ichibata ★   Matsue's best-known tourist hotel is the Hotel Ichibata in a part of town called Matsue Onsen, a hot-spring spa. Pluses include the hotel's indoor and outdoor hot-spring public baths with views over Lake Shinji and a nearby jogging path that hugs the shores of the lake. Just behind the hotel is the private Ichibata Line train to Izumo Taisha. None of the singles or doubles has a view of the lake, but the more expensive twins and all the Japanese-style rooms do, including some combination-style rooms with both beds and tatami area.

30 Chidori-cho, Matsue 690-0852. ☎ 0852/22-0188. Fax 0852/22-0230. 142 units. ¥8,500 ($71) single; ¥13,000 ($108) double; ¥15,000–¥24,000 ($125–$200) twin; from ¥19,000 ($158) Japanese-style for 2. AE, DC, JCB, MC, V. Lake Line bus: Chidori Koen (1 min., in front of the hotel). **Amenities:** 2 restaurants (Japanese, Western), 1 coffee shop, 1 bar, 1 lounge, outdoor beer garden (summer only); indoor/outdoor hot-spring baths; in-room massage; same-day laundry/dry cleaning service. *In room:* A/C, TV, minibar, hot-water pot with tea, hair dryer, washlet toilet.

⑯① **Matsue Urban Hotel Annex (Matsue Urban Hotel Bekkan)**   Although a business hotel with the usual vending machines in the lobby, this newer annex near Lake Shinji and Matsue Onsen offers large hot-spring baths and rooms with views of the lake. Rooms facing away from the lake are slightly cheaper, though some of these on higher floors do have views of Matsue Castle in the distance. All beds are semi-double in size or larger. By the way, this is the newest of four Urban hotels in Matsue. The original hotel, next door, has a convenience store, and the two you can see from the station's north exit are more worn with fewer amenities but are also less expensive.

45–2 Nishi-chamachi, Matsue 690-0845. ✆ **0852/23-0003.** Fax 0852/23-0012. 76 units. ¥6,000–¥7,500 ($50–$62.50) single; ¥9,000 ($75) double; ¥12,000–¥13,000 ($100–$108) twin. AE, DC, JCB, MC, V. Lake Line bus: Shiyakusho-mae (3 min.). **Amenities:** 1 restaurant (Western/Japanese), noodle counter, rooftop beer garden (summer only); indoor hot-spring baths; in-room massage; coin-op washers and dryers. *In room:* A/C, bilingual TV, fridge, hot-water pot with tea, hair dryer.

Tokyu Inn Part of a national business hotel chain, the Tokyu Inn is a good choice for travelers who want to spend the night close to Matsue Station. Rooms are small but have everything you need; bathrooms are a bit larger than in most business hotels. Paying slightly higher rates in each category will get you a larger bed in single rooms and a larger room in double and twin rooms.

590 Asahimachi, Matsue 690-0003. ✆ **0852/27-0109.** Fax 0852/25-1327. 181 units. ¥6,500–¥8,100 ($54–$67.50) single; ¥12,300–¥15,600 ($102.50–$130) double; ¥14,000–¥24,800 ($117–$207) twin. AE, DC, JCB, MC, V. Across the street from Matsue Station's north exit. **Amenities:** 1 restaurant (Western), 1 beer garden (summer only), 1 lounge; salon; in-room massage; same-day laundry/dry cleaning service; nonsmoking rooms. *In room:* A/C, TV with pay movies, minibar, hot-water pot with tea, hair dryer, washlet toilet, trouser press.

INEXPENSIVE

⑯ **Ryokan Terazuya** ★★ *Value* Terazuya, offers good value for your money, but it also offers something money can't buy: true hospitality. This Japanese inn has been in business since 1893, owned by the Terazu family that has shown so much kindness to foreigners that many consider their stay here a highlight of their trip. The Terazus treat guests like family, teaching them the tea ceremony in the tearoom, showing them how to make sushi in the communal dining hall, and singing karaoke with them in the tatami-matted party room. The postwar building, while nothing special on the outside, is spotless and colorfully decorated inside. Located across from a small shrine and a Lake Line stop, it's also near the Shimane Art Museum and Lake Shinji, making it convenient for watching those famous sunsets. And although it's only a 7-minute walk from Matsue Station (head west along the north side of the railroad tracks), the Terazus will pick you up if you call ahead. When faxing, please do so during Japanese business hours so as not to wake them.

60–3 Tenjin-machi, Matsue 690-0064. ✆ **0852/21-3480.** Fax 0852/21-3422. 9 units (none with bathroom). ¥4,000 ($33) per person without meals; ¥7,000 ($58) per person with breakfast and dinner. No credit cards. Lake Line bus: Shirakata Tenmangu-mae (1 min.). **Amenities:** 1 restaurant (Japanese). *In room:* A/C, TV, hot-water pot with tea.

WHERE TO DINE

Much of Matsue's regional cuisine comes from Lake Shinji, including sea bass, smelt, carp, freshwater eel, and a small black clam (*shijimi,* popular in soups). *Warigo soba,* which comes with stacked layers of noodles to which you add grated daikon radish, yam, fish flakes, seaweed and other condiments, is also popular.

MODERATE

Ji Beer Kan GRILLED MEAT In a large, airy setting beside the castle moat west of the Hearn Memorial Hall, this is Matsue's micro-brewery/restaurant (every town seems to have one now). You'll find it on the second floor above a souvenir shop; the boat dock for the Horikawa Moat Tour is just outside. Three different kinds of beer are brewed: a pilsner, a fruity pale ale, and an herb-flavored ale; a sampler of all three costs ¥880 ($7.35). The fare is beef or pork that you cook yourself at your table, with set meals including all the rice and salad you can eat. There are also a few a la carte dishes from a Japanese menu, including noodles, freshwater eel, and soup with shijimi clams.

509–1 Kurodacho. ✆ 0852/55-8877. Main dishes ¥680–¥1,200 ($5.65–$10); set meals ¥2,000–¥7,000 ($17–$58); set lunches ¥680–¥1,200 ($5.65–$10). JCB, MC, V. Daily 11am–9pm. Lake Line bus: Horikawa Fureai (1 min.).

INEXPENSIVE

⑯ **Daikichi** ☆ *Finds* YAKITORI   Daikichi means "big happiness," and judging from the English-speaking owner's smiling face, that's the order of the day. Customers seem to be content, too, as they crowd into this small counter-seating restaurant. A branch of an Osaka yakitorya, Daikichi offers an English menu of various yakitori, including chicken, minced chicken meatballs, and chicken with leek or green pepper (three sticks yakitori comes with each order), as well as its own brand of sake and wine; an evening of jovial drinking and eating here will set you back about ¥2,500 ($21), including a ¥150 ($1.25) snack charge.

491–1 Asahimachi. ✆ 0852/31-8308. Yakitori ¥80–¥250 (65¢–$2.10) per stick. No credit cards. Daily 5pm–midnight. Turn left out of Matsue Station; it will be on your right, on the street in front of the station (1 min.).

⑯ **Izakaya Ten** VARIED JAPANESE   A popular local hangout, this drinking/eating establishment is easy to spot with its high-pointed roof lined with red lanterns and its red neon sign. Inside, there are more lanterns hanging everywhere, and seating is at wooden slab tables or counters. Prices are cheap: two sticks of yakitori go for ¥240 ($2). Other items include sashimi moriawase (a platter of raw fish), tonkatsu (breaded pork cutlet), fried shrimp, and set meals depicted with photographs on the Japanese menu that include fish, eel, or pork, plus side dishes. Note, however, that there's a ¥300 ($2.50) *otsumame* (snack) charge, which means they automatically bring an appetizer to your table and charge you for it. To wash it all down, order a draft beer or try a shuhai sour— fewer calories than a beer.

113 Kataharacho. ✆ 0852/27-6880. Main dishes ¥380–¥850 ($3.15–$7.10); set meals ¥600–¥900 ($5–$7.50). No credit cards. Daily 11:30am–1:30pm and 5pm–midnight. Lake Line bus: Kyobashi (1 min.). West of Kyobashi Bridge on the south side of the moat, across from Karakoro Art Studio.

⑯ **Kaneyasu** ☆ *Value* FISH/VARIED JAPANESE   This modest one-counter place with tatami rooms upstairs has good food and is run by grandmotherly, bustling women. It has been around for more than 40 years, and most of its customers are local working people, so avoid the noontime rush. It has a great lunch teishoku—which includes a piece of yakizakana (grilled fish), vegetable, soup, tofu, rice, and tea—served from 11am to "whenever"—I came at 3pm and was still able to order it. In the evening, dishes like grilled fish, yam, bamboo, seasonal dishes, and various vegetables are placed on the counter in lieu of a menu, making ordering easy. Highly recommended.

Otesemba-cho. ✆ 0852/21-0550. Reservations recommended for dinner. Dinners from ¥3,000 ($25); lunch teishoku ¥650 ($5.40). No credit cards. Mon–Fri 11:30am–9pm; Sat 5–9pm. Closed holidays. 1 block north of Matsue Station's north exit on the street parallel to the one that runs in front, beside a restaurant with a giant crab.

⑯ **Yakumoan** ☆☆ *Finds* SOBA NOODLES   A wonderful place to stop off for lunch if you're sightseeing along Shiomi Nawate north of Matsue Castle, this lovely soba shop with a teahouselike atmosphere is surrounded by a stone wall with a large wooden entryway, a grove of bamboo, bonsai, a Japanese garden, and a pond full of prize carp. Part of the restaurant, a former samurai residence, dates from 200 years ago. Its specialty is noodles, all handmade, including the local specialty Warigo soba and udon. You'll find a plastic-food display case to the left as you step through the entryway. Seating is at either tables or tatami.

308 Kitabori-cho. ☎ 0852/22-2400. Noodles ¥500–¥1,250 ($4.15–$10). No credit cards. Daily 9:30am–4:30pm (last order). Lake Line bus: Hearn Kinenkan-mae (1 min.). On Shiomi Nawate Street, near the Buke Yashiki samurai house.

11 Hiroshima ★★

887km (554 miles) W of Tokyo; 376km (235 miles) W of Kyoto; 279km (174 miles) E of Hakata/Fukuoka

With a population of more than 1 million, Hiroshima looks just like any other up-and-coming city in Japan. Modern buildings, industry, the manufacture of cars and ships—it's a city full of vitality and purpose with a steady flow of both Japanese and foreign business executives in and out.

But unlike other cities, Hiroshima's past is clouded: It has the unfortunate distinction of being the first city ever destroyed by an atomic bomb (the 2nd city—and hopefully the last—was Nagasaki, on Kyushu island).

It happened one clear summer morning, August 6, 1945, at 8:15am, when three B-29s approached Hiroshima from the northeast. One of them passed over the central part of the city, dropped the bomb, and then took off at full speed. The bomb exploded 43 seconds later at an altitude of 1,900 feet in a huge fireball, followed by a mushroom cloud of smoke that rose 29,700 feet in the air.

There were approximately 350,000 people living in Hiroshima at the time of the bombing, and almost half of them lost their lives. The heat from the blast was so intense that it seared people's skin, while the pressure caused by the explosion tore clothes off bodies and caused the rupture and explosion of internal organs. Flying glass tore through flesh like bullets, and fires broke out all over the city. But that wasn't the end of it: Victims who survived the blast were subsequently exposed to huge doses of radioactivity. Even people who showed no outward signs of sickness suddenly died, creating a feeling of panic and helplessness in the survivors. Today, blast survivors still continue to suffer from the effects of the bomb, including a high incidence of cancer, disfigurement, scars, and keloid skin tissue.

Ironically, Hiroshima's tragedy is now the city's largest tourist draw, and visitors from around the world come to see Peace Memorial Park with its haunting museum. But Hiroshima, laced with rivers and wide, tree-lined boulevards, boasts other worthwhile attractions as well, including several excellent museums. Hiroshima is also the most popular gateway for cruises on the Seto Inland Sea and trips to nearby Miyajima, a jewel of an island considered to be one of Japan's most scenic spots, covered later in this chapter.

ESSENTIALS

GETTING THERE Hiroshima is approximately 5 hours from Tokyo by **Shinkansen** bullet train, 2 hours from Kyoto, and 1 hour and 20 minutes from Hakata Station on Kyushu. The fare from Tokyo is ¥17,540 ($146) for an unreserved seat.

A **bus** departs from Tokyo Station every night at 8pm and reaches Hiroshima Station at 8am the next morning. The one-way fare is ¥12,060 ($100.50).

VISITOR INFORMATION Before leaving Tokyo, Kyoto, or the Narita or Kansai airports, pick up a copy of the leaflet "Hiroshima and Miyajima" at the Tourist Information Center.

Upon arrival in Hiroshima, you'll find two local tourist offices at **Hiroshima Station.** The main office (℃ **082/263-6822**), on the north side where Shinkansen bullet trains arrive, is open daily from 9am to 12:30pm and 1:30 to 5:30pm. The other tourist office (℃ **082/261-1877**), in the underground passage on the station's south, is open daily from 9 to 11:30am and 12:30 to 5:30pm. A third tourist office is located in the north end of **Peace Memorial Park** in the Rest House (℃ **082/247-6738;** open daily 9:30am–6pm Apr–Sept, 8:30am–5pm Oct–Mar). All three facilities have brochures of both Hiroshima and Miyajima with maps in English. Be sure, too, to ask for the **Welcome Card,** available free to visitors; it offers discounts on member hotels, restaurants, some attractions, and more. More information on Hiroshima is available on the Internet at www.tourism.city.hiroshima.jp/.

ORIENTATION & GETTING AROUND   One legacy of Hiroshima's total destruction was its rebirth into one of Japan's most navigable cities, with wide, open boulevards instead of the usual cramped streets. Hiroshima's main attractions, including Peace Memorial Park, Hiroshima Castle, Shukkei-en Garden, Hiroshima Prefectural Art Museum, and Hiroshima Museum of Art, lie to the west and southwest of Hiroshima Station. The most convenient mode of transportation in the city is **streetcar,** which costs only ¥150 ($1.25) one-way; children pay half-fare. If you need to transfer to another line, ask the driver for a transfer card, which you then pass through the card machine upon alighting from the first bus and again when boarding the second bus. When you arrive at your destination, return the card to the bus driver. A one-day pass costs ¥600 ($5); note that it does not cover the trip to Miyajima.

It's probably easiest, however, to make the circuit to Hiroshima's centrally located attractions **on foot.** From Hiroshima Station, you can walk to Shukkei-en Garden and the Prefectural Art Museum in about 12 minutes, from which it's another 7-minute walk to Hiroshima Castle. You can walk onward to Peace Memorial Park in about 15 minutes, passing the Hiroshima Museum of Art and the A-Bomb Dome on the way. Just east of Peace Park is the **Hondori** covered shopping arcade and its neighboring streets, considered the heart of the city with its many department stores, shops, and restaurants.

SEEING THE SIGHTS

As you walk around Hiroshima today, you'll find it hard to imagine that the city was the scene of such widespread horror and destruction 50-some years ago. On the other hand, Hiroshima doesn't have the old buildings, temples, and historical structures that other cities have, yet it draws a steady flow of travelers who come to see Peace Memorial Park, the city's best-known landmark. Dedicated to peace, the city also seems committed to art—in addition to its fine art museums, you'll find statues, stone lanterns, memorials, and sculptures lining the streets.

PEACE MEMORIAL PARK & ENVIRONS

Peace Memorial Park (Heiwa Koen) ✹✹✹ lies in the center of the city. Signs in English all over the city indicate how to reach it. From Hiroshima Station, take streetcar no. 2 or 6 to the Genbaku-Domu-mae (In Front of the Atom Bomb Dome) stop. The first structure you'll see as you alight from the streetcar is just north of the park: the **A-Bomb Dome,** the skeletal ruins of the former Industrial Promotion Hall, left as a visual reminder of the death and destruction caused by the atomic bomb. Across the river is the park; it takes about 10 minutes to walk from its northern end to the museum.

Hiroshima

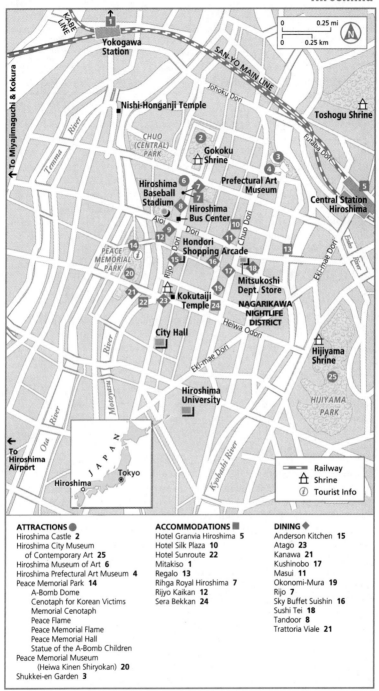

0   0.25 mi
0   0.25 km

Railway
⛩ **Shrine**
ⓘ **Tourist Info**

ATTRACTIONS ●
Hiroshima Castle **2**
Hiroshima City Museum
   of Contemporary Art **25**
Hiroshima Museum of Art **6**
Hiroshima Prefectural Art Museum **4**
Peace Memorial Park **14**
   A-Bomb Dome
   Cenotaph for Korean Victims
   Memorial Cenotaph
   Peace Flame
   Peace Memorial Flame
   Peace Memorial Hall
   Statue of the A-Bomb Children
Peace Memorial Museum
   (Heiwa Kinen Shiryokan) **20**
Shukkei-en Garden **3**

ACCOMMODATIONS ■
Hotel Granvia Hiroshima **5**
Hotel Silk Plaza **10**
Hotel Sunroute **22**
Mitakiso **1**
Regalo **13**
Rihga Royal Hiroshima **7**
Rijyo Kaikan **12**
Sera Bekkan **24**

DINING ◆
Anderson Kitchen **15**
Atago **23**
Kanawa **21**
Kushinobo **17**
Masui **11**
Okonomi-Mura **19**
Rijo **7**
Sky Buffet Suishin **16**
Sushi Tei **18**
Tandoor **8**
Trattoria Viale **21**

Impressions
In the dying afternoon, I wander dying round the Park of Peace. It is right, this squat, dead place, with its left-over air of an abandoned International Trade and Tourist Fair.
　　—James Kirkup, "No More Hiroshimas," *These Horned Islands* (1962)

Along the way you'll see its most touching statue, the **Statue of the A-Bomb Children,** dedicated to the war's most innocent victims, not only those who died instantly in the blast but also those who died afterward from the effects of radiation. The statue is of a girl with outstretched arms, and rising above her is a crane, a symbol of happiness and longevity in Japan. The statue is based on the true story of a young girl who suffered from the effects of radiation after the bombing in Hiroshima. She believed that if she could fold 1,000 paper cranes she would become well again. However, even though she folded 1,300 cranes, she still died of leukemia. Today, all Japanese children are familiar with her story, and around the memorial are streamers of paper cranes donated by schoolchildren from all over Japan. To the west of the statue is the **Atomic Bomb Memorial Mound,** which contains the ashes of 70,000 unidentified victims. On the other side of the statue is the Rest House, where you'll find a branch of the Hiroshima Tourist Office.

Also in Peace Memorial Park is a **Cenotaph for Korean Victims.** It's a little-publicized fact that 20,000 Koreans (10% of those who perished during the war) were killed that fateful summer day, most of them brought to Japan as forced laborers. The monument reads: "The Korean victims were given no funerals or memorial services and their spirits hovered for years unable to pass on to heaven." It's significant to note that, for 29 years, the cenotaph remained outside the park—even today, Koreans and their descendants face discrimination in Japan. In 1999, Hiroshima's mayor, calling for an end to prejudice against Korean residents in Japan, gave the memorial a new home within Peace Memorial Park.

Between the statue and the museum is the **Memorial Cenotaph,** designed by Japan's famous architect Kenzo Tange (who also designed the Tokyo Metropolitan Government offices in Shinjuku; see chapter 4). Shaped like a figurine clay saddle found in ancient tombs, it shelters a stone chest, which in turn holds the names of those killed by the bomb. An epitaph, written in Japanese, carries the hopeful phrase, "Repose ye in Peace, for the error shall not be repeated." If you stand in front of the cenotaph, you have a view through the hollow arch of the Peace Flame and the A-Bomb Dome. The **Peace Flame** will continue to burn until all atomic weapons vanish from the face of the earth and nuclear war is no longer a threat to humanity.

Just beyond the memorial is the main focus of the park, the **Peace Memorial Museum** (Heiwa Kinen Shiryokan) ✿✿✿, 1–2 Nakajima-cho, Naku-ku (✆ **082/241-4004;** daily 9am–6pm May–Nov, daily 9am–5pm Dec–Apr). It comprises two buildings: the East Building, which tells of Hiroshima before and after the bombing, and the West Building, which concentrates on that fateful August day. Entrance to the museum is in the East Building; admission is ¥50 (40¢). Plan on a minimum of 1 hour to tour both buildings.

The newer East Building addresses Hiroshima's militaristic past, challenging the city's former self-characterization as a blameless victim. In great detail, it explains why Hiroshima was selected as the blast site—as Imperial Headquarters, Hiroshima was home to Japan's military command center as well as a military supply base (Mitsubishi, which produced war ships, was based here). TV screens show actual footage of the bomb being dropped and its aftermath. A 360-degree photograph, taken by U.S. Navy personnel when the Allies arrived, show Hiroshima's utter destruction. The museum also documents Hiroshima's current dedication to the abolition of nuclear weapons; a globe of the world provides a chilling map of nuclear proliferation. On the ground floor is the Video Theatre where two documentaries in English are shown throughout the day. One focuses on Hiroshima and the results of the bombing, while the second film takes a more scientific look at the atomic bombs in both Hiroshima and Nagasaki. There are also booths with video screens and a selection of material for personal viewing.

The West Building concentrates on the suffering caused by the atomic bomb, beginning with panoramas of scorched earth and seared victims and photographs of the atomic bomb that destroyed the city and the intensity of the blast's epicenter. It then shows in graphic detail the effects of the blast on bodies, buildings, and materials. Most of the photographs in the exhibit are of burned and seared skin, charred remains of bodies, and people with open wounds. There's a bronze Buddha that was half-melted in the blast and melted glass and ceramics. There are also some granite steps that show a dark shadow that suggests someone had been sitting there at the time of the explosion—the shadow is all that remains. Tattered clothing and other personal effects are accompanied by short biographies of their owners, many of them children and teenagers and many of whom died in the blast.

Needless to say, visiting Peace Memorial Park is a rather sobering and depressing experience, but it's perhaps a necessary one. Every concerned individual should be informed of the effects of an atomic bomb and should be aware that what was dropped on Hiroshima is small compared to the bombs of today (in 1961, the Soviet Union tested a hydrogen bomb 3,300 times more powerful than the atomic bomb dropped on Hiroshima). From the museum, the closest streetcar stop is Fukuro-machi, where you can catch streetcar no. 1 for Hiroshima Station.

MORE SIGHTS & ATTRACTIONS

Your **Welcome Card,** available for free at city tourist offices, gives a 20% discount on admission to Hiroshima Castle, Hiroshima City Museum of Contemporary Art, and Shukkei-en Garden.

Hiroshima Castle ★★   Originally built in the 1590s but destroyed in the atomic blast, Hiroshima Castle was reconstructed in 1958. Its five-story wooden donjon is a faithful reproduction of the original, but the main reason to come here is the very good museum housed in the castle's modern interior and toured in about 30 minutes. It's devoted to Hiroshima's history as a flourishing castle town, with good presentations in English. It also gives the best description I've seen on castles in Japan, including differences in architecture between those built on hills (for defense) and on plains (mainly administrative). Videos describe Hiroshima's founding and the construction of Hiroshima Castle, while displays explain the differences in lifestyle between samurai and townspeople, the heirarchy of the feudal administration system, and other aspects of Edo life.

There's also samurai gear, models of old Hiroshima and the castle, and pictures of the past. The top of the donjon provides a panoramic view of the city.

21–1 Moto-machi, Naka-ku. ✆ 082/221-7512. Admission ¥320 ($2.65) adults, ¥160 ($1.35) children. Daily 9am–5:30pm, to 4:30pm Oct–Mar. A 15-min. walk north of Peace Memorial Park, or a 20-min. walk west of Hiroshima Station. Streetcar: 1, 2, or 6 to Kamiya-cho (10 min.); since the street car exit is underground, follow the signs to the Kencho-mae exit, continue to Jonan Dori, then take the underpass on the left-hand side of the road. The entrance to the underpass isn't marked in English, but it's the only way to cross the street.

Hiroshima City Museum of Contemporary Art 🌟🌟 Set on a hill in Hijiyama Park overlooking Hiroshima, this museum was designed by renowned Japanese architect Kurokawa Kisho in a building reminiscent of Japanese warehouse architecture. It's a great setting for the trend-setting contemporary pieces it displays, with works by established and promising Japanese artists including Okamoto Taro (famous for his faces), Ikeda Masuo, Aimitsu, Kondo Tatsuo, and pop artist Yokoo Tadanori (the Andy Warhol of Japanese art). It's a good place to explore the postwar Japanese art scene, but what makes it particularly enriching is that dossiers on individual artists are provided in English, giving a short biography and an explanation of their work. There's also an outdoor sculpture garden with works by Botero and Moore. Plan on an hour here. Incidentally, for all you cartoon fans, in Hijiyama Park is also the **Manga** Library.

1–1 Hijiyama Koen, Minami-ku. ✆ 082/264-1121. Admission ¥320 ($2.65) adults, ¥240 ($2) university students, ¥150 ($1.25) children. Tues–Sun 10am–5pm, to 7pm July–Aug. Streetcar: 5 to Hijiyama-shita (7 min.).

Hiroshima Museum of Art 🌟🌟 This private museum, housed in a modern round building in the heart of the city, has a permanent collection of some 200 paintings, half by French painters from Romanticism to Ecole de Paris and presented in chronological order. Included are works by Delacroix, Courbet, Corot, Manet, Monet, Renoir, Degas, Toulouse-Lautrec, Rousseau, Cezanne, Gauguin, van Gogh, Matisse, Braque, Chagall, and Picasso. Also on display are about 90 works by Japanese artists in the Western style from the Meiji Era to the present, including works by Kuroda Seiki and Kishida Ryusei. You can see it all in less than an hour.

3–2 Motomachi, Naka-ku. ✆ 082/223-2530. Admission 1,000 ($8.35) adults, ¥500 ($4.15) university and high-school students, ¥200 ($1.65) junior-high and elementary students. Daily 9am–5pm. Streetcar: 1, 2, or 6 to Kamiya-cho (Kencho-mae exit, 3 min.). In Chuo Park, across from the Rihga Royal Hotel (Hiroshima's tallest building).

Hiroshima Prefectural Art Museum The main focus of this museum is art created by artists who have some kind of relationship to Hiroshima Prefecture, including Aimitsu (look for his self-portrait), Minami Kunzo (*Sitting Woman*), and Kobayashi Senkou, as well as works from the 1920s and 1930s by non-Japanese artists who have influenced contemporary art in Japan such as Salvador Dali, Lyonel Feininger, Picasso, and Thomas Hart Benton. Asian decorative arts, including ceramics and lacquerware, round out the permanent collection. If you purchase a combination ticket to Shukkei-en Garden, you can enter the garden directly from the museum.

2–22 Kaminobori-cho, Naka-ku. ✆ 082/221-6246. Admission ¥500 ($4.15) adults, ¥300 ($2.50) university and high-school students, ¥100 (85¢) junior-high and elementary students. Combination ticket for museum and Shukkei-en Garden ¥600 ($5), ¥380 ($3.15), and ¥180 ($1.50) respectively. Tues–Sun 10am–6pm, to 8pm July–Aug. A 12-minute walk from Hiroshima Station, or streetcar no. 9 to Shukkeien-mae (1 min.). Adjacent to Shukkei-en Garden.

Impressions

We had found the awesome sight of a Hiroshima that was now even bigger than it had been before the bomb, far richer and more prosperous.

—James Cameron, *Point of Departure* (1967)

Shukkei-en Garden   Shukkei-en Garden, which means "landscape garden in miniature," was first laid out in 1620 by a master of the tea ceremony, with a pond constructed in imitation of famous Lake Xi Hu in Hangzhou, China. Using streams, ponds, islets, and bridges, it was designed to appear much larger than it actually is, and it is best viewed on a circular stroll. Like everything else in Hiroshima, it was destroyed in 1945, but amazingly, it looks like it's been here forever. Unfortunately, like most gardens in Japan, tall neighboring buildings detract from the garden's beauty (there ought to be a law), but it's a pleasant respite from city traffic.

2–11 Kaminobori-cho, Naka-ku. ℭ 082/221-3620. Admission ¥250 ($2.10) adults, ¥180 ($1.50) university and high-school students, ¥120 ($1) children. Combination ticket for Hiroshima Prefectural Art Museum and garden ¥600 ($5), ¥380 ($3.15), and ¥180 ($1.50) respectively. Daily 9am–6pm, to 5pm Oct–Mar. Adjacent to Hiroshima Prefectural Art Museum.

SETO INLAND SEA CRUISES

Hiroshima is also a departure point for day cruises on the Seto Inland Sea. Stretching between Honshu and the islands of Shikoku and Kyushu, the Inland Sea is dotted with more than 3,000 pine-covered islands and islets, part of which is protected as Seto-Naikai (Inland Sea) National Park. Cruises operate from March to the end of November with departures every Wednesday and Friday at 9am and returning at 5pm. The cost of the cruise, which includes lunch and drinks, is ¥14,800 ($123) for adults and ¥11,800 ($98) for children. Since times and days of cruises can change, contact the Hiroshima tourist office for updated information.

WHERE TO STAY

The **Welcome Card** available free at local tourist offices provides a 10% discount for several hotels, including the Granvia, Righa Royal, and Sera Bekkan.

EXPENSIVE

Hotel Granvia Hiroshima ⚞   Owned by JR West and Hankyu, this hotel is convenient for short stays because it's connected to the Shinkansen (north) side of the station. Inconvenient, however, is that to get to Hiroshima's sights and streetcars, which are on the other side of the station, you have to walk through an underground passage (if you have a rail pass, you can pass through the station, which is much quicker). Rooms are comfortable but are small and have no view. A plus are the hotel's many dining options.

1–5 Matsubara-cho, Minami-ku, Hiroshima 732-0822. ℭ 082/262-1111. Fax 082/262-4050. 435 units. ¥9,300–¥11,500 ($77.50–$96) single; ¥15,500–¥19,000 ($129–$158) double; ¥17,500–¥23,000 ($146–$192) twin. AE, DC, JCB, MC, V. Attached to Hiroshima Station. **Amenities:** 12 restaurants, 1 bar, 1 outdoor beer terrace (summer only); access to health club in Hiroshima Station with gym, indoor pool, and sauna (discount ticket at concierge desk ¥2,750/$23); concierge; tour desk; business center; shopping arcade; salon; room service (7–10am and 7–11pm); in-room massage; same-day laundry/dry cleaning service; nonsmoking rooms. *In room:* A/C, bilingual cable TV, minibar, hot-water pot with tea, hair dryer, washlet toilet.

167 **Mitakiso** ★★★ *Finds*   This beautiful traditional Japanese inn, part of which is more than 75 years old, has an idyllic, quiet setting. Its rooms are spread along an exquisite landscape garden with stunted pines, ponds, tiny maple trees, stone lanterns, and meandering streams. The best rooms are elegant and private with sliding doors that open onto the main garden. The least expensive rooms, on the second floor, face the front garden and street, but foreigners are often upgraded to a ground-floor room complete with a bathroom and sliding doors to a small veranda. The ryokan is well known for its excellent cuisine, served either in your guest room or in a dining hall as per your request. Although the ryokan is a bit far from the center of town, you can catch a bus just a 2-minute walk from the ryokan that will deliver you downtown near Hiroshima's attractions. A great place for a splurge.

1–7 Mitaki-cho, Nishi-ku, Hiroshima 733-0005. ℂ 082/237-1402. Fax 082/237-1403. 10 units (8 with toilet only, 2 with bathroom). ¥25,000–¥40,000 ($208–$333) per person. Rates include breakfast, dinner, and service. AE, DC, JCB, MC, V. JR Station: Yokogawa (7 min.). Taxi: 15 min. from Hiroshima Station. The entrance is past a yellow Japanese wall and a massive stone lantern. **Amenities:** In-room massage. *In room:* A/C, TV, hot-water pot with tea and coffee, hair dryer.

Rihga Royal Hiroshima ★★★   Opened in 1994, the 33-story Rihga Royal stands out as Hiroshima's tallest building and has a convenient location in the heart of the city between Hiroshima Castle and Peace Park. It's connected to a large complex called Motomachi Cred, which includes the Pacela shopping mall and Sogo department store. A sophisticated, European atmosphere makes it a favorite among foreign travelers; even the lobby lounge—with its tall ceiling and circular, glass facade—makes for a cheerful meeting place. Large rooms with luxurious furnishings come with plenty of features, including semi-double beds in the singles and twins and magnifying mirrors and lots of counter space in the bathrooms. Rates are based on floor height, but even some of the cheapest twins have great Castle views. Others face the Seto Inland Sea and Peace Park. A nice touch are the pictorial maps in each room describing the view, but the best view of all is afforded from the 33rd floor, where the Sky Buffet Rijo serves all-you-can-eat buffet lunch and set dinners (see "Where to Dine," below) and the Rihga Top provides a sophisticated setting for afternoon tea or evening cocktails.

6–78 Motomachi, Naka-ku, Hiroshima 730-0011. ℂ 082/502-1121. Fax 082/228-5415. www.rihga.co.jp. 490 units. ¥12,000–¥14,000 ($100–$117) single; ¥18,000–¥24,000 ($150–$200) double; ¥19,000–¥28,000 ($158–$233) twin; from ¥30,000 ($250) executive twin. AE, DC, JCB, MC, V. Streetcar: 1, 2, or 6 to Kamiya-cho (exit near the Astram Line, 1 min.). **Amenities:** 8 restaurants, 2 bars, 1 lounge; atrium-style pool with Jacuzzi and sauna (¥3,000/$25); health club (¥3,000/$25); concierge; shopping arcade; health and dental clinic; salon; barber; room service (7am–11:30pm); in-room massage; babysitting; same-day laundry/dry cleaning service; nonsmoking rooms; executive-level rooms. *In room:* A/C, cable TV with pay movies, minibar, hot-water pot with tea and coffee, hair dryer, bathroom scale, washlet toilet, trouser press.

MODERATE

Hotel Silk Plaza   This locally owned hotel, built in 1975, has a helpful, English-speaking, front desk staff. All rooms are very simple and small (few have closets), but cheeriness is imparted by colorful spreads. Though all single rooms have semi-double beds, note that the cheapest singles are dark and open toward a wall with windows of other guest rooms just 2 feet away. If there are two or more of you, ask for the large corner room on the ninth floor, which provides a good view of the downtown action.

14–1 Hatchobori, Naka-ku, Hiroshima 730-0013. ℂ 082/227-8111. Fax 082/227-8110. 231 units. ¥6,500–¥7,000 ($54–$58) single; ¥12,500 ($104) double or twin. AE, DC, JCB, MC, V. Streetcar: 1, 2, or 6 to the Hatchobori stop (2 min.). 2 blocks north on Hakushima Dori (there's a tram line here leading north to

Shukkein-mae) on the left. **Amenities:** 2 restaurants (Japanese, Western), 1 tavern; business center, in-room massage, same-day laundry/dry cleaning service. *In room:* A/C, bilingual TV with pay movies, fridge, hot-water pot with tea, hair dryer.

Hotel Sunroute ★★   Although most hotels in this chain are strictly business hotels, this hotel's excellent location, next to the river and catty-corner from the museum in Peace Memorial Park, makes it a popular choice for tourists as well. The highest-priced rooms have the additional advantage of views of the park; the cheapest rooms, however, are on low floors and have no views whatsoever.

3–3–1 Ohtemachi, Naka-ku, Hiroshima 730-0051. © 082/249-3600. Fax 082/249-3677. 284 units. ¥7,700–¥8,500 ($64–$71) single; ¥14,000–¥16,000 ($117–$133) double; ¥15,000–¥22,000 ($125–$183) twin. AE, DC, JCB, MC, V. Streetcar: 1 to Fukuro-machi (3 min.). Walk south (the same direction as your street-car) on Rijo Dori to Heiwa Odori (there's a small shrine on the corner) and turn right; it's on your left before the river. **Amenities:** 2 restaurants (Japanese, Italian), 1 bar; in-room massage; same-day laundry/dry cleaning service; nonsmoking rooms. *In room:* A/C, satellite TV with pay movies, minibar, hot-water pot with tea, hair dryer, washlet toilet.

⑯⑧ **Sera Bekkan** ★★   This modern ryokan is in the city center just off Namiki Dori. Although the building itself is far from traditional and resembles a hotel with its wide corridors and elevator, the rooms are Japanese style with tatami mats and shoji screens; three have views of a tiny garden. There are large public baths. Dinner is served in your room; Western-style breakfasts are available. Rates vary depending on the meal you order for dinner and the number of people staying in the room.

4–20 Mikawa-cho, Naka-ku, Hiroshima 730-0029. © 082/248-2251. Fax 082/248-2768. 35 units (all with bathroom). ¥10,000–¥20,000 ($83–$167) per person. Rates include breakfast, dinner and service. AE, DC, JCB, MC, V. Streetcar: 1, 2, or 6 to Hatchobori stop (4 min.). Walk south on Chuo Dori past Wiz Wonderland and turn right; take the 1st left and then the 1st right. It's on the corner to the left. **Amenities:** Game room; in-room massage. *In room:* A/C, TV, minibar, hot-water pot with tea, hair dryer, safe.

INEXPENSIVE

Regalo ★★ (Finds)   Opened in 1998 on one of Hiroshima's many rivers, this small, personable hotel offers great value and is a true find—nicely decorated with an Italian flair and managed by a very friendly staff (who, because of limited English, prefers fax to telephone reservations). The cheapest rooms have glazed windows facing the back, while rooms only slightly more expensive have refreshing views of the river. A very atmospheric Italian restaurant also capitalizes on the river view. A pleasant surprise compared to most inexpensive lodgings.

9–2 Hashimoto-cho, Naka-ku, Hiroshima 730-0015. © 082/224-6300. Fax 082/224-6301. 60 units. ¥6,500–¥7,000 ($54–$58) single; ¥9,500–¥10,000 ($79–$83) double; ¥9,800–¥10,000 ($82–$83) twin. Rates include breakfast, tax, and service charge. AE, DC, JCB, MC, V. Streetcar: 1, 2, or 6 to Kanayama-cho (2 min.). Walk back toward the bridge but don't cross it; turn left at the river. Or a 13-min. walk from the station. **Amenities:** 1 restaurant (Italian), 1 tea lounge; 24-hr. convenience store; in-room massage; coin-op washer and dryer; same-day laundry/dry cleaning service; nonsmoking rooms. *In room:* A/C, TV with pay movies, fridge, hot-water pot with tea, hair dryer, washlet toilet.

⎛Tips   A Note on Japanese Symbols

Many establishments and attractions in Japan do not have signs in Roman (English-language) letters. Those that don't are indicated in this guide with an oval with a number that corresponds to a number in appendix C showing the Japanese symbols. Thus, to find the Japanese symbol for, say, the **Mitakiso** ryokan (above), refer to no. 167 in appendix C.

⟨169⟩ **Rijyo Kaikan** ✿ *Value* Located close to the Hondori covered shopping arcade and Peace Memorial Park, this modern, triangular-shaped building has rooms intended primarily as lodging for government office employees, but anyone can stay here if there's space (try to make reservations 6 months in advance). Rooms are great for the price—bright, white, and cheerful. Note that check-in isn't until 4pm.

1–5–3 Otemachi, Naka-ku, Hiroshima 730-0051. ✆ **082/245-2322.** Fax 082/245-2315. 50 units. ¥5,300–¥6,000 ($47.50–$54) single; ¥9,800–¥15,000 ($82–$129) twin. Breakfast ¥800 ($6.65) extra; dinner ¥1,800 ($15) extra. No credit cards. Streetcar: 1 to Hondori (2 min.). Walk west 1 block through the covered shopping arcade and take the 1st right; it's marked "Kenmin Bunka Center" or "Hiroshima Prefectural Culture Center" on the city maps. **Amenities:** 3 restaurants (Japanese, Western, coffee shop); in-room massage; laundry service. *In room:* A/C, TV, hot-water pot with tea, hair dryer.

WHERE TO DINE
EXPENSIVE

Atago ✿✿ TEPPANYAKI This teppanyaki steak restaurant, on the ground floor of an office building on Heiwa (Peace) Odori just east of Rijo Dori, is convenient if you're visiting the Peace Memorial Museum just across the river. It's strikingly modern with its marble tables and geometric lines, and chefs prepare steak and seafood before your eyes. The ¥6,000 ($50) dinner includes salad, appetizer, sirloin or tenderloin beef, vegetables, soup, rice, and dessert.

7–20 Nakamachi. ✆ **082/241-1111.** Reservations recommended. Set dinners ¥5,000–¥16,000 ($42–$133); set lunches ¥2,500–¥6,000 ($21–$50). AE, DC, JCB, MC, V. Daily 11:30am–2:30pm and 5–9:30pm. Streetcar: 1 to Fukuro-machi (2 min.). Next to the ANA Hotel on Peace Blvd.

⟨170⟩ **Kanawa** ✿✿✿ *Finds* OYSTERS There are 10,000 rafts cultivating oysters in Hiroshima Bay with a yearly output of 30,000 tons of shelled oysters. Needless to say, oysters are a Hiroshima specialty, and this houseboat, moored east of Peace Memorial Park on the Motoyasu River at the Heiwa Odori Bridge, is one of the best places to enjoy them. Although winter is the best time for fresh oysters, the owner has his own oyster rafts and freezes his best stock in January so that he's able to serve excellent oysters even in summer. This floating restaurant has been here more than 30 years, and dining is in tatami rooms with views of the river. The English-language menu lists set meals that feature oysters prepared various ways including in the shell, fried, in soup, and steamed.

On the Motoyasu River, at Heiwa Odori Bridge. ✆ **082/241-7416.** Reservations recommended. Set dinners ¥7,000–¥15,000 ($58–$125); set lunches ¥3,000–¥4,000 ($25–$33). AE, DC, JCB, MC, V. Mon–Sat 11am–2pm and 5–10pm. Closed irregularly. Streetcar: 1 to Fukuro-machi (3 min.). Next to the Sunroute Hotel.

MODERATE

Sky Buffet Rijo ✿ CONTINENTAL This pleasant restaurant, serving inexpensive all-you-can-eat buffet lunch and set dinners, has a drawing-room ambience, but the main reason to dine here is because it's the city's highest restaurant, and has a view of Hiroshima Castle. After dinner, retire to the classy Rihga Top bar with views of the Seto Inland Sea, but note that there's a ¥1,000 ($8.35) table charge.

Rihga Royal Hiroshima, 33rd floor, 6–78 Motomachi. ✆ **082/502-1121.** Lunch buffet ¥2,500 ($21); set dinners ¥3,500–¥7,000 ($29–$58). AE, DC, JCB, MC, V. Daily 11am–1:30pm and 5:30–10pm. Streetcar: 1,2, or 6 to Kamiyacho (1 min.).

Trattoria Viale ✿ ITALIAN Convenience to Peace Memorial Park, great 15th-floor views, and good food make this an optimal choice for tourists. Though counter seats have the best views, it's nearly impossible to sit with your legs under the counter so insist on a table. The antipasto plate is a delicious way to start your meal. The wood-fired pizzas are wafer thin and flaky, while the pasta may be more al dente than you like. Still, all is forgiven as you dine and take in the view. The dinner dessert table is very tempting.

Hotel Sunroute, 15th floor, 3–3–1 Ohtemachi. © 082/249-3600. Pasta and pizza ¥1,200–¥1,800 ($10–$15); main dishes ¥2,300–¥2,500 ($19–$21); set lunches ¥1,500–¥4,500 ($12.50–$38). AE, DC, JCB, MC, V. Daily 11:30am–3pm and 5–9:30pm. Streetcar: 1 to Fukuro-machi (see directions to hotel, above).

INEXPENSIVE

Anderson Kitchen INTERNATIONAL   Occupying an old, renovated bank building in the Hondori covered shopping arcade, this popular place not far from Peace Memorial Park has a gourmet food department on its ground floor offering baked goods, wine, and sandwiches, while the second floor has a cafeteria with various counters specializing in different types of food—salads, sandwiches, pizza, stews, desserts, or drinks. Just pick up a tray and select the items you want. You pay at the end of each counter. Chinese and European restaurants with sit-down service are also on the second floor.

7–1 Hondori. © 082/247-2403. Dishes ¥550–¥1,200 ($4.60–$10). AE, DC, JCB, V. Daily 11:30am–8pm. Closed 3rd Wed of every month. Streetcar: 1 to Hondori (1 min.); in the Hondori covered shopping arcade 1 block to the east.

(171) **Kushinobo** ★★ KUSHIYAKI   This is a friendly, rub-elbows-with-the-locals kind of place, lively and crowded and decorated with Japanese knick-knacks. Skewers, prepared at the counter where you can watch, start at ¥140 ($1.15), but you should expect to pay at least ¥3,000 ($25) for dinner with drinks. I enjoyed the Kushinobo-gozen with 10 skewers of vegetables, meat, and seafood plus fresh vegetables, rice, soup, and dessert. There's a menu in English.

Parco-mae, 7–4 Horikawa-cho. © 082/245-9300. Reservations recommended. Skewers ¥140–¥450 ($1.15–$3.75); set dinners ¥2,500–¥5,000 ($21–$42); set lunches ¥830–¥1,280 ($6.90–$11). AE, DC, JCB, MC, V. Daily 11:30am–2pm and 5–10pm. Streetcar: 1, 2, or 6 to Hatchobori (2 min.). Walk south on Chuo Dori 3 blocks and turn right into a covered shopping arcade; take the 1st left and then the 1st right. It's on the north side of Parco.

Masui (Value STEAKS/SHABU-SHABU/SUKIYAKI   In business 50 years, this very popular restaurant around the corner from the Silk Plaza Hotel in the middle of town has its own butcher shop and offers great bargains: individual-size portions of shabu-shabu or sukiyaki, for example, start at only ¥1,000 ($8.35). Unsurprisingly, this two-story restaurant is especially crowded during lunchtime, when it churns out plate after plate of teishoku specials. The ¥750 ($6.25) teishoku gets you a hamburger patty, ham, omelet, pork cutlet, and rice, but you can forgo the hamburger and get the tonkatsu teishoku with rice for just ¥350 ($2.90). Masui has recently gone big time with a new sign outside advertising SUKIYAKI AND FOREIGN FOODS and an English menu, but I find it's still the same.

14–13 Hatchobori. © 082/227-2983. Set meals ¥900–¥4,000 ($7.50–$33); lunch teishoku from ¥600 ($5). No credit cards. Thurs–Tues 11am–8:20pm (last order). Closed 2nd Tues each month. Streetcar: 1, 2, or 6 to Hatchobori (2 min.). Walk north on Hakushima Dori and take the 1st left; it's on the right.

(172) **Okonomi-Mura** ★★ (Finds OKONOMIYAKI   Although the people of Osaka claim to have made okonomiyaki popular among the masses, the people of Hiroshima claim to have made it an art. Okonomiyaki is a kind of Japanese pancake filled with cabbage, meat, and other fillings. Whereas in Osaka the ingredients are all mixed together, in Hiroshima, each layer is prepared separately, which means the chefs have to be quite skilled at keeping the whole thing together. This is the best place in town to witness these short-order cooks at their trade, although the building doesn't look as though it contains restaurants. Its name means "okonomiyaki village," and that's what it is—floors of individual

stalls, dishing out okonomiyaki (the food still remains a dish for the masses). All okonomiyaki stalls offer basically the same menu—just sit down at one of the counters and watch how the chef first spreads pancake mix on a hot griddle; follows it with a layer of cabbage, bean sprouts, and bacon; and then adds an egg on top. If you want, you can have yours with udon (thick wheat noodles) or soba (thin buckwheat noodles). Helpings are enormous.

Simply wander through and stop at a stall that catches your fancy. Or, for a specific recommendation, try **Chii-chan** (*⊘* **082/249-8102**) on the second floor. It stays open until 2am (closed on Tues) and has an English-language menu. Chii-chan and his all-girl staff sell between 200 and 500 okonomiyaki a day. One of Hiroshima's most beloved establishments.

5–13 Shintenchi. *⊘* **082/241-8758**. Set meals ¥700–¥1,300 ($5.85–$11). No credit cards. Daily 11am–9pm, but some stalls stay open to 2am. Streetcar: 1, 2, or 6 to Hatchobori (2 min.). Walk south on Chuo Dori 4 blocks (you'll see Wiz Wonderland on the corner) and turn right.

⑰ **Suishin** *☆☆* RICE CASSEROLES   This is the main shop of a locally owned restaurant chain specializing in *kamameshi* (rice casseroles). First opened in 1950, this chain now has five locations in Hiroshima alone. The main shop, in the middle of town one block north of Hondori, has five floors of dining, and though the decor is rather simple, Suishin is very popular for its rice casseroles topped with such Hiroshima delicacies as oysters, mushrooms, sea bream, sea eels, shrimp, and chestnuts. It sells about 800 kamameshi per day, a number that swells to as many as 2,000 on Sunday. To deal with the demand, the owner invented his own conveyor-belt oven, which could cook 180 kamameshi in an hour. Nowadays, kamameshi are prepared fresh with each order. If you want a substantial meal, order the ¥3,000 ($25) set meal from the English menu, which comes with tempura and other side dishes. Other dishes include oysters, eel, grilled fish, and sardines. Lunch specials change daily.

6–7 Tatemachi. *⊘* **082/247-4411**. Main dishes ¥1,000–¥2,500 ($5–$21); kamameshi (rice casseroles) ¥700 ($5.85); set lunches ¥800–¥1,500 ($6.65–$12.50). AE, DC, JCB, MC, V. Thurs–Tues 11:30am–10pm (last order 8:45pm). Streetcar: 1, 2, or 6 to Tatemachi (2 min.). Walk 3 blocks south to the post office and turn left.

⑰ **Sushi Tei** *☆* *Value* SUSHI   Excellent sushi at reasonable prices is the reason this establishment is so popular. You'll be seated at the counters, as cooks shout greetings and orders back and forth. Ordering is made easy with an English menu, as well as display cases outside. There are several other Sushi Tei restaurants in town, the most convenient of which is the one near the A-Bomb Dome, one block south of Aioi Dori between Kamiyacho and Genbaku-Dome-mae stops; (*⊘* **082/545-1333**), open the same hours.

4-21 Ebisucho, Naka-ku *⊘* **082/249-1808**. 2 pieces sushi ¥160–¥600 ($1.35–$5); sushi teishoku ¥800–¥1,500 ($6.65–$12.50). Mon–Sat 5pm–midnight; Sun and holidays noon–10pm. Streetcar: 1, 2, or 6 to Ebisucho (1 min.. Take the side street next to Mitsukoshi department store and then the 1st left; it's on your left.

Tandoor INDIAN   The Pacela Building, part of the fancy Motomachi Cred (pronounced *Kuredo* in Japanese) complex, has some 30 food-and-beverage outlets, including this one with a welcoming, English-speaking staff. It specializes in tandoori, including tandoori prawns, kebabs, and chicken, as well as curries and breads. The least expensive curry set lunch is not available on weekends and holidays.

Motomachi Cred complex, 7th floor of Pacela, 6–78 Motomachi. *⊘* **082/502-3371**. Curries ¥900–¥1,200 ($6.25–$10); set lunches ¥710–¥1,680 ($5.90–$14); set dinners ¥2,000–¥5,000 ($17–$42). AE, DC, MC, V. Mon–Fri 11am–3pm and 5–10pm; Sat 11am–10pm; Sun 11am–9:30pm. Streetcar: 1, 2, or 6 to Kamiyacho (1 min.); follow the signs to the Atram Line and take the exit on your left.

12 Miyajima, Scenic Island in the Seto Sea ⟨★⟨★⟨★

13km (8 miles) SW of Hiroshima

Easily reached in about 45 minutes from Hiroshima, **Miyajima** is a treasure of an island only 1¼ miles off the mainland in the Seto Inland Sea. No doubt you've seen pictures of its most famous landmark—a huge red *torii*, or shrine gate, rising up out of the water. Erected in 1875 and made of camphor wood, it's one of the largest torii in Japan, measuring more than 53 feet tall. It guards Miyajima's main attraction, Itsukushima Shrine.

With the Japanese penchant for categorizing the "best three" of virtually everything in their country—the three best gardens, the three best waterfalls, and so on—it's no surprise that Miyajima is ranked as one of the three most scenic spots in Japan (the other two are Matsushima in Tohoku and Amanohashidate, a remote sandspit, on the Japan Sea coast). Only 12 square miles in area and consisting mostly of steep, wooded hills, it's an exceptionally beautiful island, part of the **Seto-Naikai (Inland Sea) National Park** that is mostly water, islands, and islets. Of course, this distinction means it can be quite crowded with visitors, particularly in summer.

Miyajima has been held sacred since ancient times. In the olden days, no one was allowed to do anything so human as to give birth or die on the island, so both the pregnant and the ill were quickly ferried across to the mainland. Even today there's no cemetery on Miyajima. Covered with cherry trees illuminating the island with snowy petals in spring and maple trees emblazoning it in reds and golds in autumn, Miyajima is home to tame deer that roam freely through the village and to monkeys that swing through the woods. It's a delightful island for strolls and hikes—but avoid coming on a weekend.

ESSENTIALS

GETTING THERE   The easiest way to get to Miyajima is from Hiroshima. You can travel from Hiroshima by JR train, streetcar, or bus, but the fastest and most convenient method is the **train,** which departs from Hiroshima Station approximately every 6 to 30 minutes, depending on the time of the day, and costs ¥400 ($3.35; free for JR Rail Pass holders) for the 26-minute ride to Miyajimaguchi. Otherwise, a **streetcar** takes about an hour from Hiroshima Station to Hiroden Miyajima, the last stop, and costs ¥270 ($2.25). In any case, all modes of transportation deposit you at Miyajimaguchi, from which it's just a couple minutes' walk to the **ferry** bound for Miyajima. There are two ferry companies offering the 10-minute ride to Miyajima for ¥170 ($1.40), but if you have a **Japan Rail Pass,** you can ride on the JR ferry for free.

VISITOR INFORMATION   On Miyajima, stop off at the **Tourist Information Office** (✆ **0829/44-2011;** open daily 8:30am–7pm, to 6pm in winter) located in the Miyajima ferry terminal; it has a brochure in English with a map. The staff can also make reservations for accommodations, but since they try to steer foreigners to certain places, you'll have to insist if you have a specific place in mind. Some English is spoken, and they are helpful and will show you where your accommodations are on the map. For ¥300 ($2.50), you can rent an audio guide that describes in English the 20 places of interest noted on a companion map—a great convenience.

GETTING AROUND   You can **walk** to all the sights, accommodations, and restaurants listed below. If you wish to visit one of the island's beaches or explore more of the island, there are rental **bicycles** at the JR ferry pier available 8am to

5pm costing ¥320 ($2.65) for 2 hours or ¥1,050 ($8.75) for the whole day. Inquire at the JR ticket window. Otherwise, there are shuttle **buses** traveling to the beaches once or twice an hour in July and August that cost ¥300 ($2.50). Ask the Tourist Information Office for a schedule.

EXPLORING THE ISLAND
SEEING THE SIGHTS

Miyajima's major attraction, **Itsukushima Shrine** ✿✿, 1–1 Miyajima-cho (© 0829/44-2020), is less than a 10-minute walk from the ferry pier (turn right out of the terminal) along a narrow street lined with souvenir shops and restaurants. Founded back in 592 to honor three female deities, the wooden shrine is built out over the water so that, when the tide is in, it appears as though the shrine is floating. A brilliant vermilion, it contrasts starkly with the wooded hills in the background and the blue of the sky above, casting its reflection in the waters below. If you do happen to see Itsukushima Shrine when the tide is in and it's seemingly floating on water, you should consider yourself very lucky indeed—most of the time the lovely shrine floats above a surface that's only a little more glamorous than mud. That's when some imagination comes in handy (the Hiroshima tourist offices may have a tide calendar).

The majority of the shrine buildings are thought to date from the 16th century, preserving the original style of 12th-century architecture, but they have been repaired repeatedly through the centuries. Most of the buildings of the shrine are closed, but from sunrise to sunset daily (usually 6:30am–6pm in summer, to 5pm in winter), you can walk along the 770-foot covered **dock** which threads its way past the outer part of the main shrine and the oldest Noh stage in Japan. From the shrine, you have a good view of the red torii standing in the water. If you're lucky, you might even get to see **Bugaku** (festival dances) staged for one of the many tour groups that pass through. An ancient dance performed to the accompaniment of court music, Bugaku was introduced to Japan centuries ago from India through China and Korea. The performer's costume is orange, matching the shrine around him. Admission to the shrine is ¥300 ($2.50) for adults, ¥200 ($1.65) for college and high-school students, ¥100 (85¢) for children.

Turn right upon exiting the shrine. After a few minutes, you'll come to the island's most interesting museum, the **Miyajima Municipal History and Folklore Museum** (Rekishi Minzoku Shiryokan ✿✿, 57 Miyajima-cho (© 0829/44-2019); open Tues–Sun 8:30am–5pm). It has a colorful brochure in English to guide you through the 170-year-old house, which once belonged to a wealthy soy-sauce merchant and is built around a small Japanese garden, as well as several other buildings. Packed with items donated by the people of Miyajima, the museum is a window into commoners' daily life in ages past, with farm tools, water jars, cooking objects, carved-wood boxes, furniture, lacquerware, combs, and much more. Be sure to see the narrow, three-room dwelling in the back of the museum complex, typical of the island. Admission is ¥300 ($2.50) for adults, ¥170 ($1.40) for high-school students, and ¥150 ($1.25) junior-high and elementary students. It will take about 30 minutes to see everything.

ENJOYING MIYAJIMA'S NATURAL WORLD

The other popular thing to do on Miyajima is to climb its highest peak, 1,750-foot-high **Mt. Misen.** There are signs directing you to Momijidani Park, a pleasant hillside park covered with maple trees (spectacular in autumn) and cherry trees (heavenly in spring) and marked by a picturesque stream. From here, you can take cable cars to Mt. Misen; round-trip tickets cost ¥1,500 ($12.50) for adults, ¥1,200 ($10) for students, and ¥750 ($6.25) for children. However, you might wish to enjoy some of the scenery by walking back down, in which case one-way tickets cost ¥900 ($7.50), ¥700 ($5.85), and ¥450 ($3.75) respectively. In any case, the summit of Mt. Misen, a 15-minute walk from the cable car station, offers splendid views of the Seto-Naikai (Inland Sea) National Park, and Mt. Misen itself is home to much of the island's wild monkey population.

Miyajima is also known for its beaches. If you're looking to swim, there are two beaches west of the town and shrine: **Suginoura** and **Tsutsumigaura Natural Park** (you can also camp here). Ask at the tourist office for a schedule of shuttle buses.

WHERE TO STAY

You can see Miyajima easily on a side trip from Hiroshima, but because it's such a beautiful respite from city life and because most tourists are day-trippers, you'll enjoy the island much more if you stay behind after the last ferry leaves. An added benefit of a longer stay: Itsukushima Shrine is illuminated at night, a gorgeous sight overnighters should not miss. I've therefore included a few recommendations on where to stay, but avoid Golden Week and weekends in July, August, October, and November (when maple leaves are in full color) since accommodations are usually full.

(175) **Guest House Kikugawa** ✿   Located in a quiet residential neighborhood an easy walk from the ferry pier, this guest house is modern yet adheres to traditional Japanese design with its whitewashed walls, dark timber framing, white paper lanterns, and simple elegance. The owner, Kikugawa-san, speaks English and is an accomplished chef, serving French food with a Japanese twist in his pleasant restaurant with a restful view of a maple tree (advance reservations required). Six of the guest rooms are Western style and are rather ordinary, reflected in the cheaper room rates below. The two other more expensive rooms face the front and boast flowers and washlet toilet; the smaller is a tatami room, while the larger has a tatami area and a loft with Western-style beds. Since this place is small, make reservations 6 months in advance if you want to stay here in July, August, October, or November.

796 Miyajimacho, Saeki-gun, Hiroshima-ken 739-0511. (✆0829/44-0039. Fax 0829/44-2773. http://gambo-ad.com/english/hotel/kikugawa/info.htm. 8 units. ¥6,800–¥9,000 ($57–$75) single; ¥12,000–¥16,000 ($100–$133) double; ¥15,000–¥18,000 ($125–$150) triple. ¥1,000 ($8.35) more per person holiday eves and peak season. Breakfast ¥1,000 ($8.35) extra; dinner ¥3,500 and ¥5,000 ($29 and $42) extra. DC, JCB, MC, V. A 3-min. walk from the ferry terminal; walk through the short tunnel in front of the terminal and turn right. Look for the GUEST HOUSE sign. **Amenities:** 1 restaurant; coin-op washer and dryer. *In room:* A/C, TV, hot-water pot with tea, hair dryer.

(176) **Iwaso Ryokan** ✿✿✿ *(Finds*   This is the most famous ryokan on the island, and with a history spanning more than 145 years, it was also the first ryokan to open on Miyajima, which explains its idyllic location in Momijidani Park. It's highly recommended for a splurge, with the price dependent on the room, its view, and the meals you select (when booking your room, be sure to specify any dietary needs such as vegetarian food only, whether you want a Western breakfast, or whether there are Japanese foods you cannot eat). The newest part of the ryokan was built in 1981, and though some of its newer rooms have very peaceful and relaxing views of a stream and woods, I prefer the rooms dating from about 60 years ago; they have more individuality. If you really want to go all out and live in style, there are also a couple separate cottages (*hanare*) that are more than 80 years old, are exquisitely decorated, and come with old

wooden tubs. You can open your shoji screens here to see maples, a gurgling brook, and woods, all in utter privacy. You'll be treated like royalty here, but of course you have to pay for it.

Momijidani, 345 Miyajimacho, Saeki-gun, Hiroshima-ken 739-0522. **ⓒ0829/44-2233.** Fax 0829/44-2230. 44 units (36 with bathroom). ¥21,000–¥40,000 ($175–$333) per person. Cottage, ¥35,000–¥50,000 ($291–$417) per person. Rates may be higher during peak season and nights before holidays. Rates include 2 meals and service charge. AE, DC, JCB, V. A 15-min. walk from the ferry pier in Momijidani Park. Pickup service available. *In room:* A/C, TV, minibar, hot-water pot with tea, hair dryer, safe.

⑰ **Miyajima Morinoyado** ★★ *Value*   You're forgiven for passing this place by, thinking it must be an exclusive ryokan. Indeed, if it weren't a municipally owned *Kokumin Shukusha* (People's Lodge), rates here would easily be three times as much as they are. Though modern, it has a lovely Japanese design with a lobby overlooking a carp pond. On the other hand, the many school groups and families staying here leave no doubt that it's a public lodge, and it's quite a hike from the ferry pier. Both tatami rooms and Western-style twins—simple but spacious and spotless—are available, some with views of the bay. The public baths look onto rock gardens. Although the local tourist office may indicate that the facility isn't really for foreigners ("because they won't be able to understand the Japanese way of doing things"), and not much English is spoken, it's worth persisting. Reservations should be made 1 year in advance, especially for August, The front desk is receptive to foreigners, and sometimes there are cancellations; when I dropped by on a weekday in June, rooms were available. Both Western and Japanese breakfasts are available; dinners are Japanese.

Miyajimacho, Saeki-gun, Hiroshima-ken 739-0500. **ⓒ 0829/44-0430.** Fax 0892/44-2248. 30 units (26 with bathroom, 4 with toilet only). ¥4,300 ($36) per person without bathroom; ¥4,800 ($40) per person with bathroom. ¥700 ($5.85) more per person on Sat, nights before holidays, and during peak season (Apr, May, July, and Aug). Discounts given for children. Breakfast ¥1,000 ($8.35) extra; dinner ¥2,000–¥5,000 ($17–$42) extra. No credit cards. A 25-min. walk from the ferry pier, across from the aquarium and just before the tunnel. **Amenities:** 1 restaurant (Japanese); Jacuzzi. *In room:* A/C, TV, hot-water pot with tea.

Momiji-so ★★   This small, Japanese-style house has a great location in Momijidani Park, not far from the ropeway to Mt. Misen and has been in business 85 years. Tatami rooms vary in size, though all have artwork, flowers, and views of the surrounding park; the best looks out over a koi pond. A plus is its nice outdoor Japanese restaurant serving noodles, barbecued conger eel on rice, and other dishes—weather permitting you'll dine outside. Not much English is spoken, but they're used to foreigners.

Momijidani-koennai, Miyajimacho, Saeki-gun, Hiroshima-ken 739-0500. **ⓒ 0829/44-0077.** Fax 0829/44-0076. www.gambo-ad.com. 7 units (2 with bathroom). ¥8,000 ($67) per person. Rates include breakfast. Dinner ¥3,000–¥5,000 ($25–$42) extra. No credit cards. A 25-min. walk from the ferry pier in Momijidani Park. Pickup service available.

WHERE TO DINE

⑱ **Fujitaya** ★★ *Finds* ANAGOMESHI   Although the building itself is not old, this pleasant restaurant has a history of more than 80 years and preserves a traditional atmosphere with its wooden ceiling, shoji lamps, and a back courtyard with a maple tree, moss-covered rocks, and water running from a bamboo pipe into a pool carved into a flat rock. Fujitaya serves only *anagomeshi* (barbecued conger eel on rice), which comes with side dishes (such as pickled vegetables), soup, and tea. It closes when it runs out of anago.

ⓒ 0829/44-0151. Anagomeshi teishoku ¥2,300 ($19). No credit cards. Mon–Fri 11am–3pm; Sat–Sun 11am–5pm. A 20-min. walk from the ferry pier, on the right side of the road leading toward Daishoin after exiting from Itsukushima Shrine. Look for its name written on an oversized paddle.

⑰ **Komitei** ☙ OKONOMIYAKI   Convenient to the ferry pier, this simple restaurant with counter, table, and tatami dining stays open later than most restaurants on the island and is one of the cleanest okonomiyaki restaurants we've seen. Both Hiroshima-style (which is prepared for you) and Kansai-style (which you prepare yourself) okonomiyaki are available from the English menu.

🕽 **0829/44-0177.** Okonomiyaki ¥700–¥900 ($5.85–$7.50); set meals ¥1,000–¥1,200 ($8.35–$10). No credit cards. Thurs–Tues 11am–2:30pm and 5–9pm. A 1-min. walk from the ferry pier, catty-corner to the right.

⑱ **Tonookajaya** NOODLES   Dine inside or out at this tiny teahouse-like shop next to the five-storied pagoda. The shop serves mostly udon (thick wheat noodles), including udon with tempura, but it also offers sticky rice cakes (*omochi chikara*) and a sweet rice porridge (*amazake*) is served October to May. What makes this place especially interesting is the 200-year-old pine tree out front that has been guided through the centuries in attaining its unique, horizontal shape. You can also come here just for drinks.

🕽 **0829/44-2455.** Main dishes ¥580–¥750 ($4.80–$6.25). No credit cards. Daily 10am–5pm. A 10-min. walk from the ferry pier on the hill with the 5-story pagoda, facing away from Itsukushima Shrine.

9

Shikoku

The smallest of Japan's four main islands, Shikoku is also the one least visited by foreigners. That's surprising considering the natural beauty of its rugged mountains, its mild climate, and its most famous monuments—88 sacred Buddhist temples. Many Japanese wish to make a pilgrimage to all 88 temples at least once in their lifetime as a tribute to the great Buddhist priest Kobo Daishi, who was born on Shikoku in 774 and who founded the Shingon sect of Buddhism.

This pilgrimage has been popular since the Edo Period in the belief that a successful completion of the tour exonerates Buddhist followers from rebirth. It used to take a couple months to visit all 88 temples on foot; even today, you can see the pilgrims making their rounds dressed in white—only now they go mostly by organized tour buses, which cut traveling time down to 2 weeks.

GETTING TO SHIKOKU For centuries, the only way to reach Shikoku was by boat. However, the 1988 completion of the Seto Ohashi Bridge, which links Shikoku with Okayama Prefecture and accommodates both cars and trains, changed Shikoku forever. And in 1999, a series of bridges connecting Shikoku with Hiroshima Prefecture and spanning six scenic islands in the Seto Inland Sea opened with fanfare. Complete with cycling paths offering views of the islands and Seto Inland Sea, it has since become one of Shikoku's hottest attractions. A third bridge, for cars only, connects Shikoku with Kobe.

In any case, Shikoku is no longer as far off the beaten track as it used to be, simply because access is so easy. Shinkansen travelers should simply transfer in Okayama for trains bound for either Takamatsu or Matsuyama. The energetic can cycle from Hiroshima Prefecture to Ehime Prefecture.

1 Takamatsu ★

794km (496 miles) W of Tokyo; 71km (44 miles) S of Okayama

The second-largest town on Shikoku with a population of 330,000, Takamatsu, the capital of Kagawa Prefecture, is on the northeastern coast of the island, overlooking the Seto Inland Sea. Takamatsu means "high pine," and the city served as the feudal capital of the powerful Matsudaira clan from 1642 until the Meiji Restoration in 1868. The Matsudairas are responsible for Takamatsu's most famous site, Ritsurin Park, one of the most outstanding gardens in Japan. Takamatsu also boasts more bonsai nurseries than anywhere else in Japan, while nearby is Kotohiragu Shrine, a popular mountaintop destination that requires a real workout just to see.

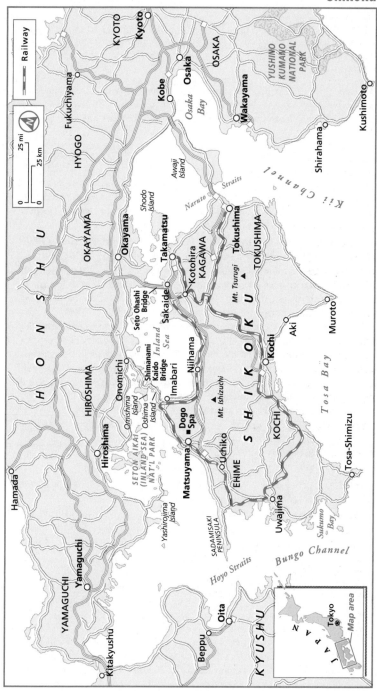

Shikoku

Railway

25 mi
25 km

HONSHU

KYOTO
Kyoto
Fukuchiyama
HYOGO
Kobe
Osaka
OSAKA
Osaka Bay
Wakayama
YUSHINO KUMANO NATIONAL PARK
Shirahama
Kushimoto
Kii Channel
Avaji Island
Shodo Island
Naruto Straits
OKAYAMA
Okayama
Takamatsu
Tokushima
TOKUSHIMA
Kotohira
KAGAWA
Mt. Tsurugi ▲
Seto Ohashi Bridge
Sakaide
Inland Sea
Niihama
Kochi
Aki
Muroto
Tosa Bay
HIROSHIMA
Onomichi
Omishima Island
Shimanami Kaido Bridge
Oshima Island
Imabari
Mt. Ishizuchi ▲
S H I K O K U
KOCHI
Hiroshima
SETON AIKAI (INLAND SEA) NAT'L PARK
Dogo Spa
Uchiko
EHIME
Matsuyama
Yashirojima Island
SADAMISAKI PENINSULA
Uwajima
Sukumo Bay
Tosa-Shimizu
Hamada
YAMAGUCHI
Yamaguchi
Hoyo Straits
Bungo Channel
Kitakyushu
Beppu
Oita
K Y U S H U
J A P A N
Tokyo
Map area

463

ESSENTIALS

GETTING THERE   By Plane   Flying time is 1 hour and 10 minutes from Tokyo (¥21,250/$177 for a one-way ticket), 1 hour and 10 minutes from Fukuoka on Kyushu island, and 1 hour and 50 minutes from Sapporo on Hokkaido.

By Train   JR's Marine Liner trains depart from Okayama Station approximately twice an hour, reaching Takamatsu in an hour; the fare is ¥1,470 ($12.25). From Matsuyama, trains take less than 2½ hours and cost ¥5,500 ($46).

By Bus   Buses depart from Tokyo Station nightly at 8:30pm, reaching Takamatsu at 6:45am the next day. One-way fare is ¥10,500 ($87.50). There are also night buses from Shinjuku.

By Boat   Hydrofoils connect Takamatsu with Osaka in 2½ hours and cost ¥6,500 ($54) one-way. Boats dock at piers just a few minutes' walk away from Takamatsu Station and the Kotoden tram.

VISITOR INFORMATION   The **Takamatsu City Information Office** (✆ 087/851-2009; open daily 9am–6pm), located outside the main exit of the train station in a small building toward the left beside a circular plaza, offers an English-language map of the city and the *Kagawa Welcome Card,* a free mini-guide complete with a discount card offering reduced rates for participating hotels, shops, restaurants, and attractions.

If you're craving a bit of news from home or are planning to remain in the area, head for **I-Pal Kagawa,** 1–11–63 Bancho (✆ 087/837-5901; open Tues–Sun 9am–6pm), located about a 15-minute walk south of Takamatsu Station on Chuo Dori in the northwest corner of Central (Chuo) Park. Here you'll find magazines and newspapers in many languages, CNN on the tube, and one computer you can use 30 minutes free of charge. This is also a good place to find out what's going on in the area and to pick up an even better map.

INTERNET ACCESS   Since I-Pal Kagawa, above, has only one machine (and a slow one at that), you're probably better off going to Queensberry@Café, 1–10–4 Tokiwa-cho (✆ 087/812-0680), across from Kotoden Kawaramachi Station's west exit (follow signs saying BUS STOP and then look for the cafe's sign to the left). It's open daily 11am to midnight and charges ¥100 (85¢) for 1 hour when you order a drink.

ORIENTATION & GETTING AROUND   Takamatsu Station, the city's ferry pier, and the local tram terminus are all clustered together on the north edge of the city on the coast of the Seto Inland Sea. All the hotels and restaurants listed below, as well as Ritsurin Park, are located south and southeast of the train station. **Chuo Dori** is the town's main avenue, running south from the train station to Ritsurin Park and beyond. Bisecting Chuo Dori and paralleling it to the east are 2.5km (1½ miles) of shopping arcade, which the city claims is the longest in Japan (several cities, however, make that claim).

Although the main attractions of Takamatsu are spread out, they're easily reached from Takamatsu Station by **JR train** or by a commuter tram called the **Kotoden Line.** The Kotoden tram terminus, called **Kotoden Chikko Station,** is a two-minute walk from Takamatsu Station's main exit, past the ANA hotel and to the right. Two stops south on the Kotoden tram (or a 25-min. walk from Takamatsu Station) is **Kawaramachi Station,** where you'll find many department stores, restaurants, and night spots.

SEEING THE SIGHTS

Ritsurin Park ⭐⭐⭐   Ritsurin Park was once the summer retreat of the Matsudaira family. Work on the park began in the 1600s and took about 100 years to complete. Using the backdrop of adjacent Mt. Shiun in a principle known as "borrowed landscaping," the 134-acre park incorporates the mountain into its overall design. Basically, the garden can be divided into two parts: a traditional, classical, southern garden, and a modern, northern garden, once a lord's private hunting grounds and with wide grassy lawns and huge lotus ponds.

The **southern garden** is the more interesting. Arranged around the prescribed 6 ponds and 13 scenic mounds, it represents what's called a strolling garden, in which each bend of the footpath brings another perspective into view, another combination of rock, tree, and mountain. The garden is absolutely exquisite, and what sets it apart are its twisted, contorted pines. On one of my visits, a mist was rolling off Mt. Shiun, lending mystery to the landscape; what better fits the image of traditional Japan than mist and pine trees? Altogether, there are 1,600 pine trees and 350 cherry trees in Ritsurin Park, which you should tour in a counterclockwise fashion to fully appreciate the changing views. Although I consider this garden just as beautiful as those in Okayama and Kanazawa, tall buildings on its Eastern periphery detract from its overall effect; without them I would give this garden top rating.

There are a couple of things you can stop and see during your tour of the park. In the northern garden are the **Sanuki Folk Art Museum** (Sanuki Mingei Kan), which is included in the park's admission and displays local folk art and handicrafts such as ceramics, lacquerware, furniture and items used in daily Edo life; and the **Commerce and Industry Hall** (Shoko Shorei-kan), which sells local products, including kites, masks, wood carvings, umbrellas, fans, and food items. But my favorite thing to do is drop by the **Kikugetsu-tei** (Scooping the Moon House) in the southern garden, with its teahouse dating from feudal days overlooking a pond. There's an extra admission for Kikugetsu-tei of ¥510 ($4.25) for adults and ¥350 ($2.90) for children, which includes green tea. Powdered tea, used in tea ceremonies, costs ¥710 ($5.90) and ¥530 ($4.40) respectively. It takes about an hour to see the southern garden; add another half hour if you also take in the northern garden.

1–20–16 Ritsurin-cho. ⓒ 087/833-7411. Admission ¥400 ($3.35) adults, ¥170 ($1.40) children. 20% discount available with the Kagawa Welcome Card. Daily sunrise–sunset (approximately 7am–5pm in winter, 5:30am–7pm June–Aug). Kotoden tram: Ritsurin-koen Station (10 min.). JR train: If you have a Japan Rail Pass, go by JR train toward Tokushima; get off at Ritsurin-koen Kita Guchi (north entrance, which closes year-round at 5pm); turn right out of the station, follow the tracks to the 1st street, and turn right (4 min.).

Shikoku Mura Village ⭐⭐   On the northeastern edge of town, this open-air museum boasts more than 20 traditional houses, sheds, and storehouses dating from the Edo Period and collected from all over Shikoku. The structures, picturesquely situated on the wooded slope of Yashima Hill, include thatch-roofed homes of farmers and fishermen, century-old cottages used by lighthouse keepers, a rustic tea-ceremony house, a 250-year-old rural Kabuki stage, rice and soy sauce storehouses, and sheds for pressing sugar and for producing paper out of mulberry bark. There's also a suspended bridge made of vines, once a familiar sight in Shikoku as a means for crossing the island's many gorges and ravines—if you look closely, however, you'll see that this one is reinforced by cables.

It takes at least an hour to stroll through the village (and there are lots of stairs). I heartily recommend a visit if you haven't had the opportunity to see similar villages in Takayama, Shirakawago, or Kawasaki, since they convey better than anything else rural life in Japan in centuries past.

91 Yashima-naka-machi. © **087/843-3111**. Admission ¥800 ($6.65) adults, ¥500 ($4.15) high-school students, ¥400 ($3.35) junior-high students, ¥300 ($2.50) children. Daily 8:30am–4:30pm (to 5pm in summer). ¥100 (85¢ discount with Kagawa Welcome Card. Kotoden tram: to Kotoden Yashima Station, about a 20-min. ride and then a 5-min. walk. JR train: Take a JR train bound for Tokushima and get off at Yashima Station (a 15-min. walk).

AN EASY SIDE TRIP FROM TAKAMATSU

If you're spending more than a day in Takamatsu, this major attraction in the surrounding countryside is worth the trek.

KOTOHIRA 🐾🐾   If you have 4 hours to spare, one of the best historical side trips you can take is to Kotohira, home of Japan's oldest Kabuki theater and **Kotohiragu Shrine** 🐾🐾, 892 Kotohira-cho (© **0877/75-2121**), one of Japan's oldest and most popular shrines. It takes about an hour to reach Kotohira by JR train from Takamatsu, but that isn't the end of it—the shrine itself is at the top of 785 granite steps, which on average take 40 minutes to ascend. If that's too much for you, you can hire one of the porters who wait at the bottom of the steps; they'll take you only to the main gate (called *Omon* in Japanese), which is reached after climbing 365 steps. The cost of riding in one of these palanquins is ¥5,000 ($42) one-way and ¥6,500 ($54) if you're carried back down. What decadence.

Otherwise, the long trek up to Kotohiragu Shrine begins by exiting from the JR Kotohira Station's only exit, walking straight past a small park with a wooden tower that served as a beacon for traveling pilgrims in the Edo Period and past the Kotoden Station (you can also travel from Takamatsu in 1 hr. by Kotoden tram), and turning left at the T-junction with a post office. You'll soon see to the right a sloping, narrow street lined with souvenir shops (though I wouldn't buy anything on the way up). Presently you'll reach the first flight of stairs. If you're making a detour to the Kabuki theater (described below), turn left after the 22nd step, from which the theater is only a 3-minute walk.

ʃFinds   Bonsai is Big in Kinashi

If you've long admired the art of **bonsai**—the crafting of miniature pines and other trees through skillful manipulation—you might wish to take a stroll through **Kinashi,** a western suburb of Takamatsu. With more than 100 nurseries, most of them cultivating bonsai, Kinashi has been a center of bonsai since the Edo Period and remains the largest bonsai-growing region in Japan. To reach it, take a local JR train from Takamatsu Station two stations to Kinashi, walk north a few minutes and then turn right onto Bonsai Street. One of the largest nurseries, ⑱ **Kandaka-Shoju-en** (© **087/881-2852**) will soon be on your right. It's owned by a fourth-generation bonsai cultivator; some of the larger pines here were started by his ancestors. You're welcome to walk through this and other nearby nurseries. From here, take the first right and then the next right again. This is the only place I've ever seen bonsai groves, with hundreds of tiny pine trees planted in rows. If you continue straight, you'll come back to Kinashi Station.

⌐ Fun Fact Doggedly Faithful

In the olden days, faithful who could not manage a trip to Kotohiragu Shrine in person would set adrift at sea a barrel, along with an offering and a plea for passing fishermen to take the offering to the shrine on their next pilgrimage. The more resourceful would even send dogs on the pilgrimage, with a tag that read "Kotohira Pilgrimage" and a pouch of money around their necks. Travelers who encountered the dogs used the money to buy the animals food and passage on boats until the dogs reached their destination.

At about the 475th step (in case you're counting), just past the stables to the right, you'll find **Shoin,** built in 1659 to receive important visitors. Its doors and alcoves contain paintings by Maruyama Okyo, a famous 18th-century landscape artist, making the building an Important Cultural Property. Especially famous is the painting of two tigers drinking from a stream. It's open daily from 8:30am to 4:30pm; admission is ¥200 ($1.65). After another 15-minute workout, you'll reach the **main shrine** where you'll be rewarded with a sweeping view of the surrounding countryside as well as the shrine itself. Popularly known as Kompira-San, Kotohiragu Shrine was originally founded in the 11th century but has been rebuilt many times, with the main shrine buildings re-erected about 100 years ago. It's dedicated to the Shinto god of seafarers and voyagers (look for the Votive Picture Pavilion with photos of ships and other vessels that have asked for blessings) and, in recent years, has even become revered as the protective god of traveling foreigners. For my part, I was thankful just for having successfully traveled the stairs to the shrine. And to be honest, the shrine itself is not the main draw; most of the 4 million annual hikers, it seems, come for the hike itself and the comradeship it inspires. If you're still game, you can continue another 583 steps to Okunoyashiro Inner Shrine.

Since you're in the vicinity, you should make every effort to see the highly recommended ⑱ **Kompira Grand Playhouse** (Kompira O-Shibai or Kanamaruza) ⊛, 241 Otsu, Kotohira-cho (© **0877/73-3846**), which was built to entertain the masses flocking to Kotohiragu Shrine. Located near the beginning of the many steps to the shrine—to the left as you approach and then up the hill to the right—it's the oldest existing Kabuki stage in Japan, stunning in its simplicity and delightful in its construction. Since there was no electricity when it was built in 1835, the sides of the hall are rows of shoji screens and wooden coverings, which can be opened and closed to control the amount of light reaching the stage. Notice the tatami seating, the paper lanterns, and the revolving stage, which was turned by eight men in the basement. You can also tour the various makeup and dressing rooms behind the stage and watch a video in Japanese. Actual Kabuki plays are staged once a year, in April, when you can see Edo-Period pieces. As you may well imagine, tickets are hard to come by. Otherwise, the stage is open for general viewing daily from 9am to 5pm and charges an admission of ¥300 ($2.50) for adults, ¥200 ($1.65) for junior-high and high-school students, and ¥100 (85¢) for children. Ask for the English handout.

WHERE TO STAY
EXPENSIVE

ANA Hotel Clement Takamatsu ⋆⋆   Opened in 2001 across from Taka-matsu Station, the city's most expensive hotel is also its most conspicuous—sleek, 21 stories high, cutting across the landscape like a white sail, and by far the best place in town. It's designed with an aquatic theme, with a cascading fountain in the sunlit lobby lounge, carpets with wavy patterns, bubbled or crackled glass in public places, and curving, seductive lines everywhere, even in corridors. It's the kind of place sightseers happily return to after a hard day's work. Room rates are based on size, view, and amenities, with the best twin and double rooms offering views of the sea or nearby Tamamo Park, even from windows in the bathroom. But the least expensive rooms are also recommendable—spacious and chic with contemporary furnishings and good bedside reading lamps; ask for a room on the highest available floor.

1–1 Hamano-cho, Takamatsu 760-0011. © **087/811-1111.** Fax 087/811-1100. www.anahotels.com. 300 units. ¥10,500–¥14,000 ($87.50–$117) single; ¥18,000–¥20,000 ($150–$167) double; ¥21,000–¥35,000 ($175–$292) twin. AE, DC, JCB, MC, V. A 1-min. walk from Takamatsu Station. **Amenities:** 6 restaurants, 1 bar, 1 lounge, 1 beer garden; concierge; room service (7–10am and 5–11pm); in-room massage; same-day laundry and dry-cleaning service; nonsmoking rooms. *In room:* A/C, cable TV with pay movies, dataport, mini-bar, hot-water pot with tea, hair dryer, washlet toilet, trouser press.

MODERATE

Rihga Hotel Zest   This beige-brick hotel, first opened in 1980 and adding an annex with more luxurious accommodations 10 years later, appeals to both business and leisure travelers with its convenient location on Chuo Dori next to Hyogo-machi shopping arcade, has an accommodating staff, and offers a variety of rooms at different price ranges. The cheapest rooms, including all singles, are located in the main building and are narrow with tiny bathrooms. More expensive annex rooms sport shoji screens and window panels that close for complete darkness, with deluxe rooms offering such extras as hair dryers, washlet toilets, and trouser presses. There are also combination rooms with both a tatami area and beds.

9–1 Furujinmachi, Takamatsu 760-0025. © **087/822-3555.** Fax 087/822-7516. rhiga@bronze.ocn.ne.jp. 122 units. ¥6,800–¥8,200 ($57–$68) single; ¥13,000–¥25,000 ($108–$208) double; ¥15,000–¥25,000 ($125–$208) twin. 10% discounts with the Kagawa Welcome Card; be sure to mention the card when making your reservation and show it when checking in. AE, DC, JCB, MC, V. A 7-min. walk south of Takamatsu Station, on Chuo Dori just past Hyogo-machi arcade. **Amenities:** 4 restaurants (Japanese, Chinese, French, coffee shop); in-room massage; same-day laundry/dry cleaning service; nonsmoking rooms. *In room:* A/C, bilingual TV, minibar, hot-water pot with tea.

Royal Park Hotel Annex   This business hotel, with imitation art-deco decor in its lobby and hallways, offers mostly single rooms in a convenient location near Kawaramachi Station in the heart of the city's shopping and nightlife district. Rooms, though small, are pleasantly decorated, but it's been a while since I've seen pink tiled bathrooms like those here. The cheapest singles are on lower floors where traffic is noisiest. The hotel's seven twins are all corner rooms, bright and large for the price with a vanity/sink separate from the—you guessed it—pink bathrooms (which also have a sink). Little English is spoken.

11–1 Fukuda, Takamatsu 760-0048. © **087/823-1111.** Fax 087/823-1123. 117 units. ¥6,700–¥7,200 ($56–$60 single; ¥14,000 ($117) double; ¥16,500 ($138) twin. AE, JCB, MC, V. Kotoden tram: Kawaramachi (5 min.). Take the west exit (in the direction of the bus stop) and walk north on Ferry Dori, turning right at the first traffic signal and crossing the tracks; you'll see it on the left. **Amenities:** 1 restaurant (Chinese); in-room massage; same-day laundry/dry cleaning service; nonsmoking rooms. *In room:* A/C, TV, minibar, hot-water pot with tea, washlet toilet, trouser press.

Tips A Note on Japanese Symbols

Many hotels, restaurants, attractions, and other establishments in Japan do not have signs giving their names in Roman (English-language) letters. Appendix C lists the Japanese symbols for all such places described in this guide. Each set of characters representing an establishment name has a number in the appendix that corresponds to the number that appears inside the oval before the establishment's name in the text. Thus, to find the Japanese symbol for, say, **Tenkatsu** (below) refer to no. 183 in appendix C.

INEXPENSIVE

Parkside Hotel Takamatsu ✿ *Value*   Japanese women favor this small, boutique-like hotel for its great location across from Ritsurin Park. Rooms are small, but who cares when you can open the window and look out over the fabled garden? Some rooms have only a partial view, so be sure to request a ringside seat on an upper floor; although slightly more expensive, it's worth it.

1–3–1 Ritsurin-cho, Takamatsu 760-0073. ☎ 087/837-5555. Fax 087/837-3000. parkside@maill. netwave.or.jp. 104 units. ¥6,500–¥7,000 ($54–$58) single; ¥7,000–¥9,000 ($58–$75) double; ¥9,000–¥12,000 ($75–$100) twin. AE, DC, JCB, MC, V. Kotoden tram: Ritsurin Koen (10 min.). Walk straight from the west exit, turning right on Chuo Dori; it will be on the right. **Amenities:** 2 restaurants (Royal Host family-style chain and Japanese noodle shop); in-room massage; same-day laundry/dry cleaning service. *In room:* A/C, TV, minibar, hot-water pot with tea, hair dryer.

WHERE TO DINE

Takamatsu is known throughout Japan for its *sanuki udon*—thick white noodles made from wheat flour. Takamatsu also has a fresh supply of fish from the Seto Inland Sea.

EXPENSIVE

Fiore ✿✿ NORTHERN ITALIAN   This top-floor, upscale restaurant in the classy ANA Hotel Clement offers dreamy views of the port and Seto Inland Sea, as well as live piano music to accompany Italian main dishes of fish or meat. If you want, you can come for just a drink in the second-level bar, which stays open till midnight.

20th floor of ANA Hotel Clement, 1–1 Hamano-cho, Takamatsu 760-0011. ☎ 087/811-1111. Main dishes ¥2,400–¥3,800 ($20–$32); set dinner ¥5,000 ($42). AE, DC, JCB, MC, V. Daily 5–9pm (last order). A 1-min. walk from Takamatsu Station.

MODERATE

⑱ **Tenkatsu** TEMPURA/SUSHI   This well-known tempura and sushi restaurant is in a modern-looking building with a plastic-food display case and a window where passersby can watch a chef prepare sushi. Inside the restaurant are tatami mats and tables, but I suggest sitting at the counter, which encircles a large pool filled with fish. As customers order, fish are swooped out of the tanks with nets—they certainly couldn't be fresher. Although the menu is in Japanese only, pictures describe some of the tempura and sushi courses, but your best bet is probably to order from the display case. If you really want to splurge, order one of the kaiseki courses beginning at ¥5,000 ($42).

7–8 Hyogo-machi. ☎ 087/821-5380. Reservations recommended; required for kaiseki. Dishes ¥1,000–¥2,500 ($8.35–$21); set lunches ¥800–¥2,500 ($6.65–$21); set dinners ¥1,500–¥10,000 ($12.50–$83). AE, DC, JCB, MC, V. Mon–Fri 11am–2pm and 4–10pm; Sat–Sun 11am–9pm. An 8-min. walk south of Takamatsu Station. Walk south on Chuo Dori until it intersects with a large covered pedestrian shopping arcade called Hyogo-machi. Turn right and walk all the way through the arcade; upon emerging, you'll find the restaurant on your left.

184 **Tokiwa Saryo** ★★ *Finds* VARIED JAPANESE This restaurant, easily spotted with its castle-like roof, occupies what was once a traditional Japanese inn and retains many of its original traditional features, including a delightful inner courtyard complete with a pond, dwarf pine trees, carp and some lanterns. You'll probably want to order one of the set meals like obento lunch boxes or tempura and sashimi teishoku, made easy with photographs in the Japanese menu. For dinner, mini-kaiseki meals are also available for ¥2,000 to ¥4,000 ($17–$33), though no photos are available for these, as they change with the season. At any rate, the food is delicious and very reasonably priced; you can't go wrong.

1–8–2 Tokiwa-cho. ✆ **087/861-5577.** Reservations required weekends. Set meals ¥1,380–¥4,980 ($11.50–$41.50); set lunches ¥1,000 ($8.35). JCB, MC, V. Daily 11am–2:30pm and 5–9:30pm (last order). Kotoden tram: Kawaramachi Station (2 min.). From the west exit (with its BUS STOP sign), take the side street south (to the left) parallel to Tokiwa-cho (a covered arcade); it will be one your right, on the corner.

INEXPENSIVE

185 **Kanaizumi** SANUKI UDON This modern cafeteria is about as casual as you can get—you even heat your own noodles by putting some in a basket of hot water as you go through the line. Tempura (costing ¥80–¥120/65¢–$1) a piece is also available, as is oden and soup. If all this is too much work for you, head to the more expensive restaurant on the second floor (its entrance is to the left, beside the display case), where you can order set meals averaging ¥1,000 ($8.35). At any rate, be prepared for slippery noodles and the good-natured slurping sounds of a noodle shop.

9–3 Konyamachi. ✆ **087/822-0123.** Sanuki udon ¥160–¥230 ($1.35–$1.90). No credit cards. Daily 7am–5:30pm. A 15-min. walk south of Takamatsu Station, off Chuo Dori to the left just past the city art museum.

186 **Maruichi** ★ YAKITORI Although a cozy and friendly drinking establishment, this is also a great place for an inexpensive meal. An English-language menu lists sashimi, *kimchee* (Korean spiced cabbage) with pork, tofu, deep-fried prawns, and, of course, a variety of yakitori costing ¥100 to ¥350 (85¢–$2.90) a skewer. An evening of eating, drinking, and merriment here should cost about ¥2,000 ($17) per person, including the obligatory ¥280 ($2.35) snack charge.

1–4–13 Tokiwa-cho. ✆ **087/861-7623.** Main dishes ¥450–¥650 ($3.75–$5.40); set meals ¥2,000–¥3,000 ($17–$25). No credit cards. Mon–Sat 5pm–midnight. Kotoden tram: Kawaramachi Station (1 min.). Take the west exit (the one with the BUS STOP signs) and look for the small street running parallel to the north (right of) the covered shopping arcade. It's on the left and is easy to spot with its huge red lantern and circle (maru) with a horizontal line (ichi) through it.

Milano No Okazuyasan ★ NORTHERN ITALIAN Beneath an Italian flag is the recessed entrance to this second-floor restaurant. Hospitable chef-owner Mr. Takeda, who speaks some English and has an English menu, serves mainly homemade pastas, from the usual spaghetti Bolognese with meat sauce to spaghetti with squid in black sauce, as well as a handful of pizzas and main dishes that might include sautéed veal with lemon sauce. Set lunches include all the salad and fresh-baked bread you can eat plus a choice of soup, dessert, or coffee. Whatever you order, don't miss the homemade bread, and be sure to top it all off with a cappuccino and dessert.

Egou Bldg., 11–14 Kamei-cho. ✆ **087/837-1782.** Main dishes ¥600–¥1,300 ($5–$11); pasta ¥750–¥1,180 ($6.25–$9.85); set lunches ¥800 ($6.65). No credit cards. Daily 11am–9pm. Kotoden tram: Kawaramachi

(4 min.). Take the west exit (the one with the BUS STOP sign) and walk through the covered walking arcade (Tokiwa-cho) until the awning ends; then start looking carefully for Milano on your left, opposite a bookstore.

187 **Shabutei Maru** *Value* SHABU-SHABU This casual, small 2nd-floor eatery has inexpensive lunches of chicken, pork, and beef, with second helpings of rice and vegetables included in the price. From 5pm, it offers all-you-can-eat shabu-shabu (and in winter, sukiyaki) with a 90-minute time limit—kind of like an "on-your-mark, get-set, go" spree of uninhibited gorging. Ditto with all you can drink if you pay ¥1,300 ($11) more. Seating is at counters or tables and, as you might have guessed, is usually very crowded.

8–8 Kamei-cho. C 087/835-9842. Set lunches ¥470–¥1,030 ($3.90–$8.60); all-you-can-eat shabu-shabu ¥2,200 ($18) for men, ¥1,800 ($15) women. No credit cards. Daily 11am–2pm and 5–11pm. Kotoden tram: Kawaramachi (5 min.). Catty-corner from the SE corner of Chuo Park, just off Chuo Dori on Kikuchikan-dori, next to JTB.

Zaigoudon-Waraya SANUKI UDON NOODLES Zaigoudon-Waraya, in a 100-year-old thatched-roof house, is another noodle restaurant you might want to try, especially if you're going to Shikoku Mura Village. The Japanese menu, written on the wall, features handmade noodles, and the combination udon and tempura dish is especially popular, as is the zaru udon (served cold) in summer.

91 Yashima-Nakamachi. C 087/843-3115. Sanuki udon ¥410–¥900 ($3.40–$7.50). No credit cards. Daily 10am–6:30pm. Kotoden tram: Kotoden Yashima Station (10 min.). Just below Shikoku Mura Village, near the entrance (look for the waterwheel).

2 Matsuyama Castle & Dogo Spa ★★

939km (587 miles) W of Tokyo; 192km (120 miles) E of Takamatsu; 211km (132 miles) SW of Okayama

Although Matsuyama is Shikoku's largest town and the capital of Ehime Prefecture with a population of more than 470,000, it has the relaxed atmosphere of a small town. Located on the island's northwest coast, Matsuyama features one of Japan's best-preserved feudal castles and what I consider to be the most delightful, historic public bathhouse in the country, located in Dogo Onsen. The nearby Shimanami Kaido Bridge, connecting Ehime and Hiroshima prefectures, has a dedicated cycling lane, with fantastic views of the Seto Inland Sea.

ESSENTIALS

GETTING THERE By Plane Flights connect Matsuyama with Tokyo, Osaka, Nagoya, Fukuoka, Sapporo, Matsumoto, Miyazaki, and Kagoshima. The flight from Tokyo takes 1 hour and 20 minutes and costs ¥27,000 ($225).

By Train The easiest way to reach Matsuyama is by **JR train** from Okayama (on Honshu island) with 15 departures daily; the trip takes 2 hours and 45 minutes, and the fare is ¥6,120 ($51). There are also hourly departures from Takamatsu, taking less than 2½ hours and costing ¥5,500 ($46).

By Bus Buses depart nightly from Tokyo Station at 8:20pm, arriving at Matsuyama Station the next day at 8:35am. The fare is ¥12,000 ($100) one-way.

By Boat Matsuyama is also linked to various ports on Honshu and Kyushu islands, including Kobe (overnight trip time: 8 hr.), Osaka (overnight: 11 hr.), Beppu (3½ hr.), and Hiroshima (1 hr. by hydrofoil). The fare to Matsuyama is ¥5,500 ($46) from Osaka, ¥2,600 ($22) from Beppu, and ¥5,800 ($48) from Hiroshima. Boats dock at **Matsuyama Port** (Matsuyama Kanko Ko), where buses transport passengers to Matsuyama Station in about 30 minutes.

VISITOR INFORMATION   The **Matsuyama City Tourist Information Office** (© **089/931-3914;** open daily 8:30am–5:15pm and sometimes closed noon–1pm) is inside JR Matsuyama Station to the left as you leave the wicket. In addition, the Ehime Prefectural International Center, or **EPIC,** located between Matsuyama Castle and Dogo Onsen (© **089/917-5678;** open Mon–Fri 9am–5pm), provides information on Ehime Prefecture, including Uchiko, Tobe, and the Shimanami Kaido Bridge cycling path, as well as a TV with CNN, English-language newspapers, and one computer you can use for 30 minutes for ¥50 (42¢). Be sure to pick up another useful map; *What's Going On,* an excellent, free English-language guide to Matsumyama's events and points of interest; and your free Seto Inland Sea Welcome Card which provides discounts to sights, hotels, and restaurants in Ehime and Hiroshima prefectures. To reach it, take streetcar no. 3, 5, or 6 heading toward Dogo Onsen to the Minami-machi stop; backtrack and look to the right for INFORMATION; it's in a barrack partially hidden behind another building.

INTERNET ACCESS   In addition to EPIC, above, you can also check e-mail at CONS on the second floor of the Matsuyama International Center, 6–4–20 Sanbancho (© **089/943-5777;** open Tues–Sat 9am–8:30pm and Sun and holidays to 5pm) for ¥100 (85¢) an hour. It's a 7-minute walk from Matsuyama Station, or take the streetcar to Minami-horibata-cho stop.

ORIENTATION & GETTING AROUND   **JR Matsuyama Station,** which serves long-distance trains, is on the west edge of town, with most attractions, hotels, shopping, and restaurants spreading to the east. **Matsuyama Castle** lies less than 2.5km (1½ miles) due east of the station. Just southwest of the castle is the **Okaido** shopping arcade, a covered pedestrian passageway lined with restaurants and shops and considered to be the heart of the city. **Dogo Onsen,** Japan's oldest hot-spring spa, is on the eastern edge of the city.

The easiest and most convenient form of transportation in Matsuyama is a **streetcar,** with the no. 5 line running from Matsuyama Station to the Okaido arcade (*Note:* the Okaido stop is marked ICHIBANCHO on some tourist maps), Matsuyama Castle, and Dogo Onsen. The fare is ¥150 ($1.25) per trip or only ¥300 ($2.50) for a **one-day pass** (*Ichinichi Joshaken*). Buy the pass at Dogo Onsen or **Matsuyama City Station** (Matsuyama Shi-eki), which serves local commuter lines and buses bound for the suburbs. If you arrive at JR Matsuyama and want to buy the one-day pass, take the streetcar to Dogo Onsen or Matsuyama City Station and tell the driver you are going to buy the Ichinichi Joshaken. An old-fashioned locomotive-style streetcar operating between Matsuyama Station and Dogo Onsen is slated to begin operation by 2002.

SEEING THE SIGHTS
The Seto Inland Sea Welcome Card gives a 20% discount for both Matsuyama Castle and Dogo Onsen.

Matsuyama Castle ★★   Right in the heart of the city, Matsuyama Castle crowns the top of a 435-foot hill, commanding an impressive view. It was built by feudal lord Kato Yoshiakira 400 years ago, later falling into the hands of the powerful Matsudaira family that ruled the surrounding region from here during the Edo Period. Like most structures in Japan, Matsuyama Castle has suffered fire and destruction through the ages, but unlike many other castles (such as those in Osaka and Nagoya), this one was renovated with original materials. There's only one entrance, a pathway leading through a series of gates that could be swung shut to trap attacking enemies. A secret gate allowed a surprise rear attack, while drop chutes could be used to pour stones onto the enemy. The three-story donjon houses some samurai gear, swords, screens, and scrolls from the Matsudaira family, as well as photographs of Japan's other castles. Allow 30 minutes to tour the inside.

Surrounding the castle is a park; if you're feeling energetic, you can walk through the park to the castle in about 15 minutes. Otherwise, the easiest way to reach the castle is to take the streetcar to the Okaido stop, walk 5 minutes on the street with the arch marked WELCOME TO MATSUYAMA CASTLE, and then take a cable car or chairlift (more fun) from the east side of Katsuyama Hill. A round-trip ticket costs ¥1,000 ($8.35) for adults and ¥400 ($3.35) for children, including admission to the castle.

© **089/921-4873.** Admission ¥500 ($4.15) adults, ¥150 ($1.25) children. Daily 9am–5pm (to 4:30pm in Jan and 5:30pm in Aug). Tram: Okaido stop, then chairlift.

DOGO ONSEN (DOGO SPA) ☆☆☆

Dogo Onsen boasts a 3,000-year history and claims to be the oldest hot-spring spa in Japan. According to legend, the hot springs were discovered after a white heron healed an injured leg by soaking it in the thermal mineral waters. Located in the northeast part of the city, about a 20-minute tram ride from Matsuyama Station (take streetcar no. 5 to Dogo Onsen, the last stop), Dogo Spa can accommodate about 10,000 people in 60 hotels and ryokan, which means the narrow streets resound at night with the slap of thonged slippers and the occasional clatter of *geta* as vacationers go to the various bathhouses dressed in yukata.

Most of the hotels and ryokan in Dogo have their own *onsen* (hot-spring bath), but I suggest that no matter where you stay, you make at least one trip to **Dogo Onsen Honkan** ☆☆☆, 5–6 Yunomachi, Dogo (© **089/921-5141**), a wonderful three-story public bathhouse built in 1894. A wooden structure with shoji screens, tatami rooms, creaking wooden stairways, and the legendary white heron topping the crest of its castle-like roof, this Momoyama-style building is as much a social institution as it is a place to soak and scrub. On busy days, as many as 4,000 people pass through its front doors. The water here is transparent, colorless, tasteless, and alkaline, helpful for rheumatism and neuralgia. At the very least, it makes your skin feel great—soft and smooth. The hottest spring water coming into the spa is 120°F; the coolest, 70°F. But don't worry—the waters are mixed to achieve a comfortable 108°F.

Bathing in the first-floor granite bath (rather ordinary looking now but considered luxurious when it was built), however, is just a small part of the experience here. Most people come to relax, socialize, and while away an hour or more, and I suggest you do the same. Although you can bathe for as little as ¥300 ($2.50) for adults and ¥120 ($1) for children 2 to 11, it's worth it to pay extra for the privilege of relaxing on tatami mats in a communal room on the second floor, dressed in a rented *yukata* (cotton robe), drinking tea from a lacquered tea set, and eating Japanese rice crackers. If the weather is fine, all the shoji screens are pushed open to let in a breeze, and as you sprawl out on the tatami, drinking your tea and listening to the clang of the streetcar and voices of people coming and going, you can almost imagine that you've somehow landed in ancient Japan. To my mind, the whole scene resembles an old woodblock print suddenly come to life.

The cost of the bath, yukata, crackers, and tea for 1 hour is ¥620 ($5.15) for adults, half price for children 2 to 11. Use of a smaller, more private bath and lounging area for an hour where tea and sweets are also served costs ¥980 ($8.15) for adults and half price for children. And if you really want to splurge, you can rent for 1 hour and 20 minutes your own private tatami room on the third floor, which also comes with tea, sweets, and yukata, for ¥1,240 ($10.35) for adults, half price for children. This differentiation in luxury probably dates back to the early days when there were separate baths for the upper class, priests, commoners, and even animals.

While at the spa, be sure to see the **Yushinden,** built in 1899 for the imperial family's visits to the spa and last used in 1952. You can take a tour of its rooms for ¥210 ($1.75) for adults and ¥100 (85¢) for children.

The spa is open from 6am (the arrival time of the 1st streetcar) until 11pm, but you must enter by 10:30pm. The second floor closes at 10pm (you must enter by 9pm) and the Yushinden at 9pm.

A NEARBY TEMPLE   After your bath, you may want to visit **Ishiteji Temple** ⟨⟩, 2–9–21 Ishite (⟨©⟩ **089/977-0870**), about a 10-minute walk east of Dogo Onsen Station; from the station, walk under the neon archway and keep going straight east. Built in 1318, it's the 51st of Shikoku's 88 sacred temples; with its blend of Chinese and Japanese styles, it is a good example of architecture of the Kamakura Period. Notice the huge straw sandals at the main gate; those with feet or leg ailments are thought to regain their health by touching them. You'll also see regular-sized sandals at the temple, donated by older Japanese in hopes of regaining new strength in their legs (who knows, maybe they've been walking the pilgrimage). The most interesting site, however, is the lit tunnel to the left behind the main temple. It contains stone statues representing the 88 temples of Shikoku, in front of which is sand from each temple location. Standing in front of each statue is a short circuit to the actual pilgrimage, convenient for those who don't have time for the real thing. Admission to the tunnel is ¥100 (85¢) and the temple is open daily 6am to 6pm.

AN EASY SIDE TRIP

UCHIKO ⟨⟩⟨⟩   If you have time for a side trip around Ehime Prefecture, I strongly recommend an excursion to the village of **Uchiko,** which has some fine old homes and buildings dating back to the Edo Period and the turn of the century. Whereas about 70% of Matsuyama was destroyed during World War II, Uchiko was left intact, and a tiny part of the old historic district is a living memorial to the days of yore, when it prospered as a production center for wax. Even the 25-minute express train ride from JR Matsuyama Station (departing every hr. or so) is enjoyable as you weave through valleys of wooded hills past grape, mikan orange, persimmon, rice, and tobacco farms. At Uchiko Station, ask for the "Uchiko Visitor's Guide" at the train station ticket window; it contains a map showing the 5-minute walk to Yokaichi, the historic part of town.

Your first stop is ⟨188⟩ **Uchikoza,** 1152–2 Kou, Uchiko-cho (⟨©⟩ **0893/44-2840**), a Kabuki theater built in 1916 (look for banners on the left after passing the creek). Though not as grand as the one near Takamatsu (described earlier in this chapter), it's a good example of how townspeople used to enjoy themselves years ago. It features a revolving stage, many windows that can be opened and closed to control the amount of light reaching the stage, and a small display of memorabilia (note the ultimate platform shoes, *geta* used by Bunraku puppeteers). Uchikoza is open daily 9am to 5pm. Buy a combination ticket for ¥700 ($5.85) for adults and ¥370 ($3.10) for children; this allows admission to the theater, Museum of Commercial and Domestic Life, and Kami-Haga Residence listed below.

A 5-minute walk farther along the main street, on the right, is the **Museum of Commercial and Domestic Life** (Akinai to Kurashi Hakubutsukan), 1082–1 Kou, Uchiko-cho (✆ **0893/44-5220**). This museum, once housing a pharmacy and built in typical Uchiko style, uses life-size figures, recordings, and authentic artifacts in its dioramas depicting various professions and scenes from daily life, from shop owner to restaurant owner. One of the dioramas, for example, is of a Taisho-Era pharmacy, with two figures kneeling on a tatami floor as they discuss the business at hand (in Japanese). Other places of interest in Yokaichi include two restored homes, **Machi-ya Shiryokan,** 1579–1 Kou, Uchiko-cho (✆ **0893/44-2111**), open free to the public; and **Kami-Haga Residence,** 1519 Kou, Uchiko-cho (✆ **0893/44-2771**). Built in 1894, the Kami-Haga Residence is especially grand, having once belonged to a merchant who made his fortune exporting wax. During the Edo and Meiji periods, Uchiko gained fame as a center of candlemaking and wax production, producing about 30% of the country's wax, used both for lighting and for the styling of elaborate Feudal-Era hairdos. You can see the traditional methods for wax production in the sheds out back, as well as tour the house. There's also an upstairs café, though you have to hunt for it and may have to rouse someone to serve you even if you do find it. All of these attractions are open daily 9am to 4:30pm.

Today, only one man carries on this wax-making tradition—a man named ⑱⑨ **Omori,** who represents the sixth generation of candlemakers. Following the same techniques as those developed by his ancestors 200 years ago, he even collects his own haze berries (a kind of sumac) and makes his candles by hand. You can observe him at work at his workshop at 1587 Sakamachi-ko, Uchiko-cho (✆ **0893/43-0385;** open Tues–Thurs and Sat and Sun 9am–5pm).

Where to Dine: ⑲⓪ **Shimohagatei,** 1090–1 Uchiko-ko (✆ **0893/44-6171;** open Tues–Sun 10am–9pm) is housed in a 130-year-old former residence/shop on the main street of the historic district, near the Museum of Commercial and Domestic Life. With an inner garden courtyard typical of Uchiko architecture and an upstairs crafts gallery, it offers noodles, tempura, and set meals costing ¥850 to ¥1,200 ($7.10–$10). No credit cards are accepted.

CYCLING THE SHIMANAMI KAIDO BRIDGE ✸✸✸

If you're a cyclist—and even if you're not—you owe it to yourself to ride one of Japan's most rewarding cycling routes: a dedicated biking and pedestrian lane that connects Ehime Prefecture on Shikoku with Onomichi in Hiroshima Prefecture on Honshu (Japan's main island). Part of the Shimanami Kaido Bridge, which is actually a series of 10 bridges that hopscotch across the Seto Inland Sea via six islands, the cycling path runs beside vehicular traffic on the bridges but often diverges from the highway on the islands. Needless to say, views of the sea and surrounding countryside are great, and the pathway, clearly marked in green, is easy to follow (though steep in some areas). If you want, you can cycle the entire 70km (43-mile) distance between Shikoku and Honshu in less than 7 hours and then return by bus. Alternatively, you can cycle for a few hours and then head back or you can go as far as you wish, leave your rental bike at one of 13 bike drop-off sites along the cycling path, and then catch a bus back.

For a fun day's outing, I suggest cycling to Omishima, an island you'll reach in about 2 hours, where another 30 minutes of cycling will bring you to **Oyamazumi Shrine.** Worshipped through the years by samurai, the shrine is home to the **Shiyoden Treasure Museum** ★★ *(Finds* (② **0897-82-0032**), with an astounding collection of helmets, armor, and swords, all donated to the shrine by warriors who wished to express thanks for victories in battle. About 80% of Japanese samurai gear designated National Treasures (look for the red mark) or National Important Cultural Assets are housed here, including items once worn by Minamoto Yoshitsune and Minamoto Yoritomo, in a building that is surprisingly dilapidated. It's open daily 8:30am to 5pm; admission is ¥1,000 ($8.35) for adults, ¥800 ($6.65) for students, and ¥400 ($3.35) for children. By the way, there's a bike drop-off center just before the shrine, where you can leave your bike, shower, and catch a bus back.

Rental bikes are available at the foot of the first bridge at **Sunrise Itoyama** (② **0898-41-3196**), which also offers simple hotel facilities and a restaurant. Bikes rent for ¥500 ($4.15) a day. There are also power-assisted bikes for ¥800 ($6.65); I rented one (in the interest of research, of course) and found it helpful on the circular ramp that climbs 65m (213 ft.) to meet the bridge. There's also a ¥1,000 ($8.35) deposit, which you forfeit if you decide to ditch your bike at one of the drop-off sites; be sure to ask the folks at Sunrise Itoyama for a bus schedule back. You'll also have the annoyance of bridge toll fees at varying distances (¥300/$2.50 total for the trip to Omishima). The cycling center is open daily 8am to 8pm (to 5pm Dec–Mar).

To reach Sunrise Itoyama, take an express train from Matsuyama Station 30 minutes to Imabari, from which there are three to five buses a day to the Sunrise Itoyama cycling center. You'll probably find it easier, therefore, to take a local train 5 minutes onward from Imabari to Hashihama, from which the cycling center is a 20-minute walk.

SHOPPING

TOBE Ehime Prefecture is famous for its Tobe pottery, called *Tobe-yaki* in Japanese, with about 100 families in the town of Tobe still engaged in the craft. An excellent way to see this pottery, noted for its thick white porcelain painted with cobalt-blue designs, is to visit ⑲⑨① **Tobe Pottery Traditional Industry Hall** (Tobeyaki Dento Sangyo Kaikan) at 335 Ohminami, Tobe-cho (②089/962-6600; open Fri–Wed 9am–5pm). In addition to displays of Tobe ware from the Edo Period to the present and a video showing the creative process, it also sells contemporary ware from local producers, making it a good place to shop for a variety of styles. Admission is ¥200 ($1.65) for adults, ¥150 ($1.25) for high-school and university students, and ¥100 (85¢) for children. To get there, take bus no. 18 or 19 from Matsuyama Shi-eki 45 minutes to the Tobeyaki Dento Sangyo Kaikan-mae stop (fare: ¥600/$5), from which it's a 7-minute walk (continue straight on and take the first right; it's at the T-intersection). A taxi costs about ¥3,500 ($29) for a 30-minute trip. There are also several kilns open to the public, the largest and best known of these is ⑲② **Umeno-Seito-sho** at 1441 Ohminami, Tobe-cho (②089/962-2311; open Tues–Sun 8am–4:50pm, closed 2nd and 3rd Sun each month and a few days in mid-Aug). Founded back in 1882 and now in its fifth generation of ownership by the Umeno family, it employs more than 100 people. You can watch all the artisans except those who do the glazing—the technique is a closely guarded secret. Inside the shop, be sure to check out the bargain corner where pieces with slight imperfections go for about half price. Get a map from the Tobe Pottery Traditional Industry Hall that shows the 20-minute walk to Umeno-Seito-Jo.

WHERE TO STAY

For more suggestions of where to stay in the Dogo Onsen area or to make a reservation in a ryokan there, contact the **Dogo Onsen Ryokan-Kumiai** (© **089/943-8342;** fax 089/943-8343), located near the Dogo Onsen streetcar stop at the entrance to the shopping arcade (on the right). It's open daily 8am to 8pm.

Your Seto Inland Sea Welcome Card provides a 10% discount on some of the accommodations below, including Yamatoya Besso, ANA Hotel Matsuyama, and Hotel Patio Dogo. Mention the card when making your reservation and be sure to show it upon check-in.

VERY EXPENSIVE

⑲ **Yamatoya Besso** ✿✿✿   The ultimate ryokan experience awaits at this famous ryokan in Dogo Onsen. It's the little things that make it special—the rustle of kimono as you're met by bowing, smiling women in the front courtyard; pillars of salt at the front door in good Shinto fashion; lit shoji lanterns guiding the way through hushed hallways; scrolls of haiku poems, in beautiful calligraphy, decorating all the rooms and changed seven times a year to fit the season. With a history dating back 120 years—it was rebuilt in 1988 as a refined, luxurious inn—it offers rooms that preserve the integrity of the past with TVs hidden behind shoji screens and old-fashioned cypress tubs that use water from the hot springs. Lavish kaiseki meals feature seafood of the Seto Inland Sea. The only thing lacking at this superb ryokan is the requisite garden.

2–27 Dogo Sagidani-cho, Matsuyama 790-0836. © **089/931-7771.** Fax 089/931-7775. 19 units. ¥39,000–¥71,000 ($325–$592) per person. Rates include two meals and service charge. AE, DC, JCB, MC, V. Tram: Dogo Onsen (5 min). **Amenities:** Public indoor and outdoor hot-spring baths; in-room massage; same-day laundry/dry cleaning service. *In room:* A/C, TV, hot-water pot wit tea, hair dryer, washlet toilet, urinal.

⑭ **Umenoya** ✿✿✿   Small, intimate, and secluded from the world behind a wall, this wonderful, 50-some-year-old inn boasts a beautiful small garden, beyond which is a canal, park, and a wooded hill in the distance (a good example of borrowed landscape). Rooms, which are graced with such architectural details as bamboo weavings and wood-carved transoms, vary in price according to amenities and view; the best have cypress tubs, washlet toilets, and views of the garden. One of the public baths is in a hut with a conical-shaped roof in the garden.

2–8–9 Kami-ichi, Matsuyama 790-0853. © **089/941-2570.** Fax 089/941-1025. umenoya@dogo.or.jp. 10 units (2 with bathrooms, 8 with toilets only). ¥20,000–¥30,000 ($167–$250). Rates include 2 meals and service charge. AE, DC, JCB, MC, V. Tram: Dogo Onsen (5 min.). **Amenities:** Public indoor and hot-spring baths; in-room massage; same-day laundry/dry cleaning service. *In room:* A/C, TV, minibar, hot-water pot with tea, safe.

EXPENSIVE

ANA Hotel ✿   Matsuyama's premier hotel (called Zenniku Hotel in Japanese) has a great location in the heart of the city, just a few minutes' walk to the Matsuyama Castle ropeway and the Okaido covered shopping arcade; streetcars heading for Dogo Onsen pass right in front of the hotel. Built in 1979 but constantly updated, it offers business-hotel-like inexpensive singles, as well as larger and well-appointed singles, twins, and doubles; ask for a double or twin with castle view.

3–2–1 Ichiban-cho, Matsuyama 790-8520. © **800/262-4683** in the U.S. and Canada, or 089/933-5511. Fax 089/921-6053. 333 units. ¥7,500–¥10,500 ($62.50–$87.50) single; ¥17,000–¥32,000 ($142–$267) double; ¥17,500–¥25,000 ($146–$208) twin. AE, DC, JCB, MC, V. Tram: Kencho-mae (1 min.). **Amenities:** 4

restaurants (Japanese, Chinese, French, coffeeshop), 1 bar, 1 tea lounge, 1 rooftop beer garden (summer only); large shopping arcade (including one selling *Tobe-yaki*); room service (7am–11pm); in-room massage; same-day laundry/dry cleaning; nonsmoking rooms. *In room:* A/C, cable TV, minibar, hot-water pot with tea, hair dryer, washlet toilet, trouser press.

MODERATE

International Hotel Matsuyama (Kokusai Hotel)   Opened in 1981 and not as spiffy as it once was, this medium-priced hotel is comfortable enough and, centrally located near the Okaido shopping arcade and Matsuyama Castle ropeway, is a good base for exploring the city. It caters almost exclusively to Japanese with its single rooms boasting double-size beds, good-sized desks, and wonder of wonders, fax machines (which are equipped only to send faxes; you'll have to receive faxes through the front desk). A few singles also have dataports. Some of the twins have castle views, and there are also "corner" doubles and twins that are spacious with lots of windows that open and let in lots of light. Ladies qualify for a 20% discount on single and twin rooms; the rest will have to content themselves with a special 10% discount offered to Frommer's readers; show this book upon checking in.

1–13 Ichiban-cho, Matsuyama 790-0001. ⒸＣ **089/932-5111.** Fax 089/945-2055. k-hotelm@cello.ocn.ne.jp. 80 units. ¥6,800 ($57) single; ¥8,000–¥20,000 ($67–$167) twin; ¥10,500–¥20,000 ($87.50–$167) double. AE, DC, JCB, MC, V. Tram: Okaido—marked Ichibancho on some tourist maps—(3 min.). Continue east on Densha Dori to the first gas station and turn left; it's on your right. **Amenities:** 3 restaurants (Japanese, Western, Chinese); room service (11:30am–10pm); in-room massage; same-day laundry/dry cleaning service. *In room:* A/C, cable TV, fax (in singles and some twins), minibar (twin rooms only), empty fridge (singles and doubles only), hot-water pot with tea, hair dryer, washlet toilet.

Hotel Patio Dogo ⓐ   With a great location just across the street from the delightful Dogo Onsen Honkan spa, this smart-looking medium-class hotel offers semi-double beds in singles and queens in the more expensive double rooms. Ah, space at last! Some rooms (on the 8th and 9th floors) have a view of Matsuyama Castle far in the distance (binoculars would come in handy), but best are rooms on the second through fourth floors whose windows overlook the historic spa. The most expensive accommodations in each category are larger, corner rooms. In the evening, be sure to join all the other tourists staying in Dogo and wear your yukata across the street for a nighttime soak in the historic spa.

20–12 Yuno-machi, Dogo, Matsuyama 790-0842. ⒸＣ **089/941-4128.** Fax 089/941-4129. www.patio-dogo.co.jp/. 101 units. ¥7,200–¥9,000 ($60–$75) single; ¥12,000–¥13,000 ($100–$108) double; ¥15,000–¥22,000 ($125–$133) twin. AE, DC, JCB, MC, V. Tram: Dogo Onsen (5 min.). Walk though the covered shopping arcade and turn left. **Amenities:** Restaurant (a branch of Sushimaru; see "Where to Dine," below); in-room massage; same-day laundry/dry cleaning service. *In room:* A/C, TV, fridge, hair dryer, washlet toilet.

INEXPENSIVE

⑲⑤ **Business Hotel Taihei** ⓚⁱᵈˢ   This business hotel has a rather inconvenient location, at the base of the Matsuyama Caste hill but on the opposite side of the city's downtown; you have to transfer trams to reach Dogo Onsen. Still, it offers very good value, and unusual for business hotels, it also offers features good for families, including a small play area in the exercise room so that mom and dad can get a workout on the treadmill and stationary bike while the kids ride the pedal car or play video games. In addition to both Western- and Japanese-style rooms, there are also four combination rooms with tatami areas and Western-style beds that sleep up to four persons, as well as two large family rooms that sleep five. Windows can be opened. The public baths and rooms facing the back look out on the mountain greenery and are quieter. Although there's an inexpensive dining room, I recommend you eat elsewhere.

3–3–15 Heiwa Dori, Matsuyama 790-0807. ✆ 089/943-3560. Fax 089/932-2525. 144 units. ¥4,800 ($40) single; ¥8,000 ($67) double; ¥8,000–¥10,000 ($67–$83) twin; ¥12,000 ($100) Japanese-style room for 2, ¥15,000 ($125) for 3; family rooms ¥25,000 ($208) for 5. No credit cards. Tram: Teppo-cho (3 min.). Going in the same direction as the streetcar, take the first right and then right again onto Heiwadori; you'll see the hotel on your left. **Amenities:** Restaurant (Japanese); exercise room with children's play area; public bath; sauna; in-room massage; same-day laundry/dry cleaning service. *In room:* A/C, TV, hot-water pot with tea, hair dryer.

⑲ **Minshuku Miyoshi**   This simple establishment is located in Dogo Onsen near Ishiteji Temple; if you call ahead, someone can pick you up at the Dogo Onsen tram stop. Although not much English is spoken, they're used to foreigners here. Clean but simple tatami rooms, all with a sink and toilet, make it a good choice for young budget travelers.

3–7–23 Ishite, Matsuyama 790-0852. ✆ 089/977-2581. Fax 089/977-2581. 6 units (none with bathroom, all with toilet). ¥4,000 ($33) single without meals; ¥7,000 ($58) twin without meals; ¥7,000 ($58) per person including 2 meals. No credit cards. Tram: Dogo Onsen (10 min.). Bus: no. 52 to Ishiteji. Across from Ishiteji Temple, set back from the road behind Cosmo gas station and parking lot. **Amenities:** Washer/dryer (free of charge). *In room:* A/C, TV, no phone.

WHERE TO DINE

Kadota, Sushimaru, and Tokuhiro all offer discounts with the Seto Inland Sea Welcome Card; be sure to present it upon ordering.

EXPENSIVE

Kadota ✿   Chef Kadota worked nine years at the venerable Okura Hotel and then at the ANA Hotel in Matsuyama before opening his own restaurant in 1993. Small and cozy with classical music playing in the background, flowers on every table, and French cuisine served on elegant tableware, it offers homemade appetizers, organic vegetables whenever possible, and—the house specialty— steaks and seafood. It offers only fixed-price meals; your dinner may start with a cold cucumber soup, followed by *ayu* (a Japanese river fish) served in a green sauce of pureed spinach and white wine or steak served in a red wine and veal sauce with sweet potato gratin.

3–4–25 Sanban-cho. ✆ **089/931-3511.** Reservations recommended. Set dinner ¥5,000–¥15,000 ($42–$125); set lunches ¥2,000–¥3,000 ($17–$25). AE, DC, JCB, MC, V. Daily 11am–2pm and 5–9pm (last order). Closed 2 days in Aug. Tram: Kencho-mae (5 min.). Take the side road to the left of the ANA hotel and continue straight, keeping a lookout for a side street with some white Christmas lights and a small sign (it's easy to miss).

MODERATE

⑲ **Kushihide** YAKITORI/GRILLED FOODS   Behind the counter of this 40-year-old-eatery are some 400 individual sake cups inscribed with the names of regular customers—the cook joked that, this way, they didn't have to wash them. Washed or unwashed, they're testimony to the popularity of this simple eating and drinking venue. As soon as you sit down, a large bowl of cabbage with a dip and an appetizer will be placed in front of you. It's most famous for its boiled chicken leg and thigh for ¥800 ($6.65), included in some of the set meals. It also offers chicken sashimi, which the restaurant claims is one of the few places you can eat it safely, as the restaurant raises its own chickens and serves them the day of their demise. Nearby is the chain's sushi restaurant, 3–2–4 Nibancho (✆ **089/921-9410**).

3–2–8 Nibancho. ✆ **089/921-1587.** Sticks ¥150–¥200 ($1.25–$1.65); set meals ¥1,500–¥4,000 ($12.50–$33). AE, JCB, MC, V. Daily 5–11pm. Tram: Okaido—marked Ichibancho on some tourist maps— (2 min.). Walk down Okaido Arcade and take the first right after the stoplights; it's 1 block farther on your left.

198 **Shinhamasaku** VARIED JAPANESE This modern restaurant has a pleasant, informal atmosphere and serves fresh seafood from the Seto Island Sea and other local specialties as well as shabu-shabu, kamameshi, and crab and eel dishes. The menu is Japanese only, but there are photos and a food display. The popular *seiro bento* (¥2,500/$21) includes about 20 different bite-size morsels, all served in a wooden box.

4–6–1 Sanbancho. ℂ **089/933-3030.** Main dishes ¥800–¥2,500 ($6.65–$21); set meals ¥1,200–¥10,000 ($10–$83). No credit cards. Daily 11am–3pm and 4:30–8:30pm. Tram: Kencho-mae or Shieki-mae (8 min.). Across the street and west of the Central Post Office.

199 **Sushimaru** SUSHI Located just east of the Okaido shopping arcade, Sushimaru has Japanese *noren* (shop curtain), a display case outside, and old-fashioned architecture. The popular *higawari* (today's lunch), served Monday through Saturday until 2pm and displayed outside the front door, offers sushi, nigirisushi (sushi rolls), salad, and soup for ¥690 ($5.75). A Japanese menu with photos shows other set meals; in the evening *kaiseki* featuring sashimi is also available.

Another Sushimaru with the same menu is located across the street from Dogo Onsen in the Hotel Patio Dogo at 20–12 Yunomachi (ℂ**089/932-6157;** open daily 11am–2pm and 5–10pm).

2–3–2 Nibancho. ℂ **089/941-0447.** Set meals ¥1,000–¥3,500 ($8.35–$29); kaiseki ¥5,000–¥10,000 ($42–$83). AE, DC, MC, V. Daily 11am–9pm. Tram: Okaido—Ichibancho on some tourist maps—(2 min.). Walk south along the Okaido shopping arcade. After you cross Nichiban-cho (the first light), take the first small street on your left; it will be on your right a few shops down.

200 **Tokuhiro** SHABU SHABU/YAKINIKU Located near the castle ropeway, this modern restaurant has tables with a view of a pond, a waterfall, and koi swimming happily about, as well as quiet tatami rooms. It offers all-you-can-eat yakiniku and shabu-shabu with a 90-minute time limit; prices depend on the quality of meat, with ¥2,900 or ¥3,900 ($24 or $32.50) charged for men and ¥500 ($4.15) less for women (because we all know who can eat more in 90 min.). The cheapest lunch, costing ¥680 ($5.65), is served until 2pm, but others are available until 4pm.

3–7–10 Okaido. ℂ **089/934-0880.** Set lunches ¥680–¥2,000 ($5.65–$17); set dinners ¥1,600–¥5,500 ($13–$46). JCB, MC, V. Daily 11am–11pm (last order 10pm). Tram: Okaido—Ichibancho on some maps—(5 min.). Walk up the street with the WECOME TO MATSUYAMA CASTLE arch; it will be on your right.

INEXPENSIVE

Dogo Beer *Finds* If you agree that "One gulp of beer taken just after a bath is the time when you feel most refreshed," as proclaimed on this microbrewery's pamphlet, then after bathing at Dogo Onsen Honkan head straight across the street for some sake or beer (the parent company has been a sake producer for more than a century; it opened a brewery in 1996 following deregulation that had long assured a beer monopoly by the major players). An upbeat establishment with an eclectic decor mixing traditional (bamboo ceilings) and the modern (artwork) and with jazz the likely background music of choice, it offers German-style beers, a stout, and sake. Although a sign outside its doors reads BREWERY RESTAURANT, its Japanese menu with pictures is limited to yakitori (¥380/$3.15 for 3 sticks), fried chicken (*senzanki*), deep-fried fish paste (*jyakoten*), and other pub foods, with most dishes priced below ¥700 ($5.85).

3–23 Dogo Kitamachi. ℂ **089/924-6616.** Main dishes ¥350–¥1,500 ($2.90–$12.50). No credit cards. Daily 11am–10pm. Tram: Dogo Onsen. Walk through the covered shopping arcade and then turn left.

Kyushu

The southernmost of Japan's four main islands, Kyushu offers a mild climate, famous hot-spring spas, beautiful countryside, national parks, and warm, friendly people. It also boasts several high-tech theme parks that make it Japan's number one destination for visitors from Korea, Taiwan, Hong Kong, and other Asian cities.

Historians believe that Japan's earliest inhabitants lived on Kyushu before gradually pushing northward. According to Japanese legend, it was from Kyushu that the first emperor, Jimmu, began his campaign to unify Japan. Kyushu is therefore considered to be the cradle of Japanese civilization. And because Kyushu is the island closest to Korea and China, it has served through the centuries as a point of influx for both people and ideas from abroad, including those from the West.

THE CIRCLE ISLAND TOUR: A SUGGESTED ITINERARY FOR SEEING KYUSHU Most of Kyushu's towns are along the coast, which means you can visit most cities and attractions by circling the island by train. You might, for example, wish to start out in Fukuoka, where Hakata Station is the terminus for Shinkansen bullet trains from Tokyo. From there you can head south to Kagoshima, stopping at Beppu and Miyazaki along the way. From Kagoshima, consider taking the bus to Chiran to visit its famous samurai gardens and continuing onward to the hot-springs area of Ibusuki, Kyushu's southernmost tip. Northward from Kagoshima along Kyushu's western coast brings you to Kumamoto and the exciting city of Nagasaki, where you can complete your tour of Kyushu by taking a bus to the mountain resort of Unzen. Complete your circuit of the island by returning to Fukuoka and boarding a Shinkansen bullet train bound for Honshu.

1 Fukuoka

1,168km (730 miles) W of Tokyo; 450km (281 miles) W of Hiroshima

With a population of 1.3 million, **Fukuoka** is Kyushu's largest city and serves as a major international and domestic gateway to the island. On the northern coast of Kyushu, it lies closer to Seoul, Korea, than to Tokyo.

During Japan's feudal days, Fukuoka was divided into two distinct towns separated by the Nakagawa River. Fukuoka was where the samurai lived since it was the castle town of the local feudal lord. Merchants lived across the river in Hakata, the commercial center of the area. Both cities were joined in 1889 under the common name of Fukuoka. Fukuoka's main train station, however, is in Hakata and is therefore called Hakata Station. Hakata Station serves as the terminus of the Tokaido-Sanyo Shinkansen Line from Tokyo.

In the 13th century, Fukuoka was selected by Mongol forces under Kublai Khan as the best place to invade Japan. The first attack came in 1274, but the Japanese were able to repel the invasion. Convinced the Mongols would attack again, the Japanese built a 10-foot-high stone wall along the coast. The second invasion came in 1281. Not only did the Mongols find the wall impossible to scale, but a typhoon blew in and destroyed the entire Mongol fleet. The Japanese called this gift from heaven "divine wind," or *kamikaze,* a word that took on a different meaning during World War II when young Japanese pilots crashed their planes into American ships in a last-ditch attempt to win the war.

Today, Fukuoka is a modern, internationally oriented commercial and business center with a highly developed port and coastal area. Although it's not a must-see tourist destination, there are some interesting museums, shrines, and a temple worth seeing if you've landed in Fukuoka on the Shinkansen.

ESSENTIALS

GETTING THERE   By Plane   Direct flights connect Fukuoka to a variety of international cities, including Honolulu and Hong Kong, as well as numerous domestic cities. Flying time from Tokyo's Haneda Airport is 1½ hours; the regular, one-way fare costs ¥31,000 ($258) on ANA and Japan Airlines. However, because of fierce competition on the Fukuoka–Haneda route, bargains do exist. **Skymark** (© 03/3433-7670 in Tokyo; 092/736-3131 in Fukuoka), for example, a small airline serving Fukuoka, offers six flights daily from Haneda to Fukuoka for as low as ¥16,000 to ¥17,000 ($133–$142) one-way, while even major airlines sometimes offer special rates of ¥16,500 ($137.50), depending on the time of day and season. To get into town, there's a subway station located directly under the domestic terminal of **Fukuoka Airport** (if you've arrived at the international terminal, take the free shuttle bus to the domestic terminal). The trip to Hakata Station takes only 5 minutes and to Tenjin takes 11; the fare is ¥250 ($2.10), or you can purchase a one-day subway pass for ¥650 ($5.40) if you plan on doing some sightseeing. Alternatively, there's a Nishitetsu bus service directly from the international terminal to Hakata Station's bus terminal; departures are every 20 to 30 minutes and cost ¥190 ($1.60).

By Train   Fukuoka's **Hakata Station** is the last stop on the Shinkansen bullet train from Tokyo, about 6½ hours away; Hiroshima is 1½ hours away. The fare from Tokyo is ¥21,210 ($177) for an unreserved seat.

By Bus   Buses depart from Tokyo's Shinjuku Station nightly at 9pm, arriving at Hakata Station the next morning at 11:10am. The fare is ¥15,000 ($125) one-way.

VISITOR INFORMATION   Before leaving Tokyo, Kyoto, or the Narita or Kansai airports, pick up a copy of the leaflet "Fukuoka" at the Tourist Information Center.

The **Fukuoka Tourist Information Office** (© 092/431-3003; open daily 9am–7pm) is in Hakata Station near the Hakata exit. It has maps and a pamphlet in English, and English speakers are almost always on hand. Pick up free copies of *Rainbow,* a monthly with concert, exhibition, events, and festival information, and *Fukuoka Now,* good for restaurant and nightlife listings. Also ask for the free *Fukuoka on Foot,* an excellent booklet of walking tours, as well as the free **Welcome Card** and accompanying guide, which gives overseas visitors discounts for selected hotels, restaurants, attractions, and shops (the card must be presented at check-in to receive hotel discount). Beside the tourist office is a counter for hotel reservations, with a ¥525 ($4.35) charge for the service. For information on Fukuoka Prefecture, including Space World in Kitakyushu, go to the **Fukuoka Information Center** on the second floor of the ACROS

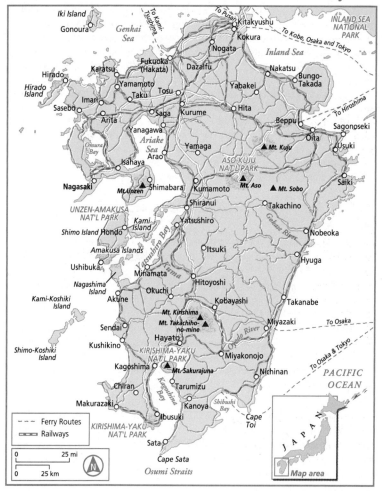

Building, 1–1–1 Tenjin, Chuo-ku (☎ **092/725-9100;** open daily 10am–7pm, closed 2nd and 4th Mon each month); English-speaking volunteers are available daily from noon to 4pm.

On the Internet, check out the Fukuoka Convention and Visitors Bureau website at **www.welcome-fukuoka.or.jp**.

INTERNET ACCESS   You can check e-mail 24 hours a day at **Kinko's,** 1–4–1 Hakata-Eki-mae (☎ **092/473-2677**), on the right side of Taihaku-dori about a 6-minute walk from Hakata Station's west side. You'll find other Kinko's on the east side of Hakata Station at 2–5–28 Hakata Eki Higashi (☎ **092/ 414-3399**) and in Tenjin-Minami near Mitsukoshi department store at 1–22–17 Imaizumi (☎ **092/722-4222**).

MAIL & ATMS   An international post office, with an ATM that accepts international credit cards and a counter for stamps and mail open 24 hours, is located next to the Hakata (west) exit of Hakata Station.

ORIENTATION Although Hakata Station is the terminus for the Shinkansen bullet train and trains departing for the rest of Kyushu, with most of Fukuoka's hotels clustered nearby, the heart and business center of Fukuoka is an area to the west called **Tenjin.** It's home to several department stores, its own train station and bus center, a large underground shopping arcade, and restaurants. Just a few minutes' walk from Tenjin is **Nakasu,** one of Japan's most famous nightlife districts, with more than 2,000 bars, restaurants, and small clubs clustered on what's actually an islet bounded by the Nakagawa River.

Across the river from Nakasu (and a 10-min. walk west of Hakata Station) is **Canal City Hakata,** an intriguingly designed (by award-winning American architect Jon Jerde) entertainment, hotel, and shopping complex with 125 shops and restaurants. Nearby and within walking distance are also Tochiji Temple, Hakata Machiya Folk Museum, Kushida Shrine, and the Fukuoka Asian Art Museum.

GETTING AROUND You can **walk** from Hakata Station to most of the attractions recommended below.

By Subway This is the easiest method of transportation because there are only two lines. One line runs from Hakata Station to Tenjin (the 3rd stop), passing Nakasu-Kawabata on the way, the stop for the Nakasu nightlife district. This same line will also take you to Fukuoka Airport. Stops are announced in English. Fares start at ¥200 ($1.65), but if you think you'll be riding a lot, purchase a one-day subway pass for ¥600 ($5).

By Train Whereas Hakata Station serves as the terminus for the Shinkansen and Japan Railways trains departing for the rest of Kyushu, Tenjin has its own station, called **Nishitetsu Fukuoka Station,** located inside the Mitsukoshi department store building and useful for trips to Dazaifu.

By Bus The city's two bus terminals are located near Hakata Station at the Kotsu Center and in Tenjin near Nishitetsu Fukuoka Station and Mitsukoshi department store; both are clearly marked in English. Buses running inside the central Hakata-Tenjin District charge a flat fare of ¥100 (85¢). Most useful for tourists is the so-called "¥100 Bus," which sports a big, ¥100 coin on its side and travels a circular route to Tenjin, Canal City, Hakata Station and the Hakata Riverain shopping/cultural complex.

EXPLORING THE CITY

About an 8-minute walk northwest of Hakata Station and located on the right side of Taihaku-dori is **Tochiji Temple,** 2–4 Gokushomachi (© **092/291-4459;** daily 9am–5pm; subway: one stop from Hakata Station to Gion, exit 1, 1 min.). This modern reconstruction of a long-established temple may not look like much, but up on the second floor is Japan's largest seated wooden Buddha, measuring 33 feet tall. Admission is free, but refrain from taking photographs. Particularly interesting is the trip through the Hells of Buddhism, which you can embark upon by entering the small room underneath the Buddha. After viewing colored reliefs of unfortunate souls burning in hell, being boiled alive, and suffering other tortures, enter the darkened passageway and walk through it guided by a rail, whereupon you'll reach the end—enlightenment! Fun for older kids.

On the other side of Taihaku-dori Avenue, down the side street marked by a large cement torii, is the ②⓪① **Hakata Machiya Folk Museum** (Hakata Machiya Furusato-Kan) ✪, 6–10 Reisen-machi (©**092/281-7761;** daily

Tips   **A Note on Japanese Symbols**

Many establishments and attractions in Japan do not have signs in Roman (English-language) letters. Those that don't are indicated in this guide with an oval with a number that corresponds to a number in appendix C showing the Japanese symbols. Thus, to find the Japanese symbol for, say, the **Hakata Machiya Folk Museum** (above), refer to no. 201 in appendix C.

10am–6pm; subway: Gion, exit 2, 4 min.). This museum celebrates the history and cultural heritage of Hakata, the old merchants' town, concentrating primarily on the Meiji and Taisho eras. It occupies three buildings, two of which are Meiji-Era replicas; the third is an authentic, 150-year-old house of a weaver. On display are items used in everyday life, including lunch boxes and combs, as well as dioramas depicting festivals, everyday street scenes, and a home typical of a Hakata merchant family. On a telephone, you can listen to Hakata-ben, the local dialect, which is quite difficult even for native Japanese speakers to understand. You can also watch artisans at work on Hakata's most famous wares, including the highly refined Hakata dolls, tops, wooden containers, and Hakata-ori cloth, used for *obi* sashes and famous for loincloths worn by sumo wrestlers. Be sure to see the 22-minute film of the Yamakasa Festival, Fukuoka's most famous festival, featuring races of men carrying enormous floats. Add another 30 minutes to see the museum itself. Admission is ¥200 ($1.65) for adults and ¥100 (85¢) for children.

Beyond the Hakata Machiya Folk Museum is **Kushida Shrine,** 1 Kamikawa-bata-machi (© **092/291-2951;** shrine grounds open 24 hr.), Fukuoka's oldest shrine. Site of the Yamakasa Festival, it has long been the shrine for merchants praying for good health and prosperity. Most interesting is a tall, towering float on view year-round that is used in the Yamakasa Festival held in mid-July and decorated with dolls made by Hakata doll makers. Incredibly, the elaborate floats are made anew every year.

Walk through Kushida Shrine and turn right into the **Kawabata-dori covered shopping arcade.** Linking Canal City Hakata and Hakata Riverain, it was once the city's main shopping street but has been overtaken by the two complexes it connects. Halfway down is another float on view year-round that's used in the Yamakasa Festival. At the end of the arcade, across the street, is Riverain, where up on the 8th floor is the **Fukuoka Asian Art Museum** 夫夫, 3–1 Shimo-Kawabatamachi (© **092/263-1100;** Thurs–Tues 10am–8pm), the only museum I've seen in Japan devoted to contemporary and modern art from around Asia. From folk pop art to political art, the permanent exhibition presents the cutting edge of art from the Philippines, Indonesia, Malaysia, Singapore, Thailand, China, Mongolia, Korea, India, and other Asian countries, with changing displays culled from the museum's own collection. It's very much worth the hour you'll spend here and the ¥200 ($1.65) admission for adults, ¥150 ($1.25) for college and high-school students, and ¥100 (85¢) for junior-high students. The closest subway station is Nakasu-Kawabata Station (exit 6) in front of Riverain.

If you're ready for dining or shopping, retrace your steps through Kawabata-dori arcade and take the escalator leading to the spectacular **Canal City Hakata,** a virtual city-within-a-city complete with hotels, shops, the Sega Joypolis amusement arcade, and a 590-foot-long canal that runs through its center.

EASY SIDE TRIPS FROM FUKUOKA
DAZAIFU

If you have 3 or more hours to spare, I heartily recommend taking a side trip to **Dazaifu Tenmangu Shrine** ⋆⋆⋆, 4–7–1 Saifu Dazaifu (☎ **092/922-8225**), which is immensely popular with the Japanese. It was established in 905 soon after the death of Sugawara Michizane, who was suddenly demoted from his position as Minister of the Right and sent here to work. He is now deified at the shrine as the god of scholarship, which explains why the shrine is so popular— high-school students flock here to pray that they pass the tough entrance exams into universities. Dazaifu has a festive atmosphere, and one of the main reasons to visit, in my opinion, is to see everyone else.

The best way to reach Dazaifu is from Nishitetsu Fukuoka Station in Tenjin (located in the Mitsukoshi department store building). Take a rapid express (*kaisoku*) of the Nishitetsu Omuta Line 10 minutes to Futsukaichi; transfer there (across the platform) for the 8-minute train ride (2 stops) to Dazaifu Station, the last stop (a few trains go directly from Fukuoka Station to Dazaifu). Otherwise, if you don't catch a rapid express, the trip to Dazaifu can take about 50 minutes. In any case, the fare is ¥390 ($3.35) one-way. The **Dazaifu Tourist Office** (☎ **092/925-1880;** daily 8:30am–5pm), located to the right inside Dazaifu Station, has an English pamphlet. Or, if you want to know more about the shrine, rent headphones with English commentary at the entrance to the shrine precinct for ¥300 ($2.50) at an information counter open daily 8:30am to 5pm.

Dazaifu Tenmangu Shrine is a 5-minute walk from the station. Take a right onto a pedestrian lane lined with shops selling souvenirs, sweets, and crafts, followed by a series of arched bridges spanning turtle-filled ponds leading to the main hall, built in 1590. On the day I was there, one-month-old babies were being blessed for good health (or maybe as insurance toward a good education?), one after the other. Behind the hall hang wooden tablets, written with the wishes of visitors—mostly for successful examination scores. Also behind the main hall is an extensive plum grove with 6,000 trees; the plum blossom, in bloom from late January to March, is considered the symbol of scholarship.

Whatever you do, don't miss **Komyozenji Temple** ⋆, just a 2-minute walk away from the shrine. This Zen temple boasts Kyushu's sole rock garden, arranged to form the Chinese character for "light." In the back is also a combination moss-rock garden, representing the sea and land and shaded by maple trees. It's a glorious sight and is almost never crowded, except in autumn when changing maple leaves make it even more spectacular. To see it, take your shoes off, throw ¥200 ($1.65) into the donation box, and walk to the wooden veranda in back where you can sit and meditate.

SPACE WORLD

One of Kyushu's most popular high-tech theme parks is **Space World** ⋆⋆, Yahata-Higashi-ku (☎ **093/672-3445**), in the town of Kitakyushu. This space-travel-themed amusement park features various thrill rides, including roller coasters, a splash ride, a 328-foot-high Ferris wheel, and Space Dome, in which visitors take a "shuttle" to a space station and from there embark on journeys to the moon, around the solar system, or through a black hole. Entertainment shows, theaters, a space museum that contains an Apollo capsule and other items, and kiddie rides are also offered. An all-inclusive pass costs ¥3,800 ($32) for adults (junior-high age and older), ¥2,800 ($23) for children 4 through

Take Me Out to the Ballgame

If you're in town March through September, consider seeing the **Fukuoka Daiei Hawks** baseball team play one of its 70-some home games in Fukuoka Dome, the first retractable-roof stadium in Japan. Tickets start at ¥1,000 ($8.35) for an unreserved seat in the outfield and are available at any Lawson convenience store up to 2 hours before the start of the game or at the box office. Personally, I find watching the spectators as much fun as watching the game, with their coordinated cheering, flag waving, trumpet blowing, and more. Oddly enough, the roof is kept closed (in case it rains and so that players aren't distracted by their shadows) except for occasional night games and during the last 15 minutes of a game if it looks like the Hawks are going to win. And this being Japan, the dome is part of a larger **Hawks Town** complex with restaurants, other amusements, and even a Backstage Tour held daily at 9am and 4pm (except on game days when it's at 10am or night games when it's at 9am and 2pm) that allows you to see the dome at close range for ¥1,000 ($8.35). To reach Hawks Town, take the subway to the Tojinmachi subway stop, from which it's about a 15-minute walk. Or, take bus no. 39 or 306 from gate 5 of the Kotsu Bus Center in front of Hakata Station to the Fukuoka-Dome Mae. On game days, there are also special shuttle buses departing from the bus centers in Tenjin and Kotsu Center near Hakata Station.

elementary school, and free for seniors (proof of age required). Minimum daily open hours are November through March from 10am to 5pm and April to October 9:30am to 5pm, with extended hours many holidays and weekends. To reach Space World, take a JR Kaisoku (express) train from Fukuoka's Hakata Station directly to Space World Station. The trip time is about 60 minutes, and the park is a 5-minute walk from the station. If you have a JR Rail Pass, it's quicker to take the Shinkansen bullet train 20 minutes from Hakata Station to Kokura Station, transferring there to a local line for the 10-minute ride to Space World. Likewise, if you're coming from Honshu via Shinkansen, transfer in Kokura.

WHERE TO STAY
EXPENSIVE

Grand Hyatt Fukuoka ✸✸   Rated among the top five hotels in Japan according to a survey conducted by a prestigious Japanese magazine (and the only Grand Hyatt in Japan), this accommodation boasts the city's most spectacular setting—in the innovative Canal City Hakata. Its black-marbled lobby has a curved facade that overlooks the shopping complex, but for guests who desire solitude, the hotel also has its own private roof garden. Service throughout the hotel is superb—along the order of "your wish is our command." Spacious rooms, with views of the private garden or the river and its night scenes, provide every luxury, but if that's not enough, the Regency Club's "hotel within a hotel" goes the extra mile, with lots of freebies thrown in—like complimentary breakfast, evening cocktails, and free use of the fitness center. But the main reason for staying at the Grand Hyatt is that it's fun, with Canal City's many shops and restaurants right next door.

1–2–82 Sumiyoshi, Hakata-ku, Fukuoka 812-0018. ⓒ 800/ 233-1234 in the U.S. and Canada, or 092/282-1234. Fax 092/282-2817. www.hyatt.com. 370 units. ¥17,000 ($142) single; ¥28,000–¥46,000 ($233–$383) double or twin. Regency Club ¥23,000 ($192) single; ¥34,000–¥52,000 ($283–$433) double or twin. AE, DC, JCB, MC, V. Subway: Nakasu-Kawabata (exit 5, 10 min.). Station: Hakata (west exit, 15 min.). **Amenities:** 4 restaurants (Continental, Cantonese, Japanese, and a sophisticated food court with 5 specialty counters), 2 bars; fitness center and spa with 25-meter indoor pool (fee: ¥3,000/$25; free to Regency Club guests); 24-hr. concierge; business center; Canal City shopping arcade; salon; room service (6:30am–midnight); same-day laundry/dry cleaning service; nonsmoking rooms; executive-level rooms. *In room:* A/C, satellite TV with pay movies, dataport, minibar, hot-water pot with tea, hair dryer, safe.

Il Palazzo ✯✯ Eye-catching with its brick-warehouse-meets-Art-Deco-temple architecture, this uniquely designed boutique hotel is the hotel of choice for artists, designers, and other creative folks. Although rooms come with all the usual amenities, the design goes beyond the usual. Rooms, even singles, are large for Japan and have marbled bathrooms thoughtfully divided by a large glass plate into "wet" areas (shower/bathtub) and "dry" areas (sink and toilet). Canal City Hakata is just across the river. The highest rates in each category above are those charged on Saturdays and evenings before holidays.

3–13–1 Haruyoshi, Chuo-ku, Fukuoka 810-0003. ⓒ **092/716-3333.** Fax 092/724-3330. 62 units. ¥13,000–¥15,000 ($108–$125) single; ¥22,000–¥25,000 ($183–$208) double; ¥21,000–¥24,000 ($175–$200) twin. AE, DC, JCB, MC, V. Subway: Nakasu-Kawabata Station (exit 1, 8 min.). Walk straight toward the river, turn left, and walk along the river to the 2nd bridge, cross it, and turn left. Bus: 68 and any other bus going down Kokutai-Doro Ave. to Minami Shinchi (4 min.). **Amenities:** 1 restaurant (Italian), a coffee shop, 2 bars; room service (4–10pm); in-room massage; same-day laundry/dry cleaning service. *In room:* A/C, bilingual TV, minibar, hot-water pot with tea, hair dryer.

MODERATE

Canal City Fukuoka Washington Hotel *Value* Though part of a nationwide business-hotel chain, this Washington is different—it has more style and lots of pluses. For one thing, it's located in Canal City Hakata, Fukuoka's number one shopping and entertainment complex, offering convenience right out the front door. In addition, its rooms come with extras not usually found in business hotels. All singles, which have semi-double beds, face the Grand Hyatt above the Canal City complex, while twins and triples have better views outward toward the city. The downside: Its good location makes it popular and you'll find the lobby crowded at check-in and check-out times.

1–2–20 Sumiyoshi, Hakata-ku, Fukuoka 812-0018. ⓒ **092/282-8800.** Fax 092/282-0757. 423 units. ¥7,900–¥9,500 ($66–$79) single; ¥16,000 ($144) double; ¥15,000–¥16,500 ($125–$137.50) twin; ¥18,000 ($150) triple. AE, DC, JCB, V. Subway: Nakasu-Kawabata (exit 5, 10 min.). Station: Hakata (west exit, 10 min.). **Amenities:** 2 restaurants (Western and Japanese); Canal City shopping arcade; nonsmoking rooms. *In room:* A/C, satellite bilingual TV, minibar, hot-water pot with tea, washlet toilet.

Dukes Hotel ✯ Flower boxes, plants, and evergreens outside the front door hint that this is no ordinary hotel. Indeed, it's an inexpensive hotel with class, with a small but very civilized lobby that exudes charm and invites you to linger with its Chinese vases, palm trees, antiques, and classical music. Most of the rooms, simple but comfy, are singles, with only nine twins and nine doubles. A thoughtful touch is the folding makeup mirror at the desk, and there's even a ladies' floor for extra security, with pink pajamas instead of the usual cotton kimono. In the world of cloned business hotels, this establishment is a welcome relief.

2–3–9 Hakataeki-mae, Hakata-ku, Fukuoka 812-0011. ⓒ **092/472-1800.** Fax 092/472-1900. 153 units. ¥7,800–¥8,700 ($65–$72.50) single; ¥12,000 ($100) double; ¥13,000 ($108) twin. AE, MC, V. Station: Hakata (2 min.). From the west (Hakata) exit, take the road straight ahead (the one between the Fukuoka City Bank and the brown, stone Center Building); it's down this street on your right in the 2nd block. **Amenities:** Coffee shop. *In room:* A/C, bilingual TV, dataport (not all rooms), fridge, hot-water pot with tea, hair dryer, washlet toilet, trouser press (except on ladies' floor).

Hotel Centraza Hakata   This hotel is just a stone's throw from the station, making it convenient if you've arrived in Fukuoka on the Shinkansen from Honshu. The singles and cheapest twins are small but packed with everything you need—a bedside light, a small desk, an easy chair, and a closet. The largest, corner twins are quite spacious and have the extras of trouser presses, washlet toilets, and two sinks. Vending machines sell socks, underwear, and other necessities, while in the basement is Gourmet City with a half-dozen tenant restaurants.

4–23 Hakataeki-Chuogai, Hakata-ku, Fukuoka 812-0012. ℂ 092/461-0111. Fax 092/461-0171. 197 units. ¥9,800 ($82) single; ¥13,000–¥18,000 ($108–$150) double; ¥14,000–¥20,000 ($117–$167) twin. Rates ¥2,000 ($17) more on Sat and nights before holidays. AE, DC, JCB, MC, V. Station: Hakata (a 1-min. walk from the east "Chikushi" Shinkansen exit). **Amenities:** 1 restaurant (serving buffet dinner), 1 coffee shop, 1 bar; small outdoor pool (free for hotel guests); a 24-hr. Lawson convenience store. *In room:* A/C, biligual TV, mini-bar, hot-water pot with tea.

INEXPENSIVE

Hakata JBB Hotel   In the heart of the city within easy walking distance of Canal City Hakata, the Asian Art Museum, and other attractions, this is a simple but very well-managed establishment under the watchful eye of friendly Yamada-san, who speaks English. Open-air passageways lead to tiny but well-kept rooms complete with a toothbrush, shampoo, and pajamas. Beds are semi-double in size and are for single use, but married couples or two women can room together for ¥6,000 ($50). You won't find anything in the city center cheaper than this.

6–5–1 Reisen-machi, Hakata-ku, Fukuoka 812-0039. ℂ 092/263-8300. Fax 092/263-8301. 48 units. ¥4,500 ($37.50) single; ¥6,000 ($50) double. No credit cards. Subway: Gion (exit 2, 4 min.). Beside the Hakata Machiya Folk Museum. *In room:* A/C, TV, hot-water pot with tea, hair dryer, no phone.

Toyoko Inn   This clean, relatively new, efficient, and inexpensive inn is popular with young travelers. Western-style rooms are simply furnished but offer a quilt-covered bed, indirect lighting, a large window that opens, a huge full-length mirror, and a free movie channel and VCR (but no video rentals). Vending machines sell drinks, and a ¥525 ($4.35) breakfast buffet is available. Book a room early for summer since rooms go quickly at these rates.

1–38 Gion-cho, Hakata-ku, Fukuoka 812-0038. ℂ 092/281-1045. Fax 092/281-1046. 176 units. ¥5,300–¥6,300 ($44–$52.50) single; ¥8,300 ($69) double or twin. AE, DC, JCB, MC, V. Subway: Gion (exit 5, 1 min.). Station: Hakata (8 min.). Take the west Hakata exit and walk down Taihaku-dori Ave.; it will be on your left. *In room:* A/C, TV with free movies, fridge, hot-water pot with tea, hair dryer.

WHERE TO DINE

For one-stop dining, head to **Canal City Hakata** 🅡, a 10-minute walk west of Hakata Station or a 10-minute walk from the Nakasu-Kawabata subway station. You'll find dozens of restaurants in this shopping complex, situated around a canal and water fountains and offering everything from Chinese, Italian, and Japanese cuisine to fast food and bar snacks. There's something for every pocketbook—you can opt for formal dining or order takeout and sit outside to watch the fountains. Set meals range from about ¥800 to ¥5,000 ($6.65–$42), and most restaurants are open from 11am to 11pm daily. Another good choice is in the adjoining Grand Hyatt Hotel's basement food court, offering ethnic cuisine from around the world.

For a bit more local flavor, head to one of Fukuoka's famous 200 *yatai* **stalls** (streetside food stalls). Most are located in Tenjin and along the Nakagawa River, on Nakasu Island south of Kokutai-Doro Avenue. Most stalls sell *ramen* (Chinese noodles) though some also serve oden, yakitori, tempura, and other simple fare. They're open from about 6pm to 2am. Many nighttime revelers stop here before or after a cruise through the Nakasu entertainment district. Simply choose a stall, sit down, and you'll be served a steaming bowl of ramen, most of which average about ¥800 ($6.65).

Aroma's EUROPEAN   Located on the lobby floor of the Grand Hyatt, which has a great location in Canal City, this upbeat, modern restaurant has a great lunch buffet serving mostly Mediterranean-inspired cuisine, including salads, antipasta, soup, and fish and meat entrees, while dinners offer various seafood and meat courses—such as fresh fish of the day or roast chicken—at varying prices.

Grand Hyatt Fukuoka, 1–2–82 Sumiyoshi. ✆ **092/282-1234.** Buffet lunch ¥1,800 ($15) weekday, ¥2,000 ($17) weekends and holidays; set dinners ¥3,500–¥8,000 ($29–$67). AE, DC, JCB, MC, V. Daily 11:30am–2:30pm and 5:30–10pm. Subway: Nakasu-Kawabata (exit 5, 10 min.). Station: Hakata (west exit, 15 min.).

Shikitei KYOTO SPECIALTIES   If you're looking for refined Japanese dining near the station, I recommend this. With the Miyako chain's most famous hotel located in Kyoto, it's not surprising Shikitei specializes in Kyoto-style dishes. Set meals center on sashimi, tempura, shabu-shabu, or sukiyaki. Kyoto kaiseki selections start at ¥5,000 ($42) for dinner and ¥4,000 ($33) for lunch; less expensive are the obento lunch boxes.

Hakata Miyako Hotel, 2–1 Hakata-eki Higashi. ✆ **092/441-3111.** Set dinners ¥5,000–¥10,000 ($42–$83); set lunches ¥1,500–¥5,000 ($12.50–$42). AE, DC, JCB, MC, V. Daily 11:30am–2pm and 5–9:30pm. Station: Hakata (1-min. walk from the east Chikushi exit).

⟨202⟩ **Ume no Hana** VEGETARIAN/TOFU   Located next to City Theater in Canal City, this low-keyed chain is known for its low-calorie, light vegetarian cuisine. It offers a variety of meals centered on tofu and vegetables, though one set meal does include meat. It's simply decorated in that sparse yet elegant Japanese way, with seating either at tables or on tatami with leg wells.

Canal City Hakata, 4th floor, 1–2 Sumiyoshi. ✆ **0120/67-1055.** Set dinners ¥2,000–¥6,000 ($17–$50); set lunches ¥800–¥2,000 ($6.65–$17). AE, DC, JCB, MC, V. Daily 11am–2:30pm and 5–9pm (last order). Subway: Nakasu-Kawabata (exit 5, 10 min.). Station: Hakata (west Hakata exit, 10 min.).

2 Beppu, King of the Hot-Spring Spas ⟨★⟩⟨★⟩

1,219km (762 miles) SW of Tokyo; 186km (116 miles) SE of Fukuoka

Beppu gushes forth more hot-spring water than anywhere else in Japan. With approximately 2,700 hot springs spewing forth 130,000 kiloliters (33.8 million gal.) of water daily (enough to fill 3,600 25m pools), it has long been one of the country's best-known spa resorts. Some 12 million people come to Beppu every year to relax and rejuvenate themselves in one of the city's 114 public bathhouses, and they do so in a number of unique ways. They sit in mud baths up to their necks, they bury themselves in hot black sand, they soak in hot springs, and on New Year's, they bathe in water filled with floating orange peels. They even drink hot-spring water and eat food cooked by its steam.

Bathing reigns supreme here—and I suggest you join in the fun. After all, visiting Beppu without enjoying the baths would be like going to a world-class restaurant with your own TV dinner.

Not a very large town, with a population of 125,000, Beppu is situated on Kyushu's eastern coast in a curve of Beppu Bay, bounded on one side by the sea and on the other by steep hills and mountains. On cold days, steam rises everywhere throughout the city, escaping from springs and pipes and giving the town an otherworldly appearance. Indeed, eight of the hot springs look so much like hell that that's what they're called—Jigoku, the Hells. But rather than a place most people try to avoid, the Hells are a major tourist attraction. In fact, everything in Beppu is geared toward tourism, and if you're interested in rubbing elbows with Japanese on vacation—particularly the older generation—this is one of the best places to do so.

ESSENTIALS
GETTING THERE   By Plane   The nearest airport is in Oita, an hour's bus ride away (bus fare: ¥1,700/$14); flights from Tokyo's Haneda airport (ANA, JAL, JAS) take about 1½ hours and cost ¥30,000 ($250) one-way.

By Train   From Tokyo, go by Shinkansen to Kokura and then transfer to a limited express bound for Beppu; the trip takes about 8 hours (not including transfers) and costs ¥22,670 ($189) for an unreserved seat. There are also a few direct trains daily from Hakata Station in Fukuoka and from Kumamoto, both taking about 3 hours.

By Ferry   Ferries make nightly runs to Beppu from Osaka (with a stop in Kobe, with fares beginning at ¥7,400 ($62); at last check, ferries departed Osaka's South Pier at 6:30 and 9pm, arriving the next morning at 6:20 and 10am respectively. Contact tourist offices in Osaka or Kobe (see chapter 8) for more information.

From Shikoku, the most practical ferry is from Yawatahama, running five times daily and costing ¥ 1,770 ($15) one-way for the 2½-hour trip; contact the **Uwajima Unyu Co.** for information (C 0894/22-2536). The ferry from Matsuyama, also on Shikoku, departs twice daily and costs ¥2,600 ($22) for the 3½-hour trip; it's run by the **Diamond Ferry Co.** (C 089/951-2266).

VISITOR INFORMATION   Before leaving Tokyo, Kyoto, or the Narita or Kansai airports, pick up a copy of the leaflet "Beppu and Vicinity" at the Tourist Information Center.

In Beppu, the **Beppu Tourist Information Office** (C 0977/24-2838; open daily 9am–5pm) is located in Beppu Station at the east (main) exit. However, no English is spoken here, so you'll be directed to the slightly less convenient **Foreign Tourist Information Office** (C 0977/23-1119; open Mon–Sat 9am–5pm), located in the north end of the station in a small shopping complex and staffed by volunteers.

ORIENTATION & GETTING AROUND   Beppu Station is located near the center of the city. Its main exit is to the east and the sea, while to the west lie the Hells and the majority of hot-spring baths. Because most destinations are not within walking distance, the easiest ways to get around Beppu are by bus and by taxi. Although there are two companies serving Beppu, the **Kamenoi Bus Company** (C 0977/23-0141) is the largest and serves most of the city. Bus fares begin at ¥140 ($1.15) and increase according to the distance, but if you plan on doing a lot of sightseeing, there's a 1-day pass called **My Beppu Free**— which nonetheless costs ¥900 ($7.50) for adults, half price for children under 12. It allows unlimited travel on Kamenoi Company buses (which are blue) in the city as well as slight discounts on a few attractions. Three-day and 5-day passes that include guided tours are also available. You can purchase the passes at the local tourist office at Beppu Station.

TAKING THE WATERS

Beppu is divided into eight hot-spring areas, each with its own mineral content and natural characteristics. Although any hot-spring bath can help stimulate metabolism and blood circulation and create a general feeling of well-being, there are specific springs with various mineral contents that the Japanese believe help in ailments ranging from rheumatism and diabetes to skin disease. The tourist office has a pamphlet to help you select the baths that will help you the most. And whatever you do, don't rinse off with plain water after taking your bath because this will wash away all those helpful minerals. You should bring your own towel and, for some places, also a *yukata* (cotton kimono), though the latter is also available for sale or for rent.

SUGINOI ★★★

Suginoi Palace (© **0977/24-1160**), a 10-minute bus ride from Beppu Station on bus no. 10 or 14, is one of the best known baths in all of Japan and also one of the largest. Although I used to consider it among the most fantastic in the country, newer, more sophisticated public baths have rendered this facility almost a relic and a rather kitschy one at that. For just those reasons, it remains one of my favorites. Two separate bathing areas are housed in what look like air-plane hangars, one for men and one for women. Filled with lush tropical plants and pools of various sizes and temperatures, one of the baths features a benevo-lent-looking Buddha sitting atop a giant fish bowl full of carp, while the other boasts a large red torii gate of Shinto shrines. If you come 2 days in a row, you can see both baths because men and women alternate facilities daily. The baths also feature a steam room, a sauna, a pit with hot sand to bury yourself in, a waterfall massage (great for shoulders and backs), and in the bath with the torii gate, a bath of stone pebbles you can tread upon to massage your feet and a Korean-style heated floor upon which you can lie down and relax.

As if that weren't enough, Suginoi Palace also has an outdoor waterfall and a pond filled with greedy carp (buy some fish food and you'll see what I mean—they almost jump out of the water in their frenzy), a small landscaped garden, a play area with amusement-park rides for children, and bowling lanes. The attached Uzone complex boasts an ice-skating rink (with plastic ice!), an in-line skating rink, arcade games, and fast-food vendors.

Admission to the Suginoi Palace bath complex, open daily from 9am to 10:30pm, costs ¥2,000 ($17) for adults and ¥1,000 ($8.35) for children 4 to 12 if you enter before 5pm. Save money by going after 5pm, when it's half price. If, however, you're staying at the Suginoi Hotel (see "Where to Stay," below), you have free use of the baths daily from 9am to 11pm.

If you're shy about disrobing in front of strangers or have kids in tow, you might want to visit Suginoi's $5 million extension of the Suginoi bathing expe-rience, **Aqua-Beat** (© **0977/26-7600**). It's a water park with water slides (great fun!), children's pools, a simulated wave pool, an artificial beach, outdoor hot springs, a sound-and-light show, and a Jacuzzi. A bar-coded locker key on a wrist band allows you to lock up your valuables, wear your bathing suit (rental suits available), and dine without having to worry about carrying money; upon exit-ing, you'll simply feed it into a machine to get your bill. Admission is ¥2,800 ($23) for adults, ¥1,700 ($14) for students, and ¥1,100 ($9.15) for children 4 to 12; guests staying in the Suginoi Hotel pay only ¥1,400 ($12), ¥800 ($6.65), and ¥500 ($4.15) respectively. General open hours are Monday to Friday 11am to 6pm, Saturday 10am to 9pm, and Sunday and holidays 10am to 7pm, except during Golden Week (end of Apr) and summer vacation (mid-July–Aug) when it's open daily 10am to 9pm. It's closed the first 3 days in June, the last week in November, the first 10 days in December, and Thursdays in September through November; but since this can change, it's best to call in advance. By the way, if you've been or are going to Ocean Dome in Miyazaki, skip Aqua-Beat—it's not as big nor as good.

HYOTAN ONSEN

If Suginoi sounds too huge and touristy, I recommend **Hyotan Onsen** *⚘*, Kannawa 159–2 (*✆* **0977/66-0527;** open daily 8am–9pm), reached by taking bus no. 20 to Jigokubaru. It's newer, smaller, and more low-key and is considered good for rheumatism, skin disease, and female disorders. It also offers open-air baths, pebble baths for your feet, steam baths, waterfall baths, and sand baths. There's a sheet with instructions in English. Admission is ¥700 ($5.85) for adults, ¥300 ($2.50) for elementary-aged children, and ¥200 ($1.65) for children 5 and younger. Yukata rentals are ¥200 ($1.65).

HOT-SAND BATHS

One of the unique things you can do in Beppu is take a bath in hot sand, considered useful for treating muscle pain, arthritis, and indigestion. Although several public baths offer hot-sand baths, one of the most atmospheric places to have one is the **Takegawara Bathhouse** *⚘⚘⚘*, 16–23 Motomachi, Beppu 874 (*✆* **0977/23-1585;** open daily 8am–9:30pm), a 10-minute walk from Beppu Station. Built in 1879 in traditional, Meiji-Era architecture, this beautiful, wooden structure is one of the oldest public baths in the city and has an interior that resembles an ancient gymnasium. Bathing areas are separate for men and women and are dominated by a pit filled with black sand. The attendants are used to foreigners here; they'll instruct you to strip, wash yourself down, and then lie down in a hollow they've dug in the sand. You should bring your own towel (or buy one here), which you should use to cover your vital parts. An attendant will then shovel sand on top of you and pack you in until only your head and feet are sticking out. I personally didn't find the sand all that hot, but it is relaxing as the heat soaks into your body. You stay buried for 10 minutes, contemplating the wooden ceiling high above and hoping you don't get an itch somewhere. When the time is up, the attendant will tell you to stand up, shake off the sand, and then jump into a bath of hot water. The cost is ¥780 ($6.50). To reach the bathhouse, take the main (east) exit from Beppu Station and walk toward the sea, turning right at the street just before the big intersection. It's a couple blocks down this street on the right with its entrance around the corner.

MORE TO SEE & DO

THE HELLS (JIGOKU)   You might as well join everyone else and go to the Hells, boiling ponds created by volcanic activity. Their Japanese name, Jigoku, refers to the burning hell of Buddhist sutras. Six of the eight Hells are clustered close together in the Kannawa hot-spring area, within walking distance of each other, and they can be toured in about an hour or so. However, since they're kind of hokey, you might just want to visit a couple. Each Hell has its own attraction. **Umi Jigoku,** or Sea Hell, is the color of sea water; **Chinoike Jigoku,** the Blood-Pond Hell, is blood red in color because of the red clay dissolved in the hot water; **Yama Jigoku** features animals living in its hot spring; **Kamado**

Jigoku, the Oven Hell, was used for cooking; and **Oniyama Jigoku** is where crocodiles are bred. **Tatsumaki Jigoku,** or Waterspout Hell, has one of the largest geysers in Japan, and with a temperature of 221°F, it's hotter than any other hot spring in Beppu. To reach Kannawa from Beppu Station, take bus no. 7 to the Kannawa bus stop. From there, you can take bus no. 16 onward to the other two Hells.

The Hells are open daily 8am to 5pm. A combination ticket, costing ¥2,000 ($17) for adults, ¥1,300 ($11) for high-school students, ¥1,000 ($8.35) for junior-high students, and ¥900 ($7.50) for children, allows entrance to all eight Hells. Otherwise, the separate entrance fee to each one is ¥400 ($3.35). You can also join a 2½-hour tour of the Hells that includes admission, but it's conducted in Japanese only. There are nine tours a day, departing from Kitahama Bus Center and costing ¥4,500 ($37.50) for adults, ¥3,800 ($32) for high-school students, ¥3,500 ($29) for junior-high students, and ¥1,830 ($15) for children. If you have a 3-day or 5-day bus pass, you can join a tour for free but must pay your own admission. For more information, contact the **Beppu Tourist Office** or the **Beppu Jigoku Association** (© **0977/66-1577**).

⟨203⟩ **JAPAN BAMBOO MUSEUM**   Beppu is famous for its bamboo crafts, and the best place to shop for bamboo ware and to learn more about this amazingly durable material is at this museum, called **Nihon Take-no-Haku-butsukan** in Japanese (6–8–19 Ishigaki-higashi (© **0977/25-7776;** open daily 8am–5pm). Exhibits explain how bamboo grows, the different varieties of bamboo, and the role bamboo has played in Japanese life; and bamboo products from all over Japan including palanquins, fish traps, lunch boxes, rakes, fans, hats, bows, and arrows, are displayed. Even Edison's electric light bulb used a bamboo filament. There are also demonstrations of basket weaving. Admission is ¥300 ($2.50) for adults, ¥200 ($1.65) for junior-high and high school students, and ¥100 (85¢) for children. To reach it, take bus no. 20 or 26 to the Kotsu Bus Center; from there, it's a 5-minute walk inland.

THE MONKEYS OF TAKASAKIYAMA MOUNTAIN   On Beppu's southern border rises Takasakiyama Mountain. Its peak, home to some 1,700 wild monkeys, is one of Japan's largest monkey habitats (© **097/532-5010**). The monkeys come down every day to feed, returning to their homes by late afternoon. They wander freely among the visitors; humans are advised not to challenge them by looking directly into their eyes. Admission is ¥500 ($4.15) for adults and ¥250 ($2.10) for children, and it's open daily 8:30am to 5pm. From Beppu Station, take an Oita Kotsu Bus for Takasakiyama (there is no bus number), a 10-minute ride; unfortunately, your My Beppu Free pass isn't accepted on this bus, so you'll have to pay a separate fare.

WHERE TO STAY

As with many hot-spring spas, Beppu levies a hot-springs tax: ¥150 ($1.25) per person, per night. In addition, some places raise their rates during New Year's, Golden Week (Apr 29–May 5), Obon (mid-Aug), Saturdays, and the evenings before holidays.

EXPENSIVE

⟨204⟩ **Kannawaen** ★★★   If it's peace and quiet you're searching for, here's the place for you: a wonderful, 110-year-old ryokan hidden away on a lushly landscaped hill not far from the Hells. It actually consists of six separate houses spread around its grounds, and its tatami rooms with shoji screens look out onto carefully tended gardens, hot springs, bamboo, streams, bonsai, stone lanterns, flowers, and different kinds of cherry trees. This is the perfect place to escape the crowds and to relax in a meandering, open-air bath set among rocks and trees; its water is said to change color seven times a day—changing with the intensity of the sunlight. The sexes bathe together here, but there are large towels you can use to wrap around yourself for modesty. Most rooms don't have a private bathroom, but the beauty of the surroundings more than makes up for that. Even members of the imperial family and prime ministers have stayed here.

Kannawa, Beppu 874-0045. ☎ **0977/66-2111.** Fax 0977/66-2113. 17 units (7 with bathroom). ¥27,000–¥40,000 ($225–$333) per person. ¥5,000 ($42) extra on weekends. Rates include 2 meals and service charge. JCB. Taxi: A 15-min. ride from Beppu Station. **Amenities:** Indoor/outdoor hot-spring baths; in-room massage. *In room:* A/C, TV, hot-water pot with tea.

Suginoi Hotel 🎿 *Kids* Probably the best-known hotel in Beppu, Suginoi is famous for the adjoining Suginoi Palace, a huge bathing complex with hot-spring baths (which hotel guests can use for free), a water park great for kids (discounts for hotel guests), skating rinks, and more. Situated on a wooded hill with a sweeping view of the city and sea below, it's a lively and noisy hotel, filled with good-natured vacationers. If you like being in the middle of the action, this is the place for you. The hotel is divided into two wings, each with its own check-in counter. The older main building is larger, catering primarily to families and groups with Japanese-style rooms and twins and including two buffet-style meals in its price. The newer Hana wing is more European in atmosphere with mostly Western-style rooms. Both wings also have combination-style rooms, featuring both beds and a separate tatami area. Rates are based on the type of room, and those facing inland are slightly cheaper than those with fantastic sea views. With all the kiddie diversions—the water park, a small amusement park, game room, cheap eats in adjoining Suginoi Palace (even a McDonald's), and more—this is a good choice for families.

Kankaiji, Beppu 874-0822. ☎ **0977/24-1141.** Fax 0977/21-0010. 574 units. Without meals, ¥12,500–¥21,500 ($104–$179) single; ¥17,000–¥25,000 ($142–$208) twin. ¥14,000–¥27,000 ($117–$225) per person including 2 buffet meals. Rates higher in peak season. AE, DC, JCB, MC, V. Bus: 10 or 14 from Beppu Station to Suginoi Palace. Taxi: 8 min. **Amenities:** 8 restaurants, 4 bars; Suginoi Palace with its hot-spring baths and other attractions (see "Taking the Waters," above); 2 24-hr. hot-spring baths for guests only; children's amusement park; game room; shopping arcade; salon; in-room massage. *In room:* A/C, TV, minibar, hot-water pot with tea; hair dryer.

MODERATE

Hotel Seawave Convenient to the station, this interestingly designed hotel is true to its name with a marine theme that includes porthole windows and nautical decor. Even the *yukata* (cotton kimono) provided in each room is imprinted with ships. Yet despite the nautical motifs, the vending machines in the halls, and the trouser presses in the rooms that give it a slightly business-hotel atmosphere, the hotel seems more feminine than masculine. Each room has individual touches such as different-colored tiles in every bathroom and original murals, some with an aqua theme. The cheapest singles have single-size beds, but all other rooms have double-size beds. You'll find the lobby on the second floor, and the reception staff speaks English. The drawback? There's no *onsen* (hot-spring bath) here.

12–8 Ekimae-cho, Beppu 874-0935. ☎ **0977/27-1311.** Fax 0977/27-1310. 92 units. ¥6,000–¥6,600 ($50–$55) single; ¥8,000–¥10,000 ($67–$83) twin. AE, DC, JCB, MC, V. Across the street from Beppu Station's main (east) exit, catty-corner to the right. **Amenities:** 1 restaurant (Japanese/Western). *In room:* A/C, TV, minibar, hot-water pot with tea; hair dryer.

(205) **Sakaeya** 🐸🐸 *Finds* The oldest minshuku in the city, this is one of the best places to stay near the Hells. There are several interesting features here that have utilized the hot springs for decades. Old radiators, for example, are heated naturally from hot springs. Another relic is the stone oven (*jigokugama*) in the courtyard, which uses steam from hot springs for cooking (many older homes in Beppu still use such ovens). Use of the oven is free in case you want to cook your own meals, but there's also a modern kitchen you can use. I recommend, however, that you opt for rates that include meals. Most of your dinner will be steamed using the hot springs and then served in a Japanese dining room with whitewashed walls and a heavy timbered ceiling. In winter, the *kotatsu* (a table with a heating element and covered with a blanket to keep legs warm) in the dining room is steam heated. Most of the rooms—all are Japanese style—have sinks, and all come with cotton yukata and a refrigerator. The oldest rooms, which don't have bathrooms but are very nice, date from the Meiji Period (1868–1912), while those with private bathroom are in a newer addition that nonetheless maintains a traditional atmosphere with sitting alcoves.

Ida, Kannawa, Beppu 874-0043. ℂ **0977/66-6234.** Fax 0977/66-6235. 12 units (7 with bathroom). Without meals, ¥3,500 ($29) single without bathroom; ¥5,000 ($42) single with bathroom; ¥7,000 ($72) double without bathroom; ¥10,000 ($83) double with bathroom. Rates with 2 meals, ¥8,000–¥10,000 ($67–$83) per person without bathroom, ¥13,000–¥20,000 ($108–$167) per person with bathroom. Rates higher during holiday periods including Golden Week (Apr 29–May 5) and New Year's. No credit cards. Bus: Kamenoi Bus no. 7 from Beppu Station's west exit 16 min. to Kannawa (6 min.; walk down the hill and take the 2nd left). Or take an Oita Bus (no number) and get off at the last stop (2 min.; take the 1st left and then the 1st left again). Sakaeya is between the 2 companies' bus stops, both of which are called Kannawa. **Amenities:** Indoor hot-spring baths. *In room:* A/C, TV, fridge, hot-water pot with tea.

INEXPENSIVE

Kagetsu Kagetsu offers what are probably the cheapest rooms in all of Beppu—in fact, its room rates are among the lowest I've come across in my travels through Japan. Even more astonishing is that each of the rooms, both Western and Japanese style, comes with its own private bathroom and central heating. Such low prices do, however, come with some drawbacks—some beds are uncomfortable, bathrooms have old tile, and telephones in the rooms cannot be used for outside calls. Avoid the beds by asking for a tatami room, and stay here only if you're counting every yen. On the bright side, the water here is supplied from the natural hot springs; and the owners, the Takayamas, who couldn't be nicer, have brightened things up with plants in the hallway. No meals are served, but there are plenty of restaurants in the area.

Tanoyucho 7–22, Beppu 874-0909. ℂ **0977/24-2355.** Fax 0977/23-7237. 11 units. ¥3,650 ($30) single; ¥6,800 ($56) double; ¥7,000 ($58) twin. Rates include tax. No credit cards. A 1-min. walk from Beppu Station; turn left out of the west exit and take the 2nd right (you'll see its sign). *In room:* A/C, TV, no phone.

Kokage In operation for almost 30 years, this minshuku, run by a friendly man who speaks a bit of English, is a member of the Japanese Inn Group. There are both Japanese and twin rooms, which are a bit worn, dark, and dreary, but they're furnished with yukata, towels, and a coin-operated heater and air conditioner (free for the first 6 hr. and then ¥100/85¢ for every 2 hr. after that). Those with bathrooms have hot-spring water. There's also a public, rock-lined, hot-spring bath, and meals are served in a homey dining room with a cluttered but interesting collection of antique lamps, clocks, and other items. If you like, the owners will fit you out in a wedding kimono and take your picture with your camera.

8–9 Ekimaecho, Beppu 874-0935. ℂ **0977/23-1753.** Fax 0977/23-3895. 13 units (10 with bathroom). ¥4,000 ($33) single with bathroom; ¥7,000 ($58) twin with bathroom; ¥9,000 ($75) triple without bathroom,

¥10,500 ($87.50) triple with bathroom. Breakfast ¥800 ($6.65) extra; Japanese dinner ¥1,800 ($15) extra. AE, MC, V. A 2-min. walk from Beppu Station's main (east) exit; walk straight ahead for 2 blocks (there's a stoplight here), turn right, and then immediately right again into a small alley. **Amenities:** Coin-op washer and dryer. *In room:* Coin-op A/C, TV, hot-water pot with tea.

WHERE TO DINE

(206) **Jin** GRILLED FOODS   If you're looking for a quick, inexpensive dinner near the train station, you'll find plenty of them in and around the main exit. Jin is one of these, a lively robatayaki featuring grilled foods including skewered meats, vegetables, and fish as well as salads and sashimi. There's an English menu, though with outdated prices.

1–15–7 Kitahama. ✆ 0977/21-1768. Main dishes ¥600–¥1,200 ($5–$10). JCB, MC, V. Daily 5pm–midnight. A 6-min. walk from Beppu Station. Walk straight down the main street leading away from the main (east) exit to the end. Jin is on the right, across the street from the Tokiwa department store and just before the big intersection; look for its sign with a monkey and "Jin" written on it.

(207) **Yakiniku Bungo** *Value* JAPANESE GRILL   This family-style restaurant near the bay offers the best deal in town. Choose what you want from a refrigerated counter with more than 20 different offerings of meat and vegetables, then take them to your table and grill them yourself. There are a dozen different kinds of meat alone, from beef and pork to skewered chicken, but the adventuresome may wish to try more unusual items such as intestines and stomach lining. There's also salad, *kimchee* (spicy cabbage), soup, curry, rice, somen noodles, Jell-O, fruit, and ice cream. If it's really busy, like on a Sunday, you may be requested to leave after an hour or so; otherwise, dig in for a marathon meal.

4–15 Shinminatomachi. ✆ 0977/21-0780. All-you-can-eat ¥1,700 ($14) for persons 13 and older, ¥1,100 ($9.15) for children 7–12, ¥400 ($3.35) for children 3–6. No credit cards. Daily noon–10:30pm. Bus: 20 or 26 to Beppu Kotsu Center (1 min.). It's 1 block inland from the center; cross the pedestrian bridge over the road, walk toward the Shell gas station, and look for the pink building to the right.

3 Off the Beaten Path: Miyazaki

1,420km (889 miles) SW of Tokyo; 407km (254 miles) SE of Fukuoka; 126km (79 miles) W of Kagoshima

The capital of Miyazaki Prefecture, **Miyazaki City** is one of the largest (population: 306,000) and most important cities in southern Kyushu. As all Japanese schoolchildren know, it boasts several famous sites relating to Japan's first emperor, Jimmu. Yet it seems isolated, even somewhat neglected, by the rest of Japan. Tokyo is far away, and Japanese honeymooners, who a couple of decades ago favored Miyazaki over most other domestic destinations, are now flocking to Hawaii and Australia.

To counter its downward spiral into touristic oblivion, in the 1990s Miyazaki developed a large resort called **Seagaia** on its wooded outskirts, complete with hotels, golf courses, a zoo, the world's largest indoor water park, and other attractions. The plan worked: Miyazaki is now a major stop for Asian tour groups making the rounds of Kyushu's theme parks. But beyond that, Miyazaki is a perfect place to relax, swim in the Pacific Ocean, get in some rounds of golf, and savor some of the local delicacies. Temperatures here are the second warmest in Japan after Okinawa (it shares the same approximate latitude with Jerusalem and San Diego), and flowers bloom throughout the year. The natives are warm and kind, maybe because they still don't see many foreigners here, particularly Westerners.

ESSENTIALS

GETTING THERE   **By Plane**   There are daily flights to Miyazaki from most major Japanese cities; ANA offers the most flights from Tokyo's Haneda

Airport. Flight time is 1½ hours from Tokyo, 1 hour from Osaka, and 40 minutes from Fukuoka. One-way fare from Tokyo is ¥31,000 ($258). From the airport, a bus travels to Miyazaki Station in 25 minutes and costs ¥400 ($3.35). Buses also travel from the airport to Seagaia for ¥800 ($6.65). There's also JR train service from the airport to Miyazaki Station; if you don't have a Japan Rail Pass, fare is ¥340 ($2.85).

By Train   From Tokyo, take the Hikari Shinkansen bullet train to Kokura and transfer there to the Nichirin limited express; the entire trip takes approximately 12 hours (not including transfers) and costs ¥25,030 ($209) for an unreserved seat. There are also direct trains from Fukuoka's Hakata Station (6 hr.), Beppu (3½ hr.), and Kagoshima (2 hr.).

By Bus   Eight buses depart daily from Fukuoka for Miyazaki (trip time: almost 5 hr.), costing ¥6,000 ($50) one-way. Buses also depart from Kagoshima's Nishi Kagoshima Station; the fare is ¥2,700 ($22.50). Long-distance buses arrive at the bus station in front of Miyazaki Station.

VISITOR INFORMATION   Before departing Tokyo, Kyoto, or Narita or Kansai airports, pick up the leaflet "Miyazaki and Vicinity" at the Tourist Information Center.

For more pamphlets on the city in English, stop off at the tourist information center at either **Miyazaki Airport** (© 0985/51-5114; open daily 7am–9pm) or the east exit of **JR Miyazaki Station** (© 0985/22-6469; open daily 9am–7pm in summer, to 5:15pm in winter). Among the various good pamphlets available, be sure to pick up *Discovering Miyazaki, A Travel Guide,* and a map.

For detailed information on Miyazaki Prefecture, drop by the **Miyazaki Prefectural Tourist Association,** or *Miyazaki-ken Kanko Kyokai,* located just off Higashi (east) Tachibana-dori at 1–9–30 Tachibana-dori (© **0985/25-4676;** open Mon–Fri 8:30am–5:15pm). It has information on Aoshima, Udo Shrine, and other prefectural attractions.

Mail & ATMs   The **Miyazaki Central Post Office,** 1–1–34 Takachiho-dori (© 0985/24-3424), is located on the right side of Takachiho-dori Avenue if you're walking from Miyazaki Station, about an 8-minute walk away. It's open Monday through Friday 9am to 7pm, Saturday 9am to 5pm, and Sunday 9am to 12:30pm. In addition to ATMs that accept foreign credit cards, it also has a money-exchange counter open Monday through Friday 9am to 6pm.

ORIENTATION & GETTING AROUND   Downtown lies west of Miyazaki Station, about a 10-minute walk away. From Miyazaki Station, take Takachiho-dori Avenue west to **Tachibana-dori,** the main street in town, which is lined with shops, department stores, and restaurants. Almost all city buses serving other parts of town, as well as buses traveling to other cities in Miyazaki Prefecture, make stops along this main thoroughfare—at Depaato-mae bus stop at the intersection of Takachiho- and Tachibana-dori; and at Tachibana-dori 3-chome bus stop, which is farther south. Otherwise, there are two major bus terminals: The **Miyazaki Eigyosho Bus Terminal** (also called Miyazaki Unko Center) is just outside the west exit of Miyazaki Station, and the **Miyako-City Bus Center** is a few minutes' walk from the JR Minami Miyazaki Station (take the south exit and turn left; you'll see the bus center 1 block ahead on your right).

Miyazaki Shrine, Miyazaki prefectural museums, and Heiwadai Park are located northwest of Miyazaki Station, while the Seagaia resort area is located on the coast northeast of Miyazaki Station. All these attractions are easily reached by bus from Miyazaki Station or Tachibana-dori. Fares start at ¥140 ($1.15) and increase according to the distance. There is also local train service from Miyazaki Station to Miyazaki Jingu Eki station near Miyazaki Shrine. For detailed instructions in English on how to use the public transportation system, ask for the pamphlet *Relax and Enjoy, Miyazaki Transportation Guidebook,* available at both area tourist offices (see "Visitor Information," above).

GUIDED TOURS Although all the sights listed below are accessible by public transportation, they're quite spread out. You may, therefore, want to join an organized tour, even though it will be conducted in Japanese only. At least the tour will get you to each destination, and you won't have to worry about time schedules and bus stops. A tour operated by **Miyazaki Kotsu Bus Company** (© **0985/52-2200**) departs at 8am daily from Miyako-City Bus Center and visits Miyazaki Shrine, Heiwadai Park, Kodomo-no-Kuni (an amusement park for children), Aoshima Island, Horikiri Pass (a scenic viewpoint taking in the lush subtropical vegetation and coast line), Cactus Park (a cactus garden that will look all too familiar to anyone from southwestern U.S. or other such climes), and Udo Shrine. The 9½-hour tour returns at 5:35pm. Called the "Nichinan Kaigan Course," it costs ¥4,000 ($33) for adults, ¥2,000 ($17) for children.

WHAT TO SEE & DO
MIYAZAKI SHRINE & ENVIRONS
The most important shrine in town is **Miyazaki Shrine** (Miyazaki Jingu) *,* 2–4–1 Jingu (© **0985/27-4004**), located about a 10-minute walk west of JR Miyazaki Jingu Station. It's dedicated to the first emperor of Japan, Emperor Jimmu, a somewhat mythical figure who established the Yamato Court in 660 B.C. and is believed to be the ancestor of every reigning emperor since. Although the shrine is thought to have originated around the time of Emperor Jimmu's reign some 2,600 years ago, either on a mountaintop or near present-day Heiwadai Park, its ancient history remains shrouded in mystery, much like the emperor himself. Peacefully surrounded by natural woods and majestic cedar, the shrine is built from cedar and is austerely plain. The grounds of the shrine are always open and there's no admission. If you don't want to walk to the shrine, you can take a bus bound for Miyazaki Jingu from Tachibana-dori Avenue or Miyako-City Bus Center.

From the shrine, take a left after passing the first torii gate (there's a map of the area here) and walk around the shrine to the east; you'll pass 200-year-old, thatched-roof Japanese homes that have been moved to the park for preservation (you can take a peek inside). North of Miyazaki Shrine on shrine grounds is the **Miyazaki Prefectural Museum of Nature and History** (Miyazaki-ken Sogo Hakubutsukan), 2–4–4 Jingu (© **0985/24-2017;** open Tues–Sun 9am–5pm). It does an excellent job of presenting the prefecture's animal and plant life, its history, and its folklore with well-designed displays and a wealth of information—what a shame it's in Japanese only. Still, it's worth spending an hour here because there's plenty to look at. Very enlightening is a replica of a home with a wood-burning stove and a bathtub heated with wood—the home dates from the 1950s. Admission is ¥300 ($2.50) for adults, ¥200 ($1.65) for high-school and university students, and ¥100 (85¢) for junior-high students and children. The closest bus stop is Hakubutsukan-mae in front of the museum; board any bus bound for Aya, Kunitomi, or Heiwagaoka from Tachibana-dori.

West of Miyazaki Shine, about a 10-minute walk away, is the **Miyazaki Prefectural Art Museum** (Miyazaki-kenritsu Bijutsukan) *,* 3–210 Funatsuka (© **0985/20-3792;** open Tues–Sun 10am–6pm). This very modern building presents works of Miyazaki artists from the Edo Period onward, those who illustrate recent artistic trends in Japan, and artists from around the world. Most famous of the local artists is probably Ei-Kyu (1911–1960), an avant-garde pioneer whose last works consisted of dots. Ai-O, a contemporary of Ei-Kyu, is known for his Rainbow series. You can see everything in less than an hour. Admission is ¥300 ($2.50) for adults, ¥200 ($1.65) for university and high-school students, and ¥100 (85¢) for children. The closest bus stop is Bunka Koen Mae; board a bus bound for Aya, Heiwagaoka, Ikeuchi, Kunitomi, or Bunka Koen.

HEIWADAI PARK   About a 15-minute walk northwest of Miyazaki Shrine is Heiwadai Park, where you'll find the **Peace Tower,** built in 1940 in celebration of the 2,600th anniversary of the mythological foundation of Japan; it purportedly contains artifacts that once belonged to the first emperor. Its pedestal is made with stones donated by Japanese expatriates from all over the world, while its copper door was created with coins donated by Japanese children. It may seem ironic that a peace tower was erected at a time when Japan was busy colonizing much of Asia; the intention was to show that the world could live peaceably, albeit with Japan as leader. Figures on the tower depict the guardians of fishery, agriculture, self-defense, and commerce.

THE MANY AMUSEMENTS OF SEAGAIA ★★

Seagaia is a convention and resort complex set in a vast national reserve of beautiful pine forest stretching 12km (7½ miles) along the coastline. In addition to hotels, it has amusements too numerous to list. **Phoenix Zoo** (© 0985/ 39-1306; open Thurs–Tues 9am–5pm) has more than 2,000 animals of 100 species from Asia and Africa; admission is ¥800 ($6.65) for adults, ¥400 ($3.35) for students, and ¥300 ($2.50) for children. **Paradise Garden** (© 0985 21-1377; open daily 10am–10pm) is an amusement park with high-tech and virtual-reality games and an orchid greenhouse. Golfers can try out their swings at the private **Phoenix Country Club** (© 0985/39-1301), a 27-hole course with visitor greens fees of ¥25,000 to ¥29,000 ($208–$242), or at the more proletarian public **Tom Watson Golf Course** (© 0985/21-1188), which has 18 holes and charges a greens fee of ¥16,095 ($134) on weekdays to ¥21,345 ($178) on weekends and holidays.

Finds   Haniwa Garden

My favorite thing to see in the park (and a good photo op) is **Haniwa Garden** ★. Archaeological digs in Miyazaki Prefecture have unearthed a multitude of ancient burial mounds and clay figures known as *haniwa;* replicas of these ancient mounds and haniwa clay figures can be seen in Haniwa Garden, where approximately 400 of the figures have been placed between trees on mounds covered with moss. There are warriors, horses, pigs, boats, and houses. I especially like the haniwa with the simple face and body and the O-shaped mouth; it's said to represent a dancing woman. A one-room exhibition house (free, open daily 8:30am–5pm) displays some items found in ancient burial mounds, and if you want you can buy a small clay replica to take home with you.

If you wish to take a bus here, board a bus from Depaato-mae bus stop on Tachibana-dori bound for Heiwadai; get off 12 minutes later at the last stop in front of the park.

Unfortunately, the coast along Seagaia is considered unsafe for swimming, but this is more than rectified by Miyazaki's most entertaining attraction, **Ocean Dome** ✦✦✦ (© 0985/21-1177), certified by the *Guinness Book of Records* as the world's largest all-weather indoor water park; it has a high-tech retractable Teflon roof (Miyazaki is one of the sunniest places in Japan). You have to see this place to believe it; children will think they've landed in heaven. At this faux tropical paradise, you can lounge on a 466-foot-long beach (covered by artificial white sand made of marble), ride waves created by the world's largest wave-making system, careen down water slides, take sophisticated adventure rides (including one that simulates shooting rapids from around the world), eat, and shop. There are also other pools, including a 666-foot flowing circular pool and children's pools, as well as daily shows that include exhibition surfing and a spectacular night show that uses water spray as a screen for lasers. There's no need to wear more than your swimsuit (rental suits are available) because your wristband key can be used to charge everything you buy or consume during your stay. Your kids will probably want to spend half a day here. Admission is ¥2,500 ($21) for adults, ¥2,000 ($17) for children 12 to 17, ¥1,400 ($12) for children 4 to 11, and free for children under 4. Several rides and attractions—the Water Crash, Adventure Theater, and Lost World—are an additional ¥600 ($5) each or ¥1,200 ($10) extra for unlimited rides. The Ocean Dome is open daily from 10am to 9pm (9am–9pm during summer vacation), but closes once or twice a month for maintenance, so check before you go.

Access to all the Seagaia attractions and hotels (see "Where to Stay," below) is by direct bus from the west exit of **JR Miyazaki Station** (¥470/$3.90 for the 20-min. trip), **Tachibana-dori** (¥490/$4.10 for the 30-min. trip), or **Miyazaki Airport** as you exit the arrival lobby (¥800/$6.65 from the ticket vending machines for the 25-min. trip). Seagaia is so large that a **free shuttle bus** loops to all its facilities including hotels, running every 15 to 20 minutes from 7am to 10pm.

AN EASY SIDE TRIP TO THE NICHINAN COAST

South of Miyazaki city is the Nichinan Coast, famous for its exposed and eroded rock sea floor, which is weirdly shaped like rippling waves. Known to the Japanese as Oniwa Sentaku Iwa, or The Ogre's Washboard, it resembles just that.

Here, too, is one of the most famous sights associated with Miyazaki— **Aoshima,** a tiny island less than a mile in circumference and connected to the mainland via a long walkway. Surrounded by rippling rock in low tide, it is covered with Betel palms and subtropical plants. It takes only 15 minutes to walk around the island. In its center is a small vermilion shrine, **Aoshima Jinja,** dedicated to first Emperor Jimmu's grandparents. According to legend, the grandfather, a hunter, was a young man when he and his brother, a fisherman, decided to trade chores. The grandfather, fishing here on Aoshima, lost his brother's hook and dove into the depths to retrieve it, only to end up on a turtle that delivered him to an undersea Dragon's Palace, where he met a fair princess. When he finally found the hook and returned to land, the princess came with him, later bearing him a son. Because of the legend, Aoshima Shrine is considered fortuitous in matchmaking; those wishing for marriage come here to be blessed. The shrine is open daily from dawn until dusk.

You can reach Aoshima in about 30 minutes from Miyazaki Station on the JR Nichinan Line; the fare is ¥360 ($3) and trains depart about every hour. Aoshima Island is about a 5-minute walk from Aoshima Station. More frequent

---

Kids   A Beach & an Amusement Park

Near Aoshima you'll find **Aoshima Beach,** popular for swimming in July and August, and **Kodomo-no-Kuni** (© **0985/65-1111**), a small amusement park known also for its year-round flowers. It's kiddie rides, Ferris wheel, roller coaster, water ride, and paddleboats are good for younger children. It's open daily 9am to 5pm with varying extended hours on holidays (to 9pm during summer vacation); admission is ¥800 ($6.65) for adults and ¥400 ($3.35) for children. Rides cost extra.

---

are buses departing from Miyazaki Station every 15 to 30 minutes, taking 49 minutes to reach Aoshima and costing ¥670 ($5.60).

Farther south on the Nichinan Coast, about 15 miles south of Aoshima and 25 miles south of Miyazaki city, is **Udo Shrine** ✿✿ (© **0987/29-1001**). Dedicated to the father of Emperor Jimmu, this vermilion-colored shrine is actually located in a cave beside the ocean—an unusual setting for a shrine, but one boasting an exhilarating view. According to legend, it was here that Emperor Jimmu's grandparents came for the birth of their son. As delivery drew near, the soon-to-be mother asked her husband not to watch. Naturally, he couldn't resist, and to his surprise, his wife turned into a dragon. Ashamed, she fled back to sea, leaving breasts on the cave ceiling to feed her newborn son.

Throughout the ages, Udo Shrine has been famous among newlyweds, who come to pray for success and harmony in marriage. In the cave are formations thought to resemble breasts; the water dripping from them is lucky "milk," considered beneficial for pregnancy, childbirth, and nursing mothers (milk candy is a specialty of the shops near the shrine). If you want to make a wish, purchase some clay pottery pieces at the shrine and try to toss them inside a rope circle that adorns a turtle-shaped rock—if you manage to land one inside the circle, you've got your wish. Women are supposed to throw right-handed, men left-handed.

You can reach Udo Shrine, open 6am to 7pm, by bus from Aoshima or Miyazaki. Get off at Udo Jingu Iriguchi, from which it's a few minutes walk to the first torii gate followed by a 20-minute walk along the coast to the shrine itself. If you're coming from Miyazaki, take a bus going to Nichinan from platform 16 of the Miyako-City Bus Center; the bus ride takes about 70 minutes and costs ¥1,350 ($11).

WHERE TO STAY
EXPENSIVE

Aoshima Palm Beach Hotel ✿✿ *Kids*   Located right on Aoshima Beach and surrounded by lovely grounds, this new and beautiful Palm Beach–style hotel was developed by the local government and is a great place for a vacation, especially for families. Hotel guests receive free admission to Kodomo-no-Kuni, an amusement park for children located right beside the hotel (and which has nightly fireworks displays during summer vacation). TVs offer pay video movies, including English films the whole family can watch. All Western-style rooms and most of the 44 Japanese-style rooms (which can sleep up to 5 persons) have huge windows facing the sea and views of Aoshima Island. During summer vacation (mid-July and Aug), reserve at least 2 months in advance.

1–16–1 Aoshima, Miyazaki 889-2162. © **0985/65-2929.** Fax 0985/65-2655. www.miyakoh.co.jp/palm/. 214 units. ¥13,700–¥15,900 ($114–$132.50) twin or Japanese-style room for 2. Extra charges during Golden

Week (Apr 29–May 5) and New Year's. Rates include breakfast and service charge. AE, DC, JCB, MC, V. Train: JR Nichinan Line to Kodomo-no-Kuni Station (3 min.). Bus: Miyazaki Kotsu Bus from Miyazaki Station or Miyako-City Bus Terminal to Kodomo-no-Kuni-hoteru-mae (2 min.). **Amenities:** 2 restaurants (Chinese, Japanese/Western), coffee shop, lounge, snack bar (handy for beachgoers); hot-spring baths fed by saltwater with ocean views; exercise room; indoor lap pool and children's pool (free for hotel guests); Jacuzzi; Kodomo-no-Kuni amusement park (free admission for hotel guests; rides cost extra); in-room massage. *In room:* A/C, TV with pay movies; fridge; hot-water pot with tea; hair dryer; safe; washlet toilet.

Hotel Ocean 45 ★★★   The most relaxing and luxurious place to stay in Miyazaki is Seagaia's crowning jewel, Hotel Ocean 45, Kyushu's tallest hotel with 43 floors. It is also the most convenient hotel to Ocean Dome, just a 5-minute walk away. Its marbled, elegant lobby stretches 11 stories high, emitting lots of light. Rooms, all of which face the sea with magnificent views, are palatial by Japanese standards and are equipped with lots of extras, including bathroom phones, vanity/sink areas separate from the bathroom (some standard twins also have separate shower stalls and tubs), both soft and firm pillows, and closets lit by motion detectors. Since you're a bit far from town, it's good to know there are plenty of dining options immediately on hand, including a French restaurant on the 42nd floor with good views and a Japanese pub specializing in local, country-style cuisine. If you're looking for a pampered getaway, this is the place.

Hamayama Yamazaki-cho, Miyazaki City 880-8545. ✆ **0985/21-1133.** Fax 0985/21-1144. www.seagaia. co.jp. 753 units. ¥19,000–¥27,000 ($158–$225) single; ¥30,000–¥32,000 ($250–$267) double; ¥30,000–¥38,000 ($250–$317) twin. AE, DC, JCB, MC, V. Bus: From JR Miyazaki Station or Miyazaki Airport; see directions for Seagaia under "What to See & Do," above. **Amenities:** 8 restaurants, 1 bar and 2 lounges; health club with 24-meter indoor lane pool, fitness room, sauna and Jacuzzi (fee: ¥2,000/$17); rental bikes, ¥500/$4.15) for 2 hr.); observation room on the 43rd floor (admission: ¥500/$4.15); library lounge exclusively for hotel guests; small video theater with 3 to 4 popular movies shown daily; mah-jongg and Go salons; small shopping arcade; business center; babysitting room for 6-week-olds to 12-year-olds; concierge; tour desk; business center; small shopping arcade; room service (6pm–midnight); in-room massage; same-day laundry/dry cleaning service; nonsmoking rooms. *In room:* A/C, cable TV with video games, dataport, minibar, hot-water pot with tea and coffee, hair dryer.

MODERATE

Miyazaki Kanko Hotel   The Miyazaki Kanko Hotel is the best of a string of hotels along the Oyodo River, which has been developed into a small waterfront park not far from Miyazaki Station. It consists of a newer east wing with higher-priced rooms featuring washlet toilets and an older west wing with fewer amenities (no washlet toilets) and cheaper prices. Rooms face either the river or town (favored for its night view) for the same price. A plus are the hot-spring baths; the hot springs were excavated from deep below the ground after much effort.

1–1–1 Matsuyama, Miyazaki City 880-8512. ✆ **0985/27-1212.** Fax 0985/25-8748. 375 units. ¥7,000–¥16,000 ($58–$133) single; ¥14,000–¥21,000 ($117–$175) double; ¥16,000–¥27,000 ($133–$225) twin. AE, DC, JCB, MC, V. A 15-min. walk from Miyazaki Station (or a 5-min. taxi ride); turn left from Miyazaki Station's west exit, walk south on Route (Kendo) 341 to the Oyodo River, and turn right. **Amenities:** 8 restaurants, 2 bars, 2 lounges; indoor/outdoor hot-spring baths; sauna; game arcade; shopping arcade; room service (9–11:30pm); same-day laundry/dry cleaning. *In room:* A/C, bilingual TV, dataport, hot-water pot with tea, hair dryer.

Sun Hotel Phoenix   Built in the early 1970s long before Seagaia was a reality, the Sun Hotel Phoenix is still surrounded by pine forest but is now part of the huge Seagaia resort complex that spreads along the coast. Catering largely to groups, which give the spacious lobby a boisterous, holiday atmosphere, it has mostly twin rooms and Japanese-style rooms. The cheapest rooms face inland and have fewer amenities, while higher-priced rooms have views of the sea and washlet toilets. Restaurants serve udon noodles, teppanyaki, sushi, and Western fare and include a 9th-floor restaurant-lounge with unobstructed views of the Pacific. Beyond, accessible by free shuttle bus, are all the attractions of Seagaia.

3083 Hamayama Shioji, Miyazaki City 880-0122. © **0985/39-3131.** Fax 0985/38-1147. www.seagaia.co.jp. 290 units. ¥15,000–¥28,000 ($125–$233) single; ¥30,000 ($250) double; ¥17,000–¥35,000 ($142–$292) twin; ¥18,000–¥30,000 ($150–$250) Japanese-style rooms for 2. AE, DC, JCB, MC, V. Bus: From JR Miyazaki Station or Miyazaki Airport; see directions for Seagaia in "What to See & Do," above. **Amenities:** 4 restaurants, 1 bar; outdoor swimming pool (free for hotel guests); souvenir/convenience store; in-room massage. *In room:* A/C, TV, fridge, hot-water pot with tea, hair dryer.

INEXPENSIVE

Cottage Himuka *Kids* Located in the Seagaia resort area, Cottage Himuka is geared toward families, groups, and longer stays with clean, bright, and functional apartments complete with kitchenettes (hotplate, microwave, refrigerator, cookware), four single beds, a sofa and two chairs, a balcony, and separated sink, toilet, and tub areas. There are also larger, more expensive apartments that sleep up to eight persons (contact Cottage Himuka for rates). Apartments occupy free-standing "cottages" on spacious grounds grouped around a restaurant (open for breakfast and dinner only), a convenience store, and an outdoor pool open July to mid-September. All the Seagaia facilities are at hand.

Hamayama, Yamazaki-cho, Miyazaki City 880-8545. © **0985/21-1355.** Fax 0985/21-1356. www.seagaia. co.jp. 72 units. ¥20,000 ($167) for up to 4 persons. Rates ¥4,000 ($33) more on Sat and evenings before holidays. AE, DC, JCB, MC, V. Bus: From JR Miyazaki Station or Miyazaki Airport; see directions for Seagaia in "What to See & Do," above. **Amenities:** 1 restaurant (Japanese); outdoor swimming pool (free for hotel guests); rental bikes (¥500/$4.15 for 2 hr.); convenience store. *In room:* A/C, TV, kitchenette, hair dryer.

Hotel Kensington The main reason most people come to Miyazaki is to relax at accommodations at Seagaia or Aoshima, but if you can't afford those prices (or didn't book soon enough), this is a good budget choice in the city center. Opened in 1994 and located on Tachibana-dori Avenue near department stores and shopping, this inexpensive establishment resembles a business hotel in its simplicity but is also popular with young Japanese women because of its location and rates. Despite its name, the only hint of English is a knight of armor guarding the drawing-room-style lobby. Rooms are tiny; ask for a room that doesn't face another building. The cheapest doubles are with semi-double-size beds, which are comfortable for one but cramped for two. Its first-floor Western restaurant attracts young diners.

3–4–4 Tachibana-dori-higashi, Miyazaki City 880-0805. © **0985/20-5500.** Fax 0985/32-7700. 160 units. ¥6,300–¥7,700 ($52.50–$62) single; ¥8,300–¥10,000 ($69–$83) double; ¥10,700 ($89) twin. AE, JCB, MC, V. A 10-min. walk from Miyazaki Station's west exit. Walk straight ahead down Takachiho-dori to Tachibana-dori and turn left; the hotel will be on your left. **Amenities:** 1 restaurant (Western); nonsmoking rooms. *In room:* A/C, TV, minibar (except in singles), hot-water pot with tea, hair dryer.

WHERE TO DINE

Miyazaki's subtropical climate is conducive to the growth of a number of vegetables and fruits, including sweet pumpkins, oranges, cucumbers, green peppers, shiitake mushrooms, and chestnuts. In summer, a popular dish is *Hiyajiru,* a rice dish topped with soup made from fish, miso bean paste, tofu, cucumbers, and other ingredients. Also popular is *shochu,* made from sweet potatoes, buckwheat, or corn.

In summer, you might want to head for Hotel Phoenix's rooftop beer garden, **Beer Island,** 2–1–1 Matsuyama (© **0985/23-6111**), open daily 5:30 to 9pm from about mid-June to mid-September. It offers a good view of the Oyodo River flowing to the ocean and serves grilled fish, skewered meats, oden, snacks, and beer. It's located about a 12-minute walk from Miyazaki Station; turn left from Miyazaki Station's west exit, walk south on Route 341 to the Oyodo River, and turn left.

⑳ **Gyosantei** LOCAL SPECIALTIES   Although the stairway leading up doesn't seem to promise much, this is actually an attractive restaurant with wooden floors, both table and tatami seating, and waitresses dressed in country-style clothing. For local food, try the *Himukazen* (facing the sun) course, which changes according to what's in season and what the cook decides to create; in summer, it might include the chef's own version of Hiyajiru such as a sesame-seed- and mint-flavored soup poured over rice. There's no English menu, but pictures show approximations of various courses. In any case, dining here is a culinary surprise; even your chopstick holder may be unusual, consisting of nothing more than a small green pepper.

Airline Hotel East Building, 2nd floor, 3–10–19 Tachibana-dori-nishi. ℂ 0985/32-3737. Set lunches ¥1,000–¥2,500 ($8.35–$21); set dinners ¥2,000–¥7,000 ($17–$58). AE, DC, JCB, MC, V. Daily 11:30am–1:30pm and 5:30–9pm (last order). A 10-min. walk from Miyazaki Station. From the station's west exit, walk straight ahead down Takachiho-dori and cross Tachibana-dori; it's immediately on your left before the small alley.

Restaurant Paris 5 FRENCH   Located to the right of the main entrance to Miyazaki Shrine and convenient if you've been visiting the many sights in the area, this delightful restaurant looks as though it was imported directly from sunny southern France. It beckons with a balcony overflowing with flowers and plants and a tall and airy dining room. Although its seasonal menu is written in Japanese, ordering is easy since only set meals—most feature seafood and Miyazaki beef—are available for both lunch and dinner. (This is the only French restaurant in Miyazaki authorized to serve Miyazaki beef, but don't ask me why authorization is necessary.) Its cheerful balcony is open year-round (weather permitting). Call beforehand, however, because its close proximity to Miyazaki Shrine makes it a popular venue for wedding receptions.

1–8–8 Jingu-Higashi. ℂ 0985/29-8039. Reservations recommended. Set lunches ¥2,200–¥4,500 ($18–$37.50); set dinners ¥3,500–¥8,800 ($29–$73). AE, JCB, V (accepted only at dinner). Wed–Mon 11:30am–2:30pm and 5:30–9:30pm. Bus: From Tachibana-dori Ave. or Miyako-City Bus Center to Miyazaki Jingu (1 min.).

4 Kagoshima ⓧ

1,483km (927 miles) SW of Tokyo; 315km (197 miles) S of Fukuoka; 197km (123 miles) S of Kumamoto; 343km (214 miles) SW of Beppu

With a population of more than half a million and capital of Kagoshima Prefecture, Kagoshima is a city of palm trees, flowering trees and bushes, wide avenues, and people who are like the weather—warm, mild-tempered, and easygoing. It spreads along Kinko Bay and boasts one of the most unusual bay vistas in the world—Sakurajima, an active volcano, rising up from the waters. During summer vacation (July 21–Aug), there are nightly fireworks displays over the bay. Kagoshima is also home to Senganen Garden, one of my favorite gardens in Japan.

Because of its relative isolation at the southern tip of Japan, far away from the capitals of Kyoto and Tokyo, Kagoshima has developed an independent spirit through the centuries that has fostered a number of great men and accomplishments. Foremost is the Shimazu clan, a remarkable family that for 29 generations (almost 700 years) ruled over Kagoshima and its vicinity before the Meiji Restoration in 1868. Much of Japan's early contact with the outside world was via Kagoshima, first with China and then with the Western world. Japan's first contact with Christianity occurred in Kagoshima when St. Francis Xavier landed here in 1549; although he stayed only 10 months, he converted more than 600 Japanese to Christianity. Kagoshima is also where firearms were introduced to Japan.

By the mid–19th century, as the Tokugawa shogunate began losing strength and the confidence of the people, the Shimazu family was already looking toward the future and the modernization of Japan. In the mid-1850s, the Shimazus built the first Western-style factory in the country, employing 200 men to make cannons, glass, ceramics, land mines, ships, and farming tools. In 1865, while Japan's doors were still officially closed to the outside world and all contact with foreigners was forbidden, the Shimazus smuggled 19 young men to Britain so they could learn foreign languages and technology. After these men returned to Japan, they became a driving force in the Meiji Restoration and Japan's modernization.

Another historical figure who played a major role during the Meiji Restoration was Takamori Saigo, who was born in Kagoshima Prefecture. A philosopher, scholar, educator, and poet, he helped restore Emperor Meiji to power, but because he was also a samurai, he subsequently became disillusioned when the ancient rights of the samurai class were rescinded and the wearing of swords was forbidden. He led a force of samurai against the government in what is called the Seinan Rebellion but was defeated. He then withdrew to Shiroyama in Kagoshima, where he committed suicide in 1877. Today, Saigo has many fans among the Japanese, who still visit the cave on Shiroyama Hill where he committed suicide.

ESSENTIALS

GETTING THERE   By Plane   You can reach Kagoshima from Tokyo (flight time: 1 hr. 40 min.), Nagoya (flight time: 1 hr. 20 min.), and Osaka (flight time: 1 hr. 5 min.) on JAL and ANA; ANA also flies direct to Kagoshima from Sapporo (flight time: 2 hrs. 35 min.) and Hiroshima (flight time: 55 min.). The fare from Tokyo is ¥33,000 ($275) one-way.

Downtown Kagoshima is linked to the airport by **limousine bus,** which departs every 10 minutes, takes 1 hour to reach Nishi Kagoshima Station, and costs ¥1,200 ($10).

By JR Train   Travel time is approximately 12 hours from Tokyo, 8 hours from Osaka, and 4 hours from Fukuoka. Tickets from Tokyo cost ¥25,350 ($211) for an unreserved seat. All trains passing through Kagoshima make two stops, at both Kagoshima Station and Nishi Kagoshima Station; be sure to check which station your hotel is closest to so you know where to get off the train.

VISITOR INFORMATION   Before departing Tokyo, Kyoto, Narita or Kansai international airports, stop by the Tourist Information Center to pick up the leaflet called "Kagoshima and Vicinity" which includes information on Ibusuki and Chiran.

In Kagoshima, there are tourist information centers at both **Nishi Kagoshima Station** (© **099/253-2500;** open daily 8:30am–6pm) and **Kagoshima Station** (© **099/222-2500;** open daily 8:30am–5pm) as well as at the airport (© **0995/58-2115**). They have good maps in English as well as a very handy booklet with suggested walking tours of the city.

The **Kagoshima Prefectural Tourist Office** is located in the Sangyo Kaikan Building, 9–1 Meizan-cho (© **099/223-5771;** open Mon–Fri 8:30am–5:15pm), where you can obtain information on the city as well as the prefecture, including

Ibusuki and Chiran. Kagoshima Prefecture is quite large, stretching 360 miles from southern Kyushu all the way to the Amami islands just north of Okinawa and encompassing some 600 islands and seven active volcanoes. Ask for the booklet *Kagoshima Travel Guide,* which contains information on Ibusuki and Chiran. To find the office, take the streetcar to the Asahi-Dori stop and then walk southeast (toward the bay); the Sangyo Kaikan Building is on your left in the second block.

INTERNET ACCESS   It has a strange name, but **eggs,** centrally located on the second floor at 20–10 Higashi Sengoku-cho (✆ **099/239-2159**), is a small enterprise offering Japanese and English lessons and Internet service, charging ¥400 ($3.35) per 30 minutes of online time. A plus is that everyone here speaks English well. **eggs** is open Monday through Saturday noon to 8pm. To find it, take the streetcar to Izuro-dori stop, walk inland in the direction of Central Park through the Nakamachi covered shopping arcade (to the left of Yamakataya department store), walk 1 block farther after the arcade ends, and turn left.

MAIL   An international post office, where you can send letters and packages and obtain cash through ATMs, is located at Nishi Kagoshima Station.

ORIENTATION & GETTING AROUND   The downtown section of Kagoshima is the area between Nishi Kagoshima and Kagoshima stations, with **Tenmonkan-Dori** (a covered shopping arcade) serving as the heart of the city. You can walk from one station to the other in less than 40 minutes, but there's also a streetcar connecting the two, running along an unnamed street that locals have nicknamed Densha Dori (tram street).

Kagoshima is served by two **streetcar lines** (fare: ¥160/$1.35), as well as two types of **buses**—City View buses and Kagoshima City buses. The **Kagoshima City buses** are regular buses used as commuter transportation by the people living here, while the **City View buses** are geared toward visiting tourists. Running every 30 minutes from 9:30am to 5pm daily (9am–5:30pm daily mid-July–Aug), the City View buses look like old-time trams, have English announcements, and travel a 9-mile circuit through the city, beginning at Nishi Kagoshima Station (with departures on the hour and half hour). They stop at all tourist sights, including Senganen, Sakurajima Ferry Terminal and Kagoshima Aquarium, and Tenmonkan covered shopping arcade. The fare is ¥180 ($1.50), half-fare for children, and you pay when you get off.

If you think you'll be doing a lot of traveling by streetcar and bus, invest in a one-day pass for ¥600 ($5), half fare for children, allowing unlimited travel on Kagoshima's two tram lines and on City View and Kagoshima City buses. Passes can be purchased at the tourist offices in Kagoshima Station and Nishi Kagoshima Station and on City View buses, Kagoshima City buses, and trams.

GUIDED TOURS   Since city tours are offered only in Japanese, more useful, perhaps, are guided tours that take you to places a bit more difficult to reach on your own. Tours of Sakurajima lasting 1½ hours will take you halfway up the volcano to a lookout observatory, with departures from the ferry pier on Sakurajima twice daily (see "What to See & Do," below for more information). In addition, there's a 9-hour guided tour that departs Nishi Kagoshima Station at 8:50am, takes the ferry to Ibusuki (the next city covered in this chapter), and then visits a shochu factory, Mt. Kaimon, Lake Ikeda, Chiran with its samurai houses and Peace Museum (see "What to See & Do," below), and other sights before returning to Nishi Kagoshima Station. The cost of this tour is ¥4,550 ($38) for adults and ¥2,360 ($20) for children (you can also join the tour in

Ibusuki; see the next section for more information). Contact the **Kagoshima Kotsu Bus Company** at ℂ **099/259-2888** for information and bookings.

Finally, from July 21 through August, boat cruises of Kinko Bay are offered every evening from 7 to 9pm (except for a few days during Obon in mid-Aug), the highlight of which are fireworks over the water. Boats depart from the Kagoshima side of the Sakurajima Ferry Terminal and cost ¥1,000 ($8.35) for adults, half fare for children. Call ℂ **099/293-2525** for more information.

WHAT TO SEE & DO
THE TOP ATTRACTIONS
MT. SAKURAJIMA ✿   With ties to Naples, Italy, as its sister city, Kagoshima bills itself as the "Naples of the Orient." That's perhaps stretching things a bit, but Kagoshima is balmy most of the year and even has its own Mt. Vesuvius— Mt. Sakurajima, an active volcano across Kinko Bay that has erupted 30 times through recorded history and continues to puff steam into the sky and occasionally cover the city with fine soot and ash. In 1914, Sakurajima had a whopper of an eruption and belched up 3 billion tons of lava. When the eruption was over, the townspeople were surprised to discover that the flow was so great it had blocked the 1,666-foot-wide channel separating the volcano from a neighboring peninsula—Sakurajima, which had once been an island, was now part of the mainland.

Magnificent from far away and impressive if you're near the top, Sakurajima can be visited by **ferry,** which departs from the Sakurajima Ferry Terminal. The terminal is about a 15-minute walk from Kagoshima Station, an 8-minute walk from the Shiyakusho-mae tram stop, or a 2-minute walk from the Kagoshima Aquarium-mae/Sakurajima-sanbashi City View bus stop. Ferries run 24 hours, departing every 15 minutes during the day and about once an hour through the night. It takes 15 minutes to reach Sakurajima and costs ¥150 ($1.25) for adults, ¥80 (65¢) for children.

A fun thing to do on Sakurajima is visit **Furusato Onsen** ✿✿, at the Furusato Kanko Hotel (ℂ **099/221-3111**), with open-air hot-spring baths set amid lava rocks right beside the sea. It also has an outdoor seawater swimming pool with a sunning terrace, an indoor 25-meter lap pool heated with hot-spring water, and indoor hot-spring baths with windows overlooking the bay. You wear your swimming suit in the pools but should put a *yukata* (cotton kimono) over your suit when using the outdoor bath (an English handout provides guidelines). It's open every day except Thursday from 6am to 10pm (you must enter by 8pm); note that on Monday the outdoor bath is closed until 2:30pm, and the indoor hot-spring bath and pool are closed on Tuesday. Admission is ¥1,050 ($8.75) including yukata; bring your own towel or buy one for another ¥210 ($1.75). You can reach Furusato Onsen by taking the **free Furusato Kanko Hotel shuttle bus** departing from the Sakurajima Ferry Terminal every 30 minutes from 8:45am to 8pm (no service from 12:20–2:20pm). Otherwise, take the **Kagoshima Kotsu Bus** that departs once an hour from the ferry terminal, costing ¥290 ($2.40) for the 15-minute trip. For more information on the Furusato Kanko Hotel, see "Where to Stay," below.

Guided Tours of Sakurajima   There are **walking paths** through lava fields close to Sakurajima's ferry pier, but because Sakurajima is sparsely populated with only limited public transportation, you might want to join a tour that visits lava fields and travels to the Yunohira lookout point halfway up the volcano.

⌈ **Fun Fact**   **Mt. Sakurajima's Produce**

Mt. Sakurajima's rich soil grows the world's largest radishes, averaging about 37 pounds but sometimes weighing in at as much as 80 pounds, and the world's smallest oranges, only 1.2 inches in diameter.

Buses depart twice daily at 9:30am and 1:30pm from the ferry dock on Sakurajima; the price of the tour, which lasts 1½ hours, is ¥1,000 ($8.35) for adults and half fare for children. Call ② **099/293-2525** for more information.

SENGANEN GARDEN ⟲⟲⟲   Whereas Sakurajima, rising dramatically out of the bay, is Kagoshima's best-known landmark, **Senganen,** 9700–1 Yoshino-cho (② **099/247-1551**), is its most widely visited attraction. The grounds of a countryside villa, it's a garden laid out more than 300 years ago by the Shimazu clan, incorporating Sakurajima and Kinko Bay into its design scheme in a principle known as borrowed landscape. There's a lovely grove of bamboo, a waterfall located a 30-minute walk up a nature trail with good views over the bay, and the requisite pond, but my favorite is a particularly idyllic spot where the 21st lord of the Shimazu family held famous poem-composing garden parties. Guests seated themselves on stones beside a gently meandering rivulet and were requested to have completed a poem by the time a cup filled with sake came drifting by on the tiny brook. Ah, those were the days! Today it remains Japan's only garden with its original poem-composing garden (called Kyokusui) still intact.

The good life is also apparent in **Goten,** which was built as a summer villa by the Shimazu clan about 350 years ago and became the family's main residence when the Meiji Restoration made feudal lords obsolete. Now only one-third its original size, Goten can be viewed by joining a tour conducted every 20 minutes and given only in Japanese (but with an information sheet in English). You'll see 8 of the villa's 25 rooms, including a bedroom, a bathroom, a dressing room, and reception rooms; throughout are furnishings and artifacts that once belonged to the Shimazu clan. Green tea and a sweet are included in the tour.

A must after visiting the garden, and included in the admission price to Senganen, is the **Shoko Shuseikan Museum** located next to the garden. Built in the mid-1850s as Japan's first industrial factory, it houses items relating to the almost 700-year history of the Shimazu clan, including family heirlooms ranging from lacquerware to tea-ceremony objects, palanquins used to carry Shimazu lords back and forth to Edo (present-day Tokyo; the trip from Kagoshima took 40 to 60 days), everyday items used by the family, and photographs. The museum shop is also quite good. In all, you'll probably spend at least 2 hours seeing everything.

Senganen and the Shoko Shuseikan Museum are open daily from 8:30am to 5:30pm (to 5:20pm in winter); Goten is open daily from 9am to 4:40pm. Admission to Senganen and Shoko Shuseikan Museum is ¥1,000 ($8.35) for adults and ¥500 ($4.15) for children. Tours of Goten are an extra ¥800 ($6.65) for adults and ¥500 ($4.15) for children, but you'll save money by buying a **combination ticket** for the garden, museum, and villa for ¥1,500 ($12.50) for adults, half price for children.

To reach Senganen, which is east of Kagoshima Station and a bit out of the city, take the City View bus to the Senganen-mae bus stop outside its front gate.

MORE TO SEE & DO

KAGOSHIMA CITY AQUARIUM The aquarium is beside the Sakurajima Ferry Terminal on the Kagoshima side, 3–1 Honko-Shinmachi (© **099/ 226-2233;** open daily 9:30am–6pm; you must enter by 5pm). It concentrates on sea life from waters surrounding Kagoshima Prefecture, including the Amami islands. The largest tank is home to sting rays, bluefin tuna, Japanese anchovy, and other creatures from the Kurushio (Black Current), which flows from the East China Sea past Kagoshima to the Pacific Ocean. Another tank contains squid, octopuses, the Japanese giant crab (the world's largest crab), and fish that inhabit the Kagoshima seas. Other highlights include the world's only display of tube worms, a 3D movie of the seas around the Amami islands, and the world's largest eel (from Lake Ikeda). Dolphins, which have access to open waters, are used only for educational shows (conducted in Japanese only). Expect to spend at least an hour here; more if you have kids. Admission is ¥1,500 ($12.50) for adults, ¥750 ($6.25) for junior-high and high-school students, and ¥350 ($2.90) for children. To reach it, take the City View bus to the Kagoshima Aquarium-mae/Sakurajima-sanbashi bus stop.

MUSEUMS For an overview of Kagoshima Prefecture including its history and folklore, visit the **Kagoshima Prefectural Museum of Culture** (Reimeikan), 5–1 Shiroyama-cho (© **099/222-5100;** open Tues–Sun 9am–5pm). It was built on the former site of Tsurumaru Castle, of which only the stone ramparts and moat remain. Upon entering the museum, you'll walk over a glass floor above a map of Kagoshima Prefecture. The museum then traces the history of the people of Kagoshima over the last 40,000 years, including the rise of the Shimazu clan in the 11th century and Kagoshima's pre-eminence as a pottery center after Korean potters were brought here in the 1500s. There are models of an 18th-century samurai settlement, Tsurumaru Castle, and best of all, Tenmonkan-Dori as it might have looked 70 years ago. The second floor is devoted to folklore with bamboo ware, festival objects, and personal items that once belonged to the Shimazu clan. The third floor has a hands-on learning room for children with old-fashioned toys, samurai outfits that can be tried on, and other amusements. Don't miss the 140-year-old thatched-roof farmer's house and pond located outside. A visit to this museum will take about an hour. Admission is ¥260 ($2.15) for adults, ¥150 ($1.25) for college and high-school students, and ¥100 (85¢) for children. To reach it, take the City View bus to the Satsuma Gishihimae stop in front of the museum. Or take the streetcar to Shiyakusho-mae stop; walking in the direction of Kagoshima Station, take the first left and walk 4 minutes straight to the museum.

Only a few minutes' walk away from the Reimeikan is the **City Art Museum** (Kagoshima Shiritsu Bijitsukan), 4–36 Shiroyma-cho (© **099/224-3400;** open Tues–Sun 9:30am–6pm), which has a collection of Western-style works by artists from Kagoshima Prefecture. Look for the portrait of Takamori Saigo, painted by Masayoshi Tokonomi, to the left upon entering the permanent gallery. A small selection of paintings by Western artists is also displayed, as well as decorative art including the famous Satsuma pottery and cut glass. You can see everything in less than an hour. Admission is ¥200 ($1.65) for adults, ¥150 ($1.25) for college and high-school students, and ¥100 (85¢) for children. To reach it, take the City View bus to Saigodouzou-mae; the museum is a minute's walk away to the right of the statue of Saigo. Or take the streetcar to Asahi-dori and take the street beside the Minami-Nippon bank; it's a 5-minute walk ahead.

Although it's not as conveniently located, the **Nagashima Museum** ✦✦, 3–42–18 Take (© **099/250-5400;** open daily 9am–5pm), is a very worthwhile private museum on a hill high atop the city with great views of Sakurajima and Kagoshima. While its focus is mostly works by Kagoshima artists like Seiki Kuroda, it also contains some works by well-known Western artists, including Picasso, Braque, Kandinsky, Renoir, and Chagall, as well as pottery from South America. But most impressive, in my opinion, is an outstanding collection of mainly 19th-century white Satsuma pottery, including many pieces that were originally imported to London, Paris, and New York, and the more utilitarian 17th- to 20th-century black Satsuma pottery. An hour is enough time to see everything, but try to time your visit during lunch so you can eat in the museum's French restaurant **Camellia** (open 11am–3pm with set meals ranging from ¥2,000–¥3,000/$17–$25), which has great views over the city. Admission is ¥1,000 ($8.35) for adults, ¥800 ($6.65) for college and high-school students, and ¥400 ($3.35) for children. You'll have to take a taxi to get here; it's about a 10-minute ride from Nishi Kagoshima Station.

A SIDE TRIP TO THE GARDENS OF CHIRAN

If you have an extra morning or afternoon, I suggest taking an excursion to **Chiran** ✦✦, a small village 19 miles south of Kagoshima. Surrounded by wooded hills and rows of neatly cultivated tea plantations, it's one of the 102 castle towns that once bordered the Shimazu kingdom during the Edo Period. Although the castle is no longer standing, seven old gardens and samurai houses have been carefully preserved.

Apparently, the village headman of Chiran had the opportunity to travel with his lord Shimazu in the mid-1700s to Kyoto and Edo, taking with him some of his local samurai as retainers. The headman and his retainers were so impressed with the sophisticated culture of Kyoto and Edo that they invited gardeners to Chiran to construct a series of modestly sized gardens on the samurai estates surrounding the castle.

Some of these gardens remain and are located on a delightful road called **Samurai Lane,** which is lined with moss-covered stone walls and hedges. Since descendants of the samurai are still living in the houses, only the gardens are open to the public. There are two types of gardens represented: one, belonging to the Mori family, is of the miniature artificial hill style, in which a central pond symbolizes the sea and rocks represent the mountains; the others are "dry" gardens, in which the sea is symbolized not by water but by white sand that is raked to give it the effect of rippling water. The gardens are masterful demonstrations of the borrowed landscape technique, in which surrounding mountains and scenery are incorporated into the general garden design. Although the gardens are small, they are exquisite and charming. Notice, for example, how the tops of hedges are cut to resemble rolling hills, blending with the shapes of mountains in the background. Entrance is through imposing gates from the era.

The seven gardens open to the public are indicated by a white marker in front of each entry gate. All seven can be visited for ¥310 ($2.60) for adults, ¥205 ($1.70) for children; it should take about 1½ hours to see them all. Pay the entry fee for all seven at the first garden you visit; you'll be given a pamphlet containing a map and a description of the gardens in English. They're open daily from 9am to 5pm and can be viewed in about 1½ hours. For more information on the samurai gardens, call © **0993/83-2511.**

Also in Chiran is the **Peace Museum** (Heiwa Kaikan; ✆ **0993/83-2525;** open daily 9am–5pm), dedicated to the kamikaze pilots who trained here for World War II suicide missions, steering bomb-laden planes into Allied warships and other targets. Although there isn't much in English and you can walk through in about 30 minutes, an English audio guide is available for ¥100 (85¢) if you want to learn more. Admission is ¥500 ($4.15) for adults, ¥300 ($2.50) for children.

Chiran can be reached in about 1 hour and 20 minutes by taking a bus headed for Makurazaki (there's no bus number) from Yamakataya Bus Station in front of the Asahi-Dori streetcar stop in downtown Kagoshima. There are 10 buses a day, including departures at 9, 9:50, and 11:10am; the ride costs ¥860 ($7.15). Although it's a long ride, the trip through the countryside with its tea plantations and wooded hills is nice. In Chiran, get off at Buke-Yashiki to see the samurai gardens. From there, you'll have to take a taxi to visit the Peace Museum.

An alternative to going on your own is to join a 9-hour **guided tour** from Nishi Kagoshima Station that includes a stop at the samurai gardens in Chiran. See "Guided Tours," under "Essentials," above for more information.

SHOPPING

Local Kagoshima products include **oshima tsumugi,** beautiful silk from Amami Oshima Island made into such items as clothing, handbags, and wallets; **shochu,** an alcoholic drink made from such ingredients as sweet potatoes and drunk either on the rocks or mixed with boiling water; furniture, statues, and chests made from **yaku cedar;** and **Satsuma pottery**—probably Kagoshima's most famous product. It has been produced in the Kagoshima area for more than 380 years. Satsuma pottery comes in two styles: black and white. White Satsuma pottery is more elegant and was used by former lords; the black pottery was used by the townspeople in everyday life.

A good place to shop for local items is the **Display Hall of Kagoshima Products,** downtown in the Sangyo Kaikan Building (the same building housing the Kagoshima Prefectural Tourist Office) at 9–1 Meizan-cho (✆ **099/225-6120;** open daily 9am–5pm; closed the 1st and 3rd Sun of the month). This one-room shop offers tinware, handmade knives, Satsuma pottery, glassware, oshima tsumugi, yaku cedar, shochu, and other locally made items. To reach it, take the streetcar to the Asahi-Dori stop, from which it's a 1-minute walk away toward the bay.

The most famous cake of Kagoshima (the one all Japanese tourists must buy before returning home) is *karukan,* a delicious spongy white cake made from rice, with Chinese and Korean origins. The most famous maker of karukan today is ⑳ **Akashiya,** 4–16 Kinseicho (✆**099/226-0431;** open daily 8am–7:30pm), which began selling the cakes 140 years ago. It has the solemnity of a first-rate jewelry store and is just as refined. It's located behind the Yamakataya department store, a 1-minute walk from the Asahi-Dori streetcar stop. Although cakes are now available made from beans and other ingredients, old-timers insist that only the plain white ones are the real thing. A small round one, good for a snack, costs ¥140 ($1.15), while a 700-gram (1½ lb.) cake goes for ¥1,800 ($15).

WHERE TO STAY
EXPENSIVE
⑳ Shigetomiso ★★   One of Kagoshima's most famous and beautiful ryokan—and once a villa of the ruling Shimazu clan—spreads along a gentle

slope in a storybook setting with views of the bay and Sakurajima. Its oldest rooms, which are no longer used as guest rooms but can be booked for lunch, date from the 1820s and exude history. One room, for example, is said to have belonged to the lord's mistress; you can see a wooden pillar marred by tiny holes—apparently made by the mistress as she stabbed it with her hairpin out of frustration with the lord's too-infrequent visits. There's a closet where the clan could hide during attack, and the ceiling of one hallway was constructed deliberately low to thwart downward blows of enemy swords. In more recent history, a sequence in the James Bond movie *You Only Live Twice* was filmed in one of the ryokan's rooms. In short, the ryokan is a museum in itself and contains antiques that once belonged to the Shimazu family. Unfortunately, guest rooms, which are located in a new wing, do not have as much character as the Edo-Era ones, but they exude simple elegance and come with a private bathroom, peace, and tranquility. Since they are all the same price, ask for one of the two facing the garden. Room prices reflect the seasons, with the highest price charged during Golden Week and New Year's. Note that reservations are not accepted by fax.

31–7 Shimizu-cho, Kagoshima 892-0802. (℃ 099/247-3155. Fax 099/247-0960. 8 units. ¥25,000–¥40,000 ($208–$333) per person. Rates include breakfast, dinner, and service charge. AE, DC, JCB, MC, V. Taxi: 5 min. from Kagoshima Station, in the direction of Senganen. **Amenities:** 1 outdoor restaurant (Japanese barbecue), kaiseki lunches served in private rooms (reservations required 1 day in advance; prices start at ¥5,000/$42); in-room massage. *In room:* A/C, TV, minibar, hot-water pot with tea, hair dryer.

Shiroyama Kanko Hotel ★★ Kagoshima's foremost hotel sits 353 feet high atop the wood-covered Shiroyama Hill and commands a great view of the city below and Sakurajima across the bay. It also has a nice garden. Opened a quarter of a century ago and recently renovated to keep it up to date, it offers pleasant and comfortable rooms, the most recommended of which face the volcano and city with the best views in town. The hotel's main drawback is its isolated location away from the city center. Taxis may add to the price of staying here, but it's a good respite from city life and restaurants offer views of the peaceful garden or sweeping panoramas of the city. Hot-spring baths are another plus.

41–1 Shinshoin-cho, Kagoshima 890-8586. (℃ 099/224-2211. Fax 099/224-2222. 313 units. ¥10,000–¥13,000 ($83–$108) single; ¥19,000–¥25,000 ($158–$208) double or twin. AE, DC, JCB, MC, V. Taxi: 15 min. from either station. Bus: City View from Nishi Kagoshima Station to Shiroyama (1 min.). **Amenities:** 4 restaurants (Western, Japanese, Chinese), 2 lounges; outdoor/indoor hot-spring baths; sauna; travel agency; large souvenir shop selling locally made crafts; salon; room service (10pm–midnight); in-room massage; same-day laundry/dry cleaning service; nonsmoking rooms. *In room:* A/C, bilingual TV, minibar, hot-water pot with tea, hair dryer, trouser press.

MODERATE

(211) **Furusato Kanko Hotel** ★ *(Finds* Although this ryokan on Sakurajima is inconvenient for sightseeing, it's great for relaxation. It boasts open-air hot-spring baths set amid rocks right beside the sea. It also has an outdoor, seawater swimming pool with a sunning terrace, an indoor 25-meter lap pool heated with hot springs, and indoor hot-spring baths overlooking the sea (see "What to See & Do," earlir for more information). Guests are charged a one-time usage fee of ¥210 ($1.75). Afterwards, retire to the shrinelike Meditation Room for spiritual cleansing as well. Rooms are all Japanese style with balconies overlooking the bay. Breakfast, featuring *kamameshi* (rice casseroles), is served in a dining room, while dinner, consisting mainly of seafood, *tonkotsu* (boiled pork), and other local specialties, is served in your room if the ryokan is not busy. A great getaway.

1076 Furusato-cho, Kagoshima 891-1592. (℃ 099/221-3111. Fax 099/221-2345. 40 units. ¥13,000 ($108) per person weekdays; ¥15,000 ($125) per person weekends and the night before holidays; ¥18,000 ($150) per person Golden Week and New Year's. Rates include breakfast, dinner, and service charge. AE, JCB, MC, V. From Kagoshima Station, a 5-min. walk to Sakurajima Ferry Terminal, then a 15-min. ferry ride to Sakurajima, then a free Furusato Kanko Hotel shuttle bus departing from ferry terminal every 30 min. from 8:45am–8pm (no service 12:20–2:20pm) or a local bus departing hourly from the ferry terminal to Furusato Onsen. **Amenities:** Indoor pool; great indoor/outdoor hot-spring baths; in-room massage; meditation room. *In room:* A/C, TV.

Kagoshima Tokyu Hotel *Kids*   This first-rate medium-priced hotel is in a newer area of Kagoshima, smack-dab on the waterfront with a good view of the volcano, even from its lobby lounge. Its twins and doubles face the water with balconies—great for watching the sun rise over Sakurajima. Note that singles, however, all face inland. Outdoor pools, including a children's pool, are open year-round free to hotel guests, making this a good bet for families. In summer, take advantage of the outdoor, seaside beer terrace.

22–1 Kamoike Shinmachi, Kagoshima 890-0064. ✆ **099/257-2411.** Fax 099/257-6083. 206 units. ¥7,800–¥10,000 ($65–$83) single; ¥17,000 ($142) double; ¥15,000–¥23,000 ($125–$192) twin. AE, DC, JCB, MC, V. Bus: 11 from Nishi Kagoshima Station to the last stop (2 min.). **Amenities:** 3 restaurants (Japanese, Western, steaks), 1 bar, summer beer garden; outdoor pool; children's pool; outdoor hot-spring bath; Jacuzzi; salon; in-room massage; same-day laundry/dry cleaning service; nonsmoking rooms. *In room:* A/C, bilingual TV with pay movies, minibar, hot-water pot with tea, hair dryer, washlet toilet (except in singles).

Sun Royal Hotel   This hotel is also located in a newer area of Kagoshima, a waterfront neighborhood of modern buildings and wide avenues. It's a bit far from the center, but city buses departing from Nishi Kagoshima reach the hotel in 20 minutes. The best rooms are those facing the sea with a small balcony, while the cheapest rooms face inland. There's a great *onsen* (hot-spring bath) with a sauna on the 13th floor, separated for men and women and free to hotel guests, where you can look out over Mt. Sakurajima as you bathe. There's also a relaxation room with a choice of therapies that promise everything from relaxation to enhanced creativity, administered after you crawl into a capsule with music, sounds, aromas, vibrations, changing temperatures, and glasses emitting flashing lights (fee: ¥1,000/$8.35). Restaurants include the Phoenix Sky Lounge on the 13th floor serving Western food and boasting a view of the sea.

1–8–10 Yojiro, Kagoshima 890-8581. ✆ **099/253-2020.** Fax 099/255-0186. www.sunroyal.co.jp. 262 units. ¥6,600–¥15,000 ($55–$125) single; ¥18,000 ($150) double; ¥16,500–¥18,000 ($137.50–$150) twin. AE, JCB, MC, V. Bus: 27 from Nishi Kagoshima Station to Shimin-Bunko Hall-Kitaguchi (1 min.). **Amenities:** 2 restaurants (Japanese, Western), 1 coffee shop, 1 bar; indoor hot-spring bath; relaxation room; salon; room service (5:30–11pm); in-room massage; same-day laundry/dry cleaning service; nonsmoking rooms. *In room:* A/C, TV, minibar, hot-water pot with tea, hair dryer.

Urban Port Hotel *Value*   Close to Kagoshima Station, the ferry to Sakurajima, and Kagoshima's market (I recommend starting your morning with a stroll through the market), this well-equipped tourist/business hotel offers good value for the price and more facilities than most in its price range. It has mostly singles, which are small but clean and bright with semi-double beds or (more expensive) double-size beds. Views are of either the city with mountains in the background or—better—the port and Sakurajima (ask for the highest floor possible).

15–1 Ogawacho, Kagoshima 892-0817. ✆ **099/239-4111.** Fax 099/239-4112. 102 units. ¥7,200–¥7,700 ($60–$64) single; ¥9,500 ($79) double; ¥14,000–¥20,000 ($117–$167) twin. AE, JCB, MC, V. Station: Kagoshima (5 min.). Streetcar: Sakurajima Sanbashi Dori (1 min.); walk down the wide avenue toward the bay (there's usually a street market here) and take the 2nd right. **Amenities:** 1 restaurant/bar (Western); health club with indoor pool, whirlpool bath, and exercise room (fee: ¥1,000/$8.35); in-room massage; same-day laundry/dry cleaning. *In room:* A/C, bilingual TV, minibar, hot-water pot with tea, hair dryer, washlet toilet.

INEXPENSIVE

Gasthof Hotel *Kids*   After traveling to Europe, the owner of this inexpensive, 30-year-old hotel decided to re-create the coziness of a German bed-and-breakfast with a comfortable lobby decorated with antique vases and rooms that vary in decor, furniture, and bedspreads, including four-poster beds in some. Although it falls short, the Gasthof has a lot more character than a regular business hotel. The location is convenient, and the rooms and baths have been freshly redone. It's also a good place for families—the owners are very nice to children. Downstairs, in Kitchen Market, are yatai-style food counters and bars, open evenings.

7–3 Chuo-cho, Kagoshima 890-0053. © **099/252-1401.** Fax 099/252-1405. 47 units. ¥5,300 ($47.50) single; ¥8,500 ($76.50) double or twin. Breakfast ¥700 ($5.85) extra. JCB, MC, V. Station: Nishi Kagoshima (3 min.). Walk down wide, tree-lined Napoli Dori 2 blocks and turn left; it's at the end of the street on the left. **Amenities:** 1 restaurant/bar (Japanese). *In room:* A/C, TV, hot-water pot with tea.

Nakazono Ryokan   A member of the Japanese Inn Group, this simple ryokan with Japanese-style rooms offers a convenient location, public baths open 24 hours, and an English-speaking owner who is knowledgeable about area sightseeing—he has even prepared handouts on how to get to Ibusuki and Chiran. No meals are served but there's a communal refrigerator, and the owner will direct you to nearby restaurants or, if you wish, help you order delivery pizza or sushi.

1–18 Yasui-cho, Kagoshima 892-0815. © **099/226-5125.** Fax 099/226-5126. www.satsuma.ne.jp/ myhome/shindon. 10 units (none with bathroom). ¥4,000 ($33) single; ¥8,000 ($67) twin; ¥11,400 ($95) triple. Rates include tax. Closed Aug. 13–15. AE, V. Station: Kagoshima (7 min.). Follow the streetcar along Densha Dori (or take the tram 3 stops to Shiyakusho-mae) for about 5 min. until you pass a temple on your left, turn left at the next alley, and then left again. **Amenities:** Coin-op washer and dryer. *In room:* A/C, coin-op TV, hot-water pot with tea.

WHERE TO DINE

While in Kagoshima, be sure to try its local dishes, known as **Satsuma cooking** (Satsuma was the original name of the Kagoshima area). This style of cooking supposedly has its origins in food cooked on battlefields centuries ago; if that's the case, it certainly has improved greatly since then. Popular Satsuma specialties include *Satsuma-age* (ground fish mixed with tofu and sake and then deep-fried), *tonkotsu* (pork that has been boiled for several hours in miso, shochu, and brown sugar—absolutely delicious), and *Satsuma-jiru* (miso soup with chicken and locally grown vegetables including Sakurajima radishes). *Kibinago* is a small fish belonging to the herring family that can be caught in the waters around Kagoshima; a silver color with brown stripes, it's often eaten raw and arranged on a dish to resemble a chrysanthemum.

EXPENSIVE

Kumasotei ★★ SATSUMA SPECIALTIES   Located in the city center, this restaurant specializes in local Satsuma dishes but carries it one step further by featuring them as part of kaiseki set meals. It reminds me more of a private home or ryokan since dining is in individual tatami rooms. If there isn't a crowd, you'll probably have your own private room; otherwise, you'll share. The main menu is in Japanese, but there's a smaller menu in English with photographs of the various set meals, which may include such local dishes as Satsuma-age, tonkotsu, Satsuma-jiru, or kibinago, as well as *zakezushi* (rice that has been soaked in sake all day and then mixed with such things as vegetables and shrimp), bonito baked with salt, and *awameshi* (rice mixed with wheat). A good choice for dinner is the ¥5,000 ($42) Taka set course, which includes several local dishes served kaiseki style.

6–10 Higashi Sengoku-cho. © **099/222-6356.** Set dinners ¥3,500–¥10,000 ($29–$83); set lunches from ¥2,000 ($17). AE, DC, JCB, MC, V. Daily 11am–2:30pm and 5–10pm (last order). Streetcar: Tenmonkan-Dori (4 min.). Walk through the Tenmonkan-Dori covered shopping arcade (the one with the movie screen) 4 blocks and turn left; it will be on your right.

MODERATE

⑫ **Ajimori** ★ BLACK PORK   This 25-year-old establishment specializes in pork from small black pigs, which the locals claim is more tender and succulent than regular pork. The restaurant is divided into two parts: the upper floors, with both table seating and private tatami rooms, serve Satsuma Kuroshabu, a Kagoshima specialty of black-pork shabu; the first floor is a casual dining room specializing in *tonkatsu,* breaded black-pork cutlet. If you order the Kuroshabu, you'll eat it just like the more common beef shabu-shabu, cooking it yourself at your table by dipping it into a boiling broth and then in raw egg or sauce. Portions are generous, but if you wish, you can also order tonkatsu as a side dish. Otherwise, go to the first floor for perhaps the lightest, best-tasting tonkatsu you'll ever have; the set lunches, available every day except Sundays and holidays, are a bargain.

13–21 Sennicho. ✆ 099/224-7634. Shabu set dinners ¥4,000–¥8,000 ($33–$67); shabu set lunch ¥3,000 ($25); tonkatsu set dinners ¥780–¥3,000 ($6.50–$25), tonkatsu set lunches ¥600–¥650 ($5–$5.40). DC, MC, V accepted only for meals costing more than ¥10,000 ($83). Daily 11:30am–2:30pm (noon–1:30pm for shabu) and 5:30–9pm (last order). Streetcar: Tenmonkan-Dori (3 min.). Walk through the Tenmonkan-Dori covered arcade (the one beside Taka Pla, opposite the movie screen) and keep going past the koban police box; it's on the left just before the 2nd arch with the eyeglass motif, in a modern building with colored photographs outside.

INEXPENSIVE

⑬ **Noboruya** *Finds* RAMEN NOODLES   This popular, inexpensive restaurant in the center of town is Kagoshima's best-known *ramen* (noodle) shop, in business for more than half a century. It's a simple place, occupying one room of a small, wooden home with one counter and an open kitchen. Since only one dish is served, there's no problem ordering. A big bowl of ramen comes with noodles (made fresh every day) and slices of pork, all seasoned with garlic. You also get pickled radish (supposedly good for the stomach) and tea. As you eat your ramen at the counter, you can watch women peeling garlic and cooking huge pots of noodles over gas flames. A great place to soak up local atmosphere.

2–15 Horie-cho. ✆ 099/226-6697. Noodles ¥1,000 ($9). No credit cards. Mon–Sat 11am–7pm. Streetcar: Izuro-Dori (1 min.). Walk down the wide street marked by stone lanterns on each side (Miami Dori) and take the 1st right; Noboruya is at the end of the 2nd block on the left, with its entrance around the corner.

5 Southern Kyushu's Top Spa: Ibusuki ★

50km (31 miles) S of Kagoshima

At the southern tip of the Satsuma Peninsula, **Ibusuki** (pronounced "ee-boo-ski") is southern Kyushu's most famous hot-spring resort. With a pleasant average temperature of 64.5°F, it's a region of lush vegetation, flowers, and palm trees. It also boasts Japan's best natural hot-sand bath.

ESSENTIALS

GETTING THERE   Ibusuki is approximately an hour from Nishi Kagoshima Station by **JR train;** the fare costs ¥970 ($8.10) one-way. There are also **buses** that depart from Kagoshima's Yamagataya Bus Center in the heart of the city (near the Asahi Dori tram stop) 10 times a day (some make stops at Nishi Kagoshima Station before traveling onward), reaching Ibusuki's train station 1½ hours later and costing ¥850 ($7.10) one-way.

Because the sights of southern Kyushu are spread out, you might wish to travel directly to Ibusuki by bus or train, spend the night, and then return to Kagoshima on a guided tour (see "What to See & Do," below for more information).

VISITOR INFORMATION   Be sure to get the leaflet "Kagoshima and Vicinity" from the Tourist Information Center in Tokyo, Kyoto, or Narita or Kansai international airports. In Ibusuki, stop by the tourist information counter at **Ibusuki Station** (© 0993/22-4114; open daily 9am–6pm) to pick up a map.

GETTING AROUND   The small town of Ibusuki is spread along the coast, and public **buses** run along the main streets. **Taxis** are also readily available.

WHAT TO SEE & DO

TAKING A HOT-SAND BATH   The most popular thing to do in Ibusuki is to have yourself buried up to your neck in black sand at Yunohama Beach, heated naturally by hot springs that surface close to the ground before running into the sea. To partake, head to the **Natural Sand Bath** ⭑⭑⭑ (Sana Mushi Onsen; © 0993/23-3900; open daily 8:30am–noon and 1–9pm), a modern facility nicknamed Saraku by the locals (*saraku* has two meanings: to walk around and to enjoy the sand). Take the elevator up to the reception, pay ¥900 ($7.50) for the baths and rental yukata (add another ¥100/85¢ if you didn't bring a towel), change into the yukata in the dressing room, and then head down to the beach. One of the women there will dig you a shallow grave. Lie down, arrange your yukata so no vulnerable areas are exposed, and then lie still while she piles sand on top of you. It's quite a funny sight, actually, to see nothing but heads sticking out of the ground. The water, a hot 185°F, contains sodium chloride and is considered beneficial against rheumatism, arthritis, gastrointestinal troubles, neuralgia, and female disorders. It is also valued as a beauty treatment for the skin. After your 15-minute sand bath, go indoors for a relaxing, hot-spring bath. The Natural Sand Bath is a 10-minute walk from Ibusuki Station; from the main exit, walk straight to the beach and turn right. You can also take a bus to the Saraku-mae stop; the bus announces it as "Sanamushi-mae."

SEEING THE SIGHTS   Southern Kyshu's main attractions are all natural wonders. **Mt. Kaimon,** rising 3,000 feet above sea level, has a conical shape that has earned it the nickname, "Mt. Fuji of Satsuma," and it affords a grand view of the sea from its peak. **Lake Ikeda,** Kyushu's largest lake, is a crater lake formed after the collapse of a volcano. With a depth of 765 feet, it's home to gigantic eels, some of which weigh as much as 33 pounds and measure about 6 feet in length. According to popular lore, it also has its own Loch Ness monster, fondly named Isshy. At **Nagasakibana Point,** Kyushu's southernmost point, is **Flower Park Kagoshima** (© 0993/35-3333; open daily 9am–5pm), Japan's largest flower garden with approximately 2,000 species of mostly subtropical flowers and plants collected from around the world. Admission is ¥600 ($5) for adults, half price for children.

Because public bus lines to areas around Ibusuki are neither extensive nor frequent, it's best to join a **group tour,** which begins in Ibusuki and ends in Kagoshima. Although conducted only in Japanese tours go to all the main sights, including a local shochu factory, Nagisakabana and Flower Park Kagoshima, Mt. Kaimon peak, Lake Ikeda, and Chiran with its Peace Museum and samurai gardens. They depart daily from Ibusuki Station at 10:30am, arriving at Nishi Kagoshima Station at 5:55pm. Costs are ¥3,800 ($32) for adults and ¥1,990 ($17) for children. For more information, call the **Kagoshima Kotsu** bus company's office in Ibusuki at © 0993/22-2211.

GOLF   In **Mt. Kaimon Natural Park** at the foot of Mt. Kaimon, you'll find the 18-hole **Ibusuki Golf Course.** Greens fees are ¥7,000 ($58) on weekdays,

¥14,000 ($117) on Saturday, Sunday, and holidays. For more information, call the golf course at ℂ **0993/32-3141.**

WHERE TO STAY
EXPENSIVE

214 **Hakusuikan Ryokan** ★★★   A driveway lined with pine trees sets the mood for this modern, elegant, and resort-like ryokan right on the beach with one of the most impressive hot-spring baths I've ever seen. Established in 1960 and expanded over the years, the ryokan seems like a village, with corridors that stretch seemingly forever and serve as galleries for an extensive collection of antique Satsuma and Chinese pottery, calligraphy, and old photographs. The public bath—a reproduction of an Edo-Period hot-spring spa—is classy and refined, also designed like a small village with a large bathing area made of cypress wood and stone with pools of varying temperatures, a huge *rotenburo* (outdoor hot-spring pool), a sand bath, a steam room, and a replica Edo-Era sauna with a round dome. Even the dressing rooms are faithfully styled after the Edo Period, though naturally they contain all the latest conveniences.

Several room types are available. Least expensive are the 30 Western-style twins, all of which face inland and are rather ordinary looking. Better are the Japanese-style tatami rooms facing the sea, but if you can afford it, spring for one of the ryokan's 100 combination rooms with both beds and separate tatami areas. Breakfasts are Western or Japanese buffets, while Japanese dinners are served as buffets only during busy seasons. The perfect getaway.

Chirinosato, Ibusuki 891-0404. ℂ **0993/22-3131**; 0993/23-3898 for reservations. Fax 0993/23-3860. 205 units. ¥15,000–¥50,000 ($125–$417) per person. Rates include breakfast, dinner, and service charge. AE, DC, JCB, MC, V. Taxi: 5 min. from Ibusuki Station. **Amenities:** 2 restaurants (Japanese), 1 lounge; fantastic indoor/outdoor hot-spring baths; outdoor swimming pool; children's pool; in-room massage. *In room:* A/C, TV, minibar, hot-water pot with tea, hair dryer.

Ibusuki Iwasaki Hotel ★   This is Ibusuki's best-known spa hotel, a self-contained resort on 125 acres of lush tropical grounds with pleasant walking trails throughout. It's very popular with Japanese tour groups, both for its facilities that include huge public baths, outdoor swimming pools, and a golf course, and for its evening entertainment. If you come during the off-season, however, you have the hotel seemingly to yourself. Another plus are the resort's own private museums, one featuring Japanese artists painting in the Western style and the other displaying crafts from Papua New Guinea as well as Satsuma pottery.

All rooms have either a full or partial view of the sea and a balcony; the best rooms also have views of the wonderful garden, one of the resort's best features and well worth a stroll. The majority of rooms are twins (there are no singles). Not quite as nice are Japanese-style rooms, which are rather small and are located in an older building. In any case, nights here are nice, with the sound of the waves and the frogs croaking in the lotus pond.

3755 Juni-cho, Ibusuki 891-0493. ℂ **0993/22-2131**; 0993/24-3888 for reservations. Fax 0993/24-3215. 366 units. ¥14,000–¥22,000 ($117–$183) twin; from ¥25,000 ($208) twin in peak season. AE, DC, JCB, MC, V. Taxi: 5 min. from Ibusuki Station. Bus: to Ibusuki Iwasaki Hotel, the last stop. **Amenities:** 5 restaurants, 1 nightclub, 1 casino/bar; outdoor swimming pool; children's pool; fitness room (fee: ¥700/$5.85); indoor/outdoor hot-spring baths overlooking the sea; hot-sand baths (fee: ¥1,050/$8.75); Jacuzzi; tennis courts; bowling arcade; rental bicycles; Ibusuki Golf Course; art and crafts museums; in-room massage. *In room:* A/C, TV, minibar, hot-water pot with tea, hair dryer.

MODERATE
Coral Beach Hotel   Coral Beach Hotel is located across the street from the waterfront and just a few minutes walk from the Natural Sand Bath (or you can

take a free shuttle service to the baths). Despite its name, most of the rooms are Japanese-style, and those facing the sea boast balconies and lovely views. The public hot-spring baths include a sauna, a waterfall bath (for massaging shoulders), and *rotenburo* (outdoor bath), but otherwise facilities here are limited.

2–12–7 Yunohama, Ibusuki 891-0406. **(** **0993/22-2241.** Fax 0993/23-3110. 51 units. ¥8,000–¥10,000 ($65–$83) per person without meals; ¥13,000–¥20,000 ($108–$167) per person including breakfast and dinner. AE, DC, JCB, MC, V. Taxi: 5 min. from Ibusuki Station. **Amenities:** Indoor/outdoor hot-spring baths; in-room massage. *In room:* A/C, TV, hot-water pot with tea.

INEXPENSIVE

㉕ **Kyuka-Mura Ibusuki** *Value* This inexpensive, government-owned lodge is located right at the water's edge (but a bit far from town) and offers reasonably priced, basic accommodations, making it a popular choice with Japanese families. During summer vacation months, on New Year's, in March during spring vacation, and in May during school trips, you should reserve 6 months in advance. At other times, it's relatively easy to get a room here. Rates are based on the type of room and meals you select. Cheapest are the eight Western-style rooms, which face inland and have toilets but no bathrooms. Most expensive are Japanese-style rooms facing the sea with a bathroom; some even have a balcony.

Higashikata, Shiomi-cho, Ibusuki 891-0491. **(** **0993/22-3211.** Fax 0993/22-3213. 65 units (7 with bathroom, 58 with toilet only). ¥6,000–¥12,500 ($50–$104) per person. Rates include breakfast and dinner. MC, V. Free shuttle buses depart from in front of Ibusuki Station after every train arrival; look for a purple bus with QKAMURA written on it. **Amenities:** Indoor hot-spring baths; sand baths (fee: ¥840/$7); tennis courts; rental bikes. *In room:* A/C, TV, hot-water pot with tea.

㉖ **Marutomi** 🌸 Located just a minute's walk from the Natural Sand Bath at Yunohama Beach, this inexpensive inn is a family-run affair. The owner is a fisherman, so you can count on fresh seafood meals. And following the ryokan tradition of naming rooms instead of assigning numbers (rooms are commonly named after flowers), rooms here are named after fish—you can stay in the Tuna room! All the rooms are Japanese style—clean and with more character than many in this price range. Meals are served communally on tatami at low tables.

5–24–15 Yunohama, Ibusuki 891-04061. **(** **0993/22-5579.** Fax 0993/22-3993. 7 units (none with bathroom). ¥5,000 ($42) per person without meals, ¥7,000 ($58) per person with dinner and breakfast. No credit cards. A 10-min. walk from Ibusuki Station. From the main exit, walk straight to the beach and turn right; after passing the Natural Sand Bath, turn right and walk uphill. Bus: Going in the direction of the Ibusuki Iwasaki Hotel (ask for the Ibusuki Iwasaki Hotel yuki bus; the bus does not have a number), get off at the Saraku-mae stop ("Sunamushi-mae" is announced in the bus) and walk inland up the hill (1 min.). It's on the right. **Amenities:** Small hot-spring bath; free washing machine. *In room:* A/C, TV, no phone.

WHERE TO DINE

If you can't get out to the countryside, **Chozjuan** (below) has a branch just a 10-minute walk from Ibusuki Station at 12–495–1 Ibusuki (**(** **0993/22-5272;** open daily 11am–3pm and 5:30–9pm). Although it doesn't have the grand setting of its country cousin, it's pleasant enough with a tall ceiling reminiscent of a traditional farmhouse. Soft jazz plays in the background. Its menu is also more varied, and specialties center on noodles, tempura, kaiseki, and local Kagoshima specialties. Soba set meals start at ¥1,000 ($8.35), a tempura teishoku is ¥2,500 ($21), and shabu-shabu ranges from ¥2,500 to ¥3,500 ($21–$29). Walk straight out of the main exit of the station, take the first right, then the first left.

㉗ **Chozjuan** ★★ *Finds* SOMEN NOODLES If you're adventurous, try this fun, open-air restaurant in the countryside near Mt. Kaimon. Serving as a lunch stop for some of the organized tours of the area, it specializes in *somen,* or cold noodles. Seating is under a pavilion beside a man-made waterfall, so you eat to the accompaniment of running water with Japanese traditional music playing in the background. In the middle of your table is a large round container with water swirling around in a circle; when you get your basket of noodles, dump them into the cold water, fish them out with your chopsticks, dip them in soy sauce, and enjoy. There are also four set menus, which come with such main dishes as grilled trout or carp sashimi along with vegetables and soup.

Kaimon-cho, Tosenkyo. © 0993/32-3156. Noodles ¥530 ($4.40); set meals ¥1,300–¥2,600 ($11–$22). No credit cards. May–June, daily 10am–7pm; July–Aug, daily 9am–9pm; Sept–Apr, daily 10am–5pm. Bus: 8 departures daily from Ibusuki Station (a 30-min. ride) including departures at 10:15am, 11:50am, and 1:55pm.

6 Kumamoto ⟨★

1,287km (804 miles) W of Tokyo; 189km (118 miles) S of Fukuoka

Located roughly halfway down Kyushu's western side, Kumamoto boasts a fine castle and a landscaped garden, both with origins stretching back to the first half of the 17th century. Once one of Japan's most important castle towns, Kumamoto today is the progressive capital of Kumamoto Prefecture, with a population of 660,000. Yet it retains a small town atmosphere, which is precisely why I like it.

ESSENTIALS

GETTING THERE   By Plane   JAL, JAS, and **ANA** fly to Kumamoto from Tokyo in 1 hour and 40 minutes, with fares averaging about ¥31,000 ($258) one-way. Airport shuttle buses operate from the airport to Kumamoto Station and the Kumamoto Kotsu (bus) Center downtown, taking about 50 minutes and costing ¥670 ($5.60).

By Train   It takes more than 9 hours to reach Kumamoto from **Tokyo,** with a change in trains at Hakata Station in **Fukuoka.** The fare is ¥23,270 ($194) one-way for an unreserved seat. Limited express trains depart from Fukuoka's Hakata Station three times an hour, reaching Kumamoto in about 1½ hours. There are also two express trains daily from **Beppu,** reaching Kumamoto in 3 hours.

VISITOR INFORMATION   The leaflet "Kumamoto and Mt. Aso," distributed by the Tourist Information Centers in Kyoto, Tokyo, Narita, and Kansai international airports, contains information on how to get to Kumamoto and places of interest in the city. In Kumamoto, there's a Kumamoto Tourist Office inside Kumamoto Station near the main exit (© **096/352-3743;** open daily 9am–5:30pm, sometimes closed 1–2pm). It has a good English map and brochure and is staffed by helpful English speakers who can make lodging reservations. In the city center, there's another Kumamoto Tourist Information Center on the first floor of the **Sanbun Kaikan Building** (which is part of the Sangyo Bunka Kaikan complex; © **096/322-5060;** open daily 9:30am–6pm, closed 2nd and 4th Mon of the month), opposite the Sunroad Shinshigai covered shopping street and in front of the Karashimacho tram stop. If you're coming by plane, stop by the **Kumamoto Airport Information Office** (© **096/232-2810;** open daily 6:50am–9:30pm).

More information is available on the city's website at **www.city.kumamoto. kumamoto.jp/**.

ORIENTATION & GETTING AROUND   **Kumamoto Station** lies far south of the city's downtown area, but transportation between the two is easy via streetcar no. 2, which departs from in front of the station and reaches the downtown area in about 10 minutes. **Downtown** centers on two covered shopping streets called Shimotori and Sunroad Shinshigai, with many department stores, shops, hotels, bars, and restaurants in the area. Here, too, is the city's bus station, the **Kumamoto Kotsu Center,** from which all buses in the city depart. Just north of downtown, within walking distance, rises **Kumamoto Castle,** which is surrounded by moats, turrets, and expansive greenery, on the edge of which are several museums and historic sites. **Suizenji Garden** lies far to the east.

Getting around Kumamoto via **streetcar** is easy because there are only two lines. Streetcar no. 2 is most convenient for tourists; it departs from Kumamoto Station and passes through downtown and near Kumamoto Castle (stop: Kumamotojo-mae) before going onward to Suizenji Garden (stop: Suizenji-Koen-mae). Fares range from ¥130 to ¥200 ($1.10–$1.65).

Because the grounds surrounding Kumamoto Castle encompass 242 acres (with a circumference of 5½ miles), you might consider visiting sights on its perimeter via one of two **Kumamoto Castle tour buses,** which depart from Kumamoto Kotsu Center and make a circular route around the castle grounds every 30 minutes (every 15 min. during peak season, weekends, and holidays), stopping at Hosokawa Mansion, Kumamoto Prefectural Museum of Art, Kumamoto Prefectural Traditional Crafts Center, and other places of interest. Nicknamed the "Musashi" and the "Toryanse," they cost ¥130 ($1.10) for a single journey or ¥300 ($2.50) for the whole day; children pay half fare.

If you plan on taking public transportation at least four times in one day, you can save money by purchasing a **1-day pass,** which allows unlimited travel on all city buses (including the Castle tour bus) and streetcars for ¥500 ($4.15) for adults, ¥250 ($2.10) for children.

THE TOP ATTRACTIONS

Kumamoto Castle ★★   Completed in 1607, Kumamoto Castle is massive— it took 7 years to build. It was constructed under the direction of Kato Kiyomasa, a great warrior who fought alongside Tokugawa Ieyasu in battle and was rewarded for his loyalty with land. The castle was built atop a hill and had 2 main towers, 49 turrets, 29 gates, and 18 two-story gatehouses; to make the walls impossible for enemies to scale, they were built with curves at the bottom and nearly vertical at the top and were crowned with an overhang. More than 100 wells ensured water even during a seige, while camphor and gingko trees were planted for firewood and edible nuts. The castle passed into the possession of the Hosokawa family in 1632 and remained an important stronghold for the Tokugawa shogunate throughout its 250 years of rule, particularly in campaigns against the powerful and independent-minded lords of southern Kyushu. During that time, 11 generations of the Hosokawa clan ruled over Kumamoto.

Much of the castle was destroyed in 1877 during the Seinan Rebellion led by Saigo Takamori, a samurai who was unhappy with the new policies of the Meiji government in which ancient samurai rights were rescinded. Saigo led a troop of samurai in an attack on the castle and its imperial troops who remained under siege for 53 days before government reinforcements finally arrived and quelled the rebellion. When the smoke cleared, most of the castle lay in smoldering ruins.

The castle was reconstructed in 1960 of ferroconcrete, and although it's not nearly as massive as before, it's still quite impressive and remains Kumamoto's star attraction. The interior houses a museum with elaborately decorated palanquins, models of Kumamoto and the castle during the Edo Period, armor, swords, former possessions of both Kato Kiyomasa and the Hosokawa family, and rifles and other artifacts from the Seinan Rebellion. You can learn more about the castle and its history by picking up an English audioguide at the west

---

(*Moments* Moonlight Dining

After 6pm (5pm in winter), there's a small door beside the main entrance to the **Suizenji Garden** that remains unlocked, allowing you to enter for free and dine at the garden's restaurants (see "Where to Dine," below). If you want to do some moon gazing, this is the place.

---

gate of the castle grounds. Because castle grounds are large, you'll probably spend more than an hour here.

1–1 Honmaru. ℭ **096/352-5900.** Admission ¥500 ($4.15) adults, ¥200 ($1.65) children. Apr–Oct, daily 8:30am–5:30pm; Nov–Mar, 8:30am–4:30pm. Streetcar: Kumamotojo-mae (10 min.) or Shiyakusho-mae (6 min.). Bus: Kumamoto Castle bus "Toryanse" or "Musashi" to Kumamotojo stop (5 min.).

Suizenji Garden 🅐 Laid out in the 1630s by Tadatoshi Hosokawa as a retreat for the tea ceremony and as the grounds of a nearby temple, Suizenji Garden took about 80 years to complete. The garden wraps itself around a cold spring–fed lake (considered particularly good for making tea). But what makes the place especially interesting is that its design incorporates famous scenes in miniature from the 53 stages of the ancient **Tokaido Highway,** which connected Kyoto and Tokyo. (The 53 stages were also immortalized in Hiroshige's famous woodblock prints.) Most recognizable is cone-shaped Mt. Fuji and Lake Biwa; near the garden's entrance is Nihon Bashi (Bridge of Japan), Edo's starting point of the Tokaido Road. The park is small—almost disappointingly so—and for the life of me, I can't figure out more than a handful of the 53 stages. Maybe you'll have better luck. On its grounds is a 400-year-old **thatched-roof teahouse** beside a pond, transported from the imperial grounds in Kyoto, as well as **Izumi Shrine,** built in 1878 in dedication of the Hosokawa lords. Near the garden's entrance is a teahouse where you can sip tea and look out over the pond. Plan on spending an hour here.

(Suizenji Jojuen). 8–1 Suizenji Koen. ℭ **096/383-0074.** Admission ¥400 ($3.35) adults, ¥200 ($1.65) children. Mar–Nov, daily 7:30am–6pm; Dec–Feb, daily 8am–5pm. Streetcar: no. 2 streetcar from Kumamoto Station or the downtown area to Suizenji-Koen-mae (about a 20-min. ride), followed by a 3-min. walk.

MORE TO SEE & DO

Hosokawa Mansion (Kyu-Hosokawa Gyobutei) A 10-minute walk north of Kumamoto Castle, this 300-year-old samurai mansion was built by a subsidiary member of the Hosokawa clan, Lord Gyobu, and was enlarged in the 1800s. Guided tours lasting 25 minutes take visitors through various rooms, including the lord's study and reception room, teahouse, kitchen, and servants' quarters, where you can see Edo-Era furnishings and personal items including an Edo clock, a suitcase, clothing, a woman's cosmetic case, lacquerware, a kimono chest, and more, giving you a good idea of how feudal lords lived during the Edo Period.

3–1 Furukyo-machi. ℭ **096/352-6522.** Admission ¥300 ($2.50) adults, ¥100 (85¢) children. Apr–Oct, daily 8:30am–5:30pm; Nov–Mar, daily 8:30am–4:30pm. Bus: Kumamoto Castle bus "Toryanse" or "Musashi" to Kyu-Hosokawa Gyobutei stop (1 min.).

Kumamoto Prefectural Art Museum (Kumamoto Kenritsu Bijutsukan)
This prefectural art museum displays a little bit of everything, including traditional and modern Japanese art (and including works by Kumamoto artists), pieces by Western old masters and contemporary artists, scrolls, screens, ceramics, lacquerware, tea utensils, and other crafts. Works from the museum's

collection are rotated in shows based on various themes, but you may see art by Noda Hideo, Katayama Nanpu, and Zenzo Sakamoto, as well as Albrecht Dürer, Renoir, and Picasso. There are better art museums in Japan, so come here only if you have an extra hour or art is your particular passion.

2 Ninomaru. ✆ 096/352-2111. Admission ¥260 ($1.90) adults, ¥160 ($1.35) students, free for children; more for special exhibits. Tues–Sun 9:30am–5pm. Bus: Kumamoto Castle bus "Toryanse" or "Musashi" to Kumamotojo stop (3 min.). Streetcar: Kumamotojo-mae or Shiyakusho-mae (10 min.). On the castle grounds, just NW of the castle.

SHOOTING THE KUMAGAWA RAPIDS 🛶🛶

If you've had enough of shrines, museums, castles, and gardens, consider boarding a boat or raft and shooting the **Kumagawa Rapids.** Compared to wild rivers in the United States, the Kumagawa seems pretty tame; people do the trip not so much for the thrill of the ride but for the scenery of a narrow river valley bordered by wooded hills. It makes for a pleasant outing. There are two companies offering rides: One uses long, traditional, wooden boats steered by boatmen fore and aft; the other has modern rafts guided by a staff of young professionals and goes through slightly rougher water. Both companies are located in Hitoyoshi City.

You can reach **Hitoyoshi** by bus from Kumamoto Kotsu Center in about 1½ hours, with fares costing ¥2,300 ($19) one-way. There are also six trains a day from Kumamoto Station to Hitoyoshi; the express train takes 1½ hours. There are trains and buses that connect Watari and Kyusendo with Kumamoto; if you're taking the Kyryu Course, head straight for Watari.

Incidentally, if you're coming to Kumamoto from **Kagoshima,** you should consider taking a bus from Nishi Kagoshima Station to Hitoyoshi; it takes almost 2 hours and costs ¥2,050 ($17). After your boat ride, you can then continue onward to Kumamoto.

The first company, **Kumagawa Kudari Kabushikigaisha,** Shimoshin-machi 333–1 (a 20-min. walk from Hitoyoshi Station), Hitoyoshi City (✆ **0966/ 22-5555**), offers two different routes in its wooden boats, both lasting 90 minutes. The **Seiryu Course** (Crystal Stream Course) goes 8km (5 miles), beginning in Hitoyoshi and ending in Watari, and covers a rather gentle stretch of the river. It's offered year-round, with one to eight trips daily depending on the time of the year; from December through February the boats have *kotatsu* (heated blankets). The cost is ¥2,835 ($24) for adults and ¥1,890 ($16) for children; winter trips with kotatsu cost ¥3,675 ($31) and ¥2,835 ($24) respectively. The **Kyuryu Course** (Rapids Course) covers 10km (6.2 miles), beginning in Watari and ending in Kyusendo, and is more exciting, though the river is still only a grade 2. This trip is offered April through October, 5 to 12 times daily and costs ¥3,675 ($31) for adults and ¥2,100 ($17.50) for children. During rainy season (mid-June to mid-July), trips are sometimes cancelled due to swollen rivers. Make reservations a day or two in advance to be assured of a seat.

The other company appeals to a younger crowd. The **Land Earth Outdoor Sports Club,** Tsuruta-machi 31–2, Hitoyoshi City (✆ **0966/22-1077**), offers a 10km (6¼-mile) white-water rafting trip from Watari to Kyusendo along a rougher route than that of the Kyuryu Course. This trip is offered daily April through November. Participants should arrive at 9am for instruction and outfitting in wet suits; put-in is at 11am. Afterwards, everyone goes to a hot-spring bath; the trip is completed by around 5:30 or 6pm. The cost is ¥12,800 ($107) and includes a Japanese-style barbecue lunch and bath. Reservations are necessary. This company is located about a 15-minute walk from Hitoyoshi Station; you can also call from the station for pickup service.

SHOPPING

One of Kumamoto's most famous products is its Higo Inlay or **damascene,** in which gold, silver, and copper are inlaid on an iron plate to form patterns of flowers, bamboo, and other designs. Originally used to adorn sword guards and armor, damascene today is used on such accessories as paperweights, jewelry, and tie clasps. Another Kumamoto product is the **Yamaga lantern,** made of gold paper and used during the Yamaga Lighted Lantern Festival held in August. Other local products include Amakusa pearls, pottery, knives, toys, and bamboo items.

A wonderful place to see Kumamoto Prefecture's products and to learn how they're made is the ⑱ **Kumamoto Prefectural Traditional Crafts Center** (Dento Kougeikan), northeast of Kumamoto Castle at 3–35 Chibajo-machi (✆096/324-4930; open Tues–Sun 9am–5pm). The center's second floor exhibits handmade crafts from all over the prefecture, along with displays showing the step-by-step procedure for producing them. Displays include toys, furniture, fans, wooden rice barrels, bamboo baskets, pottery, damascene, and kitchen knives sharp enough to chop through bone. The entrance fee—¥200 ($1.65) for adults, ¥130 ($1.10) for university students, and free for children under 18—is worth every yen. Local products are sold on the first floor in a gallery. Take streetcar no. 2 to the Shiyakusho-mae stop, from which it's a 5-minute walk.

South of Kumamoto Castle is the ⑲ **Display Hall of Kumamoto Products** (Kumamoto-ken Bussankan), located on the third floor of the Sanbun Kaikan Building (which is part of the Sangyo Bunka Kaikan complex) at 7–10 Hanabata-cho (✆ 096/353-1168; open daily 10am–6pm, closed 2nd and 4th Mon each month). It sells local products such as Higo Inlay, knives, pottery, Yamaga paper lanterns, Amakusa pearls, shochu, sake, and confections. The hall is located near the Kumamoto Kotsu Bus Center and opposite the Sunroad Shinshigair shopping arcade (the Kumamoto Tourist Information Center is in the same building). The Karashimacho streetcar stop is in front of the building.

WHERE TO STAY
EXPENSIVE

Hotel New Otani Kumamoto ★★ *Value*   This hotel has everything: a convenient location next to the station, the respected New Otani name, a perceptive staff, and the latest in design and amenities—all at reasonable rates. Although it's not deluxe compared to hotels in Tokyo or Osaka, it's the best hotel in town. The spacious rooms feature a corner sofa and a large coffee table, and the desk and counter areas are generous. All rooms come with individual reading lights with dimmer switches, window blinds to block light, double-pane windows that block noise and can also be opened, window blinds for complete darkness, a message light and bedside controls, massage shower heads, and such extras as hangers with nonslip pads and bathroom phones. Double rooms have queen-size beds.

1–13–1 Kasuga, Kumamoto 860-0047. ✆ **800/421-8795** in the U.S. and Canada, or 096/326-1111. Fax 096/326-0800. 130 units. ¥11,000–¥13,000 ($92–$108) single; ¥18,000–¥32,000 ($150–$267) double or twin. AE, DC, JCB, MC, V. A 1-min. walk from Kumamoto Station; turn right out of the station. **Amenities:** 4 restaurants (Japanese, Chinese, Western, coffee shop); 1 piano bar; small exercise room and (for men only) sauna (fee: ¥1,000/$8.35 for either); souvenir shop/convenience store; room service (6am–10pm); in-room massage; same-day laundry/dry cleaning service; nonsmoking rooms. *In room:* A/C, bilingual satellite TV (but no CNN), minibar, hot-water pot with tea, hair dryer.

Kumamoto Hotel Castle ★   This tall brick hotel is just east of Kumamoto Castle, with good views of the castle from some of its more expensive rooms. A subdued, quiet, and conservative hotel, it's popular with middle-aged Japanese, including locals who come for receptions or to dine in one of its restaurants. Rooms are comfortable with modern furniture and headboard controls; deluxe twins and singles offer semi-double-size beds and sofas in a more spacious setting.

4–2 Joto-machi, Kumamoto 860-8565. © **096/326-3311.** Fax 096/326-3324. info@hotel-castle.co.jp. 185 units. ¥8,900–¥14,500 ($74–$121) single; ¥17,000–¥21,000 ($142–$175) double; ¥16,000–¥25,000 ($133–$208) twin. AE, DC, JCB, MC, V. Streetcar: no. 2 15 min. to Shiyakusho-mae, then a 2-min. walk north 1 block. **Amenities:** 4 restaurants (Japanese, French, Chinese, coffee shop); room service (11:30am–midnight); in-room massage; laundry/dry cleaning service. *In room:* A/C, bilingual cable TV, minibar, hot-water pot with tea, hair dryer, washlet toilet.

MODERATE

Ark Hotel ✹✹   If you want to stay close to the castle, this is a great choice in a moderate price range. It has a relaxed, gardenlike atmosphere, from the bamboo garden in the lobby to the flower-patterned rooms. There's even a small rooftop garden with a path leading to a tea-ceremony house (used for private functions). Rooms are more than the usual boxes, with added architectural details like alcove ceilings and fashionable furniture. Rooms on the seventh to ninth floors look out on the Tsuboigawa River and the castle, though an unsightly NHK broadcasting tower mars the view.

5–16 Joto-machi, Kumamoto 860-0846. © **096/351-2222.** Fax 096/326-0909. 222 units. ¥8,000–¥9,100 ($67–$76) single; ¥16,000 ($133) double; ¥14,500–¥24,500 ($121–$204) twin. AE, JCB, MC, V. Just east of the castle. Streetcar: no. 2 to Shiyakusho-mae, then a 5-min. walk north 3 blocks. **Amenities:** 2 restaurants (Japanese, Western); laundry/dry cleaning service. *In room:* A/C, bilingual TV, minibar, hot-water pot with tea, hair dryer.

Chisan Hotel Kumamoto   Located in downtown Kumamoto near the Kumamoto Kotsu Center and Sunroad Shinshigai shopping street, this chain business hotel doesn't offer anything in the way of service. However, its lobby is pleasantly decorated with marble, brass railings, and stained glass, and the rooms are tasteful if tiny and simple. Essentially, this is a dependable, centrally located place to rest your head.

4–39 Karashimacho, Kumamoto 860-0804. © **096/322-3911.** Fax 096/356-5229. 201 units. ¥6,900–¥7,800 ($57.50–$65) single; ¥12,000 ($100) double; ¥12,500–¥14,000 ($104–$117) twin. AE, DC, JCB, MC, V. Streetcar: no. 2 to Karashimacho, then a 2-min. walk west in the opposite direction from Sunroad Shinshigai. **Amenities:** Restaurant (Western); coin-op washer/dryer. *In room:* A/C, TV, minibar, hot-water pot with tea, hair dryer.

INEXPENSIVE

Kajita   Two pug-nosed dogs (real) in a cage by the front door and a mongoose, a cobra, and birds (stuffed) in the lobby greet you at this friendly, family-run establishment, a member of the Japanese Inn Group. It has a central location, just a 10-minute walk to the castle grounds and a 5-minute walk to the streetcar that will take you onward to Suizenji Garden. Tatami rooms, named after flowers, are simple but clean. If you call, you'll most likely be picked up at the station, though if no car is available, someone will wait for you at the bus stop.

1–2–7 Shinmachi, Kumamoto 860-0004. © **096/353-1546.** Fax 096/353-1546. 10 units (none with bathroom). ¥4,000 ($33) single; ¥7,600 ($63) double; ¥10,500 ($87.50) triple. Breakfast ¥700 ($5.85) extra; dinner ¥2,000 ($17) extra. Bus: from Kumamoto Station to Shinmachi stop, then a 2-min. walk. Take the narrow road between a bank and a big health center (with round windows) and then take the 1st left. It's on the left. **Amenities:** Coin-op washer/dryer. *In room:* Coin-op A/C (¥100/85¢ per hr.), TV, hot-water pot with tea, no phone.

Tokyu Inn   Right in the middle of downtown near department stores and shopping, this business hotel is connected to a 24-hour convenience store and offers mostly single rooms, cramped but containing everything you need. Location is this hotel's main selling point.

7–25 Shinshigai, Kumamoto 860-0803. ℂ **096/322-0109.** Fax 096/322-3050. 138 units. ¥6,500–¥7,500 ($54–$62.50) single; ¥10,300–¥11,000 ($86–$92) twin. AE, DC, JCB, MC, V. Streetcar: no. 2 to Karashimacho, then a 1-min. walk. Next to the Sunroad Shinshigai covered shopping arcade. **Amenities:** 1 restaurant (Western). *In room:* A/C, TV, fridge, hot-water pot with tea, hair dryer.

WHERE TO DINE

Kumamoto's specialties include *dengaku* (tofu, and sometimes taro and fish, coated with bean paste and grilled on a fire), *karashi renkon* (lotus root that has been boiled, filled with a mixture of bean paste and mustard, and then deep-fried), and *basashi* (raw horse meat sliced thin and then dipped in soy sauce flavored with ginger or garlic).

EXPENSIVE

⑳ **Koshintei** ★★★ *Finds* KAISEKI   Dine here to pretend you're living in a past era. Located near the New Sky Hotel between Kumamoto Station and downtown, Koshintei is one of several establishments housed in a unique complex comprised of three Edo-Period buildings, including the eclectically decorated Cafe Shingen, an inexpensive Japanese restaurant, and a shop of European antiques. Koshintei is a traditional Japanese house with private antique-filled tatami rooms, several of which face the river. There's no additional room fee, but note that there must be two or more of you to dine here. There are three choices for kaiseki dinners, costing ¥7,000 ($58), ¥8,500 ($71), and ¥10,000 ($83); each is delivered by a kimono-clad waitress, who serves in traditional style, kneeling each time she opens and closes the doors. Meals change monthly to match the season and come exquisitely arranged on beautiful dishes, also chosen with great care to match the season and the food. Lunches are quite reasonably priced.

15 Nakatoji-machi. ℂ **096/322-4231.** Reservations required. Lunch ¥3,500–¥5,000 ($29–$42); dinner ¥7,000–¥10,000 ($58–$83). AE, MC, V. Daily 11am–2pm and 5–11pm. Streetcar: Gofukumachi, then a 1-min. walk in the direction of downtown to the 1st stoplight and fire station, turning left and then left again.

㉑ **Senri** ★★ LOCAL SPECIALTIES/VARIED JAPANESE   You can try Kumamoto's local dishes at this restaurant right in Suizenji Garden. The menu features set meals and is in Japanese only. For lunch, you can choose main dishes like eel, river fish, or tempura, served with side dishes of a vegetable, soup, rice, and tea. Or order the Kyodo-ryori Course, which includes local specialties such as fried lotus, basashi and dengaku. Dinners include the same items as lunch plus extra dishes. Dining is in small tatami rooms; choice rooms face the garden.

Suizenji Garden. ℂ **096/381-1415.** Reservations recommended. Set dinners ¥4,500–¥6,000 ($37.50–$50); set lunches ¥2,100–¥3,150 ($17.50–$26). No credit cards. Daily 11am–2:30pm and 5–8pm (last order). Streetcar: no. 2 to Suizenji-Koen-mae; Senri has its own entrance to the right of Suizenji Garden's main gate.

MODERATE

㉒ **Aoyagi** ★ LOCAL SPECIALTIES   Everyone in Kumamoto knows this restaurant, located in the downtown area just off the Shimotori covered

---

Tips **A Note on Japanese Symbols**

Many establishments and attractions in Japan do not have signs in Roman (English-language) letters. Those that don't are indicated in this guide with an oval with a number that corresponds to a number in appendix C showing the Japanese symbols. Thus, to find the Japanese symbol for, say, **Koshintei** (above), refer to no. 220 in appendix C.

shopping arcade. It has four floors of dining with seating on tatami or at low tables with leg wells. There's a plastic-food display case outside its front door, showing dishes of sushi, basashi, eel, and *kamameshi* (rice casseroles). Kaiseki and Kyodo-ryori set meals begin at ¥5,000 ($42); a Japanese menu shows pictures of the courses. You can also take out box lunches of sushi for ¥1,000 ($8.35) and up.

1–2–10 Shimotori. ✆ 096/353-0311. Set lunches ¥980–¥3,800 ($8.15–$32); set dinners ¥1,500–¥7,000 ($12.50–$58). AE, JCB, MC, V. Daily 11:30am–10pm. Streetcar: Torichosuji (2 min.). Walk through the Shimotori shopping arcade 2 blocks to Sannenzakadori St. (just past Daiei) and turn right; it's in the 2nd block on the right.

(201) **Gozan** ★★ *Finds* JAPANESE CROSSOVER   Don't miss this surreal mix of ancient Japan and modern kitsch. Although essentially another drinking establishment, Gozan is anything but typical; this is clear as soon as you see its entrance, decorated according to the season—cherry blossoms in spring, maple leaves in fall, wisteria in summer—but always in plastic. Inside, plastic bamboo mixes with tile roofs and faux mud walls, New Age/kabuki music plays in the background, and a volcano in the middle of the room erupts in lit optic fibers. A giant screen shows festivals and scenery from around Kumamoto Prefecture, as well as classic American movies such as *Casablanca,* without the sound. Come here just to check out the decor—even the bathrooms are interesting. Dishes on the English menu range from basashi and sashimi to yakitori, Kumamoto beef, seafood, and agedashi tofu, but it's easiest to order one of the set Japanese or Western courses (there must be at least 2 of you to order it). Because of its low prices, Gozan attracts a mostly young clientele.

Taigeki Kaikan Building. basement, 4–1 Tedorihoncho. ✆ 096/351-2869. Reservations recommended. Set dinners ¥3,000–¥5,000 ($25–$42). AE, JCB, MC, V. Daily 5pm–midnight (last order 11:15pm). Streetcar: Torichosuji (1 min.). In front of the tram stop, in the basement of a building with a pachinko parlor on the ground floor.

(224) **Shingen Chikai** ★★ *Finds* KAISEKI   Part of the Edo-Period complex that also houses Koshintei (see above), this basement restaurant is decorated with antiques, stone walls, a low ceiling with heavy wood crossbeams, and sophisticated black lacquered tables. It offers reasonably priced kaiseki dinners and an obento for lunch, as well as an a la carte menu written only in Japanese that includes tempura, soba, and basashi. After your meal, you may want to stop for a drink at **Cafe Shingen** on the first floor (open daily 10am–10:30pm), a cafe like none other with its two-story high ceiling, stained-glass windows, antiques, and display cases of chinaware (which is for sale), all of which conspire to give it a flea-market atmosphere. From 8pm, a piano player serenades on a century-old piano. Upstairs is a shop specializing in European antiques. All in all, not your usual dining experience.

15 Nakatoji-machi. ✆ 096/354-9583. Set lunch ¥1,500 ($12.50); set dinners ¥3,500 and ¥4,000 ($29 and $33). AE, MC, V. Daily 11am–2pm and 5–10:30pm (last order). Streetcar: Gofukumachi (1 min.). Walk in the direction of downtown to the 1st stoplight and fire station, turn left and then left again.

INEXPENSIVE

Fontana di Otani ITALIAN/CONTINENTAL   This very casual coffee shop has a very convenient location in Kumamoto's best hotel, right beside Kumamoto Station. Its menu features lighter fare such as pizza, pasta, curry dishes, risotto, and sandwiches, as well as more substantial dishes like grilled chicken, roasted lamb with thyme, steak, and seafood. There are also special seasonal menus.

Hotel New Otani Kumamoto, 1–13–1 Kasuga. ✆ 096/326-1111. Main dishes ¥1,000–¥2,000 ($8.35–$17); set lunch ¥1,300 ($11); set dinner ¥3,500 ($29). AE, DC, JCB, MC, V Daily 11:30am–10pm. A 1-min. walk from Kumamoto Station; turn right out of the station.

225 **Goemon** VARIED JAPANESE/LOCAL SPECIALTIES   Located downtown near the Shimotori shopping arcade in a building packed with other bars and restaurants, this is technically a drinking establishment, but it serves a variety of inexpensive dishes as well. The place is popular with a lively crowd, especially on weekends. A la carte dishes include dengaku, sashimi, fried lotus, basashi, fried shrimp, pizza, steak, tofu, and much more. The menu is in Japanese only, but there's a plastic-food display case. It's all tatami seating in this rustic place, but some of the tables have leg wells underneath for your feet. Take off your shoes at the front door and deposit them in a locker, just as you would at a bathhouse.

1–7–3 Shimotori. ☎ **096/354-2266.** Main dishes ¥350–¥950 ($2.90–$7.90); set dinners from ¥2,000 ($17). JCB, MC, V. Daily 5pm–midnight. Streetcar: Kumamotojo-mae (3 min.). Walk 2 blocks east on Ginzadori, turn left on Sakaedori, and then take the next right (a parking lot is on the corner); it will be on your right.

226 **Kimura-so** *Value* EEL   Just a few steps away from Senri (above) in Suizenji Garden, this restaurant specializes in *unagi* (eel) but also offers set courses with river fish, basashi, and grilled shrimp as the main dish. There's a display case outside. The best time to come here is April through October in fine weather, when you can dine on tatami in an open-air pavilion built over a pond with a partial view of the garden. In winter, diners are relegated to an ordinary tatami room with no view.

Suizenji Garden. ☎ **096/384-1864.** Reservations required. Set meal ¥2,100–¥3,150 ($17.50–$26). Prices include tax and service charge. No credit cards. Thurs–Tues noon–8pm. Streetcar: no. 2 to Suizenji-Koen-mae. If Suizenji Garden's main gate is closed, enter through the small side door to the left of the garden's main gate and then turn right.

227 **Tateki** 🗡 KUSHIAGE   Located on a street filled with striptease clubs (be sure to match the kanji in appendix C with the sign outside the door—otherwise you'll get more than skewered food), Tateki serves *kushiage,* or skewered foods. Although kushiage isn't unusual cuisine in Japan, this restaurant's method of cooking and serving it is—instead of counter seating, behind which the cook prepares your food, here you sit on tatami while a waiter in a beret kneels at your own personal hibachi and grills your meal right in front of you. The least-expensive set dinner comes with 10 sticks of meat and vegetables, appetizer, salad, and soba; the other two set dinners add one or two sticks along with more side dishes. The set lunch consists of seven sticks, two sauces, rice, soup, appetizer, and salad.

Kaishika Bldg., 1–11–8 Shimotori. ☎ **096/325-4989.** Set lunch ¥1,000 ($8.35); set dinners ¥2,000–¥4,000 ($17–$33). No credit cards. Daily 11:30am–11pm. Streetcar: Kumamotojo-mae (5 min.). Walk east on Ginza Dori 3 blocks, turn right into the Shimotori shopping arcade, and after 1 block turn right (unmarked, but the street is called Korinjidori); it will be on the left in the 2nd building next to an eyeglass shop.

7 Nagasaki ★★

1,320km (825 miles) W of Tokyo; 152km (95 miles) SW of Fukuoka

Unlike Kumamoto or Kagoshima, **Nagasaki** doesn't have a castle or a famous landscaped garden. Its charm is much more subtle. Many people in Japan—including foreign residents—consider this city to be one of the country's most beautiful. It's a place of hills rising from the deep, U-shaped harbor, of houses perched on terraced slopes, of small streets and distinctive neighborhoods, and of people extremely proud of their hometown. Without a doubt, Nagasaki is one of Japan's most livable cities, despite its population of almost half a million.

Nagasaki

Honrenji Temple

NAGASAKI PARK

Ken-ei Bus Station

Shofukuji Temple

Museum of Art

Nagasaki Station

Central Post Office

Nishi Nakamachi

City Hall

Umamachi Dori

Nagasaki River

Chamber of Commerce

Inauomachi Dori

GOTO MACHI

Kofukuji Temple

KOZEN MACHI

City Hall Street

Manzaimachi Dori

Fukuromachi Dori

Megane-bashi

Kodaiji Temple

Ohato Dori

Ohato Pier (Nagaski Port Terminal)

Kanko Dori

Prefecture

Naitajima Gowa

Hamanomachi

Kajiyamachi

Dalon

Sofukuji Temple

DEJIMA MACHI

Nagasaki Bus Station

Nagasaki Harbor

MOTOKAGO MACHI

Oura Gawa

JAPAN

Tokyo

Nagasaki

‡ Church
⊠ Post Office
▭▭ Railway
ⓘ Tourist Info

ATTRACTIONS

Confucius Shrine & the Historical Museum of China **8**

Dejima **6**

Dutch Slope **7**

Glover Garden **9**

Nagasaki Atomic Bomb Museum **1**

Nishizaka Hill **2**

Peace Park (Hirano-machi) **1**

Sofukuji Temple **5**

Spectacles Bridge **4**

Suwa Shrine **3**

Capital of Nagasaki Prefecture, Nagasaki is also perhaps Japan's most cosmopolitan city with a unique blend of outside cultures interwoven into its history, architecture, food, and festivals.

Nagasaki, which is located on the northwest coast of Kyushu, opened its harbor to European vessels in 1571 and became a port of call for Portuguese and Dutch ships; Chinese merchants soon followed and set up their own community. Along with traders came St. Francis Xavier and other Christian missionaries, primarily from Portugal and Spain, who found many converts among the local Japanese. During Japan's more than 200 years of isolation, only Nagasaki was allowed to conduct trade with outsiders and thus served as the nation's window on the rest of the world. Even today, Japanese come to Nagasaki for a dose of the city's intermingled cultures.

All of the city's major attractions are connected to its diversified, and sometimes tragic, past. Nagasaki is best known as the second city—and, I hope, the last city—to be destroyed by an atomic bomb.

ESSENTIALS

GETTING THERE **By Plane** **ANA, JAL,** and **JAS** serve Nagasaki with 10 flights daily from Tokyo's Haneda Airport. Flight time is 1 hour and 45 minutes, and the fare is around ¥33,000 ($275). Airport limousine buses connect with the Ken-ei Bus Terminal across from Nagasaki Station in about 1 hour and cost ¥1,200 ($10).

By Train Trains depart Hakata Station in **Fukuoka** approximately every half hour, arriving at Nagasaki Station a little more than 2 hours later and costing ¥4,910 ($41). It's a 3-hour train ride from **Kumamoto.** From **Tokyo,** take the Shinkansen bullet train to Hakata Station and transfer there for a train to Nagasaki; travel time is 8½ to 9½ hours, depending on the type of train and connections; the fare is ¥24,180 ($201.50) for an unreserved seat.

VISITOR INFORMATION Pick up the "Nagasaki and Unzen" leaflet from the Tourist Information Center in Tokyo, Kyoto, or Kansai or Narita international airports (see "Visitor Information," in chapters 3, 7, and 8). In Nagasaki, the **Nagasaki City Tourist Information Office** (℃ **095/823-3631;** open daily 8am–7pm, to 5:30pm mid-Nov through Feb) is located just outside the main exit of Nagasaki Station. Information on all of Nagasaki Prefecture (including Huis Ten Bosch and Unzen; described later in this chapter), is available just across the street from the train station at the **Nagasaki Prefectural Tourist Federation** (℃ **095/826-9407;** open daily 9am–5:30pm) on the second floor of the Ken-ei Bus Terminal.

ORIENTATION & GETTING AROUND Along with Kobe and Sapporo, Nagasaki is one of Japan's most navigable cities, with lots of signs in English pointing the way to attractions. City layout follows natural boundaries set by the Urakami River, the long and narrow Nagasaki Bay, and the many steep-sloped hills. **Nagasaki Station** isn't located in the downtown part of the city; rather, most nightspots, shops, and restaurants are located southeast of the station, clustered around an area that contains **Shianbashi Dori** and **Kanko Dori** **streets** and the **Hamanomachi** covered shopping arcade. Farther south is **Glover Garden,** where many foreigners settled in the 19th century. Nearby is **Hollanders Slope** (*Oranda-zaka,* also referred to as Dutch Slope), undoubtedly Nagasaki's prettiest street, a cobbled lane lined with wooden houses built by former European residents (a century ago, the people of Nagasaki referred to all

Europeans as Hollanders). **Peace Park** and its atomic-bomb museum are located north of Nagasaki Station on the other end of town.

By Streetcar   Trams have been hauling passengers in Nagasaki since 1915 and, from the looks of things, have changed little in the ensuing years; they're still the easiest—and most charming—way to get around. Four lines run through the heart of the city, and most stops are written in English. The streetcars are ancient one-wagon affairs, retired to Nagasaki from other cities that considered them too slow and old-fashioned—and yet, since streetcars have their own lanes of traffic here, during rush hour they're usually the fastest things on the road. It costs a mere ¥100 (85¢) to ride one no matter how far you go; pay at the front when you get off. You are allowed to transfer to another line only at **Tsukimachi Station** (ask the driver for a *noritsugi,* a transfer ticket, when you disembark the first tram); otherwise, you must buy a separate ticket each time you board. If you need change from, say, a ¥1,000 bill, you may ask the driver when he's waiting at a red light and isn't busy, an endearing anachronism in high-tech Japan. To avoid the hassle of individual tickets, you can also buy a ¥500 ($4.15) **pass** at both tourist offices mentioned above and at major hotels that allows unlimited rides for 1 day. Trams run from about 6:15am to 11:30pm.

On Foot   With the exception of Peace Park, you can also get around Nagasaki easily on foot, which is certainly the most intimate way to experience the city and its atmosphere. You can walk from the Hamanomachi downtown shopping district to Glover Garden, for example, in 20 minutes, passing Chinatown, Dejima, and the Dutch Slope on the way. Shianbashi Dori, located just off the streetcar stop of the same name, is just a minute's walk from the Hamanomachi shopping arcade.

By Bus   Nagasaki also has buses, but destinations are in Japanese only, and who knows where the heck they're going? Stick to the streetcars.

EXPLORING THE CITY
NISHIZAKA HILL

After Nagasaki opened its port to European vessels, missionaries came to the city to convert the Japanese to Christianity. Gradually, however, the Japanese rulers began to fear that these Christian missionaries would try to exert political and financial influence through their converts. Who was to say that conversion to Christianity wasn't just the first step toward colonization? So in 1587, the shogun Toyotomi Hideyoshi officially banned Christianity. In 1597, 26 male Christians (20 Japanese and 6 foreigners) were arrested in Kyoto and Osaka, were marched through the snow to Nagasaki, and were crucified on **Nishizaka Hill** as examples of what would happen to offenders. Through the ensuing decades, there were more than 600 documented cases of Japanese, Portuguese, and Spanish Christians being put to death in the Nishizaka area. In 1862, the 26 martyrs were sainted by the pope.

Today, on Nishizaka Hill, about a 4-minute walk north of Nagasaki Station, there's the Monument to the 26 Saints, with statues of the martyrs carved in stone relief. Immediately striking is that three of them look very young; indeed, the youngest was only 12. Behind the relief is a small **museum** (© **095/ 822-6000;** open daily 9am–5pm) housing artifacts relating to the history of Christianity in Japan, including paintings and drawings of the 26 saints, letters, and religious objects, as well as remains of Japanese martyrs returned to Nagasaki in 1995 after more than 380 years interment in Macau. Perhaps most amazing about the history of Christianity in Japan is that the religion was practiced secretly by the faithful throughout Japan's isolation policy, surviving more than 200 years underground without the benefits of a church or clergy. Admission to the museum, which can be toured in a half hour, is ¥250 ($2.10) for adults, ¥150 ($1.25) for junior-high and high-school students, and ¥100 (85¢) for children.

DEJIMA

When the Tokugawa shogunate adopted a national policy of isolation in the 1630s, only Nagasaki was allowed to remain open as a port of trade with foreigners. Since the Portuguese and Spaniards were associated with the outlawed Christian religion, they were expelled in 1639; only the Dutch and the Chinese were allowed to remain and continue trading. In 1641, all the Dutch were confined to a tiny, fan-shaped artificial island called Dejima, where they remained for 218 years (at any one time, about 15 Dutchmen were in residence; no wives were allowed). This was Japan's only official contact with the outside world; the director of Dejima was required to travel to Edo every 1 to 4 years to report to the shogun. Otherwise, the only people allowed to cross the bridge into the Dutch community were Japanese prostitutes and traders.

Today, after having long become part of the mainland through land reclamation and after decades of languishing as little more than a streetcar stop, Dejima is undergoing ambitious restoration with plans to rebuild the island as it was in the early 19th century. After alighting at either the Dejima or Tsukimachi streetcar stop (Dejima lies between them, about a 1-minute walk from each), head for the outdoor model showing how the island looked when the Dutch lived here. Across the street, in a blue, colonial-style wooden building constructed in 1877 as Japan's first Protestant seminary, is the **Dejima Museum of History,** 6–3 Dejima-machi (© **095/821-7200;** open daily 9am–5pm), which gives an excellent account of the historical development of the island, what life was like for the Dutch who lived here, and how the trading system worked. Nearby, in a replica of an old stone warehouse, is the museum's annex with folk objects from Holland and artifacts unearthed during excavations on Dejima. Admission to both museums, which can be seen in about an hour, is ¥300 ($2.50) for adults and ¥150 ($1.25) for children. Also nearby is the **Dejima Theater,** with a free, 12-minute film on the Dejima, though in Japanese only. Work is underway to add other buildings and attractions to the area.

GLOVER GARDEN & VICINITY

Glover Garden ★★   After Japan opened its doors to the rest of the world and established Nagasaki as one of a handful of international ports, Nagasaki emerged as one of the most progressive cities in the country, with many foreign residents. A number of Western-style houses were built during the Meiji Period (1868–1912), many of them on a hill overlooking Nagasaki and the harbor. Today, that hill has been developed into Glover Garden, which showcases nine Meiji-Era buildings and homes on lushly landscaped grounds. Some of the structures stand on their original site; others have been moved here and given new life. The stone and clapboard houses have sweeping verandas, Western parlors, the most modern conveniences of the time, and Japanese-style roofs. Most famous is **Glover Mansion,** Japan's oldest Western-style house, built in this location in 1863 and romanticized as the home of Madame Butterfly, the fictitious, tragic heroine of Puccini's opera. Married to a Japanese woman (and much more faithful than his Puccini counterpart), Thomas Glover was a remarkable

Scotsman who, among other things, financially backed and managed ship-repair yards in Nagasaki, brought the first steam locomotive to Japan, sold guns and ships, and exported tea.

Among the other buildings, a former boys' academy houses photographs of old Nagasaki, including portraits of foreigners who used to live here. The Mitsubishi Dock House, built in 1896 to serve as a rest house for ship crews, offers great views of the harbor. One of Nagasaki's first Western restaurants is now a quaint cafe. And don't miss the **Nagasaki Traditional Performing Arts Museum,** which displays floats and dragons used in Nagasaki's most famous festival, the Okunchi Festival, held in October. The museum's highlight is an excellent film of the colorful parade, featuring massive ships deftly maneuvered on wheels and Chinese dragon dances.

Incidentally, upon entering the grounds, you'll see a moving escalator carved into the hillside. Although an outdoor escalator in a garden devoted to Meiji-Era buildings might seem a little bizarre, the Japanese point out that it's there for the benefit of senior citizens who might find the climb up the hill too strenuous. At any rate, the views from here are among the best in the city. Plan on spending 2 hours here if you want to see everything.

8–1 Minami Yamate-machi. ✆ 095/822-8223. Admission ¥600 ($5) adults, ¥300 ($2.50) high-school students, ¥180 ($1.50) junior-high and elementary students. Daily 8am–6pm (to 9:30pm July 20 to mid-Oct). Streetcar: Oura Tenshudoshita (7 min.); cross the bridge, turn left after the Tokyu Hotel, and walk uphill following signs.

PEACE PARK (HIRANO-MACHI) 🏮🏮

On August 9, 1945, at 11:02am, American forces dropped an atomic bomb over Nagasaki, 3 days after they had dropped one on Hiroshima. The bomb, which exploded 1,600 feet above ground, destroyed about a third of the city, killed an estimated 74,000 people, and injured 75,000 more. Today, Peace Park, located north of Nagasaki Station, serves as a reminder of that day of destruction with a museum, memorials, and statues. Nagasaki's citizens are among the most vigorous peace activists in the world; a peace demonstration is held in Peace Park every year on the anniversary of the bombing.

Near the Nagasaki Atomic Bomb Museum (see below) is a black pillar marking the exact epicenter of the atomic blast; a black casket contains names of the bomb's victims. Ironically, the bomb exploded almost directly over the Urakami Catholic Church, of which a fragmented wall remains. A few minutes' farther north, separated by several streets, is the largest part of Peace Park (the nearest streetcar station to this section is Matsuyama). It occupies the site of a former prison; all 134 inmates died in the blast. A fountain is dedicated to the wounded who begged for water; many of them died thirsty. Statues donated by countries from around the world line a pathway leading to Peace Statue, a 30-foot-high statue of a male deity. One hand points to the sky from where the bomb came (meant as a warning?), and the other hand points to the horizon (representing hope? the future?).

Nagasaki Atomic Bomb Museum 🏮🏮🏮   Visiting this museum, with displays in English, is by far the most important thing to do in Peace Park. After paying admission, guests enter an empty, glass-dome foyer with a spiraling ramp—bringing to mind, perhaps, the atomic mushroom cloud? This is followed by photographs of the city as it looked before the bomb, accompanied by the ominous, loud ticking of a clock. Displays illustrate events leading up to the bombing, the devastation afterward, Nagasaki's postwar restoration, the history of nuclear weapons, and the subsequent peace movement. Objects, photos, and artifacts graphically depict the bomb's devastation, including a clock stopped precisely at 11:02am, personal belongings ranging from mangled spectacles to a student's singed trousers, hand bones encased in a clump of melted glass, and photographs of victims, including a dead mother and her baby and a 14-year-old whose face has been hideously burned. On video, survivors describe their own personal experiences on that fateful day. The museum is by no means pleasant, but something every concerned individual should see—plan on at least an hour here. (If, however, you've already seen the much larger Peace Memorial Museum in Hiroshima, this one will be largely repetitive.)

7–8 Hirano-machi. ☎ 095/844-1231. Admission ¥200 ($1.65) adults, ¥100 (85¢) children. Daily 8:30am–5:30pm. Streetcar: 1 or 3 to Hamaguchi-machi (3 min.).

TEMPLES, SHRINES & BRIDGES

Confucius Shrine and Museum of Chinese History (Koshibyo) ✫   Chinese residents living in Nagasaki built this colorful, red-and-yellow shrine in 1893, aided by the Ch'ing Dynasty in China. This is the only Confucian shrine outside China built by the Chinese. In fact, the land upon which it stands belongs to China and is administered by the Chinese embassy in Tokyo. The main hall contains a statue of Confucius, attended by courtyard statues representing his 72 disciples. More fascinating, however, is the small Museum of Chinese History located behind the main hall with bronze jars, pottery, wooden food boxes, painted enamel vases, Buddha statues, and other treasures on loan from Beijing's National Museum of Chinese History and Beijing Palace's Museum of Historical Treasures. You can see everything in about 45 minutes.

10–36 Oura-machi. ☎ 095/824-4022. Admission ¥525 ($4.35) adults, ¥420 ($3.50) students, ¥315 ($2.65) children. Daily 8:30am–5pm. Streetcar: Oura Tenshudoshita (3 min.). Walk inland (continuing in the same direction of your streetcar if coming from downtown), turning left when you reach a small playground on your right. Near the Dutch Slope.

Sofukuji Temple ✫   Sofukuji is Nagasaki's most famous temple. Distinctly Chinese with its Ming architecture, it dates back to 1629 when it was founded by Chinese residents. Its Buddha Hall, painted a brilliant red and decorated with Chinese lanterns, was designed and cut in China before transportation to Nagasaki. Erected in 1646, it's the oldest building in Nagasaki and is a National Treasure. Another National Treasure is the temple's beautiful gate, which employs a complex jointing system and features brightly painted detailing. But most fascinating, in my opinion, is the temple's gigantic cauldron, built by a priest during a terrible famine in the 1680s to cook enough porridge to feed more than 3,000 people a day.

Kayjiya-machi. ☎ 095/823-2645. Admission ¥300 ($2.50) adults, ¥200 ($1.65) students, ¥100 (85¢) children. Daily 8am–5pm. A 7-min. walk from the Hamanomachi downtown shopping district. Streetcar: Shokakuji-shita (4 min.); head back toward the bay, turning right at Sofukuji St.

Spectacles Bridge (Megane-bashi)   In addition to the temples described above, the Chinese also left their mark on Nagasaki with several bridges. Most famous is the so-called Spectacles Bridge, built in 1634 by a Chinese Zen priest. It's the oldest stone-arched bridge in Japan and is named after the reflection its two arches cast in the water; I wouldn't know, however, because I've never seen the Nakashima River larger than a trickle except once, when it rushed angrily after a heavy rain. The river does occasionally flood, as in 1982 when it wiped out several old bridges. These have now been reconstructed, along with a promenade complete with benches and children's playgrounds. Since Megane-bashi is one of Nagasaki's most photographed objects and since it's only a 5-minute walk from the Hamanomachi shopping arcade, you might wish to come here with some take-out sushi and enjoy a picnic.

Streetcar: Nigiwai-bashi or Kokaidomae.

Suwa Shrine   Although Nagasaki's famous Okunchi Festival has Chinese roots, it's celebrated at this Shinto shrine, built to promote Shintoism at a time when the feudal government was trying to stamp out Christianity. Today, with a good location on top of a hill with views over the city, the shrine symbolizes better than anything else the spiritual heart of the Japanese community. When Japanese women turn 33 and men turn 40, they come here to pray for good health and a long life. Newborns are brought 30 days after their birth to receive special blessings and then again for their 3rd, 5th, and 7th birthdays. On New Year's, the grounds are packed with those seeking good fortune in the coming year. People also visit to ask the shrine's many deities for favors—good marriage, safe childbirth, good health, and more. You can even have your automobile blessed here. The shrine sells fortunes in English. If you're satisfied with your fortune, keep it; if you're not, tie it to the branch of a tree and the fortune is conveniently negated.

18–15 Kami-Nishiyama. (℃ 095/824-0445. Free admission. Open 24 hours. Streetcar: Suwa Jinja-mae (4 min.); take the underground passage and follow the signs up many stone stairs.

CRUISING NAGASAKI'S HARBOR

If you're interested in seeing the results of Nagasaki's history as a trading port, take to the waters on one of two cruises offered by the **Yamasakaiun Company** (℃ **095/824-0088** or 822-5002). The 60-minute cruises depart three times daily throughout the year and cost ¥1,980 ($16.50) for adults and ¥990 ($8.25) for children. They pass a fishing port, huge ships at moor and in dry dock, and the Mitsubishi shipyards, where battleships and cruisers are built and repaired. The 90-minute cruises depart once a day March through November and cost ¥2,980 ($25) for adults and ¥1,490 ($21) for children. They cover the above sights and also take a spin around Battleship Island, developed by Mitsubishi in 1890 to exploit coral for energy use. Once home to 5,000 people but deserted since 1974, the concrete town stands eerily vacant and in disrepair. Commentary is in English, and boats are small, seating 40 to 100 people. Reservations are a must, with departures from both **Ohato Port Terminal** (also called Nagasaki Port Terminal; a 5-min. walk from the Ohato streetcar stop) and **Matsugae Pier** (a 2-min. walk from the Oura Kaigan Dori streetcar stop).

Another boat company, **Yasuda Sangyo Kisen Company** (℃ **095/ 821-0010**), offers 60- and 90-minute cruises departing four to five times daily from Ohato Port Terminal mid-March through December and costing ¥1,200 ($10) and ¥1,500 ($12.50) respectively; children pay half price. Routes approximate those given above, but the difference here is that meals are available on board, including a la carte dishes, obento lunch boxes starting at ¥1,050 ($8.75), and do-it-yourself barbecues.

A SIDE TRIP TO HUIS TEN BOSCH ★★★

If you're ready for some R&R but have only one day to spare, perhaps **Huis Ten Bosch,** in Sasebo (℃ **0956/27-0001**), will do the trick. This replica of a 17th-century Dutch village boasts tree-lined canals, brick houses, city squares, brick-paved roads, churches, museums, shops, restaurants, hotels, and even stately, private homes—proof at how adept the Japanese are at imitation. Many of the buildings are faithful reproductions of an original back in the Netherlands; even the bricks were imported from Holland. Although I was a bit skeptical about visiting an imitation Dutch village in Japan, I must admit the grounds and craftsmanship are beautifully done. Even Holland itself isn't this pristine. In fact, I consider it the country's premier theme park designed for adults. Although there are some rides and attractions, this is not an amusement park in disguise.

Highlights include **Paleis Huis Ten Bosch,** a replica of the formal residence of Queen Beatrix of the Netherlands, which contains an art gallery, period rooms showing how upper-class Dutch lived, a baroque garden, **porcelain** and **ornamental glass museums,** and **theaters** that re-create a ship's voyage from Holland to Japan in the 17th century and the flooding of a Dutch town. There are also cruises of Omura Bay and the village's canals; parades, dances, and other events daily; more than 60 shops; and more than 50 restaurants (including open-air beer and wine gardens and an e-mail cafe). The park is so vast that there are shuttle buses and other forms of transportation, but to really feel like you're in Holland, rent one of the park's bicycles.

A one-day pass to Huis Ten Bosch costs ¥4,800 ($40) for adults, ¥3,600 ($30) for children 12 to 17, and ¥2,600 ($22) for children 4 to 11 (under 3 are free). The best time to visit is in the spring, during—what else?—tulip season. Open March through November, daily 9am to 9:30pm (last entrance 8:30pm); December through February, 9am to 8:30pm (last entrance 7:30pm).

To reach Huis Ten Bosch, take the **JR Sea Side Liner Express** from Nagasaki Station to Huis Ten Bosch Station (1 hr. and 20 min.); the train departs every hour and costs ¥1,430 ($12) one-way. Or take a **bus** from the Ken-ei Bus Terminal (across from Nagasaki Station) to Huis Ten Bosch (65 min.); there are more than 15 departures daily, and the cost is ¥1,350 ($11) one-way.

WHERE TO STAY

Nagasaki has very reasonably priced hotels. Peak times, when a few accommodations may raise their rates, are Golden Week (Apr 29–May 5), Obon (mid-Aug), and the Okunchi Festival (Oct 7–9).

EXPENSIVE

Hotel New Nagasaki ✦✦   One of Nagasaki's deluxe hotels, the Hotel New Nagasaki has a convenient location right next to the train station. Its large, marbled lobby is light and airy, and its rooms are among the city's largest. Some even offer a view of Nagasaki's busy port, and most have been upgraded for Internet access. Add the hotel's wide range of facilities, and you have what amounts to one of Nagasaki's best choices.

14–5 Daikoku-machi, Nagasaki 850-0057. ⓒ 095/826-8000. Fax 095/823-2000. 149 units. ¥18,000 ($150) single; ¥24,000 ($200) double/twin; ¥26,000 ($217) executive double/twin. AE, DC, JCB, MC, V. A 1-min. walk from Nagasaki Station to the right. **Amenities:** 8 restaurants, 1 bar; well-equipped fitness club with indoor lap pool (and retractable roof) and sauna (fee: ¥2,000/$17); concierge; art gallery; salon; room service (7am–10pm); in-room massage; same-day laundry/dry cleaning service; nonsmoking rooms; executive-level rooms. *In room:* A/C, cable TV with 40 channels for music and radio, dataport (not all rooms), minibar, hot-water pot with tea, hair dryer.

Nagasaki Prince Hotel ✦✦✦   This is one of Nagasaki's finest hotels. Its marbled lobby, decorated with large Oriental vases, centers on an indoor pond and has a distinct Asian flair. Rooms, which combine colonial-style decor with Chinese accents, offer the usual comforts; unique is the ladies-only wing with amenities geared toward female travelers and a women's lounge complete with sofas and free tea and coffee. There are only three single rooms in the hotel,

---

Tips   A Note on Japanese Symbols

Many establishments and attractions in Japan do not have signs in Roman (English-language) letters. Those that don't are indicated in this guide with an oval with a number that corresponds to a number in appendix C showing the Japanese symbols. Thus, to find the Japanese symbol for, say, **Sakamoto-ya** (below), refer to no. 228 in appendix C.

---

though discounts are given for single use of twins and doubles. Regrettably, none of the rooms boast much of a view; for that you'll need to visit the 15th-floor Shanghai Sky Lounge with its panoramic vistas.

2–26 Takara-machi, Nagasaki 850-0045. ✆ **800/542-8686** in the U.S. and Canada, or 095/821-1111. Fax 095/823-4309. www.princehotels.co.jp/. 183 units. ¥15,000 ($125) single; ¥24,000–¥29,000 ($200–$242) double; ¥24,000–¥35,000 ($200–$292) twin. AE, DC, JCB, MC, V. Streetcar: Takaramachi (1 min.). Or an 8-min. walk north of Nagasaki Station in the direction of Peace Park. **Amenities:** 3 restaurants (Japanese, Chinese, steak/seafood), 2 lounges; Japanese roof garden; concierge; salon; room service (7am–11pm); in-room massage; same-day laundry/dry cleaning service; nonsmoking rooms. *In room:* A/C, bilingual satellite TV with pay movies, minibar, hot-water pot with tea, hair dryer, large safe.

(228) **Sakamoto-ya** ★★★ *Finds*   This beautiful 107-year-old ryokan (Nagasaki's oldest) right in the heart of the city is a wonderful place, especially when you consider how rare traditional ryokan are nowadays in major Japanese cities. Most of the rooms have a Japanese-style bathtub made of wood, as well as traditional artwork on the walls. The best room is the Pine Room (Matsu No Ma), which even has its own miniature private garden with a tiny shrine. Rates vary according to the room and the meals served; you may order a *shippoku* dinner, a Nagasaki specialty consisting of a variety of dishes showing European and Chinese influences, for ¥5,000 ($42) more. Western breakfasts are also served on request.

2–13 Kanaya-machi, Nagasaki 850-0037. ✆ **095/826-8211.** Fax 095/825-5944. 19 units (13 with bathroom). ¥15,000–¥25,000 ($125–$208) per person. Rates include breakfast, dinner, and service charge. AE, DC, JCB, MC, V. A 10-min. walk SE of Nagasaki Station. Turn right out of the station and follow the streetcar tracks south past the 1st tram stop; turn left after Nishi-Nihon Bank (just before the stoplight), walk up a slight incline, and turn left at the blinking light. It will be on your left. **Amenities:** In-room massage. *In room:* A/C, TV, minibar, hot-water pot with tea.

MODERATE

Holiday Inn Nagasaki ★★ *Value*   This hotel offers standard American convenience but with a rich mix of Asian and European design. Unlike most Holiday Inns, it keeps a low profile; it's hidden in the middle of a block and has a small, intimate lobby that resembles a rich merchant's home in old Nagasaki rather than a place to check in. As with all Holiday Inns, however, all beds are at least double size (some are even queens or kings). Note, however, that the cheapest singles face a wall 1 foot away; if you're claustrophobic, specify a room with an outside view. One of the best things about this hotel is its convenient location, close to the Hamanomachi shopping arcade in the heart of the city and Chinatown. You can walk from the hotel to most sites, including Glover Mansion and Sofukuji and Kofukuji temples. Another plus is the front desk's English-speaking staff.

6–24 Doza-machi, Nagasaki 850-0841. ✆ **800/HOLIDAY** in the U.S. or 095/828-1234. Fax 095/828-0178. holidayinn@holidayinn-nagasaki.ne.jp. 87 units. ¥8,500–¥11,000 ($71–$92) single; ¥15,000–¥16,000 ($129–$133) double; ¥16,000–¥20,000 ($133–$167) twin. Children under 12 stay free in parents' room. AE, DC, JCB, MC, V. Streetcar: no. 1 to Kanko Dori (1 min.). The hotel is hidden behind a building; look for its sign. **Amenities:** 1 restaurant (Italian); in-room massage; same-day laundry/dry cleaning service; nonsmoking rooms. *In room:* A/C, bilingual cable TV, minibar, hot-water pot with tea, hair dryer.

Hotel Majestic ✿✿✿ The Majestic is a small, charming jewel of a hotel. The beautifully appointed rooms are decorated in one of several themes—the country-living theme, for example, sports wooden floors, light-oak furnishings, and claw-footed bathtubs. All rooms have small balconies and larger-than-average bathrooms. There are no singles, the cheapest twins offer no views, and even more expensive rooms also look out over a parking lot in addition to the bay. No matter. The best things about this getaway are its small size—which means no tour-bus groups in the lobby—and its great location near Glover Garden. A tiny, cozy, European-style restaurant/bar makes you feel right at home.

2–28 Minami Yamate-machi, Nagasaki 850-0931. ✆ 095/827-7777. Fax 095/827-6112. 23 units. ¥23,000 ($192) double; ¥19,000–¥27,000 ($158–$225) twin. AE, DC, JCB, MC, V. Streetcar: no. 1 to Tsukimachi, then no. 5 to Oura Tenshudoshita (2 min.); cross the bridge and walk straight past the ANA Hotel Nagasaki Glover Hill. **Amenities:** 1 restaurant/bar (Western); in-room massage; same-day laundry/dry cleaning service; non-smoking rooms. *In room:* A/C, TV, minibar, hot-water pot with tea, hair dryer, washlet toilet.

Nagasaki Hotel Monterey ✿✿ Step into old Portugal in this whimsical place complete with whitewashed walls, imported tiles, a small chapel with decorations imported from Portugal, and hand-painted furnishings. There's even a kerosene lamp museum on hotel premises, free to hotel guests. Popular with young women, the hotel fits the historic past of Nagasaki and is conveniently located at the bottom of Hollander Slope. Rooms, too, give hints of Portugal with their terra-cotta-colored floor tiles and painted wood furniture. Although the cheapest singles have small bathrooms with no counter space, twins have lots of counter space. Only those rooms on the highest floors have views of the bay.

1–22 Oura-machi, Nagasaki 850-0918. ✆ 095/827-7111. Fax 095/820-7017. 123 units. ¥8,500–¥12,000 ($71–$100) single; ¥18,000–¥22,000 ($150–$183) twin. AE, DC, JCB, MC, V. Streetcar: no. 1 to Tsukimachi, then no. 5 to Oura Kaigan Dori (1 min.); walk inland. **Amenities:** 1 restaurant (Italian), 1 coffee shop; in-room massage; same-day laundry/dry cleaning service, nonsmoking rooms. *In room:* A/C, bilingual TV, minibar, hot-water pot with tea, hair dryer.

Nagasaki Washington Hotel This chain business hotel is in the heart of Nagasaki on the edge of the city's tiny Chinatown, about a 2-minute walk from the Hamanomachi shopping district. Its mostly single rooms are small but cheerful, with panels that close for complete darkness. Essentially, a place to lay your head at night.

9–1 Shinchi-machi, Nagasaki 850-0842. ✆ 095/828-1211. Fax 095/825-8023. 300 units. ¥6,500–¥8,600 ($54–$72) single; ¥15,000 ($125) double; ¥16,000–¥25,500 ($133–$212.50) twin. AE, DC, JCB, MC, V. Streetcar: no. 1 to Tsukimachi (1 min.); walk over the little bridge and then turn left. **Amenities:** 1 restaurant (steak), 1 coffee shop; in-room massage; same-day laundry/dry cleaning service; nonsmoking rooms. *In room:* A/C, TV, minibar, hot-water pot with tea, hair dryer, washlet toilet.

INEXPENSIVE

Hotel Wingport Nagasaki This clean and modern business hotel convenient to Nagasaki Station offers mostly singles that couldn't get much smaller. However, the fact that they're spotless, with white walls and cheerful bedspreads, helps alleviate claustrophobia, as do good bed lights. Panels close for complete darkness; note that some rooms face another building.

9–2 Daikoku-machi, Nagasaki 850-0057. ✆ 095/833-2800. Fax 095/833-2801. 200 units. ¥5,800–¥6,300 ($48–$52.50) single; ¥7,000–¥15,000 ($58–$125) twin. DC, JCB, MC, V. A 2-min. walk across from Nagasaki Station; turn right out of the station and take the pedestrian bridge over both tram tracks and continue straight. *In room:* A/C, TV, hot-water pot with tea, hair dryer.

(229) **Minshuku Tanpopo** (Value) This minshuku, a member of the Japanese Inn Group, is located north of Nagasaki Station on the east side of the Urakami River,

about a 7-minute walk from Peace Park but somewhat inconvenient to the other city sites. However, it offers simple tatami rooms at very reasonable rates.

21–7 Hoeicho, Nagasaki 852-8016. ℂ 095/861-6230. Fax 095/864-0032. www3.ocn.ne.jp/~tanpopo7/. 13 units (none with bathroom). ¥4,000 ($33) single; ¥7,000 ($58) twin; ¥9,000 ($75) triple. Breakfast ¥600 ($5) extra; dinner ¥2,000 ($17) extra. AE, V. Station: JR Urakami (15 min.). Take the pedestrian bridge over the river, turn right, turn left at the 3rd stoplight (there's a gas station on the corner), then left again, and then the 1st immediate right. Streetcar: nos. 1 or 3 to Matsuyama (6 min.). Cross the river and turn left, turn right after 3 blocks (there's a gas station on the corner), take the 1st left and then the 1st immediate right. If you let the owners know you're coming and call from Urakami or Matsuyama station, they'll pick you up if they're not too busy. **Amenities:** Coin-op washer/dryer. *In room:* A/C, TV, hot-water pot with tea.

(230) **Pension Dejima-no-Ki** 𝒦 This no-frills, five-story pension is conveniently located across the street from the Dejima Museum of History, within walking distance or an easy streetcar ride of Hamanomachi shopping arcade and Glover Garden. Ms. Ano, the congenial owner, speaks English and includes Japanese or Western breakfasts in her rates. Her Western rooms are basic and dorm-like and come with minuscule bathrooms, but a plus is that every two rooms share a small balcony. Ask for a room on a higher floor facing Dejima.

10–16 Dejima-machi, Nagasaki 850-0862. ℂ 095/822-6833. Fax 095/822-8197. 10 units. ¥6,000 ($50) single; ¥10,000 ($83) twin; ¥15,000 ($125) triple. Rates include breakfast. No credit cards. Streetcar: no. 1 to Tsukimachi (1 min.). Walk in the same direction as the streetcar (over a little bridge and then right); it will be on your right. **Amenities:** 1 coffee shop. *In room:* A/C, TV, fridge, hot-water pot with tea, hair dryer.

(231) **Sansui-so** The lobby of this reasonably priced, older accommodation features huge fish tanks with 40-year-old carp swimming about. Although concrete on the outside, the interior follows Japanese tradition with mostly tatami rooms. However, two single and four twin Western-style rooms are also available, as are Western breakfasts. Since traffic is a bit loud, try to get a room toward the back of the hotel. Like most ryokan, there's a public bath, but guests staying here may use the outdoor bath in the annex Fuji, a minute's walk away.

2–25 Ebisu-machi, Nagasaki 850-0056. ℂ 095/824-0070. Fax 095/822-1952. 28 units. ¥5,000 ($42) per person without meals; ¥7,000 ($58) per person with breakfast; ¥9,000 ($75) per person with breakfast and dinner. JCB, MC, V. A 5-min. walk SE of Nagasaki Station. Across from the station, follow the streetcar tracks that fork to the left onto Sakura-machi Street; Sansui-so is just past the post office on a corner to the right. **Amenities:** Coin-op washer/dryer. *In room:* A/C, coin-op TV, hot-water pot with tea.

WHERE TO DINE

Nagasaki's most famous food, called *shippoku,* is actually a whole meal of various courses with Chinese, European, and Japanese influences. It's a feast generally shared by a group of four or more people and includes such dishes as fish soup, sashimi, and fried, boiled, and vinegared seasonal delicacies from land and sea. Another Nagasaki specialty is *champon,* a thick Chinese noodle usually served in soup with meat, seafood, and vegetables.

Nagasaki's nightlife district centers on a small street near Hamanomachi known as **Shianbashi Dori,** which begins just off the streetcar stop of the same name and is easily recognizable by the neon arch of a bridge and palm trees that stretches over the entrance of the street. Lined with pink plastic flowers, this street shimmers with the lights of various drinking establishments and yakitori-ya, which are often the cheapest places to go for a light dinner.

EXPENSIVE

(232) **Kagetsu** ★★★ *finds* SHIPPOKU/KAISEKI If I were a woman of boundless means, this wonderful but expensive traditional restaurant is where I'd entertain all my friends—it's the ultimate Japanese dining experience. First

established in 1618, Kagetsu is one of Japan's longest-running restaurants; the oldest part of the present wooden building is about 360 years old. This is an oasis of dignified old Japan, with kimono-clad waitresses shuffling down wooden corridors and serving guests in tatami rooms. Formerly a geisha house, it has separate stairways for patrons and hostesses. It even has a stone-floored room designed for a table and chairs where foreign patrons could be entertained. Display cases exhibit treasures related to the Kagetsu's history.

Behind the restaurant, which is set back from the road, is a beautiful 300-year-old garden. I'll never forget my evening stroll here as a half-moon rose above gnarled, stunted pines. The back of the restaurant, consisting mainly of glass, was lit up, so I could see into a multitude of private tatami rooms all on different levels. It was like a woodblock print suddenly sprung to life. Needless to say, this restaurant is very popular and is sometimes entirely booked a full month in advance. There must be at least two of you if you want to eat shippoku or kaiseki.

2–1 Maruyama-machi. ☎ 095/822-0191. Reservations required at least a day (a week is better) in advance. Lunch obento (available only weekdays) ¥5,200 ($43); shippoku or kaiseki set meals ¥11,000–¥20,000 ($92–$167). DC, JCB, V. Mon–Sat noon–8pm (last order). Closed some Sun and holidays. Streetcar: Shianbashi (3 min.). Head under the neon arch of a bridge onto Shianbashi Dori, continue straight, and then take the road between the cute Koban police box and the small park; it's straight ahead where the street ends, with the traditional gate.

MODERATE

233 **Gohan** 👍👍 ORIGINAL JAPANESE   Gohan's English-speaking owner-chef, Tsunehiro Yoshimura, is also a musician, so you'll hear interesting music as you dine on creative, original meals. The interior is authentically old; salvaged beams and pieces from five different houses were given new lives here. The handwritten menu changes daily, but the set dinner more than satisfies. Included may be sashimi, new potato with sesame seed, a whole snapper, crayfish, tofu, soup, and rice. The dishes themselves are by Keisuke Iwata, a talented local potter of some renown. Hip waiters bring the food from an open kitchen. Very highly recommended.

2–32 Aburayamachi. ☎ 095/825-3600. Lunch teishoku ¥800 ($6.65); obento ¥2,000–¥3,000 ($17–$25); set dinners ¥4,000–¥6,000 ($33–$50). AE, JCB, MC, V. Mon–Sat noon–2pm and 5pm–midnight (last order 9:30pm). Closed holidays. Streetcar: Shokakujishita (1 min.). Walk 1 block down Sofukuji-dori toward the temple and take the 1st left; it's the 2nd building on your right with the name on the noren—look carefully, it's easy to miss.

234 **Hamakatsu** SHIPPOKU   This modern restaurant, just a minute's walk from the Hamanomachi covered shopping arcade, is one of Nagasaki's best known shippoku restaurants. The ground floor, with table seating, is made private with alcoves and bamboo screens; upstairs is a large tatami room with individual tables. The burabura shippoku set meal (¥2,800/$23) is for one person, making it a good place to try this unique cuisine if you're alone, while other set meals from ¥3,800 ($32) per person can only be ordered for parties of two or more. Note that shippoku is not served for lunch.

6–50 Kajiya-machi. ☎ 095/826-8321. Set lunches ¥1,000–¥2,500 ($8.35–$21); shippoku set meals ¥2,800–¥12,000 ($23–$100). AE, DC, JCB, MC, V. Daily 11:30am–8:30pm (last order). Streetcar: Shianbashi (4 min.). Walk under the arch with the clock and take the 2nd right (Lawson is on the corner); it's in the middle of the block on the left.

Harbin 👍👍👍 FRENCH/RUSSIAN   Established in 1959, Harbin is a Nagasaki tradition, one of those places you don't want to miss. Its owner was

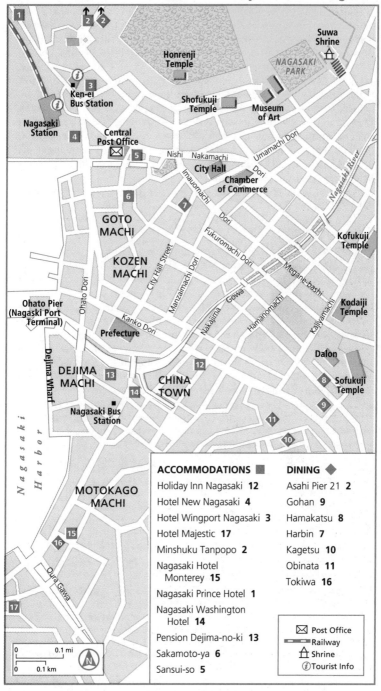

Where to Stay & Dine in Nagasaki

ACCOMMODATIONS ■

Holiday Inn Nagasaki **12**
Hotel New Nagasaki **4**
Hotel Wingport Nagasaki **3**
Hotel Majestic **17**
Minshuku Tanpopo **2**
Nagasaki Hotel Monterey **15**
Nagasaki Prince Hotel **1**
Nagasaki Washington Hotel **14**
Pension Dejima-no-ki **13**
Sakamoto-ya **6**
Sansui-so **5**

DINING ◆

Asahi Pier 21 **2**
Gohan **9**
Hamakatsu **8**
Harbin **7**
Kagetsu **10**
Obinata **11**
Tokiwa **16**

⊠ Post Office
━ Railway
⛩ Shrine
ⓘ Tourist Info

0   0.1 mi
0   0.1 km

N

born in Manchuria and named his restaurant after Harbin, a town close to his birthplace that was once an international city of Russian, Chinese, and Japanese residents. His family-run restaurant serves a unique blend of French and Russian cuisine; in recent years, his French-trained chef son has brought his own interpretations to the menu.

On the ground floor is a cafe/bar (open Mon–Sat 10am–1am), while upstairs is the more formal restaurant. Both have appropriate decor—lots of dark, polished wood and red furnishings. The changing menu, written in Japanese, English, and Russian, may include chicken liver stroganoff, fried chicken Kiev style, Georgian spicy lamb pot, and duck steak in plum sauce. The coulibiac (traditional Russian salmon pie), when available, is perhaps the best thing on the menu. The ¥1,500 ($12.50) set lunch gives a choice of entree along with soup, homemade bread, and coffee or tea.

2–27 Kozen-machi. ℂ **095/822-7443.** Main dishes ¥1,200–¥3,500 ($10–$29); set dinners ¥2,900–¥7,500 ($24–$62.50); set lunches ¥1,500–¥3,500 ($12.50–$29). AE, DC, MC, V. Mon–Sat 11:30am–1:15pm and 6–8:30pm (last order). Streetcar: Sakura-machi (3 min.). Walk uphill (to the right if coming from the direction of Nagasaki Station) and turn right onto City Hall Street; it's just past the JAL office on the right.

Obinata ⭐⭐ *Finds* ITALIAN   One of my favorite restaurants, Obinata is an oasis of old Europe in the heart of Kyushu. The place has a warm, earthy feel to it, due perhaps to its heavy wooden beams, large bouquets of flowers, oil wick lamps on each table, scattered antiques, and classical music playing softly in the background. The atmosphere is cozy, and the service is a delight. The menu, in Italian, lists such dishes as beef filet grilled with crushed black pepper with cream sauce, veal and ham served with wine sauce, risotto, spaghetti, lasagne, and pizza, all served with fresh, homemade bread. Dishes are creative and fun. Expect to pay about ¥6,000 ($50) if you go all out and order an appetizer, main dish, and wine (there's a wide selection of Bordeaux, Moselle, and Rhine wines—the owner is a wine buff), but you can eat more cheaply if you stick to pastas.

3–19 Funadaiku-machi. ℂ **095/826-1437.** Pastas and main dishes ¥1,000–¥5,000 ($8.35–$42); pizza ¥1,000–¥1,800 ($8.35–$15). AE. Mon–Sat 5–11pm (last order). Streetcar: Shianbashi (3 min.). Walk under the neon-lit arch of a bridge onto Shianbashi Dori and turn right at the Fukusaya castella cake shop (an old traditional building); it will be almost immediately on your left—look for the sign.

Tokiwa SASHIMI/TEMPURA/KAISEKI   Raw fish doesn't come any fresher than at this conveniently located restaurant between Hamanomachi and Glover Garden. Tokiwa features a wooden counter surrounding a large pool filled with live fish; when its number is up, the fish is scooped out of the water and then prepared right before your very eyes. Sometimes the fish is gutted and filleted with only the head, heart, and skeleton left intact, so that the sashimi can be arranged around the alive and still-quivering creature and be delivered to your table. Barring that, you might opt for one of the lunch *teishoku* (set meals), which range from sashimi to tempura.

Nagasaki View Hotel, 2–33 Oura-machi. ℂ **095/824-2211.** Set lunches ¥980–¥2,500 ($8.15–$21); set dinners ¥1,900–¥8,000 ($16–$67). AE, DC, JCB, MC, V. Daily 11:30am–2pm and 5–10pm. Streetcar: Ourakaigan Dori (1 min.); across the street from the stop, but entrance to the restaurant is around the back.

INEXPENSIVE

In addition to the restaurant below, another good place for inexpensive fare is the newly developed **Dejima Wharf,** a complex of restaurants, bars and shops spread along a boardwalk located near the Dejima historic district and Dejima streetcar stop.

Asahi Pier 21 VARIED   This very inexpensive restaurant, popular with students and those on a budget, is located on the second floor of Seiyokan, a European-style building filled with shops and restaurants. It's a good place for a meal if you're visiting Peace Park, just a 2-minute walk away. Lunch features an all-you-can-eat buffet of Chinese, Western, and Japanese dishes, including spaghetti, salad, pizza, fried noodles, soup, and much more. Plates are huge, encouraging gluttony, but the food is about as good as you'd expect for the price. Dinners are a la carte; choose from the display case outside showing enormous plates of omelets, pork, vegetables, and spaghetti. Unless you're big eaters, two of you can easily split a plate. Part of the fun in dining here is trying to decipher the decor—judging from its name and cavelike interior, my vote goes for an underwater nautical theme. Music ranges from rock and pop to disco and jazz.

Seiyokan, 13–1 Kawaguchi-machi. ℂ 095/846-8808. Lunch buffet ¥950 ($7.90); main dishes ¥780–¥1,080 ($6.50–$9). AE, DC, JCB, MC. Mon–Fri 11:30am–3pm, Sat–Sun 11:30am–4pm; daily 5–11pm. Streetcar: Hamaguchi-machi (1 min.).

8 Unzen Spa & Its Hells ★★

66km (41 miles) SE of Nagasaki

Unzen Spa is a small hot-spring resort town located 2,300 feet above sea level in the pine-covered hills of the Shimabara Peninsula. Thanks to its high altitude, cool mountain air, great scenery, and hot sulfur springs, Unzen became popular in the 1890s as a summer resort for American and European visitors, who came from as far away as Shanghai, Hong Kong, Harbin, and Singapore to escape the oppressively humid summers. They arrived in Unzen by bamboo palanquin from Obama, 7 miles away. In 1911, Unzen became the first prefectural park in Japan. The fact that there were foreigners here explains why Unzen has one of Japan's oldest golf courses, dating from 1913. In 1934, the area became **Unzen-Amakusa National Park** ★★, one of the nation's first national parks; it covers 102 square miles.

I like Unzen Spa because it's small and navigable. It consists basically of just a few streets with hotels and ryokan spread along them, a welcome relief if you've been spending a few hectic weeks rushing through big cities and catching buses and trains. Only 1,450 people live here, and from the town a number of hiking paths wind into the tree-covered hills. Dense clouds of steam arise from solfataras and fumaroles, evidence of volcanic activity. More evidence is the abundance of hot springs—Unzen's name derives from "Onsen," meaning "hot spring."

ESSENTIALS

GETTING THERE   The easiest way to get to Unzen is by **Ken-ei Bus** from Nagasaki. Buses leave every hour or more frequently from the Ken-ei Bus Terminal across the street from Nagasaki Station. The ride takes about 2 hours and costs ¥1,900 ($16) one-way or ¥3,420 ($28.50) round-trip. For a bus schedule, drop by the Nagasaki Prefecture Tourist Federation on the second floor of the Ken-ei Bus Terminal.

VISITOR INFORMATION   Before leaving Tokyo, Kyoto, or Narita or Kansai international airports, be sure to stop by the Tourist Information Center to pick up the free leaflet "Nagasaki and Unzen," which describes places of interest in Unzen and the Shimabara Peninsula. In Nagasaki, stop by the **Nagasaki Prefectural Tourist Federation,** across from Nagasaki Station on the second floor of the Ken-ei Bus Terminal.

In Unzen, the **Tourist Information Center,** 320 Unzen, Obamacho Minami Takaki-gun 854-06 (© **0957/73-3434;** open daily 9am–5pm), is located in the heart of Unzen Spa next to the Unzen Spa House and across from the police station (and between the Nishi-Iriguchi and Shin-yu Visitor Center-mae bus stops). It has a good map in English of Unzen and the surrounding area. Nearby is the park's **Unzen Visitor's Center** (© **0957/73-2642;** open Fri–Wed 9am–6pm, to 5pm in winter), with information on the national park.

GETTING AROUND   Buses from Nagasaki make four stops in Unzen Spa, terminating at Unzen's Ken-ei Bus Center. I've provided the bus-stop name for accommodations so you can alight at the nearest stop. Otherwise, Unzen is so small you can walk from one end to the other in about 30 minutes.

WHAT TO SEE & DO

When the area around Unzen Spa was designated a national park in 1934, it was named after what was thought to be an extinct volcanic chain, collectively called Mt. Unzen. In 1991, however, a peak in Mt. Unzen—Mt. Fugen—erupted for the first time in almost 200 years, killing several dozen people on its eastern slope and leaving behind a huge lava dome. Unzen Spa, on the opposite side, was untouched and remains the area's most popular resort town.

THE HELLS (JIGOKU)   Unzen Spa literally bubbles with activity, as sulfurous hot springs erupt into surface cauldrons of scalding water in an area known as the Hells (Jigoku). Indeed, in the 1600s, these cauldrons were used for hellish punishment, as some 30 Christians were boiled alive here after Christianity was outlawed in Japan. Today, Unzen Spa has more than 30 solfataras and fumaroles, with the Hells providing the greatest show of geothermal activity, making this spot Unzen's number one attraction. It's a favorite hangout of huge black ravens, and the barren land has been baked a chalky white through the centuries. There are pathways leading through the hot-spring Hells, where sulfur vapors rise thickly to veil pine trees on surrounding hills. Old women in bonnets sell corn on the cob and eggs that have been boiled in the hot springs. A simple cross erected on stones serves as a memorial to the Christians killed here.

CLIMBING MT. FUGEN ☆   If you feel like taking an excursion, head for Mt. Fugen, Unzen's most popular destination outside Unzen Spa. Buses depart about five times a day (more often in peak season) for **Nitta Pass,** about a 20-minute ride away. The fare is ¥740 ($6.15). From Nitta Pass, you can take a 3-minute ropeway (cable car) (¥1,220/$10 round-trip) up higher to **Mt. Myoken,** which at 4,265 feet offers spectacular panoramic views. But the best thing to do, in my opinion, is to skip the ropeway and take the footpath that runs from Nitta Pass and skirts the mountain along a tree-shaded path. It takes about 30 minutes to reach Nitta Pass, and that's all you may care to exert yourself. If you're ready for some real climbing, however, continue along a marked path another hour or so; it leads starkly uphill to the summit of **Mt. Fugen,** once Unzen's highest peak at 4,462 feet above sea level—this is the peak that erupted in 1991. Here, on a clear day, you'll be rewarded with splendid views of other volcanic peaks as far away as Mt. Aso in the middle of Kyushu. You can also see Mt. Heisei Shinzan (the lava dome), born during Mt. Fugen's last eruption and now Unzen's loftiest peak at 4,875 feet. Allow at least 2½ hours for the hike from Nitta Pass to Mt. Fugen and back so you don't miss the last bus. *Note*: Mt. Fugen has recently been closed to climbers; check with the Unzen Tourist Information Center before setting out.

HITTING THE LINKS   You can play golf at Japan's oldest public golf course (© **0957/73-3368;** open daily 8am–5pm), a 5-minute taxi ride from Unzen Spa. The total charge for 18 holes at the 9-hole course—including greens fees, tax, and caddy—is ¥9,680 ($81) on weekdays, ¥12,480 ($104) on weekends and holidays. A shorter nine-hole course (good for beginners) costs ¥3,150 ($26) on weekdays, ¥3,680 ($31) on weekends and holidays.

WHERE TO STAY

Keep in mind that, as with most resort areas in Japan, Unzen tends to be crowded and sometimes even fully booked during Golden Week, during New Year's, and from mid-July through August. The best times of year are late April to June, when the azalea bushes are in glorious bloom, and in late October and early November, when the maple leaves turn brilliant reds.

With the exception of the inexpensive accommodation listed at the end of this section, all the ryokan and hotels listed here are within an easy walk of bus stops along the route traversed by the bus from Nagasaki. Tell the bus driver where you're staying, and he'll drop you off at the nearest stop.

EXPENSIVE

Kyushu Hotel ⋆⋆   Despite its name, the Kyushu Hotel is an 83-year-old ryokan in an updated building with a view of a lovely garden from the renovated, luxurious lobby. The staff members, some of whom speak English, are very gracious and accommodating. But best of all, the Kyushu Hotel offers some of the most scenic views in town—many of its rooms boast great views of the hills as well as the Hells. Tatami rooms feature alcoves with Western-style chairs next to large windows, affording a relaxing place to take in the view. There are also a few Western-style rooms and combination rooms with tatami areas and beds.

320 Unzen, Obamacho, Minami-Takaki-gun 854-0697. © **0957/73-3234.** Fax 0957/73-3733. 98 units. ¥18,000–¥40,000 ($162–$360) per person. Rates include breakfast, dinner, and service. AE, DC, JCB, MC, V. Bus: Shin-yu Visitor Center-mae (2 min.). **Amenities:** 2 restaurants (Japanese, Western), 1 coffee shop, 1 bar, 1 lounge; indoor/outdoor hot-spring baths with great views of the Hells; in-room massage. *In room:* A/C, TV, minibar, hot-water pot with tea, hair dryer.

㉟ **Miyazaki Ryokan** ⋆⋆   One of the largest Japanese inns in Unzen, this modern ryokan with traditional service overlooks a beautiful, gracefully manicured garden with hills and sulfur vapors rising in the background—absolutely exquisite when the azaleas are in bloom. Upon arrival, you'll be served green tea and sweets here by graceful women in kimono. Afterwards, you'll want to ease into the large, marble hot-spring bath overlooking a rock-lined outdoor bath, separated for men and women. Or, if you're shy about bathing with others or want to make it a family affair, make a reservation for no extra charge at the private family bath (there's a 30-min. time limit). After bathing, relax in the peaceful tatami area with Go tables, huge flower arrangements, and a dispenser of cool *mugi cha* (wheat tea). Next comes one of the best reasons to stay here— the kaiseki meals. Although breakfasts (Western style, if desired) are served in a communal dining area, excellent dinners are served in guest rooms in true ryokan fashion. In addition to Japanese-style tatami rooms, there are also combination rooms with twin beds and a separate tatami area. Since room rates are the same regardless of which direction the rooms face, I'd advise securing one that looks out over the garden or, barring that, the Hells (views from here are not as good, however, as from the Kyushu Hotel above).

320 Unzen, Obamacho, Minami-Takaki-gun 854-0621. © **0957/73-3331.** Fax 0957/73-2313. 106 units. ¥20,000–¥30,000 ($157–$250) per person. Rates include breakfast, dinner, and service. AE, DC, JCB, MC, V. Bus: Shin-yu Visitor Center-mae (2 min.). **Amenities:** Indoor/outdoor hot-spring baths; in-room massage. *In room:* A/C, TV, hot-water pot with tea, hair dryer, tiny safe, washlet toilet.

MODERATE

Unzen Kanko Hotel ★★★ *Finds* If you're the least bit romantic, you won't be able to resist staying at this old-fashioned mountain lodge, built in 1935 of stone and wood, covered in ivy, and resembling a Swiss chalet. The lobby, main dining hall, and public spaces are little changed over the decades with their white-washed walls, dark-beamed ceilings, and inviting sofas and chairs. The rooms are rustic and old-fashioned, too, with heavy ceiling-to-floor curtains tied back to reveal a balcony, brass doorsills, a high ceiling, and wooden beams. There are 49 Western-style rooms, eight Japanese-style tatami rooms, and two combination rooms that come with both a bed and tatami area.

320 Unzen, Obamacho, Minami-Takaki-gun 854-0621. © **0957/73-3263.** Fax 0957/73-3419. www.unzenkankohotel.com. 59 units. ¥8,500–¥10,000 ($71–$83) single; ¥12,000–¥16,000 ($100–$133) double; ¥14,000–¥22,000 ($117–$183) twin; ¥25,000–¥45,000 ($208–$375) Japanese-style rooms; ¥22,000 ($183) combination rooms. AE, DC, JCB, MC, V. Bus: Nishi-Iriguchi (1 min.). **Amenities:** 1 restaurant (Japanese/Western), 1 bar; hot-springs baths (including a family bath; get the key at the reception); game room; in-room massage. *In room:* A/C, TV, hot-water pot with tea, hair dryer.

INEXPENSIVE

㉖ **Kaseya Ryokan** Located on the main street through town not far from the bus center, this economically priced ryokan dates back to 1909 but has been remodeled. All of the rooms are Japanese-style, simply decorated but with high ceilings and flower arrangements. Western-style breakfasts can be requested for weekdays but only with prior reservations.

Unzen, Obamacho, Minami-Takaki-gun 854-0621. © **0957/73-3321.** Fax 0957/73-3322. 13 units (none with bathroom). ¥6,800 ($57) per person Sun–Fri; ¥7,980 ($66.50) per person Sat and nights before holidays; more during Golden Week and New Year's. Rates include breakfast, dinner, and service. DC, JCB, MC, V. Bus: Jinja-mae (2 min.). **Amenities:** Hot-spring baths (including a private one for families). *In room:* A/C, TV, hot-water pot with tea, safe.

㉗ **Seiunso Kokumin Shukusha** *Value* Formerly a youth hostel, this public lodging recently underwent extensive remodeling and now offers as much comfort and facilities as a moderately priced resort hotel. Rooms are Japanese-style; most have a small balcony offering views of the surrounding woods, and all have sinks and toilets. There are also three combination rooms with both beds and tatami areas that are quite spacious (and handicapped-accessible) and have the best views; you can stay here, if they're not booked, for the same charge. Needless to say, you should reserve early to stay here. The main disadvantage is that it's located outside Unzen, about a 30-minute walk from the Hells.

500–1 Unzen, Obamacho, Minami Takaki-gun 854-0621. © 0957/73-3273. Fax 0957/73-2698. 63 units (none with bathroom). ¥7,400–¥9,400 ($62–$78) per person. Rates include breakfast and dinner. No credit cards. Bus: Nishi-Iriguchi (20 min.). Pickup service available from Ken-ei Bus Center. **Amenities:** 1 restaurant (Japanese); indoor/outdoor hot-spring baths; tennis courts; free washer/dryer. *In room:* TV, hot-water pot with tea, washlet toilet.

WHERE TO DINE

Even if you don't stay at the **Unzen Kanko Hotel,** you may want to come here for lunch. Its old-fashioned dining hall is large with wooden paneling and wooden floors, white tablecloths, and flowers on each table. It serves both Japanese and Western selections, with set lunches beginning at ¥1,800 ($15) and Japanese obento priced at ¥2,000 ($17). A la carte items include filet mignon and lobster or inexpensive spaghetti. Western dinners start at ¥5,000 ($42). Open for lunch from noon to 1:30pm and for dinner starting at 6pm, with last orders taken at 8pm.

Unzen Tabi no Beer Kan WESTERN   This microbrewery brews three different kinds of beer. A half liter costs ¥700 ($5.85), or you can have a sampler of all three for ¥750 ($6.25). A buffet is served daily from 11am to 3pm. After that, there's a limited a la carte menu with snacks ranging from curry rice to cheese croque. The dining hall is light and airy with large windows overlooking the wooded hills, and the music is German beer-drinking music.

Across from the Ken-ei Bus Center. 🕐 **0957/73-3113.** Main dishes ¥500–¥1,000 ($4.15–$8.35); buffet lunch ¥1,500 ($12.50). JCB, MC, V. Daily 11am–8pm. Bus: Ken-ei Bus Center (1 min.).

11

Northeastern Honshu—Tohoku

Because so many of Japan's historic events took place in Kyoto, Tokyo, and other cities in southern Honshu, most visitors to Japan never venture farther north than Tokyo. True, northeastern Honshu (called the Tohoku District) does not have the famous temples, shrines, gardens, and castles of southern Japan, but it does have spectacular mountain scenery, national parks, hot springs in abundance, excellent ski resorts, and many hiking trails. Its rugged, mountainous terrain, coupled with cold, snowy winters, has also helped preserve the region's traditions. You won't find any of Tokyo's edgy flashiness here, but rather a down-to-earth practicality, warm hospitality, and a way of life that harks back generations.

Matsushima, about 3 hours north of Tokyo, is considered one of Japan's most scenic spots, with pine-covered islets dotting its bay. Farther north, near the middle of Tohoku, is the pleasant village **Kakunodate,** once a thriving castle town and famous for its remaining samurai houses and cherry trees. Occupying 333 square miles of northern Tohoku is the resplendent **Towada-Hachimantai National Park,** best visited for its scenic lakes, rustic hot-spring spas that seem little changed over the decades, skiing, and hiking, including a trail that flanks the picture-perfect Oriase Stream. After a day of trekking or skiing, what can be better than a soothing, hot-spring soak?

TOHOKU ESSENTIALS
GETTING THERE & AROUND
Northern Tohoku's major airports are in Aomori and Akita, with fares from Tokyo's Haneda Airport costing ¥25,500 ($212) and ¥20,500 ($171) respectively. You can also travel to Tohoku via **Shinkansen** bullet train from Ueno or Tokyo Station in Tokyo as far as Akita, which stops at Kakunodate and Tawazako, a convenient springboard for travel onward to Towada-Hachimantai National Park.

Although there is bus service in the national park, frequency of buses to some of the more remote areas is infrequent or nonexistent. For that reason, Tohoku is one of the few regions in Japan where **rental cars** are a great convenience, if not a necessity. In addition to car-rental agencies at both Aomori and Akita airports, there are JR Eki Rent-A-Car offices at train stations throughout Japan, including Aomori, Morioka, Kakunodate, and Tawazako stations, which offer 20% discounts for train fares booked in conjunction with car rentals. You'll also find Toyota Rent-A-Car offices virtually everywhere. If you want to keep your driving to a minimum, I suggest taking a Shinkansen as far as Tawazako and renting a car from there. You could then visit nearby Kakunodate, Lake Tazawa, and Nyuto Onsen before continuing northward to Lake Towada. A two-day rental of a subcompact car costs about ¥18,500 ($154), including mileage and insurance. Drop-off fees can add ¥4,000 ($33). Keep in mind that Tohoku's winter season, from November to March, can bring below-freezing temperatures and up to a foot of snowfall virtually overnight. Some mountain passes are occasionally closed due to snowfall, though access is generally open to major ski resorts.

See "Getting Around Japan," in chapter 2 for more information on renting a car in Japan. Contact information for rental agencies in Tohoku are provided under individual destination listings below.

1 The Pine-clad Islands of Matsushima (★

374.5km (234 miles) NE of Tokyo

Because the trip to Northern Tohoku or onward to Hokkaido is such a long one, the most pleasant way to travel is to break up the journey with an overnight stay in **Matsushima** (★. Matsushima means "Pine-Clad Islands"—and that's exactly what this region is. More than 260 pine-covered islets and islands dot Matsushima Bay, giving it the appearance of a giant pond in a Japanese landscape garden. Twisted and gnarled pines sweep upward from volcanic tuff and white sandstone, creating bizarre and beautiful shapes.

Matsushima is so dear to Japanese hearts that it's considered one of the three most scenic spots in Japan (the other two are Miyajima in Hiroshima Bay and Amanohashidate on the north coast of Honshu)—and was so designated about 270 years ago in a book written by a Confucian philosopher of the Edo government. Basho (1644–94), the famous Japanese haiku poet, was so struck by Matsushima's beauty that it's almost as though he were at a loss for words when he wrote: "Matsu-shima, Ah! Matsushima! Matsushima!"

Unfortunately, motorboats have been invented since Basho's time, detracting from the beauty that evoked such ecstasy in Basho long ago.

ESSENTIALS

GETTING THERE   From Tokyo, you can take the **Tohoku Shinkansen** train from Ueno or Tokyo Station to Sendai, which will take from 1½ to 2¼ hours, depending on the number of stops. In Sendai, change to the **JR Senseki Line**—it's well marked in English, so you shouldn't have any difficulty changing trains in Sendai. From Sendai, it takes about 25 minutes by express train and costs ¥400 ($3.35) to reach **Matsushima Kaigan Station,** with trains departing approximately every half hour.

A more popular way to get to Matsushima is to take the Senseki Line from Sendai only as far as **Hon-Shiogama** (about 18 min. by express), where you can catch a **sightseeing boat** operated by the Matsushima Bay Sightseeing Ferry Co. (© **022/366-5111**) for a 50-minute trip to **Matsushima Kaigan Pier;** tickets cost ¥1,420 ($12) for adults and ¥710 ($6) for children. Although commentary is in Japanese only, an English pamphlet describing more than you'd ever want to know about the islets you're passing is available. You'll also pass the unsightly Tohoku Thermal Electric Power Station, which the pamphlet says was built in such a way "as not to distract from Matsushima Bay's beauty, but rather harmonize with it." I don't even have to tell you my thoughts on this. Boats depart from both Hon-Shiogama and Matsushima Kaigan piers about every half hour between 8am and 4pm, but only once an hour between 9am and 3pm December through March. From Hon-Shiogama Station it's about a 10-minute walk to the boat pier; take a right out of the station, cross the street and turn right at the first red light (crossing under the tracks), and continue straight.

VISITOR INFORMATION   Upon arrival in Matsushima, stop off at one of the two **Matsushima Tourist Association Offices,** where you can pick up a brochure with a map in English and get directions to your hotel. One is located to the right as you exit **Matsushima Kaigan Station** (© **022/354-2263;** open daily 10am–5pm, to 4:30 pm in winter). The staff here speaks English and will help you with reservations for lodgings in Matsushima; you can also make reservations for **Goodwill Guides,** volunteers who will guide you to major local attractions free of charge. Adjoining the tourist office is a left-luggage counter, useful if you're making a quick stopover (there are also lockers in Sendai Station).

If you're arriving in Matsushima by boat, you'll find another information booth at **Matsushima Kaigan Pier** (© **022/354-2618;** open daily 8:30am–5pm, to 4:30pm in winter). Note, however, that this office does not make accommodations arrangements.

ORIENTATION & GETTING AROUND **Matsushima Kaigan Station** lies to the west of the boat pier and Matsushima's main attractions; the train station and pier are about a 6-minute walk apart. All of Matsushima's major attractions are within walking distance of both the station and the pier (though the pier is more centrally located); you can cover the whole area on foot in a half day of leisurely sightseeing.

SEEING THE SIGHTS
CRUISING THE BAY Arriving in Matsushima by **sightseeing boat** is a good introduction to the bay because you pass pine-covered islands and oyster rafts along the way. Board the boat in Hon-Shiogama for the 50-minute trip to Matsushima Kaigan Pier (see "Getting There," above).

If you come by train or even if you arrive by boat, you might still want to take a **boat trip** in the bay. Regular sightseeing boats depart from the pier once an hour between 9am and 4pm, making 50-minute trips around the bay and charging ¥1,400 ($12) for adults, half price for children.

TEMPLES & HISTORIC BUILDINGS
(238) **Zuiganji Temple** ⭐⭐⭐ Matsushima's best-known structure is the most famous Zen temple in northern Japan. Located just a few minutes walk away from Matsushima Kaigan Pier and 7 minutes from the station, its entrance is shaded by tall cedar trees. On the right side of the pathway leading to the temple are caves and grottoes dug out by priests long ago; adorned with Buddhist statues and memorial tablets, they were used for practicing *zazen* (sitting meditation) and are an impressive sight. Here, too, you'll find what is probably Japan's only monument to—eels!

Now a National Treasure and the highlight of a stay in Matsushima, Zuiganji Temple was originally founded in the Heian Period (828) as a Tendai temple but became a Zen temple in the 13th century. After a period of decline, it was remodeled in 1604 by the order of Date Masamune, the most powerful and important lord of northern Honshu. Unifying the region known as Tohoku, Date built his castle in nearby Sendai, and today almost all sites in and around Sendai and Matsushima are tied to the Date family. It took hundreds of workers 6 years to build the impressive main hall, a large wooden structure that was constructed in the shoin-zukuri style typical of the Momoyama Period and that served as the family temple of the Date clan. Be sure to walk around the temple for a better look at its gorgeous, gold-plated sliding doors.

See, too, the **Homotsuden,** which houses the **Zuiganji Art Museum** (Seiryuden) with its displays of temple and Date family treasures, including painted

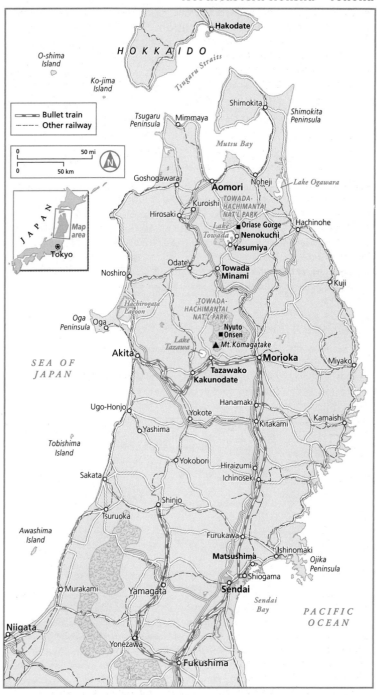

Hakodate

O-shima Island

H O K K A I D O

Tsugaru Straits

Ko-jima Island

Shimokita

Shimokita Peninsula

Bullet train

Other railway

Tsugaru Peninsula Mimmaya

Mutsu Bay

0   50 mi

0   50 km

Goshogawara

Aomori Noheji

Lake Ogawara

J A P A N

Map area

⊗ **Tokyo**

Kuroishi

TOWADA-HACHIMANTAI NAT'L PARK

Hirosaki

Lake Towada

■ **Oriase Gorge**

Hachinohe

Nenokuchi

Yasumiya

Odate

Towada Minami

Noshiro

Kuji

Hachirogata Lagoon

TOWADA-HACHIMANTAI NAT'L PARK

Nyuto
■ **Onsen**

Oga Peninsula Oga

Lake Tazawa

▲ **Mt. Komagatake**

Akita

Morioka

Miyako

Tazawako
Kakunodate

SEA OF JAPAN

Hanamaki

Ugo-Honjo

Yokote

Kamaishi

Yashima

Tobishima Island

Kitakami

Yokobori

Hiraizumi

Sakata

Ichinoseki

Shinjo

Tsuruoka

Awashima Island

Furukawa

Ishinomaki

Matsushima

Ojika Peninsula

Shiogama

Murakami

Yamagata

Sendai

Sendai Bay

PACIFIC OCEAN

Niigata

Yonezawa

Fukushima

Tips **A Note on Japanese Symbols**

Many hotels, restaurants, attractions, and other establishments in Japan do not have signs giving their names in Roman (English-language) letters. Appendix C lists the Japanese symbols for all such places described in this guide. Each set of characters representing an establishment name has a number in the appendix that corresponds to the number that appears inside the oval before the establishment's name in the text. Thus, to find the Japanese symbol for, say, **Zuiganji Temple** (above), refer to no. 238 in appendix C.

---

sliding doors, portraits of the Date clan, tea cups, scrolls, calligraphy, and woodblock prints, many of Matsushima as it looked in former times, shown on a rotating basis. In all, you'll probably spend an hour at Zuiganji Temple.

Under the supervision of Zuiganji Temple is **Godaido,** a small wooden worship hall on a tiny island not far from the pier. Connected to the mainland by a short bridge, its grounds are open night and day and are free, but there's not much to see other than the bay. Godaido is often featured in brochures of Matsushima, making this delicate wooden temple one of the town's best-known landmarks.

91 Aza-chonai. ✆ 022/354-2023. Admission for both Seiryuden and Zuiganji Temple ¥700 ($5.85) adults, ¥400 ($3.35) children. Daily 8am to between 3:30pm and 5pm, depending on the month.

⟨239⟩ **Entsuin** ★★ *(Finds*   This lesser-known temple was also built in the early Edo Period, more than 340 years ago, by the Date clan. It features a small rock garden (with seven rocks representing the Seven Deities of Good Fortune), a moss garden with six different types of moss, a lovely rose garden, an Edo-Period garden with a pond and "borrowed landscaping," and a small temple housing an elaborate statue of Lord Date Mitsumune, grandson of Lord Date Masamune, who founded the Sendai fief. Depicted here on a white steed, Mitsumune was reportedly poisoned by the Tokugawa shogunate and died at the tender age of 19 in Edo Castle. The seven statues surrounding him represent retainers who committed ritual suicide to follow their master into death. The interior walls are all covered with an overlay of gold. The painting of an occidental rose on the right-hand door is thought to be the first in Japan (hence the rose garden); other Western flowers include narcissus and corona. Be on the lookout for "hidden" crosses above the door that are slanted; because Christianity was banned in Edo Japan, the Date clan used crosses as a symbol for silent revolt. Expect to spend 45 to 50 minutes here.

67 Aza-chonai. ✆ 022/354-3206. Admission ¥300 ($2.50) adults, ¥150 ($1.25) high-school students, ¥100 (85¢) children. Daily 9am–5pm. Next to Zuiganji Temple (to the left as you face it).

Kanrantei   Another famous structure is Kanrantei, the "Water-Viewing Pavilion," just a one-minute walk from the boat pier. A simple wooden teahouse, it was used by generations of the Date family for such aesthetic pursuits as viewing the moon and watching the ripples on the tide. Originally it belonged to warlord Toyotomi Hideyoshi as part of his estate at Fushimi Castle near Kyoto, but he presented it to the Date family at the end of the 16th century; it was moved here in 1645, where it remains one of the largest teahouses in Japan.

For an additional ¥300 ($2.50), you can drink ceremonial green tea while sitting on the teahouse tatami and contemplating the bay, its islands, and the boats carving ribbons through the water. After tea, wander through the small museum containing Samurai armor, ceramics, lacquerware, and tea-ceremony utensils belonging to the Date family.

56–1 Aza-chonai. ✆ **022/353-3355.** Admission ¥200 ($1.65) adults, ¥150 ($1.25) university and high-school students, ¥100 (85¢) children. Daily 8:30am–5pm (to 4:30pm in winter).

MUSEUMS

�240 **Michinoku Date Masamune Historical Museum (Michinoku Date Masamune Rekishikan)** ⚐ This wax museum details the life and times of Masamune (1567–1636) through 25 life-size, audio-visual diorama displays. Showing everything from how Masamune lost sight in one of his eyes at age 5, to his marriage at age 13, to his victories in battle. The dioramas bring to life what might otherwise be dull history. At the very least, you get to see how people dressed back then and learn why Masamune was nicknamed the One-Eyed Dragon. Of less interest are some early 19th- and 20th-century figures of Northern Japan; be sure to ask for the English pamphlet or you won't know who the heck they are. A visit to this museum takes about an hour.

Matsushima Kaigan. ✆ **022/354-4131.** Admission ¥1,000 ($8.35) adults, ¥600 ($5) junior-high and high school students, ¥500 ($4.15) children. Daily 8:30am–5pm. Across from the Godaido temple and set back from the main street.

Matsushima Orgel Museum ⚐⚐ This is a museum within a museum: It displays the entire Belgium National Music Box Museum, which was bought and shipped lock, stock, and barrel from Bruges, Belgium. The 100 or so music boxes, dating from 1860 to 1950, are priceless; some were owned by kings, others designed for theaters, exhibitions, dance halls, cafes, or train stations and are quite huge and elaborate. The largest in the collection (and one of the largest in the world) boasts 619 wooden pipes, drums, trumpets, and xylophones. There are also phonographs, player pianos, harmoniums dating back to 1905, and other early inventions (including a 1900 Ediphone). Best of all, some of the music boxes are played on request. You can easily spend 45 minutes here.

33–3 Funendo. ✆ **022/353-3600.** Admission ¥1,000 ($8.35) adults, ¥700 ($5.85) junior-high and high school students, ¥500 ($4.15) children. Daily 9am–5:30pm, to 5pm in winter. On the main road, an 8-min. walk from the pier or a 15-min. walk from Matsushima Kaigan Station.

ISLANDS

On the southern edge of Matsushima about a 10-minute walk from Matsushima Kaigan Station is **Oshima** (also spelled Ojima), a small island once used as a retreat by priests. At one time, there used to be more than 100 hand-dug caves with carvings of scriptures, Buddhist images, and sutras, but today the island and its remaining 50 caves and stone images are rather neglected and forgotten. There's no fee, no gate, and the island never closes. Connected to the mainland by bridge, it's a nice quiet spot to sit and view the harbor; you can walk around the entire island in about 20 minutes. Because it was a Buddhist retreat, women were forbidden on the island until after the Meiji Restoration in 1868.

At the other end of Matsushima about a 10-minute walk from the boat pier is **Fukuurajima,** another island connected to the mainland, this time by a long red concrete bridge with orange-colored railings. It's a botanical garden of sorts, with several hundred labeled plants and trees, but mostly it's unkempt and over-grown—which comes as a surprise in cultivated Japan. It takes less than an hour to walk completely around the island, with many resting spots along the way, including a snack shop selling ice cream and drinks. Between 8am and 6pm

(4:30pm in winter), you must pay ¥200 ($1.65) admission (half price for children), but it's free the rest of the time.

WHERE TO STAY

Because this is a popular tourist destination, accommodations in Matsushima are not cheap, especially during the peak months of May through November. For the Tanabata Festival (Aug 6–8 in Sendai) and the Toronagashi Festival (Aug 15–16 in Matsushima), rooms are usually fully booked 6 months in advance and rates are at their highest. Rates are generally lower during the off-season months (Dec–Apr).

Almost all accommodations here are in ryokan, which means you're generally expected to take your dinner and breakfast there.

Directions are given from the boat pier or train station, whichever is closer. The pier and station are about a 6-minute walk apart.

EXPENSIVE

(241) **Hotel Ichinobo** ★★ Despite its large size, modern facilities, and having the word "hotel" in its name, this property has the atmosphere of a traditional ryokan and offers mostly Japanese-style rooms. It's surrounded by pine trees and boasts lovely landscaped grounds and ponds, with views of the sea and islands. However, its location on the northern edge of Matsushima—about a 20-minute walk from the pier—is inconvenient, though there is a free shuttle service to both the pier and train station several times every morning. A huge plus is that all rooms look out over the bay; the more expensive rooms overlook the beautiful garden as well. Rooms, 10 of which are singles and 7 twins, are comfortable and come equipped with wet bars, perfect for entertaining. Even the bathroom areas boast two sinks. Kaiseki dinners and buffet breakfasts are served in a dining room.

Matsushima Kaigan, Matsushima-cho, Miyagi-gun 981-0215. ✆ **022/353-3333.** Fax 022/353-3339. m_yoyaku@ichinobu.com. 126 units. ¥17,000–¥25,000 ($142–$208) per person Apr–Sept; ¥15,000–¥20,000 ($125–$167) per person Oct–Mar. Rates include 2 meals. AE, DC, JCB, MC, V. Free shuttle from Matsushima Kaigan Station or Matsushima Kaigan Pier; call for pickup. **Amenities:** 1 restaurant (kaiseki), 1 bar; outdoor pool (free for hotel guests); public indoor and outdoor baths; in-room massage; same-day laundry/dry cleaning service; glass museum (10% discount for hotel guests). *In room:* A/C, TV, minibar, hot-water pot with tea, hair dryer, safe, washlet toilet.

Matsushima Century Hotel ★ This white hotel, near Fukuurajima island, is popular with families. I recommend taking a Japanese-style room or combination room with both tatami area and beds, as these all face the bay with a balcony and chairs. Otherwise, if you're on a budget, the Western-style rooms, though sunny and cheerful, face only inland and have no balcony, but are the cheapest rates given below. Meals are served in a restaurant; breakfast is an all-you-can-eat buffet.

8 Aza Senzui, Matsushima-cho, Miyagi-gun 981-0213. ✆ **022/354-4111.** Fax 022/354-4191. 135 units. ¥12,000–¥16,000 ($100–$133) per person in summer; ¥10,000–¥13,000 ($83–$108) per person in winter. Rates include 2 meals. AE, DC, JCB, MC, V. A 5-min. walk east of the pier. Call for a pickup from the station or pier. **Amenities:** 2 Japanese restaurants, 1 coffee shop; outdoor pool (free for hotel guests); public baths (with sauna) overlooking the bay; in-room massage; same-day laundry/dry cleaning service. *In room:* A/C, TV, minibar, hot-water pot with tea, hair dryer, safe (in Japanese-style rooms only).

(242) **Taikanso** ★★ Able to accommodate 1,100 guests, Matsushima's largest hotel sprawls atop a plateau surrounded by pine-covered hills and offers the best view in town. To compensate for its isolation, a free shuttle bus operates between the hotel and Matsushima Kaigan Station every 20 minutes. Both Western- and Japanese-style rooms are available, though the cheapest rooms (singles and

twins) face inland. All the Japanese-style rooms face the sea, including wonderful combination rooms (the most expensive) which offer the best of both worlds with a tatami area, beds, bedside controls for curtains and lights, and wall-to-wall windows offering great views. A plus here is that you can choose which of six restaurants you wish to dine in, with rates dependent on the meal and restaurant. One of the least expensive is one of my favorites: Shiosai (see "Where to Dine," below), which has the best view in town of both Matsushima Bay and the surrounding hills. The front desk is very helpful with sightseeing information in English.

10–76 Aza Inuta, Matsushima-cho, Miyagi-gun 981-0213. © 022/354-2161. Fax 022/353-3431. www. taikanso.co.jp. 256 units. ¥12,000–¥31,000 ($100–$258) per person including 2 meals; ¥9,600–¥24,800 ($80–$207) per person double occupancy including breakfast. Winter discounts available. AE, DC, JCB, MC, V. Free shuttle bus meets trains at Matsushima Kaigan Station; or a 20-min. walk. **Amenities:** 7 restaurants and bars; outdoor pool (free for hotel guests); indoor and outdoor public baths overlooking the island-studded bay; game room; souvenir and amenities shop; room service (8pm–midnight); in-room massage; same-day laundry/dry cleaning service. *In room:* A/C, TV, minibar, hot-water pot with tea, hair dryer, safe.

MODERATE

Folkloro Matsushima *Value* Opened in 1999, this modern, simple budget hotel with Western-style rooms is located on a hill above the train station and has a nice outdoor terrace where you can have breakfast (dinner is not available). Catering mostly to couples and families, it offers only twins and larger, family rooms with two twin beds and two sofa beds, some of which have views of the sea. Note that *yukata* (cotton robes) are not standard fare, but you can rent one for ¥100 (85¢).

17 Sanjukari, Matsushima Aza, Matsushima-cho, Miyagi-gun 981-0213. © 022/353-3535. Fax 022/ 353-3588. 29 units. Peak season, ¥13,000 ($108) twin; ¥16,000 ($133) for two, ¥19,000 ($158) for three, and ¥22,000 ($183) for four people in family room. Regular season, ¥12,000 ($100)twin; ¥14,000 ($117) for two, ¥17,000 ($142) for three, and ¥20,000 ($167) for four in family room. Rates include breakfast. No credit cards. A 10-min. walk from Matsushima Kaigan Station. Take a right out of the station, then another right under the tracks, and continue straight up the hill; it will be on your left. *In room:* A/C, TV, fridge, hot-water pot with tea.

Hotel Daimatsuso Although an older, slightly worn hotel, with a lobby whose souvenir shop and vending machines make it seem crowded, but homey nonetheless, Hotel Daimatsuso has the advantage of being close to the train station. It also offers Japanese-style rooms that face the sea with balconies. Best are those on the 5th floor, some of which are also combination rooms with beds and tatami areas. The cheapest rooms (both Japanese and Western style) have no bathrooms and look unceremoniously onto another building next door; this is where you'll probably end up if you opt for a room without meals. Rooms come with the basics, and some of the built-in bathroom units are so small you have to wonder how some people fit into them. If you take your meals here, dinner will be served in your room, while breakfast is served communally in the ground-floor dining room.

Koen-mae, Matsushima Kaigan Eki, Matsushima, Miyagi-gun 981-0213. © 022/354-3601. Fax 022/ 354-6154. 41 units (4 with toilet only, 29 with bathroom). ¥7,000–¥8,000 ($58–$67) per person without meals; ¥8,000–¥15,000 ($67–$125) per person with 2 meals. AE, DC, JCB, MC, V. A 1-min. walk from Matsushima Kaigan Station. Walk straight out of the station; it will be on your left. *In room:* A/C, TV, minibar, hot-water pot with tea, safe.

243 **Matsushima Kanko Hotel** ★★ *Finds* This is my top choice if you want to stay in an old-fashioned ryokan. It's popularly called Matsushima-jo, which means Matsushima Castle. Indeed, as Matsushima's oldest ryokan (built about 120 years ago), it does rather resemble a castle with its sloping tiled roof, white

walls, and red railings. Inside it's airy and delightful, with copies of famous woodblock prints lining the wooden corridors and great detailing in some of the tatami rooms. Keep in mind that rooms tend to be drafty in winter, the communal toilets are Japanese style, and the ryokan has arguably seen better days. Yet so much of the ryokan's old character remains intact that you can easily imagine what those better days were like. For a romantic, this is the place. And some rooms have good views of the bay, though you'll have to take meals here to get one of those. The public bath uses heated cold-springs water, which is very salty.

Matsushima Kaigan Pier, Matsushima-cho, Miyagi-gun 981-0213. © 022/354-2121. Fax: 022/354-2883. 28 units (7 with bathroom). ¥10,000–¥30,000 ($83–$250) per person including 2 meals; ¥6,300–¥9,800 ($52.50–$82) per person room only. No credit cards. Conveniently located across from Godaido worship hall, a 4-min. walk east of the boat pier; turn right (east), and it's on your left up a driveway after the second traffic signal. *In room:* A/C, TV, fridge, hot-water pot with tea, safe, no phone.

INEXPENSIVE

(244) **Ryokan Kozakura** This 25-year-old ryokan is very simple but serves delicious and generous Japanese meals in your tatami room. The owners are friendly but don't speak much English. One drawback to the place is that it's on the main truck route; if you're a light sleeper, request a room at the back.

13–7 Aza Fugendo, Matsushima-cho, Miyagi-gun 981-0213. © 022/354-2518. Fax 022/354-5353. 12 units (4 with bathroom). ¥4,000–¥6,000 ($33–$50) per person without meals; ¥7,000–¥15,000 ($58–$125) per person with 2 meals. No credit cards. A 5-min. walk from the pier. Take a right onto the main street and continue past the third signal; it's just past a sake shop, on the left. *In room:* A/C, TV, minibar, hot-water pot with tea.

WHERE TO DINE

In summer, stalls up and down the main street of Matsushima sell grilled octopus, corn on the cob, and crab.

(245) **Donjiki Chaya** NOODLES/ODANGO This rustic noodle shop is a convenient place for a light, inexpensive lunch if you're visiting Zuiganji and Entsuin temples. Built about 400 years ago, it's easy to spot because of its thatched roof, with sliding doors pushed wide open in summer and tatami seating. In addition to noodles, it also serves *odango*—pounded rice balls covered with sesame, red bean, or soy sauce for ¥450 ($3.75). There's an English menu.

Entsuin-mae, Matsushima. © 022/354-5855. Noodles ¥350–¥500 ($2.90–$4.15). No credit cards. Apr–Nov, daily 9am–5pm; Dec–Mar, daily 9am–4pm. In front of Entsuin Temple, a 5-min. walk from Matsushima Kaigan Station or the pier.

Shiosai ★★ *Value* FRENCH Located atop a hill, this restaurant has the best view in town. Book a table at sunset close to the floor-to-ceiling windows overlooking Matsushima, where you can watch the day fade and lights in the town below begin to glimmer. Only set meals are available, but they're very good and surprisingly inexpensive. My ¥2,300 ($19) dinner consisted of soup, lobster ravioli and grilled fish, salad, bread, dessert, and coffee or tea. A good place for a romantic meal on a budget. Or, from 2:30 to 4pm, come for dessert and coffee or the local Matsushima Brewing Company beer and enjoy the view.

Taikanso Hotel, 7th floor, 10–76 Aza Inuta. © 022/354-2161. Set lunches ¥1,600–¥5,000 ($13–$42); set dinners ¥2,300–¥5,000 ($19–$42). Daily 11:30am–2:30pm and 5:30–8:30pm (last order). For directions, see "Where to Stay," above.

Ungai ★ *Finds* BUDDHIST VEGETARIAN Located on the grounds of Entsuin Temple (to the right after entering), this is a great place for a peaceful meal, as you dine in a modern tatami room and look out over a garden. It serves three set meals typical of Buddhist vegetarian cuisine; let your budget be your guide.

Entsuin Temple, 67 Aza-chonai. ☏ **022/353-2626.** Reservations required one day in advance. Set meals ¥3,500 ($29), ¥5,000 ($42), and ¥7,000 ($58). No credit cards. Daily 11am–3pm. Next to Zuiganji Temple (to the left as you face it).

2 Kakunodate, Town of Samurai Homes ⨀

Kakunodate was founded in 1620 by feudal lord Ashina Yoshikatsu, who chose the site for its river and easily defendable mountain. His samurai retainers settled just south of his hilltop castle, in modest thatched-roof homes behind wooden fences along wide, fine streets, which they lined with weeping cherry trees imported from Kyoto. To help support themselves, the samurai engaged in cottage industry, crafting beautiful products made from cherry bark. Meanwhile, merchants settled in their own district, in narrow, cramped quarters.

Although the castle is long gone, Kakunodate's castle-town architectural layout remains remarkably intact, with one of the country's best-preserved (though regrettably small) samurai districts in Japan. It's also famous for its cherry trees, not only in the samurai district but also along the banks of the Hinokinai River, and crafts produced from local cherry bark are still famous throughout Japan. Yet Kakunodate is an unpretentious village, with only a few of the souvenir and tourist shops that plague other picturesque towns. Many of its 14,800 residents are direct descendents of the town's original samurai and merchants.

ESSENTIALS
GETTING THERE   From Tokyo, take the **Tohoku Shinkansen train** from Ueno or Tokyo Station to Morioka and then the **Akita Shinkansen** to Kakunodate (you can travel some Shinkansen the entire distance without having to transfer in Morioka). The trip takes about 3½ hours and costs ¥14,980 ($125) for an unreserved seat. Kakunodate is just one stop before Tazawako (see "Towada-Hachimantai National Park: For the Active Traveler," below).

VISITOR INFORMATION   After exiting from Kakunodate Station, look for the **Kakunodate Tourist Information Center** to the right, housed in a replica traditional warehouse (☏ **0187/54-2700;** open daily 9am–6pm), where you can pick up an English map.

ORIENTATION & GETTING AROUND   You can walk to all the sights and lodging and dining recommendations below (though you might opt for a short taxi ride to your accommodations if you're weighed down by luggage). To reach the samurai district, about a 15- to 20-minute walk from the station, walk straight out of the station and continue until it ends at a T-intersection (you'll see a post office across the street; this is the former merchant district and the heart of the city) and then turn right.

CAR RENTALS   If you've rented a car through **JR Eki Rent-A-Car** (☏ **0187/53-2070**), you can pick it up at Folkloro Kakunodate, a JR-owned hotel beside the station to the left. For **Toyota Rent-A-Car** in Kakunodate, call ☏ **0187/55-2100.**

SEEING THE SIGHTS
Kakunodate is at its most glorious (and crowded) in late April, when its hundreds of cherry trees are in full bloom. The most popular viewing spot is along the Hinokinai River, where two rows of some 370 cherry trees form a

shimmering tunnel of blossoms for 2km (1¼ miles). They were planted in 1933 to commemorate the birth of the present emperor, Akihito.

THE SAMURAI DISTRICT (BUKEYASHIKI) ★★ Of Kakunodate's 80-some samurai mansions built during the Edo Period, only six remain. Still, the district retains its feudal atmosphere to an amazing degree, thanks to its wide streets flanked by weeping cherry trees and dark wooden fences. These fences and traditional entry gates are even employed today to conceal more modern homes, giving a clean, crisp line of vision throughout the district. It's a strong contrast to the jumble of most Japanese cities, and even to the merchant district just a short walk away.

If you're walking from the station, the first place of interest will be the ㉖ **Aoyagi Samurai Manor** (Kakunodate Rekishi-mura Aoyagi) ★★★ Higashi Katuraku-cho 26 (© **0187/54-3257**) to the right through an impressive entry gate. Its English name is misleading, since it's actually a compound of several traditional buildings spread throughout a garden, each filled with a wealth of eclectic treasures from the 17th to 20th centuries, all collected through the ages by the Aoyagi family. As you wander throughout, you'll see samurai armor, rifles, swords, dolls, kimono, sake cups, *ukiyo-e* (woodblock prints), scrolls and screens, Meiji-Era uniforms and medals, farm tools, a great collection of album covers (from Billie Holiday to Karajan conducting the Vienna Philharmonic Orchestra), antique record players, and cameras. One building serves as a fascinating antiques store (with high prices), while others hold a gift shop and restaurant. You'll want to spend at least an hour exploring here. Open daily 9am to 5pm (to 4pm in winter). Admission is ¥500 ($4.15) for adults, ¥300 ($2.50) for junior-high and high school students, and ¥200 ($1.65) for children.

Next door is the **Ishiguro Samurai House** ★★, Omotemachi (© **0187/ 55-1496**). In contrast to the Aoyagi Samurai Manor, this thatched-roof home remains almost exactly as it might have looked when it was constructed 200 years ago by the Ishiguro samurai family. After the Meiji Restoration, the family became landlords and collected rice as rent. Today, English-speaking, 12th-generation Ishiguro Naotsugi continues to live here; he has opened five simple but elegant rooms to the public in the main house. Family heirlooms, including samurai gear, winter *geta* (fur-lined and with spikes), scales for weighing rice, and old maps of Kakunodate are on display in a former warehouse. The medical illustrations (copies), by the way, are from Japan's first book on anatomy, copied from a Dutch book in 1774 by Kakunodate samurai Odano Naotake. You can see everything in less than 30 minutes, though if Ishiguro-san is on hand to answer questions, you might linger longer. Open daily 9am to 5pm. Admission is ¥300 ($2.50) for adults and ¥150 ($1.25) for children.

SHOPPING

Kakunodate has been famous for its cherry-bark crafts since the Edo Period. You can observe this painstaking craft by watching artisans at work at the ㉗ **Kakunodate-machi Denshokan,** Omotemachi Shimocho 10–1 (© **0187/54-1700**), just a couple minutes' walk from the samurai houses, above. In addition to seeing how strips of cherry bark are applied to tea canisters, boxes, vases, and other crafts, you can also tour a small museum devoted to the craft and shop for cherry-bark products in its large shop. Admission is ¥300 ($2.50) for adults and ¥150 ($1.25) for children. It's open daily 9am to 5pm (to 4:30pm in winter).

There's a smaller shop outlet of *the denshokan* at the train station, open daily 9am to 6pm.

WHERE TO STAY

Although you can easily tour Kakunodate's sights in a day, I've included a few accommodations in case you're arriving from Tokyo or seeking respite in a small town. Keep in mind that you should book well ahead if you hope to stay here during cherry-blossom season.

Folkloro Kakunodate   No English is spoken at this JR-affiliated hotel, but its location next to Kakunodate Station and simple but clean, modern, and inexpensive Western-style rooms make it a logical choice for a one-night stopover. Only two types of rooms are available: 11 twins and 15 family rooms that sleep up to four. Note, however, that the family rooms seem cramped for four but are roomy for two.

Iwaseihaza, Nakasuga-sawa 14, Kakunodate, Akita. ℂ **0187/53-2070.** Fax 0187/53-2118. 26 units. Peak season, ¥13,000 ($108) twin; ¥16,000 ($133) for 2, ¥19,000 ($158) for 3, and ¥22,000 ($183) for 4 people in family room. Regular season, ¥12,000 ($100) twin; ¥14,000 ($117) for 2, ¥17,000 ($142) for 3, and ¥20,000 ($167) for 4 in family room. Rates include breakfast. No credit cards. To the left after exiting the station. **Amenities:** 1 restaurant (Japanese and Western food); nonsmoking rooms; car-rental agency. *In room:* TV, fridge, hot-water pot with tea, hair dryer.

(248) **Ishikawa Ryokan**   One of Kakunodate's oldest ryokan, open since the Edo Period and now in its 5th generation of innkeepers, this establishment has been modernized and is a bit drab in parts. But although corridors suggest the ordinary, the Japanese-style rooms are fine, simple but with nice wood details. And the elderly couple running the ryokan, every bit as self-effacing as their ancestors must have been to traveling samurai and other high officials, couldn't be nicer (though they don't speak English). Meals are served in your room.

Iwamasemachi 32, Kakunodate, Akita. ℂ **0187/54-2030.** 12 units (2 with bathroom, 1 with toilet only). ¥9,000–¥18,000 ($75–$150) per person. Rates include two meals and tax. No credit cards. A 12-min. walk from the station. Walk straight out of the station, turning left at the 4th street (1 block before the T intersection); it will be on your right. *In room:* A/C, TV, hot-water pot with tea.

(249) **Tamachi Bukeyashiki Hotel** 🌟🌟 *Finds*   This delightful hotel is deceiving—it looks as though it has been here since the Edo Period with its white-washed walls, open wooden beams, and rustic ambiance. Built in 1999, it combines tradition with modern comfort, with gleaming wood floors, contemporary Japanese art, and Japanese- and Western-style rooms that exude class, from sensuously curving paper lampshades to ceramic tissue holders. Breakfast is served in an adjoining tatami restaurant. In short, this small, intimate establishment is a perfect choice for experiencing Kakunodate's relaxed, small-town charm.

Tamachi Shimocho 23, Kakunodate, Akita. ℂ **0187/52-1700.** Fax 0187/52-1701. 12 units. ¥10,500 ($87.50) per person. Winter discounts available. Rates include breakfast. Dinner ¥5,500 ($46) extra. JCB, V. A 12-min. walk from the station. Walk straight out of the station, turning left at the 3rd street; it will be a couple blocks down, on your right. **Amenities:** 1 restaurant (Japanese). *In room:* A/C, fridge, hot-water pot with tea, hair dryer, washlet toilet.

WHERE TO DINE

In addition to the choices below, a simple dining room at Aoyagi Samurai Manor called **Inaniwa Korai Udon** (ℂ **0187/52-8015**) offers noodle dishes priced under ¥1,000 ($8.15), including tempura soba and sansai udon (noodles with mountain vegetables).

(250) **Nishinomiyake** 🌟 VARIED JAPANESE   This pleasant inexpensive restaurant is located in the family compound of the Nishinomiya clan, a samurai family that later became merchants and built the main house and five

warehouses that are on display today. The restaurant is in a warehouse dating from 1919 and offers a limited menu of fried seafood, noodles, hash beef with rice and other dishes. Best, perhaps, is to order one of the obento lunch boxes. After your meal, be sure to wander through the other warehouses, including a small museum housing family treasures and a craft shop.

Tamachi Kami-cho 11–1. ℂ **0187/52-2438.** Obento ¥1,500–¥2,000 ($12.50–$17). JCB, V. Daily 9:30am–6pm. An 8-min. walk from Kakunodate Station. Walk straight out of the station, turning left at the 3rd street; it will be almost immediately on your right.

㉕ **Shi Chi Be Ei** VARIED JAPANESE   This airy, modern restaurant is conveniently located between the train station and the samurai disrict. It offers a variety of dishes from a Japanese menu, including noodles (the "Udon Gozen" set includes udon noodles, tempura, vegetables, and a rice ball), obento lunch boxes, and steaks (a house specialty).

Yokomachi 15. ℂ **0187/54-3295.** Set lunches ¥720–¥980 ($6–$8); set meals and obento ¥900–¥1,800 ($7.50–$15); steak set meals ¥5,000–¥7,000 ($42–$58). AE, DC, JCB, MC, V. Wed–Mon 10am–9pm. A 12-min. walk from Kakunodate Station. Walk straight out of the station, turning right at the T-intersection; it will be on your right, just past the traffic light and gas station.

3 Towada-Hachimantai National Park: For the Active Traveler

The **Towada-Hachimantai National Park,** spreading 333 square miles through north central Tohoku and shared by three prefectures, is blessed with mountain ranges, lakes, streams, and hot-spring spas. It's perfect for the outdoor enthusiast, offering hiking in summer and skiing in winter. Most easily accessible from Tokyo is **Lake Tazawa** in the southern end of the park with its nearby ski lifts, hot-springs, and biking and hiking opportunities. Far to the north, and a good choice if you're heading onward to Hokkaido, are the pristine **Lake Towada** and its delightful **Oriase Stream** with its riverbank hiking trail.

Unfortunately, bus service through Towada-Hachimantai National Park is either infrequent or nonexistent. There is, for example, no bus that connects lakes Tazawa and Towada, so you either have to choose which one to visit or make a long, circuitious journey by bus and train. If you want to see both, your best bet is to rent a car.

LAKE TAZAWA AND NYUTO ONSEN

Lake Tazawa (Tazawako) has the distinction of being the deepest lake in Japan, 423m (1,387 ft.) deep. Crystal clear, it offers swimming and cycling along its rim. Nearby are several ski resorts, as well as rustic hot-spring spas at the base of Mt. Nyuto that make good bases for exploring the area. Mt. Komagatake is a popular destination for trekkers.

ESSENTIALS

GETTING THERE   From Tokyo, take the **Tohoku Shinkansen train** from Ueno or Tokyo Station to Morioka and then the **Akita Shinkansen** to Tazawako Station (you can travel some Shinkansen the entire distance without having to transfer in Morioka). The trip takes about 3 hours and costs ¥14,190 ($118) for an unreserved seat. Tazawako is one stop before Kakunodate (see "Kakunodate, Town of Samurai Homes," above). In Tazawako you can board a bus to all the recommendations below, including Nyuto Onsen.

VISITOR INFORMATION   For information on Lake Tazawa and vicinity, including skiing and bus schedules throughout the region, stop by the

Tawazako Tourist Information Center inside Tazawako Station (© 0187/
43-2111; open daily 8:30am–6pm).

ORIENTATION & GETTING AROUND   The town of Tazawako, in Akita
Prefecture, is the transportation launching pad for visiting the southern region
of Towada-Hachimantai National Park. **Buses** depart from the Tazawako Bus
Terminal across from Tazawako Station for Lake Tazawa, area ski resorts, Mt.
Komagatake, and Nyuto Onsen hot-spring spas. Ask for bus schedules at the
Tazawako Tourist Information Center.

Lake Tazawa is just a 15-minute bus ride from Tawazako Station; note that
some buses stopping here go onward to Tazawako Skijo ski resort, Kogen Onsen,
and Nyuto Onsen, all of which lie northeast of the lake. Otherwise, a bus
departs Tazawako Station approximately every hour for Tazawako Skijo (a 30-
min. ride), Kogen Onsen (37 min.) and Nyuto Onsen (45 min.)

CAR RENTALS   Tazawako is a good starting point for driving excursions
through Towado-Hachimantai National Park. **JR Eki Rent-A-Car** (© 0187/
43-1081) is located beside Tazawako Station. For **Toyota Rent-A-Car** in
Tazawako, call © 0187/43-2100.

WHAT TO SEE & DO

SWIMMING AND CYCLING AT LAKE TAZAWA   Just 20km (12½ miles)
in circumference, Lake Tazawa is popular for its small swimming beach just a
couple minutes' walk from Tazawako Kohan bus stop. Outside the swimming
season—mid-July through August—you'll find nary a soul there. There are also
bikes you can rent at the lake, costing ¥400 ($3.35) per hour. It takes about 2
hours to ride around the lake; unfortunately, you have to share the road with
vehicular traffic, but because this is a popular cycling route, motorists know to
keep a lookout (still, it may be prudent to avoid weekends and the mid-July-
through-August vacation crunch). Except for one small stretch, the road is
mostly flat (it may be easier to circle the lake counter-clockwise) and is pleasantly wooded and relatively unspoiled. Along the way you'll pass a golden statue
of the legendary Princess Tatsuko, a nymph-like beauty just off the shoreline.

Finally, there are also sightseeing boats operating on Lake Tazawa from late
April to early November, costing ¥1,170 ($9.75) for the 40-minute trip.

There are many buses traveling the 15 minutes between Lake Tazawa and
Tazawako Station. Fare is ¥350 ($2.90); get off at the Tazawako Kohan bus stop.

SKIING   Of several area ski resorts, largest is **Tazawako Skijo** (© 0187/
46-2011), with nine lifts. A one-day lift ticket costs ¥3,400 ($28) weekdays and
¥3,900 ($32) weekends and holidays. Ski equipment rentals cost ¥5,000 ($42)
for everything; snowboarding is also available. Buses from Tazawako Station
(traveling in the direction of Nyuto Onsen) reach Tazawako Skijo in about 30
minutes and cost ¥580 ($4.85).

Smaller, with four lifts, is nearby **Tazawakokougen Assl Skijo** (© 0187/
46-2723), while **Nyuto Skijo** (© 0187/46-2244), in Nyuto Onsen, has only
one and is recommended only for beginners.

CLIMBING MT. KOMAGATAKE   Visible from Lake Tazawa, Akita Prefecture's tallest mountain is actually a 5,370-foot-high dormant volcano. It's a
popular destination for hikers, though a bus that deposits hikers at the 8th
Station makes it a fairly quick hike—you can reach the top in about 1½ hours
or so. At the peak you're rewarded with grand vistas of the surrounding

mountains, as well as continuing hiking trails. Since the path is steep at times, wear non-slip soles (all the Japanese will be outfitted in regulation hiking regalia). To reach Mt. Komagatake's 8th Station, take a bus from from Tazawako Station 37 minutes to Kogen Onsen, transferring there for a 25-minute ride to the 8th station (a few buses a day travel from Tazawa Station all the way to the 8th Station). The fare from Tazawako Station is ¥810 ($6.75), ¥410 ($3.40) from Kogen Onsen. *Tip*: "If you've rented a car, you can drive all the way to the 8th Station, though access is severely restricted. During peak season, you have to drive up before 6am (you'd be astounded by the number of people who do).

WHERE TO STAY

By far, the best place to stay in this region is **Nyuto Onsen** with its seven hot springs. In contrast to most onsen, which consist of ryokan clustered in a village or town, Nyuto Onsen is centered on an isolated, winding country road, with a handful of rustic, secluded ryokan scattered along its length. Unsurprisingly, access is a problem if you don't have a car, though there are some nine buses a day from Tazawako Station that travel the Nyuto Onsen road; it takes 45 to 50 minutes by bus and costs ¥740 ($6.15).

(252) **Kuroyu** ★★   Although I'm partial to Tsuru-no-yu (see below), some consider this Nyuto Onsen's best place to stay. A little more than 1km (½ mile or a 20-min. walk) from the main Nyuto Onsen road, this rustic inn has a secluded spot and one of the area's best outdoor baths, separated for men and women and with good views of the surrounding mountainside. Although first opened as a ryokan more than 60 years ago, its present thatched-roof accommodations were constructed in the 1990s, with small, very simple tatami rooms. Clearly, what draws most of the retirees who flock here are the baths. Meals are served in a communal dining room.

2–1 Kuroyu, Tazawako-machi, Senboku-gun, Akita 014-1201. ✆ **0187/46-2214.** Fax 0187/46-2280. 20 units (none with bathroom). ¥11,700 ($97.50) per person. Rates include 2 meals, tax, and service charge. Closed Nov–Apr. No credit cards. Bus: from Tazawako Station 50 min. to Kuroyu bus stop and then a 20-min. walk; a few buses a day go directly to the inn (ask for a schedule). **Amenities:** Indoor/outdoor hot-spring baths. *In room:* Hot-water pot with tea, no phone.

(253) **Qkamura National Park Resort Village (Kyukamura Tazawako-Kogen)**   This government-owned public lodging offers the convenience of being right on Nyuto Onsen's main road (buses from Tazawako Station stop right outside). While it lacks the wonderful ambiance of the other rustic inns in the area and has about as much charm as a dormitory, it was recently renovated and offers both indoor and outdoor hot-spring baths. In addition, it's the only place to stay if you prefer Western-style rooms, though Japanese tatami rooms are also available. Rooms are simple but pleasant, with sinks and toilets. If you stay here, you can always sample the other ryokans' hot-spring baths by paying a modest fee. Buffet-style meals are served in a communal dining room.

Komagatake 2–1, Tazawako-machi, Senboku-gun, Akita 014-1201. 38 units (all with toilet only, none with bathrooms). ¥11,000 ($92) single; ¥10,000 ($83) per person double. Rates include two meals. JCB, MC, V. Bus: from Tazawako Station 50 min. to Qkamura-mae stop. **Amenities:** Indoor/outdoor hot-spring baths, coin-op washer and dryer. *In room:* TV, hot-water pot with tea, safe.

(254) **Tsuru-no-yu Onsen** ★★★ *Finds*   By far, this is the best place to stay in Nyuto Onsen, if not all of Tohoku. Contrary to what you might think, however, it's not refined or elegant; it's not even expensive. Rather, nestled in a wooded valley more than 2.5km (1½ miles) off the already isolated main Nyuto Onsen

road, this is about as remote as you can get in Japan. And with its thatched-roof row house of tiny tatami rooms lit by oil lamps, complemented by the sound of rushing water and steam rising from the outdoor baths, it seems positively ancient. I've never seen anything like it.

Tsuru-no-yu opened as an onsen 350 years ago; its oldest building—the row house of connected rooms—is 100 years old (the biggest drawback to staying in one of these is that you have to walk outside to reach a bathroom, a definite inconvenience in winter). Additions that ramble along the hillside were added over the years; the best room, on a corner beside the rushing stream, has its own toilet and open-hearth fireplace (*irori*) where you'll have dinner (breakfast is served in a dining hall). If you're on a budget, however, you can stay in the self-cooking wing, which offers simple tatami rooms and allows you to cook your own meals in a communal kitchen. Outdoor sulfurous baths are separated for men and women but are not especially private, and unfortunately, daytrippers spoil some of the fun of staying here. Evenings, however, are magical. Another plus: This is one of the few onsen open all year, with great cross-country skiing. *Caveat*: Avoid the modern annex Yama no Dado about 10 minutes down the road. Its indoor baths are unspectacular (and its outdoor bath is for both sexes); if you've come this far, stay in the real thing.

Kokuyurin 50, Tazawako-machi, Senboku-gun, Akita 014-1204. © 0187/46-2139. Fax 0187/46-2761. 35 units (9 with toilet, none with bathrooms). ¥8,000–¥15,000 ($67–$125) per person including two meals. ¥2,500 ($21) per person in the self-cooking wing with communal kitchen. JCB, MC, V. Pick up available from Kogen Onsen bus station. **Amenities:** Indoor/outdoor hot-spring baths. *In room:* Hot-water pot with tea, no phone in cheapest rooms.

LAKE TOWADA & ORIASE STREAM ✿✿

Located on the northern end of Towada-Hachimantai National Park on the border between Aomori and Akita prefectures, **Lake Towada** (Towadako in Japanese) is considered one of the park's top scenic gems. It's certainly one of Japan's least spoiled lakes, with only two small villages on its perimeter and encircled by wooded cliffs and mountains. Best, however, is **Oriase Stream,** the only river flowing out of Lake Towada. A shaded, mountain stream that courses over boulders and down waterfalls, it is flanked by a hiking trail that offers one of the prettiest walks in Tohoku. In autumn, leaves of gold and red render the scenery truly spectacular.

ESSENTIALS

GETTING THERE   Since Lake Towada does not lie close to a train station, you must first take a **Shinkansen train** to Morioka (about 2½ hr. from Tokyo), Towada-Minami, or Aomori and then continue onward by **bus.** From Morioka, there are four buses that depart daily from in front of the train station bound for Yasumiya (also called Towadako-machi), a small village on Lake Towada with a tourist office and a few accommodations; the name of the bus stop in Yasumiya is Towadako. The bus trip takes about 2¼ hours and costs ¥2,420 ($20), though there's one JR bus daily you can ride for free if you have a JR railpass (at last check it departed Morioka at 3pm). Towada-Minami is the closest train station to Lake Towada; there are four buses daily to Yasumiya costing ¥1,130 ($9.40).

Aomori is more convenient if you're arriving from Hokkaido. Outside Aomori Station, to the left, you can board a JR bus bound for Lake Towada, with the last stop at Yasumiya. If you have a JR railpass you can ride for free. Otherwise, the 3-hour bus ride costs ¥3,000 ($25). Note that this bus travels the same road as the hiking trail along Oriase Stream (see below) and makes several stops there, with about six runs daily. Note, too, that bus service to Lake Towada is available only from April to early November; for a JR bus, you can make reservations in advance at a major JR train station or travel agency. For more information, contact the JR Bus company in Aomori at ℂ 017/773-5722.

CAR RENTALS JR Eki Rent-A-Car has offices at Aomori Station (ℂ 017/722-3930) and Morioka Station (ℂ 019/624-5212). **Toyota Rent-A-Car** also has offices near Aomori Station (ℂ 017/734-0100) and Morioka Station (ℂ 019/622-0100).

VISITOR INFORMATION At the Tokyo, Kyoto, or Narita or Kansai Airport Tourist Information Centers, be sure to pick up the leaflet "Towada-Hachimantai National Park."

In Yasumiya, the **Lake Towada Information Center** (ℂ 0176/75-2425; open daily 8am–5pm) is located next to the JR Bus Center (to the right after exiting the bus terminal's main door). Be sure to ask for your Aomori Welcome Card, free for visiting foreigners and providing discounts to several area accommodations and the sightseeing boat on Lake Towada.

ORIENTATION & GETTING AROUND Yasumiya, a village on the southwestern shore of Lake Towada, has a bus terminal, tourist office, and a handful of accommodations and restaurants. On the eastern side of the lake is Nenokuchi, trailhead for hikes along Oriase Stream. You can reach Yasumiya, Nenokuchi and several stops along the hiking trail via the same **JR bus** that connects Lake Towada with Aomori Station, with approximately six runs a day from April to early November. Otherwise, your best bet for travel between Yasumiya and Nenokuchi is via **sightseeing boat** (see below).

SEEING THE SIGHTS

In Yasumiya, the major point of interest is **Towada Jinja Shrine,** which boasts marvelous wood carvings of animals. Nearby, on the shore of Towadako, is a sculpture of two middle-aged women, whose generous proportions are a welcome sight after the golden nymph at Lake Tazawa.

SIGHTSEEING BOATS ON LAKE TOWADA The best way to enjoy the pristine beauty of crystal-clear **Lake Towada** (Towadako), a double caldera formed some 20,000 years ago by a volcanic eruption, is aboard excursion boats that cruise the waters April to mid-November. About 44km (27 miles) of undulating coastline marked by capes, inlets, cliffs, and trees that put on a spectacular autumn show make this one of Towada-Hachimantai National Park's major draws. Two cruises are available: a 1-hour cruise that begins and ends at Yasumiya, and a 50-minute cruise that travels between Yasumiya and Nenokuchi. Cost of either is ¥1,320 ($11) for adults and ¥660 ($5.50) for children (the Aomori Welcome Card provides a 10% discount). A surcharge of ¥500 ($4.15) for adults and ¥250 ($2.10) for children is levied if you wish to sit in the top lounge.

HIKING ORIASE STREAM 🐾🐾 To my mind, hiking along the Oriase Stream is the major draw for a trip to Lake Towada. A clear-running, gurgling stream that runs 67km (42 miles) on its way from the lake to the Pacific Ocean, it's at its picture-perfect best in **Oriase Gorge,** where hikers are treated to a myriad of waterfalls, rapids coursing over moss-covered boulders, and a dense wood of Japanese beech, oaks, and other broadleafed trees. A trail runs beside the stream from Nenokuchi on the lakeshore 14km (8¾ miles) to Yakeyama.

Most hikers, however, go only as far as Ishigedo, hiking the 9km (5½ miles) in about 2 hours. Disappointingly, a road runs through the gorge beside the stream, but the pathway often diverges from the road and the roar of the swift-running river and the 13 waterfalls mask the sound of vehicles.

There are 9 bus stops on the road beside Oriase Stream, including Nenokuchi, Ishigedo, and Yakeyama. Since buses run only once an hour or so, you might consider taking a bus first and then hiking back. Alternatively, if you're coming from or going to Aomori with luggage, you can take advantage of a baggage transfer service for hikers operating between Yakeyama and Nenokuchi (buses will wait for you at Yakeyama if you want to send your luggage onward but wish to begin hiking at Ishigedo). There are **luggage transfers** in both directions four times a day from Golden Week (end of Apr) to early November; the cost is ¥400 ($3.35) a bag (call ✆ **0176/76-1121**) for schedule information). In any case, the hike upstream (toward Nenokuchi) is considered the most picturesque, since it affords a full view of the cascading rapids.

WHERE TO STAY

Minshuku Himemasu Sanso and Oriase Keiryu Grand Hotel offer a 10% discount on room charges for holders of the Aomori Welcome Card. Be sure to mention the card when making reservations and to show it when checking in. Peak season is August and October; be sure to book far in advance for these months.

(255) **Himemasu Sanso** *Value*   This modest but pleasant *minshuku* has a convenient location near the JR bus terminal in Yasumiya and offers simple tatami rooms, some of which offer good views of the surrounding wooded hills. Meals are served communally and usually feature trout from Lake Towada and local wild mountain vegetables; Western-style breakfasts are available on request.

16 Aza Towada, Oaza Okuse, Towadako-machi, Kamikita-gun, Aomori 018-5501. ✆ **0176/75-2717.** Fax 0176/75-2717. 16 units (none with bathroom). ¥6,300 ($52.50) per person. Rates include 2 meals, tax, and service charge. No credit cards. A 5-min. walk inland from the JR bus station. **Amenities:** Coffee shop. *In room:* TV, hot-water pot with tea, no phone.

Oriase Keiryu Grand Hotel   The main reason for staying in this large, rather ordinary hotel is its location on Oriase Stream, making it an easy base for hiking the Oriase Gorge trail. It also offers a free bus shuttle from Aomori Station (inquire about departure times when making reservations). The hotel is divided into two sections: the older Daiichi (1st) Wing with 105 rooms and the newer Daini (2nd) Wing with 85 rooms. I prefer the Daini with its lobby overlooking the stream and maple trees and hard-to-overlook giant fireplace sculpture by eccentric Okamoto Taro. It offers both Japanese tatami and twin rooms, about half with views of Oriase Stream (which cost an extra ¥2,000/$17). Public hot-spring baths also take advantage of river views.

Oirase Keiryu Onsen, Towadako-machi, Aomori 034-0300. ✆ **0176/74-1111.** Fax 0176/74-1118. 190 units. ¥13,000–¥17,000 ($108–$142) per person. Rates include 2 meals. Off-season discounts available. JCB, MC, V. Bus: Yakeyama (1 min.). **Amenities:** 7 restaurants; 5 bars and lounges; indoor hot-spring baths; game room; souvenir shops; in-room massage; laundry room (free of charge). *In room:* A/C, TV, minibar, hot-water pot with tea, hair dryer, safe.

Towada Hotel ★★★   This imposing, elegant hotel is my top choice for a splurge on Lake Towada. Secluded on a wooded hill overlooking the lake (and practical only if you have your own car), it was built in 1938 using huge cedar logs in a mix of Western-lodge-meets-Japanese-temple style, with a modern addition added years later. Former U.S. ambassador Edwin Reischauer and Emperor Showa have stayed here; nowadays most American guests are high-ranking officers from a nearby U.S. military base. Although all rooms face the lake, best are the Japanese rooms, all in the older part of the hotel and elegant with great views. Western-style rooms, though spacious and beautifully designed, do not have as good a view; be sure to ask for a room on the top floor and be sure, too, to wander over to the older wing for a look at its beautiful wood details in the old lobby (crafted by temple carpenters). Unfortunately, the public baths do not have hot-spring waters, but they do have lakeside views and outdoor tubs. Meals, served in a communal dining room with a mix of Japanese and Western dishes, are substantial. Western-style breakfasts are available.

Gosaka-machi, Towadako Nishi-goham, Akita 018-5511l. *C* **0176/75-1122.** Fax 0176/75-1313. 50 units (46 with bathroom). Peak season, ¥18,000 ($150) per person; regular season, ¥15,000 ($125) weekends and ¥12,000 ($100) weekdays. Rates include 2 meals. AE, DC, JCB, MC, V. Pick-up service available from JR bus terminal in Yasumiya. **Amenities:** 1 restaurant and 1 lounge; indoor/outdoor public baths; Jacuzzi; sauna; in-room massage. *In room:* A/C, TV, minibar, hot-water pot with tea; hair dryer; safe; washlet toilet.

Tsuta Onsen ✦ This classic, north-country inn dates to 1918 and is one of Tohoku's most famous traditional ryokan. *Tsuta* means ivy in Japanese, a theme carried out not only in pillars, transoms, and other architectural details but also in the dense, surrounding beech forest. Rooms in the original wooden structure, up a long flight of stairs, have beautiful wood-carved details and good views but are without bathrooms (they're also cheaper). The rooms in the addition, added in 1989 and served by elevator, lack the character of the older rooms but are nice enough and have the added convenience of bathrooms; for the best views, be sure to request a room facing away from the street. For those who don't like sleeping on futon, there are three combination rooms that offer both a tatami room and beds. The hot-spring baths are new but preserve traditional bathhouse architecture, with tall ceilings and cypress walls. Breakfasts are served in a communal dining room, but for dinner you have a choice of dining communally or in your room. Although not as conveniently located as, say, the Oriase Keiryu Grand Hotel, the same JR bus that travels between Aomori and Lake Towada (it's about a 15-min. bus ride to Yakeyama) serves this hotel, and has its own 1-hour hiking course to a nearby lake.

Okuse. Towadako-machi, Kamikita-gun, Aomori 034-0301. *C* **0176/74-2311.** Fax 0176/74-2244. 50 units (30 with bathroom). ¥10,000–¥32,000 ($83–$267) per person. Rates include 2 meals. DC, JCB. Bus: From Aomori Station, a 2-hour JR bus ride to Tsuta Onsen stop (1 min.). **Amenities:** Hot-spring indoor bath; in-room massage. *In room:* TV, hot-water pot with tea.

WHERE TO DINE

Most accommodations serve breakfast and dinner. For an inexpensive meal on the Oriase Gorge trail, there's a small snack bar at Ishigedo selling ramen noodles, tempura soba, ice cream, and drinks.

Komorebi WESTERN A convenient place for lunch in Yakeyama if you're hiking the Oriase Gorge trail, this simple hotel restaurant offers set lunches that include beef or fish as their main dishes, as well as simpler choices like curry rice from a Japanese menu. There are several other restaurants in the hotel, including those serving Japanese and Chinese food.

Oriase Keiryu Grand Hotel (Daini Wing). Oirase Keiryu Onsen. *C* **0176/74-1111.** Set lunches ¥1,200–¥3,000 ($10–$25). MC, V. Daily 11am–2pm (last order). Bus: Yakeyama (1 min.).

12

Northern Japan—Hokkaido

Hokkaido, the northernmost of Japan's four main islands, has a landscape strikingly different from that of any other place in Japan. With more than 30,000 square miles and accounting for 22% of Japan's total landmass, it has only 5% of its population. In other words, Hokkaido has what the rest of Japan doesn't—space. The least developed of Japan's four islands, it's your best bet for avoiding the crowds that plague Japan's more well-known playgrounds during peak travel season.

Considered the country's last frontier, Hokkaido didn't begin opening up to development until after the Meiji Restoration in 1868, when the government began encouraging Japanese to migrate to the island. Even today, Hokkaido has a frontier feel to it, and many young Japanese come here to backpack, ski, camp, and tour the countryside on motorcycles or bicycles. There are dairy farms, silos, and broad, flat fields of wheat, corn, and potatoes. Where the fields end the land puckers up, becoming craggy with bare volcanoes, deep gorges, and hills densely covered with virgin forests and dotted with clear spring lakes, mountain ranges, rugged wilderness, wild animals, bubbling hot springs, and rare plants. And the people of Hokkaido are as open and hearty as the wide expanses of land around them.

Much of Hokkaido's wilderness has been set aside as national and prefectural parkland. Of these, Shikotsu-Toya, Daisetsuzan, and Akan national parks are the best known, offering a wide range of activities from hiking and skiing to bathing at their *onsen,* or hot-spring spas.

Hokkaido has its main tourist season in August, when days are cool and pleasant with an average temperature of 70°F. While the rest of the nation is afflicted by the rainy season, Hokkaido's summers are usually bright and clear. Winters are long and severe; still, ski enthusiasts flock to slopes near Sapporo and to resorts such as Daisetsuzan National Park, and February marks the annual Sapporo Snow Festival with its huge ice and snow sculptures.

With its Chitose Airport, the city of Sapporo—Japan's largest city north of Tokyo—serves as a springboard to Hokkaido's national parks and lakes. And yet despite all the area has to offer and despite its size and importance, I've seen few foreigners in Sapporo even in August. To most visitors to Japan, Hokkaido remains virtually undiscovered.

1 Hokkaido Essentials

INFORMATION Information on Hokkaido is available online at **www.all-hokkaido.net/marugoto/**.

GETTING THERE & GETTING AROUND The fastest way to reach Hokkaido is to **fly.** Flights from Tokyo's Haneda Airport to Sapporo's **Chitose Airport** take about 1½ hours. Although flights have traditionally cost upwards of ¥28,000 ($233) one-way, renegade airline **Air Do** (© 03/5350-7333 in Tokyo, © 011/200-7333 in Sapporo) offers one-way tickets to Tokyo for ¥20,000 ($167) or less. **ANA** also has two flights a day to **Kushiro Airport** on the eastern side of the island, with the one-way fare to Tokyo costing ¥33,000 ($275); there are discounts for advance purchase. Alternatively, you can save money on domestic flights by tying them into your international flight. If you're coming from Europe, for example, fly KLM from Amsterdam to Osaka, travel by train through Japan, and then fly back to Europe from Sapporo. Similarly, from North America you might fly ANA to Sapporo with a stopover in Tokyo.

Travel to Hokkaido by land is generally via **Shinkansen** bullet train from Ueno or Tokyo Station in Tokyo to Morioka, followed by a **limited express train** from Morioka to Aomori on the northern tip of Honshu Island. For centuries, the only way to continue from Aomori to Hokkaido was via a 4-hour ferry ride, but the opening of the Seikan Tunnel in 1988 now allows the entire trip to be made by train in little more than 2 hours—more than a fourth of which is in the 34-mile-long tunnel. At any rate, the entire trip from Tokyo to Hakodate (on Hokkaido) via train should take about 8 hours and costs ¥18,400 ($153) for a reserved seat one-way. The trip from Tokyo to Sapporo takes about 12 hours and costs ¥22,430 ($187). Your **JR Rail Pass** is good for all trains.

Public transportation around Hokkaido is by train and bus. In addition to regular bus lines, sightseeing buses link the national parks and major attractions. Although they're more expensive than trains and regular buses and commentaries are only in Japanese, they offer unparalleled views of the countryside and usually stop at scenic wonders. Keep in mind that bus schedules fluctuate with the seasons, and some lines don't run during the snowy winter months.

JR Hokkaido Passes   If you plan to do a lot of traveling in Hokkaido and you're not traveling by Japan Rail Pass, you can purchase a special pass issued by Japan Railways that allows unlimited travel on its trains and buses in Hokkaido. The **Hokkaido Free Kippu** can be purchased anywhere in Japan except Hokkaido and allows unlimited travel in Hokkaido. A 7-day pass costs ¥23,750 ($198) but is not valid May 3–5, August 13–16 or December 29–January 4.

Renting a Car   Because distances are long and traffic is rather light, Hokkaido is one of the few places in Japan where driving your own car is actually recommended. Because it's expensive, however, it's economical only if there are several of you. Rates for a 1-day rental of a compact car begin at ¥6,000 ($50) per day with unlimited mileage, and each additional day costs ¥5,000 ($42). Insurance will run another ¥1,000 ($8.35) per day. Car-rental agencies are found throughout Hokkaido, often near train stations as well as at Chitose Airport outside Sapporo and Kushiro Airport in Kushiro. In Sapporo, **Toyota Rent-A-Car** (© 011/281-0100) is located east of Sapporo Station. **JR Eki Rent-A-Car Hokkaido** (© 011/241-0931), near the south exit of Sapporo Station, offers 20% discounts for train fares booked in conjunction with car rentals. Their offices are always located near a JR Station.

A GOOD STRATEGY FOR SEEING HOKKAIDO   If you're traveling from Tokyo, your first destination in Hokkaido should be **Hakodate,** a convenient one-night stopover. From there you can board a local train bound for **Sapporo,** stopping off at **Shikotsu-Toya National Park** along the way. After spending a few days in Sapporo, take the train to Kamikawa and transfer there for a direct bus to **Sounkyo Onsen** in **Daisetsuzan National Park.** From Sounkyo Onsen, you can then continue your trip by taking a bus back to Kamikawa and

transferring there to a train to Bihoro, where you can pick up a sightseeing bus departing for **Akan National Park** and stopping at **Lake Akan.** From Akan, you may wish to return to Tokyo by plane from Kushiro Airport. To follow this plan, you need at least a week.

2 Hakodate, Southern Gateway to Hokkaido ⍟

895km (559 miles) NE of Tokyo; 283km (177 miles) SW of Sapporo

Hakodate, the southern gateway to Hokkaido, is about as far as you can get in a day if you're arriving in Hokkaido from Tokyo by train. Hakodate makes a good 1-night stopover because it has one nighttime attraction and one early morning attraction, which means you can easily see a little of the city before setting out for your next destination.

Founded during the Feudal Era, Hakodate was one of Japan's first ports opened to international trade following the Meiji Restoration. Today it has a population of over 290,300, making it Hokkaido's third-largest city. Yet it feels provincial in atmosphere—still an outpost despite the recent renovation of its former warehouse district into shops and restaurants and its wealth of century-old Western-style buildings. That's part of its charm.

ESSENTIALS

GETTING THERE From Tokyo, take the **Shinkansen** bullet train to Morioka (2½–3 hr. depending on the train), then transfer to a direct train for Hakodate (about 4 hr.). The total fare for an unreserved seat is ¥18,400 ($153). There's also a night train that departs Ueno Station in Tokyo around 7pm, arriving in Hakodate the next morning at 6:30am and costing ¥21,000 ($175); if you have a JR Railpass, you'll pay only a ¥9,450 ($79) sleeping-car surcharge. Hakodate is about 3½ hours from Sapporo, Hokkaido's largest city. See "Hokkaido Essentials," above for further details. **ANA** and **JAL** fly from Tokyo's Haneda Airport to Hakodate; one-way fare for the 1¼-hour trip is ¥26,500 ($221).

GETTING AROUND With the exception of Mt. Hakodate, the most pleasant way to see Hakodate is on foot. The city is easy to navigate, and there are many signs in English. Otherwise, streetcars are the major form of transportation, with fares starting at ¥200 ($1.67); take a ticket upon entering the back door.

VISITOR INFORMATION The **Tourist Information Centers** located in Tokyo, Kyoto, and international airports in Tokyo and Osaka have a pamphlet called "Hakodate and Vicinity." Otherwise, the **Hakodate Tourist Office** (© **0138/23-5440;** open daily 9am–7pm, to 5pm Nov–Mar) is just to the right after you exit Hakodate Station. The office provides an excellent English map of Hakodate as well as a transportation map and other information.

WHAT TO SEE & DO

In addition to the sights here, you might also want to explore the renovated **warehouse district** with its shops and restaurants and historic **Motomachi,** a picturesque neighborhood of steep slopes and turn-of-the-19th-century Western-style clapboard homes and buildings. The Hokkaido Prefectural Government's old branch office in Motomachi Park contains a small **tourist office,** open daily 9am to 7pm (to 5pm in winter).

MT. HAKODATE AFTER DARK Hakodate is probably most famous for its night view from atop Mt. Hakodate, which rises 1,100 feet just 1¾ miles southwest of Hakodate Station. Few vacationing Japanese spend the night in Hakodate without taking the cable car to the top of this lava cone, which was formed by the eruption of an undersea volcano. From the peak, the lights of Hakodate shimmer and glitter like jewels on black velvet. I wouldn't miss it, not only for the view but for the camaraderie shared by everyone making the pilgrimage. There's an informal restaurant here where you can indulge in a drink or a snack while admiring the spectacular view as well as the usual souvenir shops (time your visit just at sunset), but note that it can be chilly up here, even in August.

You can reach the foot of Mt. Hakodate via a 5-minute streetcar ride from Hakodate Station to the Jujigai stop. From there, walk about 6 minutes to the cable car that will take you to the top. It costs ¥1,160 ($10) for adults and ¥590 ($5) for children round-trip, with operating hours daily 10am to 10pm April 26 through October (from 9am during Golden Week and in Aug) and 10am to 9pm November to April 25. From April 25 to November (daily during peak season but otherwise only on weekends), you can also reach the top of Mt. Hakodate directly by bus from Hakodate Station; the 30-minute trip costs ¥360 ($3) for adults and half price for children.

THE MORNING MARKET The other famous thing to do is visit Hakodate's morning market, which spreads out just south of the train station daily from about 5am to noon (closed Sun, Oct–Apr). Walk around and look at the variety of foods for sale, especially the hairy crabs for which Hokkaido is famous. You can make an unusual breakfast of fruit, raw sea urchin, or grilled crab from the stalls here.

WHERE TO STAY

Hakodate's peak tourist season is July and August. Accordingly, some hotels raise their rates during this time.

EXPENSIVE

Hotel Sea Borne ✰✰   If you're searching for a small boutique hotel with class, this is a top pick. Its elegant lobby, with reproduction antique furniture, imparts a cozy European atmosphere, while each of its rooms is based on a different decorating theme, from modern to frilly European to rustic American (apparently, some Japanese guests are so enamored of the different styles that they request a change of rooms the second night, just for the experience). Granted, jaded travelers might find it all a bit over the top, but excellent service from a friendly staff, welcome drinks (tea, coffee or soft drink the first night, a cocktail the second night), good in-room amenities (including 4 different kinds of shampoo), and a great location near the warehouse district make this place infinitely better than your standard hotel.

14–28 Suehiro-cho, Hakodate 042-0053. ℂ **0138/27-4411.** Fax 0138/27-0028. www.dish.ne.jp/seaborne/. 20 units. ¥15,000–¥18,000 ($125–$150) single; ¥20,000–¥25,000 ($167–$208) double; ¥23,000–¥35,000 ($192–$292) twin. AE, DC, JCB, MC, V. Taxi: 5 min. Streetcar: Jujigai (2 min.). Turn right and walk 2 blocks toward the bay; it will be across the street, on your left. **Amenities:** 1 restaurant (Western) and 1 Japanese teahouse (see "Where to Dine," below); room service (5–9:30pm); same-day laundry/dry cleaning service. *In room:* A/C, TV, minibar, hot-water pot with tea, hair dryer, washlet toilet.

㉖ **Wakamatsu Ryokan** ✰✰   Here's a seaside inn worthy of a splurge. Almost a century old (grainy black-and-white photographs in the lobby memorialize Emperor Showa's 1954 visit) but renovated and with a seven-story addition added in 1994, it's the epitome of an updated but elegant ryokan. Pampering begins as soon as you enter the grand, teahouse-style entrance, where a kimono-clad hostess ushers you to your room and brings a welcome tea. After soaking in the public hot-spring baths overlooking the sea, you'll be treated to a kaiseki feast in your room (all with views of the sea). The sea is so close you'll fall asleep listening to the gentle sound of waves. Bonuses are the nearby Yunokawa public swimming beach and the night illumination of fishing boats searching for squid. The main disadvantage to staying here is location—near the airport (thank goodness, planes don't fly at night) and a long, 30-minute streetcar ride from Hakodate Station (a taxi will set you back about ¥1,700/$14).

1–2–27 Yunokawa-cho, Hakodate 042-0932. ℂ **0138/59-2171.** Fax 0138/59-3316. wakamatsu@ hakodate.ne.jp. 29 units (26 with bathroom). ¥27,000–¥74,000 ($225–$617) per person. Rates include breakfast, dinner, and service. AE, DC, JCB, MC, V. Taxi: 15 min. from Hakodate Station, 7 min. from Hakodate Airport. Streetcar: 2 or 5 to Yunokawa Onsen (6 min.). Turn right and walk along a canal until it ends; it's across the street, to the right. **Amenities:** Hot-spring indoor/outdoor baths; in-room massage. *In room:* A/C, TV, minibar, hot-water pot with tea, hair dryer, safe.

MODERATE

B&B Hakodatemura   This immaculate, mostly Western-style Japanese Inn Group member, decorated with white-washed walls, wood furniture, and live and dried flowers, is built around a courtyard where you can choose to eat breakfast. There are two tatami rooms and one triple with a loft bed; only one twin has a bathroom. Rules are similar to a youth hostel's (check in at 3pm, check out at 10am, and the door locks at 11pm), but what I like most about this place is its location near the warehouse district and Motomachi, and only a 15-minute walk from Hakodate Station.

16–12 Suehiro-cho, Hakodate 040-0053. Ⓒ **0138/22-8105.** Fax 0138/22-8925. 18 units (1 with bathroom). ¥5,300 ($44) single; ¥9,800 ($82) twin, ¥12,100 ($101) twin with bathroom; ¥13,800 ($115) triple. Breakfast ¥700 ($5.85) extra. AE, MC, V. Streetcar: Jujigai (2 min.); follow the streetcar tracks for 1 block, turn right, and then left. Closed Dec 1–Jan 15. **Amenities:** Coin-op washer and dryer. *In room:* A/C (some with fan only), TV, hot-water pot with tea.

Harborview Hotel   Location, location, location: this hotel's main selling point is its convenience to Hakodate Station. Despite its name, none of the rooms face the harbor, though those closest to the waterfront from the 7th floor up do have side water views if you stand at the window. Standard rooms are small but pleasant.

14–10 Wakamatsu-cho, Hakodate 040-0063. Ⓒ **0138/22-0111.** Fax 0138/23-0154. 200 units. ¥11,000 ($92) single; ¥18,000 ($150) double; ¥22,000–¥27,000 ($183–$225) twin. Weekends and holiday evenings May–Oct, ¥500 ($4.15) extra per person. Off-season discounts available. AE, DC, JCB, MC, V. Just to the right as you exit Hakodate Station (less than 1 min.). **Amenities:** 2 restaurants (Japanese and Western), 2 bars, 1 lounge; in-room massage; shopping arcade; same-day laundry/dry cleaning service; nonsmoking rooms. *In room:* A/C, TV, minibar, hot-water pot with tea, hair dryer, washlet toilet.

Hotel Chocolat Hakodate   I'm not sure how this hotel, opened in 1991, got its name (sometimes these things just remain a mystery), but it appeals to a mostly young female clientele with its lobby mural of frolicking cute dogs, flower arrangements, reasonable rates, and handy location halfway between Hakodate Station (a 20-min. walk away) and the Motomachi historic district. Rooms (mostly twins) are rather ordinary, with windows that open; best are the roomy deluxe corner twins on the 6th floor.

1–1 Otemachi, Hakodate 040-0064. Ⓒ **0138/26-1330.** Fax 0138/26-0393. choco330@oregano.ocn.ne.jp. 39 units. ¥8,000 ($67) single; ¥10,000–¥20,000 ($83–$167) twin. Off-season discounts available. AE, DC, JCB, MC, V. Streetcar: Uoichiba-dori (1 min.). Turn left; it will be in the next block, on the left on a corner. **Amenities:** 1 restaurant (open only for breakfast); same-day laundry/dry cleaning service; nonsmoking rooms. *In room:* A/C, TV, hot-water pot with tea, hair dryer, washlet toilet.

INEXPENSIVE

Niceday Inn *Value*   The Saitos, the kind and generous couple who run this inn, give a warm welcome and make you feel right at home. Mr. Saito, who speaks English, offers lots of tourist information and a map. Staying here is like living with a Japanese family. The inn is very simple but offers clean Japanese- and Western-style rooms. No meals are served, but free instant coffee, a refrigerator, TV, and public phone are in the small communal entry room.

9–11 Otemachi, Hakodate 040-0064. Ⓒ **0138/22-5919.** 6 units (none with bathroom). ¥3,000 ($25) per person for foreigners. No credit cards. An 8-min. walk south of Hakodate Station. Take the street that runs on the west (bay) side of the Harborview Hotel right across from the station; after crossing the wide, tree-lined avenue, take the 4th left (across from the Kokusai Hotel entrance). It's a white, 2-story building on your right. *In room:* A/C or fan, no phone.

WHERE TO DINE

Several of Hakodate's harborfront warehouses have been renovated into smart-looking shopping and dining complexes. They're about a 10-minute walk from Hakodate Station, reached by walking past the right (bay) side of Harborview Hotel and continuing along the seaside promenade.

Bay Restaurant and Market JAPANESE/WESTERN BUFFET   This is one of the largest restaurants among several in the renovated brick warehouses along the waterfront. A combination restaurant, shop, and cafe, it offers an inexpensive all-you-can-eat buffet of meat, seafood, salads and other fare.

11–5 Toyokawa-cho. ✆ **0138/22-1300.** Dinner buffet ¥2,500 ($21) adults, ¥1,500 ($12.50) children; lunch buffet ¥1,500 ($12.50) adults, ¥1,000 ($8.35) children. AE, DC, JCB, MC, V. Summer, daily 11am–2:30pm and 5–9pm (last order); winter, daily 11:30am–2pm and 5:30–8:30pm. A 15-min. walk south of Hakodate Station along the seaside promenade. Streetcar: Jujigai (4 min.); turn right and walk to the waterfront.

Hakodate Beer BAR FOOD   Near the warehouse district, this attractive, brick building with outdoor seating and an English menu offers three kinds of beer brewed in the large copper vats you can see as you dine on such fare as fish and chips, the day's pasta, Japanese-style fried chicken, or a "steamboat"—seafood, sliced meat, vegetables, and dumplings cooked in boiling broth at your table and dipped in chili sauce. Set lunches are a steal.

5–22 Ohtemachi. ✆ **0138/23-8000.** Main dishes ¥680–¥2,500 ($5.65–$21); set lunch ¥600 ($5). AE, DC, JCB, MC, V. Daily 11am–10pm. Streetcar: Uoichiba-dori, then walk 3 blocks toward the bay; it's on the corner. A 9-min. walk from Hakodate Station.

㊅ **Ika Matsuri** SUSHI   A long conveyor belt, with stools on one side and family-sized booths on the other, is loaded with different-colored saucers of sushi, each representing a different price. Just take what you want; when you're done, your plates will be tallied to figure the bill. Add ¥120 ($1) for all-you-can-drink soft drinks; it's self-serve for ginger, soy sauce, and tea. You'll recognize this clean and cheerful place by the blue marlin above the name and King Kong climbing a pole to reach—what else?—a plate of sushi. Take-out sushi is available.

24–10 Toyokawa-cho. ✆ **0138/27-5588.** 2 pieces of sushi ¥120–¥580 ($1–$4.85). No credit cards. Daily 11am–10pm. Streetcar: Uoichiba-dori, then walk 3 blocks toward the bay; it's catty-corner from Hakodate Beer, next to 7-Eleven. A 9-min. walk from Hakodate Station.

Tao Tao ASIAN CROSSOVER   This eclectic restaurant in a bright yellow building in the Motomachi District offers interesting Asian food, an amusing decor, and music videos. You might try Thai curry, a *naan* (Indian bread) sandwich, tacos with rice, or *adobocha han* (Manilla-style) pork fried rice. Salads range from tofu (very good with lots of greens and a spicy dressing) or Harbin potato salad to *Shan Shan* (it means "smells good"), hot-bacon, and lettuce salad. There's an outdoor patio for nice weather.

15–19 Motomachi. ✆ **0138/22-0002.** Main dishes ¥750–¥1,000 ($6.25–$8.35). No credit cards. Tues–Sun noon–11pm. Streetcar: Suehiro-cho (3 min); walk 2 blocks up Hachimanzaka and turn left.

3 Sapporo

1,169.5km (731 miles) NE of Tokyo; 283km (177 miles) NE of Hakodate

Sapporo is one of Japan's newest cities. A little more than a century ago, it was nothing more than a scattering of huts belonging to Ainu and Japanese families. With the dawning of the Meiji Period, however, the government decided to colonize the island, and in 1869 it established the Colonization Commission. The area of Sapporo, which comes from the Ainu word meaning "big, dry river," was chosen as the site for the new capital, and in 1871, construction of the city began.

During the Meiji Period, Japan looked eagerly toward the West for technology, ideas, and education, and Hokkaido was no exception. Between 1871 and 1884, 76 foreign technicians and experts (including 46 Americans) who had experience in colonization were brought to this Japanese wilderness to aid in the island's development.

Sapporo was laid out in a grid pattern of uniform blocks similar to that of American cities. In 1875, the Sapporo Agricultural College was founded to train youths in skills useful to Hokkaido's colonization and development.

The Sapporo of today, capital of Hokkaido Prefecture, has grown to 1.8 million residents, making it the largest city north of Tokyo. In 1972, it was introduced to the world when the Winter Olympics were held here, and its many fine ski slopes continue to attract winter vacationers, as does the Sapporo Snow Festival held every February (see the "Calendar of Events," in chapter 2). In August, when the rest of Japan is sweltering under uncomfortably high temperatures and humidity, Sapporo stays pleasantly cool.

ESSENTIALS

GETTING THERE   By Plane   Flights take 1½ hours from Tokyo's Haneda Airport, 2 hours from Hiroshima, and 2¼ hours from Fukuoka. Air Do, which flies only between Tokyo and Sapporo, charges ¥20,000 ($167) one way. Both JAL and ANA charge ¥28,000 ($233). (See "Getting There & Getting Around," under "Hokkaido Essentials," earlier in this chapter for details on international flights.)

Sapporo's **Chitose Airport** (② **0123/23-0111**), located about 43km (27 miles) southeast of the capital, is connected to downtown by either **Airport Limousine Bus,** which delivers passengers to a few major hotels in about 75 minutes for ¥820 ($6.85) one-way, or by **JR trains** operating between Chitose Airport Station and Sapporo Station, with trips taking about 36 minutes and costing ¥1,040 ($8.65).

By JR Train   Trains from Tokyo and other cities on Honshu arrive in Hakodate approximately every hour or 1½ hours; in Hakodate you'll transfer for trains departing every hour or so for Sapporo. The fare from Tokyo to Sapporo costs ¥22,430 ($187), with trips averaging 12 hours. There are also overnight trains from Ueno Station in Tokyo to Sapporo, taking about 16 hours. From Hakodate, trains to Sapporo take about 3½ hours and cost ¥8,590 ($72).

VISITOR INFORMATION   Be sure to pick up the useful leaflet "Sapporo and Vicinity" at a **Tourist Information Center** in Tokyo, Kyoto, or Tokyo or Osaka airports; it has information also on nearby Shikotsu-Toya National Park. In Sapporo, there's an **International Information Corner** (② **011/213-5062;** open daily 9am–5pm, closed 2nd and 4th Wed of most months) in Sapporo Station just across from the west ticket wicket. Multilingual volunteers provide general hotel, sightseeing, and transportation information; there's also an English-language reading corner. There's also **Plaza i** in the MN Building across from the Clock Tower (see "A Stroll Around Sapporo," below) at N1 W3, Chuo-ku (② **011/211-3678;** open daily 9am–5:30pm); it provides information on tourist attractions, daily life, and transportation, offers guidebooks and maps, and has international public telephones and fax machines. English speakers are always available. Online, you can check **www.global.city.sapporo.jp/**.

INTERNET ACCESS   You can get online at **Bon de Bon** (② **011/213-5726;** daily 10am–8:30pm), a cafe in the basement of Paseo Mall in Sapporo Station. It charges ¥200 ($1.65) for 30 minutes, and you're expected to order a drink.

POST OFFICE   Sapporo Central Post Office, N6, E1 (② **011/748-2336**), a couple blocks east of Sapporo Station, has an ATM machine for cash advances (weekdays 7am–11pm and weekends 9am–7pm) on international credit cards, as well as a 24-hour window for stamps and mail.

ORIENTATION & GETTING AROUND   After the jumble of most Japanese cities with their incomprehensible address systems, Sapporo will come as a welcome surprise. Its streets are laid out in a grid pattern, making the city easy

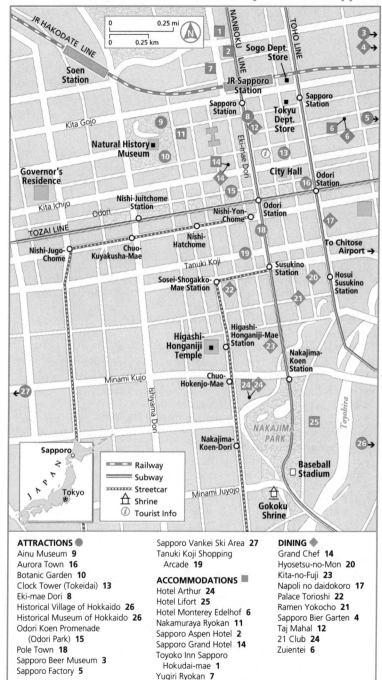

Attractions & Where to Stay & Dine in Sapporo

0 | 0.25 mi
0 | 0.25 km

JR HAKODATE LINE

Soen Station

NANBOKU LINE

TOHO LINE

Sogo Dept. Store

JR Sapporo Station

Sapporo Station

Sapporo Station

Tokyu Dept. Store

Kita Gojo

Natural History Museum

Eki-mae Dori

Governor's Residence

City Hall

Odori Station

Kita Ichijo

Odori

Nishi-Juitchome Station

Nishi-Yon-Chome

Odori Station

TOZAI LINE

Nishi-Jugo-Chome

Chuo-Kuyakusha-Mae

Nishi-Hatchome

Tanuki Koji

To Chitose Airport →

Susukino Station

Hosui Susukino Station

Sosei-Shogakko-Mae Station

Higashi-Honganiji-Mae Station

Higashi-Honganiji Temple

Minami Kujo

Ishiyama Dori

Chuo-Hokenjo-Mae

Nakajima-Koen Station

Nakajima-Koen-Dori

NAKAJIMA PARK

Toyohira

Sapporo

Tokyo

JAPAN

Railway
Subway
Streetcar
Shrine
Tourist Info

Minami Juyojo

Baseball Stadium

Gokoku Shrine

ATTRACTIONS ●
Ainu Museum **9**
Aurora Town **16**
Botanic Garden **10**
Clock Tower (Tokeidai) **13**
Eki-mae Dori **8**
Historical Village of Hokkaido **26**
Historical Museum of Hokkaido **26**
Odori Koen Promenade
 (Odori Park) **15**
Pole Town **18**
Sapporo Beer Museum **3**
Sapporo Factory **5**

Sapporo Vankei Ski Area **27**
Tanuki Koji Shopping
 Arcade **19**

ACCOMMODATIONS ■
Hotel Arthur **24**
Hotel Lifort **25**
Hotel Monterey Edelhof **6**
Nakamuraya Ryokan **11**
Sapporo Aspen Hotel **2**
Sapporo Grand Hotel **14**
Toyoko Inn Sapporo
 Hokudai-mae **1**
Yugiri Ryokan **7**

DINING ◆
Grand Chef **14**
Hyosetsu-no-Mon **20**
Kita-no-Fuji **23**
Napoli no daidokoro **17**
Palace Torioshi **22**
Ramen Yokocho **21**
Sapporo Bier Garten **4**
Taj Mahal **12**
21 Club **24**
Zuientei **6**

to navigate. Addresses in Sapporo refer to blocks that follow one another in logical, numerical order.

Sapporo Station lies at the north end of the city, with downtown and many of its attractions, hotels, and restaurants spreading to the south. The center of Sapporo is **Odori** (Main St.), a tree-lined avenue south of Sapporo Station that runs east and west and bisects the city into north and south sections. **North 1st Street,** therefore, refers to the street 1 block north of Odori. The other determinant landmark is the **Soseigawa River,** which marks addresses east and west. **West 1st Street** runs along the west bank of the Soseigawa River, while **East 1st Street** runs along the east bank.

Addresses in Sapporo are generally given by block. **N1 W4,** for example, the address for the Sapporo Grand Hotel, means it's located in the first block north of Odori and 4 blocks west of West 1st Street. If you want to be more technical about it, the entire, formal address of the hotel would read N1-jo W4-chome. "Jo" refers to blocks north and south of Odori, while "chome" refers to blocks east and west of the river. Better yet, street signs in Sapporo are in English.

Central Sapporo is easy to cover on foot. You can walk south from Sapporo Station to **Odori Park** in less than 10 minutes and on to **Susukino,** Sapporo's nightlife district, in another 7 or 8 minutes. For longer distances, transportation in Sapporo is via **bus,** three **subway** lines (which interchange at **Odori Station**), and one **streetcar** line. Fares begin at ¥200 ($1.67; ¥170/$1.40 for streetcars), but easier is the **With You Card,** available in denominations beginning at ¥500 ($4.15) and valid for city buses, subways and streetcars. One-day Cards, allowing unlimited rides in one day, are also available, costing ¥1,000 ($8.35) for all modes of transport and ¥800 ($6.65) for subways only. Children pay half fare. Cards can be purchased at subway stations and on buses and streetcars.

Finally, the Sapporo Lincle Bus is a **tourist bus** that loops around the city and stops at such sights and attractions as Sapporo Beer Garden, Nakajima Park, Susukino, and Maruyama Park, but unfortunately, it doesn't go to Nopporo Forest Park. A one-day pass (¥1,200/$10 adults, ¥1,000/$8.35 junior-high and high-school students, ¥700/$5.85 children) allows you to get on and off as many times as you want between 9am and 7pm from the end of April to November. Buses depart from the bus terminal in front of Sapporo Station's south exit, and stops are clearly marked.

A STROLL AROUND SAPPORO

One of the first things you should do in Sapporo is simply walk around. Starting from **Sapporo Station,** take the street leading directly south called **Eki-mae Dori** (which is also West 4th). This is one of Sapporo's main thoroughfares, and it takes you through the heart of the city.

YOUR FIRST STOP   Four blocks south of the station, turn left on N1; after a block, you'll find Sapporo's most famous landmark, **Clock Tower** (Tokeidai), N1 W2, Chuo-ku (✆ **011/231-0838**). This Western-style wooden building was built in 1878 as a drill hall for the Sapporo Agricultural College (now Hokkaido University). The large clock at the top was made in Boston and was installed in 1881. In summer, it attracts tourists even at night; they hang around the outside gates just to listen to it strike the hour. Inside the tower is a local-history museum, but it's only in Japanese and is not worth the price of admission. By the way, across the street is **Plaza i,** where you can obtain information on Sapporo.

ON TO ODORI PARK   If you continue walking 1 block south of the Clock Tower, you'll reach **Odori Koen Promenade,** a 344-foot-wide boulevard stretching almost a mile from east to west. In the middle of the boulevard is a wide median strip that has been turned into a park with trees, flowerbeds, and fountains. This is where much of the **Sapporo Snow Festival** is held in early February, when ice and packed snow are carved to form statues, palaces, and fantasies. Begun in 1950 to add a bit of spice and life to the cold winter days, the Snow Festival now features about 220 snow statues and 120 ice sculptures and draws about 2.2 million visitors a year. One snow structure may require as much as 300 6-ton truckloads of snow, brought in from the surrounding mountains. The snow and ice carvings are done with so much attention to detail that it seems a crime they're doomed to melt (see "Calendar of Events." in chapter 2).

Odori Park is also the scene of the **Sapporo Summer Festival,** celebrated with beer gardens set up the length of the park from mid-July to mid-August and open every evening beginning at 5pm and Saturday and Sunday from early afternoon. Various Japanese beer companies set up their own booths and tables under the trees, while vendors put up stalls selling fried noodles, corn on the cob, and other goodies. Live bands serenade the beer drinkers under the stars. It all resembles the cheerful confusion of a German beer garden, which isn't surprising considering Munich is one of Sapporo's sister cities (Portland, Oregon, is another one). Other festivals held in Odori Park are the **Lilac Festival** in late May heralding the arrival of summer and **Bon-Odori** in mid-August with traditional dances to appease the souls of the dead.

THE UNDERGROUND SHOPPING ARCADES   From Odori Park, you can continue your walk either above or below ground. Appreciated especially during inclement weather and during Hokkaido's long cold winters are two underground shopping arcades. Underneath Odori Park, from the Odori Station all the way to the TV tower in the east, is **Aurora Town** with boutiques and restaurants. Even longer is **Pole Town** with 1,300 feet of shops, almost 100 in all. Pole Town extends from the Odori Station south all the way to **Susukino,** Sapporo's nightlife amusement center where you'll find many restaurants and pubs (see "Where to Dine," later in this chapter). Before reaching Susukino, however, you may want to emerge at **Sanchome** (you'll see escalators going up), where you'll find more shopping at the kilometer-long **Tanuki-koji** covered shopping arcade with its 300 boutiques and stores.

THE BOTANIC GARDEN ✿   Backtracking now toward the station, you should stop at the 32-acre **Shokubutsu-en,** the entrance to which is at N3 W8 (© **011/221-0066**). It contains some virgin forest and more than 4,000 varieties of plants gathered from all over Hokkaido and arranged in marshland, herb, alpine and other gardens. Of greater interest, perhaps, is the section devoted to plants used by the Ainu, whose extensive knowledge of plants covered not only edible plants but also those with medicinal use and other properties including organic poison used for arrows to kill bears and other game. Unfortunately, there are no English explanations of plant usage. Still, with lots of trees and grassy lawns, it's a good place for a summer afternoon picnic, which you may have to defend from a tame fox roaming the grounds.

Worth visiting on garden grounds is Japan's oldest **natural science museum,** founded in 1882 to document the wildlife of Hokkaido and housed in a turn-of-the-century, Western-style building. Be sure, too, to visit the small, one-room **Ainu Museum,** which displays some fine examples of Ainu artifacts, including traditional costumes, jewelry, farming tools, hunting traps, harpoons, a canoe, bamboo mouth harp (played by women and children), and other items. In any case, you'll probably want to spend at least 1 hour in the Botanic Garden.

The Botanic Garden and its museums are open April 29 to November 3, Tuesday through Sunday from 9am to 4pm. Admission, which includes the museums, is ¥400 ($3.35) for adults and ¥280 ($2.35) for children. From November 4 to April 28, only the greenhouse is open; admission then is ¥110 (90¢) for both adults and children.

MORE TO SEE & DO

Sapporo Beer Museum ★★   Although it's not within easy walking distance of Sapporo Station, if you think of beer when you hear the word "Sapporo," then you should make this museum part of your sightseeing itinerary. Famous throughout the world, Sapporo beer has been brewed in this handsome brick factory ever since 1876; today, the Sapporo Beer Company is the third-largest beer producer in Japan. You can visit the handsome, brick brewery and museum only on a free guided tour. Hour-long tours explain the history of the company, show off company memorabilia (my favorite is the exhibit of advertising posters), continue with the brewing and canning process, and end in a large hall where you get to sample the product. Tours are held daily throughout the year, departing every 15 minutes or so; although you can just show up and hope there's room, it's best to make reservations in advance during peak season to avoid having to wait. Although tours are conducted in Japanese only, a few of the guides speak English; ask whether it's possible to have an English interpreter at the time you make your reservation.

You might want to cap off your tour with a meal or a mug of beer in the adjoining Sapporo Bier Garten (see "Where to Dine," below). Also, about a 12-minute walk from the Beer Museum is **Sapporo Factory.** N2 E4, Chuo-ku (✆ **011/207-5000**), a shopping complex housing a microbrewery, restaurants, 140 shops, and movie theaters.

N7 E9, Chuo-ku. ✆ **011/731-4368.** Free 1-hour tours of the museum and brewery held daily: Sept–May 9am–3:40pm, June–Aug 8:40am–4:40pm. Reservations are suggested. Bus: Higashi 63 from the north side of Sapporo Station or Higashi 3 from the Bus Terminal south of Sapporo Station 10 min. to Kita 8 Higashi 7 stop (3 min.). It's also on the Lincle Bus line.

NOPPORO FOREST PARK (NOPPORO SHINRIN KOEN)

If you have an extra half-day or more, I recommend this park on the outskirts for its two very worthwhile attractions. To reach the park, take a **JR train** to Shinrin Koen Station (a 20-min. ride), then walk 15 minutes in the direction of the tower (built in commemoration of Hokkaido's centennial). Or take the **Tozai subway line** 20 minutes to Shin-Sapporo Station, where you can then board a **JR bus** for a 10-minute ride to, the last stop. If your first stop is the historical museum, get off at the next-to-the-last stop, Kinenkan Iriguchi. It's about a 15-minute walk between the two attractions; in summer on weekends and holidays, there's a free shuttle bus connecting the two.

Historical Village of Hokkaido (Kaitaku-no Mura) ★★ *Kids*   This open-air museum of more than 50 historical Japanese- and Western-style buildings, dating mostly from the Meiji and Taisho eras and brought here from around Hokkaido, includes homes, farmhouses, a shrine, church, newspaper office, post office (from which you can mail a letter), police box (manned by a sword-wielding police officer), and many small businesses, including a blacksmith, brewery, barbershop, grocery, inn, and sleigh factory. You can easily spend 2 hours here, wandering through buildings of the fishing village, farm village, mountain village, and town. Kids like being able to run and explore; there's even an old-fashioned playground with stilts, seesaw, and other traditional play equipment.

Konopporo 50–1, Atsubetsu-cho. ℂ **011/898-2692**. Admission Apr–Nov, ¥610 ($5.10) adults and ¥450 ($3.75) university and high-school students; Dec–Mar, ¥500 ($4.15) and ¥400 ($3.35) respectively. Free for children and senior citizens. Tues–Sun 9:30am–4:30pm. Bus: Kaitaku-no-Mura (2 min.).

Historical Museum of Hokkaido (Kaitaku Kinenkan) ⋆ This museum does a great job detailing Hokkaido's development from prehistoric to modern times, with lots of information in English. The section on the Ainu displays clothing, a house, and other artifacts and describes their forced assimilation into Japanese culture. You'll also learn about Hokkaido's early contacts with Russia, life of 19th-century Japanese pioneers, the opening of Hakodate Port, establishment of Sapporo Agricultural College, and more. The Living Experience Room provides hands-on experience with tools, including a handloom, and interactive displays. If history's your thing, you can easily spend 2 hours here.

Konopporo, Atsubetsu-cho. ℂ **011/898-0456**. Admission ¥300 ($2.50) adults, ¥100 (85¢) university and high-school students, free for children and senior citizens. Tues–Sun 9:30am–4:30pm. Closed some national holidays.

HITTING THE SLOPES

Skiing is big in Sapporo, site of the 1972 Winter Olympics and easily accessible by plane from many cities in Japan—there are slopes within city limits and more than a dozen skiing areas less than 2 hours away, most open from early December to late April. On the west edge of town are Okurayama Jump Hill and Miyanomori Jump Hill, both sites of the 1972 Winter Olympics. Here, too, is the **Sapporo Vankei Ski Area,** just 20 minutes from downtown Sapporo and popular for after-work skiing. You can reach them by subway to Maruyama Koen Station and then by bus.

Farther afield, the **Teine Olympia Ski Ground** (ℂ **011/685-7000**) is about an hour's bus ride from Sapporo Station. This was the site of the alpine, bobsled, and toboggan events for the Olympics. A 1-day pass to the ski lifts goes for ¥3,500 ($29); ski-rental equipment is available for about ¥4,200 ($35), while snowboarding gear costs ¥3,500 ($29) per day. However, keep in mind that sizes are generally smaller than in the West. For further information on skiing in the region, stop by the Sapporo tourist office.

WHERE TO STAY

Sapporo has a large selection of fine hotels in various price categories. The busiest tourist seasons are in summer and during the annual Snow Festival in early February. If you plan to attend the Snow Festival, book your room at least 6 months in advance. At other times you should have no problem finding a room, but it's always wise to make a reservation in advance. In winter (excluding festival time), some upper- and medium-priced hotels lower their room rates, sometimes by as much as 40%—be sure to ask for a discount.

EXPENSIVE

Hotel Arthur ⋆⋆ This smart-looking hotel with a European atmosphere is located near Nakajima-koen Park in a quiet section of town, offering refuge from tour buses and crowds and the opportunity for early-morning jogs. The lobby looks out over a green lawn made festive with white lights. Rooms facing east have views of the park, while those facing west have views of city lights with mountains in the background. Standard rooms are rather small but are well equipped; business travelers will appreciate special rooms that allow wireless

Internet access—for free. The staff is courteous and the service excellent; ask for an address or a hard-to-find item, and they'll come up with it. But what truly sets this hotel apart are its top-notch restaurants (unusual for a hotel this size outside downtown), including a high-class kaiseki restaurant, a teppanyaki restaurant with great views, and the Manhattan Grill serving American cuisine in a hip setting.

S10 W6, Chuo-ku, Sapporo 064-8561. ℂ 011/561-1000. Fax 011/521-5522. www.hotel-arthur-sapporo. co.jp. 229 units. ¥12,500–¥14,000 ($104–$117) single; ¥23,000 ($192) double; ¥23,000–¥35,000 ($192–$292) twin. AE, DC, JCB, MC, V. Subway: Namboku Line to Nakajima-koen (5 min.). Take exit 1 and turn left at the top of the stairs into the park (well-lit even at night); walk past the children's swings and over a bridge and continue bearing right until you leave the park and see the hotel in front of you. **Amenities:** 4 restaurants (Kaiseki, Teppanyaki, American, Chinese), 3 bars, 1 lounge; business center; salon; room service (6am–midnight); same-day laundry/dry cleaning service; in-room massage. *In room:* A/C, bilingual TV, minibar, hot-water pot with tea, hair dryer.

Hotel Monterey Edelhof ★★★

Although opened in 2000, this elegant hotel embraces the architectural exuberance of early 1900s Vienna, with lots of marble, stained-glass windows, Art-Deco embellishments, and Otto-Wagner-inspired designs. Even the elevators have old-fashioned floor dials, classical music plays in public spaces, and function rooms carry names like Schönbrunn. Forgive me a sudden craving for Sachertorte. Located in downtown Sapporo, on the upper floors above an office building, it offers small but smartly decorated rooms with a slight Art-Deco motif. The hotel spa, which utilizes hot springs tapped deep below ground and has the good Austro-Hungarian Empire name Karlovy Vary, is a huge (though pricey) plus, and if you still don't think you're in the empire yet, check out the Wagner House Restaurant.

N2 W1, Chuo-ku, Sapporo 060-0002. ℂ 011/242-7111. Fax 011/232-1212. www.hotelmonterey.co.jp. 181 units. ¥15,000 ($125) single; ¥28,000–¥38,000 ($233–$317) twin. AE, DC, JCB, MC, V. An 8-min. walk southeast of Sapporo Station. **Amenities:** 4 restaurants (Japanese, Chinese, Continental), 2 lounges; hot-spring spa with sauna and Jacuzzi (fee: ¥1,800/$15); room service (9pm–midnight); in-room massage; same-day laundry/dry cleaning service, nonsmoking rooms. *In room:* A/C, bilingual cable TV, minibar, hot-water pot with tea, hair dryer, washlet toilet.

Sapporo Grand Hotel ★

This dignified hotel, open since 1934 and one of Sapporo's old-timers, has a good downtown location near the Botanical Garden and Odori Park. This is usually where VIPs stay when they come to town. It occupies three buildings constructed at various times: company executives generally stay in the main building, groups and families usually opt for less expensive rooms in the east building, and business travelers take advantage of the mostly singles in the annex. Most rooms are fairly large and nicely furnished rooms but—a sign of its time—have small windows and small bathrooms. Note, too, that some of the cheapest rooms face another building. Still, you can't go wrong staying here.

N1 W4, Chuo-ku, Sapporo 060-0001. ℂ 011/261-3311. Fax 011/231-0388. www.mitsuikanko.co.jp/sgh/. 565 units. ¥13,000–¥16,000 ($108–$133) single; ¥24,000 ($200) double; ¥23,500–¥38,000 ($196–$317) twin. AE, DC, JCB, MC, V. An 8-min. walk south of Sapporo Station. **Amenities:** 5 restaurants, 4 bars; shopping arcade; salon; room service (7am–1am); in-room massage; same-day laundry/dry cleaning service; nonsmoking rooms. *In room:* A/C, bilingual cable TV, dataport, minibar, hot-water pot with tea, hair dryer, washlet toilet.

MODERATE

Hotel Lifort ★ *Value*

Built as a getaway for school teachers and owned by a teachers' association, this well-designed hotel looks more expensive than it is and offers comfortable rooms that are open to the public when there's space (Sat is usually fully booked). Located across from Nakajima-koen Park, it offers mostly single rooms, which are small but very nicely decorated. Deluxe twins are especially spacious, separated into living and sleeping areas, though don't expect to hang more than one suit in the shallow closet. The best views are of the park. Unfortunately, not much English is spoken here.

S10 W1, Chuo-ku, Sapporo 060-0810. ⓒ 011/521-5211. Fax 011/521-5215. 195 units. July–Oct, ¥7,700 ($64) single; ¥14,100–¥19,000 ($117.50–$158) twin. Nov–May, ¥6,200 ($52) single; ¥11,400–¥17,000 ($95–$142) twin. MC, V. Subway: Nakajima-koen (3 min.). Take exit 1, turn right, cross the big street, and turn right again. **Amenities:** 1 restaurant (Japanese/Western/Chinese); same-day laundry/dry cleaning service; nonsmoking rooms. *In room:* A/C, TV, fridge, hot-water pot, hair dryer, washlet toilets (twins only).

258 **Nakamuraya Ryokan** ⭐ If you want to stay in a ryokan, this modern and comfortable Japanese inn, just a stone's throw from the Botanic Garden, is a good choice. First opened 100 years ago but now occupying a nondescript 25-year-old building, it offers pleasant Japanese-style tatami rooms, some with sitting area near the window. The hallways with eaves and slatted wooden doors to each room are a nice touch. Although rooms have their own tub, you might want to take advantage of the public baths here. To receive the low rates listed below, you must book in advance and mention the Japanese Inn Group. Western breakfasts are available.

N3 W7, Chuo-ku, Sapporo 060-0003. ⓒ 011/241-2111. Fax 011/241-2118. 27 units. Rates for foreign guests ¥7,000 ($58) single; ¥13,000 ($108) double. Breakfast ¥1,500 ($12.50) extra; dinner ¥3,000 ($25) extra. AE, JCB, MC, V. Located between the entrance of the Botanic Garden and the Old Government Building, a 10-min. walk SW of Sapporo Station. **Amenities:** 1 restaurant (Japanese); in-room massage. *In room:* A/C, TV, fridge, hot-water pot with tea.

Sapporo Aspen Hotel Built in 1996, this hotel has an English-speaking staff and a convenient location just north of Sapporo Station (its brochure says 100 steps, but I didn't count them). Otherwise, rooms are rather small for the price but are comfortable enough, with windows that open, heavy curtains to block light, sitting areas and desks, and plenty of counter space in bathrooms. The best views are from the west side overlooking Hokkaido University and a distant forest.

N8 W4, Kita-ku, Sapporo 060-0808. ⓒ 011/700-2111. Fax 011/700-2002. 302 units. June–Sept and Snow Festival, ¥10,000–¥12,000 ($83–$100) single; ¥19,000–¥23,000 ($158–$192) twin. Oct–May, ¥6,000–¥6,500 ($50–$54) single; ¥12,000–¥13,000 ($100–$108) twin. AE, DC, JCB, MC, V. A 2-min. walk straight north of Sapporo Station, on the left. **Amenities:** 1 coffee shop; concierge; in-room massage; same-day laundry service; nonsmoking rooms (reserve in advance); rental bicycles (fee: ¥1,570/$13 per day). *In room:* A/C, bilingual TV, fridge, hot-water pot with tea, hair dryer, washlet toilet.

INEXPENSIVE

259 **Toyoko Inn Sapporo Hokudai-mae** ⭐ *Finds* The motto of this inexpensive business-hotel chain translates roughly as "Eliminate unnecessary luxury but attend to guests' needs." It does so by offering free TV movies, video player (there's a video rental shop next door), free use of a lobby computer with Internet access, special bathroom amenities for women, and little extras like semi-double or double-size beds in the mostly single rooms. The twins are great for friends traveling together (or couples who wish they weren't)—the bathroom splits the room in half, with each half containing its own bed, TV, mirror, hair dryer, and more. And true to its motto, the staff is friendly. Since it's located across from Hokkaido University, rooms are understandably hard to come by during February entrance exams.

4–22–7, N8, Kita-ku, Sapporo. ⓒ 011/717-1045. Fax 011/717-1046. 180 units. June–Sept and Snow Festival, ¥6,300–¥6,800 ($52.50–$57) single; ¥8,800 ($73) double; ¥9,800 ($82) twin. Oct–May, ¥4,700–¥5,200 ($39–$43) single; ¥7,100 ($59) double; ¥8,100 ($67.50) twin. AE, DC, JCB, MC, V. A 3-min. walk north of Sapporo Station. Walk straight north, turn left at the gas station and then right; it will be on the right, on a corner. **Amenities:** Coin-op washer and dryer; lobby computer with free Internet access. *In room:* A/C, TV with free movies and video player; fridge, hot-water pot with tea, hair dryer; trouser press.

260 **Yugiri Ryokan**   Only simple Japanese-style rooms (a bit worn but comfortable) and a Japanese-style public bath are available at this simple ryokan near the station. Doors close here at midnight and check-out is at 10am. Not much English is spoken, but surprisingly, 80% of guests are non-Japanese.

N7 W5, Kita-ku, Sapporo 064-0807. © 011/716-5482. 15 units (none with bathroom). ¥3,500 ($29) per person double occupancy; ¥3,900 ($32) per person single occupancy. Rates include tax. No credit cards. Station: Sapporo (north exit, 2 min.). Take an immediate left, cross the street and turn right, then left; it's the third building on the right. *In room:* TV, no phone.

WHERE TO DINE

Hokkaido's specialties include crab, corn on the cob, potatoes, **Genghis Khan** (a dish of mutton and vegetables that you grill yourself, also spelled "Jingisukan"), salmon, and **Ishikari Nabe** (a stew of salmon and other Hokkaido vegetables, also cooked at your table). As for Western food, your best bet is to dine in one of the many fine restaurants in Sapporo's top hotels.

Sapporo is also famous for its *ramen* (Chinese noodles), and the most popular place to eat them is on a tiny, narrow street in Susukino popularly known as **Ramen Yokocho.** Located just 1 short block east of the Susukino Station, it's an alleyway of noodle shop after noodle shop. It doesn't matter which one you choose—just look to see where there's an empty seat. The shops are all very small affairs consisting of a counter and some chairs, with photos of various dishes outside the front door. Most are open from 11:30am to 3am daily. Noodles generally begin at ¥700 ($6.30) for a steaming bowlful.

EXPENSIVE

Grand Chef ★★ FRENCH   This excellent, elegantly decorated French restaurant, in Sapporo's oldest hotel and a cool oasis compared to the traffic swirling outside, specializes in Hokkaido cuisine—cooked à la Française. The menus change monthly but always include selections of steaks and seafood like scallops, salmon or lobster. There are two sommeliers here, offering French, Italian, German, Chilean, and Japanese wines.

Sapporo Grand Hotel, N1 W4. © 011/261-3311. Reservations suggested. Set dinners ¥5,000–¥10,000 ($42–$83); set lunches ¥1,800–¥5,000 ($15–$42). AE, DC, JCB, MC, V. Daily 11:30am–2:30pm and 5–10pm. An 8-min. walk south of Sapporo Station.

21 Club ★★★ TEPPANYAKI   The 21 Club mirrors the sophistication of Hotel Arthur—sleek and elegant—and it's also Sapporo's highest spot for a meal. The views of the city, Nakajima-koen Park, and the Toyohira River are lovely. If the teppanyaki dinners featuring Kobe beef are too expensive, come for the "21 Club" set lunch for ¥2,500 ($21), which consists of grilled beef or fish, vegetables, salad, pickles, rice, soup, dessert, and tea or coffee. Relax in the sophisticated bar-lounge before your dinner with a cocktail or after your lunch with coffee or tea. This is the kind of place where you're asked whether you want milk or lemon with your tea—and then whether you want your milk hot or cold. Perhaps a glass of wine would be more to your liking—the hotel has five wine advisers!

Hotel Arthur, 25th floor, S10 W6. © 011/561-1000. Reservations recommended. Set dinners ¥8,000–¥25,000 ($67–$208); set lunches ¥2,500–¥8,000 ($21–$67). AE, DC, JCB, MC, V. Daily 11am–2pm and 5–9:30pm (last order). Subway: Namboku Line to Nakajima-koen, then exit 1 and through the park (5 min.).

Zuientei ★★ KAISEKI   Although the Hotel Monterey Edelhof prides itself on its turn-of-the-20th-century decor, my favorite restaurant here is this 13th-floor escape, a soothing respite with its tall ceiling, bamboo screens and small inner garden. Although the handwritten menu is only in Japanese, ordering is easy: choose one of the kaiseki dinners that change with the seasons or, for lunch, an obento or set meal.

Hotel Monterey Edelhof, N2 W1. *(©* 011/242-7111. Set dinners ¥5,000–¥10,000 ($42–$83); set lunches ¥2,000–¥3,000 ($17–$25). AE, DC, JCB, MC, V. Daily 11am–2pm and 5–9pm (last order). An 8-min. walk southeast of Sapporo Station.

MODERATE

Hyosetsu-no-Mon KING CRAB   A well-known restaurant that specializes in giant king crab caught in the Japan Sea north of Hokkaido, Hyosetsu-no-Mon is in Sapporo's Susukino nightlife district. Its menu (in English with photos) is easy enough—it consists almost entirely of king crab dishes. Set courses include a cooked crab, sashimi, crab soup, crab tempura, and vegetables. You can also order a la carte fried king crab claws, deep-fried king crab, tempura king crab, grilled king crab, and crabmeat chowder. Each floor has different seating arrangements from tables to tatami; the best is the sixth floor where you sit on tatami in a dining hall reminiscent of an old Kabuki theater. Here you'll be treated to a performance of traditional and contemporary dances, a bit corny in parts but popular with the mostly middle-aged set. Shows start between 7 and 8pm and cost ¥630 ($5.25) in addition to dinner.

S5 W2 (next to Sluggers Batting Stadium). *(©* 011/521-3046. Reservations recommended for 6th floor. Set meals ¥2,500–¥12,000 ($21–$100). MC, V. Daily 11am–11pm. Subway: Susukino (2 min.).

(261) **Kita-no-fuji** (Finds CHANKO NABE   Located in the heart of the Susukino nightlife district, this restaurant specializes in the famous hearty stews favored by sumo wrestlers, *chanko nabe*. After putting your shoes in lockers with famous wrestler's names on them, you'll be led by kimono-clad waitresses to your table or tatami. The center of the restaurant is dominated by a sumo ring with a bear in it (your guess is as good as mine); sumo wrestler's large hand prints are on the walls. As for the nabe, which you'll cook at your table, there's a picture menu but your best bet is probably to tell them how much you want to spend per person. The more expensive nabe features crab, with prices beginning at ¥2,700 ($22.50). Unfortunately, the staff in this busy nightspot has no time for cordiality, but this is definitely a unique place to dine.

S7 W4. *(©* 011-512-5484. Reservations suggested in winter. Chanko nabe ¥1,800–¥3,000 ($15–$25). AE, DC, JCB, MC, V. Daily 4pm–11pm. Subway: Susukino (7 min.). Beside a disco with a Mayan-like facade; look for the sumo pictures.

(262) **Palace Toriyoshi** ★ (Finds YAKITORI/VARIED   In a building filled with restaurants and bars in the Susukino nightlife district, this tiny restaurant serves yakitori with a twist, including many original creations by owner/chef Mr. Okuyama. How about cherry tomatoes covered in cheese, lotus root, small onion filled with minced chicken, tofu salad, or eggplant with minced meat? Since the menu is only in Japanese, the best strategy is to tell them what you like to eat and how much you want to spend; they'll fix a course meal to suit your budget. For ¥2,500 ($21), I had sashimi, seven yakitori and original skewers, salad, one of the best savory custards I've ever eaten, and soba.

Japanland Building. 2F. S5 W5. *(©* 011-521-2002. Reservations recommended. Yakitori ¥140–¥400 ($1.15–$3.35); set meals ¥2,500–¥6,000 ($21–$50). JCB, MC, V. Mon–Sat 5–11pm (to 10pm national holidays). Subway: Susukino (3 min.).

INEXPENSIVE

㉖㊂ **Napoli no daidokoro** ITALIAN   This inexpensive basement eatery, decorated with murals but with exposed, silver-encased ductwork up above, is popular with young women for its cheap pasta. The Japanese menu with photos lists more than a dozen spaghetti choices such as chicken and mushroom with a spicy tomato sauce and—my favorite—a very spicy eggplant and minced meat. For a little more, you can add a trip to the salad bar.

S1 W1. ✆ 011/231-2035. Spaghetti ¥680–¥880 ($5.65–$7.35); set lunches ¥750–¥950 ($6.25–$7.90). JCB, V. Mon–Sat 11am–10:30pm; Sun 11am–10pm. Station: Odori (1 min.). East across the street from Marui department store; look for the tiny orange, white, and green sign.

Sapporo Bier Garten ✿ GENGHIS KHAN/BAR FOOD   I can't imagine going to Sapporo without dropping by the Sapporo Bier Garten beside the historic Sapporo Beer Museum. Go for a late tour and then stay for dinner; or, if it's winter or early in the day when the beer garden is closed, dine in the Sapporo Beer Hall, an old ivy-covered brick building built in 1889 as the Sapporo brewery. I personally prefer the second floor's Kessel Hall, where you dine underneath a huge old mash tub once used in brewing beer. You can order dishes a la carte for snacks like Japanese-style fried chicken, sausage, fried potato, or boiled soybeans (edamame), but the specialty of the house is Genghis Khan, which you cook yourself on a hot skillet at your table. The best deal in the house is the appropriately named King Viking, which for ¥3,400 ($28) gives you as much Genghis Khan and as much draft beer as you can consume in 100 minutes. Otherwise, for all you timid drinkers, draft beer starts at ¥490 ($4.10) for a small mug.

Sapporo Beer Museum, N6 E9. ✆ 011/742-1531. Reservations not required. All-you-can-eat Genghis Khan ¥2,400 ($20). AE, DC, JCB, MC, V. Garden, July–Aug, Mon–Sat 5–9pm; Sun noon–3pm and 4–9pm. Beer Hall, daily 11:30am–10pm. Taxi: 5 min. from Sapporo Station. Bus: See "Sapporo Beer Museum," under "More to See & Do," earlier in this chapter.

Taj Mahal *Value* INDIAN   This very good, second-floor Indian restaurant tries too hard with its Indian mirrored fabrics, brass lamps, Indian music, and Japanese staff in Indian dress (the cooks are Indian), as the food alone is reason enough to come here. The service is friendly and the choices are varied—in addition to tandoori and kebabs, they serve chicken, lamb, fish, seafood, and vegetable curries (but no pork or beef). Tasty lunch specials are served until 3pm, but not on Sundays or holidays.

N2 W3. ✆ 011/231-8850. Main dishes ¥850–¥1,850 ($7.10–$15); set dinners ¥1,480–¥5,200 ($12–$43); set lunches ¥580–¥880 ($4.85–$7.35). AE, DC, JCB, V. Mon–Fri 11am–3pm and 5:30–10pm (last order); Sat–Sun 11am–10pm. Station: A 6-min. walk from Sapporo Station. Walk south on Eki-mae Dori and turn left when you see JAL and JTB to the right; it's catty-corner from the post office.

4 Noboribetsu Spa & Shikotsu-Toya National Park

If you have only a couple days to spare to visit one of Hokkaido's national parks, head to **Shikotsu-Toya National Park** ✿✿, the closest to Sapporo and the first national park you'll reach if you enter Hokkaido via train to Hakodate. This 381-square-mile national park encompasses lakes, volcanoes, and the famous hot-spring resort of **Noboribetsu Onsen** ✿✿, home to 1,200 people.

Famous for the variety of its hot-water springs ever since the first public bathhouse opened here in 1858, Noboribetsu Spa is one of Japan's best-known spa resorts and is the most popular of Hokkaido's many spa towns. It boasts 11

Tips   Un-Bearable Park

As you wander around Noboribetsu Onsen, you'll see advertisements for a bear park and an Ainu village attraction. The best thing about this place is the trip via ropeway—the bear park occupies one of the tallest hills around. The 160 or so bears, however, are crowded together in concrete pens in one of the saddest sights I've ever seen, and the Ainu "village" is mainly for souvenirs. Although the bears here, many of them rescued from extermination or brought here as orphaned cubs, are luckier than some of their peers (government policy advocated the extermination of Hokkaido brown bears in the 1950s and still allows 300 of the estimated 2,000 remaining wild bears to be hunted and culled annually), the admission of ¥2,520 ($21) is too high a price for this joyless place. Skip it—you're better off spending your money elsewhere. Or, donate money for a cause: dedicated employees bent on saving brown bears here have begun a non-profit organization in hopes of moving off the mountain to a place where there's more room.

---

different types of hot water (each with a different mineral content) and gushes 10,000 tons a day. With temperatures ranging between 113°F and 197°F, the waters contain all kinds of minerals, including sulfur, salt, iron, and gypsum, and are thought to help relieve such disorders as high blood pressure, poor blood circulation, rheumatism, arthritis, eczema, and even constipation.

Also known for its seasonal beauty, Noboribetsu is an impressive sight in spring, when 2,000 cherry trees lining the road into the onsen are in full bloom. In autumn, thousands of Japanese maples burst into flame. In the nearby village of **Shiraoi** on Lake Poroto, a museum and village commemorate the native Ainu and their culture.

ESSENTIALS

GETTING THERE   Noboribetsu Onsen is about a 15-minute **bus** ride (¥330/$2.75; departures 3 or more times an hour) from the town of Noboribetsu and **Noboribetsu Station,** which is where you'll arrive if you come by train. Noboribetsu Station lies on the main **JR train** line that runs between Hakodate and Sapporo, a little more than 2 hours from Hakodate and 1 hour and 10 minutes from Sapporo. Fares for an unreserved seat are ¥3,850 ($32) from Sapporo, ¥6,190 ($52) from Hakodate.

There are also **direct buses** from Sapporo Station to Noboribetsu Onsen departing every half hour or so and costing ¥1,900 ($16) for the 2½-hour trip. Contact the **Hokkaido Chuo Bus Company** (© 011/231-0500) for more information.

VISITOR INFORMATION & GETTING AROUND   The **Noboribetsu Tourist Association** (© 0143/84-3311; open daily 9am–6pm) is on Noboribetsu Onsen's main street, just a minute's walk north of the bus depot (turn left out of the depot; it will be on your left side). There's a pamphlet, a map in English, and hot-springs information, but you may not encounter anyone who speaks English. Luckily, the town is so small you shouldn't have any problem getting around.

WHAT TO SEE & DO

ENJOYING NOBORIBETSU'S NATURAL WONDERS

TAKING THE LOCAL WATERS   Although all the spa hotels and ryokan have their own taps into the spring water, almost everyone who comes to Noboribetsu Onsen makes a point of going to the most famous hotel bath in town, **Daiichi Takimotokan** ★★ (© **0143/84-2111**), one of the first bathhouses to open at the hot springs. Now a huge, modern bathing hall with some 10 pools containing different mineral contents at various temperatures, it's an elaborate affair with hot-spring baths both indoors and out, indoor and outdoor Jacuzzis, saunas, steam rooms, and waterfall massage (this is one of my favorites—you simply sit under the shooting water and let it pummel your neck and shoulders). Although the baths are separate for men and women, there's an indoor swimming pool for families with a slide and play area for children, so be sure to bring your swimsuit. If you're staying at the Daiichi Takimotokan hotel (see "Where to Stay," below), you can use the baths for free at any time—in the evenings, don't miss bathing in the outdoor baths, where you can order beer, soft drinks, or sake and enjoy the nice mountain scenery. Otherwise, Daiichi Takimotokan is open to the public daily from 9am to 6pm (you must enter by 5pm); the charge is ¥2,000 ($17) for adults, half price for children 3 to 12.

㉖④ **Sagiriyu** (© **0143/84-2050**) is Noboribetsu Onsen's public bathhouse. On the main street next to the Tourist Information Office, it offers two types of hot-spring waters, a whirlpool bath, and a sauna (but unfortunately no outdoor bath). Taking the waters and sauna here costs ¥390 ($3.25), and it's open daily 7am to 10pm.

HELL VALLEY (Jigokudani) ★   To get an idea of what all this hot water looks like, visit Hell Valley at the north edge of town past the Daiichi Takimotokan hotel (see "Where to Stay," below). A volcanic crater 1,485 feet in diameter, the huge depression is full of bubbling, boiling water and rock formations of orange and brown. As you walk along the concrete path that winds along the left side of the crater (called Hell Valley Promenade) keep an eye down below to the right for a tiny shrine dedicated to the deity that protects eyes (those most in need are apt to miss it); local lore says that if you rub some of the protective water over ailing eyes, they'll be cured. Farther along, you'll soon reach a sign for OYUNAMA and a path leading uphill to the left through lush woods; if you follow it for about 10 minutes, you'll come to a lookout point over a large pond of hot bubbling water called Oyunama (the lookout is across the highway; it's another 5-min. walk to the pond). If you want to take a different route back, follow the path to the right just as you recross the highway. This pathway, called Funamiya (or Mt. Funami) Promenade, traces the backbone of several ridges all the way back into town, passing a number of small stone guardians along the way. If you follow it 25 minutes to the end (where it's a bit overgrown and neglected), you'll end up in front of Oyado Kiyomizu-ya ryokan (see "Where to Stay," below). But the path diverges at several points, and if you take the wrong path you'll end up at—Hell Valley.

ESPECIALLY FOR KIDS

In addition to the two theme parks listed below (which you can see on a joint, discounted ticket available only to foreigners), there's a Bear Park with 160 brown bears crowded in an enclosure of cement. Very sad; skip it.

Noboribetsu-Date Historic Village (Jidai-mura) ★★ *Kids*   A visit to Jidai-mura, a reproduction of a Feudal-Era village, is the closest you can get to taking a time machine back to the last days of the Edo Period. Shops, restaurants, theaters, the downtown, and a samurai district are built as they were of yore, staffed by people dressed in period clothing. See Ninja warriors fighting in a trick mansion, local merchants hawking their wares, Edo-Era tenements with life-size models, and courtesans performing in this Disney-esque re-creation of how Japan might have looked when the shogun reigned. Although shows are in Japanese (the Ninja show is probably the only one that would interest children), the various attractions are fun for the whole family, and if you haven't seen another historic theme village elsewhere in Japan, this rather small one is worth a 2-hour visit. To commemorate the day forever, you can don a kimono, samurai, or Ninja outfit and have your photo taken in front of a traditional backdrop for ¥2,100 ($17.50)

53–1 Nakanoboribetsu, Noboribetsu-shi. ✆ **0143/83-3311.** Admission ¥1,800 ($15) adults, ¥900 ($7.50) for children; passport (admission with all shows) ¥3,500 ($29) for adults, ¥1,800 ($15) for children. *Tip:* A foreigners-only combination discount ticket allowing passport admission to both Jidai-mura and Marine Park Nixe (see below) costs ¥3,000 ($25) for adults, ¥1,800 ($15) for children. Summer, daily 9am–5pm; winter, Thurs–Tues 10am–4pm. Bus: From Noboribetsu Onsen or JR Noboribetsu Station to Jidai-mura; note that some buses traveling between the two stop here.

Noboribetsu Marine Park Nixe *★ Kids*   Small children love this combination Danish theme park and aquarium, located near Noboribetsu Station (if you're traveling with luggage, there are lockers both at the station and here). The aquarium, one of the largest in northern Japan, is in Castle Nixe, modeled after a Danish castle (and visible from the station), where you'll see sharks, rays, salmon, sturgeon, king crab, frogs, turtles, and other sea creatures. More attractions include a dolphin show, a king penguin parade, a sea lion show, game arcade, the ubiquitous souvenir shops (selling Danish and aquarium-related gifts), and a handful of kiddie rides (which cost ¥200–¥300/$1.65–$2.50 extra). You can see everything in 2 hours.

1–22 Noboribetsu Higashi-machi, Noboribetsu-shi. ✆ **0143/83-3800.** Admission ¥2,300 ($19) adults, ¥1,150 ($9.60) children. A foreigners-only combination discount ticket allowing passport admission to both Jidai-mura (see above) and Marine Park Nixe costs ¥3,000 ($25) for adults, ¥1,800 ($15) for children. Daily 9am–5pm. A 7-min. walk from JR Noboribetsu Station; walk straight out the exit and after one block turn right.

LEARNING ABOUT THE AINU IN NEARBY SHIRAOI

Poroto Kotan and the Ainu Museum *★*   Shiraoi (an Ainu word meaning "Place of Many Horseflies") was settled by the Ainu long before the Japanese arrived; today, it's a small town of some 23,000 inhabitants, including Ainu. Poroto Kotan means "Big Lake Village" in Ainu, and nestled on the shores of Lake Poroto is a mock village of native houses made entirely from wood and reeds, a native plant garden, a dance area, probably the most important Ainu museum anywhere, and a research center dedicated to preserving Ainu culture.

After passing, regrettably, through a huge souvenir hall, you'll find yourself surrounded by traditionally built houses, where there are demonstrations of Ainu weaving techniques, woodworking, and other crafts and where native dances are performed by Ainu in traditional costume. Unfortunately, there are bears (and dogs) kept in captivity here in filthy, metal cages, but even this is an Ainu tradition—in spring, when the mother bear would leave her cave in search of food, Ainu would fetch the cubs to keep in a wooden cage in the village until they were old enough for slaughter. Bears were revered as gifts from the gods. The most important thing to see, however, is the museum, with English descriptions of Ainu history, culture, society, and traditions, and displays of utensils, clothing, jewelry, and other everyday artifacts.

If you wish, you can lunch on dried salmon, potato cakes, and herb tea bought from one of the stalls. Otherwise, although the village is small and can be toured in about an hour, it's important for those wishing to learn about Ainu culture and the indigenous people who have little left of what was once a rich heritage.

2–3–4 Wakakusa-cho, Shiraoi-cho, Hokkaido 059-0902. ⓒ **0144/82-3914.** Admission ¥650 ($5.40) adults, ¥500 ($4.15) high-school students, ¥400 ($3.35) junior-high students, ¥300 ($2.50) children. Apr–Oct, daily 8am–5pm; Nov–Mar, daily 8:30am–4:30pm. Closed 1 week over New Year's. Train: JR train 25 min. from JR Noboribetsu Station to JR Shiraoi Station, then a 15-min. walk; walk out to the traffic signal, turn left, and then turn left again at the next light. Cross the tracks; it's on your right. *Note:* Not all trains running between Hakodate and Sapporo (with stops at Noboribetsu Station) stop at Shiraoi, so make sure yours does.

WHERE TO STAY

The busiest tourist season is July through September and during New Year's, which is when hotel rates are at their highest, particularly on weekends. October, when the leaves are changing, is also popular. With the exception of Kikusui, all the places below charge a daily ¥150 ($1.25) hot-springs tax.

EXPENSIVE

㉖㊄ **Oyado Kiyomizu-ya** ⭐⭐   You'll be made to feel welcome at this elegantly modern ryokan with traditional touches, one of our favorites in Hokkaido. After entering the front gate, you'll be ushered down a long corridor decorated with plants, stones and paper lanterns to the elevator that will whisk you up to your room. Cheapest are average-looking Western-style rooms, making the simple but pleasant Japanese tatami rooms a better choice. For a splurge, combination rooms are actually two-room suites, with a tatami room where you'll dine and a separate bedroom. The ryokan is beside a roaring river, the sounds of which will sing you to sleep as you snuggle against fur-lined futon (which cost an astounding $1,000 each!) and down covers. But it's the delicious and abundant seasonal *kaiseki* meals served in your room that assure the ryokan many repeat guests, a parade of beautifully prepared dishes that includes local specialties. Service, as to be expected, is impeccable, and the second-generation owner, Mr. Iwai, speaks excellent English and can answer your questions regarding Noboribetsu and the surrounding area (a sake connoisseur, he can also recommend which of the 14 different kinds of sake he keeps on hand might go best with your meal). If you're looking for a place far from tour groups, souvenir shops, and impersonal service, you'll be happy here.

173 Noboribetsu Onsen-machi, Noboribetsu-shi, Hokkaido 059-0551. ⓒ **0143/84-2145.** Fax 0143/84-2146. 43 units. ¥10,000 ($83) single; ¥16,000 ($133) double; ¥24,000 ($200) triple. Breakfast ¥2,000 ($17) extra; dinner ¥5,000–¥10,000 ($42–$83) extra. AE, DC, JCB, MC, V. The staff will pick you up at the station if you tell them your arrival time in advance; otherwise, it's above Noboribetsu Onsen's main street, a 10-min. walk from the bus terminal. **Amenities:** Coffee shop, karaoke bar; indoor/outdoor hot-spring baths (the one outdoor bath alternates days for men and women); in-room massage. *In room:* TV, hot-water pot with tea.

MODERATE

Daiichi Takimotokan ⭐   Thanks to its long history and gigantic public baths with various pools, this is Noboribetsu Onsen's best-known ryokan. Opened in 1858 as the area's first inn and now in its 5th generation of innkeepers (a 30-something woman and probably Japan's youngest female general manager), it remains Noboribetsu's oldest accommodation, though now it's a large, modern facility with little personality and lots of noisy tour groups. Still, the most compelling reasons to stay here are its location near Hell Valley and its hot-spring baths, which hotel guests are entitled to use free anytime, night or day. As for

**Another Island, Another People:
The Ainu of Hokkaido**

Hokkaido is home to the Ainu, a people that are the native inhabitants of Japan's northernmost island. Not much is known about their origins; it's not even clear whether they're Asian or Caucasian, but they are of different racial stock than the Japanese. They're round-eyed and light-skinned, and Ainu males can grow thick beards and mustaches.

The Ainu arrived in Hokkaido approximately 800 years ago. Living in a harsh environment with few resources, they were skilled at using the plants and animals around them for everything from medicine to utensils. With no metal at their disposal, they carved arrows with wooden "knives" and then dipped them in poison to increase their efficiency. Clothes were fashioned from bark, wild rye, or even salmon skin. Traditionally, they lived as hunters and fishermen, using dogs to help in the hunt and setting up trip traps with arrows to catch wild animals. Animistic, they had gods for every object and phenomenon, whether sun, thunder, fire, or animals. Most important to Ainu culture were bear cubs, kept in captivity before being killed, with elaborate ceremonies held to send the cub's spirit to the next life. To avoid attention from demons, babies were dressed in old clothing and given temporary names like "small excrement" until they were 2 or 3 years old. Girls were tattooed around their lips, arms, and hands beginning at age 12 and were considered ready for marriage by the time they were 15 or 16.

After Hokkaido was opened for development in the late 1800s, the Ainu were forcibly assimilated into Japanese society, and many died with the spread of smallpox, measles, cholera, and other newly introduced diseases. Like Native Americans, they were often discriminated against, and their culture was largely destroyed. Hunting and fishing were prohibited, and male Ainu were taken from their families for forced labor. Eventually, the Ainu took Japanese names and adopted the Japanese language and clothing. Today, there are an estimated 23,000 Ainu still living in Hokkaido. Some of them earn their living from tourism, selling Ainu wood carvings and other crafts as well as performing traditional dances and songs.

rooms, most are simple tatami (only 10 are Western style), with repeat guests usually preferring the west wing (though glazed windows make them a bit dark and in-room meals are not available). Meals are served in a large dining room offering a Japanese, Chinese, and Western buffet or, at slightly higher prices, in some of the Japanese-style rooms.

Noboribetsu Onsen-machi, Noboribetsu-shi, Hokkaido 059-0595. ☎ **0143/84-2111.** Fax 0143/84-2202. www.takimotokan.co.jp. 399 units (342 with bathroom, 57 with toilet only). ¥10,000–¥25,000 ($83–$208) per person; peak season, Sat, and holiday evenings ¥2,000 ($17) extra. Rates include 2 meals. DC, JCB, MC, V. A 5-min. walk uphill from the bus station, beside Hell Valley. **Amenities:** Coffee shop, Japanese and Chinese noodle shops, 2 bars, 1 disco; indoor swimming pool (free for hotel guests); indoor/outdoor hot-spring baths; shopping arcade; in-room massage; laundry/dry cleaning service. *In room:* TV, minibar, hot-water pot with tea, safe.

266 **Kashotei Hanaya** ✪ This is one of the most refined members of the Japanese Inn Group ryokan, modern but with such traditional touches as a small Japanese garden off the lobby, flower arrangements, bamboo, decorative floors, and Japanese music playing softly in public places. Most rooms are Japanese style, with and without bathroom, while the three Western-style rooms are without bathroom (all rooms, however, have toilet and sink). Meals are served in your room, and the owner speaks English. It's on the edge of town, about a 5-minute walk from the bus terminal.

134 Noboribetsu Onsen-machi, Noboribetsu-shi, Hokkaido 059-0551. ✆ **0143/84-2521.** Fax 0143/84-2240. 22 units (5 with bathroom, 17 with toilet only). ¥7,000–¥7,500 ($58–$62.50) single with toilet only; ¥12,000 ($100) double with toilet only, ¥20,000 ($167) double with bathroom. Japanese or Western breakfast ¥1,000 ($8.35) extra; dinner ¥2,500–¥7,500 ($21–$62.50) extra. AE, V. Bus: From Noboribetsu Station to Byoin-mae/Kashotei Hanaya-mae (if you're arriving by bus, you'll get off before reaching the terminal—ask the bus driver to let you know where—the ryokan will be a stone's throw behind you, across the road). Pick-up service also available from Noboribetsu Onsen bus terminal. **Amenities:** Coffee shop; indoor/outdoor hot-spring baths; in-room massage. *In room:* A/C, TV, minibar, hot-water pot with tea.

Takimoto Inn If you prefer a hotel with beds to a ryokan with futon, this quiet and moderately priced hotel has the additional advantage of allowing guests to use Daiichi Takimotokan's famous baths across the street for free. All the rooms are twins (but can be used also as singles and triples) and are fairly basic with a small bathroom. There's no view, but windows open. Buffet breakfasts and dinners offer a mix of Japanese and Western food.

76 Noboribetsu Onsen-machi, Noboribetsu-shi 059-0551. ✆ **0143/84-2205.** Fax 0143/84-2645. 47 units. Off season, ¥6,000–¥8,000 ($50–$67) per person. Sat and peak season ¥2,000 ($17) extra; New Year's, Golden Week and mid-Aug ¥3,000–¥4,000 ($25–$33) extra. Rates include 2 meals. AE, DC, JCB, V. A 5-min. walk uphill from the bus station, across the street from Daiichi Takimotokan. **Amenities:** 1 restaurant; hot-spring bath (guests can use Daiichi Takimotokan's baths for free); in-room massage. *In room:* TV, fridge, hot-water pot with tea.

INEXPENSIVE

267 **Noboribetsu Tokiwaso** (Value) This cement building has as much charm as a youth hostel, but it's one of the cheapest places in town and has adequate Japanese-style rooms and a pleasant dining room. Its hot-spring bath, however, is not very inviting, so you'll probably want to go elsewhere.

96 Noboribetsu Onsen-machi, Noboribetsu-shi, Hokkaido 059-0551. ✆ **0143/84-2041.** 14 units (none with bathroom). ¥5,500 ($46) single; ¥10,000 ($83) double. Rates include 2 meals. No credit cards. A 6-min. walk from the bus terminal; walk uphill, turning left at Akiyoshi Ryokan, crossing the stream, and turning right. **Amenities:** Hot-spring baths. *In room:* TV, hot-water pot with tea.

WHERE TO DINE

268 **Fukuan** SOBA This small, traditional soba shop serves its own buckwheat noodles. Since the menu is only in Japanese, I recommend ordering the *Tenseiro,* a tempura soba meal with shrimp and vegetables, or the *Ebi-tenzaroshi* soba, a summertime meal of cold soba, shrimp tempura, seaweed, dried fish flakes, and Japanese daikon radish. Or, look around at what others are eating. There are leg wells, saviors for those errant legs that just won't fit under low Japanese tables.

30 Chuo-dori. ✆ **0143/84/2758.** Soba ¥680–¥1,200 ($5.65–$10). JCB, MC, V. Daily 11:30am–2pm and 6–11pm. A 1-min. walk from the bus terminal, on the main street across from the tourist information office.

Poplar Restaurant WESTERN If you find yourself looking for a place to stop for lunch, a draft beer, or coffee, try this restaurant, which serves inexpensive Western dishes. While they may not win any culinary awards, items on the

Japanese menu with pictures include beefsteak, pork chops, hamburger steak, fried shrimp, fried scallops, sandwiches, curry rice, shrimp gratin, and spaghetti.

Takimoto Inn. (C) **0143/84-2205.** Main dishes ¥650–¥900 ($5.40–$7.50); set meals ¥1,300–¥2,500 ($11–$21). AE, DC, JCB, V. Daily 11am–2pm (last order). A 5-min. walk from the bus terminal, near Hell Valley and across from Daiichi Takimotokan.

(269) **Tokumitsu** ⭐ SUSHI   This is a friendly, local hangout where you'll be served good, reasonably priced dishes while sitting at the long sushi counter or on tatami. A plastic-food display will help you order dishes like *Chiraishi sushi* (raw fish served over a bed of rice), *unagi* (eel), or *kani-nabe* (a crab stew you cook yourself), all priced at ¥1,500 ($12.50). Tokumitsu stays open late as a nightcap spot for locals and tourists alike.

29 Chuo-dori. (C) **0143/84-2079.** Sushi and sashimi platters ¥700–¥1,800 ($5.90–$15); set meals ¥1,000–¥1,800 ($8.35–$15). No credit cards. Daily 11am–2pm and 4:30pm–midnight. A 1-min. walk from the bus terminal, on the main street across from the tourist office.

5 Sounkyo Spa & Daisetsuzan National Park

Although I find it difficult to rank nature in terms of beauty, there are some who maintain that **Daisetsuzan National Park** ⭐⭐⭐ is the most spectacular of Hokkaido's parks. With its tall mountains covered with fir and birch trees and sprinkled with wildflowers and its river gorge laced with waterfalls and hiking trails, Daisetsuzan National Park is the perfect place to come if you've been itching to get some exercise in relatively unspoiled countryside. Lying in the center of Hokkaido (east of Sapporo), this national park—Japan's largest—contains three volcanic mountain groups, including the highest mountain in Hokkaido, Mt. Asahi, 7,513 feet high. Hiking in summer and skiing in winter are the park's primary pursuits.

Nestled at the very edge of Sounkyo Gorge, Daisetsuzan's most famous natural attraction, is **Sounkyo Onsen** ⭐ (*onsen* means "spa" in Japanese), the perfect base for exploring the national park. Once rather unattractive with a hodgepodge of ugly cement buildings, Sounkyo has reinvented itself with attractive and compatible alpine-style buildings and stone and wood paths that do justice to the magnificent scenic backdrop and its soothing hot springs. Yet it remains a mountain village, home to 600 residents and only a dozen or so accommodations, most of them small affairs. More important, Sounkyo Spa serves as the starting point for bicycle trips along Sounkyo Gorge and for the cable-car trip to the top of a neighboring peak with its hiking trails. In February, it's the scene of the Ice Falls Festival, a winter fantasyland with giant ice castles, frozen waterfalls lit with colored lights, and weekend fireworks. Need I add that Sounkyo is one of my favorite places in all of Hokkaido?

ESSENTIALS
GETTING THERE   The only way to reach Sounkyo Onsen by public transportation is by **bus.** If you're coming from Sapporo, take the **JR train** 2½ hours to Kamikawa (¥5,670/$42 one-way), transferring there for the 30-minute bus ride (¥770/$6.40 one-way) directly to Sounkyo Onsen. Buses depart about 14 times a day and generally connect with train arrivals, but it's always wise to check ahead with the tourist information center in Sapporo.

There are two buses a day connecting Sounkyo Onsen with Akanko Onsen in Akan National Park (see below), with the one-way fare costing ¥3,260 ($27) for the 3½-hour trip (reservations are required; call (C) **01658/5-3321** in

Sounkyo or © **0154/67-2205** in Akan or drop by the bus terminal in either town). All bus fares are half price for children.

VISITOR INFORMATION & ORIENTATION   The **tourist information office** (© **01658/5-3350;** open daily 10am–5:30pm May–Oct, daily 10am–4:30pm Nov–Apr) is located inside the bus terminal on the right-hand side. The window is not marked in English and spoken English is limited, but the staff can point you in the direction of your lodging or even make reservations for you. They also have a brochure in English describing the national park and its attractions and a brochure about Mt. Kurodake with hiking paths. In any case, the village is so tiny that you won't have any difficulty getting around; it's basically just two streets leading up to the ropeway and a pedestrian lane called Canyon Mall Street that wanders through the center of town (nicknamed Hot Hut).

EXPLORING SOUNKYO ONSEN

Before exploring the environs, you might want to pop into the **Daisetsuzan National Park Visitor Center,** located next to the ropeway (© **01658/9-4400**), with displays on the park's animals, plants, and geological wonders. Unfortunately, displays are in Japanese, though there's an English handout with rudimentary explanations and a video shows the park's changes through the seasons. If you plan on hiking, you might ask the staff at information counter for more details on the "Guide to Mountain Climbing" exhibit, as it alerts hikers to places brown bears are often spotted. The center is open Tuesday from 9am to 6pm.

BICYCLING THE SOUNKYO GORGE 🚴   The Sounkyo Gorge is a river valley hemmed in on both sides by rock walls rising almost 500 feet high. Almost perpendicular in places, the gorge extends for about 12 miles, offering spectacular views with each bending curve. The best way to see part of the gorge is **by bicycle** (unfortunately, a permanent rock slide prohibits cyclists from seeing the whole gorge), which you can do in about an hour or so. From Sounkyo, the first part of the trip is along a sidewalk next to a highway strung with cars. The highway winds along a rushing river past a couple of waterfalls until finally disappearing into a dark tunnel (where it belongs). From this point, the gorge belongs to cyclists and hikers and becomes quite narrow. I find this a glorious ride, especially on fine days, and look forward to it every time I come to Sounkyo Onsen. I only wish the ride were longer, especially since bicycles, available for rent at the Sounkyo bus terminal, cost ¥1,500 ($12.50) regardless of whether you keep them for 1 hour or a whole day. Bikes are available for rent daily from 6am to 6pm from Golden Week (end of Apr) through October.

GOING TO THE TOP OF MT. KURODAKE 🚶   If you're interested in hiking, or even if you're not, take the **cable car** directly from Sounkyo Onsen to the lofty peak of Mt. Kurodake. The trip takes 7 minutes, and round-trip tickets cost ¥1,650 ($14) for adults, ¥850 ($7.10) for children. From the cable-car station, walk a few minutes farther up the mountain where you'll come to a chairlift. The chairlift ride (my favorite part) takes 15 minutes, swinging you past lush forests of fir and birch. Round-trip fare for this is ¥600 ($5) for adults, ¥400 ($3.35) for children. Ropeway and lift operating hours vary; in summer it's 6am to 7pm.

Day Hikes   At the end of the lift, where the hiking paths begin, there's a hut to the left where you sign your name and give your route so that tabs can be kept on people who are on the mountain. You can also rent rubber boots here for ¥500 ($4.15), a must if you don't have hiking boots and trails are slippery and wet (small streams from winter snows cascade down the trail even in July; note that rental sizes only go up to 28cm or 11.2 inches). If you're not feeling overly ambitious but are prepared to exert yourself climbing over boulders, you can reach the peak of **Kurodake,** 6,500 feet high, in about 1½ hours, where, if the weather is clear, you'll be rewarded with views of the surrounding mountain ranges. If you feel like taking a day's hike, there's a circular path along the top of mountain ridges that you can hike in about 8 hours (be sure to get a map at the tourist information office and note lift operating hours). The tops of the mountains are really beautiful here, covered with wildflowers and alpine plant life. It would be a shame to come to Sounkyo and not spend a few hours amid its lofty peaks.

SKIING   From November to May the mountain becomes a skier's haven, especially for beginners (advanced skiers won't find the slopes here challenging). Although you can rent skis up on the mountain at the cable-car station, keep in mind that your feet may be too big (at last check, boots went up to 27cm or 10.8 inches). Skis and boots (for adults only) rent for ¥3,150 ($26), while a one day cable-car and chairlift ticket goes for ¥3,600 ($30) for adults, ¥2,100 ($17.50) for children.

TAKING THE WATERS   In the village Hot Hut Community Center, you'll find **Spa Kurodake** (✆ **01658/5-3333**), a public hot-spring bath with large, spotless, and attractive indoor and outdoor baths plus a sauna. The spa charges ¥600 ($5) for adults (half price for children) and is open 10am to 9pm in summer and 11am to 8pm in winter; buy your tickets at the entrance vending machine.

WHERE TO STAY

There are plenty of inexpensive pensions and hotels in Sounkyo. The army of college-age Japanese you see working in the area comes from other parts of Japan to work for the summer. They may not know a lot about the area, but most of them speak some English.

At all of the accommodations with hot-spring baths, you'll pay a hot-spring tax of ¥150 ($1.25) in addition to the usual government tax. If you want to stay here in August, be sure to make advance reservations.

MODERATE

㉗ **Ginsenkaku** ⭐   Opened in 1998 in the heart of Hot Hut, this modern, functional ryokan offers convenience and rather ordinary Japanese-style rooms with small bathrooms. Except during busy peak periods, Japanese meals are served in your room; buffet breakfasts in a communal dining room offer Japanese and Western choices.

Sounkyo, Kamikawacho, Kamikawa-gun 078-1701. ✆ **01658/5-3003**. Fax 01658/5-3121. 36 units. Summer, ¥12,000–¥13,500 ($100–$125) per person; off-season ¥7,000–¥8,000 ($58–$67) per person. Rates include 2 meals. JCB, MC, V. A 4-min. walk from the bus terminal. **Amenities:** Indoor/outdoor hot-spring baths; in-room massage. *In room:* TV, fridge, hot-water pot with tea, hair dryer, safe, washlet toilet.

Taisetsu Hotel ⭐⭐ *Value*   Although it's the farthest walk from the bus terminal, this hotel's ridge-top location above town gives it good views of the surrounding gorge and mountains. What makes this a top pick, however, are its gorgeous baths, of which there are three (open 24 hr.). Best are the 7th-floor indoor and outdoor baths with great views and the new outdoor baths over-looking expansive greenery. As for rooms, most are Japanese-style, and since prices are the same, no matter which way they face, ask for a room on a top floor facing the gorge (avoid the hotel's 2 twins; they have no view). The best are in the west wing (ask for a room on the 4th to 6th floor facing the river), but since guests who stay here are expected to dine in their room, you'll have to pay ¥3,000 ($25) extra per person to stay here. You'll dine in one of two restaurants, one serving Japanese set meals and the other serving a blend of Japanese and Western cuisine. Breakfasts are served buffet style with both Western and Japanese food.

Sounkyo, Kamikawacho, Kamikawa-gun 078-1701. ⓒ **01658/5-3211.** Fax 01658/5-3420. www.taisetsu-g. com. 231 units (219 with bathroom; 12 with toilet only). Summer, ¥13,000 ($108) per person; off-season ¥11,000 ($92) per person. Rates include 2 meals. AE, DC, JCB, MC, V. An 8-min. walk from the bus terminal. **Amenities:** 3 restaurants (Japanese, combination Japanese/Western, coffee shop); 1 Japanese-style pub; indoor/outdoor hot-spring baths; sauna; whirlpool baths; in-room massage. *In room:* TV, fridge, hot-water pot with tea, hair dryer, safe, washlet toilet (west wing only).

INEXPENSIVE

Northern Lodge ⭐   This small and personable European-style lodge invites with its cozy living room complete with fireplace, English-speaking staff, and spotless, mostly Japanese-style rooms, though there are a few twins with down quilts and sofas. The unit bathrooms are small, but you'll probably want to go to the public hot-spring baths anyway, which use fences for privacy, above which are views of soaring mountains. The communal dining room, decorated with natural wood, offers both European (Swiss fondue) or Japanese cuisine, as well as buffet breakfast. If you're here for the winter Ice Falls Festival, be sure to ask for a room on the 4th or 5th floor facing the river.

Sounkyo, Kamikawacho, Kamikawa-gun 078-1701. ⓒ **01658/5-3231.** Fax 01658/5-3021. 36 units. Summer, ¥11,000 ($92) per person; off season, ¥9,000 ($75) per person. Rates include 2 meals. JCB, MC V. A 1-min. walk from the bus terminal, across the footbridge over the river and up the hill. **Amenities:** Indoor/outdoor hot-spring baths; gift shop; coin-op washer and dryer; rental bikes (¥1,000/$8.35 per day). *In room:* TV, fridge, hot-water pot with tea, safe.

Onsen Pension Ginga ⭐ *Value*   Opened in 2001, this cute lodge is bright and airy, with a glass-enclosed communal dining room decorated in European drawing-room style and both Japanese- and Western-style rooms, most with large windows providing great panoramic views (best are corner rooms or rooms 208 and 210). Rooms without a bathroom do have sinks. Japanese meals, served in the dining room, feature local fish and other ingredients. Unfortunately, the hot-spring bath is small.

Sounkyo, Kamikawacho, Kamikawa-gun 078-1701. ⓒ **01658/5-3775.** 21 units (6 with bathroom. ¥6,500–¥7,800 ($54–$65) per person, including 2 meals. No credit cards. A 2-min. walk from the bus terminal. **Amenities:** Small indoor hot-spring bath; coin-op washer and dryer. *In room:* TV, hot-water pot with tea, no phone.

㉗ **Resort Pension Yama-no-ue**   This pension offers simple tatami rooms with just the basics. There are communal toilets, sinks, and showers; but for a real hot-spring bath, guests staying here are entitled to use the Spa Kurodake (see above) in the adjoining building for free. In summer, the small dining room serves ample meals of Hokkaido cuisine; if you stay more than one night or in winter, you'll dine at Beergrill Canyon (see "Where to Dine," below). Breakfast is Western style.

Sounkyo, Kamikawacho, Kamikawa-gun 078-1701. ⓒ **01658/5-3206.** Fax 01658/5-3207. 14 units (none with bathroom, 1 with toilet). TV. ¥5,500 ($46) per person. Breakfast ¥1,000 ($8.35) extra; dinner ¥2,000 ($17) extra. No credit cards. A 2-min. walk from the bus terminal. *In room:* TV, hot-water pot with tea, no phone.

(*Tips* **A Note on Japanese Symbols**

Many establishments and attractions in Japan do not have signs in Roman (English-language) letters. Those that don't are indicated in this guide with an oval with a number that corresponds to a number in the appendix showing the Japanese symbols. Thus, to find the Japanese symbol for, say, **Resort Pension Yama-no-ue** (above), refer to no. 271 in appendix C.

WHERE TO DINE

Beergrill Canyon PIZZA/PASTA Located in the same building as Spa Kurodake (identified as "Community Center" on the English map), this casual restaurant serves various pizzas and pasta from its Japanese menu. Choices include pizza with mushrooms and bacon, spaghetti in a white cream sauce with egg and bacon, and spicy curry chicken, and sirloin steak using local beef. For a complete meal, add a mini salad, bread or rice to your main dish by paying ¥200 ($1.65) extra. Wash it down with Kamikawa-brewed Hokuto beer.

Sounkyo. C **01658/5-3361.** Main dishes ¥850–¥2,000 ($7.10–$17). No credit cards. Daily 11:30am–4:30pm and 6–9pm. Closed Wed in winter.

6 Akanko Spa & Akan National Park

Spreading through the eastern end of Hokkaido, **Akan National Park** ★★ features volcanic mountains, dense forests of subarctic primeval trees, and three caldera lakes including Lake Akan.

The best place to stay in the park is at **Akanko Onsen,** a small hot-spring resort on the edge of Lake Akan and home to 2,500 residents. It makes a good base for active vacations ranging from fishing to hiking and from which to explore both Akan National Park and nearby Kushiro Marshland National Park, famous for its red-crested cranes.

ESSENTIALS

GETTING THERE   By JR Train & Bus Since there's no train station at Akanko Onsen itself, transportation to the resort town is by train to Kushiro or Kitami and then by bus to Akanko. Kushiro is about 4 hours from Sapporo by JR train; Kitami is 4½. From **JR Kushiro Station,** buses depart four or five times a day for Akanko and cost ¥2,650 ($22) one-way for the 2-hour trip. From **Kitami,** buses depart twice a day (at last check at 9:30am and 3pm) and cost ¥1,800 ($15) for the 70-minute trip (you must make a reservation for this bus by calling C **0157/23-2181** in Kitami or C **0154/67-2205** in Akanko).

If you're coming from Sounkyo Onsen, there are two buses a day connecting Sounkyo Onsen with Akanko Onsen, with the one-way fare costing ¥3,260 ($27) for the 3½-hour trip (reservations are required; call C **01658/5-3321** in Sounkyo or C **0154/67-2205** in Akan or drop by the bus terminal in either town).

All bus fares are half price for children.

In addition to regular buses, there are also sightseeing buses that take in the most important sights in both Akan and Kushiro Marshland national parks along the way. This is the best way to see the national park if you don't have your own car; for details, see "Seeing the Sights," below.

By Plane Because Akan National Park lies at the eastern extremity of Hokkaido, you may wish to fly at least one-way between here and Tokyo. The closest airport to Akanko Onsen is Kushiro Airport, with the flight from Tokyo taking about 1½ hours and costing ¥33,000 ($275) one way on ANA and JAS. From Kushiro Airport, buses travel to Akanko in about 1 hour and 20 minutes for ¥2,090 ($17).

VISITOR INFORMATION   **Akanko Onsen's Tourist Association** (① 0154/ **67-2254;** fax 0154/67-3024; open daily 9am–6pm) is located just a minute's walk from the Akanko Onsen bus terminal in the direction of the lake (turn right out of the bus terminal and take the first left; it will soon be on your right, just past the police box). Occasionally, there's an English speaker here, and in any case, you can pick up a pamphlet in English about Akan National Park with a map of the town and two foldouts on hiking. The staff will also make reservations for hotels and ryokan. For information on the park and its natural wonders, drop by the newly opened **Akankohan Eco Museum Center** (① 0154/67- **2785;** open 9am–5pm, to 7pm end of June–Aug), with free admission.

ORIENTATION & GETTING AROUND   Akanko Onsen is small, and walking is the best way to get around. It consists primarily of one main street that snakes along the lake, with ryokan and souvenir shops lining both sides.

WHAT TO SEE & DO
SEEING THE SIGHTS
SIGHTSEEING BUS TOURS OF AKAN NATIONAL PARK   If you're not renting a car, the best way to see Akan National Park is aboard a sightseeing bus departing from **Bihoro,** which is north of the park and can be reached by JR train from other parts of Hokkaido. That way, you'll travel all the way through the park and see the most important natural wonders enroute, ending up at Akanko Onsen.

The bus trip takes 5 hours, making stops at several scenic spots along the way including **Bihoro Pass** (a scenic overlook) and Kussharo and Mashu lakes. **Kussharo** is one of Japan's largest mountain lakes, but what makes it particularly interesting is its hot-spring waters right on the beach; in summer, you can see people digging holes to sit in the hot springs. **Mashu,** a crater lake that is considered one of Japan's most beautiful lakes, was called "lake of the devil" by the Ainu because no water flows either into it or out of it. Surely Mashu is one of Japan's least-spoiled lakes: Because of the steep, 660-foot-high rock walls ringing it, the lake has remained inaccessible to humans (the bus stops at an observation platform high above the water). The bus also stops at the foot of Mt. Iou with its sulfurous caldrons. *Beware:* Frequent fog often eliminates scenic views, there are tacky souvenir shops at every stop, and tours are only in Japanese.

The bus trip, called the **Panorama Course,** costs ¥5,600 ($47) for adults, half price for children. Buses depart from Bihoro twice daily, once in winter. Be sure to check departures ahead of time since bus schedules change. For more information, call the **Bihoro bus center** at ① 01527/3-4181 (Japanese only) or fax the tourist information center in Akan (fax 0154/67-3024).

RED-CRESTED CRANES & BUS TOURS OF KUSHIRO MARSHLAND NATIONAL PARK   Red-crested cranes, the official birds of Hokkaido, are traditionally regarded as both a good omen and a national symbol of Japan. Once threatened with extinction, these graceful and beautiful creatures now lead protected lives in and around **Kushiro Marshland National Park** (Kushiro Shitsugen), Japan's largest marshland and designated the country's newest park in 1987. If you don't have a car, the best way to see the marshlands and catch a glimpse of the cranes in their natural habitat is via sightseeing bus, tours are conducted only in Japanese but traverse the marshland and make stops at observatories and Tancho-Tsuru Koen (see below). The **Akan Bus Company** (© 0154/ 37-2221) offers tours that begin and end at Kushiro Station twice a day from the end of April to October that cost ¥2,340 ($19.50) for adults and ¥1,170 ($9.75) for children. The **Kushiro Bus Company** (© 0154/36-8181) offers a similar tour departing Kushiro Station June through October that includes lunch for ¥5,500 ($46) for adults and ¥3,780 ($31.50) for children, with slightly cheaper rates if you join the tour at Kushiro Airport.

During the rest of the year or if you prefer sightseeing on your own, the best place to learn about cranes is at the excellent **Akan Kokusai Tsuru Center** (Akan International Crane Center) ⚐, 23–40 Akan (© 0154/66-4011; open daily 9am–5pm, closed Mon Apr–Oct). In addition to a film showing their beautiful courtship dance and nesting habits, it has fun, interactive displays with lots of explanations in English. You'll learn just about everything you'd ever want to know about red-crested cranes, from why they fly to how much an egg weighs. Best of all, however, is adjacent **Tancho-no-Sato,** an excellent observatory on private land where 200 red-crested cranes live, court, and mate from November through March. This is a great place to photograph the birds in action, and you'll be surprised at how large they actually are. Admission for both the International Crane Center and the Tancho-no-Sato is ¥400 ($3.35) for adults, ¥200 ($1.65) for children. Plan on staying at least an hour in winter, less in summer when the birds have returned to their native marshlands. The International Crane Center is some 40 minutes from Akanko Onsen by bus; get off at the Tanchozuru stop (fare: ¥1,570/$13). Incidentally, the bus that stops here is the same one that goes from Akanko Onsen to Kushiro Airport, so it's possible to stop here, visit, and then catch the next bus to Kushiro.

In summer, your best bet for observing cranes outside the marshland is at **Tancho-Tsuru Koen** (Red-crested Crane Reserve), Kushiro-cho (© 0154/ 56-2219; open daily 9am–6pm, to 4pm in winter), a marshy area set aside in 1958 for breeding and raising cranes. It now has 24 cranes, some of them second and third generation, living in natural habitats behind high mesh fences. Admission is ¥310 ($2.60) for adults and ¥100 (85¢) for children. Also on the way to the airport but farther from Akanko, it's 1¼ hours by bus from the Akanko Onsen bus terminal; get off at the Tsuru-koen stop. If all you want is a quick look and you're on your way to the airport, note that some buses en route make a 15-minute stop at this park, which is enough time to see some of the birds before continuing on to the airport.

ATTRACTIONS IN AKANKO ONSEN   Although the Ainu originally lived near Kushiro, not Akan, they have built the **Ainu Kotan Village** in Akanko Onsen (© 0154/67-2727). Although the Ainu Kotan Village itself is just a souvenir shop–lined street, it leads to a thatched-roof lodge where you can see Ainu performing traditional dances and playing bamboo mouth harps. This is the most professional Ainu production I've seen, and since dances aren't the same as those performed at Poroto Kotan in Shiraoi (see "Noboribetsu Spa & Shikotsu-Toya National Park," earlier in this chapter), these are highly recommended even if you've already been to Poroto Kotan. Thirty-minute shows are performed six times a day in summer (including evenings), less frequently in winter. Admission is ¥1,000 ($8.35) for adults and ¥500 ($4.15) for children. Beside the performance lodge is the **Seikatsu Kinen Kan** (open May–Oct daily 10am–10pm), an Ainu home and outbuildings with displays of various Ainu utensils and crafts.

Admission here is ¥300 ($2.50) for adults, ¥100 (85¢) for children (skip it if you've been to Poroto Kotan).

ENJOYING THE OUTDOORS

BOATING For Japanese visitors, one of the most popular activities in Akanko Onsen is to take a **boat cruise of Lake Akan,** which provides a close-up view of the mountains, islands, and shoreline, all stunningly beautiful. Lake Akan is famous for its very rare spherical green algae, a sponge-like ball of duckweed called *marimo* that's been designated a Special Natural Monument. Found in only a few places in the world, marimo is formed when many separate and stringy pieces of algae at the bottom of the 144-foot-deep lake roll around and eventually come together to form a ball, gradually growing larger and larger. It takes 150 to 200 years for marimo to grow to the size of a baseball; some in Lake Akan are as much as 11½ inches in diameter—meaning they are very old indeed. Supposedly, when the sun shines, the marimo rise to the surface of the water, giving Lake Akan a wonderful green shimmer. On your boat cruise you'll make a 15-minute stop at Churui Islet to see the **Marimo Exhibition Center** with a few tanks of marimo, but my favorite part of the tour is when the boat travels through narrow passages between islands and into hamlets. Cruises, with explanations in English, operate from May to mid-November and last 1 hour and 25 minutes, costing ¥1,620 ($14.50) for adults and ¥850 ($7.10) for children. Boats depart every 30 minutes (every hour May and Nov), with the last boat departing at 5:30pm in summer.

HIKING Akanko Onsen's easiest walk begins and ends right in town. Start at the **Akankohan Eco Museum Center** on the east end of town, where you'll find an easy, 30-minute footpath leading through a primeval forest of pines and ferns, past *bokke* (volcanic, bubbling mud) and along the lakeshore. It ends at the boat dock with cruises of Lake Akan (see above)

For more serious hiking, while out on your boat trip you'll see two cone-shaped volcanoes: **Oakandake** (Mt. Oakan) to the east and **Meakandake** (Mt. Meakan) to the south. Both are popular day-long destinations for hikers. **Mt. Oakan** (called "male mountain" by the Ainu for its supposed manly features) is dormant, and it's about a 4½-hour hike to the summit from Akanko Onsen. You can reach the trail entrance, Takiguchi, in 5 minutes by bus (going in the direction of Kushiro). **Mt. Meakan** (which the Ainu called "female mountain"), the highest mountain in the Akan area, is active and is covered with primeval forests of spruce and fir. There are three hiking trails up Mt. Meakan. Closest to Akanko is from the west end of town, where you can follow the Fure-betsu Woodland Road, a former transport road to an old sulfur mine, 3 hours to the trail entrance. From the trail entrance it's another 3 hours to the peak, from which you have panoramic views of the surrounding area. Pick up English alpine guides to Mt. Oakan and Mt. Meakan at the tourist association.

A shorter hike follows a trail to **Mt. Hakutozan,** from which you also have a good view of the town and lake. It takes about 20 minutes to reach Akan's skiing area and another 50 minutes to reach Mt. Hakutozan observatory, a grassy and moss-covered knobby hill that remains slightly warm throughout the year because of thermal activity just below the surface. The woods of birch and pine here are beautiful, and what's more, you'll probably find yourself all alone. Stop at the local tourist office for directions to the trailhead and a Japanese map.

CANOEING To get a real feel for Akan Lake at duck and goose level, take a canoe trip in a two-person Canadian canoe. After a short lesson in canoeing, you'll be guided to uninhabited Yaitai Island in the lake or, if it's windy, to Shirikomabetsu, a deserted corner of the lakeshore. At either spot, you may see carp spawning, deer, or—if you are really lucky—bear. Make canoe reservations 1 day in advance at **Akan Nature Center** *(C* **0154/67-2081** or at **Emerald Hotel** *(C* **0154/67-2011**). The price is ¥4,000 ($33) per person for 2 hours including guide, lessons, and equipment.

FISHING ★★   Lake Akan is one of Japan's most famous fishing lakes. In addition to Kokanee salmon, said to have originated in the lake, sport fish include rainbow trout, steelhead trout, and white spotted char, a native fish. If you want to fish, contact **Fishing Land** *(C* **0154/67-2057**). A fishing permit costs ¥1,100 ($9.15) a day; for ¥3,000 ($25) more you can have a boat and a guide. Or contact the **Emerald Hotel** *(C* **0154/67-2011**), which has two fly-fishing advisors who will take you to an island, set you up, and then come back to get you for ¥3,000 ($25). Fly-fishing season is from May to the end of November, except from mid-July to mid-August when it's too hot. Fishing equipment is for sale in Emerald Hotel's shop. If you do not catch and release, ask your hotel if they can cook your fish for you.

In winter, you can also ice fish during the February Winter Festival; for ¥1,500 ($12.50), festival staff will dig a hole in the ice for you and supply you with fishing equipment.

WINTER ACTIVITIES   In winter, Lake Akan freezes over and becomes a play land for winter sports. International marathon ice-skating races—200km (124 miles)—held in February have brought attention to the area's natural richness. **Cross-country skiing** (rental equipment ¥1,000/$8.35 for 2 hr.), **ice-skating** (¥1,000/$8.35 an hr.), and ice fishing (¥1,500/$12.50 a day) are popular sports. For downhill skiers, the **Kokusetsu Akan-kohan ski ground** is blessed with a magnificent view of Mt. Oakan rising behind Lake Akan. The F.I.S.-certified slalom course attracts ski teams and individuals in training, while the intermediate and beginner slopes are popular with less demanding skiers. A day pass for lifts costs ¥3,000 ($25); ski-rental equipment costs ¥5,000 ($42). *Tip:* Emerald Hotel guests only pay ¥1,050 ($8.75) for a day-lift pass.

In February, illuminated ice sculptures, traditional dance, nightly fireworks over the frozen lake, and stalls selling food make for a fun midwinter festival. Contact the tourist office for more details.

WHERE TO STAY
EXPENSIVE

(272) **Yuku-no-Sato Tsuruga** ★★★ *Finds*   Extravagance is the word that comes to mind in describing Yuku-no-Sato Tsuruga, which translates loosely as "Village of eternally playing graceful cranes." Unsurprisingly, cranes are the main motif throughout, but what makes this hotel a standout are its hot-spring baths, among the most beautiful and fantasy provoking I've ever seen. One is designed as a village, spread on several levels and including a cave-like room and an outdoor bath beautifully landscaped with stones and pines overlooking the lake. The other, on the 8th floor, has the usual whirlpool, hot and dry saunas, and baths, as well as a rooftop hot-spring bath with 360-degree panoramic views. The baths, separated for men and women, are switched alternative days so guests may enjoy both. The rest of the hotel, with natural woods throughout, well-designed restaurants, and well-appointed guest rooms do not disappoint. Most rooms are Japanese style, the best of which have lakeside views, large bathrooms, bar areas for entertaining, and seating around an indoor hearth with hot

plate (it costs ¥2,000/$17 for meals delivered to your room). There are also more than 50 combination rooms with tatami area and beds, as well as 5 twin rooms that have great views of the lake from their own veranda.

4–6–10 Akanko Onsen, Akancho, Akan-gun 085-0467. ℂ 0154/67-2531. Fax 0154/67-2754. 129 units. Summer, ¥18,500–¥32,000 ($154–$267) per person; off-season, ¥9,800–¥27,000 ($82–$225) per person. Rates include 2 meals. AE, DC, JCB, MC, V. A 10-min. walk from the bus terminal; turn left out of the terminal, take the first right to the main street, and turn left. **Amenities:** 2 restaurants (Japanese and international), 1 coffee shop, 1 lounge, 1 nightclub; beautiful indoor/outdoor hot-spring baths; shopping arcade; in-room massage. *In room:* A/C, TV, minibar, hot-water pot with tea, hair dryer, washlet toilet.

MODERATE

Akan View Hotel   Despite its name, this 20-year-old hotel is one of the few around with no lake view. Most of its rooms are Western-style twins, narrow and with tiny bathrooms but with everything you need; 30 Japanese-style rooms are also available. One of the best things about this hotel are the large indoor thermal pools (you wear your bathing suit here), one for swimming laps and another with slides for children, as well as the usual hot-spring baths (open 24 hrs. except during cleaning) with a large, outdoor bathing area. I also like the glass-enclosed barbecue restaurant, open all year where you can order Genghis Kahn (lamb and vegetables), seafood, or beef meals you grill yourself (make reservations to dine here a day in advance). Otherwise, you dine buffet style in the communal dining room.

4–1–7 Akanko Onsen, Akancho, Akan-gun 085-0467. ℂ 0154/67-3131. Fax 0154/67-3139. 188 units. Summer, ¥8,000–¥12,000 ($67–$100) per person; winter, ¥6,000–¥10,000 ($50–$83) per person. Rates include 2 meals. AE, DC, JCB, MC, V. A 7-min. walk from the bus terminal. Turn left out of the bus terminal, cross the bridge, and turn right at the stoplight. **Amenities:** Lobby lounge, 1 bar; indoor swimming pool (free for hotel guests); indoor/outdoor hot-spring baths; tennis courts; game room; in-room massage; coin-op washers and dryers; rental bikes (¥500/$4.15 per hr.). *In room:* TV, minibar, hot-water pot with tea, safe.

⟨273⟩ **Hotel Emerald** ⭑   This lakefront ryokan is one of Akanko Onsen's most well-known accommodations, due in no small part to English-speaking Dameon Takada, third-generation owner who has expanded it considerably from its early days and has added all kinds of incentives. In the lobby is a tour desk that can arrange fishing, canoeing, skiing, and other adventure trips; it will even tailor day trips to other lakes and hiking destinations according to individual desires (the hotel also offers fishing and ski packages that include airfare from Tokyo). Rooms are spread in three connected buildings, cheapest of which are in the oldest part. Note, however, that none of the Western-style rooms face the lake (a mystery is the large corner room with mirrored ceiling above . . . twin beds; really, what's the point?). Best and most expensive are Japanese-style rooms facing the lake; meals served in your room cost ¥3,000 ($25) extra. There's also a so-called Ladies Floor, where all the staff are women and bathrooms and amenities are geared toward women. Regrettably, the hotel attracts tour groups, but pluses are the accommodating staff, elaborate buffet breakfasts and dinners in a large dining room overlooking the lake, and a location just a minute's walk from Ainu Kotan Village (join the many Japanese who stroll over to a nighttime performance wearing yukata).

4–6–5 Akan Onsen, Akancho, Akan-gun 085-0467. ℂ 0154/67-2011. Fax 0154/67-2864. www.hotelemerald. co.jp/. 206 units. ¥10,000–¥23,000 ($90–$207) per person. Winter discounts available. Rates include 2 meals. AE, DC, JCB, MC, V. A 9-min. walk from the bus terminal; turn left out of the terminal, take the first right to the main street, and turn left. **Amenities:** 1 buffet restaurant, 1 karaoke bar; outdoor/indoor hot-spring baths; sauna; game room; tour desk; souvenir shop (which also sells fishing gear); in-room massage; coin-op washers and dryers. *In room:* TV, minibar, hot-water pot with tea; safe.

INEXPENSIVE

274 **Onsen Minshuku Kiri** Located above a souvenir shop on the main street, this simple accommodation offers clean Japanese-style rooms and a small cypress hot-spring bath.

4–3–26 Akanko Onsen, Akancho, Akan-gun 085-0467. ✆ **0154/67-2755.** Fax 0154/67-2755. 9 units (none with bathroom). ¥5,500 ($46) per person including 2 meals, ¥3,500 ($29) per person without meals. No credit cards. A 9-min. walk from the bus terminal; turn left out of the terminal, take the first right to the main street, and turn left (it's across from Hotel Emerald). **Amenities:** Indoor hot-spring bath; coin-op washer and dryer. *In room:* TV, hot-water pot with tea.

282 **Tohoukan Ryokan** This modest ryokan, with Japanese-style rooms, is located a bit inland so there are no views from the windows, but they do open. The owner is both the head of the Marimo Protection Association and a slalom ski coach, so he is ideally suited to answer questions on those topics. Hot-spring baths are open 24 hours a day, and Japanese food is served in a communal dining room. Western breakfasts, as well as vegetarian meals, are available if you order when you make your reservation.

2–3–3 Akanko Onsen, Akancho, Akan-gun 085-0467. ✆ **0154/67-2050.** Fax 0154/67-2945. 25 units (2 with bathroom). ¥6,450 ($54) per person including 2 meals and tax, ¥3,500 ($29) per person without meals. JCB, MC, V. A 2-min. walk from the bus terminal; turn left out of the terminal and take the first right (it will be on the left). **Amenities:** Hot-spring bath; free use of washer and dryer. *In room:* TV, hot-water pot with tea.

WHERE TO DINE

Porono AINU CUISINE For a different kind of lunch, head to the Ainu Kotan Village and look on the right-hand side for a souvenir shop called Mingei Kissa with a sign reading HANDMADE FOLKCRAFT AND AINU TRADITIONAL FOOD, where in the back you'll find two tables, a counter, and funky ethnic decor. The menu lists *rataskepu,* a cold vegetable dish with beans, corn, and pumpkin; *pochimo,* a fried potato cake (a bit hard); pumpkin cakes; and drinks like bark tea (*shikerebe*). Or, order the Ainu teishoku set meal (rice with red beans and deer soup last time I was there). Not your usual meal.

Ainu Kotan Village, Akanko Onsen. ✆ **0154/67-2159.** Dishes ¥350–¥450 ($2.90–$3.75); Ainu teishoku ¥800 ($6.65). No credit cards. Daily noon–9pm.

Appendix A:
Japan in Depth

With a population of about 127 million, a history stretching back thousands of years, the world's longest-reigning monarchy, and its own unique forms of culture, art, food, etiquette, and religion, Japan merits more than this short chapter can deliver. Be sure to check "Recommended Reading," at the end of this appendix for other sources of information.

1 History 101

ANCIENT HISTORY (ca. 30,000 B.C.–A.D. 710)   According to mythology, Japan's history began when the sun goddess, Amaterasu, sent one of her descendants down to the island of Kyushu to unify the people of Japan. Unification, however, was not realized until a few generations later when Jimmu, the great-grandson of the goddess's emissary, succeeded in bringing all of the country under his rule. Because of his divine descent, Jimmu became emperor in 660 B.C. (the date is mythical), thus establishing the line from which all of Japan's emperors are said to derive. However mysterious the origin of this imperial dynasty, it is acknowledged as the longest-reigning such family in the world.

Legend begins to give way to fact only in the 4th century A.D., when a family by the name of Yamato succeeded in expanding its kingdom throughout the country. At the core of the unification achieved by the Yamato family was the Shinto religion. Indigenous to Japan, **Shintoism** is marked by the worship of natural things—mountains, trees, the moon, stars, rivers, seas, fire, animals, rocks, even vegetables—as the embodiment of gods (called *kami*), the spirits of ancestors, and by the belief in the divinity of the emperor. Along with Buddhism (see below), Shintoism is still a driving belief in Japanese life.

Although the exact origin of the Japanese people is unknown, we know Japan was once connected to the Asian mainland by a land bridge, and the territory of Japan was occupied as early as 30,000 B.C. From about 10,000 to 300 B.C., hunter-gatherers, called Jomon, thrived in small communities primarily in central Honshu; they're best known for their hand-formed pottery decorated with cord patterns. The Jomon Period was followed by the Yayoi Period, which was marked by metalworking, the pottery wheel, and the mastering of irrigated rice cultivation. The Yayoi Period lasted until about A.D. 300, after which the Yamato family unified the state for the first time and set up their court in what is now Nara Prefecture. Yamato (present-day Japan) began turning cultural feelers toward its great neighbor to the west, China.

In the 6th century, **Buddhism,** which originated in India, was brought to Japan via China and Korea, and the large-scale Chinese cultural and scholarly influence—including art, architecture, and the use of Chinese written characters—began. In 604, the prince regent Shotoku, greatly influenced by the teachings of Buddhism and Confucianism, drafted a document calling for political reforms and a constitutional government. By 607, he was sending multitudes of Japanese scholars to China to study Buddhism, and he started building Buddhist temples: The most famous is **Horyuji Temple** near Nara, said to be the oldest existing wooden structure in the world. He also built **Shitennoji Temple** in what is now Osaka.

THE NARA PERIOD (710–784)   Before the 700s, the site of Japan's capital changed every time a new emperor came to the throne. In 710, however, a permanent capital was established at Nara. Although it remained the capital for only 74 years, seven successive emperors ruled from Nara. The period was graced with the expansion of Buddhism and a flourishing of temple construction throughout the country. Buddhism also inspired the arts including Buddhist sculpture, metal casting, painting, and lacquerware. It was during this time that Emperor Shomu, the most devout Buddhist among the Nara emperors, ordered the casting of a huge bronze statue of Buddha to be erected in Nara. Known as the Daibutsu, it remains Nara's biggest attraction.

THE HEIAN PERIOD (794–1192)   In 794, the capital was moved to Heiankyo (present-day Kyoto), and following the example of cities in China, Kyoto was laid out in a grid pattern with broad roads and canals. Heiankyo means "capital of peace and tranquility," and the Heian Period was a glorious time for aristocratic families, a time of luxury and prosperity during which court life reached new artistic heights. Moon viewing became popular. Chinese characters were blended with a new Japanese writing system, allowing for the first time the flowering of Japanese literature and poetry. The life of the times was captured in the works of two women: Sei Shonagon, who wrote a collection of impressions of her life at court known as the *Pillow Book,* and Murasaki Shikibu, who wrote the world's first major novel, *The Tale of Genji.*

Because the nobles were completely engrossed in their own luxurious lifestyles, however, they failed to notice the growth of military clans in the provinces. The two most powerful warrior clans were the Taira (also called Heike) and the Minamoto (also called Genji), whose fierce civil wars tore the nation apart until a young warrior, Minamoto Yoritomo, established supremacy. (In Japan, a person's family name—here, Minamoto—comes first, followed by the given name.)

THE KAMAKURA PERIOD (1192–1333)   Wishing to set up rule far away from Kyoto, Minamoto Yoritomo established his capital in a remote and easily defended fishing village called Kamakura, not far from today's Tokyo. In becoming the nation's first *shogun,* or military dictator, Yoritomo laid the groundwork for 700 years of military governments—in which the power of the country passed from the aristocratic court into the hands of the warrior class—until the imperial court was restored in 1868.

The Kamakura Period is perhaps best known for the unrivaled ascendancy of the warrior caste, or **samurai.** Ruled by a rigid honor code, samurai were bound in loyalty to their feudal lord, and they became the only caste allowed to carry two swords. They were supposed to give up their lives for their lord without hesitation, and if they failed in their duty, they could regain their honor only by committing ritualistic suicide, or *seppuku.* Spurning the sort of life led by court nobles, samurai embraced a spartan lifestyle. When **Zen Buddhism,** with its tenets of mental and physical discipline, was introduced into Japan from China in the 1190s, it appealed greatly to the samurai. Weapons and armor achieved new heights in artistry, while *bushido,* the way of the warrior, contributed to the spirit of national unity.

In 1274, Mongolian forces under Kublai Khan made an unsuccessful attempt to invade Japan. They returned in 1281 with a larger fleet, but a typhoon

Here and *Zazen*: Buddhism in Japan

Founded in India in the 5th century, Buddhism came to Japan in the 6th century via China and Korea, bringing with it the concept of eternal life. By the end of the 6th century, Buddhism had gained such popularity that Prince Regent Shotoku, one of Japan's most remarkable historical figures, declared Buddhism the state religion and based many of his governmental policies on its tenets. Another important Buddhist leader to emerge was a priest called Kukai, known posthumously as Kobo Daishi. After studying Buddhism in China in the early 800s, he returned and built temples throughout Japan, including the famous 88 temples on Shikoku Island and those on Mt. Koya, which continue to attract millions of pilgrims today.

Probably the Buddhist sect best known to the West is Zen Buddhism. Considered the most Japanese form of Buddhism, Zen is the practice of meditation and a strictly disciplined lifestyle to rid oneself of desire so that one can achieve enlightenment. There are no rites in Zen Buddhism, no dogmas, no theological conceptions of divinity; you do not analyze rationally but are supposed to know things intuitively. The strict and simple lifestyle of Zen appealed greatly to Japan's samurai warrior class, and many of Japan's arts, including the tea ceremony, arose from the practice of Zen.

Zazen, or meditation, is practiced as a form of mental or spiritual training; laymen meditate to relieve stress and clear their minds. Zazen is achieved if one sits in a cross-legged lotus position with the neck and back straight and eyes slightly open. Usually done in a group—in a semi-dark room with cushions, facing the wall—meditation is helped along by a monk, who stalks noiselessly behind the meditators. If someone squirms or moves, he's whacked on the shoulders with a stick to help him get back to meditating. There are several Zen temples where foreigners can join in zazen (see chapter 4); if you'd like to try it for yourself, contact the Tourist Information Center in Tokyo or Kyoto or check the *Japan Times* to see whether a session of zazen is being organized with instruction in English.

destroyed it. Regarding the cyclone as a gift from the gods, the Japanese called it *kamikaze,* meaning "divine wind," which took on a different significance at the end of World War II when Japanese pilots flew suicide missions in an attempt to turn the tide of war.

THE MUROMACHI & AZUCHI-MOMOYAMA PERIODS (1336–1603)

After the fall of the Kamakura shogunate, a new feudal government was set up at Muromachi in Kyoto. The next 200 years, however, were marred by bloody civil wars as *daimyo* (feudal lords) staked out their fiefdoms. Similar to the barons of Europe, the daimyo owned tracts of land and had complete rule over the people who lived on them. Each lord had his retainers, the samurai, who fought his enemies. This period of civil wars is called Sengoku-Jidai, or **Age of the Warring States.**

Yet these centuries of strife also saw a blossoming of art and culture. Kyoto witnessed the construction of the extravagant Golden and Silver pavilions as well as the artistic arrangement of Ryoanji Temple's famous rock garden. Noh drama, the tea ceremony, flower arranging, and landscape gardening became the passions of the upper class. At the end of the 16th century, a number of castles were built on mountaintops to demonstrate a daimyo's strength, to guard his fiefdom, and to defend against the firearms introduced by the Portuguese.

In the second half of the 16th century, a brilliant military strategist by the name of Oda Nobunaga almost succeeded in ending the civil wars. Upon Nobunaga's assassination (by one of his own retainers), one of his best generals, Toyotomi Hideyoshi, took up the campaign, built the magnificent Osaka Castle, and crushed rebellion to unify Japan. Nobunaga and Hideyoshi's successive rules are known as the **Azuchi-Momoyama Period,** after the names of their castles.

THE EDO PERIOD (1603–1867)   Upon Hideyoshi's death (1598), power was seized by Tokugawa Ieyasu, a statesman so shrewd and skillful in eliminating enemies that his heirs would continue to rule Japan for the next 250 years. After defeating his greatest rival in the famous battle of Sekigahara, Tokugawa set up a shogunate government in 1603 in Edo (present-day Tokyo), leaving the emperor intact but virtually powerless in Kyoto. In 1615, he assured his supremacy by getting rid of Hideyoshi's descendants in a fierce battle at Osaka Castle that destroyed the castle and annihilated the Toyotomi clan.

Meanwhile, European influence in Japan was spreading. The first contact with the Western world had occurred in 1543, when Portuguese merchants (with firearms) arrived followed by Christian missionaries. St. Francis Xavier landed in Kyushu in 1549, remaining for 2 years and converting thousands of Japanese; by 1580, there were perhaps as many as 150,000 Japanese Christians. Although Japan's rulers at first welcomed foreigners and trade, they gradually became alarmed by the Christian missionary influence. Hearing of the Catholic church's power in Rome and fearing the expansionist policies of European nations, the shogunate banned Christianity in the early 1600s. In 1597, 26 Japanese and European Christians were crucified in Nagasaki.

The Tokugawa shogunate intensified the campaign against Christians in 1639 when it closed all ports to foreign trade. Adopting a policy of **total isolation,** the shogunate forbade foreigners from landing in Japan and Japanese from leaving; even those Japanese who had been living abroad in overseas trading posts were never allowed to return. The only exception was in Nagasaki, where there was a colony of tightly controlled Chinese merchants and a handful of Dutch, who were confined to a trading post on a tiny island.

Thus began an amazing 200-year period in Japanese history during which Japan was closed to the rest of the world. It was a time of political stability but also one when personal freedom was strictly controlled by the Tokugawa government. Japanese society was divided into four distinct **classes:** samurai, farmers, craftsmen, and merchants. Class determined everything in daily life, from where a person lived to what he was allowed to wear. Samurai led the most exalted social position, and it was probably during the Tokugawa Period that the samurai class reached the zenith of its glory. At the bottom of the social ladder were the merchants, but peace and prosperity led to the development of new entertainment forms to occupy their time: Kabuki drama and woodblock prints became the rage, while stoneware and porcelain, silk brocade for kimono, and lacquerware improved in quality. In fact, it was probably the shogunate's rigid policies that actually fostered the arts, since anything new was considered dangerous and quickly suppressed—the Japanese were forced to retreat inward, and they focused their energies in the arts, perfecting handicrafts down to the most minute detail whether it was swords, *netsuke* (small containers for medicine), kimono, or lacquered boxes. Only Japan's many festivals offered relief from harsh and restrictive social mores.

To ensure that no daimyo in the distant provinces would overrun the shogun's power, the Tokugawa government ordered each daimyo to leave his family in Edo as permanent residents (effectively as hostages) and required the lord to spend a prescribed number of months in Edo every other year. In expending so much time and money traveling back and forth and maintaining elaborate residences both in the provinces and in Edo, the daimyo had no resources left with which to wage a rebellion. Inns and townships sprang up along Japan's major highways to accommodate the elaborate processions of palanquins, samurai, and footmen traveling back and forth between Edo and the provinces.

Even though the Tokugawa government took such measures to ensure its supremacy, by the mid–19th century, it was clear that the feudal system was outdated and economic power was in the hands of the merchants. Many samurai families were impoverished, and discontent with the shogunate became widespread.

In 1853, American Commodore Matthew C. Perry sailed to Japan, seeking to gain trading rights. But the Japanese were unwilling, so Perry departed, his mission unaccomplished. Returning a year later, he forced the shogun to sign an agreement despite the disapproval of the emperor, thus ending Japan's 2 centuries of isolation. In 1867, some powerful families toppled the Tokugawa regime and restored the emperor as ruler, thus bringing the Feudal Era to a close.

MODERN JAPAN (1868–PRESENT)   In 1868, Emperor Meiji moved his imperial government from Kyoto to Edo, renamed it Tokyo (Eastern Capital), and designated it as the official national capital. During the next few decades, known as the **Meiji Restoration,** Japan rapidly progressed from a feudal agricultural society of samurai and peasants to an industrial nation. The samurai were stripped of their power and no longer were allowed to carry swords, thus ending a privileged way of life begun almost 700 years earlier in Kamakura. A prime minister and a cabinet were appointed, a constitution was drafted, and a parliament (called the Diet) was elected. With the enthusiastic support of Emperor Meiji, the latest in Western technological know-how was imported, including railway and postal systems, along with specialists and advisers: Between 1881 and 1898, about 10,000 Westerners were retained by the Japanese government to help modernize the country.

Meanwhile, Japan made incursions into neighboring lands. In 1894 to 1895, it fought and won a war against China; in 1904 to 1905, it attacked and defeated Russia; and in 1910, it annexed Korea. After militarists gained control of the government in the 1930s, these expansionist policies continued; Manchuria was annexed, and Japan went to war with China again in 1937. On the other side of the world, as **World War II** flared in Europe, Japan formed a military (Axis) alliance with Germany and Italy and attacked French Indochina.

On December 7, 1941, Japan attacked Pearl Harbor, entering World War II against the United States. Although Japan went on to conquer Hong Kong, Singapore, Burma, Malaysia, the Philippines, the Dutch East Indies, and Guam, the tide eventually turned, and American bombers reduced every major Japanese city to rubble with the exception of historic Kyoto. On August 6, 1945, the United States dropped the world's first atomic bomb over Hiroshima, followed on August 9 by a second over Nagasaki. Japan submitted to unconditional surrender on August 14, with Emperor Hirohito's radio broadcast telling his people the time had come for "enduring the unendurable and suffering what is insufferable." American and other **Allied occupation** forces arrived and remained until 1952. For the first time in history, Japan had suffered defeat by a foreign power; the country had never before been invaded or occupied by a foreign nation.

The experience had a profound effect on the Japanese people, yet they emerged from their defeat and began to rebuild. In 1946, under the guidance of the Allied military authority headed by U.S. General Douglas MacArthur, they adopted a democratic constitution renouncing war and the use of force to settle international disputes and divesting the emperor of divinity, giving power to the people instead. A parliamentary system of government was set up, and 1947 witnessed the first general elections for the National Diet, the government's legislative body. After its founding in 1955, the **Liberal Democratic Party (LDP)** remained the undisputed majority party for decades, giving Japan the kind of political stability it needed to grow economically and compete in world markets.

To the younger generation, the occupation was less a painful burden to be suffered than an opportunity to remake their country, with American encouragement, into a modern, peace-loving, and democratic state. A special relationship developed between the Japanese and their American occupiers. In the early 1950s, as the Cold War between the United States and the Communist world erupted in hostilities in Korea, that relationship grew into a firm alliance, strengthened by a security treaty. In 1956, the occupation ended, and Japan joined the United Nations as an independent country.

Avoiding involvement in foreign conflicts, the Japanese concentrated on economic recovery. Through a series of policies favoring domestic industries and shielding Japan from foreign competition, they achieved **rapid economic growth.** In 1964, Tokyo hosted the Summer Olympic Games, showing the world that the nation had transformed into a formidable industrialized power. Incomes doubled during the 1960s, and a 1967 government study found that 90% of Japanese considered themselves middle class. By the 1980s, Japan was by far the richest industrialized nation in Asia and the envy of its neighbors, who strove to emulate Japan's success. Sony was a household word around the globe; books flooded the international market touting the economic secrets of Japan, Inc. After all, Japan seemed to have it all: a good economy, political stability, safe streets, and great schools. As the yen soared, Japanese traveled abroad as never before. Japanese businessmen gained national attention as they gobbled up real estate in foreign lands and purchased works of art at unheard-of prices.

Meanwhile, a snowballing trade surplus had created friction between Japan and the United States, its chief trading partner. In the 1980s, as Japanese auto sales in the United States soared and foreign sales in Japan continued to be restricted, disagreements between Tokyo and Washington heated up. In 1989, Emperor Hirohito died of cancer at age 87, bringing the 63-year Showa Era to an end and ushering in the **Heisei Period** under Akihito, the 125th emperor, who proclaimed the new "Era of Peace" (Heisei).

In the early 1990s, shadows of financial doubt began to spread over the land of the rising sun, with alarming reports of bad bank loans, inflated stock prices, and overextended corporate investment abroad. In 1992, **recession** hit Japan, with the Nikkei (the Japanese version of the American Dow) falling a gut-churning 63% from its 1989 peak, bursting the economic bubble and plunging the country into its worst recession since World War II. In 1993, the Japanese government, under intense international pressure to liberalize its trade policies, agreed to open its rice market to imports, a move that angered many nationalists (some went so far as to maintain that the Japanese couldn't eat imported rice because their digestive systems were different). Japan also came under increasing fire from abroad for not taking a more active role in world affairs, consonant with its economic power. In 1992, bowing to international pressure, Japan agreed to take part in United Nations peacekeeping operations in Cambodia, sending a small contingent of troops (the first to serve outside Japan since World War II) and civilian police instructors. In doing so, the government went against strong public opposition.

Meanwhile, public confidence in the LDP, which had held power uninterruptedly for nearly 4 decades, eroded after its top officials were accused of participating in a series of political and financial scandals. But a revolving door of prime ministers (many of whom also became implicated in scandals) throughout the 1990s failed to revive the economy or alleviate voters' growing fears of financial doom. Indeed, in 1998 a record number of companies filed for bankruptcy; in 1999 unemployment hit a record high of 4.6%, its highest level since World War II.

But almost as frightening to most Japanese as a tightening of the economic belt was an increasing feeling of vulnerability and helplessness. The government had long assured its people that Japan's buildings, railway lines, and highways were earthquakeproof—but the **earthquake** that jolted Kobe in 1995 was a vertical shock, not the more common horizontal shock, and buildings, elevated highways, subway tunnels, and almost all of Kobe port's container lifts collapsed. The massive earthquake, which measured 7.2 on the Richter scale, killed more than 6,000 people and left 300,000 homeless. The nation received another scare in September 1999 when a nuclear plant 70 miles from Tokyo exposed dozens of people to radiation due to human error, a major concern in a country that obtains almost all its energy from nuclear power plants; two workers subsequently died from the radiation.

Crime also became a national concern, fueled by some gruesome events: Just two months after the Kobe quake, an obscure religious sect, Aum Shinrikyo, released the deadly nerve gas sarin on three different commuter lines during Tokyo's rush hour, killing 12 people and injuring more than 5,000. In 1997, a teenager killed and beheaded an 11-year-old boy in Kobe, but the worst blow of all was in 2001, when a knife-wielding man stormed into an elementary school in Osaka Prefecture, fatally stabbing eight children and wounding 15 others. For many Japanese, it seemed that the very core of their society had begun to crumble.

Even Japan–U.S. relations became strained, especially after the 1995 rape of a young teenage girl by U.S. servicemen stationed in Okinawa, followed by another alleged rape in 2001. In February 2001, a U.S. nuclear-powered submarine collided with a Japanese fishing-training vessel off Hawaii, sinking the fishing boat and killing nine Japanese.

In April 2001, after yet another prime minister resigned due to scandal, Koizumi Junichiro took the political helm. Although a member of the LDP, the long-haired, 59-year-old Koizumi had long been considered something of a maverick, battling against the long-established power brokers of the LDP and vowing to overturn the LDP's long-standing pork-barrel politics by slashing public spending on bridges, dams, and roads, forcing Japanese banks to write off bad loans, and dismantling regulations that protected large sectors of the economy. His cries for **reform,** coupled by media attention that gave him the revered status of a rock star, won Koizumi more voter support than any prime minister since the bubble economy. Following the September 2001 terrorist attacks in New York City and against the Pentagon, Koizumi quickly showed allegiance by pushing through an anti-terrorism bill that enabled Japan's military to ship supplies and provide medical and other non-combative support.

2 Japan Today

Assuming Prime Minister Koizumi Junichiro holds onto his job longer than his predecessors, he'll have his work cut out for him. Not only must he restructure an uncooperative government, but he must also maintain support from a nation that has suffered a severe crisis of confidence for more than a decade. The **economy** is stagnant, growing at a rate of less than 1% a year compared to the 6% annual growth it enjoyed in the 1980s.

On a personal level, few Japanese remain untouched by the **recession.** Fallen assets have robbed individuals of life savings, and real estate prices have fallen as much as 70% from what they were in 1990. A record-breaking number of companies have gone bankrupt, and lifetime employment is no longer a guarantee. It's especially brutal for workers older than 45 who are seeking work (there is no law against age discrimination in Japan). Yet Japan, with one of the most frugal welfare-benefit plans in the industrialized world, is ill-equipped to handle the swelling ranks of the unemployed, which some predict will reach 6 or 7% in 2002. Unemployment checks are paid out for only a limited time—sometimes only 10 weeks—and support for the poverty-stricken is granted only after the recipient has sold all assets, spent all savings, and submitted statements from family members stating they cannot or will not provide any support. Homelessness is so common that it no longer draws stares, even in the swank Ginza District.

But there are other, more troubling cracks in the societal fiber. According to recent surveys, most Japanese believe that **crime** is on the increase. Student attacks on teachers—some fatal—have dominated the news, and student bullying is common. Lurid murders, though rare, garner media attention. Even theft is a major topic, virtually unheard of only a decade ago. My former landlady fears burglary so much that she refuses to open her doors to strangers. My friend's boyfriend had a car stolen from a parking lot, one of 119 luxury cars reported stolen in Tokyo in 2000.

All these crises—the recession, unemployment, scandals, crime, and natural and man-made disasters—have been a major blow to the national psyche. Japanese fear that their country is no longer safe, predictable, and orderly—something they had always taken for granted and prided themselves in. Although it's mainly the older generation who is bewildered by this new Japan, the older generation cannot be ignored: Japan has one of the fastest-growing **aging populations** in the world; by 2020, it's predicted that one-fourth of its people will be older than 65. Meanwhile, the birth rate in Japan is at an all-time low of 1.38 per woman (the birth-control pill was legalized in 1999), prompting the Japanese Health and Welfare Ministry to announce that a predicted shortage of future workers will severely strain the country's resources for pensions and health care.

For the short-term visitor to Japan, the events that seem so overwhelming to the Japanese will make themselves readily apparent mainly in financial terms: The high yen against the dollar still makes the country seem expensive; on the other hand, **inflation** is so low that hotel rates have remained stable for the past 7 years, and many restaurants now offer meals at substantially lower prices than in the 1980s. Given the current economic climate, some predict that the yen will sink against the dollar, making the country more affordable for tourists. Regardless, Japan is affordable if you live and eat much as the Japanese do.

As for safety, **earthquakes** are a fact of life in Japan, just as they are in California and just as other natural phenomena are elsewhere. Tokyo experiences about 50 quakes a year that you can actually feel, which means I've felt quite a few of them, mostly minor tremors. But the possibility of earthquakes doesn't keep me from going to Japan; see "Fast Facts: Japan," in chapter 2 for advice on what to do in the event of an earthquake.

As for personal **safety,** crime in Japan doesn't even begin to approach the criminal level of the United States. Most victims of violent crime are known to the attacker, with incidence so low that a murder makes national news. I am more careful than I was 15 years ago—I guard my purse in crowded subways; I avoid parks after dark. For Americans, such precautions seem merely self-evident.

For the most part, life in Japan appears much as it always has—humming with energy, crowded beyond belief in its major cities, and filled with acts of human kindness. Teenagers seem less bent on following in their parents' footsteps, dressing more casually and wildly, yet they still seem very well mannered and remain captivated by innocent fads that take on larger-than-life proportions

---

⌜Fun Fact⌟ The Magical World of Vending Machines

One of the things that usually surprises visitors to Japan is the number of vending machines in the country. They're virtually everywhere—in train stations, in front of shops, on the back streets of residential neighborhoods. Most will take bills and give back change. Many have almost nonsensical English promotional lines on them, like "Enjoy Refreshing Time." Some will even talk to you.

And what can you buy in these vending machines? First, there are the obvious items—drinks and snacks, including hot or cold coffee in a can. But if you're on your way to someone's house, you might even be able to pick up a bouquet of flowers from a machine. Your Walkman is out of batteries? You may be able to find those, too, along with CDs, film, and disposable cameras. Vending machines outside post offices sell stamps and postcards.

But there are also things sold from sidewalk vending machines that would meet with instant protest in other countries around the world. Cigarettes are sold on almost every corner, where even children could buy them if they wanted to. Until recently, beer was also readily available, though in an effort to curb alcoholism and underage drinking, access is now more limited.

I remember a vending machine in my Tokyo neighborhood. By day, it was just blank with no clue as to what was inside. Come night, however, the thing would light up, and on display would be pornographic comics.

If it's available in Japan, it's probably in a vending machine somewhere.

in Japan, whether it's bleached hair, fashions, or portrait booths that will print your likeness on sheets of tiny stickers. Families spend more time together because companies are no longer willing to pay overtime. Japanese department stores are so crowded with shoppers and a dazzling array of goods that they seem to belie there's a recession (though Japanese are careful in what they buy). I'm astounded by the number of new tourist attractions that have opened throughout Japan in the past decade, and getting around the country has never been easier. There are more foreign tourists visiting Japan than ever before, mostly from neighboring Asian countries.

3 Minding Your Ps & Qs

As an island nation with few natural resources, Japan's 127 million people are its greatest asset. Hard-working, honest, and proud about performing every task well no matter how insignificant it may seem, the Japanese are well known for their politeness and helpfulness to strangers. Indeed, hardly anyone returns from a trip to Japan without stories of extraordinary kindnesses extended by the Japanese.

With almost 99% of its population consisting of ethnic Japanese, Japan is one of the most homogeneous nations in the world. That, coupled with Japan's actual physical isolation as an island nation, has more than anything else led to a feeling among the Japanese that they belong to a single huge tribe that's different from any other people on earth—that all people can basically be divided into two categories: Japanese and non-Japanese. You'll often hear a Japanese preface a statement or opinion with the words "We Japanese," implying that all Japanese think alike.

Indeed, one characteristic of the Japanese that has received much publicity—and is seen (at least by some) as a reason why Japan became so economically powerful so quickly—is this **group mentality.** Whereas in the West the attainment of "happiness" is the elusive goal for a full and rewarding life, in Japan it's satisfactory performance of **duty.** From the time they are born, the Japanese are instilled with a sense of duty that extends toward parents, spouses, bosses, coworkers, neighbors, and society as a whole. In a nation as crowded as Japan, consideration of others is essential, and consideration of the group always wins out over the desire of the individual. In fact, I have had Japanese tell me they consider individuality to be synonymous with selfishness and a complete disregard for the feelings of others.

MEETING THE JAPANESE

On a personal level, the Japanese are among the most likable people in the world. They are kind, thoughtful, and adept in perceiving another person's needs. The Japanese have an unerring eye for pure beauty whether it be in food, architecture, or landscaped gardens; I don't think it's possible to visit Japan and not have some of the Japanese appreciation of beauty rub off.

If you're invited to Japan by some organization or business, you'll receive the royal treatment and will most likely be wined and dined so wonderfully and thoroughly that you'll never want to leave. If you go to Japan on your own as an ordinary tourist, however, chances are your experiences will be much different. Except for those who have lived or traveled abroad, few Japanese have had much contact with foreigners. In fact, even in Tokyo there are Japanese who have never spoken to a foreigner and would be quite embarrassed and uncomfortable if they were confronted with the possibility. And even though most of them have studied English, few Japanese have had the opportunity to use the language and cannot (or are too shy to) communicate in it. So don't be surprised if you find the empty seat beside you on the subway the last one to be occupied—most Japanese are deathly afraid you'll ask them a question they won't be able to understand.

In many respects, therefore, it's much harder to meet the locals in Japan than in many other countries. The Japanese are simply much more shy than Americans. Although they will sometimes approach you to ask whether they might practice some English with you; for the most part, you're left pretty much on your own unless you make the first move.

Probably the easiest way to meet Japanese is to go where they play—namely, the country's countless **bars,** including those that serve *yakitori* (skewered chicken). Usually small affairs with perhaps just a counter and some tables, they're often filled with both younger and older Japanese, many of whom are regulars. As the evening wears on, you'll encounter Japanese who will want to speak to you if they understand English, and some slightly inebriated Japanese who will speak to you even if they don't. If you're open to them, such chance encounters may prove to be the highlight of your trip, or at the very least an evening of just plain fun.

Janie, who traveled around Japan with her then 3-year-old daughter, found that **traveling with children** opened up opportunities like a magic key. Other children talked freely to her child (they never seemed to have a language barrier), while she was able to talk to parents about their children. She even had complete strangers she met on the train invite her and her daughter home; in contrast, some Japanese she has known for years have never invited her home, preferring instead to meet at coffee shops or restaurants.

Another good way to meet the Japanese is to stay in a **minshuku,** an inexpensive lodging in a private home (see "Tips on Accommodations," in chapter 2).

ETIQUETTE

Much of Japan's system of etiquette and manners stems from its feudal days, when the social hierarchy dictated how a person spoke, sat, bowed, ate, walked, and lived. Failure to comply with the rules would bring severe punishment, even death. More than one Japanese literally lost his head for committing a social blunder.

Of course, nowadays it's quite different, although the Japanese still attach much importance to proper behavior. As a foreigner, however, you can get away with a lot. After all, you're just a "barbarian" and, as such, can be forgiven for not knowing the rules. There are two cardinal sins, however, you should never commit: One is you should **never wear your shoes inside a Japanese home, traditional inn, temple, or into any room with tatami;** the other is you should **never wash with soap inside a communal Japanese bathtub.** Except for these two horrors, you will probably be forgiven any other social blunders (such as standing with your arms folded or your hands in your pockets).

As a sensitive traveler, however, you should try to familiarize yourself with the basics of Japanese social etiquette. The Japanese are very appreciative of foreigners who take the time to learn about their country and are quite patient in helping you. Remember, if you do commit a faux pas, apologize profusely and smile. They don't chop off heads anymore.

Tips **The Home-Visit System**

Recognizing the difficulty foreigners may face in meeting the Japanese, the Japan National Tourist Organization has launched a super program called the **Home-Visit System,** which offers overseas visitors the chance to visit an English-speaking Japanese family in their home for a few hours. Not only does such an encounter bring you in direct contact with Japanese, it also offers a glimpse into their lifestyle. You can even request that a family member share your same occupation, though such requests are, of course, sometimes impossible to fulfill. The program doesn't cost anything, and it's offered in 14 cities throughout the country. To take advantage, all you need to do is call or apply in person at least 24 hours in advance—preferably 2 days in advance—to the local administrative authority or private organization (which is sometimes the local tourist office) that handles the home visit in each of the participating 14 towns. After contacting a local family, the office will inform you of the family and the time to visit. Most visits take place for a few hours in the evening (dinner is not served). It's a good idea to bring a small gift such as flowers, fruit, or a souvenir of some kind from your hometown. Prior to your visit, you may be asked to appear in person at the application office to obtain detailed directions, or the office may simply call with the directions. Note that application offices may be closed on weekends and holidays. In addition, it's impossible to make reservations from abroad. You're allowed only one visit during your stay in Japan. Here are a few contact numbers for cities participating in the Home-Visit System: **Tokyo** (✆ 03/3201-3331), **Narita** (✆ 0476/34-6251 or 24-3198), **Yokohama** (✆ 045/441-7300), **Nagoya** (✆ 052/581-568), **Kyoto** (✆ 075/752-3511), **Osaka** (✆ 06/6345-2189 or 06/6643-2125), **Kobe** (✆ 078/303-1010), **Okayama** (✆ 086/256-2000), **Kurashiki** (✆ 086/424-3593), **Hiroshima** (✆ 082/247-9715), **Fukuoka** (✆ 092/733-2220), **Kumamoto** (✆ 096/359-2121), and **Miyazaki** (✆ 0985/32-8457). For more information, call the **Tourist Information Center** in Tokyo (✆ 03/3201-3331) or the local tourist office.

Most forms of behavior and etiquette in Japan developed to allow relationships to be as frictionless as possible—a pretty good idea in a country as crowded as Japan. The Japanese don't like confrontations, and fights are extremely rare. The Japanese are very good at covering almost all unpleasantness with a smile. Foreigners find the smile hard to read—a smiling Japanese face can mean happiness, sadness, embarrassment, or even anger. My first lesson in such physiognomic inscrutability happened on a subway in Tokyo, where I saw a middle-aged Japanese woman who was about to board the subway brutally knocked out of the way by a Japanese man rushing off the train. She almost lost her balance, but she gave a little laugh, smiled, and got on the train. A few minutes later, as the train was speeding through a tunnel, I stole a look at her and was able to read her true feelings on her face. Lost in her thoughts, she knitted her brow in consternation and looked most upset and unhappy. The smile had been a put-on.

Another aspect of Japanese behavior that sometimes causes difficulty for foreigners, especially in business negotiations, is **the reluctance of the Japanese to say no when they mean no.** Many consider such directness poor manners. As a result, they're much more apt to say your request is very difficult, or they'll simply beat around the bush without giving a definite answer. At this point, you're expected to let the subject drop. Showing impatience, anger, or aggressiveness rarely gets you anywhere. Apologizing sometimes does. And if someone does give in to your request, you can't say thank-you often enough.

If you're invited to a Japanese home, you should know that it's both a rarity and an honor. Most Japanese consider their homes too small and humble for entertaining guests, which is why there are so many restaurants, coffee shops, and bars. **If you're invited to a home, don't show up empty-handed.** Bring a small gift such as candy, fruit, flowers, or perhaps a souvenir from your hometown. Alcohol is also appreciated. And if someone does extend you a favor, be sure to thank them again the next time you see them—even if it's a year later.

When the Japanese give back change, they hand it back to you in a lump sum rather than counting it out. **Trust them.** It's considered insulting for you to sit there and count it in front of them because it insinuates you think they might be trying to cheat you. The Japanese are honest. It's one of the great pleasures of being in their country.

Don't blow your nose in public if you can help it and never at the dinner table. It's considered most disgusting. On the other hand, even though the Japanese are very hygienic, they're not at all averse to spitting on the sidewalk. And, even more peculiar, the men urinate when and where they want, usually against a tree or a wall and most often after a night of carousing in the bars.

This being a man's society, men will walk in and out of doors and elevators before women, and in subways, they will sit down while women stand. Some Japanese men who have had contact with the Western world (particularly hotel staff) will make a gallant show of allowing a Western woman to step out of the elevator first. For the sake of women living in Japan, thank them warmly.

BOWING   The main form of greeting in Japan is the bow rather than the handshake. Although at first glance it may seem simple enough, the bow—together with its implications—is actually quite complicated. The depth of the bow and the number of seconds devoted to performing it, as well as the total number of bows, depend on who you are, to whom you're bowing, and how they're bowing back. In addition to bowing in greeting, the Japanese also bow upon departing and to express gratitude. The proper form for a bow is to bend from the waist with a straight back and to keep your arms at your sides, but if you're a foreigner, a simple nod of the head is enough. Knowing foreigners shake hands, a Japanese may extend his hand, although he probably won't be able to stop himself from giving a little bow as well. (I've even seen Japanese bow when talking on the telephone.) Although I've occasionally witnessed Japanese businessmen shake hands among themselves, the practice is still quite rare. Kimono-clad hostesses of a traditional Japanese inn will often kneel on tatami and bow to the ground as they send you off on your journey.

VISITING CARDS   You're a nonentity in Japan if you don't have a visiting card, called a *meishi.* Everyone—from housewives to bank presidents—carries meishi to give out during introductions. If you're trying to conduct business in Japan, you'll be regarded suspiciously—even as a phony—if you don't have business cards. Meishi are very useful business tools for the Japanese. Likewise, a meishi can be used as an introduction to a third party—a Japanese may give you his meishi, scribble something on it, and tell you to present it to his cousin who owns a restaurant in Fukuoka. Voilà—the cousin will treat you like a royal guest.

As a tourist, you don't have to have business cards, but it certainly doesn't hurt, and the Japanese will be greatly impressed by your preparedness. The card should have your address and occupation on it; you might even consider having your meishi made in Japan, with the Japanese syllabic script (*katakana*) written on the reverse side.

Needless to say, there's a proper way for presenting a meishi. Turn it so that the other person can read it (that is, upside down to you) and present it with both hands and a slight bow. If you can, try to deliver your card underneath the card you are receiving, to show deference. Afterwards, it's customary for both of you to study the meishi for a moment and, if possible, to comment on it (such as, "You're from Kyoto? My brother lived in Kyoto!" or "Sony! What a famous company!"). If you're at a business meeting, place the card in front of you on the table; it's considered impolite to simply put the card away.

DINING   There are several dining customs in Japan that differ from those in the West, many of them involving chopsticks or drinking. For information on dining etiquette and customs, refer to "Tips on Dining, Japanese Style," later in this chapter.

SHOES   Nothing is so distasteful to the Japanese as the bottoms of shoes. Therefore, you should take off your shoes before entering a home, a Japanese-style inn, a temple, and even some museums and restaurants. Usually, there will be some plastic slippers at the entranceway for you to slip on, but whenever you encounter tatami, you should take off even these slippers—only bare feet or socks are allowed to tread upon tatami.

Restrooms present a whole other set of slippers. If you're in a home or a Japanese inn, you'll notice another pair of slippers—again plastic or rubber—sitting right inside the rest-room door. Step out of the hallway plastic shoes and into the bathroom slippers, and wear these the whole time you're in the restroom. When you're finished, change back into the hallway slippers. If you forget this last changeover, you'll regret it—nothing is as embarrassing as walking into a room wearing toilet slippers and not realizing what you've done until you see the mixed looks of horror and mirth on the faces of the Japanese.

BATHING   On my very first trip to Japan, I was certain I would never enter a Japanese bath. I was under the misconception that men and women bathed together, and I couldn't imagine getting into a tub with a group of smiling and bowing Japanese men. I needn't have worried—in almost all circumstances, bathing is gender segregated. There are some exceptions, primarily at outdoor hot-spring spas in the countryside, but the women who go to these are usually grandmothers who couldn't care less. Young Japanese women wouldn't dream of jumping into a tub with a group of male strangers.

Japanese baths are delightful. You find them at Japanese-style inns (*ryokan* and *minshuku*), at hot-spring spas (*onsen*), and at neighborhood baths (*sento*); not everyone has his or her own bath in Japan. Sometimes they're elaborate affairs with indoor and outdoor tubs, whirlpools, plants, and statues, and sometimes they're nothing more than a tiny tub. Public baths have long been regarded as social centers for the Japanese—friends and co-workers will visit hot-spring resorts together; neighbors exchange gossip at the neighborhood bath.

Sadly, however, the neighborhood bath has been in great decline over the past decades, as more and more Japanese own private baths.

In any case, whether large or small, the procedure at all Japanese baths is the same. After completely disrobing in the changing room and putting your clothes in either a locker or a basket, hold your washcloth in front of you so that it covers the vital parts and walk into the bath area. There, you'll find basins and stools (they used to be wood but are now mostly plastic) and faucets along the wall. Sit on the stool in front of a faucet and repeatedly fill your basin with water, splashing it all over you. If there's no hot water from the faucet, it's acceptable to dip your basin into the hot bath. Soap yourself down and then rinse away completely—and I mean completely—all soap traces. After you're squeaky clean, you're ready to get into the bath. When you've finished your bath, do not pull the plug. The same bath water is used by everyone.

Your first attempt at a Japanese bath may be painful—simply too scalding for comfort. It helps if you ease in gently and then sit perfectly still. You'll notice all tension and stiffness ebbing away. The Japanese are fond of baths, and many take them nightly, especially in winter, when a hot bath keeps one warm for hours afterward. If they're staying in a hot-spring spa, they'll use the baths both at night and again in the morning.

4 Dealing with the Language Barrier

Without a doubt, the hardest part of traveling in Japan is the language barrier. Suddenly you find yourself transported to a crowded land of 127 million people where you can neither speak nor read the language. To make matters worse, few Japanese speak English. And outside big cities and the major tourist sites, the menus, signs at train stations, and shop names are often in Japanese only.

However, millions of foreign visitors before you who didn't speak a word of Japanese have traveled throughout Japan on their own with great success. Much of the anxiety travelers experience elsewhere is eliminated in Japan because the country is safe and the people are kind and helpful to foreigners. In addition, the **Japan National Tourist Organization (JNTO)** does a super job of publishing various helpful brochures, leaflets, and maps, and there are local tourist offices in almost all cities and towns, usually at train stations. The country has done a mammoth job during the past decade in updating street signs, subway directions, and addresses in Roman letters, especially in Tokyo, Osaka, Kyoto, and other major cities.

If you need to ask directions of strangers in Japan, your best bet is to **ask younger people.** They have all studied English in school and are most likely to be able to help you. Japanese businessmen often know some English also. And as strange as it sounds, if you're having problems communicating with someone, **write it down** so he or she can read it. The emphasis in schools is on written rather than oral English (many English teachers can't speak English themselves), so Japanese who can't understand a word you say may know all the subtleties of syntax and English grammar. If you still have problems communicating, you can always call the **Travel-Phone,** a toll-free nationwide English-language helpline set up by the JNTO at ✆ **0888/22-4800,** available daily from 9am to 5pm (in Tokyo, call the TIC at ✆ **03/3201-3331;** in Kyoto, ✆ **075/371-5649**). It also doesn't hurt to arm yourself with a small pocket dictionary.

If you're heading out for a particular restaurant, shop, or sight, have your destination written out in Japanese by someone at your hotel. If you get lost along the way, look for one of the police boxes, called *koban,* found in virtually every neighborhood. They have maps of particular districts and can pinpoint exactly where you want to go if you have the address with you. Remember, too, that main train stations in major cities and tourist-resort areas have **tourist information offices** (*kanko annaijo*) that can help you with everything from directions to hotel reservations. The staff may not speak any English, but you shouldn't have any trouble communicating your needs.

A glossary of simple phrases and words appears in appendix B of this book. In addition, realizing the difficulties that foreigners have with the language barrier in Japan, the JNTO has put out a nifty booklet called the *Tourist's Language Handbook.* It contains basic sentences in English, with their Japanese equivalents, for almost every activity from asking directions and shopping to ordering in a restaurant and staying in a Japanese inn. It also has a short list of useful Japanese phrases to help you get around on your own. Pick up a copy at a Tourist Information Center in Tokyo, Kyoto, or Narita or Kansai airport.

THE WRITTEN LANGUAGE No one knows the exact origins of the Japanese language, but we do know it existed only in spoken form until the 6th century. It was then that the Japanese borrowed the Chinese pictorial characters, called *kanji,* and used them to develop their own form of written language. Later, two phonetic alphabet systems, *hiragana* and *katakana,* were added to kanji to form the existing Japanese writing system. Thus, Chinese and Japanese use some of the same pictographs, but otherwise there's no similarity between the languages; while they may be able to recognize some of each other's written language, the Chinese and Japanese cannot communicate verbally.

The Japanese written language—a combination of kanji, hiragana, and katakana—is probably one of the most difficult in the modern world. As for the spoken language, there are many levels of speech and forms of expression relating to a person's social status and sex. Even nonverbal communication is a vital part of understanding Japanese because what isn't said is often more important than what is. It's little wonder that St. Francis Xavier, a Jesuit missionary who came to Japan in the 16th century, wrote that Japanese was an invention of the devil designed to thwart the spread of Christianity. And yet, astoundingly, adult literacy in Japan is estimated to be 99%.

A note on establishment names: Many hotels and restaurants in Japan now have signs in *romaji* (Roman, or English-language, characters) in addition to their Japanese character signs. For those that don't, take heart—appendix C contains the Japanese character names of those establishments I recommend that only have Japanese signs; this should help you recognize them.

OTHER HELPFUL TIPS It's worth noting that Japanese nouns do not have plural forms; thus, for example, *ryokan,* a Japanese-style inn, can be both singular and plural, as can *kimono.* Plural sense is indicated by context.

In addition, the Japanese custom is to list the family name first followed by the given name. That is the format I have followed in this book, but note that many things published in English—business cards, city brochures, and so on—may follow the Western custom of listing family name last.

And finally, you may find yourself confused because of suffixes attached to Japanese place names. For example, *dori* can mean street, avenue, or road; and sometimes it's attached to a street name with a hyphen, while at other times it stands alone. Thus, you may see Chuo-dori, Chuo Dori, or even Chuo-dori Avenue on English maps and street signs, but they're all one and the same street. Likewise, *dera* means "temple" and is often included at the end of the name, as in Kiyomizudera, or may be translated into English as Kiyomizu Temple; *jo* means castle and may appear at the end, as in Nijojo, or may be left off and appear as Nijo Castle.

WRITTEN ENGLISH IN JAPAN   I'd like to mention here that English words are quite fashionable in Japanese advertising, with the result that you'll often see it on shop signs, posters, shopping bags, and T-shirts. However, words are often wonderfully misspelled or are used in such unusual contexts that you can only guess at the original intent. What, for example, could possibly be the meaning behind "Today birds, tomorrow men," which appeared under a picture of birds on a shopping bag? In Okayama, I saw a shop whose name was a stern admonition to customers to "Grow Up," while in Kyoto there's the "Selfish" coffee shop and the "Pitiful Pub." A staff member of the Hokkaido Tourist Association whose business card identified him working for the "Propaganda Section" was probably more truthful than most. And imagine my consternation upon stepping on a bathroom scale that called itself the "Beauty-Checker." But the best sign I've seen was at the Narita Airport, where each check-in counter displayed a notice advising passengers they would have to pay a service-facility charge at "the time of check-in for your fright." I was unable to control my giggles as I explained to the perplexed man behind one counter what was wrong with the sign. Two weeks later, when I went back through the airport, I was almost disappointed to find all signs had been corrected. That's Japanese efficiency.

5 Tips on Dining, Japanese Style

Whenever I leave Japan, it's the food I miss the most. Sure, there are sushi bars and other Japanese specialty restaurants in many major cities around the world, but they don't offer nearly the variety available in Japan (and often they aren't nearly as good). For just as America has more to offer than hamburgers and steaks and England more than fish-and-chips, Japan has more than just sushi and teppanyaki. For both the gourmet and the uninitiated, Japan is a treasure trove of culinary surprises.

JAPANESE CUISINE

Altogether, there are more than a dozen different and distinct types of Japanese cuisine, plus countless regional specialties. A good deal of what you eat may be completely new to you as well as completely unidentifiable. Sometimes the Japanese themselves don't even know what they're eating, so varied and so wide is the range of available edibles. The rule is simply to enjoy.

To the Japanese, **presentation** of food is as important as the food itself, and dishes are designed to appeal not only to the palate, but to the eye. In contrast to the American way of piling as much food as possible onto a single plate, the Japanese use lots of small plates, each arranged artfully with bite-size morsels of food.

Tips **Taxes**

Keep in mind that restaurants will add a 5% tax to your bill. First-class restaurants will also add a 10% to 15% service charge, as do many hotel restaurants.

Below are explanations of some of the most common types of Japanese cuisine. Generally, only one type of cuisine is served in a given restaurant—for example, only raw seafood is served in a sushi bar, whereas tempura is featured at a tempura counter. There are exceptions to this, especially in those restaurants where raw fish may be served as an appetizer. In addition, some Japanese drinking establishments offer a wide range of foods from soups to sushi to skewered pieces of chicken known as *yakitori*.

For a quick rundown of the various types of Japanese foods and individual dishes, refer to the menu terms in appendix B.

FUGU   Known as blowfish, pufferfish, or globefish in English, fugu is one of the most exotic and adventurous foods in Japan—if it's not prepared properly, it means almost certain death for the consumer. In the past decade, some 50 people in Japan have died from fugu poisoning, usually because they tried preparing it at home. The fugu's ovaries and intestines are deadly and must be entirely removed without puncturing them. So why eat fugu if it can kill you? Well, for one thing, it's delicious; for another, fugu chefs are strictly licensed by the government and are greatly skilled in preparing fugu dishes. Ways to order it include raw (*fugu-sashi*), when it's sliced paper-thin and dipped into soy sauce with bitter orange and chives; in a stew (*fugu-chiri*) cooked with vegetables at your table; and as a rice porridge (*fugu-zosui*). The season for fresh fugu is from October or November through March, but some restaurants serve it throughout the year.

KAISEKI   The king of Japanese cuisine, kaiseki is the epitome of delicately and exquisitely arranged food, the ultimate in Japanese aesthetic appeal. It's also among the most expensive meals you can eat and can cost ¥25,000 ($208) or more per person; some restaurants, however, do offer more affordable mini-kaiseki courses. In addition, the better *ryokan* (Japanese inns) serve meals kaiseki-style, which is a primary reason staying in one costs so much. Kaiseki, which is not a specific dish but rather a complete meal, is expensive because much time and skill are involved in preparing each of the many dishes, with the ingredients cooked to preserve natural flavors. Even the plates are chosen with great care to enhance the color, texture, and shape of each piece of food.

Kaiseki cuisine is based on the four seasons, with the selection of food and its presentation dependent on the time of the year. In fact, so strongly does a kaiseki preparation convey the mood of a particular season, the kaiseki gourmet can tell what season it is just by looking at a meal.

A kaiseki meal is usually a lengthy affair with various dishes appearing in set order. First come the appetizer, clear broth, and one uncooked dish. These are followed by boiled, broiled, fried, steamed, heated, and vinegared dishes and finally by another soup, rice, pickled vegetables, and fruit. Although meals vary greatly depending upon the region it's served in and what's fresh, common dishes include some type of sashimi, tempura, cooked seasonal fish, and an array of bite-size pieces of various vegetables. Since kaiseki is always a set meal, there's no problem in ordering. Let your budget be your guide.

KUSHIAGE   Kushiage foods are breaded and deep-fried on skewers and include chicken, beef, seafood, and lots of seasonal vegetables (snow peas, green pepper, gingko nuts, lotus root, and the like). They're served with a slice of lemon and usually a specialty sauce. The result is delicious, and I highly recommend trying it. You'll find it at shops called *kushiage-ya* (ya means "shop"), which are often open only at night, like yakitori-ya. Ordering the set meal is easiest, and what you get is often determined by both the chef and the season.

OKONOMIYAKI   Okonomiyaki, which originated in Osaka after World War II and literally means "as you like it," could be considered a Japanese pizza. Basically, it's a kind of pancake to which meat or fish, shredded cabbage, and vegetables are added, topped with Worcestershire sauce. Since it's a popular offering of street vendors, restaurants specializing in this type of cuisine are very reasonably priced. At some places the cook makes it for you, but at other places it's do-it-yourself, which can be quite fun if you're with a group. *Yakisoba* (fried Chinese noodles and cabbage) are also usually on offer at okonomiyaki restaurants.

RICE   As in other Asian countries, rice has been a Japanese staple for about 2,000 years. In fact, rice is so important to the Japanese diet that *gohan* means both "rice" and "meal." There are no problems here—everyone is familiar with rice. The difference, however, is that in Japan it's quite sticky, making it easier to pick up with chopsticks. It's also just plain white rice—no salt, no butter, no soy sauce (it's thought to be rather uncouth to dump a lot of sauces in your rice). In the old days, not everyone could afford the expensive white kind, which was grown primarily to pay taxes or rent to the feudal lord; the peasants had to be satisfied with a mixture of brown rice, millet, and greens. Today, some Japanese still eat rice three times a day, although they're now just as apt to have bread and coffee for breakfast.

ROBATAYAKI   Robatayaki refers to restaurants in which seafood and vegetables are cooked over an open charcoal grill. In the olden days, an open fireplace (*robata*) in the middle of an old Japanese house was the center of activity for cooking, eating, socializing, and simply keeping warm. Therefore, today's robatayaki restaurants are like nostalgia trips back into Japan's past and are often decorated in rustic farmhouse style with the staff dressed in traditional clothing. Robatayaki restaurants—many open only in the evening—are popular among office workers for both eating and drinking.

There's no special menu in a robatayaki restaurant—rather, it includes just about everything eaten in Japan. The difference is that most of the food will be grilled. Favorites of mine include gingko nuts (*ginnan*), asparagus wrapped in bacon (asparagus bacon), green peppers (*piman*), mushrooms (various kinds), potatoes (*jagabataa*), and just about any kind of fish. You can usually get skewers of beef or chicken as well as a stew of meat and potatoes (*nikujaga*). Since ordering is usually a la carte, you'll just have to look and point.

SASHIMI & SUSHI   It's estimated that the average Japanese eats 38kg (83.6 lb.) of seafood a year—that's six times the average American consumption. Although this seafood may be served in any number of ways from grilled to boiled, a great deal of it is eaten raw.

Sashimi is simply raw seafood, usually served as an appetizer and eaten alone (that is, without rice). If you've never eaten it, a good choice to start out with is *maguro,* or lean tuna, which doesn't taste fishy at all and is so delicate in texture that it almost melts in your mouth. The way to eat sashimi is to first put *wasabi* (pungent green horseradish) into a small dish of soy sauce and then dip the raw fish in the sauce using your chopsticks.

Sushi, which is raw fish with vinegared rice, comes in many varieties. The best known is *nigiri-zushi:* raw fish, seafood, or vegetables placed on top of vinegared rice with just a touch of wasabi. It's also dipped in soy sauce. Use chopsticks or your fingers to eat sushi; remember you're supposed to eat each piece in one bite—quite a mouthful, but about the only way to keep it from falling apart. Another trick is to turn it upside down when you dip it in the sauce, to keep the rice from crumbling.

Also popular is *maki-zushi,* which consists of seafood, vegetables, or pickles rolled with rice inside a sheet of nori seaweed. *Inari-zushi* is vinegared rice and chopped vegetables inside a pouch of fried tofu bean curd.

Typical sushi includes tuna (*maguro*), flounder (*hirame*), sea bream (*tai*), squid (*ika*), octopus (*tako*), shrimp (*ebi*), sea eel (*anago*), and omelet (*tamago*). Ordering is easy because you usually sit at a counter where you can see all the food in a refrigerated glass case in front of you. You also get to see the sushi chefs at work. The typical meal begins with sashimi and is followed by sushi, but if you don't want to order separately, there are always various set courses (*seto*).

By the way, the least expensive sushi is *chiraishi,* which is a selection of fish, seafood, and usually tamago on a large flat bowl of rice. Because you get more rice, those of you with bigger appetites may want to order chiraishi. Another way to enjoy sushi without spending a fortune is at a kaiten sushi shop, in which plates of sushi circulate on a conveyor belt on the counter—customers simply reach for the dishes they want and pay for the number of dishes they take.

SHABU-SHABU & SUKIYAKI   Until about 100 years ago, the Japanese could think of nothing so disgusting as eating the flesh of animals (fish was okay). Considered unclean by the Buddhists, meat consumption was banned by the emperor way back in the 7th century. Imagine the horror of the Japanese to discover that Western "barbarians" ate bloody meat! It wasn't until Emperor Meiji himself announced more than a century ago his intentions to eat meat that the Japanese accepted the idea. Today, the Japanese have become skilled in preparing a number of beef dishes, and according to a survey conducted a few years ago by the Japan Fisheries Association, grilled meat, curried rice, and hamburger were the three favorite dishes among senior-high-school boys living in Tokyo. (Girls, by the way, still preferred sushi.)

Sukiyaki is among Japan's best-known beef dishes and is one many Westerners seem to prefer. Actually, its origins are more Western than Japanese (it was introduced in the last century as a new Western cuisine). To the Western palate, however, it seems distinctly Japanese and today is immensely popular in Japan. Whenever I'm invited to a Japanese home, this is the meal most often served. Like fondue, it's cooked at the table.

Sukiyaki is thinly sliced beef cooked in a broth of soy sauce, stock, and sake along with scallions, spinach, mushrooms, tofu, bamboo shoots, and other vegetables. All diners serve themselves from the simmering pot and then dip their morsels into their own bowl of raw egg. You can skip the raw egg if you want, but it adds to the taste and also cools the food down enough so that it doesn't burn.

Shabu-shabu is also prepared at your table and consists of thinly sliced beef cooked in a broth with vegetables in a kind of Japanese fondue. (It's named for the swishing sound the beef supposedly makes when cooking.) The main difference between the two dishes is the broth: Whereas in sukiyaki it consists of stock flavored with soy sauce and sake and is slightly sweet, in shabu-shabu it's relatively clear and has little taste of its own. The pots used are also different.

Using their chopsticks, shabu diners hold pieces of meat in the watery broth until they're cooked. This usually takes only a few seconds. Vegetables are left in longer to swim around until fished out. For dipping, there's either sesame sauce with diced green onions or a more bitter fish stock sauce. Restaurants serving sukiyaki usually serve shabu-shabu as well, and they'll usually be happy to show you the right way to prepare and eat it.

SOBA & UDON NOODLES   The Japanese love eating noodles, but I suspect at least part of the fascination stems from the way they eat them—they slurp, sucking in the noodles with gravity-defying speed. What's more, slurping noodles is considered proper etiquette. Fearing it would stick with me forever, however, slurping is a technique I've never quite mastered.

There are many different kinds of noodles, and it seems like almost every region of Japan has its own special style or kind—some are eaten plain, some in combination with other foods such as shrimp tempura, some served hot, some served cold. **Soba,** made from buckwheat flour, is eaten hot (*kake-soba*) or cold (*zaru-soba*). **Udon** is a thick, white, wheat noodle originally from Osaka; it's usually served hot. **Somen** is a fine, white noodle eaten cold in the summer and dunked in a cold sauce. Establishments serving noodles range from stand-up eateries to more refined noodle restaurants with tatami seating. Regardless of where you eat them, noodles are among the least expensive dishes in Japan.

TEMPURA   Today a well-known Japanese food, tempura was actually introduced by the Portuguese in the 16th century. Tempura is fish and vegetables coated in a batter of egg, water, and wheat flour and then deep-fried; it's served piping hot. To eat it, dip it in a sauce of soy, fish stock, radish (*daikon*), and grated ginger; in some restaurants, only some salt, powdered green tea, or a lemon wedge is provided as an accompaniment. Various tempura specialties may include eggplant (*nasu*), mushroom (*shiitake*), sweet potato (*satsumaimo*), small green pepper (*shishito*), sliced lotus root (*renkon*), shrimp (*ebi*), squid (*ika*), lemon-mint leaf (*shiso*), and many kinds of fish. Again, the easiest thing to do is to order the set meal, the *teishoku*.

TEPPANYAKI   A teppanyaki restaurant is a Japanese steak house. As in the famous Benihana restaurants in many U.S. cities, the chef slices, dices, and cooks your meal of tenderloin or sirloin steak and vegetables on a smooth hot grill right in front of you—though with much less fanfare than their U.S. counterparts. Because beef is relatively new in Japanese cooking, some people categorize teppanyaki restaurants as "Western." However, I consider this style of cooking and presentation special enough to be referred to as Japanese. Teppanyaki restaurants also tend to be expensive, simply because of the price of beef in Japan, with Kobe beef the most prized.

TONKATSU   Tonkatsu is the Japanese word for "pork cutlet," made by dredging pork in wheat flour, moistening it with egg and water, dipping it in breadcrumbs, and deep-frying it in vegetable oil. Since restaurants serving tonkatsu are generally inexpensive, they're popular with office workers and families. The easiest order is the *teishoku,* which usually features either the pork filet (*hirekatsu*) or the pork loin (*rosukatsu*). In any case, your tonkatsu is served on a bed of shredded cabbage, and one or two different sauces will be at your table, a Worcestershire sauce and perhaps a specialty sauce. If you order the teishoku, it will come with rice, miso soup, and pickled vegetables.

UNAGI   I'll bet that if you ate unagi without knowing what it was, you'd find it very tasty. In fact, you'd probably be very surprised to find out you had just eaten eel. Popular as a health food because of its rich protein and high vitamin A content, eel is supposed to help fight fatigue during hot summer months but is eaten year-round. Broiled eel (*kabayaki*) is prepared by grilling filet strips over a charcoal fire; the eel is repeatedly dipped in a sweetened barbecue soy sauce while cooking. A favorite way to eat broiled eel is on top of rice, in which case it's called *unaju* or *Unagi donburi.* Do yourself a favor and try it.

YAKITORI   Yakitori is chunks of chicken or chicken parts basted in a sweet soy sauce and grilled over a charcoal fire on thin skewers. Places that specialize in yakitori (*yakitori-ya,* often identifiable by a red paper lantern outside the front door) are technically not restaurants but, rather, drinking establishments; they usually don't open until 5 or 6pm. Most yakitori-ya are popular with workers as inexpensive places to drink, eat, and be merry.

The cheapest way to dine on yakitori is to order a set course, which will often include various parts of the chicken including the skin, heart, and liver. Since this may not be entirely to your taste, you may wish to order a la carte, which is more expensive but gets you exactly what you want. In addition to chicken, other skewered, charcoaled delicacies are usually offered (called *kushi-yaki*). If you're ordering by the stick, you might want to try chicken breast (*sasami*), chicken meatballs (*tsukune*), green peppers (*piman*), chicken and leeks (*negima*), mushrooms (*shiitake*), or gingko nuts (*ginnan*).

OTHER CUISINES   During your travels you might also run into these types of Japanese cuisine: **Kamameshi** is a rice casserole served in individual-size cast-iron pots with different kinds of toppings that might include seafood, meat, or vegetables. **Domburi** is also a rice dish, topped with tempura, eggs, and meat like chicken or pork. **Nabe,** a stew cooked in an earthenware pot at your table, consists of chicken, sliced beef, pork, or seafood; noodles; and vegetables. **Oden** is a broth with fish cakes, tofu, eggs, and vegetables, served with hot mustard. If a restaurant advertises that it specializes in **Kyodo-Ryori,** it serves local specialties for which the region is famous and is often very rustic in decor. In recent years, restaurants serving crossover cuisine—creative dishes inspired by ingredients from both sides of the Pacific—have mushroomed in Tokyo and a few major cities.

Although technically Chinese fast-food restaurants, **ramen shops** are a big part of dining in Japan. Serving what I consider to be generic Chinese noodles, soups, and other dishes, ramen shops can be found everywhere; they're easily recognizable by red signs, flashing lights, and quite often pictures of various dishes displayed right by the front door. Many are stand-up affairs—just a high counter to rest your bowl on. In addition to ramen (noodle and vegetable soup), you can also get such things as *yakisoba* (fried noodles) or—my favorite—*gyoza* (fried pork dumplings). What these places lack in atmosphere is made up for in price: Most dishes average about ¥550 ($4.60), making them one of the cheapest places in Japan for a meal.

DRINKS

All Japanese restaurants serve complimentary **green tea** with meals. If that's a little too weak, you may want to try **sake,** an alcoholic beverage made from rice and served either hot or cold. It goes well with most forms of Japanese cuisine. Produced since about the 3rd century, sake varies by region, production method, alcoholic content, color, aroma, and taste. Altogether, there are about 2,000 brands of sake produced in Japan. Miyabi is a prized classic sake; other popular brands are Gekkeikan, Koshinokanbai, Hakutsuru (meaning White Crane), and Ozeki.

Japanese **beer** is also very popular. The biggest sellers are Kirin, Sapporo, Asahi, and Suntory, with each brand offering a bewildering variety of brews. They enjoyed exclusive rights to brew beer until deregulation in the 1990s opened the gates to competition; now microbreweries are found everywhere in

Japan. Ironically enough, Budweiser is also a big hit among young Japanese. Businessmen are fond of **whiskey,** which they usually drink with ice and water. Popular in recent years is **shochu,** an alcoholic beverage usually made from rice but sometimes from wheat, sweet potatoes, or sugar cane. It used to be considered a drink of the lower classes, but sales have increased so much that it's threatening the sake and whiskey businesses. A clear liquid comparable, perhaps, to vodka, it can be consumed straight but is often combined with soda water in a drink called *chuhi;* watch out—the stuff can be deadly. **Wine,** usually available only at restaurants serving Western food, has gained in popularity in recent years, with both domestic and imported brands available. Although **cocktails** are available in discos, hotel lounges, and fancier bars at a rather inflated price, most Japanese stick with beer, sake, or whiskey.

TIPS ON DINING IN JAPAN
RESTAURANT ESSENTIALS

ORDERING   The biggest problem facing the hungry foreigner in Japan is ordering a meal because few restaurants have English menus, especially outside major cities. This book alleviates the problem to a large extent by giving some sample dishes and prices for recommended restaurants throughout Japan; we've also noted throughout which restaurants offer English menus.

One aid to simplified ordering is the common use of plastic food models in glass display cases either outside or just inside the front door of many restaurants. Sushi, tempura, daily specials, spaghetti—they're all there in mouthwatering plastic replicas along with the corresponding prices. Simply decide what you want and point it out to your waitress.

Unfortunately, not all restaurants in Japan have plastic display cases, especially the more exclusive or traditional ones. In fact, you'd be missing a lot of Japan's best cuisine if you restricted yourself to eating only at places with displays. If there's no display from which to choose, the best thing to do is to look at what people around you are eating and order what looks best. An alternative is simply to order the *teishoku,* or daily special meal (also called "set course" or simply "course," especially in restaurants serving Western food); these are fixed-price meals that consist of a main dish and several side dishes, including soup, rice, and Japanese pickles for Japanese teishoku. Although most restaurants have special set courses for dinner as well, lunch is the usual time for the teishoku.

HOURS   In the larger cities, the usual hours for restaurants are from about 11am to 10 or 11pm. Of course, some establishments close earlier at 9pm, while others stay open past midnight; the majority close for a few hours in the afternoon. The main thing to remember is that, if you're in a big city like Tokyo or Osaka, you'll want to avoid the lunchtime rush, which is from noon to 1pm. In rural areas and small towns, restaurants tend to close early, often by 7:30 or 8pm.

Another thing to keep in mind is that the closing time posted for most restaurants is exactly that—everyone is expected to pay his or her bill and leave. A general rule of thumb is that the last order is taken at least a half hour before closing time, sometimes an hour or more for kaiseki restaurants. To be on the safe side, therefore, try to arrive at least an hour before closing time so you have time to relax and enjoy your meal.

ETIQUETTE

UPON ARRIVAL   As soon as you're seated in a Japanese restaurant (that is, a restaurant serving Japanese food), you'll be given a wet towel, which will be steaming hot in winter or pleasantly cool in summer. Called an *oshibori,* it's for wiping your hands. In all but the fancy restaurants, men can get away with wiping their faces as well, but women are not supposed to (I ignore this if it's hot and humid outside). The oshibori is a great custom, one you'll wish would be adopted back home. Sadly, some cheaper Japanese restaurants now resort to a paper towel wrapped in plastic, which isn't nearly the same. Oshibori are generally not served in Western restaurants.

CHOPSTICKS   The next thing you'll probably be confronted with are chopsticks.

How to Use Your Chopsticks   The proper way to use them is to place the first chopstick between the base of the thumb and the top of the ring finger (this chopstick remains stationary) and the second one between the top of the thumb and the middle and index fingers (this second chopstick is the one you move to pick up food).

The best way to learn to use chopsticks is to have a Japanese show you how. It's not difficult, but if you find it impossible, some restaurants might have a fork as well. How proficiently foreigners handle chopsticks is a matter of great curiosity for the Japanese, and they're surprised if you know how to use them; even if you were to live in Japan for 20 years, you would never stop receiving compliments on how talented you are with chopsticks.

Chopstick Etiquette   If you're taking something from a communal bowl or tray, you're supposed to turn your chopsticks upside down and use the part that hasn't been in your mouth; after transferring the food to your plate, you turn the chopsticks back to their proper position. The exception is shabu-shabu and sukiyaki.

Never stick your chopsticks down vertically into your bowl of rice and leave them there—that is done only when a person has died. Also, don't pass anything from your chopsticks to another person's chopsticks; that's done only to pass the bones of the cremated.

EATING SOUP & NOODLES   If you're eating soup, you won't use a spoon. Rather, you'll pick up the bowl and drink from it. Use your chopsticks to fish out larger pieces of food. It's considered in good taste to slurp with gusto, especially if you're eating noodles. Noodle shops in Japan are always well orchestrated with slurps and smacks.

DRINKING   If you're drinking in Japan, the main thing to remember is that you never pour your own glass. Bottles of beer are so large that people often share one. The rule is that, in turn, one person pours for everyone else in the group, so be sure to hold up your glass when someone is pouring for you. Only as the night progresses do the Japanese get sloppy about this rule. It took me a while to figure this out, but if no one notices your empty glass, the best thing to do is to pour everyone else a drink so that someone will pour yours. If someone wants to pour you a drink and your glass is full, the proper thing to do is to take a few gulps so that he or she can fill your glass. Because each person is continually filling everyone else's glass, you never know exactly how much you've had to drink, which (depending on how you look at it) is very good or very bad.

PAYING THE BILL   If you go out with a group of friends (not as a visiting guest of honor and not with business associates), it's customary to split the dinner bill equally, even if you all ordered different things. Even foreigners living in Japan adopt the practice of splitting the bill; it certainly makes figuring everyone's share easier, especially since there's no tipping in Japan.

OTHER TIPS   It's considered bad manners to walk down the street eating or drinking (except at a festival). You'll notice that if a Japanese buys a drink from a vending machine, he'll stand there, gulp it down, and throw away the container before going on. In recent years, an increasing number of young people are ignoring this unwritten rule, much to the chagrin of their elders.

HOW TO EAT WITHOUT SPENDING A FORTUNE

During your first few days in Japan—particularly if you're in Tokyo—money will seem to flow out of your pockets like water. In fact, money has a tendency to disappear so quickly that many people become convinced they must have lost some of it somehow. At this point, almost everyone panics (I've seen it happen again and again) but then slowly realizes that, since prices are markedly different here (steeper), a bit of readjustment in thinking and habits is necessary. Coffee, for example, is something of a luxury, and some Japanese are astonished at the thought of drinking four or five cups a day. Here are some tips for getting the most for your money.

BREAKFAST   If you're on a tight budget, **avoid eating breakfast at your hotel.** Coffee shops offer what's called "morning service" until 10 or 11am; it generally consists of a cup of coffee, a small salad, a boiled egg, and the thickest slice of toast you've ever seen for about ¥550 ($4.60). That's a real bargain when you consider that just one cup of coffee can cost ¥250 to ¥500 ($2.10–$4.15). (With the exception of some hotel breakfast buffets, there's no such thing as the bottomless cup in Japan.) There are many coffee-shop chains in Japan, including Doutour, Pronto, and Starbucks.

SET LUNCHES   **Eat your biggest meal at lunch.** Many restaurants serving Japanese food offer a daily set lunch, or *teishoku,* at a fraction of what their set dinners might be. Usually ranging in price from ¥700 to ¥1,500 ($5.85–$12.50), they're generally available from 11 or 11:30am to 1:30 or 2pm. A Japanese teishoku will often include the main course (such as tempura, grilled fish, or the specialty of the house), soup, pickled vegetables, rice, and tea, while the set menu in a Western-style restaurant (often called set lunch) usually consists of a main dish, salad, bread, and coffee.

CHEAP EATS   Inexpensive restaurants can be found in department stores (often one whole floor will be devoted to various kinds of restaurants, most with plastic-food displays), underground shopping arcades, nightlife districts, and in and around train and subway stations. Some of the cheapest establishments for a night out on the town are the countless **yakitori-ya, noodle shops,** and **ramen shops.** For sushi, the cheapest places are those that deliver food via a conveyor belt; you simply reach out and take the plates that look good. **Coffee shops** often offer inexpensive Western food, including sandwiches. Japan also has American **fast-food chains,** such as McDonald's (where Big Macs cost about ¥280/$2.35), Wendy's, and Kentucky Fried Chicken, as well as Japanese chains—Morninaga, Lotteria, and First Kitchen, among them—that sell hamburgers and french fries.

PRE-PREPARED FOODS   You can save even more money by avoiding restaurants altogether. There are all kinds of pre-prepared foods you can buy; some are even complete meals, perfect for picnics in a park or right in your hotel room.

Perhaps the best known is the **obento,** or box lunch, commonly sold on express trains, on train-station platforms, in food sections of department stores, and at counter windows of tiny shops throughout Japan. In fact, the obento served by vendors on trains and at train stations are an inexpensive way to sample regional cuisine since they often include food typical of the region. Costing usually between ¥800 and ¥1,500 ($6.65 and $12.50), the basic obento contains a piece of meat (generally fish or chicken), various side dishes, rice, and pickled vegetables. Sushi boxed lunches are also readily available.

My favorite place to shop for pre-prepared foods is in **department stores.** Located in basements, these food and produce sections hark back to Japanese markets of yore, with vendors yelling out their wares and crowds of housewives deciding on the evening's dinner. Different counters specialize in different items—tempura, yakitori, eel, Japanese pickles, cooked fish, sushi (sometimes made by robots!), salads, vegetables, and desserts. Almost the entire spectrum of Japanese cuisine is available, and there are numerous samples available. There are also counters selling obento box meals. In any case, you can eat for less than ¥1,200 ($10), and there's nothing like milling with Japanese housewives to make you feel like one of the locals. Though not as colorful, **24-hour convenience stores** also sell packaged foods, including sandwiches and obento.

Streetside stalls, called **yatai,** are also good sources for inexpensive meals. These restaurants-on-wheels sell a variety of foods, including *oden* (fish cakes), *yakitori* (skewered barbecued chicken), and *yakisoba* (fried noodles), as well as sake and beer. They appear mostly at night, lighted by a single lantern or a string of lights, and most have a counter with stools as well, protected in winter by a wall of tarp. These can be great, cozy places for rubbing elbows with the locals. Fukuoka, in Kyushu, is famous for its yatai, but you'll find them in many cities, especially in nightlife districts. Sadly, however, traditional pushcarts are being replaced by motorized vans, which do not offer seating.

6 Cultural Snapshots: Japanese Arts in a Nutshell

TRADITIONAL THEATER

KABUKI   Probably Japan's best-known traditional theater art, Kabuki is also one of the country's most popular forms of entertainment. Visit a performance and it's easy to see why—in a word, Kabuki is fun! The plays are dramatic, the costumes are gorgeous, the stage settings are often fantastic, and the themes are universal—love, revenge, and the conflict between duty and personal feelings. Probably one of the reasons Kabuki is so popular even today is that it developed centuries ago as a form of entertainment for the common people in feudal Japan, particularly the merchants. And one of Kabuki's interesting aspects is that all roles—even those depicting women—are portrayed by men.

Kabuki has changed little in the past 100 years. Altogether, there are more than 300 Kabuki plays, all written before this century. Kabuki stages almost always have a revolving stage and an aisle that extends from the stage to the back of the spectator theater. For a Westerner, one of the more arresting things about a Kabuki performance is the audience itself. Because this has always been entertainment for the masses, the audience can get quite lively with yells, guffaws, shouts of approval and laughter from spectators. In fact, old woodcuts of cross-eyed men apparently stemmed from Kabuki—when things got a little too rowdy, actors would stamp their feet and strike a cross-eyed pose in an attempt to get the audience's attention.

Of course, you won't be able to understand what's being said. Indeed, because much of Kabuki drama dates from the 18th century, even the Japanese sometimes have difficulty understanding the language. But it doesn't matter. Many theaters have programs and earphones that describe the plots in minute detail, often in English as well. Thus, you can follow the story and enjoy Kabuki just as much as everyone around you. The best place to enjoy Kabuki is in Tokyo, with performances much of the year.

NOH Whereas Kabuki developed as a form of entertainment for the masses, Noh was a much more traditional and aristocratic form of theater. Most of Japan's shogun were patrons of Noh; during the Edo Period, it became the exclusive entertainment of the samurai class. In contrast to Kabuki's extroverted liveliness, Noh is very calculated, slow, and restrained. The oldest form of theater in Japan, it has changed very little in the past 600 years. The language is so archaic that the Japanese cannot understand it at all, which explains in part why Noh does not have the popularity that Kabuki does.

As in Kabuki, all the performers are men. The subject matter of Noh's some 240 surviving plays is usually supernatural beings, beautiful women, mentally confused people, or tragic-heroic events. Performers often wear masks. Spoken parts are chanted by a chorus of about eight; music is provided by a Noh orchestra that consists of several drums and a flute.

Because the action is slow, watching an entire evening can be quite tedious unless you are particularly interested in Noh dance and music. In addition, most Noh plays do not have English translations. You may just want to drop in for a short while. In between Noh plays, there are short comic reliefs called *kyogen,* which usually make fun of life in the 1600s.

BUNRAKU Bunraku is traditional Japanese puppet theater. But contrary to what you might expect, Bunraku is for adults, and themes center on love and revenge, sacrifice and suicide. Many dramas now adapted for Kabuki were first written for the Bunraku stage.

Popular in Japan since the 17th century—at times even more popular than Kabuki—Bunraku is fascinating to watch because the puppeteers are right onstage with their puppets. Dressed in black, they're wonderfully skilled in making the puppets seem like living beings. Usually, there are three puppeteers for each puppet, which is about three-fourths human size: One puppeteer is responsible for movement of the puppet's head, as well as for the expression on its face, and for the movement of the right arm and hand; another puppeteer operates the puppet's left arm and hand, while the third moves the legs. Although at first the puppeteers are somewhat distracting, after a while you forget they're there as the puppets assume personalities of their own. The narrator, who tells the story and speaks the various parts, is an important figure in the drama. The narrator is accompanied by a traditional three-stringed Japanese instrument called a *shamisen.* By all means, try to see Bunraku if possible. The most famous presentations are at the Osaka Bunraku Theater, but there are performances in Tokyo and other major cities as well.

THE TEA CEREMONY

Tea was brought to Japan from China more than 1,000 years ago. It first became popular among Buddhist priests as a means of staying awake during long hours of meditation; gradually, its use filtered down among the upper classes, and in the 16th century, the tea ceremony was perfected by a merchant named Sen-no-Rikyu. Using the principles of Zen and the spiritual discipline of the samurai, the tea ceremony became a highly stylized ritual, with detailed rules on how tea should be prepared, served, and drunk. The simplicity of movement and tranquility of setting are meant to free the mind from the banality of everyday

Fun Fact Sumo

The Japanese form of wrestling known as *sumo* began perhaps as long as 1,500 years ago, becoming immensely popular by the 6th century. Today, it's still popular, and the best wrestlers are revered as national heroes, much as baseball or basketball players are in the United States. Often taller than 6 feet and weighing well over 300 pounds, sumo wrestlers follow a vigorous training period, which usually begins in their teens and includes eating special foods to gain weight. Unmarried wrestlers even live together at their training schools, called sumo stables.

A sumo match takes place on a sandy-floored ring less than 15 feet in diameter. Wrestlers dress much as they did during the Edo Period—their hair in a samurai-style topknot, an ornamental belt-loincloth around their huge girths. Before each bout, the two contestants scatter salt in the ring to purify it from the last bout's loss; they also squat and then raise each leg, stamping it into the ground to crush, symbolically, any evil spirits. They then squat down and face each other, glaring to psych each other out. Once they rush each other, the object is for a wrestler either to eject his opponent from the ring or to cause him to touch the ground with any part of his body other than his feet. This is accomplished by shoving, slapping, tripping, throwing, and even carrying the opponent, but punching with a closed fist and kicking are not allowed. Altogether, there are 48 holds and throws, and sumo fans know all of them.

Most bouts are very short, lasting only 30 seconds or so. The highest-ranking players are called *yokozuna,* or grand champions; in 1993, a Hawaiian named Akebono was promoted to the highest rank, the first non-Japanese ever to be so honored.

There are six 15-day sumo tournaments in Japan every year: Three are held in Tokyo (in Jan, May, and Sept); the others are held in Osaka (in Mar), Nagoya (in July), and Fukuoka (in Nov). Each wrestler in the tournament faces a new opponent every day; the winner of the tournament is the wrestler who maintains the best overall record.

If you'd like to attend a sumo match while you're in Tokyo, see chapter 4. Tournament matches are widely covered on television, so try to catch one if you're in Japan while a tournament's on.

life and to allow the spirit to enjoy peace. In a way, it is a form of spiritual therapy.

The tea ceremony, *cha-no-yu,* is still practiced in Japan today and is regarded as a form of disciplinary training for mental composure and for etiquette and manners. In Kyoto, I once met a fellow guest in an inexpensive Japanese inn who asked whether she could serve me Japanese tea and a sweet after breakfast. She apologized for her ineptitude, saying she was only a mere student of tea. When I asked how long she'd been studying cha-no-yu, she replied only 7 years. That may seem like a long time, but the study of the tea ceremony includes related subjects, including the craftsmanship of tea vessels and implements, the design and construction of the teahouse, the landscaping of gardens, and literature related to the tea ceremony.

Several of Japan's more famous landscape gardens have teahouses on their grounds where you can sit on tatami, drink the frothy green tea (called *maccha*), eat some sweets (meant to counteract the bitter taste of the tea), and contemplate the view. Teahouses are traditionally quite small and have room for five or fewer people. There's one entrance for the host and another for guests, so small that guests must crawl through it to enter. In the center of the room is a small brazier for the teapot along with utensils needed for the making of tea—a tea bowl, tea caddy, bamboo whisk, and bamboo spoon. After hot water is added to powdered tea and beaten with the whisk, the bowl is passed from guest to guest. Tea etiquette requires guests to compliment the host on the excellent flavor of the tea and on the beauty of the tea implements, which of course change with the seasons and are often valuable art objects.

Several first-class hotels in Tokyo hold tea ceremonies in special tea-ceremony rooms; see chapter 4.

FLORAL & LANDSCAPE ARTS

IKEBANA   Whereas a Westerner is likely to put a bunch of flowers into a vase and be done with it, the Japanese consider the arrangement of flowers an art in itself. Most young girls have at least some training in flower arranging, known as *ikebana*. First popularized among the aristocrats during the Heian Period (A.D. 794–1192) and spreading to the common people in the 14th to 16th centuries, traditional ikebana, in its simplest form, is supposed to represent heaven, man, and earth; it's considered a truly Japanese art without outside influences. As important as the arrangement itself is the vase chosen to display it. Department store galleries sometimes have ikebana exhibitions, as do shrines; otherwise, check with the local tourist office.

GARDENS   Nothing is left to chance in a Japanese landscape garden: The shape of hills and trees, the placement of rocks and waterfalls—everything is skillfully arranged in a faithful reproduction of nature. To Westerners, it may seem a bit strange to arrange nature to look like nature; but to the Japanese, even nature can be improved upon to make it more pleasing with the best possible use of limited space. The Japanese are masters at this, as a visit to any of their famous gardens will testify.

In fact, they have been sculpting gardens for more than 1,000 years. At first, the gardens were designed for walking and boating with ponds, artificial islands, and pavilions. As with almost everything else in Japanese life, however, Zen Buddhism exerted an influence, making gardens simpler and attempting to create the illusion of boundless space within a small area. To the Buddhist, a garden was not for merriment but for contemplation—an uncluttered and simple landscape on which to rest the eyes. Japanese gardens often use the principle of "borrowed landscape"—that is, using the surrounding mountains and landscape by incorporating them into the overall design and impact of the garden.

Basically, there are three styles of Japanese gardens. One style, called **tsukiyama,** uses ponds, hills, and streams to depict nature in miniature. Another style, known as the **karesansui,** uses stones and raked sand in place of water and is often seen at Zen Buddhist temples; it was developed during the Muromachi Period as a representation of Zen spiritualism. The third style, called **chaniwa,** emerged with the tea ceremony and is built around a teahouse with an eye toward simplicity and tranquility; such a garden will often feature stone lanterns, a stone basin filled with water, and water flowing through a bamboo pipe.

Famous gardens in Japan include Kenrokuen Park in Kanazawa, Korakuen Park in Okayama, and Ritsurin Park in Takamatsu. Kyoto alone has about 50 gardens, including the famous Zen rock gardens at Daitokuji and Ryoanji temples, the gardens at both the Golden and Silver pavilions, and those at Heian Shrine, Nijo Castle, and the Katsura Imperial Villa.

7 Recommended Reading

Kodansha International Ltd., a Japanese publisher, has probably brought out more books on Japan in English—including Japanese-language textbooks— than any other company. Available at major bookstores in Japan, books can also be ordered over the Internet from www.amazon.com.

HISTORY   The definitive work of Japan's history through the ages is *Japan: The Story of a Nation* (Alfred A. Knopf, 1991) by Edwin O. Reischauer, a former U.S. ambassador to Japan. Ivan Morris' *The World of the Shining Prince: Court Life in Ancient Japan* (Kodansha, 1994) highlights the golden age of the imperial court through diaries and literature of the Heian Period (794–1192), while *Everyday Life in Traditional Japan* (Tuttle, 2000) details the daily lives of samurai, farmers, craftsmen, merchants, courtiers, and outcasts during the Edo Period. More recent history is the subject of Pulitzer Prize winners *Embracing Defeat: Japan in the Wake of World War II* by John W. Dower (W.W. Norton & Co., 1999), which paints a vivid picture of America's role in reshaping Japan and what life was like for the Japanese under American occupation, and *Hirohito and the Making of Modern Japan* by Herbert P. Bix (HarperCollins, 2000), which contends that the wartime emperor was not a passive leader controlled by the military but rather was actively involved in national policy and bore deep responsibility for the war.

For personal accounts of Japan in ages past, there's no better anthology than Donald Keene's *Travelers of a Hundred Ages: The Japanese as Revealed Through 1,000 Years of Diaries* (Holt, 1989). Written by Japanese from all walks of life, the journals provide fascinating insight into the hidden worlds of imperial courts, Buddhist monasteries, isolated country inns, and more. Lafcadio Hearn, a prolific writer about things Japanese in the late 19th century, describes life in Japan around the turn of the century in *Writings from Japan* (Penguin, 1985), while Isabella Bird, an Englishwoman who traveled alone in Japan in the 1870s, writes a vivid account of rural Japanese life in *Unbeaten Tracks in Japan* (Virago Press Limited, 1984).

SOCIETY   Reischauer's *The Japanese Today* (Tuttle, 1993) offers a unique perspective of Japanese society, including the historical events that have shaped and influenced Japanese behavior and the role of the individual in Japanese society. A classic description of the Japanese and their culture is found in Ruth Benedict's brilliant *The Chrysanthemum and the Sword: Patterns of Japanese Culture* (Houghton Mifflin Co., 1989), first published in the 1940s but reprinted many times since. For a more contemporary approach, look into *The Japanese Mind: The Goliath Explained* (Linden Press/Simon & Schuster, 1983) by Robert C. Christopher, valuable for its insight into the Japanese and the role history has played in developing their psyche. Debunking theories that have long shaped the outside world's views of Japan (many of which are espoused by the books above) is *Japan: A Reinterpretation* (Pantheon, 1997) by former International Herald Tribune Tokyo bureau chief Patrick Smith, who gives a spirited reinterpretation of Japan's economic miracle and recent demise.

For advice on Japanese etiquette, refer to *Etiquette Today: A Guide to Business and Social Customs* (Tuttle, 1994) by James M. Vardaman and Michiko Sasaki Vardaman; it covers everything from bowing and bathing to eating and dining customs, office etiquette, and the complicated art of giving gifts. Business travelers may also want to read *Business Japan: A Practical Guide to Understanding Japanese Business Culture* by Peggy Kenna and Sonra Lacy (NTC Publishing, 1994), which compares American and Japanese business styles, practices, and social customs.

CULTURE & THE ARTS   For a general rundown on the development of literature, religion, and art through the ages, see George B. Sansom's *Japan: A Short Cultural History* (Charles E. Tuttle, 1997).

The Japan Travel Bureau puts out some nifty pocket-size illustrated booklets on things Japanese including *Eating in Japan, Living Japanese Style, Festivals of Japan, Martial Arts & Sports in Japan,* and *Japanese Family & Culture,* which covers everything from marriage in Japan to problems with mothers-in-law and explanations of why dad gets home so late. My favorite, however, is *Salaryman in Japan* (JTB, 1986), which describes the private and working lives of Japan's army of white-collar workers who receive set salaries. For a cultural overview in one book, see *Introduction to Japanese Culture,* edited by Daniel Sosnoski (Tuttle, 1996), which covers major festivals, the tea ceremony, flower arranging, Kabuki, sumo, Japanese board games, geisha, Buddhism, kanji, and much more.

The history and philosophy of the tea ceremony, beginning with its origins in the 12th century, are given in *The Tea Ceremony* (Kodansha, 1998) by Sen'o Tanaka. Another worthwhile read is the *Japanese Way of Tea: From its Origins in China to Sen Rikyu* by Sen Soshitsu (University of Hawaii Press, 1998), which may well be the definitive book on tea.

A Net of Fireflies: Japanese Haiku and Haiku Paintings (Tuttle, 1960) is a charming collection of these typical Japanese art forms. Elizabeth Kiritani's *Vanishing Japan: Traditions, Crafts & Culture* (Tuttle, 1995) covers a wide spectrum of traditional Japanese crafts and professions that were once a part of daily life from potato vendors, shoe shiners, and tatami makers to Japanese umbrellas and handmade paper, many of which are fast disappearing in today's modern Japan.

CONTEMPORARY CHRONICLES   For contemporary experiences of foreigners in Japan, there's the inimitable Dave Barry, who describes his whirlwind trip to the land of the rising sun in the comical *Dave Barry Does Japan* (Random House, 1992) and solves such puzzling mysteries as why Japanese cars sell successfully (they're made of steel!). A delightful account of the Japanese and their customs is given by the irrepressible George Mikes in *The Land of the Rising Yen* (Penguin, 1973); I doubt you'll be able to find the book in the United States, but it's in major bookstores in Japan and would make enjoyable reading during your trip. Rick Kennedy, a longtime resident of Japan, gives a lighthearted view of life in the capital in *Home, Sweet Tokyo: Life in a Weird and Wonderful City* (Kodansha, 1988). A book seemingly from another era is *Geisha* (Vintage, 2000) by Liza C. Dalby; first published in 1983, it describes her year living as a geisha in Kyoto as part of a research project. Alan Booth's *The Roads to Sata* (Kodansha, 1997) chronicles the author's 2,000-mile hike through Japan's four main islands. *Traveler's Tales Guides: Japan* (Traveler's Tales, 1999) relates the first-hand experiences of Dave Barry, Pico Iyer, and other writers who tackle such issues as sand bathing and washlet toilets.

FICTION   Whenever I travel in Japan, I especially enjoy reading fictional accounts of the country; they put me more in tune with my surroundings and increase my awareness and perception. The world's first major novel was written by a Japanese woman, Murasaki Shikibu, whose classic, *The Tale of Genji* (Knopf, 1978), dating from the 11th century, describes the aristocratic life of Prince Genji.

In Tokyo bookstores, you'll find whole sections dedicated to English translations of Japan's best-known modern and contemporary authors including Mishima Yukio, Soseki Natsume, Abe Kobo, Tanizaki Junichiro, and Nobel Prize winner Kawabata Yasunari. An overview of Japanese classical literature is provided in *Anthology of Japanese Literature* (Grove Press, 1955), edited by Donald Keene. Likewise, *The Showa Anthology: Modern Japanese Short Stories* (Kodansha, 1992), edited by Van C. Gessel and Tomone Matsumoto, covers works by Abe Kobe, Mishima Yukio, Kawabata Yasunari, Oe Kenzaburo and others written between 1929 and 1984, while *Modern Japanese Stories: An Anthology* (Tuttle, 1962), edited by Ivan Morris, introduces short stories by some of Japan's top modern writers, including Mori Ogai, Tanizaki Junichiro, Kawabata Yasunari, and Mishima Yukio.

For novels, you might wish to read Mishima's *The Sea of Fertility* (Knopf), a collection of four separate works, or *The Sound of Waves* (Knopf, 1956), about young love in a Japanese fishing village. Other famous works by Japanese authors include Soseki Natsume's first novel, *I am a Cat* (Charles E. Tuttle, 1972), which describes the foibles of upper-middle-class Japanese during the Meiji Era through the eyes of a cat; and his later novel, *Kokoro* (Regnery Gateway Co., 1985), as well as Kawabata Yasunari's *Snow Country* (Knopf, 1956), translated by Edward G. Seidensticker.

Oe Kenzaburo gained international recognition when he became the second Japanese to win the Nobel Prize for Literature in 1994. In addition to such well-known novels as *A Personal Matter* (Grove Press, 1968), about a man in search of himself after the birth of a handicapped son, and *Hiroshima Notes* (Grove/Atlantic, 1996), with personal accounts of atomic bomb survivors and a moving commentary on the meaning of the Hiroshima bombing, is one of his latest works, *A Healing Family* (Kodansha, 1996), a collection of essays written over several years dealing primarily with Oe's severely handicapped autistic son, Hikari, who has become a celebrity in his own right as a composer of classical music. Favorite writers of Japan's baby-boom generation include Murakami Ryu, who burst onto the literary scene with *Almost Transparent Blue* (Kodansha, 1977) and later captured the undercurrent of decadent urban life in his best-selling *Coin Locker Babies* (Kodansha, 1995), and Murakami Haruki, whose writings include *Dance Dance Dance* (Kodansha, 1994), *Hard-Boiled Wonderland and the End of the World* (Vintage, 1993), *The Wind-Up Bird Chronicle* (Knopf, 1997), which centers on the massacre of Japanese troops in Mongolia by Soviet soldiers in 1939, *South of the Border, West of the Sun* (Knopf, 1999), the story of a bewildered man in contemporary Tokyo, and *Norwegian Wood* (Vintage, 2000), a coming-of-age story set during the 1969 student movement in Japan. Yoshimoto Banana's first novel, *Kitchen* (Washington Square Press, 1993), about free-spirited young women in contemporary Japan, created a "Bananamania" when first published in Japan in 1988.

For works of fiction about Japan by Western writers, most Westerners are familiar with James Clavell's *Shogun* (Dell, 1975), a fictional account (and later a television miniseries) based on the lives of Englishman William Adams and military leader Tokugawa Ieyasu around 1600. The best-selling *Memoirs of a Geisha* (Knopf, 1997), deftly written by Arthur Golden, is the fictional autobiography of a fisherman's daughter who was sold to a geisha house and later became one of Kyoto's most celebrated geisha of the 1930s.

For fictional yet personal contemporary accounts of what it's like for Westerners living in Japan, entertaining novels include *Ransom* (Vintage, 1985) by Jay McInerney; *Pictures from the Water Trade* (Harper & Row, 1986) by John D. Morley; and *Max Danger: The Adventures of an Expat in Tokyo* (Tuttle, 1987) by Robert J. Collins. Pico Iyer taps into the mysterious juxtaposition of the old Japan versus the new in *The Lady and the Monk: Four Seasons in Kyoto* (Knopf, 1991). *Audrey Hepburn's Neck* (Simon & Schuster, 1996) is Alan Brown's poignant portrait of Japan's mishmash of Western and Japanese culture, as seen through the eyes of a confused young Japanese comic illustrator.

Appendix B:
A Glossary of Useful
Japanese Terms

Needless to say, it takes years to become fluent in Japanese, particularly in written Japanese, with its thousands of *kanji*, or Chinese characters, and many hiragana and katakana characters. Knowing just a few words of Japanese, however, is not only useful but will delight the Japanese people you meet in the course of your trip.

PRONUNCIATION
In pronouncing the following vocabulary, keep in mind that there's very little stress on individual syllables (pronunciation of Japanese is often compared to Italian). Here's an approximation of some of the sounds of Japanese:

a   *as in* father
e   *as in* pen
i   *as in* see
o   *as in* oh
oo *as in* oooh
u   *as in* boo
g   *as in* gift at the beginning of words; like ng in sing in the middle or at the end of words

Vowel sounds are almost always short unless they are pronounced double, in which case you hold the vowel a bit longer. *Okashi*, for example, means "a sweet," whereas *okashii* means "strange." As you can see, even slight mispronunciation of a word can result in confusion or hilarity. (Incidentally, jokes in Japanese are nearly always plays on words.) Similarly, double consonants are given more emphasis than only one consonant by itself.

USEFUL WORDS & PHRASES
BASIC TERMS
Good morning   **Ohayo gozaimasu**
Good afternoon   **Konnichiwa**
Good evening   **Konbanwa**
Good night   **Oyasuminasai**
Hello   **Haro (or Konnichiwa)**
How are you?   **Ogenki desu ka?**
How do you do?   **Hajimemashite?**
Good-bye   **Sayonara (or Bye-bye!)**
Excuse me/Pardon me/I'm sorry   **Sumimasen**
Please (when offering something)   **Dozo**
Please (when requesting something)   **Kudasai**
Thank you   **Domo arigatoo**
You're welcome   **Doo-itashimashite**
Please (go ahead)   **Doozo**
Yes   **Hai**
No   **Iie**

BASIC QUESTIONS & EXPRESSIONS

I'm American   **Amerikajin desu**
I'm Canadian   **Canadajin desu**
I'm English   **Eikokujin desu**
Sorry, I don't speak Japanese   **Sumimasen, Nihongo was wakarimasen**
Do you understand English?   **Eigo wa wakarimasu ka?**
Do you understand?   **Wakarimasu ka?**
I understand   **Wakarimasu**
I don't understand   **Wakarimasen**
Can I ask you a question?   **Otazune shitaino desu ka?**
Just a minute, please   **Chotto matte kudasai**
How much is it?   **Ikura desu ka?**
It's expensive   **Takai desu**
It's cheap   **Yasui desu**
Where is it?   **Doko desu ka?**
When is it?   **Itsu desu ka?**
What is it?   **Kore-wa, nan-desu-ka?**
I like it   **Suki desu** (pronounced "ski")
Where is the toilet?   **Toire wa, doko desu ka?**
My name is . . .   [Your name] **to mo shimasu**
What is your name?   **O-namae wa, nan desu ka?**

TRAVEL EXPRESSIONS & DIRECTIONALS

Where is . . . ?   **Doko desu ka . . . ?**
Where is the train station?   **Eki wa, doko desu ka?**
Train station   **Eki**
Airport   **Kuukoo**
Subway   **Chika-tetsu**
Bus   **Bus-u**
Taxi   **Takushi**
Airplane   **Hikooki**
Train   **Densha**
Bullet train   **Shinkansen**
Limited express train (long distance)   **Tokkyu**
Ordinary express train (doesn't stop at every station)   **Kyuko**
Rapid train   **Kaisoku densha**
Local train (one that stops at every station)   **Kakueki teisha** (or **futsu**)
I would like a reserved seat, please.   **Shiteiseki o kudasai.**
I would like a seat in the no-smoking car, please.   **Kinensha no shiteiski o kudasai.**
Unreserved seat   **Jiyuseki**
Platform   **Platt-homu**
Ticket   **Kippu**
Destination   **Ikisaki**
One-way ticket   **Katamichi-kippu** (or **katamichiken**)
Round-trip ticket   **Ofuku-kippu** (or **ofukuken**)
I would like to buy a ticket.   **Kippu ichimai o kaitai no desu kedo.**
I would like to buy two tickets.   **Kippu nimai o kaitai no desu kedo.**
Exit   **Deguchi**
Entrance   **Iriguchi**
North   **Kita**
South   **Minami**

East   **Higashi**
West   **Nishi**
Left   **Hidari**
Right   **Migi**
Straight ahead   **Massugu** (or **zutto**)
Is it far?   **Toi desu ka?**
Is it near?   **Chikai desu ka?**
Can I walk there?   **Aruite ikemasu ka?**
Street   **Dori** (or **michi**)
Tourist Information Office   **Kanko annaijo** (or **kanko kyokai**)
Where is the tourist office?   **Kanko annaijo, doko desu ka?**
May I have a map, please?   **Chizu o kudasai?**
Police   **Keisatsu**
Police box   **Koban**
Post office   **Yubin-kyoku**
I'd like to buy a stamp.   **Kitte o kaitai no desu kedo.**
Bank   **Ginko**
Hospital   **Byooin**
Drugstore   **Yakkyoku**
Convenience store   **Konbiniensu stoa**
Embassy   **Taishkan**
Department store   **Depaato**
Downtown area   **Hanka-gai**

LODGING TERMS
Hotel   **Hoteru**
Japanese-style inn   **Ryokan**
Youth hostel   **Yusu hosuteru**
Cotton kimono   **Yukata**
Room   **Heya**
Do you have a room available?   **Heya ga arimasu ka?**
Does that include meals?   **Shokuji wa tsuite imasu ka?**
Tax   **Zei**
Service charge   **Saavice**
Key   **Kagi**
Balcony   **Baranda**
Hot-spring spa   **Onsen**
Outdoor hot-spring bath   **Rotenburo**
Bath   **Ofuro**
Public bath   **Sento**
Where is the nearest public bath?   **Ichiban chikai sento wa, doko desu ka?**

DINING TERMS & PHRASES
Restaurant   **Resutoran** (serves Western-style food)
Dining hall   **Shokudo** (usually serves Japanese food)
Coffee shop   **Kissaten**
Japanese pub   **Izakaya**
Western food   **Yoshoku**
Japanese food   **Washoku**
Breakfast   **Chosoku**
Dinner   **Yushoku**
I'd like to make a reservation.   **Yoyaku oneigai shimasu.**

Menu   **Menyu**
Japanese green tea   **Ocha**
Black (Indian) tea   **Kocha**
Coffee   **Koohi**
Water   **Mizu**
Lunch or daily special, set menu   **Teishoku** (Japanese food)
Lunch or daily special, set menu   **Cosu,** or **seto** (usually Western food)
This is delicious.   **Oishii desu.**
Thank you for the meal.   **Gochisoo-sama deshita.**
I would like a fork, please.   **Foku o kudasai.**
I would like a spoon, please.   **Saji o kudasai.**
I would like a knife, please.   **Naifu o kudasai.**
May I have some more, please? (if you're asking for liquid, such as more
coffee, or food)   **Mo skoshi o kudasai?**
May I have some more, please? (if you're asking for another bottle—say, of
soda or sake)   **Mo ipon o kudasai?**
May I have some more, please? (if you asking for another cup—say, of coffee
or tea)   **Mo ippai o kudasai?**
I would like sake, please.   **Osake o kudasai.**
I would like a cup of coffee.   **Koohii o ippai o kudasai.**
I would like the set meal, please.   **Seto o kudasai** or **Teishoku o kudasai.**

FOOD TERMS

Ayu   A small river fish; a delicacy of western Japan.
Anago   Conger eel.
Chu-hai Shochu   Shochu (see below) mixed with soda water and flavored
with syrup and lemon.
Dengaku   Lightly grilled tofu (see below) coated with a bean paste.
Dojo   A small, eel-like river fish.
Fugu   Pufferfish (also known as blowfish or globefish).
"Genghis Khan"   Mutton and vegetables grilled at your table.
Gohan   Rice.
Gyoza   Chinese fried pork dumplings.
Kaiseki   A formal Japanese meal consisting of many courses and served
originally during the tea ceremony.
Kamameshi   A rice casserole topped with seafood, meat, or vegetables.
Kushiage (also **kushikatsu** or **kushiyaki**)   Deep-fried skewers of chicken,
beef, seafood, and vegetables.
Maguro   Tuna.
Makizushi   Sushi (see below), vegetables, and rice rolled inside dried seaweed.
Miso   A soybean paste, used as a seasoning in soups and sauces.
Miso-shiru   Miso soup.
Mochi   Japanese rice cake.
Nabemono   A single-pot dish of chicken, beef, pork, or seafood, stewed with
vegetables.
Natto   Fermented soybeans.
Nikujaga   A beef, potato, and carrot stew, flavored with sake (see below) and
soy sauce; popular in winter.
Oden   Fish cakes, hard-boiled eggs, and vegetables, simmered in a light broth.
Okonomiyaki   A thick pancake filled with meat, fish, shredded cabbage, and
vegetables or noodles, often cooked by diners at their table.

Ramen   Thick, yellow Chinese noodles, served in a hot soup.

Sake (also **Nihon-shu**)   Rice wine.

Sansai   Mountain vegetables, including bracken and flowering fern.

Sashimi   Raw seafood.

Shabu-shabu   Thinly sliced beef quickly dipped in boiling water and then dipped in a sauce.

Shochu   Japanese whiskey, made from rice, wheat, or potatoes.

Shojin-ryori   Japanese vegetarian food, served at Buddhist temples.

Shoyu   Soy sauce.

Shumai   Steamed Chinese pork dumplings.

Soba   Buckwheat noodles.

Somen   Fine white wheat vermicelli, eaten cold in summer.

Sukiyaki   A Japanese fondue of thinly sliced beef cooked in a sweetened soy sauce with vegetables.

Sushi (also **nigiri-zushi**)   Raw seafood placed on top of vinegared rice.

Tempura   Deep-fried food coated in a batter of egg, water, and wheat flour.

Teppanyaki   Japanese-style steak, seafood, and vegetables cooked by a chef on a smooth, hot tableside grill.

Tofu   Soft bean curd.

Tonkatsu   Deep-fried pork cutlets.

Udon   Thick white wheat noodles.

Unagi   Grilled eel.

Wasabi   Japanese horseradish, served with sushi.

Yakisoba   Chinese fried noodles, served with sautéed vegetables.

Yakitori   Charcoal-grilled chicken, vegetables, and other specialties, served on bamboo skewers.

Yudofu   Tofu simmered in a pot at your table.

MATTERS OF TIME

Now **Ima**		What time is it? **Nan-ji desu ka?**	
Later **Sto de**		Daytime **Hiruma**	
Today **Kyoo**		Morning **Asa**	
Tomorrow **Ashita**		Night **Yoru**	
Day after tomorrow **Asatte**		Afternoon **Gogo**	
Yesterday **Kinoo**		Holiday **Yasumi** (or **kyujitsu**)	
Which day? **Nan-nichi desu ka?**		Weekdays **Heijitsu**	

DAYS OF THE WEEK

Sunday **Nichiyoobi**	Thursday **Mokuyoobi**
Monday **Getsuyoobi**	Friday **Kinyoobi**
Tuesday **Kayoobi**	Saturday **Doyoobi**
Wednesday **Suiyoobi**	

MONTHS OF THE YEAR

January **Ichi-gatsu**	July **Shichi-gatsu**
February **Ni-gatsu**	August **Hachi-gatsu**
March **San-gatsu**	September **Kyuu-gatsu**
April **Shi-gatsu**	October **Juu-gatsu**
May **Go-gatsu**	November **Juuichi-gatsu**
June **Roku-gatsu**	December **Juuni-gatsu**

NUMBERS

01	**Ichi**	20	**Nijuu**
02	**Ni**	30	**Sanjuu**
03	**San**	40	**Shijuu** (or **yonjuu**)
04	**Shi**	50	**Gojuu**
05	**Go**	60	**Rokujuu**
06	**Roku**	70	**Nanajuu**
07	**Shichi** (or **nana**)	80	**Hachijuu**
08	**Hachi**	90	**Kyuuju**
09	**Kyuu**	100	**Hyaku**
10	**Juu**	1,000	**Sen**
11	**Juuichi**	10,000	**Ichiman**
12	**Juuni**		

OTHER GENERAL NOUNS

Fusuma   Sliding paper doors.

Gaijin   Foreigner.

Geta   Wooden sandals.

Haori   A short coat worn over a kimono.

Irori   Open-hearth fireplace.

Jinja   Shinto shrine.

Kotatsu   A heating element placed under a low table (which is covered with a blanket) for keeping one's legs warm; used in place of a heater in traditional Japanese homes.

Minshuku   Inexpensive lodging in a private home; the Japanese equivalent of a European pension.

Nihonjin   Japanese person.

Nomi-ya   A drinking establishment.

Shoji   White paper sliding windows.

Tatami   Rice mats.

Tera (or **dera**)   Temple.

Tokonoma   A small, recessed alcove in a Japanese room used to display a flower arrangement, scroll, or art object.

Torii   Entrance gate of a Shinto shrine, consisting usually of two poles topped with one or two crossbeams.

Washlet   Bidet toilet.

Yukata   A cotton kimono worn for sleeping.

Zabuton   Floor cushions.

Appendix C:
A Japanese-Character Index
of Establishment Names

CHAPTERS 3 & 4
TOKYO

DINING

1   Sushiko
    寿司幸

2   Ohmatsuya
    大松屋

3   Donto
    どんと

4   Ginza Daimasu
    銀座大増

5   Kushi Colza
    串コルザ

6   Rangetsu
    らん月

7   Atariya
    当り屋

8   Fukusuke
    福助

9   Shabusen
    しゃぶせん

10 Tentake
    天竹

11 Edogin
    江戸銀

12 Sushi Dai
    寿司大

13 Komagata Dojo
    駒形どぜう

14 Mugitoro
    むぎとろ

15 Chinya
    ちんや

16 Daikokuya
    大黒屋

17 Namiki Yabu Soba
    並木薮蕎麦

18 Izu'ei
    伊豆栄

19 Kakiden
    柿伝

20 Kappoya Yaozen
    八百善

21 Tsunahachi
    つな八

22 Hakkaku
    八角

23 Harajuku Gyoza Lou
    原宿餃子樓

24 Heirokuzushi
    平禄寿司

25 Inakaya
    田舎屋

26 Takamura
    篁

27 Fukuzushi
    福鮨

28 Bikkuri Sushi
    びっくり寿司

29 Ganchan
    がんちゃん

Index

FROMMER'S® COMPLETE TRAVEL GUIDES

Alaska
Alaska Cruises & Ports of Call
Amsterdam
Argentina & Chile
Arizona
Atlanta
Australia
Austria
Bahamas
Barcelona, Madrid & Seville
Beijing
Belgium, Holland & Luxembourg
Bermuda
Boston
Brazil
British Columbia & the Canadian
    Rockies
Budapest & the Best of Hungary
California
Canada
Cancún, Cozumel & the Yucatán
Cape Cod, Nantucket & Martha's
    Vineyard
Caribbean
Caribbean Cruises & Ports of Call
Caribbean Ports of Call
Carolinas & Georgia
Chicago
China
Colorado
Costa Rica
Denmark
Denver, Boulder & Colorado
    Springs
England
Europe
European Cruises & Ports of Call
Florida

France
Germany
Great Britain
Greece
Greek Islands
Hawaii
Hong Kong
Honolulu, Waikiki & Oahu
Ireland
Israel
Italy
Jamaica
Japan
Las Vegas
London
Los Angeles
Maryland & Delaware
Maui
Mexico
Montana & Wyoming
Montréal & Québec City
Munich & the Bavarian Alps
Nashville & Memphis
Nepal
New England
New Mexico
New Orleans
New York City
New Zealand
Northern Italy
Nova Scotia, New Brunswick &
    Prince Edward Island
Oregon
Paris
Philadelphia & the Amish Country
Portugal
Prague & the Best of the Czech
    Republic

Provence & the Riviera
Puerto Rico
Rome
San Antonio & Austin
San Diego
San Francisco
Santa Fe, Taos & Albuquerque
Scandinavia
Scotland
Seattle & Portland
Shanghai
Singapore & Malaysia
South Africa
South America
South Florida
South Pacific
Southeast Asia
Spain
Sweden
Switzerland
Texas
Thailand
Tokyo
Toronto
Tuscany & Umbria
USA
Utah
Vancouver & Victoria
Vermont, New Hampshire &
    Maine
Vienna & the Danube Valley
Virgin Islands
Virginia
Walt Disney World & Orlando
Washington, D.C.
Washington State

FROMMER'S® DOLLAR-A-DAY GUIDES

Australia from $50 a Day
California from $70 a Day
Caribbean from $70 a Day
England from $75 a Day
Europe from $70 a Day

Florida from $70 a Day
Hawaii from $80 a Day
Ireland from $60 a Day
Italy from $70 a Day
London from $85 a Day

New York from $90 a Day
Paris from $80 a Day
San Francisco from $70 a Day
Washington, D.C. from $80 a Day

FROMMER'S® PORTABLE GUIDES

Acapulco, Ixtapa & Zihuatanejo
Amsterdam
Aruba
Australia's Great Barrier Reef
Bahamas
Baja & Los Cabos
Berlin
Boston
California Wine Country
Cancún
Charleston & Savannah
Chicago
Disneyland
Dublin
Florence

Frankfurt
Hawaii: The Big Island
Hong Kong
Houston
Las Vegas
London
Los Angeles
Maine Coast
Maui
Miami
New Orleans
New York City
Paris
Phoenix & Scottsdale

Portland
Puerto Rico
Puerto Vallarta, Manzanillo &
    Guadalajara
Rio de Janeiro
San Diego
San Francisco
Seattle
Sydney
Tampa & St. Petersburg
Vancouver
Venice
Virgin Islands
Washington, D.C.

FROMMER'S® NATIONAL PARK GUIDES

Banff & Jasper
Family Vacations in the National
    Parks
Grand Canyon

National Parks of the American
    West
Rocky Mountain

Yellowstone & Grand Teton
Yosemite & Sequoia/ Kings Canyon
Zion & Bryce Canyon

FROMMER'S® MEMORABLE WALKS

Chicago
London

New York
Paris

San Francisco

FROMMER'S® GREAT OUTDOOR GUIDES

Arizona & New Mexico
New England

Northern California
Southern New England

Vermont & New Hampshire

SUZY GERSHMAN'S BORN TO SHOP GUIDES

Born to Shop: France
Born to Shop: Hong Kong,
  Shanghai & Beijing

Born to Shop: Italy
Born to Shop: London

Born to Shop: New York
Born to Shop: Paris

FROMMER'S® IRREVERENT GUIDES

Amsterdam
Boston
Chicago
Las Vegas
London

Los Angeles
Manhattan
New Orleans
Paris
Rome

San Francisco
Seattle & Portland
Vancouver
Walt Disney World
Washington, D.C.

FROMMER'S® BEST-LOVED DRIVING TOURS

Britain
California
Florida
France

Germany
Ireland
Italy
New England

Northern Italy
Scotland
Spain
Tuscany & Umbria

HANGING OUT™ GUIDES

Hanging Out in England
Hanging Out in Europe

Hanging Out in France
Hanging Out in Ireland

Hanging Out in Italy
Hanging Out in Spain

THE UNOFFICIAL GUIDES®

Bed & Breakfasts and Country
  Inns in:
  California
  Great Lakes States
  Mid-Atlantic
  New England
  Northwest
  Rockies
  Southeast
  Southwest
Best RV & Tent Campgrounds in:
  California & the West
  Florida & the Southeast
  Great Lakes States
  Mid-Atlantic
  Northeast
  Northwest & Central Plains

Southwest & South Central
    Plains
  U.S.A.
Beyond Disney
Branson, Missouri
California with Kids
Chicago
Cruises
Disneyland
Florida with Kids
Golf Vacations in the Eastern U.S.
Great Smoky & Blue Ridge Region
Inside Disney
Hawaii
Las Vegas
London

Mid-Atlantic with Kids
Mini Las Vegas
Mini-Mickey
New England and New York with
    Kids
New Orleans
New York City
Paris
San Francisco
Skiing in the West
Southeast with Kids
Walt Disney World
Walt Disney World for Grown-ups
Walt Disney World with Kids
Washington, D.C.
World's Best Diving Vacations

SPECIAL-INTEREST TITLES

Frommer's Adventure Guide to Australia &
  New Zealand
Frommer's Adventure Guide to Central America
Frommer's Adventure Guide to India & Pakistan
Frommer's Adventure Guide to South America
Frommer's Adventure Guide to Southeast Asia
Frommer's Adventure Guide to Southern Africa
Frommer's Britain's Best Bed & Breakfasts and
  Country Inns
Frommer's Caribbean Hideaways
Frommer's Exploring America by RV
Frommer's Fly Safe, Fly Smart
Frommer's France's Best Bed & Breakfasts and
  Country Inns
Frommer's Gay & Lesbian Europe

Frommer's Italy's Best Bed & Breakfasts and
  Country Inns
Frommer's New York City with Kids
Frommer's Ottawa with Kids
Frommer's Road Atlas Britain
Frommer's Road Atlas Europe
Frommer's Road Atlas France
Frommer's Toronto with Kids
Frommer's Vancouver with Kids
Frommer's Washington, D.C., with Kids
Israel Past & Present
The New York Times' Guide to Unforgettable
  Weekends
Places Rated Almanac
Retirement Places Rated